DOCUMENTS ON BRITISH FOREIGN POLICY 1919—1939

EDITED BY

W. N. MEDLICOTT, M.A., D.Lit., D.Litt.

Emeritus Professor of International History, University of London

DOUGLAS DAKIN, M.A., Ph.D.

Emeritus Professor of History, University of London

AND

M. E. LAMBERT, M.A.

FIRST SERIES
Volume XX

LONDON
HER MAJESTY'S STATIONERY OFFICE

© *Crown Copyright 1976*

First published 1976

HER MAJESTY'S STATIONERY OFFICE

Government Bookshops

49 High Holborn, London WC1V 6HB
13a Castle Street, Edinburgh EH2 3AR
41 The Hayes, Cardiff CF1 1JW
Brazennose Street, Manchester M60 8AS
Southey House, Wine Street, Bristol BS1 2BQ
258 Broad Street, Birmingham B1 2HE
80 Chichester Street, Belfast BT1 4JY

Government publications are also available
through booksellers

PRINTED IN ENGLAND
FOR HER MAJESTY'S STATIONERY OFFICE
BY VIVIAN RIDLER AT THE UNIVERSITY PRESS, OXFORD
Dd 506514 K14 4/76
ISBN 0 11 591553 2 *

DOCUMENTS ON BRITISH FOREIGN POLICY

1919–1939

First Series, Volume XX

German Reparation and
Allied Military Control
1922
Russia
March 1921–December 1922

PREFACE

THE first part of this volume (Chapters I to IV) deals with German Reparation and Allied Military Control of Germany during the year 1922. It continues the documentation in Volume XVI, Chapters III to VII. The second part (Chapters V and VI) is concerned with Russia from the signing of the Anglo-Soviet Trade Agreement of March 16, 1921, to the end of 1922. This part continues the documentation in Volume XII, Chapter V. In both parts much of the documentation is related to that in Volume XIX, which deals with the Cannes Conference (Chapter I), the Genoa Conference (Chapters II and III), and The Hague Conference of Experts (Chapter IV). The two first-named conferences were concerned with both Germany and Russia. More directly than ever before, the German and the Russian problems came to be connected in inter-Allied negotiations and it is therefore most appropriate that the documentation of these negotiations in 1922 should be presented together.

Anglo-French antagonism, which had been considerable throughout 1921 (see Introductions to Volumes XVI and XVII), increased during the Cannes and Genoa Conferences (see Introduction to Volume XIX) and, with M. Poincaré in control at the Quai d'Orsay, continued to grow throughout the remainder of 1922 on all issues, including that of the Near East (see Introduction to Volume XVIII). On German Reparations, a problem with which the Supreme Council at Cannes had failed to come to grips and which M. Poincaré had almost totally excluded from the negotiations at Genoa, France made it clear in a Note of May 19 that, in the event of Germany's default on Reparation payment on May 31, she would demand guarantees and, if necessary, take unilateral action to obtain them, despite M. Millerand's alleged pledge of April 11, 1920 (see Nos. 23 and 25). At a meeting of British and French representatives on June 19 (see No. 30) M. Poincaré demanded the effective control of German finances in order to prevent the diversion of funds and capital to purposes other than Reparation. Following His Majesty's Government's resistance to this demand and the attempt of the Belgian Government to mediate between Great Britain and France, on August 1 Lord Balfour communicated to the French Ambassador a note (No. 45) which stated that Great Britain was prepared to abandon all further claims to German reparation and to repayment by her Allies of their debts, provided this renunciation were part of a general plan to solve the problem of international indebtedness. This note was ill-received in France (see No. 77) and met with much scepticism in America (see No. 145). At meetings of Allied representatives in London from August 7 to 14 (this conference had come about largely through the good offices of Belgium), M. Poincaré insisted on 'productive guarantees' as a condition of his agreement to the grant of a moratorium to Germany. The guarantees he proposed were: allied control of import and export licences in the occupied Rhineland; the allied exploitation of German State Mines and Forests; the expropriation of shares in German factories on the left bank of the Rhine; the establishment of a customs barrier and the allied collection of customs in that same region; and the imposition of export taxes in the Ruhr. Discussion of these proposals (see Chapter II) led nowhere. German offers to provide guarantees (see Nos. 75, 86, and 89) satisfied neither France nor Belgium (see Nos. 90 and 93) and the conflict continued not only in diplomatic exchanges but also in the Reparation Commission, to which the British representative, Sir J. Bradbury, submitted on October 6 proposals (see No. 97) which in turn provoked French counter-proposals (see No. 103). On November 13, the German Government came forward with fresh proposals to the Reparation Commission (see No. 113) but these failed to break the deadlock. Once again, largely as a result of Belgian pressure (Belgium had intimated that she might be forced to join France in coercive action (see No. 125), generally understood to be the invasion of the Ruhr), His Majesty's Government agreed to meet her allies in London on December 9 and 10 (see Nos. 120, 121, 122, 126, and 127). At this meeting (see Nos. 132 and 133) the Allied Prime Ministers rejected a German Note of December 9 (see No. 131, Enclosure, and Nos. 134, and 135) and decided to meet again in Paris in the New Year. This Paris conference, its failure, and the decision of France and Belgium to invade the Ruhr will be dealt with in Volume XXI.

At the end of 1922, the problem of the termination of the military control of Germany was, like the Reparation issue, still unsettled as a result of Anglo-French differences and of German intransigence. As early as August, 1921, the Supreme Council had discussed the possibility of modifying the Military, Naval and Aeronautical Missions of Control in Germany, but had decided to postpone the question for further consideration by the Allied Governments (see Vol. XV, Nos. 103, minute 8 and 104, minute 4). On the basis of reports submitted to the Supreme Council (see ibid., No. 103, Appendix 5 and No. 104, Appendices 6 and 7) the French claimed that the time for the complete removal of control had not arrived and held out for a new system. His Majesty's Government's plan was to substitute at the end of 1921, with German consent, a small control mission in Berlin for the Aeronautical Commission of Control and to hasten the completion of the work of the Military and Naval Control Commissions which, also with German consent, should be replaced by small commissions of limited duration (see Vol. XVI, No. 835 and Enclosures and No. 836). Throughout the winter of 1921–2 negotiations on this issue, which were closely linked with the question of the withdrawal of military sanctions and dogged by French conviction and British suspicion that Germany was not acting in good faith with regard to reparation and disarmament, made but little progress (see Vol. XVI, No. 845 and this volume Nos. 172, 175, 178, 179, 181, 183, and 188). On April 14, 1922, however, the Conference of Ambassadors notified the German Government of the constitution of a new Inter-Allied Aeronautical

Committee of Guarantee to replace the Inter-Allied Aeronautical Commission of Control, outlined the measures of military and naval disarmament still to be executed, and requested the German Government to accept, upon the withdrawal of the Military Commission of Control, a small inter-Allied supervisory body on the lines of the Aeronautical Committee of Guarantee (see No. 208). On May 1, the German Government accepted the Aeronautical Committee of Guarantee but gave no satisfaction with regard to the remainder of the Conference of Ambassadors' Note (see No. 212), and it was not until September 29, 1922, that the Allied Governments (this time through their Ambassadors in Berlin) managed to agree on a further note to the German Government on military (but not naval) control (see No. 277, n. 1). The delay had been occasioned by difficulties raised by the French, by the constant need to refer disputed details to the Service ministries, by discussions and delays on the related issue of the organisation of the German police, by the intransigence of the German Government, who made constant appeals to the Allied Government against the decisions of the Military and Naval Control Commissions, and by an attack on members of the Military Control Commission at Stettin on July 17 (see No. 267). Not until October 27 did the German Government reply to the Allies. In the meantime a further attack on Allied military personnel took place at Passau on October 15 (see No. 293).

The German reply (see No. 287) failed to satisfy the Allies. It ignored five specific demands (see No. 270, n. 5): the reorganisation of the German police; the transformation of factories; the delivery of unauthorised war material; the delivery of documents concerning existing German war material at the time of the armistice and production of war material during the war and after the armistice; and the promulgation of laws prohibiting the importation or exportation of war material and bringing the recruitment and organisation of the army into line with the provisions of the Peace Treaty. On November 17 the Conference of Ambassadors addressed a further note to the German Government (see No. 306), who replied on November 28 (see No. 328) and again on December 10 (see No. 351). In this second reply the Germans claimed that they had disarmed, complained against alleged demands of the missions of control, and pleaded that the 'transformation des usines' was not a simple question, but one affecting German economic life, both industrial and agricultural. There the matter rested at the end of 1922. On the related issue, however, of attacks on Allied military personnel at Stettin, Passau, and Ingolstadt (see Nos. 267, 273, 281, 293, 299, 301, 302, 306, and 309), the German Government, following threats (the nature of which gave rise to much altercation between the French and British Governments (see Nos. 320, 322, 326, 330, 334, and 336)) gave some satisfaction (see Nos. 340 and 349).

During the period March, 1921 to December, 1922 the execution of the Anglo-Soviet Trade Agreement of March 16, 1921, provides much of the documentation of Anglo-Russian relations. Although in April, 1921, M. Chicherin, Commissar for Foreign Affairs, had assured His Majesty's

Government that the Russian Government intended to execute strictly all engagements undertaken (see No. 356), the Foreign Office and the India Office continued to receive reports of constant contraventions. Protests against these were frequently made to M. Krassin, Head of the Russian Trade Delegation in London, and later in Moscow, through Mr. Hodgson, who arrived there in August as Head of the British Commercial Mission to Russia (see Nos. 376 and 389). In June, at the instigation of the India Office, the Cabinet approved the establishment of an Interdepartmental Committee which sat regularly in the Foreign Office to collate information on Russian activities (see Nos. 377, 379, and 383). The outcome of their labours was a long note despatched to Mr. Hodgson on September 7 for onward transmission to the Soviet Government protesting against breaches of the Anglo-Soviet Agreement (see Nos. 414, 421, 426, and 427). To this note the Soviet Government sent a long reply dated September 27, contending that His Majesty's Government were badly misinformed and on some points misguided by intelligence manufactured in White Russian circles (see No. 428). On October 27 Lord Curzon transmitted to Mr. Hodgson a further note refuting the Soviet contentions point by point (see No. 437) and making allegations which M. Chicherin denied (see No. 444).

Partly because of Mr. Hodgson's advice, partly because of the reluctance of the Foreign Office to indulge in a fruitless exchange of this kind, partly because the Prime Minister was developing his idea of handling the Russian and German problems together in a European economic conference, and partly moreover because of the problems posed by the Russian famine in the second half of 1921 and by the need to negotiate over a host of lesser issues, this acrimonious correspondence ceased and the Foreign Office continued its more humdrum task of regularising Anglo-Soviet trade relations, of dealing with problems such as fishing rights (see Nos. 364, 483, 486, 489, 491, 500, 552, and 570), of watching Russian relations with other powers, and of encouraging the Finnish Government to maintain strict neutrality in regard to the anti-Bolshevik rising in Karelia (see Nos. 447–484, *passim*).

Concurrently with these problems, the Foreign Office was concerned with the task of bringing relief to the Russian people stricken by famine. This great calamity was discussed by the Supreme Council in Paris in August, 1921 (see Vol. XV, pp. 672–6, 705, and 714) and an International Commission was set up to study the problem. From the outset it was realised that famine in Russia could not (in Lord Curzon's words) 'be fought simply by filling ships with corn and sending them to Odessa or other Russian ports'. Nor could it be adequately fought by the donations from humanitarians in America and Europe. Famine relief raised a whole train of issues—the economy and transport system of Russia; credit, which was related to the problem of Russian debts; relations between foreign personnel and the Russian civil and military authorities; and the question of how far the Soviet Government would allow intervention by the Powers. Most of these issues had come up for discussion on August 6 when British interdepartmental representatives met members of the Russian Trade Delegation at the Board of Trade (see No. 388), and it soon became clear that the Russians preferred that relief should be given by individual nations on the lines of the American (Hoover) plan (see No. 396) rather than through international action, or even by Dr. Nansen's organisation under the auspices of the League of Nations (see No. 403), provided it were accorded in a fashion acceptable to them (see Nos. 410 and 412). Neither the Russians nor Dr. Nansen favoured the International Commission's design (see No. 413) to send a Mission of Enquiry into Russia in order to study the question of immediate needs and of credit for long-term economic reconstruction. Indeed, almost from the outset the question of relief to Russia ceased to be a purely humanitarian issue and became a matter of political importance, it being realised by the International Commission in Paris that the credits which Dr. Nansen was demanding could not be given until the Soviet Government recognised Russian debts and offered, to use Mr. Leeper's words, 'real tangible security' (see No. 417).

On October 6–8, representatives of twenty-one countries met in Brussels to discuss the question of credits and related issues and passed resolutions, the most important of which were 5c (i) and (ii): that credits would be forth-coming only if Russia recognised her debts and afforded security for any credit given (No. 430). Russia accepted these conditions in principle in a Note of October 28 to the Allies (see No. 438, n. 1), but the French Govern-ment held that the Russian reply was much too vague and proceeded to expound the essential conditions for the resumption of relations with the Soviet Government (see No. 443, Enclosure). This issue was caught up in the discussions preceding the meeting of the Genoa Conference in April, 1922 (see Volume XIX, Chapters II and III), which was designed to deal concurrently with the Russian and German problems and the economic situation of Europe as a whole. These discussions tended to overshadow the question of famine relief, which was dealt with largely by the American Relief Organisation, by Dr. Nansen and the League of Nations, by voluntary efforts and to some extent by the Soviet Government itself. By July, 1922, the prospects of a good harvest had removed the fears of an intensification of famine conditions and the Russian delegation at The Hague Conference (see Volume XIX, Chapter IV) firmly refused to accept the Allied conditions with regard to credits and the resumption of relations. It was, therefore, left to creditors and commercial firms to fend for themselves and to obtain what concessions they could under the New Economic Policy that had been introduced in Russia in 1921. Some idea of how the British financial and commercial interests fared in comparison with German concerns will be gained from documents scattered throughout the volume (see, for example, Nos. 367, 399–401, 423, and 432).

There will also be found in this volume documents on Soviet commercial relations with Afghanistan (Nos. 358 and 366), Czechoslovakia (No. 512), Norway (No. 415), Italy (Nos. 459, 504, 509, 571, and 573), Poland (No. 431) and Sweden (Nos. 476, 567, and 575); on Soviet-German commercial, political, and military relations (Nos. 362, 492, 495, 502, 505, 513, 519, 537,

551, 553, and 559); on Soviet-Roumanian relations (Nos. 368, 420, 439, 530, 544, and 545); on Soviet-Polish relations (Nos. 420 and 424) and on the Warsaw Conference of March, 1922 (Nos. 477–9 and 488). Several documents deal with M. Herriot's visit to Russia in October 1922 and with Franco-Soviet relations (Nos. 540–576, *passim*). Of considerable interest are the reports of Mr. Hodgson from Moscow on political and social conditions in Russia, on the Red Army and on the Russian Church. Only a few of these reports have been printed but attention has been called to others in the footnotes.

I have to thank Mr. B. Cheeseman, O.B.E., Head of the Library and Records Department of the Foreign and Commonwealth Office, and his staff for all their help. In preparing this volume I have had unrestricted access to all the papers in the Foreign Office records. I also have to express my gratitude once more to the staff of the Public Record Office for their unfailing co-operation. Finally, I have to acknowledge my debt to Mrs. R. Warman, B.A., Mrs. G. Bennett, B.A., and Miss Kathleen Jones, B.A., for their invaluable assistance in the preparation of this volume.

March, 1975   DOUGLAS DAKIN

CONTENTS

LIST OF ABBREVIATIONS

B.F.S.P.	*British and Foreign State Papers* (London).
Cmd.	Command Paper (London).
Degras	*Soviet Documents on Foreign Policy*, selected and edited by Jane Degras, 3 vols. (London, 1951 ff.), vol. i.
F.R.U.S.	*Papers relating to the Foreign Relations of the United States* (Washington).
H.C. Deb. 5 s.	*Parliamentary Debates (Hansard), Official Report 5th Series,* House of Commons (London).
Slusser and Triska	Robert M. Slusser and Jan F. Triska, *A Calendar of Soviet Treaties 1917–1957* (Stanford, 1959).

An asterisk following the file number of a document indicates that the text has been taken from Confidential Print.

CHAPTER SUMMARIES

CHAPTER I

Reparation by Germany: Germany's Default and Events leading to the Fifth London Conference, January 19–August 5, 1922

xvii

CHAPTER II

Proceedings of the Fifth Conference of London and Records of Conversations connected therewith, August 7–14, 1922

CHAPTER III

Reparation by Germany: Events leading to the French and Belgian Invasion of the Ruhr, August 17–December 31, 1922

xxix

CHAPTER IV

Military Control of Germany and German Problems other than Reparation, January–December, 1922

xxxix

xliii

1

CHAPTER V

Russia, March 22–December 31, 1921

CHAPTER VI

Russia, January–December, 1922

CHAPTER I

Reparation by Germany: Germany's Default and Events Leading to the Fifth London Conference

January 19–August 5, 1922

No. 1

Memorandum by Mr. Wigram[1] on the position of the reparations negotiations at the close of the Cannes Conference[2]

[*C 968/99/18*]

FOREIGN OFFICE, *January 19, 1922*

[1] At the Downing Street discussions in December 1921[3] the British and French governments agreed to recommend to the Cannes Conference a scheme providing for

(a) the limitation during the year 1922 of German cash payments to 500 millions gold marks (£25 millions gold)

(b) the limitation of the recoverable annual costs of the armies of occupation to 220 millions gold marks (£11 millions gold)

(c) certain guarantees by the German government for the re-establishment of a sound financial system

(d) the operation of the Wiesbaden agreement[4] subject to certain amendments needed to safeguard the interests of the allies other than France and the operation of the August agreement[5] subject to certain amendments designed to meet French objections.

2. Owing to the fall of the French government[6] it was not possible to secure the acceptance by the Cannes Conference of any of these recommendations. The only definite decision taken at Cannes in the sphere of reparation was that of the Reparation Commission which was formally approved on January 13th.[7] This decision provided for

(a) provisional postponement of the January and February payments

---

[1] A member of the Central European Department of the Foreign Office.

[2] See Vol. XIX, Chap. I.   [3] See Vol. XV, Chap. VII.

[4] This agreement was signed on October 6, 1921 (see Vol. XVI, Nos. 681 and 711). For the text, see Cmd. 1547 of 1921.

[5] See Vol. XV, No. 104.

[6] M. Briand had resigned on January 12. M. Poincaré formed a government on January 15, and on January 18 succeeded M. Briand as President of the Council and Minister for Foreign Affairs.

[7] See Vol. XIX, No. 25.

(b) a cash payment by the Germans of 31 millions of gold marks (£1,550,000 gold) every ten days dating from January 18, 1922 and continuing during the period of provisional postponement

(c) the submission by the German government to the Reparation Commission, within fifteen days from January 13th, 1922, of a scheme of budget and currency reform with appropriate guarantees as well as a complete programme of cash payments and deliveries in kind for the year 1922. This scheme, immediately upon receipt by the Reparation Commission, must be transmitted to the allied governments who will then decide whether to deal with it themselves or to refer it back to the commission for the necessary action.

3. The next step in the reparation negotiations, therefore, waits upon the receipt of the German government's scheme. It appears from Lord D'Abernon's telegram No. 11[8] that we may expect this scheme very shortly.

4. The memorandum (A.J. 331)[9] which was considered by the allied financial experts at Cannes, and which it is understood received general approval,[10] may be taken, subject to any sudden change in French policy, to foreshadow the kind of offer which the Germans must make if it is to be acceptable to the allies. In its main lines the allied financial experts' memorandum provides for

(a) cash payments by Germany during the year 1922 amounting to 720 millions gold marks (£36 millions gold)

(b) value of deliveries in kind (including reparations recovery act) not to exceed 1450 millions gold marks (£72½ millions gold), during 1922

(c) limitation of annual recoverable costs of armies of occupation to 220 millions gold marks (£11 millions gold) from May 1, 1922. These costs from May 1, 1921 to December 1, 1922 to be charged against the deliveries in kind actually in the hands of the allied governments. (N.B. This is an improvement on the Downing Street agreement, and balances the increase of the cash payment from 500 to 720 millions gold marks.)

(d) the guarantees decided upon by the Anglo-French Downing Street conference in December 1921 for the re-establishment of sound German governmental finance to be given by the German government. These guarantees included fixation of German customs duties on a gold basis, abolition of subsidies, adequate coal tax, railway and postal rates, effective prohibition of export of capital, limitation of note issue and grant of autonomy to the Reichsbank.

5. It appears also from the allied financial experts' memorandum that, subject to certain amendments, the Wiesbaden and August financial agreements are now likely to enter into operation and that, for the moment at any

[8] Of January 18 (C 909/99/18), not printed.
[9] Not printed. A draft English text of this memorandum is preserved at C 2044/99/18. For the final text, dated January 11, communicated to the Germans, see *Documents relatifs aux Réparations*, Tome Premier (Paris, Ministère des Affaires Etrangères, 1922), No. 20 (1).
[10] See Vol. XIX, No. 22.

rate, no more will be heard of the injury done to French rights by the latter or of the interference with Belgian priority involved by its acceptance in its amended form.

No. 2

Lord Hardinge[1] *(Paris) to the Marquess Curzon of Kedleston*
(Received January 21, 8.30 a.m.)
No. 35 Telegraphic: by bag [*C 990/99/18*]

PARIS, *January 20, 1922*

My immediately preceding telegram.[2]

Monsieur Poincaré's ministerial declaration was succeeded by interpellations of which a full report follows by despatch.[3] Socialist party expressed hostility to new régime, and demanded that an end should be made of the 'dogma of eternal war'. President of the Council made important statement in reply. He demanded the 'integral application' of the Treaty of Versailles: France's sacrifices must be rewarded by the payment of her just due. She was not rich enough to renounce it. Germany was responsible not only for the war but for her conduct of it. She must be punished and must make amends for her systematic destructions on French territory. He again criticized the system of Conferences which, he said, ought only to be the preparation for negotiations. The war criminals must be given up, otherwise Germany would expose herself to a prolongation of the occupation. The supervision of German finances required by the Reparations Commission must be efficacio[u]s. 'We will not sacrifice anything essential in order to obtain immediate advantages.' As for the Genoa Conference, 'we will not admit that the Treaty should be discussed ("mis en cause") at Genoa[4] in a Conference attended by Russia, who has nothing to do with the Treaty, and Germany, who signed it. This Conference has been summoned by Monsieur Bonomi.[5] I shall take steps to prevent Germany raising the question either of the revision of the Treaty or of reparations.' Monsieur Briand[6] here intervened to point out that this had been already decided at Cannes.[7] Monsieur Poincaré replied that he suspected Germany's intentions, and that France would oppose any German attempt to raise the question of the revision of the Treaty. Monsieur Briand retorted that the Allies had been agreed on this point and that, if Germany attempted anything of the kind, France would be entitled to withdraw from the Conference. Monsieur Poincaré went on to say that the French Government would demand precise engagements and sure guarantees in regard to the participation of Russia, who had been invited without being made to agree to conditions beforehand.

[1] H.M. Ambassador Extraordinary and Plenipotentiary at Paris.
[2] Of January 19, not printed.
[3] No. 192 of January 20 (W 684/50/17), not printed.   [4] See Vol. XIX, No. 34.
[5] Italian President of the Council and Minister of the Interior.
[6] See No. 1, n. 6.   [7] See Vol. XIX, No. 20.

3

The French Government would consider with their Allies the means of putting an end to the Greco–Turkish conflict.[8] 'I will resume the study of the Tangier question[9] with a view to a prompt and complete solution.' Turning to the Anglo-French pact,[10] he said that the French Cabinet were desirous of dissipating all divergences of views between the two countries, but that the situation between them must first be cleared up. The pact would be as valuable to England as it would be to France and Belgium. It was not a case of protector and protected; it was a case of friends vigilant in face of threats or dangers. There were not two Germanies. They must realize that there was only one Germany, who aimed at revenge. As was clearly proved by General Nollet's[11] reports, Germany had not disarmed either materially or morally. The Commissions of Control had discovered arms even in the factories which employed socialist workmen. To an enquiry from the Left as to why he had not insisted on the disarmament of Germany in 1918 when he was President of the Republic, Monsieur Poincaré replied that the armistice did not bear his signature. This statement was received with cries of 'Pontius Pilate!' from the Extreme Left. Monsieur Poincaré concluded his speech by expressing the conviction that the Allies, who had signed the Treaty, would understand France's attitude and would support her in seeing it carried out.

After a speech by Monsieur Herriot, the Socialist Radical deputy for the Rhone, and a discussion as to the relations of Marshal Pétain[12] with the Minister of War (both of which are reported by despatch),[3] a vote of confidence in the Government was passed by 434 votes to 84.

Monsieur Poincaré's ministerial declaration and subsequent speech are received with almost unanimous approval by the Press (with the exception of the Socialist newspapers). It seems to be felt that his firm and decided statements have upheld the national dignity of France. Particular interest is attached to his statement in his declaration regarding the postponement of the evacuation of German territory.

[8] See Vol. XVII.

[9] See *Survey of International Affairs, 1925*, vol. i (1927), p. 169, and Graham H. Stuart, *The International City of Tangier* (Stanford, 1955), pp. 56–77.

[10] See Vol. XIX, Nos. 1, 10 and 17.

[11] General Nollet was President of the Inter-Allied Military Commission of Control in Germany.

[12] Commander-in-Chief of the French army.

No. 3

Lord D'Abernon[1] (Berlin) to the Marquess Curzon of Kedleston
(Received January 28, 9.50 a.m.)
No. 17 Telegraphic [C 1328/99/18]

BERLIN, *January 27, 1922, 8.30 a.m.*

Following is summary of reply[2] of German government to reparation commission:

(A) Budget and note circulation reform.

Measures taken to increase taxation and reduce expenditure will balance budget. Direct taxes have been increased and new measures which will be passed shortly will increase German indirect taxation to level of foreign countries.

Extraordinary expenditure will be covered by loans in future.

Energetic measures have been taken against flight of capital and non-payment of taxation.

German government is endeavouring to make international arrangements for purpose of reaching German capital abroad.

From 1st April, 1922, expenditure on post and railways will be met by actual takings. Goods tariffs have been increased thirty-two times and post and telegraph tariffs twenty-one times as compared with 1914.

Subsidies for food will be abolished in course of financial year 1922.

Extraordinary civil service expenditure will be reduced to three milliard paper marks.

Two milliard gold marks in excess of exports.

German government is aware that following figures were considered at Cannes[3] for year 1922.

720 million gold marks and deliveries in kind to extent of 1150 [*sic*][4] million gold marks.

In spite of internal financial reform a large portion of these deliveries could only be effected by increasing floating debt and German government request that cash payments should be reduced, if necessary, by increasing deliveries in kind.

German government propose following programme for 1922:

Cash payments and deliveries in kind made in connection with 15th January and 15th February instalments should be credited against amounts due for 1922.

---

[1] H.M. Ambassador Extraordinary and Plenipotentiary at Berlin.

[2] This reply to the Note of the Reparation Commission of January 13 (see No. 1, n. 7) was dated January 28, 1922. The text is printed in Reparation Commission III, *Official Documents Relative to the amount of Payments to be effected by Germany under Reparations Account* (H.M.S.O., 1922), No. 12.

[3] See Vol. XIX, Nos. 7 and 12, and No. 22, n. 12.

[4] Cf. No. 1, para. 4b. The figure communicated (see No. 1, n. 9) to the Germans was 1450.

Remaining cash payments for year 1922 should be met by equal monthly payments.

German government request

(A) that cost of army of occupation paid in foreign currency shall be included in calculation of year 1922,

(B) that occupation costs paid in paper marks be reduced considerably,

(C) that other obligations which must be met in foreign currency especially clearing house payments[5] be reduced to a reasonable extent by special agreements.

Germany is prepared to conclude agreements similar to Wiesbaden[6] with all other allied governments.

As deliveries in kind by Germany require foreign raw material German government request that deliveries for each country should be separately fixed and limited to actual requirements for 1922.

German government is of opinion that settlement of reparation deliveries for 1922 is merely first step towards solution of reparation problem. General settlement can only be effected by credit operations on large scale. German government request reparation commission to re-establish trust of world in German credit at home which is indispensable for fulfilment of reparation obligations.[7]

[5] See Vol. XVI, No. 422, n. 6.   [6] See No. 1, n. 4.

[7] In a letter of January 27 to Sir B. Blackett (Controller of Finance at H.M. Treasury), Sir John Bradbury (Principal British Representative on the Reparation Commission) commented on the German reply as follows: 'The document generally strikes me as thoroughly disappointing. . . . I am pretty clear that either the German financial reform proposals are ludicrously insufficient, or the Cannes figures [see n. 3] belong to fairyland—or both. At any rate, it is obvious that the Germans do not believe the Cannes figures feasible and do not intend to make any serious effort to reach them. If, therefore, we embark on a policy of "guarantees" to secure the Cannes figures, we shall certainly have to try to impose on the German Government measures which they regard as impracticable, and shall find ourselves either without a German Government or with a large number of kettles of inedible fish on our hands. . . . Personally, I am more than ever convinced that Germany cannot get on to her financial legs without a period in which no cash shall be taken for reparation, and only very moderate deliveries in kind. The only other alternative is Reparation crises every six months.' In a further letter (January 31) to Sir B. Blackett, Sir John Bradbury stated: 'In my last letter about the German proposals I think I failed to do justice to the very serious efforts which [the Germans] express their intention of making towards the improvement of the budget position. Their undertakings in regard to railway and postal rates and the bread subsidy are indeed so drastic that I am disposed to doubt whether they do not go beyond what will prove to be practicable.

'Until the main annexes [not printed] have been translated (I hope to receive copies tonight) I do not feel able to express any definite opinion on the *tout ensemble*. There are many indefinite elements which will probably not be elucidated even by the annexes but on the whole my general impression is one of *bonne volonté*.' The annexes referred to were received in translation in the Foreign Office on February 1 (C 1524/99/18).

No. 4

Lord D'Abernon (Berlin) to the Marquess Curzon of Kedleston
(Received January 28, 9.30 p.m.)
No. 19 Telegraphic [C 1341/99/18]

BERLIN, *January 28, 1922, 7 p.m.*

In connection with German reply to reparations commission,[1] state secretaries Schroeder and Fischer make following observations which they desire to be regarded as confidential:—

1. Difficulty of arriving at a compromise between socialists on the one side and People's Party on the other was immense. Success was only achieved by intense personal pressure by Chancellor[2] and President[3] of the Republic.

2. German reply takes up all points but one contained in memorandum[4] handed by [allied] representatives to German delegation at Cannes.

Point omitted was that limiting note issues to amount not greater than December. Limitation suggested would have been of no benefit to anybody as December was a record issue.

3. Deliveries in kind amounting to [14]50 millions will inevitably lead to further increases of note issues in 1922. German government will not be able to avoid printing notes in order . . .[5] German producers of deliveries in kind.

German experts desire that there should be no misunderstanding or misapprehension on this point.

[1] See No. 3.   [2] Dr. Wirth.   [3] Herr Ebert.
[4] See No. 1.   [5] The text is here uncertain.

No. 5

Sir J. Bradbury (Reparation Commission) to Treasury
(Received in the Foreign Office, February 2)
[C 1580/99/18]

Copy

Confidential   PARIS, *January 31, 1922*

May it please your Lordships,

With reference to the decision of the Reparation Commission of the 13th instant,[1] upon the application of the German Government for a partial postponement of the instalments under the Schedule of Payments[2] falling due on the 15th instant and the 15th proximo and the letter from the commission of yesterday's date[3] on the same subject, I have the honour, on behalf of my colleagues and myself, to make the following observations:—

The members of the Reparation Commission desire respectfully to impress

[1] See No. 1, n. 7.
[2] Drawn up at the Fourth Conference of London in May, 1921 (see Vol. XV, No. 83, Appendix 2, and No. 86, n. 6).
[3] Not printed. A copy of this document is preserved at C 1524/99/18.

upon their respective Governments the importance of making at the outset a definite choice between the alternative procedures indicated by the commission.[4]

If for reasons of policy, of which the Allied Governments must be the judges, those Governments prefer to deal with the matter directly, retaining the ultimate decision in their own hands, we venture to express a hope that the commission will not be called upon to intervene in the matter until the Governments have taken their decision.

If, on the other hand, the Allied Governments should be of opinion that the proper course is to refer the question back to the commission, we trust that the full discretion given to that body by the treaty will be left unimpaired.

The commission can only hope to possess the authority necessary to deal effectively with the questions which come before it, if it retains the full responsibility for the decisions at which it may arrive.

Representations in an identic sense are being made by the other delegates on the commission to their respective Governments.

Copies of this report and of the letter from the commission of yesterday's date are being forwarded to His Majesty's Embassy.

I have, etc.,
JOHN BRADBURY

[4] In a letter to Sir B. Blackett of January 31 (see No. 3, n. 7), Sir John Bradbury stated: 'My own feeling is that it is better that the question should be dealt with by the Governments, if this can be arranged without a quarrel with France. If it cannot, we might perhaps be left to try our hands at it. We *may* be able (if it is left in our hands) to hammer out a temporary compromise. Failing this we shall either differ *coram publico* (which is probably a less objectionable way of beginning the quarrel than its initiation by the Governments) or shall secure formal unanimity by reporting Germany for default. In the latter alternative you will have secured a deferment of the crisis at the expense perhaps of some weakening of your strategic position.

'If Genoa is really coming off and you want to play for time, the reference to the R[eparation] C[ommission] may help you. But in any case I hope it will be a reference "to settle". In practice the question will inevitably come back to the Governments in one way or another if we fail to reach a settlement which is acceptable both to France and to Great Britain. But if we are asked to deal with the question subject to reference back to the Governments, we shall merely have an acid squabble about the attributes of the Commission and no results of any kind.'

No. 6

Memorandum by Mr. Wigram comparing the reparation proposals drafted by the financial experts at Cannes[1] and the German reply of January 2[8],[2] 1922

[C 1591/99/18]

FOREIGN OFFICE, February 1, 1922

Although no definite reparation settlement was reached at Cannes, the allied financial experts were in general agreement respecting (1) the method

[1] See No. 1, n. 9.   [2] See No. 3, n. 2.

of reducing the payments due, under the London ultimatum,[3] during the year 1922, and (2) the financial reforms which the German government ought to introduce in return for the partial moratorium implied by such reduction. It will be convenient to contrast a summary of the experts' proposals with a general summary of those contained in the German government's note of January 2[8]th, 1922.

2. Cannes proposals	German reply
A. *Financial reforms*	A. *Financial reforms*
The Cannes experts insisted upon the importance of:—	The German government insist upon:—
(a) The balancing of the German budget and the creation of a budget surplus by means of increased taxation and decreased expenditure. They instanced especially the necessity for placing the customs duties on a gold basis, for the raising of the internal price of coal, for increased railway, postal, telegraph and telephone rates, for the suppression of subsidies, for the covering of any budgetary deficit by the raising of internal loans.	(a) The efforts which they are making to balance their budget and to create a budget surplus. Direct taxation has been largely increased, though even the allied financial experts at Brussels in 1920[4] considered an increase in direct taxation difficult. When the new taxes are in operation, German indirect taxation will, it is alleged, be as heavy as any in Europe. Customs duties will be collected on a gold basis. The internal price of coal will be raised. (N.B. It is believed not as heavily as allied experts have considered possible.) Postal, railway and telegraph rates are being heavily increased. Subsidies are being abolished. Internal loans, in addition to a forced loan, are to be raised.
(b) Effective measures for the prohibition of the export of capital.	(b) Measures to prevent export of capital will be taken.
(c) The grant of autonomy to the Reichsbank and, pending the grant of such autonomy, the limitation of monthly uncovered paper issues to the December 1921 figure as a maximum.	(c) Autonomy will be granted to the Reichsbank. (N.B. No mention is made of limitation of uncovered paper issues though, in Lord D'Abernon's telegram No. 19,[5] it is pointed out that, the December 1921 issue being a record one, there would be no benefit to anyone in such limitation.)
(d) The publication of financial and trade statistics according to pre-war practi[c]e.	(d) Financial and trade statistics will be published in the pre-war manner.

[3] See Vol. XV, No. 87.

[4] This conference, held under the auspices of the League of Nations, met in September, 1920. The eighty-six delegates from thirty-nine countries were appointed as experts and not as spokesmen of official policy. See Hans Aufricht, *Guide to League of Nations Publications* (New York, 1951), pp. 218–19; see also Vol. XIX, No. 49, Appendix 1.

[5] No. 4.

B. *1922 payments*

(a) Cash payments equivalent to 720 millions gold marks (£36 millions gold).

(b) Payments in kind maximum value 1450 millions gold marks (£72½ millions gold).

(c) Recoverable costs of armies of occupation to be charged against deliveries in kind.

(d) Lump sum for those occupation costs payable by Germans in first instance to be fixed.

B. *1922 payments*

(a) Germany, being at present faced with an annual import surplus of some 2 milliards gold marks (£100 millions gold), can meet the deficit so caused in her trade balance only by the purchase of foreign exchange. Such purchase tends naturally to depress mark exchange, a tendency which is increased by every cash reparation payment and to a lesser extent by all deliveries in kind insofar as such deliveries necessitate corresponding import of raw material.

(b) A falling mark exchange implies increasing difficulty in revenue collection, increasing difficulty in balancing the budget with the inevitable consequence of further inflation, and a further fall in the mark exchange.

(c) The practical result of the execution of 1922 cash payments, and indeed to some extent of the deliveries in kind, recommended by Cannes experts, must therefore eventually be a fresh crisis in the mark exchange, a renewed reparation crisis and this time probably no reparation in 1923.

(d) The German government, without naming any definite figure, therefore ask for smaller cash payments and the limitation of deliveries in kind to the quantities actually to be used in 1922.

(e) Beyond (d) reparation is only possible as a result of international cooperation and after the successful negotiation of a foreign loan which, in the present state of affairs, is not forthcoming.

No. 7

Sir J. Bradbury (Reparation Commission) to Sir B. Blackett (Treasury)
(Received in the Foreign Office, February 9)

[C 1938/99/18]

Copy   PARIS, *February 7, 1922*

My dear Blackett,

I hear that the official suggestions of the French Government[1] as to the manner in which the 1922 Reparation payments should be dealt with were formulated last evening.

I am told that they are in the shape of a letter to 'the Chairman' of the Reparation Commission, of which a copy is being sent to the Allied Powers. This seems a curious procedure, since the obvious intention of our letter of the 30th ultimo[2] was that the Governments should agree amongst themselves and tell us their joint decision. It is probably intended as a diplomatic manœuvre, but, if so, it is a somewhat childish device, and I do not think that it will help the French or seriously inconvenience anyone else.

Dubois[3] has not communicated the letter to me or even told me he has received it. If it were really the official reply of the French Government to the Commission's letter of the 30th, he would of course be wrong in not doing so. But I gather that, notwithstanding its being addressed to the Chairman, it is in reality merely an explanation to the French Delegate of the point of view of his own Government.

If, however, as I gather, a copy has been sent to you, I should like to have it as soon as possible.

The communication, I understand, is to the effect that, in the opinion of the French Government, the amount of the direct payments by Germany in 1922 is a question of minor importance, but that steps should be taken to facilitate the early raising of a loan by Germany for Reparation purposes.

I hear from a confidential source that Poincaré has been urging Dubois to accept the Cannes figures,[4] but has encountered strenuous resistance. I had a long talk myself with Dubois yesterday and expressed my grave doubts as to the policy of having the matter referred back to the Commission unless there were a reasonable prospect of our being unanimous, emphasizing at the same time the improbability of unanimity either for figures higher than

---

[1] A Note of February 2 from the French Ambassador (Count de Saint-Aulaire) to Lord Curzon ran as follows: 'La Commission des Réparations a demandé aux Gouvernements Alliés s'ils entendent traiter eux-mêmes la question des réparations — telle qu'elle ressort du rapport déposé par le Gouvernement allemand pour l'année 1922 — ou s'ils préfèrent la lui renvoyer pour être résolue par elle.

'Le Gouvernement français est d'avis de répondre qu'il estime que le travail de préparation des échéances et des garanties à demander à l'Allemagne doit être envoyé à la Commission, seule qualifiée pour traiter ces questions avec l'Allemagne comme le veut le Traité de Paix. Il aimerait, toutefois, à connaître l'opinion du Gouvernement de Sa Majesté Britannique.'

[2] Not printed (see No. 5, n. 3).

[3] M. Louis Dubois, President of the Reparation Commission.   [4] See No. 6.

Cannes or guarantees involving direct interference in German administration.

Dubois' attitude was somewhat sphinx-like. I think that his discussion with Poincaré (which I gather was somewhat acrimonious) has for the moment hardened him. But I still think he will come to the Cannes figures in the end. We shall have even more trouble over the guarantees than the figures, and there I admit I do not see daylight. The German Government, if they are clever, will give us without much resistance those which are most likely to burn our fingers, and fight those which might be practicable and useful to us, some of which are politically difficult, as damaging to national self-respect.

We may therefore have a very awkward three-cornered battle.

Nevertheless, I remain on the whole of opinion that the question had better be left to the Commission on an open reference, provided that the Allied Governments first agree:—

(1) that the arrangements of the Cannes *projet*[5] as regards inter-Allied distribution are to stand whatever the decision of the Reparation Commission may be as to the amount

(2) that the Cannes proposals in regard to Armies of Occupation expenses in 1922 are adopted and the Reparation Commission is requested to give effect to them.

As regards (1), Belgium is not unlikely to want some safeguarding proviso to operate in the event of the Commission going below the Cannes figures.[6]

I have indicated this as the direction in which your minds are travelling—though of course without in any way committing you—both to Dubois and

[5] See No. 1, n. 9.

[6] In a memorandum of February 6 (enclosed in a letter of February 7 from Sir G. Grahame, H.M. Ambassador Extraordinary and Plenipotentiary at Brussels, to Sir E. Crowe, Permanent Under-Secretary of State for Foreign Affairs), Mr. Spring-Rice, First Secretary in H.M. Embassy at Brussels, reported as follows: 'M. Gutt (Chef de Cabinet of M. Theunis [Belgian President of the Council and Finance Minister], and his right-hand man for several years past) in the course of conversation yesterday evening made some remarks about the present position of the reparation problem which may be worth recording, as his views probably reflect or coincide with those of his chief.

'He is clearly not inclined to accept the Poincaré thesis that the solution of the problem, as now presented by the Cannes decision and the German answer, should be left to the sole discretion of the Reparation Commission. The latter could of course be asked by the Governments to deal with the German reply in the first instance, so that "the decencies might be observed" as regards strict adherence to the procedure laid down by the Treaty of Versailles; but ultimately the question must be referred back by the Commission to the Governments, since (a) the divergence between the Allies' requirements and the German offers was so wide, and the Reparation Commission could not reasonably be expected to "statuer" on so grave a political issue and (b) the question is now inextricably bound up with the revision of the August 13 agreement [see Vol. XV, No. 104, minute 2]—a matter which the Commission itself had referred to the Governments, the distribution of German payments among the Allies being outside its competence. M. Gutt thought one of the most unfortunate results of the premature breaking up of the Cannes Conference had been to put this revision (a matter of vital concern to Belgium) back two stages; all that had been achieved in this respect since last August was now back in the melting pot.'

Delacroix.[7] I have also told them that the Chancellor of the Exchequer[8] envisages the possibility of a preliminary conference of Finance Ministers if this is thought desirable.

Dubois indicated that de Lasteyrie[9] has by no means abandoned his intention of going to London. There is great activity in French reparation circles and I should not be surprised if he arrives with a comprehensive plan for the future, embodying the new 'credit operations' ideas.

Yours sincerely,
JOHN BRADBURY

[7] Belgian delegate to the Reparation Commission.   [8] Sir Robert Horne.
[9] French Minister of Finance.

No. 8

Sir J. Bradbury (Reparation Commission) to Sir B. Blackett (Treasury)
(Received in the Foreign Office, February 18)

[*C 2423/99/18*]

Copy   PARIS, *February 10, 1922*

My dear Blackett,

I hear from the Belgians that the French note[1] on the question whether the German request for postponement should be dealt with by the Governments or referred back to the Reparation Commission has not reached Brussels. On the other hand, Dubois understands from the French Foreign Office that Jaspar[2] has replied to it!

The truth appears to be, probably, that the French Ambassador at Brussels has had a conversation with Jaspar without handing him an official note and Jaspar has told him that the Belgian Government is favourable in principle to leaving the matter to the Commission provided that a preliminary agreement is reached between the Governments as to repartition (i.e. much on the lines we discussed in London).[3]

Dubois tells me that he gave de Lasteyrie, in conversation, the substance of the talk I had with him (which I reported to you in my letter of the 7th instant)[4] and that he (Dubois) thought that there would probably not be much difficulty in the French Government falling in with our views. This was an impression based on his conversation with de Lasteyrie but was subject to modification as Poincaré had not yet been consulted.

I think from some other remarks he made to me yesterday that Dubois now appreciates much more fully than he did a while ago the importance to France of securing a settlement of the Reparation question which will be acceptable also to Great Britain. I have some hopes, therefore, that if the responsibility of dealing with the matter is left to the Commission he may prove less intransigent than I previously feared. I am, however, still very

[1] See No. 7, n. 1.   [2] Belgian Foreign Minister.
[3] See Vol. XV, No. 105.   [4] No. 7.

nervous about this aspect of the matter, as Dubois' previous record and political associations make anything like a moderate line very difficult for him.

Yours sincerely,
JOHN BRADBURY

No. 9

The Marquess Curzon of Kedleston to the Belgian Ambassador[1]
[*C 2044/99/18*]

FOREIGN OFFICE, *February 15, 192*

Your Excellency,

With reference to your memorandum of February 2nd,[2] I have the honour to inform Your Excellency that the question of the procedure to be followed for the consideration of the German government's note of January 28th[3] a to the German reparation liabilities for the year 1922 has been carefully considered, with the result that His Majesty's Government, while they are disposed to believe that a preliminary discussion between the finance ministers of the powers represented on the Supreme Council would be useful as regards the whole of this question, and in particular in respect of certain matters arising thereon and requiring settlement, which are outside the competence of the Reparation Commission, are ready to accede to the proposal which has been made to them by the French government that these questions should be considered by the Reparation Commission. The consent of His Majesty's Government to this course is, however, conditional upon its being clearly understood that the distribution of the reparation receipts among the allied governments and the fixation for the future of the amount to be charged to Germany in respect of the armies of occupation shall be upon the footing contemplated by the Supreme Council at Cannes;[5] and that the financial agreement of August 13th, 1921,[6] shall be ratified forthwith, subject to the modifications required by the Cannes proposals.

2. For convenience of reference, a copy of the draft provisionally agreed upon at Cannes is enclosed.[7] The articles of this draft which, in the opinion of His Majesty's Government, should be regarded as finally settled and outside the competence of the Reparation Commission, are: article 8 (cost of occupation) article 15 (deliveries in kind)—subject to any modification in regard to the total value of deliveries to be demanded from Germany, which may be required in consequence of the decisions reached by the Reparation Commission; article 16 (inter-allied accounting for deliveries in kind for 1922); article 17 (coal); article 18 (allocation of receipts), subject to any modification in the figure of cash which may be necessitated by the judgment of the Reparation Commission; and article 19 (correction of clerical error in the Paris agreement).

[1] Baron L. A. G. Moncheur.   [2] Not preserved in the Foreign Office archives
[3] See No. 3, n. 2.   [4] See No. 7, n. 1.   [5] See No. 1
[6] See Vol. XV, No. 104.   [7] Not printed (see No. 1, n. 9)

3. In conveying to the French government[8] the views of His Majesty's Government as set out above I have at the same time communicated to them the following suggestion, which I desire to submit to the Belgian government also. At the same time as the agreement containing these clauses is signed, it seems desirable that a subsidiary agreement should be signed by all the powers entitled to reparation determining the reparation percentages to be allocated to Serbia,[9] Greece and Roumania. In order to make this possible, the French government have been reminded that it will be necessary for them to give their formal adherence to the percentage provisionally agreed to by Greece (i.e. 4%). I should be glad if you would draw the attention of your government to this proposal.[10]

4. A similar note[11] has been addressed to the Japanese and Italian Ambassadors at this Court.

I have etc.,
(for the Secretary of State)
S. P. WATERLOW[12]

[8] In a note of February 15 to the Count de Saint-Aulaire (C 2044/99/18), not printed.

[9] In a letter of February 23 to M. Gavrilovitch, Serb-Croat-Slovene Minister in London, Lord Curzon stated: 'With reference to your memorandum No. 43 of February 2nd [not printed], I have the honour to inform you that His Majesty's Government have no intention of departing from the terms of the agreement made [on June 20, 1921] between them, the Serb-Croat-Slovene government and the French government on the subject of the percentage of reparation receipts to be allotted to Serbia. This percentage, in common with the other percentages agreed upon at the Spa Conference [see Vol. VIII, Chap. VIII], will not come into force until the prior claim for Belgian priority has been satisfied. His Majesty's Government are however aware that in the meanwhile your government desire to obtain deliveries in kind to the fullest possible extent in order to assist in the reconstruction of the devastated regions of Serbia, and they will not fail to bear this in mind in the course of any further discussions as to the distribution of deliveries in kind to be made by Germany during 1922.'

[10] In Article 14 of the Financial Agreement of March 11, 1922 (see No. 11, below), it was stated: 'The Powers signatory to the present agreement will endeavour to secure the early adherence to this Agreement of the other Allied and Associated Powers concerned.' See also No. 15, nn. 4 and 5, below.   [11] Not printed.

[12] A senior member of the Central European Department of the Foreign Office.

No. 10

Lord D'Abernon (Berlin) to the Marquess Curzon of Kedleston
(Received March 16, 5.35 p.m.)
No. 78 Telegraphic [C 3928/99/18]

BERLIN, March 16, 1922, 5.20 p.m.

My telegram No. 75.[1]

I understand that Cabinet has had long discussion regarding financial position. Although majority were of opinion that after March 18th ten day

[1] Of March 16. This ran: 'Payment of 31 million gold marks due March 18th has been covered with greatest difficulty.

'It would be unwise to count on further payment under Cannes decision [see No. 1] as

payments could not be maintained, it was decided not to make any official communication on this subject to entente governments, or to reparations commission before March 20th or March 21st. It is anticipated that before then reparations commission will have come to some decision, and will have made a communication.

means to make required remittances are asserted not to exist. Further purchases of exchange under present conditions will, it is believed, cause heavy fall and create [financial panic].

'Committee of guarantees [see Vol. XV, No. 81, Appendix] will report situation fully to reparations commission and presumably German government will make an official communication. But I have thought it expedient to inform Your Lordship in advance of what is probably about to occur.'

No. 11

Record by Mr. Wigram of Conversation with Sir B. Blackett respecting Allied Finance Ministers' Meeting

[*C 3943/99/18*]

FOREIGN OFFICE, *March 16, 1922*

[1] Sir Basil Blackett gave me this morning the following observations on the recent allied finance ministers' meeting in Paris.[1]

2. Three matters were considered by this meeting:

(a) the distribution amongst the allies of certain reparation payments,
(b) the amount of the German reparation payments for 1922, and
(c) the general question of the eventual settlement of the methods of the payment of reparation after 1922.

3. The first question—the distribution amongst the allies of certain of the reparation payments—was brought to a satisfactory conclusion by the signature of the agreement, the text of which is in paper 2.[2] This agreement covered the question of the limitation of the costs of the armies of occupation to 220 millions of gold marks per annum; the distribution of this sum amongst the French, British and Belgian governments; the shares of the various allied governments in the deliveries in kind to be made by Germany; the acceptance by the allied governments, other than France, of the Wiesbaden agreement[3] and the recognition of the right of the allied governments, other than France, to conclude similar agreements; the method of distribution amongst the allied governments of the cash payments made to date by the German government, notably the 'first milliard'; certain minor matters arising out of the relation to Austrian, Hungarian and Bulgarian reparation of certain of the bonds to be issued by the German government under the schedule of payments.[4]

[1] The delegates to this meeting were Sir R. Horne (Great Britain), M. Theunis (Belgium), M. de Lasteyrie (France) and Signor Peano (Italy).

[2] Not printed. This agreement, signed on March 11, 1922, is published in Cmd. 1616 (1922).

[3] See No. 1, n. 4.

[4] See No. 5, n. 2.

4. As regards the amount of the 1922 payments to be made by Germany, each of the allied finance ministers took the opportunity to discuss this question with their representatives on the reparation commission. These representatives were given to understand that the reparation commission, to whom has now been referred the settlement of the amount of the 1922 payments, were not to fix a higher figure than that decided upon at Cannes.[5] The French government are, it is understood, afraid that they will have considerable difficulties with their representative on the reparation commission, M. Dubois, in this matter, but, in the event of his proving recalcitrant, he will be called upon to resign.

5. The third question considered by the allied finance ministers, that of the general settlement of the methods of paying reparation after the year 1922, was only discussed in a very general manner. The Italian delegation put forward a proposal which was based on a proposal put forward by Sir B. Blackett to the Chancellor in December last.[6] This proposal was to the effect that the German capital debt should be divided into two parts, and that the payment of one part, which would correspond to the amount of interallied indebtedness (viz. about 65 out of 130 milliards) would be indefinitely suspended and finally waived. There was a general discussion of this proposal but of course no decision of any kind was taken. The Italian delegation, however, proceeded to communicate a general résumé of the discussion on this point to the press, with the result, in Sir B. Blackett's opinion, that the American government are not likely to be particularly pleased, and that the whole position with regard to interallied indebtedness will not be improved.

6. The only other matter, which arose in the course of the recent discussions and which calls for comment here, is the American memorandum[7] in which the American rights to the repayment of the costs of their armies of occupation prior to May 1, 1921, were specially reserved. The American memorandum has been met by the inclusion of a special clause[8] in the finance ministers' agreement reserving the rights of the United States government. Apparently, in consideration of this clause, there is today in *The Times*[9] a statement from Washington to the effect that the United States government having 'established its case' does not intend at the moment to press any further for payment of the army costs. Sir B. Blackett, however, points out that the Washington statement, even though it may indeed emanate from the United States government, is a very incorrect one, for the allied governments have certainly *not* recognised the right of the United States 'to share in the German reparation payments'. All the allied governments have done is to safeguard the 'rights of the United States of America, whatever they may

---

[5] See No. 1.
[6] No other record of this proposal has been found in the Foreign Office archives.
[7] Of March 10 (see *F.R.U.S.* 1922, vol. ii, pp. 218–19).
[8] Article 13. This ran: 'The present agreement is made subject to any rights of the United States of America.'
[9] See *The Times*, March 16, p. 12.

prove to be' which is a very different thing. In these circumstances, Sir B. Blackett thinks it would be very useful to have an opinion from Sir Cecil Hurst[10] on the following point: 'What are the rights of the United States government under the treaty of Versailles to recover the costs of their army of occupation out of the payments collected from Germany by the reparation commission under the treaty?' Sir B. Blackett is inclined to think that the United States government, not being a party to the treaty of Versailles, can enjoy no rights under that treaty. He is inclined, however, to consider that, as a matter of equity, the United States, having, by the presence of their army of occupation in the Rhineland, assisted to recover from Germany the reparation payments to date, ought to be allowed to collect from Germany on their own account the expenses of their army of occupation up to May 1, 1921. In such circumstances, it would be necessary for the allied governments to waive their right to further reparation payments for the time being and until the United States had been reimbursed for their army costs. The allies should of course await definite representations from the United States gov[ernmen]t before taking action.

P.S. It is interesting to note that Sir B. Blackett considers the attitude of the French to have been less unreasonable during the recent discussions.[11]

[10] Legal Adviser to the Foreign Office.

[11] In his despatch No. 695 of March 18, Sir M. Cheetham (H.M. Minister at Paris) reported as follows: 'With regard to the [Financial Agreement of March 11], Monsieur de Lasteyrie stated [at a meeting of the Financial Committee of the Chamber on March 17] that, in the opinion of the French Government, Germany ought to float an international loan to be secured on tangible assets such as the products of mines, customs and railways etc. Monsieur de Lasteyrie is reported to have stated that while France had no intention of repudiating interallied debts, she was unable at present to pay them; and he was of opinion that some agreement on the subject should be reached among the Allies. He added that the Inter-Allied Financial Agreement of the 11th March would be submitted to the Chamber for ratification.'

No. 12

Lord D'Abernon (Berlin) to the Marquess Curzon of Kedleston
(Received March 24, 8.30 a.m.)
No. 82 Telegraphic [C 4374/99/18]

BERLIN, *March 23, 1922, 8 p.m.*

Note of reparations commission[1] has caused acute political and financial excitement. Exchange has fallen from 1,335 to 1,448.

Political crisis is not improbable. It is held that Wirth[2] and Rathenau[3]

[1] The reference is to two letters of March 21, one addressed to the German Government, the other to the Chancellor of the Reich. Both are printed in Cmd. 1634 (1922) (*Reparation: Decision of the Reparation Commission on the subject of Payments to be made by Germany in 1922*) and in Reparation Commission III, op. cit., pp. 113–21.

[2] See No. 4, n. 2.   [3] German Minister for Foreign Affairs.

cannot survive unless they take strongly negative attitude regarding several of reparations commission's demands.[4]

Resistance centres round demand for new taxation of 60 milliard marks. At a moment when government has only just succeeded in passing a taxation compromise which approximately doubled previous taxation, it is thought unreasonable and clumsy to demand 60% increase on top of 100% increase. Whether any government in any country would be strong enough to pass such a measure may be doubtful: it is practically certain that the present government cannot pass it here and that no alternative government will get necessary support for acceptance.

The first effect of reparations commission decision will be to break up coalition which supported fulfilment and which stood behind Wirth and Rathenau.

Peoples Party want to break away from taxation scheme which they had just accepted and Democrats are inclined to follow.

---

[4] These were summarised by Mr. Wigram in a memorandum of March 28 (C 5153/99/18) as follows: 'The reparation commission

(a) insisted upon the payment by the German government during the year 1922 of 720 million gold marks (£36 millions gold) in cash and of deliveries in kind to the value of 1450 million gold marks (£72·5 millions gold);

(b) demanded that the German government should

(i) by April 5, 1922, take the necessary legislative measures for the enactment of the financial reforms for which a date was fixed in the German note of January 28, 1922, e.g., notably 75% increase in price of bread, balancing of railway and posts revenue and expenditure,

(ii) by April 30, 1922, take the necessary legislative measures for the execution of the "taxation compromise" reached in the Reichstag on January 26, 1922.

(iii) by May 31, 1922, increase taxation by a further 60 milliards of paper marks,

(iv) by April 21, 1922, revise the expenditure as now contained in the draft 1922 budget,

(v) by April 30, 1922, issue an internal loan sufficient to cover any budgetary deficit,

(vi) by April 30, 1922, present to the reparation commission a scheme for preventing the export of capital,

(vii) by May 31, 1922, take the necessary legislative measures to ensure the independence of the Reichsbank,

(viii) by May 31, 1922, make the necessary arrangements for the publication of pre-war financial and economic statistics;

(c) informed the German government that full details respecting the execution of the measures taken in accordance with (b) above must at once be communicated to the reparation commission in order that the latter, through the committee of guarantees, should be in a position to control the state of execution of the above measures;

(d) warned the German government that the partial moratorium granted for the year 1922 was dependent upon the satisfactory execution of the measures outlined in (b) above, and that if on May 31, 1922, the reparation commission found that these measures had not been taken, the moratorium would be suspended, the London agreement would re-enter into force and payments thereunder would become due as from June 15, 1922. If the London payments were not forthcoming at that date (viz., June 15) the reparation commission would, under paragraph 17 of annex 2 to the reparation clauses of the treaty of Versailles, report the German government for default. The allied governments would then have the right to take "such measures as they determined to be necessary".'

Extreme Right claim to be the only party justified by event since they said from the first that only sound policy was to refuse fulfilment.

It would be unwise to take the first impressions too tragically as public here and (? still more) politicians are inclined to despair on inadequate grounds but outlook is unquestionably grave.

Repeated to Paris for the information of Lord Curzon.[5]

[5] Lord Curzon was attending the Paris Conversations on the Near Eastern question (see Vol. XVII, Chapter IV).

No. 13

Sir J. Bradbury (Reparation Commission) to the Treasury
(Received in the Foreign Office, April 5)

[C.P. 3916][1]

Copy

PARIS, *March 24, 1922*

May it please your Lordships,

I have the honour to invite your attention to the decision of the Reparation Commission of the 21st instant and the letter addressed to the German Government on the same date,[2] copies of which I have already transmitted to you,[3] on the subject of the payments to be made by Germany in 1922 and the conditions subject to which a provisional postponement of a part of the liability under the Schedule of Payments[4] has been granted.

Your Lordships will observe that the amounts prescribed both for cash payments and deliveries in kind are those which were the outcome of the deliberations of the Allied Governments at the Cannes Conference.[5]

Although by the recent decision of these Governments the question whether, and, if so, to what extent and subject to what conditions a postponement should be allowed was referred back to the Commission to be determined by it in virtue of its Treaty Powers, the effective discretion enjoyed by the Commission was, in fact, apparent rather than real.

The figures in question had not merely already been substantially agreed by the Allied Governments themselves as representing the minimum which they would be prepared to accept, but they had formed the subject of direct, if informal, negotiations between the representatives of some, at any rate, of the Allied Governments and those of the German Government.

The letter of the German Government of the 28th January[6] in reply to the Commission's demand for a programme of payments for 1922, though not accepting these figures, clearly contemplated the probability that they would

[1] This document (C.P. 3916) was printed for the Cabinet. A copy is preserved in the Foreign Office archives at C 5022/99/18.

[2] Not printed (see No. 12, n. 1).

[3] A copy of the Reparation Commission's letter of March 21 to the German Government was communicated to the Foreign Office by the Treasury on March 21.

[4] See No. 5, n. 2.   [5] See No. 1; see also Vol. XIX, Chap. I.

[6] See No. 3, n. 2.

be imposed by decision either of the Allied Governments or of the Commission, and offered no conclusive evidence that they represented a measure of performance of which Germany would be incapable.

In these circumstances it would have been difficult for the Commission, having regard to the terms of Article 234 of the Treaty of Versailles, to decide that a more extensive postponement was necessary, and almost impossible for us to refuse what had virtually already been offered by the creditor Powers.

The figures should not, however, be taken as representing the considered judgment of the Commission as to the economic capacity of Germany to make reparation in the year in question. Such a judgment, in the face of the present disorganisation of the German finances and exchanges, would be an impossible task, nor had the Commission under the Treaty the duty of attempting to discharge it.

The Treaty liability of Germany for 1922 is determined by the Schedule of Payments. The Commission was merely called upon to consider the degree of postponement necessitated by the facts disclosed in the application of the German Government. The decision must, in my view, be regarded as representing the minimum postponement consistent with the avoidance of an immediate breakdown, granted experimentally and without clear assurance that it will constitute a final settlement even for the period for which it aims at providing.

While, however, as I have indicated, there was no real question for the Commission to decide as to the figures, the conditions of the postponement constituted a more difficult problem.

The deliberations of the Cannes Conference were of great assistance to us as indicating broadly the views held by the Allied Governments, and it will be seen that our decisions follow very closely the general outlines sketched by the Cannes memorandum.[7] It was, as that memorandum indicated, a matter of common agreement that any concessions made to Germany should be conditional upon early and drastic steps being taken to remedy the budgeting and other financial abuses which if unchecked must rapidly undermine the whole economic fabric of the country, not only destroying the hope of exacting reparations in future but even endangering the social structure itself.

Although such reforms are obviously essential in the interests of Germany herself, there is a general consensus of opinion that German initiative alone cannot be relied upon in existing circumstances to bring them about. The memorandum clearly contemplated the imposition on Germany of a measure of supervision or even actual control by representatives of the Allied Powers.

On the other hand, it gave no very precise guidance as to the manner in which such control should be enforced, the intention being to invite proposals from the German Government before formulating a definite plan.

Such proposals were, in fact, asked for in the Commission's letter to the German Government of the 13th January,[6] but the response, as contained

[7] See No. 1, n. 7.

in the reply of the 26th idem [*sic*],[6] cannot be held to represent any substantial progress.

The Commission had therefore itself to formulate a plan.

Two distinct lines of procedure might be envisaged.

Under the one the responsibility of the German Government for the initiation of fiscal legislation, the regulation of Government expenditure and general administration would be left unimpaired, the Reparation Commission, as the agent of the Allied Powers, concerning itself primarily with the results to be achieved and the limits of time within which they must be obtained.

Under the other the German Government would be required to accept the directions of the Commission as to the taxes to be imposed, submit its estimates on expenditure for the approval of the Commission, both in gross and in detail, and carry on its administration under the supervision of controllers appointed by the Commission and invested with executive authority.

Under the former procedure the performance of the German Government would be judged entirely by the results achieved. The penalty for failure would be the withdrawal of the concessions granted, with the result that Germany would inevitably be placed in default in respect of her Treaty obligations and exposed to the coercive measures which the Allied Powers are entitled to adopt in that contingency—which, however disastrous in their results they may be to all parties concerned, are the only ultimate sanction for intractability.

Under the latter procedure, a large part, at any rate, of the responsibility for results would, where the directions of the Commission had been acted upon, devolve upon the Commission. If the directions of the Commission were ignored, recourse would have to be had to the same sanctions as those contemplated under the former procedure.

As to the choice between these alternatives, the Cannes memorandum, for the reasons I have indicated, gave no precise guidance. The arguments which can be advanced in favour and against each are familiar to your Lordships, and I do not propose to repeat them.

The Commission has, as will be seen from its decision, elected for the time being, at any rate, for the first.

The German Government, however, should cherish no delusions that if reasonably satisfactory results are not forthcoming without delay, we shall have any alternative but to refer the problem (which will then necessitate steps beyond our competence) to the Allied Governments or that it will then be possible for the Allied Governments to refrain from action which, apart from other grave consequences, cannot leave intact the fiscal autonomy of the German people.

Of the conditions imposed by the Commission, the one with which compliance will be most difficult is undoubtedly that for an immediate and drastic increase of German taxation. I am fully conscious of the considerations of internal politics involved, as well as of the real economic and social embarrassment which will necessarily be created.

The continuance, however, of the vicious practice of meeting a high percentage of the total Government expenditure by the creation of fictitious money during a period for which the Reparation burden is temporarily reduced for the very purpose of enabling a commencement to be made of serious financial reform would be a *reductio ad absurdum* of the moratorium policy.

Even if the additional taxation asked for by the Commission is imposed and all possible economies are made in the estimates of expenditure, the dimensions of the remaining deficit are likely materially to exceed the amount which a country with Germany's present internal and external credit can reasonably hope to raise by genuine loans, and there is no certitude that the general financial situation at the end of the moratorium period will not be worse than it is at present.

While I recognise the enforcement of such taxation as is proposed requires a high degree of courage on the part of the German Government and heavy sacrifices by the German people, I cannot resist the conclusion that either it must be forced or the Allied Governments must be prepared to receive substantially smaller reparation payments in 1922 than those at present contemplated, or the position in 1923 will be even more difficult to handle than that which now confronts us.[8]

I have, etc.,

JOHN BRADBURY

[8] Foreign Office minutes, which were initialled by Lord Curzon, ran as follows: 'It is all very well for the reparation commission to continue indefinitely their present policy, which so far as one can judge, is to keep on demanding the impossible, allow it to be proved impossible by force of circumstances and then to demand a little less, which in itself, by the time it is demanded is also impossible. But there is always the chance, of which we seem again to be in measurable distance now, that events will get out of hand, and that either the German government will be overthrown and something like chaos will ensue, or else that the German government will refuse the impossible, when the allied governments will be faced with the choice between military coercive measures and the "ottomanization" of Germany. It is unnecessary to add that any of these results would be disastrous, so far as our immediate interests are concerned.' (Mr. Wigram, March 28.)

'Sir J. Bradbury's guarded language scarcely veils his opinion that the present demands are impracticable. Meanwhile Lord D'Abernon [see Nos. 10 and 12] continues to play, to an audience whose attention is diverted to the more stimulating but more unreal problem of Russia, his rôle of Cassandra.' (Mr. Waterlow, March 28.)

'The most natural course to adopt would seem to be that the opportunity should be taken of the presence at Genoa of the Prime Minister [Mr. Lloyd George] and Sir R. Horne [see Vol. XIX, Chap. II] to sound the French *outside the Conference* as to whether the whole question of Germany's ability to pay should not be studied afresh. But it would be necessary to make it quite clear that there was no intention whatever of bringing the subject up formally at Genoa.' (Mr. Lampson, March 29.)

'I do not know how far such a procedure may prove practicable. It is evident that unless the reparation question is tackled afresh, there will be a crisis in Germany which the French may wish to utilize in order to resort to further "sanctions".' (Sir E. Crowe, March 29.)

No. 14

Lord Hardinge (Paris) to the Marquess Curzon of Kedleston
(Received March 31)
No. 801 [C 4756/99/18]

PARIS, *March 30, 192*

My Lord,

With reference to my despatch No. 800[1] of yesterday's date, I have the honour to inform Your Lordship that the debate on the budget of the devastated regions came to an end yesterday. A separate despatch[2] is being addressed to Your Lordship on the financial aspects of this debate.

Monsieur de Lasteyrie, Minister of Finance, closed the debate by stating that although a loan from Germany, supplemented by deliveries in kind, was most desirable in the interests of the devastated regions, he feared that very little would be extracted from Germany in the course of the year 1922, and that to meet the requirements of the moment it would be necessary to have recourse once again to an internal loan, much as he deprecated this solution. He hoped that it would be the last of such expedients, but in order to ensure this, it was essential that the problem of reparations should be settled. Germany must keep her engagements and pay. If she was not willing to pay, France would force her to be willing, and to be willing to establish order in her finances. The interested Governments would find means to take the necessary steps to this end once the Reparations Commission had given its verdict on the German reply to its last note. This statement was received with loud applause in the Senate.

As a further indication of the fact that French patience is coming to an

[1] This ran as follows: 'In the course of a long speech [in the French Senate on March 28] Monsieur François-Marsal, who was Minister for Finance in Monsieur Millerand's Cabinet, after attributing the blame for France's present financial difficulties to the terms of the Treaty of Versailles, suggested that it was unfortunate that the Allied Ministers in the agreement signed on March 11th last [see No. 11, n. 2], had undertaken that no reparations in kind received by the various allied countries should be re-exported. Monsieur Poincaré interrupted with the remark that this argument might have been valid before the Spa agreement, but was not so now. Monsieur François-Marsal, who Your Lordship will recollect was one of the French representatives at Spa, replied that he could defend the arrangements reached there, but only in a secret session. The Senate thereupon decided by a large majority to go into secret session.

'I understand that in the course of this session Monsieur Poincaré made a strong and almost violent attack on Monsieur Millerand [French President from September 1920] and incidentally on the part played by Great Britain at the Spa meeting. According to the "Action Française", Monsieur Poincaré is reported to have stated that the attitude taken up by Mr. Lloyd George in regard to the French demand for the occupation of the Ruhr was entirely wrong as under the treaty each allied power had the right to act alone in case of non-execution by Germany of the clauses of the treaty. It is currently reported in political circles here that the tension between Monsieur Poincaré and Monsieur Millerand has considerably increased of late and further developments are expected this afternoon in the event, as seems likely, of the Chamber of Deputies deciding to follow the example of the Senate and hold a secret session.'

[2] No. 852 of April 4 (W 3039/185/17), not printed.

end, I have the honour to report that in today's papers Monsieur Dubois, President of the Reparation Commission, is quoted as having stated yesterday in the course of a speech that if France, who was the greatest sufferer from the war, could not obtain from her Allies their consent to forcible measures, she was strong enough to act alone, even if it was necessary to have recourse to guns and bayonets.

'Pertinax'[3] in the 'Echo de Paris' urges that France made a mistake at Spa[4] in not occupying the Ruhr. For the future she must either obtain definite pledges from her Allies, or remain under the crushing burden of a gigantic debt. The Reparation Commission has fixed May 31 as the limit after which will come the time for action.

The above indicates, I think, accurately the general feeling as expressed in the press which bases its argument on the assumption that the Reparation Commission was set up to give legal justification for action against Germany as soon as the Commission has notified the Governments concerned of a final refusal by the Germans.

The 'Temps' tonight, in a leading article of which I enclose the text,[5] after accusing Herr Rathenau of being entirely under the influence of Lord D'Abernon, remarks that the figure of sixty milliards of marks and the guarantees to be exacted from Germany, were in reality the proposals of the British delegate on the Reparation Commission. It reminds its readers that Sir John Bradbury is also the author of a project for the institution of an international committee to examine the conditions under which an international loan could be floated on Germany's behalf. The guarantees for this loan would have to be essentially the same as those which the Reparation Commission demanded from the German Government; but, in face of the definite refusal of the German Government supported by the German people to agree to the demand of the Reparation Commission, who would be found to lend the money on so poor a security and to a debtor so unwilling to pay? In short, Herr Rathenau has 'torpedoed' Sir John Bradbury's project.

I have, etc.,

HARDINGE OF PENSHURST

[3] M. André Géraud.   [4] See Vol. VIII, Chap. VIII.   [5] Not printed.

No. 15

The Marquess Curzon of Kedleston to Sir R. Graham (Rome)[1]
No. 295 [C 4373/99/18]

FOREIGN OFFICE, *April 4, 1922*

Sir,
    With reference to my telegram No. 94 of March 24th,[2] I transmit to you herewith three copies of the English text of the financial agreement signed

[1] H.M. Ambassador Extraordinary and Plenipotentiary at Rome.
[2] Telegram No. 106 to Paris, No. 20 to Brussels, No. 94 to Rome, not printed.

by the allied finance ministers on March 11th, 1922, together with the covering note accompanying the agreement.[3]

2. In communicating a copy of this text to the government to which you are accredited, you should state that in accordance with article 14 thereof copies of the agreement have been communicated to the Greek, Polish, Portuguese, Roumanian, Jugo-Slav and Czecho-Slovakian Governments, and that these Governments have respectively been invited to adhere to the agreement at an early date.[4]

3. It will be observed that under article 1 (5) of the agreement it will be necessary for the Belgian, British and French governments before May 1st, 1922, to decide (1) upon the total of the sums in paper marks required to cover the cost of the services to be furnished by Germany under articles 8 to 12 of the arrangement of Versailles of 28th June, 1919, and (2) upon the method by which this total sum shall be divided between the three armies. I therefore request that Your Excellency will propose to the government to which you are accredited that the ambassadors' conference should be asked to appoint a committee of military and financial experts to report to the conference on the method of settling this question.[5] It will probably be desirable that certain members of the commission on the cost of the armies of occupation appointed in accordance with the decision of the Supreme Council of August 13th, 1921,[6] should be reappointed forthwith as a committee for this purpose.

4. Similar despatches have been addressed to His Majesty's representatives at Paris and Brussels.[7]

I am, etc.

(For the Secretary of State)

MILES W. LAMPSON[8]

[3] Not printed. See No. 11, n. 2.

[4] The Greek government adhered to the Agreement (despatch No. 314 of June 20 from Mr. Lindley, H.M. Representative to the Greek government). The Portuguese government refused to accept the Agreement unless the percentage allotted to Portugal at the Spa Conference (see Vol. VIII, Chap. VIII) was maintained (despatch No. 174 of May 20 from Sir L. Carnegie, H.M. Minister at Lisbon). The Czechoslovak government refused to agree outright to the Agreement (despatch No. 163 of July 7 from Sir G. Clerk, H.M. Minister at Prague). No reply had been received from Roumania by the end of 1922. For the attitude of the Jugo-Slav government, see No. 47, below. The request made in error to the Polish government was withdrawn.

[5] In his telegram No. 176 of May 12 to Lord Hardinge, Lord Curzon stated: 'Invitation to Italian government who are not really interested in committee was due to departmental oversight. In view of short time available it seems hardly possible now to invite Japanese and American representation on committee. We would therefore suggest that you should consult Sir J. Bradbury and act according to his views. Treasury concur.'

[6] See Vol. XV, No. 104, minute 2 (3) and Appendix 3.

[7] No. 965 to Paris, No. 225 to Brussels.

[8] Head of the Central Department of the Foreign Office.

No. 16

Memorandum respecting the French Budgetary Situation
[*C 5466/99/18*]

Confidential   FOREIGN OFFICE, *April 4, 1922*

The annexed statement[1] shows the figures of (1) the French ordinary budget, (2) the expenses recoverable under the Peace Treaty, and (3) the French extraordinary budget.

A review of the estimates of the amount of the French national debt will give an idea of the present poor state of French finances.

According to figures supplied by the French Government to the Finance Commission of the Senate, the national debt amounted on the 15th November last to 326 milliard francs inclusive of the external debt, calculated at the rate of exchange of the day. The Government's estimate may well err on the side of moderation on account of the uncertainty as to the precise amount of the floating debt. It has been increased by 104 milliard francs since the armistice, and the burden of the external debt has become much heavier on account of the depreciation of the franc during the period. It is considered that on the 31st December last year the debt amounted to 328 milliards.

It is estimated that the debt will reach the sum of 427 milliard francs, involving an annual charge in interest of 21,350,000,000 fr., a sum not far short of the whole expenditure of the State at the present time. This formidable sum is reached on the assumption that the present debt will be increased by 72 milliards on account of expenditure for the liberated regions at the rate of 9 milliards a year, 28 milliards for pensions, 4 milliards for the liquidation of the special accounts and 4 milliards in Treasury bonds. It is assumed, on the other hand, that 8 milliards are realised out of the 14 milliards which are owed to France by various foreign countries, the debts being calculated at par. It is also assumed that during the period under review Germany will pay 45 milliard francs. On these hypotheses the final estimate of 427 milliards allows a considerable margin, i.e., 32 milliards, for the payment of interest on the external debt, for extraordinary expenditure on public works and national defence and for meeting possible deficits in the ordinary budgets.

These estimates, even although they are challenged in some quarters as too pessimistic, have produced a considerable impression on public opinion.

The opinion prevalent in France in respect to reparation payments from Germany and the degree to which she relies on these payments for the restoration of the devastated areas can be clearly seen from a speech made by the Minister of Finance on the occasion of the passing of the 1922 budget of expenses recoverable under the Peace Treaties.

The Minister of Finance reviewed the general position as regards reparations, and observed that the problem, so far as it concerned France, might be summarised under three heads:—

1. In accepting the London schedule of payments,[2] France had agreed to

---

[1] Not printed.   [2] See No. 5, n. 2.

a sum which amounted to about one-third of that which she was entitled to demand from Germany under the Treaty of Versailles.

2. Up to the present time Germany had only paid the cost of the French armies of occupation, and not one single centime on account of reparations.

3. France had borne, from her own resources, the cost of the reconstruction of the liberated regions, and also of pensions and military allowances.

The total expenditure involved amounted to 80 milliards, namely, 45 milliards as compensation for damage to property, 29 milliards as compensation for damage to individuals, and 6 milliards for interest on the debts contracted under these two heads. It was because Germany had not carried out her undertakings that France had been obliged to incur this expenditure. If Germany, as she was bound to do under the treaty, had paid 20 milliards of gold marks on or before the 1st May, 1921, France would have received 5 or 6 milliards of gold marks, or a sum equivalent to from 15 to 18 milliard francs. Her situation would consequently have been very different from what it was now.

M. de Lasteyrie insisted that the question of reparations was to France a question of life and death, and that it was no less so for Belgium, which was faced with the same difficulties as France. Although Germany had made a considerable effort recently to balance her budget, it could not fairly be asserted that the German tax-payer supported a burden comparable to that of the tax-payer in France or in England. A considerable proportion of German revenue was applied to subsidise private persons, and this fact should be taken into account in any comparison of taxation. Moreover, it should not be forgotten, in any attempt to estimate the burden of taxation in France, that the devastated regions had not yet recovered their power to pay their share.

M. de Lasteyrie went on to say that the French Government, as had been emphasised in M. Poincaré's declaration on his assumption of office, were anxious that the Reparations Commission should exercise the functions which devolved on it under the Treaty of Versailles, and that the commission should be recognised as the only authority qualified to settle with Germany questions regarding reparations. He referred to the financial agreement of the 13th August[3] and to the agreements reached at Wiesbaden,[4] London[5] and Cannes,[6] and expressed the fear that, as regards these questions, there was a certain misunderstanding between France and England.

The Minister of Finance pointed out that the estimated receipts under the budget submitted to the Chamber amounted to 7 milliards, of which $4\frac{1}{2}$ milliards would be provided by German annuities and $2\frac{1}{2}$ milliards by the negotiation of German bonds. He considered that this estimate was extremely hazardous. In the first place, the figure of $4\frac{1}{2}$ milliards was probably much too high, as account should be taken of Belgian priority and of the

[3] See Vol. XV, No. 104.   [4] See No. 1, n. 4.
[5] See Vol. XV, No. 111, Appendix 3.   [6] See Vol. XIX, No. 25.

28

effect of the moratorium. It might be said that, although France would not receive the sum which she expected, yet she would be compensated by delivery in kind under the Wiesbaden Agreement. He observed, however, that the Wiesbaden Agreement had not yet been ratified by the Governments concerned, and, further, that the situation had changed since the agreement was concluded. At that time there was a considerable difference between German and French prices. Recently, however, these prices had tended to coincide, and he feared that the increase in German prices left an insufficient margin for the normal working of the agreement.

As regards the negotiation of German bonds, he drew attention to the loss which would inevitably be supported by the French taxpayer in order to negotiate these bonds in foreign countries.

He concluded that, to his extreme regret, the only means of meeting the expenditure involved in the budget of recoverable expenses would be to resort once more to loans. There were, in the first place, the loans of the Crédit national. The Government also contemplated the possibility of converting the amount of compensation due to persons who had suffered during the war into life annuities. Lastly, the Government would continue the issue of Treasury bonds or would have recourse to a loan. He admitted that this policy of borrowing was deplorable, but he saw no other solution of the problem except by compelling Germany to meet her undertakings and pay what she owed. He assured the House that the Government would make every effort to insist on the execution of the conditions of the Treaty of Peace and the disbursement of the sum arrived at under the schedule of payments.

No. 17

Lord D'Abernon (Berlin) to the Marquess Curzon of Kedleston
(Received April 18)

No. 294 [C 5584/99/18]

Confidential   BERLIN, *April 10, 1922*

My Lord,

I have the honour to transmit herewith to your Lordship the translation of a memorandum, which I have received unofficially from the Ministry of Finance. As your Lordship will observe, the memorandum purports to give in a concise form a review of the sums paid out by Germany in connection with the Peace Treaty since the signing of the armistice.

I have, etc.,
D'ABERNON

ENCLOSURE IN No. 17

Memorandum

(Translation)

In indirect and direct connection with the execution of the Peace Treaty in the period from the 10th November, 1918, until the 31st January, 1922, a total of about 93,180,000,000 M. had to be expended. This sum is composed of the following main items of expenditure:—

		Million Marks
1. Acquisition of foreign currency for reparation	. .	32,000
2. Payments in Clearing House transactions	. . .	5,900
3. Deliveries of seeds and cattle (*pœna*)	. . . .	4,112
4. Delivery of coal and coal by-products	. . . .	13,200
5. Delivery of dyes and pharmaceutical products, &c.	.	2,700
6. Handing over of army and war material. Transfer of airships	. . . .	1,140
7. Other deliveries to the Committee of Guarantees	. .	2,479
8. Compensation by the State for the surrender of mercantile marine ships	. . . .	1,947
9. Liquidation of Alsace-Lorraine matters, inclusive of compensation to the people of Alsace and Lorraine who have been expelled .	. . . .	1,672
10. Work by the railway administration in the execution of the Peace Treaty	. . . . . .	32
11. Costs of the Reparations Commission	. . . .	583·8
12. Costs of the Inter-Allied Commission in Upper Silesia	.	70·7
13. Costs of the Inter-Allied Commissions of Control	. .	411·3
14. Costs of occupation (inclusive of other cost incurred by the Treasury)	. . . .	9,394

Circulation of bank-notes, inclusive of 'Darlehnskassenscheine'—

On the 23rd October, 1918	. . . . .	25,571
On the 23rd January, 1922	. . . . .	119,901

Total of Treasury bills discounted by the State—

On the 31st October, 1918	. . . . .	48,200
On the 31st January, 1922	. . . . .	255,900

No. 18

Lord D'Abernon (Berlin) to the Marquess Curzon of Kedleston
(Received April 25, 8 p.m.)

No. 103 Telegraphic [C 6077/99/18]

BERLIN, *April 25, 1922, 6 p.m.*

Nothing is being done here by competent department to prepare answer to reparation commission's letter of April 13th.[1] It would seem unwise to

---

[1] Not printed. This was a reply to the German Chancellor's letter of April 7, not printed, in answer to the Reparation Commission's communication of March 21 (see No. 12, n. 1). Both letters are printed in Reparation Commission III, op. cit., vol. i, pp. 121–6. Copies of these communications (that of April 7 in translation) are preserved in the Foreign Office archives at C 5863/99/18. German answers (C 7367/99/18 and C 8325/99/18) to the Reparation Commission's letter of April 13 were given on May 9 and May 28 (Reparation Commission III, pp. 128–32).

delay negotiations with reparation commission too long. Hint to German delegation at Genoa might be opportune.[2]

² This telegram was repeated as No. 46 to the British Delegation at Genoa on April 27.

No. 19

Memorandum respecting British Central European Policy in its relation to Genoa[1]

[*C 6875/6200/18*]

FOREIGN OFFICE, *May 9, 1922*

I.—THE PRESENT REPARATION SITUATION AND THE THREAT OF INDEPENDENT ACTION BY FRANCE AFTER MAY 31

[1] The result of Cannes[2] was to impose on Germany, in substitution for the Schedule of Payments under the London Agreement of May 1921[3] (which experience had shown to be impracticable), a moderate schedule of monthly payments, totalling 720 million gold marks for the current year, in addition to deliveries in kind. But this was accompanied by a demand for the immediate imposition of further taxation to the amount of 60 milliard paper marks, in addition to the new taxes of more than 110 milliards just voted. The German Government have declared this to be impracticable, and the Reparation Commission have returned an unyielding reply.[4] Possibly this deadlock may be relaxed before the 31st May by the development of a scheme to provide Germany with a loan, which would put the reparation question on a new footing. This possibility is being explored at Genoa; and the Reparation Commission have appointed a committee[5] to investigate the conditions under which the German Government can raise loans abroad. Sir R. Kindersley is the British member of this committee, and American finance is represented by Mr. Pierpont Morgan. But it may be doubted whether the political conditions are very favourable to any such scheme, which would require for its ripening an atmosphere of leisure and security. Failing this or some other new development, the moderate Schedule of Payments will be automatically withdrawn again on the 31st May, and the London Agreement (fixed annuity of 2,000 million gold marks, payable quarterly, and variable annuity equivalent to 26 per cent. of the value of German exports) comes into force again. Germany will be formally declared to have defaulted as from that date.

2. Such are the circumstances in which M. Poincaré, in his speech at Bar-le-Duc on the 24th April,[6] said that the Allies will have the right and the duty to take for the protection of their interests measures that it would

¹ i.e. the Economic Conference at Genoa (see Vol. XIX, Chap. III).
² See Vol. XIX, No. 25.   ³ See No. 5, n. 2.   ⁴ See Nos. 3, 4, 6, 12 and 13.
⁵ The 'Loan' or 'Bankers' Committee was composed of M. Delacroix (Belgium), Signor d'Amelio (Italy), M. Sergent (France), Mr. J. P. Morgan (U.S.A.), Sir R. Kindersley (Great Britain), M. Vissering (Netherlands), and Herr Bergmann (Germany).
⁶ See Annex I.

undoubtedly be 'infinitely desirable' to adopt and to apply by common mutual agreement, but which, by the terms of the treaty, can, in case of need, be taken respectively by each of the nations interested, and which Germany is bound by the Treaty of Versailles not to consider as an act of hostilities. He added that, although earnestly desiring Allied co-operation, 'we shall defend in full independence the French cause'.

3. This declaration, although a subsequent speech[7] by the President of the Republic was evidently designed to tone it down, may be, and, indeed, has been, interpreted as meaning that, whatever the result of Allied consultation, France intends that coercive measures shall be applied to Germany in the event of Germany's being declared in default on the 31st May; jointly by the Allies, if possible, but, if not, by herself. There is evidence that the measures contemplated include the occupation of the Ruhr Basin, and that Belgium will participate in this operation. Evidently the question what our attitude should be, if the French Government commit themselves to a step of this moment, will be decided on broad political grounds rather than on points of law or precedent. The gravity of the present crisis is that it contains the germs of forces, fostered by the course of events at Genoa, that may easily impel France so to commit herself, and thereby presumably to make further British co-operation with her to enforce the reparation clauses of the treaty impossible.

4. This note is intended to suggest a policy which, if adopted in time, might perhaps counteract those forces. It appears that the Prime Minister wishes to conjure them by discussion at a meeting of the States signatory of the Treaty of Versailles; but it may be confidently expected that the French Government will, as they are perfectly entitled to do, prefer to leave the matter to the Reparation Commission, and to enter into no discussion until that body has reported after the 31st May. Certain considerations relevant to our case against France if, when that stage has been reached, she should still resort to independent action, are set out in the annex to this note; they relate to the legal basis of independent action, to our own previous record, and to the history of similar occasions in the past.

II.—The Apparent Failure of British Policy

5. The aim of British foreign policy since the armistice has been to reconcile and mediate. That we have been quicker than France to recognise economic facts and to work for the wiping out of the past is no credit to ourselves; we have not been invaded, and the longer Europe continues in a state of economic nightmare, dominated by the fluctuations of fear and revenge, the more our business suffers. The powers of the Reparation Commission are such that economic reconstruction is theoretically possible within the four corners of the Treaty of Versailles, and our whole effort has accordingly been to apply the treaty in a spirit at once just and reasonable—to

[7] This is a reference to M. Millerand's speech of April 26 at Philippeville, a summary of which was transmitted to the Foreign Office in Paris telegram No. 239 of April 27, not printed.

permit that economic recovery of Germany which is a necessity for ourselves, and at the same time to secure the disarmament which is equally a necessity if French fears are to be allayed. The radical difference between our point of view and that of France, to say nothing of our respective national histories, traditions and methods, is such that in any case this task must have been one of extreme difficulty, calling not only for much patience (which has been abundantly displayed), but for the highest political sagacity in the adaptation of means to ends. The series of difficulties that have been overcome, or postponed, or glossed over need not be enumerated; the Genoa Conference was designed to resolve them all. It was to be our crowning effort, the culmination of the policy by which we have striven to turn the Versailles settlement into a real peace. It is significant that its opening stages should have coincided with the occurrence of two events which, taken together— and their simultaneous occurrence is not fortuitous—are the direct negation of our whole post-armistice policy, if, indeed, they do not threaten its complete collapse. These events are the reparation deadlock and the conclusion of the separate Russo-German Agreement.[8]

6. Consequently, M. Poincaré's speech, with its hint of independent action and its conclusion that France must set her face against any further concessions to Germany and Russia, provokes in ourselves an instinctive and quite justifiable reaction. It is intolerable that the intransigence of one Power, whose military strength dominates the Continent, and whose aerial and submarine projects are a potential threat to ourselves, should frustrate our efforts to bring Russia back into the economic orbit of Europe, to restore the general, commercial and financial conditions that are vital to the British Empire, and to avoid any return to the European group system that provided the conditions of the last war. It is especially intolerable at the moment when all the threads of our policy converge upon a conference which must do something to promote these ends, on pain of making them more difficult of attainment than ever. For if the result of Genoa is to confirm France in her refusal to treat Germany and Russia other than as pariahs, then sooner or later, we feel, those two great populations will be cemented into a union of hostility to Western Europe. In particular, the repeated postponement of a practical reparation settlement, for which French policy is responsible, although all reasonable people now understand the necessity for such a settlement, can only make Germany turn reluctantly but despairingly eastwards—a process of which the Easter Treaty[8] stands as a symbol and a warning, and which the independent action threatened after the 31st May is likely to complete. The contrast between this prospect and what Genoa was intended by us to do is striking; instead of the international economic co-operation that British opinion demands, a grouping of opposed Powers that may well 'turn Europe into a shambles' once more. Has not the moment come to make it clear that France must choose between this picture and that? And that, if she chooses the second, this country must refuse further responsibility and must dissolve a partnership productive of no results, but

[8] The Treaty of Rapallo, signed on April 16, 1922 (see Vol. XIX, No. 75, n. 1).

such as are repugnant to British instincts? To judge from the Prime Minister's utterances, His Majesty's Government are asking themselves these questions, while trying to save the situation by pushing forward an international agreement to renounce aggression.

7. A general non-aggression agreement, whatever its usefulness, cannot, however, alter the fundamental facts from which the present situation has arisen. Nor is it enough merely to react, however justifiably, against the influences that thwart us. To denounce France as a wrecker, to cut loose from her, to leave her to act alone, to her own eventual damage (so we believe) as well as to that of Europe and ourselves, and incidentally to make trouble for us throughout the Mahommedan world—this is not a policy. For the moment our post-armistice policy of reconciliation and mediation seems to have failed, and there is a real danger that it will produce results precisely the opposite of those we intended. But that fact is no reason for abandoning it in favour of no policy at all; on the contrary it should stimulate us to enquire, first, whether the failure may not be due to mistakes rather of method than of conception, and, secondly, whether, if so, it may not be possible to change our methods before it is too late. But before approaching this two-fold enquiry it will be desirable first to bring out a point which is perhaps not always fully appreciated—namely that, if we leave France to act against Germany alone, and thereby in effect dissolve the Alliance, there will be little moral prestige to be got from our attitude of detachment. Possibly to a certain extent American feeling would support us; but even here there would be cross-currents, and it is certain that an Anglo-French breach would end all hope of practical American help in European reconstruction.

III.—Objections to a Breach with France

8. Our case against France seems overwhelming. If an agreed peace with Turkey, and consequently a settlement of the Middle Eastern regions, is not in sight, the fault is hers.[9] If the Moroccan question and the long-standing difficulty of Tangier[10] are as far from settlement as ever, the cause is her treachery and duplicity. The periphery of French policy would afford other illustrations of the way in which disturbance is propagated wherever British interests require tranquillity; they need not be enumerated here, since the clash proceeds from a single central point. That point is Germany. If the clash could be resolved as regards Germany, the settlement would radiate outwards through Europe to the periphery; but to concentrate our energies on outlying problems, even on one of such importance as the Russian problem, while leaving the central difficulty to settle itself, is to court disaster. A breach with France, if it comes, may be ostensibly on Russia; it will really be on Germany. For it is here that French and British policies are most deeply and vitally opposed. Our need for the security of sea communications implies instinctive opposition to any Power erecting a hegemony of force in Europe. Our need to trade implies a prosperous Germany. A prosperous

[9] See Vol. XVII.   [10] See No. 2, n. 9.

Germany implies, in its turn, a politically stable and independent Germany; which means, in plain language, the early development of a German Government based on the genuine play of internal German forces, and not, as all German Governments have hitherto been based, on the question of compliance or non-compliance with the reparation and military demands of the Entente. The creation of such a Government in Germany is, in a word, the essential and central requirement of British policy, the first condition to which our national recovery is subject. To pursue anything else in Europe, except as means to this end, is to pursue a mirage. Now it is precisely to the attainment of this end that French opinion, even moderate and reasonable opinion, is deeply opposed. The grounds of its opposition are twofold. France must have security against the war of revenge that Germany will undoubtedly organise, if she can do so with any prospect of success; and she must have immediate financial relief to save her national finances from bankruptcy. These two demands, which are as vital and deep as ours, combine to solidify French opinion at each recurrent crisis against the political and economic recovery of Germany, which British opinion on the whole is now prepared to welcome. We may think that the result is to make France's own demands incapable of fulfilment; but that does not alter their profound and permanent character, and to recognise that character clearly is to doubt whether the case for a breach with France is really so overwhelming as it seems. It might be justified on grounds of expediency, if the solution of the German problem, which is our central problem, would be promoted by a breach. It might be justified on grounds of morality, if our political conscience were perfectly clear. Under either head qualms are permissible. Unrestrained, France's power to perpetuate disturbance would be much enhanced; nor is there reason to believe it would not be exercised, for Russo-German rapprochement, combined with British aloofness, would give every French military chauvinist the appearance of reason, and would transform every French moderate into a militarist. And the case against ourselves would be automatically strengthened by the emergence of certain blots which, like the chemical changes in an exposed photographic plate, are only awaiting the application of the appropriate acid to become visible. The two following paragraphs deal with these blots.

9. In the first place, we are as much, or even more responsible than France for imposing on Germany a reparation burden now generally admitted to be far beyond her capacity to pay. The requirement that Germany should pay the Allied war pensions, in addition to making good the direct damage caused by the war, was due not to French but to British action at Paris in 1919. It was General Smuts, it will be remembered, who succeeded in persuading President Wilson that this claim was no contravention of the terms upon which Germany signed the armistice.[11] We may deplore the deafness of France to our preaching of sound economics; we may be convinced that she is frustrating herself when she thinks to retrieve her own bankruptcy

[11] See H. W. V. Temperley (ed.), *A History of the Peace Conference of Paris* (London, 1920–4), vol. ii, p. 14 and p. 45, n. 1.

by extorting forcibly from bankrupt Germany wealth that from the nature of things cannot be forcibly transferred across a frontier; but it remains the fact that we solemnly put our hand to a bond which, but for ourselves, would have been less onerous. Our motive was of course that, having no devastated regions, we required the pensions to swell an indemnity which otherwise might have disappointed the constituencies. The practical result, since the total is fantastic, is to make it more difficult for France to be paid her direct damages than it might otherwise have been. Thus, if we desert France now, it will be for causes partly attributable to what will be represented as British greed.

10. That will be sufficiently unpleasant; but there is more. If France does not feel secure, we are ourselves partly responsible. The Guarantee Agreement, signed at Versailles in 1919[12] as part of the general peace settlement, was not open to the objection commonly and forcibly urged against a comprehensive alliance with France. It could not have drawn us into a war in which direct British interests might not have been involved (e.g., for the defence of Poland), or which might have been avoided had not our ally been encouraged by the alliance to adopt an unbending attitude. Its operation was conditional upon the single contingency of an unprovoked movement of aggression by Germany; and it was placed under the ægis of the League of Nations as consistent with the Covenant. A similar agreement was signed at the same time between France and America, and each was made contingent upon the operation of the other. The tripartite arrangement thus reached was the inducement which persuaded France to give up the claim to the Rhine frontier; only by this solution was one of the more serious crises of the Peace Conference resolved. When the United States failed to ratify the Treaty of Versailles, and consequently the Guarantee Agreement also, the arrangement automatically fell to the ground so far as we were concerned. It seems probable that, had our agreement not thus proved abortive, we might not have been struggling today against a psychological background that makes it as difficult for France to return to sanity as the conflexes of a neurotic introvert make it for him to enjoy normal health. Fear of German revenge and self-absorption in her own wounds are the main features of that background. It can hardly be doubted now that a generous gesture at the time would have paid us a hundred times over; and that, had we said 'America, for her own good reasons, has not come in; we nevertheless intend to go beyond the letter and to maintain our agreement,' Parliament would have endorsed that action. The effect in France would have been electrical. As it is, the argument that M. Clemenceau was led, as regards the safety of France on her eastern flank, into a characteristic British trap, is one which, even if it is not expressly formulated (for even the French have their generous reticencies), lies not far below the level of the French consciousness. To confute it by any reply that will not seem coldly technical and verbal is not easy. Whether it is too late to confute it by an act will be discussed below.

11. It may be said that we have already retrieved this point by offering to

[12] See Temperley, op. cit., vol. iii, pp. 337–8.

conclude a pact of guarantee with M. Briand at Cannes in January,[13] and that the continued postponement of this proposal has been due to no fault of our own. To some extent this is true, although it may be doubted whether the offer was made in the right way or the right spirit. In any case, nothing practical has been done to meet the French demand for some assurance that some day she will not have to meet Germany alone. This fact, coupled with the fact that we are in some measure responsible for the excessive size of the Reparation Bill, makes our moral position, in the event of our being obliged to break with France, not as strong as might be wished. We may denounce France as the wrecker; but all that we say will be infected by this subtle poison, and the force of public and parliamentary opinion, on which the breach must rest, will be proportionately sapped. It is therefore doubly desirable to examine afresh the possibility of avoiding a breach.

IV.—Have our Methods been Wrong?

12. The first step is to ask whether mistakes of method have not been partly responsible for the failure to attain our ends. This can never be proved; whatever our methods, we were bound to be handicapped by the two points just discussed, and it is possible that no methods would have produced better results. But, if it can be shown that we have consistently misused or neglected the machinery that might have secured what we want, a presumption will be created that we might do better if we changed our methods.

13. The Treaty of Versailles created two new and unprecedented international bodies—the League of Nations and the Reparation Commission—on the operation of which it was manifest from the beginning that the fortunes of Europe would, for good or for evil, largely depend. The following observations are designed to suggest that an important reason why our policy has not produced its full fruit is to be sought in our failure to make the best use of the machinery provided by these bodies. The Reparation Commission will be briefly dealt with first.

14. On the use made by the French Government of the Reparation Commission it is unnecessary to dwell in detail. While maintaining, whenever it suited their purpose to do so, that the commission was an independent and judicial body, the French Government have in practice always seen to it that their representative should accept their views, and, as far as possible, impose them upon his colleagues. Had the commission really been an independent body, the task of nursing European finance back to convalescence might safely have been left to it; it would have fixed the total of Germany's indebtedness at the present relatively moderate figure, but much earlier, thereby facilitating credit operations; and, the total once fixed, its power under article 34 to postpone (but not to cancel) payments would have given elasticity enough for the purpose. But the independence was, of course, a fiction, except, perhaps, so far as we were concerned; it is childish to imagine that a body of this importance will not act as an organ of the Governments, if only because its actions must, unless it is superseded by the Governments at every

[13] See Vol. XIX, No. 1.

moment, have far-reaching political effects. In these circumstances, there were two possible lines of action that we might have followed. The critical period began with the fixation of Germany's total indebtedness a year ago.[14] We might at that moment have made up our minds that the commission was henceforth to be treated as a cypher, as a convenient façade behind which, while it was busy with the unrealities of the reparation chapter of the treaty, the Governments were arranging a real settlement; or, we might have tried systematically to use it as the instrument through which to translate into practice our conception of a real settlement. Of these two policies, while the French Government have on the whole used the commission as the instrument to enforce *their* idea of a real settlement, we have on the whole inclined to the former, but not wholeheartedly, with the result that we have fallen between two stools. Logically, the position assigned to the British delegate, responsible to the Treasury alone, although the only real importance of the Reparation Commission is political, is all in the direction of treating the commission as a cypher. But, if that was to be the arrangement, the logical corollary was that the Foreign Office should be responsible for policy at every stage of the commission's work, whereas in fact questions of policy, as well as of detail, have been deliberately left to Sir J. Bradbury and to the Treasury. The result has been the maximum of friction with the French, who at each successive crisis have had reluctantly to accept the substitution of the Supreme Council for the Reparation Commission, combined with the minimum of power to secure due weight for the British point of view in the working of the commission. It seems likely that the future historian will attribute the failure of British policy in no small degree to this circumstance; he will in any case be amazed at the departmental incoherence which was permitted, nay, which was encouraged, to produce this result in a matter of such moment. He will ask why the British representative was not a man of ripe political experience, versed in negotiations with foreign Governments, and endowed with those qualities of the British character which seldom fail to influence the French mind; he will enquire why it was supposed necessary that he should be a financial expert and no more; and he will find no intelligible answer.

15. While our policy as regards the Reparation Commission has been to treat it as a cypher, without following up the logical consequences of that attitude, our policy as regards the League of Nations has been similar, but more consistent. Except on paper, and as an expedient for minor purposes or an escape from some dilemma, we have not taken the League seriously. The French Government, who at first would not have been reluctant to kill the League, were not slow to take advantage of this fact, and to use it, as they have used the Reparation Commission, as an instrument for the promotion of French policy. There would have been nothing improper in our competing with them in this respect, and in our using the machinery of the League to push British policy, because the objects of British policy happen, broadly speaking, to be genuinely identical with those of the League.

[14] At the Fourth London Conference, April 30–May 5, 1921 (see Vol. XV, Chap. IV).

16. It may be objected that we have in point of fact, whenever suitable occasions arose, encouraged resort to the machinery of the League, as in the cases of the Aland Islands,[15] Vilna,[16] Albania[17] and Silesia[18] (to mention only European cases); that it was not in our power to do more than this; and that this is more than the French Government have done. But these very examples illustrate the contention that we might have done more than this, and might still do more. In the cases of Albania and the Aland Islands reference to the League was obvious and easy; they were minor matters, not directly involving British interests or any central problem of European policy. It is otherwise with the cases of Vilna and Silesia. The League has so far failed to solve the Vilna question, precisely because a major problem of policy is involved; nor have we put ourselves in a position to contribute to its solution through the League machinery. The case of Silesia is especially instructive. Here what was really at issue was the fundamental clash between French and British policy that forms the subject of this note, and here it was possible to reach a solution with the help of the League—not wholly satisfactory perhaps, but still a solution—because we did not wish to break with France on this question, and because we took the initiative in remitting it to the League. But this was done on no system and with no premeditation; it was a decision spontaneously and suddenly taken by the Prime Minister, as an escape from an *impasse*, at Paris in the night of the 10th August, 1921. What is required is machinery for doing systematically what was done haphazard[ly] in the single case of Silesia—namely to obtain, through the machinery of the League, the settlement of questions that have baffled not merely the Ambassadors' Conference, but the Supreme Council. If we were seriously to apply ourselves to using the League for this purpose, and to increasing its power and prestige, it is reasonable to suppose that we could secure a settlement of these major questions, and in a sense more satisfactory to our interests than was the Silesia settlement.

17. Detailed suggestions for such machinery cannot be made here. All that can be pointed out is that it is not enough for His Majesty's Government to be represented on the Council of the League by any Minister, however eminent, who is not directly responsible for the conduct of British policy. Unless the British representative is the Prime Minister or the Secretary of State for Foreign Affairs the League must remain an anæmic body, so far as the promotion of British policy, and consequently of European peace, is concerned. On the other hand, the British section of the League, actively directed by the Cabinet through the Foreign Office as the most important wheel in the machinery by which foreign affairs are conducted, would afford an instrument more likely to attain success than our present methods. It would bring into play a whole new set of opportunities for shepherding French public opinion and French Governments along the path of reason.

[15] See Vol. XI, Nos. 250 and 296.   [16] See ibid., Nos. 189 and 526.
[17] See *Survey of International Affairs 1920–1923*, p. 345.
[18] See Vol. XV, No. 102, minutes 1 and [6] and appendix, and Vol. XVI, Nos. 296–347 *passim*.

Into the scope of such a policy the Franco-German problem, which is the real centre of disturbance, could be gradually drawn. Such a policy would be more likely to settle that problem than our present methods, for at the moments of tension it would have behind it a united force of opinion both here and abroad to which in the long run France would be bound to yield genuine compliance. A breach with France must in present circumstances, as this note has tried to show, have a dubious moral basis, and consequently a division of British opinion behind it. But a breach, should a breach be necessary, would command the support of the whole country, if it were to come as the result of energetic action on our part through the League of Nations, the prerequisite of which is departmental organisation in London. That America has recoiled from the covenant, and especially from article 10, is not a valid objection. The present suggestion presupposes a real development of the League and its activities on lines which, by contributing to European reconciliation and reconstruction, would be more than anything else calculated sooner or later to enlist American co-operation in some practical form.

18. The best way of initiating this policy would be to combine it with a renewed offer of the defensive pact to France, to which should be coupled an offer to write down our reparation claim against Germany, and perhaps a prospective reduction of France's debt to us, against a reasonable settlement of the whole reparation problem. To postpone a settlement with France on these lines until such questions as those of Russia, Tangier and the Near East have been settled is to put the cart before the horse; no progress is possible on that method, whereas if we settle the central question we may in time find things easier at the periphery, and shall certainly find them no worse. It would not be difficult to frame detailed proposals if this general line of policy were approved. Politically, they would take the form of a complex of agreements centring round the Franco-British pact, with the adhesion of Belgium and Italy, and eventually of Germany, the whole under the special charge of the League of Nations. Financially, there should be no difficulty, so far as British public opinion is concerned, in remitting the whole question of inter-Allied debts to the League, subject to suitable precautions to safeguard American susceptibilities. The League again, if properly nourished by us under these conditions, could deal with the question of an international loan for Germany. But for all this, systematic diplomatic preparation between His Majesty's Government and the French Government is necessary. It may be doubted whether faulty methods have not gone too far, and whether the time at our disposal is sufficient.

Annex

Our Position as regards Independent Action

The relevant paragraph of M. Poincaré's speech at Bar-le-Duc, as published in the 'Temps' of the 25th April, reads as follows:—

'Si l'Allemagne résiste, et si, à l'heure fixée, la commission constate un manquement volontaire, les Alliés auront le droit, et par conséquent le devoir, de prendre pour protéger leurs intérêts des mesures qu'il serait, sans aucun doute, infiniment désirable d'adopter et d'appliquer d'un commun accord entre eux, mais qui, aux termes du traité, peuvent, en cas de besoin, être prises respectivement par chacune des nations intéressées, et que l'Allemagne s'est obligée, par le Traité de Versailles, à ne pas considérer comme des actes d'hostilité. Nous souhaitons ardemment de maintenir, en cette occasion capitale, le concours de tous les Alliés, mais nous défendrons, en pleine indépendance, la cause française et nous ne laisserons tomber aucune des armes que nous a données le traité. Nous ne souffrirons pas que notre malheureux pays succombe sous le poids des réparations, aux côtés d'une Allemagne qui ne consentirait pas à faire l'effort nécessaire pour se libérer de sa dette.'

2. The claim, which these words contain, that the Treaty of Versailles gives France, in case of need, the right to take independent action against Germany rests entirely on the word 'respective' in the second of the two following paragraphs:—

Annex II to Part VIII (Reparation), Paragraphs 17 and 18.
(17.)

'In case of default by Germany in the performance of any obligation under this part of the present treaty, the [Reparation] Commission will forthwith give notice of such default to each of the interested Powers and may make such recommendations as to the action to be taken in consequence of such default as it may think necessary.'

(18.)

'The measures which the Allied and Associated Powers shall have the right to take, in case of voluntary default by Germany, and which Germany agrees not to regard as acts of war, may include economic and financial prohibitions and reprisals, and in general such other measures as the respective Governments may determine to be necessary in the circumstances.'

3. At first sight, it looks as if this passage of the treaty must be interpreted as making it possible for one of the Allied Powers to determine itself what action is necessary, and to take it, whatever the nature of the action contemplated. It will be noted that the word 'respective' is used only in the sentence now in question. In paragraph 17 notice of default is to be given to 'each of the interested Powers'; paragraph 18 begins, 'The measures which the Allied and Associated Powers shall have the right to take'; and then at the end we have the phrase, 'such other measures as the respective Governments may determine to be necessary'. Some meaning must be given to the word 'respective,' and the only meaning seems to be that each Government can determine for itself. If this were not the intention, one would have expected some phrase like 'the Governments of the said Powers may determine,' which would have suggested that they were to determine in common.

4. Moreover, it may be said that it is unnecessary to labour the point, because this interpretation has in fact been adopted (albeit in a different context) by His Majesty's Government themselves, and used in a discussion with the French Government.

5. In October 1920 British shipping and banking interests made strong representations as to the detrimental effects of paragraph 18 of Annex II. It appeared that apprehensions that German post-war deposits and goods in the United Kingdom would, in the event of Germany's default, be liable to seizure under this paragraph were hitting British shipping by driving cargoes, that we should otherwise have carried, to neutral and Japanese bottoms, and were injuring British finance by causing the transference of German bank deposits to America and Holland. It was even said at the time that this process appreciably affected the dollar exchange. The result was that we declared that, as regards post-war deposits and goods in the United Kingdom and under United Kingdom control, we did not intend to exercise our rights under the paragraph. This caused an agitation of some violence in France, to allay which the Chancellor of the Exchequer (Mr. Chamberlain) dealt with our action in the House of Commons on the 28th October[19] in the following terms:—

6. After explaining the origin of the decision and the circumstances which justified it, he used these words:—

'With regard to the criticism that this action was taken by His Majesty's Government on their own responsibility without obtaining the concurrence of the Allied Governments, I would say that the words of the paragraph (of the treaty) clearly leave it "to the respective Governments" to determine what action may be necessary under the paragraph. In the opinion of His Majesty's Government, it would have been both unnecessary and undesirable to seek to share the responsibility of the decision they have taken with the other Allies, thus both limiting their own freedom of action under the treaty and giving the appearance of desiring to dictate to other Governments as to their action under the paragraph. As a matter of courtesy, the decision reached was immediately communicated to the other Powers through the Ambassadors' [Conference] and also to the Reparation Commission through the British delegate.'

In telegraphing[20] this statement beforehand for the information of the French Government, the following instructions were added for the guidance of Lord Derby:—

'Please explain to the French Government that, as stated at the end of the answer, His Majesty's Government regarded as both unnecessary and undesirable to create a precedent which might have seemed to limit the unfettered responsibility of each Allied Government under the paragraph or to involve an attempt to dictate to other Governments.'

[19] See 133 *H.C. Deb*, 5 *s.*, cols. 1921–2 (see also Vol. X, No. 397).
[20] Foreign Office telegram No. 1165 of October 28, 1920, not printed. See, however, Vol. X, No. 397, n. 3.

7. The French Government, who seemed throughout this incident to have been actuated in some degree by a fear that His Majesty's Government by their action might have prejudiced the application of the penalties provided for under the treaty to other parts of the treaty besides the reparation clauses, placed themselves on record in these terms:—

'Le Gouvernement français estime qu'un des signataires du traité ne saurait s'autoriser d'une action individuelle *vis-à-vis* de l'Allemagne pour renoncer au détriment de ses Alliés aux droits qu'il tient du traité.'[21]

And about the same time the French press, clearly under official inspiration, emphasised the understanding reached between the British and French Governments at the time of the occupation of Frankfort[22] (see below) that the Allied Governments had no intention of acting in any inter-Allied question raised by the execution of the treaty save in agreement with their Allies. The line of argument was that complete agreement between the Allies was indispensable in every sphere, and that no Allied Government should take any action whatever arising out of the treaty without previous agreement with the others.

8. It is thus clear that, if we wish to make the text of the treaty a ground for resisting or reprobating independent French action in the event of Germany's default, we can only do so if we can demonstrate that, when the relevant passage was drafted, what its authors had in mind was exclusively commercial action analogous to 'blockade pressure'. If this can be proved, our position merely on treaty grounds will be strong, and will have been in no way invalidated by Mr. Chamberlain's explanation of our own action under paragraph 18. As it happens, the history of the drafting of paragraph 18 shows conclusively that this was in fact intended.

9. On the 23rd April, 1919, the Council of Four had before them a draft prepared by a committee, of which the clause dealing with sanctions ran as follows:—

'18.

'In case of voluntary default by Germany in the performance of any obligation, of whatever kind, to comply with and satisfy its decisions, the commission will forthwith give notice of such default to each of interested Powers, and may make such recommendations as to the action to be taken in consequence of such default as it may think necessary.

'These measures, which the Allied and Associated Powers shall have the right to take, and which Germany agrees not to regard as acts of war, may be in particular the following:—

(1) Prohibition against German vessels entering ports situated in the territory of the Allied and Associated States or of their possessions and dependencies and from utilising any coaling stations belonging to the said States.

[21] See Vol. X, No. 397, Enclosure.   [22] See Vol. IX, No. 294.

(2) Seizure, whether in the ports of the Allied and Associated States, whether on the high sea, of all German vessels, under reserve of the rights of neutrals, which should be safeguarded.

(3) Prohibition from entering into the territories of the Allied and Associated States or of their possessions and dependencies to all German subjects and all goods of German origin.

(4) Prohibition of the negotiation on the territories of the said States of German securities of any kind.

(5) Suspension of all postal, telegraphic and telephonic communication with Germany.

(6) Seizure on the territories of the said States of all German goods.

'These rights shall not be exclusive of the exercise of any others.

'The engagement of the German Government in the financial protocol in the armistice signed at Trèves on the 13th December, 1918, shall be maintained until Germany has paid the first 20,000,000,000 mark bonds referred to in article   , unless the commission should previously accept some other guarantee in lieu thereof.'

The following is the record of the discussion which took place when this article was reached:—

'*President Wilson* pointed out that the United States representatives had accepted the principle of Sanctions, but were not prepared to approve the form of words proposed in the draft. He then read a shorter and simpler formula.

'*M. Klotz*[23] said that he would accept, with the addition of the words (underlined below) "or financial" after "economic". The following substitute for the second and third sub-paragraph of this article was adopted:—

"The measures which the Allied and Associated Governments shall have the right to take, and which Germany hereby agrees not to consider as acts of war, may include economic or financial prohibition and reprisals, and in general such other measures as the respective Governments may determine to be necessary in the premise."

'*Note.*—Just as the meeting was breaking up, it was agreed in addition to omit the last paragraph of article 18.

'In accordance with this, the revised draft, dated the 24th April, reads as follows:—

"17. In case of voluntary default by Germany in the performance of any obligation, of whatever kind, to comply with and satisfy its decisions, the commission will forthwith give notice of such default to each of the interested Powers, and may make such recommendations as it may think necessary.

"The measures which the Allied and Associated Powers shall have the right to take, and which Germany agrees not to regard as acts of war,

[23] French Finance Minister (September 1917–January 1920).

44

include economic and financial prohibitions and reprisals, and in general such other measures as the respective Governments may determine to be necessary in the circumstances." '

10. This shows conclusively that what was intended was not acts of military force, but acts to be taken by one or all of the Powers on their own territory; and that it was precisely this point that the word 'respective' was designed to bring out. Thus, if we are to go by intention, M. Poincaré's position cannot be maintained. This point may prove useful if it should become necessary to resort to an argument of a legal character to reinforce our position, which must be based ultimately on broad political considerations.

11. Those considerations will always reduce themselves to this. In matters of grave moment no question of independent action will arise until there has been a discussion by the Supreme Council, resulting either in a semblance of agreement or in a definite disagreement; and, failing definite disagreement, it is an act of disloyalty to take independent action while the machinery of Allied discussion is still available and working. The two leading cases where the French Government have strained our relations by taking independent action in European affairs of the first moment were preceded by the semblance of agreement, or at any rate by an attempt to reach agreement. This was so in April, 1920 when the French Government, supported by the Belgian Government, occupied Frankfort and four other towns in the basin of the Main;[24] and again in August 1920, when they recognised the Government of General Wrangel as the *de facto* Government of South Russia.[25]

12. The Frankfort case was a peculiarly insidious blow at Allied solidarity, because the action was taken at the very moment that His Majesty's Government and the French Government were endeavouring to reach agreement as to the terms on which the German Government might be allowed to move troops into the neutral zone to suppress the Communist rising in the Ruhr; the French Government suddenly took alarm, and, on the plea of urgency, proceeded to the occupation without the sanction of their Allies. So grave a view was taken of this action that Lord Derby was instructed[26] to take no further part in the deliberations of the Ambassadors' Conference, in so far as the execution of the Treaty of Versailles was concerned, until an adequate assurance should be given that in no circumstances would one of the Allies act in future in such important matters except with the knowledge and concurrence of the remainder. This drew from the French Government the following declaration:—

'As regards the future, the Government of the republic repeat that in all inter-Allied questions raised by the execution of the treaty it has no intention of acting save in accordance with its Allies.'[27]

This declaration was made on the 11th April, and the following day His Majesty's Government took formal note of it as meaning that, 'in the future,

[24] See Vol. IX, Chap. IV
[25] On August 11, 1920. See J. Bradley, *Allied Intervention in Russia* (London, 1968), p.179.
[26] See Vol. IX, No. 322.　　　　　　　　　　　　　　　　　[27] See ibid., No. 357.

in all inter-Allied questions raised by the execution of the treaty, the French Government had no intention of acting save in agreement with their Allies'.[28] With that the incident closed.

13. The French recognition of General Wrangel was liquidated by no such clear-cut declaration. This affair was complicated by its connection with the counter-charge that we on our side had broken Allied solidarity, and failed to give effect to the agreement of the Supreme Council at Lympne,[29] by independently advising the Poles to accept the Bolsheviks' peace terms.

14. But both this and the Frankfort case were similar in that they were examples of independent action following immediately upon an attempt by the Supreme Council to decide upon a course of joint action. The real objection to any such proceeding is not that the action may be ill-conceived in itself, but that no independent action ought to be taken by any Ally until the resources of agreement have been exhausted. The preservation of unity is so important that it may require the sacrifice of individual views. That must always be the strength of the British position as against French tendencies to break away.

15. The force of this argument, supported as it is by the unequivocal declaration by the French Government after the Frankfort incident, will doubtless be felt when the Supreme Council (or the signatories of the Treaty of Versailles) meet to discuss the situation created by the impending default of Germany. But the argument is one which must always be felt by the French to operate unfairly, because it is always they who desire action, whereas we should be quite satisfied with passivity. Now it does not do to rely exclusively or overmuch on a weapon that is felt to be unfair. That is why it is desirable to have a second and a more positive string to our bow.[30]

[28] See ibid., No. 367.   [29] See Vol. VIII, Chap. XI.
[30] For a further discussion of points in this Memorandum, see Annex III to Enclosure in No. 23, below.

No. 20

The Marquess Curzon of Kedleston to Lord Hardinge (Paris)
No. 180 Telegraphic: by bag [C 7007/99/18]

FOREIGN OFFICE, *May 13, 1922*

My telegram No. 176[1] and your telephone message of today.[2] Constitution of committee on distribution of costs of armies of occupation.[3]

We understand that at Ambassadors' Conference on Wednesday, French government will suggest that committee shall consist of French, British and Belgian representatives only. If Italian Ambassador then requests Italian representation we do not wish to oppose it. But we deprecate any further additions to committee as tending to make it unwieldy, and we see no reason

[1] Of May 12, not printed.
[2] The record of this message is preserved in the Foreign Office archives at C 7007/99/18.
[3] See No. 15 and No. 21, below.

for suggesting inclusion of Japanese and American representatives. Japan is not interested in committee and United States Government was not a party to agreement of March 11th.[4] Treasury concur.

Please act accordingly.

[4] See No. 11, n. 2. See also No. 196.

No. 21

Sir R. Graham (Rome) to the Marquess Curzon of Kedleston
(Received May 22)

No. 437 [C 7455/99/18]

ROME, May 17, 1922

My Lord,

On receipt of Your Lordship's despatch No. 295 (C 4373/99/18) of the 4th April last,[1] relative to the Financial Agreement signed by the Allied Finance Ministers on March 11th 1922,[2] I at once addressed a Note[3] to the Italian Ministry for Foreign Affairs in accordance with Your Lordship's instructions, and have now received from them a reply[3] to the effect that the Italian Government sees no objection to the Conference of Ambassadors at Paris taking steps for the nomination of a Committee to decide on the question of the application of Section V of Article I of the Agreement. The Italian Government also shares the view that the members of the Commission on the cost of the armies of occupation nominated in accordance with the decision of the Supreme Council of the 13th August last,[4] should form part of the new Committee for the consideration of the question of the application of Articles VIII and XII of the Agreement of the 28th June 1919.

I have, etc.,
R. GRAHAM

[1] No. 15. [2] See No. 11, n. 2.
[3] Not traced in the Foreign Office Archives. [4] See Vol. XV, No. 104, Appendix 3.

No. 22

The Marquess Curzon of Kedleston to M. Tadić[1]

[C 7157/99/18]

FOREIGN OFFICE, May 18, 1922

Sir,

With reference to your memorandum of May 12th,[2] I have the honour to inform you that, according to a report which has just been received from His Majesty's Ambassador at Rome,[3] the Italian Government have now

[1] Chargé d'Affaires, Serb-Croat-Slovene Legation in London. [2] Not printed.
[3] The reference is to Sir R. Graham's despatch No. 417 of May 11 (C 7153/99/18), not preserved in the Foreign Office archives.

adhered to the agreement concluded on June 20th, 1921,[4] by the Serb-Croat-Slovene Government with His Majesty's Government and the French Government in regard to the percentage of reparations from ex-enemy states to be assigned to Jugo-Slavia.

I have, etc.,
(For the Secretary of State)
MILES W. LAMPSON

[4] See No. 9, n. 9.

No. 23

Memorandum communicated by the Marquess Curzon of Kedleston to Mr. Lloyd George

[*C 7546/99/18*]

FOREIGN OFFICE, *May 22, 1922*

Attitude of French Government in the Event of the Failure by Germany to meet her Reparation Obligations

Prime Minister,

These papers and the advice in which they culminate are the result of a conversation between Sir Eyre Crowe, Sir Cecil Hurst,[1] Mr. Wigram and myself this afternoon.

The legal ground on which we stand is strong (*vide* Sir C. Hurst's note), though not absolutely impregnable. We may be sure, however, that, strong as it is, it will not convince the French, and we may go on arguing the matter in interminable notes.

It is preferable, therefore, to regard the question from the political stand-point.

Here, we are in a position not without advantage:—

1. The situation demanding action cannot arise on the 31st May, nor before the 15th June. It may conceivably not arise until a little later.

2. M. Poincaré has indicated his willingness to concert with the Allies upon the situation produced by the probable German default.

3. The right thing to do is to take him at his word and propose or agree to such a consultation.

4. In it, the French and the Belgians will be, or may be, on one side. The British, Italians and Japanese will be on the other.

5. Should the French decide to break away after such a consultation and to act on their own the onus and odium of breaking the Entente will then devolve publicly upon them.

They will not do it.

For Poincaré would at once fall.

I have not here discussed the German action either on the 31st May or the 15th June, because I am not familiar with their intentions. But it is obvious that a move on their part might throw a different light on the situation.

[1] See No. 11, n. 10.

48

Memorandum [on] M. Poincaré's Note of May 19[2] respecting the Attitude to be adopted by the French Government in the Event of the Failure by Germany to meet her Reparation Obligations

FOREIGN OFFICE, *May 22, 1922*

(A brief summary of the recent history of the reparation negotiations and a note on the state of execution of the Allied ultimatum of the 5th May,

[2] This Note, transmitted by Lord Hardinge under cover of his despatch No. 1215 of May 20 (not printed), ran: 'Des informations de presse rendent compte d'une question posée hier à la Chambre des Communes par M. le Député Kenworthy, pour demander si le Gouvernement britannique a reçu l'assurance que le Gouvernement français participera à une conférence ayant pour objet de discuter la question des réparations, avant de prendre de nouvelles mesures militaires contre l'Allemagne.

'Mr. Chamberlain [Lord Privy Seal] avait répondu, au nom du Gouvernement britannique, que celui-ci avait déjà reçu du Gouvernement français des assurances nettes et explicites après l'occupation de Francfort, et il a fait état de la déclaration, alors faite au Gouvernement britannique, d'après laquelle le Gouvernement français, en ce qui concerne l'avenir, a l'intention de n'agir qu'en accord avec ses Alliés sur toutes les questions interalliées soulevées par l'exécution du traité.

'Je n'ai pas besoin de vous rappeler les conditions dans lesquelles la déclaration du Gouvernement français mentionnée par l'Honorable A. Chamberlain a été faite. C'était après l'occupation de Francfort et de quatre autres villes allemandes, occupation motivée par l'entrée de troupes allemandes en surnombre dans la zone neutralisée, sans l'autorisation préalable des Puissances alliées, en dérogation à l'article 43 du Traité de Versailles.

'Des explications ayant été échangées à ce sujet entre le Gouvernement britannique et le Gouvernement français, celui-ci, après avoir justifié son action et constaté son plein accord avec le Gouvernement britannique sur la nécessité de maintenir l'unité des Alliés, non seulement, d'ailleurs, vis-à-vis de l'Allemagne, mais en présence de tous les vastes problèmes qui se posaient dans le monde, fut amené à déclarer que "dans toutes les questions interalliées que soulève l'exécution du traité, il n'envisage aucun cas où il ne soit heureux, avant d'agir, de s'assurer de l'assentiment de ses Alliés".

'Cette déclaration, dans une note subséquente et après un nouvel échange de vues, fut confirmée de la manière suivante: "Pour l'avenir, le Gouvernement de la République répète que, dans toutes les questions interalliées que soulève l'exécution du traité, il n'entend agir que d'accord avec ses Alliés."

'Il y a lieu d'observer que l'occupation de Francfort a été motivée par une infraction de l'Allemagne à une clause du traité ayant un caractère général et intéressant l'ensemble des Alliés. Le Traité de Versailles ne prévoyait aucune procédure spéciale dans le cas d'une infraction de ce genre. Aussi, le Gouvernement de la République s'est-il toujours réclamé, pour prendre les mesures qu'il a alors jugées utiles, non point d'une disposition du Traité de Versailles, mais bien des principes et des précédents du droit international.

'En ce qui concerne la question des réparations, le Traité de Paix contient des dispositions spéciales, parmi lesquelles les paragraphes 17 et 18 de l'Annexe II de la Partie VIII du Traité de Versailles, qui fixent la procédure à suivre en cas de manquement par l'Allemagne à l'exécution qui lui incombe de l'une quelconque des obligations visées à cette partie du traité.

'Le Gouvernement français entend, pour sa part, se conformer strictement à cette procédure; il attend donc que la Commission des Réparations ait signalé à chacune des Puissances intéressées le manquement éventuel de l'Allemagne à cette obligation, et, ainsi qu'il l'a déclaré, il est prêt à se concerter avec ses Alliés pour examiner alors la situation tant en ce qui concerne les propositions que la Commission des Réparations jugerait opportun de joindre à sa communication aux Puissances intéressées, qu'en ce qui touche les mesures à prendre en raison de l'inexécution des obligations de l'Allemagne.

'Toutefois, aux termes du paragraphe 18, les Gouvernements respectifs ont le droit de prendre telles mesures qu'ils peuvent estimer nécessitées par les circonstances. Il ne s'agit plus là de mesures interalliées, mais de dispositions qu'il appartient à chaque Gouvernement d'arrêter pour la défense de ses intérêts propres. Cette éventualité, que le Gouvernement français — qui souhaite ardemment la réalisation du plein accord entre tous les Alliés — espère bien ne pas voir se produire, est donc tout à fait étrangère aux cas envisagés dans les notes échangées en avril 1920 entre les deux Gouvernements. Le droit de se prévaloir ou non du paragraphe 18 appartient, en effet, à chaque Gouvernement, et nous sommes fondés à penser que cette opinion est entièrement partagée par le Gouvernement de Sa Majesté britannique, comme en témoigne la décision prise par lui, de sa propre initiative, et sans concert préalable avec ses Alliés, en octobre 1920, à l'effet de renoncer en ce qui le concerne au droit qu'il tient du paragraphe 18 susdit de saisir les biens des ressortissants allemands. Si cette décision a motivé alors la protestation du Gouvernement français, c'est qu'en agissant ainsi le Gouvernement britannique avait par avance restreint publiquement la portée des sanctions éventuelles en diminuant l'efficacité d'un des moyens de pression prévus à l'égard de l'Allemagne, puisqu'il supprimait la possibilité d'une action concertée entre les Alliés pour l'application collective de la mesure de saisie.

'Le Gouvernement français n'a, quant à lui, jamais renoncé aux droits qu'il tient du traité et auxquels il lui aurait été, du reste, constitutionnellement impossible de renoncer sans un vote du Parlement.

'J'ai tenu à rappeler ces différents éléments de la question, estimant que, dans l'intérêt même de l'étroite entente entre les Gouvernements français et britannique, à laquelle le Gouvernement de la République tient vivement, il était désirable que la position des Gouvernements respectifs fût bien précisée à cet égard.'

In a minute of May 21 to Lord Curzon, Sir E. Crowe wrote: 'The attached note from Monsieur Poincaré was handed by Sir M. Cheetham to our delegates as they passed through Paris yesterday morning [on their way back from the Genoa Conference]. Mr. Wigram translated it in the train for the Prime Minister, who begged to have it circulated to the Cabinet on Monday (tomorrow) morning for discussion by the Cabinet on Tuesday. It was apparently this note which caused the Prime Minister to telegraph a message to Lord D'Abernon last night that he should come to London at once.

'I will get the Department, immediately tomorrow morning, to go into the whole question once more (we have papers, fully discussing it, in hand), and will then submit a memorandum to you, in case you wish to send a message to the cabinet.

'An opinion is held by some that we can successfully traverse the legal argument on which M. Poincaré relies in his interpretation of the terms of the treaty of Versailles. I personally doubt this, and my first impression is that we should leave aside all legal quibbling, and take our stand very firmly on the definite and unconditionally-worded assurance given by M. Millerand at the time of the French occupation of Frankfort and the 4 other German towns [see n. 7]. The words were:

' "As regards the future, the government of the Republic repeat that *in ALL inter-allied questions raised by the execution of the treaty*, it has no intention of acting save in accordance with its allies."

'It is therefore M. Poincaré who is quibbling when he tries to make out that this assurance is strictly limited to cases where the treaty does not contain specific provisions authorizing the allied governments to impose "sanctions". Our simplest and most effective reply to M. Poincaré may be to say: that the reason why in the case of the occupation of the 5 towns H[is] M[ajesty's] G[overnment] took so grave a view of the French action, was that it was taken in direct violation of a definite undertaking given by the French government shortly before that they would not so act without previous consultation with H[is] M[ajesty's] G[overnment]. The incident was closed, as between the two governments, by M. Millerand's definite and, as was then understood, unambiguous, pledge above quoted. We cannot admit the legal quibble by which M. Poincaré now endeavours to justify a clear breach, both in the spirit and in the letter, of the honourable undertaking then given; and if the French Gov[ernmen]t persist in this attitude, H[is] M[ajesty's] G[overnment] cannot but place

1921,[3] as modified by the Reparation Commission's decisions of the 13th January, 1922,[4] and the 21st March, 1922,[5] are appended to the present memorandum as Annexes I[6] and II.)[6]

The purpose of M. Poincaré's note is to explain—

1. That the French Government will—

    (a) in accordance with the procedure contemplated in paragraphs 17 and 18 of Annex 2 to Part 8 of the Treaty of Versailles, await the announcement to each of the interested Powers by the Reparation Commission of the actual failure of Germany to fulfil any of her obligations; and

    (b) then be ready to concert with their Allies in examining the position.

2. That the French Government consider that under paragraph 18 of Annex 2 to Part 8 of the Treaty of Versailles the respective Governments nevertheless retain the right to take such measures as they may consider necessitated by circumstances; and

3. That the French Government do not consider themselves in the last resort debarred from taking separate action despite the pledge which M. Millerand gave to the British Government after the occupation of Frankfurt on the 6th April, 1920.[7]

The procedure contemplated by the Reparation Commission in the event of the failure by Germany to accept the demands set out in the commission's note to the German Government of the 21st March, 1922[5] is clearly set out in the last section of the decision which accompanied that letter. The following procedure is there laid down:—

    (a) On the 31st May, 1922, the commission will examine the progress made by the German Government towards satisfying the conditions laid down in the commission's letter of the 21st March 1922.[5]

    (b) Should the progress made be judged unsatisfactory, the provisional arrangement contemplated for the year 1922 will be cancelled and the payments due under the London ultimatum of the 5th May,

formally on record, and protest firmly against, such a renewed failure on the part of the French government to respect their solemnly-given word.

'I will however go more carefully into the whole question with the assistance of the department and of Mr. Wigram, who had a conversation with Sir E. Grigg [Private Secretary to Mr. Lloyd George] in the train after the Prime Minister had spoken with Lord Hardinge and Sir John Bradbury at the Paris railway station.'

Lord Curzon minuted on May 22: 'A little while ago I wrote a note and F[oreign] O[ffice] I believe drew up a [memorandum] (which however I never saw in its final form) dealing with the question of our isolated action in respect of enemy property and the pleas by which we defended it.

'We are not on very certain ground and shall have to differentiate, if we can, between the action that we took and justified (while the French attacked it) and the action which the French apparently contemplate now. I think there is a distinction *in kind* between the two but Hurst will have to be consulted. I can see you any time tomorrow after your conference.'

    [3] See No. 6, n. 3.   [4] See Vol. XIX, No. 25.   [5] See No. 13.
    [6] Not printed.   [7] See Vol. IX, Nos. 353 and 357. Cf. No. 19, Annex.

1921,[3] but not paid to date, will become due within fourteen days of the foregoing cancellation, i.e. about the 15th June.

(c) Should these payments not be forthcoming, paragraph 17 of Annex 2 to Part 8 of the Treaty of Versailles will immediately operate, i.e., the Reparation Commission will forthwith give notice of the default of Germany to each of the interested Powers.

(d) Paragraph 18 of Annex 2 to Part 8 of the Treaty of Versailles, which reads as follows, will then operate:—

'The measures which the Allied and Associated Powers shall have the right to take in case of voluntary default by Germany, and which Germany agrees not to regard as acts of war, may include economic and financial prohibitions and reprisals, and in general such other measures as the respective Governments may determine to be necessary in the circumstances.'

The interpretation of paragraph 18 is discussed in the accompanying note (Annex III). It will be apparent from this that, from the point of view of strict legality, it will be possible to dispute the contention put forward by M. Poincaré. But that the French would finally accept the legal argument is obviously most improbable.

In view, therefore, of this, and of the fact that immediate independent action by the French is not in question, it is for consideration whether the reply which we should return to M. Poincaré should not be on some such general lines as the following:—

M. Poincaré is at pains to argue that the solemn pledges, given to His Majesty's Government in April 1920, that the French Government would, for the future, only act in agreement with its Allies in all inter-Allied questions which are raised by the execution of the treaty, do not apply in the present case, for various technical and legal reasons.

His Majesty's Government do not admit the soundness of M. Poincaré's argument, and are fully prepared to show conclusively why it is faulty. An outline of their counter-argument is given in the annexed memorandum.

They are, however, loath to follow M. Poincaré in the path of legal controversy in regard to a matter touching, as this does, the very heart of the alliance. They prefer to dwell on the definite intimation given in his note that the French Government will in fact be ready, if and when the Reparation Commission has declared Germany to have defaulted, to concert with their Allies for the purpose of considering the position as regards the measures to be taken.

His Majesty's Government think it unnecessary at this moment to pursue the theoretical and hypothetical question as to what isolated action, if any, might legitimately be taken by one or the other of the Allied Powers in the event of their failing to come to an agreement among themselves for common action. They would fain believe that in this, as in all previous instances, the loyal co-operation of the Allied Governments will ensure the successful pursuit of a common policy on the basis of unanimity.

It is in this conviction that they now ask the French Government to arrange for a meeting of representatives of the four Allied Powers as soon as possible after the Reparation Commission have made their report.

Annex III to Enclosure in No. 23

Memorandum by Sir C. Hurst on the Legal Situation

FOREIGN OFFICE, *May 22, 1922*

The French rely on paragraph 18 of Annex 2 to the reparation section of the Treaty of Versailles as justifying independent action, such as an advance into the Ruhr, in case the Reparation Commission notify under paragraph 17 that Germany is in default.

Paragraph 18 is as follows:—

'The measures which the Allied and Associated Powers shall have the right to take, in case of voluntary default by Germany, and which Germany agrees not to regard as acts of war, may include economic and financial prohibitions and reprisals, and in general such other measures as the respective Governments may determine to be necessary in the circumstances.'

The interpretation of this paragraph is not very easy, but to my mind the intention was that the action was to be taken by the individual Governments, and that the individual Governments had a discretion as to the action they would take, but the fact that the action is to be decided on by the individual Governments shows that it must be action of the type which it is proper for Governments to take individually. Economic and financial prohibitions, &c., constitute measures which would be taken within the territory of the individual Allied State concerned, and the proper deduction to be drawn from the presence of the word 'respective' is that the 'other measures' referred to are also such as individual Governments would take within the limits of their own sovereignty.

The occupation of German territory is not such a measure as an individual Government is entitled, consistently with the spirit of the Treaty of Versailles, to take for the purpose of enforcing the execution of the treaty. Article 428 provides for a joint Allied occupation of certain territory west of the Rhine as a guarantee for the execution of the treaty, and article 430 provides for the reoccupation of any such territory, if part should have been evacuated, on a finding by the Reparation Commission that Germany refuses to observe the whole or part of her obligations under the present treaty.

The foregoing interpretation of paragraph 18 is corroborated by the other provisions of the Treaty of Versailles. The last paragraph of article 233 provides as follows:—

'The commission shall concurrently draw up a Schedule of Payments prescribing the time and manner for securing and discharging the entire obligation within a period of thirty years from the 1st May, 1921. If, however, within the period mentioned, Germany fails to discharge her obligations, any balance remaining unpaid may, within the discretion of the commission, be postponed for settlement in subsequent years, or may be handled otherwise in such manner as the Allied and Associated Governments, acting in accordance with the procedure laid down in this part of the present treaty, shall determine.'

It will be noticed that default in the discharge of a payment due is here regarded as producing a situation to be handled by the Allied and Associated Governments in common. It seems unreasonable that a particular Power should have a more extended right of individual action in respect of the non-payment of a particular instalment than in respect of the whole sum due, of which the instalment forms but a part.

Paragraph 18, the provision on which the French rely, merely forms part of one of the annexes to the reparation section. It is an annex which may even be amended by the Allied Powers represented on the Reparation Commission without the consent of Germany (see paragraph 22: 'Subject to the provisions of the present treaty, this annex may be amended by the unanimous decision of the Governments represented from time to time on the commission.')

Viewed in its proper setting as a provision in an annex to the reparation section, paragraph 18 does not seem to justify a claim by France to take independent action against German territory in case of a default by Germany in payment of an instalment due under the treaty.[8]

[8] In a letter of June 7 to Sir E. Crowe, Mr. M. A. Robertson (H.M. Agent and Consul-General at Tangier) commented: 'With reference to Hurst's memorandum of May 22 on the legal situation in regard to the attitude to be adopted in the event of failure by Germany to meet her Reparation obligations, it may possibly be of interest and of use to you to know the view of Baron Rolin Jaequemyns (who was my colleague at Coblenz [Mr. Robertson had been High Commissioner on the Inter-Allied Rhineland High Commission] and, if I remember right, Belgian Secretary General at the Peace Conference) in regard to the famous para[graph] 18 of Annex 2 to the Reparation Section.

'He thought that the paragraph was badly drafted but that its intent was quite clear. "Such other measures" was never intended to mean further invasion of German territory, but merely measures of an economic or financial nature in the spirit of the paragraph. Invasion of the territory of a Power with which one was at peace was, of course, an act of war, and so serious a matter that, had it been deliberately intended, it would have formed the subject of a special article in the main body of the Treaty, instead of being included vaguely among "other measures" in a small print paragraph of an Annex to a Section of the Treaty.

'I have no doubt that he informed his Gov[ernmen]t of this view and I know that they pay considerable attention to him. We discussed the matter on the last occasion that the French were threatening to occupy the Ruhr in April of last year. The military guarantee for the execution of the Treaty was the occupation of the Rhineland which can continue until the Treaty is executed.'

In a minute of May 24 to Mr. Waterlow, Mr. J. Headlam-Morley (Historical Adviser to the Secretary of State for Foreign Affairs) wrote as follows: 'Have you seen the attached article from the "Manchester Guardian" on clauses 17 and 18? The point against the French is put with great vigour and skill, but the writer . . . really knows the treaty and knows what he is talking about; his argument would of course have been very much strengthened had he had the original draft which I sent you the other day [see No. 19, Annex], and had he known that this paragraph was actually drafted by the Americans. The passage which I have marked dealing with the general attitude of this treaty towards sanctions is particularly important. Throughout the whole of the Treaty, throughout all the discussions at Paris, and throughout the later discussions between the French themselves as to the interpretation of the Treaty, there cannot be found anywhere a single suggestion, apart from this, that it was contemplated including the invasion of Germany among the sanctions. I should like also to call attention to the fact that the point which M. Poincaré is now taking up has clearly been suggested to him by M. Klotz. It is certainly not going too far to say that this alone was sufficient to make the point suspect, for his whole record on these matters is extremely bad. Of course we cannot say this, but it may be worth while keeping in mind in any correspondence that takes place. M. Poincaré is in this matter dealing with something of which he has no first hand knowledge, as he has himself often complained. . . .'

No. 24

Lord Hardinge (Paris) to the Earl of Balfour[1] *(Received May 30)*
No. 1280 [C 7848/99/18]

Confidential   PARIS, *May 29, 1922*

My Lord,

The Belgian Ambassador called on me this morning and told me that his Government are continually pressing him to ascertain from the French Government what action they propose to take in the event of the German Government failing to carry out their treaty obligations on the 31st May. He said that a fortnight ago he put the question to M. Poincaré, in consequence of the latter having expressed to him the hope that, in any complication that might arise from the default of Germany on the 31st May, Belgium would be found to be acting in support of the French Government. It appears that Baron Gaiffier told M. Poincaré that the last thing that the Belgian Government desired was any active operations in the Ruhr. He reminded him that in the Belgian Chamber there are at present sixty-eight Socialists and forty Flemish Deputies, all of whom would oppose active operations in the Ruhr or elsewhere, and that the consent of Parliament would be necessary before the Belgian Government could take action. It was clear to the Belgian Government that they would find themselves, in that eventuality, in a minority or with a very small majority, and in the latter case it was certain that the Flemish Ministers would resign. This would precipitate a Cabinet crisis of which it would be impossible to foresee the outcome.

M. Poincaré expressed to him his great concern at what he had told him, but added that, in the event of Germany giving an unsatisfactory answer to the Reparation Commission on the 31st May, he intends to ask the Allies what action they propose to take in order to enforce their claims, and that, should they come to no decision, he intends to throw the entire responsibility upon the Allies for taking no action to vindicate the treaty which they have signed. He expressed the hope that no action would be necessary, but added

[1] The Earl of Balfour was temporarily in charge of the Foreign Office during Lord Curzon's illness, from May 25 to August 8.

that, if the Allies failed in their duty, the French Government would not do so. It was in consequence of this conversation that the Belgian Government are so anxious to find out what action the French Government have in contemplation.

There is little doubt that public opinion in this country is veering round[2] against active operations in the Ruhr as a means of compulsion against Germany, for it is realised that the occupation of the Ruhr would be a source of endless trouble, entailing great expense, and that it would bring in nothing. Still, it is thought that the present Chamber would not be hostile to the idea, and that in this matter they do not represent public opinion in this country. There is, however, an optimistic feeling at the present moment that the Germans will make a serious effort to meet their treaty engagements and that no further action will be really necessary for the time being.

I have, etc.,

HARDINGE OF PENSHURST

[2] In a letter of May 25 to Mr. Wigram, Mr. R. S. Hudson, First Secretary in H.M. Embassy at Paris, had commented: 'You will have noticed that there has been within the last few days an interesting hardening of opinion here against separate military adventures after May 31. Some people say it's public opinion, others that it is governmental opinion. I'm inclined to think it's the former pushing the latter. You will remember I hazarded the opinion to you a little time ago that the mass of the people were against war and that in time they would make their voice heard. It's come sooner than I thought as we are told that politicans returning from the recent cantonal elections (which resulted in a *slight* gain by the Left) have been greatly impressed and more so than the mere figures warranted by the feeling among the peasants and petit bourgeois against any course of action that may lead to mobilisation or war. I doubt whether this movement has yet attained its full volume or whether it is yet safe to count on Poincaré not daring to run counter to it.'

No. 25

The Earl of Balfour[1] to Lord Hardinge (Paris)
No. 1657 [C 7648/99/18][2]

FOREIGN OFFICE, *May 30, 1922*

My Lord,

I have received and laid before the Cabinet your despatch of the 20th

[1] See No. 24, n. 1.

[2] This despatch was drafted by Sir E. Crowe in circumstances which are described in his minute of May 23 to Lord Curzon as follows: 'The Prime Minister summoned me to attend at the cabinet meeting this morning after it had sat for about an hour.

'I ascertained afterwards that there had been some rather animated, not to say heated, discussion arising out of the attitude taken up by Sir John Bradbury in regard to M. Poincaré's argument based on clause 18 of Annex II to the Reparation chapter of the treaty of Versailles. It appears that Sir J. Bradbury not only disagreed with Sir C. Hurst's views [see No. 23, Annex III to Enclosure] but (rather losing his temper) stigmatized as unpermissible the intervention of any government lawyers in a matter which was exclusively within the competence of the Reparation Commission. The Commission, he pointed out, had sole authority, under the treaty, to interpret these Reparation clauses.

'The second point of interest, I understand, was Sir J. Bradbury's statement that it was by no means certain that the Reparation Commission would declare Germany in default on May 31. Lord D'Abernon [see No. 3, n. 1] was of opinion that the German Minister of Finance [Dr. Hermes] would before May 31 put forward such definite proposals as would justify the Commission in holding that there was no "wilful default". If necessary, he thought, we could, with Italy's support, count upon getting a majority vote on this point in the Commission, opposed to the French view. Sir J. Bradbury however, so I understand, expressed the opinion that it was quite possible to get a unanimous vote in the Commission in favour of prolonging the German moratorium.

'All this passed before I came into the room. It was then being arranged that a meeting should take place between Sir J. Bradbury, Sir C. Hurst, and the Solicitor General [Sir Leslie Scott], to discuss the legal point.

'After that, the Prime Minister spoke about the proposed reply to M. Poincaré's note [see No. 23, n. 2]. He thought that the line suggested in the Foreign Office paper [No. 23] was not nearly strong enough. He saw no reason for not expressing our point of view with vigour and protesting against M. Poincaré's attempt to justify a breach of the pledge given in 1920 by M. Millerand [see No. 23, n. 7].

'Mr. Chamberlain [Lord Privy Seal] strongly supported the Prime Minister in demanding a very stiff note to M. Poincaré, mainly on the ground that the French pledge had been communicated to parliament [see 127 *H.C. Deb. 5 s.*, col. 1382]; that he had recently [May 18] made explicit reference to our reliance on that pledge [see 154 *H.C. Deb. 5 s.*, col. 536]; and that the House of Commons would undoubtedly, in view of M. Poincaré's published communication to M. Klotz [former French Minister of Finance], ask what view H[is] M[ajesty's] G[overnment] took of the French contention.

'I explained that what the Prime Minister and Mr. Chamberlain now suggested as the line of reply practically coincided with our own original view. We had at first contemplated a note which, after brushing aside the legal arguments, would end with a formal protest against the breach of the Millerand pledge. What had influenced the Secretary of State in suggesting the less direct and milder form of reply were two considerations:

'1. Sir C. Hurst had pointed out that whilst we were claiming to put aside altogether the legal argument, we should in fact be pursuing the legal argument in appealing to the pledge when answering M. Poincaré's contention that the legal argument was the very ground on which the pledge must be held to be inapplicable to the present case. For M. Poincaré's argument was, precisely, that the pledge referred specifically to "all *inter-allied* questions raised by the execution of the treaty", and that the question now at issue was, according to M. Poincaré's legal exposition, not an interallied one, but was a matter in which the treaty expressly authorized the allied gov[ernmen]ts to take isolated action.

'2. An over-acid note might, in the present heavily charged atmosphere, easily cause an undesirable explosion. It would, in any case, involve the danger of rallying to M. Poincaré much of French public opinion which at present acted as a restraint upon him as regards embarking on military action. Neither the Prime Minister nor Mr. Chamberlain—nor the rest of the Cabinet—were in any way moved by the above explanations to change their view, and I was asked to prepare a draft note in stiff terms, leading up to a strong protest and a declaration that had H[is] M[ajesty's] G[overnment] in 1920 understood the pledge then given in the sense which M. Poincaré now attributed to it, they would never have accepted it, and that if the present French government insisted on narrowing the pledge in the manner now proposed, and intended to act accordingly, they would assume a very grave responsibility for the difficulties in Anglo-French relations to which such a decision might lead.

'The meeting broke up very rapidly after this, and, as I heard only afterwards from Lord D'Abernon of what had passed in regard to the legal arguments, I am a little bit in the dark as to what exactly should be said in the note on that important point.

'Sir C. Hurst, having had his interview with Sir J. Bradbury and the Solicitor General, tells me that the latter altogether concurred in the opinions and arguments set out by Sir C. Hurst in his note which was attached to the papers circulated to the Cabinet this instant[3] forwarding copy of a note addressed to Sir M. Cheetham by M. Poincaré under date of the preceding day,[4] in which he gives a most unexpected interpretation of the pledge given to His Majesty's Government by M. Millerand in April 1920[5] on behalf of the French Government.

2. The pledge is in the following terms:—

'In all Inter-Allied questions raised by the execution of the treaty it has no intention of acting otherwise than in accord with its Allies.'

M. Poincaré now contends that it has no application to the case of any coercive measures which the French Government may wish to take if and when the Reparation Commission declare Germany to have voluntarily defaulted in the manner contemplated in paragraphs 17 and 18 of annex 2 to Part VIII of the Treaty of Versailles.

3. To support this contention M. Poincaré enters upon an elaborate legal argument as to the precise meaning of the paragraphs quoted, endeavouring to show that, in any case falling under these clauses, each one of the Allied Powers has the right, separately, to take isolated action, without agreement with the other Allies, and if necessary in opposition to their opinion.

4. I do not propose to follow M. Poincaré into these legal disquisitions. I would only say that His Majesty's Government do not agree with them, and consider that it would be easy to traverse them by cogent counter-argument. But they refrain from embarking upon such a controversy, in which neither they nor M. Poincaré are really competent to pronounce a decisive opinion. In accordance with paragraph 12 of the same annex to Part VIII, authority to interpret the provisions of that part of the treaty is expressly conferred on the Reparation Commission, whose decision under paragraph 13 (f), must be unanimous. I need only add that His Majesty's Government would be much surprised if it were found that the interpretation on which M. Poincaré relies represented the unanimous view of the Reparation Commission.

5. His Majesty's Government must express their sincere regret that M. Poincaré should have thought it necessary officially to express views which he can hardly have expected, after Mr. Chamberlain's statement in the House of Commons,[2] would be shared by His Majesty's Government. This seems the less necessary because the situation dealt with was hypothetical, and could only arise if the Reparation Commission were to report Germany in voluntary default, and if, thereupon, no agreement were to be arrived at between the British and French Governments as to the action to be taken in that situation. But whatever view M. Poincaré may take of the technical point, His

morning [see No. 23]. Sir J. Bradbury admitted that they also practically coincided with the views of his own legal adviser [Mr. J. Fischer Williams] on the Reparation Commission.

'I have nevertheless, in the draft reply to M. Poincaré's note, which I submit herewith, as a tentative effort, thought it right to leave out the legal argument on the ground which I understand to have been taken by the Cabinet, that the matter of interpreting the reparation clauses is within the exclusive competence of the Reparation Commission.'

Sir E. Crowe added on May 24: 'Lord Curzon has approved the draft. It has been submitted to the Cabinet.' [3] No. 1215, not printed (see No. 23, n. 2).

[4] See No. 23, n. 2. [5] See ibid., n. 7.

Majesty's Government cannot admit that this affects the undertaking given by M. Millerand in 1920,[5] which they continue to regard as dominating the whole field of Allied policy touching German infractions of the Treaty of Peace. M. Poincaré in his note gives a summary account of the situation out of which the pledge arose. In the concise form in which he states the case, the real facts do not, however, clearly emerge. It may therefore be well to recapitulate a little more fully what actually passed in April 1920 between our two Governments.

6. The occasion was the occupation by French troops on the 6th April of Frankfort and four other German towns in pursuance of orders issued by the French Government[6] without the knowledge of their Allies, and in spite of reiterated and explicit declarations made by the French Ambassador in London, by the Director-General of the French Ministry for Foreign Affairs and by M. Millerand himself, that the French Government would not in any circumstances take independent action, but would only act in concert with their Allies, who had consistently opposed the despatch of French or Allied troops.

7. In these circumstances, His Majesty's Ambassador at Paris was instructed[7] to refrain from any further participation in the Ambassadors' Conference, in so far as it dealt with the execution of the German Treaty, until an adequate assurance had been given that in no circumstances would one of the Allies act on such important matters except with the knowledge and concurrence of the remainder.

8. In answer to a communication to the above effect, M. Millerand wrote on the 9th April a note to Lord Derby, claiming that he had acted strictly in accordance with the assurance given by him on the 1st April, inasmuch as he had notified them on the 3rd April that 'Marshal Foch[8] was studying the military measures which can now no longer be avoided or postponed'. The note, however, concluded with the assurance that 'the French Government do not hesitate to declare that, in all Inter-Allied questions which are raised by the execution of the treaty, they do not contemplate any case in which they will not be happy, before acting, to assure themselves of the assent of their allies'.[5]

9. This assurance was not considered satisfactory by His Majesty's Government, for the reason clearly stated in the following passage of a communication made to M. Millerand by Lord Derby on the 10th April:—[9]

'The French Government appear to think that it is sufficient, before taking isolated action, to have warned and consulted their allies, and that, if, after such consultation, they have failed to convince the latter of the wisdom of the proposed course, they are nevertheless free themselves to follow it. His Majesty's Government must say definitely that they cannot accept this view, which is incompatible with the entire spirit upon which the

[6] See Vol. IX, Chaps. III and IV.
[7] See ibid., No. 322.
[8] President of the Allied Military Committee of Versailles from January, 1920.
[9] Ibid., No. 349.

alliance has hitherto been maintained, and that, until there is a complete understanding on this point, the British Ambassador in Paris cannot attend meetings of a conference which exists to concert Allied measures for the enforcement of the treaty.'

10. M. Millerand replied in a further note dated the 11th April,[10] which finally closed the incident, by recording that—

'As regards the future, the Government of the Republic repeat that, in all Inter-Allied questions raised by the execution of the treaty, it has no intention of acting otherwise than in accordance with their Allies.'

11. This is the assurance to which the Lord Privy Seal referred in his reply given in the House of Commons on the 18th May to a parliamentary question,[2] and which M. Poincaré now endeavours to represent as having a restricted meaning tending to deprive it of all practical importance.

12. It will be clearly seen from the above narrative of events that the whole end and object pursued by His Majesty's Government in pressing for an unequivocal understanding on the entire question of coercive measures for the execution of the treaty was to prevent any recurrence of such incidents as the occupation by one of the Allies against the wishes of the others of German territory beyond the area authorised by the treaty, or similar one-sided military acts. They accepted M. Millerand's assurance in its final form under the impression that it gave them complete satisfaction on this all-important point. Had His Majesty's Government entertained the least suspicion that the assurance, in the opinion of those who gave it, was capable of a legal interpretation wholly different from its obvious meaning, they would never have agreed to accept it as a settlement of the acute difference which had so unhappily arisen between them and the French Government.

13. An assurance of the attenuated scope attributed to it by M. Poincaré would not have had then, and cannot have now, any value for His Majesty's Government. If the French Government really consider themselves definitely committed to this restricted interpretation, His Majesty's Government feel constrained to enter their emphatic protest against a procedure which they cannot but regard as utterly inconsistent with the honourable understanding on which they have hitherto confidently relied.[11]

14. Your Excellency is authorised to read this despatch to the French Minister for Foreign Affairs and to hand him a copy.

I am, etc.,
BALFOUR

[10] Vol. IX, No. 357.

[11] In the original draft of this despatch, the following passage was included: 'and if the French government should proceed to act on the view of their pledge as presented in M. Poincaré's note, H[is] M[ajesty's] G[overnment] must warn them that they would be assuming a heavy responsibility in entering on a path which can have no other issue but to break the hitherto happily maintained harmony between the allies in their task of defending by common effort the sanctity of the treaties.' The draft was considered by the Cabinet on May 30, and it was decided that the terms of the despatch to be sent to the French government should be left to Lord Balfour's discretion.

No. 26

Lord Hardinge (Paris) to the Earl of Balfour
(Received June 3, 8.30 a.m.)
No. 299 Telegraphic: by bag [C 8035/99/18]

PARIS, *June 2, 1922*

Immediately upon receipt of Your Lordship's despatch No. 1657[1] referring to Monsieur Millerand's assurances that France would take no action without the co-operation of the allies, and Monsieur Poincaré's interpretation of the same, I asked for an interview yesterday in order to carry out your instructions. Monsieur Poincaré informed me that he had a Cabinet meeting in the morning and had to be in the Chamber of Deputies in the afternoon, and asked whether it would not be sufficient if I had some conversation with him in the evening as he was dining with me at the Embassy. To this I agreed, but as I ascertained that Monsieur Poincaré was to make a long speech in the afternoon, in which he intended to deal with the question of reparations and his correspondence with Monsieur Klotz,[2] I thought it desirable that he should be aware of the contents of Your Lordship's despatch before he made his speech. I therefore asked Sir Milne Cheetham to take a copy and to make sure that he received it before he went to the Chamber of Deputies. As a matter of fact Monsieur Poincaré received a copy of the despatch while sitting in the Council of Ministers, and its contents came under discussion at once.

The official report of Monsieur Poincaré's speech, which I am sending in a despatch,[3] will show the extent to which Your Lordship's arguments affected his pronouncement. After dinner last night, Monsieur Poincaré told me that the contents of Your despatch required such careful examination that he preferred to answer it in writing, but he observed that no reference was made by Your Lordship to two important communications made by Monsieur Millerand on the same subject. These I have not yet had time to trace.

I remarked that it was a pity that this controversy should have been provoked at a moment when the Germans appear to be ready to meet the demands of the reparations commission.[4] He replied that he did not agree

---

[1] No. 25.   [2] A former French Finance Minister (see No. 19, n. 23).
[3] No. 1317 of June 2, not printed.
[4] On May 31, the Reparation Commission, in reply to the German Chancellor's letter of May 28 (see Reparation Commission III, op. cit., pp. 129–38), communicated to the German Government 'Decision No. 1976A'. This confirmed that the provisional postponement granted on March 21 of a portion of the payments due under the schedule of payments in respect of the year 1922 would become definitive for the year 1922, as from June 1, in accordance with the last paragraph of the commission's decision No. 1841 of March 21, 1922, which stated that the postponement remained liable to be cancelled at any time if the commission were subsequently satisfied that Germany had failed to carry out the conditions laid down. The text (English translation) of 'Decision No. 1976A' continued as follows: 'Without prejudice to the generality of its powers under that paragraph, the commission expressly reserves its right to cancel the postponement if at any time it becomes

with me since the situation would probably become critical once more within six months, all the more so as under the present arrangement France would practically get nothing at all from the payments that Germany was ready to make.

dissatisfied with the progress made in the settlement of the matters still outstanding, or, if, in the event of Germany, through being unable to obtain the desired assistance by way of a foreign loan, failing to carry through the arrangements in regard to the floating debt specified in the Chancellor's letter of May 28, 1922, alternative arrangements satisfactory to the commission are not arrived at for dealing with the budget deficit and the floating debt.' (See Reparation Commission III, op. cit., pp. 140–2.) Copies and translations of these communications are preserved in the Foreign Office archives at C 8326/99/18.

No. 27

Sir J. Bradbury (Reparation Commission) to Treasury[1]
[C 8375/99/18]

Confidential   PARIS, *June 7, 1922*
Report No. 292

May it please your Lordships,

I have the honour to transmit herewith, for your Lordships' information, the minutes of a meeting of the Reparation Commission,[2] held this morning, in which appears a copy of a letter[3] which has today been addressed by the Reparation Commission to the chairman of the Committee on German Foreign Loans in reply to an enquiry raised by that committee as to the interpretation to be placed on its terms of reference,[4] as well as copies of

[1] A copy of this report was received in the Foreign Office on June 12, 1922.

[2] Not printed.

[3] This ran: 'The commission intends that nothing in the terms of reference should be held to preclude the committee from examining any of the conditions which may be necessary for the raising of external loans by Germany, including such as relate to the general re-establishment of her external credit.

'Indeed, any suggestion which the committee may be able to offer from this point of view, without, of course, engaging the responsibility of the commission, could not fail to be of the greatest value.'

[4] In its Report to the Reparation Commission of June 10, 1922 (not printed), the Loan Committee [see No. 19, n. 5] stated its terms of reference as follows: 'An expert committee would be appointed to consider and report to the commission on the conditions under which the German Government, regard being had to its obligations under the Treaty of Versailles, and in particular under the Schedule of Payments of the 5th May, 1921 (French text: "en l'état de ses obligations telles qu'elles sont définies par le Traité de Versailles et en particulier par l'état des paiements du 5 mai 1921"), could raise foreign loans to be applied to the redemption in part of the capital of the reparation debt.

'The committee would in particular consider—

1. The terms on which such loans could be raised, and the amount which might reasonably be expected to be obtained in the near future, and in particular in the course of each of the next two years;
2. The security which could be made available for potential lenders without undue prejudice to the future interest of reparation;
3. The manner in which the revenues and other assets assigned to the service of the loans

the statements made by my colleagues and myself before the decision was taken.

It is regrettable that this decision had to be taken by a majority,[5] more particularly since, in view of the statement made by the French President of the Council in the Chamber last week, it remains doubtful whether the majority decision of the commission will be regarded by the committee as indicating the degree of inter-Allied co-operation which they will probably consider essential to any fruitful deliberation on the basis which they contemplated.

On the other hand, the situation has been somewhat eased by the statement made by the president immediately after the decision of the commission was taken, which may perhaps be taken as indicating a willingness on the part of the French Government to accept the commission's decision and a hope that the labours of the committee will be continued on that basis with useful results. My general impression is that the French Government has come to realise that to require the Loan Committee to deliberate without giving it freedom to consider all questions relevant to the re-establishment of German foreign credit would have created an absurd situation. On the other hand,

should be controlled and administered, and the relations to be established as between the German Government, the representatives of the lenders and the Reparation Commission.

'The committee was instructed to consult with persons having practical experience in connection with the issue of Government loans in New York, London, Paris, Rome and Brussels, Amsterdam, Berne, Berlin and elsewhere, with a view to the formation of a practical plan to be submitted for the approval of the German Government and the Reparation Commission.' A copy of this Report of the Loan Committee, which was transmitted to the Treasury by Sir J. Bradbury under cover of his despatch No. 294 of June 12 (not printed), will be found in the Foreign Office archives at C 8534/99/18.

[5] In a Memorandum of June 14 (C 8545/99/18), Mr. Wigram commented: 'But despite and indeed largely because of this majority decision, the committee reported on June 10, 1922, that a foreign loan was impossible. A foreign loan was impossible because, taking into account the attitude of the French delegate on the reparation commission, the committee of bankers [the Loan Committee] felt that the favourable atmosphere essential to the successful flotation of a foreign loan by Germany was not present. France, who was after all Germany's chief creditor, did not yet "desire any enquiry into the more general conditions necessary for the re-establishment of Germany's external credit" and the committee did not therefore "feel justified in making such an enquiry".

'The committee of bankers further categorically declared that the flotation of a German foreign loan, whilst the May 1921 schedule of payments remained suspended over the head of Germany, was impossible. No one, either in the United States, Great Britain or the ex-neutral countries would subscribe to such a loan so long as it was felt that the reparation payments were beyond the capacity of Germany to pay, and whilst therefore there remained the possibility that economic collapse and social disorder in Germany might still be brought about as the result of insistence on such payments.

'The bankers added that were Germany herself to make a real and substantial effort to put her public finances in order, and were the present uncertainty in regard to the future reparation payments to be removed, and were it practicable to approach the reparation question in conjunction with that of the settlement of the war indebtedness of Germany's creditors, then the question of the flotation by Germany of a foreign loan might again be considered.'

it was impossible for political reasons for the French Government to agree to any procedure which suggested that it would be willing to consent to a reduction of the French *créance* without compensating adjustments of inter-Allied debts.

The arrangement under which the present decision of the Reparation Commission has been taken by a majority against the French vote is therefore probably not regarded by them as wholly unsatisfactory.

On the other hand, the absence of active French support undoubtedly makes the task of the committee more difficult, and it is by no means certain that the committee itself will think it worth while to continue its labours in these circumstances.

I have, etc.,
JOHN BRADBURY

No. 28

Sir J. Bradbury (Reparation Commission) to Sir R. Horne
[*C 8593/99/18*][1]

PARIS, *June 14, 1922*

My dear Chancellor,

In view of Monsieur Poincaré's visit to London[2] it may be useful if I give you an account of the situation here as I see it.

The majority decision of the Reparation Commission[3] and the Bankers' report[4] have undoubtedly given both the French Government and French public opinion a salutary shaking up.

It is hardly too much to say that it is coming to be generally realised that a considerable writing down of the German obligations under the Treaty is inevitable, but the objective now is to tie up this writing down with the grant of a larger share of the reduced amount to France and a general revision of inter-allied debts.

The prevailing opinion is that if France is to make 'concessions' to Germany she must receive compensations in the form of concessions by America and Great Britain to herself. This point of view—though I am afraid it has been encouraged in past inter-allied discussions—appears to me to be wrong in principle and likely to lead to an impasse in practice.

No one proposes any 'concession' to Germany. The only object in writing down the German obligation is to turn a bad debt into a good one and so *increase* the amount which Germany's creditors (of whom France is the largest) will receive. France is far more likely to need extensive remissions of her own debts if she wastes her substance in a wild goose chase after an

---

[1] A copy of this letter was communicated by the Treasury to the Foreign Office on June 15, 1922.

[2] M. Poincaré made an unofficial visit to London from June 17 to 19 (see No. 30, below).

[3] See No. 27.   [4] See No. 27, nn. 4 and 5.

irrecoverable créance than if she fortifies her financial position by accepting a reasonable composition.

If we are to treat the debts owing by France to Great Britain and America as a purely business proposition, i.e., on the basis on which we want the German debt to be treated we must first of all know what France's assets are likely to be before we can decide how much we can reasonably hope to recover from her, and so long as she tells us (however little we may be disposed to believe it) that she values the German créance at 100 per cent, there is really no basis for discussion.

Again if we want to be generous to France, we shall still want the same information to enable us to decide the measure of generosity which the situation requires. On the other hand, if we want to discuss on purely moral grounds the propriety of arrangements under which a particular part of the contributions which different Allies made during the war to the common cause gives rise to a permanent tribute payable by one to another, the question is then solely one of right and justice as between Allies to be considered on its merits without any relation to Germany at all.

Whatever therefore there may be to be said in favour of a proposal to write down (or even to write off) inter-allied debts on its own merits—and I have always thought and continue to think that the case in favour of it from the point of view both of abstract equity and practical necessity will ultimately become conclusive—is really quite irrelevant to the question at any rate at its present stage.

The first step is to find out what we, the Allies generally, can in fact extract from Germany as a business proposition. It has now become evident that nothing substantial can be got except by agreement—an agreement into which no doubt Germany will only be prepared to enter lest worse befall her, but an agreement which she really believes she can carry out and which is not so disadvantageous to her as to leave her under the perpetual temptation to revert to the policy of inviting the allies to do their worst.

If the French and Belgians (for Theunis' statement yesterday[5] means that political considerations are forcing the latter back towards solidarity) really mean that they will be bankrupt unless they recover 100 per cent of their German créances or receive substantial concessions from America and Great Britain, it is obvious that a policy in regard to the German créance which can only mean throwing good money after bad will make the bankruptcy inevitable even with the concessions, while we at any rate shall be less able to afford the concessions since it will have made our créance against Germany irrecoverable along with their own—quite apart from the general mischief done to our foreign trade.

I am pretty sure that there is no chance of America considering a readjustment of inter-allied indebtedness until at any rate a provisional agreement has been reached with Germany. In this connection Boyden's remarks at the discussion of the widening of the Loan Committee's reference are very

---

[5] Details of this statement were transmitted to the Foreign Office by Sir G. Grahame in his despatch No. 405 of June 14 (C 8852/99/18), not printed.

illuminating (copy annexed[6]). Indeed it is not impossible that America will insist not only upon a provisional agreement but a substantive one as an indispensable preliminary to any such discussion. This seems to me logical though a little hard and I doubt if such an attitude could be persisted in, if a definite settlement between the Allies and Germany were actually in view, provided only some readjustments could be made in regard to inter-allied indebtedness.

In that event my own view is that we could safely even go a bit ahead of America—though that is a delicate question and outside my province. But what I *am* here about is that not a penny or a cent (either in respect of inter-allied debts or British and American claims against Germany) ought to be given or promised to France until we and America are quite sure that the concession will result in a general settlement.

I believe that in the present state of French public opinion an attitude of this kind on our part will be much more likely to result in real business than if we lend ourselves to the French attempt to do a 'hors[e]-trade'. If we encourage[7] the French to think that their stiffness towards Germany is so much more damaging to us than to themselves that we shall be willing to buy them off, they will persist in this line in the hope of getting something out of us which (even if we were prepared to give it them on merits) we shall be prevented from giving them by reason of the attitude of America.

If on the other hand we tell them firmly that a provisional settlement with Germany is an indispensable preliminary to any discussion of inter-allied debts it will not be long now before they become practical.

We must, however, at the same time make it clear to them that if they are

[6] Mr. R. W. Boyden was the United States unofficial delegate to the Reparation Commission. His statement ran as follows: 'While I have always regarded the mandate of the Loan Committee as instructed, and felt that only a negative answer would be possible under its terms, I have always expected that if this proved to be the case, the Commission would be glad to receive suggestions from the Committee as to any changes in conditions which, in their judgment, would make a loan possible. My personal judgment therefore is that the Committee should now be given liberty to make such suggestions.

'As my colleagues have indicated that in their minds there is a close relation between changes in Germany's indemnity obligations and the Inter-Allied debt, I must add that this subject is not within my competence. The Inter-Allied debt has already been the subject of legislative action by the United States Congress, and a Committee appointed under that legislation is alone competent to deal with it.

'I am of opinion that any emphasis on a possible relation between the two subjects is likely to make more difficult the result which seems to be hopeful. I note that the declaration of the French Delegate contains a just appreciation of this point of view.

'I will further add that personally I have never seen any connection between the two matters. No one is likely to suggest that Germany should be relieved of any obligation which she can reasonably meet. The only effect of a change in the indemnity will, therefore, be to increase not to diminish the amounts likely to be received from Germany. I feel that the Allies have already lost considerable sums which under a different policy might have been obtained from Germany, and that more will be lost unless the policy is changed. If this opinion is well founded, the changes likely to be suggested cannot result in any sacrifice by any Power.' For the attitude of the United States Government to the problems of Inter-Allied debt and German reparation, see *F.R.U.S.* 1922, vol. i, pp. 396–417.

[7] This word was substituted for 'discourage' in the Foreign Office.

prepared to treat the German situation on business lines we will back them up in the necessary pressure upon Germany—even to the point of a Ruhr occupation in the event of real recalcitrance. I have felt much sympathy with German resistance while it has been resistance to impossible demands, but as soon as it becomes resistance to a tolerable settlement, it is mischievous, even from the point of Germany herself, unless successful. The best security therefore against its being undertaken is to make it obvious beforehand that it is hopeless. For myself I have not that degree of faith in German 'bonne volonté' as to regard this as by any means an unnecessary precaution.

Yours sincerely,
JOHN BRADBURY

No. 29

Mr. Addison[1] (Berlin) to Lord Balfour (Received June 20)
No. 456 [C 8817/99/18]

BERLIN, *June 14, 1922*

My Lord,

I have the honour to transmit to Your Lordship herewith, translation of an official communiqué[2] which appeared in this morning's press defining, in vague and general terms, the attitude of the German Government with regard to the question of reparation and the financial position of this country.

The decision of the Bankers' Conference in Paris[3] to the effect that present conditions do not allow of the grant of a loan, would appear to have placed the German Government in a position of some difficulty since the concessions made in their reply to the Reparation Commission on the 29th [*sic*][4] ultimo, were based on the assumption that foreign credits to some substantial amount would be available. Now that the German Government are faced with the same problem as before, they appear to be in a condition of resigned fatalism. I hear from many quarters that confusion prevails and that although there is a multiplicity of counsel on side issues, no definite plan has been formed as to how to deal with the main situation complicated as it is by political considerations from which ordinary commercial transactions are fortunately free. In short, the German Government would appear to be 'waiting for something to turn up'.

As Your Lordship is no doubt aware, the Committee of Guarantees[5] will shortly be visiting Berlin for the express purpose of studying the situation on the spot and of coming to an agreement with regard to the practical working of the system of control to which the German Government gave a general assent in their note of the 29th [*sic*][4] ultimo above mentioned. The

---

[1] Counsellor to H.M. Embassy at Berlin, acting as Chargé d'Affaires from May 22 to June 27, and from September 11 to October 5, 1922.

[2] Not printed.   [3] See No. 27, nn. 4 and 5.

[4] This communication was dated May 28 (see No. 26, n. 4).

[5] See Vol. XV, No. 81, Appendix.

magnitude of the task of elaboration of the practical application of this general principle will be seen from a mere perusal of the agenda of this Conference, copy of which is enclosed herein.[2] This document may, no doubt, have reached Your Lordship from another source.

I understand that considerable opposition has been aroused in the Ministry of Finance and other Governmental quarters by the perusal of this agenda and that, in particular, great resistance is to be expected to that part which relates to the collaboration with the special Commissary of Economies. In short, the obvious fact has become patent that financial supervision means financial control and that proper financial control carries with it a right of interference in the internal administration of the country, which, if granted, would imply a partial abandonment of full sovereign rights.

In addition, therefore, to many obvious subsidiary difficulties the German Government are now faced with a situation in which they have admitted a principle, whose logical consequences it is almost impossible for them to accept, if only on the ground of lack of support in Parliament and in the country. It is therefore difficult to see how the negotiations between the Committee of Guarantees and the German Government are to lead to any useful result, except in so far as they may mark a step in the direction of slow progress towards a solution of this economic problem on a purely economic basis.

I have, etc.,

JOSEPH ADDISON

No. 30

I.C.P. 249c] *British Secretary's notes of a Meeting between Mr. Lloyd George and M. Poincaré, held at 10, Downing Street, London, on Monday, June 19, 1922, at 2.45 p.m.*

[*C 8998/99/18*]

PRESENT: *Great Britain*: The Prime Minister (*in the Chair*); Lord Balfour, Sir Robert Horne (*for part of Item 1*); EXPERTS, Sir Basil Blackett (*for part of Item 1*), Mr. Vansittart[1] (*from Item 2 onwards*).
France: M. Poincaré (President of the Council); M. S[ain]t-Aulaire (French Ambassador).

SECRETARY: Sir Maurice Hankey.[2]

INTERPRETER: M. Camerlynck.

Reparations

(1) M. POINCARÉ said that just before, at luncheon, he had indicated to Mr. Lloyd George the general view of the French Government on the subject of Reparations. The Prime Minister had then expressed a desire that he should repeat it in the presence of Sir Robert Horne, and he congratulated himself on the opportunity to do so. He thought the matter

[1] Private Secretary to Lord Curzon.   [2] Secretary to the Cabinet.

could be summed up in a few words. Like the Reparation Commission, he thought that the most important and urgent subject was the establishment of control, first, over the budget and expenditure of Germany; second, over the currency and circulation of notes in Germany; and, third, over exportations from Germany.

(During the translation of the above statement MR LLOYD GEORGE asked whether M. Poincaré referred to the exportation of capital.

M. POINCARÉ replied that he referred to two forms of exportation; first, the exportation of goods in connection with the general balance of trade, and, second, the exportation of capital in the form of foreign bank notes, securities, etc., which, he was informed, were leaving Germany in the ordinary course of trade.)

Continuing, M. Poincaré said that perhaps it had been a mistake to ask the Committee of Bankers[3] to meet before control was realised and had become effective. It was very important that control should not be established and the loan should not be launched before the German finances were on a sound basis and not in the state of chaos in which they were today. He hoped then that the question of an International Loan would be discussed again after Germany had carried out what the Reparation Commission demanded.[4] At this moment there was no question of an international loan, and the consideration of the question could not be resumed. In the unanimous view of the French Government, however, there was no question of abandoning any part of the French debt from Germany. Hence, the control must be established in the conditions foreseen, whether by the Treaty of Versailles or laid down by the Reparation Commission. On this point he thought there was no difference of opinion, and the French Government was in agreement with the British Government.

MR LLOYD GEORGE said that Sir Robert Horne was in continuous contact with the British representative on the Reparation Commission; perhaps, therefore, he would explain the present position.

SIR ROBERT HORNE said that, as M. Poincaré realised, the Committee of Bankers appointed by the Reparation Commission had failed to reach practical conclusions. The reason for this was that the question of reparations had become mixed up with the question of inter-Allied indebtedness, and both were involved with the fact that no foreign financier would grant a loan while the question of reparations remained undetermined. In fact, no foreigner would produce the money for Germany to pay her creditors until he knew what was the total amount that Germany would have to pay. Without this knowledge he could not judge whether the security was good enough. Consequently, they were back in the position in which they were before the Committee met, namely, that the Reparation Commission had to deal with the question. The position was, first, that Germany must balance her budget; second, that she must stop the increase in the circulation of paper money, which was one of the root causes of her present trouble;

³ See No. 27, nn. 4 and 5.   ⁴ See No. 26, n. 4.

third, as M. Poincaré had suggested, that they must try and regain some of the capital which German industrialists were exporting from Germany, thereby rendering Germany less capable of fulfilling her obligations. The difficulty was that they were in a vicious circle. Germany said she could not stop the emission of paper money and repay her obligations unless she was able to raise a foreign loan, and she could not raise a foreign loan unless she could pay her obligations. This was the vicious circle they were in. His view was that Germany should meet her expenditure by the normal means of raising revenue to meet expenditure. Germany had undertaken to restrict her paper if she could obtain a loan. But, as she could not obtain a loan, he feared that the promise to restrict the paper circulation was only a pious aspiration.

MR LLOYD GEORGE asked as to the possibilities of an internal loan for the purpose of balancing the budget.

SIR ROBERT HORNE said that the Reparation Commission had advised that Germany should raise an internal loan,[5] and he understood that the question was now being discussed.

MR. LLOYD GEORGE asked if the Reparation Commission was prepared to sanction an internal loan for the purpose of balancing the budget?

SIR ROBERT HORNE replied that that was the case. But the difficulty of reparation payments was that they could not raise enough money to make these payments without a foreign loan.

MR. LLOYD GEORGE asked if they could not do so by payments in kind?

SIR ROBERT HORNE replied that they could not pay them in full. The amounts were restricted to £37,500,000 in cash and £72,500,000 in kind. In reply to the Prime Minister, he doubted if Germany could meet this obligation. She had the capacity to raise the amount, whether in raw materials and in kind, or in cash, but he doubted if she could deliver the amount in France.

MR. LLOYD GEORGE remarked that this was a question of the French capacity of absorption and of transport.

SIR ROBERT HORNE agreed. He thought she might raise the restricted amount this year if it could be delivered. He thought that the full amount of her obligations could only be raised if Germany had time to recover herself. He had given a good deal of thought to the question of exportation of capital. The only way to get back the exported German capital was, he thought, to make Germany a more attractive place for Germans to invest their capital in. It was the old story of the goose and the golden egg. You could not get the egg if you killed the goose.

MR. LLOYD GEORGE asked Lord Balfour to describe his conversation with Mr. Jack Morgan.[6]

LORD BALFOUR said that he ought to begin by explaining that his conversation was perfectly informal, unofficial and private. (M. Poincaré interpolated that it had been exactly the same in Paris.) Continuing, Lord Balfour

[5] In a letter of March 21 to the German Chancellor (see No. 12, n. 1).

[6] Mr. J. P. Morgan was an American banker who served on the Committee of Bankers appointed by the Reparation Commission in April, 1922.

said that as Mr. Morgan was in London on his return from Paris he had taken advantage of meeting him to ask his view on the whole question. Put shortly, his view, which also was that of the financial authorities with whom Mr. Morgan had discussed the matter, was that nothing could be obtained from the American lenders, or, for the matter of that, from lenders in any other country, if there was any doubt in regard to the solidity of the Entente between Great Britain and France. The commercial and lending world thought that this was the only hope of Europe, and was the solid basis of the existing state of affairs. If they thought that the Entente was in any dangerous or dubious state, it would have a most adverse influence upon them. Reconstruction, in their view, could not take place if England and France were to quarrel. That was Mr. Morgan's first proposition. His second proposition was a fairly obvious banker's declaration:— they would not risk their money unless the debt was a first charge on the German resources; that is to say, if a way was to be found of putting an end to the present reparations situation by means of a foreign loan, it would be necessary that that loan should be put in front of the other obligations of Germany.

(Sir Robert Horne had to leave at this point, for Parliamentary reasons.)

The third point was that Germany could not obtain a loan unless Germany could be rehabilitated economically. Mr. Morgan had appeared to take a gloomy view as to the economic situation. So long as she was in her present position, Germany was not, in his view, in a position to pay her obligations under the Treaty of Versailles and as fixed by the Reparation Commission. The only chance was that Germany should know the total amount of what she had to pay. So long as that was an uncertain quantity, liable to be increased if Germany was prosperous and to be diminished when she was not, a state of depression would be produced in Germany which would, in Mr. Morgan's view, prevent her from putting herself in a position to pay. At this point Lord Balfour said he ought to remind his hearers of what they probably knew, namely, that Mr. Morgan was very far from being a pro-German; he took the view that Germany ought to be able to pay, and he was not in favour of cutting down her obligations. He considered, however, that Germany could only pay if she was prosperous and economically efficient. He was conscious of the argument that the total amount could not be fixed until it was known whether Germany was going to be prosperous. If she was prosperous she could pay a great deal of money; otherwise she could not. Broadly speaking, Mr. Morgan appeared to think that the Allies must make up their minds as to whether they wanted a weak Germany who could not pay, or a strong Germany who could pay. If they wanted a weak Germany they must keep her economically weak; but if they wanted her to be able to pay they must allow Germany to exist in a condition of cheerfulness, which would lead to a successful business. This meant, however, that you would get a strong Germany, and a Germany that was strong economically would, in a sense, be strong from a military point of view also. That was the general impression he had formed of the conversation, and which he understood Mr. Lloyd George wished him to explain.

71

Mr. LLOYD GEORGE said he thought it was a very important statement, as this was the view of a very strong friend of the Allies.

(Sir Basil Blackett entered at this point.)

M. POINCARÉ said that in Paris several members of the French Government, as well as he himself, had had long discussions with the American Bankers, and they had derived much the same impression as Lord Balfour. While he laid great stress on those statements, nevertheless, in spite of all, it had to be remembered that bankers were only bankers and that they did not pretend to represent the United States Government. They could not give any sort of undertaking in regard to inter-Allied claims and debts. They could give certain hints and suggestions, but they could give no kind of engagement on the subject of these debts. Hence he stood by his first statement, and accepted Mr. Morgan's words as a general indication of his attitude. After these general remarks M. Poincaré said he would come to the various points suggested in the conversation between Mr. Morgan and Lord Balfour.

The first point related to the importance of the solidity of the Entente. It was quite obvious that on this the financiers were right. If the Entente were to disappear or become feeble, the security of Europe and, indeed, of the world, would be compromised. There would then be no further question of a foreign loan, but he thought that that would be the least of the ill results to follow from a rupture of the Entente. Everyone must agree that by maintaining the Entente they were doing much more than giving satisfaction to the bankers and safeguarding far loftier and more noble interests.

The second point in Mr. Morgan's conversation had been that the loan must be a first charge on German resources. The Reparation Commission had not excluded that, but he thought that an essential condition was that the produce of the loan should, in the main, be devoted to reparations and only a small part should be devoted to the balancing of the German budget. The Reparation Commission, indeed, would fail in its duty if it allowed any large proportion of the loan to be devoted to Germany. Germany must pay her creditors. That was the basic idea of the Treaty of Versailles.

The third observation of Mr. Morgan had been that an International Loan could only be envisaged if it were possible to expect the economic restoration of Germany. He agreed. If the lenders thought that the German economic position could never be restored, this would be a bad opinion and would probably discourage the public from taking up the loan. All this, however, was a matter of proportion, and on this question he could bring to the notice of the British Government some facts which would enlighten them and help them to form an opinion. At the present time Germany was constructing railways and was doubling and quadrupling the permanent way on existing railways. He could supply definite information to the British Government on this subject, which he had derived from the Inter-Allied Military Commission. Germany was also developing her mercantile marine in a manner which would before long make it a severe competitor not only to the French but also to the British mercantile marine. Germany was also spending money freely in order to ameliorate her economic position, which would help her in her future competition with Great Britain and France. Some of this money should be diverted towards the fulfilment of her obligations. He was told that the fixation of the German debt was an essential. It was fixed already. Of course the payments could be postponed on the decision of a majority of the Reparation Commission, but the debt could not be reduced. The amount was fixed and could only be altered by a majority of the nations concerned. France was not prepared to grant any reduction. Already 90 milliards of francs had been spent on assisting Germany. Germany was aware of this, and so were the American bankers. The amount that Germany had to pay had been fixed at 132 milliard gold marks, and could not be reduced. He did not propose to refer to the question of Inter-Allied debts, as he did not know the position of the United States of America on the subject, but his country was a creditor for a sum of 2 milliards. He understood Mr. Morgan to say that they were in front of a dilemma. They were told that if they wanted to be paid it was necessary that the German situation should be restored not only from an economical but from a military point of view.

(During the interpretation of this part LORD BALFOUR intervened to say that this was not what Mr. Morgan had said. What he had suggested was that the fact of economic strength carried with it military strength.

M. POINCARÉ said it was only another form of saying the same thing. He had understood his view to be that she must have military strength.

LORD BALFOUR said that the military strength only followed on the economic strength.

M. POINCARÉ said that this reasoning would apply to any other situation. If Germany was powerful economically she would exercise her economic strength against other countries, and the Allies would then have to consider what was to be done.)

Continuing, M. Poincaré said that the situation was singularly difficult, as the suggestion was that if Germany was restored to the extent necessary to enable her to pay the Allies she would reach the point where, from the military point of view, she became redoubtable. He thought, however, that the matter need not be managed in that way and that it might be arranged that little by little Germany should be in a position to pay her creditors. Consequently he did not think they were in such a vicious circle as had been suggested. He now asked for control. Why? Because he was certain that Germany was wasting her money. She was using in Governmental luxury expenditure money which ought to be devoted to other purposes—to develop her finances systematically and to pay her debts. Also, Germany was husbanding her resources in order to stimulate her exports and improve her position as a competitor with France and Great Britain. It had been noticed that every time the Mark showed a tendency to rise the German merchants did something to bring about its collapse, in order that they might profit by the fall in the Mark to improve their exportation. Were the Allies to arrange to prolong this state of affairs? Could not the Reparation Commission manage so as to make Germany put her house in order and get rid of waste and this enormous note circulation? The desired International Loan was in reality only to enable Germany to pay her obligations. He would say clearly to the British Cabinet that the French Government favoured payment in kind. He thought that Germany could probably do a good deal more in that respect than at present. She was in a position to deliver certain kinds of raw materials for the devastated regions. He thought that arrangements might be made for greater assistance in the form of labour and material in these regions. As regards exportation of capital, he would ask how these investments took place? The men who exported were exactly the same persons who contributed to the fall of the Mark, namely, the great industrialists who invested in foreign undertakings, and more particularly in neutral countries from which it was very difficult to secure the return of the capital. It had been suggested that it might be a good plan to render Germany more attractive for the investment of capital by German financiers. As the German Ambassador had remarked to him a few days ago in Paris, the German industrialists exported capital in order to escape from their own taxation. They would neither pay their own taxation nor enable their Government to pay its creditors. Bank-notes would only come back to Germany if the German Government suppressed its taxes. They were clear, therefore, that they had before them a country that had no intention of paying, and the French Government were absolutely of opinion that the money could only be obtained if all the Allies acted together.

MR. LLOYD GEORGE asked what was the nature of the agreement which the Reparation Commission had entered into with the Germans as regards control.

SIR BASIL BLACKETT said that the Commission [Committee] of Guarantees[7] had the right of examination and inspection of German finances without any control of administration in Germany. This had been settled on May 31st.[8] After first objecting[9] to the control proposed the German Government had agreed to this, and the question was now settled. The Commission [Committee] of Guarantees was entitled to full knowledge of German finances, but not to take any executive action.

M. POINCARÉ said that in the present state of affairs he thought the view of the Reparation Commission was that it was in a first stage as regards control. He did not wish to prejudge the question in any way, but it might later become necessary to ask if this control was sufficiently effective. It was not yet an organised control. It was only organised as regards the emission of Notes, but it was not organised in regard to exportation and very little organised in regard to the German budget. He was not certain that the Reparation Commission in the present state of affairs had sufficient personnel to exercise its powers. The Commission [Committee] of Guarantees

[7] See Vol. XV, No. 81, Appendix. [8] See No. 26, n. 4.
[9] In a letter to the Reparation Commission of April 7 (see Reparation Commission III, op. cit., pp. 121–4).

was mostly in Paris and very rarely in Berlin. Consequently it could not exercise in full the right of inspection which Sir Basil Blackett had described. To exercise these powers properly he thought that the Commission [Committee] of Guarantees should have a Delegation in Berlin or that it should sit permanently in Berlin. In fact at the moment they were in a provisional period. He would take the liberty to call the kind attention of the British Government to the importance of making this control a reality.

MR. LLOYD GEORGE said he was trying to find out exactly what was the proposal of the French Government. All were agreed on a certain measure of control in order to ascertain if the German budget was being drawn up in a bona fide manner; whether the deficiencies were beyond the control of the German Government or whether there was some expenditure they ought to suppress; and whether they were really spending money on what M. Poincaré had described as Governmental luxury. If so, such expenditure ought to be stopped since they were not fulfilling the Treaty. Personally he did not think that the creation of a Mercantile Marine was a luxury. He did not see how they could conduct their business without it. He knew nothing of the Railway expenditure of Germany, but if the construction was required for the development of industries it might be argued as necessary to the life of Germany and ought to be allowed to develop. If, however, it was for military purposes of course it should be forbidden. He understood that the immediate step to be taken was a matter on which the two Governments were agreed, namely that there should be a thorough investigation of the German budget under the auspices of the Reparation Commission; that they should ascertain what was the German expenditure and that there was no unnecessary expenditure; and that they were doing all they could to confine themselves to a permissible expenditure. That much was agreed. If the Reparation Commission required strengthening it ought to report this matter and the Governments could consider the mechanism.

SIR BASIL BLACKETT in reply to the Prime Minister said that this was a matter within the com[p]etence of the Reparation Commission.

MR. LLOYD GEORGE continuing said that on this point there was no fundamental disagreement. If the Reparation Commission reported that Germany was deliberately and fraudulently manipulating her accounts with a view to defrauding her creditors M. Poincaré would find no difficulty in inducing the British Government to agree to reasonable steps being taken. If, however, the report was of a different character and to the effect that Germany was doing her best, then he thought probably there would be no difference between the two Governments. It was obvious that if the Reparation Commission reported that Germany was for purposes not under its control unable to balance its budget, then there could be no question of coercion. On the first step, however, the two Governments were agreed. His view was that the present difficulties were temporary; he had always believed that Germany could make substantial payments and he was still of that opinion. He admitted that he was disappointed as to the time taken for Germany to be in a position to do so. Looking back, however, he saw that his expectations had been too sanguine. In order to pay outside Germany must sell outside her own country. The only exception was in regard to payments in kind. He agreed with M. Poincaré that it would be a good thing if Germany could increase her payments in kind, but he did not see how this could be done without direct assistance from Government Departments in France, Belgium and Great Britain. He was all in favour of an increase in material payments, but outside of that he did not see how there could be any increase. Germany's sales in foreign countries were exactly 25 per cent. of what they were before the War. Like all other countries Germany was suffering from the impoverishment of consumers in other countries. Great Britain was finding that Europe and Asia could not buy, and the same applied in South America. Unless the trade of the world improved there was no chance of Germany being able to pay the instalments fixed in the London agreement.[10] This difficulty, however, was temporary. This was the reason why he thought there should be no abatement of German payments fixed in relation to the present economic position which was at its worst. As the general position improved so the capacity of Germany to pay would increase. Secondly he did not believe that there could be a settlement of Reparations until there was a settlement of inter-allied indebtedness, and this would not take place until the United States of America was ready to discuss it.[11] Great Britain could not forego her claims on her Allies or on Germany until the United States of America would also forego her claims. This she was not prepared to do, certainly not this year and he could not speak as regards next year.

(M. Poincaré interpolated that next year there was an Election).

Continuing Mr. Lloyd George repeated that the difficulty was temporary. The trade of the world was at the lowest level, worse than in 1920 or 1921. As Germany had always been an exporting country her capacity to pay abroad was also at bottom. It would not improve until the world position improved. Hence he was opposed to any alteration in payments based on present conditions. If some means could be found of tiding over present difficulties until the world position was restored, then substantial payments might be obtained. This brought him to his next point.

The moment was bad to examine the powers of coercion. Such consideration at the present moment would be made at a time when Germany could make out a case for her inability to pay. Perhaps she might be made to pay a little more here or there, but Germany could make out a case at present that she could not carry out the whole of the payments in the schedule. Hence to apply coercion now would be to exercise this right at a time when the whole world would be against the Allies. He recalled that some time ago coercion had been applied by the occupation of Dusseldorf and other towns.[12] A fine piece of paper had been obtained by this coercion, but the cost of the Army of Occupation had been increased. What was required now was not paper but payment. If means of coercion were adopted it would

---

[10] See No. 5, n. 2.   [11] See No. 28, n. 6.
[12] See Vol. XV, Nos. 45–7, and Vol. XVI, No. 458.

merely mean that the cost would be still further increased. He would be more willing to consider coercion if he were really convinced Germany was shamming and could be made to pay, but he was not convinced of that. He was certain that Germany, like the rest of the world, was suffering from general depression, and was not in a position to make large payments outside her borders. Hence he agreed in [sic] the first proposal of M. Poincaré that the Reparation Commission should examine the finances of Germany, and the British Government would support anything that was required to ensure a searching report on the whole position. When the Report was received they would see what sort of a Report it was, and then consider what further action was required to adapt themselves to the situation.

He himself had never believed in an external loan for Germany. The Germans had been sanguine, and thought they could obtain the money in Great Britain, America, and France. He had thought the conditions were far too uncertain to justify any financier in advising his clients to invest in such a loan. He was certain Germany would obtain no foreign loan until, first the economic position of the world improved, and second until German exports recovered. He observed that as competitors we were not afraid of the revival of her exports, because such a revival would mean there would be a recovery, and our own exports would recover at the same time. Until that time he was certain that no loan could be obtained.

(During the interpretation of the above remarks, Mr. Lloyd George interjected that the British Government had received no Report from Sir John Bradbury on the staff of the Reparation Commission. M. Poincaré replied that neither had the French Government. They had instructed their Delegate on the subject, and he would like the British Government to do the same in order that there might be an increase.)

M. Poincaré said that he was pleased to find that on many points there was full accord between Mr. Lloyd George and himself, especially on the essential point—that we were now passing through a provisional period. At present it was clear that the position for Germany was at its worst, and there was no need to envisage the future on the basis of the present. The French Government would never agree to a reduction of German debt based on present conditions, because it believed that Germany would recover. If they agreed to reduce the debt, they would expose themselves to the most terrible consequences in a few years' time, because Germany would recover, and French public opinion would never forgive a Government which had reduced its debts and abandoned part of its rights.

He also agreed, in fact it was almost a truism, that the German Government could not pay unless there was a development of its exports, or else an international loan. He was less optimistic [sic] than Mr. Lloyd George as to the prospects of a loan. At first he had not believed in it, but Mr. Morgan[13] had suggested that in four months' time the bankers might return in a more optimistic frame of mind to make a proposal more favourable to the Allies. They might see that Germany was becoming more prosperous. Hence he

[13] See n. 6, above.

saw the necessity of being patient. In the interval he would like to get more payment in kind. The French industrials would object, but perhaps this difficulty might be surmounted.

As for sanctions, of which Mr. Lloyd George had spoken, the French Government would never employ them lightly, or without necessity. He was, however, expressing the view of the whole French Government, when he said they did not wish to give up the right of using the sanctions allowed by the Treaty of Versailles. They might find themselves tomorrow in the presence of a Germany who could not pay, but if the Reparation Commission granted a delay for payment, of course there would be no question of sanctions.

Further, if the Reparation commission declared that Germany could not pay no one would dream of applying sanctions. But they might come up against a different position. The Reparation Commission might make certain demands on Germany either in regard to the investigation or on the question of note issues or questions of exportation, and if Germany would not execute the wishes of the Reparation Commission or if she would not allow the exercise of the agreed control this would be a proof of bad faith. It was evident that in such eventualities it might be necessary to intervene to compel Germany to accept the control or to carry out what the Reparation Commission demanded. He repeated, however, that they must have patience. They were not in a position of having to demand a payment today but they wished to know if they had in front of them a Germany who wanted to balance her budget; who was not wasting her resources; who was not issuing an excessive paper currency. If they were in front of a Germany who could not pay and sanctions were applied then, as Mr. Lloyd George had said, the world would be against them. But if they were in front of a Germany who refused to pay what she could pay then there would be no public opinion against them and sanctions might have to be applied. If they ever were applied he hoped they would be applied in common.

Mr. Lloyd George said that perhaps the question could be reduced to one of definitions. He understood that the present control was confined to an investigation of the financial position of Germany. It was not proposed to set up something corresponding to the Ottoman Debt Commission[14] which possessed certain executive and administrative authority. It was only an investigation into financial conditions in Germany with a view to report to the German Government and the Allied Governments. The report would point out to Germany whether she was extravagant and in what respect she was failing to place her finances in a sound position.

M. Poincaré agreed that this was the present significance of the decision of the Reparation Commission. He reserved the opinion of the French Government, however, in case the measures at this first stage did not prove adequate or in case Germany did not prove her *bona fides* by assisting the

---

[14] An institution consisting of the holders of Turkish bonds which, by the Decree of Moharrem (December 20, 1881), was granted the right to collect and administer certain State revenues (see Vol. XVII, No. 565, n. 1).

enquiry with the necessary information. For the moment he must maintain this position. He thought that perhaps a misunderstanding had arisen from the difference of meaning of the word 'control' in the two languages. In French the word 'control' implied no executive authority (Mr. Lloyd George interpolated that in English it did imply a certain executive authority). Continuing, M. Poincaré said that in French it only involved a supervision. It might be, however, that on the morrow it might have to be exercised more freely in Germany if the Germans showed bad faith in preventing the execution of the decision. One of two things might happen. Either Germany would hinder free surveillance or else the investigations would result in the discovery of mismanagement. In either of these two hypotheses Germany would be failing to execute her obligations. If she closed the door to the enquiry or if deliberate mismanagement were discovered the two Governments would have to consider the question and decide what was to be done to make Germany fulfil her obligations.

Mr. Lloyd George said that there seemed to be general agreement as regards the present and the immediate future and he hoped that they might also be able to agree when the next stage was reached. If Germany refused information or to meet her obligations when it was known that she possessed resources then M. Poincaré would find that the English view was the French view and the French view was the English view. In the meantime the Reparation Commission would pursue its investigations in regard to the real position of German finance and report to the Governments. Then they would put their heads together to consider what was to be done.

M. Poincaré thought that that was the best procedure. When the time came he would be at Mr. Lloyd George's disposal to discuss the matter again. It would be easier for him than for Mr. Lloyd George because the French Parliament adjourned before the British. Then he would be at his disposal to come to England for further and freer conversations on this subject.

Mr. Lloyd George said he would be quite ready to discuss the matter. He asked if he might now pass on to another question.

M. Poincaré said he was leaving for Paris that evening at 8.0 p.m. and he thought the question of reparations was now exhausted.[15]

---

[15] The Conference then discussed (item 2) Russia (see Vol. XIX, No. 162), and (item 3) the Near East (cf. Vol. XVII, No. 659).

No. 31

Note of Interviews between Sir Basil Blackett and Dr. Ernst von Simson,[1] on Friday, June 30, 1922 from 6.15 p.m. to 6.45 p.m. and on Saturday, July 1, 1922, from 10.30 a.m. to 11.45 a.m.

[C 9523/99/18][2]

TREASURY CHAMBERS, *July 3, 1922*

PRESENT: Sir Basil Blackett and Mr. S. D. Waley[3] (on Saturday only); Dr. von Simson and Herr Dufour-Feronce.[4]

Dr. von Simson explained that he had been asked to come to England by Dr. Wirth to see Sir Basil Blackett semi-officially and discuss with him the question of an early application by Germany for an extension to cover 1923 and if possible 1924 of the Moratorium for German Reparation at present limited to 1922.[5] Dr. Rathenau had been contemplating such an application at the moment of his murder.[6] The German Government was led to consider this by the difficulty which it forsaw in meeting the instalment of 50,000,000 gold marks due on August 15th and the subsequent instalments during 1922. It also felt that Monsieur Poincaré's recent utterances[7] suggested that the French were no longer so insistent on immediate cash payments as they had hitherto been and might be willing to consider a Moratorium for 1923 and 1924 as a means of escaping from further pressure to reduce forthwith the gross total of the reparation debt. The Germans hoped that a Moratorium might be granted for 1923 and 1924 which would release them from any further *cash* payments on account of reparation during 1923 and 1924 and thus limit their cash payments during the next 30 months to the 320,000,000 gold marks due between now and December 1922. The Germans would be ready to go to the utmost limit during that period in regard to deliveries in kind. Dr. von Simson suggested 1,750 million gold marks as the annual figure for 1923 and 1924 deliveries in kind.

Dr. von Simson stated that it was really impossible for Germany to pay the 320 million gold marks cash during the rest of 1922 unless Germany were relieved of any cash liability for reparation in 1923 and 1924. Such a relief would enable Germany to make banking arrangements with foreign banks for meeting the 1922 payments.

But Dr. von Simson added that a release from cash payments for reparation during 1923 and 1924 would not be enough. There must also be relief in respect of cash payments due under other heads. He estimated that up to the end of 1924 Germany would, as things stand, have to find 580 million gold marks for the Enemy Debts Clearing House,[8] and 75 million gold marks

---

[1] A State Secretary in the German Foreign Office.
[2] This document was communicated by the Treasury to the Foreign Office on July 4.
[3] A Principal in H.M. Treasury.   [4] Counsellor of the German Embassy in London.
[5] See No. 26, n. 4.   [6] Dr. Rathenau was assassinated on June 24.
[7] For example, M. Poincaré's speech in the Senate on June 29 (see *The Times*, June 30, p. 9).
[8] The Enemy Debts Clearing House was established under article 296 of the treaty of Versailles; see Reparation Commission V, *Report on the Work of the Reparation Commission from 1920 to 1922* (H.M.S.O., 1923), pp. 53–5.

under the Mark Agreement with Belgium[9] if it was accepted (and he thought it would be necessary to come to an agreement with Belgium on this mark question in order to secure Belgian assent to the proposed moratorium) and in addition there was a potential liability of enormous amount (Dr. von Simson said on [a] certain hypothesis it might reach £1,000 million sterling) in respect of German requisitions in occupied territory and sequestration etc. of Allied property in Germany if the Mixed Arbitral Tribunals[10] (especially the French Tribunal) accepted certain claims.

Dr. von Simson stated that he did not look for any official statement of the British Government's probable attitude towards an application from Germany for a Moratorium on these lines, but solely to discuss the matter with Sir Basil Blackett personally. It was made plain to him that beyond a momentary conversation with the Chancellor of the Exchequer preparatory to these interviews Sir Basil Blackett was entirely without guidance from the British Government as to what he should say and could only express a purely personal opinion. He recognised that, in the absence of any broad plan for settlement of international indebtedness at the present time, it was most desirable that the German Government should do what it could to prevent a complete collapse of the mark, and that if the German Government was satisfied that a Moratorium for 1923 and even for 1924 also was essential to prevent an immediate crisis, there were obvious advantages in the question being raised at once rather than after the crisis had developed. He thought for his own part that the British Government would be sympathetic to any plan which offered a real prospect of stabilising the mark and leading to a real balancing in the near future of the German Budget and the cessation of new issues of uncovered paper by Germany. Much would depend naturally on the character of the report brought back from Germany by the Committee of Guarantees.[11] Moreover if the German Government were to avoid a wide extension of the existing supervision by the Committee of Guarantees, it was necessary that the German request for a further Moratorium should be accompanied by some definite undertakings by the German Government as to balancing of its Budget and cessation of new issues of currency. It would also be necessary to make it clear that the grant of a Moratorium for 1923 and 1924 would not in any way prevent the German Government from forwarding to the utmost of its ability any practicable suggestions as to an international loan and a broad solution of the Reparation problem in the interim.

Dr. von Simson said that nothing would please the German Government better than to be able to give a promise as to balancing its Budget by means of taxation and internal loans, provided it felt that the promise was one it could perform. He thought that some undertaking might be given to fix an absolute limit to the maximum issue of fiduciary currency by Germany, if the Moratorium were granted on terms that really limited the cash liabilities of

[9] A copy of the draft of this agreement, dated September 1, 1921, is preserved in the Foreign Office archives at W 625/625/4 (1922).
[10] The Mixed Arbitral Tribunals were set up under articles 304–5 of the treaty of Versailles.
[11] See No. 29.

Germany up to the end of 1924. He said that this promise and indeed all the German Government did could be immensely facilitated if the present German Government could obtain at the same time a conspicuous political success, such as the withdrawal of the Armies of Occupation from Dusseldorf and Ruhrort.[12]

Dr. von Simson added that, in view of these interviews, he was disposed to recommend to his Government to make an application for an extended Moratorium without delay. He would consider the desirability of sounding the Reparation Commission and the French, Belgian and Italian Governments in advance, but was inclined to think it would be better to launch the application without further parley. His idea was that the application should be addressed to the Reparation Commission but that it should simultaneously be sent direct to the Principal Allied Powers and to Belgium, in view of the fact that concessions would be asked in matters not wholly within the purview of the Reparation Commission such as the Clearing House and the Mixed Arbitral Tribunals.

[12] See Vol. XV, Nos. 45–7, and Vol. XVI, No. 458.

No. 32

The Earl of Balfour to Lord Hardinge (Paris)
No. 2044 [C 8661/99/18]

Confidential   FOREIGN OFFICE, July 4, 1922

My Lord,

I have received your despatch No. 1430 of the 16th June, 1922,[1] forwarding copy of a note addressed to you on that date by M. Poincaré, in which his Excellency contends that the pledge given to His Majesty's Ambassador at Paris on the 11th April, 1920,[2] cannot be held to exclude the possibility of independent action by France under paragraphs 17 and 18 of Annex 2 to Part VIII of the Treaty of Versailles in the event of a default by Germany in her reparation obligations.

2. So far as His Majesty's Government are concerned, they do not feel able to abandon the opinion, which the Lord Privy Seal expressed in the House of Commons on the 18th May, 1922,[3] that the French Government are definitely committed by M. Millerand's pledge of the 11th April, 1920, not to resort to new military coercive measures against Germany, save with the consent of and in agreement with their allies. In these circumstances, I have noted with great pleasure the hope which M. Poincaré expressed on behalf of the French Government in the course of his recent conversation at 10, Downing Street[4] that sanctions, if they had again to be applied, would be applied in common by the Allied Governments concerned.

[1] Not printed.   [2] See No. 23, n. 7.   [3] See No. 25, n. 2.
[4] See No. 30.

3. Your Excellency should, however, explain to M. Poincaré that, whilst His Majesty's Government are unable to express any final or authoritative opinion upon the interpretation of paragraphs 17 and 18 of Annex 2, which (as has already been pointed out in paragraphs 4 and 5 of my despatch No. 1657 of the 30th May, 1922)[5] is, in their opinion, under paragraph 12 of the same annex, expressly entrusted to the Reparation Commission, they hold strongly to the view that all reparation questions must be regarded as matters of common interest to the Allies. Not only is the whole subject of reparation entrusted to an Inter-Allied Commission, but the obligation which Germany undertakes in the treaty is not to pay reparation to individual Allied Powers, but to hand over her successive payments in satisfaction of the reparation claims for division among the Allied Powers as they may agree. It is expressly laid down in article 233 that, on failure by Germany to discharge her obligations, any balance remaining unpaid may within the discretion of the commission be postponed, or may be handled in such manner as the Allied Governments, acting in accordance with the procedure laid down in the reparation section of the treaty, may determine. This clearly contemplates common action by the Allies.

4. It is evident, nevertheless, that some uncertainty exists upon the proper construction of the reparation provisions of the treaty, and any difference of opinion between the Allied Governments on this question would be so unfortunate that I would suggest that the Reparation Commission should be invited to accompany any notification which may be made by them to the interested Powers under these paragraphs with a considered opinion as to their meaning, and the type of action they justify. His Majesty's Government are inclined to think that action taken by any individual Allied Government thereunder would have to be confined to measures which such a Government could properly take within its own jurisdictional limits. An example of such action is to be found in that taken by His Majesty's Government on the 28th October, 1920, when they declared that they would not, in the event of the case arising, seize post-war German deposits and goods in the United Kingdom.[6]

5. There is one other passage in M. Poincaré's note to which I am reluctantly compelled to call attention. It is that in which M. Poincaré denies that the military measures taken by the French Government on the 6th April, 1920[7] were taken without the knowledge of the Allies. As proof of the justice of this denial M. Poincaré quotes the instructions sent by the French Government to the French Ambassador in London on the 3rd April, 1920,[8] the final paragraph of which read: 'Marshal Foch is studying the military measures which now can no longer be avoided or delayed.' In communicating these instructions to Mr. Bonar Law on the 5th April, 1920[9] the French Ambassador, speaking on behalf of the French Government, stated that if His Majesty's Government were unwilling to take part in the proposed military measures, the French Government asked to be allowed to act alone. Mr.

[5] No. 25. [6] See No. 19, Annex. [7] See Vol. IX, Nos. 294–7.

[8] See ibid., No. 278. [9] See ibid., No. 292.

Bonar Law, in replying to this request and after stating that he was speaking on behalf of the Prime Minister, explained the reasons for which His Majesty's Government felt it to be unwise and dangerous to adopt the course proposed, and requested the French Ambassador to propose to his Government that 'the position should be regularised by the Allies agreeing to the presence in the Ruhr of the German troops—without actually specifying numbers—for the limited time necessary for restoring order; the German Government on their part to undertake to withdraw the troops at the end of such time (which might be put at a fortnight), after which, failing such withdrawal, the German Government would allow the Allied occupation of the five towns'. No reply to this proposal was ever received from the French Government, and indeed subsequent information shows that, at the time when it was being made, M. Millerand was practically admitting to His Majesty's Minister in Paris[10] that orders had already been given by the French Government for the advance of the French troops. It is therefore strictly accurate to say that the occupation of Frankfurt and the four other towns was undertaken by the French Government 'without the knowledge of the British Government'.

6. As, however, I feel that a further exchange of notes on this point and at this period of time could serve no useful purpose, I request that you will suggest to M. Poincaré that the best course would be for the two Governments to publish the whole correspondence on the matter. Public opinion, both in France and in Great Britain, will then have ample opportunity to form an opinion upon the exact merits of the controversy.

7. You are authorised to read this despatch to M. Poincaré and to leave with him a copy.

I am, etc.,
BALFOUR

[10] See ibid., No. 291.

No. 33

The Earl of Balfour to Lord Hardinge (Paris)
No. 2077 [C 8256/99/18]

FOREIGN OFFICE, *July 5, 1922*

My Lord,

I request that Your Excellency will inform the French Government that His Majesty's Government desire to obtain their consent to the communication to Parliament of the recent correspondence exchanged between the two governments relating to the interpretation of paragraphs 17 and 18 of Annex 2 to Part VIII of the Treaty of Versailles. This correspondence comprises Monsieur Poincaré's note of May 19th, 1922[1] (Germany print, May 23rd,

[1] See No. 23, n. 2.

section 1), my despatch No. 1657 of May 30th,[2] 1922 (Germany print, May 30th, section 1), Monsieur Poincaré's note of June 16th, 1922[3] (Germany print, June 17th, section 1), and my despatch No. 2044[4] of July 4th, 1922.

2. Copies of correspondence with the French Ambassador at this Court on the subject of the publication of certain notes exchanged between the British and French Governments after the occupation of Frankfurt in April 1920 are enclosed herewith.[5] The whole of the Frankfurt correspondence will be found in the printed collection of documents enclosed in my despatch No. 1926 of June 23rd.[6]

I am, etc.,
(For the Earl of Balfour)
MILES W. LAMPSON

[2] No. 25.   [3] Not printed (see, however, No. 32).   [4] No. 32.
[5] Not here printed (see, however, Vol. IX, Chap. IV).   [6] Not printed.

No. 34

Lord Hardinge (Paris) to the Earl of Balfour (Received July 8)
No. 1581 [C 9714/99/18]

PARIS, *July 7, 1922*

My Lord,

At an interview which I had with Monsieur Poincaré this morning, I communicated to him the contents of Your Lordship's despatch No. 2044 of the 4th July,[1] and in view of Monsieur Poincaré's knowledge of English, I gave him Your Lordship's despatch to read and left with him a copy. At the same time I explained to him that His Majesty's Government, without expressing any final or authoritative opinion upon the interpretation of paragraphs 17 and 18 of Annex II of Part VII[I] of the Treaty of Versailles, hold strongly to the view that all reparation questions must be regarded as matters of common interest to the Allies. I told him, at the same time, that in Your Lordship's opinion, a further exchange of Notes would serve no useful purpose, and that the best course would be for the two Governments to publish the whole of the correspondence[2] in order that public opinion in France and Great Britain should be in a position to judge the merits of the controversy.

In reply Monsieur Poincaré stated that the French Government shared entirely the view that all reparations questions must be regarded as matters of common interest to the Allies, especially in view of the necessity for the complete execution of the Treaty of Versailles. As regards the publication of the correspondence which has passed between the two Governments, he asked me to inform Your Lordship unofficially that he considers it would be

[1] No. 32.   [2] See No. 33.

very undesirable, since it would open a controversy which might affect the position of the Chief of the State in France.[3]

I have etc.,
HARDINGE OF PENSHURST

[3] Sir E. Crowe commented (July 10): 'We must keep a watch on the French press now. If M. Poincaré continues the practice of giving his own versions to the newspapers, we may have to consider publishing, in self-defence, the correspondence in full even without his consent.'

No. 35

The Earl of Balfour to the French Ambassador
[C 9285/1729/18]

FOREIGN OFFICE, July 7, 1922

Your Excellency,

With reference to your memorandum of May 25th,[1] I have the honour to inform Your Excellency that note has been taken of the fact that the French delegate on the Reparation Commission proposes to raise in the commission the question of the compensation paid to German shipowners by the German Government in respect of ships delivered to the allies under the Treaty of Versailles, and whether such compensation constitutes an infringement of the second paragraph of section (1) b of the Reparation Commission's note to the German Government of March 21st, 1922.[2]

2. The view which His Majesty's Government hold on this question has already been communicated to you in my note of May 16th, 1922;[3] and as the matter appears to be one entirely within the competence of the Reparation Commission, His Majesty's Government hardly feel that any useful purpose would at the moment be served by the issue of special instructions to Sir J. Bradbury thereon.

3. Copies of this correspondence have, however, been communicated to Sir J. Bradbury.

I have, etc.,
(For the Earl of Balfour)
MILES W. LAMPSON

[1] Not printed.   [2] See No. 12, n. 1.

[3] Not printed. The relevant part of this note ran as follows: 'His Majesty's Ambassador at Berlin has been instructed to make careful enquiry and to report to me whether financial assistance in any form is being given to German shipbuilding out of government funds. In the meantime I have the honour to submit the following observations on the subject. To the extent, at any rate, to which the expenditure referred to by the French Government represents compensation for the expropriation of vessels delivered to the allies under annex III to the reparation chapter of the Treaty of Versailles, it would appear to be justifiable in principle even on the strictest interpretation of Germany's treaty obligations to the Allied and Associated Powers. So far, on the other hand, as it constitutes a subsidy, the payment of which would conflict with provision by Germany for the payment of reparation, it is apparently one of the items on the expenditure side of the German budget the suppression of which is already being urged by the Reparation Commission. In these circumstances I would suggest that it is not necessary to issue any special instructions to the British delegate on that body.'

No. 36

Note by Mr. Wigram
[*C 9928/99/18*]

FOREIGN OFFICE, July 10, 1922

I was present this afternoon at a meeting at the Treasury between the German Ambassador and Sir Basil Blackett. This meeting was held at the request of M. Sthamer who, upon the instructions of his government, communicated to Sir Basil Blackett the drafts of two notes which were respectively to be presented by the German Government to the Reparation Commission and to the allied governments on Wednesday next, July 12th.[1]

M. Sthamer explained that these drafts were to the following effect:

(1) The Reparation Commission was to be asked to agree to the cash payments due from the German Government during the remainder of the year 1922 under the 1922 moratorium,[2] and amounting to 320 millions of gold marks, being spread over the years 1923 and 1924 in addition to the remainder of the present year.

(2) The Reparation Commission was to be asked to demand no further cash payments for this period, i.e. from the present date to the end of 1924; and the allied governments were to be asked to limit all cash demands upon Germany in excess of this (i.e. clearing office balances, payments under decisions of the Mixed Arbitral Tribunal[3] and armies of occupation) to five hundred thousand pounds sterling per month.

M. Sthamer added that the German gov[ernmen]t would be glad of any observations, which the British gov[ernmen]t might wish to make on these drafts.

Sir Basil Blackett enquired whether this demand was intended to include the payment due by the German Government on Saturday next, July 15th. M. Sthamer said the German Government have the money to pay this, but that they hoped that the Reparation Commission would not demand it but would leave it for the present in the hands of the German Government, in order to assist them in their effort to stabilise the exchange position.

Sir Basil Blackett also pointed out that the German Government had not said anything in their notes about the measures which they intended to take to stabilise their financial position during the period of the extended moratorium for which they were asking. M. Sthamer replied that the German Government had designedly omitted all reference to this, and that for internal political reasons they preferred to leave it to the Reparation Commission to make what demands they saw fit in this connection. Sir Basil Blackett pointed out one other apparent omission in the German notes. The German Government had not said anything about the value of the deliveries in kind which they were prepared to make during the years 1923 and 1924. M. Sthamer seemed to think that the German Government had thought it better

[1] See No. 38, below.   [2] See No. 26, n. 4.
[3] See No. 31, n. 10.

to leave this matter over for negotiations between the Kriegslastenkommission[4] and the Reparation Commission.

Sir Basil Blackett undertook to refer both drafts to the Chancellor of the Exchequer.[5]

[4] The German War Burdens Commission.

[5] These drafts were circulated to the Cabinet by Sir R. Horne on July 10. Mr. Wigram commented: 'I understand that two representatives of the German government, Herr Fischer and Herr Schroeder, will communicate copies of these drafts unofficially to Sir John Bradbury and M. Delacroix, the Belgian representative on the reparation commission, today for their comments. Herr Sthamer was clear that no communication similar to that made to the British government through Sir Basil Blackett was being made either to the Belgian or to the French government, though a somewhat similar communication is apparently being made to the Belgian government in connection with a German-Belgian financial agreement relating, I think, to Belgian holdings of German paper marks. I am not at all clear how far the French representative on the reparation commission is being kept informed of the progress of events, but, as everybody knows Messrs. Schroeder and Fischer are in Paris, I suppose the French government know pretty well what is going on.'

No. 37

The Treasury to the Foreign Office (Received July 12)
[C 9961/99/18]

TREASURY CHAMBERS, *July 11, 1922*

The Lords Commissioners of His Majesty's Treasury present Their compliments to the Secretary of State for Foreign Affairs, and beg to transmit herewith for information and guidance copy of a letter of today's date which They have caused to be addressed to the British Delegate, Reparation Commission.

ENCLOSURE IN No. 37

The Treasury to Sir J. Bradbury (Paris)

TREASURY CHAMBERS, *July 11, 1922*

Sir,

I have laid before the Lords Commissioners of His Majesty's Treasury your Report of the 5th instant (B.R. No. 436/22[1]), relative to the discrepancy between the percentages of deliveries in kind attributed to the various Allied Powers by Article 3 of the Agreement of Finance Ministers signed at Paris on the 11th March last,[2] and those established by the Commission's decision (No. 1841)[3] according a provisional moratorium to Germany in respect of Reparation payments in 1922.

In reply, I am to state that Their Lordships concur in the view which you stated to the Commission in regard to this question, and am to authorise you

[1] Not printed.   [2] See No. 11, n. 2.

[3] i.e. the decision transmitted to the German government in the Reparation Commission's letter of March 21 (see No. 12, n. 1).

to inform the Commission that His Majesty's Government would be content to accept the slight modification of the percentages laid down in the Financial Agreement which would result from following the moratorium decision.[4]

4 See No. 26, n. 4.

No. 38

Sir J. Bradbury (Reparation Commission) to Sir B. Blackett (Treasury)
(Received in the Foreign Office, July 14)
[*C 10032/99/18*]

Copy   PARIS, *July 12, 1922*

My dear Blackett,

The German demand was received today. I am sending the text[1] under separate cover.

We discussed it semi-officially this afternoon. Neither the French nor Belgians would agree to my suggestion that the Germans should be allowed to retain the 32 millions (balance due 15th July) until our decision upon their application.

We shall probably reply tomorrow recognising the gravity of the situation and promising careful consideration as soon as the Committee of Guarantees return.[2] Delacroix is drafting and will try to make the tone as reassuring as possible.

Dubois is still nervously intransigent. I think Poincaré is playing for a majority decision against the French Delegate, but Delacroix will probably not play that game again,[3] and, personally, I rather doubt the wisdom of it. I feel pretty sure that if I decline to make a proposal except with the concurrence of the French, we shall ultimately be unanimous for granting a postponement, but it means a certain amount of time—which is, of course, dangerous.

Anyhow, I hope we shall get out a fairly reassuring letter tomorrow.[4] We can discuss the next step on Friday.[5]

Yours sincerely,
JOHN BRADBURY

1 Not printed. See Carl Bergmann, *The History of Reparations* (London, 1927), pp. 139–40.
2 The Committee of Guarantees had gone to Berlin (see No. 29).   3 Cf. No. 27.
4 This letter, dated July 13, addressed to the *Kriegslastenkommission* from the Reparation Commission, ran as follows: 'The Reparation Commission has the honour to acknowledge the receipt of the Kriegslastenkommission's memorandum of the 12th July, and will study it with all the care which the serious situation therein described requires. At the same time the commission is satisfied that the reparation payments are only one, and not the most important, of the causes of the present depreciation of the mark, and that stability can only be definitely re-established if the financial reforms which the Reparation Commission has for a long time demanded are immediately put into force.

'So long as the report of the Committee of Guarantees on the application of these measures has not reached it, the commission cannot take any decision. In view of the

[*See overleaf for note 4 cont. and note 5*

urgency of the problem, it hopes to take and to intimate its decision to the German Government before the 15th August next.

'As regards the payment due on the 15th instant, the Kriegslastenkommission was notified, in a letter dated the 11th instant, that the amount of this payment has been reduced by reason of certain credits which fall to be made against it to 32,107,397·70 gold marks (about 1,605,000*l.*). This balance, which, according to the declaration of the German Government, is held at the disposal of the commission, should be paid over on the 15th July.'

⁵ July 14.

No. 39

Lord D'Abernon (Berlin) to the Earl of Balfour
(Received July 19, 8.30 a.m.)
No. 136 Telegraphic [C 10305/99/18]

BERLIN, *July 18, 1922, 11.58 p.m.*

Committee of Guarantee[s] has come to agreement with German government represented by Hermes¹ regarding the future control over flight of capital and other points. This agreement takes the form decided by Committee of Guarantees to which German government will notify their assent in a few days after certain formalities. Terms agreed upon appear satisfactory to English representatives and are considered to constitute a fair compromise of a practical nature between opposing standpoints. I understand, confidentially, that Committee's report as to fiscal administration of Germany will admit the difficulties past and will recognise both present efforts as well as determination to secure future improvement.

¹ German Finance Minister.

No. 40

Sir M. Cheetham¹ (Paris) to the Earl of Balfour
(Received July 19, 4.40 p.m.)
No. 381 Telegraphic [C 10314/99/18]

Urgent   PARIS, *July 19, 1922, 2.15 p.m.*
Part 1
My telegram No. 374.²
I have received personal letter³ from French prime minister, copy of which

¹ Sir M. Cheetham acted as Chargé d'Affaires at Paris from July 16 to August 15.
² Of July 17. This ran: 'Date of Monsieur Poincaré's arrival in London.
'I understand Monsieur Poincaré, who has been away from Paris, will shortly send me a reply to Lord Hardinge's enquiry on this point.
'Reply may not, however, be very definite, since Political Director informs me that Monsieur Poincaré considers Reparations issue infinitely more important than other questions to be discussed. He will probably therefore await both report of Committee of Guarantees and decision of Reparations Commission thereon before finally fixing date of his departure.'
³ Not printed. This letter, dated July 18, was transmitted to Lord Balfour by Sir M. Cheetham under cover of his despatch No. 1682 of July 19.

goes by bag tonight, stating that he cannot yet fix date for conversation which was proposed during course of his last interview with Mr. Lloyd George[4] as he considers it necessary to await report of committee of guarantees[5] on which will depend discussion of measures for ensuring execution of treaty and payment of reparations. He adds that he will be at disposal of Mr. Lloyd George and Signor Schanzer[6] as soon as moment comes and that the three prime ministers could then take opportunity of their meeting in London, Paris or Italy to discuss eastern question, though it seems to him unnecessary to meet to discuss latter until impending conference near Constantinople[7] has finished its labours.

As for Tangier[8] he would prefer a previous study of question by ambassadors and experts at Foreign Office in London who should prepare an agreement for approval of heads of governments. If, however, he were to meet Mr. Lloyd George about reparations he would be ready to set apart a day for discussion, with him and Spanish prime minister, of principles which should guide Tangier discussions in London. He points out that the three prime ministers would not have time to . . .[9] question at length.

Part 2[10]

Following is a continuation of my immediately preceding telegram.

French prime minister evidently wishes to avoid discussing any subject at present.

I gather, however, from political director[11] whom I saw this morning that when Monsieur Poincaré does make up his mind to attend a conference he will have no objection to its being held in London. The vagueness of phrase in his letter regarding place of meeting is due to the fact that Italian prime minister[12] has suggested Italy or Paris.

I told political director that in my private opinion Poincaré's letter would cause His Majesty's Government some surprise.

---

[4] See No. 30.   [5] See No. 39.   [6] Italian Minister for Foreign Affairs.
[7] See Vol. XVII, Nos. 676, 680, 690, 692, 699, and 700.   [8] See No. 2, n. 9.
[9] The text is here uncertain.
[10] This section of Sir M. Cheetham's telegram was despatched at 4.30 p.m. and received in the Foreign Office at 5.40 p.m. on July 19.
[11] Count de Peretti de La Rocca.   [12] Signor Facta.

No. 41

Sir G. Grahame (Brussels) to the Earl of Balfour (Received July 24)
[*C 10448/99/18*]

Private & Confidential   BRUSSELS, *July 19, 1922*

Dear Lord Balfour,

M. Jaspar[1] said to me today, speaking of the reparation question, that he hoped a meeting of Inter-Allied Ministers would take place at the earliest

---

[1] Belgian Foreign Minister.

possible occasion. He seems afraid of a deadlock at the Reparation Commission about the moratorium question, and renewed ill-feeling between the Allies. I presume that he and M. Theunis would wish to go to London if and when M. Poincaré goes there.[2] If such a meeting were to come off, he (M. Jaspar) would probably first go to Paris[3] in order to placate the French for they are always suspicious of the Belgian Ministers' dealings with His Majesty's Government. He thinks that M. Poincaré does not like either M. Theunis or himself. He is not sure about his sentiments as regards M. Theunis, but he knows that he himself is an object of suspicion to M. Poincaré.

[2] See No. 40.

[3] In his despatch No. 512 of July 24, Sir G. Grahame stated: 'The Paris correspondent of the Brussels newspaper "Le Soir" makes the following statement with regard to Germany's request for a moratorium:—

"It would only be natural that the Governments of Paris and Brussels should examine together the situation with which they are confronted. Their interests and their immediate needs are identical; both are animated with the same desire to maintain peace and at the same time a full respect of their rights. Both in Paris and in Brussels the view is taken that it is not possible to grant Germany a long moratorium without guarantees and compensation, for to do so would mean a practical abandonment of the prospect of obtaining reparation. Both in Paris and in Brussels the reduction of the German debt is considered as dependent upon a corresponding annulment of inter-Allied debts; and in both capitals there is a wish to facilitate the conclusion of an international loan. The way is thus open for maintaining, by parallel action, the solidarity of the two friendly nations, each acting in full independence. Such co-operation would greatly conduce towards clearing up the diplomatic situation."

'It is difficult for the Belgian Ministers openly to dissociate themselves from the French Government with regard to the moratorium question. M. Theunis and M. Jaspar probably do not see eye to eye with M. Poincaré in this matter, and doubtless have ideas of their own as to the best manner of proceeding; but, in view of public opinion here, they would have to be cautious so as not to give the impression that they are deserting the French. This does not mean that at an inter-Allied conference the Belgian Government would necessarily adopt or support any French scheme in its entirety. They are even capable of making overt opposition with regard to proposals put forward by the French Government if it could be shown that they were not fully in accordance with Belgian interests.

'The Belgian Government, for example, entirely endorsed the action of M. Delacroix, the Belgian representative on the Bankers' Committee, in dissociating himself from the French attitude, and successfully justified their action in the eyes of Belgian public opinion. The Belgian Government were not seriously criticised in Belgium on that occasion, except by a small and noisy group whose political creed is that the policy of Belgium should always be identical with that of France in every question affecting Germany.

'Whenever the policy of the Belgian Government does not coincide with that of the French Government, the former take every precaution to ensure themselves, so far as is possible, against criticism at home. No Belgian Minister would willingly place himself in the position of having to meet the joint onslaught of the French and Belgian press for failing to act energetically in order to make Germany pay what she owes. The above-quoted statement in "Le Soir"—which I observe has been given prominence by the Paris "Temps" —is probably designed to produce some pronouncement from the Belgian Ministers which can be interpreted in France as an indication that the French Government have the Belgian Government with them in meeting the issues raised by the German request for a moratorium.'

He observed that he did not think that he was actuated by national *amour propre* in believing that M. Theunis was more likely to lead the Allies out of the reparations *impasse* than anyone else. In the first place, from his having dealt with this question in various capacities for so long a time, he had a knowledge of the details of the question such as only experts had, with the possible exception of M. Loucheur.[4] M. Theunis was a trained financier before entering public life and his political experience, joined to this expert knowledge, placed him in an exceptional position. In addition to these qualifications, he had an accurate knowledge of both the English and the French points of view, and was an unrivalled negotiator, and, by nature, a fair-minded man.

I asked M. Jaspar whether M. Theunis had a plan of his own. He gave me to understand that he had but that he did not intend to produce it prematurely.

M. Jaspar says that recently the French Government were thoroughly rattled (*affolé*) about Germany. The murder of Rathenau[5] and the fall of the mark etc. upset them altogether.

M. Jaspar told me that he was exceedingly pleased that the allied front had not been broken during the Hague Conference.[6] The British and Belgian delegations had acted in perfect accord. The French, who had not sent men of any considerable authority, had, to some extent, taken a back seat. The bad faith of the Soviet Government had once more been shown. He had hopes that before long changes would take place at Moscow. M. Vandervelde,[7] when he came back from Moscow, had told him definitely that Lenin[8] was doomed, as he had some disease of the spinal cord. M. Jaspar evidently thinks that once the titular head disappears, factions will fight for supremacy and finally some kind of disruption will come about.

Yours very truly,

GEORGE GRAHAME

[4] Former French Minister for Reconstruction and the Liberated Regions.
[5] See No. 31, n. 6.   [6] See Vol. XIX, Chap. IV.
[7] M. Emile Vandervelde, former Belgian Minister of Justice and Socialist leader.
[8] President of the Soviet Russian Council of People's Commissars.

No. 42

The Earl of Balfour to the French Ambassador[1]
[*C 10708/99/18*]

FOREIGN OFFICE, *July 25, 1922*

My dear Ambassador,

I have consulted the Prime Minister on the subject of your letter[2] and Monsieur Poincaré's proposed visit to this country.

I need hardly say that the British Government would welcome a conversation with the French Prime Minister; indeed, we had hoped that this could

[1] The Count de Saint-Aulaire.   [2] Of July 23, not printed.

have taken place in the second half of the present month, as was originally indicated by Monsieur Poincaré on the occasion of his last visit;[3] but we quite recognise that the pressure of domestic affairs upon any Prime Minister may require the reconsideration of the best-laid plans.

The only objections which I see to the present scheme arise out of the difficulty of assembling in the course of next week the Representatives of the three other nations who have to take part in our discussions. As regards Tangier, we must have the Spaniard; as regards the Near East, we must have the Italian; and as regards Reparations, we must have both the Italian and the Belgian.[4]

Have you any information as to whether the Representatives of these various States are in a position to come here at such short notice?

I have no special reason for thinking that the Spanish and the Belgian Representatives would have any difficulty in being present, although August is not a favourable month for asking hard-worked Ministers to undertake any new business. As regards Italy, however, I should greatly fear that the present crisis[5] may render it impossible to form a new Government within the next few days, and that, when it is formed, the new Prime Minister may require some little time before he sees his way to discussing the important and difficult subjects with which the Conference will have to deal.

I do not know whether Your Excellency or Monsieur Poincaré have considered these points or have arrived at a conclusion upon them. I can only say, on behalf of Mr. Lloyd George, that, so far as he is concerned, he would be delighted to have an opportunity of discussing with Monsieur Poincaré and other Prime Ministers, Foreign Ministers and Finance Ministers, the three important subjects which it was agreed in June should be discussed at this Conference, as well as a fourth subject, not referred to in your note, namely the present economic and political position of Austria.

BALFOUR

[3] See No. 30.

[4] In a letter to Lord Balfour of July 25, Sir M. Hankey wrote as follows: 'This is to remind you of the conclusion reached by the Cabinet this morning in regard to M. Poincaré's proposal to visit England on or after August 1st, which was that the Acting Secretary of State for Foreign Affairs should reply to M. Poincaré to the effect that the British Government had understood at the time of his last visit that M. Poincaré would be able to pay a further visit to England during the last half of July, which would have suited them better than a visit in August. Nevertheless, the British Government would be glad to welcome M. Poincaré any day during next week for the purpose of discussing:

Reparations—though no indication should be given that we had any plan to propose;
The Near East;
Tangier.

'This, however, should be subject to the understanding that the questions of Reparations and the Near East could not be discussed in the absence of a representative of the Italian Government, and to the date being convenient to the Spanish Government for the discussion of Tangier.'

[5] A reference to the ministerial crisis in Italy following the defeat of the Facta government on July 19.

No. 43

Mr. Kemball-Cook[1] (*Reparation Commission*) *to Treasury*
[C 10707/99/18]

PARIS, *July 26, 1922*

Report No. 304[2]

May it please Your Lordships,

I have the honour, in the absence of Sir John Bradbury, to acknowledge the receipt of Treasury paper No. F 4377/01,[3] (which is herewith returned) on the subject of the execution of Articles I and II of the Financial Agreement of the 11th March 1922,[4] with special reference to the practice hitherto followed by the Allied Governments of requisitioning paper marks to meet the expenses of their Armies of Occupation, and to state, for Your Lordships' information, that this practice was discussed by the Reparation Commission yesterday in connection with the Report by its Finance Service contained in Annex 1495.[5]

The Commission was unanimous in the opinion that the value of the paper mark requisitions if and in so far as they have been made since the 1st May 1922 must be accounted for against the 'forfaits' fixed by Article I of the 11th March Agreement.

In the course of the discussion, the President[6] stated that the arrangements under which the Allied Armies procured paper marks by requisitioning was in his view convenient and practical. The Treaty imposed on the German Government the obligation of paying the costs of these Armies, and the French Government would not be prepared to adopt any system involving the necessity of its making cash advances to meet the cost of the French Army of Occupation. He proposed, therefore, that the opinion of the minority of the Finance Service should be adopted, i.e., that the Commission should decide that these paper mark requisitions should continue.

I stated that the present system of requisitioning appeared to me as a practical question to involve considerable risk of abuse. Further, it seemed impossible to find any formal justification for the practice in existing circumstances, having regard to the provisions of Article II of the Agreement of the 11th March, under which the costs of occupation from the 1st May 1921 to the end of the present year fall to be met out of the value of deliveries in kind made to each Power during that period. If marks were requisitioned from Germany to meet these costs, the object of the foregoing provision would be, in fact, pro tanto defeated.

I stated that His Majesty's Government had already issued instructions to the effect that such requisitioning should cease, so far as the British Army

---

[1] British assistant delegate on the Reparation Commission, and British delegate on the Committee of Guarantees.

[2] A copy of this Report was transmitted to the Foreign Office by the Treasury on July 27.

[3] Not traced in the Foreign Office Archives.   [4] See No. 11, n. 2.

[5] Not printed. This Annex, received in the Foreign Office from the Reparation Commission on August 10, is preserved at C 11375/899/18.

[6] See No. 7, n. 3.

of Occupation is concerned, that any marks requisitioned on British account since the 1st May last should be repaid to the Reichsbank, and that any marks required in future by the British Army should be purchased on the market. I considered that it would be right for the same course to be followed by the French and Belgian Governments, but I was prepared, in view of the opinion expressed by the majority of the Finance Service, to agree that the value of marks already requisitioned for the needs of the French and Belgian Armies should, as from the beginning of the present year, be credited against Germany's obligations in respect of deliveries in kind in 1922, provided that it was agreed that such requisitions should cease at a reasonably early date.

The Belgian Delegate[7] stated that he was disposed to agree with the French Delegate's opinion. He saw no difficulty in treating requisitioned paper marks as deliveries in kind for the purposes of the moratorium account in 1922. He did not think there was any risk of abuse, but if there was, some form of supervision might be arranged to obviate it. If the requisitioned marks were not assimilated to deliveries in kind, they must be regarded as cash payments, and their equivalent should accordingly be handed over to Belgium in pursuance of Article 8 of the Agreement of the 11th March.

The unofficial American Delegate[8] pointed out that his Government is not a party to the Agreement of the 11th March, and reserved its position in general terms.

After further discussion it became evident that unanimity would not be reached at the meeting and the question was adjourned at the request of the Belgian Delegate to enable the French and Belgian Delegates to consult their Governments.

I would be glad to know that Your Lordships approve the attitude which I adopted in the matter, and to receive any further instructions which it may be thought desirable to send to me as a result of the discussion in the Commission as reported above. As it is advisable that the question should come before the Commission again at an early date, I would be glad if I might be favoured with a reply as soon as possible.

A copy of this Report has been communicated to His Majesty's Embassy, Paris.

I have, etc.,
B. A. KEMBALL-COOK

[7] See ibid., n. 7.   [8] See No. 28, n. 6.

No. 44

The Earl of Balfour to Mr. Lloyd George
[*C 10933/99/18*]

[FOREIGN OFFICE], *July 29, 1922*

My dear Prime Minister,

The French Ambassador insisted on seeing me this afternoon and discussing with me the question of Monsieur Poincaré's visit.[1]

The situation as I understand it is this:—

1. There is no question of having a Conference without the Italians on any subject except the answer which has to be given to the Germans about Reparation on August 15th.[2]

2. From the very nature of the case this is a subject which must be dealt with at once and M. Poincaré thinks it absolutely necessary, before dealing with it, that he should have a conversation with you.

3. The Germans ought to make payments on the 15th, but cannot do so. They request, therefore, a moratorium.[3]

In the opinion of the Ambassador, accurately reflecting, I have no doubt, the opinion of his Government, French public opinion would never admit a moratorium simply and without conditions. It is, presumably, these conditions which M. Poincaré wishes to discuss with you.

I pointed out that after an appeal made to me by Baron Moncheur[4] on behalf of the Belgians, I did not think that any discussion could take place on reparation in which Belgium did not take part, and that as regards Italy I quite recognised that it was impossible to defer the question of the answer to Germany until an Italian Government was formed,[5] for that answer had to be given by the 15th August. At the same time I thought it very desirable that the Italian Ambassador, M. de Martino, though necessarily without full powers from Rome, should be present and, if necessary, take part in the discussion.

To these propositions I did not gather that M. de Saint-Aulaire took any exception.

There can, I think, be no question of discussing any subject except the answer to be given to Germany on the 15th.

In all the circumstances of the case I do not think it possible for you to refuse to see the French Prime Minister, and if you share this view the sooner you see him the better for all of us, and I suggest that you should telephone to the French Embassy at once suggesting the 2nd of August as the time for the meeting.

If you share this view please send a duplicate of your message to the French Ambassador to this Office. I will make arrangements that on receipt of your

---

[1] See No. 42.   [2] See No. 38, n. 4.

[3] Germany had again applied for a moratorium (see No. 36 and No. 38, n. 1) in a letter of July 12 to the Reparation Commission (see No. 38).

[4] See No. 9, n. 1.

[5] See No. 42, n. 5. Signor Facta agreed to re-form his government on July 30.

message they should immediately communicate with the Belgian Government.[6]

I shall of course be here on Wednesday and Thursday,[7] though this restricted discussion is more the affair of the Chancellor of the Exchequer than of myself, who has no intimate knowledge of the reparation problem.

If you see Poincaré *now* [it] will, I fancy, clear you till October at earliest, perhaps [t]ill November.[8]

Yours,

BALFOUR

[6] In a letter of July 31 (not preserved in the Foreign Office archives) the Belgian ambassador told Sir Eyre Crowe that his government had been informed of Mr. Lloyd George's proposal to M. Poincaré for a meeting on August 7 (cf. n. 8, below).

[7] i.e. August 2 and 3.

[8] In a letter to Lord Balfour of July 31, Sir M. Hankey wrote as follows: 'This is to remind you of the decision taken at the short Conference of Ministers held after the meeting of the Committee of Imperial Defence this morning, as to the reply to be made to M. Poincaré.

'The understanding was—

(a) That you should inform the French Ambassador that the Prime Minister agrees that it is necessary for the question of Reparations to be discussed with M. Poincaré before the 15th August. You should remind the Ambassador that the British Government have throughout attached importance to the presence of Italian representatives at this discussion, but that you do not at present know whether it will be possible for them to come before August 15th; consequently, that the Prime Minister proposes that the meeting should take place on August 7th;

(b) That the Belgian Government should be asked to send a representative;

(c) That the Japanese Ambassador should be warned that these meetings are to take place.

'I presume that you will also make some communication to the Italian Government, though I did not record anything to this effect.'

In a minute of August 4, Mr. Lampson wrote: 'The Japanese Embassy telephoned this morning to ask whether or not the Ambassador was expected to attend the meetings next week. I replied that I had understood that H[is] E[xcellency] had already been invited (see C 10933), but would make quite sure.

'I cannot quite make out what has happened, but from what is ascertainable it appears that the [invitation] . . . never actually reached Baron Hayashi.

'In accordance with authorisation received this morning from the Private Secretary I have telephoned to M. Tokugawa [First Secretary] and informed him that Baron Hayashi is invited to attend the meetings. He asked if there would be any written invitation. I replied in the negative and that he could take my message as formal and official. There had been no written invitations to attend.

'M. Tokugawa said he would ask the Cabinet Secretariat for details as to hour and place of meeting etc.'

The Earl of Balfour to the Count de Saint-Aulaire[1]
[W 6402/2618/50]

FOREIGN OFFICE, *August 1, 1922*

Your Excellency,

As your Excellency is aware, the general question of the French debt to this country has not as yet been the subject of any formal communication between the two Governments, nor are His Majesty's Government anxious to raise it at the present moment. Recent events, however, leave them little choice in the matter, and they feel compelled to lay before the French Government their views on certain aspects of the situation created by the present condition of international indebtedness.

Speaking in general terms, the war debts, exclusive of interest, due to Great Britain at the present moment amount in the aggregate to about 3,400,000,000*l.*, of which Germany owes 1,450,000,000*l.*, Russia 650,000,000*l.* and our Allies 1,300,000,000*l.* On the other hand, Great Britain owes the United States about a quarter of this sum—say, 850,000,000*l.* at par of exchange, together with interest accrued since 1919.

No international discussion has yet taken place on the unexampled situation partially disclosed by these figures; and, pending a settlement which would go to the root of the problem, His Majesty's Government have silently abstained from making any demands upon their Allies, either for the payment of interest or the repayment of capital. But, if action in the matter has hitherto been deemed inopportune, this is not because His Majesty's Government either underrate the evils of the present state of affairs, or because they are reluctant to make large sacrifices to bring it to an end. On the contrary, they are prepared, if such a policy formed part of a satisfactory international settlement, to remit all the debts due to Great Britain by our Allies in respect of loans, or by Germany in respect of reparations.

Recent events, however, make such a policy difficult of accomplishment. With the most perfect courtesy, and in the exercise of their undoubted rights, the American Government have required this country to pay the interest accrued since 1919 on the Anglo-American debt, to convert it from an unfunded to a funded debt, and to repay it by a sinking fund in twenty-five years.[2] Such a procedure is clearly in accordance with the original contract. His Majesty's Government make no complaint of it; they recognize their obligations and are prepared to fulfil them. But evidently they cannot do so without profoundly modifying the course which, in different circumstances, they would have wished to pursue. They cannot treat the repayment of the Anglo-American loan as if it were an isolated incident in which only the United States of America and Great Britain had any concern. It is but one of a connected series of transactions, in which this country appears sometimes

---

[1] This despatch was also addressed to the Italian, Serb-Croat-Slovene, Roumanian, Portuguese and Greek representatives in London, *mutatis mutandis*. It is printed as Cmd. 1737 of 1922.　　[2] See *F.R.U.S.* 1922, vol. i, pp. 396–417.

as debtor, sometimes as creditor, and, if our undoubted obligations as a debtor are to be enforced, our not less undoubted rights as creditor cannot be left wholly in abeyance.

His Majesty's Government do not conceal the fact that they adopt this change of policy with the greatest reluctance. It is true that Great Britain is owed more than it owes, and that, if all inter-Allied war debts were paid, the British Treasury would, on balance, be a large gainer by the transaction. But can the present world situation be looked at only from this narrow financial standpoint? It is true that many of the Allied and Associated Powers are, as between each other, creditors, or debtors, or both. But they were, and are, much more. They were partners in the greatest international effort ever made in the cause of freedom; and they are still partners in dealing with some, at least, of its results. Their debts were incurred, their loans were made, not for the separate advantage of particular States, but for a great purpose common to them all—and that purpose has been, in the main, accomplished.

To generous minds it can never be agreeable, although, for reasons of State, it may perhaps be necessary, to regard the monetary aspect of this great event as a thing apart, to be torn from its historical setting and treated as no more than an ordinary commercial dealing between traders who borrow and capitalists who lend. There are, moreover, reasons of a different order, to which I have already referred, which increase the distaste with which His Majesty's Government adopt so fundamental an alteration in method of dealing with loans to Allies. The economic ills from which the world is suffering are due to many causes, moral and material, which are quite outside the scope of this despatch. But among them must certainly be reckoned the weight of international indebtedness, with all its unhappy effects upon credit and exchange, upon national production and international trade. The peoples of all countries long for a speedy return to the normal. But how can the normal be reached while conditions so abnormal are permitted to prevail? And how can these conditions be cured by any remedies that seem at present likely to be applied?

For evidently the policy hitherto pursued by this country of refusing to make demands upon its debtors is only tolerable so long as it is generally accepted. It cannot be right that one partner in the common enterprise should recover all that she has lent and that another, while recovering nothing, should be required to pay all that she has borrowed. Such a procedure is contrary to every principle of natural justice, and cannot be expected to commend itself to the people of this country. They are suffering from an unparalleled burden of taxation, from an immense diminution in national wealth, from serious want of employment, and from the severe curtailment of useful expenditure. These evils are courageously borne. But were they to be increased by an arrangement which, however legitimate, is obviously one-sided, the British tax-payer would inevitably ask why he should be singled out to bear a burden which others are bound to share.

To such a question there can be but one answer, and I am convinced that

Allied opinion will admit its justice. But while His Majesty's Government are thus regretfully constrained to request the French Government to make arrangements for dealing to the best of their ability with Anglo-French loans, they desire to explain that the amount of interest and repayment for which they ask depends not so much on what France and other Allies owe to Great Britain as on what Great Britain has to pay America. The policy favoured by His Majesty's Government is, as I have already observed, that of surrendering their share of German reparation and writing off, through one great transaction, the whole body of inter-Allied indebtedness. But, if this be found impossible of accomplishment, we wish it to be understood that we do not in any event desire to make a profit out of any less satisfactory arrangement. In no circumstances do we propose to ask more from our debtors than is necessary to pay to our creditors. And, while we do not ask for more, all will admit that we can hardly be content with less. For it should not be forgotten, though it sometimes is, that our liabilities were incurred for others, not for ourselves. The food, the raw material, the munitions required by the immense naval and military efforts of Great Britain, and half the two thousand million sterling advanced to Allies were provided, not by means of foreign loans, but by internal borrowing and war taxation. Unfortunately a similar policy was beyond the power of other European nations. Appeal was therefore made to the Government of the United States; and under the arrangement then arrived at the United States insisted, in substance if not in form, that, though our Allies were to spend the money, it was only on our security that they were prepared to lend it. This co-operative effort was of infinite value to the common cause; but it cannot be said that the rôle assigned in it to this country was one of special privilege or advantage.

Before concluding I may be permitted to offer one further observation in order to make still clearer the spirit in which His Majesty's Government desire to deal with the thorny problem of international indebtedness.

In an earlier passage of this despatch I pointed out that this after all is not a question merely between Allies. Ex-enemy countries also are involved; for the greatest of all international debtors is Germany. Now His Majesty's Government do not suggest that, either as a matter of justice or expediency, Germany should be relieved of her obligation to the other Allied States. They speak only for Great Britain; and they content themselves with saying once again that, so deeply are they convinced of the economic injury inflicted on the world by the existing state of things, that this country would be prepared (subject to the just claims of other parts of the Empire) to abandon all further right to German reparation and all claims to repayment by Allies, provided that this renunciation formed part of a general plan by which this great problem could be dealt with as a whole, and find a satisfactory solution. A general settlement would, in their view, be of more value to mankind than any gains that could accrue even from the most successful enforcement of legal obligations.

I have, etc.,
BALFOUR

Sir J. Bradbury (Reparation Commission) to Sir B. Blackett (Treasury)
(Received in the Foreign Office, August 5)

$[C \ 11104/99/18]$

Copy

Confidential   PARIS, *August 2, 1922*

My dear Blackett,

I came up from the country today and find that my colleagues were disposed to take no action in regard to the extension of the moratorium until
after the London Conference.[1]

I saw them individually this morning and told them that this was a policy
in which I could not acquiesce. It was the duty óf the commission under
article 234 to decide whether or not the German capacity for payment neces-
sitates a postponement, and before the Governments could be in a position
to come to any decision they would necessarily have to ask what conclusion
the commission had arrived at.

If we were able to be unanimous, our decision would clearly be of the
greatest assistance to the Governments; if we were not unanimous, either a
majority decision (if we should think it wise to take one), or, failing that,
a communication of our individual views, would not be without utility.

In the end I insisted on an official meeting this afternoon at which I proposed a resolution, a copy of which I enclose.

Dubois deprecated any decision being taken until after the London meeting, but did not combat my view that an extension of the moratorium was
necessary. Delacroix and Raggi[2] sat vigorously on the hedge. Both of them
are anxious to receive guidance from their Governments before taking up
a definite position.

In the end we adjourned until tomorrow. I indicated at the close of the
meeting that I was prepared to consider as a possible compromise, in the
event of our failing to be unanimous, that, instead of taking a majority
decision, we should transmit officially to the Governments before the 7th
the minutes of our discussions with such reports thereon as we might individually see fit to make, on the understanding that the Governments would
be at liberty to publish these reports if they saw fit.

We agreed at the end of the meeting to keep secret for the moment the fact
that a discussion has taken place at the commission on the question of the
moratorium, and to ask our Governments to do the same. Previous experience makes me sceptical as to the possibility of effecting this.

As regards my visit to London, unless you really want me before Sunday,[3]
I think I shall be more usefully employed here for the rest of the week.
Whether I should come next week or not is for you to decide. I want to get

---

[1] See Chap. II, below.
[2] Marquis Salvago Raggi, Italian delegate on the Reparation Commission.
[3] August 6.

back to Pornichet as soon as may be, but, of course, I am entirely at your disposition.

I will let you know tomorrow what happens at the adjourned meeting.[4]

Yours sincerely,

JOHN BRADBURY

[4] In a letter of August 3 to Sir B. Blackett, Sir J. Bradbury wrote as follows: 'The meeting today was mainly taken up by statements by Delacroix and Dubois.

'Delacroix painted a gloomy picture of the present state of Germany, representing it indeed as so hopeless that no moratorium would do any good. The only hope was that the Allied Governments would discover some method of providing international credits to cure a situation which the Reparation Commission was powerless to deal with.

'Dubois returned to the old thesis that the German nation was perfectly well able to pay and the present situation was the result of the German State having wilfully reduced itself to bankruptcy to avoid its reparation liabilities.

'Both Delacroix and Raggi indicated pretty clearly that they regarded the extension of the moratorium to be unavoidable but obviously wished to leave the responsibility of deciding on it to the Allied Governments—no doubt with the idea that the French would be able to get something in London in exchange for their consent in the nature of further interallied debt concessions or credits, in which Belgium and Italy would share.

'Dubois himself did not definitely commit himself against an extension but talked of suspension of one or two payments only and seizure of "gages" on lines, with which you are familiar.

'But you will have the full text of the declarations by Monday [August 7].

'In the end Delacroix proposed to adjourn the consideration of my proposal until after the London meeting and moved the adjournment against my vote.

'I thought it best to have a vote taken on the question of adjournment and to insist on the publication of my draft resolution, and the fact that the Commission had adjourned the decision upon it until after the London Conference. I agreed, however, that in order to avoid premature public discussion the publication should be delayed until Monday morning.

'The Minutes of the discussions are to be communicated officially to the Governments before the London meeting. They will, I hope, be of some help to the British point of view. Some remarks of Delacroix's on ["responsabilités"] may be quite useful.

'I am sorry I could not get a definite decision to grant the moratorium, but, of course, I scarcely hoped for this.

'I will come over on Sunday.'

In a Memorandum of August 5 (C 11160/99/18) Mr. Lampson stated: 'I raised with Sir B. Blackett this morning the point whether it was opportune or not for the Reparation Commission to publish on Monday morning [August 7], as proposed, the draft Resolution proposed by Sir J. Bradbury on the subject of the German moratorium.

'He was not very responsive at first but finally admitted that if left to his own judgment he did not think that he would have advocated publication. As it was however the whole Reparation Commission had voted in favour of publication together with an explanatory statement, and as the Commission were a sovereign body entitled to take such action as they thought fit, he saw no possibility of now restraining them from publication.

'I said that in those circumstances there was nothing more for me to say, but I still maintained my point of view that publication would probably have an adverse effect upon French public opinion and to that extent prejudice the prospects of success at the meeting with M. Poincaré. I felt however that having spoken to him and raised the point I had at least achieved an "acquis de conscience".'

Resolution

Having regard to the existing financial situation of Germany and the collapse of the mark exchanges, the Reparation Commission is of opinion that it has become necessary to suspend all cash payments by Germany in foreign currencies in respect of Peace Treaty charges for the remainder of the calendar year 1922.

It accordingly recommends to the Allied Governments that payments in respect of the clearing offices should be suspended, on condition that the sum of 500,000*l.* sterling per month offered by the German Government under that head should be paid to the Reparation Commission to be disposed of as the commission may hereafter determine.

In the event of the Allied Governments agreeing to this recommendation, the commission agreed to suspend the remaining instalments of the payments to be made in cash in respect of reparation for the year 1922. The amount of the payments so suspended to be carried forward in the same manner as the amount postponed under the decision of the commission of the 21st March, 1922.[5]

In view of the urgency of the present situation the commission has not thought it necessary to impose new conditions for the further moratorium to be granted in respect of 1922.

It will, however, become necessary at a very early date to determine the amounts of the payments to be required from Germany in the years 1923 and 1924 and the whole question of the conditions to be imposed in respect of any postponement of these payments (which will necessarily be more stringent than those of the existing moratorium) will be considered in connection with that decision.

[5] See No. 12, n. 1.

No. 47

Mr. Cadogan[1] to M. Gavrilović

[C 10551/99/18]

Copy FOREIGN OFFICE, *August 3, 1922*

Sir,

With reference to Monsieur Tadić's memorandum No. 267 of the 11th July,[2] I have the honour to inform you that there is no objection on the

[1] A senior member of the Central Department of the Foreign Office.

[2] Not printed. In a minute of July 22 to Sir B. Blackett, Mr. Waley (see No. 31, n. 3) wrote as follows: 'Mr. Boshkovich, the Serbian Delegate on the Reparation Commission, discussed with me this morning two points.

'(1) Article XI of the Agreement of March 11th 1922 and the Annex [see No. 11, n. 2]. The Serbian Government wishes this Article to be interpreted so as to mean that Serbia's debt in respect of ceded State property and Liberation Bonds can be satisfied not only by the C Bonds to be received in respect of the debt of Austria, Hungary and Bulgaria and to

part of His Majesty's Government to the manner in which the Serb-Croat-Slovene Government desire to interpret article 11 of the Paris agreement of March 11th 1922, provided that this interpretation is concurred in by the other powers concerned.

2. It has been proposed that article 3 of the agreement should be formally interpreted by the National Delegates on the Reparation Commission, and upon the interpretation of this article His Majesty's Government do not therefore at the present stage desire to express any formal opinion. They are disposed however to consider that it will eventually be found possible for the Serb-Croat-Slovene Government to obtain the deliveries in kind which it is understood that they require in 1922, without having to make a cash payment in respect thereof to the Reparation Commission.

I have, etc.,

(For the Earl of Balfour)

ALEXANDER CADOGAN

be distributed in the percentages fixed by Article II of Spa [see Vol. VIII, No. 77, n. 3] but also from the C Bonds to be received in respect of the debt of Germany and to be distributed in the percentages fixed by Article I of Spa. I said that the provisions of Article XI were notoriously obscure but that I did not think that the British Government would object to their being interpreted in this sense. The consent of Serbia to the release of the liens on Austrian Assets is conditional on their being satisfied that they will be able to use all the C Bonds to which they will ultimately be entitled to meet their debts in respect of ceded property and Liberation Bonds and their adherence to the Agreement of March 11th is also conditional on this.

'(2) Article III of the Agreement of March 11th. Mr. Boshkovich thought that the British Government had possibly changed their mind on the question whether this country is entitled to take any share in the unused surpluses on the 380 million gold marks of deliveries in kind. I said that this Article was also notoriously obscure and it was quite possible that there had been a misunderstanding but we had now authorised Sir John Bradbury to interpret the Article for us so we could not discuss the interpretation with him. It appeared, however, that he agrees that we should interpret the Article so as to give us a right to unused surpluses but would like us to make a private arrangement with the Serbian Government to hand over to them part of the surpluses to which we may be entitled in order to enable them to avoid paying cash for the railway material which they are obtaining from Germany in 1922. I said that this might involve an additional cash payment by us to the Reparation Commission and it was rather a difficult matter and suggested that the question might be left over until we see how the situation finally develops.'

No. 48

Mr. Phipps[1] (Brussels) to the Marquess Curzon of Kedleston
(Received August 5, 8.30 a.m.)

No. 57 Telegraphic [C 11141/99/18]

BRUSSELS, *August 4, 1922, 7.30 p.m.*

The principal organs of the Belgian press criticize, but on the whole with moderation, your note on war debts.[2] The usually very pro-French Paris

---

[1] Chargé d'Affaires in Brussels.　　　[2] See No. 45.

correspondent of the 'Soir' even admits the proposals contained therein are not wanting in generosity.

The Catholic 'Libre-Belgique' greatly deplores the isolated French ultimatum[3] to Germany without previous consent of British or Belgian governments. France has thereby placed herself in a position of either having to retreat or to follow isolated (?policy) of sanctions. It deprecates simultaneous demand of His Majesty's Government for payment of allied war debts and reduction of German debt and their apparent desire to save Germany from bankruptcy at the cost of that of the unfortunate countries devastated by the German army; the article expresses the hope that Belgian delegates will urge this consideration in London.

[3] A reference to M. Poincaré's Note to the German Government of July 26. In an entry in his diary of July 31, Lord D'Abernon commented: 'Poincaré's note . . . is couched in the terms of an Ultimatum and reminds one of nothing so much as the Austrian Ultimatum to Serbia in 1914. It would seem to indicate a determination on his part to bring matters to a crisis. Finding it impossible to obtain a majority in the Reparation Commission, and determined to secure a declaration that Germany has made wilful default, he has seized the opportunity offered by the German request for a partial moratorium on the Clearing House payments. The situation created here is of extreme gravity. Although the German Government only published a summary of Poincaré's Note—a summary so mild that it was misleading—the effect on the financial position has been disastrous. It seems very probable that when the exact text is known—and this cannot be long delayed—a further aggravation of the crisis is certain.

'It is by no means improbable that the extreme parties will demand the re-assembly of the Reichstag and will attack the Government on the ground that the fulfilment policy has completely failed. Since concession has only led to further attacks and demands by France, there is considerable justification for the view that it was a mistake ever to have entered upon the Wirth policy. I do not hold this view myself, but it will certainly be held by very large sections here.

'Poincaré has done more to assist the Nationalists and more to destroy the fulfilment policy than could fairly have been expected from a special envoy from the Prince of Darkness.'

No. 49

Sir J. Bradbury (Reparation Commission) to Treasury[1]
[*C 11157/99/18*]

Copy
Confidential   PARIS, *August 4, 1922*
No. 309

May it please your Lordships,

The Reparation Commission has had before it the report of the Committee of Guarantees[2] on the results of its recent visit to Berlin for the purpose of organising a supervision over German finance, and also the demand recently received from the German Government for an extension of the moratorium in regard to cash payments for reparation.

[1] Communicated to the Foreign Office on August 5.
[2] See Reparation Commission V, op. cit., Appendix XXXVIII.

On my return to Paris on Wednesday, the 2nd instant, I found that the general disposition of the members of the commission was in favour of abstaining from taking any definite action until the whole situation had been considered by the Allied Governments at the forthcoming London Conference.

This course did not commend itself to my judgment for the following reasons:—

1. The catastrophic course of the German exchange is making every day's delay in adopting such remedial measures as are still possible, not merely extremely expensive from the point of view of the ultimate prospects of reparations, but highly dangerous to the general welfare of Europe.

2. The Reparation Commission has, under the Treaty of Versailles, a clear duty to adjust the payments to be required from Germany on account of reparation from time to time, according to the conclusions at which it may arrive in regard to German capacity, and to whatever extent it may be proper, and even necessary, for the Allied Governments on occasions to deal with reparation questions directly and not through their representatives upon the commission; it is clear that the considered judgment of the commission on matters to which it has given special study, and in regard to which it is entitled under the treaty to pronounce with authority, cannot but fortify the Governments for the decisions they are called upon to take.

I am satisfied that any attempt to insist on further cash payments in respect of Peace Treaty obligations between now and the 31st December next (the end of the period covered by the existing partial moratorium) will inevitably produce a catastrophe which will go far towards destroying any prospect of obtaining reparation for many years to come, if not for all time.

I accordingly requested the chairman to summon a meeting at 4 p.m. on Wednesday afternoon,[3] and proposed that the commission should immediately and as a matter of urgency take a decision in the terms of the draft enclosed herewith.[4]

The discussion at this meeting and the further sitting on Thursday afternoon is fully reported in the minutes which I append.[5]

In the end my colleagues, while recognising the extreme gravity and urgency of the situation, were unwilling to take the responsibility of coming to a decision of any kind until after the London Conference, and decided by a majority in favour of a simple adjournment of the discussion.

It was further resolved that the statements made in the course of the discussion should be communicated by the delegates to their respective Governments.

The proposal embodied in my draft resolution is, of course, no more than an emergency palliative. While the adoption of it without delay might for the moment cause some recovery of confidence, and give a breathing space

[3] See No. 46. [4] Not here printed (see No. 46, Enclosure).
[5] Not printed: see, however, No. 46, n. 4.

in which future arrangements could be considered, it will be of little utility unless followed by a practical plan to deal with the whole situation created by the breakdown of the schedule of payments.[6]

That the full obligation under that schedule can in the near future be enforced is a proposition to which I doubt whether any serious economist or man of affairs in any country would now be found to subscribe. As regards the remote future it is more difficult to speak with confidence, but my own judgment, for what it is worth, is that the burden resulting from the automatic criterion which it lays down will be an impossible one unless the volume of German foreign trade assumes dimensions which seem at the moment improbable—a development which in itself presupposes a restoration of German credit, to which the existence of the present obligation offers an effective barrier.

There are—or perhaps it would be more accurate to say that two months ago there were, since recent events have made the restoration of German credit much more difficult—two alternative methods of handling the reparation problem with some prospect of financial advantage. One was to create conditions favourable to the restoration of German credit under which substantial amounts might become available for Germany's creditors by means of German foreign loans. The failure of this policy through the interruption of the proceedings of the Bankers' Committee[7] in circumstances with which your Lordships are familiar, has made it necessary to have recourse to the other alternative, i.e. Germany's creditors must content themselves for the time being with the amounts which represent the exportable surplus of current German production, plus the proceeds of such German assets of a capital nature as can be realised abroad.

In present conditions little can be hoped for in the near future under the last head. That part of the capital wealth of the country which is capable of physical exportation without crippling the machinery of production is relatively insignificant, while the acquisition by foreigners of assets to be retained in Germany is unlikely to take place on any important scale until general credit can be restored.

The problem thus resolves itself in the main into one of creating an exportable surplus of production and making that surplus available for reparation.

The only machinery by which it can be solved is the incorporation of the cost of whatever reparation is made, either in cash or kind, in a State budget covered by real resources—that is to say, unless and until internal State credit can be restored by taxation.

Unfortunately the bringing into operation of this machinery must inevitably, in the first instance, have a prejudicial effect on production itself, and, until the period of acute depression which will follow a stoppage of new inflation has been passed, any attempt to include a substantial provision for reparation in the budget without again destroying its equilibrium is probably foredoomed to failure.

[6] See No. 5, n. 2.   [7] See No. 27, n. 5.

The events of the last few weeks have rendered the task of maintaining budget equilibrium, even without any reparation provision, very much more difficult. Until the plans of the German Government for 1923 have been formulated it is difficult to form any adequate appreciation of the possibilities, but, if these plans indicate that a real effort is being made to cope with the situation, the Reparation Commission and the Allied Governments would be wise in exercising the greatest moderation in respect of reparation demands, both in cash and kind, during the critical period.

Indications were given by the French delegate, in the course of the recent discussions, that his Government contemplate the possibility of making the suspension of the remaining cash payments for 1922 conditional on the acceptance by the German Government of more stringent provisions in regard to financial control and on the transfer to the Reparation Commission of certain German State assets by way of security.[8]

A very early opportunity will arise for enforcing such conditions, if they are deemed to be desirable, in connection with the arrangements for 1923 and subsequent years, and it would, in my opinion, be undesirable to attempt to settle so difficult and delicate a problem under the conditions and urgency which govern the decision in respect of the 1922 payments.

I am myself strongly of opinion that effective guarantees must be obtained for the stoppage of further inflation, and I believe this can be done if the Allied Governments are content to moderate the reparation demand on the lines above indicated.

I remain, however, completely sceptical as to the usefulness of endeavours either to dictate the details of German fiscal legislation, to exercise a veto over public expenditure or actively to interfere in administration. Control on such lines would, if it were made really complete, involve the government of Germany by the Allies as a conquered country: if incomplete it would be ineffective.

The only reparation policy likely to be fruitful is, in the first place, to set Germany a task which is capable of accomplishment and to leave her responsible for the precise methods by which it is to be accomplished, but to take drastic action if she fails to carry it out.

The adoption by the Allies of measures of coercion can, without a doubt, inflict the gravest injury upon—possibly bring complete destruction to—Germany, but such measures will, from the financial point of view, for the Allies be wholly unproductive.

A settlement of the reparation problem by the free consent of all the nations concerned cannot be hoped for in the present temper of the world. If results therefore are to be obtained, the Allies must be prepared in the last resort to apply coercion, at whatever cost to themselves. Necessity for actual resort to it will probably be avoided if the alternative offered to Germany is not—as it has been up to the present—to attempt to perform an impossible task, but to carry out a policy of sane financial reform which is essential in her own interests, and to assume for the purposes of reparation only such

[8] Cf. No. 51, below.

burdens as are consistent with the maintenance of her national solvency and the preservation of a tolerable standard of life for her people.

If coercion has to be applied, the method should, if possible, be sharp and short. It will be effective only in so far as it is damaging, and in so far as it is damaging it will diminish the power of Germany to make payment in the future.

The same considerations apply to most of the schemes which have been outlined for taking securities ('gages'). The hypothecation of customs or railway receipts, the taking over of State forests or blocks of shares in industrial undertakings could not be carried out without creating serious economic friction and impairing the efficiency of German administration. On the other hand, it is doubtful how far such pledges, if obtained, could be turned by the Allies to practical account.

Measures of coercion should, in my opinion, be resorted to only in the event either of deliberate defiance or real negligence on the part of the German Government. I am quite aware that the opinion is widely held, particularly in France, that these conditions exist. My own conclusion, on the contrary, is that the present German Government has made, and is continuing to make, a genuine effort to carry out, under disheartening conditions, the obligations which it assumed in May 1921. There has, it is true, been a considerable measure both of active and of passive resistance on the part of large sections of the German people. The question whether, by the display of a higher degree of political courage, the Government could have done more in the direction either of increasing its reparation performance or of restoring order in internal finance is a very difficult one to answer, but whatever shortcomings can be laid to its charge have been to a large extent condoned by the Reparation Commission in its final decision in regard to the 31st May moratorium.[9]

I am satisfied, as I have already indicated, that the task set to the German Government in May 1921 was an impossible one—at any rate, in regard to the earlier years. The Allied Governments would have been wiser to content themselves with much smaller reparation payments at the commencement and to concentrate the efforts of the German Government upon restoring order in their internal finance. The political difficulties of the German Government have undoubtedly been enhanced by the conviction prevalent in Germany that the policy of 'execution' was hopeless and by the often inconsiderate attitude of the Allied Governments and of the Reparation Commission.

It is certainly true that the expenditure side of the German budget has not been curtailed in the manner which prudence should have dictated after an exhausting war, and that the reorganisation of taxation has been slow and incomplete. The difficulties under the latter head were largely the inevitable consequence of administrative changes resulting from the revolution, and considerable progress is now being made towards remedying them. The

[9] A reference to the letter of June 14 from the Reparation Commission to the German Chancellor: see Reparation Commission III, op. cit., pp. 142–4.

former error is not peculiar to Germany. Almost all countries immediately after the conclusion of peace attempted to accelerate material reconstruction by means of Government credits. The vice has persisted in Germany longer than elsewhere, largely because currency depreciation which other countries recognised as a danger signal was attributed to reparation demands. For the future, a ruthless cutting down of State expenditure should certainly be insisted upon; but as regards the past, I see no evidence that extravagant expenditure has been deliberately undertaken by the German Government in order to absorb money which otherwise would have had to be devoted to reparations.

Recourse to measures of force at the present moment would, in my judgment, be unjustifiable. It would further have the effect of destroying what remains of German credit, and might easily create a situation in which not only would the abandonment of the whole reparation claim become inevitable, but in which the Allied Governments might find themselves confronted with a problem similar to that which has arisen in the case of Austria, but upon a scale which would render it wholly intractable.

A copy of this report has been addressed to His Majesty's Embassy, Paris.

I have, etc.,
JOHN BRADBURY

CHAPTER II

Proceedings of the Fifth Conference of London and Records of Conversations connected therewith

August 7–14, 1922

No. 50

S. 55] *Minutes of a Conference of Ministers held at 10, Downing Street, S.W.1, on Monday, August 7, 1922 at 10.30 a.m.*

[*C 12075/99/18*]

PRESENT: The Prime Minister (*in the Chair*); The Rt. Hon. A. Chamberlain, M.P., Lord Privy Seal; The Rt. Hon. Sir Robert Horne, G.B.E., K.C., M.P., Chancellor of the Exchequer; The Rt. Hon. Sir Laming Worthington-Evans, Bt., M.P., Secretary of State for War; Sir John Bradbury, G.C.B., Principal British Representative, Reparation Commission; Sir Basil Blackett, K.C.B., Controller of Finance; F. Leith Ross, Esq.,[1] Reparation Commission; Sir Edward Grigg, K.C.V.O., C.M.G.; SECRETARY, Sir Maurice Hankey, G.C.B.

After some preliminary discussion during which the Prime Minister explained that he had summoned this meeting to compare notes as to the present position in regard to German Reparations, which was to be discussed half-an-hour later with representatives of the Allies,[2] the PRIME MINISTER read a personal message which he had received from the German Chancellor, dated August 5th, 1922 (Appendix).

SIR JOHN BRADBURY agreed with the Prime Minister that Dr. Wirth's statement was a very fair one. He agreed with what Dr. Wirth said about deliveries in kind. He thought that the German Government had been inclined to over-estimate the capacity of Germany for delivery in kind.

THE LORD PRIVY SEAL raised the question of how German wages compared with British wages. M. Theunis had said that the British wages in the coal industry were the lowest in Europe.

THE CHANCELLOR OF THE EXCHEQUER said that British coal was actually going to Germany because in some parts of Germany it was cheaper to buy British than German coal.

THE PRIME MINISTER pointed out that this was perhaps due to sea transport.

[1] A member of the Finance Service Managing Board of the Reparation Commission.
[2] See No. 51, below.

SIR JOHN BRADBURY said that after the Armistice, German wages had been very low and there had been a good deal of distress, but matters had then improved and up to three or four months ago wages had gone ahead of the rise in prices. Now, however, prices were going ahead of wages. He did not think, however, that there was much real distress among the German working classes.

MR. LEITH ROSS, in reply to the Prime Minister, said that it was very difficult to estimate the purchasing value of wages in Germany as compared with Great Britain. The purchasing power of the mark varied with every day. At present, however, prices were going steadily against wages.

After some exchange of views as to the amounts already paid by Germany and their economic effect, the PRIME MINISTER said that the two questions which had to be considered were first, at what stage would the Allies be justified in taking a step which would upset the German Government and paralyse the German administration and internal economy, and second, whether it was worth while taking such steps.

APPENDIX

Personal message from the German Chancellor to Mr. Lloyd George, communicated by the German Ambassador, August 5, 1922.

[C 11159/99/18]

Within a few weeks conditions in Germany have fundamentally deteriorated. This deterioration of the economic situation has been accompanied by a growing crisis in the political situation. Owing to the unbearable rise in prices an extraordinary exasperation has seized large sections of the population. It is commonly alleged that the catastrophic condition of the German exchange and the general pauperisation and misery is due to the government's 'policy of fulfilment', which, it is said, has exceeded the limits of possibility. This exasperation of the people can unfortunately not be ignored and it constitutes a fact, which must be seriously considered by the German government. The most extensive measures of precaution cannot preclude the possibility of further political assassinations. In view of this growing exasperation a further delay in the solution of the Reparation question would be fatal; social and political upheavals could scarcely be avoided. I am personally conscious of tremendous responsibilities and have, therefore, consistently followed the policy of fulfilment within the last year: acknowledging Germany's liabilities I have patiently borne all demands, so cruel to the German people, in the hope of better times to come. But today it is no more a question of patience but of exhaustion.

In my opinion it is the German democratic government, which, after the catastrophe of the war, has saved the bourgeois society of Central Europe from Bolshevism, and has, therefore, from the point of view of history, deserved well of the world social order. A policy looking to Europe as a whole can, however, not be continued in face of the complete pauperisation of the German people.

I desire to draw attention to the fact that, should the present fall in the exchange continue, deliveries in kind will shortly have to be restricted, as it would become impossible to finance them internally. In any case the deliveries of coal imposed upon us are excessive and cannot be continued. However, I will exert the greatest energy to continue the present line of German policy, but this policy, I am bound to state, will collapse, owing to the plain fact of the depreciation of the mark, unless external help is given *in time*. I must emphasise our *non possumus* as far as payments in gold and exorbitant deliveries in coal are concerned.

The German democracy is doomed unless a stop can be put to the further pauperisation of the German people. The laments of all members of the middle classes, who have become beggars owing to the currency depreciation, is indescribable. I must therefore implore you—

(1) Not to allow the evident evolution of the Reparation question towards a solution to be disturbed by forcible measures calculated utterly to ruin the finance and economic strength of Germany.

(2) To work towards a reduction of Reparations to figures definitely bearable by the German national economy, towards allowing Germany sufficient breathing space to consolidate her utterly ruined exchange and thus to create the only basis of German economic efficiency.

I venture to address this forcible exposition of the situation to Mr. Lloyd George as conscientious deliberations have convinced me that this is the last decisive moment.

No. 51

I.C.P. 250.] *British Secretary's Notes of an Allied Conference held at 10, Downing Street, on Monday, August 7, 1922, at 11 a.m.*

PRESENT: *Belgium*: M. Theunis, M. Jaspar, Baron Moncheur; EXPERTS: M. Bemelmans,[1] M. Gutt, M. Furst; SECRETARY: Vicomte Davignon.[2]

British Empire: The Right Hon. D. Lloyd George, O.M., M.P., Prime Minister (*in the Chair*); The Right Hon. A. Chamberlain, Sir Robert Horne, Sir L. Worthington-Evans; EXPERTS: Sir William Tyrrell,[3] Sir Basil Blackett, Mr. R. G. Vansittart, Sir Edward Grigg, Mr. F. Leith Ross, Mr. S. D. Waley, Mr. P. J. Grigg;[4] SECRETARIES: Sir Maurice Hankey, Mr. R. B. Howorth,[5] Mr. T. St. Quintin Hill.[6]

France: M. Poincaré, M. de Lasteyrie, M. le Comte de Saint-Aulaire; EXPERTS: M. le Comte de Peretti della Rocca, M. Tannery, M. Avenol, M. de Margerie; SECRETARY: M. Massigli.[7]

Italy: Signor Schanzer, Signor de Martino; EXPERTS: Signor Giannini,[8] Signor d'Amelio,[9] Signor Conti Rossini, Signor

[1] Assistant Belgian delegate to the Reparation Commission.
[2] Chef du Cabinet in the Belgian Ministry of Foreign Affairs.
[3] Assistant Under-Secretary of State for Foreign Affairs.
[4] Private Secretary to the Chancellor of the Exchequer.
[5] An Assistant Secretary in H.M. Treasury.
[6] A Principal in the Cabinet Secretariat.
[7] Secretary to the Conference of Ambassadors.
[8] Secretary in the Legal Department of the Italian Foreign Office.
[9] Assistant Italian delegate to the Reparation Commission.

Ciarrocca, Signor Mercurio; SECRETARY: Count Vannutelli Rey.
Japan: Baron Hayashi; EXPERTS: M. T. Sekiba,[10] M. G.
Nishigawa, M. S. Arai; SECRETARY: M. T. Tokugawa.
INTERPRETER: M. Camerlynck.

Procedure

1. MR. LLOYD GEORGE, after welcoming the Allied delegates, informed the conference that M. Poincaré was anxious that there should be an interchange of views before the 15th August,[11] having regard to the fact that an instalment of the annual payment from Germany would fall due on that date, and having regard also, no doubt, to the general situation in Germany itself. In the circumstances, although it would have been preferable for the conference to have had before it the report of the Reparation Commission on Germany's application for a moratorium,[12] yet there were undoubted advantages in having a discussion of the general position at the present moment. With a view to initiating the discussion, he (Mr. Lloyd George) thought that the best plan would be for him to call upon M. Poincaré to develop his views as to the general situation.

M. POINCARÉ remarked that he had responded to the very kind invitation extended to him by Mr. Lloyd George on the last occasion on which he had come to London for the purpose of discussing outstanding questions between Great Britain and France.[13] On that occasion both Mr. Lloyd George and himself had thought that it would be useful to renew the conversations regarding reparations when Germany had submitted her reply to the Reparation Commission. That reply had now been received, and was at the moment under the consideration of the commission, and its tenor was well known. The most important question on the reply was the precise nature of the control which it would be necessary in future to exercise over German finances, and, having regard to the complexities of the matter, he (M. Poincaré) was very glad to have this opportunity of discussing the whole question with the Allies of France. It must, however, be remembered that since he was last in London, new events had happened which had a most important bearing on the situation. There was, for example, the report of the Commission of Guarantees,[14] and there was also the note issued by the British Government on the question of inter-Allied debts.[15] This latter document was a most momentous contribution to the problem. There was also, of course, the recent application made by the German Government for a substantial moratorium. He (M. Poincaré) was in no special position, and certainly had no peculiar right or privilege to open the discussion: in fact, he personally would much prefer to hear, in the first place, what the Allies of France had to say regarding the situation.

SIGNOR SCHANZER remarked that the reparation question was one in which all the Allies were concerned, and at the present meeting it would

---

[10] Assistant Japanese delegate to the Reparation Commission.   [11] See No. 38, n. 4.
[12] See No. 36 and No. 38, nn. 1 and 4.   [13] See No. 30 and Vol. XVII, No. 659.
[14] Of July 18, 1922 (see No. 39): see also Reparation Commission V, op. cit., pp. 267–76
[15] i.e. the Balfour Note of August 1, 1922 (see No. 45).

be possible for the Allies to feel their way by initiating a discussion. M. Poincaré had indicated the new factors in the situation, such as the report of the Commission of Guarantees and the British note, and he agreed with M. Poincaré that the present discussions could be regarded as a resumption of former conversations. He (Signor Schanzer) was of opinion that it would, in all the circumstances, be best for M. Poincaré to open the discussion.

BARON HAYASHI and M. THEUNIS agreed with the remarks of Signor Schanzer.

MR. LLOYD GEORGE then requested M. Poincaré to open the discussion, indicating that he did so at the unanimous request of all the Allied representatives.

German Reparations—The French Point of View

2. M. POINCARÉ said that it would, of course, be very ungracious on his part if he did not yield to the unanimous request of the Allied representatives to open the discussion. The Allied delegates must excuse him if he found it necessary to begin at a point anterior in date to the last Conversations with Mr. Lloyd George.[13] He could not hide from the Conference the fact that France was in a state of the deepest anxiety, due not only to the developments of the Reparation question in recent years, but also to the events which had happened in Germany in the last two months. In the view of French public opinion the Treaty of Versailles had, during the last three years, been less and less carried into effect. So much was this the case that at the moment the Treaty might be said hardly to be in process of being carried out at all. For example, the Allies had agreed, though with some hesitation, to the war criminals being tried in Germany by the Leipzig Court.[16] That Court had undertaken certain trials and had passed either ridiculous sentences on the prisoners or had released them altogether. The question of war criminals was now before the Conference of Ambassadors, who were engaged in seeing whether some other method of dealing with the matter could not be devised. On the question of Disarmament, Germany had given very great trouble throughout, and she was showing more and more ill-will as time went on. The proceedings of the Allied Military Commission of Control were being thwarted, and blood had been shed recently in consequence. As regards Reparations, the hopes and expectations of France and her Allies had not been realised. It should be remembered that the Treaty of Versailles had excluded from the purview of Reparations purely war expenditure; but the Allies were to be indemnified in respect of damage to property, and for pensions and allowances payable to soldiers and civilians who had suffered in person through the War, including those unfortunate French and Belgian civilians who had been deported and put on to forced labour. There was some danger of these provisions of the Treaty being forgotten. As regards damage to property, the Reparation Commission had fixed the amount of Germany's liability in April, 1921, at 132 milliards.[17] The Allies had them-

[16] See Vol. XVI, No. 555.

[17] See ibid., No. 546, and see also Reparation Commission V, op. cit., p. 35.

selves reduced this amount by 12 milliards, and France had then hoped that payment would be made of the residue by means of the instalments contemplated in the Schedule of Payments of May, 1921,[18] and that Europe would enter upon an era of the realisation of the Treaty.

On 1st May 1921, France had for the second time asked her Allies to agree to an Allied occupation of the Ruhr.[19] Both at Spa[20] and in London France had encountered very strong objection to her proposals respecting the Ruhr, and under pressure of circumstances she had reluctantly accepted the amount, 132 milliards, fixed by the Reparation Commission, and the provisions of the Schedule of Payments and the percentage division of receipts among the Allies, hoping that by making these great concessions to Germany in a conciliatory spirit an end would be brought to the policy of concession and weakening of the Treaty which had been so constantly urged in the last two or three years. The three series of Bonds provided for in the Schedule of Payments would have furnished a basis for the settlement of Inter-Allied Debts. The French Government had carefully examined this aspect of the matter and but for recent events would have been prepared to formulate proposals based on the utilisation of the 'C' Bonds for the purpose of liquidating these debts. In spite of the new situation he, M. Poincaré, still hoped that negotiations on these lines might be opened on some future date. Today, France was forced by the pressure of circumstances to concentrate on the most urgent and pressing points of difficulty. The Allies had, it was true, a Schedule of Payments, but this Schedule was of a theoretical rather than a real character. The German Government had obtained a moratorium.

Mr. Chamberlain, interrupting, remarked that the German Government had applied for a moratorium to the 31st December 1924.[21]

Sir Robert Horne added that the Moratorium granted as a result of the Cannes decisions was an incomplete moratorium.

M. Poincaré said that what he meant was that Germany was applying for an extension of the moratorium to the 31st December 1924. M. Poincaré, resuming, said that on the other hand the whole question of Inter-Allied indebtedness had assumed a new character. In the view of France, no useful purpose would be served by treating the question of Inter-Allied debts until German Reparation payments had been placed on a settled basis and the payments themselves were being regularly made. He, M. Poincaré, reminded the Conference that France was not claiming monies which she had advanced to certain of her Allies. France, indeed, had almost forgotten these advances which had been made for the common benefit. The United States of America and Great Britain, had, however, reminded their Allies of their indebtedness. The United States of America, it was true, was not asking for payment of debt, but had requested its debtors to confer at Washington on the best methods of arranging for payment at some future time. The Note recently issued by the British Government[22] to the debtors of Great

---

[18] See No. 5, n. 2.   [19] See Vol. XV, No. 78.   [20] See Vol. VIII, Chap. VIII.
[21] See Nos. 1, 36, and 38.   [22] See n. 15, above.

Britain was couched in lofty and courteous terms, but indicated without possibility of doubt that Great Britain proposed to insist some day on payment. The result, so far as France was concerned, was very cruel. France had ten of her Departments devastated and she had advanced more than 80 milliards in respect of German Reparations.

MR. LLOYD GEORGE enquired what this 80 milliards included.

M. POINCARÉ said that in addition to Reparations proper it also included money for pensions and allowances.

MR. LLOYD GEORGE enquired whether M. de Lasteyrie could give the actual figures.

M. DE LASTEYRIE said that at the end of the present year the French Government would have advanced about 55 milliards for Reparations proper, about 30 milliards for pensions and allowances under the Treaty, making a total of about 85 milliards. In addition, there would be the interest on loans raised for the purpose of making these advances, which would bring the total sum up to about 95 milliards. He undertook to furnish the Conference with a statement of the exact figures.

M. POINCARÉ, resuming, pointed out that in the events which had happened France was incurring a financial responsibility in respect of Reparations on account of Germany which was steadily and rapidly increasing. As a result, France had to face a deficit, not only on her Extraordinary Budget but on her Ordinary Budget. The situation was full of peril and could not possibly last. No one desired to drive France—or for that matter Germany—to despair, but if the present financial situation continued—and he, M. Poincaré, weighed his words carefully—France would find herself in an absolutely hopeless position.

It seemed to him that certain persons did not quite realise the great danger with which France was threatened. Germany cried out loudly and by doing so attracted everyone to her side; France had refrained from crying out and both in France and Belgium the financial position was very serious indeed. It was alleged that France was actuated in her present policy by a militaristic spirit, and these allegations had occurred in newspapers in Allied and friendly countries. It had even been suggested that France was in favour of the dismemberment of Germany. He, M. Poincaré, would take this opportunity of repeating, in the most absolute manner, the assurances given by his predecessors on this subject. There could be no more mendacious slander than the statement that France was in favour of the annexation of German territory or that she desired to crush Germany. France had no wish to annex permanently territory inhabited by German nationals. At the same time, France desired to escape from ruin, and she had given recent proofs of her desire to treat the whole question in a conciliatory manner. She had, however, never shared in the optimism which some persons had held regarding Germany, and she was of opinion that the future reconstruction of Europe depended on the just settlement of the Reparations question. The Conference of financial experts at Brussels[23] had

[23] See No. 6, n. 4.

come to this conclusion, and he, M. Poincaré, was certain that if the Reparation question could be finally disposed of the reconstruction of Europe would automatically follow.

It had been urged that France should reduce her armaments and should tax her people more. As regards taxation, it would be interesting to know how taxation in Germany compared with taxation in France. The French Government had very materially reduced their military and naval expenditure, and had recently reduced by 50% the period of military service; but further reductions could only be made if guarantees were secured—and what guarantees had France against the menace of a revived Germany? In Germany, the spirit of revenge was growing stronger every day, and it must be remembered that Germany was not fully disarmed. If France—and, he would like to add, Belgium—further reduced their armaments, undoubtedly they would be threatened by Germany.

Certain British newspapers had enquired why France did not disarm at sea. Why did France require submarines when Great Britain was there to assist her? France fully realised that in the event of renewed trouble with Germany Great Britain would be on her side, but it should be remembered that France would have to bear the brunt of the contest at the outset, and—what was often forgotten—a large part of France's army was situated in Africa and it was necessary to maintain a fleet of submarines for the purpose of convoying the transports across the Mediterranean. As regards a reduction of taxation, the French Government [were] doing everything they possibly could to secure this end. The French Government would be willing to take up this matter when they knew precisely what Germany was going to do in the same matter. The Chancellor of the Exchequer had said that Great Britain was more heavily taxed than any other Allied country. It was, however, a most difficult matter to compare the taxation in one country with that in another, and he, M. Poincaré, had found such comparisons very misleading. It must be remembered that France had ten devastated Provinces, 1,400,000 dead and as many mutilated, and that matters of this kind meant national weakness from the taxation point of view. The French system of taxation differed materially from that of Great Britain. In addition to the Income Tax collected by the French Government there were rates and taxes of various kinds collected by the Province, the Department, and the Commune, and in certain Communes the local rates were very high indeed. Again, the social structure of the French population was essentially different from that of the population of Great Britain. The lower middle, and poor, classes in France were far more numerous in proportion to the whole than was the case in Great Britain, while the number of very rich persons was very small in France. France was financially almost out of breath and morally and socially it was quite impossible for the French Government to contemplate the imposition of heavier taxation. Before this could be done France must be given a breathing space. At present she existed largely on her credit, and it was essential for her to exact from Germany her just and proper claims in respect of reparations. This work of reconstruction which is being carried out now, that is the work of repairing houses and buildings in French Provinces, could not be interrupted. It would be most damaging to the French inhabitants of the devastated Provinces if houses were left unfinished, and would spell ruin to millions of the inhabitants of the Department of the Nord. This Department was densely populated and was equal in size to four or five average French Provinces.

But the French Government would be told that of course France was in a sorry plight and the situation was very bad; but Germany was in a terrible position, the mark was now worth nothing, and Germany was unable to find gold or foreign securities for her foreign payments. He admitted that there was no doubt Germany was facing a very serious situation but there was a considerable difference between the situation of France and Belgium on the one hand and of Germany on the other. He would not refer to the original cause of the present state of affairs in Germany or to the responsibility for the War, but in regard to the cause of the present situation he would say that Germany was herself to blame on account of her actions since the Armistice. In the last three years the German Government had spent money recklessly and without count. Germany had behaved as perhaps a victorious nation might behave and had indulged in luxury expenditure. He would point to the steps which Germany had taken to restore her Mercantile Marine. Those present had seen the German programme for the construction of navigable waterways and he was prepared to circulate a map which would show what Germany was doing in this respect and a statement of the money which she was spending and proposed to spend. It had been found necessary to refer certain questions to the Inter-Allied Military Committee with a view to intervention to prevent the construction of railway lines in Germany which, although being built apparently for commercial purposes, were in reality intended for strategic purposes. Besides, it was only sufficient to travel in Germany in order to see the new stations which have been erected there and German railway development. Further, in the German Budget there were sums included as a subsidy for reducing the price of bread. All those facts showed that Germany had spent money and was continuing to spend money without restraint. Had Germany taxed her people and tried to raise the level of taxation to that ruling in Allied countries? No; she remained in a permanent state of violation of the Treaty of Versailles. She had increased her money in circulation enormously and had regarded this as the only means of getting out of her financial embarrassments. If France had done the same she would at this moment be a ruined nation, but she had done exactly the reverse, and had reduced both her expenditure and her monetary circulation. Germany on the other hand had put into circulation many milliards of paper marks and was continuing to do so. The Committee of Guarantees[24] should stop this kind of thing and should establish a control over the estimates and the carrying out of the German budget. There should also be a control of exports. The Germans claim that the control should only be provisional and conditional, that is that it should

[24] See No. 10, n. 1, and Nos. 29, 38 and 39.

continue only as long as the moratorium and should be established only if the moratorium were granted in a form acceptable to her. The French Government thought that control would be illusory if it were not permanent and designed to carry out a plan which would put German finances on a sound basis. It would also be illusory as long as the Committee of Guarantees did not sit in Berlin and did not carry out the control on the spot. He desired to draw the attention of the meeting to these considerations.

There was also a lacuna which required to be filled up. On this point so far nothing had been said by him or by M. de Lasteyrie. The lacuna consisted of the absence of control of the Reichsbank. If the collapse of the mark were to be stopped a means must be found of putting an end to the operation of the printing press and of reducing the circulation of paper money. In the opinion of France a moratorium could only be granted under conditions which had been strictly determined. These conditions should be fixed as strictly as possible and should begin with the taking of guarantees. As regards the granting of a moratorium, without an equivalent, this would be a dangerous and unwise step. Germany would see in such action a proof of weakness which she could use to her advantage. Besides, a moratorium without an equivalent would prove unacceptable to French public opinion and would damage the credit of France which would experience difficulties in issuing on the International market loans to carry on the work of reparations. Moreover, the Allies must obtain guarantees susceptible of immediate realisation. If France were alone and could act without taking account of the opinion of her Allies, she would have no hesitation in undertaking the occupation of the Ruhr because that in her opinion was the only effective step, but she wanted to make a serious attempt to come to agreement with her Allies and she thought that this agreement might be made on the basis of guarantees other than that referred to above. Until Germany could redeem her pledges, these pledges should act as guarantees for the loans which France needed to issue in order to supply her need for reparations. He would now indicate some of the measures which appeared to the French Government to be necessary and practicable.

In the first place the French Government thought that it would be advisable to keep on the controls over export which were now in the hands of the Inter-Allied Committee. The question of a change in policy in regard to this had been brought before the Conference of Ambassadors in Paris, but he was opposed to the idea of altering the present arrangement which was satisfactory and more and more necessary. Belgium and France knew very well in their dealings with Germany what lack of goodwill on the part of Germany meant. Germany had begun by saying that she could not fulfil all her payments in cash or securities but that she would be liberal in deliveries in kind. An agreement had therefore been signed by M. Loucheur and Herr Rathenau at Wiesbaden,[25] but this agreement had now become a dead letter. There were daily difficulties experienced in getting the Germans to carry out such agreements.

[25] See No. 1, n. 4.

He had a second proposal to make and in making this proposal he put all his cards on the table. He did not wish to hide anything in regard to the French point of view which he desired fully to explain. This point of view had been fully discussed in Paris and the proposals he had to make were considered to be necessary by France. His next suggestion was that the control over the Custom Houses on the eastern frontier of the occupied provinces should be re-established. This control, which had been established under the Treaty, had been enforced for some time and had proved satisfactory. It had been given up because it had resulted in a number of millions of marks being placed in the hands of the French and Belgians, but these were only paper marks.

Thirdly, the French Government desired to suggest that Germany should be asked to hand over to the Allies certain State properties. Provision was made for this under the Treaty of Versailles. These State properties would include State mines and *inter alia* the mines in the Ruhr. The State mines could, when handed over, be ceded to a third party or let out on lease by the Allies. Further, there was the cession of State forests. If the information of the French Government was accurate, before the war the revenue derived from these forests amounted to 120 million gold marks a year. The timber produced by these forests could be sold abroad and paid for in gold or securities and not in paper marks.

Lastly, on the left bank of the Rhine there were a number of factories of all kinds. These were very important. For instance, there were the factories engaged in the manufacture of dye-stuffs. They represented 95% of the total number of factories in Germany which were engaged in the manufacture of dye-stuffs and they could, in case of war, be utilised for the manufacture of poisonous gases. The French Government thought that a proportion of their capital, say 60%, should be handed over to the Reparation Commission and he thought that, in this way, the Allies would be able to obtain effective guarantees.

This was not all. At the end of the war of 1870–71, when France had shown reluctance to pay her indemnity, Germany had threatened to raise and collect the taxes in the regions which she occupied. It was true that if the Allies did this in the occupied areas they would be collecting taxes in paper marks, but these paper marks would enable them to pay for German products which they wished to purchase and to pay certain expenses in Germany. This was a means of raising money which was not negligible.

Lastly, he suggested that an effective control of the German Customs should be established under the Committee of Guarantees.

It was necessary, in the opinion of the French Government, that all the Allies should impose their conditions on Germany before the granting of a moratorium and should not postpone the imposition of those conditions to some future date. The French Government had discussed the whole question of the action to be taken in regard to Germany several times and on each occasion they had been unanimous. Every member of the French Cabinet had assented and, therefore, he had a definite Mandate from the French

Government on the subject and he could not accept anything less than the proposals which he now put forward or a compromise on these conditions. (*Note*. During the translation of the above passage of his speech, M. Poincaré interrupted to say that his remarks had not been correctly interpreted and that he had not said that every one of the conditions stated by him must be accepted. Mr. Chamberlain remarked that he understood then that M. Poincaré did not mean to say that every one of his proposals must be accepted. M. Poincaré replied that the principle that was irreducible was that no moratorium could be granted without an equivalent consideration, but he had not said that all these conditions must be accepted outright. If he had said such a thing, it would have meant precluding any discussion with the Allies.) All this was without prejudice to the verdict on the defaults which Germany had committed in other directions. These defaults were being considered by the Reparation Commission. They were numerous and Germany was now haggling with the Reparation Commission on the subject of control and was trying to introduce certain conditions which would defeat control and make it dependent on the granting of a moratorium. Germany was in default in respect of para[graph] 12 of Annex II, Part VIII of the Treaty of Versailles which required the Reparation Commission to examine the German system of taxation to the end that the sums for reparation which Germany is required to pay shall become a charge upon her revenues prior to the service or discharge of any domestic loan. Germany should, therefore, pay her debts to foreign countries before paying the interest on internal loans, but she had carried out the service of internal loans and took no care about paying her foreign debts. In the same way, Section (b) of para[graph] 12 of the same Annex also required the Reparation Commission to examine the German system of taxation so as to satisfy itself that the German scheme of taxation was fully as heavy proportionately as that of any other of the powers represented on the Commission, but the Commission had found that the German taxpayer was not being heavily taxed and when Germany said that she could not pay, we might perhaps believe that she was acting in good faith, but we should change our opinion if she refused to allow control to be imposed and to carry out the provisions of the Treaty of Versailles.

He had stated the French point of view as shortly as possible. He desired to apologise for the length of his statement. He had expressed the views of the French Government in regard to the problems which would have to be faced immediately in regard to Germany.

As regards the general European situation, the French Government had completed a scheme and remained at the disposal of its Allies with a view to concerting measures for avoiding the immediate danger which faced them.

MR. LLOYD GEORGE said that M. Poincaré had stated with great lucidity the point of view of the French Government. There was no need for him to apologise for the length of his statement, having regard to the seriousness of the situation. He could not have spared one word from his statement.

The statement was of so serious a character that, speaking on behalf of the

British Government, he was not disposed to give an answer at once, but he would wish to consider the statement in conjunction with his colleagues, and would, therefore, prefer an immediate adjournment. If, however, any representative of the Allied Governments wished to speak, he would not press for such an adjournment. So far as the British Government were concerned, he would not reply till he had time to discuss the matter with his colleagues and make a considered reply to M. Poincaré's proposals.

SIGNOR SCHANZER stated that he had followed M. Poincaré's statement with great attention. It deserved very careful consideration. The Italian Government would consider the situation of France with very great sympathy, the more so that it was analogous to the situation of Italy. Though all might be agreed that it was important not to sacrifice Allied interests to German interests when one was disposed to examine the means of averting a crisis in Germany, the question of method became important. The proposals of M. Poincaré would require careful consideration. On behalf of the Italian Government he was not in a position to concur with them at once, and he agreed with Mr. Lloyd George's proposal for an adjournment.

BARON HAYASHI and M. THEUNIS signified their agreement with the proposal for an adjournment.

At Mr. Lloyd George's suggestion the time for the resumption of the meeting was fixed at 4.30 p.m.

Press Communiqué

3. MR. LLOYD GEORGE suggested that the press should merely be told that M. Poincaré had made a statement.

M. POINCARÉ said that if the press were told this they would immediately ask what the statement was.

MR. LLOYD GEORGE said that at 4.30 p.m. a statement would have to be made on behalf of the British Government. If, therefore, M. Poincaré's statement were communicated to the press, the British statement would have to be given in reply, and also the statements of the Belgian, Italian and Japanese Governments. A statement on behalf of one Government implied statements on behalf of other Governments.

M. POINCARÉ replied that French public opinion would wish to know what his statement was. He could not keep it from the French public indefinitely. He had carefully refrained from telling the press, or persons outside, of his views, because he had wished to see the representatives of the Allies first, but it would be very difficult to keep his statement from the French public. He was quite willing to maintain silence until tomorrow, however.

MR. LLOYD GEORGE said that it all depended what the Allies proposed to do. If they wished to evolve a common policy they would have to carry on discussions until they reached it, but, if there were debates with definite proposals on one side and definite proposals on the other, it would be impossible to come to agreement. The press would begin to take sides.

M. POINCARÉ replied that he quite agreed, and he was ready to undertake, on behalf of himself and the French delegation, that the strictest secrecy would be maintained until the conference released the French delegation from this obligation; but he would like to recall what had happened when Lord Curzon came to Paris in the spring to discuss Near Eastern questions,[26] and when there had been an indiscretion. He had accused the French press, first of all, but it had turned out that others were responsible for the indiscretion. He was prepared to maintain absolute secrecy in regard to what had passed at the conference, but he desired to give formal notice that at the slightest indiscretion he would consider himself at liberty to make a full disclosure.

The conference agreed—

That no information should be communicated to the press beyond the fact that the conference would hold a further meeting the same day.

2, Whitehall Gardens, August 7, 1922.

[26] See Vol. XVII, pp. 705–6.

No. 52

S. 56] *Minutes of a Conference of Ministers held at 10, Downing Street, S.W. on Monday, August 7, 1922 at 1 p.m.*

[*C 11256/99/18*]

PRESENT: The Prime Minister (*in the Chair*); The Rt. Hon. A. Chamberlain, M.P., Lord Privy Seal; The Rt. Hon. Sir Robert Horne, G.B.E., K.C., M.P., Chancellor of the Exchequer; The Rt. Hon. Sir Laming Worthington-Evans, Bt., M.P., Secretary of State for War; Sir John Bradbury, G.C.B., Principal British Representative, Reparation Commission; Sir Basil Blackett, K.C.B., Controller of Finance; F. Leith Ross, Esq., Reparation Commission; P. J. Grigg, Esq., Treasury; R. G. Vansittart, Esq., C.M.G., M.V.O., Foreign Office; S. D. Waley, Esq., Treasury; Sir Edward Grigg, K.C.V.O., C.M.G.: SECRETARY, Sir Maurice Hankey, G.C.B.

N.B. This meeting followed immediately after the Allied meeting.[1]

THE PRIME MINISTER commented on what appeared to be an extraordinary change of front in M. Poincaré's attitude. He recalled that M. Poincaré had first been interpreted as indicating that he could not compromise on any of the proposals he had made, as every member of the French Government had expressed his agreement in them and he was not entitled to give way. Then he had interrupted the interpreter to explain that the point on which he could not compromise was the principle that there could be no moratorium without some counterpart.

MR. VANSITTART said his impression had been that M. Camerlynck's original translation had been correct. All depended, however, upon whether M. Poincaré had used the words 'ces conditions' or 'cette condition'.

[1] See No. 51.

The Prime Minister said the proposals appeared to be quite hopeless. M. Briand had suggested something similar before he had seen clearly that they were impracticable. Supposing, for example, the Allies were to seize the forests. He had put the position to M. Theunis and M. Jasper and asked, if they, as Theunis-Jaspar and Co., had to handle the German forests as a commercial proposition, what would they do with it? M. Theunis had made a very sensible proposal, namely, that the question should be put to experts to work out how many gold marks would be obtained from the proposals— how much cash would the Allies obtain.

Sir Basil Blackett said that there was a certain amount of money in the proposal for a customs barrier.

The Prime Minister remarked that this would only be paper money.

Sir Basil Blackett said that before, the French and Belgians had made the mistake of keeping the marks, which only depreciated, instead of disposing of them at once.

Sir John Bradbury entered at this point.

Mr. Leith Ross said that, at the values then obtaining, half-a-million sterling might have been obtained.

Sir John Bradbury, in reply to the Prime Minister, said that out of all the proposals made by M. Poincaré, the Allied Governments might obtain a little cash, but it would make the bankruptcy of Germany complete.

The Prime Minister remarked that Marshal Foch had always said that seven divisions would be required for the occupation of the Ruhr. If the French occupied the Ruhr, it would take a good deal of the proceeds to pay the cost. He then reverted to M. Theunis's proposal to remit the proposals to experts, which he thought should be adopted.

The Secretary of State for War agreed that this was a good proposal.

The Prime Minister said he objected to the constant allusion to the sufferings of Belgium and France, without a word being said about the British Empire's losses and casualties and without a word about the Italian losses and casualties.

Sir Basil Blackett said that a very considerable figure could be built up as to what Great Britain had advanced to Germany if calculated on the same lines as M. Poincaré's statement.

The Prime Minister said he thought he ought to say something on the subject of what M. Poincaré had said about disarmament, for he felt convinced that whatever was said would be published and it was necessary to state the facts.

The Chancellor of the Exchequer asked whether the Prime Minister would like to say something about M. Poincaré's remarks that French taxation was not comparable with British.

The Prime Minister said he would be glad if Sir Robert Horne, who had gone into the question, would say something about this.

The Chancellor of the Exchequer pointed out that the Committee on Guarantees had just returned from Germany[2] and the German Govern-

2 See Nos. 38 and 49.

nent had undertaken to do all that they wished. He felt that what they
needed was to get the co-operation of Germany, and that the use of the iron
hand was of no use.

After some further discussion, the Conference adjourned after agreeing:—

(a) To meet again at 4.0 p.m.[3]
(b) That Sir Basil Blackett should by then furnish an estimate calculated
    on the same lines as M. Poincaré's estimate as to what advances had
    been made to Germany;
(c) That the Chancellor of the Exchequer should be prepared to make
    a reply to what M. Poincaré had said on the subject of British and
    French taxation.

2, *Whitehall Gardens, S.W.1, August 7, 1922.*

[3] See No. 53, below.

No. 53

5. 57] *Minutes of a Meeting held at 10, Downing Street, on Monday, August 7,*
1922 at 4 p.m.
[*C 12076/99/18*]

PRESENT: The Prime Minister (*in the Chair*); The Rt. Hon. A. Chamberlain,
M.P., Lord Privy Seal; The Rt. Hon. Sir Robert Horne, G.B.E., K.C.,
M.P., Chancellor of the Exchequer; The Rt. Hon. Sir Laming Worthington-
Evans, Bt., M.P., Secretary of State for War; Sir John Bradbury, G.C.B.,
Principal British Representative, Reparation Commission; Sir Basil Blackett,
K.C.B., Controller of Finance; F. Leith Ross, Esq., Reparation Commission;
S. D. Waley, Esq., Treasury; P. J. Grigg, Esq., Treasury: SECRETARY, Sir
Maurice Hankey, G.C.B.

SIR ROBERT HORNE handed the Prime Minister a paper, as requested at
the morning meeting,[1] giving figures of British expenditure recoverable from
Germany, drawn up on the same basis as the French figures produced by
M. Poincaré at the meeting the same morning[2] (Appendix).[3]

THE PRIME MINISTER commented that this resulted in a British figure of
50 milliards as compared with the French 80 milliards. He then gave a
resumé of the figures taken from a report by the Bankers' Trust Company
of New York, which he proposed to utilise the same afternoon in reply to
M. Poincaré.

SIR ROBERT HORNE said that, if a comparison was made between the
British War Debt and the French War Debt, it would be found that the difference was greater than what the French claimed to be disbursing on recoverable expenditure.

[1] See No. 52.　　　[2] See No. 51.　　　[3] Not printed.

THE PRIME MINISTER asked how the Bankers' Trust Company came upon their figures.

SIR BASIL BLACKETT said he thought that their representative had worked closely with the representative of the French Treasury. A similar book had been produced by the Bankers' Trust Company in regard to Great Britain.

THE PRIME MINISTER said he had that book with him.

SIR ROBERT HORNE raised the question of whether it would be wise to take unverified figures such as those of the Bankers' Trust Company.

THE PRIME MINISTER said he had tried to find some neutral and unbiassed basis from which to quote his figures. He said he proposed to repeat a figure Sir Robert Horne had mentioned at the morning meeting—that Germany had in one form or another handed over the value of £425,000,000 to the Allies for reparation, cost of armies, etc.

SIR ROBERT HORNE said that, if the cost of billets in occupied territory were included, the figure was nearer £500,000,000. This would include State properties handed over in the ceded territories, ships, coal, and other deliveries in kind.

THE PRIME MINISTER said he also proposed to mention that Germany had had no less than three revolutions, namely, the original revolution which upset the Kaiser,[4] the famous putsch,[5] and the Spartacist revolution.[6]

SIR ROBERT HORNE then quoted the actual figures from a paper by Mr. Leith Ross of the Reparation Commission.

SIR LAMING WORTHINGTON-EVANS then handed the Prime Minister a document containing a number of draft resolutions setting out counter-proposals to M. Poincaré's proposals.

THE PRIME MINISTER said he thought the first thing to be done was to dispose of M. Poincaré's proposals and show them to be impracticable.

MR. CHAMBERLAIN said he had not written anything out nor completed anything so useful as Sir Laming Worthington-Evans's proposals. His impression when he left the morning meeting had been that the intention was that the Prime Minister should knock to pieces M. Poincaré's proposals, which were impracticable. He wondered, however, whether it would not be advisable in the first instance to say that he had discussed the matter with his colleagues and took a grave view of M. Poincaré's proposals, and that before speaking he would like to hear what the other Allies had to say.

THE PRIME MINISTER thought the other Allies would be unwilling to speak until he had spoken. Signor Schanzer, he said, had already asked him to speak first. He agreed that Mr. Chamberlain's proposal was the right policy if we could rely on the other Allies to express their opinions, but he was confident they would not speak freely until he had spoken.

MR. CHAMBERLAIN asked whether the Prime Minister thought it worth while to refer to the Air question. This was one branch of the French expenditure on defence which was also putting us to a great deal of expense.

4 Of November, 1918.
5 The Dr. Wolfgang Kapp putsch of March, 1920 (see Vol. IX, Chap. II).
6 Of January, 1919.

Sir Laming Worthington-Evans thought it would be better not to raise this question as the French feared the revival of Germany in the air more than anything else.

The Prime Minister, after mentioning that he proposed to answer M. Poincaré on the subject of disarmament, remarked that the first thing to be done was to dispose of M. Poincaré's proposals. He thought the best plan would be to submit them to the experts for a report. If the experts reported that they would not produce much money, he did not think M. Poincaré could press them.

Sir John Bradbury remarked that M. Poincaré's proposals had never been put to the Reparation Commission, which was the proper body to deal with them.

2, Whitehall Gardens, S.W.1, August 8, 1922.

No. 54

I.C.P. 251[A].] *British Secretary's Notes of an Allied Conference, held at 10, Downing Street, on Monday, August 7, 1922 at 4.30 p.m.*

Present: *Belgium*: M. Theunis, M. Jaspar, Baron Moncheur; Experts: M. Bemelmans, M. Gutt, M. Furst; Secretary: Vicomte Davignon.

British Empire: The Right Hon. D. Lloyd George, O.M., M.P., Prime Minister (*in the Chair*); The Right Hon. A. Chamberlain, Sir Robert Horne, Sir L. Worthington-Evans; Experts: Sir William Tyrrell, Sir Basil Blackett, Mr. R. G. Vansittart, Sir Edward Grigg, Mr. F. Leith Ross, Mr. S. D. Waley, Mr. P. J. Grigg, Mr. H. Brittain;[1] Secretaries: Sir Maurice Hankey, Mr. R. B. Howorth, Mr. T. St. Quintin Hill.

France: M. Poincaré, M. de Lasteyrie, M. le Comte de Saint-Aulaire; Experts: M. le Comte de Peretti della Rocca, M. Tannery, M. Avenol, M. de Margerie; Secretary: M. Massigli.

Italy: Signor Schanzer, Signor de Martino; Experts: Signor Giannini, Signor d'Amelio, Signor Conti Rossini, Signor Ciarrocca, Signor Mercurio; Secretary: Count Vannutelli Rey.

Japan: Baron Hayashi; Experts: M. T. Sekiba, M. G. Nishigawa, M. S. Arai; Secretary: M. T. Tokugawa.

Interpreter: M. Camerlynck.

1. Mr. Lloyd George said that he and his colleagues had had an opportunity of examining the proposals submitted to the conference by M. Poincaré.[2] Before he came to deal with these proposals he felt that he must make some observations on the statement with which M. Poincaré had led up to his proposals.

[1] An Assistant Principal in H.M. Treasury, and Private Secretary to Sir B. Blackett.
[2] See No. 51.

If Germany had failed in meeting the reparation claims—and he understood that she had not succeeded in doing this at present—the matter was
one in which all were concerned; it was not the concern of one of the Allies
or of two of the Allies, but of all the Allies, and the loss was the loss of all.
If he were to offer any criticism of M. Poincaré's statement, it would be that
he had treated the failure of Germany and the consequent loss as the loss of
France and Belgium alone. This was not the case. All the Allies had suffered in the war, and all very heavily. M. Poincaré had referred to the very
heavy casualties which the French had suffered. He understood that France
in that respect had suffered more grievously than any of the Allies, except,
of course, Russia; but the British Empire had casualties which ran to $3\frac{1}{2}$
millions, and the casualties of Italy were placed at $2\frac{1}{2}$ millions. He had tried
to get an impartial statement, and so he took the figures issued by the Bankers'
Trust of the United States of America. As regards expenditure, the Bankers'
Trust of the United States of America had put the French expenditure in
the war at $37\frac{1}{2}$ milliards of dollars; the Italian expenditure at $14\frac{1}{2}$ milliards,
and the British Empire's expenditure at 49 milliards. These were the facts.
The debt of the British Empire was heavier than of any of the Allies but, in
addition, this country had raised 3,000,000,000l. during the war and after,
by means of extra taxation. The United States of America and ourselves
were the only countries which had raised by taxation large sums during the
war towards the military expenditure. So this country had far and away
the highest expenditure; and if to this were added the cost of reparations and
the equivalent cost to Great Britain, the cost of the war to Great Britain
was heavier than it had been to any of the other belligerents.

M. Poincaré had stated that since the war 80 milliards of francs had been
advanced to Germany in respect of the reparations which could be claimed
under the Treaty of Versailles. If the equivalent due to Great Britain were
taken, this country had advanced—if such a calculation could be referred
to as an 'advance'—a sum of 50 milliards of francs.

> (*Note.*—During the translation of this passage Mr. Lloyd George explained
> that he had given the latest figures for reparations, but that the rate of
> exchange at which they had been converted was 50 fr. to the £. At the
> present rate of exchange the figures would be higher.)

As regards devastation, the trade of the United Kingdom had been completely devastated. The test of devastation was that it should be something
which shattered the machinery of production, and whether this machinery
were factories or were organisation, the population suffered equally. The unemployment in this country had risen to a figure of 2,000,000 persons, and
it now stood at 1,400,000. Great Britain was facing a winter with the prospect
of between 1,400,000 and 1,500,000 unemployed. Just as France had paid
money towards the unhoused population of the devastated areas, this country
had had to support the unemployed and their families. He understood
that the population of the devastated areas was 2,000,000, but the number of
unemployed and their dependants in this country was between 4,000,000

and 5,000,000 persons, and these were maintained exclusively at the public expense. Huge grants had been made from the Exchequer, and, in addition, the localities had been obliged to find equivalent sums. He wished to point out that the question could not be treated as if the failure of Germany were something which concerned France and Belgium alone. He had already ventured to call the attention of the French Government to this fact some time ago.[3] This country had heavier taxes and a heavier debt. It was not a question whether taxes produced more or less than the taxes of Allied countries because this country was richer, but it was a question of scale, and the British scale of taxation was heavier; and the people of this country paid with astonishingly few arrears. He thought that it was necessary to make these facts quite clear before the conference proceeded to examine the next question.

He thought that when M. Poincaré had reviewed the past he had been unnecessarily hard on the Treaty of Versailles. The treaty had been more successful than M. Poincaré was prepared to admit. For instance, there was disarmament, which he would have thought was of fundamental importance to France. In fact, M. Poincaré had treated the question of the security of France as vital to her, and rightly so; he therefore would have thought that, whether disarmament was more important than reparations, or whether reparations were more important than disarmament, disarmament was one of the two things vital to France. He would have thought that disarmament was the more important of the two. M. Poincaré had skimmed lightly over this question by saying that Germany had not disarmed. This was not a complete statement of what had been done, and anyone not possessing a knowledge of the facts, who had heard him, would have received a false impression. The latest figures available (they were only up to July 20—he had not been able to obtain later ones, since this was a bank holiday and it was difficult to obtain this information) showed that of heavy guns and gun barrels Germany had surrendered or destroyed 33,478; that was practically all her equipment of heavy guns. There might be, it was true,[4] a few more hidden away in different parts of Germany; in fact, it was quite possible. M. Poincaré thought that it was so, but it was impossible and inconceivable that Germany should have available any guns to equip a formidable army. She had, in fact, surrendered her artillery equipment. The figures for other weapons and military stores surrendered or destroyed by Germany were as follows:—

Shells	38,000,000
Minenwerfer . . .	11,597
Machine-guns . . .	87,400
Small arms	4,389,000
Small arms ammunition .	459,000,000[4]

When Germany had surrendered all that quantity she had clearly not the equipment available to spring a surprise on Europe again. He had himself

---

[3] See Vol. XIX, No. 62.   [4] Cf. Nos. 242 and 263, below.

been engaged as a Minister[5] in the manufacture of guns and rifles, and he knew how long it took to produce these articles. This country had not been able to supply rifles to its own troops under three years. We had entered the war in 1914, and the first artillery equipment which we had produced had been used two years later, at the battle of the Somme, and this was manufactured only by means of turning every factory in the kingdom into a munition factory. If he had had to do this secretly, keeping the knowledge away from France, Italy and other nations, he could not have done it, not even in thirty years—and in the meantime his attempts would have been discovered. Germany had not the equipment left for a formidable army, and he defied any soldier of any race or nation to say otherwise. She could not equip an army strong enough to stand up to Czechoslovakia, let alone France, and she could not manufacture in two years, even with the knowledge and consent of the Allies, the quantity of munitions equivalent to what she had given up to the Disarmament Commission. Therefore, it was no use creating anxiety and disquietude in the hearts of people, who were naturally anxious because of their memory of the terrible period through which they had passed, by not telling them the fact that Germany as a military Power was broken, prostrate and in the dust; that she could not become so for many years, and without challenging the intervention of more powerful nations in the meantime.

Therefore, it was necessary, when they were talking about the Treaty of Versailles not being carried out—in fact, it was fair to the Allies—this might be a small thing—it was fair to Germany—this might also be a small thing— but it was fair to the whole world that it should be known that the German army of 3,000,000 to 4,000,000 men had become an army of 100,000 men. Supposing there were a few small auxiliary forces scattered up and down Germany, if all these were added together the result would only be a police force barely sufficient for a great Empire, a police force for a great Empire hardly sufficient to repress a rebellion within its own boundaries. He would add that conscription was now at an end. Young men now growing up in Germany received no military training, and every year the reserves of men available for mischief which Germany might be meditating were becoming less powerful. There was also the fact, important for France as well as Great Britain, that the German navy had been destroyed.

As regards cash payments by Germany, it was true that Germany had not paid what we had expected and what we had demanded, but every time the question had been investigated by the commission set up for this purpose— a commission, let it be remembered, in which there was no uninterested Power in the juridical sense, since all Powers represented were directly interested in recovering reparations—this commission representing the Powers definitely interested in recovering reparations had found Germany, for reasons believed to be adequate, unequal to discharging her full obligations on each occasion; but Germany had, in cash and in kind between the cost of the armies of occupation and payments for reparations, parted with the

[5] Mr. Lloyd George had been Minister of Munitions from 1915 to 1916.

equivalent of £500,000,000, or 10 milliards of gold marks. She had lost two or three of her richest provinces and had three revolutions. She had no complete control over her provinces now. One had only got to watch what was happening in Bavaria to realise this. Most of the difficulties of disarmament came from the refusal of Bavaria to carry out the orders of the Allied Powers. These were the difficulties which Germany had got to encounter. The Committee of Guarantees appointed by the Reparation Commission had reported, on the whole, favourably on the efforts of the Germans to collect taxes.[6] The collecting of income tax was proceeding more satisfactorily in Germany than in some Allied countries. M. Poincaré had said that Germany was crying out. No doubt she was, and the Allies were not bound to take statements made by a debtor in order to avoid payment without enquiry into them, but it was not a question of crying out only. The exchange was like a clinical thermometer, which indicated the financial temperature of a country. A man may cry out that he is very sick or in pain, and you might say that he was malingering; but if the thermometer showed that his temperature was 104, then you would believe that there was something in his sickness. It was the same with the mark, the thermometer of which had risen to 3,000–4,000. This showed there was something wrong in Germany. That was a fact which the Allies must take into account. All the Allies were interested in getting as much from Germany for reparations as they could, and it was all a question whether the methods they adopted were likely to bring trouble or cash. It was no use applying sanctions unless they produced money, gold for the French to use in restoring their devastated areas and for us with which to recoup our losses. All sanctions were subject to that test. M. Poincaré suggested that France had once or twice wished to apply sanctions, but the Allies had not agreed. He could only recall one occasion—at Spa—at which time the question of occupying the Ruhr had been discussed.[7] Why had not this been done? Because Marshal Foch said that the Ruhr would require seven divisions, and the Allies concluded that one thing was certain, namely, they would have to pay the cost of these divisions, whilst it was not certain that they would get back this cost. He remembered that the Chief of the Belgian Staff had been very much opposed to the occupation of the Ruhr. He had represented [sic] the expense involved and the fact that the army would get into difficulties with the local workmen, and had shown great opposition to it. The Allies had acted on the figures produced by Marshal Foch and on the advice of the Belgian Chief of Staff. His recollection was that the French delegates did not press for occupation when the figures had been produced. But when M. Briand had pressed for the occupation of Düsseldorf, Duisburg and Ruhrort, and for the erection of customs barriers, the Allies had consented.[8] They had never refused to apply sanctions when they thought that these would prove a means of exacting a fair and just claim from Germany. He wished to add that, at the request of the French Government, the British Government at that time

[6] See No. 51, n. 14.   [7] On July 14, 1920 (see Vol. VIII, No. 71).
[8] See Vol. XV, Nos. 45–7, and Vol. XVI, No. 458.

had stated that they would use the navy if the sanctions then applied did not prove sufficient. As a matter of fact, they had achieved their purpose, which was the acceptance by Germany of a certain programme. M. Poincaré had said that, before a moratorium were granted to Germany, the Allies should get from Germany the acceptance of a number of counter-proposals. He would have thought that under the Treaty of Versailles it was for the Reparation Commission to examine the question whether there was a case for a moratorium. He would have thought that the Reparation Commission had full power to decide this question, and it was certainly a part of their duty to examine it. The Treaty of Versailles was a document which the Allies had signed, and under it they claimed reparations and disarmament. The document was their title to these claims, and, if a slur were to be cast on the title of a body which they had set up, surely the Allies should not act so as to infringe the terms of the document. He would have thought that when sanctions were discussed the first step to be taken would have been to refer to the Reparation Commission the following questions: Was Germany unable to pay reparations? If she was unable to do so, was it for reasons over which she had no control? Was there a case for a moratorium? If as a result of the examination by the Reparation Commission it appeared that there was a case for a moratorium, the Allies could not sell justice by saying that they would do something to Germany if she would do something in return. Under the document Germany had a right to a moratorium or she had not. He thought that the Allies should act as the Reparation Commission decided.

But what were M. Poincaré's counter-proposals? Was there any one of them which would produce as much money as they would cost? He ventured to predict that, if there were a balance at all, in the end there would be an adverse balance, and that would not be a creditable decision for the representatives of five great nations to come to after months of reflection, i.e., to take steps which would produce no cash and cost more, and this by way of getting money for the devastated provinces. He would now take M. Poincaré's proposals in turn.

Firstly, there was the occupation of the Ruhr. This proposal had been examined at Spa, and after examination the French delegation did not press it. He did not say that they withdrew the proposal. Unless Marshal Foch had altered his view of it, it would require seven divisions.

M. POINCARÉ intervened to say that seven divisions would not be required today.

MR. LLOYD GEORGE replied that he did not know why this should be so.

M. POINCARÉ replied that the French were already occupying three of the towns.

MR. LLOYD GEORGE, continuing, said that it would be necessary to persuade the German miners to work. Those best acquainted with the psychology of labour realised that it made all the difference whether labour worked reluctantly or with a goodwill. If German labour was reluctant, the occupation of the Ruhr would not produce sufficient money to pay for its own expenses, and this was so whether it was found necessary to employ five or seven or ten divisions of troops. He (Mr. Lloyd George) was judging the matter from what he was sure would be the case if a mining district in Great Britain were put under foreign administration. Overwhelming force would be necessary, and the more overwhelming the force, the greater its cost.

Next, he would like to consider another of the propositions, which was no new proposal, since it had been mooted by M. Millerand two years ago. This was the suggestion that 60 per cent. of the capital of factories on the left bank of the Rhine should be handed over to the Reparation Commission, so that out of the profits reparations might be paid. The difficulty here was that the profits would be made in paper marks. The receipts and payments of these businesses would be all in paper, and, if they showed any surplus at the end of the year, this would be a paper surplus. It was true that in so far as these factories exported abroad they received for such export payment on a gold basis, but then part of this payment would be taken under M. Poincaré's customs proposals. The Allies could not hope to get the double benefit out of the same transaction. He (Mr. Lloyd George) could understand utilising the customs proposals to the full, but as regards sales in Germany itself, nothing would be forthcoming but paper money. In point of fact, nearly all M. Poincaré's proposals involved paper transactions—the seizure of the forests and mines, the extension of the customs service—all involved management and administration, and if the policy was to use the factories and mines and forests for export purposes, then Germany would be deprived of her raw materials and would most certainly collapse.

Under the 1921 sanctions[9] $1\frac{1}{2}$ milliards of paper marks had been collected by the German customs on Allied reparation account, but the Reparation Commission had decided that it was undesirable to cash these paper marks. This decision was probably a wise one inasmuch as the cashing of marks would have resulted in their further depreciation. M. Poincaré's proposals now involved the collection of customs and taxes and profits of a vast quantity of paper marks which could not possibly be cashed and which would have to be locked up with a view to possible appreciation. It was, however, most improbable that the mark would appreciate if the Allies retained large quantities of paper marks in hand. This fact would in itself hinder appreciation. M. Poincaré's proposals involved much trouble and practically no cash. Their success depended almost entirely on the goodwill of the German workmen, who could easily convert a profitable undertaking into a bankrupt one. The employment of forced labour was, of course, unthinkable. This particular proposal (taking 60 per cent. capital of certain businesses) had always been rejected in the past. Prima facie, the general idea was an attractive one, and it was easy to say 'here are these businesses and forests and mines representing thousands of milliards of gold marks' and to add them up and say they are more than sufficient to pay for reparations, but, as soon as the matter was looked into, one was brought up against the old proposition, namely, how to transmit across the frontier these natural resources, which was the whole

[9] See Vol. XV, No. 46, Appendix, and Nos. 47 and 49.

crux of reparations. He (Mr. Lloyd George) did not wish to reject any proposition without full examination. The view of the British delegates was that these particular proposals would produce no money, but would almost certainly precipitate a catastrophe in Germany. The mere fact that it was proposed to impose on Germany conditions which had never been suggested even in the case of Turkey would cause Germany to go over the precipice, and he assured the conference that there would not be much reparations saved from the fragments. Unless M. Poincaré's plans contained a very promising chance of securing large sums, he (Mr. Lloyd George) thought them too risky for the Allies to adopt. M. Poincaré had suggested that his proposals might form the basis of, and security for, a loan. He (Mr. Lloyd George) would like to consult the bankers on this aspect of the matter, but if, by the use of force, the Allies were to seize German property and take over the administration in the way proposed, he had a shrewd suspicion that no banker would lend even a ten-dollar bill on the German assets in question.

It should not take long for the Belgian, French, Japanese, Italian and British experts to examine whether or not there was any cash in the proposals. The experts might examine the question at once and report tomorrow (Tuesday afternoon), or on Wednesday, whether, in their judgment, there was any prospect of getting any substantial sum out of the proposals of the French delegates. If the reply of the experts was in the affirmative, then the conference would discuss the proposals on their merits. If, however, the reply was in the negative, he (Mr. Lloyd George) was sure that M. Poincaré would agree that it was quite useless to investigate the proposals further. He was sure that M. Poincaré had no desire to take measures which would have no other effect than the destruction of the financial stability of Germany.

Mr. Lloyd George, in conclusion, said that he had suggested that the heads of the other Allied delegations should speak first, but, in accordance with their express wishes, he had followed M. Poincaré. Perhaps Signor Schanzer would now state the views of Italy.

SIGNOR SCHANZER said that he desired to express in a few words the point of view of Italy. He had listened that morning with great attention and sympathy to the remarks of M. Poincaré. In many respects, Italy found herself in a position very similar to that of France. Italy had suffered greatly in consequence of the war; much of her national wealth had been dissipated and she had made no war profits. Italy had a large devastated area and a very heavy bill for pensions and allowances. There was a large deficit on the budget, amounting, directly after the war, to 24 milliards, and even now amounting to 6 milliards. The army had been reduced to a minimum compatible with national safety, and now numbered 175,000 men. The burden of taxation was very high and had risen from 2 milliard lire in 1913–14 to 13 milliards in 1921–22, an increase of 637 per cent. War profits had been confiscated and a very heavy income tax had been imposed. The public debt had increased from 13 milliards pre-war to 113 milliards, an increase of 833 per cent. The cost of the war, 133 milliards, had been met as to 100 milliards by means of loans and as to 33 milliards by taxation.

These sacrifices meant far more for Italy than they would mean for a more prosperous country. Italy was not rich and was destitute of national resources. As regards inter-Allied debts, the point of view of Italy closely coincided with that of France. Italy did not think that these debts should be regarded as ordinary debts, but that they should be treated as part of the general reparation question. Italy had no desire whatever to give Germany any assistance if by so doing any of her Allies were injured; she was firmly of opinion that Germany must pay to the best of her ability. The only question was the best method of extracting payment. M. Poincaré had given figures showing Germany's extravagant expenditure, and Italy considered that Germany should be restricted to absolute necessities. On the other hand, Italy was very dubious about the wisdom of imposing coercive measures which might easily have the effect of making the serious situation in Germany worse. It would be a great mistake to put undue humiliations on the German people, and the political consequences of so doing might be very serious. The question was, therefore, whether the Allies ought to adopt the measures proposed by M. Poincaré notwithstanding that these measures might be very troublesome to administer and might prove very expensive, or whether it would not be better to give Germany relief in some other way so that later on she might be in a better position to pay reparations. The important thing was the re-establishment of German credit.

After these preliminary remarks, he (Signor Schanzer) proposed to examine very briefly the propositions of M. Poincaré that no moratorium should be granted to Germany except on certain conditions. In regard to the question of the control of deliveries in kind, Italy had had precisely the same difficulties which France had experienced. Italy was in favour of the retention of the control of these deliveries, and it was understood that there had been negotiations for administering the control through a mixed commission.

M. POINCARÉ, interrupting, said that the negotiations had been adjourned pending a decision of the conference on the general question.

SIGNOR SCHANZER, continuing, said that M. Poincaré, while disposed in principle to the granting of a moratorium, on the other hand was putting forward proposals for forcing immediate payment of large sums out of Germany. These two policies seemed to him not quite consistent. The proposed re-establishment of the customs barrier probably meant the collection of little cash valuable for reparations. He was dubious about the proposals regarding State forests and mines and the 60 per cent. share of the factories on the left bank of the Rhine. There was already in operation a general fiscal control of the customs, and to substitute actual administrative control would mean very heavy expense and great friction. Mr. Lloyd George had suggested that the question of the moratorium should be remitted for decision to the Reparation Commission. The question of a long moratorium involved very full and careful examination. As regards a brief moratorium, he (Signor Schanzer) was in favour of accepting the report of the Commission of

Guarantees. Italy would be prepared to give a moratorium until the 31st December next in respect of all cash payments, not for payments in kind. He did not give up all hope of an international loan, and later on he thought that the Committee of Bankers should be called together with a view to a reconsideration of the prospects of such a loan. This briefly represented the Italian point of view on the general question. As regards Mr. Lloyd George's immediate proposal, he (Signor Schanzer) saw no objection to the suggested examination of M. Poincaré's proposals by the Allied experts.

BARON HAYASHI said that he agreed with Mr. Lloyd George's proposal.

M. THEUNIS said that this morning he had listened to the eloquent statement of M. Poincaré in which had been described the devastation of France and the absence of reparation. This statement had brought forth a reply from Mr. Lloyd George, and the Foreign Minister of Italy had indicated the Italian point of view. He desired shortly to inform the conference of the position of Belgium, and in this connection he could not do better than refer to the reply given recently in the House of Commons by Mr. Lloyd George when he had indicated that Germany must be made to repair the damage done by her.[10]

Before the war the finances of Belgium had been prosperous and her budget had balanced. Including railway expenditure the debt was 5 milliards of francs, and had now risen to 34 milliards. Notwithstanding the provisions of the Treaty of Versailles, under which Belgium should have obtained repayment from Germany, her finances were far from prosperous. She had had to advance 16 milliards of francs for reparation purposes and had bought 5 milliards of gold marks at par at a cost of 7 milliards of francs. Belgium had suffered from the war as much as, if not more than, other countries. It should be remembered that she had no raw materials except coal of a somewhat poor quality. As had been truly said, the raw material of Belgium was her labour, and, of course, from an industrial point of view, she occupied a favourable geographical position. Belgium, however, had to import 75 per cent. of the wheat consumed in the country, and, in order to exist, her population had to work very hard. Belgium had been four and a half years in German occupation, and, while the actual devastated region was small, yet in a sense it could be said that the whole of Belgium had been ravished inasmuch as the Germans had destroyed or carried away machinery and other needed material. In 1921 there had been 328,000 unemployed, involving a very heavy charge on the Belgian Exchequer. The taxation was five or six times the pre-war taxation, and the Belgian Parliament had just increased by 50 per cent. the taxation on movables and on professional profits. This, then, was briefly the position of Belgium.

As regards the execution of the Treaty of Versailles and the position in regard to reparations, he would not retell the sad story of the experiences of the Allies and the disappointment which they had undergone. This had been done this morning. He would pass to the present situation. There were many

[10] A reference to Mr. Lloyd George's speech in the House of Commons on August 3 (see 157 *H.C. Deb. 5 s*, cols. 1787–95).

different views as to the possibility of payment, but all economists would agree that Germany could pay a great deal of money. This morning there had been a comparison of the Allied debts. It would be interesting to compare Germany's debt in gold with that, for instance, of the United Kingdom and France. Fifteen months ago in London there had been a just and severe indictment of the Reich for extravagant expenditure.[11] Only a few weeks ago something had happened, but he had never received the impression that Germany had decided to act fairly. He said 'only a few weeks ago' because control was now actually functioning. He would be very glad for it to continue.

He proposed not to deal with payments in cash, but to consider the situation in regard to payments in kind. It had been said that there had been enormous payments in kind. With this he disagreed, and in regard to these payments he would state that Germany had shown nothing but ill-will. Her attitude was more than that of inertia. She was indulging in passive resistance. He desired his hearers to remember what had happened at Spa. There was then a great dearth of coal in Italy and France and all over Europe. When Germany was asked if she could supply sufficient coal, she had replied that it was absolutely impossible. The Allies demanded 2,000,000 tons, and put such pressure on Germany that it was forthcoming. The Allies had not noticed that German industries had been hampered as the result of this in any way.

On another point in regard to the Spa Conference, he would like to correct the recollection of Mr. Lloyd George. M. Jaspar and he were both present in different capacities at that conference. The opposition of the Belgian Chief of Staff to the proposal for the occupation of the Ruhr was not so much based on military grounds, but on certain social difficulties which were expected to arise in relation to the population. The Ruhr was a densely-populated area, and the population possessed a special mentality.

Mr. LLOYD GEORGE (intervening during the course of the translation) said that he quite agreed with M. Theunis's statement of what had happened.

Mr. CHAMBERLAIN also remarked that this was what Mr. Lloyd George had really said.

M. THEUNIS said that there had been many complaints to the Reparation Commission about deliveries in kind. For instance, the Germans had delivered railway sleepers in the proportion of only one out of a hundred. This was a ridiculous delivery, and its smallness was obviously due to ill-will on the part of Germany. It was rather disheartening when the Allies were trying to put before Germany reasonable proposals and Germany never approached them in a reasonable spirit. The Allies should therefore make her understand now that she had got to undertake reasonable obligations. She had never been made to understand that so far.

He understood very well in these conditions the reasons of M. Poincaré, who thought that the moratorium should be granted subject to payment by

11 Presumably a reference to the Allied Note of May 5, 1921, which accompanied the Schedule of Payments (see Vol. XV, No. 85, Appendix 2).

Germany on the 15th August, and he desired to impose certain guarantees and obtain certain securities. It was very disheartening that at each concession which had been granted there had been more resistance on the part of Germany. He instanced the Bemelmans–Rathenau agreement for deliveries in kind.[12] The agreement had hardly been made before the bad faith of Germany was evident and she had commenced haggling about the way in which it should be put into force. It was therefore necessary to put moral pressure on Germany to remind her of her obligations. This morning M. Poincaré put forward a series of measures which could be taken against Germany. He had not had time to examine these fully in the interval between the morning meeting and the present meeting, and to see the exact character of the proposals and the practical effect which they would have on the state of Germany. The proposals were of great importance to Belgium, for she was not only interested in the payment of her priority but was closely concerned with all reparation payments. In spite of Belgium's immediate cash interest, in regard to which he could not help feeling, as Finance Minister, the greatest concern, he thought that the subsequent effect of M. Poincaré's proposals should not be lost sight of, and he hoped that when these proposals were submitted for examination to the experts, those gentlemen would bear in mind not only their immediate, but their more distant effects. He hoped that the Allies would have the question examined by technical experts, who would be able to let them know tomorrow or the day after their opinion and would render their advice as to what should be done to deal with the present situation and to cope with the ill-will which Germany was exhibiting.

BARON HAYASHI stated that he had listened with the greatest interest to the proposals made to the conference. He gathered that the principal object of these proposals was to get money within practical limits without creating further trouble, and, with that view, he fully agreed with the suggestion made by the Prime Minister of Great Britain to have the matter examined by experts, subject, of course, to the concurrence of M. Poincaré in this proposal.

M. POINCARÉ said that if it were a question of reserving his approval or giving his agreement to the proposal of Mr. Lloyd George, he would, of course, give his consent, and he would do it in two words. This would avoid a reversion to the discussion of that morning. He desired, however, to enter a general reservation against the figures given by Mr. Lloyd George. He did not agree with the figures quoted on the authority of the Bankers' Trust of New York in regard to the total casualties during the war. The figures which he had quoted that morning had referred only to the losses suffered by France in killed and mutilated. If the wounded were to be included, at least 1,000,000 more would have to be added to these figures.

As regards disarmament, he thought that Mr. Lloyd George was optimistic. He would be very glad if he could be shown to be wrong, but the information which he had received was most serious. General Nollet had told him

[12] A reference to the Bemelmans–Cuntze Agreement of June 2, 1922 (see Carl Bergmann, op. cit., p. 94).

(M. Poincaré) a few days before that Germany had never shown so bad a spirit as at present and that the difficulties were on the increase.

The discussion had so far been of a general character and had no very direct bearing on the question before the conference. He had thought that it was necessary to explain that the situation in which France found herself was one of inexorable necessity. Every representative present had followed his example and had explained the position of his country. This was what he had expected would happen. Each representative had painted his separate picture in equally dark colours. The conclusion was that they were all in a very sad and unfortunate position, and it was more and more important for the Allies to march together in agreement. If he had said that France had set forth certain principles on which he could not compromise, it was not, he could assure those present, without having reflected upon them. He hoped that it would be possible to reach agreement on these principles, and he agreed that the experts should consider the practical application of them. But the question of the practical application of these principles was only one question. If he proposed today certain measures, it was because they were called for by the needs of France. He had said that morning that certain measures should be taken and certain guarantees exacted, and this was necessary in order to keep France in a state of confidence in the French Government. He had referred to a loan, and perhaps he had not made himself clear. His proposal was not that Germany should raise a loan, but that France and the other Allied countries should raise loans on the basis of guarantees furnished by Germany. These guarantees were wanted in order to show France that the Allies were not being duped. He agreed with the statement of M. Theunis in regard to the difficulties of exacting reparations from Germany.

Mr. Lloyd George had referred, not without some irony and humour, to the proposal made by him, and had alleged that this proposal deprived the Reparation Commission of its undoubted right. This statement of Mr. Lloyd George's was all the more to the point since he remembered that he himself had charged Mr. Lloyd George on one occasion with similar behaviour towards the Reparation Commission. But all he was asking was that similar instructions should be given to each of the Allied delegates on the Reparation Commission. That commission would meet under the inspiration of certain political ideas. If the commission met and expressed an opinion in favour of the moratorium, the Allies knew that the moratorium would be granted without guarantees. The present conference was summoned in order to prevent this and to obtain guarantees for a moratorium. With this reservation he accepted the proposal that there should be a meeting of experts to examine the suggestions he had made. He desired, however, to nominate as the French expert the French Minister of Finance, since M. Seydoux, the principal expert of the French Government, had been detained by business in France, and, moreover, the state of his health made it necessary for him to be spared as much as possible.[13]

[13] The text of this sentence has been supplied from Confidential Print.

Signor Schanzer said that he desired to ask one question regarding the mandate of the committee of experts. He was of the opinion that the mandate should be precise. It could not, however, be simply to enquire into the possibility of obtaining money through the measures suggested by M. Poincaré. He had no doubt that the Allies could obtain money—for instance, from German mines and forests—but he thought that the measures suggested by M. Poincaré should be considered from the point of view of their effect on political life in Germany, and their effect on her capacity of making payment in future. He also thought that the possibility of applying them for a short period only should be considered. He would be grateful if the conference would decide that the mandate to the experts should include the above questions. He would also be glad if the Italian Minister of Finance,[14] who was travelling here, and would arrive, he hoped, in two days' time, could be a member of the committee of experts. Would it be possible for each nation to be represented by two experts instead of one only?

Mr. Lloyd George said that he thought there was a great deal to be said in favour of having two experts for each of the nations represented on the committee. He did not know, however, if M. Poincaré agreed to this.

M. Poincaré said that Signor Schanzer had suggested that the terms of reference to the Committee of Experts should be widened. He had heard with the greatest satisfaction the statement by Signor Schanzer that it would undoubtedly be possible to get money from Germany by means of the measures suggested. It was the first time that he had been told that, and it was a very pleasant thing for him to hear. He was quite sure that the Allies could get money in this way. Signor Schanzer, thinking this, had considered it to be superfluous to refer this question to the experts, and had suggested, therefore, that the experts should deal with something else. But the question to be referred to the experts was a difficult one, and the question of the political and economic effects of these measures was one for the representatives of the Allies in this conference. Signor Schanzer, in a previous statement, had suggested that there was a contradiction between granting a moratorium and taking possession of German resources. He did not see this. There would be one if the Allies had granted a moratorium with a view to pleasing Germany, but they were only proposing to do it because of the difficulty Germany had in paying them. The question of the social and political effect of the measures proposed by him in Germany was not one for the experts, but was one which should be reserved for discussion at the present conference.

Signor Schanzer said that all he wished to establish was the necessity of studying not only the monetary point of view, but the political, economic and social consequences of the measures proposed by M. Poincaré. If it was proposed to discuss these questions at the conference there was no necessity to remit them to the experts.

Mr. Lloyd George said that the first question for the experts should be: What money will be produced by the proposals of M. Poincaré? Of course,

[14] Signor Bertone.

142

this enquiry would involve an enquiry into the expense of these proposals, since only the balance would be available for reparations. He also thought that the experts should be invited to consider the question whether these proposals were preferable to those which had already been adopted, i.e., those relating to customs, etc. He agreed that the political and moral effect of the proposals was one for consideration by the conference. Signor Schanzer had, however, been quite right in saying that the Allies must take these into consideration. The question the conference proposed for the experts was a specific one, namely, to see what cash would be obtained by M. Poincaré's proposals if they were adopted. With regard to the numbers of the Experts' Committee, he suggested that each Power should nominate two representatives.

M. Poincaré remarked that he agreed to two experts being nominated by each Power. He suggested that they should have assistance.

Mr. Lloyd George replied that he had assumed that. The meeting would take place tomorrow in the board room at the Treasury.

The Constitution of and terms of reference to the Committee are as follows:—

> Belgium: M. Bemelmans and M. Gutt.[15]
> France: M. de Lasteyrie and M. Tannery.
> Italy: Signor d'Amelio and Signor Conti Rossini.
> Japan: M. Sekiba and M. Arai.
> United Kingdom: The Right Hon. Sir Robert Horne, G.B.E., K.C.,
> M.P., and Sir Basil Blackett, K.C.B.

to study and report on—

(a) The sums which would be made available for reparations if the measures proposed by M. Poincaré were adopted by the Allied Governments.

(b) The question whether the measures proposed by M. Poincaré were preferable to those which had already been adopted in order to obtain reparations from Germany.

2. Press Communiqué

Mr. Lloyd George said that there was a good deal to be said for a literal statement of what had happened at the conference being communicated to the press. Each country would in this statement give an explanation of its financial position, and that would be interesting at least to the inhabitants of the country concerned.

Signor Schanzer said that it would be necessary to have an understanding as to what should be communicated to the press in view of the undertaking given by M. Poincaré this morning. It would be difficult to keep things quiet. Public opinion was nervous, especially in more distant countries, which desired to know what was going on at the conference. It would be difficult to avoid leakages. He asked, therefore, that the members of the

[15] See No. 7, n. 6.

conference should be released from the pledge which they had given at the meeting in the morning and should be free to state what had taken place at the conference that day.

Mr. LLOYD GEORGE agreed, and said that there was nothing to keep secret. Would, however, M. Poincaré prefer that it should simply be stated that he had made certain proposals, which were to be examined by a committee?

M. POINCARÉ replied that, if the conference agreed, he saw no objection to every member of it stating what his proposals were and that a committee had been appointed to examine the practicability and productivity of the proposals made by himself.

M. JASPAR said that it would be very regrettable if each member of the conference was free to inform the press what had been said. All those present had attended meetings of the Allies which had achieved practical results. Those results would, in the present meeting, be obtained sooner and better if the discussions did not appear in the press. If it was agreed that each member could communicate his proposals bit by bit to the press, it was important that the proposals should be published in the light of the remarks made at the conference. This was a very daring suggestion and he begged the conference to reflect before adopting it.

M. POINCARÉ asked whether M. Jaspar would agree to a joint communiqué?

M. JASPAR assented. This had always been the practice of Allied conferences.

Mr. LLOYD GEORGE remarked that to publish all the proceedings of the conference would be to put the French delegates in a difficult position. The proposals would have been published, and if the committee had got to report whether the proposals were practicable, it would put the French delegates in a difficult position and might necessitate their going back on what they had said.

M. POINCARÉ said that personally he had no objection to divulging his proposals, but what M. Jaspar had suggested would be more in conformity with regular procedure, and he was ready to keep the secret if everyone else did the same.

Mr. LLOYD GEORGE said that there was no harm in an exposition of the general financial position of each country. It would interest the public and would satisfy them. He suggested that the general statements made by all the heads of the delegations should be published.

M. JASPAR agreed.

M. POINCARÉ said he had not come to England to make statements of the financial situation of France. If a statement were made, and it did not include definite proposals by him, everyone in France would be disappointed and would wonder what he had come here for. He would prefer that nothing should be said at all than that the secret should be partially divulged.

SIGNOR SCHANZER said that each proposal before the conference had inconveniences, but he thought that public opinion could not be left ignorant of what was being done at the conference. He did not think that the public would be satisfied merely with a statement of the financial position of each country. He thought that the conference should agree that a measure of caution should be exercised in what was said to the press, and that the members of the conference should avoid making things public which would create difficulties later on.

MR. LLOYD GEORGE stated that it should be left to the discretion of each delegate to decide what he should communicate to the press.[16]

2, Whitehall Gardens, Whitehall, August 7, 1922.

[16] An account of this meeting appeared in *The Times*, August 8, 1922, pp. 6 and 12.

No. 55

Foreign Office Memorandum on the relation of the proposed French 'Guarantees' to the French policy in the Rhineland

[*C 11669/99/18*]

FOREIGN OFFICE, *August 8, 1922*

[1] It will be noted that of the six 'guarantees' proposed by Monsieur Poincaré on August 7, 1922[1] four relate to the Rhineland.[1] These four are:—

(a) The continuance of allied control of the German import and export licensing system in the occupied territories.

(b) The re-establishment under allied control of the customs barrier on the eastern frontier of the occupied territories.

(c) The surrender to the Reparation Commission of a certain proportion —say 60%—of the share capital of certain of the factories and works in the occupied territories.

(d) The collection by the allied governments of the taxes in the occupied territories.

2. It will be well in the first place to consider the details of these four proposals.

(a) *The continuance of allied control of the German import and export licensing system in the occupied territories.* This control dates from the establishment of the so-called customs sanction in March 1921.[2] When this sanction was imposed the Rhineland Commission, acting on its own responsibility, assumed control of the German import and export licensing system with the object of preventing the German authorities from rendering impossible the collection of customs duties by refusing licences for the occupied territory. When, in September 1921, the customs sanction was abolished in accordance with the decision of the Supreme Council of August 13th 1921,[3] this control was continued 'as a transitional measure for the purpose of avoiding any disturbance of the economic life of the occupied territories' pending the establishment of the allied committee which was to supervise the administration of the German import and export licensing system in so far as the occupied territories were concerned. The German government had accepted

[1] See No. 51.
[2] See Vol. XV, No. 46, Appendix.
[3] See ibid., No. 104, Appendix 8.

the continuance of this control upon the clear understanding that it was intended only for 'the liquidation of matters negotiated when the sanctions were in force, i.e. the disposal of the funds collected at that time', and there is no doubt that the continuance of the control, which was inconsistent with the removal of the customs sanction, would never have been accepted by the British government, if they had ever supposed the control would continue for nearly a year after the abolition of the sanction. It is clear further from information received from the British representative in the Rhineland[4] that the control has in fact been used largely for the advancement of allied and particularly French trade in the Rhineland, a purpose bearing no resemblance whatever to that which the Supreme Council had in view, and which was to prevent only discrimination against allied trade in the Rhineland. It is thus important to note that it is not, as Monsieur Poincaré's speech implies, merely a question of the continuance of an existing legal organisation but of the legalization of an existing illegal organisation which ought, unless sanctions are to be applied under paragraph 18 of Annex 2 to part 8 of the treaty or as an act of force majeure, or unless 'guarantees' are to be taken with the consent of the German government, to be removed. (N.B. In any case it is for consideration whether the opportunity provided by M. Poincaré's speech ought not to be taken to clear up the whole question of the substitution for the allied control of the German import and export licensing system in the Rhineland of the allied supervisory body foreshadowed in the Supreme Council's decision of August 13, 1921.)

(b) *The re-establishment under allied control of the customs barrier on the eastern frontier of the occupied territories.* This barrier was originally set up by the allied governments on March 8, 1921 as part of the sanctions which were imposed at that time. It remained in force until September 29 [30][5] 1921, when it was withdrawn upon the acceptance by the German government of an allied committee to supervise the administration of the German import and export licensing system in the occupied territory, and because it was considered that the German government had at that date made adequate progress with their reparation and disarmament obligations.[6] The amount of money collected on the eastern customs barrier during a period of six months amounted in all to 187,170,655 paper marks, or, at the average rate of exchange current at the time, to some £693,000 or some 15 millions of gold marks, (i.e. less than one-third of each monthly cash payment due under the existing moratorium). It cannot therefore be said to have been a very lucrative measure from the financial point of view. It will however be remembered that its specific object at the time of its imposition was to hit the Germans and compel them to make adequate reparation proposals. It was never supposed that its effects would be anything but prejudicial to trade, and its financial effects were never considered to be anything but secondary. Its establishment as a 'guarantee' therefore appears to be a somewhat surprising proposal.

(c) *The surrender to the Reparation Commission of a proportion of the share capital of certain factories and works in the occupied territory.* It will be remembered

---

[4] Lord Kilmarnock.   [5] See Vol. XVI, No. 708.   [6] Ibid., Nos. 696–709.

hat somewhat similar proposals have been made at various dates by various German theorists but it has never before been suggested that these proposals should be applied to the Rhineland only. Why should not the proposals be extended to the whole of Germany?

(d) *The collection by the allied governments of the taxes in the occupied territories.* The occupied territories, with the exception of the small area comprised within the Düsseldorf bridgehead and occupied as a sanction in March 1921,[7] are administered under the Rhineland agreement.[8] This agreement lays down that 'the civilian administration of the province, government departments, urban circles, rural districts and communes shall remain in the hands of the German authorities and the civilian administration of these areas shall continue under German law and under the authority of the central German government except in so far as it may be necessary for the high commission by ordinance and for the purpose of securing the maintenance, safety and requirements of the armies of occupation to adapt that administration to the needs and circumstances of the occupation'. The allied governments could not assume the right of taxation under the Rhineland agreement, the exercise of which right would necessitate the establishment of an entirely different régime, such, for instance, as that which would normally be set up in a conquered country, or which, in fact, was set up in Upper Silesia.[9]

3. The *general effect* of the French proposed 'guarantees' as regards the occupied territories may now be considered. These territories comprise an area of some 12,000 square miles supporting a population of some 7,000,000. They are very rich in agricultural and industrial resources, and contain at least four towns with populations of over 100,000 and at least seven towns with populations of 50,000 to 100,000. Of the whole area comprised within their limits the British occupy some 660 square miles with 7,500 men; the Americans occupy the town of Coblenz with one battalion; the Belgians occupy some 1,520 square miles with 12,000 men; and the French some 9,670 square miles with 104,000 men. There are in addition in the Rhineland serving under the High Commission some 146 British officials, some 60 American officials, some 153 Belgian officials, and some 888 French officials. There can be little doubt that French influence in the Rhineland has been increased by this predominant share which the French exercise in the administration of the occupation.

4. As will be apparent from the accompanying note by the Historical Adviser to the Foreign Office (Annex I),[10] the French government during the Peace Conference, aimed not merely at securing the right to exercise this predominant influence, but at securing rather the formal separation from Germany of the greater part of the area now comprised within the occupied territories. Since the Treaty of Versailles closed for the moment the path to the realisation of this aim, there is little doubt that the French Government have endeavoured, through their agents, to reach the same goal through the agency of political propaganda. This endeavour has however so far been

[7] Ibid., No. 458.   [8] Of June 28, 1919 (see *B.F.S.P.*, vol. 112, pp. 219–24).
[9] See Art. 88, Annex, of the Treaty of Peace.   [10] Not printed.

attended with little success, and in May 1922 the British representative in the Rhineland stated that the one chance of securing serious support for the Separatist movement in the Rhineland seemed to be by the use of the bait of economic advantage.[11]

5. There is reason to believe that it is this bait which the French government is now in fact endeavouring to use, and there is little doubt that the acceptance by the allied governments of the above-mentioned four of M. Poincaré's proposed 'guarantees' might be used to make this bait considerably more attractive. Continuance of allied control of the German import and export licensing system in the Rhineland would give the French government an admirable opportunity of watching the activities and markets of Rhineland firms and of securing 'pickings' in the Rhineland for French interests. The re-establishment of the eastern customs barrier on what might be expected to be something approaching a permanent basis would do much to increase in the Rhineland the sense of economic separation from Germany. Viewed from this standpoint, the financial proceeds of the barrier would not be a matter of paramount importance. The surrender to the Reparation Commission of part of the share capital of Rhineland factories and works would obviously be of far greater importance to France, with her closer economic ties with the Rhineland, than to the other allied governments concerned. The collection of the Rhineland taxes by allied officials would necessarily imply the virtual disappearance of the Rhineland agreement and would provide an admirable hunting-ground for French separatist intrigue. It would probably not in practise be found that the Rhenish population groaned beneath the yoke of the foreign taxpayer or that the proceeds of these taxes were quick to fill the coffers of the reparation commission.

6. In estimating the political results of M. Poincaré's proposed 'guarantees', the above considerations will no doubt be borne in mind and the possible reaction of French economic domination of the Rhineland on British interests in the widest sense of the term will no doubt be considered.

[11] Cf. No. 219, Enclosure, below.

No. 56

I.C.P. 251B.] *Record of Conversation[1] between the Prime Minister and M. Jaspar at 10, Downing St[reet], August 8, 1922, 6.30 p.m.*

German Reparation:

After his conversation with M. Schanzer on August 8th, 1922,[2] the Prime Minister had a conversation alone with M. Jaspar, lasting from 6.30 p.m. until after 7.30 p.m.

[1] This record was made by Sir Maurice Hankey.
[2] No record of this conversation has been found in the Foreign Office archives.

M. Jaspar had, earlier in the afternoon, seen M. Poincaré, and the object of the conversation was to compare notes on the latest developments of the Reparations situation.

Immediately after his conversation with M. Jaspar the Prime Minister was joined by Sir Robert Horne, and the two went to 11 Downing St[reet] to discuss matters privately with Mr. Chamberlain.

On the conclusion of this conversation the Prime Minister was joined by Lord Rothermere,[3] with whom he dined.

There was no opportunity either for Sir Edward Grigg or myself to ascertain what had transpired.

[3] Newspaper proprietor: formerly Air Minister (1917–18).

No. 57

I.C.P. 251C.] *Notes*[1] *taken during a conversation at the French Embassy at London on August 9, 1922 at 9.30 a.m. between M. Poincaré, Mr. Lloyd George and M. Theunis*

[*C 12104/99/18*]

Interpreter: M. Camerlynck

Confidential

M. Theunis, the Prime Minister of Belgium, having brought with him one copy of a draft report of the financial experts,[2] which had just been given to him, and the other Ministers not having copies with them, this report was read in English.

With regard to the first question, *the control of granting of import and export licences* for goods destined for or originating in the occupied part of the Rhineland, it was decided that it was not necessary to consider it.

2. *The collection of 25 per cent of the value of German exports*

M. THEUNIS, at the request of his colleagues, gave certain explanations. He agreed with Mr. Lloyd George in recognising that the collection of 25 per cent upon exports being made in gold is a source of real revenue for the Allied Governments. The German buyer pays for that which he has to buy in paper marks, but the seller sells in gold.

3. *Collection of Customs receipts*

An exchange of explanations also taking place with regard to this matter, it was recognised that it is no real source of revenue.

MR. LLOYD GEORGE asked that the experts should come to a conclusion upon this point. They had left to the Prime Ministers the task of finding out what use should be made in the present circumstances of the paper

[1] According to a note made by Sir M. Hankey, these notes were supplied to Mr. Lloyd George by M. Camerlynck. For Mr. Lloyd George's account of the conversation, see No. 59, below.

[2] See No. 58, below.

marks thus obtained. Mr. Lloyd George remarked that it was for the experts to make suggestions on this point. This remark applied equally to the former question.

It was understood that the experts had been asked to add to their report certain explanations with regard to this point.

4. *The exploitation and possible alienation of State Mines and Forests*

(a) *State Mines*

MR. LLOYD GEORGE asked how it was proposed to organise the exploitation of State mines and what form the 'control' should take.

M. THEUNIS replied that the term 'control' might give rise to misunderstandings, and that it was probably that which had prevented the French and British experts from agreeing, because they were probably not thinking of the same thing.

M. POINCARÉ remarked that this was not the first time in the history of the Treaty of Versailles and subsequent negotiations that the term 'control' had given rise to misunderstandings.

M. THEUNIS pointed out that the possession of a majority of the shares in a mining business did not imply any particular consequence so far as the exploitation and even the management were concerned. He instanced mines which from the financial point of view, belonged to a great majority of shareholders, French, Germans, or Belgians, a fact which did not prevent the administrative and working staff, and even the management from being purely German (see with regard to this point the explanations and examples given by the experts, and particularly, by M. Bemelmans, at the meetings held at the Treasury the day before).[3]

MR. LLOYD GEORGE declared that he always felt anxious about the financial product of an operation of this kind. He was afraid that the substitution of one majority of shareholders for another, or the arrival of new proprietors, would influence the work of the labourers, the output of the mines, and consequently the advantages gained by the Allies, assuming that they should exploit the mines.

He also pointed out that the coal would always be sold in [*sic*] paper marks, anyhow in the interior of Germany, and it was not paper marks that the Allies needed; they had already amassed a sufficient quantity.

No decision was come to on this point, and the second paragraph of this part of the report, was then examined, that is to say:

(b) *State Forests*

The Prime Ministers took note of the unanimous conclusion of the experts upon this point, when they considered that the Reich could easily carry out the deliveries of wood with a minimum charge to its budget, since the majority of its forests are the property of the German States and the Reich could apply to them.

[3] No record of these meetings has been found in the Foreign Office archives.

They also noted that the experts proposed to draw the attention of the Reparation Commission to the possible exploitation, or even alienation of the State forests, so as to assure the deliveries in kind, according to the quantities drawn up by the Reparation Commission itself.

Mr. Lloyd George here expressed doubts with regard to the product of an operation of this kind. He found this new method of procedure much inferior to the already existing mechanism which permitted the seizure of 26 per cent of the foreign exchanges received for export.

M. THEUNIS explained that when sugar or manufactured products were exported, it was certain that 26 per cent could be levied on it when it left the country; but the question here was one of exploiting forests which would have been handed over to them and that was a means for the Allies to procure directly foreign exchanges in excess of a levy of 26 per cent.

M. POINCARÉ: 'It is in fact in order to have a particular guarantee that we do not include the production of a sale of wood in the levy of 26 per cent. If we are led to make concessions in placing at the disposition of Germany, for her own needs, the whole or part of the product of this 26 per cent, we are attempting, on the other hand, to extract a revenue from the State forests, firstly by obtaining requisitionings of wood and then by exporting foreign exchanges.'

MR. LLOYD GEORGE asked for information concerning the manner in which it was proposed to exploit these forests. Were the Allies to undertake to cut down and sell the wood? Whatever they did they would be forced to have recourse to German labour. That would amount to seizing the goods of foreigners and forcing the workmen to work for foreigners. They might obtain results, if the labour were given with good will, otherwise the work would be of bad quality and the output would be mediocre. It would also be necessary to find buyers; it would be necessary to buy and sell and it would be infinitely preferable to work with people or with States who collaborated with good will. Otherwise exploitation would be bad and costly. For instance, the woodman would cut down one tree for every three that they ought to. They would have to be paid all the same, and where would the profit come in? It would completely disappear. After the labour had been paid, it would be found that money had been lost, while if 26 per cent were merely taken off this article, like all other articles, when it left Germany, reliable resources in gold would be gained, without speaking of the deliveries in kind, which would certainly be obtained. He was for solutions which attained the substance, for realities and not for chimeras. What was needed was cash.

M. POINCARÉ: 'Of course; what we want to obtain is, as you say, cash, that is to say, the substance. But if in order to obtain money we await the good will of the Germans, or their collaboration in the exploitation of enterprises, they will do nothing, just as they have done nothing up to now. It would be an illusion to expect voluntary execution on their part. If the Germans know that we have in our hands the means of exploiting, for instance, their forests, we shall arrive very quickly at an arrangement. Otherwise we shall be completely disarmed. In Mr. Lloyd George's reasoning I always find the same misunderstanding and psychological failure to appreciate German mentality. Mr. Lloyd George believes that in order to obtain results it is enough to appeal to the good will of the Germans; but they will only consent to work for us if they know that we possess the means of acting for ourselves.'

Mr. Lloyd George: 'I do not think that I am mistaken about the psychology of the Germans. You certainly have to make them clearly understand *that they must* pay, *that they must* work, but within the limits of their capacity. If you go beyond that, it will be no use saying to these people "you must"; it is useless to tell anyone to bear a burden, even if you threaten him with a whip, if he is not capable of doing so; consequently, it is necessary to discuss their capacity and to take account of it.

'On the other hand, how shall we be able to force the Germans to exploit their forests properly, simply b[y] telling them that we have the means to do it ourselves? You do not intend to send ten thousand woodmen, either from France or from Belgium, any more than we shall send them from England. As I have told you, in the end you will always be obliged to have recourse to German labour and to pay it. And who will pay? The workmen will not work until you have come to an arrangement with Germany; instead of direct and private exploitation, I should rather understand that you wish to exercise measures of coercion. If they do not carry out properly their obligations for providing wood, we might well threaten them with general measures. That is what we did last year. One can imagine measures of blockade, or the occupation of certain towns, which France has already carried out. But as for applying direct measures of coercion by the exploitation of forests already fixed upon, I do not believe in it, and once more, it will only bring you in paper; we have already on our hands four and a half milliards of paper marks, and as for getting more of them, it really would not be worth the trouble.

'I do not therefore think that I am mistaken about German mentality; and if we can agree about what she can do, I shall then be ready to assist M. Poincaré in taking all general measures of coercion which may appear suitable.'

M. Theunis: 'I have frequently had occasion to observe that the differences of opinion, especially the theoretical ones, which separated the Allies, disappeared quite quickly if the questions were thoroughly examined; and if we should apply this method here, if each should indicate how he views the measures proposed and their practical application, we should certainly arrive more quickly at an arrangement. Thus it is quite certain that M. Poincaré's idea is not to send into Germany French woodmen, or even overseers, that he takes into account that it would certainly be necessary to utilise German labour, the German staff which probably is conversant with the conditions of exploitation. All that he demands is doubtless the possibility of giving orders to the leaders and seeing that these orders are executed. Whether the system envisaged by Mr. Lloyd George or by M. Poincaré is accepted, it clearly will always be necessary to utilise the services of the people on the spot. But we could limit ourselves to directing them from very high up by means of a controller and inspectors, very few in numbers, who would give a general order, saying: "we need such and such a quantity of wood by such or such a date". It would be for the German technical experts to choose the trees to be felled, and to order and supervise the execution. Thus from whatever point of view one started, one would arrive at the same result.'

M. POINCARÉ: 'I must observe that so far as the left bank of the Rhine is concerned, which possesses considerable forests, we can dispose of efficacious methods of action, and that the exploitation of forests could easily be carried out under the supervision of the allied military authorities.'

M. THEUNIS. 'Pursuing my idea, I must point out that the experts to whom we have entrusted the task of preparing the report upon these questions, however qualified they may be, from the financial and economic point of view, are not, nevertheless, experts in matters appertaining to coal and forests. If we should ever call in specialists, they would very soon agree, for after all, there are not two ways of exploiting mines or forests. A forester knows very well what it would be necessary to do in order to obtain the amounts required by the devastated regions, or the quantities of sleepers demanded by such and such a country.'

M. POINCARÉ: 'The Reparation Commission has thoroughly studied this question, and the Belgian Institut Solvay has brought out a very complete report upon the value of the State forests in Germany, the methods of exploitation before the war, and those which could be applied now.'

M. THEUNIS: 'The same thing happens in the case of deliveries of coal. When discussions take place at Paris, it seems extremely difficult to arrive at conclusions; when the debate is removed to the Central Bureau at Essen, and conversations take place between the German Coal Syndicate and the French representatives of the devastated coalfields, as well as Belgian merchants, these gentlemen very soon come to an agreement on practical grounds.'

MR. LLOYD GEORGE: 'I still do not understand how you will succeed in procuring resources by these means. After all, the value of the paper mark is the value that it may have on the Belgian, French or British market. Let us assume that your share is one milliard of paper marks. How are you going to make that cross the frontier? You will find no one to buy them, while once again a tax upon exports brings you in gold; if it is wood for building that comes out of Germany, it is gold; if it is coal that comes out, it is again gold. But any operation which could result in the production of enormous quantities of paper marks would put us in a ridiculous situation, because we should not be able to get rid of them. We should be laughed at.'

M. POINCARÉ: 'It is true that today the paper mark is not worth much, but we must consider this question in connection with the totality of the measures to be taken for relieving the financial situation in Germany. We must resolve to take measures to restore to the paper mark part of its value. We French and our Belgian friends, we think that the first thing to do would be to organise the control of the Reichsbank and of the fiduciary issue, in order to arrive at some stabilisation of the mark.

'When a customs line was established, it obviously brought us in paper marks, but in a very appreciable quantity. You cannot say that that was nothing, especially when at that time the mark still had an average value of about six to eight centimes. Thus if the mark were more or less stable, we should still be able to convert it into gold marks. It is evident that whatever we may do, no useful result will be obtained if we have not begun by establishing supervision over the Reichsbank, and fixing the limits of the fiduciary issue. That will not be done in a week, but at the end of several months. We shall be able to obtain results if we begin at the same time by controlling the Reichsbank and taking guarantees which will quickly become productive.'

MR. LLOYD GEORGE: 'The trouble will always come at the moment when you realise your marks. If you throw them upon the market, the rate of exchange will inevitably fall. All the control which you may be able to exercise upon the Reichsbank will not stop that. It would be the same thing if, for example, we were obliged to sell large quantities of sterling abroad; their value would immediately sink.'

M. THEUNIS: 'When in the past we succeeded in getting a milliard and a half of paper marks, we never thought we should have to realise them. The mentality of the members of the Reparation Commission was scarcely different from that which we have today. The rate of 6·7 centimes, which we would like to see the mark recover, appeared at that time so disastrous that no one was ready to assume the responsibility of conversion. But I return to the more important point which has just been raised by M. Poincaré. I am of his opinion, and I do not see any solution of the problems which are now confronting us, until the question of the value of the mark has been settled. I have just read a document, the existence of which was previously unknown to me. It is a letter dated the 14th of June last, and addressed by the Reparation Commission to the German Government.[4] I believe that it is almost entirely in the hand of Sir John Bradbury. It deals with the measures considered indispensable in order to establish the autonomy of the Reichsbank. Unfortunately, the suggestions of this letter were never acted upon. But it is certain that until the finances of Germany have been put in order, and until her money has been stabilised, all the measures which may be taken will only augment the economic disorder and, in any case, will not have improved the possibilities of payment. We must always return to this question of the mark; it is the very heart of the matter.

'We have not even been able to obtain from Germany the deliveries in kind by applying the agreements of Rathenau or Gillet.[5] The Reparations Commission should really adopt a severer attitude in order to oblige Germany to carry out the deliveries in kind. If they are not carried out with the system which has been decided upon, the situation is desperate, and we really have grounds for being annoyed.'

[4] See Reparation Commission III, op. cit., pp. 142–4.
[5] A reference to the Wiesbaden agreement of October 6, 1921 (see No. 1, n. 4), and the Gillet–Ruppel agreements of March 15 and June 6–9, 1922 (see Reparation Commission II: *Agreements Concerning Deliveries in Kind* (H.M.S.O., 1922), pp. 32–5).

The Prime Ministers then discussed the working of the levy of 26 per cent on exports and the amount which this levy had brought to England (about 5 milliards of gold marks). Having arrived at this point in the conversation M. POINCARÉ stated that he thought it would be useful to summarise the experts' answer and to draw upon it the inevitable conclusions.

M. Poincaré summarised the answer as follows:

1. The experts were unanimously of the opinion that they should ask the Reparation Commission to accept the 26 per cent recommended by the proceeding [sic] decisions, leaving it to the Reparation Commission to decide what part of this 26 per cent could be utilised at once for the payment of allied credits or returned to Germany for her own needs, which would amount to the application of the moratorium determined upon. He noticed that there was nothing new in that and that they would be simply faced by the putting into practice of theories already enunciated.

2. The experts had been unanimous in their opinion that it would be advisable to take over the product of German customs, he imagined under the same conditions as the levy of 26 per cent. That would not constitute a positive guarantee since while taking this product they would expose themselves to having to return the whole or part of it. How then could this control be carried out? They would allow him therefore to say that up to this point he could not consider that these proposals satisfied the demand which he had formulated.

3. By a majority, contrary to the opinion expressed by the British experts (the question was therefore not entirely finished with) the experts appeared to accept the placing of the state mines in the hands of the Reparation Commission, who would of course represent the Allies and act as a delegation appointed by them. But would the Commission be the owner and would it have the right to dispose of these mines?

4. As far as the woods were concerned the experts had only arrived at a solution which he found a little vague and which did not satisfy him completely.

5. No reply had been made about the gathering of taxes in the occupied countries.

6. With regard to the point to which he attached the greatest importance, that was to say the re-establishment of the customs line such as has already existed and the creation of a certain number of customs posts along the boundary of the Ruhr in order to control coal and metal products, the experts were of the opinion that they should not absolutely reject but that they should adjourn these methods as not being useful and as possibly being harmful at the present moment.

'I think that that is all. Well, I should say to my great regret that this reply is not such as to give satisfaction to France. This very morning I have received a telegram from the President of the Republic telling me that any concession on the essential points of our demands would be, in his opinion, as in mine, quite inacceptable. And if I cannot obtain satisfaction regarding the customs line I should be obliged to ask for time to consider the matter and to refer it to my colleagues of the Cabinet and to the President of the Republic. But now I must say that I do not think that the French Government could be contented with the very modest concessions obtained in the first part of the report of the experts.'

MR. LLOYD GEORGE: 'Without entering into the discussion of the body of the question I ask M. Poincaré whether he means that he would return to France to consult his colleagues.' M. POINCARÉ replie[d] that that was not what he meant and that he could await their reply in London.

M. THEUNIS: 'Will you allow me to say with reference to that that for two years I have attended a good number of Inter-Allied meetings. I am in a position to say that for a long time I have been an advocate of the Entente and a convinced advocate of the necessity of reparations. We have already had some differences as difficult as this one. I understand M. Poincaré perfectly when he says that the accumulation of the delays caused by Germany in the reparation question and the successive deceptions which have been inflicted on France have rendered the opinion of the country and of the Parliament more unfavourable to any arrangement which would not at last bring substantial results. The difficulties which we have already encountered in 1921 have perhaps become still more serious this year because time has not improved the situation; but I have nevertheless the impression that we were further from one another in 1921 than we are now in reality. I have already told you my experience; it is that every time a question of principle is raised between French and British experts if the general political point of view which one adopts is in appearance totally different, nevertheless when one commences to discuss the application of the British or French principles strangely enough an understanding takes place; as soon as one goes into details the points of view cease to be so far apart as they appeared at first. It must also be remembered that the experts although some of them may be good linguists speak two different languages and furthermore that their thoughts do not take the same form. The example has already been given of the word "control" in French and in English. It is possible that regarding the State mines this word may have been the cause of a complete misunderstanding. A control could be exercised perfectly well without giving rise to the legal objections suggested by this word in English. It is the same thing with the forest question. I understand very well that the French Minister of Finance wishes to be able both from the moral point of view and from the financial point of view to show that he has some real guarantees in hand, particularly as in the opinion of the public they would be new resources. On the other hand I recognise that the collection of the 26% provided for in 1921 and the yield of the customs could give sufficient resources. But that has remained more a theoretical than a practical question. We have loyally endeavoured, following certain statements made to Germany at the time of the signature of the Peace Treaty, to avoid all interference in her internal affairs. We had at that time illusions as to the good will, the power or the authority of the Central Government. We thought that the Wirth Government would be better than that of Simons. But little by little we have seen our illusions disappear and our experts, the members of the Reparation Commission and the Allied Ministers yield to the evidence. We should consider the absolute control of the customs and imports and exports. The unfortunate thing is that this is all very well in theory but that in practice these measures amount to what has been called the "turkification" of the country. When all the revenue of a country must pass through the hands of foreign controllers, when it must hand over 26% in gold on its exports, that is really the strongest control which can be exercised over the general economy of a country. In actual practice this system would amount to something so strong that the Allies would become to some extent the tutors of Germany, who alone could receive the revenues of their pupil and give him what is necessary to carry on his economic life. The only point of view in regard to which differences remain (and it does not appear that in regard to this point the French experts have given practical examples) is the question of the customs posts to be set up around the Ruhr basin. The best reason which has been given for it is that it would be a means of direct action on the large industrials who are responsible for the present situation. This would therefore be rather a measure of coercion than a real guarantee for obtaining cash, that is to say a means of pressure of a political nature which could be considered as a second line of attack, a further turn of the screw which would allow us to see whether we could not bring Germany to a state of good will or at least of resignation. But for the moment we could leave this point in the background as it divides us and consider it only as a further step which would not be taken at first. This would be something like the system followed by the French Government quite recently in regard to the clearing-houses. We would agree on a list of sanctions on an ascending scale to be applied gradually and, step by step, up to complete satisfaction. This would be the best method to adopt because really I no longer have much doubt about the ill will of Germany or the inertia of its Government through fear of the People's Party. The German Government will not, or cannot, give the least satisfaction in a question so simple as that at present under consideration.

'At the point where we are now,' continued M. Theunis, 'permit me to say that after having successfully overcome so many difficulties between us, it would be really unfortunate at the end of three years to arrive at a rupture which (both Mr. Lloyd George and M. Poincaré have said it) would mean in practice not only an avowal of a total difference of opinion on the Reparation Question but the end of the Entente. I know perfectly well how grave and formidable the question must appear to the two Prime Ministers to whom I am now speaking, and I know also what that would mean for Belgium. When I think of all that we have seen and suffered in the past eight years, of all the sacrifices which we have made together, of all the moral suffering undergone, of all our dead, I have really the feeling that a breach between us would be a frightful catastrophe for humanity.'

After having paused for some moments, M. Theunis added:—

'Mr. Lloyd George has given in the course of the last few months so many proofs of patience, of wisdom, and of diplomacy as to solve a problem so thorny as the Irish problem[6] that I do not think that facing a man like M. Poincaré, filled with an ardent desire to save the world from Prussian domination, one could not finally find a common ground for conciliation and understanding.'

M. POINCARÉ: 'Permit me to add a few words to what M. Theunis has just said. For my part, I desire very heartily that we may succeed in finding a common ground for agreement. I fully share the emotion and the anxiety felt by our colleague and friend M. Theunis, but I must state that it does not appear to me possible to consider as he has suggested the division of the measures taken into two successive lines. I do not think that they could be compared with the measures recently taken by France in regard to the clearing-houses. The latter are fixed for certain dates chosen in advance with a view to their being applied gradually. Germany is warned that these are not hypothetical and vague measures like those which have so often been announced (and never applied) in London,[7] Paris[8] and Spa,[9] which were sanctions which looked well in a programme but have never been realised in practice. Germany knows what is meant by further measures. She would not believe in them. If one wished to relegate to the background certain measures regarding Customs asked for by us [sic].'

M. THEUNIS: 'These measures have already been applied and Germany would therefore not believe them impossible.'

M. POINCARÉ: 'The argument could be used the other way; Germany could consider it as an enormous concession that we hesitated to apply measures which have already been tested and have given satisfactory results. Germany would not understand why they are not re-established, since nothing would be easier.

'Moreover, I am not free. I have to bear in mind the decisions of the Council of Ministers and the opinion of the President of the Republic himself. I have just received a telegram in reply to one which I sent him. He tells me that resistance was expected, but that, whatever may be the attitude of our Allies, he is still fully in agreement with me in maintaining our decisions and that any other attitude would be disastrous. When I refer to the President of the Republic it is not with the object of introducing his personality into the debate and attributing to him a responsibility which must be mine, but in order to show you that this is not the decision of one particular government nor the opinion of one day, this is not a personal policy which is expressed before you, but a profound and permanent belief of my country. I have the conviction that no other government in France could adopt any other attitude. I have the ardent desire to maintain in fact the intimate relations which we have always had with Belgium and England and it would really break my heart to leave friendly and Allied countries on the question of reparations. I do not wish to be compelled to act in isolation, at the very moment when we entertained the most friendly relations on which is founded

6 See Cmd. 1502 of 1921. 7 See Vol. XV, Chaps. II and IV.
8 Ibid., Chaps. I and VI. 9 See Vol. VIII, Chap. VIII.

the solidity of the Entente. I beg you to believe that, if France insists on her demands being satisfied, it is because it is not possible for her to do otherwise from the financial point of view, not to speak of the political point of view. It would be impossible for her to escape from her present extremely serious situation if we gave French public opinion the impression that in view of the difficult financial situation of Germany and the pressure recently brought to bear upon us by Great Britain and the United States for the payment of Inter-Allied debts,[10] we did not immediately take all the guarantees that we could get.'

Mr. LLOYD GEORGE: 'I have been deeply touched by the powerful appeal addressed to me by M. Theunis and I should respond to it with joy but, to speak friendly [? frankly], there is nothing in M. Poincaré's reply which encourages me to do it, and it is with deep regret that I am compelled to say so. I have always done my best to understand the demands of France and to accept them in spite of that it is continually said that France allows herself to be dragged in the train of England. Now, precisely the contrary has been said in the House of Commons, where I have been attacked, where I have been accused of allowing England to be dragged in the train of France. The demands to which I have several times given my consent have not yielded the results which were expected. It is really time that we considered proposals representing realities. My deep conviction is that the present French proposals are unreal. They would produce tons of paper marks, nothing else, and [if] that is what M. Poincaré balances against the Entente and nothing else, it is for him to decide. As for me I should have rated the Entente with Belgium, Italy and Great Britain higher than a mountain of paper-marks. I understand that M. Poincaré and the President of the Republic are of a different opinion. They are the best judges.

'I cannot, however, allow to pass without remark a statement just made by M. Poincaré; he said that the London, Paris and Spa agreements did not produce anything. That is really leaving the facts out of account. Owing to the Spa agreement millions of tons of coal have been delivered; thousands of guns, millions of rifles have been surrendered and destroyed, and the German army has been reduced to some hundreds of thousands of men. The London agreement has produced millions and, please understand, millions of gold marks, not to speak of deliveries in kind. I venture to say that what has been received thanks to the Spa and Paris agreements will in the end be found to be much greater than the yield of all these new proposals which the experts have just rejected. Perhaps France is of a different opinion. M. Poincaré evidently knows her and I cannot venture to speak in her name; but what I can say is that France will think differently before long and that she will regret having broken a friendship for which we have sacrificed 900,000 human beings and 10 milliards of pounds. I can quite understand that nothing that I can say will change the decision of M. Poincaré and M. Millerand; all that I venture to attempt is to make it quite clear that our proposals would produce substantial sums for reparations. I have not the

10 See No. 28, n. 6, and No. 45.

least doubt that in the long run France will realise that our proposals were wise and that they did not deserve to bring about a quarrel, because one can never say what the end may be, a misunderstanding may grow, a disagreement may extend, once it has commenced. M. Poincaré speaks of a breach as though it were a breach between individuals, but it is a question of two great nations, each of which will then have to follow its own path. If that should occur, I should be happy in any case to be able to say to myself that the responsibility did not rest on me.'

M. Poincaré: 'My conscience is quite clear that the responsibility for the disagreement would not be on our side. It is not we who spoke of the breach, it was the English who first pronounced the word. Even in the presence of M. Theunis it has been said that our demands would bring about a breach but this statement does not come from us. That is for the first point.

'As to the second, I have just understood Mr. Lloyd George to say that his proposals would yield more than ours. But I should like to ask him: "Where are the British proposals"? What I do know is that Great Britain has accepted some of my proposals but that she has not made any for her part. That is even the reason why I am here.

'I do not wish to go back to the question of responsibilities and I do not wish to say anything which could embitter the discussion. Let us confine ourselves therefore to discussing the experts' report: I have explained as well as I could the nature and extent of the French proposals and I have spoken in all that in the name of France; if one misrepresented her opinions, I would undertake to explain and that not only for France, but for the whole world; France would not have any responsibility for what might occur if her demands were rejected.'

M. Theunis: 'Do you not think that before taking decisions we should await the final report of the experts; they are meeting at this moment and it might be advisable to ask them to examine more thoroughly the question of the Reichsbank and the fiduciary circulation. There is also a question which has not been discussed, that of the taxes which could be collected in the Rhenish territories. We should obtain their opinion about this. There is also the first question which we have to discuss, that is an opinion of the experts on the method of utilising the paper marks representing the customs-receipts.'

Mr. Lloyd George [asked][11] what would [be] the effect produced if one endeavoured to place these paper marks on the market.

M. Poincaré: 'I am compelled to reserve the question of the internal customs line which in our opinion is the most important of all. This is only, I would repeat, a question of taking again a measure provided for by the Treaty. To give it up would be equivalent to the abandoning of one of its clauses.'

M. Theunis: 'I suppose that M. Poincaré has in mind the customs line along the Rhine; he is not referring to the question of the customs line which as a matter of economic strategy, if I may so express it, would control the

[11] This word has been substituted for 'Adding'.

production of the Ruhr. Are these two questions connected together in the opinion of M. Poincaré or should we discuss them separately?'

M. POINCARÉ: 'The two questions are not necessarily connected. The line which you have called economic strategy would obviously be preferable; but one could argue that this question is not absolutely connected with the other.'

M. THEUNIS: 'I see clearly the advantages which this latter arrangement would have in your opinion. The idea of exercising in this way a salutary pressure on the lords of the Ruhr who are responsible for all the evil is moreover not new. But frankly, I have the very definite feeling that, if we talk of measures to be taken regarding the Ruhr basin, we shall cause, in at least a portion of public opinion in the country of our English friends, a fear that purely economic measures taken at certain stations or at the junction of the waterways might finally bring about a military occupation of the Ruhr. It is useless to recall the discussions which have taken place in regard to this. But it is undeniable that the very name of the Ruhr could at the present moment give rise to certain ideas which it would be better to avoid by giving up this project. Moreover, we cannot say of this measure that it was provided for by the Treaty. It would be an entirely new sanction and it would perhaps be better to leave the Ruhr out of it.'

MR. LLOYD GEORGE: 'It remains to establish a distinction between simple measures of coercion and reasonable measures intended to produce money. All these measures which you propose may be useful as means of pressure, but you would do better to give up at once the idea that they would bring you anything; the experts tell you so, Belgium is of this opinion, France will see it soon, perhaps [not] immediately, but, in a few months, French opinion will see that its satisfaction in seeing its proposals triumph will vanish completely after they have entered into effect. It was always in this spirit that we made proposals and that we were, for example, in favour of a high export tax, which would yield gold. We remain in favour of all measures which would force Germany to deliver raw material for reparations. We are ready to confirm this engagement, even in writing, if desired. But we cannot associate ourselves with a project which, once more, looks very well on paper, but which would not give us anything but paper and once more paper.'

M. POINCARÉ: 'It will not be only paper if we commence by re-establishing the German monetary system and the control of the Reichsbank. If this control is not established today, it never will be, and, if one establishes it, the moment will come sooner than one thinks when the paper can be converted into gold. If we do not get it tomorrow we shall obtain it soon.'

MR. LLOYD GEORGE: 'Nothing prevents you from doing it, if you think you can get it. Before concluding, I should also like to suggest that we ask the experts to explain to us what has prevented France and also Belgium and Italy from obtaining substantial receipts, as we have done, from the collection of 26% on German exports. France could have obtained in this way 270,000,000 francs per annum. Why has she not obtained them? It is really of no use to make fresh proposals, when with the old ones you could succeed in getting payment in gold.'

Conclusions:

It is decided that the following points will be sent to the experts for more thorough examination:

(1) Question of the utilisation of the paper marks obtained by means of the various collections of customs duties.

(2) Control of the Reichsbank and the fiduciary issue.

(3) Collection of taxes in Rhineland.

(4) Explain how it is that the system of collections of 26% has not functioned for countries other than Great Britain.

In the interval, M. Poincaré will consult his colleagues in Paris and Mr. Lloyd George will summon the members of his Cabinet. The conversation will be resumed at the point where it was left today.

The conversation was concluded at 11.45 a.m.

No. 58

A.J. 362.] *Report of the Committee of Experts appointed in accordance with the Decision taken by the Allied Prime Ministers on August 7, 1922*[1]

TREASURY, *August 9, 1922*

The committee was constituted as follows:—

British delegation: The Right Hon. Sir Robert Horne, G.B.E., K.C., M.P. (*Chairman*); Sir Basil Blackett.
French delegation: M. de Lasteyrie, Ministre des Finances; M. J. Tannery.
Italian delegation: Signor d'Amelio, Signor Conti Rossini.
Japanese delegation: M. Sekiba, M. Arai.
Belgian delegation: M. Bemelmans, M. Furst.

The task entrusted to the Committee of Experts was to examine the measures of 'productive guarantees' proposed by M. Poincaré, the Prime Minister of France, at the meeting of the 7th August,[2] and to study their financial bearing and the amount which they would yield, in comparison with other resources.

I.—*Control by an Inter-Allied Commission of the Grant of Import and Export Licences for Goods entering or going from the Occupied Rhineland Territories*

This measure was not intended to produce any cash, and accordingly calls for no observations from the Committee of Experts.

II.—*Exploitation and possible Transfer of State Mines and State Forests*

(a) *State Mines*—The mines in question are the mines in the Ruhr belonging to the Prussian State. The output of these mines is about 9,000,000 tons a year.

It was admitted that the exploitation of these mines by the Allies would not result in any increase in the output of coal in Germany, and that consequently

---

[1] See No. 54.   [2] See No. 51.

it would not increase Germany's capacity to pay, but the Italian and Belgian delegates were of opinion that the French proposal might constitute a means of ensuring a more reliable execution of the coal deliveries prescribed by the Reparation Commission, since the mines, which would be worked under the control of the Allies, produce about 50 per cent. of the quantity of the coal deliverable under the decisions of the Reparation Commission.

On the question as to whether it would be practicable for the Allies to take control of these State mines, the French and Belgian delegates thought that it would be practicable to carry out such operations without undue cost. On the other hand, the Italian delegate was of the view that the Allies should not take control of the State mines, but that the Reparation Commission should set up, on the basis of article 248 of the Treaty of Versailles, some other system whereby a sufficient guarantee might be obtained for the deliveries of the coal which the Germans were under obligation to send to the Allies. The Japanese delegate was of the opinion that the matter required further investigation, and that it should be referred to the Reparation Commission to decide whether the operation of the States mines by the Allies was practicable. The British delegate was of the opinion that the operation of the Ruhr State mines by the Allies was entirely impracticable; that it would be more difficult to induce the German miners to work the mines successfully under the management of the Allies than under their own system, and that such an attempt on the part of the Allies would inevitably end in reducing production.

If the alienation of the State mines should be contemplated, that is to say, the transfer of the property in them to the Reparation Commission, the capital value might be of the order of magnitude of 400,000,000 gold marks, but it is impossible to say what sum would actually be realisable. The British experts were of opinion, that any such sale would be very difficult to effect, that it would necessarily bring in only paper marks, and that it could not be regarded as a financial guarantee of any importance. The French delegate again observed that the proposal would fulfil the object which the French Government have in view, i.e., it would constitute an asset which would be at the disposal of the Allies in case of default by Germany in the fulfilment of her obligations.

(b) *State Forests*—Although the British representatives considered that timber deliveries from Germany could never be regarded as being in principle economically sound, the Committee of Experts unanimously agreed that the delivery of timber on reparation account was a delivery which the German Government could carry out with comparative ease and with the minimum burden on the German budget, in view of the fact that a large proportion of the German forests are the property of the German States. Although the question of timber deliveries was not directly submitted to the committee, the committee was unanimous in proposing to call the attention of the Reparation Commission to the question.

The French delegation considered it necessary to take efficacious measures to place at the disposal of the Reparation Commission the State Forests, both to ensure the full delivery to the Allied countries of the timber for which they have asked, and which the Reparation Commission has considered that Germany can deliver, and in addition to constitute a guarantee.

The other delegations considered that the difficulties of realising the State mines applied with even greater force to the forests, and they were therefore of opinion that these forests could be regarded rather as a guarantee for the timber deliveries than a financial guarantee, the capital value of which could be realised.

III.—*Factories on the Left Bank of the Rhine*

It was stated that before the war the capital invested in these factories amounted to a total of 1 milliard gold marks. If 60 per cent. of this capital accordingly was expropriated for the benefit of the Allies the value of the shares obtained would nominally be 600,000,000 gold marks.

The British, Italian, Japanese and Belgian delegates were of opinion that as the German Government would have to indemnify the holders of these securities which would involve an expenditure of 70 milliards paper marks at the present rate of exchange, this would have the effect of weakening the financial position of the German Government, and still further depreciating the mark, and that accordingly this suggestion was, in present circumstances, impracticable.

The French delegation indicated that if it obtained sufficient guarantees by the application of other measures proposed by M. Poincaré it would be able to fall in with the views of the majority on this question.

IV.—*Collection of Customs on the Western Frontier of Germany (Left Bank of the Rhine), Establishment of a Customs Barrier on the Rhine, and of Export Taxes in the Ruhr District*

(a) *Collection of Customs on the Western Frontier of Germany*—The total of the paper marks obtained during the six months during which this measure was in force in 1921 was 1,177,000,000 paper marks, which, at the average rate of exchange of the year, would be equal to about 58,000,000 gold marks, while the cost of the Allied control was only 29,000,000 paper marks.

It is worthy of note, however, that during the last month, in which the system was in force, i.e., September 1921, the receipts amounted to 16,000,000 gold marks.

The experts, with the exception of the French representative[s], recognised that the control of the collection of these customs formed part of the question of the control of the collection of the customs of Germany as a whole, provided for in the Schedule of Payments, and that it was not necessary to deal with the collection of these particular customs separately. The question of the collection of customs duties is dealt with below.

The French representative[s] observed, on the contrary, that the control by the Allies of the Rhine customs enabled the Allies to obtain an important asset, and they considered that it is impossible to disassociate the control of the customs on the western frontier of Germany from the question of the proposed customs line on the Rhine.

(b) *Customs Frontier to be Established on the Rhine*—The French experts remarked that during the last three months, during which a special customs system was established for the left bank of the Rhine (i.e., July, August and September 1921), 20 per cent. of the customs receipts came from the customs houses established along the Rhine, being an amount of 145,000,000 paper marks, which are still in the hands of the Reparation Commission.

The British, Italian, Japanese and Belgian experts were of the opinion that the institution of a customs frontier in the interior of Germany would be liable to result in serious embarrassment of Germany's economic life, and that it was rather a measure of compulsion, having consequently only a provisional character and being such as would not easily form a security for an important financial operation.

(c) *Installation of a Customs Ring round the Basin of the Ruhr*—The French experts stated that the establishment of customs posts at the points of exit from the Ruhr had especially as its object the collection of taxes on the exportation of goods from the Ruhr Basin (principally coal, metallurgical products, &c.). They stated that the value of the metallurgical products from the Ruhr Basin amounted to about 578 milliards of paper marks, so that the collection of an export tax of only about 5 per cent. on these products could realise a quantity of paper marks corresponding to several hundred million gold marks.

The British, Italian, Japanese and Belgian experts were of opinion that the application of this measure of guarantee could not be contemplated as a step actually to be taken in view of the present situation in regard to the payments demanded from Germany and having regard to the fact that the establishment of a special customs line around the Ruhr Basin would seriously embarrass Germany's economic life, and consequently decrease her capacity to pay reparation.

The French delegate, on the contrary, was of the opinion that, in view of the influence which such a measure might exercise on the large industrials of the Ruhr Basin, who possess an enormous influence over the German Government, the actual organisation of this form of guarantee would make it obtain an important security which would be susceptible of further development and which might have a favourable influence over the disposition of Germany in regard to the Treaty of Peace.

V.—*Export Levy and Collection of Customs*

It was pointed out that the Committee of Guarantees appointed by the Reparation Commission under the Schedule of Payments of May 1921[3] had already the right to take certain guarantees.

In the first place, it had the right to require payment to it of the produce of all customs and export duties collected not only in the Rhineland, but at all the frontiers of Germany. This payment had actually been effected by the German Government from October 1921 to January 1922, and had only been suspended owing to the grant of the moratorium at Cannes.[4] The yield

---

[3] See No. 5, n. 2.   [4] See Vol. XIX, No. 25, Appendix II.

from this source amounted to about 1,700,000,000 paper marks per month, which was equivalent to nearly 300,000,000 gold marks per annum. The Committee of Guarantees still controlled the collection of these revenues, and could, if necessary, exercise its right to payment without any friction or difficulties.

In the second place, the Committee of Guarantees had a right to a levy of 25 per cent. on the value of all German exports, to be paid in gold or foreign currencies. In pursuance of this provision, German exporters were required to hand over to the Reichsbank (against payment in paper marks) a proportion of their foreign bills. This had yielded in recent months over 100,000,000 gold marks, and the German Government had agreed that these bills should be held for the account of the Committee of Guarantees up to the amount due for payment to the Reparation Commission each month, the balance being released for the current needs of the German Government.

It was pointed out that the arrangement leaves the Reparation Commission to decide whether these bills can be applied in existing circumstances to reparations or not, but these two resources give a total of about 1,500,000,000 gold marks per annum, paid for the most part in foreign currencies, which more than covers the total obligations at present prescribed for the current year.

In conclusion, the committee unanimously agreed that the receipts already under control of the Committee of Guarantees, viz., the customs revenues and the export levy would constitute excellent resources for the Allied Governments if their proceeds were paid to accounts in the name of the Committee of Guarantees.

The French delegation observed that the application of the two measures referred to above had been requested by M. Poincaré and offered assured advantages. It consider[ed], however, that these measures could not be considered as sufficient. The proposals of M. Poincaré must not be considered from the point of view only of their present financial yield, but from the point of view also of the guarantees they provide[d] in the event of ill-will on the part of Germany. In this connection, the French delegation pointed out that these proposals, as compared with those contemplated above, offered the decided advantages—

(a) that they create during the continuance of a moratorium a means of securing payment which would be available in case of need, and would produce the best results if Germany failed to execute the reforms required of her;

(b) that they place in the hands of the Allies German assets which could immediately be made to produce revenue and could ultimately be realised.

The British, Italian, Japanese and Belgian delegates, on the contrary, took the view that the alternative guarantees proposed by M. Poincaré were superfluous in so far as they were intended as security for the cash payments now required, and that the disadvantages they involved more than outweighed the value of the proceeds which might be obtained from them. These proceeds would be paper mark proceeds, the realisation of which would present difficulties, whereas the export bills represent sums in foreign currencies.

No. 59

S. 58.] *Conclusions of a conference of Ministers, held at 10, Downing Street, S.W. 1, on Wednesday, August 9, 1922, at 12.30 p.m.*

[C 12077/99/18]

PRESENT: The Right Hon. D. Lloyd George, O.M., M.P., Prime Minister; The Right Hon. A. Chamberlain, M.P., Lord Privy Seal; The Right Hon. Sir Robert Horne, G.B.E., K.C., M.P., Chancellor of the Exchequer; The Right Hon. Sir L. Worthington-Evans, Bart., G.B.E., M.P., Secretary of State for War; Sir Maurice Hankey, G.C.B., (Secretary, Cabinet); Sir Edward Grigg, K.C.V.O., C.M.G.

German reparations

THE CHANCELLOR OF THE EXCHEQUER said that the proceedings of the Committee of Allied Experts, over which he had been presiding,[1] had become somewhat confused. At the request of the French the Report had been drafted by the Belgian Delegation, and he did not feel that it was a very satisfactory document.

THE PRIME MINISTER said that M. Poincaré had expressed a good deal of dissatisfaction with the Report.[2] He had taken the various recommendations and had condemned all of them in turn. The first two he said were merely a repetition of what was already being done, the next pair of recommendations was vague, and so forth. The Prime Minister then gave an account of a three-hours' conversation he had had with M. Poincaré and M. Theunis that morning.[2] It was, of course, impossible for him to recount all that had happened in such a long conversation. He had therefore asked that M. Camerlynck, the Interpreter, might send a full note of the conversation. M. Poincaré had rather demurred at first, but had eventually consented. In the course of the conversation M. Theunis had made what was in the nature of an emotional appeal to M. Poincaré, at the end of which he had almost broken down. He had referred to what an indescribable catastrophe to humanity it would be if the Entente broke down after the immense sacrifices of the War. M. Poincaré had not responded to this appeal in the very least. He said that all this had been tried at Spa and at London, and so forth,[3] and nothing had ever come out of it all. The Prime Minister himself had challenged M. Poincaré on this point, and had reminded him that the Spa Conference had resulted in millions of tons of coal being handed over by the Germans, as well as other deliveries in kind. The London Conference, he had pointed out, had resulted not merely in deliveries in kind but in actual

[1] See No. 58.   [2] See No. 57.   [3] See No. 57, nn. 7, 8, and 9.

gold. He had pointed out it was useless to make statements of that kind. M. Poincaré had spoken of a rupture. He himself had replied that M. Poincaré seemed to talk quite calmly of a rupture and he could not understand how he could do so after the sacrifice of millions of lives in the War. He had further pointed out that the rupture was to take place merely for a few million German paper marks. The Allies were in agreement on everything which would produce actual cash. He had thought that M. Poincaré was just a little staggered at this. Mr. Lloyd George himself had then said that he did not pretend to know the state of public opinion in France, which might be behind M. Poincaré at the moment. Six months hence, however, when it was discovered that the only result was paper marks, French public opinion would see things differently. In the end M. Poincaré had said that he must consult his colleagues. Mr. Lloyd George had asked him if this meant going back to Paris, and he had replied that it did not; he could consult them from London. He himself had said that he would have to consult on the matter with his colleagues, and he thought it would be necessary to summon the Cabinet.

THE LORD PRIVY SEAL suggested that a Cabinet Meeting should be summoned by telegram.

THE PRIME MINISTER, continuing, said that M. Theunis had been quite first-rate at the conversation that morning. He had shown that all M. Poincaré's proposals, if not adopted now, could be held in reserve as, so to speak, a second line of attack. If the Germans did not respond to what was done now, M. Poincaré's measures could be adopted as means of coercion: for example, the control of the customs, the exploitation of the forests, and so forth. Mr. Lloyd George had then pointed out that the London proposals,[4] such as the 26 per cent. on customs and the Reparations Recovery Act,[5] had produced actual gold. M. Poincaré had been rather surprised at this. Mr. Lloyd George had then pointed out that the Reparations Recovery Act was producing 100,000,000 gold marks a year, and he had asked why France and Belgium were getting nothing. He had suggested that before measures were adopted to produce more paper marks, the existing plan should be put into operation. M. Poincaré had then suggested that the British were privileged. He himself had replied that this was not the case, that the decision was available for all the Allies, only France and Belgium had not put it in operation. M. Poincaré then suggested that the Germans played fair for the British but would not do so for the other Allies. Eventually M. Poincaré had agreed to refer the question to the Experts, viz., as to why the Reparations Recovery Act had produced 100,000,000 gold marks for Great Britain, which was equivalent to nearly 250,000,000 francs. After the meeting he had driven away with M. Theunis, and they had discussed the desirability of putting the British and Belgian proposals in writing, together with what these proposals would produce.

[4] See Vol. XV, No. 83, Appendix 2, and Vol. XVI, No. 556.

[5] German Reparation (Recovery) Act, 1921, 11 Geo. 5, Ch. 5 (see Vol. XVI, Nos. 459, 469 and 471, and No. 495, n. 3).

The Chancellor of the Exchequer pointed out that the system in operation produced £70,000,000 a year, but that the Germans now said that if continued it would mean a financial collapse, and had asked for a moratorium.[6] M. Poincaré's attitude was that he would agree to a moratorium but only on conditions which would bleed Germany in another way. This appeared very illogical.

The Prime Minister thought that, subject to the moratorium, a memorandum should be put forward showing how much our proposals would produce. This would make it harder for M. Poincaré to effect a rupture, particularly as he himself had told M. Poincaré that six months hence the French proposals, if adopted, would produce nothing but paper.

(At this point there was some discussion on the value of paper marks if converted into foreign currency immediately they were received. During this discussion Sir L. Worthington-Evans entered.)

The Prime Minister suggested that it would be useful to prepare a memorandum setting forth the British proposals in regard to reparations.

The Lord Privy Seal stated the British position as follows:— The sum which Germany could pay for foreign reparations was the difference between German exports and German imports, reduced to the lowest possible minimum. That could be presented in the form of a percentage on German exports. What that percentage should be was a matter for Experts to decide.

The Prime Minister said that M. Poincaré was willing to accept 26 per cent.

Sir L. Worthington-Evans said that 26 per cent. was more than the difference to which Mr. Chamberlain had referred. He quite agreed with Mr. Chamberlain's statement of the British case.

The Chancellor of the Exchequer said that £500,000,000 of exports before the War had enabled Germany to invest about £50,000,000 a year. He had investigated the matter recently, and previous estimates on the subject were incorrect.

The Lord Privy Seal, continuing, said that this could be stated as a percentage on exports, and it should be somebody's business to find out what this percentage should be. It appeared to him that, under the Treaty, the Reparation Commission was the proper body to fix the percentage. If that percentage could be obtained, and if his premise was correct that that was all that could be obtained, it would be the best method available. Was there in fact a better plan than that adopted in the London Agreement,[7] whereby the trader paid over his percentage to the Reichsbank in foreign currency or its equivalent, and the Reichsbank handed the proceeds over to the Committee of Guarantees? Was there any plan so simple or so easy to put in operation?

The Chancellor of the Exchequer said that this system had been adopted, though its full operation had been checked as the result of the Cannes meeting.[8]

[6] Cf. No. 26, n. 4, and Nos. 36 and 38. [7] See Vol. XV, No. 83, Appendix 2.
[8] See Vol. XIX, Chap. I.

THE LORD PRIVY SEAL said that if M. Poincaré accepted the premise he did not see how he could avoid the conclusion.

THE PRIME MINISTER said that M. Poincaré was not in the mood to accept anything. He thought the first point was to decide whether to summon the Cabinet. He was particularly anxious that Lord Curzon should be present, if possible, and he instructed Sir Maurice Hankey to send a communication to Lord Curzon saying that, if his health permitted, he attached importance to his being present, since vital questions of foreign policy were raised. He also thought it important that Mr. Churchill, who, he understood, was in France, should be present.

SIR MAURICE HANKEY pointed out that this involved telegrams *en clair*.

THE LORD PRIVY SEAL thought there was no objection to sending the proposed telegram *en clair* to Lord Curzon under present conditions.

THE PRIME MINISTER said the next point was that he would like the Chancellor of the Exchequer to ask Sir Basil Blackett to produce a memorandum showing the British plan.

(At this point there was some discussion on Allied Debts and the amounts that would be remitted under the Balfour Note.)

THE LORD PRIVY SEAL suggested that if the Prime Minister asked M. Theunis to write a paper he should suggest that he should begin by pointing out that all were agreed that Germany must pay what she could, though they were not agreed on the question of when and how the payment should be made, and before there was any question of a rupture they ought to consider seriously whether any of the new methods proposed would produce more than existing methods.

THE PRIME MINISTER said he would speak to M. Theunis about this at lunch. He thought that if agreement could be reached as to the proposals, the best plan would be to treat them as instructions to be given by each Government to its representative on the Reparation Commission. The alternative plan, which would probably be the quicker one, would be to send for Dr. Wirth and communicate the proposals to him, but he felt sure M. Poincaré would never agree to this. If, however, the proposals were made to the German Government by the Reparation Commission and discussed by them with the representatives of the German Government, the Reparation Commission could report that some of the proposals would not work, and a fresh conference could be held.

THE CHANCELLOR OF THE EXCHEQUER pointed out that the Committee of Guarantees had done this some time ago. Though their Report had not been received, he had received a communication regarding their conclusions.[10]

THE PRIME MINISTER said he would like to have a copy.

THE CHANCELLOR OF THE EXCHEQUER said he would ask Mr. Leith Ross to write down what the conclusions were.

---

[9] Secretary of State for the Colonies.   [10] See No. 49.

The Conference agreed—

(a) That the Cabinet should be summoned for 3 p.m. on the afternoon of Thursday, August 10, 1922, and that Lord Curzon should be asked to make a point of attending if his health permitted.
(b) That the Chancellor of the Exchequer should instruct Sir Basil Blackett to prepare a Memorandum setting forth the British proposals and their financial effect.
(c) That the Chancellor of the Exchequer should send the Prime Minister a summary of the conclusions of the Committee of Guarantees.

2, Whitehall Gardens, S.W.1, August 9, 1922.

No. 60

Memorandum[1] on certain Political Aspects of the 'Guarantees' proposed by the French Government

[*C 11430/99/18*]*

Confidential   FOREIGN OFFICE, *August 10, 1922*

1. The 'pledges' or 'guarantees,' of which, in addition to the imposition of a stricter inter-Allied financial control, M. Poincaré, at the Allied

[1] In a minute of August 10, Mr. Lampson explained: 'The Experts' Report [No. 58] upon the French proposals [No. 51] only reached us after 11 p.m. last night. Consequently it has only been possible to put together the annexed memorandum very hastily if it was to be available before the Cabinet Meeting fixed for 3 p.m. today [see No. 59].

'In putting together these notes we have had the advantage of the local knowledge and experience of Mr. Troughton [Economic Adviser to the Rhineland High Commission] who, at our request, was sent over by Lord Kilmarnock in case expert advice should be required in Rhineland matters by the Conference. The attached memorandum has been prepared in collaboration with Mr. Troughton who is available to give fully detailed opinion upon each or any point if required.

'There can, I imagine, be no doubt at all that behind these ostensible "financial" measures there are deeper schemes on the part of the French. If there were any doubt, the history of the events leading up to the existing arrangements for the occupation of the Rhineland would suffice to dispel them. We are fortunate in having M[r.] Headlam-Morley to tell the story and this he has done in a memorandum [not printed] of the actual facts at the Peace Conference which I am having printed and which will be submitted as soon as possible.

'France wanted the Rhine frontier in 1919. She did not get it but got the Treaties of Guarantee instead. Even so her more ardent spirits were bitterly opposed to the compromise which was eventually reached—thanks to the good sense of M. Clemenceau. But when the treaties of guarantee were wrecked, the opposition to the settlement increased; and it is significant that the most violent critic and opponent of the compromise agreed to by Clemenceau was, and is, M. Poincaré—the man who now makes these "financial" proposals which, so he urges, are to be applied to the Rhineland.

'We may therefore take it as axiomatic that there is a political motive behind the French proposals and that that political motive is to speed up the process of detaching the Rhineland from the Reich and absorbing it into France as in Napoleonic days.

'It has not been easy to put up anything helpful in the circumstances surrounding the Conference. In the first place there is complete uncertainty as to the line of policy which

171

Conference of the 7th August, 1922,[2] demanded the exaction from the German Government, are as follows:—

(1) Continuance of Allied control of the German import and export licensing system in the occupied territories (i.e., the Ems organisation).[3]

(2) The re-establishment of the customs barrier on the eastern frontier of the occupied territories, and the establishment of a customs barrier around the Ruhr.

(3) The cession to the Allies of certain State properties (i.e., Ruhr mines and State forests throughout Germany).

(4) The surrender to the Allies of 60 per cent. of the share capital of certain of the factories and works in the occupied territories.

(5) The collection by the Allies of certain taxes in the occupied territories. (N.B.—The only such tax specifically discussed in the experts' report of the 9th August, 1922,[4] is the customs on the western or external frontier of the Rhineland, but there is nothing to show that M. Poincaré contemplated any such limitation.)

(6) The establishment of an effective Allied control of the whole of the German customs (i.e., not only those on the western frontier of the occupied territory but throughout the German Reich).

2. The instructions issued to the Allied experts by the Allied Conference on the 7th August, 1922, were—

'to study and report on—

(a) The sums which would be made available for reparations if the measures proposed by M. Poincaré were adopted by the Allied Governments.

(b) The question whether the measures proposed by M. Poincaré were preferable to those which had already been adopted in order to obtain reparations from Germany.'

3. The experts reported on the 9th August, 1922, [as follows:]

(1) The Allied control of the German import and export licensing system in the occupied territories [is] not a financial measure at all. It will be

H.M.G. are tending towards. If, for instance, the answer to the French proposals is to be a definite negative, then the attached memorandum loses any point which it might otherwise have had. For what it envisages is a decision by the Cabinet that the Entente is to be maintained, even at the cost of coming to some form of compromise with the French involving the adoption of some, or all, of the Poincaré proposals. What the memorandum endeavours to do is to suggest certain palliatives—no doubt inadequate if they are to be looked upon as total cures—of the results of the French proposals if they are accepted and applied to the Rhineland.

'French policy in the Rhineland has a bad record. How bad we can easily, with the help of Mr Troughton, demonstrate. But that form of criticism would be purely destructive. It has accordingly been considered wiser to take as our point of departure the assumption that the Cabinet will decide upon some form of compromise with France. It is not for the Department to advise whether such an attitude on the part of the Cabinet is desirable or not. That is a matter of the highest policy which hardly falls within the orbit of Departmental opinion.'

[2] See No. 51.   [3] See Vol. XVI, Chap. VI, *passim*.   [4] No. 58.

remembered that this was imposed concurrently with the Rhineland Customs sanction in March 1921,[5] and was intended ostensibly to prevent the Germans from reducing that sanction to an absurdity by the refusal of all import and export licences for the occupied area. Its maintenance at this period of time is, in fact, contrary to the Supreme Council's decision of August 1921.[6]

(2) *Customs Barrier on the Rhine and around the Ruhr.* All the experts other than the French opposed these measures on the ground that they would embarrass Germany's economic life and diminish rather than increase the main reparation receipts.

(3) *Cession of State Properties.* Whilst the French and Belgian delegates considered Allied operation of the Ruhr mines to be practicable without undue cost, and whilst the Italian and Belgian delegates considered such operation might provide a more reliable means of due execution of the German treaty coal deliveries, the British experts thought the whole proposal impracticable. All the experts except the French considered that, though timber reparation deliveries were capable of increase, the cession of the State forests should be regarded as a guarantee for the timber deliveries rather than as a financial guarantee.

(4) The experts other than the French considered the cession of part of the share capital of the factories on the left bank of the Rhine to be impracticable.

(5) and (6) The experts other than the French considered the customs collection on the western frontier of the Rhineland to be part of the general question of the collection of customs throughout Germany. The proceeds of these customs, together with the export levy, might well be paid to the account of the Committee of Guarantees.

4. This report can scarcely be said to be favourable to the adoption of M. Poincaré's proposals. But should the Conference, nevertheless, consider it expedient for reasons of high policy to accept any of these measures, the following points should be clearly defined:—

(1) *The duration of the 'guarantees'.*
(2) *The exact purpose of the 'guarantees'.*
(3) *The economies by which their effect might be supplemented.*

5. *Duration of the guarantees.* In March 1921 after the imposition of the sanctions the French Government were under the impression that the sanctions were to continue more or less indefinitely. The British Government understood that they would be withdrawn when Germany accepted the Allied demands. No opening should be left for a similar misunderstanding now.

6. *The purpose of the 'guarantees'.* The ostensible object is financial. But it is not inherently improbable that underlying them there is a political motive, for the financial yield will be small. Four of them apply to the Rhineland, the

[5] See Vol. XV, Nos. 47 and 49.   [6] See ibid., No. 104, Appendix 8.

objective of French expansionist policy. Might not the following palliative, inadequate though it possibly may be, be considered? The British army in the Rhineland at present holds only 660 square miles of occupied territory with 7,500 men. The French army holds 9,670 square miles with 104,000 men. The Belgians hold 1,520 square miles with 12,000 men. There are 146 British officials on the Rhineland Commission as against 888 French and 153 Belgians. An enlargement of the British Zone of Occupation[7] and a decrease in the French army and officials might afford some slight check upon expansionist designs on the Rhineland.

7. *Possible economies.* But the avowed purpose of the 'guarantees' is increased reparation receipts. Could not economies be effected in certain directions for the same purpose? For example, could not the numbers of the occupying forces be reduced? Need the occupation of the three towns (Duisburg, Ruhrort, Düsseldorf) under the military sanction of March 1921 be continued? The cost of the occupation of this additional territory is a charge against the German Government, and, apart from other and political considerations, reduces *pro tanto* the funds available for reparation. A further question is the possible withdrawal of the existing commissions of naval and military control in Germany and their replacement by less expensive machinery, i.e., the so-called Committee of Guarantee. Negotiations with that object have already been initiated[8] by the Allied Governments and these might now be expedited.

8. If for reasons of high policy the Conference decides upon the application of any of the French proposals, the above suggestions might be considered.

[7] A note on the Memorandum runs: 'To this there would presumably be no military objection as no increase of troops need, so far as is known, be involved.'
[8] See Chap. IV, *passim.*

No. 61

I.C.P. 251E.] *British Secretary's Notes of a Conversation at 10, Downing Street, on Friday, August 11, 1922, at 9 a.m.*

PRESENT: *Belgium*: M. Theunis.
        British Empire: The Right Hon. D. Lloyd George, O.M., M.P., Prime Minister; SECRETARY: Sir Maurice Hankey.
        France: M. Poincaré.
        INTERPRETER: M. Camerlynck.

German Reparations—Proposed reference to Reparation Commission or League of Nations

1. MR. LLOYD GEORGE said that the British Cabinet had met on the previous day and had decided to put forward a memorandum, which he then handed round (Appendix).[1] If this memorandum did not prove acceptable to

[1] In his diary of the conference, August 10 (I.C.P. 251D), Sir Maurice Hankey recorded:
'At 9.15 a.m. M. Theunis and M. Jaspar had breakfast with the Prime Minister. After breakfast they adjourned to the Cabinet Room, where in due course they were joined by

M. Poincaré, the Cabinet felt that there was no alternative but to suggest that the question should be referred to the Reparation Commission, which was in accordance with the Treaty of Versailles, or, as an alternative, to the League of Nations. The memorandum had been put forward with a sincere desire to meet M. Poincaré's difficulties. Frankly, it must be admitted that they all had their difficulties. The Cabinet had borne this in mind, and had put the memorandum forward in a sincere desire to meet M. Poincaré's difficulties. He would repeat that if the memorandum did not prove acceptable there was no alternative but to refer the question to the Reparation Commission or the League of Nations.

M. POINCARÉ said that before expressing his opinion on the memorandum he must ask Mr. Lloyd George a question on one point, for the sake of precision. He wished to know whether the document must be taken as it stood, without any alteration, or if, on the contrary, it was put forward as a basis for discussion. If no change was possible, then there was no object in discussing it, and the same had applied to his own proposals.[2] Such proposals were useless if they could not be discussed. He wished, besides this, to add that he could not accept for any reason reference to the League of Nations of a question which was essentially one for debate first between the Allies themselves and afterwards between them and the German Government. Such a question could not be referred to the League of Nations or settled outside the circle of the Allies. He hoped, however, that they would be able to settle the question themselves, though it would be necessary for him to enter this caveat.

Mr. Chamberlain, Sir Robert Horne and Sir L. Worthington-Evans. No Secretary was present.

'At this meeting the general lines of a memorandum, giving the British terms, [to] which the Belgian Delegate agreed, were settled. Immediately after the meeting Mr. Leith Ross, who had been present at the end of the meeting, drafted the memorandum, the first edition of which is attached (Appendix I) [not printed].

'This was shown by Sir Robert Horne to M. Theunis at lunch, and in its general lines was accepted by M. Theunis. It was also shown to M. Schanzer, who wished, in the last paragraph, to omit all the words after "31st December, 1922".

'The memorandum was reproduced just before the Cabinet meeting and laid before the Cabinet during the meeting, the results of which are recorded in Cabinet 44 (22) [not printed].

'After the Cabinet, Mr Chamberlain, Sir Robert Horne and Sir L. Worthington-Evans, with Sir Maurice Hankey and Mr P. Grigg (of the Treasury) as Secretaries, met to revise the draft, and a second edition was produced (Appendix II) [not printed].

'At 6.30 [p.m.] M. Theunis and M. Jaspar came to 10, Downing Street, and the Prime Minister showed them the memorandum. They made a few alterations, and a third draft was produced (Appendix III) [not printed, but see a further revised draft of August 12 at Appendix to No. 62].

'During this meeting the Prime Minister arranged for M. Poincaré and M. Theunis to breakfast with him at 9.15 a.m. on the following day. He instructed Sir Maurice Hankey also to be present and to bring with him copies of the revised draft in English and French.

'M. Theunis undertook to send his Private Secretary to 2, Whitehall Gardens, at once to translate the document.'

2 For M. Poincaré's proposals, see No. 51.

Mr. Lloyd George agreed that it was no use for the two sides to fire ultimata at each other. The memorandum he had handed round was an indication, in substance, of the extreme limit to which the British Cabinet were prepared to go. It was not necessary that every word should remain, but in substance it represented the limit to which the Government could go. As regards the League of Nations, this was not a question merely between Germany and the Allies, but between the Allies themselves, and it especially affected France and Great Britain. If a question arose between France and Great Britain, surely it affected the League of Nations; otherwise the League would be merely a sham. However, he did not wish to take up this point at the moment, as, like M. Poincaré, he hoped it would be possible to reach agreement.

M. Poincaré said that, though he was as hopeful as Mr. Lloyd George as to reaching agreement, nevertheless he hoped it would not be necessary to raise the question of remitting the matter to the Reparation Commission or to the League of Nations. If the question was one between the Allies relating to any subject other than Germany, he would agree that it would fall within the jurisdiction of the League of Nations. This, however, was a question of the interpretation of the Treaty of Versailles bearing on the common relations of the Allies to the Germans. He could not admit that the execution of the Treaty of Versailles could be submitted to an assembly, of which neutrals were members, such as the League of Nations.

Mr. Lloyd George said it was perhaps premature to discuss this matter in detail at the moment, but he had felt it desirable to put this proposal of the British Cabinet before M. Poincaré before he read the memorandum. He hoped that it would not be necessary, but he must give warning that he would return to the question of referring the matter to the League of Nations later, if necessary.

M. Poincaré, referring to the memorandum, said that he had just glanced through it and would make some general remarks. At first sight it seemed to result that the proposals to which the French Government attached the greatest importance had been set aside. For example, the proposals that 60 per cent. of the shares of the factories on the left bank of the Rhine, including the dyestuff factories, should be made over to the Reparation Commission; the collection of taxes on the left bank of the Rhine; and the control of the grant of import and export licences, which had already been in operation, had all been set aside. The same was true of the idea of a customs line at the exits of the Ruhr, and the re-establishment of a special organisation in the Rhineland for a customs barrier on the Rhine and for the collection of the customs on the western frontier of Germany. If all these demands which France had made were set aside, it followed that the French programme was considerably mutilated in essential clauses. This would be extremely difficult to accept, at first sight. It must be remembered that he could not be regarded as having a 'clean slate' in approaching the question. Supposing he were ready to start from the assumption that he was ready to accept the various proposals, he must still reserve the right of asking for satisfaction on he other points he had raised. On the question of the forests and the State mines of Germany, the formula proposed by the British Government was unacceptable and hypothetical. He was ready to discuss the other points. He observed that on one point of great importance, namely, the full autonomy of the Reichsbank, the British and French Governments were in agreement.

MR. LLOYD GEORGE observed that this was a very important point.

M. THEUNIS said that it was really the beginning of everything.

M. POINCARÉ, continuing, said he would now be ready to discuss the memorandum point by point, but he was not prepared to say that he had abandoned the French proposals, and he must reserve full liberty in regard to these points, since, if he did not get some compensation for them, he would be placed at a disadvantage.

MR. LLOYD GEORGE agreed that it would be useful to take the memorandum paragraph by paragraph and see if M. Poincaré could accept the various items of the document so far as it went. M. Poincaré had said that the British Government had set aside the French demands. They had, however, put this document forward, not as a criticism of M. Poincaré's proposals, but in response to M. Poincaré's suggestion that they should formulate counter proposals, and they had tried to accept as much as possible of the French proposals. In fact, they had strained their own position in order to accept some of these. As regards M. Poincaré's document, the Cabinet view of the clauses which they had not included in this document was much the same as the view of the majority of the Committee of Experts[3] namely, that those particular proposals would produce a certain number of paper marks, a great deal of trouble, but no money. Other points, however, had been included in the memorandum. He and his colleagues had thought that the best thing that could be done was to work up a position in which a loan could be obtained from the bankers. If the French proposals were adopted they felt that no banker could advance anything. On the other hand, if the British proposals were adopted and Germany accepted them— and if Germany did not accept the British Government would be willing to stand in with the French Government on any sanctions that were necessary —if, however, the German Government accepted, he thought that by the end of the year such an improvement would have been made that the bankers would be prepared to give a loan. He wished to call attention to one important point, namely, the proposal in paragraph 10 that the annual payments should be so adjusted that they would work progressively towards the flotation of a loan by the German Government which would enable them to pay a good sum in reparations. Supposing the Reichsbank were given autonomy and the Committee of Guarantees were given control in the French sense of the word, it was estimated that Germany might get a loan of 4 milliards of gold marks, a good part of which would be paid to reparations. This would enable France to stabilise her finances and to get a considerable sum towards reparations. Moreover, this would not interfere with the deliveries of coal and timber which stood outside. He thought that the

[3] For the Report of the Committee of Experts, see No. 58.

concessions to M. Poincaré which the British Government had accepted, taken in conjunction with the other proposals, would lead up to a position when France could obtain something substantial for reparations within the next six months.

M. Poincaré said that on this last point he might find it necessary not to commit himself without conferring with M. de Lasteyrie, the Minister of Finance. There might be technical points in the memorandum on which he would require M. de Lasteyrie's advice. Under this reserve, however, he was prepared to proceed to read the document, taking each of the ten clauses.

Mr. Lloyd George said that before they began to consider the document in detail there was one figure which he would like to mention to show how substantial these proposals were. The figure related to German exports before the war and he supposed that the increase in price might be taken as double pre-war.

M. Theunis thought that the increase would be 60 per cent. gold.

Mr. Lloyd George said that in sterling the price might be taken as double. Taking that as a basis, 26 per cent. on German pre-war exports would yield $4\frac{1}{2}$ milliard gold marks; that is to say, nearly 13 milliard to 14 milliard francs paper at the present rate. That showed that when these proposals began to get into operation and German export trade was moving again, there would be a lot of money obtained apart from deliveries in kind.

(The Prime Minister then instructed the secretary to read the memorandum paragraph by paragraph in English, M. Poincaré and M. Theunis following on French copies.)

M. Poincaré pointed out that the statement that 'the German Government has now expressed its inability to continue the reduced cash payments fixed for 1922,' though quite correct, was incomplete, since Germany had also demanded a moratorium for 1923 and 1924.[4]

Mr. Lloyd George agreed that this should be added.

M. Poincaré, referrring to the first of the opening paragraphs on page 1, said that he would not contest the general statements contained in it, with which he was in general accord. He noted, however, that they omitted what was the logical conclusion for any country, and certainly for France, namely, that Germany ought to be declared in voluntary default.

Mr. Lloyd George said that under the Treaty it was only the Reparation Commission that could decide this.

M. Poincaré said that the Governments could instruct their delegates on the Reparation Commission.

Mr. Lloyd George said the British Government could not give such instructions to its delegate.

M. Poincaré said that if he was to speak all that was in his mind, he would have to say he would be reproached because the French Government did not instruct the French delegate to declare Germany in voluntary default. He thought it ought to be done, and French public opinion expects it.

[4] This demand had been made on July 12, 1922 (see No. 36 and No. 38, n. 1).

Mr. Lloyd George said he did not know the attitude of the French delegate, but if the British Government were to instruct Sir John Bradbury[5] he would say that it was not their business. He considered that he was there in a judicial capacity. The only thing the Government could do would be to dismiss him, but it would be a bad thing to dismiss a man because he was doing his duty.

M. Theunis said that Germany was not at the moment in default from the point of view of cash, but only as regards deliveries in kind. Before the 15th August they would not be technically in default as to cash.

M. Poincaré agreed, and said his general observation would be that the opening paragraph was very exact and the premises were severe, but the conclusions were not severe.

Mr. Lloyd George said that if M. Poincaré would read on he would find the conclusions were severe. Supposing, for example, Germany and Austria were in a position to take control of the Bank of England or the Bank of France, and to say that it must not issue notes without their permission, would not that be regarded as severe?

M. Poincaré drew attention to the translation in the French text of the word 'conditions' in the second of the opening paragraphs. The French word 'abus' was much stronger and, in his view, preferable.

Mr. Lloyd George pointed out that the word 'abuses' in English would mean something quite different. This was one of the difficulties that was constantly cropping up.

M. Poincaré, referring to paragraph 1 of the Guarantees, and more particularly to the words 'all measures required,' asked whether this was intended to refer to the past or to the future as well.

Mr. Lloyd George thought the intention was to refer to the future, and suggested it should be redrafted to read: 'all measures which may be required by the Reparation Commission'.

M. Poincaré asked if that included the right of vetoing fiduciary circulation.

Mr. Lloyd George said that point was dealt with in paragraph 2. He agreed that it was quite useless to stop the issue of paper by the Reichsbank if the German Government were free to do this.

Sir Maurice Hankey then read paragraph 2 of the Guarantees.

M. Theunis said that this was a very important paragraph, which went to the core of many of the difficulties.

M. Poincaré agreed, and said he had put this first among the French proposals.

Mr. Lloyd George said the British Government had accepted the French proposals in this respect.

Sir Maurice Hankey then read paragraph 3.

M. Poincaré said he had a good deal to say on this paragraph. As it stood the Allies would have to accept blindly the German valuation of the German exports. The fact was that the Allies had not sufficient control

5 See No. 3, n. 7.

(in the French sense of the word) on German exports. In the present state of affairs he could affirm with certainty that frauds existed, and, if necessary, he could bring the proofs of this with him to a meeting in the afternoon. The fact of fraud was established by the correspondence between the German Government and the Committee of Guarantees.[6] The German Government had declared that it was unable to say whether the local officers were doing their duty or not. Even if there were no evidence of fraud, prima facie it was clear that in all probability it existed. German exporters were certainly interested in undervaluing their exports in order to avoid taxation. It was certain that the German Government had not exercised decisive control. That was why he had insisted so strongly on the importance of customs control, not only on the east, but also on the west of the Rhineland. If this were done, the Allies would be able to see how the system of export licences worked. He knew that the British Government did not like these licences, because they thought that the system of import licences had not worked well. The control of licences, however, would have at least this advantage, that it would enable the Allies to see how the system was working in other parts of the country. Being on the spot, the Allies could effect a personal sounding of the system, which would enable them to ascertain, or at any rate to guess, what was happening in the rest of the customs system of Germany. That is why he had been pressing for the maintenance of the control of these licences and of the body at Ems that grants them. If Mr. Lloyd George wished, he could write down a formula in regard to this.

M. Theunis said he did not wish so much to discuss the detail of M. Poincaré's proposal as to go to the root of the idea behind it. It was certain that anyone who went about in Germany or read the newspapers was struck by the industrial activity in that country. As people said, all the chimneys they saw from the railway carriage were smoking. Moreover, there was not much unemployment. The German Government stated officially that there were 30,000 or 40,000 unemployed, but this was almost a negligible figure. How was it, then, that so much activity was going on, and yet no reparations were furnished by Germany? One could not help being struck by the official figures of the German Government, according to which exports were only 40 per cent. of pre-war. As Mr. Lloyd George had pointed out, this figure was not exact, because prices were double, so that in reality the amount of the exports only came to 20 per cent. to 25 per cent. of pre-war if the figures were correct. This made him suspect the statistics. He had the deepest suspicion of statistics drawn up by pure minds, and people could juggle with figures and do what they liked with statistics. M. Poincaré had said, and it was easy to understand, that the merchants would understate their exports, first owing to the tax on exports, and second because they had to deliver part of the payment in foreign bills. It was difficult to realise the attraction of foreign bills in Germany or in other countries with a low exchange. Since payment of reparations was made on a percentage of exports the German

[6] For the correspondence between the Committee of Guarantees and the German Government, July 18–21, 1922, see Reparation Commission V, op. cit., pp. 267–78.

Government had no object in overestimating the amount of exports. He recalled that last January at Cannes there had been a controversy between Dr. Rathenau and M. Bemelmans,[7] in the course of which M. Bemelmans had suggested that the German exports were 50 per cent. above the figures given to the Reparation Commission. There was probably a good deal of truth in that. It would be quite normal in such circumstances not only in Germany, but elsewhere, that the figures for exports should be undervalued. Therefore, any measures which would enable the Allies to verify more exactly the value of exports would be useful as a basis for the system of checking reparations. M. Poincaré had suggested the continuance of the supervision over the Export Licences Bureau, which was now in the hands of the High Commission of the Rhine. By this means a supervision would be obtained at the point where trade crossed the frontier, i.e., at rather an active point, and the result of such supervision would enable the Allies to know what was happening on the other frontiers. The same, as M. Poincaré was just remarking, applied to the exterior customs. M. Poincaré had said it would be interesting to see what took place in the bureaux which were under supervision. He would call Mr. Lloyd George's attention to the fact that he (Mr. Lloyd George) himself had always been a partisan of any measures enabling the Allies to fix the debt and that he had always said that the capacity of Germany to pay outside Germany could be measured only by her exports in gold. He was certain that if the Germans were trying to falsify the basis of calculation Mr. Lloyd George would agree that this was intolerable. He asked Mr. Lloyd George, therefore, to examine the proposal as to whether the supervision of licences was not one of the simplest methods of obtaining a check. He was not, generally speaking, in favour of any system of licences, and the system of import licences had been abused by the Allied authorities. The merchants of every nationality—British, French and Belgian—had been able to abuse this system by bringing in luxury goods contrary to the wishes of the German Government, who were the best judge of this question. He would, however, like to have the question examined as to whether export licences were not a very useful condition for the purpose of verifying the amount of the exports. This supervision, he pointed out, was within the powers of the Committee of Guarantees.

M. Poincaré said that undoubtedly the supervision now exercised by the Committee of Guarantees was inadequate. Anyhow, he would like to alter the first sentence of paragraph 3. In its present form it looked as though the German Government was collecting the levy on its own initiative, instead of under the surveillance of the Committee of Guarantees. As regards the customs, he understood the Committee of Guarantees only had a staff of fifteen. The staff for supervising exports had been strengthened, but was still inadequate. He would like to establish a régime of control in the districts which were now occupied, and where control should present no difficulty. That would give a means of checking control in the remainder of Germany.

Mr. Lloyd George demurred to the idea that the phrase at the outset of

[7] See Vol. XIX, No. 23.

paragraph 3 'The German Government shall continue to collect' suggested that Germany was doing it of her free will. As a matter of fact, they were doing it under the terms imposed in May 1921,[8] and the only modification since made had been made by the Reparations Commission. No doubt there had probably been some evasion of these taxes. Income tax had been collected in Great Britain for some eighty years. It had taken a long time to establish the collection properly. On the whole, however, at the present time there was very little evasion because, as the result of a long struggle between the State and the merchants, traders and private capitalists, an efficient system had been established. Probably France and Belgium were now going through the earlier British experience. Secondly, he would not like to say that there was not a certain amount of evasion by German traders and others of their export taxes. The German Government, however, collected for their own account, and if the moratorium were granted would still continue to collect for their own account, and consequently it was to their interest to collect the tax. He thought that perhaps the amount of evasion was exaggerated. As an illustration, he would point out that before the war British imports from Germany had been worth £80,000,000 sterling, which was, at present values, equivalent to £160,000,000. At the present time Great Britain was only receiving £20,000,000, only one-eighth. In this case the collection was made in Great Britain, and yet that was all they were receiving. The fact was, the Germans were not exporting very much. Their chimneys were kept smoking and their factories alive owing to the large home consumption which was due to the falling mark. As M. Theunis had observed to him, when the mark was falling people would rather buy half a dozen pairs of boots than save marks. This, however, would bring a day of reckoning in due course. This system of depreciating the currency might have been adopted here. If Great Britain had not been deflated there would not have been the one and a half millions unemployed and the factories would have been full of work. Great Britain, however, would not have been exporting. The moment Germany stopped this increase of paper, the Germans would have to take to exportation again, and German exports would increase. He must say that he did not like the control of licences by the Allies, as such licences constituted an artificial barrier on trade, which the Allies had an interest in stimulating. If, in the British interest, he wished to destroy German industry, he would do it by instituting some such system. He agreed, however, with M. Poincaré that it was necessary to prevent fraud, and that some study should be instituted of the question how to prevent such fraud. He was prepared to refer this question to the Reparation Commission, who might be asked to devise measures to make sure that there should be no fraud, and manage either from time to time or permanently to prevent it.

M. POINCARÉ asked permission to reply on two points. If he asked for an addition to paragraph 3 it was because a form of supervision already existed under the Committee of Guarantees. It might not be a very good super-

[8] See Vol. XV, No. 83, Appendix 2.

vision, but they had their agents on the spot, and if the Allies were to record their views they must give the impression that they were standing energetically by what existed. Secondly, he thought that what existed was insufficient to stop fraud, and he maintained that there was a plan by which effective supervision could be obtained.

Mr. Lloyd George had said rightly that the licensing system was not a good one, but it did exist, and the Allies ought to supervise it. In present conditions, the German Government speculated on these licences. There was undoubtedly traffic in these licences by the German Government, [and] profit [for] the great industrials. Consequently the Allies ought to see what was happening, and where they were on the spot they might as well inform themselves. He did not wish to insist on his argument but he was trying to put himself in the position which Mr. Lloyd George had taken up and to insert as much as possible in the present memorandum of points where they were in agreement.

Mr. Lloyd George asked if M. Poincaré could not agree to refer the question to the Reparation Commission.

M. Theunis said that up to the present they were in agreement as regards the 26 per cent., and they were in agreement that the supervision should be strengthened.

Mr. Lloyd George asked if they could not agree on referring the question to the Reparation Commission. He would accept M. Poincaré's view that the existing supervision of the Committee of Guarantees should not be reduced, but he would like to refer to the Reparation Commission to consider if any further steps should be taken to tighten up the supervision. He suggested that M. Theunis should frame something. At the present time he did not know enough about the details to be able to agree to any particular draft, and he would rather leave the framing of the words to Sir Robert Horne and M. de Lasteyrie and others who understood the question. He would not object, however, to any strengthening of supervision which would ensure that the Allies would not be cheated.

M. Poincaré then produced the following draft of an addition to paragraph 3:—

'La Commission de Réparations sera invitée à fortifier le contrôle qu'exerce aujourd'hui le Comité de Garanties sur la perception du prélèvement de 26 pour cent, notamment en utilisant dans les pays occupés le contrôle existant des licences d'exportation.'

Mr. Lloyd George said he would not like to say that he refused this, but he would like to refer it to others who were more in touch with the technical sides of the question.

M. Poincaré asked if Mr. Lloyd George accepted the idea of strengthening the supervision.

Mr. Lloyd George replied that he did.

Sir Maurice Hankey then read paragraph 4 of the conditions.

M. Poincaré said that he would like to scrutinise this formula carefully.

M. THEUNIS pointed out that the money would go to a body on which veto could be imposed. The Reparation Commission could impound the money collected at any time.

M. POINCARÉ pointed out that this was only so long as Germany fulfilled her obligations. He pointed out that the memorandum had begun by stating that Germany did not. He then proposed that the phrase in the middle of the sentence should read 'so long as the Reparation Commission is satisfied that *the German Government* fulfils the obligations that *may be* imposed upon it'. (The words italicised were an addition proposed by M. Poincaré.)

MR. LLOYD GEORGE felt some doubt whether this alteration really strengthened the paragraph, but said that he had no particular objection to it.

M. POINCARÉ then said he did not think the words at the end of paragraph 4 made the meaning quite clear. It transpired, however, that this was due to a mistranslation into the French.

During the above discussion, reference was made to the fact that in French the 'Reparation Commission' is feminine, and the 'Committee of Guarantees' is masculine, and to some jokes that had been made in regard to the desirability of wedding them.

M. POINCARÉ said he thought it would be better if in this case the wife were to live a little apart from the husband, viz., at Berlin.

M. THEUNIS said it was absolutely necessary that the Committee of Guarantees should be at Berlin.

MR. LLOYD GEORGE said he was inclined to agree.

M. THEUNIS said that arrangements would have to be made to prevent too many letters passing between them. There would have to be some very close system of liaison.

MR. LLOYD GEORGE said that Sir John Bradbury would like the whole Reparation Commission moved to Berlin.

M. THEUNIS thought that would be a great thing, but he thought that the French delegates had objections.

M. POINCARÉ considered it was necessary for the Committee of Guarantees to go to Berlin, and if agreement could be reached on this point he said he would make it his business to impose it.

M. THEUNIS again insisted on the importance of some very careful arrangement as regards communication between the two so as to avoid a vast correspondence.

MR. LLOYD GEORGE thought that it would be better if the Reparation Commission itself were moved to Berlin, but if this were impossible, at least they should visit it frequently.

M. POINCARÉ said he would willingly accept the change that the Committee of Guarantees should be moved to Berlin, and that the Reparation Commission should go there every two months to visit the Committee of Guarantees. He asked if all were agreed that the Committee of Guarantees should be established in Berlin. If so, it would have a good effect if it could be inserted in the document.

Mr. Lloyd George said that he personally was in favour, but he would like to discuss the matter with Sir John Bradbury before committing himself.

M. Poincaré suggested that there should be a new article between 4 and 5, stating that the Committee of Guarantees should reside at Berlin.

Mr. Lloyd George undertook to discuss the matter with his experts.

M. Poincaré pointed out the advantage which the commissions of control possessed in the facility to go and discuss matters and settle them quickly by personal contact.

Mr. Lloyd George observed that in his experience no useful business could be done by letter.

M. Theunis observed that it took two days to distil a lawyer's letter in a matter which could be settled by conversation in a quarter of an hour.

M. Poincaré summed up that although the three were in agreement that the Committee of Guarantees should go to Berlin, they would reserve it to enable Mr. Lloyd George to consult his advisers.

Sir Maurice Hankey then read paragraph 5.

M. Poincaré said he preferred the English word 'investigation' for the French word 'enquête' which had been used in the last line but one. A committee of enquiry in France usually meant the shelving of a question.

Mr. Lloyd George agreed that 'investigation' was a better word. In English it involved business.

M. Poincaré then drew attention to the phrase at the beginning of paragraph 5, 'The German Government shall carry into effect the arrangement made with the Committee of Guarantees'. Did not this mean arrangements 'which may be made?'

Mr. Lloyd George said this was not the case; they were referring to something which had already been settled, and it was important not to weaken this.

M. Poincaré proposed the phrase 'which have been or may be made'.

Mr. Lloyd George said that that was all right.

Sir Maurice Hankey then read paragraph 6.

M. Poincaré asked why at the outset of this paragraph the words used were, 'The German Government shall proceed to carry into effect'. Why was not the same phrase used as in paragraph 5, 'The German Government shall carry into effect'?

Mr. Lloyd George said that this was because paragraph 5 dealt with something that had already been settled, whereas paragraph 6 related to the necessity of the German Government to carry out further legislation. He thought M. Poincaré's point could be met by inserting the word 'forthwith' before 'proceed'.

M. Poincaré agreed.

M. Poincaré, referring to the last part of this paragraph, said that the use of an imperative formula would be approved by some of the Germans. The German Ambassador in Paris[9] had told him that the German Government

9 Dr. W. Mayer.

would like their hands strengthened in the matter of preventing the export of capital.

Mr. Lloyd George observed that no legislation would stop the exportation of capital, but only economic conditions which would attract it back.

Sir Maurice Hankey then read paragraph 7.

M. Poincaré said that at this point they were coming to the deeper causes of discord. So far, there had been general agreement on the various points in the memorandum, but on paragraph 7 he felt it was impossible to accept the point of view of the British Government. As he had told M. Theunis, he had been given definite instructions and a definite mandate from the French Government on this subject. It was impossible for the French Government to grant any moratorium, however short, without some new previous counterpart in the form of guarantees, that is to say, fresh guarantees. So far, the memorandum merely consecrated decisions which had already been taken. There was really nothing new in it at all.

M. Theunis said that an exception to this was the control of the Reichsbank, which was very important.

M. Poincaré said that had been agreed to before.[10] It was only now proposed to apply the agreement. Public opinion would say that up to now the Allies had been asleep and that they ought to have done it months ago. Nothing new at all was being given. Hence the French Government attached capital importance to their proposals in regard to State mines and forests, and he would have to examine this matter at some length. In the British draft they were not given the measures which the French Government had suggested, but the supervision over the State forests was only to be considered if there was a voluntary default by Germany. What he demanded was that the measures should be applied immediately. However short the moratorium, these measures must be applied completely. It was not sufficient to say, 'The Reparation Commission shall consider the establishment by article 248 of the Treaty of Versailles of a supervision over the State forests, &c.' Nor was it sufficient to speak of the delivery of timber. The essential point was that article 248 gave a first charge, both general and absolute, on the German goods, and gave the Reparation Commission the right to apply these measures to a certain number of specific properties which included forests and mines. He asked for the immediate execution of this article, and not for a mere threat. The French Government wanted the immediate execution of the article in regard to these two classes of property. That was an irreducible condition, and he hoped that agreement would be reached on this. Otherwise it was no good going on to discuss the memorandum.

Mr. Lloyd George said that he also had definite instructions from his Government.

M. Theunis said he was well aware of the points of view held by the British and French Governments respectively, and he had also considered the report

[10] A reference to the Reparation Commission's letter of April 16, 1921, to the German Government (see Reparation Commission V, op. cit., p. 21).

of the Committee of Experts. Both the Belgians and the Italians had seen great advantages in the development of reparations in kind, but he would leave this point aside for the moment, and put some considerations with a view to diminishing the difference which existed between the points of view of the British and French Governments. Yesterday, he and M. Jaspar had discussed the question with M. Poincaré, and when they came to discuss details with greater precision they seemed, contrary to the usual experience, to bring the two points of view closer together. M. Jaspar, who was a lawyer, had hastily dictated a memorandum on this subject, which he would like to read. He then read the following memorandum by M. Jaspar:—

'The French delegation insists in particular, from the point of view of public opinion, on the inclusion in the arrangements of special rights conferred on the Reparation Commission over the mines of the Ruhr and the forests of the German States. It cannot content itself with giving the character of a sanction to these rights.

'The interpretation of M. Poincaré in this respect is only the strict application of the clauses of the treaty. In virtue of article 248, the Reparation Commission possesses, in fact, privileges of the first importance over all the property of the German Empire and States. These privileges have not, up to the present, been specifically determined to the extent of allotting the Reparation Commission such and such claim over such and such German State property. What M. Poincaré asks is that it should be specifically determined in this way for the mines and forests.

'In other words, he does not ask at all that the property of these mines and forests should be from now on transferred to the Reparation Commission. The property would remain the capital of the actual owners, i.e., Prussian or other States, but a claim in the name of the Reparation Commission would be laid down in regard to the mines and forests. It would include, moreover, the products of these mines and forests under the same condition as the receipts from the 26 per cent. levy on the customs. The exploitation of these properties would remain with their owners. It would be merely controlled by the Reparation Commission, and that commission, like every privileged creditor, where an immovable property is concerned, would only have the right of realising the said mines or forests in the event of the non-execution by Germany of reparation payments due by the State, or of agreements signed with the Allies.

'The result of the preceding will be that, providing Germany executes with loyalty and precision the conditions laid down by the Reparation Commission in regard to the payment of reparation, and providing she turns over to the account of the Reparation Commission the products, duly exploited, of the mines and forests, there will be no change in the actual situation except over its control, or in the usual character of the exploitation of the properties referred to. In consequence, there will be no establishment in the Ruhr or elsewhere for a property belonging to the

Reparation Commission, or to any Allied Power, taking the place of a German property; from the political as well as the judicial point of view, the present situation will undergo no modification, and there would be no violation of the treaty. The treaty, on the other hand, would be executed both in the letter and the spirit.'

M. POINCARÉ said he would like to rectify some parts of M. Theunis's statement. What he asked for was the application of article 248 of the Treaty of Versailles. The Allies had a first charge on all German property, so they had the right of realisation in certain cases on particular properties. He asked that they should take advantage of this right in the two cases of forests and national mines, and, as M. Theunis had said, he did not demand an immediate transfer of ownership. It might involve the hypothesis of supplementary sanctions, but he did not ask it immediately. He limited himself to asking for 'gages' to which the Allies were entitled under the Treaty of Versailles, and the execution of the guarantees in these two particulars of State mines and forests. As M. Theunis said, there would be an actual legal registration of the pledge against Germany, and there would be a first charge in this sense on the State forests and mines. What would be the result? At the slightest default the Reparation Commission could put these properties in adjudication; that is to say, they could put them up for sale. He did not ask that the Allies should take them themselves, but that they should offer the property to buyers in the whole world. That was what he meant by the 'realisation' of the properties. For the moment he would merely keep the position of a privileged creditor. He was in favour of control in the English sense of the word, and as the Belgians understood it. The Allies might have a majority of directors. He knew Mr. Lloyd George's difficulties—that the administration and exploitation of these properties would create a certain embarrassment for the foreign directors. On the left bank of the Rhine, however, there were cases where coal mines were worked in collaboration by French and German owners, and no special difficulties arose. He quoted the case of a French Deputy, M. de Wendel, who had direct interests in one of these mines and who said that no difficulty was encountered. If this was the case between French and Germans, *a fortiori* when the collaboration was between French, Belgian and British direction, there should be no difficulty. If it were merely a collaboration between the French and German Governments there might be painful incidents, but this ought not to apply to a Franco-Belgian-British direction. He asked that the first charge on these properties should be acknowledged and established, and that a plan for their exploitation should be drawn up immediately, and that it should be put immediately in operation. The French Government had discussed and decided this question, and they had just discussed it again under the chairmanship of the President of the Republic, and had reaffirmed their previous decision. He had gone so far as to show to M. Theunis the telegram he had received from the French Government on this subject. Consequently, he could not contemplate any compromise on this question. M. Theunis had gone beyond his position. He might give up ownership, but he could not give up what he was pressing for.

Mr. Lloyd George said that it was because they stood by the Treaty of Versailles that the British Government could not agree to M. Poincaré's proposal. He would be deeply pained if they had to disagree on this question, the more so because he was convinced that they were disagreeing on a sham and not on a reality. Here was the position. M. Poincaré did not wish to take possession of the mines, but to have a 'gage', a guarantee, or a security. He [Mr. Lloyd George] happened to have an exceptional experience in this kind of question, because he had spent his youth in a conveyancing firm and had had some twenty years' experience. He did not know if there was much difference between French and British law on this question. Under British law it was possible to take a charge on a property, that is to say, a guarantee for some sum of money. If there was a default you could take possession and sell it, or work it yourself, but there was no intermediate stage. You could either leave the goods in the hands of the proprietor or enter into possession and sell. The Treaty of Versailles gave a first mortgage on all the assets of Germany—mines, forests, buildings, railways, &c. The Allies had a first charge on all German goods. If they were to pick out one class of goods, for example, mines, forests or railways, it would weaken their authority on the whole property, and would imply that they had not a good title on the remainder. He objected, therefore, to M. Poincaré's proposal because it would weaken the general rights which the Reparation Commission exercised on the whole of the German assets. If a client who had a mortgage on a property came to him and said he wanted a special charge on, say, categories 'A' and 'B', he would advise him that he was weakening his whole claim, since he had rights over the whole property from 'A' to 'Z'. He objected to picking out one or two items, because it would weaken the general position in regard to the mortgage as a whole. If the Allies were to say that Germany was in default, that would be contrary to the treaty, for under the treaty there was only one body which could declare Germany in default, namely, the Reparation Commission. Hence, the Allies would be breaking the treaty themselves and ruining their juridical position. They would be tearing up the only deed they possessed. If they were to tear it up now they would never get another treaty, since the whole world would be against them. Hence, their object would really be weakened by M. Poincaré's proposal. If the Reparation Commission were to declare Germany in default and were to say they must exercise their rights over German assets, he would think it a mistake. Supposing they were to enter the Ruhr for the purpose of administering it, it would be necessary to have soldiers, and it would be necessary to pay wages to the workmen, and this would swallow the profits. It was no use assuming that workmen would work the same for everyone. Workmen here in England did not ask who[m] they were working for; but supposing the German Government came and took possession, the workmen would not be willing to work in the same way, and so, instead of obtaining a profit, they would get a loss. He objected to M. Poincaré's proposals, in the first place, because they weakened the general security of all the signatories to the treaty—of Great Britain just as much as of Belgium and France. Article 248 was an effective document in itself. The only way to apply it was to take possession and sell. M. Poincaré had said that he only wished to apply article 248 to the extent of taking the right. What was the use of asking for a right which the Allies already possessed? By doing so the Allies would be disputing the validity of the title they already possessed. He had never heard of anyone going into court to say that the whole of their title was not good and consequently they wanted rights over a part only. He stood by the treaty, which gave a guarantee and gave a title. There was only one thing which could be done under the treaty, and that was to go in and sell the properties, but no one proposed to do that. He was told that in the opinion of the French Cabinet and of the President of the Republic the Entente was going to be broken because the French delegation proposed to limit itself to 2 or 3 pledges. If France wanted to cast doubt on the title over German properties they must do it on their own responsibility. The British Government could take no part in this. That was the definite opinion of the British Government. If the Reparation Commission proposed to sell the mines and forests—incidentally, he would observe that it would require a French army and would be a very foolish thing—nevertheless, if the Reparation Commission were to say they must sell these things, he would back them up, because he had signed the Treaty of Versailles; but if he was asked to take action which would break up the Treaty of Versailles, he must refuse. The British Cabinet had met for two hours on the previous day,[11] and had reached quite a unanimous decision. If the French Government insisted on doing this now it must do it on its own responsibility, and the Alliance, which had cost all so much, would cease to operate.

M. POINCARÉ said he would like to observe at first that it would be better if the question of the Alliance were not constantly being brought up. He could perhaps give instances where the British Government had taken the initiative without breaking the Alliance. He did not understand this perpetual menace of the breakup of the Alliance. He could not accept the position that because the Allies were all differing and one of them was to act independently, the Alliance must be broken. He could give many instances where the British Government had taken isolated action even on questions relating to reparations, but France had never suggested that the Entente must therefore be broken. For the rest, he could not, of course, dispute Mr. Lloyd George's experience on the question of mortgages, but the Paris lawyers were not entirely ignorant on this question, and he himself was not entirely inexperienced. He could not, however, admit [Mr. Lloyd George's] juridical interpretation of article 248 of the Treaty of Versailles. Moreover, he could prove that Mr. Lloyd George did not agree in his own interpretation. He would make one preliminary observation, however. He was told that in the matter of declaring Germany in default and of sanctions being required, it was a matter for the Reparation Commission alone to

<hr>

[11] See n. 1.

settle it. He was not speaking of a default or sanctions. If it were a matter of default he agreed it would be for the Reparation Commission to decide.

(Sir Edward Grigg entered at this point to tell Mr. Lloyd George that the Italian delegation were making persistent enquiries as to what was going on. He then withdrew.)

M. POINCARÉ, continuing, said that if the Reparation Commission declared a default it would not be a question of sanctions under article 248 of the treaty, but under articles 17 and 18 of annex 2 of Part VIII of the Treaty of Versailles. The position would be entirely different. In this part of the treaty they spoke of sanctions of a different character, including economic sanctions, blockade, and even military sanctions were not excluded. He did not envisage those. He was only discussing article 248 of the treaty, which gave a floating charge on all the properties. Mr. Lloyd George had said that he was acting contrary to the treaty, but what about the customs, the most important of these sanctions? There was a time when Mr. Lloyd George had agreed to use the customs as a first charge[12] under article 248, and he had been perfectly right. Did Mr. Lloyd George imagine that an article which gave a first charge on the whole of the assets did not enable them to exercise this first charge on each item separately? If so, it would be an impossibility and an absurdity. It was obvious that in applying these sanctions they must begin somewhere. That was what had been done in the case of the customs. He only asked to take two more classes of property as a condition of the present moratorium, namely, State mines and forests. He asked that these should be taken as a guarantee. He asked that the Reparation Commission should have the right to use these properties as a guarantee in a general manner. All he asked for was some control in the widest sense of the word so as not to be confronted with something null and void. He realised that they had now come somewhere near a deadlock, and he would ask Mr. Lloyd George if he would continue the conversation in the afternoon. Perhaps after reflection they might see if some compromise were possible. So far they were practically agreed on the first six points of the memorandum, but this was not the case as regards Nos. 7 and 8, which they had under their eye at present. He thought, however, that they should not be too precipitate, as they might reach a resolution which would produce an irreducible difference between them.

MR. LLOYD GEORGE said he did not wish to argue whether he had given away his case by the agreement in regard to customs. It was always the case when a concession was made to the opposite point of view, which had been done in this case for the sake of reaching agreement with France, the general case was weakened. He agreed that logically the concession as regards the customs had weakened his position, but this was true of every compromise. He would, however, like to make a suggestion, not for an immediate reply, because he agreed with M. Poincaré that it would be advisable to have an adjournment for consideration. He would, however, be willing to agree that paragraph 4 relating to customs should be applied also

[12] Under the Schedule of Payments.

to the mines and forests; that is to say, the proceeds of the mines and forests should be applied by the German Government to a special account and that the Reparation Commission should have power to seize these proceeds at the moment when there was default. He must make a reserve, however, that he did not know how this would affect the States. There might, for example, be a forest in Bavaria the proceeds of which would be paid, not into the Reichsbank, but into a bank at Munich. This might involve the Allies in difficulties which they would rather avoid, but if there were State forests the proceeds of which would be paid into the Reichsbank, he would agree that, subject to there being no question of getting into difficulties with the States, that the sums raised from them should be at the disposal of the Reparation Commission. This was only a suggestion for consideration which they might discuss in the afternoon.

M. Theunis thought this last proposal of Mr. Lloyd George met one of M. Poincaré's ideas, namely, that revenues should be collected from State properties, viz., forests and mines. He thought there would be no difficulty as regards the States because the States were in permanent relations of debit and credit with the Reich.

M. Poincaré proposed that they should resume the question at the afternoon meeting. He must say at once that the suggestion Mr. Lloyd George had made did not meet the thought of the French Government. It only related to the case of some later default by Germany, but what they had in mind was some immediate counterpart for a moratorium.

Mr. Lloyd George said that he must enter a caveat against the statement that the British Government had acted on their own responsibility in regard to the execution of the treaty. He believed that the basis of this was that they had taken action in regard to German goods in Great Britain.[13] He did not want to go into the question at present, but he must ask to have it placed on the *procès-verbal*.

M. Poincaré said that he would have a reservation on the reservation, because he thought he could adduce other instances where the British Government had acted independently.

M. Theunis alluded to a speech made by Mr. Lloyd George in regard to the moratorium.[14]

Mr. Lloyd George said that if every speech M. Poincaré had made was to be taken as a breach of the treaty, there would be no end to the cases of breach he could raise.

2, Whitehall Gardens, August 11, 1922.

[13] See No. 19, Annex, paragraph 5.
[14] Presumably a reference to Mr. Lloyd George's speech in the House of Commons of August 3 (see No. 54, n. 10).

I.C.P. 251F.] *British Secretary's Notes of a Conversation held at 10, Downing Street, London, on Friday, August 11, 1922, at 4 p.m.*

PRESENT: *Belgium*: M. Theunis.
          British Empire: The Right Hon. D. Lloyd George, O.M., M.P., Prime Minister; SECRETARY: Sir Maurice Hankey.
          France: M. Poincaré; SECRETARY: M. Massigli.
          INTERPRETER: M. Camerlynck.

German Reparations

M. POINCARÉ said that his reflections during the luncheon interval had resulted in a series of points. He had collaborated with M. de Lasteyrie, to whom he had read the whole of the text of the first six articles of Mr. Lloyd George's memorandum.[1] Even on these, M. de Lasteyrie had had several objections, some of which were rather strong. The first related to the control of the Reichsbank (article 1). The British proposals appeared to give something in substance, but he wanted something in reality. If they did not provide for the control of the note issue by the Reichsbank they would not get much. No doubt that had been the idea of the British draughtsmen, but he did not think the article gave effect to it. He proposed some such condition as the following:—

'The Reichsbank shall be submitted to the permanent supervision of the Committee of Guarantees, which shall fix the amount of the issues of paper notes.'

Apart from that there was no fresh point of substance, and M. de Lasteyrie's criticisms were rather questions of drafting. He thought that the British proposals should be examined article by article by, say, two experts of each Power who were accustomed to work with each other, and would carefully compare the differences in the two languages.

M. THEUNIS, referring to M. de Lasteyrie's proposals, pointed out that in any case it would be as well to keep control of the floating debt, which was even more vast than the emission of notes. The floating debt had considerable influence in the price of the mark and the exchange.

M. POINCARÉ said that as regards the collection of the 26 per cent. which he thought had been accepted in principle at the morning meeting, the Minister of Finance had a certain number of points to make which were not without interest. There was a presumption that the Allies were being deceived. Information had been given to the German Committee of Socialisation[2] to the effect that traders declared their exports on their internal value. This was clearly a subterfuge for understating the values. If the statistics

---

[1] Not printed: for the text as revised by the Committee of Allied Experts, see Appendix.

[2] The German Committee of Socialisation was set up soon after the war by the Social Democratic Government to make recommendations for the nationalisation of German industry (see Erich Eyck, *A History of the Weimar Republic* (London, 1962–4), vol. ii, p. 109).

for September 1921 were compared with the statistics for December 1920, it was found that the former surpassed the latter by 5 per cent., while the value expressed in gold marks was inferior by one-third. [This seemed rather incomprehensible. If the statistics for May and April 1922 were compared with 1913, it was found that articles were being sold below their cost in 1913. For example, automobiles were being sold at a price 50 per cent. below the pre-war price. This seemed incomprehensible. He gave other instances of the same kind. There was an office in Germany devoted to keeping down internal prices.

(*Note*—Several examples read by M. Poincaré from a typewritten paper at this point were imperfectly understood, and no attempt was made to record them.)]*

Then there was the question of legislation to prevent the exportation of capital from Germany. The experts thought that the legislation was illusory in the terms in which it had been made. The German law in reality left the control of the law to the Chambers of Commerce. That was the reason why he had asked for a firmer control than was contemplated in Mr. Lloyd George's draft. If they stuck to the terms of this draft they would be doing something extremely dangerous, and would obtain no kind of result. He thought that the German Government ought to submit to something analogous to what existed in France, and that German legislation should be at least as strict as that of France. [Germany had not the same interest to prevent the exportation of capital, and if the last word rested with the Chambers of Commerce the persons concerned would find means to evade it.] He proposed the following draft:—

'The German Government shall immediately pass the necessary legislation to forbid the export of capital in the following conditions:—

'(*a*) The purchase of foreign bills shall only be effected through the medium of a limited number of banks which shall communicate to the Minister of Finance a periodical statement of the operations that have been effected.

'(*b*) The said banks shall be authorised to sell to private individuals foreign bills only for the purpose of paying for imported goods except with the permission of the Minister of Finance visé by the Committee of Guarantees.³

'(*c*) An extract from the ledger of banks relating to these operations shall be communicated to the Committee of Guarantees.'

He was not asking for an immediate answer. These were rather technical matters, and should no doubt be referred to the experts.

M. THEUNIS said that similar measures had been applied in Great Britain and other countries during the war.

M. POINCARÉ said that they were applicable and something must be done. The present control was inadequate to the situation. He thought this point

* The text of the passages between square brackets is supplied from Confidential Print.
³ See Vol. XV, No. 83, Appendix 2.

might be reserved and that they might start where they left off at the end of the morning[4]

Mr. Lloyd George agreed that these were very important questions. M. Poincaré's proposals might produce some result, but they might only tend to strangle trade and reduce reparations. They should be referred to the same committee as had examined M. Poincaré's proposals.[5]

M. Poincaré said he would now come to the point where he had left off at the morning meeting. The Minister of Finance, when reading the British counter-proposals, had received exactly the same impression as he had at the morning meeting, namely, that as far as article 6 inclusive they contained nothing new. The memorandum merely completed measures which had already been decided on and partially applied. In some respects it completed them, but it did not modify the general situation. Hence the Minister of Finance had the impression that they did not meet the French demand that any grant of the shortest moratorium must be accompanied by some counterpart.

Hence, although broadly speaking there was agreement on articles 1 to 6, they did not in the least meet the present situation in regard to a moratorium. The Reparation Commission instead of declaring a default was under these proposals to give a moratorium. That meant that the Reparation Commission would be giving an excessive advantage to Germany, yet Germany, who is [sic] largely responsible for the financial and economic situation in which she found herself, was to give no new securities. This is [sic] the situation which the French Government could not accept. The French Government had made a series of demands, including the participation in the factories on the left bank of the Rhine, including the dyestuff factories, including the establishment of customs control on the exits of the Ruhr Basin on the line of the Rhine—the latter being nothing new, but merely what had previously been applied and had existed and functioned under the Treaty of Versailles. This, it was true, would only supply paper marks, but as the fiduciary circulation was reduced and the state of the mark improved, their proposals would have produced gold marks. In other words, they were proposing precautions for the future which would give results later on. Perhaps at the moment their value was illusory, but later they would produce results. All this was being refused to France, or rather was being refused to all the Allies since the French propositions had been made in the common interest. In these circumstances and in every reserve as to the consequences as to this first refusal, it was at least indispensable to be entirely in agreement on the other pledges demanded, i.e. the State mines and the forests.

M. Poincaré then returned to articles 7 and 8 for which he proposed the following new text:—

'In consideration of the moratorium granted to Germany, as well as with a view to guaranteeing the execution of the plan of deliveries in kind to be effected for the Allies, the Commission of Reparation means to exercise on and from this day as regards the German State forests and the fiscal mines

[4] See No. 61.   [5] See No. 58.

of the Ruhr the right to make use of the first charge referred to in article 248 of the Treaty of Versailles. Consequently, and without prejudice to any measures that may be taken later on with a view to the alienation of the property, the management of the forests and mines shall be carried out under the authority of the Reparation Commission.'

So much for the principle. Now he would explain how it would be applied under the Reparation Commission. Before discussing details, he did not conceal that his proposals were at variance with articles 7 and 8 of the British draft, but he wished to draw attention to this fact at once. M. Theunis, he said, had asked him to read the remainder of the document as well.

M. Poincaré declared himself ready to do it, adding, however, that in the details so far as concerned the forests and State mines the project was by way of suggestion and was susceptible of modification in detail. As a conclusion to reading the document he added the following formula: 'The whole is subject to the reserve of the right of alienation provided by the Treaty.'

M. Poincaré then read the following:—

'*Forests*—As regards the forests, the Reparation Commission will every year inform the Government of the Reich what are the forests which the commission intends should be exploited in order to obtain the timber deliveries required by the Allied Governments. By this notification the Reparation Commission will automatically replace the owner of the forest as to the management ("ménagement") and the right to sell the trees. The Reich Government shall settle direct with the owner the value of the timber, and shall pay according to the indications given by the Reparation Commission the contractors or buyers who are responsible for the output of timber. The amounts thus paid by the Reich to the contractors or buyers shall be written to the credit of Germany on account of reparations.

'*Fiscal Mines in the Ruhr*—The Reparation Commission shall appoint a committee of three members whose chairman will be French. This committee shall enjoy all the powers of a board of directors in a limited company, notably as regards the right of appointment or dismissal of the general manager and higher staff; they will ensure that the whole of the coal produced by the mines is either directly or by way of exchange put at the disposal of the Allied Governments on account of reparations. Until the time when it might become necessary to proceed with the alienation of the mines, these mines shall be operated at the expense and risk of the Prussian Government.'

M. Poincaré said he recognised that this view was rather different from that of the British Government, and it corresponded rather to the view of the Belgian experts on the Expert Committee.

M. Theunis said he could not say what the Belgian expert had said in regard to the actual control. He was mainly concerned with the question of ownership.

M. Poincaré asked if the Belgian experts had not contemplated representation on the board of directors.

M. Theunis said that perhaps he had contemplated a rather less direct intervention.

M. Poincaré said he had not contemplated taking over the management at first, but only later on, when some high officials might have to be appointed.

M. Theunis said he had been under the impression that the experts were not concerned in the destination of the timber and deliveries in kind. He adverted to the possibility of influencing [*sic*] coal deliveries to the Reparation Commission more directly than through the medium of the German Government and the Coal Syndicate. Mr. Lloyd George had that morning come to the point of suggesting the delegation to the Reparation Commission of the revenue on the mines. In the case of the mines, this plan produced something very similar to a title of ownership. If the Reparation Commission received all the proceeds of the mines, they would end by utilising all the property in the mines. It was a form of ownership which appeared to provide the possibility of a compromise.

M. Poincaré said that the French Minister of Finance had remarked that Mr. Lloyd George's plan did not tend to assist the deliveries of timber and coal. He thought that possibly a compromise might be found providing for a certain right of control to ensure deliveries in kind of timber and coal with the right of eventual action under article 248 of the treaty.

M. Theunis [thought that if these two ends were kept in view it might not be impossible to come to some understanding. In the case of the coal-mines, for example, they might leave the Reparation Commission to collect the proceeds under some general plan similar to that adopted in the case of the 26 per cent. customs levy. This would practically amount to a leasehold of the mines. This would be a form of ownership which could not give rise to the same objections as the actual transfer of ownership. M. Poincaré had asked for the usufruct on deliveries of coal. This might be understood as giving the Reparation Commission an option on the mines. By this means M. Poincaré's object might be obtained without running counter to the British view.]

M. Poincaré said that, before he could say whether he would agree, there was a previous question to be considered. The strongest objection to the British articles 7 and 8 was that they began by referring to a certain date— that is to say, the date when there was a failure by Germany to carry out the programme of timber deliveries fixed by the Reparation Commission. This date had to be ascertained before the article came into operation, and it would be necessary for the Reparation Commission to declare a default. The Commission would not do this unless all the Governments desired it. [The Reparation Commission, however, would always compromise on such a question. Consequently, instead of immediate action, everything was subject to a later decision.]

M. Theunis did not think that this was Mr. Lloyd George's proposal. He did not think his intention was that the right of action by the Committee of Guarantees should only be granted in the case of ultimate default, but that his intention was for the Committee of Guarantees to collect at once from the proceeds of the State mines. He asked Mr. Lloyd George what his intention had been.

MR. LLOYD GEORGE said that he had made a suggestion in favour of the application of the principle adopted in the case of the customs. If there was to be a default, the Reparation Commission could alone declare it. What M. Poincaré proposed was to smash the treaty and write a new one. He gave a most extraordinary reason for this. The Germans had asked for a moratorium.[6] They had a perfect right under the treaty to do this. The Allies were asked by M. Poincaré to reply that because the Germans had asked for a moratorium this was a justification for them to smash the treaty. Article 248 of the treaty gave the Allies as security the assets of Germany. If a default was declared, the Allies were entitled to enter into possession of these assets. M. Poincaré said he did not want to wait for the Reparation Commission to declare the default, but he wanted to do it right over the heads of the Reparation Commission. The Germans had never asked for the Reparation Commission; the Allies had put it into the treaty. All its representatives were Allied representatives. It contained no impartial persons at all. All its members were representatives of the creditor countries. M. Poincaré said he could not trust the Reparation Commission to do what he wanted, so he would brush it aside and act without Germany having been declared in default. He wished to go straight into Germany and get his own reparations. If he liked to break the treaty, he must do it alone. He (Mr. Lloyd George) himself had always said that the first to break the treaty would be those who depended on it most. France, who depended on it more than anyone else, was saying that, whether the Allies agreed or the Reparation Commission agreed, they would take action. If the Treaty of Versailles did not fit in with their wishes they would alter it. He (Mr. Lloyd George) stood by the treaty. The moment the Reparation Commission declared that Germany was in default, and that the mines must be seized, he would stand by it, but to do this without a declaration of default was to take the responsibility of breaking the Treaty of Versailles. When the treaty suited Germany there was to be no treaty; when it did not suit the Allies, apparently there was to be no treaty. It could not be admitted that each of the Allies was free to apply the Treaty according to the circumstances of the moment. This was not a question of the Alliance. It was rather a question whether the only guarantee of France's security and her right to reparations should be maintained. At present France could depend on overwhelming power, but she could not count on this for ever. The time might come when Germany, possibly not with her own power, but with some Power behind her, such as Russia, might point to France as the country which had broken the Treaty of Versailles. He (Mr. Lloyd George) would stand by the treaty himself, and therefore he could only assent to a reference to the Reparation Commission of the question whether, under the terms of the treaty, they could take action under article 248 in regard to the administration of forests and mines. It was

6 See No. 36 and No. 38, nn. 1 and 4.

a matter on which the Reparation Commission should declare the position. Perhaps the French and Belgian Governments could give orders to their representatives on the Reparation Commission. The British Government could not. They regarded it in the same way as they would regard putting a matter to a judge, not merely to a clerk or a messenger. That was his proposal—to refer the question to the Reparation Commission. If M. Poincaré could not agree to that, there appeared nothing to be done but to adjourn to the following day, when a full meeting of the Allies could be held and the position could be stated by M. Poincaré and himself. He was sorry he could not go beyond this point. Even as regards the proposal he had made at the morning meeting he felt doubtful. He would put the matter to experts, and ascertain if his proposal could be carried out legally under the treaty. His other proposal was to request the Reparation Commission to consider the possibility of taking over, in virtue of the first charge referred to in article 248 of the Treaty of Versailles, the administration of the German State forests and State mines in the Ruhr. If neither proposal could be agreed to by M. Poincaré, there was no object in further discussion; it would be better to adjourn and to have a full meeting on the following day, when each could define his position. That was as far as he could go. He would add one word. M. Poincaré had said that morning that he (Mr. Lloyd George) had agreed to similar proposals in connection with the customs and the 26 per cent. He would point out, however, that these were agreed to by the Reparation Commission and the German Government, so that no breach of the treaty was involved.

M. Theunis said that before M. Poincaré replied in a general manner to Mr. Lloyd George's observations, he would like to say a few words on the subject of the forests and mines. That morning Mr. Lloyd George had been in agreement to exercise the first charge in regard to forests and mines under article 248 of the treaty in a certain form by demanding that the German Government should delegate the collection of the proceeds from the fiscal mines to the Committee of Guarantees in a similar manner to that adopted in the case of the customs and the 26 per cent.

Mr. Lloyd George interpolated that the 26 per cent. was in rather a different category.

M. Theunis said that this plan might be utilised to obtain coal, and the delegation of powers to the Reparation Commission might be so organised as to constitute almost a form of leasehold, and he thought that this might give satisfaction to M. Poincaré as well. The majority of the exports to the Allies were obtained from the State-owned mines, and if formal instructions were given that the proceeds were to be delivered effectively for this purpose the monthly difficulty in regard to coal deliveries might be diminished. This might result in proper deliveries of the coal. He would like to ask Mr. Lloyd George if he saw any objection to the first charge under article 248 being exercised in the manner he suggested, that is to say, to exercise the first charge on the fiscal mines so as to have a first call and option on their produce. These were two proposals which, considered together, might provide a compromise.

MR. LLOYD GEORGE said he saw no objection in principle, but he would like to refer the question to the experts. He was specially anxious not to break the treaty. Whatever was done ought to be done legally and making use of the Reparation Commission. At the meeting in London in 1921[7] a similar situation had arisen, but it had been realised that the Allies could only act through the Reparation Commission, which had been invited to come to London; otherwise the treaty would be broken, which would be a fatal error. If they were not careful the day might come when people might say that all the trouble had arisen because on the 11th August, 1922, Mr. Lloyd George, M. Poincaré and M. Theunis had broken the treaty and had made a treaty of their own.

M. POINCARÉ assured Mr. Lloyd George that he was not thinking of violating the Treaty of Versailles. France had always stood by the treaty. If any modifications, changes or softening of the treaty had been made in favour of Germany it had not taken place on the initiative of France. France remained faithful to the maintenance of the treaty in the greatest possible degree, and had always decided to respect the treaty. Consequently, France did not expose herself to that criticism. Mr. Lloyd George had suggested that Germany, at some future date, might revive with some great nation behind her. He supposed that Mr. Lloyd George referred to the Bolsheviks.

MR. LLOYD GEORGE interpolated that he had been thinking of a period twenty years hence. M. Poincaré gave the Bolsheviks a longer life than he did.

M. POINCARÉ replied that he hoped twenty years hence Germany would be isolated again and would have no other country to help her. This was a nightmare that he was doing his best to get rid of. Continuing his main statement, he said he did not think of violating the Treaty of Versailles. This was merely a difference of interpretation. It was true that Germany had applied for a new moratorium and appeared likely to obtain it. The question was on what conditions Germany could obtain the moratorium. The British representatives had clearly stated that Germany had not fulfilled her obligations, to prove which he read in full the first preliminary paragraph of the British memorandum (Appendix to I.C.P. 251E[1]). These words, he said, expressed the situation perfectly. It was difficult to see how they could be more just or more severe. He admitted that in regard to the moratorium France was in an exceptional position. The majority of the Allies apparently wished to grant it; he did not, but he saw that the Reparation Commission was going to grant a moratorium by a majority vote and was not going to declare Germany in default. What was his position? He did not ask for sanctions, but only for guarantees. His position rested on article 248 of the Treaty of Versailles. This [article] did not involve sanctions. If a voluntary default was declared article 248 would give a first charge on certain German assets to all the creditors. These assets could be used by the sole fact that Germany was in a deficit. The case of a default arose under paragraphs 17 and 18 of annex 2 to part VIII of the treaty. That article came into play if the Reparation Commission declared Germany in default and reported to the

[7] See Vol. XV, Chap. IV.

Governments, who would then apply such sanctions as were necessary. There was no reason for that at present. We were in the presence of article 248 and not paragraphs 17 and 18 of annex 2. It was a case of voluntary default and not fraudulent bankruptcy. Germany was merely a bankrupt who had a deficit and could not make both ends meet. He repeated that the treaty had never been violated by France. He had been told that France had not respected the prerogatives of the Reparation Commission. He did not deny that the Reparation Commission had its prerogatives. These had not always been recognised by the Allied Governments previous to the arrival in power of the present French Cabinet. The commission had complained several times, and he recalled that at Cannes the commission had passed an unofficial but, nevertheless, unanimous resolution that its prerogatives must be better respected in the future.

Mr. Lloyd George, during the translation, [interpolated] that the British Government had never received this resolution, which must have been passed owing to something the French Government had done.

M. Poincaré replied that he believed it had been communicated to all the Governments.

Mr. Lloyd George said he had never received it.

M. Poincaré said that perhaps the reason was that the commission felt better able to approach the French Government, because they knew that the French Government never had infringed its prerogatives. It had been an unofficial resolution which had been passed by the commission after its return to Paris from Cannes. The resolution had been couched in polite terms and had asked that the prerogatives of the commission should be respected.

Continuing his main statement, M. Poincaré said he, for his part, was quite disposed wholly to respect the prerogatives of the Reparation Commission, but were they, he asked, not entitled even to prescribe to their own delegates the principles on which they should act? He agreed that they could not instruct the commission on such a subject as declaring Germany in default.[8] In such a case, as Mr. Lloyd George had said, the commission had a juridical status and instructions could not be given.

Mr. Lloyd George said that instructions could not be given to the delegates.

M. Poincaré said that he thought they were entitled to give general directions (directives). To show that this was the view of the British Government also, he referred to Mr. Lloyd George's article 10 of the British proposals, which directly encroached upon the prerogatives of the Reparation Commission. When they came to discuss that, it would be his turn to say that Mr. Lloyd George was violating the prerogatives of the Reparation Commission. It was by means of the Reparation Commission that the Governments could exercise the first charge on German assets given by article 248. They should ask their delegates for the execution of this article. Perhaps it would be useful at this point for him to discuss the relations of the Governments to the Reparation Commission. He was quite in agreement with

[8] Cf. No. 7, n. 6.

201

Mr. Lloyd George and M. Theunis that in certain cases the Reparation Commission had a juridical status. In such cases they could not give imperative [instructions], but in matters relating to the application of the treaty the Governments had the right to give instructions to their delegate, and each delegate was made responsible to his own Government under the very terms of the treaty. He thought he could remember a time when the British Government did not favour too much liberty being given to the delegates. They had even objected to their making statements to the press.

Mr. LLOYD GEORGE, during the interpretation, interpolated that the reason for this was that the delegates on the Reparation Commission were in a position similar to that of judges, who, in Great Britain, could not make statements to the press.

M. POINCARÉ, continuing his main statement, said that the British action in this matter restored him to full liberty, and now he could say that he thought the British Government was right and that the members of the Reparation Commission were under the orders of their Government, except on such matters as the adjournment of payments, in which they were judges.

Mr. LLOYD GEORGE said that they were judges in the first instance, but that the Governments had to express their assent or dissent.

M. POINCARÉ said he would go rather further than Mr. Lloyd George. The Governments, for example, could dismiss their representatives on the Reparation Commission.

Mr. LLOYD GEORGE agreed that they could do so under clause 21 of the annex, which made the members of the commission responsible to the Governments.

M. POINCARÉ said that they adjudicated in the first instance. If the Reparation Commission were unwilling to declare Germany in default the Governments had no means to bring this about.

Mr. LLOYD GEORGE said that the only means was by appointing new members of the commission.

M. POINCARÉ said that the French Parliament was strongly of his opinion. He had only recently been asked by a Deputy to remind the French delegate of the existence of article 12 of annex 2, and he had had to write to the representative on the Reparation Commission on this subject. Nearly every day he found it necessary to send instructions to the French delegate. The Chamber was always asking him to have some instructions given. The Allies at this moment were trying to agree on joint instructions.

Mr. LLOYD GEORGE said he was afraid it was impossible to carry the matter much further. They would have to have a full meeting. The Italian delegation were uneasy as to what was going on and had been asking for news all day. He felt they must have a plenary session. There was a very fundamental difference between the British and French delegations. He had sent M. Poincaré's various proposals up to the Treasury during the meeting and they took rather a strong view against them. Sir Robert Horne had said that the application of article 248 was a matter for the Reparation Commission, and he himself believed that that was the case. M. Poincaré was trying to drive a distinction between default and wilful default. He represented that the Governments could act under a mere default, but the Reparation Commission could only act under a wilful default. He did not think [he] was right in this. Article 248 gave the Allies the rights of a mortgagee. Article 18 of annex 2 of part VIII provided for sanctions. He did not see any distinction between the two. He was willing to refer the question to the Reparation Commission. He was prepared to have the commission here in London to discuss the matter. They had the perfect right of access to the commission, and he would be very willing to see the commission invited to come and discuss the matter and get their view. He objected, however, to giving instructions to the members of the commission. They had no right to do this. He had just received a further note from the Treasury, and their notes seemed to be getting stronger and stronger on these matters. Sir John Bradbury held that the Allies had no right to exercise the powers under article 248 until a default had been declared under the treaty by the Reparation Commission. If this was the case, it would be breaking the treaty to take action under this article.

M. Poincaré said he must acknowledge that he was entirely of a different opinion. Only that morning the British Government had been of his opinion, because in article 10 of the British proposals they favoured giving instructions to the Reparation Commission in a case where unanimity was essential.

Mr. Lloyd George said that the Governments had the right to advise and suggest, but not to give instructions. If article 10 was so drafted as to give instructions, he must admit that this was not justified.

M. Poincaré said that paragraph 10, to which he would revert later, used an imperative form to the Reparation Commission. If Mr. Lloyd George would like, they could leave the present subject of discussion and work through articles 9 and 10 of the British draft.

M. Theunis, reverting to articles 7 and 8, said that there was so much discrepancy between the British and French points of view that Mr. Lloyd George seemed to have come to the conclusion they could not continue the discussion. They now knew the views of both sides. Mr. Lloyd George, before lunch, had made certain proposals, and M. Poincaré had given his views that afternoon. He himself had tried to reconcile the two points of view. Except that he wished to refer the matter to experts, Mr. Lloyd George had appeared to have no objection to his view. He asked M. Poincaré to give his opinion.

M. Poincaré said that it could only be considered as a possible basis of compromise if it was not subjected to the condition of ascertaining definitely that Germany was in default.

M. Theunis said he was trying to put together, first, Mr. Lloyd George's proposal to delegate to the Committee of Guarantees the produce of the mines, and, second, the idea of having a first call on the coal under article 248, so as to get deliveries in kind. At first sight Mr. Lloyd George had seemed to have no objection, subject to examination by experts, and M. Poincaré perhaps would agree that a recommendation could be made to the Reparation Commission to be put in operation within a definite time.

MR. LLOYD GEORGE said that at the morning meeting he had reserved the possibility of difficulties owing to the States owning the properties. He then read the following note he had received from Sir Robert Horne, which he rather thought emanated from Sir John Bradbury:—

'The German Government could not accept this without prior consent of Prussia, Bavaria, Saxony, which actually own these properties. It would need legislation and would make the internal dispute with Bavaria still more acute.[9] There is grave doubt whether article 248 could legally be construed to justify such a measure, and it certainly gives no power to manage the properties, whatever that may mean.'

If the German Government could not give control over the forests, perhaps the same idea could be stated in the form of their giving an equivalent. He suggested that that idea should be examined at the same time. It did not matter to the Allies whether it was the equivalent or the actual proceeds of the forests and mines that were paid into the account. He did not object to M. Theunis's further proposal to examine the question of a first call on the coal of the mines. He did not object to that, combined with a recommendation to the Reparation Commission.

He then pointed out the difficulty which would arise. Supposing the Bavarian Government was to refuse the order from the Reichs Government and was to refuse to pay. The Allies could not bring pressure on Prussia to obtain payment from Bavaria, but would have to bring pressure on Bavaria itself, which would be very difficult. This would be avoided by adopting his proposal to put it in the form of an equivalent.

M. POINCARÉ said he knew of the difficulties between the Reich and Bavaria. Germany, however, was centralised and the Allies only knew the Reich. It was the Reich they would approach in regard to article 248 of the Treaty. He said that after discussion with M. de Lasteyrie he had tried to put Mr. Lloyd George's thought into words, and the following was the result which did not represent his (M. Poincaré's) views, but which he set out as an indication of the attitude taken by Mr. Lloyd George:—

'In consideration of the moratorium granted to Germany as well as in order to guarantee the execution of the programme of deliveries of timber and coal the Reparation Commission will exercise supervision of the fiscal mines of the Ruhr and of the forests belonging to German States with a view to ensuring the complete execution of the deliveries of timber and coal as fixed by the Reparation Commission.

'The surplus of the receipts shall be paid into a special account at the Reichsbank in the name of the Committee of Guarantees, all this prejudicing in no way the rights held by the Reparation Commission under article 248.'

MR. LLOYD GEORGE asked if the discussion of articles 7 and 8 might be adjourned to enable him to ascertain if there was any objection in principle

[9] Cf. Nos. 262, 264, and 305, below.

to this proposal. He was most anxious to meet M. Poincaré if possible. He suggested that they should continue by the discussion of articles 9 and 10 of the British draft while he sent M. Poincaré's draft to Sir Robert Horne to obtain an expression of opinion.

M. Poincaré then read article 9 of the British draft. He objected to the words in the middle of paragraph 9: 'The German Government shall undertake to give effect'. He thought it would be better to omit the words underlined.

Mr. Lloyd George said that M. Poincaré had shown him that they had gone too far in regard to the wording relating to the Reparation Commission. He had used this wording to try and meet the Belgian point of view, but he thought that to adopt this wording would be only to add to their difficulties, and he suggested that the sentence should begin as follows: 'The Reparation Commission and the Committee of Guarantees shall be invited to direct their attention to,' &c.

M. Poincaré and M. Theunis agreed to this.

Mr. Lloyd George then said he would not object to leaving out the words 'undertake to'. This was adopted.

M. Poincaré then adverted to article 10, some points of which he found obscure.

Mr. Lloyd George suggested that the opening sentence should read, 'Subject to the acceptance by the German Government of these guarantees the Reparation Commission will be recommended to grant a moratorium,' &c.

M. Poincaré said that he would never recommend the Reparation Commission to grant a moratorium. He might put up with a moratorium, but he would never recommend it.

M. Theunis suggested the following wording, 'Subject to the acceptance by the German Government of those guarantees it will be for the Reparation Commission to grant,' &c.

Mr. Lloyd George agreed.

M. Poincaré said that so far the article was all right, but that there were other difficulties. He thought that the article as worded would be likely to have dangerous results equivalent, first, to tearing up the schedules of May 1921,[10] second, to suppressing the totality of the fixed annuities, and, third, to a reduction in the amount of the claims. He then alluded to differences between the British and French texts in the phrase 'shall as soon as possible fix the annual payments in cash in respect of all treaty charges for the succeeding period'. The British wording would appear to include payments under the clearing house scheme and the costs of occupation.

Mr. Lloyd George said that had not been intended.

M. Theunis said that in any event the sentence was too long.

M. Poincaré [said that he had not spoken yet of the clearing house scheme which was not part of reparations, but they would have to exchange views on this also. He confessed that he did not understand this article 10, which

<hr/>

[10] See No. 5, n. 2.

had appeared to him to involve a reduction of German payments in cash. In view of the technical character of this article he thought it should be referred to the Experts Committee.

Mr. LLOYD GEORGE agreed.]

M. POINCARÉ suggested therefore that instead of holding a plenary meeting on the following day they should first bring the experts together.

Mr. LLOYD GEORGE agreed.

M. THEUNIS raised the question of the time.

Mr. LLOYD GEORGE then sent a message asking Sir Robert Horne to join the meeting.

M. THEUNIS pressed strongly for a meeting that evening.

M. POINCARÉ was quite agreeable, but asked that there might be a meeting of experts on the morrow also. He also asked that M. Fromageot[11] might attend the meeting to give an interpretation of article 248.

Mr. LLOYD GEORGE agreed and directed Sir Maurice Hankey to invite Mr. Malkin[12] also to attend.

Sir Robert Horne entered at this point.

Mr. Lloyd George explained to Sir Robert Horne that it was proposed that the experts should meet the same evening to go through the British draft, their special attention being drawn to articles 7, 8 and 10. M. Fromageot and Mr. Malkin should be present to advise as to article 248 of the treaty. He hoped that the experts would start that evening and continue on the following day. There was also a point for the experts to consider which M. de Lasteyrie wished to raise concerning the exportation of capital.

It was agreed that the experts should meet at 9 p.m. that evening.

(A copy of the British proposals, revised in accordance with the above meeting, the alterations to which have been underlined, was prepared for the use of the experts at their meeting at 9 p.m., and is attached as an appendix.[13])

2, Whitehall Gardens, London, August 11, 1922.

APPENDIX TO No. 62

A.J. 364 (Revise)]

Reparation: Revise by Committee of Allied Experts of the Document discussed by the Allied Prime Ministers at the Meetings held on August 10 and 11, 1922 (Communicated by Cabinet Offices; received in Foreign Office, August 16)

[*C 11634/99/18*]

Confidential   *August 12, 1922*

NOTE.—Deletions made by the Committee from the document as submitted to them (see Appendix[14] to I.C.P. 251 F)[15] are shown in square brackets. Additions by the Committee are in *italics*.

[11] Legal Adviser to the French Ministry of Foreign Affairs.
[12] Assistant Legal Adviser to the Foreign Office.
[13] Not printed. The text printed below is a revise by the Allied experts.
[14] See n. 13.   [15] No. 62.

Secret.

The obligations imposed upon Germany by the Schedule of Payments of the [5]th May, 1921,[10] have not been fulfilled. The cash payments due under the schedule were only effected in full during 1921, and the German Government has now expressed its inability to continue the reduced cash payments fixed for 1922, and has in fact demanded a moratorium in respect of all cash payments up to the 31st December, 1924.[6] The deliveries of coal and of timber required by the Allied Governments and ordered by the Reparation Commission have not been effected in full. The German Government has, since the armistice, balanced its budgets by the issue of Treasury Bills and covered its payments by the increase of the fiduciary circulation, thus depreciating the mark and destroying its gold value. Meanwhile, it has incurred large expenditure *especially on public works which were not urgent and* on subsidies, which it has only recently taken steps to abolish.

The Allied Governments will only agree to the grant of a further moratorium to the German Government if effective guarantees are secured that these conditions will not recur. These guarantees are as follows:—

1. The German Government shall proceed to the execution of all the measures which *have been or* may be required by the Reparation Commission to ensure the full autonomy of the Reichsbank [and shall give the Reparation Commission the fullest power of scrutiny to ensure the efficacy of these measures].

2. The German Government shall forthwith proceed to carry out the decisions of the Reparation Commission and the Committee of Guarantees with regard to the measures required to secure an effective control of the arrangements made for keeping down the floating debt. It shall further carry out the decisions of the Reparation Commission and the Committee of Guarantees with regard to the measures required for putting a complete stop at an early date to further increases in the floating debt and for beginning its reduction, and shall submit *as soon as possible to the Reparation Commission the proposals already requested in the Commission's letter of the 14th June, 1922,*[16] *with a view to limiting the fiduciary circulation and stabilising the German currency* [as soon as possible to the Reparation Commission the proposals already requested by the commission with a view to the reform and stabilisation of the German currency].

3. The German Government shall continue to collect the levy payable in gold or foreign currencies amounting to at least *25 per cent.* [26 per cent.] of the total value of German exports. The proceeds of this levy shall be paid into an account in the Reichsbank standing in the name of the Committee of Guarantees.

The Committee of Guarantees will be invited to strengthen the supervision which it exercises over the value of German exports, especially by making use in the occupied territory of the present supervision of export licences, so long as it is in operation.

[This was adopted in place of the article 3 proposed by M. Poincaré for consideration by the Committee of Experts:—

'La Commission des Réparations sera invitée à fortifier le contrôle qu'exerce le Comité de Garanties sur la perception du prélèvement sur le 26 pour cent. notamment en utilisant dans les pays occupés le contrôle existant des licences d'exportation.']

4. The produce of all German import and export duties other than the levy shall be paid monthly to a special account at the Reichsbank which shall be under

[16] See No. 49, n. 9.

207

the scrutiny of the Committee of Guarantees. The German Government shall have the disposal of the sums standing to the credit of this account so long as the Reparation Commission is satisfied that the German Government fulfils the obligations that *have been or* may be imposed upon it *by the Reparation Commission.* If at any time the commission is not satisfied that this is the case, the Committee of Guarantees shall have the right to take over the sums standing to the credit of this account and to secure the payment to it of the produce of these duties thereafter.

[(The following additional paragraph was not adopted by the Committee of Experts:—4 (*a*). The Reparation Commission shall be invited to consider the permanent transfer of the Committee of Guarantees to Berlin.)]

5. The German Government shall carry into effect the arrangements that have been or may be made with the Committee of Guarantees for the supervision both of the receipts and of the expenditure of the budget, and shall give the representatives of that Committee the fullest facilities for investigating and reporting on all proposals affecting either side of the budget.

6. The German Government shall *before the 31st December, 1922* [forthwith] proceed to carry into effect the proposed legislation agreed upon with the Committee of Guarantees with a view to preventing the export of capital, and shall give the representatives of the Committee of Guarantees the fullest facilities for observing and reporting on the execution of this measure.

Paragraphs 7 and 8. No agreement was arrived at on these paragraphs. The original text was as follows:—

7. In the event of any failure to carry out the programme of timber deliveries fixed by the Reparation Commission for the restoration of the devastated areas or otherwise, the Reparation Commission shall consider the establishment by application of article 248 of the Treaty of Versailles of a supervision over the State forests so as to ensure the full execution of these deliveries.

8. In the event of failure to carry out the programme of coal deliveries the Reparation Commission shall similarly consider the establishment of a supervision over the State mines in the Ruhr.

The British and Japanese delegations accepted this text as it stood.

The Italian delegation proposed the substitution for these paragraphs of the following text:—

'In case of a default by Germany in the deliveries of coal and timber prescribed by the Reparation Commission, the Reparation Commission will be invited to establish a system of supervision over the State mines in the Ruhr and the public forests belonging to the German States, with a view to ensuring the complete execution of the coal and timber deliveries. This provision is without prejudice to the powers held by the commission in virtue of article 248 of the Treaty of Versailles.'

The Belgian delegation proposed the following text:—

'The Reparation Commission will collect and utilise the net profits of the State mines in the Ruhr and of the State forests in the same way as article 4 prescribed the collection and utilisation of the customs and export duties. If it considers it necessary the commission shall have power to give direct instructions to the director of these mines and forests as regards the destination of their output. In the event of these instructions not being strictly obeyed, the German Government shall cause the dismissal of the director and the appointment of a successor.

'Without prejudice to the exercise of the other rights which the commission possesses in virtue of article 248 of the Treaty of Versailles, the Reparation Commission in application of that article and on finding a default by Germany in the coal and timber deliveries prescribed by it, shall specially apply the first charge it possesses on the State mines in the Ruhr and in the State forests, by requiring the transfer of the property in these mines and forests to the commission.'

The French delegation proposed the following text:—

'In consideration of the moratorium granted to Germany, and with a view to guaranteeing the execution of the programme of coal and timber deliveries, the Reparation Commission shall exercise control over the State mines in the Ruhr and the public forests of the German States so as to ensure the complete execution of the deliveries of coal and timber. The surplus recipts from these undertakings shall be paid into a special account at the Reichsbank, standing in the name of the Committee of Guarantees.

'Without prejudice to the exercise of the rights which the Reparation Commission exercises in virtue of article 248 of the Treaty of Versailles, the Reparation Commission on finding a default by Germany in the deliveries of coal prescribed by it shall specially apply the first charge which article 248 gives to the Allied creditors on the State mines in the Ruhr by effecting the transfer of the property in these mines to the Reparation Commission as the representative of the Allied Government.'

9. The Reparation Commission and the Committee of Guarantees shall be invited to direct their attention to the measures to be taken to secure a real surplus of the receipts over the expenditure of the German budget, and the German Government shall give effect to the requirements of the Reparation Commission with a view to securing that such surplus shall be brought into existence at the earliest possible moment and to the maximum amount feasible.

Subject to the acceptance by the German Government of these guarantees it will be for the Reparation Commission to grant a moratorium in respect of all cash payments remaining due from Germany *on account of reparation* up to the 31st December, 1922 [and further the commission shall as soon as possible fix the annual payments in cash in respect of all Peace Treaty charges for the succeeding period at such an amount not exceeding 26 per cent. of the value of German exports as they may find to be proper with a view to the early flotation of a loan by the German Government, the major portion of which loan shall be devoted to the payment of reparation].

In lieu of the words in square brackets the British, Japanese and Belgian delegations accepted the following text:—

'The Reparation Commission will pronounce as soon as possible on the request made by Germany for a moratorium for the years 1923 and 1924, and will fix the annual payment to be made on account of reparations in the succeeding period at such amount as they may find proper with a view to the early flotation of a loan by the German Government the major portion of which shall be devoted to the payment of reparation.'

The Italian delegation proposed to invite the Reparation Commission to fix the cash payments of Germany after the 31st December, 1922, at an amount not exceeding 25 per cent. of the value of German exports, on the following conditions:—

(1) The moratorium should only be granted up to the 31st December, 1923.
(2) Deliveries in kind to the various Allies should be determined by the Reparation Commission at their discretion.
(3) The schedule of payment and the subsequent decisions of the Reparation Commission should remain in force.

The French delegation considered that no moratorium should at present be granted for the period after 31st December, 1922; they added the following declaration:—

'The French delegation state that they are as anxious as the other Allies that a loan should be issued as soon as possible in Allied and other countries, but they consider that it is impossible to prejudice by the grant of a moratorium for two years the general settlement of the question of reparation and inter-Allied debt.'

In regard to this declaration the British, Japanese and Belgian delegations took the view that their proposal did not prejudice the general question of reparation and of inter-governmental debts, and that the issue of a loan afforded the best if not the only prospect of getting any substantial payments on account of reparation.

[10] The Committee of Guarantees shall during the period of the moratorium, and to the extent decided upon by the Reparation Commission, transfer each week to the German Government the amounts standing to the credit of the account referred to in paragraph 3, so long as the Reparation Commission is satisfied that the German Government is carrying out the reforms required of it. If at any time the Reparation Commission is not satisfied that the German Government is fulfilling its obligations the Committee of Guarantees shall on receipt of notification from the Reparation Commission transfer to the Commission the sums standing to the credit of its account and all further sums paid to that account.

The following new paragraph was adopted:—

'As regards the cash payments due from Germany under sections III and IV of the economic clauses, the Allied Governments propose to require the payment by Germany of the 2,000,000*l.* due on the 15th August within four weeks from that date. As from that date they propose to denounce the agreement of the 10th June, 1921,[17] and to take steps to negotiate arrangements separately with the German Government for the settlement of any balances due to them under the economic clauses, any such arrangements being submitted for the prior approval of the Reparation Commission.'

---

[17] See Reparation Commission V, op. cit., p. 55. This agreement between the Allied Clearing Offices and the German Government settled the monthly payments to be made by Germany to these offices.

[1.C.P. 252.] *British Secretary's Notes of a Conversation held at 10, Downing Street, on Monday, August 14, 1922, at 11 a.m.*

PRESENT: *Belgium*: M. Theunis.

    British Empire: The Right Hon. D. Lloyd George, O.M., M.P., Prime Minister; SECRETARY: Sir Maurice Hankey.

    France: M. Poincaré; SECRETARY: M. Massigli.

    Italy: Signor Schanzer; SECRETARY: Count Vannutelli Rey.

    Japan: Baron Hayashi; SECRETARY: M. I. Tokugawa.

    INTERPRETER: M. Camerlynck.

Death of Lord Northcliffe[1]

1. MR. LLOYD GEORGE, at the outset of the meeting, said he had just received information of the death of Lord Northcliffe.

German Reparations

2. MR. LLOYD GEORGE asked whether the weekend had brought any useful reflections.

M. POINCARÉ said that his reflections were not of a very consoling and optimistic order. He had, rather, found that the Allies could not put themselves in agreement in regard to articles 7, 8 and 10 of what he would call the British counter-proposals.[2] He was even of opinion that it would be useless to take up the proposals on this subject again. On the previous day he had learned that Signor Schanzer had elsewhere made certain proposals to Mr. Lloyd George, which would have been to leave matters as they were; that is to say, there would be no moratorium for three months, after which they should resume the conversations under more satisfactory conditions, and perhaps contemplate more usefully and with better prospects of success the question of a loan to Germany, on the one hand, and of Inter-Allied debts on the other. Signor Schanzer, however, said that the British Government could not accept this, and so he did not see what could be done. To him the proposals seemed acceptable, because three payments of 50,000,000 M. each seemed to be something by no means unrealisable to Germany. With a little good-will she ought to be able to get round the corner. If, however, the proposals were to be modified and a provisional moratorium were to be granted to Germany during this interval, he could not accept it without *gages* and guarantees. He had always taken this position, and it was precisely on the question of *gages* and guarantees that they were in disagreement. It was true that the Allies [were in agreement on a part of the arrangement, but this only meant putting into operation something which had already been agreed.]* There was no new *gage* proposed. To accord a moratorium

---

* The text of the passages between square brackets is supplied from Confidential Print.

[1] Proprietor of *The Times*, and Director of Propaganda in Enemy Countries in 1918.

[2] See No. 62, Appendix.

without some new counterpart of guarantee was to give a favour to Germany without receiving anything in return, and was unacceptable to France.

Signor Schanzer placed on record that the Italian delegation had made every possible endeavour to reach an agreement, because it realised the serious consequences for the whole world if this was not achieved. In this spirit their representatives had tried, in the Committee of Experts, to bring about an approach with the French point of view on the question of guarantees. Disagreement, however, had been reached in regard to the questions of forests and mines. He had had a discussion with the Belgian delegates and M. Poincaré, and he had made [a proposal for using the forests as a guarantee.] This proposal did not prove acceptable. He had then advanced a proposal similar to what M. Poincaré had in mind, with a view to suspending the discussion, and to relegating to a later conference the whole question of reparations, inter-Allied debts, and guarantees, this new conference to be held in November, when the situation in Europe and the United States of America would be less aggressive. M. Poincaré and the Belgian delegates had seemed in favour of this, but M. Poincaré had laid down certain conditions. In particular, he would not concede in the interval any kind of moratorium. He had informed Mr. Lloyd George of this, and Mr. Lloyd George had said that he could not wholly accept a proposal of this kind because he had in mind the consequences of the next payments on the political and economic situation in Germany. He had also expressed an idea that the discussion should be suspended, but that they should remit to the Reparation Commission to discover to what extent Germany could [pay and face the next dates of payment.] This was not accepted by the French delegation. Today he had the honour to make another suggestion, which he had that morning made to Mr. Lloyd George, and had just hastily communicated to M. Poincaré (appendix). He would propose to delay the next two payments in cash, taking into consideration Mr. Lloyd George's apprehension that Germany could not continue to pay without very grave consequences. He had proposed to adjourn to a later date all M. Poincaré's proposals on which no agreement had been reached; also, immediately to put in operation all the guarantees proposed by M. Poincaré and accepted at this conference, remitting to a later conference all the proposals which were not yet agreed to. That was the proposal he had the honour to submit this morning. He had no particular authority to do so, but he wished to make an appeal to all to avoid drifting into a situation that would have the gravest consequences.

M. Poincaré said he would like to thank Signor Schanzer for making his proposal, but he was afraid he could not possibly accept it because, under this agreement, a moratorium would be granted for two months more without any new *gage* or guarantee, and the future would be compromised. As a counterpart he would only obtain the matters [*sic*] on which agreement had been reached the previous day, but all of which were covered by previous agreements.

Signor Schanzer pointed out there would be the 26 per cent. and the customs.

M. Poincaré said that both of these had been in the schedule of payments.[3] The control over the Reichsbank of fiduciary circulation had already been discussed for months by the Reparation Commission and had been decided. If a moratorium was to be granted to Germany he must repeat it could not be granted without some new counterpart. To accord a moratorium to Germany in other conditions would be to give to the world a proof of the weakness and complacency of the Allies and he could not take part in such a policy. As regards the proposal for an adjournment, he would lend himself to it very willingly and with a good heart; that is to say, to leave things as they are, to execute the control proposed by the Committee of Guarantees,[4] and at the same time not to accord a moratorium to Germany. Neither Signor Schanzer nor M. Theunis had appeared to have any objection to this on the previous day.

Signor Schanzer said he had reserved his liberty in the matter.

M. Poincaré said of course he realised this.

M. Theunis said that at the point which had been reached there were certain points, technical in appearance, on which there were opposing points of view. In order to try and avoid a rupture or separation without agreement, he would like to start rather further back and to examine the question from a general point of view. In the previous March the Allies had given a moratorium to Germany.[5] Without altering the total payments the moratorium was a transitional arrangement, and it was noticed that it was not a proper solution of the immediate difficulties, much less of the economic difficulties of Europe. The truth was that this question went a good deal beyond reparations and was a great question of inter-Allied policy. The question of the debts must be settled, for otherwise the economic unrest ('malaise') of Europe could not really be ameliorated. It had been decided at Cannes, and the Reparation Commission had agreed, that there should be convened a meeting of bankers.[6] This had been no new idea. It has been mooted for two or three year past. It was hoped, however, that it would enable Germany to reconstruct herself and to put her finances in order, and that the Allies, who were most pressed, would receive sums of which they had great need to enable them to carry out their reconstruction. The loan would be based on the future capacity of Germany to pay, and all were agreed that Germany had a great future capacity for payment. The question arose, therefore, as to whether we could discount the capacity for payment of this rich industrious country. The bankers had met.[7] He must admit that this first attempt had not succeeded, but in fact there had been great advantages in so much as it had resulted in posing the questions and in showing the difficulties. It was proved also that if a solution was to be reached the question must be examined comprehensively. Then the present meeting of London had been

[3] See No. 5, n. 2.

[4] In its correspondence with the German Government of July 18–21, 1922: see No. 61, n. 6.

[5] See Reparation Commission V, op. cit., pp. 154–5.   [6] See No. 19.

[7] See No. 27, n. 4.

arranged. He did not conceal that when he had heard that the questions were to be limited within such narrow bounds, he had not felt that there was very much hope of a successful issue. The position of the Belgian delegation was peculiar in so much as they were less concerned in inter-Allied debts, and on the other hand more interested than any other country in immediate payment by Germany. Consequently he [had a special discretion and particularly the object of trying to exact payments due for reparations].[8]

After alluding to the undesirability of a rupture of which he did not like to speak, M. Theunis said that he wished to approach the question not merely from the point of view of technical details such as forests and mines, but rather from that of general policy. The policy adopted had no real value unless accepted by the other side. There would be great value in any arrangement which was accepted by the other party as well. A sanction would have a double value if the arrangement had been accepted by both parties. Hence he very much regretted that the matter had been discussed on a very limited ground, that no agreement had been reached, and a dead point, that is to say, a deadlock had been arrived at. He then reviewed the position of the different countries towards dealing with the question comprehensively. England was absolutely convinced of the necessity of a general settlement, not only of reparations, but also of Allied debts. The Balfour note on the question of inter-Allied debts[9] which he himself could perhaps discuss in a wider spirit than some others, was not intended, he felt certain, to block the way to a general settlement, but to lead to a settlement later. He might add that France realised perfectly well the necessity for a general settlement on a much broader issue than a settlement with Germany alone and including all questions of debt. Italy was also of this point of view as he felt sure Signor Schanzer would agree.

Belgium was less interested in the question of debt, but realised that there was an unavoidable connection between all these questions. Belgium which was essentially an industrial country attached more importance than other countries to the establishment of economic peace in the world; consequently Belgium was more than ever convinced of the need of a general settlement because business suffered more from general doubt and uncertainty than from settled facts. He was persuaded therefore that the general question of reparations and all other questions could be dealt with more easily on the day on which they were considered on a higher level and from a more comprehensive standpoint. When that day was reached a solution would be found and the technical differences resulting from political differences and discrepancies would assume their proper importance and everything would fall into line in its proper place. Questions as to the control of forests or mines or the supervision of Germany, would then not prevent a settlement. In all sincerity M. Theunis thought it deplorable that it should be possible to have any question of a rupture between the Allies, not on some great matter, but

[8] A note to the text of the Confidential Print indicates that part of this statement was missed by the British Secretary.

[9] See No. 45.

arising out of an aspect of the question which appeared to be quite of secondary importance to the majority of mankind and the technical details of which only had importance in the eyes of the Allies because they showed two distinct lines of policy, of which the rest of the world could not understand the issue. Evidently, therefore, the conclusion of his remarks was that the question must be taken up from a higher standpoint. Perhaps the question had not been sufficiently prepared for this to be done immediately. Time must be gained. Perhaps two or three months hence it would be possible to produce a plan of a more general kind. Perhaps the contacts which were being established with the American Treasury might produce some supplementary ideas from which to get to work for the settlement of inter-Allied debts. Whether they accepted the British or the French proposal, it would only be a temporary solution. It would not give the Allies much to live on, but it would maintain a general peace for three months and then they could see whether they could not settle the questions with a better chance of winning the prize they desired, namely, the economic peace of Europe. It was worth running a risk to achieve that. Let them, therefore, gain a few months and at the end of this they would try and reach a final agreement. Was it not possible, he asked, to find some provisional solution for three months? Naturally for a provisional solution it would be necessary to be less hard on Germany than for a permanent solution. There was, of course, the risk which M. Poincaré had foreseen that a provisional agreement might commit the Allies as to the future. He agreed that that was true unless they kept in mind the necessity for a more general arrangement and did not merely regard the matter from the point of view of the monthly payments. He had indicated just now that Belgium had a difficult situation in this respect. He had indicated that in spite of internal difficulties and the need for the Belgian priority, the Belgians would put the maintenance of the Entente above this question. He did not wish to be misunderstood. In no discussion had he ever pronounced the word 'priority'. He merely wished to convince his colleagues of the necessity of a solution and of making sacrifices to reach one. He need not emphasise the economic upheavals which would be created if agreement was not reached and if separate action were taken by one party and separate arrangements made. Moreover, the political and economic points of view were much mixed up. If separate action was taken by any of the Allies the effects might last a long time and prolong the economic difficulties from which the world was suffering. Moreover, such action would make a future agreement infinitely more difficult to reach and, what was most serious of all, would destroy the confidence of the world. It was because of lack of confidence that the world was undergoing so much economic difficulty.

MR. LLOYD GEORGE said he would be prepared to prolong the discussion if he was sure that there was any chance of reaching accord, but after M. Poincaré's reception of Signor Schanzer's proposal, he thought the last ray of hope had disappeared and that nothing was to be gained by prolonging the discussion. As to Signor Schanzer's proposal he would have accepted it in principle, though he would have made some suggestions in regard to it.

It was no use his doing so, however, because M. Poincaré had not been able to accept it. It was idle to discuss the continuation of the conference if the Allies were demanding the continuation of a payment which they knew Germany could not pay. Was the conference to demand that Germany should pay 50,000,000 gold marks for reparations and perhaps another 50,000,000 for the liquidation of private debts? It was evident that Germany could not pay these; on the other hand if Germany failed to effect the payment, what were the Allies to do in the meantime? Were they to allow the German default to continue without taking any action, or were they to take sanctions? It was idle to talk of an adjournment for three months without any solution of what was the most urgent problem before them. So far as Great Britain was concerned, he would leave the matter to the treaty. There was a machinery provided in the treaty for dealing with a situation of this kind. If the treaty was broken it would be a serious matter which would have to be taken into account. If, however, the Allies could not agree among themselves there remained the Treaty of Versailles which contained most elaborate provision for a situation of this kind. Hence he would propose a plenary meeting for the afternoon to which they would have to report their failure to come to agreement and take note of the consequent situation. There was one personal point on which he wished to make an explanation. He had seen it suggested that in leaving London at 5.30 o'clock on Saturday he had been guilty of some discourtesy to the other members of the conference. He felt sure that this was not their view. He had notified his colleagues beforehand. He recalled that in this country there were many people who objected to work on Sunday, and questions had even been asked in Parliament on the subject. An exceptionally strenuous Parliamentary session had only just concluded when this conference had begun. A few weeks before Mr. Chamberlain's health had broken down and he had been absent for three weeks, during which Mr. Lloyd George had had to undertake much of his duty. He had a strong physique, and no doubt he might have worked throughout a Sunday conference. If he had thought that his colleagues felt it was any discourtesy to them his not doing so, he would never have left London. It was alleged that the discourtesy was increased by his having played a game of golf. This was wholly untrue. The only pleasurable circumstance to alleviate his Sunday had been two hours' conversation with Signor Schanzer on the question of reparations. For the rest he had done little but contemplate the greyness of British skies. He had, however, also felt that there would be some advantage in twenty-four hours for reflection in the difficult position that had been reached. He would now propose that they should meet in the afternoon at any time which suited his colleagues. He ended by asking Baron Hayashi to speak.

Baron Hayashi said he noticed the endeavours of the Prime Ministers of the Powers concerned to come to an agreement. If they were unable to do so, he could only express his great regret. It seemed to him that a conference of a general character concerning the appraisement of the German debt and inter-Allied debts would be useful. It might prove that their present difficulties under articles 7 and 8 of the British counter-proposals were merely temporary. If the Reparation Commission was trusted, why should they not refer the matter to that commission? He gathered that there were Belgian, French and Italian proposals, as well as the British proposals, in which the Japanese expert had concurred. Why should not these be remitted to the Reparation Commission to consider? There only remained article 10 of the British counter-proposals. If they were to agree that a general conference should take place, the French view, as he understood it, would seem to be accepted, namely, that a moratorium for 1923–24 could not be granted unless a conference took place. Hence, if his humble opinion was taken, he thought that they might find some final solution. If no solution could be reached, it would be very regrettable.

MR. LLOYD GEORGE at this point read the following telegram received from Paris recording a communication[10] sent by the Reparation Commission this morning to the German Government:—

> 'Notwithstanding the hope expressed in its letter of the 13th July,[11] the commission is not in a position to notify its views before the 15th August or its decision on your memorandum of the 12th July.[12] It will, however, acquaint you of its decision at a very early date, and will at the same time settle the question of the payment due on the 15th August, which will be suspended until a decision has been taken.'

M. POINCARÉ said it was hardly necessary for him to say—and he was sure he was speaking for all those present—that he had not seen any act of discourtesy in Mr. Lloyd George's absence on Sunday. Mr. Lloyd George had had the kindness to consult him on Saturday morning on the matter, and he had agreed. In the circumstances, he quite understood Mr. Lloyd George's wish to conform to the traditions of his country in regard to the observation of the Sabbath. In France also they liked to enjoy a weekly rest. He thought, however, that the Sunday's rest had not been particularly enjoyable either to Mr. Lloyd George or himself, owing to the very serious matters with which they had been faced. He was quite agreeable to their making an affirmation of their regrettable disagreement at a plenary session in the afternoon, although he saw no necessity for it. [He must say one word as to one of Mr. Lloyd George's remarks, which seemed to suggest that he was responsible for this disagreement. After Signor Schanzer's proposal had been rejected, it had been useless to continue the discussion. He himself had refused Signor Schanzer's last proposal only after his own proposal had been rejected. His own proposal had not seemed so bad to Signor Schanzer or M. Theunis at the time. He realised, however, that Signor Schanzer had reserved liberty of action, and that no engagement had been taken by either party.[13]

[10] A copy of this communication was received in the Foreign Office on August 17 (C 11673/99/18).

[11] See No. 38, n. 4.   [12] See No. 36 and No. 38, n. 1.

[13] A note to the text of the Confidential Print read: 'This speech, which was very rapidly delivered and translated, was imperfectly understood.'

As regards Signor Schanzer's proposal of that morning (appendix), if Mr. Lloyd George had found it reasonable he would have accepted it, but apparently he did not. He thanked Signor Schanzer for his effort to bring about an agreement. Mr. Lloyd George did not think that Germany could pay for the next three months. Yesterday Signor Schanzer, M. Theunis and he had rather come to the conclusion that Germany could pay.

SIGNOR SCHANZER nodded assent.

Continuing, M. POINCARÉ said he was not reproaching Signor Schanzer. He was not trying to maintain ideas that were ridiculous, but ideas which the previous day had seemed sensible. He could not accept any responsibility for the present rupture. On the previous day he had gone to the extreme limits of conciliation. However, nothing which he had asked for at London had been granted to France.]

SIGNOR SCHANZER said it was indispensable for him to give a little more detail of what had happened on the previous day. He had never made any suggestion that M. Poincaré's proposals were ridiculous. He must recall the facts. On the previous morning M. Poincaré, the Belgian delegates and he had consulted, and he had dwelt on the necessity for reaching practical conclusions. He had then put forward a proposal to adjourn for a new conference in November, to which should be put all the outstanding questions. That had been his proposal. The exclusion of a moratorium had been a limitation proposed by M. Poincaré to the idea which he himself had put forward. He did not say he would refuse to put this to Mr. Lloyd George. If M. Poincaré did him justice, he would remember that he had raised the same objection as Mr. Lloyd George, namely, that Germany could not pay.

M. POINCARÉ said he did not recollect this, but if Signor Schanzer was sure of this, he had no doubt he was correct.

SIGNOR SCHANZER said he could assure him frankly that he had made these observations as to Germany's capacity to pay, and that he had added that it would be difficult for him to get Mr. Lloyd George to accept. He merely said this to show that his idea had been a plan for a future conference, and he was still of the same opinion.

M. THEUNIS [said he would like to add a few words to drive away any possible misunderstanding. When at the conference the previous day it had been discovered that it was impossible to reconcile the British and French points of view in regard to forests and coal, they had looked round for something else, and it had occurred to them that a conference might meet three months hence to consider the question as a whole. M. Poincaré had said that, unless he could get the essential guarantees, he could not accede to a moratorium. The disagreement on this subject accounted for the misunderstanding between M. Poincaré and Signor Schanzer. In another private conversation, after he had reflected on the situation, he had suggested that perhaps the difficulties in regard to the German payments during the three months might be avoided by some system similar to that adopted in May 1921, and that, instead of paying in cash, Germany should hand over three months' bills. His idea was that in three months the Allies could arrive at some general arrangement, and in that case Germany would have no difficulty in honouring the bills, because there would be such an improvement in the situation that these payments would become insignificant; or, alternatively, there might be no agreement, either of a general or particular character, and in that case the situation would neither be better nor worse. Hence, they had tried every effort at compromise, and had suggested an adjournment.]

Mr. Lloyd George said that as M. Poincaré did not think it necessary to have a plenary session, he thought it was essential there should be no misunderstanding as to what the points are on which the break was arising, so he would indicate the British point of view. He wished to make it clear, not only that the British Government accepted the proposal to adjourn the question until November, but that they had not desired the present meeting. They had thought it was premature to meet until the Reparation Commission had adjudicated upon the whole position. They would have preferred to hold the meeting later. For that reason they approved the principle of an adjournment. They also approved it for the reason given by Signor Schanzer, namely, that by that time the position of the United States of America would be better known. France had already sent a representative to America.[14] Great Britain would be sending the Chancellor of the Exchequer[15] very shortly, and, he understood, Signor Schanzer was also sending a representative. These representatives could not return until November. The American Secretary of State[16] would not be back at Washington until the end of October, as he had gone on a visit to South America. It was impossible to settle the question of the American debts without him. This would take a long time, especially as an election was pending in America, which would distract the attention of the politicians. Hence the delegates to Washington would not be back before November.[17] He would have been very glad when they returned to have met again to discuss the question, taking higher ground, as M. Theunis said, and making a more comprehensive survey. The question was: What was the situation in the meantime? If Germany could pay, why was the present conference being held? If there was a wilful default, then the Reparation Commission could declare this. If the default was not wilful, then why were they all in London to discuss whether Germany could pay 50,000,000 gold marks a month? What was the use of getting more paper from Germany? It would merely increase the stacks of paper which these conferences had produced. He was prepared, on behalf of the British Government, to leave to the Reparation Commission the settlement of the question. The machinery of the treaty left such questions to the Reparation Commission

[14] M. Parmentier, Director of the General Handling of Funds of the French Ministry of Finance.

[15] By the time the British mission left England (December 1922), Mr. Stanley Baldwin had become Chancellor of the Exchequer.

[16] Mr. Hughes.

[17] On the negotiations on behalf of the World War Debt Commission for the Settlement or Refunding of Debts Owed the United States by Foreign Governments, see *F.R.U.S.* 1922, vol. i, pp. 396–417, and 1923, vol. i, pp. 272–7.

to settle after they had heard what the Germans had to say. His proposal would be to adjourn until the representatives of the three countries had come back from the United States of America. The British Chancellor of the Exchequer would have to be back by November for his own duties. The British Government could agree to a meeting the moment they came back. In the meantime it was necessary to decide if Germany could continue to pay the 50,000,000 gold marks. The Reparation Commission could discuss that. The mark was at about 4,000 to the £ sterling. He could not say how much to the dollar. The British proposal was that this should be decided by the Reparation Commission. It was true that under the Balfour note payments from the Allies would fall due. Certainly, however, this could be put off until the discussion on the general question took place and no payment would be required till then. That, at any rate, would not aggravate the problem. To leave things as they were meant a default by Germany, and in the meanwhile someone might be taking separate action. Much had been said of the British objections. Great Britain had no objection except to bringing trouble and chaos without obtaining any compensation. Great Britain had no objection to making Germany pay everything she could. The difficulty was to find out how much she could pay. M. Theunis said that the Allies had had many makeshifts, but had never settled what Germany could pay. He would ask frankly, why? The British Government were blamed in Great Britain because they were alleged to have agreed under French pressure to things which they really knew Germany could not carry out; in fact, that they had agreed to what M. Theunis called a makeshift. That was the accusation in Great Britain. What was the accusation in France— he did not know whether M. Poincaré had or had not made it himself— anyhow the suggestion was that France would have received great sums in reparation but for the objections of Great Britain; that Great Britain had prevented them from receiving their fair due. That was the view which French opinion held. The views were irreconcilable. If France knew some way in which she could get reparations from Germany without loss, let her get them. The British Government could not go with them, because they were convinced that if France embarked on that course she would not get the tons of gold she thought that Great Britain was hindering her from getting. He would have been very glad to have tried to reconcile the two points of view. It was no use trying, however, to reconcile them. He had been trying for three years, and it was only in order to avoid a rupture that he had given way against his better judgment time after time. He was suffering the reproaches of his friends in England because he had given way, and of France because he had not given way along the whole line. If France thought that she could get more, he was convinced that it was necessary to let her be disillusioned in her own way. In the war he had been one of those who, in the interests of the common victory, had worked very closely with French Ministers, and he would be deeply grieved to see a failure now to reach agreement. He had always been an advocate of close working together of the British and French democracies. He had advocated this for thirty or forty years before the war, and it was still his opinion. He was deeply grieved at the thought of any estrangement between two democracies whose ideas were alike in so many respects and both of whom could claim to be the guardians of liberty. It would be a disaster not only to themselves, but to the whole world that, merely for a question of a four months' moratorium, they should destroy an alliance that had meant so much and had cost so dear. The following were the four proposals of the British Government:—

1. An adjournment of the conference until the return of the Allied delegates from the United States of America.
2. In the meanwhile the question of German payments, until the conference took a decision, should be left to the Reparation Commission.
3. The guarantees decided upon by the Committee of Guarantees to be put into effect immediately.
4. During the interval no demands to be made for payment of interest on inter-Allied debts.

M. POINCARÉ said he feared that Mr. Lloyd George had misunderstood one of his remarks. He had said that he had no objection to a plenary session, only he did not see the necessity for it. They could not expect to reach agreement today. In that event, in a plenary session they would merely say in set speeches what they had discussed already in greater familiarity in this smaller meeting. The position would not be improved by a plenary conference, and he did not see any particular object in it. If, however, his colleagues pressed for such a meeting he would not refuse, though he regarded it as waste of time. Also, he had not said that he had objections to a general conference on reparations and Allied loans. His position was that he could not accept it if it involved the status quo with a continuation of the moratorium admitted in March and a new moratorium, unless certain conditions were fulfilled. Mr. Lloyd George's suggestion to remit the question of German monthly payments to the Reparation Commission seemed to him to be illusory. The commission would merely reproduce in itself the difficulties encountered at this table, unless the delegates received instructions. Why had they met on this occasion? Mr. Lloyd George had said that he had not been in favour of the meeting and that he himself had been. France asked that either they should refuse the moratorium until the end of the year, or that it should only be granted against new *gages* and guarantees. There it seemed they could not agree. He doubted if they ought to employ the word 'disagreement' ('désaccord'). There was a difference of opinion on one specific point. What was the result? Either that France must agree in the British view or that it must keep to its own opinion. There was no other consequence. France kept her own opinion and could not accept that of Great Britain. Mr. Lloyd George had spoken of French opinion as democratic. French opinion was democratic. He belonged to a country that had adopted democracy right through. He was the only representative there of a country which had become a republic and had carried democracy to extreme limits. Hence, France would yield to no one and would learn lessons from no one in regard to democracy. He himself in particular had always been a strong believer in the friendship of the two democracies. He had never entertained any other thought, and he had spoken to all parties and on all occasions to the effect that it would be infinitely deplorable if any estrangement arose between the two countries. He had never entertained the thought that France could obtain more alone than she could with her Allies. He had always thought it would be much more difficult, and he would repeat this. As for the Entente, he had given proofs of his attachment and fidelity to the Anglo-French Entente. He had had thirty-five years of political life, even longer than that of Mr. Lloyd George, and he had always cultivated the idea of the Entente. Moreover, he had served the alliance for even longer than Mr. Lloyd George. He had assisted in the *Accord* of 1912, of which Mr. Lloyd George had spoken, and in 1912 and 1913 he had done his best to defend it.[18] In the course of the war, Mr. Lloyd George had given many examples of courage and he thanked him for them. He had, however, perhaps served the common cause himself with as much fidelity. What would France do tomorrow or the day after? He had heard the word 'disagreement' used. The Government would deliberate. It had taken no decision. He could not agree to discuss decisions that had not yet been taken. He simply stood by his opinion and claimed the right to exercise it.

SIGNOR SCHANZER said that if there were to be no plenary session he must ask permission to make a declaration. He observed with pleasure that M. Poincaré had excluded the idea of a rupture and had given an interpretation which indicated that there was no rupture, but merely a divergence of view on a particular point.

M. POINCARÉ observed that it might lead to a different line of action.

SIGNOR SCHANZER said that, anyhow, M. Poincaré's declaration tended to tranquillise matters and to prevent the present disagreement having the character of a rupture. They had discussed a definitely limited question, namely, the grant of a short moratorium to Germany, and proposals had been multiplied for trying to alleviate it. He would declare, on behalf of Italy, that he did not despair that another conference might be proposed later. He thanked Mr. Lloyd George that he had practically accepted the idea of convening such a conference. He would express the hope that M. Poincaré would not exclude it from his mind. M. Poincaré had said that he would accept a moratorium only on certain conditions. He would ask him not to let this prejudice the idea of a meeting, after the lapse of a few months, to consider the question of reparations and Allied debts together. This view corresponded to Italian public opinion. Signor Schanzer then read the following declaration:—

> 'It will be necessary to consider this problem in its whole. If we do not find, within the shortest possible time, a satisfactory solution to this problem, it will be vain to hope for the accomplishment of the European

[18] See G. P. Gooch and H. W. V. Temperley, *British Documents on the Origins of the War 1898–1914*, Vol. X, Part II, Chap. XCVI.

pacification or to believe that confidence between the nations may grow again, or that Europe may come back to a normal and settled economical life. Certainly, the condition of the vanquished peoples is difficult, and it is fair to give them facilities, within the limits of the possible, for the fulfilment of their engagements arising from the treaties. But it is not less fair and indispensable to consider the plight of the countries which, even belonging to the group of nations that won the war, have more bitterly suffered from the economic consequences of the war itself.

'As I have said in one of our previous sittings, the reparations question is closely connected with the question of the inter-Allied debts. One can even say that today one great question dominates and weighs upon European life: the general question of the debts. So long as this question will be unsolved Europe will not be able to breathe freely, and a true economical, as well as political, *détente* in Europe will not be possible.

'The debts in question cannot be considered as the ordinary debts between business people. Lord Balfour has rightly exposed this idea in his note.[19] Debts have been contracted—Lord Balfour has said—and loans have been floated not in the particular interest of one State or of another, but for a great aim, common to all, which has been reached. The question, then, is—we can add—of means put in common for a common enterprise. Every one of the Allies, having contracted loans, has not spent their amount only in its own interest, but in the interest also of the other Allies and Associated [Powers].

'Moreover, this amount has been almost exclusively spent in the countries which had granted the loans, and not for productive purposes in the debtor countries. Everybody desires that the European reconstruction could be accomplished, but this reconstruction is to remain a formula devoid of value if we have not the courage to tackle the problem of the reparations and of the inter-Allied debts in their close connection and to solve it in a fair manner. When the war broke out Italy was not attacked, and found herself not in need to defend herself from enemies. The Italian neutrality saved the common cause of the Allies. Afterwards Italy joined the Allies in the war at one of the gravest moments of the immense struggle.[20] As it was then looked forward to [*sic*], the war seemed to be of short duration, and Italy only asked Great Britain for a loan of £50,000,000. Today the Italian foreign debt, caused by the war, reaches £900,000,000 sterling. Italy has suffered during the war the most cruel sacrifices of lives and properties without obtaining, after the victory, any economic advantages. No country (considering the respective national wealth) has produced, during and for the war, an economic effort superior to that of Italy. It is only right that for us, and for the other countries which find themselves in conditions similar to ours, means should be found in order to avoid that peace should result in economic disaster and in the endless depreciation of our currency, depreciation which would not be either in the interest of the creditor countries.

[19] See No. 45.   [20] Italy had entered the war in 1915.

'The economic destruction of those who have fought for justice and liberty and who have won cannot be the final result of the great war. The nations which, thanks not only to their economic and industrial development but also to their intellectual and moral value, have raised themselves to the highest degree of power in the world, certainly have such deep feelings of fairness not to allow that such should be the final results of the war which ended with our common victory.'

Mr. LLOYD GEORGE said there would be no use in convening a conference if by that time each had gone his own way.

M. POINCARÉ said he would repeat, let each one try and march with the other, but at present their points of view were irreconcilable, and it was impossible for them to reach agreement. He did not give up hope that they might meet again in the future, and for his part he would be very happy to try, but for the moment they were revolving within the same circle. None of his proposals had been accepted, and it was impossible to reach a result.

Mr. LLOYD GEORGE said they were revolving in different circles.

M. POINCARÉ said they might try to bring their circles to the same centre.

M. THEUNIS said that Signor Schanzer had indicated the possibility of a future conference, but that did not seem enough. They must make sure that it was to happen if Europe was not to remain in its present economic situation. Mr. Lloyd George's observations, however, gave him some fears as to the prospects of such a conference taking place. The present circumstances were not very terrible in themselves, but raised rather sad reflections. It was not merely a difference of view, which could be ameliorated with time. Time in this case was the enemy. Three or four months might quite well prevent a solution of the problem, and might result in setting friends apart from one another. He would say friends because he had been so profoundly impressed with the words used successively by Mr. Lloyd George and M. Poincaré, who had done so much for victory in the common cause. These made him hope that a sincere effort would be made, not only to reconcile differences of view, but what was really a misunderstanding. M. Poincaré had said that he reserved his opinion, but he had not given any details.

M. POINCARÉ said he had not given details because the French Government had not deliberated.

M. THEUNIS said that the French Government would have to take its decision, but, given the gravity of the situation, unlike Signor Schanzer, he was not so reassured as to the probable results. He therefore begged the two parties before parting to find some means by which they could alleviate a situation which, he confessed, alarmed him.

M. POINCARÉ said he did not refuse, for his part, to reflect on the matter until the evening, but he did not see very much use in having a continuation of the present meeting, which would merely lead to repeating their respective standpoints. He would propose, therefore, to adjourn in quite a friendly way, and that each party should reflect separately on the situation. If no one could see any solution, he saw no object in meeting again. In any case he must reserve entirely his liberty, or rather the liberty of the French Government.

2, Whitehall Gardens, August 14, 1922.

APPENDIX

Signor Schanzer's Proposals

The conference could decide that every Government would give instructions to their representatives on the Reparation Commission—

(a) To grant to Germany a respite for cash payments of August and September. Consequently, Germany would pay only on the 15th October.

(b) This concession would be granted under the condition of the acceptance by Germany of the guarantees judged necessary by the Reparation Commission amongst those considered by the Committee of Experts of the present London Conference.

The mentioned guarantees are the following:—

1. Full autonomy of the Reichsbank.
2. Prohibition to increase furthermore the floating debt and limitation of paper circulation.
3. Payment into account in the Reichsbank of the 25 per cent. of total value of the German exports in foreign currency.
4. The same for all customs duties.
5. Supervision by the Committee of Guarantees of all receipts and revenues and expenses of Germany.
6. Laws to prevent the evasion of capital.

No. 64

I.C.P. 253.] *British Secretary's Notes of an Allied Conference, held at 10, Downing Street, on Monday, August 14, 1922, at 5 p.m.*

PRESENT: *Belgium*: M. Theunis, M. Jaspar; EXPERTS: M. Bemelmans, M. Gutt, M. Furst; SECRETARY: Vicomte Davignon.

British Empire: The Right Hon. D. Lloyd George, O.M., M.P., Prime Minister (*in the Chair*), The Right Hon. A. Chamberlain, Sir Robert Horne, Sir L. Worthington-Evans; EXPERTS: Sir William Tyrrell, Sir Basil Blackett, Sir Edward Grigg, Mr. F. Leith Ross, Mr. P. J. Grigg; SECRETARIES: Mr. Thomas Jones,[1] Mr. T. St. Quintin Hill.

France: M. Poincaré, M. de Lasteyrie; EXPERTS: M. Avenol, M. de Peretti della Rocca.

Italy: Signor Schanzer, Signor Paratore, Signor de Martino; EXPERTS: Signor Giannini, Signor D'Amelio; SECRETARY: Count Vannutelli Rey.

Japan: Baron Hayashi; EXPERTS: M. T. Sekiba, M. S. Arai; SECRETARY: M. I. Tokugawa.

INTERPRETER: M. Camerlynck.

[1] Principal Assistant Secretary in the Cabinet Secretariat.

Financial Situation in Austria

1. Mr. Lloyd George said that he was sorry to trouble the conference again, but the conference had received a note from the Austrian Legation dated the 7th August (see A.J. 361),[2] and this afternoon the Austrian Minister had visited him and given him a document, which he desired to bring to the knowledge of the conference. He therefore had ventured to ask the conference to assemble again.

Mr. Lloyd George then read to the conference the note from the Austrian Minister, which is reproduced in the Appendix.

On being informed that the members of the conference had received copies of this note, Mr. Lloyd George said that there would be no need to have it translated. He had felt bound to bring the matter to the notice of the conference because the situation was serious. It was not the first time the Austrian situation had been discussed. This country had advanced between 10 and 15 millions sterling to Austria and this advance had not had the slightest effect; they had only seemed to make the krone worse, and the situation was one which ought to be considered very carefully.

M. Poincaré said that the French Government had also made an advance to Austria amounting to 50 million francs, and he was not aware that this advance had improved the situation to any appreciable extent. The French point of view was that if the Allied Governments were disposed to make another effort, the French Government would co-operate, but it would be very difficult for the French Government to take effective action. He had experienced the greatest difficulties in getting the last vote through the French Parliament. There had been strong objections in the Senate to it and many criticisms had been made. Still, the Austrian note disclosed a serious threat to European peace, and the situation was particularly grave since it indicated a danger of Germany and Austria being brought together with a resultant breach of the Treaty of Versailles. Personally, he would be favourably disposed towards the making of another effort, and he would be ready to bring in a Bill if the Allies were agreed that such an effort should be made, but he would point out that the Austrian Government was only asking for guarantees and not for the payment of any sum.

Signor Schanzer stated that the Italian Government had also been seriously considering the Austrian situation. Italy had granted various sums to Austria. At the moment he did not remember the exact figure, but Parliament had recently passed a Bill granting further credits to Austria this year of 70 million lire. This was a big effort for Italy considering her unfavourable economic situation. He was ready to consider the granting of further assistance to Austria, but could not commit the Italian delegation. He would have to bring the matter before the Italian Cabinet, and eventually the Italian Chamber, before a decision could be reached.

The question was whether the Allies could give a limited guarantee. Herr Schuller,[4] who had seen him, had said that the guarantee would be limited

---

[2] Not printed. [3] Herr G. Franckenstein.
[4] *Chef de Section* in the Austrian Foreign Office.

to a sum of 10 millions sterling, and not 15 millions sterling, so that the risk for each of the Great Powers would be diminished in proportion. Moreover, there were substantial securities which could be used as a basis for loans, but the British House of Parliament [*sic*] was not in session, and there was the same difficulty in France and Italy.

BARON HAYASHI, in reply to Mr. Lloyd George, said he was not in a position to make any statement of substance, beyond the fact that he was reporting on the matter to his Government.

MR. LLOYD GEORGE said that all the Allies seemed to be in the same position. They were not disposed to advance sufficient sums for the purpose of keeping Austria up. Each would like to do something, but none of them was prepared to advance the large sums required. He did not know who would be able to do so. Certainly not the United States. Neither France, Italy nor Great Britain would vote 10 or 15 million pounds for Austria, and it was, moreover, very doubtful whether they should do so in any case. He had expressed his opinion to M. Briand last year.[5] The present position was an impossible one. Vienna had formed the capital of a country of 53 million people, and it was now the capital of a country of $6\frac{1}{2}$ million people. This small population could not support a capital like Vienna. Moreover, Austria had internal difficulties. Her army was Communist, more Communist than Socialist. Wages were extraordinarily high—higher than they had ever been, and no one possessed authority to keep them down because of the Communist tendencies of the army. How could Austria possibly be maintained? Great Britain alone had pumped into Austria a sum of $12\frac{1}{2}$ millions sterling. This had been done for a very small State, and all the money had been paid in cash. There was no State in Europe which had had the same support. The British Government were not prepared by calling on their heavily-taxed nationals to create further credits for Austria. This did not, however, solve the question. The Austrian Government threatened to resign; no other Government could be formed he had been told. In the event of there being no Government in Austria, an offer had been made to place the destiny of Austria in the hands of the Allies. What would happen then? The Communists would no doubt try to seize Austria. Then Hungary, Czechoslovakia and the neighbouring States would be looking at Austria and at each other, anxious lest their neighbours should seize Vienna; and there would be Italy looking over the Alps to see what was going on. There might, in fact, be quite a little trouble, and there was just as much trouble in Europe now the Allies could negotiate. In fact, they had more trouble than they could negotiate after hours and hours of sitting down together. What was to be done, then? Some decision had to be reached, for the conference would not be meeting again, at any rate, immediately. There was a threat of converging armies, and the situation had to be dealt with. It was one which might end in a clash. He would ask for the Italian opinion—Italy was nearer Vienna than England, thank God.

SIGNOR SCHANZER said that as Mr. Lloyd George had asked for his opinion

5 See Vol. XV, No. 3.

it was necessary for him to define the situation more clearly. Mr. Lloyd George had said that there were good reasons against making further sacrifices which might be useless in the end, but he had said that the Austrian Government would resign and that would produce an extremely dangerous situation. According to the note which he had received, however, the threat to resign had only been made if the Powers did not give guarantees for a loan of 10 millions sterling. The League of Nations had formally [*sic*] studied the question of financial assistance to Austria,[6] but it was not possible to adopt their plan now. The Austrian Government had put forward a financial scheme, part of which would be the carrying out of a levy and included in this scheme was a plan for a loan. In respect of the money raised by this loan there would be guarantees such as the tobacco monopolies. The bankers had thought a guarantee by the Powers was necessary, but this guarantee had been reduced to a sum of 10 millions sterling and would be shared out among the Powers. The situation was therefore that there was a threat to European peace unless the Powers gave financial support. What would happen then? He thought it necessary to declare in the name of the Italian delegation that the Italian Government was very exercised as to the danger which would arise if there were a Bolshevik movement or similar political movements in Austria such as an attempt to reunite with Germany or to create a Danubian Confederation. Italy would be opposed to such movements which would be dangerous to her. If a Danubian Confederation were formed, Austria would be a member of it and it would consist of nations not very friendly disposed towards Italy.

As regards the other troubles which Mr. Lloyd George had referred to, that is to say, the danger of movements by countries neighbouring on Austria, he desired to say that [in such a case the Italian Government for reasons of safety, reserved to itself liberty of action. It should be necessary for the Italian Government to do so. Intervention was not inevitable, but if necessity arose it would have to be resorted to for the sake of Italy's safety. He thought it better, in order to avoid such a disaster, for Italy and for the other countries to continue financial sacrifices in order to assist Austria, but the situation would be a very serious one in the case of the resignation of the Austrian Government.]*

MR. LLOYD GEORGE said that he did not see that any of the Allies were prepared to come forward with any proposal. He asked how much money Austria had been given altogether. The United Kingdom had given Austria £12,500,000.

M. POINCARÉ replied that the first French instalment had been given in conjunction with the United States of America. He did not remember the exact figures. The second French instalment had been given this year and amounted to 55,000,000 francs.

* The text of this passage between square brackets is supplied from Confidential Print.

[6] See Vol. XV, No. 61 and for further allied discussions of the Austrian financial problem, see Nos. 62–4, 67 and 68.

SIGNOR SCHANZER said that Italy had given Austria 280,000,000 lire and had passed a Bill for the grant of 70,000,000 lire more. This made a total of 350,000,000 million lire. In addition to these sums there were the sums granted by the American Relief Fund which amounted to 21,000,000 dollars.

MR. LLOYD GEORGE said that the United Kingdom had just given Austria £2,500,000. The country was a sink. Moreover, the Allies must envisage what would happen if there were no arrangement in regard to reparations. The mark would get worse. This would affect the krone and eventually other currencies. It was no use settling things piecemeal in Europe. He did not see that anyone was prepared to lend anything and if there was trouble, well, Italy was nearer Austria than anyone else.

SIGNOR SCHANZER said that he had not given any undertaking in regard to Austria. He had only wanted to make a reservation as to liberty of action on the part of Italy. He had given no undertaking.

MR. LLOYD GEORGE replied that he did not see how Italy could disinterest herself in movements in Austria.

SIGNOR SCHANZER agreed, but he desired to point out that this was a matter which affected all the Great Powers. If a serious crisis arose in Austria, it would be a great menace to European peace and this was a matter of general European concern.

M. POINCARÉ stated that he noted that the Italian Government reserved its liberty of action and against this he did not protest at all.

MR. LLOYD GEORGE said that it would be useful for all the Powers concerned to know that any general scramble in Austria would not be regarded by the Great Powers with indifference.

M. POINCARÉ said that he thought this was an opportunity for the League of Nations perhaps. It had already dealt with Austria in some respects, but the League of Nations could do nothing on its own initiative. The Allies might ask the League to take some action and the League might perhaps do more than the Allies would be able to do separately. The League might be able to put forward a scheme for financial reorganisation. Such a scheme had already been worked out and was in fact in the possession of the French expert, M. Avenol.

MR. LLOYD GEORGE said that he was in favour of referring the question to the League of Nations, but it was only fair to inform the League beforehand that there was no hope of money from the Great Powers. It would be putting the League on a false scent if they started enquiries into schemes for buttressing up Austria based on international credits, that is credits furnished by the Allied Governments, when in the end there would be no such credits, but if there were any other schemes the Allies could invite the League to consider them and the League would be very usefully employed in doing so. Was this proposal agreed to?

SIGNOR SCHANZER asked what the proposal was.

MR. LLOYD GEORGE replied that it was M. Poincaré's proposal to refer to the League of Nations for investigation and report the Austrian financial situation and to make it clear to the League that there was no prospect of obtaining credits from the Great Powers. It would only be fair to inform the League of this.

General agreement was expressed with the above proposal.

Clearing House Payments

2. MR. LLOYD GEORGE said that the Chancellor of the Exchequer had called his attention to the fact that in their report of the 12th August (A.J. 364)[7] the Allied financial experts had made a unanimous recommendation as to cash payments due from Germany under sections 3 and 4 of the economic clauses of the Treaty of Versailles. This recommendation had been reported to the conference, but it had not been taken cognisance of. If the conference agreed, it could approve the recommendation, because action would have to be taken on it, one way or the other.

M. DE LASTEYRIE said he had not the experts' report before him, but if he remembered rightly they had agreed on imposing an obligation to carry out the first payment of £2,000,000. One point was not agreed, however, and that was the date. Some of the Allies had suggested a delay of one month, but the French had reserved this point.

SIR ROBERT HORNE said that his impression was that the period of one month [had] been agreed on.

MR. LLOYD GEORGE asked that the article should be read, and the article was then read in French.

M. POINCARÉ said that the delay of one month suggested by the article seemed a little long to the French representatives, because of the office at Strassburg which had been crowded with requests and was now suffering from a shortage. The French experts had expressed a wish for a shorter period and this had in fact been suggested by the Belgian delegation. He would like this shorter period, but if the conference did not agree he would consent to the other.

MR. CHAMBERLAIN asked if the French Government would make separate arrangements.

SIR ROBERT HORNE agreed [*sic*] that they would.

M. POINCARÉ suggested that the date should be the 1st September.

SIR ROBERT HORNE said that the arrangements would require a month and he thought a month ought to be given.

MR. LLOYD GEORGE asked if this was agreed.

M. THEUNIS said that he wished to give the Belgian point of view on this subject. It had been known for over a year, and it was to the effect that the German Government were acting illegally in taking the place of their nationals. Owing to the fall in the value of the mark, it happened that 99 per cent. of the instalments were paid by the Reich and not by private persons in Germany. This was a clear infringement of article 251 of the treaty, which granted payment of reparations first. When the experts had discussed this proposal, for the sake of harmony the Belgians had agreed to

[7] No. 62, Appendix.

230

it, and only for that reason. He did not think that the proposition of the Belgian Government was debateable.

M. Poincaré said that this proposition was not debateable and it was not debated. The French delegation quite agreed with the Belgian delegation, and thought it outrageous that priority should be given by the German Government over reparation payments.

M. Theunis replied that this was still more regrettable when the Allies had been discussing stopping other German reparation payments.

Sir Robert Horne said that the terms of the agreement, to which all the Allies had agreed, left it to the Reparation Commission to supervise individual arrangements made with Germany.

Mr. Lloyd George asked if there were anything more? Did the Belgian delegation desire to press their objection?

M. Theunis replied that they would not do so, because of the delegation's sheer love of peace.

In reply to Mr. Lloyd George, Signor Schanzer and Baron Hayashi signified their assent to the wording of the paragraph as approved by the Allied experts.

(*The conference then adjourned.*)

2, Whitehall Gardens, August 14, 1922.

Appendix

Herr Franckenstein to Mr. Lloyd George

AUSTRIAN LEGATION, *18 Belgrave Square, August 13, 1922*

Mr. Prime Minister,

I have been instructed by the Austrian Government to make to your Excellency, as president of the inter-Allied meeting in London, the following declaration, and to beg you to bring it to the knowledge of the conference:—

If, contrary to expectations, the Allied Powers, during the present meeting in London, should not come to a decision to give definite assurances to Austria that it will obtain adequate foreign credits on the assets just realised, the Austrian Government will have to summon Parliament immediately after the conclusion of the London Conference, and would have to make the following declaration:—

The finance plan of the Austrian Government, worked out on its own initiative and sanctioned by the Federal Parliament—a scheme which is almost identical with the plan set up by the Powers for the financial reconstruction of Germany—cannot be carried out and will have to be dropped, because, in spite of the release of the liens, the foreign credits which are an essential part of it cannot be obtained, although they have been repeatedly promised to Austria since the signing of the Peace Treaty of Saint-Germain.

For this reason the Austrian Government must resign. No other Government can be constituted. The further destinies of Austria must be placed in the hands of the Allied Powers. The responsibility for all the consequences must rest with them.

I have, etc.

FRANCKENSTEIN

Reparation by Germany: Events Leading to the French and Belgian Invasion of the Ruhr

August 17–December 31, 1922

No. 65

Lord Kilmarnock (Coblenz) to the Marquess Curzon of Kedleston
(Received August 17, 9.30 p.m.)
No. 20 Telegraphic [C 11710/99/18]

Confidential   COBLENZ, *August 17, 1922, 5.40 p.m.*

General Allen[1] expressed to me last night considerable apprehension as to action which France might take in view of result of London conference.[2] Although he had no definite information he seemed to be under the impression that a military advance was not improbable. If such should take place question would arise as to whether French should be allowed to carry out requisitions in American and British areas and General Allen would be very glad to know what attitude His Majesty's Government would adopt in regard to our area. He has not as yet reached a decision as to American area but his attitude will, I believe, largely depend on ours. He thinks that if French knew that no requisitions would be allowed by ourselves and Americans it would have strong restraining influence on any contemplated action.

It seems to me that this question affords an opportunity of common action with Americans which might have far reaching effects and exercise considerable influence on American policy as a whole. I strongly recommend that I be authorized to tell General Allen that His Majesty's Government will on no account allow requisitions by French in British area with a view to facilitating military (?measures).

I should be grateful for immediate answer.

[1] General Henry T. Allen, Commander of the American Forces in Germany.
[2] See Chap. II.

No. 66

Lord D'Abernon (Berlin) to the Marquess Curzon of Kedleston
(Received August 18, 8.30 a.m.)
No. 150 Telegraphic [*C 11733/99/18*]

BERLIN, *August 17, 1922, 8.20 p.m.*

In confidential conversation this morning, Chancellor told me that certain negotiations between French and German industrial magnates had come to his knowledge. Object was an arrangement for co-operation between Ruhr district and France—a result which would have a considerable political effect. These negotiations appear to be closely connected with French Minister for Foreign Affairs' specific demands in London[1] and were certainly known to French government. Chancellor showed me certain documents confirming fact of negotiations and alleged that principal [participants] on one side were Senator Japy and Herr Spiess who is half French half German; on the other side Stinnes, Thyssen and other big coal and iron masters.

Chancellor said he did not know whether to encourage negotiation or to stop it. He had sent for Herr Thyssen and would inform me further when he had seen him. It was no use questioning Stinnes.

Meanwhile he wished to be in close touch with His Majesty's Government to keep them fully informed and to ascertain their impression.

I replied that I would telegraph for instructions. Without more precise knowledge as to position of negotiations and of objective, it appears difficult to form an opinion.

Chancellor urged utmost secrecy regarding the matter.[2]

[1] See No. 51.
[2] In his telegram No. 77 of August 21, Lord Curzon replied:
'I am consulting the Treasury and Board of Trade to ascertain whether such a deal as foreshadowed in your telegram would benefit British interests or not.
'In the meantime I should like you to bear in mind that we should avoid becoming advisers to the Germans in this matter until we can settle upon a clear policy.'

No. 67

Lord Hardinge (Paris) to the Marquess Curzon of Kedleston
(Received August 18, 8.30 a.m.)
No. 425 Telegraphic: by bag [*C 11711/99/18*]

PARIS, *August 17, 1922*

My telegram No. 422 of yesterday.[1]

Official communiqué states that at second meeting of Cabinet Council latter examined in detail the different eventualities which may arise according to the decisions of the reparation commission.[2]

On Monsieur Poincaré's return from Rambouillet he had a long interview with French representative on that commission. Press, which remains

[1] Not printed.   [2] See No. 63.

moderate in tone, recognizes that centre of interest has now shifted to deliberations of reparation commission. Attitude of Belgian representative is awaited with interest. This evening's 'Temps' maintains that article 437 of treaty of Versailles is decisive as to casting vote of president.[3]

[3] On August 19 (C 11625/99/18) the Foreign Office referred the question whether the chairman of the Reparation Commission had a casting vote to the Treasury, who consulted Sir John Bradbury. On August 28, Sir John Bradbury stated: 'In my opinion the right of the Chairman of the Reparation Commission in the event of equality of votes to give a second vote is not open to question and I have in fact accepted decisions by a majority created by this vote on several occasions.

'Article 437 is, however, not within the competence of the Reparation Commission to interpret and I imagine that it is within the rights of any Government affected by decisions of the Reparation Commission so taken to challenge their validity by whatever means may be open to it.

'If the British Government should desire to reserve this right it might be desirable that I should make a statement to this effect in any future case in which a decision may be so taken.

'I shall be happy to do this, if so desired.'

To this communication Mr. Niemeyer, Deputy Controller of Finance in the Treasury, sent the following reply, a copy of which was transmitted to the Foreign Office on August 29: 'I am to inform you that Their Lordships do not consider that it would serve any useful purpose to reserve the right of His Majesty's Government to challenge the validity of decisions taken by a majority created by the casting vote of the Chairman, more especially as such decisions have, in fact, been accepted in the past.'

No. 68

The Marquess Curzon of Kedleston to Lord Kilmarnock (Coblenz)
No. 15 Telegraphic [C 11710/99/18]

FOREIGN OFFICE, *August 20, 1922, 5 p.m.*

Your telegram No. 20 (of August 17th).[1]

We cannot assume that French have no right to requisition in our zone, although it might perhaps be argued that right of requisition is conferred on 'armies of occupation' and that right could not be exercised as result of introduction of fresh French troops object of which is advance into unoccupied area.

But if French have decided on advance, protest, which could not be enforced, would not deter them. Even if it could be enforced I am advised that such advance would not be seriously hampered by inability to requisition.

I consider it, therefore, undesirable to make any protest at this stage.

You should explain confidentially to General Allen, making it clear that while we should deprecate any independent French action of the nature which he apprehends, we consider that, from the practical point of view, his proposal would be ineffective.

[1] No. 65.

No. 69

Lord D'Abernon (Berlin) to the Marquess Curzon of Kedleston
(Received August 22, 8.30 a.m.)
No. 153 Telegraphic [C 11878/99/18]

BERLIN, *August 21, 1922, 11.45 a.m.*

I have had long conversation with Bradbury regarding his mission here.[1] We appear to have same views.

I desire, however, to emphasize the following opinion. The points raised by French Minister for Foreign Affairs regarding fiscal mines and state forests are of little immediate practical utility.[2] The essential thing is to establish equilibrium in budget and some control of Reichsbank and issue fiduciary currency on lines of articles 1, 2 and 9 of London proposal of His Majesty's Government.[3] If this could be done in an effective and striking form, there might be some chance of stopping the panic. Otherwise I see little hope. The immense urgency of measures on the lines above and relative non-urgency of other measures appear to me essential characteristic of the position.

I have discussed these views privately with Bradbury who is in complete accord but who for obvious reasons cannot press them personally.[4]

---

[1] Sir J. Bradbury had left Paris for Berlin on the evening of August 19. Before leaving he had written (August 18) to Sir B. Blackett as follows: 'Ostensibly of course we are going merely to inform ourselves of the present conditions in Germany and report to the Commission. There is an off chance that we may be able to find some solution of the immediate difficulty in agreement with the German Government but I am particularly anxious not to excite hopes only to have them disappointed.

'The French delegation (with encouragement I am pretty sure from the Quai d'Orsay) has been vigorously pressing the mission. . . . From the press, however, it looks as if Poincaré was going publicly to decline to associate himself with it and there is of course a danger that the whole French attitude (apart from Dubois's in whose complete sincerity I retain full belief) is a manœuvre to try to get me buttoned up to the policy of "no further moratorium without new guarantees". I am confident, however, that I can avoid this—unless of course the Germans make a bloomer. In any case I think the advantages of the "détente" are worth the risk.

'The French press on obvious official inspiration is returning today to the Ruhr occupation. This is not necessarily unfavourable to the prospects of our mission.'

[2] See No. 62.   [3] See ibid., Appendix.

[4] In his telegram No. 154 of August 22, Lord D'Abernon reported: 'Bradbury informs me no definite progress in negotiations today. He expects crisis in discussion will come tomorrow, or more probably Thursday.

'German government have categorically refused any concession regarding control of mines and forests, but have indicated the possibility of some deposit in foreign banks as guarantee against possible deficiency in delivery of coal and wood up to the end of the year.'

No. 70

Lord Hardinge (Paris) to the Marquess Curzon of Kedleston
(Received August 23)
No. 1951 [C 11935/99/18]

PARIS, *August 22, 1922*

My Lord,

Monsieur Poincaré's speech at Bar-le-Duc yesterday, the text of which was enclosed in my despatch No. 1941 of August 21st,[1] has been received by the entire Paris press (with the exception of course of the Socialist organs) with the most rapturous applause. I am unable to say how much of this applause is the result of a *mot d'ordre* from the Government, but the fact remains that none of Monsieur Poincaré's previous utterances [has] ever elicited such unanimous approval. His eloquence is compared to that of Cicero, while the substance of his speech is acclaimed as statesmanlike and (what is perhaps more surprising) as moderate and in no way calculated to displease British public opinion.

To me Monsieur Poincaré's speech appears singularly ill-judged. It will not have escaped Your Lordship's notice that the complaints in which it abounds are all addressed to Great Britain, to the entire exclusion of France's other Allies. Monsieur Poincaré has thus thought it politic entirely to ignore the fact that the policy of seizing guarantees for which he pressed in London met with the opposition, not only of His Majesty's Government, but of the Italian and Belgian Governments.[2] It can hardly be agreeable to them to see their opinions and even their presence at the Conference in London, so consistently ignored by Monsieur Poincaré. But indeed the whole of his speech, bitter and disappointed in tone as it is, conveys to me the distinct impression that he is biassed by personal animosity to the British Prime Minister which it is beyond his power to suppress. Monsieur Poincaré evidently regards Mr. Lloyd George as his only serious opponent. In this sense his speech may be taken as a highly flattering testimony to the power and prestige of Great Britain and her Prime Minister at the present moment.

Monsieur Poincaré once more repeats his assertion that France is not militarist and aims at no hegemony. Such assertions as these are, it seems to me, mere idle words so long as France, in spite of her impoverishment and inability to balance her budget, maintains a standing army of eight hundred thousand men and is organising to be ready by next spring an air force of two hundred and forty squadrons against an enemy whom she cannot name. The reference by the *Daily Chronicle*[3] to the money spent on French submarines has, as Your Lordship is aware, aroused much indignation in the French press. I do not consider that this indignation is justified; for the submarine question is but a symptom of the militarist disease which, as it seems to me, is at present poisoning French policy and infecting thereby the whole body politic of Europe. I should have been happy to see, in Monsieur Poincaré's

---

[1] Not printed.   [2] See Chap. II, *passim*.   [3] In an article of August 18.

latest declarations, some sign of a return to a more sane and pacific attitude; but I cannot accept as such his assertions as to the existence of a state of mind which is, unfortunately, contradicted by plain facts.

I have, etc.,

HARDINGE OF PENSHURST

No. 71

Sir G. Grahame (Brussels) to the Marquess Curzon of Kedleston
(Received August 24)
No. 571 [C 12004/99/18]

Confidential   BRUSSELS, *August 22, 1922*

My Lord,

On returning to Brussels from a short absence on leave, I went to see the Belgian Minister for Foreign Affairs who, with the Prime Minister, had come back from London a day or two previously.

M. Jaspar, in a long and informal conversation, described for my benefit much of what had happened at the recent Allied Conference.[1] The following observations which I have the honour to make respecting Belgian policy are largely but not entirely based on what M. Jaspar said to me during this conversation:—

The two Belgian Ministers did not go to London with many illusions as regards the likelihood of the conference coming to decisions which would really prove helpful to Europe in general. They would have liked to have set about unravelling the tangled skein of European difficulties in a way which, owing to circumstances beyond the control of any one Government, was not practicable either immediately before or during the conference. The disappointment which they felt at the sterile result of their labours in London was, however, none the less keen from having been partially anticipated. The actual spectacle of the deadlock produced by the sharply divergent attitudes of the British and French Governments evidently produced the most serious disquietude in the minds of both M. Theunis and M. Jaspar. Intensely anxious as the Belgian Government have always been to receive cash payments from Germany—and this anxiety is especially comprehensible in the case of M. Theunis who is Minister of Finance—the apprehension of a break or split in the Entente nevertheless caused the Belgian Ministers to relegate their financial needs to a second place. M. Jaspar, in particular, has always regarded the possibility of a rupture of the Anglo-French Entente as a kind of nightmare. It is the very essence of his foreign policy to avoid having to choose between French and British friendship. For one thing, he foresees the internal complications which would arise if Belgium had to turn her back on one or other of her Allies, for such a proceeding would stir up in the most unhappy manner the antagonism

[1] See Chap. II.

between Flemings and Walloons who would frequently be found in opposite camps. He realises also the general consequences likely to ensue if Great Britain and France were no longer to co-operate the one with the other; and he no doubt reflects on the probable fate, in such case, of what is his real and ultimate aspiration, namely to see England, France, and Belgium all bound together in some form of alliance—*un bloc occidental*, as he has more than once described it.

Since the return of the two Ministers to Brussels, they have been warily playing a waiting game. They have abstained from formulating at a Ministerial Council instructions or recommendations to be given to the Belgian delegate on the Reparation Commission as regards a moratorium. He has merely been requested to do all that is possible with a view to inducing agreement within the Commission between conflicting policies and principles. The Belgian Ministers were strongly in favour of sending a deputation of the Reparation Commission to Berlin, and they cherish the expectation that something may result from the journey there of Sir John Bradbury and M. Mauclère of a kind to ease the situation.[2] M. Jaspar apparently clings to the hope that the Germans may still make a payment of some sort, for he said to me that they would be very well advised to do so as in such case the favourable effect on world opinion would be striking. He alternatively seems to hope that they may be induced to offer some kind of *gages* which would take the edge off M. Poincaré's asperity.

As regards M. Poincaré's political activities, one might hazard the opinion, without much fear of being far from the mark, that the two Belgian Ministers privately regard them as being pernicious from the point of view of the prospects of an early European settlement. I should say that, at the back of their minds, there exists a suspicion that M. Poincaré's obsession with regard to the delinquencies of Germany has brought him very near to a condition in which he is unable to survey the general situation sanely and calmly.

M. Jaspar mentioned to me that, since M. Theunis and he had returned to Brussels, they had been given to understand that M. Poincaré was not, on reflection, in favour of the offer put forward by M. Theunis at the last stage of the conference to accept from Germany six months' bills under certain conditions instead of cash.[3] I understand that M. Poincaré considers such an agreement would amount to granting Germany a disguised moratorium. M. Jaspar told me that M. Theunis had only contemplated making this offer apply to a period of three months, but he (M. Jaspar) had persuaded him to make a sacrifice in the interests of the Entente and to extend it to six months.

The Belgian press has been debating whether the Belgian Government would allow such an offer to be put before the Reparation Commission in spite of their knowledge that M. Poincaré regarded it with disfavour, but the Government have said nothing one way or the other beyond letting it be known that they are not bound by any undertaking towards France. On the

[2] See No. 69, n. 1.   [3] See No. 63.

other hand, they have not made a secret of the fact that they sympathize to a certain extent with France in her desire to obtain some tangible guarantees before granting a moratorium, and that they think that England is wrong in refusing to consider the principle of such guarantees. It would, however, probably be found that there was a notable difference between what the Belgian Ministers and M. Poincaré considered as satisfactory in this respect.

On several occasions within the last few months, the Theunis Cabinet has refused to conform its ideas and acts to those of the French Government. The attitude of the Belgian Delegate, acting on instructions, at the Committee of Bankers in Paris;[4] the view taken by the Belgian Government[5] with regard to the Clearing-House payments;[6] the refusal to support the proposals for lines of Customs round the Ruhr basin and on the eastern frontier of the German occupied regions[7] are some recent cases in point, and show the readiness of the Belgian Ministers to act in accordance with their own view of the necessities of the situation without regard to the wishes of the French Government. Such an attitude must appear to M. Poincaré, who, more than any one, has laid himself out in the past to please Belgian sentiment, as highly deplorable and as a sad back-sliding from the level set by M. Jaspar's predecessor, M. Hymans, who joyfully consented to join the French in their advance into Frankfort,[8] and dragged the somewhat reluctant Delacroix Cabinet along with him. Fortunately for M. Theunis and M. Jaspar—who are associated in a personal and political comradeship of exceptional intimacy—their position is now so well-established at home that they can, as a rule, face, without much misgiving, the criticisms directed against them from nationalist quarters both in Paris and in Brussels. They have none the less to be careful for they are often in the position of moving against the popular current in Belgium when they appear to favour less severe measures than those advocated by M. Poincaré, whose tirades against Germany find a sympathetic echo in this country where the German invasion and all its attendant miseries are still fresh in the public mind.

I believe that the principal aim of the Belgian Government at present is to prevent the divergence between British and French policy from becoming more accentuated. If the Reparation Commission cannot find some means of satisfying all parties, the Belgian Government will continue to try to gain time by one expedient or another, their chief hope being that a conference will be summoned before the end of this year to deal with all the elements of the financial problem, including reparations, inter-allied debts and an international loan. They evidently think that a conference of this kind and on the broadest lines may still achieve satisfactory settlement and deliver Europe and the world from the intolerable strain of an uncertain present and from the dire apprehension of a tragic future.

I have, etc.,
GEORGE GRAHAME

---

[4] See No. 41, n. 3. [5] See No. 64. [6] See Vol. XVI, No. 422, n. 6.
[7] See Nos. 57 and 58. [8] See Vol. IX, Chap. IV.

No. 72

Record by Sir W. Tyrrell[1] of a conversation with the Italian Ambassador
[*C 12028/99/18*]

FOREIGN OFFICE, *August 22, 1922*

In the course of conversation today[2] the Italian Ambassador told me that Monsieur Schanzer was rather perturbed by reports ascribing to the French Government the serious intention of intervening in the Ruhr, and it had occurred to him that we might be disposed to join the Italians in a joint protest at Paris against French intervention in Germany. Signor de Martino asked me my opinion and I unhesitatingly replied that my personal view was that such a step would secure for Monsieur Poincaré and the Marshals of France a twenty years' lease of power, and that I did not imagine that either the British or Italian Governments desired such a consummation. His Excellency entirely agreed with me and on my remarking that I would report Monsieur Schanzer's suggestion to the Secretary of State, [Signor] de Martino exclaimed: 'That would be very cruel.'

In this connection I should like to add that both Monsieur de S[ain]t-Aulaire and Monsieur de Montille (the counsellor of the French Embassy) have assured me that, whatever action with regard to Germany Monsieur Poincaré decided upon, it would not be of a nature to destroy German capacity to pay reparations or injure the relations of France with her Allies.[3]

W. T.

[1] See No. 51, n. 3.

[2] That same day, as reported (C 12251/99/18) by Mr. Shakespeare (the Prime Minister's Private Secretary) to Mr. Leeper (Assistant Private Secretary to the Secretary of State for Foreign Affairs), Signor de Martino called 'to obtain for Schanz[er']s benefit the attitude of the P[rime] M[inister] in case the French without consultation occupied the Ruhr Basin or enforced any of the other sanctions separately'. Mr. Lloyd George instructed Mr. Shakespeare as follows: 'Reply verbally to Signor de Martino that the Prime Minister is in the country and hopes to be in town early next week.

'They (the Italians) know that any isolated action of this character taken by the French would be regarded by us as giving rise to a situation of great gravity. We should regard it as a breach of the Treaty and a definite break of the Entente.

'What steps we should take in such an eventuality would have to be very carefully considered.'

[3] Lord Curzon commented (August 23): 'What then will it be?'

No. 73

Lord D'Abernon (Berlin) to the Marquess Curzon of Kedleston
(Received August 28)

No. 680 [C 12175/99/18]

BERLIN, *August 24, 1922*

My Lord Marquess,

My telegrams will have kept Your Lordship informed as to the course of the negotiations between the German Government and the Delegation of the Reparation Commission.[1]

Up to the hour of writing (11 a.m. August 24), not much progress can be reported. Both sides appear to be anxious to find a compromise but the German Government has categorically refused to agree to any hypothecation of the mines and forests, and the Reparation Commission delegates have not, so far, admitted the possibility of any alternative solution.

I gather from Sir John Bradbury that the Minister of Finance, Dr. Hermes, has been more practical than Dr. Wirth, the latter confining himself largely to dilating upon the appalling difficulties of the German situation, the large amount of foreign exchange which Germany must find to pay for food, and the generally gloomy outlook resulting from the rapid and continuous fall of the mark.

An alternative suggestion has been put forward by Herr Bergmann, somewhat hesitatingly endorsed by Dr. Hermes, and so far resisted by Dr. Wirth. It is to the effect that to guarantee possible deficiencies in the deliveries of coal and wood, foreign exchange to an amount of 2½ millions sterling should be deposited in some Entente Bank. It is not quite clear whether this guarantee fund would have to be made good if drawn upon, nor is it clear whether the deposit of 2½ millions sterling would be prolonged beyond the end of the year, i.e. the presumed period of the Moratorium now under discussion.

The French delegate, M. Mauclère, appeared not unfavourably impressed by this proposal, and is supposed to have telegraphed to Paris for instructions. These have not yet arrived, so that thorough examination of the proposal has not been entered upon.

Sir John Bradbury appears somewhat surprised at the friendly attitude of M. Mauclère to the proposal, and is inclined to doubt whether it will be endorsed by M. Poincaré.

Meantime the mark continues to fall rapidly, and is quoted today at 7,800 to the £, as compared with 5,600 last Saturday.[2] The outlook could not be more serious. As I stated in my telegram No. 153 of the 21st instant[3] the essential thing is to establish equilibrium in the Budget, and some control over the Reichsbank and the issue of fiduciary currency. I doubt whether any of the measures now under discussion will do much to clear the horizon.

I have, etc.,

D'ABERNON

[1] See No. 69.   [2] August 19.   [3] No. 69.

No. 74

Lord D'Abernon (Berlin) to the Marquess Curzon of Kedleston
(Received August 25, 8.30 a.m.)
No. 158 Telegraphic [*C 12041/99/18*]

BERLIN, *August 25, 1922, 12.15 a.m.*

No progress has been made towards solution of reparation question. French delegate today refused German proposals[1] regarding deposit of 50,000,000 marks gold in foreign exchange in Entente banks.

German government maintain their refusal of French Minister for Foreign Affairs' proposal regarding mines and forests.[2]

They have also refused variation of this proposal brought forward by Sir J. Bradbury[3] and which appears to offer considerable advantages.

German government will propose tomorrow to guarantee deliveries of coal and wood by contracts signed by leading German industrials with binding clauses and penalties.

Sir J. Bradbury and Monsieur Mauclère propose to leave tomorrow and will submit this proposal to bureau of reparations commission but they do not hold out any assurance of acceptance.

Financial crisis is getting rapidly worse.

[1] See No. 73. [2] See No. 69, n. 4. [3] See No. 76 below, Enclosure.

No. 75

Lord D'Abernon (Berlin) to the Marquess Curzon of Kedleston
(Received August 26, 11 a.m.)
No. 159 Telegraphic [*C 12109/99/18*]

BERLIN, *August 25, 1922, 8.10 p.m.*

Bradbury and Mauclère left today taking with them last German proposal[1] viz. that deliveries of coal and wood during moratorium should be guaranteed by leading German industrial firms.

German government came yesterday to an agreement in principle with these firms regarding this notably with Stinnes, but precise terms will require some days to elaborate.

Impression of delegates appeared slightly less unfavourable today.

German government deserve credit for obtaining assent of industrialists to financial endorsement and would possibly not have obtained it but for fact that political negotiations went on simultaneously under which Volkspartei will shortly join coalition.

Probable effect of this double agreement would appear favourable and tend to enhance prospect of obtaining reparation from Germany after requisite breathing space. It would, however, be unwise to underrate either duration or completeness of moratorium now required.

[1] See No. 74. In his despatch No. 687 of August 26 (C 12180/99/18), Lord D'Abernon transmitted to Lord Curzon a translation of this German proposal.

No. 76

Lord D'Abernon (Berlin) to the Marquess Curzon of Kedleston
(Received August 28)
No. 686 [C 12179/99/18]

BERLIN, *August 25, 1922*

My Lord,

I have the honour to enclose a suggestion which was put forward by Sir John Bradbury yesterday as a possible modification of the French claims regarding mines and forests.

Before submitting this proposal to the Germans, Sir John Bradbury consulted M. Mauclère, who did not like the proposal, and considered that important modifications would have to be made in it before it could be considered acceptable to the French Government.

The proposal was subsequently submitted to the German Government, and a Cabinet meeting took place regarding it. The unanimous opinion appears to have been that public opinion here would not agree to any transfer of ownership, however remote, of German forests.

In Sir John Bradbury's view the proposal is favourable to Germany, and even Ministers, who are against the proposal on the ground of internal politics, admit that economically no harm could result to Germany from acceptance.

As to the political effect, it is difficult for a foreigner to judge. German forests have a great sentimental value here, and anything that touches them stirs deep feelings. It is indeed stated that the Cabinet thought that, not only would they encounter a hostile Reichstag, but that their own personal safety would be endangered if they surrendered any mortgage or proprietary rights on so cherished a national possession.

Looked at on less emotional lines, Sir John Bradbury's proposal would appear to possess unquestionable merit in that it would be agreed to by the Reparation Commission while to German rights of property it is in some senses less dangerous than the Treaty of Versailles.

I have, etc.,
D'ABERNON

ENCLOSURE IN No. 76

Mines and Forests

(The following suggestions are put forward by Sir John Bradbury merely as a possible basis for discussion. He is not himself at present clear whether they would be fair or practicable.)

The German Government to agree that in the event of the coal or timber deliveries falling short of the programmes presented from time to time by the R[eparation] C[ommission], the Reparation Commission shall have a first call on the output of the fiscal mines and State forests up to a quantity not exceeding deliveries in arrear until such time as the arrears are overtaken.

In the event of this arrangement coming into operation the German Government will give facilities to experts appointed by the Reparation Commission to inspect the mines and forests in question and draw up programmes of deliveries.

Superintendents of deliveries—one for coal and one for timber—will be appointed, who shall be persons neither of German nor of Allied nationality selected by agreement between the Reparation Commission and the German Government.

The programme of deliveries prepared by the Reparation Commission's experts will be examined by the superintendents of deliveries who shall have power to reduce them if, in their opinion, the quantities asked for from any particular mine or forest exceed the quantities which can reasonably be gotten or felled within the prescribed period, regard being had to the proper technical and commercial exploitation of the mine or forest in question.

The programme of deliveries, as approved by the superintendents, shall be executively binding on the respective mines and forests administration and the execution of them shall be supervised by the superintendents.

Any failure to carry out the approved programme in respect of any mine or forest (not being in the opinion of the superintendent wholly due to causes outside the control of the administration or of the Government of the Reich or of the Government of the State concerned) shall forthwith be reported by the Superintendent to the Reparation Commission, which shall thereupon enter into possession of the mine or forest in respect of which the failure has occurred.

As from the date of entering into possession the full rights of ownership in the mine or forest in question shall vest in the Reparation Commission free of all charges and encumbrances.

The German Government will thereafter be entitled to be credited on account of reparation at the option of the Reparation Commission with either:—

(a) the capital value of the mine or forest, as determined by the Reparation Commission at the date of entry into possession; or
(b) the net receipts arising from time to time from sale, lease or exploitation by the Reparation Commission, subject, where necessary, to such adjustments as may be equitable in respect of produce delivered under part VIII of the Treaty of Versailles.

Lord Hardinge (Paris) to the Marquess Curzon of Kedleston
(Received August 29)

No. 1997 [C 12244/99/18]

PARIS, *August 28, 1922*

My Lord,

It will be within your recollection that Sir Milne Cheetham's telegram No. 390 of July 24th[1] last drew Lord Balfour's attention to the existence, as reported in the Press here, of a constructive plan to be put forward by Monsieur Poincaré, on his arrival in London, as a solution of the reparations and inter-allied debt problems. As Your Lordship is aware, it has been consistently maintained by Monsieur Poincaré and by the French press that the issue of the Balfour Note[2] on the inter-allied debts precluded the French Government from putting forward this plan, and forced them to insist on less conciliatory measures being adopted towards Germany than would have been the case if the Balfour Note had not been issued. The responsibility for the present unfortunate situation is thus thrown upon His Majesty's Government. This standpoint is, I observe, taken up by the 'Times' and its correspondent here,[3] who, while admitting Monsieur Poincaré to be much to blame in the matter, yet contend that His Majesty's Government are still more so.

In these circumstances it will doubtless be of interest to Your Lordship to see the details of this French plan, now reproduced for the first time by the 'Temps'.[4] It seems scarcely reasonable to blame His Majesty's Government

---

[1] Not printed.   [2] No. 45.   [3] See *The Times*, August 2, 1922, p. 8.

[4] The French plan was summarised in the *Temps* of August 27 as follows: 'Le projet français partait de cette constatation: d'après les stipulations du traité et les décisions prises par la Commission des Réparations, l'on peut considérer que la dette allemande de réparations, payable à partir du 1er août 1922, représente environ 120 milliards de marks or.

'De ces 120 milliards, le projet français faisait deux tranches.

'Une première tranche de 50 milliards devait jouir d'une priorité absolue et produire un intérêt de 5 pour cent, plus 2 pour cent d'amortissement, à partir du 1er août 1922. Avec des taux ainsi fixés, l'amortissement serait terminé en vingt-cinq ans environ.

'Pour aider l'Allemagne à amortir sa dette par anticipation, au moyen d'emprunts, les versements en espèces qu'elle effectuerait pendant les quatre premières années devaient lui être escomptés à des taux favorables.

'Dans l'ensemble, 70 pour cent au moins de la première tranche devaient être payés en espèces et 30 pour cent devaient être payés par des prestations en nature. Toutefois les créanciers n'étaient tenus d'accepter les prestations en nature, jusqu'à concurrence des trois quarts de la part de chacun d'eux, que jusqu'au 1er août 1926.

'Passons à la seconde tranche de la dette allemande, tranche évaluée à 70 milliards de marks or.

'La dette constituée par cette seconde tranche devait être annulée au fur et à mesure des payements effectués par l'Allemagne sur la première tranche et des annulations de créances que les Puissances alliées s'accorderaient réciproquement. Ces deux causes d'annulation ne devaient se cumuler qu'à partir du moment ou l'Allemagne aurait intégralement acquitté la première tranche de sa dette.

'En pratique, voici comment le projet français prévoyait l'application de ces principes.

[*Footnote 4 continued overleaf*

for having failed to take into account a scheme with which they had, so far as I am aware, never been acquainted by the French Government, and the mere existence of which they were left to gather from statements in the French press.

I also enclose an article from last night's 'Temps'[1] putting forward, on its own account, a scheme for dealing with the present situation, based on the transfer to a foreign bank of the gold reserve in the German Reichsbank.

I have, etc.,
(For the Ambassador)
MILNE CHEETHAM

'La Grande-Bretagne, la France, l'Italie, le Portugal, la Roumanie, et la Yougoslavie décidaient immédiatement d'annuler leurs créances réciproques.

'Comme le montant de ces créances représente environ 30 milliards de marks or, il aurait été convenu que la seconde tranche de la dette allemande serait annulée jusqu'à concurrence de 30 milliards, à mesure que l'Allemagne amortirait, pour un montant égal la première tranche de sa dette.

'Après cette opération, les éléments du problème auraient été les suivants:

'L'Allemagne aurait eu à amortir les deux derniers cinquièmes de la première tranche, soit 20 milliards de marks or.

'Les Alliés auraient eu à régler leurs dettes envers les États-Unis.

'Enfin, il serait resté 40 milliards sur la seconde tranche de la dette allemande, et l'on avait à se demander comment cette dette de 40 milliards pourrait être annulée.

'Voici la solution que suggérait le projet français: la dette allemande de 40 milliards, formant le solde de la deuxième tranche, devait être annulée dans la proportion des payements que l'Allemagne effectuerait pour amortir le solde de la première tranche (20 milliards) et dans la mesure où les États-Unis consentiraient à la réduction de leurs créances. En tout cas les Alliés ne prendraient pas l'initiative de fixer à l'Allemagne pour le solde de la seconde tranche, des conditions d'intérêt et d'amortissement. Ils se contenteraient d'adopter les conditions appliquées par les États-Unis eux-mêmes aux créances que ce solde compenserait.

'Le projet français s'occuperait enfin de répartir, entre les Alliés qui ont droit aux réparations, les payements que l'Allemagne effectuerait pour acquitter la première tranche de sa dette.

'Sans entrer dans le détail des deux combinaisons qui étaient envisagées, disons simplement qu'elles aboutissaient l'une et l'autre aux résultats ci-après:

'La Grande-Bretagne touchait, de toute façon, 10 pour cent des payements allemands; les autres Alliés se trouvaient recevoir, approximativement, des sommes correspondant aux dépenses qu'entraînent la restauration des régions dévastées et, d'une manière générale, la réparation des dommages aux biens.'

No. 78

Lord Hardinge (Paris) to the Marquess Curzon of Kedleston
(Received September 2, 8.30 a.m.)
No. 454 Telegraphic: by bag [*C 12404/99/18*]

PARIS, September 1, 1922

Following official communiqué was issued at close of this morning's meeting of Cabinet council at which Monsieur Poincaré explained present situation of questions of foreign policy.

'The Reparation Commission not having granted Germany the moratorium she requested,[1] the council considered that, for the moment, it had only to take act of this decision. As to the future payments, Belgium (who, in virtue of her right of priority, is entitled to receive the whole of them) having not only accepted but herself proposed the arrangements adopted by the commission, the council considered it desirable to reserve its liberty of action until the operation ("mise en œuvre") of the conditions contemplated.

'The council, faithful to the idea maintained by the President of the Council in London,[2] also decided to press for the meeting, as soon as possible, of a conference to which all the allies without exception should be summoned, and which should study the whole question of inter-allied debts and reparations.'

It is also stated that the council decided upon the text of the reply to Lord Balfour's note of August 1 respecting inter-allied debts.[3]

The press is in doubt as to whether to hail the decision of the Reparation Commission as a victory for France or to deplore it as another concession to Germany. Much is of course made of the rejection of Sir John Bradbury's motion, but the more Left papers are not slow to point out that the satisfaction obtained by France is one of form and not of substance. The 'Temps' observes that the decision is merely provisional, and only forms a stage on the way to a general and permanent settlement. On the whole there appears to be, except in the extremist papers, a distinct feeling of relief that a crisis has once more—if only temporarily—been avoided.

[1] In a note of September 1 (C 13088/99/18), Mr. Waley summed up the situation as follows: 'On August 26th, the Reparation Commission gave a hearing to Sir John Bradbury and M. Mauclère, but there was no discussion. Complicated unofficial negotiations then took place. The French were not prepared to agree to a moratorium on the terms of the German offer.

'Sir John Bradbury could not obtain majority support for a complete moratorium accompanied by the appointment of a "neutral" financial adviser to control German finances. The Belgians finally put forward a plan for the acceptance by Belgium of six-month German Treasury Bills to be guaranteed in a manner to be agreed by the Belgian and German Governments in lieu of the cash payments due from August 15th onwards, pending a decision on the German request for a moratorium till the 31st December, 1924, this decision being reserved until the completion of its scheme for the radical reform of German public finances to include (a) the balancing of the Budget, (b) in the event of the Governments represented on the Reparation Commission giving their prior consent thereto in conformity with Article 234 of the Treaty of Versailles, the reduction of the foreign obligations of Germany to the extent necessary to restore her credit, (c) currency reform, and (d) the flotation of foreign and internal loans.

'On August 30th the German Government were given a formal hearing at which nothing fresh emerged, and Sir John Bradbury decided with reluctance to support the Belgian plan (to which the Italians adhered) even if the French opposed it and no unanimous decision was possible.

'On August 31st the Reparation Commission rejected Sir John Bradbury's proposal to grant a moratorium till December 31st, 1922, and unanimously adopted the above Belgian proposal.'

The decision of the Reparation Commission, No. 2119 (for the text see *The Times* of September 1, p. 8), was communicated to the German Government on August 31.

[2] See Chap. II.   [3] No. 45.

No. 79

Mr. Phipps (Brussels) to the Marquess Curzon of Kedleston
(Received September 5, 3 p.m.)

No. 68 Telegraphic [*C 12574/99/18*]

BRUSSELS, *September 5, 1922, 12.45 p.m.*

Minister for Foreign Affairs sent for me this morning. I found His Excellency somewhat upset at declaration[1] made last night by British delegate, Reparation Commission, to British press representatives, stating that it would be unfortunate in the interests of Germany and of reparations to remove as guarantee large portion of gold reserve of Reichsbank. Belgian Minister for Foreign Affairs considers such a declaration, however true it may be, ill-timed and calculated to stiffen German resistance and to cause German government to think that it can count on British support in its negotiations with Belgian delegates on Reparation Commission who left for Berlin last night.

He feels that the very fact that Belgium has been so moderate throughout will cause Belgian public opinion to get quite out of hand if it sees that Belgium is being trifled with, nor could he, in such event, attempt to restrain it. Suggestion in German press that only Reichsbank signature should be given as guarantee was perfectly futile and if that were the last word of Germany Belgian delegates would have to leave Berlin and declare Germany in default.

Minister for Foreign Affairs on his own behalf and on that of Prime Minister earnestly begs that urgent instructions be sent to His Majesty's Ambassador at Berlin to give all possible moral support to Belgian delegates and to make German government realise absolute necessity of showing itself reasonable and giving satisfaction to just Belgian requirements.[2] Belgian

---

[1] See *The Times* of September 5, p. 9. On September 8, Sir W. Tyrrell communicated to Sir Robert Horne Sir J. Bradbury's declaration as reported in *The Times*, and continued: 'It is hardly open to doubt that such public utterances, however sound the opinions expressed may be (as to which we cannot of course claim to be any judge), are apt to lead to misunderstanding and even, as in the present instance, to friction with our Allies. Might it not, in the general interest of our international relations, be possible to drop a hint to Sir J. Bradbury that at critical times such as the present, silence, so far as the press is concerned, has its advantages? After the extremely conciliatory line of policy which the Belgian Government have adopted in the matter of reparations, it seems at the least ungracious publicly to run counter to their wishes.

'It is of course true that we have in some degree met the specific request of the Belgian Government and instructed Lord D'Abernon [see No. 80, below] to urge the Germans in general terms to be reasonable in their negotiations with Belgium. But Lord Curzon considers that we should do more than this and he accordingly desires me to submit, for your concurrence, the enclosed draft of a telegram [for an amended text, see No. 82, below] which he would propose to address to Sir G. Grahame at Brussels.'

[2] In his telegram No. 69 of September 5, Mr. Phipps reported: 'Minister for Foreign Affairs told me very confidentially that arrangement which Belgian delegates would probably propose at Berlin would be to obtain payment of first two monthly instalments due from German government in foreign currency, third and fourth instalments being

government set particular store on support of His Majesty's Government in this matter.

His Excellency has made a similar request to United States ambassador here for American support at Berlin.

Repeated to Berlin.

guaranteed by the three D. banks and two others, leaving last two instalments, only due after next conference, to be guaranteed by gold deposits.'

(N.B. There were four D. banks: Deutsche Bank, Disconto-Gesellschaft, Dresdner Bank and Darmstädter Bank.)

No. 80

The Marquess Curzon of Kedleston to Lord D'Abernon (Berlin)
No. 81 Telegraphic [C 12574/99/18]

FOREIGN OFFICE, *September 6, 1922, 6.5 p.m.*

Brussels telegrams Nos. 68[1] and 69[2] (of September 5th).

Without advocating particular measures you should urge German government in general terms to make reasonable proposals to the Belgians.

Private and Confidential

His Majesty's Government are aware of certain suggestions[3] made informally by Sir J. Bradbury both to Bergmann[4] and Delacroix: these do not include the export of Reichsbank gold which His Majesty's Government do not favour.

[1] No. 79. [2] No. 79, n. 2.
[3] In a minute of September 6 Mr. Lampson wrote: 'Mr. Niemeyer, with whom I have spoken, is particularly anxious that we should do nothing at Berlin which would prejudice a scheme which Sir J. Bradbury has in hand whereby instead of German gold, certain *Belgian* bonds which we hold might to some extent be used as guarantee for the proposed German bonds to Belgium. The scheme is very involved and we have not got its text, but in the circumstances he would like the attached telegram [here printed] sent to Berlin.'
[4] Reparations expert. President of the Kriegslastenkommission, 1919–21.

No. 81

Lord D'Abernon (Berlin) to the Marquess Curzon of Kedleston
(Received September 9, 8.30 a.m.)
No. 166 Telegraphic [C 12735/99/18]

BERLIN, *September 8, 1922, 9.40 p.m.*

German government intend to propose to Belgian delegation that 60 or 70 per cent bills of exchange should be guaranteed by Reichsbank, a second guarantee, in addition to that of Reichsbank, being given by German industry if necessary arrangements can be made. Reichsbank has already accepted this proposal under pressure.

249

Industry have not yet agreed to give second guarantee demanded. They are out for considerable concessions regarding coal deliveries on reparation account.

Regarding balance of 40 or 30 per cent German government is anxious [that] Germany together with Belgium should approach England for some arrangement similar to that discussed privately with E. . . .[1] So far Belgians have vigorously resisted this proposal on the ground that they will not mix merchandise reparations with elapsed indebtedness.

Belgian delegation propose to leave Berlin Sunday[2] either with or without an arrangement.

Presumably they would be ready to return at later date if Belgian government accepted German basis.

[1] The text is here uncertain.   [2] September 10.

No. 82

The Marquess Curzon of Kedleston to Sir G. Grahame (Brussels)
No. 35 Telegraphic [C 12738/99/18]

FOREIGN OFFICE, *September 11, 1922, 6.45 p.m.*

Berlin telegram No. 169.[1]

You should convey substance of Lord D'Abernon's statement to Belgian government.

Attitude of His Majesty's Government in this matter will be clear to you from my telegram to Berlin No. 81[2] which through an error was not repeated to you but goes to you today. You should endeavour to remove any feeling of soreness under which Belgian government may be labouring. His Majesty's Government have acted throughout in complete loyalty to Belgium.

Repeated to Berlin No. 88.

[1] This telegram, dated September 10 and repeated to Brussels, ran as follows: 'This Embassy has given Belgian delegation constant, energetic, and to a large extent effective support. I have been in close touch with Monsieur Delacroix during critical days of negotiations and he has expressed recognition of good offices.

I should be glad for these facts to be known to Belgian government. They can be stated categorically and without reserve or qualification.'

[2] No. 80.

No. 83

Sir G. Grahame (Brussels) to Sir W. Tyrrell (Received September 15)
[C 13052/99/18]

Private and Confidential   BRUSSELS, *September 12, 1922*

My dear Tyrrell,

I had some conversation after dinner at the American Embassy on Friday last[1] with both M. Theunis and M. Jaspar. When it took place, it was not

[1] September 8.

yet known whether the German Government would come to terms with the Belgian Delegates at Berlin about the guarantees for their Treasury Bills.[2] M. Theunis was angry with the German Government for their obstinate attitude and exceedingly anxious as to the outcome of the negotiations. He considered it to be essential that this cape should be safely circumnavigated and seemed to think that there would be smoother water beyond. He knew how difficult and disagreeable it was for the German Government to come to terms, but, on the other hand, if they did not do so, infinitely worse would befall them. M. Poincaré would certainly take action as soon as he had a good excuse and would either go into the Ruhr or occupy Munich and Frankfort or something of that kind. No tangible benefits to the Allies would ensue but that would not stop M. Poincaré. He, M. Theunis, did not say that this German Ministry was exactly responsible for the present economic crisis, fall of the mark, etc. They had found themselves on a slippery slope, but, as Mr. Lloyd George had said on more than one occasion in public, this and other German Cabinets were to blame for having allowed matters to get into such a state as made the present conditions possible.

M. Theunis spoke more than once of a conference which would have to undertake a general settlement and for which the success of the present Belgo-German negotiations would be a happy augury. I asked him whether he thought that matters would be ripe for such a conference before the end of the year, observing that some people did not think that a general 'clean-up' was practicable at so early a date. The settlement would have to be made on somebody's back and the general opinion abroad seemed to be that it must be done on that of the already sorely-burdened British taxpayer. M. Theunis did not give any very definite answers to these remarks beyond observing that we considered the restoration of Europe was of such value to us that we seemed to be willing to forego hopes of getting reparation from Germany in order to hasten the process. The same reason might make us feel that it was worth while to let the French off their debt to us. He did not think that Great Britain had much chance of obtaining from the continental nations what they owed her. I observed that we might all be surprised later by the rapidity with which France recovered. In a decade or two, she might be well on her way, with the splendid resources which she now had at home and in Africa, to regain her pre-war position of one of the richest peoples in the world.

Some remarks of M. Theunis about the so-called Balfour Note[3] were rather lost owing to interruption. I understand, however, that M. Theunis does not agree with most of the criticism brought against the Note. Indeed, he recently stated in an interview that he did not think that the Note precluded all prospect of a settlement as some people argued.

M. Theunis believes that the Americans will ultimately have to reduce the rate of interest which they were asking from Great Britain. He told me, however, that all Americans who came to see him declared that we could pay in full. One of these visitors, apparently a person of some consequence,

2 See No. 81.   3 No. 45.

had stated that we had used a portion of the sums borrowed from America, not for war purposes, but to foster and reinforce British trade in South America at the expense of American trade. I observed that this was a quite novel accusation to me.

M. Theunis mentioned that he had had to engage himself to M. Poincaré not to permit the Belgo-German negotiations to take the form of a disguised moratorium. He had given M. Poincaré an assurance that he would insist on such guarantees from the German Government as would enable the Belgian Government to discount the German bills as they were received. This is borne out by a passage in M. Poincaré's speech at Meaux yesterday [*sic*][4] in which he is reported as having said that the Belgian Cabinet had expressly assured the French Government that the conditions which it would require from the German Government would preclude the arrangement from being a disguised moratorium and from prejudicing the future for the sake of the present.

M. Jaspar seems to think that M. Poincaré's power is wilting away. He even said to me that, if the Belgo-German negotiations succeeded, the indirect effect on M. Poincaré's position would be such as to mark the beginning of the end of his tenure of power. It may be that the wish is father to the thought, but both M. Theunis and M. Jaspar said that they had seen signs of trouble coming to M. Poincaré in France. M. Theunis said laughingly: 'Un pur trouve toujours un autre pur plus pur que lui.'

Yours, etc.,
GEORGE GRAHAME

[4] This speech, on the eighth anniversary of the first battle of the Marne (September 10), is summarised in Lord Hardinge's despatch No. 2134 of September 11 (C 12939/99/18), not printed.

No. 84

Sir G. Grahame (Brussels) to the Marquess Curzon of Kedleston
(Received September 15)
No. 631 [C 13019/99/18]

BRUSSELS, *September 12, 1922*

My Lord,

Having to see Herr Landsberg, the German Chargé d'Affaires in Brussels, about a minor matter, I took advantage of this occasion, and of an opening which he gave me by alluding to the present difficult situation caused by the interruption of the negotiations between Berlin and Brussels with regard to guarantees for six months Treasury Bills, to tell him that I was quite sure that the Belgian Ministers were very much in earnest. They were bound by the decision of the Reparation Commission, and, as he would have observed in reading the speech of the French President of the Council at Meaux[1] two days ago, by assurances given to the French Government that they would not accept an arrangement which would amount to a disguised

[1] See No. 83, n. 4.

moratorium and thus affect ulterior payments. Moreover, I added, the state of public opinion in Belgium must also be taken into account. It was pressing strongly upon the Belgian Ministers.

Herr Landsberg, who is a person of some consequence, having been a Majority Socialist Deputy and having been mentioned as a possible candidate to succeed Herr Rathenau, listened attentively to what I said. He observed that he was not acquainted with the details of the negotiations, but he did not see how the German Government could force the Reichsbank to act in a way contrary to what its strong-minded President[2] considered proper, for a law had recently been passed making the Reichsbank autonomous.

In taking leave of Herr Landsberg, I advised him once more not to under-estimate the strength of the determination of the Belgian Ministry to obtain satisfaction in the present controversy.[3]

I have, etc.,
GEORGE GRAHAME

[2] Dr. R. Havenstein.
[3] In his despatch No. 632 of September 12, Sir G. Grahame transmitted to the Foreign Office the following *Note Verbale* of September 11 from the Belgian Government:

'Le Gouvernement belge a l'honneur de porter ce qui suit à la connaissance du Gouverne-ment anglais:

'Conformément à la décision de la Commission des Réparations, en date du 31 août 1922, le Gouvernement belge s'est mis en rapport avec le Gouvernement allemand, à l'effet de se faire remettre, par ce dernier, des bons du Trésor allemand à six mois, payables en or, et a cherché à se mettre d'accord avec le Gouvernement allemand sur les garanties destinées à assurer le paiement de ces bons.

'Les délégués du Gouvernement belge, MM. Delacroix, Bemelmans et Philippson, se sont à cette fin rendus à Berlin, où ils ont discuté avec les représentants du Gouvernement allemand, du mardi 5 au samedi 9 septembre.

'L'offre du Gouvernement allemand a consisté à proposer au Gouvernement belge de lui remettre des bons du Trésor allemand, pour les versements du 15 août au 15 décembre, à l'échéance de six mois; la Reichsbank, par un instrument de garantie spéciale, prenait l'engagement de garantir la bonne fin de ces bons; quant aux échéances des 15 octobre–15 novembre et 15 décembre, et moyennant l'accord du Gouvernement belge, il pourrait être substitué à la garantie de la Reichsbank celle d'un consortium d'industriels et de banquiers à constituer dans les quatre semaines. Toutefois, le Gouvernement allemand mettait comme condition essentielle à sa proposition l'engagement, par le Gouvernement belge, de consentir à proroger de six mois l'échéance des bons pour les deux tiers et une seconde fois pour le dernier tiers, en manière telle que le premier tiers serait payé au bout de six mois, le second tiers au bout de douze mois et le troisième tiers après dix-huit mois.

'Sans s'arrêter à la discussion de la garantie offerte par le Gouvernement allemand, sous la forme d'un aval de la Reichsbank ou, éventuellement, d'un consortium d'industriels, le Gouvernement belge a estimé que, la décision de la Commission des Réparations limitant à six mois le délai d'échéance des bons, il ne pouvait consentir à la prorogation de ceux-ci pour un délai de douze et dix-huit mois.

'En conséquence, les pourparlers ont été rompus.

'La Commission des Réparations ayant décidé qu'à défaut d'accord sur les garanties à attacher au paiement des bons, ceux-ci devraient être garantis par un dépôt d'or dans une banque étrangère agréée par la Belgique, le Gouvernement belge, exécutant cette décision, notifie au Gouvernement allemand qu'il lui demande de lui remettre immédiate-ment deux bons du Trésor allemand à six mois, payables en or, chacun de 50 millions de marks-or, représentant les échéances des 15 août et 15 septembre 1922 et garantis par un dépôt d'une somme correspondante en or à la Banque nationale de Belgique.'

No. 85

Mr. Addison (Berlin) to the Marquess Curzon of Kedleston
(Received September 16)

No. 737 [C 13092/99/18]

BERLIN, *September 12, 192*

My Lord Marquess,

It may be considered that my telegram No. 173[1] of today exceeded the scope of my duties inasmuch as I had not been invited to make any comment or suggestion with regard to the question at issue. In reply I can only plead the urgency of the problem, as revealed in the telegrams from his Majesty', Ambassador at Brussels Nos. 71[2] and 72,[2] and the fact that any suggestion may possibly be of some use at such a time. The urgency is obvious, for an ultimatum of the nature indicated in Sir George Grahame's telegram No. 71 is likely, so far as prophecy is permissible, to lead to an aggravation of the present serious economic situation, and might render almost impossible the solution which it will be the aim of the forthcoming Reparation Conference to attain. As time is also of the essence of the contract, I thought it not out of place to indicate that the German negotiators might not be unwilling to yield, as the result of pressure, where they had not done so of their own free will, and that a warning as outlined in Sir George Grahame's telegram No. 72[2] might induce in them a better understanding of the interests of their country.

So far as could be ascertained from conversations with the Belgian delegates during their visit to Berlin, their attitude was exceedingly moderate and sensible, and corresponded entirely to the general position of the Belgian Government, as set out at length in Sir George Grahame's despatch to Your Lordship, No. 571 of the 22nd ultimo.[3] M. Bemelmans in particular told me that the object of the Belgian proposal, which had been accepted by the Reparation Commission,[4] had been merely to avoid a breach between England and France, the policy of Belgium being based on the cardinal fact that the Entente between these two countries must be maintained in the interests of European peace in general, and of a proper settlement of the reparations question in particular. The Belgian Government had therefore practically taken upon their own shoulders the burden of granting a six months' Moratorium to Germany, and would alone incur the loss consequent upon a failure of the German Government to pay at the proper time, the instalments due during that period. They quite realised that paper guarantee and the endorsement of the bills by German banks, or by a German Consortium, could not increase the value of the bills as a marketable asset, but they were quite willing to agree to some such compromise merely in order to grant a respite, thus enabling the forthcoming conference to deliberate in comparative peace and freedom of mind.

---

[1] Not printed.   [2] Of September 11, not printed.   [3] No. 71.
[4] See No. 78, n. 1.

It is indeed clear that no guarantee from this country can be of any use to ensure payment of the bills of exchange which do not include a mortgage of the German gold reserve, and in accepting, as they practically did, such illusory guarantees as that of the Reichsbank or of a consortium of German businessmen, the Belgian delegates showed clearly that they were willing to come to an arrangement which, while satisfying public opinion in Belgium and, to a certain extent, in France, would in reality amount to nothing more than a respite, during which the whole problem could be settled by the Allied Statesmen in Council. Obviously if the German Government cannot find at the present time the necessary sums in foreign currency to enable them to pay debts accruing at present and in the near future, they are not likely to be in a better position to do so after the month of February next when, if matters are allowed to take their course, conditions will probably be worse than they are now, and *a fortiori* will this argument apply to the Reichsbank or to any other Association in this country (except insofar of course as German business men might be willing to part with a portion of their unknown reserves in foreign countries, which is unlikely). To accept a German promise to pay, unaccompanied by the tangible support of gold, is clearly equivalent to the action of a private bank accepting as cover for an overdraft a cheque drawn on itself by the person who has incurred such overdraft. Instead, however, of realising that the true meaning of the negotiations was to make Germany a free gift of breathing time, coupled with such outward conditions as would satisfy allied public opinion, and that the question of the real date when the bills of exchange must be met could conveniently be left till such time as they matured, and would probably be settled in some way between now and that moment, the German Government appear to have adopted a course which is characteristic of their lamentable lack of diplomatic skill and to have allowed the negotiations to be wrecked over a point which common sense should have warned them was of little practical importance. Experience should have taught the German Government that the policy of uttering an emphatic and despairing 'No' on every possible occasion is one which is not to be commended and that the most practical way of effecting an end is often to appear to yield on the immediate point at issue. Above all they should keep in mind during negotiations the warning addressed by Mirabeau to the National Assembly: 'la banqueroute, la hideuse banqueroute, est là: elle menace de consumer vous, vos propriétés, votre honneur,—et vous délibérez'.

It would appear to be imperative, for the furtherance of British interests which require that the reparation problem be studied and settled with the calm of an ordinary business discussion, that some direct understanding between Belgium and Germany, however illusory, should create the atmosphere appropriate to this end. It would seem to be equally necessary that, in the interval, no further depreciation of the mark should be occasioned by outside complications, a depreciation which will be serious enough owing to the frenzied activity of the printing press in this country. It is for these reasons that I ventured to invite Your Lordship's instructions as to whether

I should take action which I hope might not be entirely devoid of success in view of the inability of German official circles to see the obvious, unless it be emphatically pointed out to them.

I have, etc.,
JOSEPH ADDISON

No. 86

Lord Hardinge (Paris) to the Marquess Curzon of Kedleston
(Received September 13, 7 p.m.)
No. 462 Telegraphic [C 12977/99/18]

PARIS, *September 13, 1922, 4.40 p.m.*

Following for Chancellor of the Exchequer from Sir John Bradbury:—
Sir G. Grahame's telegram No. 71 to Foreign Office.[1]

I consider German proposals made to representatives of Belgian government for guarantee of German Treasury six months bills entirely reasonable. There is nothing in my opinion in decision of reparation commission[2] which precludes Belgian government from giving indulgence in respect of time to guarantors if their liabilities should become operative. In any event sudden rupture of negotiations on the part of Belgian government and peremptory demand for deposit of gold in Brussels has created on my mind worst possible impression. The last-mentioned demand is in any case wholly unjustified under terms of decision of reparation commission itself which on default of agreement between the two governments required a deposit of gold by way of guarantee in a foreign bank approved by Belgian government.

Suggest strong pressure should be brought to bear on Belgian government to secure immediate withdrawal of demand and to agree that question of adequate guarantees offered by German government should be submitted to arbitration of America or neutral banker.

Repeated to Brussels.

[1] Of September 11, not printed.   [2] See No. 78, n. 1.

No. 87

Sir G. Grahame (Brussels) to the Marquess Curzon of Kedleston
(Received September 14, 3.15 p.m.)
No. 75 Telegraphic [C 13009/99/18]

Immediate   BRUSSELS, *September 14, 1922, 12.45 p.m.*

Lord Hardinge's telegram of September 13th.[1] Sending message from Sir J. Bradbury to Chancellor of the Exchequer.

Belgian demand on Germany having been made public and having

[1] No. 86.

received warm approval of country, it would be useless for His Majesty's Government to endeavour to make Belgian government recede from position taken up, especially in absence of any German counter concession. Endeavour would be deeply resented and be calculated to throw Belgium altogether into the arms of France.

Possibly discreet [intervention] might induce Belgian government to substitute non-Belgian Bank for National Bank here but I cannot be sure.

Repeated to Paris.

No. 88

The Marquess Curzon of Kedleston to Sir G. Grahame (Brussels)
No. 37 Telegraphic [C 12977/99/18]

FOREIGN OFFICE, *September 14, 1922, 2.5 p.m.*[1]

Your telegram No. 71[2] and Sir J. Bradbury's telegram to Chancellor of Exchequer of September 13th.[3]

Treasury take very serious view of the effect the transfer of gold from Germany to Belgium may have on exchange situation. We thoroughly appreciate the public spirited effort Belgium has made to ease matters in connection with reparations and especially her latest efforts in Berlin: but we cannot help thinking that it is not quite realised locally what consequences may follow owing to her present demand for the deposit of gold.

We hope you will make every effort to induce Belgian government to waive this requirement thus giving time for other expedients to be explored, and we leave it to your discretion to use as much of the arguments supplied by Sir J. Bradbury as you think opportune.

[1] This telegram crossed No. 87.   [2] Of September 11, not printed.
[3] No. 86.

No. 89

The Marquess Curzon of Kedleston to Mr. Addison (Berlin)
No. 92 Telegraphic [C 12872/99/18]

FOREIGN OFFICE, *September 14, 1922, 7 p.m.*

Brussels telegram No. 72[1] (of September 11th: German Belgian reparation negotiations).

On September 11th the German ambassador made two proposals.

1. He asked that Sir John Bradbury might be instructed to move the reparation commission to intimate to the Belgian government that they were at liberty to accept the German proposal to extend the period for the maturity of the German bills handed to Belgium from six months to eighteen months.

[1] Not printed.

2. He suggested a scheme under which English banks were to offer collateral security for the German bills up to 25%. He stated that the German government had asked the Belgian government to apply to His Majesty's Government to obtain this security for them but Belgian government had refused. German government accordingly suggested that His Majesty's Government should approach the Italian or Japanese governments with a view to their putting forward the proposal.

After consultation with Treasury M. Sthamer was informed on September 12th that as regards first proposal German government's view would be communicated to Sir J. Bradbury but that he could not, owing to his judicial position, be sent instructions suggested. As regards second proposal His Majesty's Government could not entertain it. M. Sthamer was also informed that in our view it would be in the best interests of Germany to do everything that was possible to meet the Belgian requirements.

Repeated to Brussels No. 38.

No. 90

Sir G. Grahame (Brussels) to the Marquess Curzon of Kedleston
(Received September 15, 8.30 a.m.)
No. 77 Telegraphic [C 13054/99/18]

Confidential   BRUSSELS, *September 14, 1922, 7.56 p.m.*
Your telegram No. 37.[1]

I happen to know that Minister for Foreign Affairs is somehow aware of Sir John Bradbury's views as expressed in his telegram to Chancellor of the Exchequer[2] and that he refuses to believe that His Majesty's Government would go so far as to adopt . . .[3] course of action suggested therein.

I will endeavour to see him again tomorrow and mention serious view taken by Treasury of what would happen if German gold were transferred, but I know beforehand that his answer will be 'then help us in getting Germans to withdraw demand for prolongation'. If German government agree to do this, demand for gold will of course be relinquished as agreement will have been reached (see my telegram No. 76, last paragraph).[4]

Not repeated.

[1] No. 88.   [2] No. 86.   [3] The text is here uncertain.
[4] Of September 14, not printed.

No. 91

Mr. Addison (Berlin) to the Marquess Curzon of Kedleston
(Received September 15, 8.30 a.m.)
No. 175 Telegraphic [C 13042/99/18]

BERLIN, *September 14, 1922, 8.20 p.m.*

President of Reichsbank leaves for London tonight.

I gather from Ministry of Foreign Affairs that he desires to obtain some form of guarantee from Bank of England that latter will assist should Reichsbank find difficulty in meeting six months bills when due. He would then be willing to endorse six months bills without insisting on prolongation.

Proposal is not that Bank of England should also guarantee payment but that private arrangement be made as between the two banks based on deposit of fifty million gold marks of Reichsbank which Bank of England already holds. President of Reichsbank might even be willing to provide Bank of England with further gold guarantee failing possibility of any other arrangement but neither he nor German government will consent to transfer gold to Belgian or French bank.

No. 92

Mr. Addison (Berlin) to the Marquess Curzon of Kedleston
(Received September 18, 10.15 p.m.)
No. 177 Telegraphic [C 13191/99/18]

BERLIN, *September 18, 1922, 8.15 p.m.*

I hear from Ministry for Foreign Affairs that President of Reichsbank having concluded satisfactory private arrangement in England,[1] note will be sent to Belgian government tomorrow agreeing to Reichsbank's guarantee of six months bill[s] without condition of prolongation.

Repeated to Brussels.

[1] See No. 91.

No. 93

Sir G. Grahame (Brussels) to the Marquess Curzon of Kedleston
(Received September 21)
No. 640 [C 13275/99/18]

Confidential   BRUSSELS, *September 19, 1922*

My Lord,

As I had the honour to inform Your Lordship by my telegram No. 81 of today's date,[1] the Belgian Minister for Foreign Affairs informed me this

[1] Not printed.

morning that the German Government had made known to him through the German Chargé d'Affaires in Brussels that they withdrew the condition of prolongation beyond six months of the period within which the German Treasury Bills, to be tendered to Belgium in settlement of the reparation payments due to her from August 15 to the end of the year, should be met. In this way satisfaction was given to the Belgian desiderata and the matter was settled.

I told M. Jaspar that I felt that the successful conclusion of these ticklish negotiations might properly be the occasion for offering congratulations to him and to the Prime Minister. They had already received encomiums from various quarters for having opened out an issue from the deadlock which had arisen in the Reparation Commission at the end of August.[2] The fact of having now achieved an agreement with Berlin would bring them added prestige, and Belgian public opinion would surely not fail to recognize the success of the Belgian Cabinet in obtaining satisfaction. Last, but not least, two hundred and seventy million gold marks would now, by the discounting of the Germany Treasury Bills as received, be paid into the coffers of the Belgian Treasury. It was these considerations among other things which induced me to offer him my congratulations. I felt sure that he would agree with me that this sum would not have been obtained for Belgium if the course which I understood was favoured by the French Government, namely military sanctions, had been adopted. In the general upset which would have ensued from these measures, cash payments might have been whistled for.

M. Jaspar thanked me for my congratulations and said that there was truth in my remarks.

I ventured to remind M. Jaspar that British support during these negotiations had been forthcoming in Berlin, in Brussels and in London.[3] In all three capitals, the German Government or German Representatives had been urged from the British side to meet the reasonable demands of Belgium, and warned that the Belgian Ministers were in earnest. These various efforts on the part of His Majesty's Government to bring about a settlement between Brussels and Berlin seemed—if I might say so—all the more deserving of appreciation as the fact could not be ignored that in the British view the best course would have been a moratorium pure and simple. His Majesty's Government were therefore, when giving support to the Belgian policy, not supporting the one which appealed to them the most.

M. Jaspar said that he sincerely appreciated the assistance which had been afforded to the Belgian Government. No doubt his appreciation would have been more spontaneous if he had not been aware—presumably through the Belgian Delegate—that the British Delegate on the Reparation Commission had suggested at a critical moment of the negotiations with Berlin that His Majesty's Government should induce the Belgian Government to withdraw the demand publicly made that the Reichsbank should deposit one hundred million gold marks at the National Bank in Brussels. But as His Excellency

<hr />

[2] See No. 78, n. 1.   [3] See Nos. 79–92.

had no indication that Sir John Bradbury's proposition was endorsed by His Majesty's Government he can have no grievance against them.

The French Ambassador, who left M. Jaspar as I arrived had, so I learnt from the latter, brought a message straight from the French President of the Council apparently to the effect that he considered that the Belgian Government ought not at this stage to be satisfied with anything less than the delivery of the gold demanded from Germany.

I gathered that this unsolicited advice was not appreciated by M. Jaspar and that a somewhat sharp discussion, going beyond the immediate question at issue, followed its delivery.

I have, etc.,

GEORGE GRAHAME

No. 94

Sir J. Bradbury (Reparation Commission) to Sir R. Horne (Treasury)
(Received in the Foreign Office, October 12)

[C 14129/99/18]

Copy   PARIS, *September 22, 1922*

My dear Chancellor,

Here is my Swan-Song.[1]

Having satisfied myself by my conversations with the Prime Minister and yourself that my ideas were generally in accordance with those of the Government, I had intended to sing it to the Commission on my own responsibility. My doing so will, however, inevitably mean a certain amount of friction with our French friends which may, regard being had to the Eastern situation,[2] be inopportune, although the friction could no doubt be alleviated, if necessary, by the sacrifice of an already moribund British Delegate—a willing and even an enthusiastic victim.

Further the acceptance yesterday by Mr. Fisher at Geneva of M. de Jouvenal's motion[3] about reparation and inter-allied debts seems to indicate a higher degree of hopefulness in regard to the possibility of an early

---

[1] It had been arranged that Sir J. Bradbury should retire from the Reparation Commission on November 30 (see below). On September 29, however, Sir Warren Fisher (Permanent Secretary of H.M. Treasury) wrote to him as follows: 'The Chancellor and I have had more than one serious conversation on the subject of 30th November. The fact that I am writing on his behalf is only because, in common with other Ministers, he is continually engaged with the problems arising out of the Near East and he knows that you and I are old friends. The Chancellor, while fully realising the strength of your wish to be freed from the incessant work and responsibility which has been yours so long, asks me to put it to you that you might be willing to defer, until the end of March 1923, your severance from the Reparation Commission. He knows, as I do, how distasteful the delay will be to you personally; and he would not have dreamt of making a request involving such inconvenience to you if the circumstances of the immediate future had left him any reasonable alternative.'

[2] See Vol. XVIII, Chap. I.

[3] At the Eighth Meeting of the Committee on the Reduction of Armaments. See *League of Nations: Records of the Third Assembly: Meetings of the Committees, 1922*, pp. 41–4.

comprehensive settlement than I possess myself or than I have hitherto been disposed to credit to H[is] M[ajesty's] G[overnment].

In these circumstances, I think that I ought to consult you—at any rate unofficially—before launching my offensive, and that, in the case of your thinking it unwise, I ought to abandon it. I put the question to you in this negative form because if I am to launch it I think it is better that it should be on my own responsibility as it might be dangerous in the present unstable conditions of international politics for H[is] M[ajesty's] G[overnment] to be irretrievably committed to it.

If I abandon the offensive, I do not think there is much that the Commission can usefully attempt pending the result of the inter-allied conference which will presumably take place in December.[4] The French will probably indulge in guerilla operations with a view to securing a declaration of 'manquement' in regard to the coal deliveries and the carrying out by the German Government of the control agreements with the Committee of Guarantees but these ought to be contained without any great effort; and, except for the danger of an internal debacle in Germany—which may not be obliging enough to wait for the conference—we ought to have a fairly placid time until the end of the year. I would therefore (regarding the settlement of the Belgian bond question as the 'end of the present crisis'[5] within the meaning of my letter of the 27th June[6]) with your permission propose to go away on leave shortly after Kemball-Cook's return on the 2nd proximo (say about the 14th) and not return to active work unless before my successor is available anything should arise with which you would wish me to deal.

Six weeks' leave would bring us to 30th November—the date originally fixed for my retirement—but if it is convenient for my successor to take over at an earlier date I am quite agreeable. If on the other hand he is not available by the 30th November I could, if you wish, remain titular Delegate for a few weeks longer without pay. This is of course not in any way intended as a threat of resignation if I am not given my way about the offensive. Frankly I am myself very doubtful as to the wisdom of launching it in existing circumstances—indeed I should be certain of its unwisdom if I could see any other way of avoiding the danger of our being blackmailed at the inter-allied conference.

On the other hand, I do feel very strongly the responsibility of the Reparation Commission under the Peace Treaty for seeing that the reparation claims are not pressed to the point of destroying the financial and economic fabric of Germany, and, as I am convinced that an immediate and generous moratorium is essential, I find it very difficult to remain an active member of

---

[4] Inter-Allied conferences on Reparations and Inter-Allied Debts were held in London (December 9–11) and Paris (January 2–4, 1923). Reports and Secretaries' Notes of Conversations are printed in Cmd. 1812 (Miscellaneous No. 3 (1923)). These Reports and Notes will not be published in this Series.

[5] See Nos. 79–93.

[6] Not traced in the Foreign Office Archives.

the Commission without making every effort to enforce such a policy without delay.

If I am to make a move in the Commission I think I ought to do it as soon as possible, since, though early agreement on the lines I advocate is clearly out of the question, the making of the move might help the mark and check the progress of the mischief in Germany. It will of course be necessary in any case to wait until we are through the acute phase of the Eastern crisis but that I imagine is not likely to last very long.

Yours sincerely,
JOHN BRADBURY

No. 95

Mr. Niemeyer (Treasury) to Sir J. Bradbury (Reparation Commission)
(Received in the Foreign Office, October 12)

[C 14129/99/18]

Copy   *September 27, 1922*

My dear Bradbury,

The Chancellor, who is very much occupied with Turkey,[1] has asked me to tell you his views on your letters of 22nd[2] and 25th September.[3]

To deal with the latter first. He doesn't favour the idea that a Minister might be the Reparations Delegate. He much prefers the present system which has the great advantage that the Commission can, on occasion, speak as an expert judiciary, and at all times function at least nominally independently of politicians.

As to the swan song, the Chancellor agrees that you should proceed with the offensive, though it might be well not to go over the top for a few days yet.

It will clearly be best for you to put forward the scheme on your own authority and without therefore criticism of it in general from us: but there are one or two points which the Chancellor would prefer to see omitted, at any rate at the present stage. I don't think they interfere with anything but the frills.

They are as follows:—

(1) The specific reference to the Reparation Recoveries Act.[4] As you know this is very dear to certain persons here and though we should ultimately have to repeal it if a complete moratorium went through, we should like to leave this in the background for the moment.

(2) The 80% advances[5] from State Banks. We should in fact much dislike this and would prefer that it should not be suggested to the other countries.

(3) The hypothecation of State mines and forests. We have so recently made this a cardinal point of difference, that a volte face so soon would be very awkward. If you suggest it, it will be thought that His

---

[1] See Vol. XVIII, Chap. I.   [2] No. 94.   [3] Not printed.
[4] See No. 59, n. 5.   [5] Cf. No. 97, Enclosure, below.

Majesty's Government are really weakening on it and that all the pother in August[6] was really unnecessary.

Warren Fisher at the Chancellor's request will be writing to you[7] on the personal points in your letter of the 22nd.

Blackett will probably be here from Monday onward.

Yours sincerely,

O. E. N[IEMEYER]

[6] See Chap. II.   [7] See No. 94, n. 1.

No. 96

Mr. Cadogan to the Treasury
[C 13843/99/18]

FOREIGN OFFICE, *October 4, 1922*

Sir,

I am directed by the Marquess Curzon of Kedleston to inform you that the German Ambassador called at the Foreign Office on October 2nd to express the uneasiness of his government at the apparent delay that is taking place in dealing with the question of reparations.

2. His Excellency pointed out that there were only three months remaining up to the end of the year, in the course of which some solution would have to be found. It had occurred to the German Government that it might now be possible to resuscitate the Bankers' Committee, whose sittings were not formally terminated but only adjourned in June last.[1]

3. Monsieur Sthamer said that the German Government fully realised that they could not themselves make the first move in this direction, but that they were anxious to know whether His Majesty's Government would be prepared to sound their allies on the proposal. Monsieur Sthamer added that he had reason to believe that the Belgian Government were very favourable to the foregoing suggestion.

4. Lord Curzon would be glad to know what answer should, in the opinion of the Lords Commissioners of His Majesty's Treasury, be returned to Monsieur Sthamer.

I am, etc.,

ALEXANDER CADOGAN

[1] See No. 27, nn. 4 and 5, and No. 28, n. 6.

Sir J. Bradbury (Reparation Commission) to the Treasury
(Received in the Foreign Office, October 10)
Report No. 316 [C 14075/99/18]

Copy   PARIS, *October 6, 1922*

May it please your Lordships,

I have the honour to transmit, for Your Lordships' information, a copy of a memorandum which I have laid before the Reparation Commission on the subject of the steps which ought, in my opinion, to be taken in regard to the payments to be demanded from Germany under the Treaty of Versailles in the years 1923 and 1924, and the general policy to be adopted in view of the serious situation created by the collapse of the mark exchanges.

I have, etc.,
JOHN BRADBURY

ENCLOSURE IN No. 97

Memorandum on the Future of Reparation

I am convinced that unless immediate steps are taken to improve and stabilise the exchange value of the mark, a breakdown of the German financial structure which will be destructive to all hopes of obtaining reparation, either in cash or kind, for many years to come, if not for ever, is inevitable.

If action is delayed until German internal prices have adjusted themselves to the present exchange of 2000 marks to the dollar (even if the rate goes no worse, as it almost certainly will do unless early remedial action is taken), the difficulties of establishing budget equilibrium, even if Peace Treaty payments both in cash and kind are suspended altogether, will be very great.

I am definitely of opinion that if matters are allowed to drift, such entire suspension will before very long become unavoidable, and that the longer the grant of it is delayed, the longer the period of suspension will have to be.

If it is delayed until the collapse of the German foreign exchanges is complete, I believe a break-up of economic and social order in Germany will follow, and, if this takes place, the process of rebuilding will be a very long and painful one, involving in all probability as an indispensable preliminary the entire remission of the reparation liability.

If any further increase of the floating debt could be stopped, there would at the present moment be no serious difficulty in the way of stabilising the exchange value of the mark at any reasonable figure (say, between the limits of 500 marks and 1000 marks to the dollar) which those responsible might see fit to select. All that is necessary is that the Reichsbank should sell gold freely for paper marks at the rate selected.

Such a policy (always on the assumption that there will be no further addition to the floating debt) involves no serious risk of depleting the gold reserve.

The present circulation is, even at an exchange of 500 marks to the dollar, quite inadequate to the needs of the country. Once the creation of new floating debt comes to an end, there are only three ways in which additional currency can be obtained by the public:—

(a) By the discounting with the Reichsbank of German Government Treasury bills now held by the public (amounting on 23rd September 1922 to about 75 milliard marks).

(b) By the withdrawal of existing deposits in the Reichsbank (which inclusive of liabilities classified under 'miscellaneous' at the same date stood at 83 milliards).

(c) By the creation of new credit by the Reichsbank.

The maximum amount theoretically obtainable under (a) and (b) is 158 milliards; in practice, it would be much less, for, though no doubt the bulk of the Treasury bills still held by the public would either be presented for discount or have to be replaced at maturity by new bills discounted with the Reichsbank, the deposits are not capable of unlimited reduction.

It is certain, therefore, that recourse would have to be had on a very considerable scale to (c),[1] and, as the creation of new credits by the Reichsbank is entirely optional, the control of the bank over the currency would be complete. The bank would then be able to protect its gold and maintain the foreign exchanges by the time-honoured methods—though necessarily in the first instance at the cost of an acute credit crisis. Such a crisis has, however, to be faced in any case if serious attempts at financial reform are to be taken in hand.

The above plan is, however, only feasible if further inflation can be avoided—otherwise it will merely result in the Reichsbank gradually losing its gold without acquiring the control necessary to stop the rot.

Unless and until the credit of the German Government is re-established, inflation can only be stopped by covering Government outgoings by taxation.

With an exchange anywhere in the neighbourhood of 500 marks to the dollar, this condition could be secured without serious difficulty if Peace Treaty charges were completely suspended. I doubt, however, whether it is possible if any appreciable provision has to be made for Peace Treaty charges in 1923, or anything more than quite a modest provision in 1924.

Quite apart from payments in foreign currency, the paper mark payments in respect of deliveries in kind, even on the scale of this year, would make the task a difficult one, while any increase in the deliveries in kind above the present level would almost certainly make it impossible.

With an exchange of 1,000 marks to the dollar the task of balancing the budget would be still more difficult but not I think hopeless if the Peace Treaty charges could be entirely suspended.

[1] A note to the Memorandum runs as follows: 'Indeed this is in fact already happening notwithstanding the continued expansion of the floating debt, by reason of the decline in the value of the mark having for the moment outstripped the progress of inflation. The Reichsbank's holding of Bills and Cheques increased between 30th June and 23rd Sept. from 4·8 milliards to no less than 43 milliards.'

On the other hand, a complete moratorium in respect of all Peace Treaty obligations, both in cash and kind, not only is impossible for political reasons but economically might have serious consequences to the Allied countries principally interested in reparation.

Is there no way out of the *impasse*?

There is one way, and I think only one. To the extent to which Peace Treaty payments, either in cash or kind, are called for in excess of the provision which can be made for them in the budget, credit facilities must be provided for the German Government.

In present circumstances, the only countries which have any inducement to provide such facilities are those receiving the payments.

My proposal is:—

(1) That all cash payments for Peace Treaty charges (including costs of armies of occupation, reparation, compositions for restitution, clearing offices balances, and miscellaneous obligations) falling due between 1 January, 1923, and 31 December, 1924, should be met by German Treasury five-year bonds to be delivered to the Reparation Commission and distributed to the respective Governments interested in the same manner as the cash would have been distributed if payment had been made in cash.

(2) That in respect of all deliveries in kind, services rendered etc., within the same period for which credit has to be given to Germany under the Peace Treaty the German Government should be notified month by month of the amounts debited to each Allied Government, and should be allowed to obtain from each such Government a guarantee of German Treasury five-year bonds to the amount so debited, less such percentage, if any, as the Reparation Commission may from time to time decide can be met without creating a deficit in the German budget.

The bonds under paragraphs (1) and (2) would be identical in every respect. They would be expressed in gold marks and should be payable by the agents of the German Government in the capital of the recipient or guaranteeing Power in the currency of that Power, at the option of the holder, either at the rate of exchange ruling at the date of issue (which should be stated on the bond) or at that ruling at the date of payment.[2]

The liability of the guarantors however should be limited to payment in currency at the rate of exchange at the date of issue, the holder to accept in the event of a German default such payment by the guarantor as a full

[2] A note runs as follows: 'This option would no doubt in the event of a considerable improvement taking place in the gold value of the currency of a guaranteeing country be very costly to the German Government. In all the circumstances, however, I do not think it is unreasonable to ask the German Government to take the risk in consideration for the guarantee. If the bonds are to be readily negotiable in the guaranteeing countries it is obviously essential that their value in terms of the national currency should be assured. If, in addition to this, they are gold bonds (even though the marginal gold value is not guaranteed) they would have a certain element of attractiveness (which would become considerable as German credit improves) as investments in countries of which the exchanges are not very stable.'

discharge, all claims against the German Government in respect of the defaulted bonds to pass to the guarantor. If instead of claiming payment under the guarantee, the holder prefers to retain the defaulted bond as a gold claim against the German Government he should be at liberty to do so, the guarantee thereupon lapsing.

The bonds should bear interest at a rate high enough, regard being had to the credit of the guaranteeing countries, to enable them to be readily negotiated at par (say, 6 or even 7 per cent.). They should have on their face a space for endorsement thereon of the guarantee of the recipient Government. Those under paragraph (1) would be retained by the Governments concerned, and would be negotiable by them only under their respective guarantees; those under paragraph (2) would be returned, after the endorsement thereon of the guarantees of the recipient Government, to the German Government, and would be negotiable by that Government.

In order to increase the attractiveness of the bonds to investors it is for consideration whether the State Banks of the respective guaranteeing countries might not undertake at any time during the currency of the bonds to make advances against them up to (say) 80 per cent. of their guaranteed face value, receiving authority if necessary from their respective Governments to treat them as cover for their note issues.

Any country called upon to guarantee bonds under paragraph (2) should be given the option of retaining the bonds on payment to the German Government of their face value in cash.

It should be announced that, provided that the German Government carry out the requirements of the Reparation Commission in regard to balancing the budget and reform of the finances of Germany, similar arrangements will, to such extent as the Reparation Commission may think them necessary, be made for the years 1925 and 1926, and that, as soon as the position becomes sufficiently clear, and in any case not later than 1 July 1926, the Allied Governments will consider the whole question of the aggregate liabilities of Germany under the Peace Treaty with a view to their permanent adjustment to her capacity of payment and to their liquidation by a series of foreign loans.

Subject to the above arrangements, the reparation liabilities of Germany from 1 January, 1923, would be governed by the Schedule of Payments,[3] under which the cash liability for each year is the difference between the value of the deliveries actually effected and the full annuity liability. This would have the result of giving an inducement to Germany to increase the deliveries in kind to the maximum possible figure, since the guaranteed bonds representing the value of the deliveries in kind would be placed at her disposal, while those representing the cash liability would remain with Allied Powers.

From the point of view of the Treasuries of the Allied Powers, the plan has the advantage of providing the same measure of budget relief as would have been derived from a complete execution of the Schedule of Payments

[3] See No. 5, n. 2.

provided they are prepared to guarantee, and to find a market for, the German bonds.

No alternative policy seems likely to secure anything like so satisfactory a financial result.

The policy of insisting on reparation payments and deliveries in kind without regard to their effect on the budget has already made the continuance of payments in foreign currencies impossible and jeopardised the deliveries. To continue it will soon make the cessation of even the deliveries in kind inevitable and will create conditions in which measures of coercion, if applied, will not even cover their own cost.

On the other hand, the difficulties in which the Treasuries of the Allied Powers find themselves by reason of the disappointment, now inevitable, of the extravagant hopes formerly entertained in regard to the possibilities of reparation payments are very real difficulties. They will indeed be mitigated—not aggravated as some seem inclined to contend—by a prudent handling of bad and doubtful assets and a recognition of the unwisdom of throwing good money after bad; but even so they will remain serious, and just as it would be suicidal for the Allies to press their claims against Germany to the breaking point of the latter, so it would be suicidal for the creditor Allies to press inter-Allied claims to the breaking point of the debtor.

It is suggested therefore that in order to ease the general situation the Allied Governments should be invited to reconsider the existing inter-Allied financial arrangements with a view to:—

(1) The grant of indulgence in respect of inter-Allied war indebtedness during the period up to the maturity of the last issued German guaranteed bonds.

(2) The acceptance of the guaranteed bonds as between Allied Governments in lieu of cash for the purpose of adjustment of accounts.

(3) The taking into account of any losses incurred by the guaranteeing Governments by reason of their guarantee becoming operative in the ultimate arrangements for dealing with inter-Allied indebtedness, which should be made at the same time as the German liability is permanently adjusted.

If the above plan commends itself to my colleagues, I would suggest that the Commission should pass a resolution approving it in principle subject to the observations of the German Government and the approval of the Allied Governments.

The approval of the Allied Governments is, I think, desirable before the plan is adopted because, though more favourable to them than a simple postponement for five years of the payments falling due in 1923 and 1924 (which would be within the competence of a majority decision of the Reparation Commission), it undoubtedly involves new elements, such as the guarantee of the bonds by the Allied Governments, which are not contemplated by the Treaty of Versailles.

Its adoption should be made conditional on the German Government undertaking to impose by law upon the Reichsbank the obligation to sell gold at a fixed price—the figure to be determined by a mixed commission of three, one member to be appointed by the German Government, one by the Reparation Commission, and the third to be an American financial expert agreed by the other two; the price, once fixed, to be incapable of increase, but to be subject to diminution on the demand of the German Government with the approval of the Reparation Commission.

The figure should have regard to the internal purchasing power of the mark,[4] as determined by a comparison of average German and American prices for staple commodities, at the time the rate is fixed in order to avoid complicating the credit crisis which will certainly follow the introduction of the arrangement by a fresh disturbance of internal values. Two or three weeks ago, a rate of 500 marks to the dollar would, I believe, have been suitable and practicable. Now it may be necessary to go as high as 750 or even 1,000. In a very few weeks' time a very much higher rate will almost certainly be inevitable.

Although I think it desirable that the German Government should retain the power, subject to the approval of the Reparation Commission, to lower the rate (i.e. to raise the exchange value of the mark), if in future it is thought wise to do so, it will probably be found that a new parity, once established, will be permanent. It will be convenient, therefore, to select a mark-price for gold which will make the mark-dollar or mark-pound parity a round figure.

The new Reichsbank law should also make suitable provisions, in accordance with recommendations to be made by the Committee above suggested, for the control of the note issue by requiring any new expansion to be covered in suitable proportions by gold or approved foreign currencies and commercial bills. It should also prohibit any further issues of legal tender money otherwise than by the Reichsbank.

Such an arrangement would give the best possible guarantee for the rehabilitation of the German budget position, since Germany would know that, unless the increase of the floating debt were arrested, she would lose her gold reserve and with it the last barrier between herself and final financial collapse.

If further guarantees on the part of Germany are thought to be necessary, I should see no serious objection to requiring the German Government to agree to pledge specific State assets of a suitable character to the service of the guaranteed bonds and to invest the Reparation Commission with powers of foreclosure in the event of default. The problem of finding assets suitable for pledging will obviously be greatly simplified if the mark can be stabilised.

I do not myself believe that such guarantees would really improve the security, but they might have a certain political value, not only in the eyes

[4] A note runs as follows: 'Some elasticity may be desirable in applying this principle. A fall in paper mark prices if it comes before the recent catastrophic rise has become stereotyped would probably be salutary rather than otherwise.'

of public opinion in Allied countries, but as indicating to the German people that any failure on their part to carry out the new arrangement will be followed by drastic action. I have never myself opposed the use of coercion to enforce obligations which Germany is really capable of carrying out—indeed, in the last resort it is the only alternative—but from the point of view of the restoration of German credit the fact of menaces of this character being regarded as necessary is an element of weakness rather than of strength, and unless the political advantages of indulging in them are thought to outweigh the financial disadvantages, I should prefer that recourse to them should be avoided.

I would further suggest that, in the event of the adoption of the new plan, the Allied Governments should at the same time consider the question of the desirability of reconstructing the Reparation Commission and transferring it to Berlin.

The interests of Germany and Germany's creditors are, in my opinion, on a long-sighted view, identical. Recent history has, however, shown pretty clearly that the Reparation Commission as at present constituted is too much disposed to sacrifice the interests of Germany, both present and future, and the ultimate interests of her creditors to the immediate necessities of the latter, while the German Government tends to sacrifice the immediate interests of Germany's creditors and the ultimate interests of Germany herself to the pressing financial exigencies of the moment.

If German sovereignty is to be preserved—and unless the Reparation Commission is to undertake administrative responsibility for the government of Germany and be given an army to support its authority, no other basis is possible—very intimate co-operation between the German Government and the commission is indispensable.[5]

[5] A copy of this Memorandum (CP 4272: FO/C 14179/99/18) was circulated to the Cabinet on October 11.

No. 98

Sir J. Bradbury (Reparation Commission) to Sir B. Blackett (Treasury)
(Received in the Foreign Office, October 14)
[*C 14216/99/18*]

Copy

 Confidential   PARIS, *October 11, 1922*
My dear Blackett,

 We had a long semi-official discussion this afternoon on my memorandum.[1] It was criticised acutely by Delacroix on points of detail, but he accepted the general principle that the effective payments of Germany during the next year or two must be limited to what could be provided consistently with budget equilibrium. As regards the stabilization of the mark he wanted to

[1] No. 97, Enclosure.

create a foreign exchange reserve by means of a loan instead of using the existing gold reserve. He ended up with the somewhat indefinite proposal to have an immediate Committee of Reparation Commission, League of Nations and Bankers to make a report on German capacity from a 'technical' point of view. In the end he undertook to present a proposal of his own in the course of the next few days.

Barthou lay very low. He recognised the seriousness of the situation but emphasised the difficulties of my suggestions from the point of view of the French 'man in the street'.

In the end he proposed to adjourn the discussion until Friday afternoon,[2] the proposals in the meantime and indeed the fact of my having made them to be kept entirely confidential. I expressed scepticism as to the possibility of preventing Press indiscretions and said (quoting Poincaré in London)[3] that in the event of such indiscretions I must reserve my liberty to publish them in full.[4] Barthou said that he had specially cautioned the French Government against any premature disclosure, and appealed to me to try the experiment of non-disclosure, once again.

The reception of the proposals has on the whole been rather better than I expected—of course my hopes were not very high. I think Barthou realises that the time has gone by for a policy of mere stone-walling.

It is possible that we may decide on publication on Friday. In any case I think that it might be useful if I came over to London this weekend. I should very much like to see the Chancellor before he leaves for America.[5] Would there be any chance of my catching him on Saturday?

Yours sincerely,

JOHN BRADBURY

---

[2] October 13.   [3] See No. 51.

[4] Commenting on minutes by Sir W. Tyrrell and Sir E. Crowe, Lord Curzon stated (October 12): 'I most emphatically object to publication without my consent and I think a telegram should be sent at once to Sir J. Bradbury to that effect. He acts as though he were an independent State.'

On October 13, Lord Curzon sent the following unnumbered telegram to Lord Hardinge

'Please give following message to Sir John Bradbury at once:—

'Unless reparation commission themselves decide to publish Sir John Bradbury's scheme of October 4th, Lord Curzon and Chancellor of the Exchequer are both strongly of opinion that publication is undesirable.

'Effect upon our relations with France would at present juncture be in Lord Curzon's opinion disastrous.'

[5] See No. 63, n. 15.

Sir J. Bradbury (Reparation Commission) to Sir B. Blackett (Treasury)
(Received in the Foreign Office, October 23)

[*C 14509/99/18*]

Copy   PARIS, *October 13, 1922*

My dear Blackett,

We had a long discussion this afternoon at a semi-official meeting of the Commission on my memorandum.[1]

Barthou criticised it in by no means hostile terms but, at the same time, firmly turned down the proposals as unacceptable to the French Government.

He ended by agreeing with Delacroix as to the desirability of appointing a 'technical' committee and promised to submit to the Commission substantive proposals on behalf of the French Government by next Friday.

Rumour has it that these proposals on which the French are now hard at work will concentrate on extended control over the German currency and German budget, possibly to the length of taking over the financial administration of Germany, though no doubt it will not be put so bluntly as that. They will presumably dodge the question of the grant of a moratorium by leaving it to the new control authority to get out of Germany what it can.

Barthou's general attitude was most conciliatory and the whole proceedings were very cordial. There was, however, I think an underlying feeling on both his side and mine that we are travelling towards a breaking-point.

As regards publication, he expressed himself as anxious to be guided by my views, saying indeed that while he had objected to publication until he and the French Government had had the opportunity of studying the memorandum that objection no longer held and, indeed, he thought it was practically impossible, now that the fact that there was a memorandum and that the Commission was considering it was public property, to avoid giving the public at any rate a resumé of the contents. After some discussion we agreed that the Secretary General should send out a short précis of my proposals and accepted the principle that, if it becomes necessary, in view of the developments of the discussion, to publish the full text (of the memorandum, not the covering note), the Commission will publish it.

In the meantime the text of the document itself as submitted to the Commission remains confidential, though this of course does not make it improper to make use of it when necessary for the purpose of explaining points which may be obscure in a short précis.

I hope this arrangement will meet the wishes of the Chancellor and Lord Curzon as explained in the telegram I received through the Embassy today.[2]

I enclose a copy of the draft of the précis[3] which may, however, be altered before publication.

Yours sincerely,
JOHN BRADBURY

[1] No. 97, Enclosure.   [2] See No. 98, n. 4.   [3] Not printed.

No. 100

Lord Hardinge (Paris) to the Marquess Curzon of Kedleston
(Received October 16, 8.30 a.m.)

No. 521 Telegraphic: by bag [C 14221/99/18]

PARIS, *October 15, 1922*

A summary of Sir John Bradbury's proposals[1] in regard to Germany has been officially published by the Reparation Commission and has aroused unanimous disapproval in Paris press. Comments vary in hostility according to the tone of the paper, but general attitude is that they are quite [u]nacceptable to France. M. Millet, in today's 'Petit Parisien', can find nothing better to say of them than that their author does not apparently consider them final or incapable of revision.

Last night's 'Temps' enquires why Great Britain has taken this initiative in favour of Germany, instead of starting an inter-allied discussion on reparations and inter-allied debts, and why she does not practice herself the inter-allied solidarity for which she so often appeals.

[1] See No. 97, Enclosure.

No. 101

Lord Hardinge (Paris) to the Marquess Curzon of Kedleston
(Received October 23)

No. 2466 [C 14537/99/18]

Urgent

PARIS, *October 21, 1922*

My Lord,

I have the honour to transmit to you herewith the full text[1] of the French counter-proposal to Sir John Bradbury's proposals[2] which was submitted to the Reparation Commission yesterday, and is now published in this evening's 'Temps'.

The leading article in that newspaper, of which I also enclose the text,[1] while welcoming the statement at the commencement of this document that nothing should be done by the Reparation Commission to interfere with the work of the approaching international Conference,[3] goes on to explain that the time has gone by for a system of control of the German finances such as is advocated by the present French proposal, and to point out the dangers and responsibilities which the Allies would incur if they were to undertake it.

Your Lordship will see, from my despatch No. 2467[4] of today's date, that Monsieur Reynaud, speaking yesterday in the Chamber of Deputies, expressed much the same opinion. 'Pertinax,'[5] looking at the matter from his, the French Nationalist, point of view, has come to the same conclusion, though for different reasons. He declares that the proposal to exercise this

[1] Not printed. [2] No. 97, Enclosure. [3] Cf. No. 63.
[4] Not printed. For an extract, see n. 6, below. [5] See No. 14, n. 3.

extent of control over a conquered country is a mere chimera, and that it is neither possible nor desirable for the Allies to undertake it. He pleads once more for the seizure of 'productive guarantees' and for the organization of the Ruhr and of the left bank of the Rhine until such time as the Germans have put their affairs in order.[6] The question of guarantees should, he declares, be at once raised in London, instead of summoning at Brussels a conference which, he maintains, will produce no immediate result.

I would add that, in Sir John Bradbury's opinion, the new French scheme has no constructive merit whatever, and that it appears to have been drawn up by somebody without knowledge or experience of budgets and financial economics.

I have, etc.,
HARDINGE OF PENSHURST

[6] In his despatch No. 2467, Lord Hardinge reported: 'Monsieur Reynaud produced his own solution—viz. to force the great industrial magnates (the only people in Germany who possess money and influence) to pay the reparations due to France. To do this he would take 30% of the shares of their various industries and would exercise the right of surveillance which this would give, with the object of sharing in the subsequently reviving prosperity of Germany. As for the German currency, the present mark must be consolidated and a new currency issued to be called "the gold mark". The only result of the present policy, or lack of policy, of the French Government was, he said, to embitter the already starving middle classes in Germany and to make France appear before the world as responsible for Germany's ruin. Germany would never recover until the two countries had come to an agreement. In order to force the industrial magnates to consent to some such arrangement as he had proposed, he would be prepared to see the French Government make a definite and final threat to seize the Ruhr. He could not but condemn the practice of making empty threats to seize it every two months; but he reminded the Chamber, amidst applause, that the "coal of the Ruhr is the base of the industrial pyramid of which Stinnes' electric lamp is the apex", and that the fear of a real French occupation of the district could not but operate powerfully on the industrial magnates.'

No. 102

Sir J. Bradbury (Reparation Commission) to Mr. Bonar Law[1]
(Received in the Foreign Office, October 30)
[C 14819/99/18]

Copy   PARIS, *October 23, 1922*

My dear Prime Minister,

One of the first—and I fear of the most troublesome—questions to which you will have to give attention is the proposal of the French Government that an early inter-allied conference should be held to deal with Reparation and Inter-Allied Debts.

I am afraid that in view of recent developments in the German situation, such a conference if held can only result in a fiasco.

Monsieur Poincaré is obsessed by the notion that Great Britain is so anxious to reduce the German liability that by stone-walling us he can induce

[1] Mr. Bonar Law had formed a government on October 23.

us to give up our share of reparations and write off the French debt as the price of his consent to such a reduction.

I am told that he still wants to produce the plan[2] which he had in his pocket at the last London Conference but that he is likely to be ready, in return for a complete abandonment of our share of reparations and cancellation of European inter-allied debts, under severe British pressure to come down to 40 milliards of gold marks for the German liability.

In my opinion there is now no chance of reviving German external credit until the mark can be stabilised and the budget balanced and made to cover whatever reparation charges may be imposed—now probably a two-year job without a reparation charge and a five-year job with anything above a very modest reparation charge.

I do not believe that any advantage would be gained by attempting to fix the aggregate German liability at the present moment of chaos. Any such figure as 40 milliards would do more harm than good from the credit point of view. The present total of 132 milliards (or rather something like 70 milliards—the nearest estimate which can be made of the present value of the Schedule of Payments liability)[3] has the advantage of being ridiculous as well as absurd and has ceased to be, psychologically at any rate, any real incubus but if the Allies really set themselves to attempt to recover 40 milliards we should be passing from pure to applied lunacy.

I am pretty sure that at the present moment no figure above 25 milliards (for all Peace Treaty charges not merely reparations) would be of any help at all from the point of view of credit reaction. On the other hand any such figure as 25 milliards is quite impossible politically for the French and probably bad business for the Allies generally as I am convinced that the asset if properly nursed is worth more.

It seems to me, therefore, that a Conference runs the risk either of leading to nothing at all or of causing us to give away claims, which however valueless they may be in themselves are extremely valuable for bargaining purposes when a real general settlement becomes possible, in exchange for a purely fictitious settlement, and at the same time getting us committed to joining in 'energetic action' against Germany to enforce demands which though reduced are still impossible.

If this diagnosis of the situation is right, the problem is how to avoid the conference without quarrelling with France.

I venture to suggest that before committing yourself to the principle of the proposed conference you should meet Poincaré à deux. I imagine the French Government will now press for a summoning of the conference immediately. In any case I presume this is impossible for you, and the personal meeting would be a natural alternative.

I would then tell him quite frankly that any attempt at a general settlement by conference in the face of the present condition of Germany, without a preliminary agreement between France and Great Britain, will inevitably lead to a row (which I am certain he is as anxious as you are to avoid). I

[2] See No. 77.   [3] See No. 5, n. 2.

would ask him what his plan is. If you can agree, well and good. If not, I would insist on deferring the conference until the Reparation Commission has settled the 1923 payments. If Barthou is brought up against this, I do not think that even he can resist a fairly complete moratorium. Indeed his tactics will probably be to forestall the discussion by insisting on the Commission reporting Germany to the Powers under paragraph 17 of Annex II of Part VIII of the Treaty of Versailles for failure to make the coal and timber deliveries. I shall oppose this as I am of opinion that Germany is doing her best under very difficult conditions—indeed the coal deliveries have recently shewn a substantial improvement—but he will probably get a majority.

You can then either deal with the question by conference, or by diplomatic discussion, or leave him if he sees fit to take independent action—I doubt whether he will do anything serious if he is left to himself. In any case you will I think be in a much stronger position if the issue is raised in the form of how much can be recovered of a bad debt than if it is raised in the form of the writing the worst part of the bad debt off British claims.

All this of course is on the assumption that America is still unwilling to join officially in a conference to consider a general settlement. If Boyden is to be believed, the Chancellor of the Exchequer may find progress in that direction possible when he goes to Washington.[4] If so, that will change the whole situation. But even in that case it would greatly facilitate matters to get a German moratorium first, and probably the French objections to this would be greatly diminished if they saw a chance of getting America in.

I hear that Theunis is contemplating private visits to both Paris and London in about a fortnight's time. These can do nothing but good but I expect that you will have great pressure from the French side to agree to the summoning of a conference without waiting for them. Delacroix tells me privately that Theunis is much more complaisant to the French point of view than he is himself and he even talks of concerting a line of action with me which may involve his own resignation. Barthou (who is not reported to be on the best of terms with Poincaré) will also find it difficult to carry intransigence to the Poincaré lengths. It is therefore I think very desirable from the tactical point of view that the Reparation Commission should be required to try to deal with 1923 payments before a conference is held.

Yours sincerely,
JOHN BRADBURY

---

[4] See No. 63, n. 15.

No. 103

Sir J. Bradbury (Reparation Commission) to Sir B. Blackett (Treasury)[1]
[C 14818/99/18]

Copy   PARIS, October 24, 1922

My dear Blackett,

We completed our semi-official discussions on the British and French
projets[2] this evening and decided to leave for Berlin on Sunday evening[3] 'to
discuss with the German Government the steps which the Commission may
judge necessary to secure the balancing of the budget and the stabilization
of the mark'. Barthou has admitted frankly in these conversations (of which
of course there is no *procès verbal*) that reparation must *if necessary* give way
to the necessity of balancing the budget, but professes to believe that taxation
can be increased and expenditure diminished in such a way as to provide
an immediate surplus, and that when this is done it will be possible to raise
internal loans to finance deliveries in kind. I said I did not want to rule out
the possibility of this—though I was very sceptical of it—until we had discussed the situation with the German Government but that, if after such
discussion we were satisfied that reparation payments and deliveries were
only possible at the expense of further creation of floating debt, they must be
suspended. I could only go to Berlin on the understanding that we were free
to exercise our powers of postponement under Article 234 both as to cash
payments and as to deliveries in kind if we came to the conclusion that it
was necessary to do so. He tacitly accepted this and agreed to my suggestion

---

[1] A copy of this letter was communicated to the Foreign Office on October 25.
[2] For the British proposals, see No. 97, Enclosure. The French proposals were put
forward by M. Barthou on October 22. They are summarised in a Foreign Office memorandum of November 2 (C 15425/99/18) as follows:

  '(a) The imposition upon the German Government by the Reparation Commission of
     much stricter measures of financial control, the Committee of Guarantees of the
     Reparation Commission being empowered to compel the German Government to
     impose or increase any particular tax and to diminish or put an end to any par-
     ticular item of expenditure.
  (b) The balancing of the German budget and therefore the stabilisation of the mark
     being rendered possible by these measures, early consideration by the Allied Govern-
     ments of the questions of German currency reform and of the floating by the German
     Government of loans destined to facilitate the resumption of the reparation pay-
     ments.'

In a memorandum enclosed in his despatch No. 827 of October 27 (C 14877/99/18), Lord
D'Abernon criticised the French scheme as follows: 'It has no chance of willing acceptance
by the German Government. In the absence of willing acceptance by the German Government, it is improbable that it can be carried out, and still more improbable it will produce
any financial improvement. The defect of the scheme is that it is too extended; that it does
not concentrate attention and action on the really essential point. It spreads control over
so large a field that it will require, or will be said to require, a large foreign personnel,
greatly increasing friction and difficulty. It will displace responsibility for German administration, and will make the Entente appear the cause of inadequate salaries and of all the
social trouble which the winter is sure to bring.'

[3] October 29.

that Delacroix should draft a note specifying precisely the object of our journey.

He also agreed that both in the press notification of our journey and the Delacroix marching orders phraseology should be employed implying that the Commission had an open mind in regard both to the British and French proposals and other suggestions which had been made, and that nothing should be said which would suggest the 'triumph of one thesis over the other'.

It is a little difficult to say how far we have got, but my impression is we have got a long way in securing a unanimous decision in the above sense and if you can keep the discussions on the proposal for an inter-allied Conference long, we ought to be able to secure an atmosphere of greater reality before the conference meets.

I asked yesterday for Barthou's authority for the statement in the French *projet* that the Allied Governments had accepted the principle of an early international conference to deal with reparations and inter-allied debts as closely connected problems, and today he referred me to the proceedings of the London Conference of 14 August.[4] I pointed out that the only statement which could be regarded as a commitment of Mr. Lloyd George was contained in a proposal which Monsieur Poincaré had rejected, but added that while I had thought it desirable in order to avoid any danger of misunderstanding to challenge the categorical statement in the French *projet* I was of course content to leave the construction to be placed on the proceedings of 14 August to the Governments themselves.

I have since seen the F[oreign] O[ffice] note of 9th October[5] which places the present attitude of the British Government beyond doubt and I trust that it will be possible to avoid being more precise until we come back from Berlin. If we can without undue friction insist on getting the urgent aspect of the German situation dealt with as far as possible by the Reparation Commission before a conference, I am convinced that there is a much better chance of the conference itself having fruitful results.

I suppose that by the time this reaches you we shall have a Chancellor of the Exchequer.[6] If he thinks there is any advantage in my coming over to London before going to Berlin, I will cross on Thursday or Friday night. We meet on Thursday afternoon to consider Delacroix's draft marching orders.

Yours sincerely,
JOHN BRADBURY

[4] See No. 63.
[5] This is a reference to Lord Curzon's despatch No. 3064 of October 9 (C 13977/12995/62) to Lord Hardinge, in which Lord Curzon stated that he had informed the Belgian Chargé d'Affaires as follows: 'His Majesty's Government are prepared to examine the proposal for such a conference in the most sympathetic spirit, but that at any rate until they are in a position to appreciate the results of the negotiations of the various Allied missions which are shortly proceeding to the United States [see No. 63] to discuss the funding of the various Allied debts to the United States, they consider it would be premature to attempt to define the conditions under which such a conference could usefully be convoked, or to prepare the programme of its proceedings.'
[6] Mr. Stanley Baldwin became Chancellor of the Exchequer on October 25.

No. 104

The Marquess Curzon of Kedleston to Sir G. Grahame (Brussels)
No. 998 [*C 15067/12995/62*]

FOREIGN OFFICE, *November 1, 1922*

The Belgian Ambassador called upon me this afternoon with a message from his Government. He began by referring to the suggested conference on reparations and inter-Allied debts at Brussels,[1] the acceptance of the invitation to which by Great Britain had been deferred until the result had been made known of the proposed British Mission to the United States on the subject of the repayment of the debt due to that country.[2] The sending of that mission had had to be postponed for political reasons, and no envoy had yet started. In these circumstances the French Government had approached the Belgian Government, and urged them to issue immediate invitations to the conference in Brussels in the opening days of December, threatening them that, if Belgium did not do so, France would not hesitate to take the initiative herself. His Excellency impressed upon me the importance of holding the conference before the end of the year, because the Governments would have to decide before the 31st December upon the payments to be demanded from Germany in 1923. He further pointed out to me the superiority of the political atmosphere of Brussels to that of Paris for any such discussions. He wished to know what reply His Majesty's Government would advise his own Government to return.

I told him that, only ten days ago, the French Ambassador had come to me with a somewhat similar message from the French Government,[3] although the threat with which it had concluded had assumed a rather different form. To me, M. Poincaré had not given any hint of an intention to summon a conference himself: he had merely said that, unless a conference were convened, France must claim the right to act on her own account. I informed Baron Moncheur that I did not think that either of us need be much disturbed by these threats, because, whether a conference was summoned or not, and wherever it was summoned, it could not take place until the principal parties had agreed to accept the invitations to it. For the moment, it was obviously impossible for His Majesty's Government to give a decided answer on this point. In the first place, I should require to consult the Chancellor of the Exchequer on the point whether he still regarded the visit to America as an essential preliminary to the holding of a reparations conference in Europe. Secondly, in view of the elections now proceeding in this country,[4] it seemed to me very unlikely that the British Government, whether represented at the conference by the Chancellor of the Exchequer or by anyone else, would be in a position to take part as early as the first week in December. Thirdly,

[1] See No. 102. [2] See No. 63, n. 15.

[3] A record of Lord Curzon's conversation with the French Ambassador on October 19 is to be found in Lord Curzon's despatch No. 3176 of October 19 (C 14441/12995/62) to Lord Hardinge, not printed.

[4] A general election was held on November 15 (see Vol. XVIII, No. 132, n. 2).

until the result of the elections was known, it would be impossible for the present holders of office to commit the British Government in any of these respects, since it was conceivable, though perhaps not likely, that within three weeks' time other people might be occupying their posts. On all these grounds I recommended that the Belgian Government should express their inability to reply at the present juncture to the veiled threat which they had received from the French. For my own part, I added that I did not intend to be in the least degree deflected by the latter from the most expedient course of action.

Baron Moncheur then went on to ask me whether his Government, without making any claim to take a regular part in the Peace Conference about to be convened at Lausanne[5] to draw up a new Treaty of Sèvres, might notwithstanding, as signatories of the original treaty, be permitted to state their views on any points in the new treaty in which Belgium was vitally interested. He reminded me of the very large share of the Ottoman Debt in the hands of Belgian bondholders, and of the interest felt by Belgium in the general financial position of Turkey. He recalled that, when the meetings of the Supreme Council at which the first outlines of the former Treaty of Sèvres were drawn up had been held in Downing Street in 1920,[6] he himself had been admitted to the council table on more than one occasion to state the claims of Belgium. In these circumstances, he enquired whether a similar privilege might not be accorded to Belgian representatives in Lausanne.

I said that, as the conference was to meet on neutral territory, it would not, on the present occasion, rest with any individual Power to control the issue of the invitations, and these could be sent only by common consent. For my own part, I was disposed to consider the request of the Ambassador as reasonable, and, without giving a definite pledge at the moment on a matter which he now brought before me for the first time, and which I had not yet had the opportunity to examine carefully, I would consult my advisers as to the manner in which it might be possible to respond to his wishes.

I am, etc.,

CURZON OF KEDLESTON

[5] See Vol. XVIII, Chap. I.   [6] See Vol. VII, *passim*.

No. 105

Lord D'Abernon (Berlin) to the Marquess Curzon of Kedleston
(Received November 5, 7.5 p.m.)

No. 196 Telegraphic [*C 15136/99/18*]

BERLIN, *November 5, 1922, 2.40 p.m.*

Numerous meetings have been held during the week both between reparations commission and German government and between German government and committee of foreign experts.[1]

[1] In Berlin telegram No. 189 of October 17, Lord D'Abernon had reported: 'German Government contemplate inviting Professor Cassel, Professor Keynes, and probably an

In former case no very definite result has been attained but a fairly accommodating spirit has been shown.

Barthou seems anxious to be reasonable but is cramped by instructions and is apprehensive at tone of Paris press.

Hermes yesterday presented a plan for stabilization of the mark but as this involved a loan and did not provide measures likely to be radically effective, it did not offer a very promising basis. Hermes has now undertaken to present a modified and more precise plan on Monday[2] or Tuesday after consulting committee of experts.

The latter have so far not elaborated their proposals but expect to be able to do so today or at latest on Monday. Considerable divergences of opinion originally existed between different [expert]s, but they are endeavouring to arrive at some joint modus vivendi and present a report which will achieve end in view, namely stabilization. They hold that a complete moratorium is indispensable until stabilization is assured.

As far therefore as immediate negotiations are concerned, everything depends on what experts committee recommend and how far German government accept their recommendations.

American and French expert to come to Berlin in order to advise them as to measures to prevent further fall of mark.'

[2] November 6.

No. 106

Lord Hardinge (Paris) to the Marquess Curzon of Kedleston
(Received November 9)
No. 2601 [C 15331/99/18]

PARIS, *November 8, 1922*

My Lord,

I have the honour to transmit to Your Lordship herewith a summary[1] of a speech which was delivered by Monsieur Loucheur in the Chamber yesterday in the course of the debate on the French budget.

I should perhaps explain that another deputy, Monsieur Léon Blum, had on the previous day made a most interesting speech analysing the financial situation arising out of the treaty of Versailles. Monsieur Blum traced the history of events and successive reparations crises since 1919 and came to the conclusion that the authors of the treaty should not be blamed too much as they were only human and they drew up the financial and reparation clauses of the treaty under the (as events proved) mistaken idea that the world would see an immediate resumption of production on a scale greater than that of pre-war days in order to make up for the exhaustion of commercial stocks caused by five years' war. Monsieur Blum went on to state that no Government in France had so far had the courage to tell the people the

[1] Not printed.

truth and it was necessary now that someone should 'tear the veil'. No country could pay another country in gold; it could only do so by the export of goods and in present conditions the class of goods which Germany could export must be carefully chosen in order that they might not compete with the produce of French manufacturers in the French domestic market. The various schemes which have been advocated by successive French Governments for the payment of reparations by Germany were illusory for the reason that ultimately all the French Government received were paper marks and the problem had not been solved of converting those paper marks into cash for the restoration of the devastated regions. The occupation of the Ruhr would be merely an expense to France as would also the annexation of the Left bank of the Rhine, while the system of payments in kind had the insuperable drawback that it merely resulted in a further inflation of the currency circulation in Germany. Turning to the remedy, Monsieur Blum suggested the formation of an international institute of credit somewhat on the lines suggested by Mr. Vanderlip, details of which will be found on page 2964 of the 'Journal Officiel' enclosed in my despatch No. 2603.[2] Unfortunately Monsieur Léon Blum is an extreme Socialist credited with Communist leanings and yesterday's press omitted all mention of his able analysis of the situation and confined itself to pouring ridicule on his proposed solution.

Monsieur Loucheur in the course of yesterday's speech confessed himself in agreement with many of Monsieur Blum's arguments and thought that some portions of his suggested remedy might be adapted to his own scheme. Monsieur Loucheur's speech met with a favourable reception in the Chamber and I shall have the honour at a later date to inform Your Lordship of its reaction on public opinion. It is in any case interesting as it is generally regarded as an attempt by Monsieur Loucheur to define the programme which he would endeavour to follow in the event of his attaining his ambition and succeeding Monsieur Poincaré as President of the Council.

I have, etc.,
HARDINGE OF PENSHURST

[2] Of November 8, not printed.

No. 107

Lord D'Abernon (Berlin) to the Marquess Curzon of Kedleston
(Received November 14)

No. 861 [*C 15606/99/18*]

Confidential   BERLIN, *November 9, 1922*

His Majesty's Ambassador presents his compliments to His Majesty's Secretary of State for Foreign Affairs, and has the honour to forward a private Note regarding conversations with M. Barthou and others.

Note by Lord D'Abernon

Confidential   BERLIN, *November 8, 1922*

Barthou has been active and skilful during his visit here. He has seen a large number of leading Germans, both politicians and industrials. He has formed what are probably quite erroneous impressions regarding most of them—but that is not the point: it is that he has seen them and talked things over with them in a more or less friendly way. Up to the present, French representatives have been quite out of touch with all but a small section. Barthou is no doubt extremely clever and agreeable. I had a long talk with him and the Chancellor last night at dinner at the American Embassy. The following are passages in the conversation:—

Barthou: 'You have a very heavy task, Mr. Chancellor, but you should not make heavy weather of it. Take my advice, do not read the papers, particularly do not read those that attack you. The most important thing for a political leader is to have a reliable friend who can be trusted to sift the papers, and only give one what is really essential, suppressing all offensive attacks. I have a man who does this for me. I did not bring him to Germany as he does not know the language, but I never read any newspaper he does not give me. Old Clemenceau told me this dodge years ago. He said "Les journaux—je m'en fous—je ne les lis pas".'

Wirth: 'I begin reading the papers at 7 in the morning, and I go through them all myself.'

Barthou: 'That is why you look worried. You are a much younger man than Lord D'Abernon and myself, but you won't last as long if you go on those lines.

'There is another thing I strongly advise, namely, keep off the question of the responsibility for the Great War. What is the good of stirring up this question? Leave it to history. Your speech the other day brought out Poincaré in a bitter attack: further, it has induced Viviani to write his infernal memoirs.[1] What is the good of that? These recollections merely stir up animosity and prolong hate.'

Wirth: 'I assure you my speech the other day was absolutely necessary. Internal politics required it. How many speeches on the same subject has not Poincaré made? I have only made one in reply.'

Barthou: 'I hope that means, Mr. Chancellor, that you will not make another. Believe me it is a sterile and a dangerous discussion. Let us bury it.'

The Chancellor was anxious that the Reparation Commission should not leave Berlin too soon. He pressed Barthou to remain here until the Reparation Commission had received the German reply, and there had been time to discuss it. Barthou was not very forthcoming on this point, but finally

[1] See *The Times*, October 3, 1922, p. 9, and December 12, p. 11.

agreed to wait until Friday, provided the German Government sent in a specific detailed answer by this (Wednesday) evening.

In further intimate conversation with Barthou I gained the impression that he thinks Wirth is sure to fall. Also he thinks, although he did not say it, that he has contributed a good deal to his downfall, and that France will be able to get on better with the Volkspartei, Stinnes and Company. Quite a doubtful opinion.

I said to Barthou: 'What do you expect to achieve during your visit to Berlin?' He was not very explicit in his answer, saying he could decide nothing, that he had to report, etc., but he appeared impressed when I told him, as my private opinion, 'the best—probably the only—definite result the Reparation Commission can achieve is the stabilisation of the mark. If you take back that and nothing else you will have done a great work: even if you lay the foundation of it, you will have deserved well of the world. Can you not concentrate on this?'

Talking of Poincaré, he said, 'Don't mention him—I might be tempted to agree with you.'

No. 108

Message telephoned to Lord Curzon from Mr. Bonar Law on November 9 in reply to Lord Curzon's letter of November 9[1]

[C 15574/99/18]

'As regards the courtesy visit[2] nothing could have been more formal, or more indefinite than our conversation. I told the French Ambassador that I had really not had any time to find out anything about the difficulties beyond what I knew while I was still outside the Government.

'As regards reparations, what I said was that I hoped it would be possible for the whole thing, before I expressed any view about it, to stand over until after the election as while it was on I could not deal with it. That, you will see, tended towards a delay in the time of the Conference. Not a word was said about having a Conference at Brussels[3] or of my attending it. The interview only lasted about ten minutes.

'The most definite thing which occurred was that on his part the Ambassador told me that there were two schools of thought in France: one, that they might get what they wanted by industrial co-operation with the Germans, but that he and most Frenchmen detested it for they thought the Germans would get the better of them: the other, that they might get something by more sanctions, and he added the very alarming remark to me that even the

[1] Not traced in the Foreign Office archives (see, however, n. 4).

[2] On November 6, the *Daily Telegraph* had reported that the Prime Minister, Mr. Bonar Law, had received a visit on November 1 from the French Ambassador.

[3] The *Daily Telegraph* of November 6 had further reported that the Belgian Government intended to convene a conference at Brussels on December 5 to discuss reparations and inter-allied debts.

Frenchmen who realised that no good would come of it thought the French would never be satisfied until it had been tried.

'My only observation on this was to say that of course during the last months I had watched the talk about the invasion of the Ruhr and the question I always put to myself was "Suppose today the French Government announce that they are going to march into the Ruhr, what will be the value of the franc tomorrow?"'

(Mr. Bonar Law also spoke to Lord Curzon in regard to the interview.)[4]

[4] Lord Curzon's record of this conversation will be found at C 15136/99/18.

No. 109

Sir J. Bradbury (Reparation Commission) to Mr. Baldwin
(Received in the Foreign Office, November 28)
[C 16250/99/18]

Copy

Confidential   PARIS, *November 11, 1922*

My dear Chancellor,

I saw Hermes privately just before we left Berlin yesterday and he told me he was sending Bergmann to Paris next week when he hoped the German Government would be able to make a proposal which would be more satisfactory to me. The truth is that Barthou's conciliatory attitude—more particularly in private conversation—has given Hermes hopes that either Barthou will stand up to Poincaré or bring him over, and he wants to see which way the cat jumps before taking a more definite line.

Barthou has also indicated to me that he hopes to be able to modify the attitude of the French Government. Indeed, he almost besought me in Berlin not to do anything to upset Poincaré so as to give him (Barthou) a chance when he got back to Paris.

For my own part, I am very sceptical about all this. French public opinion is still in no mood to grant concessions to Germany, either as regards the total debt or as regards an adequate moratorium, which would appreciably help the credit situation. Nine-tenths of Poincaré's speech in the Senate yesterday was mere reiteration of the old nonsense and the other tenth, though interesting as indicating a desire to be sensible, was so tentative and obscure as to be nearly valueless for practical purposes. Barthou will only come out against Poincaré if he is satisfied that he will get enough popular support—and I can see no sign that this will be forthcoming.

The only educational influence which can now operate sufficiently rapidly on French public opinion is a further fall in the franc exchange. This is essential in any case sooner or later for the purpose of reducing the real burden of the internal debt—as they will never be able either to get reparation or to raise taxation to the extent necessary to enable them to carry the burden on the basis of the present value of the franc—and the sooner it comes the better. Unfortunately, however, it cannot be counted on. The present fall is mainly the result of loss of external credit, and it has already gone further than the existing state of French currency and economic conditions justify. Until internal credit suffers and the French Government are unable to renew their short-date bonds I doubt if there will be any sensational collapse.

As regards the proposed Brussels Conference,[1] I become more certain every day of its inutility. There is absolutely no basis at the moment for a permanent settlement with Germany. The existing German Government is clearly hopelessly at variance internally as regards its reparation policy, and even if it were agreed it has not sufficient public support to make any policy it might adopt effective.

An inter-allied conference at the present moment would either resolve itself into an attempt by France to get inter-allied debt concessions as a bribe for abandoning a policy of coercion which she herself now knows would be suicidal, or would have to confine itself to attempting to arrange foreign credits for the stabilisation of the mark, which in the absence of any resolute policy on the part of the German Government combined with a liberal Peace Treaty moratorium would be frittered away without any permanent advantage.

Until the German Government—or rather *a* German Government, for I doubt whether anything can be hoped from the present combination—really takes the situation in hand remedial measures are useless and coercive measures would only precipitate the catastrophe.

I believe the best course would now be to give them (say) six weeks to formulate a plan for dealing with the stabilisation of the mark, gradual stoppage of the increase of the floating debt and budget reform, suspending *all* Peace Treaty payments and deliveries during that period and undertaking to consider sympathetically the grant of whatever reparation concessions might be necessary to give the plan a reasonable chance of success.

The French ought to be able to agree to this without a Conference in return for a moratorium for interallied debts of the same scope and duration as would be ultimately given to Germany. But if they have not the nerve to do this, except under pressure of an interallied conference, I would give them their Conference—but only if you have a private understanding with them beforehand as to what the outcome of the Conference is to be.

I assume in what I have written above that the general lines of your policy are likely to differ in manner rather than matter from those of the policy of the late Government.[2] This seems to me to be indicated by the public utterances of Ministers, but it is in order that I may have further light as to this that I am anxious to come to London as soon as you have time to spare to see me.

Yours sincerely,
JOHN BRADBURY

[1] See No. 108.   [2] The Lloyd George Government.

P.S. I enclose a copy of today's 'Temps' containing the full text of Poincaré's speech in the Senate.[3] The passage I have marked if read literally—and Poincaré as a rule weighs his words—suggests that he contemplates inviting the ex-enemy Powers to take part in the Conference. This would make it a really international conference to revise the Peace Treaties. I have always believed that such a Conference will be necessary sooner or later but it would be futile until Germany has a Government which can really speak in her name and is in a position to make a real offer.

I observe that he said that the new British Government has accepted with 'empressement' the invitation of Brussels. At first sight this rather alarmed me, but the reply to Ribot's question below seems to make it clear that it is not intended to hold the Conference unless a previous Anglo-French Agreement is arrived at.

J. B.

[3] Not printed.

No. 110

Lord D'Abernon (Berlin) to the Marquess Curzon of Kedleston
(Received November 16)
No. 866 [C 15685/99/18]

BERLIN, *November 11, 1922*

His Majesty's Ambassador presents his compliments to His Majesty's Secretary of State for Foreign Affairs, and has the honour to forward herewith Note of a conversation with Dr. Wirth.

ENCLOSURE IN No. 110

Note by Lord D'Abernon of conversation with Dr. Wirth

BERLIN, *November 11, 1922*

I called on the Chancellor this morning and discussed the recent negotiations with the Reparation Commission and the Foreign Experts.

The Chancellor said that the last fortnight had not given any satisfactory result. The members of the Reparation Commission seemed all to have different views. The Belgian Delegate had urged the German Government at all costs to avoid using the word 'moratorium', and had said that the essential point was to arrive at the convocation of a Bankers' Committee: if this was called together all would be well, but the word 'moratorium' must not be breathed above a whisper. Sir John Bradbury had taken precisely the opposite standpoint, and, speaking in his own name alone, had expressed the view that unless the German Government took its courage in both hands, and demanded a moratorium for two years, no serious progress would be achieved.

The Chancellor had the greatest regard for Sir John Bradbury, and for his opinion, but the advice he gave did not even purport to come from the English Government, and the Chancellor did not know how far the English Government would support Germany if she took the bold step advocated by Bradbury.

The German Government could not afford altogether to neglect Delacroix's advice, because, if the Belgian voted with the Frenchman, it was more than probable that the Italian would agree with them, so that Sir John Bradbury would be left in a minority of one. This was not only undesirable but dangerous.

I took the opportunity of pointing out to the Chancellor that the correspondence with the Reparation Commission[1] appeared somehow to have got wrong. The German letter to the Reparation Commission of November 8 was confined entirely to a minor issue, and based upon a subsidiary report of minor importance. The really important documents,[1] viz.—the two Memoranda of the Keynes—Cassel Experts (dated November 7), and the Dubois—Vissering Experts (dated November 8)—were not mentioned in the correspondence between the German Government and the Reparation Commission. They appeared to have been either ignored or side-tracked by the German Government. A very false basis for the discussion was thus created.

The Chancellor explained that everything had been done in a great hurry; the experts' report had only been received at the last minute; some confusion had apparently existed between the first Vissering Report (dated November 8), and the second Vissering Report (dated November 10). He would discuss the matter with the Minister of Finance and endeavour to get things straight.

[1] Copies of this correspondence and of the reports of the international financial experts to the German Government were transmitted to the Foreign Office by Lord D'Abernon in his despatch No. 867 of November 11, not printed. A part of this correspondence is printed in Cmd. 1812 (Miscellaneous No. 3 (1923)), No. 1.

No. 111

Mr. Lampson to Baron Moncheur

[*C 15465/99/18*]

FOREIGN OFFICE, *November 16, 1922*

Your Excellency,

I have the honour to refer to your note No. 4086 of the 13th instant,[1] in which Your Excellency was good enough to inform me that Monsieur Theunis and Monsieur Jaspar had decided to proceed to Paris on the 17th or 18th instant, and to visit London immediately afterwards in order to confer with His Majesty's Government on the subject of the proposed conference at Brussels.[2]

[1] Not printed.   [2] See No. 108.

2. I have since heard from His Majesty's Ambassador at Paris that the visit of Monsieur Theunis and Monsieur Jaspar to Paris has been postponed, and I presume that in the circumstances Their Excellencies intend to postpone their visit to London also. I need scarcely add that, when at a later date it is convenient for them to come to London, His Majesty's Government will be very happy to receive them and to discuss with them matters arising out of the Belgian Government's proposal to hold a conference at Brussels.

I have, etc.,
(In the absence of the Secretary of State)
MILES W. LAMPSON

³ In Paris telegram No. 598 of November 14, not printed.
⁴ The Foreign Office informed Lord Curzon at Lausanne (telegram No. 4 of November 20, not preserved in the Foreign Office archives) that the Belgian Ambassador had stated that the Belgian ministers would visit M. Poincaré in Paris on November 23 and proceed to London on November 24, but the Prime Minister had suggested that Lord Curzon should ask M. Poincaré to postpone his meeting with the Belgians. Lord Curzon replied (telegram No. 8 of November 21, not preserved in the Foreign Office archives) that it was too late for him to stop the Paris meeting and that it would be for the Prime Minister to postpone, if he wished, the visit of the Belgians to London.

No. 112

The Marquess Curzon of Kedleston to Lord Hardinge (Paris)
No. 3430 [C 15237/99/18]

Confidential   FOREIGN OFFICE, *November 16, 192*

My Lord,

With reference to paragraph 4 of your despatch No. 2586 of the 6th November,[1] I request that your Excellency will inform M. Poincaré that entirely reciprocate the hope, expressed in the concluding paragraph of his note of the 6th November,[1] that our two Governments will be able to maintain the most complete and cordial agreement in all future developments of the question of reparations. His Excellency can confidently rely upon it that His Majesty's Government appreciate the importance attached to this question by the French Government, and that they will do their best to ensure the adoption of a common course of action for its solution.

I am, etc.,
CURZON OF KEDLESTON

¹ Not printed.

No. 113

Lord D'Abernon (Berlin) to the Marquess Curzon of Kedleston
(Received November 23)

No. 891 [C 16001/99/18]

BERLIN, *November 19, 1922*

My Lord Marquess,

I have the honour to enclose a translation of the Note of the German Government of November 13,[1] to the Reparation Commission. This document has already reached His Majesty's Government through the Reparation Commission, but its importance is such that a second translation may not be without utility.

The Note has importance, for the following reasons:—

(*a*) the German Government adopt the fundamental principles contained in the two Memoranda[2] of the Financial Experts; these principles being in marked contrast, if not in direct contradiction, with the German Government's past practice;

(*b*) the German Government adopt a new position regarding

   (i) the importance they attach to the stabilisation of the Mark as a precondition of financial reform;

   (ii) the decision to devote a large portion of the gold reserve of the Reichsbank to stabilisation—a measure previously declined;

(*c*) notwithstanding the fall of the Wirth Government,[3] this—their last act—has been endorsed by all Parties in Germany, with the exception of the Extreme Right, and the Communists;

(*d*) notwithstanding the necessity which they assert of a long moratorium in respect of direct payments, the German Government agree to devote to Reparation the whole money they may receive from foreign loans, and half the money they may receive from internal loans.

Thus, a new state of affairs is created, and an opportunity occurs to examine the situation on new lines. This position has resulted in the main from the Mission of the Foreign Experts who were called to Berlin. Their deliberations and their Reports have thrown a flood of light on the financial position. In particular, as regards the German Government, they have shown that Germany is herself to a large extent responsible for the disorder in which her currency now is. Further, that Germany has it in her own power, either with or without external assistance, to correct the position.

The fact that these pronouncements were made by friendly advisers selected by the German Government itself lends them an authority and—still more—assures them an acceptance with German opinion which would

---

[1] Not printed. A translation of this Note was communicated to Lord Curzon by Herr Sthamer on November 14 (C 15643/99/18).

[2] See No. 110.

[3] Dr. Wirth resigned as Chancellor on November 14.

not be accorded to any verdict by a body like the Reparation Commission—a body that has been imposed from without.

As regards the Entente and the body of Germany's creditors, the Expert Reports suggest, if they do not prove, that the policy followed in the past has not been on the most practical lines; an equal amount of pressure exerted in a different direction by different methods would probably have led to a better result.

If these views are correct, a new departure is required.

The question is in what direction? Are the proposals of November 13[1] an acceptable basis of negotiation between the creditors of Germany and the German Government?

I have already expressed the view in my telegram No. 203 of November 14,[4] that, while open to obvious criticism, the German proposals offer a favourable basis for discussion. Further study of the document convinces me that I might have expressed this opinion with even greater emphasis.

The difficulty has always been to adjust the demands of France to the capacities of Germany, or to the willingness and ability of the German Government to impose sacrifices on Germany. The system hitherto followed has been to demand large immediate payments or, in default, large deliveries in kind—an alternative hardly less burdensome to the German Government than payments in cash. In default of payment and delivery, various sanctions have been threatened—some have been enforced.

Today this system has irretrievably broken down. It has only been possible to continue it so far because the payments and deliveries demanded were met by inflation. But inflation has now reached such a level and has caused so vast a depreciation of German currency that a continuance of this method no longer produces adequate results in Foreign currency—apart from the fact that it has destroyed the basis of German solvency.

Something must be done to meet the immediate requirements of France. The suggestion of the Note of November [13] is that these requirements should be met by internal and external loans, under the preliminary condition of a stabilised German currency. Is this proposal acceptable or not?

It would appear from Poincaré's speech[5] and more clearly from the 'Temps' of November 18, that the general idea of payment by loan is not now rejected in principle. It is further recognised that no loan is possible except after stabilisation.

There would thus appear to be no direct antagonism as to the underlying principles of a possible settlement. A great deal clearly depends upon how soon the requisite loans can be realised. That again depends upon the question how soon stability can be attained. If stabilisation could be achieved rapidly, the necessary basis for foreign credits would be reached, and loans might be realised in time to meet the necessities of France.

In my judgment there is no valid reason why stabilisation should not be

[4] Not preserved in the Foreign Office archives.
[5] This speech of November 17 was reported in Lord Hardinge's despatch No. 2701 of November 18 (C 15804/99/18), not printed.

achieved almost immediately, provided in the first place that the future receipts and disbursements of the Government can be adjusted without recourse to the printing press—a point on which the German authorities are confident—and provided in the second place that the recommendations of the Majority Experts are adopted in their entirety, and confided to some administrative organisation of adequate science and resolution.

The event clearly depends upon the adoption and maintenance of a fixed and unalterable ratio of exchange. This is the essential point of the Majority Scheme. If the Minority Report by MM. Vissering, Dubois and Kamenka, which substitutes for a fixed ratio the uncertain operation of a Stabilising Syndicate, is followed, no permanent success is probable. The result will merely be a series of ups and downs according as official intervention or hostile speculation gets the upper hand.

While, therefore, the general views put forward by the two bodies of Experts are not dissimilar, it should be realised from the outset that there is on this question of the fixed ratio a vital difference, and that it is essential to the success of the whole plan for stability, and to the execution of the Reparation scheme which is admitted to pivot upon stability, for the scheme of the Majority Experts to be followed.

Should this programme be adopted by the German Government voluntarily, or should it be imposed upon them by the Entente, with adequate guarantees for its effective execution, there is no reason why a completely successful result should not be attained at Brussels.

Since the above was drafted, the fact that President Ebert has again made the Note of November 13[1] the essential basis of policy on which a new German Government has to be formed, reinforces what is said as to the vital importance of that document.

I have, etc.,
D'ABERNON

No. 114

Note by Mr. Wigram on a discussion between the Prime Minister and Sir John Bradbury, held on November 22, 1922

[C 16116/99/18]

FOREIGN OFFICE, *November 23, 1922*

There was a discussion last night at No. 10, Downing Street, at which Sir John Bradbury explained his views on the reparation question to the Prime Minister. The Prime Minister having informed Sir J. Bradbury that he was trying to avoid for the present discussing the question of the Brussels conference[1] with the Belgian Ministers, Sir John Bradbury strongly advocated

---

[1] See No. 108.

indefinite postponement of the Brussels conference itself pending at least a preliminary agreement between the allies.

The Prime Minister having endeavoured to elicit from Sir John Bradbury the form that such an agreement would take, Sir John appeared to advise in the first instance some kind of fresh 'bankers' conference' which would consider the terms on which an international loan would be floated by Germany.

No reference was made by Sir John Bradbury to the period which must presumably elapse before such a loan could be floated, and Sir John seemed to be fairly definite that, in the matter of the capitalized value of the German debt itself, there was no chance of the Germans making an offer such as the allied governments could accept.

When the question was broached of the action to be taken to compel the Germans to submit a reasonable offer, Sir John Bradbury appeared to agree that the French could advocate vigorous measures in the Rhineland or in the Ruhr. The Prime Minister enquired whether there was not something to be said for giving the French their heads on this point, but Sir John seemed to deprecate measures of force on the ground that the allies had no right to take them under the treaty and that it would spell the ruin of the French exchange, and so of Europe. The Prime Minister asked if the latter part of this statement was not a slight exaggeration.

It will be noted that Sir John Bradbury did not give any indication of the results to the French exchange if vigorous action was not taken against Germany and if money for France was consequently not forthcoming at all. Whilst moreover Sir John apparently hoped eventually for a general international conference (at which Germany would be represented) to revise the treaty of Versailles, he did not explain what was to happen as regards the benefits accorded the allies by the treaty of Versailles in the event of Germany continuing to refuse to execute the treaty. Nor did Sir John refer to the increasing danger of a communist outbreak in Germany if the Germans, in pursuance of their policy of rendering the payment of reparation impossible by means of the depreciation of the mark, were not compelled to stabilize before the remnants of the German middle classes and intelligentsia themselves joined the ranks of low-paid labour.

Sir John Bradbury concluded his lecture—for from the tone in which his remarks were delivered, they can be described as little else—by a clear indication that he had a policy of his own in these matters which he intended to pursue on the commission, that it might not always be that of H[is] M[ajesty's] Gov[ernmen]t, but that if the Prime Minister thought Sir John's policy was likely to embarrass him, he was ready to resign forthwith. The Prime Minister said that he hoped that Sir John Bradbury would in future keep in very close touch with the Government.

Sir John Bradbury's views, so far as he developed them verbally to the Prime Minister, seem to me to portray such an incomplete view of the situation that I submit in a separate memorandum[2] a few brief points which Sir John appeared last night entirely to neglect.

[2] This ran: '. . . It would be unreasonable to expect that the French government will

I would add that the impression left on my mind by the views which Sir John Bradbury outlined to the Prime Minister only served to intensify and to throw into still stronger relief the conviction which I have long held of the extreme danger of allowing a question of the prime political importance of reparation to be dealt with by a few Treasury officials and ex-officials acting in complete independence of the Foreign Secretary.[3] It

accept these proposals [see No. 113]. . . . What they oppose is the grant of a moratorium without, among other things, some guarantee of future payment.

'The guarantee which they primarily require is not apparently control of German finance or of German administration. It is much more probably complete economic, military and political control of the left bank of the Rhine. . . . But it will be well to remember also the strain to the Entente which will be involved by continuance of the opposition to the French standpoint in this matter. The advocacy of further concessions to Germany may force France to act in Germany alone. . . . It will be well also not to forget the meagre results of the so-called "change of heart" in post-war Germany, and the manner in which Germany has during the last few months repaid the British government for the efforts made to mitigate the fate which Germany had brought upon herself. . . .'

[3] In a memorandum dated November 14, Mr. Wigram had stated: 'It is clear that this situation will not be remedied until (a) adequate and up-to-date information is supplied to the Foreign Office in respect of the reparation question, as in respect of all other matters affecting the foreign relations of this country. . . . (b) Sir John Bradbury observes complete silence so far as the press is concerned on all matters arising out of the proceedings of the commission. . . . (c) an arrangement is adopted either that (i) Sir John Bradbury shall obtain through the channel of the Foreign Office the instructions which (despite the fact that it is sometimes claimed that, as a delegate to the reparation commission, he occupies under the treaty a judicial position) he does at the moment obtain from the Treasury, or (ii) that whenever he asks for instructions from the Treasury officially or unofficially he shall communicate at the same time a copy of this request to the Foreign Office and that the Treasury shall agree not to reply to such requests without first obtaining the concurrence of the Foreign Office.'

On November 18 Mr. Lampson minuted: 'We should go a little warily over this or we shall find ourselves landed with the whole responsibility for Reparations, and that seems unwise now that they have become hopelessly tangled up as the result of actions and decisions taken on the initiative of others. . . . As the Treasury is the Department more immediately under the Prime Minister, should not that Department rather than the Foreign Office remain responsible to the British public for Reparation policy? It certainly seems more logical. But clearly that does not mean that the Treasury are absolved from consulting the Secretary of State before issuing any instructions to the British Delegate on the Commission that have a political bearing—which in effect means practically all instructions, for reparations and politics are so intertwined that even the most technical financial decisions have come to exercise a political effect. . . . Finally, and in addition to the above official action, I would submit that the Secretary of State might see his way to write *privately* to Mr. Bonar Law somewhat on the lines that if and when the time comes to appoint a new British Delegate to the Commission he would like to be given full opportunity of putting forward the name of any candidate for the post whose qualifications seem in [His Lordship's] opinion especially strong.'

Sir E. Crowe added on November 20: 'I do not altogether agree. . . . The fact that the financial problems engaging the attention of the Reparation Commission concern primarily the Treasury, is not a reason against letting the British Representative address his reports to the Foreign Office. Such reports would be passed on to the Treasury in the same way as reports from the Naval and Military Attachés are passed on to the Admiralty and War Office respectively, and reports on commercial negotiations, or shipping questions are passed on to the Board of Trade, extradition cases to the Home Office. . . . I do not know

may be worth mentioning, as evidence of the strange results of this procedure, a remark made by Sir John Bradbury last evening to the effect that he considered that if he could postpone the outbreak of a reparation crisis for another week, the Eastern question[4] would be solved and the immediate necessity for propitiating France removed. I cannot but imagine such an estimate of the situation to be based upon somewhat exaggerated optimism.

I am afraid it is but repetition to point out that the relations of questions of high finance to politics are precisely similar to the relations to politics of technical military and naval and economic matters. The Secretary of State does not allow War Office, or Admiralty or Board of Trade officials to dictate foreign policy or to neutralize a diplomatic position. It is difficult to understand why this privilege should be reserved for an ex-Treasury official.

R. F. WIGRAM

how the question of Sir J. Bradbury's resignation [see No. 94, n. 1] stands. I am under the impression that he has been asked to stay on.

'I have grave doubts as to whether the choice of Lord D'Abernon as his successor would be acceptable to the French.'

4 See Vol. XVIII.

No. 115

Sir G. Grahame (Brussels) to the Marquess Curzon of Kedleston
(Received November 25)

No. 100 Telegraphic [C 16098/99/18]*

Very Confidential BRUSSELS, *November 25, 1922*

I had a short conversation with Belgian Prime Minister and Foreign Minister yesterday evening shortly after their return from Paris, and a long one this morning with latter. My two following telegrams[1] give the substance of these conversations.

Belgian Minister asked that His Majesty's Government shall observe great discretion and not let French Government know what they have learned of M. Poincaré's views in this way, as he would probably resent that information had reached them indirectly instead of directly at a later date from himself.

1 Nos. 116 and 117, below.

No. 116

Sir G. Grahame (Brussels) to the Marquess Curzon of Kedleston
(Received November 25, 9.35 p.m.)

No. 101 Telegraphic [C 16099/99/18]

Very Confidential BRUSSELS, *November 25, 1922, 7.08 p.m.*

My immediately preceding telegram.[1]

Belgian Minister found French President of the Council in markedly optimistic mood. No trace of past resentment towards them appeared. He

1 No. 115.

informed them he had brought back from Lausanne extremely encouraging impressions. In the first place Italian Prime Minister[2] had acknowledged need for stronger action against Germany. In second place French President of the Council had been greatly struck by language of Sir W. Tyrrell which had encouraged him to believe that new Cabinet was likely to lighten restraining pressure on French policy in the matter of forcible measures against Germany.

Monsieur Poincaré announced that French government would demand at Brussels conference abolition of all question of moratorium and reversion to schedule of payments as arranged [in] May, 1921, entailing payment by Germany without delay, of three milliard gold marks. If this were not at once accepted by Germany he would propose:—

1. That a loan should be floated, part of which should be used for stabilizing German mark, and another but larger part to relieve urgent financial needs of the allies.

2. That Essen should be provisionally occupied by the allies in order to control coal production, and as means of pressure on German industrialists. Marshal Foch has been consulted, and he had given opinion that in order to do so it would not be necessary to occupy the whole of the Ruhr Basin with a large force, and that French army could do its part without fresh classes being called up.

Poincaré indicated that if the allies refused, France could carry out this operation alone.

If Brussels conference failed, French government would propose in addition to these two measures a third one, namely change in status of Rhineland, entailing dismissal of all Prussian functionaries and what would practically amount to taking over of Rhineland administration by the allies.

[2] Signor Mussolini had become President of the Council and Minister for Foreign Affairs *ad interim* on October 31.

No. 117

Sir G. Grahame (Brussels) to the Marquess Curzon of Kedleston
(Received November 26, 9 a.m.)
No. 102 Telegraphic [C 16100/99/18]

Very Confidential   BRUSSELS, *November 26, 1922, 12.35 a.m.*

My immediately preceding telegram.[1]

Belgian Minister for Foreign Affairs considers situation very serious. He is quite in the dark as to what the policy of British cabinet is likely to be in face of Monsieur Poincaré's attitude. He doubts whether rhodomontades of Italian Prime Minister are to be taken quite at face value. When he gets back to Italy anti-French influences there may somewhat affect him. But

[1] No. 116.

on the other hand if he goes to Paris it is likely that he will be given a great popular reception which may go to his head.

Belgian Minister for Foreign Affairs is strongly of opinion that if French government are to be stopped from carrying out policy announced by Monsieur Poincaré something must be done at once. His suggestions are:

1. that German government should immediately float a loan with aid of some big industrialists to produce 500 million gold marks for stabilisation of mark and a similar sum for reparations account. He has already told Herr Bergman[n] of this suggestion.

2. that His Majesty's Government should announce at allied meeting previous to Brussels conference that they will cancel debts of European allies. He thinks this action may greatly conduce to stop Monsieur Poincaré as it would have marked effect on French public opinion.

3. [that] Belgian Prime Minister [should suggest] to Monsieur Poincaré as alternative to his proposals that a demand should be made on German government to grant allied participation in profits of big German industries. Shares in these would be deposited with reparations commission and accrued dividends paid to it for distribution. German government or German industries would have the faculty of re-purchasing them out of their overseas investments at a gold standard. In this way allies would have their share if and when German industries increased in prosperity and it would be a safeguard against the world market being captured by German industries to detriment of allied exporting countries.

Belgian Minister for Foreign Affairs believes it is most urgent to take measures at once for dealing with Monsieur Poincaré's plan. Though latter is strongly pressed by French internal situation he still believes that it is possible to prevent him from breaking loose.

Belgian Ministers think that it is most important that they should get into personal touch with British Ministers at earliest possible moment.[2]

[2] Sir E. Crowe minuted (November 27): 'This raises important political as well as economic problems.

'A letter is being written to the Treasury, sending copies of all the recent papers and inviting them to furnish, after consultation with Sir J. Bradbury if necessary, their observations on the economic side of the question, which the Secretary of State would desire to have before him when considering the political aspect.'

Lord Curzon (who was at the Conference of Lausanne) added on November 28: 'I sent a telegram to F[oreign] O[ffice] yesterday saying that it is quite impossible for me to deal with this case here. I have also written to the P[rime] M[inister] asking if he is prepared to take it in hand since at present we are drifting and merely making everyone angry by our assumed indifference. Would it not be well to submit the papers as they come in to the P[rime] M[inister] so that he may be familiar with its political aspect?'

No. 118

Sir G. Grahame (Brussels) to the Marquess Curzon of Kedleston
(Received November 26, 1.15 p.m.)
No. 103 Telegraphic [C 16688/99/18]

Very Confidential   BRUSSELS, *November 26, 1922, 11.25 a.m.*

Belgian Prime Minister while expressing more indignation about German shortcomings than Minister for Foreign Affairs seems almost more troubled than latter at result of conversations in Paris.

I asked him whether he thought that if coercive measures were applied to Germany they would produce enough in the way of reparations to counterbalance shock which might thus be caused to European situation. He shrugged his shoulders and said that France owing to her particular economic conditions was likely to suffer shock less than exporting countries such as England and Belgium; but that even if there were prospects of material loss for France it must be remembered that nations like individuals sometimes ran such risks in order to satisfy sentiment or passion.

In the course of this conversation he interjected a remark that if situation were to develop in a certain way Belgium might conceivably find herself forced to accompany France in action against Germany so as to avoid result to Belgium of having to let her take it alone.

In any case such partnership with France is regarded by Belgian Ministers absolutely as a *pis aller* and they view prospect with the utmost misgiving.

No. 119

Sir G. Grahame (Brussels) to the Marquess Curzon of Kedleston
(Received November 30)
No. 782 [C 16338/99/18]

Confidential   BRUSSELS, *November 27, 1922*
My Lord,

A Cabinet Council is being held today at which the Prime Minister and Minister for Foreign Affairs will explain to their colleagues what they were told by the French President of the Council last week in Paris as regards the demands which he intended to make at the Brussels Conference.[1]

Several of the Ministers have already learnt what these demands are.

M. Franck, Minister of the Colonies, who is Deputy for Antwerp and therefore particularly in touch with Flemish and business circles, spoke to me confidentially on the subject yesterday. He said that we seemed to be approaching the most serious crisis which had occurred within the last two years. M. Poincaré appeared to hold better cards in his hands than hitherto. It would require clever generalship on the part of the other Allies to prevent him from pursuing a course of action which he believed might not be in their

---

[1] See No. 116.

best interests and would be fraught with disadvantages and dangers. There were many people in Belgium who disliked the French policy of sending troops further into Germany, but there was, at the same time, an exceedingly strong body of opinion which would in certain circumstances be in favour of joining with France. He considered that it was absolutely necessary that a plan should be evolved which would offer France and Belgium, at any rate, substantial advantages. This plan should include the partial proceeds of a loan and a really satisfactory control over German finances. It would be highly desirable that the cancellation of the debts of the European Allies to Great Britain should form part of it. Possibly also an arrangement for participation in profits of German industries could be reached; and, if this were feasible, the question of the defensive pacts should be reconsidered.

M. Franck believes that the best way to deal with M. Poincaré would be to put forward advantages of this kind, and then make it an absolute condition of granting them that the French Government should renounce its proposal for further territorial sanctions. If French public opinion were to see that in the one scale there lay such benefits and in the other the sterile prospect of action by the army, M. Poincaré might lose much support in France.

M. Franck thought that a majority of his countrymen, who were more reasonable people than the French, would, if satisfactory offers were made and accepted by Germany, cease from agitating to induce their Government to accompany France on a military adventure. He is of opinion that, if it should happen that France were to break away from her Allies and take isolated action, she would not be able to maintain herself long in such an advanced position. Her moral isolation would be complete; she would have drawn upon herself the hostility of the organised workers of the world and a hostile Anglo-American opinion[2] in particular would render her position highly unpleasant, not to mention the defection of Belgium. On the other hand, if Belgium were to be forced into accompanying France, the moral prestige of Belgium—the first victim of German oppression and innocent sufferer of the Great War—would cover and act as a condonation of French policy which, as many people thought, harboured an *arrière pensée* not shared by her Allies. It would, however, be difficult and dangerous for a Belgian Cabinet to disassociate itself from French coercive measures, and that was why he thought that a plan should be rapidly arranged and measures conjointly taken to ward off the peril; but nothing would avail unless substantial measures of material relief were devised as an offset to the French policy.

I have, etc.,

GEORGE GRAHAME

[2] In his telegram No. 104 of November 27 Sir G. Grahame reported: 'Belgian Minister for Foreign Affairs has told American ambassador for confidential information of his government what French President of the Council proposes to do at Brussels conference.

'American ambassador believes his government will be most disagreeably impressed by proposal to send troops further into Germany and that public opinion if aware of it would be markedly hostile until the measure became necessary after all other methods to overcome German obstruction had clearly been exhausted.'

Memorandum by Mr. Bonar Law of an Interview with the French
Ambassador, held on November 28, 1922
(Received in the Foreign Office, November 29)

[*C 16247/99/18*]

Copy

Confidential   *November 28, 1922*

The French Ambassador called today, reading to me a telegram which M. Poincaré had sent regarding a conversation with Lord Curzon to the effect that, as Lord Curzon would be away,[1] I would probably take the question of reparations in hand myself, as even the Chancellor of the Exchequer would be away.[2] M. Poincaré therefore wished me to be informed that it seemed to him a necessity that the conference at Brussels should be held on the 15th, and he was very desirous that there should be a meeting of the Prime Ministers before.[3] I said to him that it was quite impossible for me to leave London until the House was up, but that I would not refuse to have a meeting in London at the end of next week, i.e., Saturday and Sunday, the 9th and 10th December, but that I would very much prefer—and I hoped that he would make this plain to M. Poincaré—that the meeting should take place in Paris the week after our House had risen. I suggested to him also that it would seem to me very desirable that before the meeting he should send me particulars of the propositions which he proposed to make at the conference.[4] We did not go into any discussion as to the proposals, but I said to him that it seemed to me in any case almost impossible that we could come to any agreement which could be carried out in the short interval between now and the end of the year, and suggested, as at least a possibility, that in order to enable a meeting to be held without an impossible pressure as regards time a moratorium of a month should be given without its affecting the big question. The Ambassador thought that M. Poincaré would have great objection to this, and this was practically the end of the conversation.

A. B. L.

[1] At the Conference of Lausanne (see Vol. XVIII).

[2] See No. 63, n. 15. In the event, however, Mr. Baldwin did not leave for Washington until December 27.

[3] In a minute of November 25, Sir E. Crowe had stated: 'The Prime Minister has abandoned the idea of arranging for an early discussion of the whole problem with M. Poincaré at a personal interview, to be held in London. The Prime Minister has learnt from Sir J. Bradbury that M. Poincaré is issuing invitations for a meeting at Paris (preliminary to Brussels) to British and Italian as well as Belgian ministers.'

[4] Cf. No. 116.

No. 121

Sir E. Crowe to the French Ambassador

[*C 16343/99/18*]

FOREIGN OFFICE, *November 29, 1922*

My dear Ambassador,

The Prime Minister, who is still busily engaged in the House of Commons, begs me to write to you in reply to your kind note[1] of this evening.

He would be much obliged if you would convey his sincere thanks to M. Poincaré for his friendly message. He will hold himself entirely at M. Poincaré's disposal on the 9th and 10th of December, trusting that this will be found convenient.

Mr. Bonar Law thinks it unavoidable that he should ask the Belgian Prime Minister to be present at the proposed meeting, if only for the reason that the latter had already arranged to come to London for a conversation on the subject of the proposed Brussels conference and that this intended visit was only deferred at Mr. Bonar Law's request.

M. Poincaré will no doubt see no objection to the presence of the Belgian Prime Minister, and as soon as Mr. Bonar Law receives M. Poincaré's assent,[2] he will address invitations to both the Italian and Belgian Prime Ministers to come to London on the 9th of December for the purpose of the meeting.

Yours sincerely,
EYRE A. CROWE

[1] Not printed.

[2] In a letter of November 30 to Sir E. Crowe, Mr. F. G. Agar-Robartes, Assistant Private Secretary (Diplomatic) to the Secretary of State, reported: 'The French Embassy have telephoned to say that M. Poincaré accepts the 9th and 10th December as the dates of the conference, and asks Mr. Bonar Law to be good enough to send invitations to M. Theunis and Signor Mussolini.

'The French Embassy would be grateful if we could give them further details, as soon as possible, as to the procedure which the Prime Minister proposes to adopt for the conference, e.g., whether M. Poincaré should bring an expert, when he should arrive in London, &c.

'The French Ambassador is not sending a written reply to your letter.'

No. 122

The Marquess Curzon of Kedleston to Sir R. Graham (Rome) and Sir G. Grahame (Brussels)

No. 407[1] Telegraphic [*C 16343/99/18*]

FOREIGN OFFICE, *November 30, 1922, 5.45 p.m.*

Monsieur Poincaré has proposed[2] a meeting of allied prime ministers preliminary to the Brussels conference on reparations which he desires to see

[1] No. 407 to Rome and No. 53 to Brussels.　　　[2] See No. 120.

assembled on December 15th. As Mr. Bonar Law could not owing to parliamentary engagements leave England before that date he has suggested that meeting should take place here in London on December 9th.

Please inform government to which you are accredited and express Mr. Bonar Law's hope that Italian/Belgian Prime Minister will be able to take part in this meeting, bringing with him such other ministers or experts as he may desire.

Repeated to Lausanne No. 36.

No. 123

Lord D'Abernon to the Marquess Curzon of Kedleston (*Received December 5*)
No. 917 [*C 16610/99/18*]

BERLIN, *November 30, 1922*

My Lord Marquess,

I have the honour to forward to Your Lordship herewith a Memorandum by Mr. Thelwall[1] on a conversation with Dr. Stresemann[2] and other prominent German politicians concerning the reparation question.

I have, etc.,
D'ABERNON

ENCLOSURE IN NO. 123

Memorandum

BERLIN, *November 29, 1922*

1. Yesterday evening I had a conversation with several Germans who are actively engaged in politics, more particularly with Dr. Stresemann and Herr Otto Wolff.

All were unanimous in describing Dr. Wirth's fall[3] as the most astounding case of political suicide which had ever come to their notice. The late Chancellor had secured the support of all the Parties from the Volkspartei to the Social-Democrats inclusive; the only thing he was asked to do was not to bring forward his reconstructed Cabinet under the name of the 'Grosse Coalition'. Everything had been satisfactorily arranged when suddenly, without any warning, Dr. Wirth changed his mind and insisted upon doing the very thing which everybody had agreed to avoid. He is said to be doing himself harm at the present moment by staying in Berlin and frequenting the Reichstag and making himself generally conspicuous instead of retiring to the country until the whole matter has blown over.

2. I said to Dr. Stresemann that, as his Party was presumably supporting the present Cabinet[4] and as the former contained practically all the leaders of finance and industry, it was high time that they made some concrete

---

[1] Commercial Secretary in H.M. Embassy at Berlin.
[2] Leader of the German People's Party (*Deutsche Volkspartei*).
[3] See No. 113, n. 3.   [4] i.e. that headed by Dr. Cuno.

proposal in the reparation question. Stresemann and Wolff both agreed about this and said that the Cabinet would probably offer to raise one milliard gold marks at once, guaranteed by German Industry and German landed property, and to pay a total of from 20 to 30 milliard gold marks for reparations; on the larger amount interest and a certain rate of amortisation would be paid annually. The chief conditions which the Germans would attach to such an offer would be the complete withdrawal of the Armies of Occupation within a short period and full liberty to conclude commercial treaties without being hampered by the obligation to accord the Allies one-sided most favoured nation treatment.

I do not think that the Germans themselves have much hope of the French agreeing to these terms, but apparently they are the only ones the former are inclined to put forward.

3. Dr. Stresemann emphasised the extremely unsatisfactory nature of his conversation with Barthou.[5] The latter seemed much more concerned at the possibility of a German attack upon France than at the difficulty of arriving at any sort of financial settlement, and when Dr. Stresemann finally pointed out that Germany had hardly any Army and Navy and no Air Force at all, Barthou replied that in all probability the German chemists would produce some invention which would be more deadly and more effective than any armed force.

4. As on several other occasions recently, I found that even well-informed people in Germany are convinced that England and France have arrived at an arrangement by which the latter is to be given a free hand in Germany in return for non-interference in the Near East. Further colour is lent to the German view by the latest French attitude which inclines more and more towards the policy outlined in Monsieur Dariac's report.[6]

5. Dr. Stresemann said that, in view of the difficult situation between Germany and France, he had proposed some arrangement between French and German industry as a possible solution. He thought for instance that a fair sum of money could be raised by a Franco-German Potash Combine and some similar scheme in the mining, iron and steel industries. I think, however, that in any case it would be difficult to use industrial agreements of such a nature for the payment of State debts and, further, there does not seem much prospect of a settlement being arrived at on these lines. As we know, the Potash negotiations have failed, and Herr Stinnes himself has told Dr. Stresemann that he finds the demands of the French much too exorbitant as far as his own particular line is concerned.

F. THELWALL

[5] Cf. No. 107, Enclosure.

[6] An extract from the *Manchester Guardian* of November 2, giving the text of this secret report on the Rhineland presented by M. Dariac (Chairman of the Finance Committee of the French Chamber of Deputies and Special Commissioner on the Rhine) is filed in the Foreign Office archives (C 15071/336/18). The *Manchester Guardian* stated that M. Dariac had been sent by M. Poincaré to report on the economics and industry of the Rhine Province.

Sir W. Tyrrell (Lausanne)[1] *to Sir E. Crowe (Received December 6)*
[*C 16688/99/18*]

LAUSANNE, *November 30, 1922*

My dear Crowe,

I am sending you under flying seal a letter which I have written to Grahame, by Lord Curzon's direction, in reply to a letter of his showing the improper use which Poincaré has made of a very informal talk which he had with me here, in his subsequent conversations with Theunis.

I leave it to you to decide whether you would think it necessary to let the Prime Minister see this correspondence previous to any talks he may have with Poincaré or Theunis.

Yours ever,
W. TYRRELL

ENCLOSURE I IN No. 124

Letter from Sir W. Tyrrell (Lausanne) to Sir G. Grahame (Brussels)

LAUSANNE, *November 30, 1922*

My dear Grahame,

Lord Curzon has shown me your letter[2] to him in which you describe what passed between Monsieur Poincaré and Monsieur Theunis on the strength of a conversation between me and Monsieur Poincaré.

Lord Curzon thinks the best plan would be if I explained to you what had passed.

To start with, there is no doubt that Poincaré, for obvious reasons of his own, had vastly exaggerated my position and influence, or else Theunis would have asked him 'what is the use of quoting Tyrrell?' Secondly, Poincaré describes our conversation from the wrong angle. It did not start with my saying to Poincaré that he would find the new Ministry more favourable to forcible measures against Germany than its predecessor. It started with Poincaré saying that his impression was that such was the case, and on my asking him how he had formed that impression, he alluded to a conversation which our Prime Minister is supposed to have had with French journalists. In this connection I rem[em]bered a conversation in which Mr. Bonar Law told 'Pertinax' that he had not made up his mind that the recovery of Germany would be an unmixed blessing, and secondly that we must always remember that nobody was in the habit of paying their debts unless forced to do so.

Remembering this conversation, I thought it best to impress upon Poincaré that if he were able to submit to Mr. Bonar Law a businesslike plan for the exaction of reparations out of Germany, he would find that his scheme would

---

[1] Sir W. Tyrrell was a member of the British Empire Delegation at the Conference of Lausanne.
[2] Enclosure 2.

be considered in a sympathetic and businesslike spirit, and that if it ultimately entailed coercion I did not think that the new Ministry would shrink from applying it, provided it were convinced that it would yield reparation payment. I then repeated my now familiar jargon that, in my opinion, the French Government would find in our new Prime Minister a man who would be both friendly and businesslike in his dealings, and who would look at things as they really were, and never become involved in far-reaching Utopian schemes.

There is no doubt in my mind that Poincaré, in his desire to associate Belgium with a policy of sanction, placed an exaggerated interpretation upon our conversation. I am surprised, however, that he should have succeeded in taking in Monsieur Theunis. It seems to me that personal intercourse with foreign statesmen is becoming increasingly difficult considering the very inaccurate versions to which they give currency. It is not very long ago, when I was in Paris, that Poincaré told Lord Hardinge that Mr. Bonar Law had agreed to all kinds of reparation conferences in a conversation with Saint-Aulaire.[3] When this report was brought to the Prime Minister's notice it turned out that his conversation had lasted about ten minutes and had been confined to the merest superficialities.

I hope, however, you will succeed with the help of this letter to disabuse Monsieur Theunis both as regards my position and influence in the Foreign Office and the tenor of my remarks to Monsieur Poincaré.

Yours ever,
W. Tyrrell

Enclosure 2 in No. 124

Sir G. Grahame (Brussels) to the Marquess Curzon of Kedleston (Lausanne)

Brussels, November 28, 1922

Dear Lord Curzon,

You will have received my reports[4] of the result of the visit of MM. Theunis and Jaspar to Paris.

Both Ministers emphasized the effect made on M. Poincaré by Signor Mussolini's apparent readiness to give his blessing to a forward policy on the part of France, and by what was said by Tyrrell. He eulogized the latter and told the Belgian Ministers that he was the official who had predominating influence in the Foreign Office. He, M. Poincaré, was glad to think that that department was coming rapidly round to a more just appreciation of French policy and French needs.

I questioned MM. Theunis and Jaspar as to whether M. Poincaré had mentioned any expression of opinion from *you* in regard to the allied attitude towards Germany. They both replied that he had only spoken of Tyrrell.

Although Signor Mussolini's declarations seem to have been highly agreeable to M. Poincaré, the former's personality seems to have taken his

---

[3] Cf. No. 108.   [4] Nos. 116, 117, 118, and 119.

breath away. He remarked to the Belgian Ministers that he was 'un Napoléon de café-concert'.

I met last night M. Delacroix (Belgian Representative on the Reparation Commission). He had seen Marchese Salvago Raggi on his return from Rome where he had spoken with Signor Mussolini since his return from Lausanne. The latter had said that it was not of supreme importance to Italy if the French did go into the Ruhr, but that if other proposals more likely to improve the situation were put forward, they would have his preference and probably his support.

Yours very truly,
GEORGE GRAHAME

No. 125

Lord Hardinge (Paris) to Sir E. Crowe (Received December 3)
[C 17361/99/18]

PARIS, *December 1, 1922*

My dear Crowe,

The Belgian Ambassador[1] came to see me this morning, and in the course of conversation, he told me that he had had a long interview with Poincaré, yesterday evening, who talked at length on the subject of Reparations and the forthcoming meeting in London next week.[2] As I foresaw at the time, when in accordance with my instructions,[3] I addressed a note[4] expressing the desire of His Majesty's Government to arrive at an agreement respecting Reparations, and asserting the necessity of making Germany pay, Poincaré has got into his head that we are ready now, since Lloyd George has disappeared, to back him up in all his enterprises to obtain money from Germany. Poincaré told the [Belgian] Ambassador that he was very sanguine of arriving at a complete accord with Mr. Bonar Law. Both he and Theunis were agreed that a change of method was absolutely necessary and that the Allied Powers should take Germany by the scruff of the neck and make her pay. He had discussed the whole question in the Cabinet recently and had decided that the best and most satisfactory manner of exerting pressure on the German industrials and on the German Government would be the occupation of Essen, for which the French Government would in London produce definite plans. Essen, so Poincaré said, was a centre through which all the canals passed, bringing coal from the mines, and all the railways converged there also, consequently when in possession of Essen it would be very easy to have complete control of the export of coal from the Ruhr. This he regarded as an essential guarantee if a moratorium was to be given to Germany. He had hopes that England would agree to joint action with France and Belgium in this direction, but if for military or other reasons, England was indisposed to take military action, France would be quite

---

[1] Baron de Gaiffier d'Hestroy.   [2] See No. 121.   [3] See No. 112.
[4] Not printed.

ready to act as a Mandatory of the other Powers. In the event, however, of there being disagreement between the Powers, France claimed, as her inalienable right, to act alone to secure the Reparations which are due to her. France, he said, was in such a position that it is now absolutely essential to obtain productive guarantees, especially as any moratorium to be given to Germany would not be one of months but of years. He told Gaiffier that he was very sanguine of obtaining complete success at the Brussels Conference and that he had no illusions as to success being the outcome of that being held at Lausanne.[5]

I asked Gaiffier whether Theunis had agreed to Poincaré's scheme when he was here a few days ago. He said that he had been present at the conversations which took place and his impression was that Theunis had agreed to nothing. On the other hand, Poincaré told him that Theunis had agreed to his scheme and that he counted on his co-operation and support in Brussels.

Gaiffier observed that in view of the strong body of Socialists in the Belgian Parliament, he thought that Theunis would hesitate before embarking on a military enterprise in the Ruhr, but he thought that the Belgian Government would probably go with France rather than allow the French to go there alone.

Till a few days ago, my impression has been that, although Poincaré would bluff a great deal about going into the Ruhr, he would never have the courage to do so. But I am not now so sure that he will not do so if provoked, as public opinion is hardening against the bad faith of Germany, and Poincaré, who has been losing ground very rapidly in the Chamber, sees in an excursion into the Ruhr, the means of recovering his position in the country, and especially with the Bloc National in the Chamber. Still, whatever happens in the next month, I doubt if Poincaré will last much longer than the end of January as there is so much dissatisfaction with him in the Chamber on internal questions.

I think perhaps the Prime Minister would like to know this in view of his meeting next week.

Ever yours,
HARDINGE OF P[ENSHURST]

[5] See Vol. XVIII, Chap. II.

No. 126

Lord Hardinge (Paris) to the Marquess Curzon of Kedleston
(Received December 5)
No. 2839 [C 16565/99/18]

Confidential   PARIS, *December 4, 1922*

His Majesty's Ambassador at Paris presents his compliments to His Majesty's Principal Secretary of State for Foreign Affairs and has the honour to transmit herewith a copy of a summary of statement made to English press correspondents by M. Poincaré dealing with the London meeting[1] between Prime Ministers, and [the] Lausanne Conference.

(Copy sent to Lausanne.)

ENCLOSURE IN No. 126

Summary of Statement made by M. Poincaré to English Press Correspondents, December 4, 1922

The English press was received by M. Poincaré this morning, and he told them it was simply to give information to the English press on the eve of his visit to London, but he did not wish them to mention his name or the fact that he had received them.

He said that no definite reply had yet been received from the Italian Premier, but he hoped he would come. The opinion of the French Government, however, was that even if Mussolini did not come, the conversations between Mr. Bonar Law, M. Theunis and himself (M. Poincaré) should proceed.

He went on to say that he was going to London to talk over his 'plan[2] for presentation at the Brussels Conference, if it is held,' and to lay the foundations for that conference; but that, of course, neither Italy, Britain nor France had a programme (as distinct from a plan) for the conference.

He said that the ideas which he would develop in London were those he had already expressed in the Chamber of Deputies[3] and the Senate. The great importance of the Brussels Conference made these preliminary conversations necessary; and it would have to be held very soon before the 15th January, when the Reparation Commission would have to reply to Germany's request for a moratorium. That meant that the Allies must reach an understanding before the 15th January; they are *au pied du mur* and cannot delay.

He strongly urged that the Brussels Conference should meet at the beginning of the latter half of December, without regard to Christmas or other holidays.

He then said: 'I do not know whether His Majesty's Government desires to have a reply from Washington before broaching the main issues. Their financial delegation has not even started, but in my view no matter what the United States of America does or does not do, the European nations must settle among themselves and agree upon what they intend to do with reference to inter-Allied debts, irrespective of Washington. I shall talk to Mr. Bonar Law of this, but, of course, our conversations must be preparatory for Brussels.'

Turning to the Near East, M. Poincaré said that the conference[4] has its ups and downs, but it seemed to him to be in a fair way. The general impression he had was fairly good. He continued: 'I had that impression when

[1] See No. 121.   [2] See No. 116.
[3] In a speech of November 17 (see No. 113, n. 5).
[4] See Vol. XVIII, Chap. II.

309

I was at Lausanne. We have given the Turks to understand that France is first of all "d'accord avec ses Alliés". France has been able to act, if not as conciliator, at least as intermediary between England and Turkey.' But he warned them that the conference would last a long time, and there was no possibility of its ending before Christmas, for many important technical, financial and economic matters would have to be settled by experts—always a lengthy method, he added.

One thing was certain, in the Near East, the more time goes by, the more impossible becomes the resumption of hostilities.

In answer to a question, M. Poincaré said that Cuno's speech[5] was 'un discours de pure illusion,' and that France cannot and will not permit the present situation to continue.

In conclusion, he repeated that he was going to London, and the conversations would doubtless be held in the most cordial and confident atmosphere.

[5] A translation of Dr. Cuno's speech of December 3 to the Berlin Press Association was transmitted to the Foreign Office in Berlin despatch No. 933 of December 5, not printed.

No. 127

Record by Sir E. Crowe of a conversation with the Italian Ambassador
[C 16750/99/18]

FOREIGN OFFICE, *December 4, 1922*

The Italian Ambassador asked me today whether any detailed programme had been fixed for the discussions between the allied Prime Ministers on the subject of reparations, to be held in London on December 9. He said that M. Mussolini was most anxious to have this information, so as to prepare himself for the meeting.

I explained that no detailed programme was in existence. The meeting arose out of a proposal, on the part of M. Poincaré,[1] that the allied Prime Ministers should have an informal talk between themselves before the meeting of the conference which was to be called by the Belgian Government at Brussels for December 15. I said that Mr. Bonar Law entirely agreed with M. Poincaré that it was desirable, nay indispensable, that, before the allies met in conference to discuss with Germany how to solve the reparation problem, an agreement should be arrived at, at least as regards the general principles on which the allies should proceed.[1] I added, speaking confidentially, that Mr. Bonar Law had at one time suggested to M. Poincaré the desirability of having an indication before the Prime Ministers' meeting of any plan that M. Poincaré might have in his mind for dealing with the situation as it now stood.[1] But M. Poincaré had replied[2] that he thought it would be better not to start with discussing a definite plan arranged beforehand, but let the views of the several Prime Ministers emerge in the course

[1] See No. 120.   [2] Cf. No. 121, n. 2.

of the informal discussions which were to be held. I observed to the Marquis della Torretta that, according to a telegram[3] we had received from our Ambassador at Rome, M. Mussolini hesitated to come to London for this meeting unless he could be given a clear idea of the programme, and I asked whether, in the circumstances, it would be likely that M. Mussolini would come. The Marquis della Torretta, speaking for himself, said he had no doubt whatever that M. Mussolini would make the journey.[4]

[3] No. 392 of December 3 (C 16474/99/18), not printed.
[4] A note on this document in Sir E. Crowe's hand states: 'Seen by the Prime Minister.'

No. 128

Record by Mr. Lampson of a conversation with Herr Dufour-Feronce
[C 16762/99/18]

FOREIGN OFFICE, *December 5, 1922*

M. Dufour, Counsellor of the German Embassy, with whom I lunched today, spoke very seriously about the situation in Germany. He said that he and the Ambassador were deeply distressed at the situation over reparations which was evidently evolving. Was it a fact that the French wished to detach the Rhineland from the Reich, and if so, did His Majesty's Government view that possibility with equanimity? He could only say that if the idea was in fact entertained by the French, it would be storing up the seeds of future war, for the inhabitants of the Rhineland would never rest under foreign rule. I told him that I was not in a position to discuss what the proposals of the French or any other Allied Government would be when the case of reparations came up for discussion, nor could I possibly hazard any view as to how the British Government would act in the event of France making any such proposal. As he knew, the French were the Allies of Great Britain, and our relations were those natural to Allies.

The talk then turned on general lines, and I put it to him frankly that the attitude of the French, as outlined in the press, was perfectly intelligible. Germany was pledged by the Treaty to pay reparation, but so far, to all intents and purposes, her payments had been small. France might reasonably say that if Germany was to have a further moratorium, she (France) must have some earnest of Germany's good faith. That was the origin of the phrase 'productive pledges'.

M. Dufour then enquired whether any alternative pledges would not be acceptable? I asked what particular alternative he had in mind. He replied that he thought the customs under foreign supervision might be adequate. There were also the state railways which could undoubtedly be made to pay, though they were not doing so at present. I pressed him as to state mines and forests, also as to participation of German industry, but he gravely doubted whether these were feasible. Finally he begged that if the German Embassy in London could be of any assistance, directly or indirectly, in letting the

German Government know any means whereby they might meet the threatening situation, I would let them know. He added that there was a very real danger of a social upheaval in Germany, unless she were able in a given time to stabilise the mark, and get her finances in order; the communists were already active, and though his Government were determined to preserve law and order to the best of their ability, yet the very fact that the solid middle class had, through impoverishment, to a large extent ceased to exist, militated against their power to resist subversive elements.

No. 129

Lieut.-Colonel Ryan[1] (Coblenz) to the Marquess Curzon of Kedleston
(Received December 7, 4.40 p.m.)
No. 37 Telegraphic: by wireless [C 16775/99/18]

Urgent   Confidential   COBLENZ, *December 7, 1922, 9.45 a.m.*
Sir G. Grahame's telegram No. 101.[2]

I had opportunity of discussing this morning question of reparations with Monsieur Tirard,[3] who was present at recent conference in Paris on this subject.

Tirard said that a large body of French opinion which [two] years ago believed Germany could pay everything, had now gone to the other extreme and believed that nothing in the shape of reparations could ever be obtained from Germany. France had seen Germany's financial position, in spite of alleviations granted by allies, steadily growing worse and even if allies granted further alleviations there appeared no prospect of any improvement in view of manifest ill-will of German people towards reparations. Government circles realised that Germany could at present moment pay nothing except as a result of large foreign loan, success of which was doubtful. France was now more apprehensive than ever for her safety in view of growth of reaction in Germany. Many people on the one hand felt that security for the future must be obtained at all costs and on the other hand that whatever action was taken by allies, no money could be obtained from Germany. Their policy was therefore to break entirely with the past by obtaining definite (amount of) security and by foregoing slight chance there was of securing substantial payment.

I asked Tirard if French government realised danger which such policy entailed for France and Europe. He replied that there was also a strong body of opinion in France that fully saw the danger and whose policy was a constructive one directed towards strengthening of Germany economically

[1] Deputy British High Commissioner on the Inter-Allied Rhineland High Commission.
[2] No. 116.
[3] French High Commissioner and President of the Inter-Allied Rhineland High Commission.

with a view to obtaining ultimately money which France needed. Of the two bodies of opinion in France, he believed latter would prevail provided guarantees were forthcoming. Such guarantees were, however, essential as French government would be unable to hold its position unless it could show to the French people that tangible assets were held in the event of Germany's default, and that France's position was secure. In this last respect he thought pact guaranteeing against German aggression would have great influence.

With regard to Ruhr, I understand the French plan is occupation of Essen and levying of coal tax which would be paid to allied instead of to German officials. This would presumably entail no radical change at first but would place the French in position of being able to increase tax later and to take over the mines and control entirely distribution of coal.

In regard to Rhineland, Tirard reiterated that France had no annexationist intentions. He himself felt a Rhineland irredenta was dangerous and that measures directed towards separation of Rhineland from Germany by force would be doomed to failure. The replacing of Prussian officials by Rhinelanders would also have no practical effect as attitude of new officials towards France would be same as that of old. The purpose of proposal was, however, to calm public opinion in France which is much influenced by events in Rhineland.

Tirard has, I think, been impressed by numerous manifestations of loyalty which have taken place within the last few days in the Rhineland and I agree with his views and probable effects of proposed measures.

Proposal as to allied participation in German industry has advantage that France and allies as a whole would be directly interested in economic recovery of Germany and its adoption would probably help to restore confidence of the world in Germany's future.

Tirard gave me to understand that His Majesty's Government (*sic*? his government) might be prepared in principle to adopt plan. He said one of conditions would be that allies should also have a proportionate measure of control over industry but that German legislation might . . .[4] this difficult.

[4] The text is here uncertain.

No. 130

Lord Hardinge (Paris) to the Marquess Curzon of Kedleston
(Received December 8)
No. 2687 [C 16803/99/18]

Very Urgent   PARIS, *December 7, 1922*
My Lord,

The eve of the London Conference brings into prominence two different forecasts of Monsieur Poincaré's attitude. On the one hand the French press believe that he intends not to disclose before Brussels the comprehensive plan which he is credited with having elaborated. On the other hand Monsieur

Millet reports that during his interview with Monsieur Poincaré last night (see my telegram No. 645 of today)[1] the latter stated that he intended to open his mind to the Prime Minister and keep nothing back. It is permissible to suppose that this change is due in large measure to the criticism which his earlier attitude met with in the English and Belgian press and to a realisation that he could never have faced French public opinion had he returned from London with the confession that the Brussels Conference, on which such high hopes have been built, was not to be held owing to his not being willing to discuss the problem à fond with the Allied Prime Ministers.

Whatever may prove to be Monsieur Poincaré's attitude, there is I think one point on which he will insist, and which will I believe prove to be the crux of the whole discussion: namely that in view of the bad faith shown by successive German Governments France cannot consent to any further concessions being made to Germany unless 'pledges' are taken with a view to exercising material pressure on the great industrialists who are believed here to control the nominal government of Germany.

My recent despatches[2] will have informed Your Lordship of the campaign that has been carried on in the press of Paris for the last few weeks for the adoption of a policy of 'no moratorium without productive pledges'. Those which Monsieur Poincaré has in mind appear to consist of the occupation of two-thirds of the Ruhr including Essen and Bochum and the expulsion of all Prussian officials from occupied territory.

I do not of course know how far, if an agreement can be reached on broad lines of the reparation and inter-allied debts problem, His Majesty's Government would be prepared to go in taking measures of constraint against Germany in the event of a further failure on her part to carry out her obligations. If, however, His Majesty's Government refuse to join Monsieur Poincaré in his plans for the taking of pledges, the question will arise whether Monsieur Poincaré will make up his mind to act alone. The answer will depend largely on the course which the previous discussion has taken. In a memorandum (C 16643/99/18) dated December 5th[1] Confidential Print Germany December 5, Section 2, the suggestion is I see made that a satisfactory solution would consist in:—

(a) Stabilisation of the mark.
(b) A moratorium of substantial duration for Germany.
(c) Scaling down of reparation payments to an amount generally accepted as being within Germany's capacity to pay.
(d) Some immediate relief for the French budget—which probably can only be obtained in an effective degree through a loan.
(e) A settlement of the question of inter-allied debts, which has now become inextricably entangled with that of reparation.

Such conditions go further than the French Government have hitherto had reason to hope for from the late Government.

[1] Not printed.
[2] e.g. despatch No. 2819 of December 1 (C 16431/99/18), not printed.

Monsieur Poincaré's personal position is more difficult: he came into power as Your Lordship is aware on the cry that Monsieur Briand was not strong enough to carry out a policy of making Germany pay: he has been freely criticised for having done no better than his predecessor: the occupation of the Ruhr would unquestionably be a popular move with the existing Chamber and Monsieur Poincaré may well feel that there is no sufficiently vocal public opinion outside the Chamber on which he could rely for support in carrying out a liberal programme distasteful to the majority of the Bloc National. He may therefore well prove not sufficiently courageous to abandon his policy of 'pledges'.

On the other hand I think that the French nation, so shrewd where their own pockets are concerned and in the main so genuinely desirous of peace, might well hesitate when faced with a choice between the substantial benefits contained in a settlement on the lines indicated in the Foreign Office memorandum referred to above and the barren satisfaction of occupying the Ruhr, possibly in isolation coupled with the clear implication that such action might involve a definite breach with England and possibly Belgium.

I therefore venture to urge that, if it is seen that Monsieur Poincaré's obstinacy is likely to make a comprehensive settlement in London impossible, the widest publicity should be given to the terms offered by His Majesty's Government to the French Government instead of the unsubstantial policy of 'productive pledges' advocated by Monsieur Poincaré more especially as the French public has hitherto been in complete ignorance of the limits to which His Majesty's Government are prepared to go if the above mentioned memorandum may be regarded as a guide to their policy.

HARDINGE OF PENSHURST

No. 131

The Marquess Curzon of Kedleston to Mr. Addison (Berlin)
No. 1708 [C 16736/99/18]

Confidential   FOREIGN OFFICE, *December 9, 1922*
Sir,

The German Ambassador called upon Sir Eyre Crowe at the Foreign Office on the 6th instant, in order to enquire confidentially whether the Prime Minister would be likely to see any objection to the new German Chancellor addressing to him a letter in the terms of the draft note of which a copy is enclosed herewith. Sir Eyre Crowe undertook to ask the Prime Minister.

2. Mr. Bonar Law subsequently authorised Sir Eyre Crowe to inform the Ambassador that he would gladly receive such a letter and the communication therein referred to. He could not, however, promise to give a personal interview to the German expert who would be charged with the communication of the letter. Moreover, he would be glad if the fact that such a mission was being sent should be kept out of the newspapers. He added that

of course it would be better not to have the German plan submitted to him if it were of a kind obviously unacceptable to the Allies.

3. M. Sthamer has been informed accordingly.

I am, etc.,

CURZON OF KEDLESTON

ENCLOSURE IN No. 131

Draft Note from German Chancellor

Translation

I have declared my readiness to undertake the direction of German policy, because as a man with practical experience of economic life I am imbued with the conviction that Germany and Europe can only be rescued from the present economic disorder by a clear, decisive pronouncement. The fate of Europe depends upon a swift solution of the reparation question which will be satisfactory to all parties.

Since the first day, therefore, that the new Cabinet entered upon its duties, in order to carry out the conditions of the note of the 13th November,[1] it has been occupied with practical suggestions for the solution of the question of the stabilisation of the mark and the final settlement of the reparations problem.

The bearer of this note has received instructions to communicate immediately to the president of the conference our proposals to the Allies respecting the stabilisation of the exchange.[2]

[1] See No. 113.

[2] In a letter dated December 9 to Mr. Bonar Law (C 16892/99/18), Dr. Cuno communicated a *Tentative Plan of the German Government for a Provisional Settlement of Reparations* (see Cmd. 1812, op. cit., pp. 57–9).

No. 132

Sir E. Crowe to the Marquess Curzon of Kedleston (Lausanne)

No. 69 Telegraphic [C 17026/99/18]

FOREIGN OFFICE, *December 10, 1922, 10 p.m.*

I am sending by bag tonight minutes of two meetings of allied Prime Ministers yesterday and a summary in telegraphic form[1] of what passed yesterday and today.[2] France insist[s] categorically on occupation in any event of Essen and Bochum by allies together if possible but by France alone if necessary. In order to avoid immediate and definite impasse, Poincaré has agreed and Cabinet will be asked to approve tomorrow adjournment of meeting to assemble again at Paris beginning of January.[3] Meanwhile no Brussels conference.

[1] See No. 133, below.

[2] The British Secretary's minutes of these three meetings (I.C.P. 254, 255, 256) are printed, together with other documents, in Cmd. 1812, op. cit., pp. 18–60.

[3] The British Secretary's minutes of the Paris meetings of January 2, 3 and 4, 1923 (I.C.P. 258, 259, 260), are printed, together with other documents, in Cmd. 1812, op. cit., pp. 67–195.

Sir E. Crowe to the Marquess Curzon of Kedleston (Lausanne)
No. 68 Telegraphic: by bag [C 17026/99/18]

FOREIGN OFFICE, *December 10, 1922*

Allied Prime Ministers met in conference twice yesterday and again today.[1]

In the course of a preliminary discussion there was general agreement that it would be useless to send delegates to proposed Brussels conference unless an understanding could be arrived at as to common line of policy to be followed by the allies at that conference.

The questions to be covered by such understanding were defined by Belgian Prime Minister as:

(1) connection between reparations and allied debts;

(2) moratorium;

(3) reduction of total of reparations debt.

A short discussion ensued on the subject of the inter-allied debts, in the course of which Mr. Bonar Law made a declaration to the effect that if an agreement could be reached which would lead to a complete and definite settlement of the reparations question Great Britain would be prepared to agree to a remission of the allied debts owing to her even to an extent which might leave His Majesty's Government exposed to the risk of having to pay to the United States in liquidation of the British debt more than she received from Germany and the allies.

Monsieur Poincaré warmly welcomed this announcement. He briefly explained the critical situation in which French finance was placed by Germany's failure to pay reparations. Fresh heavy taxation must be imposed and a large loan raised to safeguard France's own financial stability but such measures would never receive the necessary support in France unless coercive measures were applied to Germany to ensure observance of her treaty obligations. He therefore proposed as bases of present discussions (1) general question of reparations in connection with inter-allied debts, (2) stabilisation of the mark and question of loans internal and external, (3) moratorium and questions of guarantees and pledges in return for which it might be granted.

[Signor] Mussolini tabled a memorandum[2] concluding with a series of proposals of which most important are:

(1) scaling down of German reparations debt to 50 milliards gold marks;

(2) a two years' moratorium;

(3) loan to Germany of three to four milliards gold marks to be utilised partly for stabilisation of mark and partly [for] payments to allies during period of moratorium;

(4) German revenues pledges for reparations to be taken over as security for loan;

(5) deliveries in kind to continue;

---

[1] See No. 132, n. 2. [2] See Cmd. 1812, op. cit., pp. 28–31.

(6) reparation commission and committee of guarantees to contro method of German internal reforms.

General discussion soon reached stage where possibility of inter-allied agreement for common policy at Brussels conference became more and more problematical.

Monsieur Poincaré declared in the most emphatic manner that the French Government are [sic] determined to proceed to the occupation of Essen and Bochum—jointly with the allies if possible, but alone if necessary—i: Germany insisted on a fresh moratorium after January 15th next. He explained that the occupation was to serve a double object:

(1) To compel Germany to submit acceptable proposals. If such proposals are submitted, the occupation to be maintained as a guarantee for their being carried out.

(2) If Germany does not submit acceptable proposals the allies—or France if acting alone—will make use of the pledges they hold to enforce such payments as may be possible, it being admitted that in no case would such payments approach anywhere near the amounts due by Germany under the treaty.

Monsieur Poincaré added an assurance that in case France had to act alone, whatever she obtained in payment by means of coercion would not be payment for herself but placed at the disposal of the allies.

A note received from the German chancellor today submitting a tentative plan of a reparation settlement[3] was found unanimously to be altogether unsatisfactory.

Discussion was adjourned in order to allow Prime Minister to consult the Cabinet.

He will ask latter to approve a proposal which Monsieur Poincaré has privately and in advance declared his readiness to accept[4] that as in the time available it is impossible to arrive at definite conclusion meeting of allied Prime Ministers will now be adjourned to meet again at Paris at the beginning of January.[5]

[3] See No. 131, n. 2.   [4] See No. 132.   [5] See No. 132, n. 3.

No. 134

Memorandum by Lord D'Abernon[1] on the German proposals of December 10,[2] 1922

[C 16906/99/18]

Confidential   LONDON, *December 10, 1922*

The tentative plan of the German Government of the 10th December for a provisional settlement of the reparations problem constitutes a decided

[1] Lord D'Abernon had left Berlin on November 30 on leave.

[2] The tentative plan of the German Government dated December 9 (see No. 131, n. 2) was received on December 10.

advance on previous offers. The main point appears to be that the German Government undertakes to proceed at once with stabilisation, without waiting for the international bankers' credit, which they previously considered an indispensable preliminary. This offer enables the intentions of the German Government to be tested at once, without subjecting them to the necessarily long negotiations indispensable to raising any international advance.

On the second point, namely, the raising of internal and external loans and the payment of reparations, it would not be expedient to base too much hope before getting closer to details. So far as the outline is concerned, I see nothing specific to criticise, but it depends upon the details which presumably Herr Bergmann is ready to fill in. It has always been a favourite idea of his that Germany could raise large sums from German subjects abroad, provided that adequate exemption from taxation and adequate indemnities for past evasions of taxation were granted. I have less confidence than he has regarding the result of the attempt, but there can be no objection to trying it.

The most objectionable feature of the German proposal is that the German Government would ask that an additional year of moratorium should be granted for every milliard of gold marks paid to the Reparation Commission. This appears to me excessive.

If negotiations are taken up on the basis of the German proposal, the first points to ascertain are (1) what precise measures of stabilisation the German Government would contemplate; (2) what precise guarantees they will furnish for the internal and external loans; (3) will these guarantees be sufficiently serious to enable money to be raised. It is clear that some form of international control might increase the validity of the guarantees offered. A test of the value of the guarantees demanded from Germany would be afforded by the fact whether or not they facilitated the placing of the proposed external loan, i.e., a *gage* which improved the prospect of the loan being placed on the public market would be *prima facie* beneficial; conversely, a *gage* which diminished the chances of the success of the loan would be *prima facie* undesirable.

D'A.

No. 135

Mr. Bonar Law to Dr. Cuno (Received in the Foreign Office, December 11)
[*C 16892/99/18*]

Copy

Confidential   10, DOWNING STREET, *December 10, 1922*

Your Excellency,

I have the honour to acknowledge the receipt of your note of the 9th instant,[1] submitting a plan for a provisional settlement of the difficulties connected with the question of reparations.

The note was considered at a meeting of the Allied Prime Ministers held here today, and it is with sincere regret that I have to say that the plan

[1] See No. 131, n. 2.

submitted does not, in their opinion, offer a solution which could, in the existing situation, be considered satisfactory to the Allied Governments.[2]

I have, etc.,

A. BONAR LAW

[2] This letter is printed in Cmd. 1812, op. cit., p. 60.

No. 136

Sir E. Crowe to the Marquess Curzon of Kedleston (Lausanne)
No. 71 Telegraphic [C 17084/99/18]

FOREIGN OFFICE, *December 11, 1922, 7.30 p.m.*

Meeting[1] of allied Prime Ministers adjourned today after passing resolution to continue conversations at Paris on January 2nd on the understanding that, if agreement is then reached, the conference originally contemplated at Brussels shall at once assemble at Paris so as to allow of definite decisions being taken before January 15th.

Monsieur Poincaré, whilst firmly upholding French government's decision to occupy Ruhr after January 15th, was throughout extremely courteous and conciliatory in tone and manner, and parting was on entirely friendly terms.

Signor Mussolini has not so far made any attempt to open discussion on political questions outside reparation problem.

[1] The British Secretary's minutes of this meeting (I.C.P. 257) are printed in Cmd. 1812 op. cit., pp. 60–80.

No. 137

The Marquess Curzon of Kedleston to Sir A. Geddes[1] (Washington)
No. 356 Telegraphic [C 17084/99/18]

FOREIGN OFFICE, *December 11, 1922, 3.40 p.m.*

In fulfilment of a promise, which I have given to the United States Embassy here, that I would acquaint United States Government with the course of proceedings of the meeting of allied Prime Ministers, I beg you to inform State Department confidentially that the meeting at several sittings[2] went fully into present position of the problems of reparations and inter-allied debts. Various suggestions were put forward for dealing with the German demand for a fresh moratorium. The questions of guarantees and sanctions, more particularly the well-known French proposals for the occupation of the Ruhr, were considered.

A note[3] presented by the German government submitting a tentative plan for a provisional settlement of the reparations question was examined, but

[1] H.M. Ambassador Extraordinary and Plenipotentiary at Washington.
[2] See Nos. 133 and 136.   [3] See No. 131, n. 2.

found unanimously not to offer any practical solution that the allies could accept.

It was found impossible in the time available to arrive on these several points at definite conclusions, and it is therefore now proposed to adjourn the meeting to assemble another conference at Paris at the beginning of January, with the view of arriving at a definite understanding between the allies before January 15th, when present moratorium expires.

No. 138

Mr. Addison (Berlin) to the Marquess Curzon of Kedleston
(Received December 16)
No. 953 [C 17231/99/18]

BERLIN, *December 12, 1922*

My Lord Marquess,

It had generally been assumed that the latest proposals of the German Cabinet, contained in the Chancellor's letter to Mr. Bonar Law of the 9th instant,[1] had been drawn up as the result of an understanding with the leading industrialists consequent upon the negotiations, which formed the subject of my despatch No. 945 of the 8th instant.[2] Considerable surprise has therefore been caused by the statement published by Herr Stinnes in the *Deutsche Allgemeine Zeitung*, a translation of which is enclosed herein,[3] that Industry had neither been consulted as to the preparation of the Note, nor informed of its contents, and that industrial circles considered the proposals to be unsuitable and incapable of fulfilment. This statement has given rise to much criticism, examples of which are also enclosed, in the organs of the press which are not under the control of Herr Stinnes.

It is quite possible that neither Herr Stinnes nor his personal friends were consulted, and it is interesting to note that this omission, in his opinion, means that German Industry was not consulted. It should also not be forgotten that the relations between the Chancellor and Herr Stinnes are not likely to be cordial in view of their business transactions over their mutual share interests in the Hamburg America Line.

I have, etc.,

JOSEPH ADDISON

[1] See No. 131, n. 2.

[2] Mr. Addison had reported as follows: '*Die Zeit*, the official organ of Herr Stresemann, and consequently of the Volkspartei, announces that the Government are carefully considering what further proposals should be made to the Entente Powers in regard to reparations and that discussions are taking place with the leaders of industry concerning a plan whereby "German industrial forces should combine with France with a view to a final settlement, which would not only include a definite fixation of the total sum of reparation, but would also place liquid funds at the disposal both of France and of Germany".'

[3] Not printed.

No. 139

Lord Hardinge (Paris) to the Marquess Curzon of Kedleston
(Received December 14, 8.30 a.m.)
No. 660 Telegraphic: by bag [C 17146/99/18]

PARIS, *December 13, 1922*

Monsieur Poincaré in interview with press correspondents, after paying tribute to cordiality of atmosphere in which conference[1] was held, claimed a success on three points (1) that the Balfour note[2] had been virtually withdrawn, (2) that England was prepared to consider accepting 'C' bonds in payment of French debt, (3) that German note[3] was unanimously regarded as unsatisfactory. On the question of 'pledges', he denied that he ever mentioned in London the occupation of the Ruhr and refused to indicate what 'pledges' he would take if he had to act alone. He affirmed, however, that he had returned with a definite impression that if France did take isolated action, it would involve no rupture of the Entente.

Millet[4] and 'Pertinax' in telegrams from London again call attention to the conditional nature of Mr. Bonar Law's offer about cancellation of debt, and Prime Minister's answer in House of Commons[5] yesterday is widely reproduced. It does not, however, get the same prominence as Monsieur Poincaré's remark above referred to in which all mention of any condition is omitted. Both Millet and 'Pertinax' think that British public opinion is gradually coming round to a realisation that France must be allowed if necessary to take satisfactory 'pledges'.

A number of papers including *Matin, Victoire, Eclair* and *Œuvre* publish articles interpreting Monsieur Poincaré's denial that he ever mentioned an occupation of the Ruhr as an indication that he intends, in view of the criticisms which this proposal has aroused here and abroad, to abandon the Ruhr as a *gage* and content himself with the pledges of August last, namely customs, forests and fiscal mines.[6]

Monsieur Poincaré, it is announced, will make a declaration in the Chamber on Friday.[7] Should he announce a firm intention of occupying the Ruhr, he will undoubtedly receive the support of the Right and the Bloc National. There is, however, a very strong current of public opinion which is opposed to any such adventurous policy, and the more the conditional character of the Prime Minister's promise to cancel the French debt becomes generally known the more likelihood there is of a solution which would be satisfactory to His Majesty's Government. A definite scheme of control and payments should be prepared and submitted for examination before the New Year.

---

[1] See Nos. 133 and 136.   [2] See No. 45.   [3] See No. 131, n. 2.
[4] Diplomatic Correspondent of the *Petit Parisien.*
[5] See 159 *H.C. Deb. 5 s*, cols. 2585–6.   [6] See No. 62.   [7] December 15.

No. 140

The Governor General of the Union of South Africa[1] to the Secretary of State for the Colonies[2]

(Communicated to the Foreign Office, December 18)

[C 17314/99/18]

Secret   December 13, 1922

Your Secret telegram 11th December.[3] Following from my Prime Minister[4] for Prime Minister. Begins.

Secretary of State for the Colonies has sent me message regarding the results of the London Reparations Conference.[5] I sincerely trust that the French coercive proposals and further occupation of Germany will not be agreed to by British Government. Unwise policy of France in the Near East[6] has already lost us fruits of the Great War in that region and done grave damage to British prestige.

Poincaré seems bent on pursuing even more fatal policy as regards Germany. If this policy is persevered in the British Empire should be clearly and unequivocally dissociated from it as ruin it will cause will not be confined to Central Europe. Lausanne Conference[7] seems already to be leading to rehabilitation of Turkey which must be severe threat to British interests. And if France succeeds in addition in dragging the British Empire into Central European catastrophe results for us too will be most disastrous. In the summer of last year when similar drastic action over Upper Silesia question was threatened by France, Imperial Conference which was then sitting[8] passed unanimous resolutions warning France of attitude of United British Empire. This was communicated to the French Ambassador by Lord Curzon[9] and immediately had great effect. If the position at adjourned Conference becomes desperate I suggest that similar united warning in name of the whole Empire should be made to France and should be followed if necessary by open dissociation from France. I would make this further suggestion that while France threatens further occupation of Germany practically tearing up of Peace Treaty no concession should be made her in respect of her war loan liability. War debts of Allies to Great Britain should be used as weapon to secure policy of real appeasement in Europe and should only be foregone for that purpose and in that event. That reparation sum must be reduced to reasonable amount and moratorium granted against stabilisation of mark is now generally admitted.

If Allies at Paris Conference[10] cannot agree on details question should be remitted to Council of League or other impartial authority. It might be even politic for us to suggest President of the United States as arbitrator.

---

[1] H.R.H. Prince Arthur of Connaught.   [2] The Duke of Devonshire.
[3] Not printed.   [4] General The Rt. Hon. J. C. Smuts.
[5] See Nos. 132, n. 2, 133 and 136.   [6] See Vols. XVII and XVIII.
[7] See Vol. XVIII, Chap. II.
[8] The Imperial Conference met in London from June 20 to August 5, 1921.
[9] See Vol. XVI, No. 272.   [10] See No. 132, n. 3.

Any remission of war debts which the British Government may be disposed to make should be conditional on France desisting from isolated coercive measures and agreeing with Allies to a policy of appeasement. Public opinion will universally approve policy of this sort. Only chaos and ruin from which none will escape least of all France will be produced by Poincaré's policy. Ends.

No. 141

Lord Hardinge (Paris) to the Marquess Curzon of Kedleston
(Received December 15)
No. 662 Telegraphic: by bag [C 17198/99/18]

PARIS, *December 14, 1922*

The Belgian Ambassador informed me this afternoon that at luncheon at the Elysée today, the President of the Republic had told him that it was absolutely decided by the French Government to go into the Ruhr immediately after the 15th January. Monsieur Gaiffier expressed his surprise and consternation, whereupon the President stated that it would not be a military operation but that they would establish a customs cordon around the Ruhr and thus levy duties on the coal proceeding from it. The Belgian Ambassador pointed out that such an operation could not be performed against the will of Germany without the presence of military forces. To this the reply was that if possible the assent of Germany would be obtained, but if otherwise the operation, which was a small one, would be carried out by the installation of a few military posts and the occupation of the town of Essen. The Belgian Ambassador showed me his telegram to his Government reporting this conversation.

This evening I called upon the President of the Council. He at once asked me to let the Prime Minister know how touched he had been by his friendly reception in England and by the cordial and frank manner in which all the questions relating to the Conference had been discussed in London.[1] He remarked that although there were differences between the two Governments of policy, that nevertheless even if agreement was not arrived at and action was taken by the French Government, the Entente would not be impaired although there might be some painful moments to pass through.

I told Monsieur Poincaré that as an ardent friend of the Entente during the past twenty years, I should regret very much if the French Government took any action in the immediate future which would embitter the sentiments of a large section of English public opinion against France. There was no doubt that in England there was a strong feeling against an invasion of the Ruhr and if this should take place, there would undoubtedly be bitter words and hostile criticism which would tend to alienate mutual sympathies on both sides of the Channel. Surely, I said, if a plan giving guarantees of control or

[1] See Nos. 133 and 136.

supervision so that Germany would be compelled to pay such sums as she was able to pay, was instituted at Berlin, the necessity for an invasion of the Ruhr would in that case disappear. To this Monsieur Poincaré replied that he did not want guarantees but what he wanted [was] money. I asked him how he proposed to get it, for, I remarked that a tax on coal going out of the Ruhr would bring in a comparatively small amount and surely other means could be devised which would be more profitable, while it was always possible that there would be strikes and troubles in the Ruhr entailing the despatch of considerable French military forces to maintain order amongst a very virile and hostile population. Further in the event of a strike, it would be incumbent upon the French Government to feed the population. To this Monsieur Poincaré replied that there were other means of finding money and if the Allies would agree to Monsieur Mussolini's proposal[2] for the exploitation of the mines and the forests, etc. in Rhineland and the formation of a control barrier on the east and west banks of the Rhine, he would be quite ready to consider the question of not going into the Ruhr unless and until the German Government took action to starve Rhineland by preventing the export of coal westwards from the Ruhr.

He believed that such an exploitation of Rhineland would be productive of considerable financial resources and it would avoid the appearance of advancing further into Germany and of dealing with any other territory than that which was under Allied occupation.

I told Monsieur Poincaré that I had no authority to give any opinion on the subject and that my remarks had been of a personal nature, but that I believed that they represented the views of public opinion in England.

[2] See Cmd. 1812, op. cit., pp. 54, 59–60.

No. 142

Sir J. Bradbury (Reparation Commission) to Mr. Baldwin
[C 17463/99/18][1]

Copy
Confidential   PARIS, *December 15, 1922*
My dear Chancellor,
   I send you herewith a new edition of my scheme for a comprehensive settlement of reparation and European and inter-Allied debts.
   In substance (i.e., as regards the amount and incidence in point of time of the financial burdens on Germany and sacrifices asked of the respective Allies) there is no great variation from my original plan,[2] but I have made considerable alterations of form and machinery, which I hope make it more easy to grasp.

[1] This document was communicated by the Treasury to the Foreign Office on December 20.
[2] See No. 97, Enclosure.

I have got rid of the perpetual annuities originally proposed, and taken as my point of departure Signor Mussolini's proposal[3] to cancel the existing 'C' bonds and retain the 'A' and 'B' bonds. I have then modified the 'A' and 'B' bonds so as to reduce the burden on Germany in the earlier years within what I regard as tolerable dimensions. It is to be observed, however, that the deferred interest is compounded and recovered later unless an impartial tribunal decides that the payment of this deferred liability is beyond the capacity of Germany.

As regards the treatment of inter-Allied debts, I have introduced a new principle (without substantially altering the final result from a financial point of view), viz., that all except a small percentage of the debts to Great Britain should be written off at once, but that the deferred and contingent German obligation, in so far as it materialises, should be treated as a common fund for the discharge of the European indebtedness to America to be shared by the various debtors in proportion to their American debts as ultimately determined.

This goes a long way towards meeting, so far as we can meet it without the help of America, M. Poincaré's point of view that the settlement of inter-Allied indebtedness should be deferred until the Powers entitled to reparation have received substantial payments from Germany for their own restoration.

I believe that if France accepted the proposal in its present form she would do far better than she can hope to do by any measures of coercion, even if such measures were given our whole-hearted support.

There is, I fear, little likelihood that Germany would accept it readily—a great pity from the credit point of view. At the same time I am pretty certain that she would recognise it as preferable to a joint attempt at coercion by France and Great Britain, and that the constant terror of such an attempt being made would keep her up to the mark in carrying it out.

I believe that the best British and American financial opinion would regard the burden upon Germany as low enough to be consistent with the revival of her credit, though how soon such a revival could be hoped for would of course depend on the degree of willingness or unwillingness with which Germany herself accepts the settlement, and the energy with which she tackles the immediate financial problems during the breathing space which the plan allows her.

Personally, I think it would be more prudent to put the minimum burden somewhat lower (say 20 per cent.) in order to allow a margin of safety; but we shall be lucky if we can get our Allies as far as I propose, and I have no hopes of getting them any farther.

In any case, however, in my judgment, the minimum obligation I have suggested cannot be increased without serious risk of wrecking the whole plan.

I attach very great importance to making the liability on Germany a fixed amount, to include all peace treaty charges. Every reduction of reparation

[3] See No. 133.

326

liabilities hitherto made has been followed by a determined effort on the part of the French to nullify it as far as possible by increased exactions in respect of other treaty liabilities. If the opportunities for doing this are not taken away, all our efforts to obtain a comprehensive settlement and make the restoration of German credit possible will be frustrated.

Yours sincerely,
JOHN BRADBURY

ENCLOSURE IN NO. 142

Plan for General Settlement of Reparation and European Inter-Allied Debts

Reparation

1. The existing German bonds of Series 'A', 'B' and 'C', to be cancelled, and the schedule of payments annuities[4] to be reduced to the amounts required year by year to provide the interest payable on new bonds to be issued under paragraph 2.

2. Germany to issue to the Reparation Commission new bonds to be divided into two series:—

(a) *First Series.*—Bonds to the amount of 50 milliard gold marks to be issued forthwith, repayable at par on the 31st September, 1954, and bearing interest at the rate of 5 per cent. per annum, payable half-yearly; the interest to be suspended in its entirety for the first four years (until the 1st January, 1927), and to the extent of 1 per cent. per annum for the next four years (until the 1st January, 1931).

(b) *Second Series.*—Bonds to the amount of 17.31 milliard gold marks (being the amount of the deferred interest on the bonds of the first series compounded at 5 per cent. to the 1st April, 1933), or such lesser amount (if any) as the arbitral tribunal provided for in paragraph 3 may determine, to be issued on the 1st April, 1933, repayable at par on the 31st March, 1965, and bearing interest at 5 per cent. per annum, payable half-yearly.

3. If before the 1st April, 1933, Germany proves to the satisfaction of an arbitral tribunal that the payments required to meet the interest upon the second series of bonds exceed her capacity, her obligation to issue such bonds to be cancelled in whole or in part as the tribunal may decide.

The arbitral tribunal to be appointed upon application by the German Government, to be made not later than the 1st October, 1932, and to consist of one person nominated by the Reparation Commission, one person nominated by the German Government, and a third by agreement between the other two, or in default of agreement by the President of the United States of America.

4. The bonds issued and to be issued under paragraph 2 to be accepted by the Allied Governments in commutation of all financial liabilities of

[4] See No. 5, n. 2.

Germany remaining undischarged on the 31st December, 1922, under the Treaty of Versailles to Powers which have ratified that treaty, including all liabilities under agreements with particular Powers in commutation of treaty obligations, but excluding the Treasury bills issued to Belgium in respect of the last five instalments of the cash payments due in 1922.

Germany to pay at maturity the bills issued to Belgium in respect of the first two of these five instalments, those issued in respect of the remaining three instalments to be cancelled and the amounts thereof re-credited to Belgium.

Treaty obligations to make deliveries of coal, dye-stuffs and timber to continue, subject to new annual maxima to be agreed. Other deliveries in kind to be by agreement between Germany and the Powers concerned. The receiving Power to pay for all deliveries in kind by set-off against the interest receivable upon the bonds held by it, or (until such interest payments have begun, or in so far as they may be insufficient), by surrender at redemption price of bonds for cancellation.

5. Germany to have the right to redeem bonds of the first series as on any interest date after the 30th June, 1923, at the price shown in the schedule hereto.

As soon as but not before the first series of bonds has been redeemed Germany to have the right to redeem bonds of the second series as on any interest date at a discount of $\frac{1}{2}$ per cent. for each unexpired half year.

Redemption of both series at more favourable rates to be permissible by agreement between Germany and the respective Powers interested, subject to the approval of the Reparation Commission.

6. Eighty per cent. of the bonds of the first series to be distributed forthwith to the Powers entitled to reparation in the Spa Agreement percentages.[5]

The remaining 20 per cent. to be retained by the Reparation Commission as a reserve for adjustment of accounts between Powers and for the payment of miscellaneous charges as provided below.

7. Belgium to discharge her existing debit in respect of her priority adjusted in accordance with paragraph 4 by surrender to the Reparation Commission reserve of bonds of the first series to a face value equal to the amount of the debit plus 25 per cent.[6]

Belgium to waive her claims to priority of payment over other Powers in so far as they have not already been met.

8. The United States (subject to the consent of that Power), Great Britain and France to receive out of bonds of the first series retained as a reserve by the Reparation Commission amounts to a face value equal to their respective credits arising out of the last paragraph of article 232 of the treaty (Belgian war debt).

9. All other outstanding debits and credits as between Powers entitled to reparation and the Reparation Commission to be cleared as on the 1st

---

[5] See No. 47, n. 2.

[6] A note on the original runs: 'The present value of the bonds on the 5 per cent. table being 80 per cent.'

January, 1923, by transfer of bonds of the first series at redemption price. Debits to be adjusted by transfer from the debtor Power to the Reparation Commission reserve and credits by transfer from the reserve to the creditor Power.

10. As from the 1st January, 1923, costs of armies of occupation and Clearing Office[7] and other miscellaneous charges up to such amount per annum as the Reparation Commission may approve, except in so far as they can be met from cash accruing to the Reparation Commission reserve in respect of interest on bonds in that reserve, to be discharged by transfer of bonds at redemption price from the Reparation Commission reserve to the Powers entitled to the payments. Any bonds remaining in the reserve when its liabilities have been liquidated to be distributed to the various Powers entitled to reparation in the Spa Agreement percentages.[5]

11. Germany to agree, in the event of any failure to pay the interest due upon the bonds at any due date, forthwith to hand over to the Reparation Commission or to any Allied Power authorised to act on its behalf whatever revenues or assets of the German Empire or German States the commission or such Power may select.

In the event of such failure, the Powers represented on the Reparation Commission shall be entitled to adopt whatever measures may, in their unanimous judgment, appear necessary to enforce their rights. Such measures may include the occupation of German territory outside the treaty occupation area and the taking over of German fiscal machinery.

12. All loans raised by Germany in the national market of any Power, which is a holder of any of the bonds, to be applied to the redemption of bonds held by that Power unless and except to such extent as the Government of that Power may otherwise agree.

European Inter-Allied Debts

13. The deposits of gold which are held by Great Britain as security for loans made to France and Italy for the purpose of carrying on the war to be applied forthwith towards the repayment of these loans.

The French share of the German bonds applicable to the repayment of Belgian war debt to be transferred to Great Britain and accepted by her as satisfaction of an equal amount of the French debt to Great Britain.

$1\frac{1}{2}$ milliards first series German bonds to be transferred by Italy to Great Britain and accepted by Great Britain in discharge of an amount of the Italian debt to Great Britain equal to the face value of the bonds.

The balance of the French and Italian debts to Great Britain to be written off, all counter-claims at the same time being abandoned.

The Italian debt to France to be written off.

Great Britain and France to transfer to the Reparation Commission as trustees the war debts owing to them by Serbia, Roumania, Greece and Portugal to be dealt with as provided below.

---

[7] See Vol. XVI, No. 422, n. 6.

On the 1st April, 1933, the bonds of the second series to be distributed as follows:—

Great Britain	⎫	
France	⎬	The aggregate Spa Agreement
Italy	⎬	percentages of these Powers.
Any other Powers which may accept the arrangements referred to below ..	⎭	

Belgium	⎫	Their respective Spa Agree-
Japan	⎬	ment percentages.
Any other Powers which may not accept these arrangements	⎭	

The aggregate share assigned to the first-mentioned group of Powers to be divided in proportion to the respective payments and obligations of these Powers to the United States of America in respect of war advances.

For the purpose of this calculation, payments already made to be capitalised at 5 per cent. compound interest to the 1st April, 1933, and undischarged obligations as on that date to be taken at their present value on the 5 per cent. table.

Powers other than Great Britain, France and Italy which are indebted to America to have the option[8] of coming into the above arrangement and having their debts to European Allies written off, or of discharging their European inter-Allied debts and retaining their Spa Agreement percentages of the second series bonds.

Portugal, who is indebted only to Great Britain, to have the option of ceding her interest in the second series bonds to be dealt with as part of the joint share and having her debt cancelled, or of discharging her debt and retaining her Spa Agreement percentage of the second series bonds.

Any payments made in respect of uncancelled European inter-Allied indebtedness to be invested by the Reparation Commission in German bonds, such bonds to be retained by the Reparation Commission until the 1st April, 1933, and then to be distributed amongst the group of Powers first mentioned above in the same proportion as the second series German bonds.

14. Powers to which a remission of debts is granted by Great Britain under paragraph 13 to agree to support any proposals made by Great Britain for mitigating the liabilities of ex-enemy Powers other than Germany under the Treaties of Saint-Germain, Trianon and Neuilly.

---

[8] A note on the original runs: 'In the event of Serbia opting not to come into the group, her debts to France and Great Britain should, on transfer to the Reparation Commission, be written down by the amounts necessary to give her the compensation provided for in the Serbo-Franco-British Percentage Agreement of the 20th June, 1921—say, the equivalent in French francs of 70 per cent. and the equivalent in sterling of 30 per cent. of 250 million gold marks.'

Schedule

First Series Bonds

Interest Date						Price
December 31, 1923	..	..	..	..	..	50
June 30, 1924	..	..	..	..	..	53
December 31, 1924	..	..	..	..	..	56
June 30, 1925	..	..	..	..	..	59
December 31, 1925	..	..	..	..	..	62
June 30, 1926	..	..	..	..	..	65
December 31, 1926	..	..	..	..	..	68
June 30, 1927, to December 31, 1930				..	..	69

(rising by 1 point per half-year to 76)

June 30, 1931, to maturity (December 31, 1954) .. 76½

(rising by ½ per half-year to par at maturity)

Note.—The scale allows redemption on an 8 per cent. basis at the start, gradually falling to a 5 per cent. basis at the end of the thirty-two-year period.

The following examples show the annual saving in the interest charge for future years resulting from redemptions effected at particular dates.

			Annual Interest Saving on Bonds Cancelled by each 100 g.m. Cash applied to Redemption	
			1927–30	Thereafter
Redemption at 50 on December 31, 1923 .			8	10
„ 56 „ 31, 1924 .			7.14	8.93
„ 62 „ 31, 1925 .			6.45	8.06
„ 68 „ 31, 1926 .			5.88	7.35
„ 76 „ 31, 1930 .			.	6.58
„ 80 „ 31, 1934 .			.	6.25

The Schedule is arranged so as to enable Germany, if her credit is re-established, to provide interest and sinking fund on loans raised for redemption out of the saving effected on the interest of the cancelled bonds, and to give special inducements for redemption in the earlier years.

Note (A)

The governing principles of the plan are—

1. To fix a minimum German liability which is well within the less sanguine estimates which have been made by financial experts of German capacity and a supplementary liability which is *prima facie* not

unduly onerous, but which can be reduced or cancelled by an impartial tribunal if it should prove in the event to be excessive.

2. To substitute for the present fixed obligations of the European Allies to Great Britain arrangements under which all, except a small percentage (which would be accepted in the form of a transfer of German or other inter-Allied obligations), would be remitted, but under which the contingent German payments in excess of the fixed minimum would be applied to discharging European debts to America generally.

3. To give very liberal terms to Germany for the early redemption of the annual payments by anticipation.

The primary obligation of Germany is put into the form of 50 milliard gold marks thirty-two-year bonds, bearing no interest for four years, 4 per cent. for the next four, and 5 per cent. thereafter. No provision is proposed for a sinking fund, but the bonds can be redeemed on terms which, if German credit recovers, will enable the interest and sinking fund on the loans required for redemption to be met out of the resultant saving on the interest on the bonds.

Germany is thus given a double inducement to borrow from the public to redeem the original bonds.[9]

(a) She frees herself from her direct liability to the Allied Governments and so has a chance of accelerating the date of termination of Allied military occupation.

(b) She substitutes without additional cost a terminable for a perpetual liability.

The merits claimed for the plan are that its adoption will make the restoration of German credit possible and lead to the recovery of very substantial sums for reparation, while persistence in the policy of attempting to enforce impossible claims will end in the destruction of the *créance* altogether.

The present value of the primary obligation under the plan cannot be precisely estimated owing to the redemption options.

If the adoption of the plan led to a rapid revival of German credit and Germany were able by raising loans to pay off the whole of the fixed annuity in the first few years the present value might not be more, and might possibly be even less, than 30 milliards.

But if this happened the Allies would have actually received this 30 milliards and Germany would undoubtedly be in a position to pay for the service of the second series of bonds when they fall to be created ten years hence and redeem that series also very rapidly. In that event this second series would be worth at least its present value on the 6¼ per cent. table (7.4 milliards), so that on this supposition the whole indemnity would have been collected in twelve or fifteen years (mainly in the first ten) and a present value of over 37 milliards realised.

On the worst assumption, that no German loans became possible either now or in the future, that the second series of bonds has to be cancelled altogether

---

[9] A note on the original runs: 'These are not intended for issue to the public, but merely as security for the annual payments and as counters for purposes of accounting.'

and Germany merely pays the interest on the first series as a perpetual annuity, beginning four years hence at 2 milliards and rising four years later to $2\frac{1}{2}$ milliards, the present value on the 5 per cent. table is $39\frac{1}{2}$ milliards.
The annual burden on Germany under the plan is—

For the first four years . .	Nil.
,, second four years .	2 milliards.
,, next two and quarter years	$2\frac{1}{2}$ milliards.
Thereafter . . .	$2\frac{1}{2}$ to $3\frac{1}{2}$ milliards, according to the decision of the Arbitral Tribunal

This burden (which will be reduced if Germany raises redemption loans on favourable terms) covers all financial liabilities under the treaty.

Note (B)

Position of Great Britain, France, Italy and Germany under the Plan

Position of Great Britain

The present value of the first series bonds on the 5 per cent. table is $39\frac{1}{2}$ milliards. On the inconceivable hypothesis that Germany is able to raise loans to redeem the whole of them next year, the liability would be extinguishable for 25 milliards. On any plausible hypothesis as to progress of redemption, the present value is somewhere between 30 and $39\frac{1}{2}$ milliards, according to the dates at which redemption is effected.

The present value of the second series on the 5 per cent. table is about $10\frac{1}{2}$ milliards, assuming that the obligation to issue them is not modified by the Arbitral Tribunal. Allowing for the risk of such modification and the privileges of redemption at a discount, the series could not prudently be held to be worth more than 5 or 6 milliards (present value).

If we take the present value of the first series at 34 milliards and of the second at 6, the British share (22 per cent. of 80 per cent. of the first series and (say) 42 per cent. of the second) would amount to 8.5 milliards. Adding 1.4 milliards for gold deposits and 3.2 milliards for the Belgian debt (including the portion to be ceded by France) and 1 milliard for the $1\frac{1}{2}$ milliards (face value) first series bonds to be ceded by Italy, we reach a total of 14.1 milliards as against our American debt of 20 milliards.

The British share of the second series would, however, be materially increased if the Continental Allies obtained relief in respect of their American debts, so that the plan may be regarded as giving us a fair chance of covering from 70 to 80 per cent. of our capital liability to America.

If our American debt takes the form of long-date bonds at $8\frac{1}{4}$ per cent. interest, its value on the 5 per cent. table might be reduced by anything up to 15 per cent., raising the percentage of cover to 80 or possibly to 90 per cent.

On the assumption that there is no cancellation of any of the debts owing to America, either British or Continental, the distribution of second series bonds proposed gives Great Britain only about 1.2 milliards (60,000,000*l*.)

more than would be given by a simple remission of the balance of inter-Allied debts not adjusted on the first series bonds and the retention of the British Spa Agreement percentage (22 per cent.) in respect of second series bonds.

It is highly improbable, however, that within the next ten years America will be able to avoid either cancelling a large part, if not the whole, of the Continental indebtedness to her, or following the British example and dealing with the bulk of it in terms of second series German bonds. In the former event, practically the whole of the second series bonds would, under the plan, become assignable to Great Britain; in the latter, practically the whole of them would be divided between Great Britain and America. In either event, the Continental Allies would retain a very small interest, with the result that reasonable concessions to Germany, if such concessions should be necessary, would be much easier to secure.

Position of France

	Milliards
The position of France under the status quo (taking M. Bokanowski's[10] estimate of the value on the 5 per cent. table of the schedule of payments annuities— 'Chambre des Députés, No. 4820,' p. 125) is 52 per cent. of schedule of payment annuities (present value on 5 per cent. table 65 milliards)	33.8
Debts due to France in respect of war advances to Italy, Serbia, Roumania and Greece (3.89 milliard francs at 3.3 fr. to the gold mark).	1.2
	35.0
Deduct net debt to Great Britain	10.5
Net *créance* (leaving out of account debt to America) .	24.5

This is upon a valuation of the paper assets at 100 per cent., notwithstanding that in fact the arrangements of the schedule of payments have already hopelessly broken down and the chances of receiving anything appreciable from the Allied debtors is somewhat remote. No allowance is made for the cost of 'mobilisation' of the German debt, which (if such mobilisation became possible at all) would undoubtedly be very considerable.

The position of France under the plan (again estimating on the 5 per cent. table) is—

	Milliards
52 per cent. of 80 per cent. of 39.5 milliards (present value of 50 milliards first series bonds after allowing for interest suspensions)	16.43
About 30 per cent. of 10.5 milliards (present value of second series bonds after allowing for deferment of issue)	3.15
Total . . .	19.58

[10] M. Bokanowski was president of the French commission of finance.

This valuation makes no allowance for the cost of the advantages allowed to Germany on early redemption (comparable with the loss on 'mobilisation'[11] not allowed for in the estimate under status quo) or for the risk of cancellation of the second series of bonds in whole or in part by the Arbitral Tribunal.

The adoption of the plan would thus mean a reduction in the French net paper *créance* (leaving out of account the French debt to America) from 24.5 to 19.58, i.e., by 4.92 milliards or 20 per cent. As against which France obtains a reasonably good asset against a bad one: complete release from her debt to Great Britain, acceptance of the principle, which is of great value for purposes of negotiation with America, that inter-Allied indebtedness, in so far as it is discharged at all, should be dealt with in the main by redistribution of the deferred German obligations, leaving the bulk of the primary obligations for reparation.

Position of Italy

Under the status quo the whole of the Italian share of the present value of the schedule of payment annuities (65 milliards), 6.5 milliards, would be insufficient to cover the Italian net debt to Great Britain and France, 9.64 milliards.

Under the new plan Italy is relieved of the greater part of these debts and receives:—

First Series Bonds—

	Milliards
10 per cent. of 80 per cent. of 50 milliards (face value) = 4 milliards, less 1½ milliards, to be ceded to Great Britain. Net 2½ milliards, of which the present value on the 5 per cent. table is	1.97

Second Series Bonds—

	Milliards
About 18 per cent. of 6 milliards	1.03
Total	3.05[*sic*]

Position of Germany

Under the status quo the liabilities of Germany on the 5 per cent. table are—

	Milliards
Schedule of payment annuities (present value)	65
Other Peace Treaty charges (say)	5
Total	70

[11] A note on the original runs: 'This loss would, under the existing arrangements, materialise in the form of having to issue the 5 per cent. bonds to the public at a discount, or having to allow them to be released to the German Government at a price sufficiently attractive to make it worth the while of that Government to raise loans on its own account to effect the redemption.'

Under the new plan the minimum liability (leaving out of account savings by redemption) is—

	Milliards
The present value of the first series bonds, viz. . . .	$39\frac{1}{2}$
And the maximum liability is	50

There is therefore a minimum reduction of nearly 30 per cent. and a maximum reduction (leaving out of account possible savings on redemption) of nearly 44 per cent.

The saving is likely in any event to be nearer the maximum than the minimum, since either German credit will not be restored, in which case the second series bonds are likely to be cancelled by the tribunal or it will be restored, with the result that Germany will be able to effect considerable savings by redemption on favourable terms.

Apart from the actual reduction in the present value of the obligation, Germany secures the enormous advantages of—

(*a*) a complete relief for four years;

(*b*) a fixed moderate charge for the next six;

(*c*) a definite annual maximum of reasonable amount thereafter;

(*d*) freedom from indeterminate charges for Peace Treaty obligations other than reparation; and

(*e*) a chance of being able to discharge the whole liability by raising foreign loans in a comparatively short period and so obtaining the early withdrawal of the armies of occupation.

No. 143

The Marquess Curzon of Kedleston to Sir A. Geddes (Washington)
No. 363 Telegraphic [C 17368/99/18]

FOREIGN OFFICE, *December 16, 1922, 4.30 p.m.*

As you know the American government desired to be kept informed of the Prime Minister's Conference.[1]

The view taken by the Prime Minister is that agreement between France and Great Britain is not possible and that Monsieur Poincaré, if he is still in office, will take coercive steps of some kind against Germany at once and in the opinion of His Majesty's Government such steps taken to enforce claims which at present are quite impossible will hasten the complete collapse of Germany and be in the highest degree disastrous to the world.

In our opinion the only possibility of avoiding this catastrophe is by the intervention of the United States.

If the United States government would at once offer to send an observer empowered to express the views of the United States to the Conference in Paris[2] as they did at Lausanne[3] it would, we think, greatly help but without American assistance the prospect is almost hopeless.

[1] Cf. No. 137.   [2] See No. 132, n. 3.   [3] See Vol. XVIII, Chap. II.

Mr. Phipps[1] *(Paris) to the Marquess Curzon of Kedleston*
(Received December 17, 8.30 a.m.)

No. 667 Telegraphic: by bag [C 17265/99/18]

PARIS, *December 16, 1922*

Lord Hardinge's telegram No. 664.[2]

In the debate which followed Monsieur Poincaré's speech Monsieur Tardieu[3] made a long speech which is regarded as important here as being an effort to define the policy of the Bloc National in view of the elections next year.

Monsieur Tardieu commenced by criticising Monsieur Poincaré's lack of leadership. The recent budget was the first which any Government had presented to Parliament in France with a large deficit and no programme for meeting that deficit. In foreign policy Monsieur Poincaré, in spite of his criticisms of Monsieur Briand, had not achieved anything more than his predecessor. As long as Mr. Lloyd George was in power his task was admittedly difficult. Monsieur Poincaré had not, however, taken adequate advantage of the conciliatory spirit shown by the new Government in England. He should have struck out a new line instead of following well-worn paths. He should have submitted to Mr. Bonar Law before the Conference[4] his plan for dealing with the Reparations question. It was doubtful whether he had sufficiently studied the difficulties of any military operation in the Ruhr or whether the financial results would be worth the risks. He did not seem to have given adequate consideration to the alternatives among which were according to M. Tardieu:—

1. Acceptance of Herr Cuno's offer to surrender 500 million gold marks[5] of German-held foreign securities.

2. The seizure of a percentage of German Customs receipts.

3. Seizure of 30 or 40 per cent. of the fiscal revenues of occupied Rhineland.

4. Levies on the commerce passing through Düsseldorf, Duisburg, and Ruhrort.

5. A renewal of the arrangement made in 1919[6] by Monsieur Clemenceau for a large French loan on the London market. (This latter [*sic*] proposal met with some opposition in the Chamber on the ground that it would involve financial subordination to the United Kingdom.) Monsieur Poincaré had never endeavoured to come to some general settlement with England such as was reached between Monsieur Delcassé and King Edward VII.[7] The Entente

[1] Mr. Phipps (see No. 48, n. 1) had become Counsellor of H.M. Embassy at Paris on November 1, 1922 and a Minister Plenipotentiary on November 20. He took charge of the Embassy from December 16, when Lord Hardinge left Paris, until the appointment of the Marquess of Crewe as Ambassador Extraordinary and Plenipotentiary on December 31.

[2] Of December 15, not printed.   [3] Deputy for the Department of Seine et Oise.

[4] See No. 132.

[5] This is presumably the construction which M. Tardieu placed on the German plan of December 9 (see No. 131, n. 2).

[6] See Vol. II, No. 61, Appendix A.   [7] A reference to the Entente of 1904.

had existed in name but not in deed for the last three years; the policies of the two countries had been different. England had shown by the recent parliamentary elections[8] that she realised that she had obtained no advantages from the policy Mr. Lloyd George had pursued. Without some general settlement with England, American confidence in the sanity of Europe would never be restored.

Between the policy of isolation of the extreme Right and the pro-German policy of the extreme Left Monsieur Tardieu was convinced that his party was right when it advocated distinguishing clearly what was essential to French interests and what was secondary and insisting on the former and yielding to the latter.

Monsieur Poincaré was unable to follow such a policy because he felt he had not the wholehearted support at home of a homogeneous majority. In foreign affairs he counted for support on the Right, in internal affairs he inclined to the Left and endeavoured to buy the support of the Socialist Radicals. There had been much talk and complaints about the action of the Prefects. This was only an incidental result of the real disease. What was necessary, if the present members of the Chamber were to face their electors with chances of success, was that they should be able to point to the execution of some definite legislative programme while they had been in power. New methods were necessary, not new men, and the Chamber must take whatever steps were needed to ensure these.

A vote of confidence in the Government was passed by 486 to 66.

The note which ran through the entire debate was the extreme desirability of maintaining the Entente with England.

Full text of speeches goes to Your Lordship by bag tonight.[9]

[8] See No. 104, n. 4.
[9] In Paris despatch No. 2942 of December 16 (C 17268/99/18), not printed.

No. 145

Sir A. Geddes (Washington) to the Marquess Curzon of Kedleston
(Received December 19, 8.30 a.m.)

No. 499 Telegraphic [C 17399/99/18]

WASHINGTON, *December 18, 1922*

Your telegram No. 363[1] and my telegram No. 498.[2]

I have been in close touch with Secretary of State over the whole matter of reparations and have again seen him today.

Position of United States government is as follows:—

1. It is quite impossible for administration to discuss question of debts owed to United States except through debt funding commission within limitation imposed by act setting up commission. At present Congress will not relax conditions which it has imposed.

[1] No. 143.   [2] Of December 16, not printed.

2. United States government holds that there is no connection between amount of reparation which Germany should be compelled to pay and debts owed by allies to United States. Their position is purely academic one—that as Germany ought to pay what she can pay, it makes no difference whether nations she pays it to are in debt or not.

3. United States government have already conveyed to French government their strong sense of disapproval of any project to take military coercive steps of any kind against Germany. This was done through French Ambassador here.[3]

4. United States government have made some proposals to French government which they hope will enable Monsieur Poincaré to build a bridge for his retreat from his position. Mr. Hughes has urgently asked me not to press him for details of this proposal until he hears from Paris. Without knowing details therefore I can only say that I understand they are to the effect that Monsieur Poincaré should announce that, as there is difference of opinion as to what Germany can pay, he proposes an impartial enquiry and that he suggests United States as the impartial enquirer or an international body for enquiry.

Mr. Hughes is I understand under some promise to French Ambassador that he will tell no one of this so that if M. Poincaré approves he can announce it as his own idea.

5. Secretary of State thinks that if M. Poincaré adopts his suggestion, there will be no trouble at Paris meeting even if it is necessary to hold it.

6. If M. Poincaré rejects his suggestion, Secretary of State thinks that Paris meeting will have no result.

7. Secretary of State understands that French government do not wish United States to be represented at inter-Allied meeting. I also understand that American Ambassador in London has reported that His Majesty's Government were unwilling that an American observer should be present at London meeting.

I have assured him His Majesty's Government will welcome an American representative at forthcoming meeting.

8. Secretary of State is at present unwilling to agree to send such a representative. If M. Poincaré makes suggestion . . .[4] above American participation would be unnecessary. If he declines to make such a suggestion, American participation would not only be useless but harmful as it would place America in position of having publicly urged France to refrain from taking coercive measures and of being publicly rebuffed or at least ignored.[5]

This is his argument.

I have pointed out more than once that French public opinion is not reached by secret representations of which no one knows. The true reason for administration being unwilling to run the risk of having a public expression of their views ignored is of course political. They think that such a result might have, probably would have, unfortunate reactions at next elections.

3 M. Jusserand. See *F.R.U.S.* 1922, vol. ii, pp. 188–92.
4 The text is here uncertain.   5 Cf. *F.R.U.S.* 1922, vol. ii, pp. 192–5.

9. There is no doubt that a strong tide of popular American sentiment is flowing against France and it is also beyond doubt that this administration may be forced by public opinion to declare publicly their views.

10. The whole newspaper hysteria of last few days about America's coming intervention in Europe has been due to President's[6] desire to placate farmers who under steady stream of educational publicity directed at them are tending to realize that Europe is their market.

President vaguely hinted 'something was doing'. Doubtless he had in mind idea that France should ask for a United States commission to determine reparations Germany could pay which he had heard Secretary of State was suggesting.

11. There is no other suggestion that I know of in mind of administration. They are frightened of their own political shadows and terrified by new radical senators who whether they are republican or democratic are more strongly isolationist than the men they displaced. In spite of this, and para- doxically, country is becoming more interested in Europe and more inclined to help. Still the ship subsidy bill is in the hands of Senators and President has pinned his political future beside [sic] ship subsidy which is in badly troubled waters. So he dare do nothing to offend Senators.

12. I shall not fail to do all that is possible to persuade United States government to state publicly its position and to take part in the conference in Paris but my hopes are not high.

13. I wish to raise a question. Will it be possible for our debt commission to negotiate with Americans while Paris conference is in progress or to enter into definite undertaking as to payment if France adopts coercive measures? I can imagine nothing much more unfortunate at the present moment than for our commission to arrive and then be unable to say what Britain can or cannot do. On the other hand, further postponement would also be un- fortunate though in my judgment less so than if commission were to come and be unable to state Britain's position precisely.

[6] Warren G. Harding.

No. 146

Record by Sir E. Crowe of a conversation with the German Ambassador
[C 17482/99/18]

FOREIGN OFFICE, *December 18, 1922*

The German Ambassador called on me today for the purpose of discussing situation as regards the reparations problem. He was very anxious to learn whether there was anything that the British Government would desire the German Government to do between now and the 2nd of January. He expressed the great disappointment and regret of the German chancellor at seeing his last proposal again summarily rejected,[1] like all previous German

[1] See No. 135.

proposals. He wished once more to assure the British Government that the German Government would do their very best to find a way out of the difficulty, but the difficulty was very great, and they themselves were in the greatest uncertainty of what exactly the allies wished them to do, and what they could do. I said that I had no authority, nor was I competent, to give advice as to what Germany should now do. It was clear to me that something more practical and more concrete was required from them than the proposal they had recently put forward, which was found unanimously by all the allied Prime Ministers to offer no real solution of the problem before them. The Ambassador asked whether I could not indicate in what way precisely the German proposal was considered unsatisfactory. I said I was under the impression that the German representative, Mr. Bergmann, had been in communication, both before and after the meeting of the allied Prime Ministers with Sir J. Bradbury, and I presumed he must have been enlightened in this way as to the points on which the German plan fell short of expectations. I myself was not in a position to offer such detailed criticism; nor was it, I conceived, really the business of the Allied Governments to prompt the German Government as to what they should perform. I might, expressing my own private opinion, say that there was a universal impression —which the Ambassador no doubt would himself have seen reflected, even in the public press—that, whilst the allied Governments, and particularly the French Government, were very much preoccupied with the question of what securities or pledges could be obtained from Germany, effectively guaranteeing payments in future, if she were granted a prolonged moratorium, the German plan was altogether vague and sketchy on this point. Yet the German Government must realise that French uneasiness on this subject was both deep and reasonable; and I should have thought it was in Germany's own interest to come forward with definite proposals, giving satisfaction in regard to this important aspect of the problem.

The Ambassador replied that this had not occurred to him; and he felt sure that, if his Government realised that some definite proposals on this point of effective guarantees and pledges were really desired, they might very well endeavour to elaborate a scheme for consideration by the allies. But he wished to point out that this very suggestion would only strengthen the view of the German Government that it was really hopeless to arrive at a solution if the present procedure continued to be followed, by which the two parties—Germany on one side and the allies on the other—never met to exchange ideas, but fired notes or rejoinders at each other, often running on opposite but parallel lines, which could never never meet. His Government could not too earnestly urge that the best, if not the only, way to come to an arrangement, which they on their part honestly and eagerly desired, was that German and Allied representatives should meet together and discuss frankly what they wished, on one side, and what could be done, on the other. Given the disposition of the present Government, the Ambassador said he felt sure that, once a businesslike meeting of this kind could be arranged, there was every prospect of reaching a solution, provided there was goodwill on either side. What made the German Government despair was that they did not see the goodwill on the French side. He added that, if the proposals put forward by Germany from time to time were always found to be unsatisfactory, not only was this generally discouraging, but it added to the timidity with which the German Government put forward anything at all. They were under the impression that, without knowing why, whatever they advanced gave offence somewhere, and this made them shy to advance.

I listened to all this with a certain amount of sympathy, but I had to confess that I was not very much impressed; I still thought it was open to the German Government, and it was really their duty, to seek rather more seriously a solution which they could put before the allies, with a genuine expectation that it would prove acceptable. But I repeated that it would never do for any one speaking on behalf of this country to appear as the adviser of the German Government as to particular measures they should adopt; and, if it were to become known that the German Government, in putting proposals before the allies, were acting in pursuance of British advice as regards the terms proposed, it would not only place Great Britain in a false position towards her allies, but it would ensure the failure of any plan so advocated.

The German Ambassador said he quite understood, and promised that he would regard all I said as a private and personal conversation between him and me. All the same, he would not fail strongly to advise his Government to make another effort to prepare a plan, and to do so with more regard to the concrete question of guarantees and pledges.

No. 147

Sir R. Graham (Rome) to the Marquess Curzon of Kedleston
(Received December 22)
No. 1143 [C 17543/99/18]

ROME, *December 18, 1922*

My Lord,

This morning I had my first interview with Signor Mussolini since his return from London,[1] although I had exchanged a few words with him at the Station on his arrival in Rome last Friday.

His Excellency referred to his visit to London in terms which were almost enthusiastic. He said that nothing could have exceeded the warmth of his reception both in official circles and by the British public and he had especially appreciated the kindness with which he had been received by the King. He had greatly enjoyed his brief stay, although practically the whole of his time had been taken up by the pressure of official business. He had come away with sentiments of gratitude and admiration. London had given him a sense of the strength and stability of the British Empire which

---

[1] See No. 136.

corresponded to his own ideals. He hoped to return and to make himself master of the English language which he was now studying.

As regards the results of the Conference, His Excellency declared that he had never expected that much more could be attained. A step had been taken in the right direction. There had been a general goodwill and spirit of conciliation and he looked forward with a certain degree of optimism to the further meeting on January 2nd,[2] for had not Monsieur Poincaré's last speeches[3] shown that he was prepared to put water into his wine and to adopt a more reasonable attitude?

In the course of further conversation, a reference was made to the flight of German capital abroad and to the natural irritation which must be felt in France, when the Germans, professing themselves unable to meet their obligations, were yet spending large sums on the erection of national theatres at Berlin or the construction of an elaborate system of metropolitan railways. Signor Mussolini said that no method had yet been devised nor could one ever be evolved to stop the flight of capital abroad or to recover it once it had flown. His own view was that the only course open to the Allies would be to name a sum which Germany could pay (his own estimate was about 50 milliards of gold marks) and then to insist on its payment. If Germany proved recalcitrant, united allied action should then be taken and action of the strongest character. This might involve a joint occupation of the principal centres in Germany or even fresh hostilities, but the question must be ended once and for all. In reply to an enquiry on my part as to how the French could be induced to agree to such a reduction of the German obligations, he declared that the answer lay in the attitude of Great Britain. A discussion of this point proceeded on lines familiar to Your Lordship, and Signor Mussolini said that, as he had asserted to Mr. Bonar Law, if England renounced allied debts, the United States would be bound to follow suit, as they would be unable to bear the moral odium of appearing to the world in the light of the sole profiteers from the war. I expressed my fears that His Excellency was over sanguine, that the political position in the United States made it difficult for the American Government to show generosity and that whatever the feeling in New York and the East might be the pressure of world opinion would not make itself felt to the same degree in the West and on the bulk of the American people. His Excellency said that he was much interested in the press reports of impending American intervention in the problem of reparations and debts and of a proposed American loan to Germany. They even caused him some misgiving. He asked me whether I had any information tending to throw light upon the matter, but I had not.

Referring to the existing cordiality of Anglo-Italian relations, His Excellency seized an opportunity to state that it would be greatly enhanced if early steps could be taken to settle some of the outstanding questions[4] between the two countries. The most important of these was that of Jubaland, and he endeavoured to brush aside a reference by me to the interdependence of this question with that of the Dodecanese. He added that he had instructed the

[2] See No. 132, n. 3. [3] See No. 139. [4] See Vol. XVII, No. 650, n. 1.

Italian Ambassador in London to reopen the subject of Jubaland at the Foreign Office, and earnestly hoped that a satisfactory settlement might be reached.

As regards Lausanne,[5] Signor Mussolini expressed himself in hopeful terms, and he referred with warm appreciation to the skill with which Your Lordship had handled the Conference. You had succeeded in the difficult task of separating the Russians and the Turks and the latter now appeared to be amenable to reason. He did not believe that once Ismet Pasha[6] had been persuaded there was any danger that the intransigence of Angora would succeed in frustrating your efforts.

I have, etc.
R. GRAHAM

[5] See Vol. XVIII, Chap. II.   [6] Head of the Kemalist Delegation at Lausanne.

No. 148

Memorandum by Mr. Wigram on the legal position under the Treaty of Versailles in the event of the default of the German Government in the payment of reparation

[C 17313/99/18]

FOREIGN OFFICE, December 18, 1922

1. Between the 5th May 1921 and 31st December 1922 Germany's obligation under the schedule of payments[1] amounted approximately to 4378 million gold marks (£219 millions gold). Of this amount, owing to the 1922 moratoriums granted by the reparation commission on January 1[3]th[2] and March 21st 1922,[3] approximately 2124 million gold marks (£104 millions gold) only had on September 30th been entered to Germany's credit in the reparation account.

2. Germany will therefore on January 1st 1923 be in arrears in the discharge of her obligations under the schedule of payments by some 2254 million gold marks (£113 millions gold) less whatever sum is placed to her credit in the reparation account between October 1st and December 31st 1922. This sum could under the reparation commission's decisions of March 21st[3] and May 31st[4] at any time become due for immediate payment on the cancellation by the reparation commission of the postponement of the 1922 payments granted to Germany on the foregoing dates.

3. In addition, in the absence of the grant of any fresh moratorium, the first instalment of the 1923 fixed annuity, viz., 500 million gold marks (£25 millions gold), will become due for payment on January 15th 1923.

4. Before, however, any German default can properly give rise under the treaty to punitive measures by the allied powers under the provisions of the

[1] See No. 5, n. 2.   [2] See No. 1.   [3] See No. 12, n. 1, and No. 13.
[4] See No. 26, n. 4.

treaty of Versailles, action must apparently be taken by the reparation commission on the following matters:

(a) the reparation commission having, under article 234 of the treaty, 'discretion to extend the date and modify the form of payments' must answer the German request of July 12th 1922[5] (supplemented by the note of November 14th)[6] for a moratorium on the 1923 and 1924 payments;

(b) the reparation commission must, in accordance with paragraph 17 of annex II to the reparation clauses, notify 'each of the interested powers of default by Germany';

(c) the reparation commission who, under paragraph 12 of annex II to the reparation clauses, 'have authority to interpret the provisions' of those clauses must decide that the default is 'voluntary', after which the allied powers will have the right to take the punitive measures contemplated under paragraph 18 of the same annex;

(d) the reparation commission must also if there is to be 'default' in respect of the 1922 payments, as well as in respect of that falling due on January 15th 1923, decide to cancel the provisional postponement of the 1922 payments granted to Germany on March 21st[3] and May 21st 1922.[4]

5. In the event of a single power desiring to take punitive measures against Germany alone and in contradiction to the wishes of the other powers, the reparation commission, under the powers of interpretation conferred upon it by paragraph 12 of annex II to the reparation clauses, would also presumably have to decide the meaning of the words in paragraph 18 of the same annex, which provides that 'the measures which the allied and associated powers shall have the right to take, in case of voluntary default by Germany may include economic and financial prohibitions and reprisals *and in general such other measures as the respective governments may determine to be necessary*'. On the interpretation of these words the British and French governments hold different views. The French government consider that in the event of voluntary default by Germany they have individually the right to take 'such measures' (including apparently military measures) 'as they consider necessitated by the circumstances'. They hold also that in these circumstances their right to act independently is not affected by the pledge given to the British government by M. Millerand on April 11th 1920 that 'as regards the future, the government of the Republic have no intention of acting save in accordance with their allies in all interallied questions raised by the execution of the treaty'.[7] The British government, on the other hand, consider that 'action taken by an individual government under paragraph 18 would have to be confined to measures which such a government could properly take within its own jurisdiction limits'. The British government have also declared that action taken independently by the French government for the recovery of reparation, which is a matter of interest to the allies as a whole, would be inconsistent with the French government's pledge of April 11th 1920 as well as with article 233 of the treaty itself which lays

[5] See Nos. 36 and 38.   [6] See No. 113.   [7] See No. 23, n. 7.

down that 'if Germany fails to discharge her obligations, any balance remaining unpaid may within the discretion of the reparation commission be postponed for settlement in subsequent years, or may be handled otherwise as the allied and associated government shall determine'.

6. On the questions dealt with in paragraphs 4 (c) and 5 above (which are questions of the interpretation of the reparation clauses of the treaty) the decisions of the reparation commission must under paragraph 13 of annex II to the reparation clauses be unanimous. The other questions 'shall' under the same paragraph 'be decided by the vote of a majority'.

No. 149

Mr. Phipps (Paris) to the Marquess Curzon of Kedleston
(Received December 21)
No. 2966 [C 17471/99/18]

Very Confidential   PARIS, *December 20, 1922*

My Lord,

I have the honour to inform Your Lordship that I showed to Lord D'Abernon yesterday the reparations plan of which copies[1] were forwarded to you in my despatch No. 2944, Very Confidential, of the 17th instant.[2]

Lord D'Abernon is favourably impressed by the plan, apart from the paragraph suggesting the allied occupation of the Ruhr coal fields, and has set forth his views in the memorandum enclosed herein.

I have, etc.
ERIC PHIPPS

ENCLOSURE IN No. 149

Memorandum by Lord D'Abernon

PARIS, *December 20, 1922*

The note of December 2nd[2] is a vast improvement on any previous French proposal.

1. It recognises the necessity of a long moratorium.
2. It is based in the main on the reports of the financial experts.
3. It recognises stabilisation as the pre-condition of any improvement.

Once this latter [*sic*] point is admitted with all its consequential conclusions one can begin to discuss with hope of agreement.

Confining attention and criticism to the summary of conclusions[3] formu-

[1] Not printed.

[2] Mr. Phipps wrote (C 17273/99/18): 'I have the honour to transmit to your Lordship, herewith, copies of a reparation scheme drawn up on the 2nd instant by a highly placed French expert. I request that the fact of this document having reached the hands of His Majesty's Government may not be divulged.'

[3] These ran:

'1. La Commission des Réparations d'accord avec un Comité de Banquiers, entend le Gouvernement allemand (le Ministre des Finances) pour établir un programme détaillé

lated at the end of the paper and excluding the detailed arguments which precede these conclusions I have no fundamental objection to any of the points summarised except No. 10. This, which provides that the Allies take possession at once of the Ruhr coalfields as a guarantee of diligence, would be fatal. But its position at the tail of the paper suggests that the writer of the note does not regard it as essential to his proposal and further encourages the hope that it might be thrown over.

It is clearly essential that the Ruhr coalfields should be held over as an eventual sanction in the case of failure by Germany to carry out obligations. A 'fortissimo' which may be required at a given moment cannot be produced by sitting stolidly on the piano from the prelude.

The other point in the conclusions which demands further discussion is that regarding deliveries in kind. These are only possible in so far as they do not demand further issues of paper money; in other words the currency problem must have absolute priority over everything else. Any other course would be quite inconsistent with the general thesis of the note as well as destructive of any good results.

Taking the proposal as a whole, it shows a wider and more correct comprehension of the position than any of its predecessors. If the broader

comportant les mesures législatives, et qui devra être approuvé dans les deux mois par le Reichstag, celui-ci s'engageant à ne pas le modifier pendant les deux années nécessaires à son exécution.

'2. Aussitôt le programme rédigé et approuvé le Comité des Garanties et un représentant du Comité des Banquiers s'installent à Berlin pour surveiller le vote des lois et la mise à exécution des réformes législatives et administratives.

'3. Ce comité reçoit dans ses caisses 25 pour cent au moins des devises provenant des exportations allemandes et les taxes de douanes prélevées en or; il ne remet ces devises à la Reichsbank qu'autant qu'il est satisfait de l'attitude du Gouvernement allemand et de le mise à exécution du programme.

'4. Aussitôt le programme voté la Commission des Réparations et le Comité des Banquiers préparent la stabilisation du mar[c] en réunissant les fonds nécessaires soit 500 millions en or, prélevés sur l'encaisse de la Reichsbank et un crédit d'une somme égale fait par le Comité des Banquiers: les industriels allemands donnent une garantie effective pour le remboursement de crédit, cette garantie consistant soit en avoirs à l'étranger, soit en une hypothèque prise sur leurs biens.

'5. Le Comité des Garanties et le Comité des Banquiers fixent le taux de stabilisation du mar[c] et créent l'organisme bancaire nécessaire pour racheter les mar[c]s papier à l'étranger.

'6. La Reichsbank rendue complètement indépendant du Gouvernement allemand est pourvue d'un directeur non allemand nommé par la Commission des Réparations d'accord avec le Comité des Banquiers.

'7. La Commission des Réparations et le Comité des Banquiers fixant, d'accord avec le Gouvernement allemand, la date et les modalités de l'emprunt intérieur or ils étudient également les possibilités des emprunts extérieurs gagés sur les avoirs allemands.

'8. La Commission des Réparations prépare un programme de réparations en nature qui sera exécuté pendant les deux années du moratorium.

'9. Sous les conditions qui précèdent, un moratoire de deux ans est accordé à l'Allemagne pour les versements en espèces.

'10. En même temps que la Commission des Réparations notifiera ces dispositions au Gouvernement allemand, les Gouvernements alliés prennent possession des charbonnages de la Ruhr, de manière à être assurés que le Gouvernement allemand fera toute diligence pour exécuter le programme ci-dessus.'

spirit which has inspired it is allowed adequate scope, agreement on a join
programme should not be impossible.

The note of December 2nd proposes to add a member of the Bankers
Committee[4] to the Committee of Guarantees[5] at Berlin. This is quite a
sensible idea. But the evident intention is to name either Vissering or Dubois
Nothing can be said against either of these gentlemen, who were signatories
of the Minority Report[6] of the financial experts.

But the essential point is to obtain the continued assistance of the majority
experts, not of the minority. The former authorities would carry much more
weight with public opinion especially in the United States. They would be
free from any connection with German Banks and they have moreover a much
clearer conception of the measures necessary to secure rapid stabilisation.

[4] See No. 19, n. 5. [5] See No. 10, n. 1. [6] See No. 110, n. 1.

No. 150

Lord D'Abernon (Berlin) to the Marquess Curzon of Kedleston
(Received December 23, 10.15 p.m.)

No. 225 Telegraphic [C 17579/99/18]

BERLIN, *December 23, 1922, 9 p.m.*

French memorandum of December 2nd,[1] if officially endorsed by French
government, would profoundly alter the situation.

Subject to reserves and modifications indicated in my memorandum from
Paris of December 20th[2] it might form promising basis for negotiation.

I do not believe that German government would accept it integrally but they
might be brought a good way along the road so that final divergence would
be circumscribed.

If His Majesty's Government consider above-mentioned memorandum of
December 2nd suitable basis of discussion it might be well to steer discussions
here in this direction.

If left unguided German departments concerned will wrangle until the
last minute on points of secondary importance and minor relevancy.

Turning from negotiation to administration most urgent step is to commence measures for stabilisation.

This can best be achieved on lines of four experts and can only be achieved
successfully with foreign advice and assistance preferably, though not
necessarily, with advice and assistance of experts themselves. Local talent is
either inadequate or unwilling—perhaps both.

I believe that German government would be well advised to bring experts,
or some of them, back to Berlin.

Compared with local lights they would have the advantage of greater
currency experience and knowledge. Compared with committee of guarantees

[1] See No. 149, n. 2. [2] No. 149, Enclosure.

they would have, as having been originally selected by Germany, the superiority of one's own doctor over a doctor imposed by the parish.[3]

[3] Sir E. Crowe minuted (December 28): 'In my opinion it would have been well if the Germans could have been induced to produce a really practical and comprehensive plan and I still think it was a pity that Lord D'Abernon dissuaded them from making the attempt. But this tel[egram] is now 5 days old. Meanwhile I understand Sir J. Bradbury has been in communication with M. Bergmann direct and given some useful advice.
'In these circ[umstance]s I agree that this tel[egram] may now be left unanswered.'

No. 151

The Marquess Curzon of Kedleston to Mr. Phipps (Paris)
No. 3863 [C 17594/99/18]

Confidential   FOREIGN OFFICE, *December 27, 1922*

Sir,

I transmit to you herewith copy of a record of a conversation which took place between the Prime Minister, the French Ambassador and Sir Eyre Crowe on the 24th instant on the subject of German reparations.

I am, etc.,
CURZON OF KEDLESTON

ENCLOSURE IN No. 151

Memorandum

FOREIGN OFFICE, *December 24, 1922*

The French Ambassador called on the Prime Minister today in order to explain the views of M. Poincaré on the present aspect of the reparation problem. At the Prime Minister's request Sir Eyre Crowe was present at the interview.

The Ambassador went over the whole ground very much in the same way as M. Poincaré himself had done at the recent London meeting.[1] He dwelt on the three principal points requiring consideration at the forthcoming conference in Paris.[2] One was the fixation of the definite amount which Germany should be asked to pay, closely connected with which was the question of the inter-Allied debts. The second point was the stabilisation of the mark, the rehabilitation of Germany's credit and her economic position. These two points, the Ambassador declared, presented no real difficulties that could not be overcome rapidly by a friendly understanding between the Allies, and he expressed himself in an extraordinarily confident manner on the ease with which such an understanding could be promptly arrived at. It was the third point which alone appeared to present obstacles, and that was the question of pledges (*gages*). On this subject he repeated what M. Poincaré had clearly and repeatedly stated, that no French Government

[1] See Nos. 132, 133, and 136.   [2] See No. 132, n. 3.

could in any circumstances agree to a fresh German moratorium without taking pledges. M. Poincaré was determined to establish control over the exports from the Ruhr district, exports not only of coal, but of all industrial produce. No military occupation was contemplated; the plan was to send a number of customs officers and engineers to Essen and Bochum. These would establish a small organisation for the purpose of levying export duties and fixing the price of coal. It was calculated that by these means a sum of 500,000,000 gold marks per annum would be obtained. This might not be much when compared with the amounts due from Germany under the treaty, but it was something, and would afford relief, however small, to the French taxpayer. The Ambassador wished, however, at once to meet an objection which had been raised in various quarters in England, more particularly in articles which had appeared in the 'Manchester Guardian'. There appeared to be a suspicion that France would use the machinery of control in the Ruhr for the purpose of securing special economic advantages for herself and notably to fix the price of German coal in such a way as seriously to hamper the British coal trade. The Ambassador said he could not be too emphatic in declaring that the French Government most ardently desired the participation of their Allies, and especially of England, in the measures to be taken as well as in any profits to be derived therefrom. Even if Great Britain should unhappily refuse to take part in the measures contemplated the French Government would regard any payments or pecuniary benefits obtained as a result of those measures as belonging to the Allies in common, each receiving his proper share.

The Prime Minister interjected that whatever might have been said in the 'Manchester Guardian', the British Government harboured no such ideas as the Ambassador had indicated. He pointed out, however, how small even according to the French calculation was the pecuniary benefit anticipated. For the purpose of affording immediate financial relief to France it was negligible. But what were the chances that even this negligible amount would be obtained without producing a situation in which the prospects of a German economic recovery, sufficient to make the more substantial payments which the Allies had a right to claim, would be reduced to zero?

It was the unanimous expert opinion in this country that only through the restoration of German credit could large German payments on account of reparations be hoped for. But who would lend money to Germany if coercive measures in the Ruhr now taken foreshadowed the continuance of the uncertain conditions and prevented the growth in the measurable future of any confidence of healthy economic conditions? The Prime Minister asked whether M. Poincaré really believed that his handful of customs officers and engineers would be allowed to function peacefully and levy the desired contributions without having armed force at their back.

Count Saint-Aulaire replied that Essen was only about 15 kilom[etres] further than Düsseldorf, up to which point the French occupation already extended. The Germans would surely realise, therefore, that the Allied officials at Essen had force behind them. He quite admitted that their position would be difficult and might require the support of armed force on the spot if France were left to act alone; and this was an additional reason why the French Government were so anxious for Allied co-operation. M. Poincaré was convinced that so long as the measures taken in the Ruhr were seen and understood to be taken by the Allies standing together the Germans would not dare to make effective opposition. Count Saint-Aulaire quoted in this connection the analogy of the Military Control Commission in Berlin,[3] whose officers were actively interfering in all parts of Germany; showing themselves in uniform, and dealing with matters which more than any others were calculated to excite patriotic effervescence. These officers were far removed from any contact with Allied troops and were from a military point of view 'in the air'. Yet although there had been now and then isolated disagreeable incidents the Germans had not tried to prevent them from fulfilling their mission.

Sir Eyre Crowe thought it ought to be remembered that the Allied Military Commission acted in virtue of treaty stipulations recognised by the German Government, who had fully accepted responsibility for ensuring the safety and unhampered movements of the officers in the discharge of their duty. These were not the conditions under which—under M. Poincaré's scheme——his civilian agents, to be established at Essen and Bochum, would have to function.

The Prime Minister added that the Military Control Commission had to deal chiefly with Government and municipal authorities. In the Ruhr it would be a question of dealing with the mining and industrial population. If we were for a moment to imagine ourselves placed in the position that we had been defeated in the war by Germany and that German inspectors and officials were stationed in the English or Welsh or Scottish coalfields to control output and prices, it was as certain as anything that there would be strikes followed by general disorganisation.

Count Saint-Aulaire replied it was probably a mistake to look upon the attitude of German workmen as if it would be the same as that of Welsh miners in similar circumstances. All experience showed that the psychological factors were very different. German workmen were not accustomed to the traditional and extended liberty prevailing in this country. They were brought up to obey orders and could be relied upon with some confidence to recognise authority when imposed. Everything therefore depended on the Allies showing unmistakably that they were in earnest, and above all that they were united, and M. Poincaré still hoped that by some means or other the British Government could see their way to join in the proposed action.

The Prime Minister said he felt sure that M. Poincaré could not be under any misapprehension as to this; for it had been explained to him with the utmost clearness that public opinion in this country would not permit any British Government to take part in measures of coercion by which it was intended to compel Germany to do something which it was physically impossible for her to do. It was essential first of all to settle definitely what

[3] See Chap. IV, *passim.*

351

Germany must be called upon to pay. It was one thing to insist, even to the point of constraint, on due compliance with a reasonable and just demand not disproportionate to Germany's power of fulfilment, and another thing to use force in order to exact submission either to unspecified conditions or to claims long ago abandoned by practical people as unrealisable. The view taken even in the most conservative quarters in England, as has been shown by a recent meeting of prominent business men in the city, that the total sum which Germany was able to pay must now be fixed as low as 1,200,000,000*l*. The Prime Minister said he himself did not accept that figure; he considered it much too low; but he mentioned it as indicating the trend of opinion among those in England who were by instinct and policy the most remote from the point of view of a Labour Party and others certainly less friendly to France than the present Government.

The Ambassador agreed that the low figure mentioned would be quite unacceptable, but he reiterated that at whatever figure the amount was fixed Germany would never do anything unless under compulsion. He was aware of the force of British opinion in England, but in the same way public opinion in France compelled the Government to act. Owing to Germany's failure to carry out her obligations French finances were on the brink of ruin. Whatever happened, it would now be necessary to impose still further taxes in France and to get the French public to subscribe to fresh loans. But the feeling in France was such that neither imposition of taxes nor an internal loan could be carried, unless public opinion was satisfied that the French Government had exhausted every means by which the alternative remedy of obtaining payment from Germany could be applied.

The Prime Minister ventured to point out that no doubt under the conditions the Ambassador had described, the French government would be likely to have the support of French opinion in taking measures which had the appearance of promising relief, but people in England were convinced that these measures would almost immediately lead to disastrous results. Not only would the German economic situation continue with increasing speed in the path leading to the inevitable final catastrophe, but the consequent exclusion of all hope of any prospect of an alleviation of the financial condition of France would be sure to react fatally on the exchange value of the franc, French investors being driven to place their money abroad where stable currencies were to be found. When this came to be realised, as it must be very soon, the Government responsible for such disastrous consequences would be long remembered in France as the origin of their financial disasters.

In no case would a British Government associate itself with such a policy.

Count Saint-Aulaire claimed that some risks must be run to achieve anything. He would ask, since the taking of pledges was for the French Government a *sine qua non*, whether the British Government could think of others than the control of the Ruhr which were free from the objections which had been urged.

The Prime Minister confessed that he was unable to suggest any means by which Germany could be made to pay, except to devise a plan which would have the willing support of the German Government. This presupposed that the plan was both reasonable in itself and capable of execution with due regard to actualities. He thought the French were making the great mistake of looking at the problem to be solved from the point of view not of what could possibly be obtained from Germany but of what France needed to set her finances in order. He was reminded of what passed at a recent interview he had with a deputation of unemployed in his constituency at Glasgow. He had said to them something very much of the same kind, pointing out how foolish they were in dwelling exclusively on the amount of money they thought was necessary for their needs, and left out of account altogether what was the amount which could in practice be made available.

In face of the apparently irreconcilable divergence of these points of view Sir Eyre Crowe asked whether he might make a practical suggestion. It seemed to him both unfortunate and unnecessary that the whole discussion should be allowed to centre [o]n the dispute about the taking of pledges to the neglect of the other really far more important issues, of which at the best the taking of pledges was only a corollary. Count Saint-Aulaire had explained that the French Government anticipated not the slightest difficulty in arriving at an understanding as to the scaling down of the total German reparation debt, the stabilisation of the German mark and the rehabilitation of German credit. Ought not all efforts, in the first instance, to be concentrated on arriving at that understanding? We had three weeks before us in which to achieve this. Why begin with the one point on which agreement seemed impossible and so conjure up an immediate rupture deplored by all parties without making the attempt to see whether the question of pledges might not present itself in a somewhat different light if it were attacked after a general plan had been adopted which might possibly promise much more favourable financial results? It might even be suggested that if a plan so elaborated were to meet with wholehearted acceptance by Germany, the German Government itself might be induced to offer, as an earnest of its good faith, pledges which would satisfy the French Government. Even the French Government must admit that, unless the pledges they proposed to take were to have the effect of making Germany really willing and eager to co-operate in a scheme of payment, nothing of value would be achieved. Therefore let first place be given to the effort to evolve an acceptable scheme, and let the means of enforcing its working be left to subsequent discussion.

The Prime Minister added that if the German Government could be brought to accept a reasonable plan and give a formal undertaking—perhaps fortified by pledges—the British Government would probably be quite ready to declare that, if Germany failed to give due effect to such an arrangement, Great Britain would associate herself with France in any coercive measures which could be devised to compel her to do so. This would practically be presenting an ultimatum, and he thought that such ultimatums had on previous occasions proved effective. But whilst previous ultimatums had produced German acceptances, they had unfortunately not led in practice to the fulfilment of the demands made, for the reason that the demands were found not to be executable. This difficulty would be avoided if in the present instance care were taken that the demands put forward were of a reasonable and practical kind, and acknowledged to be such by the German Government itself.

Count Saint-Aulaire said he regretted he had to repeat that it was impossible for the French Government to rest content with presenting an ultimatum, thereby once more postponing to a future date the measures of coercion which in their opinion would alone yield practical results. He undertook, however, faithfully to lay before M. Poincaré all that the Prime Minister had said, and though he fully realised the grave divergence which had manifested itself between French and English public opinion, he said he for one did not despair of an agreement being somehow arrived at; for to him a break between France and England was something quite inconceivable. An understanding must be arrived at, and therefore would be arrived at.

No. 152

Sir J. Bradbury (Reparation Commission) to the Treasury[1]
[C 17771/99/18]

Copy　　　　　　　　　　　　　　　　　　　　　　　PARIS, *December 26, 192*

May it please your Lordships,

I have the honour to transmit, for the consideration of His Majesty's Government, a letter from the Reparation Commission reporting under paragraph 17 of Annex 2 of Part VIII of the Treaty of Versailles a failure of Germany to carry out her treaty obligations in respect of deliveries of timber to France in 1922.

Your Lordships will observe that the decision to declare this default was taken by a majority of three to one, and that I voted in the minority.

My reasons for differing from my colleagues were:—

1. The delays of delivery of which complaint was made by the French Government are in my opinion very largely due to the economic difficulties arising out of the desperate condition of German finances, which in their turn have been greatly aggravated by the failure of the Allied Governments and the Reparation Commission to take timely steps to deal by adequate temporary mitigation of the German treaty obligations with a situation which called urgently for that remedy early last summer. No decision has been taken upon the proposals submitted to the commission by myself on the 4th October last,[2] which, if they had been promptly put into force, would probably have enabled the deliveries in kind to proceed on a considerable scale, the French delegate having pressed that the matter should be referred for consideration to the Allied Governments.

---

[1] A copy of this letter was communicated to the Foreign Office on December 28.
[2] See No. 97.

In these circumstances, it appears to me that the current performances of the German Government during the period of difficulty and uncertainty which must necessarily exist until the decision by the Allied Governments could be taken ought to have been judged with some degree of indulgence.

2. The procedure of a report under paragraph 17 of Annex 2 appeared to me to be wholly inappropriate to the circumstances of the present case.[3]

The protocols directing the deliveries in question provided that the French Government should have the right to refuse deliveries tendered out of time.

The Reparation Commission reserved the right to fix penalties for any failure to deliver by the prescribed date, and did actually, at the request of the French Government, exercise this right in the case of sawn timber by claiming the liberty to reduce the credit to be given for late deliveries 'unless it considers that Germany is not responsible for the delay'.

Further, under the decision of the Reparation Commission of the 21st March, 1922,[4] fixing the deliveries in kind to France for 1922 at a maximum limit of 950,000,000 gold marks, it was expressly provided that 'if the Reparation Commission finds that, in the course of the year 1922, the deliveries called for within the limit of that figure have not been effected by reason of obstruction on the part of the German Government . . . additional cash payments shall be exacted from Germany at the end of 1922 in replacement of the deliveries not effected'.

In view of these decisions it appeared to me to be impossible to have recourse to the procedure of paragraph 17 in regard to the delays in question (even on the assumption that that paragraph were otherwise applicable) until the specific remedies contemplated by the protocols under which the deliveries were called for and the commission's own decision of the 21st March had been exhausted.

In my view the object of paragraph 17 is to give an arm to the commission in the event of defiance by the German Government.

On the two previous occasions on which recourse was had to it, viz., in the summer of 1920, when the German Government deliberately reduced the coal deliveries from the Ruhr as a protest[5] against the treatment of the Upper Silesian supply by the Plebiscite Commission, and again in April 1921,[6] when it declined to send 1 milliard marks in gold from the Reichsbank reserve, which the commission had called for, these conditions were satisfied.

The use of the paragraph, not upon the initiative of the commission itself to enforce its authority, but upon the demand of an Allied Government which is dissatisfied with the steps which the commission has taken to safeguard its interests in respect of what in proportion to reparation figures generally is a comparatively minor failure in regard to a particular requisition, seems to me to be open to grave objection.

I have, etc.,

JOHN BRADBURY

[3] Cf. Nos. 148 and 154, below.   [4] See No. 12, n. 1.
[5] See Vol. X, No. 164.   [6] See Vol. XVI, No. 528.

The Reparation Commission to the British Government

PARIS, *December 26, 1922*

The Reparation Commission has the honour to inform you that, at its 343rd meeting, held on the 26th December, 1922, it took the following decisions:—

1. The commission unanimously decided that Germany had not executed, in their entirety, the orders placed under Annex 4, Part VIII of the Treaty of Versailles, for the delivery of timber to France in the year 1922.

2. The commission decided by a majority, the British delegate recording an adverse note, that this failure in execution constituted a default by Germany in the performance of its obligations within the meaning of paragraph 17 of Annex 2.

3. The commission decided by a majority, the British delegate abstaining from voting, to remind the Governments concerned that, in its letter of the 21st March, fixing the payments to be made by Germany in the current year, the commission stated:

'If the Reparation Commission finds, in the course of the year 1922, that deliveries in kind called for by France or her nationals or by any other Power entitled to reparation or its nationals in accordance with the procedure laid down by the treaty or in virtue of a procedure approved by the Reparation Commission and within the limits of the figures above indicated have not been effected by reason of obstruction on the part of the German Government or on the part of its organisations, or by reason of a breach of the procedure of the treaty, or of a procedure approved by the Reparation Commission, additional equivalent cash payments shall be exacted from Germany at the end of 1922 in replacement of the deliveries not effected.'

In accordance with the terms of paragraph 17 to which reference is made above, the commission has the honour to notify the default thus declared to the Governments concerned.[7]

The British Government is requested to find herewith enclosed copies of memoranda[8] by the competent service of the commission on the deliveries in question, and extracts[8] of the minutes of the meeting at which the German Government was heard on the insufficiency of these deliveries, and of the meeting at which the default was declared as above.

LOUIS BARTHOU
LÉON DELACROIX

[7] The French text of these decisions, issued by the Reparation Commission as an official communiqué on the afternoon of December 27, was transmitted to the Foreign Office by Mr. Phipps in his telegram No. 690 of December 27 (C 17740/99/18), not printed.
[8] Not printed.

No. 153

The Marquess Curzon of Kedleston to Mr. Phipps (Paris)
No. 3879 [C 17747/99/18]

Confidential　　　　　　　　　　　FOREIGN OFFICE, *December 28, 1922*

Sir,

I transmit to you herewith copy of a record of a conversation which took place on the 27th instant between the French Ambassador and Sir Eyre Crowe on the subject of German reparations.

I am, etc.,
CURZON OF KEDLESTON

ENCLOSURE IN No. 153

Note by Sir Eyre Crowe

FOREIGN OFFICE, *December 27, 1922*

The French Ambassador called today in order to inform me of the substance of a telegraphic message he had received from M. Poincaré, replying to a report which the Ambassador had addressed to him recording his conversation with Mr. Bonar Law on the 24th December.[1]

The Comte de Saint-Aulaire read out certain passages of the telegram, but would not give me a copy. The essential points in M. Poincaré's observations are the following:—

1. M. Poincaré takes note with great satisfaction of the evidence of the British Government's continued anxiety to treat the difficult question of reparations in a spirit of the utmost friendliness to France, and their appreciation of the latter's peculiar difficulties. He has no doubt that, if the discussions at the forthcoming meeting in Paris are conducted in this spirit, an agreement between the Allies will be reached.

2. There can be no question of France receding in any way from her policy of the seizure of remunerative pledges as one of the conditions on which any grant of a moratorium can be executed. M. Poincaré has commissioned his experts to prepare a detailed plan of the pledges which he proposes to take, showing the method of application and execution, and giving as precise an estimate as can be made of the financial benefits to be obtained.

3. M. Poincaré fully realises that the question of pledges must be considered in connection with a comprehensive general plan dealing with the amount to be fixed for the total German debt, the stabilisation of the mark, the raising of loans and the general restoration of German credit and of Germany's economic position. He must, however, continue to claim that the question of pledges stands in the foreground, and its consideration cannot be allowed to stand over whilst the general problem of reparations is attacked. The Comte de Saint-Aulaire added on his own behalf the observation that it

[1] See No. 151.

357

would be easy to devise an arrangement by which the several aspects of the whole problem could be studied simultaneously by a number of committee of delegates or experts on the different questions involved.

4. M. Poincaré, feeling convinced that nothing but the seizure of pledge will advance matters, regrets to find that the British Government, whils very frankly and loyally expressing their condemnation of this particula policy, maintain a negative attitude of criticism, but do not themselves offe any alternative plan by which the desired object could be attained. M. Poincar cannot but believe that the British Government must have something definit in their mind, which they would be ready to substitute for the French plan o effective pledges, and he ventures to express the earnest hope that they will b able and ready to submit their alternative proposition for the consideratio of the French Government.

No. 154

Opinion by the Solicitor-General on the Interpretation of Paragraph 18 o
Annex II to Part VIII of the Treaty of Versailles
(Received in the Foreign Office, December 29)

[*C 17791/99/18*]

Confidential   *December 28, 192.*

1. Does the expression 'in general such other measures' in paragraph 18 o Annex II to Part VIII of the Treaty of Versailles signify any measure other than measures such as 'economic and financial prohibitions an reprisals' which fall within the limits of the sovereignty of the individua Governments?

I think paragraph 18 of Annex II to Part VIII of the treaty contemplate action by an individual Government only within its own jurisdictional limits The fact that each Government is given a separate discretion as to th measures it may deem necessary in the circumstances indicates clearly to m mind an intention to restrict 'other measures' to such measures as com within the above description.

2. Is it for the Reparation Commission, under paragraph 12 of Annex II t Part VIII of the Treaty of Versailles, to interpret paragraph 18 of tha annex?

I think it is the duty of the Reparations Commission to interpret th provisions of paragraph 18. I see no warrant for the view that there is distinction, for the purposes of paragraph 12, between interpretation a against the German Government and interpretation as between the Allie Governments. The explicit language of paragraph 12 in giving the Repara tion Commission authority to interpret the provisions of Part VIII appears t exclude the possibility of a rival authority, even in a case under paragraph 1 (if such could ever arise), in which the interests of the German Governmen were not affected.

T. W. H. INSKIP

No. 155

The Marquess Curzon of Kedleston to Sir R. Graham (Rome)
No. 425 Telegraphic [C 17828/99/18]

FOREIGN OFFICE, *December 29, 1922, 2 p.m.*

Your telegram No. 402 (of December 28th)[1] (Paris Conference).[2]

Prime Minister proposes to table a complete and detailed plan[3] dealing with the whole problem of reparations and rehabilitation of German credit as well as with question of inter-allied European debts. Please inform Monsieur Mussolini. It may possibly influence his decision not to come to Paris, if as we understand that decision was largely caused by impression that no comprehensive scheme would be before the conference.[4]

[1] Not printed.   [2] See No. 132, n. 3.

[3] This plan (Paper C.P.—4376) is printed in Cmd. 1812, op. cit., pp. 112–19. It was discussed in a meeting of the Cabinet at 3.30 p.m. on December 29, when the Cabinet agreed (Cabinct 72(22)):

'(*a*) To approve the general principles of the "Plan for General Settlement of Reparation and European Inter-allied Debts" laid before them by the Prime Minister (Paper C.P.— 4376), leaving discretion to the Prime Minister and the President of the Board of Trade [Sir Philip Lloyd-Greame] to make such alterations in detail as they might deem necessary in the course of the negotiations at the forthcoming meeting in Paris on the subject of Reparations by Germany.

'(*b*) That, from the point of view of the presentation of the plan to the French Government, it would be useful to introduce into the above plan some words to show that France would obtain from the proceeds of the loan to be raised during the proposed moratorium some advantage to meet a part of the expenditure incurred on the reconstruction of the devastated areas, provided that this could be effected without serious detriment to ourselves and without antagonising Belgium and Italy. The question of introducing a clause to this effect was left to the Prime Minister and the President of the Board of Trade in consultation with Sir John Bradbury and Mr. Niemeyer, of the Treasury.

'(*c*) That, if in the course of the negotiations the Prime Minister thought it advisable, he should be at liberty, in order to accentuate the generosity of the scheme from a public point of view, to table the proposals with the omission of the suggestion that France should transfer to Great Britain the first Series German Bonds to be received by France in respect of the Belgian War Debt.

'(*d*) That the plan should not immediately be presented to the French Government, but that full discretion should be left to the Prime Minister and President of the Board of Trade as to the right moment for its presentation.

'(*e*) That, in the event of insistence by the French Government on "Gages productives", the Prime Minister and President of the Board of Trade should be at liberty to agree to proposals, which were not seriously mischievous, even though they were not likely to prove productive. It was considered preferable in this event that the enforcement of such pledges should be left to the French.

'(*f*) In the event of a fixed determination on the part of the French Government to take independent coercive action against Germany, and a refusal to discuss any reasonable proposals, the Cabinet agreed with the course proposed by the Prime Minister, namely, that he should state that large questions were raised, such as the future participation of the British Government in the Conference of Ambassadors and in the Reparation Commission, and the retention of a British garrison on the Rhine—questions on which it would be necessary for him to consult the Cabinet.'

[4] In his telegram No. 406 of December 31, Sir R. Graham replied: 'I made communication at once but Signor Mussolini is still unwilling to go to Paris.'

No. 156

Sir A. Geddes (Washington) to the Marquess Curzon of Kedleston
(Received December 29, 11.20 p.m.)
No. 508 Telegraphic [A 7832/77/45]

WASHINGTON, *December 29, 1922*[1]

My telegram No. 505.[2]

Debate on Borah amendment[3] has been proceeding in Senate without any important development until yesterday when a letter from President to Senator Lodge was published in which administrations view was stated. Letter may be summarised as follows:—

Begins. President considers amendment undesirable because of false impression which might thereby be conveyed both to European and to American people. State Department if approached could have given confidential information in regard to situation 'in which we are trying to be helpful' and such enquiry 'would have revealed futility of any conference called until it is understood that such conference would be welcomed by nations concerned within limits of discussions which the express will of Congress compels this government to impose'. If Congress really desires to facilitate task of government first practical step would be to free hands of American debt funding commission 'so that helpful negotiations may be undertaken'. Reparations cannot be settled without consent of governments concerned and United States cannot assume to decide amounts. Present and past administration have insisted that question of European debts to United States is distinct from question of reparations, but European nations hold a contrary view and it is inconsistent to summon conference for consideration of questions in dealing with which government is denied authority by act of Congress.

As for land armaments there seems at this time to be no more promising prospect than when Washington conference[4] met. As regards limitation of auxiliary types of naval craft such agreement is much to be desired but further endeavours along that line can reasonably be postponed until final ratification of Washington agreements.[5] Ends.

In view of attitude of administration it seems likely that Borah amendment will be defeated though voting will be close if there is a division.

---

[1] The time of despatch is not recorded.

[2] Of December 22, not printed.

[3] Senator Borah's amendment, introduced on December 22, to the United States Naval Appropriation Bill provided for the summoning of a conference on world economic problems and disarmament.

[4] See Vol. XIV, Chap. VI.

[5] See Cmd. 1627 of 1922, *Conference on Limitation of Armament, Washington, 1921–22 (Treaties, Resolutions, etc.)*.

No. 157

Sir A. Geddes (Washington) to the Marquess Curzon of Kedleston
(Received December 30, 8.30 a.m.)
No. 509 Telegraphic [C 9/1/18]

WASHINGTON, *December 29, 1922*[1]

My telegram No. 499.[2]

State Department have communicated to me an extract from a speech which Secretary of State will deliver tonight at Newhaven. Extract relates to economic conditions in Europe and amounts to an elaboration of President's letter summarized in my immediately preceding telegram.[3] Views expressed coincide with Secretary of State's statements made in frequent conversations with me and fully reported to Your Lordship. I think it well to give below however a summary of certain passages of this speech.

Begins.

Crux of European situation lies in settlement of reparations. No American demand stands in the way of a proper settlement of this question. There has been persistent attempt since the armistice to link up debts owing to American government with reparations or with projects of cancellation. This attempt has been resisted. In American view capacity to pay is not affected by indebtedness of the allies to America. 'That indebtedness does not diminish Germany's capacity and its removal would not increase her capacity.' Moreover capacity of America's debtors to pay cannot be properly determined until amount that can be realised on their unsettled credits for reparations can be determined. There is not the slightest desire that France should lose any part of her just claims. On the other hand we do not wish to see a prostrate Germany and there can be no economic recuperation in Europe unless Germany recuperates. American government view with disfavour measures which instead of producing reparations would threaten disaster. There should be no question of America assuming the rôle of arbiter unless she was invited and it would be unprecedented for her to seek such an invitation.

First condition of a satisfactory settlement is that question should be taken out of politics. Opinion of experts is that forcible measures to obtain reparations would not achieve that end but might tend to destroy basis of those payments which must be found in economic recuperation. Merits of question as an economic one must alone be regarded. If statesmen cannot agree why should they not invite men of highest authority in finance in their respective countries to propose financial plan for working out payments? Governments need not bind themselves in advance to accept recommendations but they can at least approve of enquiry and free men who may represent their country from any duty to obey political instructions. Secretary of State does not believe any general political conference would answer purpose better. It would be time enough to consider forcible measures after such opportunity had been exhausted.

[1] The time of despatch is not recorded.   [2] No. 145.   [3] No. 156.

United States has most friendly and disinterested purpose and wishes to aid in any practical way. 'There lies open broad avenue of opportunity if those whose voluntary action is indispensable are willing to take advantage of it. And once this is done the avenues of American helpfulness cannot fail to open hopefully.'

Ends.

There can be no doubt that this speech of Mr. Hughes is intended to be helpful to British plans[4] at forthcoming conference.[5]

[4] See No. 155.   [5] At Paris (see No. 132, n. 3).

No. 158

Letter from Mr. C. Mendl[1] (Paris) to Sir. E. Crowe (Received December 30)

[C 17866/99/18]

PARIS, *December 29, 1922*

Dear Sir Eyre,

I saw Philippe Millet[2] this evening. He had had an interview with M. Millerand last night. There is no question that the French plan is an immediate occupation of the Ruhr which, if undertaken with ourselves, will require, they believe, no military force; but if undertaken by themselves alone will perforce necessitate a certain number of troops. The French profess to believe, however, that there is bad feeling between the German workmen and Industrialists in the Ruhr, and that consequently strikes are not to be feared, the workmen being perfectly willing to get the better of the magnates.

The only compromise formula which Millet believed would be acceptable to France's present rulers was as follows:— Though they believe that the occupation of the Ruhr would be the best thing, they are prepared to waive this for the present, providing there were an immediate confiscation of certain revenues outside the Ruhr, to be defined (e.g. the Customs in the big harbours); providing also that the revenues pass directly to the Reparation Commission and not through the German Gov[ernmen]t, it being understood that this is a temporary measure and that directly Germany meets certain obligations to be defined (e.g. the production of a certain sum of cash by the Industrialists on a given date), this confiscation would automatically cease. But if Germany did not bow to this arrangement, or if, through her fault, the confiscated pledges did not prove productive, then the French desired that we should agree to their going into the Ruhr after, say, three or four months.

This is the solution put forward by M. Millerand as being the only one which would obviate the more drastic measure of a Ruhr occupation.

Afterwards 'Pertinax' came to see me. He, of course, represents that section of the Press which ardently desires the occupation of the Ruhr. He had seen M. Poincaré last night and the Président du Conseil had given

[1] Mr. Charles Mendl was the Paris representative of the News Department of the Foreign Office, 1920–4.

[2] See No. 139, n. 4.

him assurances that he intended to go into the Ruhr. 'Pertinax', however, from previous experience professed to doubt whether M. Poincaré, when it came to the point, would prove strong enough to carry out these promises and he recalled how, last August, M. Poincaré accepted the Belgian compromise after first refusing it in London.[3]

At the same time I found 'Pertinax' much more pleased than usual, and I fear he really thinks that, this time, they have got the Président du Conseil thoroughly frightened for his Parliamentary position if he does not go into the Ruhr, and that they will be able to hold him to it. For, as 'Pertinax' pointed out, if he mounts the Ruhr horse he may be in the saddle for a great many months more—until, as I remarked, it proves a failure.

I found both Millet and 'Pertinax' highly incensed against Sir John Bradbury, and their strictures were no less strong than those of Tardieu this morning in the 'Echo National'. Though they admitted that the French may have made a mistake in pyschology *vis-à-vis* ourselves, their point was that, all the same, Bradbury must have known long before this particular session of the Commission, that the matter was coming up. They recalled M. Poincaré's statement in the Senate on December 22nd in which he referred to the fact that Germany's deliveries of sawn wood and telegraph poles were considerably short of the figures stipulated by the Reparation Commission. He went on to say: 'We have asked for the default to be declared, and the Reparation Commission is to decide shortly—if I am not mistaken, before the end of the month—about the demand which the French Gov[ernmen]t has made.'

In addition, Millet says that already last Saturday[4] or Sunday Sir John Bradbury knew what was coming up on Tuesday's session for it was an open secret in the Reparation Commission. Millet was told about it while playing golf on Sunday morning with Bergery.[5] They consider that Bradbury went over to England to incense the Prime Minister and the Press against what had been done.

M. Poincaré professed to 'Pertinax' great pessimism regarding the coming conference,[6] though he thought it even chances that some arrangement would be arrived at.

'Pertinax' told me that Marshal Foch was not against the occupation of the Ruhr, provided it was done on a modest scale. He offers (in his own words) to build a game-keeper's house but he would not undertake to build a palace; and he guarantees to put his feet on the German coal in the first stage, and after a short while to exploit it.

Speaking of Lausanne,[7] 'Pertinax' expressed himself in pessimistic terms and said that M. Poincaré had displayed much uneasiness, believing that the situation could not improve. M. Poincaré told 'Pertinax' something which surprised him very much, namely that, owing to the turn things had taken

---

[3] Cf. Nos. 71, 78, and 83.   [4] December 23.
[5] An Assistant General Secretary on the Reparation Commission.
[6] At Paris (see No. 132, n. 3).
[7] For the Conference of Lausanne, see Vol. XVIII, Chap. II.

in the East, some weeks ago France had elected a Syrian Mahomedan as Président du Conseil of the Federated States of Aleppo, Damascus and Aliot—Lebanon, as a Christian country, not being included. And 'Pertinax' expressed the opinion that should these Federated States wish to be separated or freed from the French mandate, France would not lift a finger to stop it. This Mahomedan Président du Conseil has asked to be allowed to come to Paris and is expected here sometime in the New Year.

Yours sincerely,
CHARLES MENDL

No. 159

Lord D'Abernon (Berlin) to the Marquess Curzon of Kedleston
(Received December 30, 7.50 p.m.)
No. 229 Telegraphic [C 7/1/18]

BERLIN, December 30, 1922, 1 p.m.

After long and difficult discussion leaders of industries agreed last night to furnish guarantees for loan.

Germany will send no written offer but will ask to be heard by conference when German scheme will be submitted.

Details of scheme are kept secret here but Secretary of State informs me that they will be communicated very confidentially to Prime Minister and His Majesty's Government by London Embassy as soon as Sthamer gets back.

Basic feature of scheme is a fixed minimum capital sum of reparation subject to an increment determined by an independent commission. This commission to examine and report as soon as stabilisation affected and a clearer view of Germany's real position possible. Creditors will, therefore, have something comparable with a debenture interest and a share interest.

Chancellor speaks tomorrow in Hamburg and will prepare German public for new position but will not give details.

No. 160

The Marquess Curzon of Kedleston to the Marquess of Crewe[1] (Paris)
No. 3918 [C 17835/99/18]

Confidential   FOREIGN OFFICE, *December 30, 1922*
My Lord,

With reference to my despatch No. 3911 of the 29th instant,[2] I transmit to your Lordship herewith copy of a record of a further conversation[3] between

---

[1] See No. 144, n. 1.   [2] Not printed.

[3] Sir E. Crowe's record of the previous day's conversation ran as follows: 'He [the French Ambassador] was, of course, not authorised to say—and he thought he made this clear yesterday—that M. Poincaré could ultimately agree to any plan which did not include the taking of pledges, but that was quite a different thing from saying that he would not discuss any general plan unless the principle of immediate pledges had been previously agreed to.'

he French Ambassador and Sir Eyre Crowe, on the 29th instant, on the ubject of German reparations.

I am, etc.,

CURZON OF KEDLESTON

ENCLOSURE IN No. 160

Note by Sir E. Crowe

FOREIGN OFFICE, *December 29, 1922*

The French Ambassador called today to bring me M. Poincaré's answer o the message from Mr. Bonar Law, which he undertook to convey esterday.[3] The Ambassador read to me a telegram, of which the following s the substance:—

M. Poincaré attaches much less importance to the order in which the everal points arising in connection with the reparation question are to be liscussed at the Paris Conference, than to the actual solution and to the precise results to be obtained. But he must emphasise that, in his opinion, it s the German demand for a moratorium which is the cause of the meeting, ind that this question of a moratorium is indissolubly connected in French eyes with that of the pledges (*gages*).

No. 161

Record by Mr. Lampson of a conversation with M. Roger Cambon

[*C 115/1/18*]

FOREIGN OFFICE, *December 30, 1922*

M. Roger Cambon, of the French Embassy, called this afternoon and read a collection of papers just received from Paris.

These dealt with the attempt at direct negotiations made by German ndustrialists to which M. Poincaré had alluded in the course of the recent London conversations[1] and which had also been touched upon in the conversation between Mr. Bonar Law and the French Ambassador on Sunday last.[2] Such negotiations as had taken place had been direct with French industrialists and all attempts by German industrialists to open reparation negotiations with the French Government had been turned down by the latter.

The gist of the papers was that it was not till December 9th that the German Ambassador made his first official move. Before that date there had been several attempts by German industrials through the Marquis de Lubersac[3] to get into direct touch with the French Government on the

---

[1] See Cmd. 1812, op. cit., pp. 51–2.   [2] See No. 151.
[3] President of the French General Federation of Co-operative Societies for Recon-struction.

subject of reparations; but these attempts had been refused by M. Poincar
(see his letter to the Marquis of Oct[ober] 21, of which M. Cambon left
copy, attached hereto).[4] On December 9 the German Ambassador had a con
versation with the Director of the Political Section of the Quai d'Orsay whe
he was told that the proper method was to make his suggestions to the Frencl
Government in writing. On December 16 the Ambassador (whether i
writing or not I am not clear) made his proposals to M. Poincaré: these wer
that Messrs. Stinnes, Silverberg and Kloeckner should visit Paris abou
December 22 and lay their reparation proposals before the French Goverm
ment. This drew from M. Poincaré his note of December 21 (copy herewith[4]
to the effect that the French Government were ready to receive any repara
tion proposals that might be sent to them through the official channe
but that they were not prepared to see the German industrials named above
the negotiations between those industrials and French interests concerne
merely deliveries of coal and minerals and did not refer to reparations.

M. Poincaré wished to emphasise to His Majesty's Government that suc
negotiations as there had been with these German industrials had bee
between them and French industrials and were concerned solely with coa
and mineral deliveries. The French Government had refused to see then
and no reparation proposals had ever been accepted by the French Govern
ment through that channel.

M. W. LAMPSON

[4] Not printed.

No. 162

Record[1] *by Sir E. Crowe of a conversation with the German Ambassado*

[*C 104/1/18*]

FOREIGN OFFICE, December 30, 192.

The German Ambassador came to see me today immediately on his returi
from Berlin, whence he arrived this morning. He wished to tell me tha
he found his Government in a state of the greatest anxiety, if not alarm, a
the prospects of what might result from the Paris Conference. The new
Chancellor was, if anything, more determined than ever to go to the utmos
limit of concession in order to facilitate a solution of the reparations question
but the Ambassador pointed out that, neither the present, nor any, Germai
Government could possibly give their consent to the measures which the
French Government clearly contemplated taking in the Ruhr. They there
fore still hoped that this contingency would be avoided. The Ambassadoi
referred to a remark I had made in the course of a conversation[2] with him
before he left for Berlin, to the effect that it might be in the power of the

[1] A copy of this record was transmitted to Lord D'Abernon in despatch No. 4 of January 2
1923.
[2] See No. 146.

German Government—and would in that case certainly be in their interest—that they themselves should put forward proposals, under which certain securities or pledges could be offered to the Allies as a guarantee for German payments. The German Government, he said, had from time to time been considering this matter. Everything, to their mind, depended on what was meant by pledges in this connection. Any political pledges, such as occupation of territory, establishment of separate customs in the occupied areas, or the installation of Allied officials to control German Government institutions, they did not consider possible, but guarantees or sureties in the ordinary or commercial sense of the word might perhaps be devised. At any rate, the Ambassador was now able to tell me—and he laid particular stress upon this—that at last the German industrials had definitely come to terms with the German Government, and were now standing behind them, and would assist, directly and indirectly, so far as was in their power in enabling the German Government either to make or to meet reasonable proposals. I asked the Ambassador whether this meant that the industrials were ready to guarantee certain payments to be made. He said he could not tell me, but that it was more likely that these industrial guarantees would take the form of securities for loans, but, of course, it would remain open to what purpose the loans would be applied.

The Ambassador then referred to the question which, he said, had been . much discussed in Berlin, whether the German Government should put forward a fresh comprehensive proposal, including a suggested figure representing the total amount of debt which the German Government could pay for reparations. Unfortunately, he said, the German Government were suffering from a multitude of counsellors, and advice on this point had been very conflicting. He rather suggested that he had himself derived the impression from his former conversations in this Office that we did not favour the putting forward of a fresh German proposal, and this harmonised with the advice the Chancellor had received from Lord D'Abernon.[3] I said I

---

[3] In his despatch No. 17 of January 6 (C 594/1/18) Lord D'Abernon enclosed a memorandum which ran as follows: 'I notice in Sir Eyre Crowe's note of the 30th December that the German Ambassador in London suggested that the Foreign Office did not favour the putting forward of a fresh German proposal, and that "this harmonised with the advice the Chancellor had received from Lord D'Abernon". Sir Eyre Crowe corrected this impression as far as regards the Foreign Office. I must also correct it as far as regards myself. I never gave general advice to the German Government not to present a fresh proposal. Apart from not having received instructions on the subject, I had no opinion myself as to whether a fresh German proposal was expedient in principle or not. Everything depended upon what the new German proposal was.

'What I said to the Chancellor on the 22nd December was not to submit a new proposal without feeling the ground in London. This is totally different from not presenting a new proposal. As a matter of fact, for ten days after the 22nd December the German authorities were in almost continuous session day and night discussing what the terms of their new proposal should be, a course they presumably would not have adopted had definite advice not to present a new proposal at all been tendered to them.

'The matter has a purely retrospective interest, but it is perhaps well to correct a misunderstanding on the part of Dr. Sthamer.'

must correct this impression. I remembered the Ambassador speaking to me on the subject at the time when I knew that Lord D'Abernon had given the advice mentioned. I was, personally, then not in a position to judge whether this advice was really sound; it had not been given on instructions from here, and, in these circumstances, I carefully refrained, when speaking to him, from expressing any opinion of my own. The Ambassador readily accepted my explanation, but said that he had certainly, when at Berlin, thought that Lord D'Abernon's advice represented our considered view, and had therefore helped to dissuade his Government from putting forward a new plan. Since then it had come to his knowledge that this was hardly the view of Sir John Bradbury; and other indications had reached him from various quarters to the effect that it would, after all, be to Germany's interest to have a proposal ready to put before the conference at Paris. He had therefore immediately telegraphed to Berlin, and begged them, disregarding his previous advice, to make an effort to get a proposal ready. He did not know whether there would be time to do this, but expected a telegram from Berlin today, which would enable him to say something more definite on this point. Meanwhile, he was looking forward to meeting Sir John Bradbury himself this afternoon; and I strongly advised him to be quite frank in the discussion with Sir John, in whom, I assured him, he would find a good and sympathetic listener to any reasonable suggestions.

Finally, the Ambassador once more laid stress on the desirability of German representatives being received and heard in the course of the Paris Conference.[4] He felt sure—and it was only human—that if the German Government were shown that they would be received with confidence in their loyal and honest intentions, it would be made much easier for them to come forward with suggestions and ideas, which they might well hesitate to lay before the conference if they felt all they said was treated with suspicion. He said an immense amount of newly worked-up material—statistical and other—had been prepared in Berlin, and it would be possible for the German representatives to give an accurate and convincing account of the actual state of their country's financial position. This alone, in his opinion, would be worth more than the mere mention of a total figure for reparations, for, after all, it was on such material that the total could alone be arrived at. I understood that this material would be ready to be produced in Paris next week.

4 See No. 132, n. 3.

No. 163

Lord D'Abernon (Berlin) to the Marquess Curzon of Kedleston
(Received January 1, 1923, 8 a.m.)
Telegraphic[1] *[C 103/1/18]*

BERLIN, *December 31, 1922, 9.30 p.m.*

Chancellor's speech today[2] contained no details of German proposal. He stated that fate of previous German proposal[3] prevented government from publishing details before meeting of conference. They had requested that an opportunity should be afforded to representative of Germany to lay proposal in writing before the conference and to explain it verbally.

Germany would offer definite sum as final settlement. This sum would be raised by loan as far as possible.

A condition for execution of German proposal would be evacuation of Rhine ports and reduction of garrison in Rhineland as military occupation prevented free development of Germany's economic forces.

He went on to affirm that application of policy of *gages (pfaender)* meant death of all economic reparations.

As regards French view that Rhine had to be occupied as a protection against war-like intentions on the part of Germany this apprehension was erroneous.

'In order to prove this we have informed French government through intermediary of a third power, that Germany is ready in conjunction with France and with other Great Powers interested in the Rhine to enter into an agreement not to make war on one another during a generation unless empowered by a plebiscite. A Great Power not interested in Rhine to be trustee of this arrangement.

France has declined this offer to my regret.'

Repeated to Paris No. 25.

---

[1] This telegram was unnumbered. The text here given is that amended by Berlin telegram No. 1 of January 1, 1923.
[2] At Hamburg (see No. 159).
[3] See No. 135.

CHAPTER IV

Military Control of Germany and German Problems other than Reparation January–December, 1922

No. 164

Lord Hardinge (Paris) to the Marquess Curzon of Kedleston
(Received January 3, 8.30 a.m.)
No. 3 Telegraphic: by bag [C 114/6/18]

PARIS, *January 2, 1922*

Your despatch No. 3453 (Future aeronautical control in Germany).[1]

It is clear as a result of further informal conversations with the French military authorities that they will insist upon acceptance of rules 8 and 9,[2] thus involving a form of control which will be more elaborate and inquisitorial than that which seemed to be contemplated in scheme defined in your despatch No. 2796 of October 29th.[3]

It is also probable that French will want the new control body to execute not only article 198 but also article 202, thus giving it the functions of the present commissions of control regarding German disarmament.

All this shows, as pointed out in my telegram No. 981,[4] the importance o the Supreme Council[5] defining the precise organization and the duties of the future control body, at the same time as they deal with the questions o principle as set forth in Your Lordship's despatch above mentioned.

Copy of this telegram will be given to Mr. Vansittart on his way through Paris.

---

[1] Of December 30, 1921, not printed.
[2] See Vol. XV, No. 95, minute 2. See also Vol. XVI, Nos. 838 and 842.
[3] See Vol. XVI, No. 835.
[4] Of December 31, 1921, not printed.
[5] The Supreme Council was to meet at Cannes on January 6 (see Vol. XIX, Chap. I)

No. 165

Lord D'Abernon (Berlin) to the Marquess Curzon of Kedleston
(Received January 9, 5.50 p.m.)
No. 8 Telegraphic [C 451/6/18]

BERLIN, *January 9, 1922, 4 p.m.*

Following is reported to be the position regarding different commissions of control.[1]

Naval commission.

Has reduced personnel 50% and should complete destruction by April. Factories will take rather longer.

Military commission.

Has reduced personnel by 33%. Should finish destruction in from 3 to 5 months.

Air commission.

Has completed its task and is merely waiting decision regarding 'constant supervision' and its installation.

Delay in closing up by military and naval commissions is to some extent caused by Germany, as minor obstructions and minor discoveries of arms constantly occur and are not visited with adequate punishment.

Repeated to Cannes.[2]

[1] See Vol. XVI, Chaps. IV and VII.
[2] The Inter-Allied Conference had opened on January 6 at Cannes (see Vol. XIX, Chap. I).

No. 166

Lord Hardinge (Paris) to the Marquess Curzon of Kedleston
(Received January 13)
No. 18 Telegraphic: by bag [C 602/602/18]

PARIS, *January 11, 1922*

The Conference of Ambassadors met this morning under the presidency of Monsieur Jules Cambon, the Belgian ambassador being also present, and considered the following questions:—

. . .[1]4. In accordance with instructions contained in Your Lordship's telegram No. 724 of the 20th December[2] I proposed to the Conference that in order to facilitate German reparation payments, the Commission of Control should be instructed to hand over to Germany the partially constructed light cruiser so that the latter may complete its construction, instead of building an entirely new light cruiser for inclusion in the new German Navy. I was supported in this view by the Belgian Ambassador who stipulated however that, in return for this concession, the German

[1] The sections omitted referred to other matters.   [2] Vol. XVI, No. 855.

Government should pay to the Reparation Commission the difference between the cost of building a new cruiser and the value of the partially constructed cruiser which is to be handed over to them. On the other hand the French naval authorities, strongly supported by General Weygand, opposed the proposal on the ground that it was a violation of the spirit and letter of the Treaty and that it constituted a dangerous precedent which might be used against the allies in connection with the military disarmament of Germany. The Italian Ambassador[4] likewise supported this view. It was eventually decided to adjourn the question in order to enable M. Cambon and the Italian Ambassador to consult their Governments on the subject

[3] Chief of Staff to Marshal Foch and French representative on the Allied Military Committee of Versailles.

[4] Count Bonin Longare.

No. 167

Lord Hardinge (Paris) to the Marquess Curzon of Kedleston
(Received January 26, 8.30 a.m.)
No. 43 Telegraphic: by bag [C 1236/1229/18]

PARIS, January 25, 192.

The Conference of Ambassadors met this morning under the chairmanship of Monsieur Jules Cambon, the Belgian ambassador being also present and considered the following questions:—

...[1] 3. The Allied Military Committee of Versailles have submitted to the Conference a scheme for the distribution between the Principal Allied Associated Powers of the eight million two hundred and fifty thousand gold marks payable by Germany as compensation for the zeppelins destroyed in 1919. This scheme, copy of which is enclosed in my despatch No. 219 of today's date,[2] has been in abeyance pending a decision by the Conference as regards the claim of the United States Government to receive from Germany a military airship as their share of this compensation (see my telegram No. 956 of December 16th 1921, section 2).[3] As the airship which the United States Government have now been authorised to order in Germany will cost far more than the sum allotted to her under this scheme i.e. one million six hundred and fifty thousand gold marks, it is proposed that the United States Government shall pay the difference direct to the German Government. The United States Ambassador[4] informed the Conference that he was awaiting instructions from his Government and asked that the matter might be adjourned.

[1] The sections omitted referred to other matters.   [2] Not printed.
[3] Vol. XVI, No. 853.   [4] Mr. Myron T. Herrick.

No. 168

Lord D'Abernon (Berlin) to the Marquess Curzon of Kedleston
(Received January 30, 9 p.m.)
No. 21 Telegraphic [C 1414/6/18]

BERLIN, *January 30, 1922, 6.40 p.m.*

German government is pressing aeronautical commission to declare air clauses executed, and thus permit of construction of civil aircraft commencing in three months from date of such declaration.[1]

German government, with a view to facilitate a resolution, offer to maintain present commission of control for three months after declaration of execution, if made now.

Air Commodore Masterman[2] emphasizes difficulty of present situation since execution is actually complete as far as possible, and yet he is at present unable to declare it so.

A solution is clearly dependent upon agreement respecting permanent supervision of German civil aviation and such agreement would appear urgent to put an end to anomalous situation.[3]

[1] In June 1920 at the first conference of Boulogne (see Vol. VIII, No. 36, minute 3) the Allied powers decided that Germany should not be permitted to resume the manufacture of civil aircraft until three months after the Aeronautical Commission of Control had certified the complete execution of article 202 of the Treaty.

[2] President of the Aeronautical Commission of Control and of the Chalais–Meudon Committee (see Vol. XVI, No. 586, n. 3).

[3] Mr. Wigram commented on February 1: '... continued delay in the settlement of this question always increases the risk that the German constructors will eventually start manufacturing civil aircraft on their own, thereby placing us face to face with a breach of an allied decision and increasing our difficulties.'

No. 169

Lord Hardinge (Paris) to the Marquess Curzon of Kedleston
(Received February 3, 8.30 a.m.)
No. 53 Telegraphic: by bag [C 1639/1639/18]

PARIS, *February 1, 1922*

The Conference of Ambassadors met this morning under the chairmanship of M. Jules Cambon, and considered the following questions:—

...[1]2. The Military Committee of Versailles has had under consideration the proposal of the German Government reported in Lord D'Abernon's telegram No. 21[2] regarding the date on which Germany should be allowed to recommence the construction of civil aircraft. On the recommendation of the Versailles Committee, copy of whose despatch is enclosed in my despatch No. 279,[3] the Conference decided that the 5th February shall be fixed as the

[1] The section(s) omitted referred to other matters.　　　[2] No. 168.

[3] Of February 1, not printed.

373

date on which Article 202 shall be considered as having been completely executed. I made a point of getting the Conference to take note of the complete execution of Article 202, so as to prevent any future attempt to enforce this Article after the withdrawal of the Commission of Control. The present decision will mean that on the 5th May (i.e. three months after that date) Germany will be allowed to build civil aircraft. On the other hand, the German Government are to undertake that notwithstanding the complete execution of Article 202, they will raise no objection to the continuance of the Aeronautical Commission of Control until the 5th May. Before that date, the Conference will have to decide on the rules which are to distinguish civil from military aircraft, and communicate them to the German Government. As your Lordship is aware, it has been impossible up to now to come to a decision with regard to these rules,[4] as their application depends on the nature of the supervision which the Allied Governments intend to set up in Germany after the withdrawal of the Commission of Control. The question, moreover, has recently been further complicated by the reported acceptance at Washington of the principle that no effective steps can be taken to impose a limitation of aerial armaments owing to the difficulty if not impossibility of distinguishing between military and civil aircraft.[5]

Marshal Foch took the opportunity to urge that the Allied Governments should be warned that it is essential that a definite settlement should also be reached before the 5th May as regards the form of aeronautical supervision which will have to be set up in Germany after that date, when the present Commission of Control will cease to have any *locus standi*. Hitherto the French Government have been inclined to shelve this question and to keep on the present Commission of Control indefinitely. Now that a time limit has been fixed they will be anxious to reach a settlement as quickly as possible. Your Lordship instructed me in your despatch No. 2796 of October 29th 1921,[6] to submit definite proposals on the subject to the Conference of Ambassadors, but on that occasion the French Government preferred that the question should be dealt with by the Supreme Council. As the Supreme Council at Cannes[7] were unable to take up the question, it is probable that the French Government will now propose that it should be dealt with by the Conference of Ambassadors. The latest aspect of the question is set forth in my telegrams 3[8] and 4[9] of this year, and I should be grateful if I could be furnished with the views of His Majesty's Government on the points raised in those telegrams, so as to be ready to discuss the question if and when raised at the Conference of Ambassadors . . . .[1]

[4] See Vol. XVI, No. 859.
[5] See *Conference on the Limitation of Armament, Washington, November 12, 1921–February 6, 1922* (Washington, 1922), pp. 752–82.
[6] Vol. XVI, No. 835. See also ibid., Nos. 838, 842, 843, 845, and 846.
[7] See Vol. XIX, Chap. I.   [8] No. 164.
[9] Of January 3, not printed.

Record by Sir E. Crowe of a conversation with the German Ambassador
[*C 1821/555/18*]

FOREIGN OFFICE, *February 3, 1922*

I asked the German Ambassador to call upon me today in order that I might speak to him on the question of the war criminals sentenced by the Supreme Court at Leipzig for various outrages committed during the war.

I told him I had been directed by the Secretary of State to ask him to convey to the German Government the deplorable impression which had been created in this country by the escape of two of the principal offenders, and the extraordinar[il]y lenient treatment meted out to the three others. In two of the cases the prisoners had been released by the German authorities, one for reasons of ill-health on the strength of a medical certificate, and the other for the extraordinary reason that it was desired to enable the man's former employer to keep open the situation so that his family might not be deprived of their means of support. These were men who were serving short terms of imprisonment for cruelties perpetrated on British prisoners of war. The third culprit serving a similar sentence appeared to be the only one still in prison. The two remaining had escaped. These escaped prisoners had been convicted on one of the most foul charges imaginable, namely, the deliberate firing on and sinking the boats of a British hospital ship which they had previously torpedoed, and this after having ascertained by the use of their telescopes that the boats were full of nurses and wounded. The court had passed totally inadequate sentences of four years' imprisonment. On the top of this, the German authorities, on their own admission, allowed at least one of the prisoners during the period of his confinement to carry on his business, read his own books and papers, wear his own clothes and provide his own food. He has now escaped.

The fourth officer guilty of the same crime and equally sentenced, and presumably treated with the same extraordinary leniency during his imprisonment, had followed his friend by escaping also. I said the German Government must not be surprised if the result of these incidents made the most painful of impressions in this country, and made it difficult for the British Government to believe in the sincerity of the German authorities in dealing with the prisoners.

The German Ambassador began by expressing the most profound regret for himself and his Government at the escape of the two officers. He said he would furnish the fullest particulars which were now available concerning the means which had been applied by the prisoners to gain their liberty. He felt sure the evidence would convince His Majesty's Government, as it would any impartial judge, that, however deeply the escape of the prisoners was to be deplored, it was not due to any fault on the part of the German Government and he thought even of the superior prison authorities. They were quite alive to the fact that these escapes must throw discredit on the German

Government, and that alone must have sufficed to induce the authorities to take every possible precaution. Unfortunately, their vigilance had been circumvented by the ingenuity of the prisoners and the associates which they evidently had outside the prison walls. The Ambassador said he must protest very strongly against any suggestion that the German Government was responsible for the sentences pronounced by the Leipzig Court. Not only were the judicial authorities entirely independent, but even the prosecuting counsel had, by a special arrangement, been freed from all Government control in conducting the prosecution, and had been placed entirely under the orders of the court. The Ambassador thought it was not his duty to discuss the alleged leniency of the sentences. He could not go behind the judicial decision. The sentences were in accordance with German law, which had to be impartially applied.

I remarked that although this was not the point immediately at issue, I felt it impossible to refrain from observing what a mistake had apparently been made by the Allied Governments when agreeing to the trial of the culprits by a German court, and accepting the assurances of the German Government that they could absolutely rely on full justice being done. It was impossible, I thought, to convince opinion in this country that the sentences imposed by the court represented justice. But, leaving aside this question, there was the treatment of the prisoners after sentence by the German authorities. It seemed to me that the treatment, as I stated to him, constituted a practically open declaration to the German people that, in the eyes of the German Government, the convicted prisoners had not done anything seriously wrong. That officers guilty of sinking defenceless open boats full of nurses and wounded should be considered sufficiently punished by living like private gentlemen at their ease within the precincts of the prison, conducting their private affairs and attending to their business, was, I thought, a matter which we had every reason to resent as outrageous. After that it was really hardly surprising that the officers should find their way out. They had, apparently, every means of communicating with the outside freely, and the vigilance of the prison authorities can hardly be believed to have been sufficiently strict. The matter was made infinitely worse by the second case happening so soon after the first. As for the prisoner who had been released on medical certificate, I could only say that we were not in a position to judge of the merits of the certificate, but, taking the whole attitude of the German authorities into account, the Ambassador must not be surprised if we looked on the reasons put forward for authorising release with a good deal of scepticism. The release of the other man merely for the purpose of enabling him to earn his living was, so far as we could judge, a gross violation of all sense of justice. I begged the Ambassador to leave his Government in no doubt that the effect produced by these events was such that would have a most unfortunate repercussion on the sentiments of this country towards the German people, who appeared to be wholly on the side of the convicted German criminals.

The Ambassador said he must take grave objection to my remarks, which he considered were not justified. He was under the impression, he said, that what we called the lenient treatment of the civil prisoners was in accordance with one of the principles of German jurisprudence, which authorised all persons to receive such treatment in prison as would correspond to their conditions in private life. I said if this were indeed the principle of German justice it still further deepened my feeling that what we call justice in this country was not understood in Germany. The German Ambassador had tried, on each point of our indictment, to give explanations tending to absolve the German Government from any responsibility or fault. I said it was frequently possible to bring forward excuses and explanations for a series of regrettable events, but I begged him to place himself a little in our position and ask himself what would be the accumulative effect on his mind of the several incidents which, put together, gave such distressing a picture of the situation.

Many of the original culprits, never brought to justice, were said to have disappeared. Those tried had been condemned, but given ridiculously mild sentences, and then imprisoned under conditions which gave them an extraordinary amount of liberty and enabled them to live almost in comfort; a number of them were released on grounds which we could not accept as justifiable, and the principal culprits escaped one after the other.

I said I did not want to complicate the present case by bringing in extraneous matters, but it was difficult for us not to remember the exceedingly unsatisfactory attitude displayed on numerous occasions by the German authorities as regards the surrender of arms, and the frequency with which hidden stores of guns and rifles were discovered, in each of which cases we were invariably treated to exactly the same excuses as were made by the German Government now: that they were filled with the best of intentions; that they honestly tried to carry out the obligations under the treaties; but that unfortunately, there were all sorts of reasons why, in each particular case, something had gone wrong, without the Government itself ever being in any way to blame. When all this happened so frequently, and over such a wide field, it would not indeed be surprising if we entertained considerable doubt as to the real sincerity of the German Government in their dealings with us over these matters, and I thought that, if this doubt was confirmed and deepened, the result would be most unfortunate.

The Ambassador, in the end, made a personal appeal to me, explaining how difficult was his position. It was his duty to defend the actions and the *bona fides* of his Government, and he begged me to believe he did this with sincere conviction. He felt sure that in due time we would recognise this. Meanwhile, he hoped that I did not charge him with any want of straightforward dealing. I said I was glad to be able to say that nothing I had said flowed from any such intention, that I quite understood and, to a certain extent, sympathised with the difficulty of his position, and nothing was further from my mind than to find fault with the manner in which he treated this and other questions when he discussed them with me; but what I told him of the impression created by the attitude of his Government expressed the opinion of the Secretary of State and of the British Government. I relied upon his making this clear in reporting what I had said to his Government at Berlin.[1]

[1] In telegram No. 5 of February 2, not printed, Lord Curzon instructed Lord D'Abernon to address a strong protest to the German Government against the lenient treatment of convicted war criminals. A copy of Lord D'Abernon's note of protest to the German Government, dated February 10, was enclosed in Berlin despatch No. 125 of February 10 (C 2176/555/18), not printed.

No. 171

Lord Hardinge (Paris) to the Marquess Curzon of Kedleston
(Received February 16, 8.30 a.m.)

No. 85 Telegraphic: by bag [*C 2294/180/21*]

PARIS, *February 15, 1922*

The Conference of Ambassadors met this morning under the chairmanship of Monsieur Jules Cambon, the Belgian ambassador being also present, and considered the following questions:—

. . .[1]3. I called the attention of the Conference to the alleged export of German war material from Germany to Finland as reported by Mr. Rennie in his telegram No. 21 of the 23rd ultimo,[2] and invited the Conference to remind the Finnish Government that the importation of such war material from Germany is in violation of the Treaty of Versailles (see my telegram No. 956 of the 16th December 1921,[3] section 6), and to instruct the Military Commission of Control to take up the matter with the German Government. This was agreed to.

4. The German government have maintained that the treaty of Versailles places no restriction on the calibre of guns that can be mounted on the war vessels that Germany is allowed to construct in the future. The Naval Commission of Control have appealed to the Conference of Ambassadors. The Naval Advisers however have been unable to reach a unanimous decision on the subject. It is true that articles 181 and 190 which make provision for the future German fleet lay down no restriction with regard to the guns which the various vessels are to be allowed to carry. On the other hand, it can be argued, as do the French and Italian Naval Advisers, that the stipulations in article 192 regarding the allowance of arms and munitions to be allotted to German warships apply not only to the fleet left to Germany as the result of the treaty, but also to any future fleet which Germany may construct. It is further argued that the Principal Allied Powers in fixing the quantity of arms for each warship can *ipso facto* limit the calibre of the guns to be carried. I understand that the Admiralty dispute this point of view and consider that the only method allowed to the allied powers under the treaty,

[1] The sections omitted referred to other matters.

[2] Not printed. Mr. Rennie was H.M. Envoy Extraordinary and Minister Plenipotentiary at Helsingfors.

[3] Not printed.

of restricting the armament of future German warships, is by setting a limit to the tonnage of these vessels. I put forward these views to the Conference, but being unable to convince my colleagues, it was decided to refer the matter in the first instance to the legal advisers for their opinion.

Marshal Foch took the opportunity to point out that the construction of heavy guns for German warships would constitute a serious danger from the military point of view as their manufacture in German factories would enable the German government to manufacture similar guns for the army. It was also pointed out that if the armament of German warships was not restricted, the effect would be that Germany would be placed in a privileged position in relation to the allied powers who, at the Washington conference,[4] have undertaken to limit the size of the guns carried by their warships. These practical considerations are, I venture to think, sufficiently weighty to over-ride the strict legal interpretation which the legal advisers may feel compelled to give to the stipulations of the treaty and I shall be glad to learn whether I am authorised to co-operate with my colleagues in endeavouring to arrive at some method of restricting the armament of the German fleet, even if the legal advisers decide that the treaty does not give the allied governments the power to do so. Copy of the reports of the Commission of Control and of the Naval Advisers on this subject are enclosed in my despatch No. 378 of today's date[3] . . . .[1]

[4] See No. 169, n. 5.

No. 172

The Marquess Curzon of Kedleston to Lord Hardinge (Paris)
No. 535 [C 2460/6/18]

FOREIGN OFFICE, *February 22, 1922*

My Lord,

The accompanying papers (enclosures 1 to 3 below)[1] respecting the future organisation of the control of naval, military and aeronautical armament in Germany are transmitted to your Excellency with reference to section 2 of your telegram No. 53 of the 1st February,[2] and to your despatches Nos. 403[3] and 434[4] of the 17th and 18th February.

2. With special reference to your despatch No. 434, it is necessary to remark that the proposals on this subject submitted by your Excellency at the Ambassadors' Conference on the 2nd December, 1921,[5] represented, on the part of His Majesty's Government, a very real concession to the French government in that they were intended to secure the acceptance by the German government of the establishment of allied aeronautical and military

[1] Enclosures 2 and 3 are not printed.   [2] No. 169.
[3] Not printed. This transmitted a copy of the French Note of February 14 to the Conference of Ambassadors.
[4] Not printed.   [5] See Vol. XVI, No. 845.

control inside Germany. The French government have so far made no corre
sponding concession. Indeed, it is not at all clear from their note to the Ambas
sadors' Conference of the 14th February[6] that they are not endeavouring to
secure the indefinite continuance of the existing military commission of control
It is evident that they are still trying to secure the acceptance by His Majesty'
government of an interpretation of the reference in the May ultimatum[7] to
the future of aeronautical control, which they are fully aware His Majesty'
government have definitely repudiated.

3. Whilst leaving it, therefore, to your Excellency's discretion to draw the
attention of your French colleague to the foregoing considerations, I reques
that your Excellency will propose at the conference a settlement of the futur
of control in Germany on the lines developed in the memorandum forming
enclosure 1 to this despatch.

4. The questions raised in paragraphs 4 and 6 of your despatch No. 43.
are discussed in that memorandum. There is no objection to the acceptance
of the French government's stipulation respecting certain naval armaments
as reported in paragraph 5 of your despatch. This stipulation is, however
not covered by the treaty, and your Excellency should accordingly bear in
mind the necessity of its inclusion in any agreement that may be made with
the German government respecting the powers of the military commission o
guarantee. Your Excellency will no doubt in this connection also conside
the bearing of the proposals reported in section 4 of your telegram No. 8.
of the 15th February[8] concerning the possibility of the restriction of the
calibre of German naval guns.

I am, etc.,
CURZON OF KEDLESTON

ENCLOSURE 1 IN No. 172

Memorandum

FOREIGN OFFICE, *February 22, 192.*

The views of the French government on the future organisation of allie
control of naval, military and aeronautical armament in Germany are
disclosed in the French memorandum to the Ambassadors' Conference of the
14th February, 1922.

2. The French government accept in principle the British proposals for the
future organisation of naval and aeronautical control as outlined in Foreig
Office despatch to Paris No. 2796 of the 29th October, 1921.[9] On the othe
hand, they consider, in opposition to the British view, that the Germai
government are bound by the acceptance of the allied ultimatum of May
1921,[7] to accept without any *quid pro quo* this new aeronautical control
They also contend, in opposition to the British view, that the time is not ye
ripe for the settlement of the future organisation of military control or for the

---

[6] See n. 3.   [7] See Vol. XV, No. 85, Appendix 2.   [8] No. 171.
[9] Vol. XVI, No. 835.

withdrawal of the military sanction. The points upon which the French are in disagreement with us call for the following comments:—

3. In the first place, as regards the proposal to postpone a decision as to military control, there does not appear to be any reason why the allied governments should not, upon the advice of the existing control commission, notify to the German government the action on their part which is still necessary to complete the execution of the military clauses. They should at the same time inform the German government that the withdrawal of the existing commission is dependent and will follow upon the effective completion of such action.

4. Secondly, we cannot accept the French view that the German government are bound by the allied ultimatum of May 1921 to accept the new aeronautical control. What we contemplated by the 'constant supervision' which the Germans undertook under the ultimatum to accept was a commission outside Germany. The fact that we have now conceded to the French a control inside Germany cannot place the Germans under a legal obligation to accept the latter.

5. Thirdly, as regards the proposed offer of the withdrawal of the military sanction, although the French government say they are not yet prepared to discuss this, it is desirable to use the present opportunity to obtain its cancellation, if possible. The tactics of this policy are discussed in paragraphs 8 and 10 below. In any case, the concession must be made conditional upon the completion of the execution of the military disarmament clauses.

6. The whole attitude revealed by the French in their note of the 14th February is, indeed, nothing new. It had been expected, and it had been felt that it would be necessary and possible to resist it. An important concession has already been made to the French government by the British acceptance of permanent control inside Germany. The ambassadors' decision of the 2nd February, 1922 [*sic*][10] (automatically liquidating the existing aeronautical control on the 5th May, 1922), has produced a situation in which further concessions, in addition to being undesirable, are for the moment unnecessary. Advantage can now be taken of the fact that, failing agreement between the allies, air control in Germany will automatically lapse after the 5th May, 1922. The future of air and military control and the question of the military sanction can perhaps, therefore, now be settled—as we have urged during the last six months—as a whole.

7. The allies, it is true, can no longer very effectively use the removal of the existing system of aeronautical control and the right of resumption of the manufacture of civil aircraft as inducements to the German government to accept the new system of aeronautical and military control. On the other hand, the French government have now, as is evident from their memorandum of the 14th February, a strong motive for agreeing to an early settlement of the future organisation of air control, at least. May not that motive have an even wider effect? May it not, since the French government are understood to have special anxieties about the air question, facilitate

[10] This decision was reached on February 1 (see No. 169).

agreement between them and His Majesty's government respecting the future organisation of military control also? If so, the best way of dealing with the French note at the Ambassadors' Conference will be to agree that it is desirable to settle the future organisation of air control without delay. As regards its form, the British scheme, as outlined below, should be recommended, and the discussion should be led to the point where it becomes evident that no scheme can be imposed upon the German government, and that their acceptance of any scheme without some *quid pro quo* is improbable.

8. Once the situation is seen in that light, it should be possible to suggest that the British scheme (which represents a considerable concession to the French point of view) might, as regards control of land as well as air armament, be recommended to the German government by an offer to cancel the 'military sanction'. Should the French government continue to recoil from a comprehensive solution of this kind, we shall only have to remain inactive, to expose them to a pressure, which should operate with rapidly-increasing force—that of time. For no organisation of air control in the future is possible without the co-operation of His Majesty's government, and agreement as to air control is now felt by the French government to be a matter of practical urgency.

9. In these circumstances, proposals on the following lines should be submitted to the conference by the British representative.

(a) The conference to be asked to accept the new British scheme of aeronautical and military control comprising:—

   (i) The acceptance by the German government of the establishment at Berlin of inter-allied aeronautical and military missions of guarantee organised in the manner and with the powers outlined in annexes 1 and 2 below.[11]

   (ii) The recognition by the German government of the right of the allied governments at any time immediately to reinforce the missions of guarantee for the purpose of conducting a specific enquiry or a specific purpose. This right could, however, only be exercised upon the joint request of the allied governments, and the period of such reinforcement, together with its extent, would be notified to the German government by the allied governments concurrently with the notification of their intention to exercise this right.

   (iii) The charging of the whole cost of the military and aeronautical missions of guarantee to the allied governments.

   (iv) The limitation of the period of acceptance by the German government of the military and aeronautical missions of guarantee to the period of occupation of the Cologne bridgehead, when the whole matter will again come under review, and the question of the possibility of reliance on article 213 of the treaty of Versailles will be considered.

[11] Not printed. For the scheme communicated by the British Embassy in Paris to the Conference of Ambassadors on March 1, 1922, see No. 179, below, Enclosure 2.

(b) The conference to be asked to accept the British proposal to notify the German government that the allied governments will, upon the completion of the work of the existing naval commission of control, be content to rely in the matter of control of naval armament in Germany upon the guarantees afforded them by article 213.

(c) The Ambassadors' Conference to be asked to accept the British proposal to issue immediate instructions to the existing naval and military commissions of control, to state in detail their remaining work and to estimate the exact time required for its execution (such estimates being of course dependent upon the co-operation of the German government). These statements and estimates to be communicated to the German government with the further notification in the following sub-paragraph (d).

(d) The conference to be asked to notify the German government that, in return for their acceptance as a pledge of good faith of the military and aeronautical missions of guarantee (outlined in section (a) above), the allied governments will be prepared to withdraw the military sanction immediately upon the completion of the acts specified in (c) above.

10. This last proposal will evidently be opposed by the French government. In that event it will be for consideration whether an attempt should not be made to recommend it by stiffening the conditions which the Germans are to satisfy before the military sanction can be withdrawn. The French may possibly suggest, as possible conditions, prior acceptance of the forthcoming allied arrangements respecting 1922 reparation payments, and compliance with any demands the allied governments may decide to make as regards war criminals. But such a suggestion would raise difficult questions of policy. Any proposal to link the cancellation of the military sanction with questions of reparation or war criminals will require reference to London before it can be discussed.

No. 173

The Marquess Curzon of Kedleston to Baron Moncheur
[C 2426/483/18]

FOREIGN OFFICE, *February 23, 1922*

Your Excellency,

With reference to your note No. 675 of the 17th instant,[1] I have the honour to inform Your Excellency that the German Ambassador addressed to me on January 6th last a protest,[1] apparently similar to that which has been received by the Belgian government, against the action of the French military authorities in the occupied territory of Germany in requisitioning land for the establishment of a military training ground.

2. His Majesty's Government see no reason to intervene in this matter either by questioning the opinion of the French authorities that the occupation

---

[1] Not printed.

of the land in question is a military necessity, or by reviewing the inter-pretation placed by the Inter-Allied Rhineland High Commission on article 8 (b) of the Rhineland agreement to which the German government object. The matter appears to be one that concerns the local military and civil authorities exclusively, and no reply has accordingly been returned to Monsieur Sthamer's above-mentioned communication.

I have, etc.,
(In the absence of the Secretary of State)
S. P. WATERLOW

No. 174

Lord Hardinge (Paris) to Sir E. Crowe (Received March 1)

[*C 3037/6/18*]

PARIS, *February 24, 1922*

My dear Crowe,

I have been shown by Sackville-West[1] the letter which the War Office wrote to the Foreign Office on the 17th February,[2] respecting the future of control in Germany. This letter is so misleading, not to say pernicious, that I feel bound to make a few remarks on it.

The burden of the War Office's argument is that as the French Government have been reasonable enough to agree to wind up the Aeronautical Com-mission of Control on May 5th,[3] and are naturally anxious to settle the form of future control before that date, we ought at once to take advantage of this fact to compel them to settle at the same time the question of military control on our lines. This seems to me rather a dirty game to play. But apart from that, do we really, any more than the French, wish at the present moment to negotiate with the German Government for the withdrawal of the Military Commission of Control? The daily discoveries of hidden arms in Germany make the moment most unsuitable and I take it that even the War Office do not contemplate removing the Commission of Control so long as the present unsatisfactory state of affairs continues. If so, why give the German Government, and German public opinion, the idea that we are preparing to do so?

The War Office go on to argue that if the future military control is dealt with by itself later on, the French will never agree to the withdrawal of military sanctions being offered to Germany in exchange for her consent to a permanent control, and that, even if the French did agree, Germany on her part will reject any *quid pro quo* we may offer, as she will have no inducement to get rid of the present Commission of Control.

As for the first argument I would refer the War Office to the French memorandum enclosed in my despatch No. 403,[4] which shows that the French do not refuse to consider the withdrawal of the sanctions in connection

---

[1] Major-General Hon. Sir Charles Sackville-West was British representative on the Allied Military Committee of Versailles and Military Attaché to H.M. Embassy at Paris.
[2] Not printed.　　　　[3] See Nos. 169 and 172.　　　　[4] See No. 172, n. 3.

with the withdrawal of the Military Commission of Control. Of course we may disagree as to when the moment will have arrived to carry out these two withdrawals but this is a risk which we must face. Its existence does not justify our treating the whole of the question of control in the huckstering spirit recommended by the War Office.

As for the argument that the Germans would have no inducement to get rid of the Military Commission of Control, I cannot conceive Germany wishing to keep the present commission a moment longer than she need, and there is every indication that the German Government are most anxious to be rid of them. The inducement on which the War Office pin their faith, namely that she won't be able to begin the manufacture of civil aircraft until she has agreed to the new forms of Control, is a myth, as the German Government have, whatever happens, the right to begin the manufacture of civil aircraft three months after the aeronautical clauses of the Treaty have been declared to be completed, that is to say three months from 5th February. Consequently the whole of the structure upon which the War Office argument is based falls to the ground.

I sympathise with the desire of the War Office that the whole question should be referred to His Majesty's Government for settlement. No doubt it would be a much more satisfactory method, but unfortunately we can't eliminate our allies and the question must, alas, be dealt with by some Inter-allied body, either the Supreme Council or the Conference of Ambassadors.[5]

Ever yours,
HARDINGE OF P[ENSHURST]

[5] In a private letter of February 28, 1922, Sir E. Crowe replied: 'Your letter of February 24th seems to have crossed our despatch No. 535 [No. 172]. That despatch and the telegram [No. 176, below] which we are sending in reply to your telegram of February 25th [No. 175, below] have probably cleared up most of the difficulties which you found in the War Office arguments as to what our policy should be in dealing with the future of disarmament control in Germany.'

No. 175

Lord Hardinge (Paris) to the Marquess Curzon of Kedleston
(Received February 26, 8.30 a.m.)

No. 105 Telegraphic [C 2830/6/18]

Urgent   PARIS, *February 25, 1922, 7.50 p.m.*
Your despatch 535.[1]

I will put forward Your Lordship's proposals at meeting of conference of ambassadors on March 1st, but am not sanguine of an amicable settlement on the lines laid down in your despatch. French government and French public opinion will bitterly resent any attempt to tie them down at present moment to policy of withdrawing military sanctions, and if I succeed in

[1] No. 172.

doing so it will, I am afraid, be done not by persuading them that allies must buy German consent to establishment of future air control, but by exploiting their anxiety to get this future air control settled before the summer. Public opinion will not be slow to accuse His Majesty's Government of taking an unfair advantage of concessions made by France in agreeing to withdrawal of aeronautical control; and if the impression gets about that French government have been tricked, the irritation against His Majesty's Government will be intense.

When I advocate immediate opening of negotiations with German government for ultimate withdrawal of military commission of control, French will insist that the moment is inopportune, in view of recent discoveries of hidden arms in Germany, and will argue that it would be more suitable to tell German government that this evidence of bad faith and ill-will makes it impossible to contemplate withdrawal of commission of control. Is it, in face of these facts, considered desirable to take action for . . .,[2] and to encourage Germany in the hope of the early withdrawal of commission of control, and thereby incur the resentment and hostility of France and the French government at a moment when we are endeavouring to come to a friendly agreement with them on other matters of grave political importance? I may remind Your Lordship that disarmament of Germany is a subject on which French are particularly sensitive, and not without reason.

[2] The text is here uncertain.

No. 176

The Marquess Curzon of Kedleston to Lord Hardinge (Paris)
No. 75 Telegraphic: by bag [C 2830/6/18]

Urgent   FOREIGN OFFICE, *February 28, 1922*

Your unnumbered [*sic*] telegram of February 25th[1] and your telegram No. 110 (of February 26th. German disarmament control).[2]

Object we are primarily anxious to secure is simultaneous and connected settlement of future organisations for control of land, air and naval armaments. My despatch No. 535[3] is designed to supply Your Excellency with materials for reaching a comprehensive agreement as to the form those organisations should take and as to the method of inducing German government to accept them.

A subsidiary aim is the cancellation of the military sanction, for the continuance of which after German acceptance of the ultimatum of May 5th, 1921,[4] you will remember that there has never been, in the opinion of His Majesty's Government, any justification. If, therefore, our agreement to a settlement as to the future of the control organisations can be used to attain this end also, so much the better. Precise date when sanction should lapse

[1] No. 175.   [2] Not preserved in the Foreign Office archives.
[3] No. 172.   [4] See Vol. XV, No. 85, Appendix 2.

would, on the argument of my despatch No. 535, be matter for agreement between Allied governments and German government. We do not contemplate that a date should be fixed prior to date upon which work of military and naval commissions is notified to be complete. Probably it should be simultaneous with, or not much later than, that date.

I fully realise that recent evidences of German bad faith and ill-will make it difficult for the Allied governments to hold out to the German government the prospect of an early withdrawal of the military control commission. But it is not clear that this fact necessarily increases the difficulty either (1) of reaching inter-allied agreement as to the form that future control is to take when the commission's work is complete, or (2) of obtaining now German acceptance of such modified form of control. It must always be remembered that the continuance of any form of control, after the date accepted as that upon which the disarmament clauses have been executed, must be accepted by, and cannot be imposed upon, the German government. If this is borne in mind, the policy explained in my despatch No. 535 should even be facilitated by the present unfavourable conditions emphasised by Your Excellency. For those conditions justify the Allied governments in addressing a strong remonstrance to the German government, the effect of which, if coupled with an announcement of the modified form of control that they may expect when, and not until when, they have mended their ways, should both expedite the work of disarmament and incline the German government to accept the proposed post-disarmament control.

If, in order to bring them to the latter point, it should prove necessary to offer to them the withdrawal of the military sanction, surely none but the grossest misrepresentation could describe the policy of my despatch No. 535 as an attempt to tie the French government down at the present moment to the withdrawal of the military sanction.

No. 177

The Marquess Curzon of Kedleston to Lord Hardinge (Paris)
No. 603 [C 2697/6/18]

FOREIGN OFFICE, *February 28, 1922*

My Lord,

I transmit to Your Excellency herewith copy of a letter from the War Office[1] asking that strong representations may be made to the German government to remove forthwith the existing obstructions that are being offered to the work of the Military Control Commission in Germany.

2. Effect has already been given to this proposal by the general instructions conveyed to Your Excellency in my telegram No. 75 of the 28th Feb[ruary].[2] You should, however, make clear that, so far as His Majesty's Government

---

[1] Of February 22, not printed.   [2] No. 176.

are concerned, the existing system of control cannot be modified until the work of the Military Commission has been effectively carried out.[3]

3. His Majesty's Ambassador at Berlin is being instructed to address a communication on these lines to the German government.[4] It would be well so to inform the French government.

I am, etc.,

CURZON OF KEDLESTON

[3] In a letter of March 11 to the Foreign Office, the War Office, referring to their letter of February 22 (see n. 1) and to a further report by General Nollet, stated: '... as the reductions carried out in the Inter-Allied Military Commission of Control in the last few months have merely had the effect of encouraging the Germans to obstruct and procrastinate, seemingly in the hope that the commission will be withdrawn before the military clauses of the Peace Treaty can be fully executed, the Army Council cannot recommend any further reductions in the Inter-Allied Military Commission of Control in Germany until the Germans, by their actions and spirit, show a better inclination than at present to carry out the Allies' demands.'

[4] Despatch No. 228 of March 1 (C 2697/6/18), not printed.

No. 178

Lord Hardinge (Paris) to the Marquess Curzon of Kedleston
(Received March 3, 8.30 a.m.)

No. 117 Telegraphic: by bag [C 3131/602/18, C 3132/6/18]

PARIS, *March 1, 1922*

The Conference of Ambassadors met this morning under the chairmanship of M. Jules Cambon, the Belgian ambassador being also present, and considered the following questions:—

...[1]3. The question of handing over to Germany a partially constructed light cruiser to be embodied in the new German Navy, again appeared on the Agenda (see my telegram No. 18, section 4).[2] I stated again the point of view of His Majesty's Government, to which the French again objected. Among other things they argued that this concession would constitute a precedent and lead to further applications from the German Government. The Italian Ambassador supported the French, and the Japanese Ambassador merely said that he would agree to the concession if desired by the Conference. No real attempt was made to reach a settlement and the question was again adjourned. I should be glad to know how far Your Lordship desires me to press for a decision, or whether I am to leave the initiative to my French and Italian colleagues.

4. I submitted to the Conference the views of His Majesty's Government with regard to the future system of control to be established in Germany as set forth in Your Lordship's despatch No. 535.[3] I enclose in my despatch No. 532 of today's date[4] the text of the statement which I made. I also

[1] The sections omitted referred to other matters.   [2] No. 166.   [3] No. 172.
[4] No. 179, below.

388

communicated to the Conference the substance of Your Lordship's telegram No. 75,[5] and of Your Lordship's despatch No. 603 of February 28th.[6] I likewise submitted a scheme defining the constitution, functions and rights of the proposed aeronautical and military Missions of Guarantee, and asked that it should be considered by the Allied Military Committee of Versailles, which was agreed to. This scheme, which is likewise enclosed in my despatch No. 532, embodies the text of Annex 2 to enclosure 1 of Your Lordship's despatch No. 535 of February 22nd, but as regards the aeronautical Mission of Guarantee, I substituted for the proposals contained in Annex 1 to Enclosure 1 of above despatch a revised version drawn up by my Aeronautical Adviser,[7] after consultation with the Air Ministry.

I endeavoured as far as possible to direct the discussion to the main point, namely the desire of His Majesty's Government to treat the three forms of control simultaneously. M. Cambon, however, refused to commit himself, and requested that the question should be adjourned to enable the Conference to obtain the views of the Allied Governments. The French attempted to argue again, with the assistance of M. Fromageot, that the consent of the German Government was not required to set up the proposed aeronautical Mission of Guarantee. I reaffirmed the views held on the subject by His Majesty's Government as set forth in Your Lordship's despatch No. 2796 of October 29th, 1921,[8] but urged that the simplest manner of getting round this divergence of opinion would be by dealing with the three questions simultaneously, and by offering the German Government the withdrawal of the sanctions without specifying that this concession was in return for the establishment of one Mission of Guarantee rather than the other. The French did not enter into a discussion as regards using the military sanctions in order to obtain the German Government's consent, but I took the opportunity of pointing out that strictly speaking the German Government were justified in arguing that the military sanctions ought to have been withdrawn as soon as the London Ultimatum[9] had been accepted. The other members of the Conference took practically no part in the discussion.

It appears to me now that the best course for this Embassy to pursue in relation to this question is to await the next move on the part of the French Government, while doing all that is possible to obtain the concurrence of the Versailles Committee with the two technical schemes of control put forward this morning. . . .[1]

[5] No. 176.   [6] No. 177.
[7] Group Captain Hearson succeeded Group Captain Groves as a member of the Inter-Allied Military Committee of Versailles on February 3, 1922.
[8] Vol. XVI, No. 835.
[9] See Vol. XV, No. 85, Appendix 2.

No. 179

Lord Hardinge (Paris) to the Marquess Curzon of Kedleston
(Received March 2)
No. 532 [C 3079/6/18]

PARIS, *March 1, 1922*

Lord Hardinge of Penshurst presents his compliments to the Secretary of State for Foreign Affairs, and has the honour to transmit herewith copies of a statement made at the Conference of Ambassadors on the 1st March, 1922, and of a scheme submitted by the British Embassy respecting the future system of control to be established in Germany.

ENCLOSURE 1 IN No. 179

Statement by Lord Hardinge at the Conference of Ambassadors, March 1, 1922

On the last occasion that this question was on the agenda I was compelled to ask for it to be adjourned,[1] as I wished to obtain instructions from my Government on the fresh proposals made in the French memorandum.[2] I regret this delay, but I would remind my colleagues that I submitted a definite scheme as far back as the 26th November,[3] and if it has not been discussed by the Conference of Ambassadors till now, it is chiefly because the French Government asked that it should be taken off the agenda.

I am pleased to say that an examination of the memorandum presented by the French Government to the Conference of Ambassadors on the 14th February[2] regarding the future of military, aeronautical and naval control in Germany shows that the British and French Governments are in general agreement on the policy to be adopted.

My Government agree that there is no need for the creation of a 'main body' established in Allied or occupied territory. They also agree to the inspection by the bodies to be established in Germany of naval constructions on the occasions indicated in the French memorandum. In order that there may be no doubt as to the general scheme which the Allied Governments propose to establish, I desire to submit to the conference a statement defining the constitution, functions and rights of the bodies to be set up in Berlin (which the British Government propose to name 'Missions of Guarantee'). My Government consider that the maintenance of these Missions of Guarantee should coincide with the period of the occupation of the Cologne bridgehead, at the end of which the question of their continuance will be considered. The Allied Governments have the right to reinforce them when need arises. But in such cases the Conference of Ambassadors should notify the German Government in advance, and specify the extent and duration of the reinforcements.

[1] This was reported by Lord Hardinge in his telegram No. 99 of February 22, not printed.
[2] See No. 172, n. 3.
[3] See Vol. XVI, No. 845.

There appear, however, to be two points on which there is still a divergence of opinion:—

1. The French Government wish to deal with the question of aeronautical control separately from that of military and naval control, whereas the British Government have proposed, and still maintain, that the whole question of future control must be treated as a whole and simultaneously, and that the agreement to be made between the Allied Governments and the German Government for instituting the proposed scheme must cover all three forms of control. The British Government trust that the French Government, appreciating the difficulties and dangers of treating this question piecemeal, will agree with this point of view. There ought to be no difficulty in making it abundantly clear to the German Government that these preparations for the eventual withdrawal of the Military Commission of Control do not imply in any way the condonation of the unsatisfactory progress which is at present being made in German disarmament. On the other hand, the prospect of being able, by the prompt and loyal execution of the military clauses, to procure the early withdrawal both of the Commission of Control and of the military sanctions will act as an incentive to the German Government and people to co-operate vigorously with the Commission of Control in bringing its work to a satisfactory and complete conclusion.

2. The French Government still hold that the consent of the German Government need not be obtained in order to set up a system of aeronautical control in Germany after the withdrawal of the present Commission of Control. For the reasons given in the British Embassy's memorandum of the 26th November,[4] the British Government cannot subscribe to this view. If, however, the question of control is dealt with as a whole and simultaneously this divergence of opinion will lose its importance, since it is generally recognised that the German Government's consent will have to be obtained in order to apply the proposed scheme in the case of military control (and of the occasional naval control desired by the French Government), and that some concession will have to be made to the German Government in order to obtain their consent. The British Government have proposed that this concession should take the form of the withdrawal of the military sanctions. The British Government fully appreciate the objections of the French Government to an immediate withdrawal of the military sanctions, but it is understood that the proposed concession would only require the withdrawal of the sanctions if and when the German Government had, by their loyal co-operation, executed the military clauses of the treaty in such a way as to render possible the withdrawal of the Commission of Control.

I trust therefore that the conference will deal with this question as a whole, and that they will agree to make use of the military sanctions in order to

4 Not traced in the Foreign Office archives. See, however, Vol. XVI, No. 835, Enclosure I.

obtain the consent of the German Government to the whole system of future control.

ENCLOSURE 2 IN NO. 179

Scheme Proposed by the British Embassy and communicated to the Conference of Ambassadors on March 1, 1922

CONSTITUTION, FUNCTIONS AND RIGHTS OF THE PROPOSED
MISSIONS OF GUARANTEE

Aeronautical Mission of Guarantee

(An Allied Aeronautical 'Mission of Guarantee' to be located in Germany, operating from a headquarters in Berlin.)

(a) *Constitution*

1. This mission to consist of—

British	..	1 senior officer as president and 2 other officers and 2 clerks.
French	..	2 officers and 2 clerks.
Italian	..	2 officers and 2 clerks.
Japanese	..	2 officers and 2 clerks.
Belgian	..	2 officers and 2 clerks.

(*Note.*—The above assumes that the president will be British as it is understood that the Military Commission of Guarantee will be under the presidency of a French officer.)

2. The intelligence services of the Powers represented will forward to the president of the mission all information relevant to the duties of the mission. Such information will then be pooled within the body of the mission.

3. The mission will not maintain any secret intelligence service of its own, but the Allied Governments will arrange for certain funds to be available for payments to informants by results.

4. The mission shall take its decisions by vote, on the basis of one vote for each of the five Powers represented on it. At the discretion of the president, action may be taken on a majority vote, but in all cases where there is not a unanimous vote a report must be made to the C[omité] M[ilitaire] A[llié] [de] V[ersailles] setting out the point at issue, the majority and minority opinions, and any action taken.

(b) *Finance*

The pay and allowances of all ranks of the mission to be borne by the respective Governments. The scale of allowances to be estimated by the Conference of Ambassadors. Other expenses, such as hire of buildings, stationery, travelling allowances, transport, &c., to be borne by a common fund provided by the various Governments in equal shares.

(c) *Duties and Powers*

1. The supervision of German aeronautical activities, in order to assure to the Allied Governments that article 198 of the Treaty of Versailles and the eight rules defining the difference between war and commercial aircraft are being loyally observed. Questions relative to article 202 of the Treaty of Versailles not to be dealt with, as the Conference of Ambassadors has declared this article to have been completely accomplished (see note (A) at end).

2. The president or his representative to address the German Government direct.

3. The mission, or any deputed member or members of it, to be empowered to proceed to any part of German territory at any time and for any period which may appear advisable to the president.

4. The mission, or any deputed member or members of it, to have the right, on the written authority of the president, to visit and inspect any factory, aircraft establishment, or any works capable of being utilised for the manufacture, storage or sale of aircraft material.

5. The mission to take its orders from and report to the C[omité] M[ilitaire] A[llié] [de] V[ersailles], or such other authority as the principal Allied Governments may hereafter appoint.

(d) *Date of Establishment and Duration*

The mission to reach Berlin on the 21st April, 1922; to commence to function on the 5th May, 1922, and continue to do so until the withdrawal from the Cologne bridgehead, at which date the question to be the subject of further review.

(e) *Additional Expert Inspection*

Subject to the sanction of the Conference of Ambassadors in each instance, on advice of the C[omité] M[ilitaire] A[llié] [de] [Versailles], the mission to have the assistance of additional inspection by not more than four experts at any one time from each Allied country. The duration of such inspections and the number of experts to be determined by the Conference of Ambassadors on advice of C[omité] M[ilitaire] A[llié] [de] V[ersailles]. These additional expert inspections, together with a statement as to their extent and duration, are to be notified to the German Government in advance. The experts are to be drawn from personnel normally employed on other duties.

(f) *Requirements from the German Government*

1. To recognise officially the 'Mission of Guarantee' on the departure of the I[nter-] A[llied] A[eronautical] C[ommission] [of] C[ontrol] from Berlin.

2. To designate an authority which shall represent the German Government *vis-à-vis* the commission.

3. To supply the president with passports or other written authority and with all such information and permits as he may consider necessary to carry out the duties as above defined.

4. To guarantee the unmolested and untrammelled accomplishment of the additional expert inspections detailed under (e) above.

5. To ensure suitable accommodation for the mission.

6. To grant to the headquarters buildings of the mission a diplomatic status.

7. To provide, when called upon to do so, a liaison officer to accompany mission personnel carrying out inspections.

Note (A)—The Mission of Guarantee to be invested with the powers of the late I[nter-] A[llied] A[eronautical] C[ommission] [of] C[ontrol] under article 202 of the Treaty of Versailles in so far as concerns the destruction in due course of the Zeppelin shed at Friedrichshafen[5] and the disposal of the extra personnel employed on the construction of the American Zeppelin.[6]

Military Mission of Guarantee

(a) *Officers*

	Colonels or Lieut-Colonels	Majors or Captains	Total
French officers . . .	3*	4	7†
British officers . . .	2	2	4†
Italian officers . . .	2	I	3
Japanese officers . . .	2	I	3
Belgian officers . . .	2	I	3
Total . . .	..	..	20

* Including one general officer, president of the mission.

† The preponderance of French as compared with British officers is accounted for by the assumption that the presidency of the mission will remain in French hands.

(b) *Other Ranks*

	French	British	Italian	Japanese	Belgian
Military clerks	4	2	2	2	2
Orderlies	4	3	2	2	2
M[otor] T[ransport] drivers .	2	I	I	I	I

Notes—(1) This establishment allows of the following division of duties in the manner shown, thus utilising to the best advantage the experience gained by individual officers employed with the present Commission of Control:—

[5] See Vol. XVI, No. 843, Enclosure.
[6] Ibid., Nos. 832 and 853.

Nationality (1)	Headquarters (2)	Senior Officers for Study of 'Effectives' Questions (3)	Senior Officers for Study of 'Armament' Questions (4)	Junior Officers to assist or replace Officers in columns 3 and 4 as required (5)
French . .	3‡	1	1	2
British . .	1§	1	1	1
Italian . .	..	1	1	1
Japanese . .	..	1	1	1
Belgian . .	..	1	1	1
Total . .	4	5	5	6

‡ One general officer; one 'chef de cabinet', secretary to the mission; one A[ide] D[e] C[amp].
§ Assistant or joint secretary to the mission.

No more than 50 per cent. of the officers comprising the Mission of Guarantee should, at the beginning, consist of officers of the present Military Control Commission. Within three months these 50 per cent. must have been replaced by officers who have taken no part in the Military Control Commission in Germany.

(2) This establishment also allows of the simultaneous formation of two visiting missions, comprising representatives of all the Powers concerned, or of several smaller parties, if desired, while leaving a fully representative body at headquarters.

Procedure, &c.

(a) The object of the mission is to afford a guarantee to the Allied Powers that the military clauses of the Treaty of Versailles are being faithfully observed. The mission shall have the right to address such communications to the German authorities as the execution or continued enforcement of the military clauses may necessitate.

Any question, however, of a political character shall be referred to the Allied Governments through the established channels.

(b) The Mission of Guarantee shall establish itself at the seat of the central German Government, who will be responsible for ensuring suitable accommodation.

The headquarter building in Berlin must be granted diplomatic status.

(c) The mission shall be entitled, as often as it may think desirable, to proceed to any point whatever in German territory, or to send sub-commissions, or to authorise one or more of its members to go to any point, and shall be granted written authority by the German Government to cover all such journeys and the legitimate purposes of the mission.

(d) The mission or any of its members shall have the right to visit and inspect any arsenal, military establishment or factory capable of being utilised for the manufacture, preparation, storage or deposits of arms, munitions or war material of any kind, or to carry out such inspections as may be considered necessary for the control of the effectives and armament of the German military and police forces, and any unauthorised organisations which are alleged to be of a military character, so long as accompanied by the representative of the German Government as mentioned in paragraph (e) below.

(e) The German Government must give all necessary facilities for the accomplishment of its duties to the Mission of Guarantee and its members.

It shall attach a qualified representative to the Mission of Guarantee for the purpose of receiving the communications which the mission may have to address to any German authorities, and of supplying or procuring for the mission all information or documents which it may require. It shall attach a liaison officer, when required, to any visiting sub-commission.

The upkeep and cost of the various delegations comprising the Mission of Guarantee shall be borne by the Governments concerned. Any duly authorised incidental expenses involved by the work of the mission as a whole shall be borne in equal shares by the Powers represented on the mission.

Constitution

(a) The intelligence services of the War Offices of the Powers represented will forward to the chiefs of the Allied delegations on the missions all information relevant to the duties of the mission. Such information will then be pooled within the body of the mission.

(b) The mission will not maintain any secret intelligence service of its own, but the Allied Governments will arrange for certain funds to be available for payments to informers by results.

(c) So far as possible, no visiting party will consist of less than three officers, each representing a separate nation.

(d) The mission shall take its decisions by vote, on the basis of one vote for each of the five Powers represented on it. At the discretion of the president, action may be taken on a majority vote, but, in all cases where there is not a unanimous vote, a report must be made to the Ambassadors' Conference setting out the point at issue, the majority and minority opinions and any action taken.

(e) The mission will address its reports to such authority as the principal Allied Governments may hereafter designate.

No. 180

Lord Hardinge (Paris) to the Marquess Curzon of Kedleston
(Received March 6, 8.30 a.m.)

No. 127 Telegraphic: by bag [C 3207/6/18]

PARIS, *March 4, 1922*

The Conference of Ambassadors met this afternoon under the presidency of M. Jules Cambon, a representative of the Belgian ambassador being also present, and considered the following questions:–

1. M. Cambon communicated the views of his government with regard to the proposals I had made at the last meeting on the subject of future control in Germany.[1] He agreed, on behalf of his government, that the three forms of control shall be dealt with simultaneously. On the other hand, the French government declined to link the question of military sanctions with that of future control. The military sanctions had, so M. Cambon argued, been intended to guarantee the execution of a whole series of obligations undertaken by Germany and not merely those relating to disarmament. For this reason it would be very dangerous to take up the question of the eventual withdrawal of these sanctions at a time when Germany on so many points has failed to carry out her undertakings and when it therefore would be unwise for the allied governments to deprive themselves of this means of bringing pressure to bear on Germany to carry out the undertakings to which she prescribed in the ultimatum of May last year.[2] Moreover, it would be injudicious to inform the German government in advance that the allies were prepared to give up the military sanctions in certain circumstances, before knowing whether the German government are going to accept the principle of the missions of guarantee. It is for the German government rather in the first instance to say whether they have any objection to the establishment of these missions, and for the allies then to negotiate with them. M. Cambon made no reference to the French point of view that the allied governments can impose the aeronautical mission of guarantee without the consent of the German government.

In replying to M. Cambon I welcome the decision of the French government to treat the three questions simultaneously. I have no doubt that this concession has been made easier by the fact that I was at the last meeting, thanks to Your Lordship's despatch No. 603,[3] able to reassure them as to the determination of His Majesty's Government to insist upon the strict and complete execution of the military clauses of the treaty of Versailles.

I went on to express regret that the French government did not see their way to present the German government with a complete scheme such as would include a counter concession in return for their agreement to the constitution of the proposed missions of guarantee. I feared that this omission might lead to protracted negotiations and I warned the conference that should these negotiations be still incomplete by the 5th May, my government would certainly not agree to the establishment of the proposed aeronautical mission of guarantee on that date without the express consent of the German government. In these circumstances I trusted that the French government would not refuse to reconsider my proposal to offer straight away, as compensation to the German government, the eventual withdrawal of the military sanctions. If the French government could not accept this suggestion, I was afraid my government would be somewhat disappointed. It would be felt that the British government had made important concessions to meet the French point of view by accepting their proposal to establish a system of

[1] See Nos. 178 and 179. [2] See Vol. XV, No. 85, Appendix 2.
[3] No. 177.

allied control in Berlin although there is nothing to this effect in the treaty of Versailles. In return the British government had expected that the French government would respond by agreeing once and for all as to the concession on which the military sanctions would be withdrawn. As is well known, the British government have always held that after the acceptance by the German government of the ultimatum of last May,[2] the maintenance of the military sanctions was no longer justified, and if the British government have not insisted upon this point of view, it has been out of deference to the wishes of the French government who desired to retain provisionally this means of pressure. All the same, at the Supreme Council last August, the French government undertook to discuss at the next meeting the withdrawal of the military sanctions,[4] and I should much regret if my government were now to have the impression that the French government were trying to avoid this discussion.

As M. Cambon held out no hope of the French government reconsidering their decision in the light of my remarks, and as I received no support from the other members of the conference, I agreed in principle that the scheme of the missions of guarantee should be communicated to the German government without being accompanied by any offer of a *quid pro quo*, thus leaving it to the German government to make their own proposals on this head.

In the meanwhile the allied military committee of Versailles are to be asked to complete as quickly as possible their examination of the scheme for the constitution and functions of the two missions of guarantee, which I submitted at the last meeting.[1] I understand that an agreed scheme is in process of elaboration, which is practically identical with that sent to me by Your Lordship. On only two points is there likely to be a serious departure from the scheme: (1) on authority from the Air Ministry, my aeronautical adviser has agreed to a modified form of rule 9[5] for distinguishing between civil and military aircraft; and (2) Marshal Foch objects to making the duration of the missions of guarantee coincide with the occupation of the Cologne bridgehead, on the ground that there is no connection between the two. On the other hand, he is quite prepared to fix a definite date on which the further continuance of the missions of guarantee shall be considered. As there is, I believe, disagreement between the French and British governments as to the date from which the five years' occupation of the Cologne bridgehead is to run, it would perhaps on the whole be preferable to take a date on which there is no such uncertainty. I shall be glad to have your Lordship's views on this point. . . .[6]

[4] See Vol. XV, pp. 745–6.
[5] See ibid., No. 95, minute 2. See also Vol. XVI, Nos. 838 and 842.
[6] The sections omitted referred to other matters.

No. 181

Lord D'Abernon (Berlin) to the Marquess Curzon of Kedleston
(Received March 7, 10 p.m.)

No. 63 Telegraphic [C 3414/6/18]

BERLIN, *March 7, 1922, 7.50 p.m.*

Lord Hardinge's telegram No. 6 of March 3rd.[1]

Meeting was held today at which French, Italian and Japanese ambassadors were present with myself and Belgian chargé d'affaires.

We agreed upon text of a communication to German government concerning complete execution of disarmament. Only difference of opinion was concerning first sentence. French draft proposed following:–

'Conference of ambassadors has noted during last months that the German authorities have adopted towards inter-allied military commission of control an attitude of obstruction notably on following points.'

I objected to this text as implying a general policy of obstruction on the part of German government which in my opinion does not exist.

I proposed therefore to read '*certain* German authorities' instead of '*the* German authorities'. Italian and Japanese ambassadors supported me. French ambassador said he could not accept modification without reference to Paris. Belgian chargé d'affaires took no part in the discussion.[2]

Repeated to Paris.

[1] This telegram to Berlin repeated Paris telegram No. 125 of March 3 to the Foreign Office (not printed) concurring in the view (see No. 177) that Lord D'Abernon, in concert with French and Italian representatives, should urge the German Government to remove obstructions being offered to the work of the Military Control Commission.

[2] In his telegram No. 20 of March 13, Lord Curzon replied: 'The difficulty seems one which you would do well to waive in view of the importance of acting with your French colleague on the present point.'

No. 182

Lord Hardinge (Paris) to the Marquess Curzon of Kedleston
(Received March 9, 8.30 a.m.)

No. 130 Telegraphic: by bag [C 3481/6/18]

PARIS, *March 7, 1922*

My telegram No. 127 of March 4th,[1] section 1.

At my interview today with the president of the council, he said he wished to speak to me on the subject of the military sanctions which had been discussed at the council of ministers held this morning. He said that public opinion in France would not tolerate for an instant the withdrawal of the sanctions in the near future, in view of the fact that, when they were imposed, it was in order to compel Germany to carry out her engagements in connection with war criminals, reparations and disarmament, all of which Germany

[1] No. 180.

had so far failed to fulfil. He reminded me that the trial and punishment of war criminals had been one of the planks in the electioneering programme of His Majesty's Government and no real satisfaction had been obtained so far,[2] nor was it likely that Germany would be more complaisant in this respect in the future. As for reparations, Germany had failed not only to pay the cost of the military occupation but also the sums due for reparations, while every day discoveries were being made of arms and war materials concealed in Germany and military formations, which are forbidden by treaty, were still in existence in that country. It would be quite impossible for the French government at the present time to discuss the fixing of any date for the withdrawal of the sanctions, in view of the fact that public opinion in France had already been greatly disturbed last May, when it was found that the occupation of the Ruhr was not to be permitted. The position of the allied troops in the three occupied towns[3] was in Monsieur Poincaré's opinion quite as useful as the occupation itself of the Ruhr, but there could be no question at the present time of the withdrawal of those troops.

I reminded Monsieur Poincaré that at the supreme council meeting of August last at which I happened by chance to have been present, Monsieur Briand had distinctly promised that the question would be brought up for further discussion at the next meeting of the supreme council.[4] Monsieur Poincaré replied that he had foreseen that I would raise this point and he had this morning asked Monsieur Barthou, who was a member of Monsieur Briand's cabinet, whether to his knowledge Monsieur Briand had ever contemplated such a withdrawal. Monsieur Barthou declared that Monsieur Briand had always declared to his cabinet that the withdrawal of the military sanctions was out of the question and could not possibly be accepted by the French Government. Monsieur Poincaré added that Monsieur Briand had used similar language before the foreign affairs commission at the senate and chamber of deputies.

I then asked the president of the council how it would be possible to induce the German Government to accept a new system of control if we had nothing to offer them. He replied that he considered there was plenty of room for discussion with the Germans since the establishment of a new control would be distinctly advantageous to them as being less costly than the existing controls, and although the substitution of the present controls in Germany had not been foreseen in the treaty of Versailles, the German Government could be reminded that there were other points such as the increase of the gendarmerie, etc. where concessions have been made to Germany that are not provided for in the treaty and if they are obdurate over the new controls they can be told that the allies will maintain the existing controls and will revert to the fulfilment of the treaty in other details by withdrawing the concessions they have already made. He assured me that he had gone very far to meet His Majesty's Government over the Genoa conference[5] and that he is being attacked in the press and amongst his party for doing so, but that

[2] See No. 170.   [3] Duisburg, Ruhrort and Düsseldorf (see Vol. XVI, No. 458).
[4] See Vol. XV, pp. 745–6.   [5] See Vol. XIX, Chap. III.

it would be quite impossible for him to make any concessions to His Majesty's Government at the present time as regards the withdrawal of the military sanctions.

As a matter of fact I am convinced in my own mind that the feeling in this country would be so strong over the withdrawal of the sanctions that no government would be able to withstand it.

No. 183

The Marquess Curzon of Kedleston to Lord Hardinge (Paris)
No. 85 Telegraphic: by bag [C 3207/6/18]

FOREIGN OFFICE, *March 8, 1922, 6 p.m.*

I cordially approve Your Excellency's handling of the German disarmament and control question, as reported in section 1 of your telegram No. 127 of March 4th.[1] In particular I agree that the right moment for pressing the cancellation of the military sanction further will probably not arrive until the German reply to the scheme for missions of guarantee gives a concrete opportunity for bargaining.

Marshal Foch's objection to making the duration of the missions of guarantee coincide with the occupation of the Cologne bridgehead is based on a somewhat surprising ground. Surely the connection between the two is real and close. The object with which Cologne is occupied, and that with which a form of control within Germany is to be prolonged, is one and the same— namely to secure the execution of the treaty as a guarantee against future aggression. It therefore seems only logical that the first stage in evacuating the Rhineland should be taken as the moment when the whole question of the missions of guarantee will be brought under review, especially as the evacuation of Cologne is, in its turn, dependent, by the terms of article 429 of the Treaty of Versailles, upon the faithful execution of the treaty.

As to the date from which the five years occupation of Cologne is to run, I am not aware of any disagreement between His Majesty's Government and the French Government. The wording of article 429 is perfectly precise: Cologne is to be evacuated on January 10th, 1925, 'if the conditions of the present treaty are faithfully carried out'. Possibly Your Excellency alludes to the view held, I believe, in some quarters, that the five years do not begin until the treaty has been executed. I should be reluctant to impute this view to the French government. The period prescribed by the treaty is indeterminate in so far as its end, being future and conditional, is uncertain. To read the treaty as implying that it is indeterminate in respect of its beginning also would be the height of paradox. The question, however, seems to have little bearing on that discussed in the preceding paragraph.

[1] No. 180.

No. 184

Lord Hardinge (Paris) to the Marquess Curzon of Kedleston
(Received March 10, 8.30 a.m.)
No. 135 Telegraphic: by bag [C 3527/6/18]

PARIS, *March 9, 1922*

Your telegram No. 85.[1]

If you will refer to my telegram No. 34 of the 19th January,[2] Your Lordship will observe that Monsieur Poincaré in his ministerial declaration to the chamber of deputies definitely stated as the view of the present French government that the period which will end with the evacuation of the Rhineland cannot be held to have begun until certain provisions of the Treaty of Versailles have been carried out. If therefore I am still to insist that the duration of the proposed missions of guarantees shall coincide with the occupation of the Cologne bridgehead, I think it right to warn Your Lordship that the French government do not consider that this bridgehead is to be evacuated on the 10th January 1925 even if at that date 'the conditions of the present treaty are faithfully carried out'.

[1] No. 183.   [2] Not printed.

No. 185

Mr. Post Wheeler[1] to the Marquess Curzon of Kedleston (Received March 13)
[C 3662/1229/18]

UNITED STATES EMBASSY, LONDON, *March 9, 1922*

My Lord,

I have the honour to transmit to your Lordship copies of two notes[2] which have been recently submitted to the Allied Military Committee of Versailles outlining the position of the Government of the United States on the questions of the evaluation and allocation of sums due by Germany in compensation for destroyed Zeppelins.[3] In transmitting these notes, my Government desires me to point out that, in addition to the absolute fairness of its claim as set forth in the accompanying communications, there is a further consideration involved to which it is desired that I call your Lordship's attention—namely, the distinct obligation that exists to compensate the Government of the United States for the share of the airships in Germany at the time of the signing of the armistice to which it was entitled, but which was instead apportioned among the Allies. An examination of the pertinent records fails to reveal any justification for this action. On the contrary, there is every indication that the ships in question were disposed of without the consent of

[1] Counsellor of the United States Embassy in London.   [2] Not printed.
[3] See Vol. XVI, Nos. 829 and 832.

ny Government, without any provisions being made for the replacement of his material, and in spite of the reservation of the American representative maintaining the rights of the American Government to participate in this distribution on the same basis as other Governments in accordance with the decision taken at H.D.–63, the 29th September, 1919.[4] It would thus appear reasonable that some adequate form of compensation to the Government of the United States should be provided by common understanding.

I am instructed to say that, under the circumstances, the arrangement which would be most acceptable to the Government of the United States, and apparently to the Allies, would be to allocate to the American Government a sufficient portion of the sum due from Germany under the protocol of the 30th June, 1921,[5] to cover the cost (approximately, 4,000,000 gold marks) of the Zeppelin which is about to be built[6] by Germany for the United States Government. In this connection, I have the honour to point out to your Lordship that the fulfilment of the request of the Government of the United States requires only that Germany's assessment be placed at a more adequate figure than that recently proposed by General Masterman's[7] Commission, and this the Allied Governments have full authority to do. In this way the obligation towards the United States Government can be discharged without any cost whatever to the Allies and, moreover, without imposing any obligation on the German Government which might be considered unfair or for which she is not fully responsible. The Government of the United States has so far refrained from bringing forward the consideration described in the preceding paragraph, as it is not believed that the Allies wish to deprive the United States Government of its fair share in this distribution or intend to dispute the equity of its present claim, but it is moved to do so at this juncture because it feels that this important consideration may possibly escape the attention of the various technical experts on the Committee of Versailles and on General Masterman's Commission, who are charged with the examination of this case.

I wish, therefore, to take this occasion to express to your Lordship the earnest expectation of the Government of the United States that, in view of the important considerations outlined herein, the Government of Great Britain will be disposed to examine this matter in a spirit of indulgence, and accordingly will favourably instruct its representative on the above-mentioned committee to support the request of the Government of the United States and thus arrive at a satisfactory and acceptable adjustment in the premises.

I have the honour to request your Lordship's early consideration of the above matter, with a view to enabling me to transmit a reply to my Government with the least delay possible.

I have, etc.,

POST WHEELER

[4] See Vol. I, No. 67, n. 4.   [5] See *F.R.U.S.* 1921, vol. ii, p. 59.
[6] See Vol. XVI, Nos. 832, 846, 847 and 853.
[7] Air Commodore E. A. Masterman (see No. 168, n. 2).

No. 186

Lord Hardinge (Paris) to the Marquess Curzon of Kedleston
(Received March 14, 8.30 a.m.)
No. 148 Telegraphic: by bag [C 3769/434/18]

PARIS, *March 13, 1922*

As reported in my telegram No. 117,[1] section 2,[2] of March 1st, conference of ambassadors decided that remaining Diesel engines should be placed at disposal of allies in occupied territory. Admiral Charlton,[3] who has been called to Paris to discuss procedure for carrying out this decision, sees not only technical but political difficulties in obtaining German cooperation for removal of engines. In fact he considers that it would arouse as much opposition as destruction of the engines and even suggests that military pressure might be required to enforce the decision. He therefore proposes further delay in settling this question, which will consequently make it impossible to fix date of withdrawal of naval commission of control.

As His Majesty's Government are I know particularly anxious for early withdrawal of naval commission, I hesitate to agree with Admiral Charlton's proposal, and would prefer that conference of ambassadors should abide by its decision to intern engines at once. Admiral Charlton's forebodings, however, have led foreign naval advisers to recommend further delay for conversion and installation for commercial purposes. Even so they can only recommend ultimate internment if conversion is not accepted within a given period.

Before committing myself at ambassadors' conference, I should like to have Lord D'Abernon's view as to whether it would not be possible to obtain an assurance of German government acquiescing in internment on the ground that by so doing they would be hastening the withdrawal of naval control.[4]

Repeated to Berlin.

---

[1] See No. 178. [2] Not printed.
[3] President of the Naval Inter-Allied Commission of Control.
[4] In telegram No. 80 of March 19, Lord D'Abernon stated: 'I have seen Admiral Charlton on his return from Paris and have also spoken unofficially to German government. Latter appear to hold no strong objection to internment solution and certainly prefer it to destruction but before saying anything positive they are anxious to get precise figures as to number of diesel submarine engines not yet converted to commercial purposes. ... My opinion is that pressure on German government should practically clear up whole business by the end of May or at any rate so reduce number of unconverted engines that no naval danger will exist. If the question of conversion has not made satisfactory progress by the end of May, I should advocate internment.'

No. 187

The Marquess Curzon of Kedleston to Lord Hardinge (Paris)
No. 93 Telegraphic: by bag [C 3527/6/18]

FOREIGN OFFICE, *March 13, 1922*

Your telegram (No. 135 of March 9th. Period of continuance of missions of guarantee).[1]

I do not desire to modify the terms of my telegram No. 85 of March 8th.[2]

---

[1] No. 184.

[2] No. 183. In reply to a suggestion in Mr. Wigram's minute of March 10, Mr. Waterlow had stated (and Lord Curzon had concurred): 'I think we should stick to our guns . . . there is no chance whatever of getting an assurance of reasonableness from the present French Government. Either we must wait for a new Government, or we must break with this one.'

No. 188

Lord Hardinge (Paris) to the Marquess Curzon of Kedleston
(Received March 17, 8.30 a.m.)
No. 151 Telegraphic: by bag [C 3953/6/18, C 3963/434/18]

PARIS, *March 15, 1922*

The Conference of Ambassadors met this morning under the chairmanship of M. Jules Cambon, the Belgian ambassador being also present, and considered the following questions. Count Sforza, the new Italian ambassador, attended for the first time:—

. . .[1]5. The Conference had before it the two revised schemes drawn up by the Allied Military Committee of Versailles regarding the constitution, functions and privileges of the proposed military and aeronautical Committees of Guarantee (see my telegram No. 127, paragraph 1 of March 4th).[2] These schemes (copies of which I enclosed in my despatch No. 603)[3] are, except for a few points, in conformity with those I originally submitted to the Conference. They have, however, been completely redrafted so as to fall into two parts, only the first of which is intended for communication to the German Government. The following departures from the original schemes are to be noted:—

a. As reported in my telegram No. 127,[2] last paragraph of section 1, Marshal Foch refused to agree that the duration of the Committees of Guarantee should coincide with the occupation of the Cologne Bridgehead, and the Versailles Committee has proposed instead a definite period of eight years. On the other hand the Italian Embassy has suggested that the Committees of Guarantee should cease on the day that the Allied Governments shall decide that the League of Nations can apply Article 213 of the

---

[1] The sections omitted referred to other matters.   [2] No. 180.

[3] Of March 13, not printed.

Treaty of Versailles.[4] The Conference decided to combine this proposal with the eight years' limit, so that it would be open to the Allied Governments at any time within the eight years to withdraw the Committees of Guarantee, and hand over its work to the League of Nations. I informed the Conference that pending further instructions I was unable to express any opinion on these proposals, but promised if possible to communicate the views of His Majesty's Government to the Conference at the next meeting. I should be glad therefore to have an early reply to my telegram No. 135 of March 9th.[5]

b. The Allied Military Committee of Versailles declined to accept the British proposal that only 50% of the staff of the Committee of Guarantee shall be composed of staff of the present Military Commission of Control, and that at the end of three months this staff shall be replaced by a staff which shall not have belonged to the Commission of Control. In view of French opposition to this restriction I agreed, after consultation with my military and aeronautical advisers, not to insist upon it. My reasons for doing so were that since each Government is to pay its own staff it is difficult to insist on restricting its composition, and that it will always be open to His Majesty's Government to change their staff when they wish. On the other hand, in the case of the Aeronautical Committee, both the Air Ministry and the French aeronautical authorities state that they would be unable to find the requisite technical staff.

c. In the scheme dealing with the Military Committee of Guarantee a paragraph has been added to Part 1, paragraph B (c), in order to enable the Military Committee to inspect naval constructions when they consider there is danger of these being used for military purposes. The paragraph has been worded so as only to apply to guns and runs as follows: 'The expression "arms, munitions and war material of every kind" includes guns of every description capable of being utilised on land.'

The Conference approved the two schemes subject to my reserve with regard to the question of duration, and decided that as soon as a decision on this latter point is reached, a note shall be addressed to the German Government informing them of the decision of the Conference of Ambassadors and communicating to them the first part of each scheme.

On my proposal the Conference agreed to instruct the Military and Naval Commissions of Control to prepare for the Allied Governments estimates as to the exact acts and time necessary to complete the various disarmament clauses of the treaty, such estimates being subject to German co-operation in their execution.

. . .[1]15. Admiral Charlton, President of the German Naval Commission of Control, explained to the Conference the views of his Commission as regards the decision of the Conference of Ambassadors to intern the

---

[4] This article ran: 'So long as the present Treaty remains in force, Germany undertakes to give every facility for any investigation which the Council of the League of Nations, acting if need be by a majority vote, may consider necessary.'

[5] No. 184.

unconverted diesel engines in occupied territory, as reported in my telegram No. 117 of March 1st[6] section 2.[7] As foreseen in my telegram No. 148 of March 13th,[8] Admiral Charlton deprecated this course and recommended in a memorandum, copy of which is enclosed in my despatch No. 653 of today's date,[9] that a further delay should be granted for the conversion of these engines to commercial uses. He urged, moreover, that no further time limit should be imposed on the German Government as hitherto on each occasion that this had been done the German Government had been allowed with impunity to exceed the time limit. In return he proposed that the Conference should for its own convenience fix the 30th June as the date after which the Conference should revert to its previous decision of interning any engines still unconverted. He at the same time proposed that the disposal of the submarine motors and clutches should be dealt with in the same manner as the engines themselves, thereby annulling the final time limit fixed for the conversion of these motors and clutches as reported in my telegram No. 29 of January 18th, section 4.[9]

In arguing against the immediate internment of the engines, Admiral Charlton enlarged on the various practical difficulties of transport and storage, and on the small likelihood of the Germans ever buying for commercial purposes any of the engines when once they have been interned. His arguments however did not appear to me to be very convincing on the point in which I understand His Majesty's Government to be chiefly interested, namely a prompt settlement of this question so as not to delay the early withdrawal of the Naval Commission of Control. The immediate internment of the engines would, according to Admiral Charlton, take two months, whereas according to his proposal this internment is to be postponed until the end of June. In these circumstances I declined to agree to Admiral Charlton's proposal. The rest of the Conference however, supported by their Naval Advisers, were in favour of accepting Admiral Charlton's scheme. On a majority decision being carried in this sense I made a reserve to the effect that no action should be taken on the decision pending a further communication on my part. I should be glad therefore to be furnished with the views of His Majesty's Government at an early date.

Admiral Charlton also called attention to the fact that the German Government have persistently refused to destroy the special parts removed from diesel engines on their conversion to commercial uses on the ground that these parts can themselves be used commercially. Under the internment scheme these parts would have been interned with the engines, thereby solving, at any rate provisionally, an awkward question which is delaying the winding up of naval control. By Admiral Charlton's scheme the German Government are again to be called upon to destroy these parts. They will probably again refuse, and their refusal will be quoted by the French Government as a violation of the naval clauses of the Treaty of Versailles, which will justify the continued maintenance of the Naval Commission of Control.

[6] No. 178.   [7] This section is not printed.   [8] No. 186.
[9] Not printed.

No. 189

The Marquess Curzon of Kedleston to Lord D'Abernon (Berlin)
No. 305 [C 3657/6/18]

FOREIGN OFFICE, *March 17, 1922*

My Lord,

I transmit to Your Excellency, herewith, copy of a correspondence with the War Office[1] on the subject of the completion of military disarmament in Germany.

2. I request that, unless you see objection, you will supplement the representation reported in your telegram, No. 74 of the 14th instant,[2] by impressing upon the German Government the strong views entertained by His Majesty's Government on the points indicated in this correspondence. It would be well to inform your allied colleagues of your action.

3. Copy of this despatch and its enclosures has been sent to His Majesty's Ambassador at Paris[3] for his information and guidance.

I am, etc.,
(For the Secretary of State)
ALEXANDER CADOGAN

[1] Not printed (see, however, No. 177, n. 3).   [2] Not printed.
[3] No. 781 of March 18, not printed.

No. 190

Mr. Lampson to Mr. Tufton[1] (Cabinet Office)
[C 3949/116/18]

Confidential   FOREIGN OFFICE, *March 17, 1922*

Sir,

I am directed by the Marquess Curzon of Kedleston to transmit to you herewith copies of a memorandum on problems of the Saar Valley administration,[2] prepared by the Historical Adviser to the Foreign Office, together with copies of a despatch from His Majesty's consul-general at Cologne,[3] of

[1] Mr. C. H. Tufton had been seconded from the Foreign Office to be Assistant Secretary to the Cabinet.
[2] Of February 8 (C 1963/116/18), not printed.
[3] Mr. Thurstan had visited Saarbrücken between January 25 and 28. In a long despatch (C 2469/116/18) of February 10, having described the situation in the Saar Valley, he had stated: 'The Government of the Saar Basin is in the hands of the French rather than in those of the League of Nations, and the whole trend of the Government's legislative and administrative policy has been to make the basin an entity, as completely separated from Germany as possible. . . . practically all the leading officials in the Administration are, for some reason not known to me, French. . . . The Treaty of Versailles provides for administrative action "after consultation with the elected representatives of the inhabitants", but such consultation has hitherto proved to be a mere formality. I do not profess to say whether the Treaty of Versailles meant it to be ineffective, but in that case it was a mere farce to insert the relevant clause. In any case, the fact remains that, in these

408

whose district the Saar territory forms part, reporting on conditions in the territory as observed by him during a recent visit. These papers may be useful to the British representative on the Council of the League of Nations, since it is understood that questions relating to the Saar are coming before that body at its next meeting. The Secretary of State does not desire to suggest that His Majesty's Government should make themselves responsible for any of the views expressed therein. In particular, Mr. Thurstan's despatch should, in Lord Curzon's opinion, be merely communicated confidentially to Mr. Fisher for the sake of the information that it contains.[4] Written after a visit of three days, it would not be surprising if it should prove to represent a somewhat superficial view. In any case, it does not, so far as can be judged, indicate any definite breach of the Treaty of Versailles on the part of the Governing Commission.

2. According to information communicated informally[5] by the director of the section of the League secretariat which deals with Saar questions, the following three matters are to come before the next meeting of the Council: (1) the question of arrangements for the plebiscite of 1935 under chapter 3 of the annex to article 50 of the treaty; (2) a proposal of the Governing Commission to associate an elected advisory council with the work of the commission; and (3) a proposal, designed to give enhanced stability to the government of the territory, that the Council of the League should declare that, apart from exceptional circumstances, the appointments of members of the Governing Commission should be renewable for periods of five years.

3. The Secretary of State knows no reason why the first two of these proposals should give any occasion for opposition on the part of His Majesty's

days when one of the principal causes of the world's unrest may seemingly be ascribed to the yearning for self-expression and self-determination, it seems to me extremely unfortunate that the Saarlanders should be able to say, with some show of reason, that they have not the slightest effective voice in the management of their affairs, and that the Government imposed on them by the Treaty of Versailles, and the League of Nations is the most arbitrary one existing in the world today. . . .'

On March 4 Sir E. Crowe minuted: '. . . The league is entrusted by the treaty of Versailles with the duty of controlling the administration of the district. They have set up an organ for this purpose in accordance with the provisions of the treaty. Full responsibility rests upon that organ. Anyone who wants to complain of the action of the administration must address the league or its organ. . . .

'Unless H[is] M[ajesty's] G[overnment] are to take the place or assume the duties of the league itself, they should not meddle with its business. We shall be accused of meddling, and with justice, if we inform the league that we have got our consul-general to investigate the proceedings of the league's organ of administration and to bring forward an indictment against them.'

[4] On March 12 Lord Curzon had minuted: '. . . I do not want . . . our representative to take the matter up personally at the next meeting of the Council. What I think we ought to do is to place him [Mr. Fisher] in possession of the case, tell him that it seems a matter for consideration by the Council, and invite his opinion as to the best manner of bringing it before the Council, whether it be by personal action or by supporting an interrogation from someone else.'

[5] To Mr. Waterlow, who recorded his conversation with M. Colban in a memorandum of March 14 (C 3949/116/18), not printed.

Government. On the contrary, it seems desirable to welcome measures calculated to remove causes of dispute, both by settling as soon as possible the arrangements for the plebiscite of 1935 and by associating the inhabitants with the work of the Government to such extent as the Council of the League may deem proper. As regards the first of these points, it will be observed that Mr. Headlam-Morley's memorandum draws attention to the importance of avoiding delay in compiling the registers on which the vote of 1935 will be taken.[6]

4. The third of the above-mentioned proposals seems more open to dispute. Whether increased security of tenure can be conferred upon the members of the Governing Commission without attendant political disadvantages is a question which the British representative on the Council will doubtless consider in all its bearings. The Secretary of State, as at present advised, does not feel called upon to express an opinion on the point, and he would be reluctant to make any suggestion that might fetter the discretion of the British representative.

I am, etc.,
MILES W. LAMPSON

[6] Mr. Headlam-Morley had stated: '. . . The existence of the plebiscite clauses is in fact the surest guarantee that the existing Government will have regard to the feelings of the people and place their interests first. Everything, however, depends upon the plebiscite, when the time comes, being carried out with the strictest honesty and in particular on the avoidance of any attempt to 'pack' the voting list. . . . The list of voters, although it will not be used for nearly thirteen years, can be drawn up now; I should venture strongly to urge that it should at once be drawn up. . . . Thirteen years hence it will not always be easy to get evidence as to whether in each particular case the conditions of residence were complied with in June 1919; the sooner the list is made out the less the difficulty will be. I think, therefore, that the British member on the Council of the League should take the first opportunity to move that the list be now made.'

No. 191

Lord Hardinge (Paris) to the Marquess Curzon of Kedleston
(Received March 22, 8.30 a.m.)

No. 163 Telegraphic: by bag [C 4227/434/18]

PARIS, *March 21, 1922*

Berlin telegram No. 80.[1]

In view of Lord D'Abernon's opinion that whole business could be practically cleared up by end of May, if pressure were brought to bear on German government, I would suggest as a compromise that I should be authorised to try, in return for withdrawing reserve on decision taken on 15th March (my telegram No. 151, paragraph 15)[2] to persuade the conference to agree that the time limit be advanced to 31st May, and that immediate pressure be

[1] See No. 186, n. 4.   [2] No. 188.

brought to bear on German government by informing them officially and at once of this time limit, and of fact that engines and parts will be interned f it is exceeded.

I should be grateful for reply in time for next meeting of conference on 25th March.

Repeated to Berlin.

No. 192

Lord D'Abernon (Berlin) to the Marquess Curzon of Kedleston
(Received March 25)
No. 240 [C 4398/6/18]

BERLIN, *March 21, 1922*

My Lord,

In obedience to instructions transmitted by your Lordship's despatch No. 305 of the 17th March,[1] I beg to report that I have today had a long interview with Dr. Rathenau, in which I brought strongly before him the views of His Majesty's Government on the question of disarmament. I went through the main points, regarding which the position is unsatisfactory, and I urged that the German Government should not only issue orders regarding these, but should take effective measures to see that the execution of its orders is not retarded by dilatoriness or ill-will on the part of subordinate officials. I pointed out to Dr. Rathenau that failure to comply with the desires of His Majesty's Government on this question was in every way detrimental to German interests. His Majesty's Government had given many proofs of their good-will towards Germany; on no point had they been more definite than in the desire to remove or reduce the commissions of control as soon as it was possible to do so, but their friendly intentions were frustrated by the inaction or ill-will to which I had called attention.

Dr. Rathenau, while repeating on lines similar to those reported in my despatch No. 237[2] that the system of perpetual small complaints was an intolerable one and was unjustified and unfair in that it left out of account the enormous work of disarmament already carried through by the German Government and the commissions of control, promised to do his best to deal with the matter on sensible and satisfactory lines. He appeared fully to realise the force of the argument that non-compliance can in no sense operate in Germany's interest. He contemplates making a general reply on the principal points raised, and asked me for a list of the subjects to which His Majesty's Government had drawn special attention.

I have, etc.,
D'ABERNON

[1] No. 189.   [2] Of March 20 (C 4397/6/18), not printed.

No. 193

The Marquess Curzon of Kedleston to Lord Hardinge (Paris)
No. 831 [C 4236/2285/18]

FOREIGN OFFICE, *March 23, 1922*

My Lord,

With reference to Sir M. Cheetham's despatch, No. 662 of the 17th instant,[1] and to your despatch, No. 713 of the 21st instant,[2] I transmit to Your Excellency herewith copy of a letter from the War Office,[3] from which it will be seen that the Army Council are inclined to agree with the opinion expressed in the letter from the Admiralty of the 6th instant,[2] copy of which was enclosed in my despatch, No. 712 of the 11th instant,[2] that the Treaty of Versailles does not limit the number or calibre of the guns to be mounted on warships built by Germany in the future.

2. In these circumstances, I request that, when this matter again comes before the Ambassadors' Conference, you will support the views expressed in these letters, unless they should prove to be incompatible with the opinion of the legal advisers to the conference, to whom it is observed from section 4 of your telegram, No. 85 of February 15th last,[4] that the question has been referred.

I am, etc.,
(For the Secretary of State)
S. P. WATERLOW

[1] Not preserved in the Foreign Office archives.   [2] Not printed.
[3] Of March 11 (C 3656/2285/18), not printed.   [4] No. 171.

No. 194

The Marquess Curzon of Kedleston to Lord Hardinge (Paris)
No. 840 [C 4266/6/18]

FOREIGN OFFICE, *March 23, 1922*

My Lord,

I have received your despatch No. 603 of March 13th,[1] and section 5 of your telegram No. 151[2] relating to the proposed aeronautical and military mission of guarantee in Germany.

2. Subject to the following considerations Your Excellency may consent to the communication to the German Government by the Ambassadors' Conference of the schemes for the aeronautical and military missions of guarantee enclosed in Marshal Foch's note to the Conference of March 10th.[1]

3. The following words should be inserted after the opening sentence of the two draft notes to the German Government relating to the military and aeronautical missions of guarantee: 'On the date accepted by the allied

[1] Not printed.   [2] No. 188.

governments as that upon which the military/aeronautical clauses of the treaty are to be regarded as having been completely executed'. The insertion of these words will make it clear that the proposed arrangement is one entirely outside the treaty, and will define the legal status of the missions of guarantee as something which the German Government cannot be forced to accept.

4. The proposals respecting the period of duration of the military and aeronautical missions of guarantee should be maintained on the basis put forward in my telegram No. 85 of March 8th.[3] As explained in that telegram, the Cologne bridgehead is, under article 429 of the Treaty of Versailles, to be evacuated on January 10th 1925, 'if the conditions of the present treaty are faithfully carried out'. It is evident that the faithful execution of the conditions of the treaty should also automatically involve the withdrawal of the missions of guarantee, which will exist only for that purpose.

5. Copy of a letter of March 15th from the War Office[1] is enclosed drawing attention to the points which have been omitted from paragraph B.b of Part I of the protocol relating to the military mission of guarantee. It will be seen however from the memorandum from the Director of Military Intelligence of March 22nd[1] (of which a copy is also enclosed) that there is no objection to these omissions, provided that the paragraph, drafted by General Sackville-West,[4] is inserted in part II of the same protocol.

6. Finally Your Excellency should insist on the original British proposal relating to the personnel of the military mission of guarantee being inserted in part II of the military protocol. This proposal read 'No more than fifty per cent. of the officers, comprising the mission of guarantee, should, at the beginning, consist of officers of the present military control commission. Within three months these fifty per cent. must have been replaced by officers who have taken no part in the military control commission in Germany'. There is no objection, in the case of the aeronautical mission of guarantee, to the text adopted by the conference.

I am, etc.,
(For the Secretary of State)
S. P. WATERLOW

[3] No. 183.   [4] See No. 174, n. 1.

No. 195

Lord Hardinge (Paris) to the Marquess Curzon of Kedleston
(Received March 27, 8.30 a.m.)
No. 172 Telegraphic: by bag [C 4431/6/18]

PARIS, *March 25, 1922*

The Conference of Ambassadors met this morning under the chairmanship of Monsieur Jules Cambon, and considered the following questions:—
. . .[1]3. On the strength of Your Lordship's despatch No. 840 of 23rd

[1] The sections omitted referred to other matters.

March 1922,[2] I informed the Conference that His Majesty's Government maintained their view that the continuance of the Military and Aeronautical Committees of Guarantee should come up for consideration on the evacuation of the Cologne bridgehead. As M. Cambon stated that he would have to consult his Government, no decision was taken.

At the same time the Conference agreed on my suggestion to insert in the schemes for constituting the two Committees of Guarantee a paragraph making it clear that these Committees are only to correspond with the German Government on purely military and aeronautical questions.

I carefully considered the proposal made in the third paragraph of Your Lordship's despatch No. 840[2] for the insertion in the draft scheme of words making it clear that the Military Committees of Guarantee shall come into existence on the date accepted by the allied Governments as that upon which the military clauses of the Treaty are to be regarded as having been completely executed. As the French Government have never disputed the necessity of obtaining the German Government's consent to the establishment of the Military Committee of Guarantee, it seems unnecessary on this account to insert this particular form of words. On the other hand, I have no doubt the French Government would welcome this addition, since they would thereby be enabled to postpone indefinitely the withdrawal of the Military Commission of Control on the ground that the military clauses of the Treaty have not (and are never likely to be) completely executed, for they will always be able by applying the strict letter of the treaty to point to the incomplete execution of one or other of these clauses.

If, however, nothing is said about the complete execution of the military clauses, there is a prospect of His Majesty's Government being able to get the Commission of Control withdrawn as soon as, roughly speaking, its work is more or less completed. In these circumstances, I have ventured not to carry out Your Lordship's instructions on this particular point. In the case of the Aeronautical Committee of Guarantee the Conference has already recognised that the aeronautical clauses of the Treaty have been completely executed as from the 5th February 1922 (see my telegram No. 53, section 2 of February 1st).[3] I will see that this statement is repeated in the covering note which has still to be drafted in order to communicate the two schemes to the German Government.

I regret that I was unable to submit to the Conference again the proposal to allow only 50% of the staff of the Military Committee of Guarantee to consist of officers of the present Military Commission of Control. The reasons given in my telegram No. 151, section 5,[4] which led Sir M. Cheetham to withdraw this proposal at the last meeting, are so strong that it would have been useless for me to have re-opened the question. . . .[1]

[2] No. 194.   [3] No. 169.   [4] No. 188.

No. 196

Record by Sir E. Crowe of a conversation with the American Ambassador

[*C 4846/1188/18*]

FOREIGN OFFICE, March 31, 1922

The American Ambassador called today at my invitation to discuss further the question raised by him in his conversation with the Secretary of State on the 1[7]th instant[1] on the subject of the American claim to reimbursement of the cost of their army of occupation on the Rhine, as the first charge upon Germany's reparation payments. I reminded His Excellency that Lord Curzon had desired to consult with his legal advisers as to the exact position under the Treaties, before answering the request of the United States Government for the recognition of the justice of the American claim. The legal advisers had now furnished their opinion.[2] It was now of importance to us to be quite clear as to the nature of Mr. Harvey's request. Did his Government desire to receive an official assurance from His Majesty's Government that the United States claim was recognised by them to be formally and legally valid, or was the object of the United States Government to assure themselves that the British Government acknowledged that in equity the American demand for repayment of the expenses of their army of occupation could not be questioned? If the former, we should be put to some difficulty, because we should be obliged to explain that, under a strict construction of the Treaty of Versailles, the claim of the United States Government that they stood, as regards repayment of the expenses of the army of occupation, on exactly the same footing as the Allied Governments, was not justified. Nor was this position altered if the United States Government rested their claim rather on the terms of the armistice than on those of the Treaty of Peace. For although the terms of the armistice entitled the American Government to claim payment from Germany, the German Government had subsequently, by concluding the Treaty of Versailles, put it out of their own power to pay, until their obligations to the Allies, as regards reparations, had been fulfilled. The practical result was that payment of the American claim cannot at present be made, with due regard to

---

[1] Lord Curzon reported this conversation to Sir A. Geddes in Washington in despatch No. 343 of March 19, not printed.

[2] In his Memorandum of March 24 Sir Cecil Hurst had stated: 'In strict law the pledges which Germany has given in the Treaty of Versailles to the Powers which ratified that instrument exclude the payment by her to the United States of America of the costs of the American army of occupation until the reparation payments to the Allies are completed. . . .

'In short, the payment of the American claims for the cost of her army of occupation cannot be made at present without Allied consent.

'It would be most inequitable that Allied consent should not be given.

'The presence of the American army on the Rhine is due to the co-operation of the Americans in the defeat of Germany by which alone the Allies are in a position to exact any reparation at all: their troops have remained there at the urgent request of the Allied Powers and their participation in the occupation has been a continued warning to Germany of the uselessness of all attempts to sow dissension between the Allies.'

legality, without the consent of the Allies. I explained to the Ambassador that Lord Curzon would sincerely regret that a formal statement on the foregoing lines should constitute our answer to the question which the United States Government had raised, and I earnestly hoped that they would not really desire to insist on a categorical answer on the purely technical and legal aspect of the question. His Majesty's Government were quite clear that, in equity, the American claim to repayment must be fully admitted, and, far from wishing to stand on any legal rights which they might derive from the Treaties, they would welcome any arrangement by which they could enter upon a friendly discussion with the American Government as to the best and most practical way of doing justice to their demand. This being so, I would ask of the Ambassador whether he or his Government had any view as to the method of achieving this end. Having regard to the technical aspect of the problem, the essential matter seemed to be to find a practical solution without raising points of theory. Perhaps the United States Government would come forward with some suggestion?

The Ambassador said he quite understood, after hearing my explanation, what the technical difficulty was. He thought he could say at once that what his Government desired, when they asked for the recognition of their claim, was not necessarily a formal declaration that their scheme was founded on a correct interpretation of the terms of the armistice, but an assurance that the British Government would in practice admit America's right of repayment. If we were willing to give this, he thought there ought to be no difficulty in arriving at an understanding. He had himself thought of a plan, which he proceeded to expound. I had some difficulty in following what he proposed, but as the result of much questioning and repetition, I understand his idea to be this: Under the recent arrangement arrived at by the Reparation Commission, Great Britain is to receive the sum of twenty-five million pounds in cash, in repayment of the cost of her army of occupation, France paying herself out of the proceeds of the deliveries in kind already made by Germany.[3] Mr. Harvey thought that this twenty-five million was the first cash payment made under reparations. The Reparation Commission had taken note of the American claim, and had declared that its adjustment was a matter for the several Governments. This meant that the sum of 25 millions could not be disposed of without the British Government coming to some understanding with the United States. Now, if the British Government recognised the equity of the American contention, they might make an offer that they would let some proportion of the sum go to the United States Government. The latter would content themselves with a minimum proportion of this sum, but the mere fact of such a transaction having been agreed upon would, for the moment, settle the whole question of the justice of the American claim, since they would have received what they would declare to be a fair proportion of the only cash payment yet made by Germany. It would leave over for future settlement the question in what

[3] See Reparation Commission I: *Statement of Germany's Obligations ... April 30th, 1922* (H.M.S.O. 1922), pp. 32-5.

manner the remainder of the American claim for the repayment of the expenses of their army of occupation should be adjusted; but, as further cash payments in the near future seemed now out of the question, it would put off this matter indefinitely.

I asked the American Ambassador whether I was to regard what he had just put forward as a proposal on the part of his Government. He said: no, it was merely a suggestion which he was making on his own personal initiative.[4] He could in no way guarantee that Mr. Hughes, whom he had not consulted on the point, would make it his own, although he felt very confident that his scheme would strongly recommend itself at Washington. For, he said, it presents very great advantages. There was a strong feeling in America at present in favour of close co-operation with Great Britain on the lines first started at the Washington Conference.[5] Here was a practical way of giving effect to the spirit of co-operation, and it would be possible for the American Government to justify before their public opinion the acceptance of a minimum proportion of the twenty-five millions, by using the argument that at a time when Great Britain was making provision for the first payment of the interest on the war loans, it would be good policy not to discourage her by being in any way exacting, as regards immediate payments for the army of occupation.

I said that I would not fail to explain Mr. Harvey's suggestion carefully to Lord Curzon, but I should be glad to know how, in Mr. Harvey's opinion, the question would be put before the other Allies, because Mr. Harvey must remember that, in regard to reparations, Great Britain could not very well take isolated action, however great her desire to come to a friendly understanding with the United States Government. Difficulties might arise, as he might well imagine, if, in a matter of this kind, Great Britain laid herself open to the charge of making an arrangement for herself without regard to the way in which such an arrangement might affect her Allies, even if only by way of creating precedents. I asked whether, in fact, the American Government contemplated making proposals to the French and Belgian Governments. So far as I could form an opinion, I did not believe that those two Governments would take a view concerning the equity of the American claim different from ours.

Mr. Harvey replied that he saw no difficulty in informing the other Governments, or entering into discussions with them on similar lines. He thought, however, that this was, for practical purposes, unnecessary; for, if such an arrangement as he had outlined could be arrived at with the British Government, the United States Government would rest satisfied; and as the French Government had received no cash which could be divided, there was no object in bringing them into the suggested arrangement. On the other hand it seemed to him clear that the French and other Allied Governments could not possibly object to Great Britain entering into an arrangement which was entirely to their advantage, since it would result in

[4] Cf. *F.R.U.S.* 1922, vol. ii, pp. 225–6.
[5] See Vol. XIV, Chap. VI.

the provisional settlement of the American claim without any demand being made upon them.

I finally asked the Ambassador how exactly he thought that his proposal should be handled. He suggested that we might answer his note to Lord Curzon of the 22nd of March[6] by stating in some such form as I had indicated our recognition of the equity of the American contention, and our willingness to come to an arrangement satisfactory to the United States Government before settling such claim. We might then refer to our receiving, under the terms of a resolution passed by the Reparation Commission, the sum of twenty-five million pounds in cash, in respect of the cost of the British army of occupation, and we might intimate our willingness to consider, in consultation with the United States Government, whether a proportion of that sum should be handed over to the American Government, asking at the same time what proportion they would consider fair.

I carefully refrained throughout the interview from expressing any opinion on the merits of this American proposal, and merely undertook to lay it before the Secretary of State.[7]

[6] For text of this note and supplementary note of March 23, see *F.R.U.S.* 1922, vol. ii pp. 220–5.

[7] Lord Curzon minuted on March 31: 'I must say I regard this suggestion with a good deal of suspicion. It looks to me rather like a device on the part of America or Mr. Harvey to secure at one blow (a) a recognition of their claim (b) a payment in cash (c) the avoidance of any trouble with the other Powers. I should like the opinion of Sir E. Crowe [and] the Dep[artmen]t upon it. But is it not also a question for the Reparation Commission?'

On April 3 Mr. Waterlow minuted: 'In order to answer the Secretary of State's minute . . . I consulted Sir B. Blackett this morning.

'Broadly speaking, the circumstances in which Mr. Harvey proposes that we should intimate our readiness to hand over to his Gov[ernmen]t a proportion of the cash we have received from Germany, are that our total receipts, both cash and kind translated into cash, fall short by £3 million sterling of covering the costs of our army of occupation up to March 31; while France and Belgium have received amounts (in cash and kind) which after paying for their armies of occupation, leave plus balances of £28 million sterling in the case of France and £575 million sterling in the case of Belgium, as against our minus quantity of £3 million sterling. These figures are calculated on the assumption that the allied agreements stand. This being so, Sir B. Blackett thinks—and I cannot but agree—that, apart from such technical difficulties as that our cash has already been paid into the exchequer, Mr. Harvey's suggestion cannot possibly be entertained. In itself the possibility of satisfying the American claim by a cash payment by one or more allies might be considered; but, if so, it will not be for us to make the payment; equity would probably require it to be made a charge on the Belgian priority.

'Nor do I see from the political point of view any reason why we should sacrifice ourselves in order to help the Americans to avoid unpleasantness with France and Belgium. We are already making sacrifices to satisfy America: we alone of the allies are to pay £25 million of our debt to them this year. To ask that we should make them a further payment in order to act as their lightning conductor is to ask too much.

'For these reasons I think it must be verbally explained to Mr. Harvey that his suggestion is not practicable. He might at the same time be told that before replying formally to his note we propose to discuss with our allies the best method of meeting the desires of his Gov[ernmen]t.

'Mr. Harvey's proposal for a separate arrangement may perhaps be the more safely cleared out of the way, [in] that it is only put forward on his personal initiative. If so we need have no further misgiving in adopting the more regular method of joint allied action, and the next step will be to communicate to the French Gov[ernmen]t, in reply to [the Count de Saint-Aulaire's note of March 28 communicating the text of the preliminary French reply, not printed] the heads of a draft reply to the American note.'

On April 5 Sir W. Tyrrell recorded: 'I spoke today to Mr. Harvey as authorized by the S[ecretary] of S[tate] who accepted our reasons for not adopting his plan, but he urged we should lose no time in sending an interim reply on the lines of the French note.

'I urged upon His Excellency the desirability of appointing an American Rep[resentati]ve on the Reparation Commission. He quite agreed a[nd] held out an expectation of an early appointment.'

No. 197

The Marquess Curzon of Kedleston to Lord Hardinge (Paris)
No. 922 [C 4244/289/18]

FOREIGN OFFICE, *March 31, 1922*

My Lord,

I transmit to Y[our] E[xcellency] herewith copy of a note[1] from the Belgian Ambassador suggesting that the Ambassador's Conference should deal with the report[2] of the expert committee appointed, in pursuance of the decision of the Supreme Council of August 13 last, to draw up a scheme, in consultation with German experts, for an organisation to supervise licensing in the Rhineland.[3] Copies of three despatches from H[is] M[ajesty's] High Commissioner at Coblenz are also enclosed.[4]

2. The negotiations of the experts having reached a deadlock, I share the opinion of the Belgian Gov[ernment] that the most convenient method would be that the Ambassadors' Conference should now attempt to solve this difficult problem, and I have replied to the Ambassador accordingly.[5] As Y[our] E[xcellency] will doubtless wish to have some indication of the attitude of H[is] M[ajesty's] Gov[ernment] towards it when the matter comes before the conference, the following observations are submitted for your guidance.

3. Under the decision of the Supreme Council of August 13[3] last the economic sanction in the Rhineland, which included the erection of a customs barrier along the frontier between occupied and unoccupied Germany, was withdrawn on September 25, 1921.[6] The withdrawal was subjected by the Supreme Council to two conditions, which were to be previously accepted by the German Government, namely, the constitution of the supervisory organisation mentioned above, and the recognition by the German Gov[ernmen]t of the validity of acts done during the existence of the sanction. In order to meet the difficulties of the transition period, the

[1] Of March 20, not printed.
[2] Enclosed in Lord Kilmarnock's despatch No. 61 of March 3, not printed.
[3] See Vol. XV, No. 104, Appendix 8, and Vol. XVI, No. 670.
[4] Coblenz despatches Nos. 48 (of February 23), 61 (of March 3), and 68 (of March 4), not printed.
[5] The reply, which was drafted on March 27, was not despatched until April 13.
[6] See Vol. XVI, Nos. 706–8.

Supreme Council at the same time conferred upon the Inter-Allied Rhineland High Commission (who had been originally entrusted with the administration of the sanction) the power 'to order and to carry out all executive measures and all measures during the period of transition as regards the decisions set out above'. Among the steps taken by the High Commission under these powers was the enactment of article 11 of Ordinance No. 98 (since amended by Ordinance No. 105), which provides that 'as a transitional measure, and for the purpose of avoiding any disturbance of the economic life of the occupied territories, the department for the investigation and issuing of import and export licences for the occupied territories shall be maintained until such time as the inter-Allied body referred to in the decision of the Supreme Council of August 13, 1921, shall be ready to enter on its duties'. Under this provision the licensing organisation set up at Ems for the administration of the sanction survived the withdrawal of the sanction, and is still in existence. The Italian delegation, which had been specially added by the Supreme Council to the High Commission for the purpose of administering the economic sanction, has survived with the Ems organisation, and continues to this day to be paid out of the customs receipts collected under the sanction. The Italian delegation is also represented on the committee of experts.

4. The experts began their work not long after the withdrawal of the sanction, but from the beginning they made slow progress owing to the difficulty of confining the French experts to the one object which the Supreme Council had in view as the purpose of the proposed licensing organisation, namely, the prevention of commercial discrimination in violation of the treaty. Agreement has, however, now been reached, except on the points explained in the report of the experts[2] (see enclosure in Lord Kilmarnock's despatch No. 61 of March 3[4]). Although—and this opinion is shared by the B[oard] of Trade—the position on these points adopted by the British members of the expert committee appears to be entirely reasonable, the attitude of the French delegation remains uncompromising.

5. The result is that the economic sanction is, apart from the actual collection of customs duties, still in existence six months after its abolition. This entails various evils: the practical inconveniences of the organisation at Ems set out in the last paragraph of Lord Kilmarnock's despatch No. 61; the frittering away of the customs receipts in an exorbitant salary paid to the Italian delegate (see Lord Kilmarnock's despatch No. 68);[4] and, in general, the failure of the Allied Gov[ernmen]ts to give effect to the spirit of the Supreme Council's August decision, although it has never been suggested that the German experts have not made serious efforts to collaborate with the Allied experts for the purpose contemplated by the Supreme Council. What that purpose was is not in doubt—it was to substitute for a general control over imports and exports in the Rhineland supervisory machinery in which the Germans were to be associated with the single object of safeguarding, so far as the occupied territory is concerned, the anti-discrimination clauses of the treaty. That this purpose has not yet been achieved is solely due to the

420

obstructive tactics of the French experts at Coblenz. Y[our] E[xcellency] should therefore, when the matter comes before the Ambassadors' Conference, make it clear that H[is] M[ajesty's] Gov[ernmen]t, for the above reasons, view the present position with much dissatisfaction, and that they are not prepared to instruct their experts, whose attitude is entirely approved, to make further concessions, which could only have the effect of travelling beyond the purpose that the Supreme Council had in view.

6. Should the French representative on the conference prove obdurate on this point, it may become necessary for H[is] M[ajesty's] Gov[ernmen]t to raise the whole question of the legality of the activities of the Ems organisation. It is true that the life of that organisation was prolonged by the Inter-Allied Rhineland High Commission in accordance with the desire of the Supreme Council to bridge the transition period before the supervisory licensing organisation should be established. But that period has now been so long drawn out, and with so little show of reason, that it can hardly be maintained that the Ems organisation any longer fulfils the intention of the Supreme Council; indeed, the question arises whether the Ordinance of the High Commission, under which it works, has not become void by the mere effluxion of time. Further delay in replacing the Ems licensing office by a purely supervisory organisation on the lines originally contemplated may well make it necessary for H[is] M[ajesty's] Gov[ernmen]t to instruct their representative at Coblenz to press for the abolition of the Ems organisation on these grounds. The object of H[is] M[ajesty's] Gov[ernmen]t is to promote a modification of the attitude of the French experts, which alone impedes this replacement. Whether that end will be best served by making an intimation to the above effect before or after the present deadlock has been discussed I must leave to Y[our] E[xcellency's] discretion.

7. Lord Kilmarnock informs me that the French, Italian and Belgian members of the committee of experts are expecting to be summoned to Paris at an early date, and he suggests that, as the whole question is somewhat complicated and local in character, Y[our] E[xcellency] may wish one of the officers of his staff to proceed to Paris at the same time in order to be available should you desire to consult him in the course of the discussion. You will doubtless make the necessary arrangements with Lord Kilmarnock if this suggestion commends itself to you.

8. Copy of this despatch has been sent to Lord Kilmarnock and to His Majesty's Ambassador at Berlin.

I am, etc.,
Curzon of Kedleston

No. 198

Sir A. Geddes (Washington) to the Marquess Curzon of Kedleston
(Received April 10)

No. 377 [C 5324/336/18]

WASHINGTON, *March 31, 1922*

My Lord,

I have the honour to transmit to Your Lordship herewith a report[1] by the Assistant Military Attaché to this Embassy respecting the recent decision to withdraw the United States forces in occupation of the Coblenz bridgehead.[2]

I concur generally in the view expressed in the last paragraph of Major Bridge's despatch in regard to the motives which probably prompted this decision.

Although no very reliable information is available, the fact that this decision followed almost immediately upon the reply of the Allied Finance Ministers[3] to the demand for the $241,000,000 in respect of the expenses of the American troops on the Rhine makes it safe to conjecture that the two events were not unconnected. The reports in the press alleging reluctance on the part of the Allied Governments to admit the validity of the United States' claim raised a storm of comment in the press, most of which was far from complimentary to the supposed attitude of America's former associates in the war. By these means, the proponents of immediate withdrawal found their case suddenly strengthened to an unexpected extent and the Administration no doubt felt it wise to take time by the forelock and to announce the decision to withdraw before time had been given for a new storm to gather and break in Congress.

I have, etc.,
(For the Ambassador)
H. G. CHILTON[4]

[1] Not printed.   [2] See *F.R.U.S.* 1922, vol. ii, pp. 211–15.
[3] See ibid., pp. 218–20.
[4] Mr. Chilton was Counsellor at H.M. Embassy at Washington.

No. 199

Lord Hardinge (Paris) to the Marquess Curzon of Kedleston
(Received April 3)

No. 818 [C 4830/6/18]

PARIS, *April 1, 1922*

My Lord,

With reference to my telegram No. 172, section 3, of March 25th,[1] I have the honour to transmit herewith the draft of the Note[2] which it is proposed to address to the German Government on the subject of the Aeronautical and Military Committees of Guarantee to be set up in Germany on the

[1] No. 195.   [2] Not printed.

withdrawal of the present Commissions of Control. This draft is the result of direct discussions between this Embassy and the Ministry for Foreign Affairs and I venture to think meets the requirements of His Majesty's Government on all points to which they attach importance. I would more particularly draw Your Lordship's attention to the last paragraph which lays down in accordance with the wishes of His Majesty's Government that the continuance of the Committees of Guarantee shall be considered on the evacuation of the 1st Zone as described in Article 429 of the Treaty of Versailles. This zone includes both the bridgehead and the northernmost section of the occupied Rhineland, which according to the treaty are to be evacuated simultaneously.

In urging the Conference at the last meeting to agree to linking up the Committees of Guarantee with the question of the evacuation of the Cologne bridgehead, I availed myself of the arguments used in Your Lordship's telegram No. 85 of the 8th March[3] in which the occupation of the Cologne bridgehead is described as having for object to secure the execution of the treaty as a guarantee against future aggression. The French Government have considered it necessary to forward to the Conference a short memorandum,[2] copy of which is enclosed herewith, making it clear that the occupation of the Cologne bridgehead is intended not only to act as a guarantee against future aggression but as a guarantee for the execution of the Treaty of Peace as a whole.

The acceptance by the French Government of the evacuation of the Cologne bridgehead as the date for reconsidering the question of the Committees of Guarantee represents a considerable concession on the part of the French Government and in return for it I agreed to the insertion of the penultimate paragraph which contains a vague threat in the event of the German Government proving obdurate. As was to be foreseen from my interview with Monsieur Poincaré, as reported in my telegram No. 130 of 7th March,[4] the French Government originally wished to threaten the German Government with the withdrawal of the various concessions which have from time to time been made in the sense of modifying the strict application of the military clauses of the treaty. I objected to any such specified threat and pointed out that I could not agree to the use of this particular threat, since in practice it would not be possible to reverse all the various decisions which have benefited Germany and which represent departures from the strict military letter of the treaty. On the other hand, in its present vague indefinite form I consider the threat to be i[n]nocuous and not to commit His Majesty's Government to any particular course of action.

The draft note will be formally submitted for approval to the Conference of Ambassadors at its next meeting on the 5th April.[5] It is hoped that by then the Military and Naval Commissions of Control will have furnished the timetable which is to be communicated to the German Government at the same time.

I have, etc.,

HARDINGE OF PENSHURST

[3] No. 183.   [4] No. 182.   [5] See No. 203, below.

No. 200

The Marquess Curzon of Kedleston to Lord Hardinge (Paris)
No. 118 Telegraphic: by telephone [C 4990/6/18]

Very Urgent   FOREIGN OFFICE, *April 4, 1922, 9.15 p.m.*

Your telegram No. 191 (of April 4th. Future of military control in Germany).[1]

My doubts about proposed note to German government do not arise from any desire to dispute conclusions of yourself and your colleagues as to recent evidences of German *mala fides* or to secure insertion of reference to withdrawal of military sanctions.

In the first place the Admiralty have some objection to raise which we have not yet received.

Secondly a much more important point is raised by the form in which the draft is couched. This has the appearance of being an ultimatum framed in terms of extreme severity. We feel we must be fortified by legal advice before we assent to a course which *prima facie* we have no right under the Treaty of Versailles to pursue but which is a matter for negotiation with the German government rather than for dictation to them.

But there is a third and not less serious consideration. Would such a demand be wise at a moment when the Genoa Conference[2] is about to assemble, and when the latest requirements of the Reparation Commission[3] have already produced an acute crisis at Berlin?

I am sure you will recognise in these circumstances that some caution on our part is required, and that you can make out an excellent case for postponement until we are in a position to give our carefully considered opinion.

---

[1] This ran: 'Note to German Government is the result of long and arduous negotiations with French Government, resulting in a compromise where all main points of His Majesty's Government's policy have been safeguarded. I have agreed to the note being presented as an Anglo-French draft at meeting of conference tomorrow. The French Government are anxious as to the delay which is rapidly expiring. They will not admit any reference in the note to the withdrawal of the military sanctions. This policy received approval in your telegram No. 85 of March 8th [No. 183]. I trust that under the circumstances, I may be authorised to accept the joint draft tomorrow morning.'

[2] See Vol. XIX, Chap. III.   [3] See No. 12, n. 1.

No. 201

Memorandum respecting the German Disarmament Position
[C 5151/6/18]

FOREIGN OFFICE, *April 4, 1922*

Aeronautical—The Ambassadors' Conference decided on the 1st February, 1922, to declare the air clauses of the Treaty of Versailles executed as from the 5th February, 1922.[1] The German Government have, however, consented to the maintenance in Germany of the existing Inter-Allied Aeronautical Commission of Control until the 5th May, 1922.

Negotiations are now in progress between the Allied Powers respecting the establishment in Germany after the 5th May, 1922, of an Inter-Allied Mission of Guarantee to ensure the observance by Germany of article 198 of the treaty, which forbids the construction in Germany of any military or naval aircraft. When an Allied agreement on this matter has been reached, German consent will have to be obtained to the establishment within Germany of this mission, which is not covered by the treaty.

Naval Clauses—The execution of these clauses is practically complete. The British Admiralty are anxious to withdraw from Germany the existing Inter-Allied Naval Control Commission within the next two or three months. They will then be content to rely on the League of Nations' enquiry provided for by article 213 of the Treaty of Versailles. No opposition to the views of the British Admiralty is expected from any of the Allied Governments.

Military Clauses—The military disarmament of Germany may, in general, be said to be complete, i.e.:—

1. Vast quantities of war material have been surrendered and destroyed, and Germany does not at the moment possess the armament or material necessary for a modern European war.
2. The German regular forces have been reduced to the strengths laid down in the treaty.
3. The civil population have been disarmed and the unauthorised forces broken up to a very large extent. It is not believed by the War Office that Allied control can, in this respect, accomplish very much more.

The work of the existing Inter-Allied Military Commission of Control is, however, still incomplete, and no date can as yet be given for its disappearance. Considerable difficulties are being met with respecting the future organisation of the police. Hidden war material is still being discovered, and the checking of certain statistics is still to be carried out.

Negotiations are, however, now in progress between the Allied Governments respecting the establishment in Germany of an Inter-Allied Military Mission of Guarantee after the disappearance of the existing military control. When these negotiations have been completed the German Government will be asked to accept the principle of this mission of guarantee, which is not covered by the treaty. It is proposed simultaneously to warn the German Government that the existing military control will not be withdrawn until the execution of the military clauses is complete.

(P.S.—For full details of military disarmament of Germany, see General Staff memorandum amended to the 31st March, 1922.)[2]

[1] See No. 169.   [2] See No. 202, below.

425

No. 202

General Staff Memorandum respecting the Execution by Germany of the Military Articles of the Treaty of Versailles, February 24, 1922, amended to March 31, 1922

[C 5019/6/18]

Secret   WAR OFFICE[1]

PART I.—GENERAL

(*a*) The following papers contain a brief résumé of the present situation as regards the disarmament of Germany, in accordance with the military articles of the Treaty of Versailles:—

Part II contains a note on the disarmament of Germany and a statement regarding the evasions of the military articles of the treaty.

Part III consists of an appreciation of the progress in execution of the military articles of the treaty up to the 23rd February, 1922.

(*b*) The following appendices are attached:—

Appendix 1—Table showing the surrender and destruction of war material in Germany up to the 9th March, 1922.

Appendix 2—A War Office note on the 'Times' article of the 21st February, 1922, on 'Germany not disarming'.[2]

Appendix 3—A General Staff memorandum on the disarmament of Germany, dated 1st November, 1921.[3]

This paper was prepared for the Washington Conference, and contains an exhaustive review of the progress in the execution of the military articles of the treaty, and very complete details and statistics relating to the work of control in Germany.

It is included to provide any details which cannot be elaborated in the brief review given in Part III of this paper.

Appendix 4—Letter from General Nollet, president of the Inter-Allied Military Commision of Control to the German Government, regarding obstructions to control.[4]

PART II.—THE DISARMAMENT OF GERMANY AND EVASIONS OF THE MILITARY ARTICLES OF THE TREATY BY GERMANY

(A)—*The Disarmament of Germany*

1. In general, it can be taken that Germany has been effectively disarmed as far as material is concerned, and that her authorised forces have been reduced

---

[1] This Memorandum is not dated. It was communicated to the Foreign Office on April 4.

[2] Not printed.   [3] See Vol. XVI, No. 836.

[4] This letter, dated February 10, 1922, is not here printed. Lord Curzon commented on April 8: 'I have read all the papers and the situation which they depict does not seem to me as serious as I had been led to suspect. General Nollet is likely to have stated the case in its extreme form. But he does not succeed in making my flesh creep.'

to the establishments laid down in the treaty, although control and decentralisation of the police will take several more months to accomplish completely.

The civil population and the unauthorised forces have been disarmed to a very considerable extent, and the semi-official organising staffs of the unauthorised forces and societies have been prohibited and broken up. It is more than probable, however, that private persons are still engaged in organising, in secret, the prohibited unauthorised forces and societies.

Germany is at the moment quite powerless to fight a war with any fully organised great military power; the armament and material requisite for an army in European war on a great scale have been surrendered and destroyed, and could not be reconstructed for a considerable period, even admitting that the reversion to war production could possibly escape the vigilance of the Allied representatives in Germany.

The vast quantity of war material surrendered and destroyed is shown in Appendix 1; if destruction proceeds at the present rate it should be practically complete by the 30th June, 1922.

2. Germany for the next ten or fifteen years is bound to have a large reservoir of trained man-power. She has excellent cadres for the expansion and training of a national army in the Reichsheer (100,000 army) and Schutzpolizei (armed constabulary).

Owing to her system of national organisation, and the characteristics of her people, Germany will always be able to mobilize her available manpower, although all official measures of mobilisation are forbidden.

No action by the Allies can deprive Germany of her manpower and possibility of expansion for war. On the other hand, the terms of the treaty and the work of control have placed great obstacles in the way of future mobilization, and the reserve of trained manpower will decrease with each year of peace and the continuance of voluntary service in Germany.

3. From the above it is considered that Germany has now been effectively disarmed, and presents no military menace to the Allies at the moment; Germany cannot wage an aggressive war in the present condition of her armament.

The Inter-Allied Military Commission of Control have made very great progress in the disarmament of Germany, and have accomplished far more than the members of the commission at the outset considered would ever be possible.

The Allied Governments were therefore fully justified in deciding to reduce the Inter-Allied Military Commission of Control progressively from August 1921.

(B)—*Evasions of the Military Articles of the Treaty*

1. Although Germany has on broad lines been effectively disarmed, the work of the Inter-Allied Military Commission of Control is by no means completely finished.

2. Disarmament for many months met with considerable opposition in Germany, partly owing to the attitude of the German Government, but

mainly owing to continual obstruction by subordinate authorities and the extremist elements in the country.

On the 5th May, 1921, the London Conference sent an ultimatum to the German Government demanding the complete execution of the military clauses of the treaty and the cessation of all obstruction.[5]

For some months far less obstruction was reported by the Inter-Allied Military Commission of Control, and the German Government kept obstructive officials in check.

3. During the autumn and winter of 1921 obstruction again increased, and at the present time the commission is meeting with considerable difficulties. It is considered that the increase in obstruction is partly due to the reduction of the Inter-Allied Military Commission of Control, and the consequent hopes of the German authorities that by delaying the decision on the various questions still outstanding with control they may be enabled to retain certain organisations and material which the commission are determined to have changed or surrendered.

Obstruction is also probably partly due to the feeling of the German workmen against control, which has been aroused by skilful propaganda over the Deutsche Werke question;[6] it is also, no doubt, due to a certain extent to a genuine revival of national sentiment in Germany during the past year, which makes individuals more hostile to the presence of Allied officers in the country.

4. There have been instances in the past six months of the discovery of considerable quantities of hidden war material in Germany; the most flagrant case was the discovery of a number of finished and partly manufactured 10·5 cm. howitzers at the Rockstroh Werke.

This case is being fully investigated by the commission and the German Government, and the latter have promised to take legal action against any guilty parties

5. The most recent summary of German evasions of the treaty is given in a letter sent on the 10th February by General Nollet, president of the Inter-Allied Military Commission of Control, to the German Government, calling attention to the continued obstruction met with by control, and demanding that outstanding questions should be settled. An English translation of this is attached as Appendix 4.[4]

He stated that, owing to obstruction, delay was being caused in the surrender of war material, the transformation of factories and the readjustments in the organisation of the army and administrative services.

Owing to the refusal of the necessary documents it has been found impossible by the commission to check whether recruiting for the army is being carried out in accordance with the military law.

As regards training, the German cavalry were still being trained with dummy light machine guns, which are forbidden; the army also retains its gas masks and the forbidden gas-testing centre at Hanover, which, moreover, is being extended.

[5] See Vol. XV, No. 85, Appendix 2.   [6] See Vol. XVI, No. 853.

Finally, satisfaction has not yet been obtained by the commission regarding the removal from Spandau of certain documents relating to the manufacture of war material in war-time munition factories.

PART III.—PROGRESS IN EXECUTION OF THE MILITARY ARTICLES OF THE TREATY OF VERSAILLES

(A)—ARMAMENTS

1. *Surrender and Destruction of Surplus Arms and War Material*

Treaty of Versailles, Articles 164, 165, 166, 169, and 171 (164 and 166 modified by Spa Protocol)[7]

(a) *Army*—The German Government has handed over to the Inter-Allied Mission of Control the bulk of the material surplus to that allowed under the articles referred to above. The destruction of this material has reached an advanced stage, as shown in Appendix 1.

The German Government has refused to surrender about 550,000 gas-masks, which, they maintain, are not forbidden by the Peace Treaty.

Surrenders are still incomplete as regards signal material, certain stocks of explosives, and certain transport and engineer vehicles.

Discussions with the German Government are in progress as to the scales of equipment of certain stores which Germany is to be permitted to retain for her army.

Article 162, modified by Boulogne Note of June 22, 1920[8]

(b) *Police and Gendarmerie*—The police and gendarmerie have handed over the material surplus to that allowed by the Military Inter-Allied Commission of Control with the exception of certain signal stores, transport, vehicles, reserve equipment and arms for traffic guards.

Up to the 26th January, 1922, the police had surrendered the following to the Commission of Control:—

Guns	702
Machine guns	5,301
Rifles and carbines	125,621

Articles 169, 177 and 178

(c) *Disarmament of Unauthorised Forces and of the Civil Population*—The following figures show the quantities of arms surrendered to the Commission of Control by the civil population, including various unauthorised formations whose disarmament was ordered by control. Few arms are now coming in, and it is not considered that further efforts by the German Government to complete the disarmament of the civil population will yield any considerable results, although a certain number of rifles are still scattered about the country.

[7] See Vol. VIII, No. 52.   [8] See ibid., No. 36, n. 4.

Totals surrendered up to the 26th January, 1922:—

Guns	171
Machine guns	12,245
Rifles and carbines	1,473,720

Article 167

(d) *Disarmament of Fortresses*—The armament and stocks of ammunition in the fortresses left to Germany have been reduced to the figures prescribed by the commission.

2. *Control of Factories*

(a) *Factories*—On the 26th November, 1921, General Bingham[9] reported that out of 6,942 factories known to have manufactured munitions, 6,503 had been visited. Fourteen had been authorised to continue to produce munitions. The annual quantity to be allowed is still the subject of discussion between the commission and the German Government.

Six thousand and ninety-seven factories have been transformed for the production of non-military material, and finally passed by the commission.

Nearly 15,000 machines used for the production of munitions remain to be disposed of.

The transformations ordered in the factories will, it is estimated, take five to six months more, but those in the three factories known as the Deutsche Werke will not be finished till the end of the year.

Articles 171 and 172

(b) *Gas Warfare*—The particulars supplied by Germany with regard to the production of explosives, toxic substances and similar chemical substances used by her in the war are considered by the commission to be insufficient.

The factories of Reinsdorf and Plauen have not yet been transformed to the satisfaction of the commission.

3. *Import and Export of War Material*

Articles 170 and 171

The German Government has drawn up decrees to supplement those already issued to give effect to these clauses of the Peace Treaty. These new decrees are being examined by the commission.

(B)—Effectives

Articles 157, 160 and 163, modified by the Spa Protocol of July 9, 1920[7]

1.—(a) *Reduction of the Army to 100,000 Men*—The German army was reduced to the total of 100,000 prescribed by the treaty of the 1st January, 1921.

---

[9] Major-General Hon. Sir F. R. Bingham was Chief of the British section of the Inter-Allied Military Commission of Control and President of the Subcommission for Armaments and Material.

The commission is pressing the German Government to amend certain details of organisation, including the excess of officers on divisional staffs; the excess of senior officers and of non-commissioned officers; the presence of civilian paymasters with units; the liquidation of surplus establishments of the administrative services.

Articles 173, 174 and 175

(b) *Voluntary Long Period Service*—The Wehrgesetz (Army Act) of the 23rd March, 1921, has been accepted by the commission as fulfilling the terms of the treaty with regard to recruitment and enlistment, but the German authorities are obstructing the Control Commission in its efforts to check the execution of this law.

Article 176

(c) The military schools have been reduced in accordance with this article.

Article 43

(d) All troops have been withdrawn from the neutral zone.

Articles 43 and 162

2. *Police and Gendarmerie*—The present strengths of the German police and gendarmerie, viz., 150,000 (police) and 17,000 (gendarmerie) are those fixed by the Boulogne Conference.

Of the police, about 90,000 are constabulary (Schutzpolizei), armed on a scale laid down by the Commission of Control, and about 60,000 are communal, administrative and criminal police.

It has not yet been definitely established by control that the establishment is down to 150,000 police, but it is not considered that there is any important excess of strength. It is reported, however, that there are 5,000 ex-army officers in the police above the 150,000 establishment.

The organisation of the police has, however, been objected to by the Commission of Control on the ground that it is over-centralised and includes quasi-military staffs. Further, the commission refuses to allow the continuance of aerial police units (said to consist of ex-aviators) stationed at aerodromes. These matters are under discussion between the commission and the German authorities.

On the 17th January the Prussian Minister of the Interior promised to carry out the alterations demanded. No adequate steps have, however, been taken, and, in consequence, the police question has now been raised in an acute form.

On the 27th February, 1922, the Inter-Allied Military Commission of Control sent an ultimatum to the German Government, demanding that edicts should be issued by the German States to bring the organisation, &c. of the police into conformity with the decisions of the Inter-Allied Military Commission of Control.

On the 15th March, 1922, the German Government replied to the Inter-Allied Military Commission of Control, stating the points of the control ultimatum which they would accept, namely, surrender of war material and transport, dissolution of technical Schupo units, and removal of certain police from barracks. The German Government appealed to the individual Allied Governments against the remaining points.

The Inter-Allied Military Commission of Control have now sent a fresh note to the German Government, demanding that the German police organisation be reconstituted on the lines of the regional and municipal police organisations existing in 1913, in accordance with the Boulogne note of June 1920: 'the Inter-Allied Military Commission of Control demand the breaking up of the existing constituted police companies and Abteilungen.'

The Germans will probably make considerable difficulties before complying with the demands of the Inter-Allied Military Commission of Control, and consequently it is considered that this matter will take several months to settle.

(C)—FORTIFICATIONS AND MATERIAL FACILITIES FOR MOBILISATION

Articles 42, 180, 195 and 196

The dismantling of the fortification in non-occupied territory is practically finished.

In occupied territory about six months' work remains to be done, excluding the work which the armies of occupation are retaining temporarily for their own use.

Article 43

With the sole exception of a short railway siding at Darmstadt, the destruction of material facilities for mobilisation ordered by the Commission of Control has been completed in unoccupied territory. In occupied territory some of these facilities for mobilisation are being retained for use by the Allied armies until the period of occupation ends.

APPENDIX 1 to No. 202

Table showing Surrender and Destruction of War Material

War material surrendered and destroyed since the commencement of control up to the 9th March, 1922:—

1. *Guns and Barrels of all kinds*

Surrendered to the Inter-Allied Military Commission of Control up to March 9, 1922	33,452
Surrendered by the Germans under the armistice conditions, November 11, 1918	5,000
Guns, under construction, destroyed by the Germans prior to control, the records of which have been checked	8,618

Captured by the Allied armies between July 18, 1918, and
November 11, 1918 6,615

Total German guns captured, surrendered and destroyed
between July 18, 1918, and March 9, 1922 . . 53,685

Destroyed by the Inter-Allied Military Commission of Control
up to March 9, 1922 33,330

Remaining for destruction on March 9, 1922 . . 122

2. *Trench Mortars*

Surrendered to the Inter-Allied Military Commission of Control
up to March 9, 1922 11,596

Destroyed by the Inter-Allied Military Commission of Control
up to March 9, 1922 11,588

Surrendered by the Germans under the armistice conditions,
November 11, 1918 3,000

Total surrendered up to March 9, 1922 . . . 14,596

Remaining for destruction on March 9, 1922 . . 8

3. *Machine Guns*

Surrendered to the Inter-Allied Military Commission of
Control up to March 9, 1922 87,076

Destroyed by the Inter-Allied Military Commission of Control
up to March 9, 1922 86,968

Surrendered by the Germans under the armistice conditions,
November 11, 1918 28,000

Total surrendered up to March 9, 1922 . . . 115,076

Remaining for destruction on March 9, 1922 . . 108

4. *Small Arms (Rifles and Carbines)*

Surrendered to the Inter-Allied Military Commission of Control
up to March 9, 1922 4,366,090

Destroyed by the Inter-Allied Military Commission of Control
up to March 9, 1922 4,340,781

Remaining for destruction on March 9, 1922 . . . 25,309

5. *Shells, loaded*

Surrendered to the Inter-Allied Military Commission of ⎰tons 11,410·5
Control up to March 9, 1922 . . . . ⎱ 37,652,603

Destroyed by the Inter-Allied Military Commission of ⎰tons 10,678·3
Control up to March 9, 1922 . . . . ⎱ 37,051,620

Remaining for destruction on March 9, 1922 . . ⎰tons 732·2
⎱ 600,983

6. *Small-Arm Ammunition*

Surrendered to the Inter-Allied Military Commission of
Control up to March 9, 1922 450,584,000

Destroyed by the Inter-Allied Military Commission of Control
up to March 9, 1922 407,458,400

Remaining for destruction on March 9, 1922 . . . 43,125,600

No. 203

Lord Hardinge (Paris) to the Marquess Curzon of Kedleston
(Received April 7, 8.30 a.m.)

No. 198 Telegraphic: by bag [C 5130/6/18]

PARIS, *April 5, 1922*

The Conference of Ambassadors met today under the chairmanship of Monsieur Jules Cambon, the Belgian ambassador being also present and considered the following questions:—

...[1] 3. On the note to the German Government[2] relating to the Committees of Guarantee being brought forward by Monsieur Cambon for consideration by the Conference, I asked for its postponement in view of my expecting further instructions from his Majesty's Government. This was agreed to, but Marshal Foch drew the attention of the Conference to the fact that the delay is to expire on the 5th May and that today is the 5th April.

The Conference had also before it the timetables submitted by the Military and Naval Commissions of Control indicating the dates on which their remaining work can be finished. These timetables (copies of which are enclosed in my despatch No. 866 of today's date)[3] will be communicated to the German Government as enclosures to the above mentioned Note to the German Government.

...[1] 14. In accordance with the instructions contained in Your Lordship's despatch No. 53 of January 5th,[3] I invited the conference to refer back to the civilian members of the Special Committee appointed by the Supreme Council last August,[4] the question of reducing the expenditure of the Rhineland High Commission. Copy of my memorandum on the subject is enclosed in my despatch No. 847.[5] Monsieur Cambon refused to agree to this proposal and in support of this attitude read out a long statement which I had not seen before the meeting.[3] I did not fail to tell Monsieur Cambon privately that I considered this memorandum offensive and misplaced and that I could not allow the matter to rest there. I protested strongly against a reference to British commerce and an insinuation that our action had been inspired by such motives, pointing out that my memorandum contained no allusion whatever to British commercial interests. I added that I hoped he would tell Monsieur Poincaré what I had said to him. Monsieur Cambon promised to repeat my observations with which he told me privately that he agreed. The subject is therefore to come up for further discussion at the next meeting and I shall be glad of Your Lordship's instructions.

Since drafting this telegram I have received what purports to be a copy of the declaration made by Monsieur Cambon, but from which the particular offensive paragraphs have been expunged. This is enclosed in my despatch No. 847[5] in which I deal further with this question. I am informing Lord Kilmarnock of the above.

---

[1] The sections omitted referred to other matters.   [2] See Nos. 199 and 200.
[3] Not printed.   [4] See Vol. XV, No. 104.   [5] Of April 6, not printed.

No. 204

The Marquess Curzon of Kedleston to Mr. Harvey[1]
[*C 4308/1188/18*]

FOREIGN OFFICE, *April 7, 1922*

Your Excellency,

I have the honour to acknowledge the receipt of the memorandum enclosed in your note of the 22nd March,[2] in which are set out the views of the Government of the United States as to the payment of the expenses incurred by them in respect of the American army of occupation on the left bank of the Rhine.

2. I am anxious to lose no time in assuring Your Excellency that the claim put forward by the United States Government that these expenses should be reimbursed to them is one which His Majesty's Government would not in any circumstances desire to question. It would be impossible to do so without an indifference to manifest considerations of justice and without a failure to recognise the part played by the United States in the war and in the subsequent occupation, such as I am confident that your Government would not think of imputing to His Majesty's Government. It is the earnest desire of His Majesty's Government that means should be found with as little delay as possible to give practical effect to the desires of the United States Government as explained by Your Excellency, and I am accordingly placing myself in communication with the Governments of France and Belgium in the hope that a speedy agreement may be reached as to the most convenient method by which the Allied and Associated Governments may concert together to secure the desired end.[3]

I have, etc.,
CURZON OF KEDLESTON

---

[1] United States Ambassador in London. [2] See No. 196, n. 6.

[3] In his letter of April 7 in reply to the Count de Saint-Aulaire's communication of March 28 (see No. 196, n. 7), Lord Curzon stated: 'I have . . . returned to the note of March 22nd, in which the United States Ambassador submitted that claim to me, an interim reply similar in terms to that which has been made by the French Government. I hope to be able to submit to Your Excellency very shortly proposals which might, in the opinion of His Majesty's Government, form the basis for a definitive reply to the United States note to be made in identic terms by the allied governments concerned. I would suggest that the task of concerting final agreement as to the terms of this reply might be entrusted to the Ambassadors' Conference, who, for this purpose, should avail themselves of the advice of representatives of the Reparation Commission. I have the honour to request that Your Excellency will inform me as soon as possible whether the French Government are in agreement with this suggestion. If so, I will communicate it also to the Belgian Ambassador at this Court, together with the above-mentioned proposals for the lines which the definitive reply to the United States note should follow.'

No. 205

Lord Hardinge (Paris) to the Marquess Curzon of Kedleston
(Received April 13)[1]

No. 209 Telegraphic: by bag [C 5429/6/18]

Very Urgent   PARIS, *April 12, 1922*

Sir Eyre Crowe's letter to me of April 7th.[2]

French Government accept draft note to German Government regarding future Military Mission of Guarantee subject to two alterations.

1. *3rd paragraph of draft, 2nd sentence* add:— 'et qu'en conséquence ils se voient obligés de veiller par eux-mêmes à la fidèle observation de ces clauses tout au moins pendant un certain temps.' This alteration was suggested by Marshal Foch and Monsieur Poincaré states he insists thereon. As the addition of this phrase to the sentence seems to involve the use of the argument to which Your Lordship took exception[3] in the note as originally drafted, I have informed the Quai d'Orsay that I must refer the matter to you but that I anticipate little hope of your accepting it.

2. *3rd paragraph of draft 4th sentence* should be eliminated and be replaced by insertion of following paragraph between existing penultimate and last paragraphs:—

'Sous réserve de cette adhésion les gouvernements alliés seraient prêts à substituer la mission alliée de garantie à la Commission Militaire Interalliée de Contrôle dès que celle-ci aurait achevé les travaux essentiels dont la liste figure à l'annexe C et qui, si le gouvernement allemand y prête son concours, peuvent être terminés dans les délais également indiqués dans la dite annexe.' The title of Annex C will require a slight alteration.

The French pointed out that as the draft stood there was a danger of the Germans replying that they refused to accept the mission of guarantee but that they would take steps to assure the completion of the programme set out in Annex C. If this were accomplished the Allies would have no option but to withdraw the Commission of Control without any possibility of securing the institution of a mission of guarantee. This change accordingly seems to me an improvement on the original draft and I propose to accept it unless I hear that Your Lordship has an objection to it.

I should be glad of an answer as soon as possible in order that the revised draft may be circulated to the members of the Conference before the meeting on Friday morning.[4]

---

[1] The substance of this telegram was telephoned to Mr. Waterlow at 12.15 p.m. on April 12.

[2] Not preserved in the Foreign Office archives. This letter enclosed a copy of the revised draft note to the German Government.

[3] See No. 200.

[4] April 14. For the final text of the note, see No. 208, below.

No. 206

The Marquess Curzon of Kedleston to Lord Kilmarnock (Coblenz)
No. 8 Telegraphic [C 5469/725/18]

Urgent   FOREIGN OFFICE, *April 14, 1922, 5.30 p.m.*
Your telegram No. 10.[1]

Matter is primarily one for decision by High Commission, but should they decide in favour of prohibition, His Majesty's Government would certainly raise no objection.

[1] Of April 13. This ran: 'Cologne branch of German Communist party have notified their intention to hold meeting of Third International at Cologne on April 23rd. . . . Belgian High Commissioner is strongly in favour of forbidding meeting as he fears effect on Belgian zone where Communists are strong. French High Commissioner is also inclined to this course, but both show disposition to take our views into consideration. American representative agrees with French and Belgian High Commissioners. . . .'

No. 207

Lord Hardinge (Paris) to the Marquess Curzon of Kedleston
(Received April 15, 8.30 a.m.)
No. 212 Telegraphic: by bag [C 5482/5483/6/18]

PARIS, *April 14, 1922*

The Conference of Ambassadors met this morning under the chairmanship of Monsieur Jules Cambon, the Belgian ambassador being also present and considered the following questions:—

. . .[1] 3. The conference agreed, after inserting an unimportant modification, to the revised draft of the Note to be addressed to the German government on the future of aeronautical and military control in Germany. Copies of the Note in its final form are enclosed in my despatch No. 938 of today's date.[2] In order to facilitate the acceptance by the German government of the allied proposals, it was decided that the text of the Note should not be published and that if possible the fact of its presentation should not be allowed to leak out in the allied press. The conference were of the opinion that it would be well for the allied ambassadors in Berlin to be informed of the course that the negotiations had taken in order, if their assistance were subsequently required, that they would be fully informed. They should not at present however mention the matter to the German authorities. I should be glad if Your Lordship would inform Lord D'Abernon accordingly.[3]

4. In connection with the previous question at the suggestion of my Naval Adviser I proposed, and the Conference agreed, that the Allied Military Committee of Versailles should consider and report whether the Military

[1] The sections omitted referred to other matters.   [2] See No. 208, below.
[3] This information was transmitted to Lord D'Abernon in Foreign Office telegram No. 419 of April 19, not preserved in the Foreign Office archives.

Commission of Control in Berlin can supervise any work connected with Articles 168, 169 and 196 of the Treaty that may be outstanding on July 31st and thus enable the Naval Interallied Commission of Control to be withdrawn as soon as it has completed the purely naval work of the disarmament clauses of the Treaty . . . .[1]

No. 208

Lord Hardinge (Paris) to the Marquess Curzon of Kedleston
(Received April 18)
No. 938 [C 5515/6/18]

PARIS, *April 14, 1922*

Lord Hardinge of Penshurst presents his compliments to the Secretary of State for Foreign Affairs, and has the honour to transmit herewith a copy of a note from the Conference of Ambassadors to the German Ambassador in Paris, dated the 14th April, respecting future Allied control in Germany.

ENCLOSURE 1 IN No. 208

M. Poincaré to M. Mayer

PARIS, *le 14 avril, 1922*

M. l'Ambassadeur,

Dans sa note du 11 mai 1921,[1] le Gouvernement allemand a notifié son acceptation de la demande faite par les Alliés, le 29 janvier 1921,[2] aux fins d'obtenir qu'en vue d'assurer l'application de l'article 198 du traité, interdisant à l'Allemagne de posséder une aviation militaire et navale, l'Allemagne acceptât les définitions établies par les Puissances alliées, définitions qui distingueront l'aviation civile de l'aviation militaire prohibée par l'article 198. Les Gouvernements alliés se sont réservé le droit de s'assurer eux-mêmes par un contrôle constant que l'Allemagne remplissait cette obligation.

Après avoir pris connaissance d'un rapport de la Commission aéronautique de Contrôle, la Conférence des Ambassadeurs a décidé, le 1er février dernier,[3] que le Gouvernement allemand était considéré comme ayant complètement exécuté l'article 202 du Traité de Paix à partir du 5 février, et qu'il serait permis, trois mois après cette date, au Gouvernement allemand de reprendre la fabrication d'appareils civils, aux termes de la décision contenue dans la note de Boulogne du 22 juin 1920.[4] Les Gouvernements alliés, après un examen attentif, ont arrêté les définitions nécessaires pour distinguer les appareils aériens civils des appareils aériens militaires et navals; ces définitions sont énoncées à la fin de la présente note à l'Annexe (A). Les Gouvernements alliés ont également considéré les meilleures méthodes pour assurer le 'contrôle constant' mentionné plus haut, et il a été décidé que ce but serait atteint de la meilleure manière par la création d'une mission aéronautique

---

[1] See Vol. XVI, No. 619, n. 2.   [2] Vol. XV, No. 11, Appendices 1 and 2.
[3] See No. 169.   [4] See Vol. VIII, No. 36, n. 4.

alliée de garantie, dont la constitution, les fonctions et les droits sont également spécifiés dans l'Annexe (A). Conformément à cette décision, cette mission commencera ses travaux à partir du 5 mai et prendra ainsi immédiatement la succession de la Commission de Contrôle aéronautique.

Je serais obligé à votre Excellence de bien vouloir accuser réception de cette communication dans le plus bref délai possible, au nom du Gouvernement allemand.

Il est également apparu aux Gouvernements alliés, qui désirent revenir le plus tôt possible à des conditions normales dans leurs relations avec le Gouvernement allemand, que la décision de retirer la Commission de Contrôle aéronautique et de lui substituer la petite mission de garantie mentionnée plus haut offrait une occasion opportune d'examiner la question de l'avenir de contrôle militaire en Allemagne. Le Gouvernement allemand comprendra aisément l'inquiétude que les Governements alliés éprouvent à ce sujet, eu égard aux difficultés qu'ils ont rencontrées en poursuivant l'exécution des clauses militaires du Traité de Versailles. Ils estiment que ce contrôle, le moment venu, pourrait être exercé le plus efficacement et avec le minimum de froissements et de danger en adoptant un système semblable à celui qui a été institué pour le contrôle aéronautique. Ils ont en conséquence élaboré un projet dont les détails sont exposés à l'Annexe (B) de la présente note. Après avoir consulté les Commissions militaire et navale de Contrôle, ils estiment que les commissions existantes pourraient, à condition que la collaboration du Gouvernement allemand soit assurée, achever leur travail dans le temps prévu à l'Annexe (C). Il ne semble pas nécessaire d'exposer avec beaucoup de détails les multiples avantages qui résulteraient pour les Gouvernements alliés et pour le Gouvernement allemand, et, en particulier, pour ce dernier, de l'adoption de ce projet. L'économie manifeste et très grande qui serait obtenue par le Gouvernement allemand serait un encouragement à l'accomplissement immédiat du reste des parties inexécutées des clauses militaires du Traité de Paix, et beaucoup de froissements, avec leur répercussion inévitable sur les relations internationales, seraient évités en comparaison de ce que l'on peut attendre de l'état de choses actuel qui risque de continuer indéfiniment.

Dans ces conditions, les Gouvernements alliés sont persuadés que le Gouvernement allemand se rendra compte de l'avantage que représente pour lui l'institution d'une telle mission militaire de garantie et qu'il notifiera aux Alliés son acceptation de ce projet le plus tôt possible.

Sous réserve de cette adhésion, les Gouvernements alliés seraient prêts à substituer la Mission alliée de Garantie à la Commission militaire interalliée de Contrôle dès que celle-ci aurait achevé les travaux essentiels dont la liste figure à l'Annexe (C) et qui, si le Gouvernement allemand y prête son concours, peuvent être terminés dans les délais également indiqués dans ladite annexe.

Il est entendu que le Comité de Garantie aéronautique et le Comité de Garantie militaire resteront en fonctions dans les conditions indiquées, au moins jusqu'au jour où, conformément à l'article 429 du Traité de Paix, la première zone d'occupation pourra être évacuée; les Gouvernements alliés examineront alors si les circonstances rendent nécessaire de prolonger le fonctionnement desdits comités ou, au contraire, permettent d'y mettre fin.

La question analogue qui se présente du fait que, sur certains points, les clauses navales du traité n'ont pas été complètement exécutées est réservée pour un examen ultérieur; toutefois, sous réserve de la collaboration spontanée des autorités allemandes à l'exécution des clauses navales encore en jeu, les Alliés ont l'espoir qu'il sera possible de retirer complètement la Commission navale de Contrôle à une date non éloignée.

Veuillez agréer, etc.,
POINCARÉ

ANNEXE (A)

Constitution, Fonctions et Droits du Comité de Garantie aéronautique

Un Comité de Garantie 'aéronautique' sera établi en Allemagne après le départ de la C[ommission] A[éronautique] I[nteralliée] [de] C[ontrôle]; il aura son siège à Berlin.

(A)—Composition

Le Comité se composera de:

(a) Officiers:

Anglais	. .	1 air commodore ou group captain.
		3 officiers.
Français	. .	3 officiers.
Italiens	. .	2 officiers.
Japonais	. .	2 officiers.
Belges	. .	2 officiers.
Total	. .	13 officiers.

(b) Sous-officiers et soldats:

	Anglais	Français	Italiens	Japonais	Belges
Secrétaires . . .	2	2	2	1	2
Ordonnances . .	2	2	1	1	1
Automobilistes . .	2	1	1	1	1
Automobiles . . .	2	1	1	1	1

(B)—Fonctions et Pouvoirs

(a) La mission du 'Comité de Garantie aéronautique' est de donner aux Puissances alliées la garantie que l'article 198 du Traité de Versailles et l'article 170 en tant qu'il vise le matériel aéronautique ainsi que les neuf règles définissant les différences entre l'aviation militaire et l'aviation civile sont loyalement observés.

La Conférence des Ambassadeurs ayant déclaré que l'article 202 du Traité de Versailles a été complètement exécuté, les questions relatives à cet article ne seront pas traitées par le Comité de Garantie, à l'exception des trois questions suivantes dont l'exécution a été reportée à une date ultérieure:

(i) Destruction en temps voulu du hangar de Friedrichshafen et utilisation du personnel en excédent employé à la construction de dirigeables.
(Résolution de la Conférence des Ambassadeurs, No. 157–11, du 16 décembre 1921.)[5]

(ii) Règlement de la question des installations à conserver pour l'aviation civile internationale.

(iii) Travaux de démontage et de transport des hangars d'aviation de Gleiwitz.

(*b*) Pour l'exécution de cette mission, le Comité de Garantie aura le droit d'adresser aux autorités allemandes les communications et les demandes de renseignements qui lui paraîtront nécessaires.

(*c*) Le comité ou tout membre ou membres délégués pourront se rendre en tout point du territoire allemand, en tout temps et pour la durée qui semblera utile au président.

Avec l'autorisation écrite de leur président, ils pourront visiter et inspecter toute usine ou établissement aéronautique ou tous établissements pouvant être utilisés pour la fabrication, l'emmagasinage ou la vente du matériel d'aviation.

(C)—*Inspections spéciales faites par un Personnel supplémentaire*

Après décision de la Conférence des Ambassadeurs dans chaque cas, la mission pourra être renforcée par un personnel supplémentaire chargé de faire une inspection spéciale, en cas de besoin.

La Conférence des Ambassadeurs déterminera le personnel supplémentaire, strictement limité aux besoins, à envoyer en Allemagne. Ces inspections spéciales, ainsi qu'une déclaration concernant l'étendue et la durée éventuelle de l'inspection seront notifiées d'avance au Gouvernement allemand, qui accordera toutes facilités nécessaires à l'exécution complète des travaux en vue.

(D)—*Date d'Entrée en Fonctions et Durée*

Le Comité de Garantie sera rendu à Berlin au plus tard le 21 avril 1922. Il commencera à fonctionner le 5 mai 1922 et continuera jusqu'au jour où conformément à l'article 429 du Traité de Paix la première zone d'occupation pourra être évacuée. Les Gouvernements alliés examineront alors si les circonstances rendent nécessaire de prolonger le fonctionnement desdits comités ou au contraire permettent d'y mettre fin.

(E)—*Conditions exigées du Gouvernement allemand*

(i) Reconnaître officiellement le 'Comité de Garantie' quand la Commission aéronautique interalliée de Contrôle quittera Berlin.

[5] The resolutions of December 16 were reported by Sir M. Cheetham in his telegram No. 956 of December 16, 1921, extracts of which are printed in Vol. XVI, No. 853.

(ii) Désigner une autorité qui représentera le Gouvernement allemand vis-à-vis du comité.

(iii) Fournir au président tous les passeports ou autres autorisations écrites, tous les renseignements et permis qu'il pourra juger utiles pour exercer les fonctions définies ci-dessus.

(iv) Garantir de ne gêner, ni entraver l'accomplissement des inspections d'experts supplémentaires exposées au paragraphe (C) ci-dessus.

(v) Assurer au comité un logement convenable.

(vi) Accorder aux membres du comité les privilèges diplomatiques et aux locaux du comité un statut extra-territorial.

(vii) Envoyer, lorsqu'il en sera prié, un officier de liaison chargé d'accompagner le personnel du comité au cours d'inspections.

(F)—*Dépenses*

L'entretien et les frais des diverses délégations composant le Comité de Garantie sont supportés par les Gouvernements intéressés. Toute dépense accidentale, dûment autorisée et entraînée par les travaux du comité considéré comme un tout, sera supportée en parties égales par les Puisssances représentées.

Règles de Discriminations des Appareils civils et des Appareils militaires[6]

(A)—*Appareils volants plus lourds que l'Air*

Règle No. 1—Tout monopla[n]e ayant une puissance supérieure à 60 H.P. sera considéré comme militaire, donc matériel de guerre.

Règle No. 2—Tout appareil pouvant voler sans pilote sera considéré comme militaire, donc matériel de guerre.

Règle No. 3—Tout appareil ayant soit:

Un blindage ou un moyen de protection quelconque;

Une installation lui permettant de recevoir un armement quelconque: canon, torpille bombe, avec des aménagements de visée pour les engins ci-dessus,

sera considéré comme militaire, donc matériel de guerre.

Les limites suivantes seront les maxima pour tous les appareils plus lourds que l'air et tous ceux qui dépasseront ces limites seront considérés comme militaires, donc matériel de guerre.

Règle No. 4—Plafond maximum à pleine charge 4,000 mètres (un moteur ayant une installation permettant la surcompression fera rentrer l'appareil qui en sera muni dans la catégorie militaire).

Règle No. 5—Vitesse à pleine charge et à une altitude de 2,000 mètres, 170 kilom. à l'heure (les moteurs à pleine charge et par conséquent donnant le maximum de force).

Règle No. 6—La quantité maximum d'huile et de carburant à emporter (meilleure qualité d'essence d'aviation n'excédera pas $\dfrac{800[\times]170}{V}$ grammes

---

[6] See Vol. XVI, No. 804.

H.P., *V* étant la vitesse de la machine à pleine charge et à pleine puissance à 2,000 metres d'altitude.

Règle No. 7—Tout appareil capable d'emporter une charge utile dépassant 600 kilog., pilote, mécanicien et instruments compris, alors que les conditions des règles 4, 5 et 6 auront été remplies, sera considéré comme militaire, donc matériel de guerre.

(B)—*Dirigeables*

Les dirigeables dont le cube dépassera les chiffres ci-dessous seront considérés comme militaires, donc matériel de guerre :—

1. Dirigeables rigides	.	.	.	.	30,000 m³
2. Dirigeables semi-rigides	.	.	.		25,000 m³
3. Dirigeables non rigides	.	.	.		20,000 m³

Règle No. 8—Les usines fabriquant du matériel aéronautique devront être déclarées. Tous les appareils et pilotes ou élèves-pilotes devront être immatriculés dans les conditions prévues par la convention du 13 octobre 1919. Ces listes seront tenues à la disposition du Comité de Garantie.

Règle No. 9—Les stocks de moteurs d'aviation, de pièces détachées, d'accessoires de moteurs ne seront pas autorisés au delà de ce qui sera apprecié nécessaire pour satisfaire aux besoins de l'aviation civile. Ces quantités seront déterminées par le Comité de Garantie.

Remarques générales

On estime que les définitions ci-dessus auront à être revisées tous les deux ans, afin de considérer les modifications que les progrès de l'aéronautique auraient à y faire apporter.

Annexe (B)

Constitution, Fonctions et Droits du Comité de Garantie militaire

Un 'Comité de Garantie militaire' sera établi en Allemagne après le départ de la Commission militaire interalliée de Contrôle. Il aura son siège à Berlin.

(A)—*Composition*

(a) *Officiers*

	Colonels ou Lieutenants-colonels*	Commandants ou Capitaines	Total
Officiers français . . .	3	4	7
Officiers anglais . . .	2	2	4
Officiers italiens . . .	2	1	3
Officiers japonais . . .	2†	1	3
Officiers belges . . .	2	1	3
	11	9	20

* Y compris un officier général, président de la mission. † Ou commandants.

(b) *Sous-officiers et Soldats*

	Français	Anglais	Italiens	Japonais	Belges
Secrétaires militaires .	4	2	2	2	2
Ordonnances. . .	4	3	2	1	2
Automobilistes . .	2	1	1	1	1
Total . . .	10	6	5	4	5
Automobiles . . .	2	1	1	1	1

(B)—*Fonctions et Pouvoirs*

(*a*) La Mission du Comité de Garantie militaire est de donner aux Puissances alliées la garantie que les clauses militaires du Traité de Versailles et les décisions complémentaires prises par les Gouvernements alliés en vue de leur exécution sont fidèlement observées.

(*b*) Pour l'exécution de cette mission, le Comité de Garantie aura le droit d'adresser aux autorités allemandes les communications et les demandes de renseignements qui lui paraîtront nécessaires.

(*c*) Le comité ou tout membre ou membres délégués pourront se rendre en tout point du territoire allemand, en tout temps, et pour la durée qui semblera utile au président.

Avec l'autorisation écrite de leur président, ils pourront visiter et inspecter tout arsenal, établissement militaire ou usine pouvant être utilisés pour préparer, fabriquer, emmagasiner les armes, les munitions et le matériel de guerre de toute espèce, ou faire les inspections considérées nécessaires pour le contrôle des effectifs et de l'armement de l'armée allemande et des forces de police, ainsi que pour le contrôle de toute organisation non autorisée que l'on soupçonnera d'avoir un caractère militaire. Ils devront être accompagnés par le représentant du Gouvernement allemand visé ci-dessus au paragraphe (E).

NOTE.—Dans l'expression ci-dessus : 'armes, munitions et matériel de guerre de toute espèce,' il faut comprendre 'les canons de tous modèles susceptibles d'être utilisés sur terre'.

(C)—*Inspections spéciales faites par un Personnel supplémentaire*

Après décision de la Conférence des Ambassadeurs dans chaque cas, le comité pourra être renforcé par un personnel allié supplémentaire chargé de faire une inspection spéciale, en cas de besoin. La Conférence des Ambassadeurs déterminera le personnel supplémentaire strictement limité aux besoins, à envoyer en Allemagne. Ces inspections spéciales, ainsi qu'une déclaration concernant l'étendue et la durée éventuelle de l'inspection, seront notifiées d'avance au Gouvernement allemand, qui accordera toutes les facilités nécessaires à l'exécution complète des travaux en vue.

(D)—*Date d'Entrée en Fonction et Durée*

Le Comité de Garantie militaire commencera à fonctionner à une date qui sera fixée ultérieurement. Il continuera ses fonctions jusqu'au jour où, conformément à l'article 429 du Traité de Paix, la première zone d'occupation pourra être évacuée; les Gouvernements alliés examineront alors si les circonstances rendent nécessaire de prolonger le fonctionnement desdits comités ou, au contraire, permettent d'y mettre fin.

(E)—*Conditions exigées du Gouvernement allemand*

(i) Reconnaître officiellement le Comité de Garantie quand la Commission militaire interalliée de Contrôle quittera Berlin.

(ii) Désigner une autorité qui représentera le Gouvernement allemand vis-à-vis du comité.

(iii) Fournir au président tous les passeports et autorisations écrites, tous les renseignements et permis qu'il pourra juger utiles pour exercer les fonctions ci-dessus.

(iv) Garantir de ne gêner, ni entraver l'accomplissement des inspections d'experts supplémentaires exposées au paragraphe (C) ci-dessus.

(v) Assurer au comité un logement convenable.

(vi) Accorder aux membres du comité les privilèges diplomatiques et aux locaux du comité un statut extra-territorial.

(vii) Envoyer, lorsqu'il en sera prié, un officier de liaison chargé d'accompagner le personnel du comité au cours d'inspections.

(F)—*Dépenses*

L'entretien et les frais des diverses délégations composant le Comité de Garantie seront supportés par les Gouvernements intéressés. Toute dépense accidentelle, dûment autorisée, et entraînée, par les travaux du comité, considéré comme un tout, sera supportée en parties égales par les Puissances représentées au comité.

Annexe (C)

Travaux essentiels restant à effectuer par les Commissions de Contrôle militaire et navale et Délais dans lesquels ils peuvent être achevés si le Gouvernement allemand prête son Concours à ces Commissions

(A)—*Commission de Contrôle militaire*

(a) *Armement*

Livraison et destructions de matériel de guerre restant à accomplir	15 juillet 1922.
Transformation des usines	1er octobre 1922.

(b) *Effectifs*

Rattachement au Ministère de la Reichswehr et compression des organes administratifs cédés à des administrations civiles . . . .

Réorganisation de la police:
Acceptation par le Gouvernement allemand des conditions indiquées par la C[ommission] M[ilitaire] I[nteralliée] [de] C[ontrôle] . 5 avril 1922.
Fin de l'exécution des mesures de réorganisation 25 mai 1922.
Contrôle de l'exécution de ces mesures . . 25 mai au 1er octobre 1922.

Réorganisation du Ministère de la Reichswehr . ⎫
Réglementation du recrutement des employés de l'Administration militaire . . . . ⎬ Avant le 1er octobre 1922 aux dates à fixer par la C[ommission] M[ilitaire] I[nteralliée] [de] C[ontrôle]
Suppression des cours spéciaux d'É[tat] M[ajor].
En général, exécution de toutes mesures ayant pour objet de conformer exactement l'organisation militaire allemande aux stipulations du traité . ⎭

(c) *Fortifications*

Destruction des ouvrages à démanteler immédiatement en territoire occupé . . . . 1er septembre 1922.

(d) *Législation*

Mise en concordance de la législation allemande avec ⎫
les stipulations de la Partie V du traité, en particulier au sujet de:
    La réorganisation de la police . . . ⎪
    Les services administratifs . . . . ⎪ Avant le 1er octobre
    Les pensions . . . . . . ⎬ 1922 aux dates à fixer par la C[ommission] M[ilitaire] I[nteralliée] [de] C[ontrôle]
    La démobilisation . . . . .
    Le désarmement de la population civile . ⎪
    Les fortifications . . . . . ⎪
    L'importation et l'exportation des armes .
    Le budget ('Haushaltrecht') . . . ⎭

(B)—*Commission de Contrôle navale*

Article 115—Fortifications d'Héligoland . . 30 avril.
Article 168 . . . . . . ⎫ Date antérieure au 30 septembre à fixer par la Commission de Contrôle
Article 169 . . . . . . ⎭
Article 189—Transformation des moteurs Diesel et des moteurs électriques; destruction des parties militaires . . . . . 31 mai.
Article 192—Matériel de la flotte d'après-guerre. 31 juillet.

Article 196—Matériel naval en excédent sur ⎫ Subordonné à la fin de la vérification en cours d'accord avec la Commission de Contrôle militaire. Au plus tard le 30 septembre
les quantités autorisées pour les fortifications . . . . . . ⎬
⎭

En ce qui concerne les autres articles des clauses navales, la mission de la Commission de Contrôle est terminée.

Matériel à livrer en compensation de Scapa Flow, matériel des croiseurs, etc.—

A la date du 30 septembre, il ne devra rester à achever que la construction du matériel de port dont les contrats ne prévoient l'achèvement total que fin 1922. Une commission de réception composée d'un petit nombre d'officiers des marines intéressées pourra être envoyée pour connaître et prendre livraison de ce matériel, sa mission étant exclusivement limitée à cette opération.

Si le matériel encore dû par l'Allemagne à la France et à l'Italie pour les bâtiments remis à ces Puissances ne leur a pas été entièrement livré au moment du départ de la Commission navale de Contrôle, une commission de recette franco-italienne très restreinte sera maintenue en Allemagne pendant le temps nécessaire avec cette mission exclusive.

No. 209

Lord Hardinge (Paris) to the Marquess Curzon of Kedleston
(Received April 22, 8.30 a.m.)
No. 227 Telegraphic: by bag [*C 5815/6/18*]

PARIS, *April 21, 1922*

My despatch No. 938 of April 14th.[1]
French government inform me that German ambassador here has acknowledged receipt of note in his own name but not in that of his government. French are considering what should be our next step if nothing further is heard from German government in the course of next few days. They suggested that allied ambassadors in Berlin should be instructed to warn the German government that if there is any delay existing aeronautical commission of control will be maintained after May 5th until the aeronautical mission of guarantee enters on its work.

I suggested as an alternative that we should assume that, as we heard nothing from the German government, they proposed to raise no difficulties, and that the allied governments should in the course of next week officially notify to the German government the names of the officers appointed to serve on the mission of guarantee.

I should be glad of an expression of Your Lordship's views on the procedure to be followed. I assume that you agree with the French government on the importance of avoiding any hiatus between the work of the aeronautical commission of control and the mission of guarantee.[2]

[1] No. 208.
[2] In telegram No. 149 of April 24 Lord Curzon replied: 'The assumption contained in

the last sentence of your telegram No. 227 of April 21st (Future of aeronautical control in Germany) is correct.

'But the Air Ministry point out that representations at Berlin on the lines proposed by the French government would imperil the smooth working of the new supervisory body.

'The alternative line of action suggested by Your Excellency is, therefore, fully approved.

'Names of British officers for aeronautical guarantee committee are:

'Group Captain A. B. Burdett, D.S.O., President.
Wing Commander J. R. W. Smyth-Pigott, D.S.O.
Squadron Leader J. H. Herring, D.S.O., M.C.
Flight Lieutenant R. S. Booth, A.F.C.'

In despatch No. 1051 of April 28 (C 6251/6/18), not printed, Lord Hardinge transmitted a copy of a note of April 28 from the Conference of Ambassadors informing the German Embassy of the names of the Allied officers appointed to the Aeronautical Mission of Guarantee.

No. 210

Mr. Lampson to the War Office
[C 5780/3589/18]

Immediate   FOREIGN OFFICE, *April 25, 1922*

Sir,

With reference to the War Office letter No. 0154/5938 (M.I.3) of April 7th,[1] I am directed by the Marquess Curzon of Kedleston to transmit to you herewith copy of a memorandum[2] from the French ambassador enquiring the attitude of H[is] M[ajesty's] G[overnment] towards the appeal of the German Gov[ernmen]t to the allied Gov[ernmen]ts on the question of the reorganisation of the German police on a 1913 basis. A similar note to that referred to by Count de Saint-Aulaire was addressed to the Foreign Office by M. Sthamer on April 13th,[1] and a translation was forwarded to the War Office in Foreign Office letter No. C 5694/3589/18 of April 20th.[1]

2. I am to enquire whether, in the light of the arguments contained in M. Sthamer's note, the Army Council desire to modify the view expressed in the War Office letter under reference, and what attitude they consider that H[is] M[ajesty's] G[overnment] should adopt towards the German government's appeal to the allied governments on this question.[3]

---

[1] Not printed.   [2] Of April 20, not printed.
[3] In their letter of May 1, the War Office replied: '. . . the arguments contained in Herr Sthamer's note of 13th April, have not caused the Army Council to alter their views as expressed in War Office letter No. 0154/5938 (M.I.3.) of 7th April. . . . The Army Council . . . suggest that His Majesty's Government should adopt an attitude to the German Government's appeal similar to that of the French, as stated in the memorandum of the French Ambassador. The Army Council also suggest that the German Government should be made to realize that the Inter-Allied Military Commission of Control in Germany has full authority from the Allied Governments to supervise the execution of the military clauses of the Peace Treaty and that appeals to the Allied Governments against decisions of the Commission will serve no useful purpose and simply serve to postpone the day when it will be possible to withdraw the Commission from Germany.'

No. 211

Mr. Wigram[1] to Mr. Lampson
[C 6278/6217/18]

April 27, 1922

Dear Lampson,

With reference to my telegram to you of today,[2] the possibility of taking the opportunity of the meeting of states signatory to the Treaty of Versailles (for which the Prime Minister asked Barthou yesterday)[3] to try to settle at the same time all the big points outstanding between the French and ourselves in the matter of Germany will no doubt already have occurred to you.

2. I spoke to Hankey[4] about the matter last night, and he said he thought it most important that we should be prepared, at any rate with up-to-date briefs, on all these questions. As explained in my telegram, the chief points appear to be: (1) the question of the missions of guarantee;[5] (2) the date of the commencement of the [evacuation] of the Rhineland;[5] (3) Rhineland licensing;[6] (4) the military sanction,[7] and (5) the war criminals.[8] Possibly also it would be well to take the opportunity to try to settle any questions in which the Germans are proving particularly recalcitrant, such as the emigration licences;[9] though I do not know exactly how this matter stands.

3. As regards questions 2, 3 and 4 above, I have most information here, at any rate up to March 15, since when I am not aware that these questions have progressed in any way. I have not, however, the latest information respecting guarantee commissions, nor have I anything recent about the war criminals, except Sir E. Crowe's recent interview with Sthamer, which is in print.[8]

4. Whether it would be desirable that we should take the initiative in raising the war criminals question at all, I am very uncertain. But it is quite likely that the French will raise it, seeing that, technically at any rate, the report of the war criminals commission is still waiting to be passed by the Supreme Council. Were the question not raised, and therefore left unsettled, we should have to remember that it would remain a weapon in the hands of the French, which they might at any moment decide to use, and thereby again provide an element of uncertainty, in the whole German, and consequently European, situation.

As regards missions of guarantee, I think you already know that it is at present understood to be the Prime Minister's intention to try to get the

---

[1] Mr. Wigram was a member of the British Delegation at the Conference of Genoa (see Vol. XIX, Chap. III).

[2] Genoa telegram No. 108 (C 6217/6217/18), not printed.

[3] See Vol. XIX, No. 96.

[4] Sir M. Hankey acted as secretary to the British Empire Delegation at Genoa.

[5] See Nos. 180 and 183.

[6] See No. 197.

[7] See No. 176.

[8] See No. 170.

[9] A note on the original runs: 'This is already settled.'

Russian armaments referred to the Disarmament Commission of the League, and that for this purpose some representation will presumably have to be given to Russia on the League Disarmament Commissions. Whether the question of the participation of Germany in these League Disarmament Commissions will also be raised is not yet, as far as I can make out, decided. I think that, despite the fact that German armaments have already been limited under the treaty, there would be a good deal to be gained by roping Germany also into the League Disarmament Commissions. The work of these commissions will, we must hope, be taken up more seriously after this conference comes to an end; and we may therefore suppose that the commissions themselves will be correspondingly strengthened. In these circumstances, the need for separate allied control of German armaments might then be lessened, and it might be possible to rely on the right of verification of German armaments accorded to the League by article 213 of the treaty. In any case, this possibility should, I think, be remembered, and if the Germans jib at accepting the aeronautical or military guarantee commission, or both, we might be well advised not to press them too hard at Paris for the next two or three weeks. I cannot believe that it is really vital whether the aeronautical commission of guarantee enters upon its duties on May 5, or a month later.

I enclose a copy of the latest draft[10] of the suggested resolutions about the extension of the League's disarmament enquiries. This draft is, of course, nothing but a suggestion at the moment.

Y[ou]rs ever,
R. F. WIGRAM

[10] Not printed.

No. 212

Lord Hardinge (Paris) to the Marquess Curzon of Kedleston
(Received May 3, 8.30 a.m.)
No. 249 Telegraphic: by bag [C 6468/6/18]

PARIS, May 2, 1922

My telegram No. 212 of 14th April, section 3.[1]

Note was received last night from German ambassador stating that his government accepted Aeronautical Mission of Guarantee (copy of note is enclosed in my despatch No. 1072).[2]

I understand that Marshal Foch is telegraphing to General [*sic*] Masterman in Berlin instructing him to take formal leave of the German authorities on May 5th, and at the same time to introduce Group-Captain Burdett[3] as the president of the new Mission of Guarantee.

[1] No. 207.   [2] Of May 2 (C 6523/6/18), not printed.
[3] See No. 209, n. 2.

I hope that arrangements can be made for the presence of the latter office in Berlin on the date mentioned.

No. 213

The Marquess Curzon of Kedleston to Count de Saint-Aulaire and to Baron Moncheur

[*C 6148/1188/18*]

FOREIGN OFFICE, *May 2, 1922*

Your Excellency,

In my note of the 7th April[1] I had the honour to inform you that I had returned an interim reply[2] to the note[3] in which the United States Ambassador had set out the claim of his Government that the costs of their army of occupation on the left bank of the Rhine should be reimbursed to them, and I foreshadowed the submission of proposals which might form the basis for a definitive reply to be made in identic terms by the Allied Governments concerned.

2. The draft note which I now have the honour to communicate to your Excellency herewith is an attempt to formulate the line of argument which, in the opinion of His Majesty's Government, the Allied Governments would be well advised to follow in framing their reply to the United States Government. It will be observed that it avoids a discussion of the legal grounds upon which the United States claim is ostensibly based. Those grounds are, I am advised, of doubtful validity; but, both the French and the Belgian Governments having, like His Majesty's Government, expressed their desire that the claim of the United States Government should be satisfied, the question is one upon which controversy, undesirable in any case, is now unnecessary.

3. I should be glad to learn whether the French Government are so far in agreement with the terms of this draft as to be ready to accept it as a basis for discussion, and, if so, whether they would be prepared to refer it to the Ambassadors' Conference with instructions to prepare on this basis, and with the assistance of representatives of the Reparation Commission, a joint communication to the United States Government, which should presumably be addressed by the conference to the United States Ambassador at Paris.

4. I have addressed a similar note to the Belgian/French Ambassador at this Court.

I have, etc.,

CURZON OF KEDLESTON

[1] See No. 204, n. 3.
[2] No. 204.
[3] See No. 196, n. 6 (see also No. 198).

Proposed Reply to the United States Notes as to the Reimbursement of the Costs of the United States Troops in Germany

The memorandum of the 22nd March[3] and the supplementary note of the 23rd March,[3] containing the views of the Government of the United States concerning the reimbursement of the costs of their army of occupation on the left bank of the Rhine, have received the fullest consideration by the Allied Governments concerned. These Governments have already indicated their willingness to find a practical means of meeting the manifestly just desires of the United States Government in this matter, so that it does not seem necessary at present to subject the reasoning contained in the United States notes to a detailed examination. The following observations to which the Allied Governments desire to confine themselves are therefore of a purely practical order, designed to expedite the solution of a problem as to which disagreement, if it exists at all, can only relate to the means and not to the end.

2. In the first place it must be explained that receipts from Germany up to the present date, whether in cash or in kind, have already been actually distributed, and were for practical purposes so distributed as far back as August 1921. Deliveries in kind have been made to specific countries and debited to those countries against the cost of their armies of occupation. The United States Government will doubtless recognise that such deliveries have in general terms been made for such specific purposes as the reconstruction of devastated areas. Deliveries in cash have been distributed to avoid useless and even dangerous accumulation in the hands of the Reparation Commission.

3. In the second place, to give effect to the claim of the United States Government in the precise form in which it is put forward would involve the complete reopening *ab initio* of all the complicated and difficult negotiations which eventually led to the solutions embodied in the Spa Agreement of July 1920[4] and the Paris Agreement of March 1922.[5]

4. These difficulties, however, detract nothing from the completeness with which the Allied Governments concur in the equity of the claim of the United States Government to obtain payment of their costs of occupation from Germany in priority to further payments to other countries on account of reparations. The Allied Governments welcome the expressed readiness of the United States Government to consider suggestions for the reasonable adjustment of the matter, which will clearly have to take into account the *de facto* position and the financial and economic questions involved, regard being had in particular to the considerable proportion of Germany's payments in the near future, which will be made in kind rather than in cash.

5. The Allied Governments would suggest that the most effective machinery for the purpose would be the appointment of an official United States delegate on the Reparation Commission. If such an appointment were made, there is little doubt that the Reparation Commission, who are the body

---

[4] See Vol. VIII, No. 77, n. 3.   [5] See No. 11, n. 2.

most competent to consider it in all its aspects, would be able to produce a satisfactory solution for the consideration of the Governments concerned. The latter therefore hope that the United States Government will take this suggestion into early and favourable consideration.

No. 214

The Marquess Curzon of Kedleston to British Delegation (Genoa)[1]
No. 66 Telegraphic [C 6544/6347/66]

FOREIGN OFFICE, *May 3, 1922, 4.15 p.m.*

Following for Prime Minister from Lord Privy Seal:[2]
Balfour[3] is due to attend council of League of Nations at Geneva on May 12th and has consulted Fisher[4] as to line to be taken.

Fisher asks me to put following question to you:

'Would you approve of an announcement being made in the House by way of question and answer that His Majesty's Government would be disposed to support the admission of Germany to the League of Nations next September, in the event of her making application and assuming that no untoward event intervenes? The arguments in favour of such an announcement are that Germany is unlikely to apply without an assurance of our support, and that the sooner that assurance is given, the greater the probability of an application. You alone can estimate whether the hour is opportune but in any case I am inclined to think that as the French are certain to resist admission, whenever proposed, we had better take our own course. The continued exclusion of Germany for another year would undoubtedly seriously injure the reputation of the League. If an announcement had been made before council meeting Balfour could bring it to the notice of his colleagues if he thought fit.'

[1] For a documentation of the Genoa Conference, see Vol. XIX, Chap. III.
[2] Mr. Austen Chamberlain.
[3] The Earl of Balfour was President of the Council and British Delegate to the League of Nations.　　　　　　　　　　　　　　　　　　　[4] See No. 190.

No. 215

Minute by the Marquess Curzon of Kedleston
[C 6656/6347/18]

FOREIGN OFFICE, *May 4, 1922*

Lord Privy Seal,
I have always been in favour of the admission of Germany to the League and still am on general grounds. But I do not quite see why it is necessary to make an announcement in Parliament now.[1]

[1] See No. 214.

Germany undoubtedly was guilty of a very shabby trick in making the agreement with Russia[2] behind our backs. She has been caught out in some bad deceptions about disarmament. She is probably more deeply involved than we know. She has not at all a clean bill of health.

If we announce our support *now* it will look as though we condone all these offences, and she may do what she likes.

If Balfour is asked as to his attitude or thinks fit to mention the matter at Geneva, I think he might be authorised to say that His Majesty's Government will be disposed to support the proposal if it is put forward at the Assembly in September and if nothing wrong happens in the interval.[3]

But for the reasons named I see no reason why we should commit ourselves in the House of Commons four months in advance. Further, on the last occasion[4] we consulted all our Dominions, through their special Delegates in London. I think they would expect the same compliment now.

[2] The Treaty of Rapallo (see Vol. XIX, No. 75).

[3] In a minute of May 9 to the Lord Privy Seal, Mr. Fisher made the following comments: 'I acknowledge the strength of the Foreign Secretary's argument against an immediate declaration of our intention in view of what has happened at Genoa, but I do suggest that some means should be found before very long of conveying to Germany something in the sense of the penultimate paragraph of the Foreign Secretary's Minute. I suggest, in other words, that it is not France or the World at large whom it is important that we should apprise of our general attitude but the German Government, and, as I am disposed to think that the German Government is unlikely to go, in a matter of so great importance without the support of the public opinion of its Nationals, it will be necessary some time before September, that the attitude of the British Government on this subject should be known in Germany.'

[4] In September, 1921, when Latvia, Esthonia, and Lithuania were admitted to the League.

No. 216

Lord D'Abernon (Berlin) to the Marquess Curzon of Kedleston
(Received May 8, 8.30 a.m.)
No. 109 Telegraphic: by bag [C 6733/6/18]

BERLIN, *May 8, 1922*

Following sent to Genoa today No. 23.

Government publish official order establishing rules for aeroplane construction, in conformity with decision of Conference of Ambassadors of April 14th.[1]

The only hostile comment in the press is in *Zeit*, which says it had hoped for an energetic negative from the government.

The prompt acceptance by Germany of these limitations appears important, and suggests that speedy negotiations for modifications of military control should have good chance of success.

[1] See No. 207.

A negotiation resulting in reduction of present Commission of Control with appropriate safeguards and complementary measures would greatly strengthen position of moderate parties.

Would it not also assist non-aggression pact?

No. 217

Mr. Gregory[1] *(Genoa) to the Marquess Curzon of Kedleston*
(Received May 10, 8.30 a.m.)
No. 170 Telegraphic [C 6869/6347/18]

GENOA, *May 9, 1922*

Following from Prime Minister for Mr. Chamberlain.
Your telegram No. 66.[2]
I cordially approve announcement in the House regarding admission of Germany to League of Nations which Mr. Fisher suggests.

[1] Head of the Northern Department of the Foreign Office, and a member of the British Empire Delegation at the Genoa Conference.
[2] No. 214.

No. 218

The Marquess Curzon of Kedleston to Mr. Gregory (Genoa)
No. 90 Telegraphic [C 6869/6347/18]

FOREIGN OFFICE, *May 10, 1922, 3.30 p.m.*

Following for Prime Minister from Mr. Chamberlain.
Confidential
Your No. 170.[1] Admission of Germany to League of Nations.
In view of delicate situation arising out of recent events at Genoa and after consultation with Curzon I think it would be a mistake to make formal announcement in Parliament at this moment. I fear it would be treated as evidence of estrangement from France and new orientation of policy. I propose therefore if possible to defer any statement till after your return but to inform Balfour through Fisher that if he is asked as to his attitude or thinks fit to mention the matter at Geneva he might say that the government will be disposed to support the proposal if it is put forward at the Assembly in September and if nothing wrong happens in the interval.

[1] No. 217.

Consul-General Thurstan (Cologne) to the Marquess Curzon of Kedleston
(Received May 15)
No. 102 [C 7146/336/18]

COLOGNE, *May 10, 1922*

My Lord,

I have the honour to transmit herewith, for your Lordship's information, copy of a despatch, No. 60, which I have this day addressed to His Majesty's Ambassador at Berlin.

I have, etc.,
E. W. P. THURSTAN

ENCLOSURE IN No. 219

Consul-General Thurstan to Lord D'Abernon

No. 60   *Confidential*   COLOGNE, *May 10, 1922*

My Lord,

With reference to my previous despatches, ending with No. 53 of the 26th April[1] last, on the subject of the Rhineland separatist movement, I think it necessary that I should call your Excellency's attention to the serious stage which this movement has now in my opinion reached.

The movement may be classified under three heads: the most modest of these envisages a form of home rule under the Weimar Constitution; the middle course comprises a Rhineland Republic, which, while it might be titulary independent, would, in the opinion of most Rhinelanders at least, constitute a French protectorate; the extreme possibility is that of a frank annexation by France.

The limitations put upon my powers of observation of the progress and possibilities of this movement by the present necessity for economy preclude me from furnishing your Excellency with all the information which I might otherwise well be able to put at your disposal. Nevertheless, I think it desirable to state my views on the subject for what they are worth, since I believe that this is a matter which may engage the very serious attention of His Majesty's Government at a later date, and possibly even in the near future.

I do not think that the question of Home Rule, as conceived under the Weimar Constitution, however interesting it may be to Rhinelanders, is a matter for concern to His Majesty's Government, or is, at any rate, of more than academic interest. In any case it will presumably be settled constitutionally when the occupation ceases, if the present will of the political parties concerned is observed. The second and third contingencies that I have mentioned above are, however, far more serious. In my opinion they may, for all practical purposes, be considered as one single problem, since

[1] Not printed.

I cannot see that from the point of view of the future peace of Europe there can be any distinction possible between a Rhineland republic erected under the *de facto* or *de jure* protection of France and a Rhineland frankly annexed by that country.

It seems to me that there are three postulates for the success of a Rhineland separated from the rest of Germany, namely, the consent of the Rhinelanders, the consent of the rest of Germany and the possibility of the maintenance of the Rhineland as a separate economic entity. The absence of any one of these three conditions would cause the scheme to be a failure in the end. I am doubtful, however, whether any single one of the three is possible of fulfilment, otherwise I am inclined to suppose that the creation of a separate Rhineland would constitute an ideal solution of the Franco-German problem from the point of view of His Majesty's Government, since it seems clear that a buffer State, taking no particular interest in either Germany or France, but solicitous only for its own security, would undoubtedly constitute to a great degree a pledge of security on this continent. Unfortunately, however, quite apart from the question of Germany's consent and of the economic difficulties involved, I cannot see that there is any desire on the part of serious Rhinelanders to form themselves into any such buffer State. The French had, in my opinion, a certain opportunity of furthering their ends when they advanced into the Rhineland in 1918, but all this has been gratuitously thrown away. In fact, the somewhat vague traditions of the benefits conferred upon the Rhineland by the Napoleonic occupation have been more than obliterated by measures such as the employment of coloured troops and by the arbitrary methods generally adopted.

In my opinion, a free plebiscite held now to decide whether the Rhineland should constitute a separate political and economic entity would, as I have stated in previous despatches on this subject, result in an overwhelming majority for continued unity with the German Reich. To such an extent is this the case that the mere idea of holding such a plebiscite is ridiculous. There remains, however, the possibility that force of circumstances would decree otherwise. The separatist movement in 1918 and 1919 had its origin in fear of Spartacism rather than in any desire for an orientation towards France. The events which have ocurred during the intervening period have swayed the more serious Rhinelanders in the opposite direction. They have not been blind to French policy and they have at the same time recognised that the ultimate salvation of Germany, and possibly of Europe, lies in unity and not in disintegration. At the same time the existing apathy, nervous tension and complete lack of pride or confidence in the Berlin Government all tend to keep the path open for the leaders of the separatist movement, however ridiculous a figure Herr Smeets[2] or his colleagues may for the moment cut. It is for this reason that the movement constitutes a danger. The events of the last few years have gone to prove that a small minority can, in given circumstances, gain complete mastery over the rest of the community. I have been confidentially informed from a German

[2] See No. 288, below.

457

source, for the accuracy of which I cannot of course vouch, that successful separatist propaganda is now being conducted in the Eifel and the country districts west of Cologne between Aix-la-Chapelle and Trèves. The Germans accuse the French and Belgian Kreis officers of the High Commission of participation in this and do not hesitate to allege that French money is being freely spent in the cause. I understand that the principal inducement held out to the peasant is that he will be paid in francs instead of marks at par and that the Saar basin is dangled before his imagination as an enviable example. To the more intelligent farmers the prospect of a reduction in taxation and freedom from the burden of reparations is equally alluring. The movement seems to be insignificant in the city of Cologne and probably has few adherents in the larger towns of the Rhineland. That does not, however, necessarily mitigate its danger. In my despatch No. 244 of the 2nd December[1] last I alluded to the possibility of a separatist minority declaring a Rhineland republic under the ægis of the French and Belgi[an] troops of occupation. The events which have intervened since that date have by no means lessened this risk. Indeed, there is a probability that the greater the opposition to the designs of the French against the Rhur, the more they will be tempted to encourage Smeets and his adherents to risk a coup in the Rhineland. The local officials, the Rhineland press, and the Rhineland political parties have certainly been showing alarm on this score recently. I have the honour to transmit herewith, for your Excellency's information, a translation of a resolution[1] recently adopted by the Right and Middle Parties at Königs-winter. Similar manifestoes have been issued by the Centre Party from Königswinter, by the Democratic Party at Essen and by numerous trade organisations.

The German authorities seem to be afraid of interfering in any way with Herr Smeets's activities, as they regard him as being under the open protection of the French and financed by the latter. Indeed, I am credibly informed that he is now frequently to be seen using a French military automobile. The decision of the inter-Allied Rhineland High Commission, reported in my despatch No. 246 of the 12th December last,[1] that proceedings against Herr Smeets should be suspended, may prove to have far-reaching consequences, if this movement develops further.

I have sent copies of this despatch to His Majesty's Secretary of State for Foreign Affairs and to the British High Commissioner at Coblenz.

I have, etc.,
E. W. P. THURSTAN

No. 220

The Marquess Curzon of Kedleston to Lord D'Abernon (Berlin)
No. 45 Telegraphic [C 6733/6/18]

FOREIGN OFFICE, *May 11, 1922, 6 p.m.*

Your telegram to Genoa No. 23.[1]

Has there been any hitch with German government in negotiations for eventual substitution of Committee of Military guarantee for existing Commission of Military Control? Or is your idea merely that pressure at Genoa may expedite matters?

I had hoped that prompt acceptance by German government of aeronautical control (see your telegram No. 107)[2] might be taken as good augury and that we should soon hear of similar acceptance of committee of military guarantee. In short I am not quite clear why you have referred matter to Genoa at this stage.

Repeated to Genoa No. 99.

[1] See No. 216.
[2] Of May 1, not printed.

No. 221

Lord D'Abernon (Berlin) to the Marquess Curzon of Kedleston
(Received May 13, 8.30 a.m.)
No. 112 Telegraphic [C 7033/6/18]

BERLIN, *May 12, 1922, 8.35 p.m.*

Your telegram No. 45.[1]

There has been no hitch.

On the contrary prompt acceptance by German government of aeronautical control is of good augury for similar acceptance of committee of military guarantee.

This is stated in my telegram No. 23,[2] the object of which was to confirm the view that a successful negotiation on the subject is probably attainable in the immediate future.

Event must however depend in a large measure on Genoa.[3]

Repeated to Genoa.

[1] No. 220.
[2] No. 216.
[3] See Vol. XIX, Chap. III.

No. 222

Lord Hardinge (Paris) to the Marquess Curzon of Kedleston
(Received May 19, 8.30 a.m.)
No. 278 Telegraphic: by bag [C 7311/3589/18]

PARIS, *May 17, 1922*

The Conference of Ambassadors met this morning under the chairmanship of M. Jules Cambon, the Belgian ambassador being also present, and considered the following questions:—

. . .[4]. The German Government having addressed to the Conference of Ambassadors a similar note to that addressed to His Majesty's Government on the subject of the organisation of the German police (enclosed in your Lordship's despatch No. 1352),[2] the conference decided to reply to the German Government that the Military Commission of Control was fully authorised to settle this question without appealing to the Allied Governments direct. This is in accordance with instructions contained in your Lordship's despatch No. 1339 of 5th May[3]. . . .[1]

---

[1] The sections omitted referred to other matters.

[2] Of May 6, not printed. See, however, No. 210, n. 3.

[3] Not printed. In a letter of May 5 to the Count de Saint-Aulaire, Lord Curzon wrote: 'His Majesty's Government . . . are disposed to think that the most effective method of dealing with this protest will be that the Ambassadors' Conference should impress upon the German Government that the Commission of Control has full authority from the allied governments to supervise the execution of the military clauses of the Treaty of Versailles and that appeals to the allied governments against decisions of the Commission will serve no useful purpose, but will merely serve to postpone the day when it will be possible to withdraw the Commission from Germany. . . .'

No. 223

Mr. Gregory (Genoa) to the Earl of Balfour (Geneva)
No. 214 Telegraphic [C 7329/6347/18]

GENOA, *May 18, 1922*

Addressed to Geneva No. 2, repeated to Foreign Office.[1]
Following for Lord Balfour from Prime Minister.

German Chancellor tells me while he is personally strongly in favour of League of Nations, it is not possible in present state of German feeling regarding League for Germany to apply for admission and he begged that question might not be raised at present. He mentioned decisions of League in regard to Upper Silesia[2] and Saar[3] as causes of this feeling.

---

[1] This telegram was received in the Foreign Office at 8.30 a.m. on May 19.

[2] See Vol. XVI, No. 329.

[3] See No. 190.

No. 224

The Marquess Curzon of Kedleston to Mr. Harvey
[*C 6950/1229/18*]

FOREIGN OFFICE, *May 18, 1922*

Your Excellency,

With reference to your note No. 110 of the 9th March,[1] I have the honour to inform you that on the 10th May the Ambassadors' Conference at Paris approved a scheme[2] which had been unanimously submitted to them by the Allied Military Committee at Versailles, in concurrence with the technical representative of the United States Government, for the distribution of the amount to be paid by the German Government for the illegal destruction of German Zeppelins. Under this scheme the German Government will be requested to pay a total of 9,550,000 gold marks, which will be divided amongst the Allied and Associated Powers in the following proportions:—

	Marks
United States	3,031,665
Italy	1,031,667
England	1,631,667
Japan	1,581,667
Belgium	1,531,667
France	741,667
	9,550,000

2. In communicating the above information to your Excellency, I would express my gratification that a settlement of this question has been reached in a manner which I trust will be regarded as satisfactory by the United States Government.

I have, etc,
CURZON OF KEDLESTON

[1] Not printed.
[2] This was reported by Lord Hardinge in his despatch No. 1123 of May 10, not printed.

No. 225

The Earl of Balfour[1] to Lord Hardinge (Paris)
No. 1623 [*C 7402/555/18*]

FOREIGN OFFICE, *May 27, 1922*

My Lord,

With reference to the Marquess Curzon's despatch No. 1521 of the 19th May,[2] in regard to the war criminals question, I transmit to Your Excellency

[1] See No. 24, n. 1.
[2] This ran: 'The French Ambassador spoke to Sir Eyre Crowe on the 12th May of the

herewith copies of two memoranda from the French Ambassador at this Court,[3] together with a note to the French Ambassador[3] and a copy of a memorandum[4] summarising the history of the negotiations between the Allied Governments and the German Government respecting the extradition of the war criminals.

2. Your Excellency is authorised to consent to the discussion at the Ambassadors' Conference of the report of the Allied War Criminals Commission dated the 7th January, 1922, and you are authorised to co-operate in the preparation of a draft note to the German Government. You should, however, only agree to such draft *ad referendum*. It should be submitted to me for the approval of His Majesty's Government before it is definitely adopted and despatched.

3. The observations contained in the accompanying memorandum may be of assistance to you in any discussion which may take place. It will be observed that there is a difficulty in the way of the suggestion made by the French Government that the communication to be addressed by the Ambassadors' Conference to the German Government should take note of the refusal of the latter to execute article 228 of the Treaty of Versailles, namely, that the German Government, never having been invited by the Allied Governments to give specific effect to that article, can hardly be said to have refused to do so.

4. I would add, for your information and guidance when the terms of the note to the German Government are under discussion by the Ambassadors' Conference, that His Majesty's Government are anxious that no form of words should be used which could be interpreted as meaning that the Allied Governments thereby make a demand for the surrender of the criminals under the powers conferred upon them by article 228 (2) of the treaty.

I am, etc.,
BALFOUR

present position of the question of the war criminals who, under the Treaty of Versailles, were originally to have been surrendered by the German Government for trial in the Allied countries. His Excellency recalled that, as a result of the gross miscarriage of justice at Leipzig, the French Government had decided to withdraw from the German tribunal any further cases. Since then the unsatisfactory attitude of the German authorities had been further illustrated by the escape of some of the prisoners which the Leipzig court had sentenced to imprisonment and by the utter failure of the German authorities either to recapture the fugitives or to punish anybody for their evasion. The French Government considered that the time had come for the Allied Governments to come to some decision as to what they should now do, and they thought the best method of procedure would be to charge the Ambassadors' Conference at Paris to discuss the matter and to submit a report and recommendations.'

[3] Not printed.

[4] Of May 24 (C 7723/555/18), not printed. See, however, No. 170.

Memorandum respecting the Definition of Arms, Export of which from Germany is prohibited by Article 170 of Treaty of Versailles, and necessity for stricter Control to prevent their Export

[*C 7806/32/18*]

FOREIGN OFFICE, *May 29, 1922*

1. The question of the scope of the prohibition contained in article 170 has been raised at various times in connection with sporting rifles, pistols, revolvers, swords and daggers. The following is a history of the attitude of the Commission of Control in the application of article 170 in these cases.

2. On the 30th June, 1920, the Allied Military Committee of Versailles instructed the Commission of Control to inform the German Government that the import or export of all revolvers was prohibited so long as German disarmament was incomplete, and that the import or export of sporting rifles capable of firing ammunition of any war pattern actually in use was also prohibited.

3. In August 1921 the Control Commission interpreted the above decision as covering revolvers and pistols of all calibres, and further decided that the prohibition also covered sporting rifles of military calibre, even though incapable of taking military ammunition.

4. The Commission of Control also defined sporting rifles as those which did not possess a chamber of a design allowing the use of ammunition used by the German or any foreign armies. This definition was thus based on the chamber rather than on the calibre of the rifle, the latter not being restricted in any way.

5. On the 10th February, 1922, the Commission of Control modified their decision of the 30th June, 1920, in regard to revolvers and decided to prohibit the export from Germany of all automatic pistols and revolvers of a calibre greater than 6·5 millim[etres].

6. On the 13th March, 1922, the Commission of Control again changed their view and decided that export should be prohibited in the case of all automatic pistols and revolvers whose barrel was longer than 10 centim[etres].

7. On the 21st March the Allied legal advisers to the Ambassadors' Conference, who had been asked to advise on the interpretation of article 170, gave an opinion that at the present stage no extension of the meaning of the article to cover 'arms of war' outside the definitions fixed by the Control Commission in regard to manufacture in Germany (article 168) was feasible.

8. Early in April the Belgian Government suggested that export should be prohibited of pistols and revolvers above 8·2 millim[etres] in calibre and 8 centim[etres] in length of barrel. The Belgian Government subsequently amended these dimensions to 6·5 millim[etres] in calibre and 10 centim[etres] in length of barrel.

9. On the 5th April the Ambassadors' Conference decided to refer the whole matter back to the Allied Military Committee of Versailles for further study.

10. As regards swords and daggers, the Ambassadors' Conference have never come to any decision. The War Office view is that article 170 definitely applies to both, while the India Office desire that article to be interpreted as meaning the widest possible prohibition.

11. On the 11th May Lord D'Abernon reported that the Control Commission had sanctioned the export from Germany of officers' swords and fancy daggers, but had forbidden the export of ordinary swords and bayonets.

12. The Control Commission are reconsidering the question of the limitation of the calibre of pistols for export to 6·5 millim[etres]. They are also presumably considering the inclusion in this limitation of some definition in regard to length of barrel as suggested by the Belgian Government (see paragraph 8 above).

13. As regards the attitude of the various Allied Governments in regard to the execution of article 170, the Belgian Government clearly interpret its terms more broadly than His Majesty's Government. The attitude of the other Allies is unknown. At the instance of the Board of Trade we have already communicated to the Ambassadors' Conference the policy of His Majesty's Government, which is to allow the import of German arms from any country unless there is reason to think that the arms in question ought never to have been exported from Germany. The Belgian Government point out the difficulty at this late stage of a strict and uniform enforcement by the Allies of the terms of article 170, and have suggested that the only real method is to make control in Germany stricter, and therefore to eliminate the necessity for any investigation as regards arms upon their importation into Allied countries.

14. The difficulty of making control in Germany efficient is especially great in the case of the eastern frontier and the free port of Hamburg. In the former case, Lord D'Abernon has, in fact, reported that it is practically impossible to make the control efficient and that there is undoubtedly a considerable amount of smuggling of arms from Germany into Russia. Of this we have had many reports, but it has been impossible to prove any facts regarding smuggling of any important consignments. The case of Hamburg is difficult because the German Government have always the excuse that they have insufficient powers there to stop smuggling of arms owing to the special status of the port.

15. It is most important to secure two things:—

(1) That the Ambassadors' Conference, after consultation with the Military Committee of Versailles, shall fix definitely what arms are governed by article 170 of the treaty, and give detailed instructions to the Control Commission accordingly.

(2) In communicating these instructions to the Control Commission the conference should press for a more efficient control.

16. Unless we can obtain this, it is useless for His Majesty's Government to be more strict in regard to the import of German arms into this country than

the other Allied countries, e.g. Belgium. It will simply mean that we shall drive away trade from this country without in any way promoting the execution of article 170 of the treaty.

No. 227

Lord Robert Cecil[1] to the Earl of Balfour
(Received in the Foreign Office, June 13)
[*C 8506/6347/18*]

June 7, 1922

My dear Arthur,

I saw Edgar D'Abernon last Friday.[2] He was most helpful. At his request I prepared the enclosed memorandum which I have sent to him. Please read it if you have time.

Y[ou]rs ever,
ROBERT CECIL

ENCLOSURE IN No. 227

Memorandum on the Admission of Germany to the League of Nations

June 6, 1922

For the purposes of this memorandum it is unnecessary to insist on the general arguments in favour of bringing Germany into the League. It is common ground that the League, to fulfil properly its purpose, ought to be universal and in particular that Germany and the United States, and less urgently Russia should be made members of it as soon as possible. Only so will the League obtain the necessary prestige and authority to enable it to deal with first rate international crises.

In the case of Germany there are besides special reasons for her admission. For one thing in Poland and Czecho-Slovakia and to a lesser extent in some other states there are German racial minorities the protection of which has been guaranteed by the League under the so-called Minorities treaties. The only sanction provided by these treaties is that in case of any breach the matter may be brought before the Council by any member of that body, and if thought desirable any question arising on the subject can be referred to the Permanent Court of International Justice. By these means an appeal based on an authoritative exposition of the facts of the case can be made to the public opinion of the world. It is of great importance to the peace of Europe that the present unrest of these minorities of a vigorous race should be allayed and it is clear that their grievances can best be understood and championed by men of their own blood from within the League.

Again, a number of territorial questions were left half solved by the Treaty of Versailles and a varying degree of responsibility for their solution has been

---

[1] A delegate representing South Africa at the League of Nations.   [2] June 2.

placed on the League. In some cases such as [Schleswig][3] and the districts of Eupen[4] and Malmedy[4] a more or less acceptable decision has been given. In other cases like those of Dantzig,[5] the Saar Valley[6] and Upper Silesia,[7] administrative and political problems are continuous. Decisions are constantly being given affecting German interests, and even more German sentiment as to which her views are either not heard at all or are only heard by favour and precariously. The results even when intrinsically defensible enough—as I think the Silesian decision was—are regarded by Germany as grossly unjust to her. Were she a member of the League she could urge her own views for herself and even if the decision went against her it would, as in the case of other litigants who have been fully heard, lose half its bitterness. Moreover, it is not improbable that in many cases—particularly in the Saar— she would secure valuable modifications.

It is of no less importance that in the non-contentious jurisdiction of the League, i.e. its humanitarian, social and economic side, Germany should be given a position of complete equality such as by treaty she is given in the International Labour Office. This is especially true in economic matters where almost every serious step towards reconstruction depends on the adjustment of the German difficulties. I feel certain that these could be much better dealt with in a League atmosphere. Even the thorny reparations question might thus be brought to a settlement.

Beyond these considerations there are two of outstanding moment. In the first place the admission of Germany would remove one of the stumbling blocks in the way of the United States' progress towards full international co-operation. Not only do the German Americans—a powerful section—at present form a centre of anti-League feeling in America, but there is a widely spread opinion that the League as at present constituted is dominated by the Entente. The Hearst press constantly gird at it as being a purely British concern. And the intellectuals who resent the Versailles Treaty point to the exclusion of Germany as a typical example of the extent to which Europe is still controlled by the war mind.

More important still is the danger long obvious and emphasised by the Rapallo treaty[8] of a new grouping of Europe in which a Russo-German alliance gradually absorbing Austria and Hungary not to speak of Turkey and Bulgaria and perhaps Sweden, Holland, Spain and even Switzerland, will be opposed to the Entente weakened, it may be, by internal dissensions. At present German political fears of Bolshevism prevents any very large steps in this direction. But who shall say how long Russian Bolshevism will last? True it may be succeeded by anarchy for a time. On the other hand it may not, and in any case sooner or later—possibly in a few months—it will almost certainly develop into an ordinary military despotism with which the rulers of Germany will joyfully enter into the closest relations. As far as I can see

[3] See Vol. X, Chap. VI.
[4] See S. Wambaugh, *Plebiscites since the World War* (Washington, 1933), vol. i, pp. 518–38.
[5] See Vol. XI, Chap. II.   [6] See No. 190.
[7] See Vol. XVI, Part I.   [8] See Vol. XIX, No. 75, n. 1.

the only precaution open to us against this danger is to bring Germany into the orbit of the Western powers, and this can only be done by admitting her to the League, unless we are prepared to break with France which would be disastrous.

For it is now reasonably clear that though France will struggle instinctively against any direct renewal of friendly relations between her and Germany, and will, as at Genoa,[9] nullify by her action any open attempt to bring such a renewal about yet her Government is ready to accept the admission of Germany into the League largely perhaps because she knows she could not prevent it. Nothing is more certain than that if the admission of Germany were avowedly supported by the British Empire the Assembly would grant it by an overwhelming majority even against France. Whether this be the reason or not, Nobelmaire's[10] recent speech at Lyon handed to Lord D'Abernon, which I am told was approved beforehand by Poincaré, is strong evidence that France would not now resist Germany's entry, and this evidence is confirmed by what I understand is said by the French members of the Secretariat.

There still remains the chief difficulty, namely, the reluctance of Germany to apply for admission. In 1919 Germany was anxious to come in. She was quite ready to do so in 1920. But during 1921 her attitude changed. There had always been in Germany as elsewhere certain sections of opinion hostile to the League; the older officials who dislike new-fangled proposals, the men of the world who distrust anything with an idealistic twang, the fanatics who still believe in the purifying influence of war, and especially in Germany the militarists who worship the army, and the communists who resent any rival to the Third International. These have recently had considerable reinforcement from Germans who have been persuaded that the League is dominated by France. They point to the decisions about Eupen and Malmedy where they say the plebiscite was gerrymandered, and about Silesia, where they appear to have persuaded themselves that Lord Balfour was bamboozled by Monsieur Bourgeois.[11] They are also very indignant about the Government of the Saar Valley, where they are perhaps on stronger ground and about the refusal of the League to insist on the withdrawal of the French black troops of occupation which is silly. The answer of course to all these grievances is that so far as they are legitimate Germany would be in a far better position to cure them if she were a member of the League. As to the League being in the hands of the French, the common and more plausible charge in Paris is that it is in the hands of the English. Certainly the Covenant is a purely English document, the first local habitation of the League was in London, the Secretary-General[12] is an Englishman and no one who has attended the Assemblies can doubt that British influence there is far stronger than French. As a matter of fact so far no member of the League is predominant.

[9] See ibid., Chap. III.
[10] M. Georges Nobelmaire was a French delegate at the League of Nations.
[11] French representative on the Council of the League of Nations.
[12] Sir Eric Drummond.

Then the Germans ask whether if they were admitted to the League they would also have a seat on the Council. They certainly ought to have one, and they could be told that we would support their claim. But since the permanent members of the Council can only be increased by the unanimous vote of the existing Council we cannot guarantee to them a permanent place, though personally, I do not believe the French would be so ill-advised as to refuse it. If they did I feel morally certain that with British help they could secure election as one of the non-permanent members—a position to which next year permanence would assuredly be given.

A possibly more formidable difficulty is one put by a leading German to a friend of mine; viz. that Germany would scarcely like to apply for membership without the assent of Russia. For the reasons already given the closeness of German relations with Russia is likely to grow. At present it is not probable that it has got as far as my friend's informant indicated. Indeed, the argument might as things are be turned round and it might be suggested that if Germany did not apply she would be generally thought to be influenced in her attitude by Russian Bolshevism. Still no doubt it is true that all the classes in Germany who look for an ultimate war of Revenge—and Allied policy during the last three years must, one would think, have greatly swollen their numbers—look also to Russia as their chief hope for assistance in this object. That, as has already been said, constitutes one of the principal reasons why it is so urgent to get Germany into the League without further delay. If she is not admitted at the next Assembly it may well be that she will never come in.

German soreness with Allied policy and the Treaty of Versailles creates another and perhaps the strongest obstacle to her application for membership. It is said that to enter the League would be to recognise the Treaty of which it forms a part, and so to amount to a re-signature of it under conditions free from duress, and therefore more morally binding than in 1919. This seems a somewhat far-fetched argument. The League exists and has been constantly acknowledged by Germany. She has appealed for its help—fruitlessly it is true—on more than one occasion; as, for instance, when France occupied Frankfort,[13] against the Belgian arrangements for the Eupen and Malmedy plebiscite. She has, also, attended its Economic Conference at Brussels,[14] and its hygienic conference at Warsaw.[15] And she has been co-operating with Poland in the Commission under League Chairmanship about the Economic settlement of Upper Silesia.[16] Moreover, the Covenant is the chief antidote to the more deleterious provisions elsewhere found in the Treaty. This was well brought out by General Smuts when he published[17] his reasons for signing a Treaty many of the articles of which he disapproved. After pointing out various provisions in the Treaty which would require revision he said:—

'The real peace of the peoples ought to follow, complete, and amend the peace of the statesmen. In this Treaty, however, two achievements of far

[13] See Vol. IX, No. 294.   [14] See Vol. XIX, No. 2, n. 3 and No. 15.
[15] See ibid., No. 121.   [16] See n. 7, above.
[17] See *The Times*, June 30, 1919, p. 11.

reaching importance for the world are recorded. The one is the destruction of the Prussian militarism; the other is the institution of the League of Nations. I am confident that the League of Nations will yet prove the path of escape for Europe out of the ruin brought about by this war. . . . And the enemy peoples should at the earliest possible date join the League, and in collaboration with the Allied peoples learn to practise the great lesson of this war, that not in separate ambitions or in selfish domination, but in common service for the great human causes, lies the true path of national progress. This joint collaboration is especially necessary today for the reconstruction of a ruined and broken world.'

There may be other German reasons for refusing to apply for admission to the League. But there is also without doubt a considerable body of opinion in Germany favourable to her application. It is submitted that British influence if strongly exerted could easily persuade the German Government to apply, and if so, the sooner the better. Germany cannot afford to quarrel with us just now and for this and other reasons everyone agrees that our influence with her is very powerful. She must be desperately anxious on many grounds to be restored to full membership of the European community. Nothing would help her more in this direction than membership of the League. Nothing would do more to remove the suspicion still widely entertained that she is not genuinely anxious to co-operate in restoring to Europe that real peace which she so sorely needs.[18]

[18] Sir E. Crowe minuted on June 19: 'I would suggest whether the best course, as regards procedures, would not be that one of the States neutral in the great war, but on friendly terms with France—say Switzerland, or Norway, or Holland—should be asked by Germany to sound the French government confidentially whether they would approve Germany's reception into the league if proposed at its next meeting. I do not think we should say anything about Germany's entering the Council.'

On June 27 Mr. Vansittart added: 'Lord Balfour spoke to Lord Hardinge and to Lord D'Abernon about this. There was agreement—anyhow for the present—in the last sentence of Sir E. Crowe's minute. It was further decided that Lord D'Abernon should first further sound the Germans on the matter, as there had been some German opposition to the idea, headed by Dr. Rathenau, and this might be changed by his death.'

No. 228

Sir A. Geddes (Washington) to the Earl of Balfour
(Received June 19)

No. 691 [C 8724/336/18]

WASHINGTON, *June 9, 1922*

My Lord,

On receipt of Marquess Curzon's despatch No. 437 (C 4769/336/18) of April 8th last,[1] I communicated with my French and Belgian colleagues and

[1] This transmitted a copy of Coblenz despatch No. 93 of March 28, not printed, relative to the representation of the United States Government in the Rhineland and continued: 'It would be useful if you could ascertain informally what steps your French and Belgian

ascertained that they had not yet received any instructions to make a communication to the State Department in regard to the representation of the United States Government on the Rhineland. Since that date I have kept in close touch with M. Jusserand and Baron de Cartier with regard to this matter but they are still without instructions and indeed, on the 3rd instant, M. Jusserand informed me that he considered as useless any further action with a view to inducing the American Government to modify their decision to withdraw completely from any representation on the Rhineland.

The position was then completely changed by the decision of the American Government to retain about one thousand officers and men of the American forces [i]n the Rhineland, as I had the honour to report in my telegram No. 257 of the 6th of June.[2] Major General Allen will remain in command of these troops and it is not the present intention of the Secretary of State to make any modification in existing arrangement under which General Allen attends the meetings of the Rhineland High Commission in an unofficial capacity.

I did not fail to carry out the instructions contained in the last paragraph of Marquess Curzon's despatch under reference and I requested the Secretary of the Embassy to convey verbally to the State Department the views of the British represented on the Rhineland High Commission in regard to the question of the United States being officially represented on that body. Mr. Craigie[3] was informed that, if General Allen were to be appointed an unofficial representative on the Commission with power to vote, it would be necessary first to obtain congressional sanction and any such move on the part of the State Department might have the opposite effect to what is desired and might lead to the complete withdrawal of General Allen from any association whatever with the Commission. The Secretary of State, therefore, considered that the present position of the matter should be left unchanged.

I fully endorse the view of the State Department that considerable difficulties would be likely to arise were it necessary to submit to Congress any proposal to appoint General Allen as the official American representative on the Rhineland High Commission and, in the circumstances, Your Lordship will no doubt consider it preferable to leave the matter as it stands.

I have, etc.,

(For the Ambassador)

R. A. CRAIGIE

colleagues have taken in this matter; and I would suggest that you might, at your discretion, convey verbally to the State Department the views of the British representative on the Rhineland High Commission.'

[2] Not printed. Cf. *F.R.U.S.* 1922, vol. ii, p. 218.

[3] First Secretary at H.M. Embassy at Washington.

No. 229

Mr. Orme Sargent[1] (Paris) to Mr. Lampson
(Received June 13)

[*C 8445/3589/18*]

PARIS, *June 10, 1922*

Dear Lampson,

I enclose herewith copies of some Memoranda[2] which we have sent to Hankey on the various points raised by Wirth and Rathenau in their conversation with the Prime Minister as reported in S.G. 33 of May 18th.[3]

Yours ever,
ORME SARGENT

ENCLOSURE IN No 229

Note with reference to the German Memorandum[4] on 'Schutzpolizei and [Allied] Commission of Control'

Points contained in the German Memorandum	Comment
1. Protests against the large number of Notes sent to the German Foreign Office by the Inter-Allied Military Commission of Control.	The remedy for this rests in the hands of the German Government. A knowledge of the correspondence between the Commission and the German Government, since the former came into being, gives a clear impression that the German Government has consistently sought to delay the execution of the Military Clauses by entering into long discussions on minor points.
2. States that the 'Schutzpolizei' is constitutionally under the administration of the German States.	This does not alter the fact that the German Government is responsible for ensuring the execution of the Treaty stipulations which it signed.
3. States that the 'Schutzpolizei' has retained its local character and is not centralised.	In his discussion with the Prime Minister, Dr. Rathenau clearly admits that the control of the 'Schutzpolizei' *is* centralised for each State, and that in the Towns the police is not under the Municipalities.
4. States that the 'Schutzpolizei' in all Germany numbers 85,000 men and that the States are willing to reduce this total to 50,000.	If, as appears from the interview, this is meant to imply that the total strength of the police is 85,000 only, instead of 150,000 authorised by the Boulogne Conference,[5] the statement is

[1] Mr. Orme Sargent was attached to H.M. Embassy at Paris for the work of the Conference of Ambassadors.

[2] This enclosure consists of notes on one of the German Memoranda.

[3] See Vol. XIX, No. 140.

[4] See ibid., Appendix I.

[5] See Vol. VIII, No. 33, Appendix 2.

471

certainly false. At no time has the German Government ever suggested to the Commission that the strength of the police was below 150,000. The following is a quotation from a long German Memorandum dated 15th March 1922,[6] addressed to the Commission of Control:—

'As regards the authorised effectives, it appears from returns dated September 1st 1921, addressed to the Commission of Control and comprising all categories of police, that the total effectives at that date (Schutzpolizei, Administrative Police and Criminal Police) did not exceed the figure of 150,000 men.'

Again, in its Note dated March 18th/25th[7] 1922 addressed to the Allied Governments, reference is made to the authorised establishment of 150,000 without any suggestion that this establishment has not been filled.

5. Pleads the necessity of maintaining the police in units in barracks, mentioning among other arguments, that this is necessary to ensure an appropriate use of rifles, machine pistols and tanks. At the same time it classifies as 'absolute nonsense' the suggestion that the 'Schutzpolizei' is a 'second army'.

In a Note dated May 5th 1922[6] to the Commission of Control, the German Government states that 'the Governments of the States are already engaged upon preparations for the transformation of the organisation of the police'. This implies recognition of the fact that transformation is necessary.

The arguments used by the Germans with regard to the use of arms is really an admission that the police are trained and intended for military action. Police units are moved about the country just as military units might be, and a map recently supplied by the Commission of Control showing the organisation of the 'Schutzpolizei' in East Prussia in a complete cordon of frontier posts, with mobile detachments stationed at the several group Headquarters, is convincing proof of the military organisation of the police, which could not be more unsuitably disposed from the point of view of the maintenance of internal order.

---

[6] Not printed.
[7] This would appear to be a reference to representations made to the Inter-Allied Military Commission of Control in the German note of March 15 (see n. 6) which Herr Sthamer communicated to the Foreign Office under cover of a note of March 28 (C 4797/3589/18), not printed.

Lord Hardinge (Paris) to the Earl of Balfour (Received June 16, 8.30 a.m.)

No. 324 Telegraphic: by bag [C 8602/6/18]

PARIS, *June 14, 1922*

The Conference of Ambassadors met this morning under the chairmanship of M. Jules Cambon, the Belgian Ambassador being also present, and considered the following questions:

. . .[1] 7. When the draft Protocol relating to the manufacture of certain aeronautical installations in Germany for the use of international civil aviation was presented to the German Government last year negotiations were suspended (as reported in my telegram No. 462, paragraph 11 of July 6th)[2] owing to the fact that the rules for regulating German civil aviation had not been made known by the Allied Governments.

As construction has now recommenced in Germany the Conference of Ambassadors has now decided that the Protocol should again be presented to the German Government, but with an additional stipulation to the effect that the German Government are to afford equality of treatment to the aeroplanes of all nations entering or flying over Germany.

. . .[1] 10. The Conference approved the unanimous report of the Naval Advisers enclosed in my despatch No. 1412[3] recommending that the period permitted to the German Government for the installation of the Diesel submarine engines should be extended to the 31st July, in view of the special circumstances set forth by the German Government. This report takes cognizance of the stipulation which I made on the 25th March (see my telegram No. 172, section 4)[4] that the settlement of this question shall not be used as an excuse for the maintenance of the Naval Commission of Control after the date on which the Commission of Control would otherwise be withdrawn. A further report is to be submitted to the Conference by the Naval Interallied Commission of Control on the 15th July showing the actual state of the question. Assuming that the present rate of progress in installation is maintained, and that the German Government continue to co-operate in this matter, the Naval Advisers anticipate that this question will be concluded by 31st July next. . . .[1]

[1] The sections omitted referred to other matters.
[2] Vol. XVI, No. 810.
[3] Of June 15 (C 8624/434/18), not printed.
[4] This section is not printed.

No. 231

The Earl of Balfour to Mr. Addison (Berlin)[1]

No. 976 [C 7839/324/18]

FOREIGN OFFICE, *June 19, 1922*

Sir,

With reference to Lord D'Abernon's despatch No. 284 of the 7th April[2] respecting the German foreign trade control, I transmit to you herewith a copy of a letter from the Board of Trade,[3] and also of a note[4] which was recently considered at the Foreign Office by an inter-departmental committee consisting of representatives of the Foreign Office, Treasury, Board of Trade and Department of Overseas Trade.

2. The committee approve both the proposals contained on page 3 of the enclosed note. I therefore request that you will address an enquiry to the German Government in order to ascertain whether or not the German control offices actually have the power to, and do in practice, prevent German exporters from delivering goods in accordance with the terms of contracts with foreign buyers in cases w[h]ere (*a*) the terms as to purchase price, currency, etc., satisfied the export control regulations in force at the date of contract, but where (*b*) the official regulations have varied between the date of the contract and the final delivery of the goods.

3. The question of the difficulties met with by British travellers as the result of the existing German export regulations is dealt with in a separate despatch.[5]

I am, etc.,
BALFOUR

[1] See No. 29, n. 1.   [2] Not printed (C 5517/324/18).
[3] Of May 29 (C 7839/324/18), not printed.
[4] Of June 9 (C 8491/324/18), not printed.
[5] No. 970 of June 17 (C 8098/324/18), not printed.

No. 232

Sir M. Cheetham[1] (Paris) to the Earl of Balfour (Received June 23, 8.30 a.m.)

No. 333 Telegraphic: by bag [C 9005/592/18]

PARIS, *June 21, 1922*

The Conference of Ambassadors met this morning under the chairmanship of Monsieur Jules Cambon, the Belgian ambassador being also present, and considered the following questions:

. . .[2] 6. In accordance with the instructions contained in Your Lordship's despatch No. 1535 of the 19th May,[3] I requested that the Military Committee

[1] Sir Milne Cheetham acted as Chargé d'Affaires from June 21 to July 1 and from July 16 to August 15.
[2] The sections omitted referred to other matters.   [3] Not printed.

of Versailles should make a further effort to clear up the confusion existing with regard to the enforcement of Article 170 of the Treaty of Versailles, which forbids the export of war material from Germany. This was agreed to. I pointed out that His Majesty's Government attached considerable importance to settling this question, as it was their policy to enforce strictly Article 170. At present, however, the whole question is in such a confused state that it seems impossible to enforce the article. In order to clear up the question it is most important to secure a definite statement as to what arms are governed by the article—a point on which the Commission of Control seems to have changed its mind repeatedly.[4] As soon as a definite list is in existence the Commission of Control should be able to insist upon the German Government enforcing an efficient control over the export of arms from Germany.

It was decided at the suggestion of the Italian Ambassador that the Versailles Committee should at the same time deal with the export of war material from other ex-enemy countries. . . .[2]

[4] See No. 226.

No. 233

Letter from Sir M. Hankey to the Earl of Balfour
(Received June 23)
[C 9024/6347/18]

June 22, 1922

Dear Lord Balfour,

The Prime Minister thinks that the question of the admission of Germany to the League of Nations should be mentioned at the Cabinet and he authorised me to circulate the note of the conversation yesterday,[1] which is attached herewith.[2] I was not quite sure as to the last conclusion on this subject,

[1] This conversation took place at 10, Downing Street at 11.15 a.m. Those present were: The Right Hon. D. Lloyd George, O.M., M.P., Prime Minister; The Right Hon. The Earl of Balfour, K.G., O.M., Acting Secretary of State for Foreign Affairs; The Right Hon. A. Chamberlain, M.P., Lord Privy Seal; The Right Hon. The Lord D'Abernon, G.C.M.G., British Ambassador in Berlin; Sir Maurice Hankey, G.C.B. (Secretary to the Cabinet); Sir Edward Grigg, K.C.V.O., C.M.G.

[2] Not printed. It was agreed to make to the Cabinet the following recommendations:

(a) 'That it was desirable that Germany should be admitted as a Member of the Assembly and of the Council of the League of Nations.

(b) 'That a direct proposal on these lines to the French Government was bound to lead to a refusal.

(c) 'That the most hopeful plan appeared to be to let the French Government know that we were generally in favour of the admission of Germany to the League, without entering into discussions with them on the subject.

(d) 'That the Acting Secretary of State for Foreign Affairs should discuss with the

namely, as to whether Lord D'Abernon was to be authorised to encourage the Germans to apply for membership of the League, but the Prime Minister thought there was no doubt about the matter. I am sending a similar letter to Mr. Chamberlain.

Yours sincerely,
M. P. A. Hankey

British Ambassador in Paris, now on a visit to this country, the best manner of approaching the French Government on the subject.

(e) 'That the Acting Secretary of State for Foreign Affairs should authorise the British Ambassador in Berlin to encourage the German Government to apply for membership of the League of Nations before the next meeting of the Assembly, and to let the German Government know that the representatives of the British Government on the League would support the admission of Germany to membership of the C cil.'

No. 234

The Earl of Balfour to Mr. Addison (Berlin)

No. 60 Telegraphic [*C 9061/725/18*]

FOREIGN OFFICE, *June 26, 1922, 12.50 p.m.*

Please convey following message to the German Chancellor from Mr. Lloyd George:—

I have learnt with deep regret of Doctor Rathenau's death,[1] and wish to express my horror at the abominable crime which has deprived the German people of one of its most distinguished representatives. The whole world must honour men who face the risks of public hate as he did from devotion to his country's good. Please convey my profound sympathy to his family.

[1] In his telegram No. 121 of June 24 Mr. Addison had reported: 'Rathenau was murdered this morning about eleven o'clock while in his motor on the way from his house to Ministry of Foreign Affairs. Murderers were three men who overtook him in another motor, shot at him with revolvers and also threw a hand grenade.'

No. 235

Sir M. Cheetham (Paris) to the Earl of Balfour (Received June 28)

No. 1500 [*C 9245/1188/18*]

PARIS, *June 27, 1922*

My Lord,

I have the honour to report that a meeting of the Conference of Ambassadors, under the chairmanship of M. Jules Cambon, was held on the 22nd instant in accordance with the arrangements made between your Lordship and the French Ambassador in London, as set forth in your Lordship's

476

despatch No. 1744 of the 9th instant,[1] in order to deal with the demand made by the United States Government for the reimbursement of the costs of their army of occupation in the Rhineland. In conformity with the arrangements made, the United States Ambassador was not present. On the other hand, the Reparation Commission deputed their secretary-general[2] to attend. It had been at first proposed that the delegates of the principal Allied Powers on the Reparation Commission should be invited, but they considered that, if they attended, the meeting would have the appearance of a joint session of the Conference of Ambassadors and the Reparation Commission, and as such attract undue attention and perhaps also hamper the Reparation Commission if called upon subsequently to pronounce on the question as a body. Copy of the note[3] from the Reparation Commission on the subject is enclosed herewith.

I submitted to the conference, as a basis of the discussion, the draft note which your Lordship communicated to the French and Belgian Ambassadors in London on the 2nd May.[4] Both the Italian and Belgian Ambassadors stated that they were without instructions and would have to refer to their Governments. The French, on the other hand, made it clear at once that they disliked the proposal in the last paragraph of your Lordship's draft note, to the effect that the United States Government should be invited to appoint an official delegate on the Reparation Commission. They protested that, inasmuch as the question must be settled on equitable and not on juridical lines, it is undesirable that the settlement should be negotiated by the Reparation Commission, who could but apply the Treaty of Versailles. In these circumstances, the question of inviting the United States Government to appoint an official delegate to the Reparation Commission did not arise on the present occasion, and in any case it was too important a matter to be dealt with as a side issue of the question under discussion. If the Allied Governments desire the United States Government to be officially represented, they ought to deal with the matter as a distinct question. In order to establish the French point of view, M. Cambon submitted a counter-draft,[5] in which the United States Government are merely requested to appoint a representative to negotiate an equitable settlement with the Conference of Ambassadors.

A further point made by the French Government was to the effect that the Allied Governments should, in their reply to the United States Government, suggest that the latter should examine whether German sequestrated property in the United States could not be used to cover the costs of their army of occupation. The general feeling of the meeting was opposed to this proposal being put forward at this stage of the negotiations, especially in the written reply of the Allied Governments to the United States Government. It was felt that to retort in this manner to the United States demand for payment would create friction with the United States Government and antagonise American public opinion. Eventually the French yielded so far

[1] Not printed. See, however, Nos. 196, 204, and 213. [2] Sir Arthur Salter.
[3] Of June 20, not printed. [4] See No. 213. [5] Not printed.

as to modify their draft note, on the suggestion of the Italian Ambassador, in such a way that the question of the sequestrated property in the United States should not be put forward as a definite method of solving the question, but merely as an instance of a solution which it might be worth while to examine in the course of the negotiations. I have the honour to enclose herewith the draft French note as thus amended.[6] The first paragraph of this note calls for no special comment. It is intended to reproduce the first paragraph of your Lordship's draft, although differently worded.

As regards the second paragraph, the French argued that it was preferable to avoid as far as possible the detailed explanations set forth in paragraphs 2 and 3 of your Lordship's draft. I understand, however, from Sir John Bradbury that the French draft, in laying stress on the difficulties of reimbursement, goes a good deal further than either His Majesty's Government or the Belgian Government have hitherto gone in the direction of admitting the principle of non-reimbursement to the common fund of excesses of deliveries in kind over the recipient Power's proper share, and seeks to lay down a sort of sister principle of non-reimbursement of cash receipts, though in point of fact the two notions are quite unrelated.

The secretary-general of the Reparation Commission explained to the meeting that the cost of the American army of occupation fell into two categories, namely, the expenses incurred before and those incurred after the 1st May, 1921. The amount of the costs of the first category is by far the greater, and their refund will be much more difficult to effect both for this reason and also because the greater part of the corresponding costs of the Allied armies of occupation has already been met for this period. There is, I believe, a possibility (though it was not suggested at the meeting) that in the course of the negotiations the United States Government may be prepared not to insist upon the immediate payment of the costs of this category so long as their right to refund is duly recognised. If this is so, the question will be considerably simplified. The costs for the second category being very much smaller, it may be possible, in Sir Arthur Salter's opinion, to pay them in part out of the armistice material received by the United States Government (which, however, should be more appropriately applied to the pre-1st May, 1921, costs) and out of the dye-stuffs, which are at the present time being sold to that Government.

After this exchange of views the conference adjourned in order to enable the Italian and Belgian Ambassadors to receive definite instructions, and in order to give all the Embassies time to consider the fresh proposals of the French Government. I have since consulted Sir John Bradbury, and in his opinion it would be inadvisable to raise the question of the sequestrated properties at this stage, although it will, of course, have to be raised when the oral discussions begin. There remains the French Government's refusal to invite the United States Government forthwith to appoint an official delegate on the Reparation Commission. I should be grateful to have the views of His Majesty's Government on this subject, and to learn whether your

[6] Enclosure 3.

Lordship wishes me to press the point in the face of the arguments advanced in opposition to it. I would mention that, although without instructions, the Italian Ambassador generally supported the point of view of His Majesty's Government, but admitted a distinction between the appointment of an official United States delegate to the Reparation Commission for all purposes, and the appointment of such a delegate to carry out the arrangement come to between the Governments for the settlement of this particular United States claim. This last suggestion, viz., the appointment of a United States official delegate to the Reparation Commission with a limited mandate, would, however, obviously require very careful consideration from the judicial point of view before it could be entertained.

Sir John Bradbury has sounded Mr. Boyden, the unofficial United States representative on the Reparation Commission, privately on the subject of the note to be addressed to the United States Government, and gathers from him that it would produce a better impression if a definite suggestion were made in the note itself that the cost of the period before the 1st May, 1921, should be held over for the moment, and the later costs dealt with on the same lines as the Allies' costs for the same period. This would have the appearance of actually giving the United States Government something, however little, whereas the drafts which have hitherto been prepared leave the question still entirely in the realm of platonic good intentions. I will bear this in mind when the question is next discussed at the Conference of Ambassadors.

I have, etc.,

MILNE CHEETHAM

ENCLOSURE 3 IN NO. 235

Second Amendement au Projet britannique de Réponse aux Notes des États-Unis relatives au Remboursement des Dépenses des Troupes américaines en Allemagne

Le 24 juin, 1922

Le mémorandum du 22 mars[7] et la note complémentaire du 23 mars,[7] contenant les vues du Gouvernement des États-Unis au sujet du remboursement des dépenses de l'armée américaine d'occupation sur la rive gauche du Rhin, ont été l'objet d'un examen approfondi de la part des Gouvernements alliés intéressés.

Ces Gouvernements ont déjà indiqué qu'ils étaient prêts à rechercher les dispositions à prendre pour qu'il soit donné satisfaction au Gouvernement des États-Unis.

Ils sont heureux de noter que le Gouvernement des États-Unis est prêt à accueillir toute suggestion tendant au règlement raisonnable de cette question. Laissant donc de côté les aspects juridiques du problème, ils entendent se placer à un point de vue purement pratique pour hâter le plus [tôt] possible la solution.

2. A cet égard, les Gouvernements alliés font remarquer qu'ils ont pu, jusqu'à présent, trouver des bases de répartition des paiements allemands

[7] See No. 196, n. 6.

sans obliger jamais l'un quelconque des Gouvernements intéressés à reverser aux fonds communs la valeur des prestations en nature reçues par lui, et que, même pour les paiements en espèces, ils ont pu éviter jusqu'à présent les réajustements comportant reversement. Ils espèrent que le Gouvernement des États-Unis sera d'accord avec eux pour reconnaître que cette règle de bonne entente doit continuer à recevoir une application aussi large que possible.

3. A l'effet d'examiner l'ensemble du problème, les Gouvernements alliés seraient heureux que le Gouvernement des États-Unis voulût bien désigner un représentant qui pût se réunir à Paris avec leurs propres délégués. La présence d'un délégué américain permettrait aux Gouvernements alliés de compléter leurs informations sur certains éléments de la question au sujet desquels ils sont actuellement renseignés d'une manière insuffisante, comme, par exemple, le point de savoir si, et dans quelles conditions, il pourrait être fait état, pour le règlement des frais de l'armée américaine d'occupation, de disponibilités résultant de l'application par le Gouvernement des États-Unis de l'article 297 du Traité de Versailles, retenu par l'article 2 du Traité de Berlin du 25 août 1921.

Les Gouvernements alliés ne doutent pas que cette procédure permette d'élaborer un projet à soumettre aux Gouvernements intéressés, qui serait de nature à résoudre dans des conditions satisfaisantes le problème qui fait l'objet de la présente communication.

No. 236

Sir M. Cheetham (Paris) to the Earl of Balfour (Received July 8, 8.30 a.m.)

No. 349 Telegraphic: by bag [*C 9440/8315/18*]

PARIS, *June 30, 1922*

The Conference of Ambassadors met this morning under the presidency of Monsieur Jules Cambon, the Belgian ambassador being also present, and considered the following questions:—

. . .[1] 8. Monsieur Cambon invited the conference to address a protest to the German government against the statement recently made by Herr von Kahr, late Bavarian prime minister, to the effect that Germany ought to aim at re-creating her army despite the treaty of Versailles (see Your Lordship's despatch No. 1830 of 16th June).[2] As the newspaper reports appear to constitute sufficient evidence that Herr von Kahr did make this statement, I agreed to this course on the understanding that the German government is not asked to do anything more than reprimand von Kahr. Monsieur Cambon took the opportunity of inviting the conference at the same time to protest against the speech which has since been made in the Bavarian parliament by Herr Schweyer, Bavarian minister of the interior, against the policy of the allied governments with regard to the re-organisation of the German police and in which he more particularly advocates that the

[1] The sections omitted referred to other matters.   [2] Not printed.

Bavarian government should carry on the struggle against the 'basis of the treaty of Versailles and more especially against the lie about German responsibility'. I agreed to a protest being equally made in this case since this speech by an actual Bavarian minister in the Bavarian parliament constitutes a far more flagrant attack on the treaty of Versailles than that of Herr von Kahr. Monsieur Cambon wished at the same time to reprove Doctor Wirth for the statements made in his speech in the Reichstag of the 25th June in which he protested against the Upper Silesian decision[3] and deplored the suffering of the populations of the Saar and of the Rhineland. I objected strongly to this course and was supported by the Italian ambassador who pointed out the manifest objections in the present circumstances to treating on the same footing the statements made by Doctor Wirth and those made by Bavarian ministers. Monsieur Cambon in these circumstances suggested that at any rate the allied ambassadors when presenting their written protest to the German government against the Bavarian speeches, should verbally call the attention of Doctor Wirth to the bad impression produced in the allied governments by this recent speech of his. The French are going to submit draft instructions in this sense, but I made it clear that I could not agree to any such procedure without definite instructions from Your Lordship. I enclose in my despatch No. 1516[2] of today's date the text of the statement made by Monsieur Cambon on the whole of this subject.

[3] See Vol. XVI, No. 329.

No. 237

Lord D'Abernon (Berlin) to the Earl of Balfour (Received July 6)

No. 511 [C 9623/725/18]

BERLIN, *July 2, 1922*

[My Lord,]

On the broad question whether the position of the republic has been strengthened or not by the assassination of Rathenau,[1] opinion here is almost unanimous that the democratic position has improved. The camp of reaction is disconcerted and surprised by the energy of the Government and the efficiency of the police. If the assassins had all escaped it is probable that further assassinations would have taken place. It was hoped by the reactionaries that the Reichswehr would then take part against the Government and promote some kind of restoration.

Probably this was always a misconception. Anyhow, as events have turned out, viz., one culprit arrested and important papers seized, the danger of a Hohenzollern 'Putsch' is widely considered to have disappeared for the moment. Munich, which is the head centre of monarchist intrigues, favours the Wittelsbachs; Berlin favours the Hohenzollerns. This does not facilitate co-operation in conspiracy.

[1] See No. 234.

Nobody quite knows how the Government have come to be so energetic, or why the police has been so unexpectedly efficient. Wirth has certainly risen considerably in public estimation, and a new police director—by name, Weiss—whom nobody heard of before, has shown marked ability. There are still big fences for the Government to get over. It may be difficult to secure the necessary two-thirds majority of the Reichstag for the exceptional measures required for the defence of the republic. The measures proposed are stringent, involving death penalty for membership of, or subscription to, organisations like the organisation 'C'.[2] But I anticipate that Wirth some-how or other will get the necessary parliamentary support, and he has already arrived at a compromise regarding the Wheat Bill. There is, therefore, a fair chance that a general election may be avoided.

[I have, etc.,
D'ABERNON]

[2] i.e. 'Consul'. In despatch No. 506 of June 30, Lord D'Abernon explained: 'This association consisted largely of young men spread all over Germany. It is supposed to have been supported by leading politicians of the Right and to have been supplied with funds by reactionaries mainly of the landed classes. It had a special bomb and murder branch for the execution of political personalities.'

No. 238

The Earl of Balfour to Lord Hardinge (Paris)

No. 2101 [C 8493/6/18]

FOREIGN OFFICE, *July 7, 1922*

My Lord,

With reference to your despatch No. 938 of the 14th April,[1] I transmit to your Excellency herewith three letters[2] from the War Office relating to the military disarmament of Germany, a Foreign Office memorandum on the history of the negotiations relating to the organisation of the police,[3] and a minute by Sir Cecil Hurst[4] on the scope of the functions of the control commissions.

2. The present position of this question may be summarised as follows: General Nollet's report of the 19th May[5] (enclosed with War Office letter of the 13th June) has been the subject of informal discussions between representatives of the War Office and the Foreign Office and His Majesty's Ambassador at Berlin. At these discussions the grave situation resulting from the slow progress which has of late been made in the work of the Military Control Commission was fully recognised. It must, however, be observed that further representations to the German Government by the Ambassadors' Conference on the lines of General Nollet's report are not likely to have any great effect, seeing that representations on almost the

[1] No. 208.
[2] These were dated June 13 (Enclosure 1), July 1 (Enclosure 3, not printed), July 4 (Enclosure 4, not printed) enclosing a Memorandum of June 27 (Enclosure 5, not printed).
[3] Enclosure 6.   [4] Enclosure 7.   [5] Enclosure 2, not printed.

same lines have already been made to the German Government by the Ambassadors' Conference as recently as the 14th March[6] and the 14th April,[7] by Lord D'Abernon himself on the 21st March,[8] and no doubt by the French Ambassador at Berlin on numerous occasions.

3. The difficulty of the present situation is to some extent due to the fact that General Nollet's report contained indiscriminately a whole mass of questions, some of primary importance, some of less importance and some mere matters of detail. The first essential, it would therefore seem, is to decide which matters, still outstanding under the military clauses of the treaty, were of primary importance to the Allied Governments. The selection of these matter is of special importance, because, if the Germans are constantly plied with notes from the Ambassadors' Conference and from the Control Commission, demanding the execution of innumerable minor points of detail, the real object for which the Control Commission was established in Germany under the treaty tends to be ultimately forgotten. That object was to disarm Germany, and not—however desirable it might be—to see that Germany remained disarmed. This latter function was expressly entrusted by article 213 of the treaty to the League of Nations, and it was because the Allies are not satisfied with the degree of control that could at present be exercised by the League that they are now trying to persuade the German Government to accept the Military Mission of Guarantee,[9] which would itself be charged with the function of seeing that Germany remained disarmed (in this connection I would draw your Excellency's attention to the enclosed minute by Sir C. Hurst). Moreover, the demand for the complete execution of a mass of minor points of no real importance implies the indefinite continuance in Germany of the existing Military Control Commission, against which—provided the Military Mission of Guarantee is established—there are political objections.

4. In these circumstances the War Office undertook to indicate the important points upon the execution of which it was, in their opinion, necessary for the Allied Governments to insist before consenting to the withdrawal of the existing Military Control Commission. These points, which are four, are contained in the War Office letter of the 13th June, which is supplemented, in the matter of the police, by the further letter of the 4th July.

5. I request that your Excellency will propose to the French Government–

---

[6] As reported in Lord Hardinge's telegram No. 150 of March 14, not printed.

[7] See No. 208.   [8] See No. 192.

[9] On July 24 Mr. Orme Sargent wrote to Mr. Wigram as follows: 'I notice that in your despatch No. 2101 about the winding up of the Military Commission of Control in Germany, you speak of it as being succeeded by a Military Mission of Guarantee. In order to avoid future confusion, may I remind you that this is not the correct title of this future body. It has already before its birth been christened *Committee of Guarantee* (*Comité de Garantie*) and its brother is already living and flourishing, under the name of the Aeronautical Committee of Guarantee. Both these Committees have of course been named after their first cousin the Financial Committee of Guarantee, so that shortly, if all goes well, we shall have a whole family of Committees of Guarantee living happily together in Berlin.'

whether in the Ambassadors' Conference or through M. Poincaré, I leave it to your Excellency's discretion—that—

(a) Strong pressure should be brought to bear upon the German Government completely to execute without delay the four points to which attention is drawn in section 3(a) of the War Office letter of the 13th June, point (1) being understood in the sense of the War Office letter of the 4th July, and

(b) That the German Government should be informed that the existing Military Control Commission will be withdrawn, if and when these demands have been complied with, provided that, by that date, the German Government have accepted the new Military Mission of Guarantee.

6. In making this proposal to the French Government your Excellency should lay especial stress on the considerations advanced in the enclosed minute by Sir C. Hurst, pointing out that the purpose of the establishment of the existing Military Control Commission was to disarm Germany and not to maintain the disarmament of Germany, which latter duty is, under the treaty, entrusted to the League of Nations, and which duty it is now hoped to confer upon the Military Mission of Guarantee. Your Excellency may also suggest that by ceasing to insist on a number of points of minor detail, which are of little practical importance, the Allied Governments will offer a useful bait wherewith to induce the German Government to accept the new Military Mission of Guarantee.

7. Should the French Government agree to this procedure, it will remain to decide upon the method of approaching the German Government in the matter. His Majesty's Ambassador at Berlin is inclined to doubt the usefulness of further approaches to the German Government through the Ambassador's Conference or through the Military Control Commission, and I therefore request that your Excellency will suggest to the French Government that representations to the German Government should in this case be made individually through the Allied representatives at Berlin acting in co-operation. Such representations could no doubt be reinforced by similar representations to the German Ambassadors in the Allied capitals.

I am, etc.,
BALFOUR

ENCLOSURE 1 IN No. 238

War Office to Foreign Office (Received June 13)

LONDON, *June 13, 1922*

Sir,

I am commanded by the Army Council to refer to previous letters[10] on the subject of obstruction offered to the work of the Interallied Military Commission of Control in Germany, dated the 22nd February, 1922,[11] the 11th

---

[10] See No. 177.   [11] See No. 177, n. 1.

March, 1922,[12] and the 1st May, 1922,[13] and to forward herewith, for the information of the Acting Secretary of State for Foreign Affairs, General Nollet's report, No. 39, dated the 19th May, 1922.[5]

2. I am to point out that General Nollet considers that very little progress has been made by the Interallied Military Commission of Control in the last four months, and I am particularly to draw the attention of the Acting Secretary of State for Foreign Affairs to the list of outstanding questions relating to the execution of the military terms of the treaty, enumerated on pp. 2 to 4 of General Nollet's report under review.

3. As regards the outstanding military terms of the treaty mentioned above, the Army Council consider that these questions can be divided into three categories, in order of their importance:—

(a) *Outstanding questions, the complete execution of which is considered of the utmost importance by the Army Council.*

    (1) The reorganisation of the German police forces (article 162, and decision of the Boulogne Conference, June 1920).[14]

    (2) The transformation of munition factories (article 168).

    (3) The surrender of outstanding unauthorised war material (article 169).

    (4) The surrender of the documents relating to munitions manufactured in factories in Germany during the war, and the state of German war material in November 1918 (article 206, paragraph 2).

(b) *Outstanding questions, the complete execution of which the Army Council consider desirable, but which are actually of secondary importance only*

    (1) Measures have not been taken by the German Government to prevent the illicit possession of war material (articles 169, 178, 204 and 211).

    (2) The present German law prohibiting the export and import of war material is practically valueless (articles 170 and 211).

    (3) Administrative establishments of the former German army, not used by the 100,000 army, have not been alienated (articles 161 and 178).

    (4) The control of recruiting for the 100,000 army (articles 174, 175 and 206).

(c) *Outstanding questions, the complete execution of which is demanded by the French, but which the Army Council consider of no real importance*

    (1) The prohibition of German Military Missions in foreign countries, and the prevention of the enlistment of German nationals in foreign armies (article 179).

       The War Office have no information of any German Military Missions being at present in foreign countries; no effective steps

---

[12] See No. 177, n. 3.   [13] See No. 210, n. 3.
[14] See Vol. VIII, No. 33, Appendix 2, and No. 36, n. 4.

can be taken to stop the enlistment of isolated individuals by foreign Powers.

(2) The abrogation of the law of the 13th June, 1879, relating to requisitions in time of mobilisation (article 178).

This is valueless, as the measure can be re-enacted in war-time with ease.

(3) Retention of certain powers appertaining to mobilisation and of the archives dealing with mobilisation by local authorities (article 178).

It is impossible for control to check effectively the archives retained by local authorities, or to prevent these authorities retaining in some camouflaged form or other their possible duties on mobilisation.

(4) The legal enactment of the German Government's declaration regarding obsolete and dismantled fortifications (articles 180, 195 and 211).

This is of no importance, as the fortifications are obsolete.

(5) The retention of excess staffs and non-commissioned officers in the 100,000 army (articles 160 and 161).

It is impossible to guard against the German authorities making changes in the distribution of officers and other ranks within the 100,000 army; the Interallied Military Commission of Control have recognised that it was impossible for them to prohibit the German Government retaining non-commissioned officers whose period of service had not expired.

(6) The military organisation of the German railway system (article 178).

The German Government can always take over the railways in time of war.

(7) The Versorgungsämter (Pensions Offices) contain the documents of all the men who served in the army up to 1919 (article 178).

It is impossible for the German pension authorities to do their work without retaining many documents valuable for mobilisation.

(8) The reduction of the German police in the plebiscite areas of Allenstein and Marienwerder (article 162).

The Germans maintain that the Boulogne note does not limit local variations in proportional police strengths from the 1913 establishment.

4. I am to add that the Army Council will be unable to recommend the substitution of a Mission of Guarantee for the Interallied Military Commission of Control as contemplated in War Office letter dated the 11th February, 1922,[15] and Foreign Office despatch No. 535 of the 22nd February, 1922,[16] until such time as the important points referred to above in list (a) shall have been satisfactorily settled.

I am, etc.,
H. J. CREEDY[17]

---

[15] Not printed.   [16] No. 172.   [17] Secretary of the Army Council.

Memorandum respecting Negotiations between the German Government and the Military Control Commission respecting the Organisation of the German Police[18]

FOREIGN OFFICE, *June 19, 1922*

The Allied demands with regard to the German police are to be found (1) in articles 162 and 178 of the Treaty of Versailles, and (2) in the Boulogne and Paris notes of the 22nd June, 1920,[18] more explicitly interpreted in the Military Control Commission's note of 12th August, 1920.[15] The treaty stipulations, which were:–

(*a*) Limitation of numbers to the 1913 figure, except in localities where population had increased since 1913, and where a corresponding increase in police numbers was to be permitted.

(*b*) Prohibition of assembly for military training.

(*c*) Prohibition of all 'measures of mobilisation' were modified by the Boulogne and Paris notes of the 22nd June, 1920, as follows:—

    (*a*) Total strength increased to 150,000 in return for—

    (*b*) Prohibition of any 'centralised organisation' i.e., police to 'remain a regional and municipal organisation';

    (*c*) Prohibition of all armament, except that permitted by Military Control Commission.

The questions of strength and armament are now no longer at issue. The matters in dispute concern details arising almost entirely out of (*a*) the prohibition of assembly for military training, and (*b*) the prohibition of any 'centralised organisation'.

The history of the recent negotiations respecting these matters is as follows:—

On the 27th February, 1922, the Military Control Commission fixed the 15th March, 1922, as the date by which the different German States must have passed the measures necessary for complete execution of the Allied decisions on the subject of the police.[19] On the date fixed, the German Government announced[19] the measures proposed and with respect to the two points specifically in dispute declared that:—

(*a*) The right of increasing the number of State in relation to Municipal police would, subject to the agreement of the majority of the States concerned, only be used for the future to an extent which would be agreed upon between the German Government and the Control Commission.

(*b*) The number of formed police units would be considerably reduced.

(*c*) The accommodation in barracks of police officials employed in individual service would cease.

[18] Papers relating to this question (June 22, 1920 to May 30, 1922) are in a Foreign Office dossier printed in Confidential Print 12006 (Germany, Part VII, January to June 1922), pp. 595–623.   [19] See No. 202, Part III.

On the 23rd March, 1922, the Military Control Commission replied[19] that:—

(a) All the German States must by the 5th April, 1922, formally recognise the principle of a return to the 1913 organisation (N.B.—This, except in a few of the large States, would exclude a State police), and that any extension of this organisation in the direction of the creation in any State of a State police could only be made with the express permission of the Control Commission; and

(b) That, amongst other measures, which must be taken by the 25th May, 1922:—

1. The number of formed units must not exceed the 1913 number without the express permission of the Control Commission.
2. Higher police staffs and administrative police services must be suppressed.
3. Military exercises must be forbidden.

On the 5th April, 1922, the German Government, on behalf of all the German States, recognised the 'conditions of 1913 as the basis for the organisation of the police'.[15]

On the 24th May, 1922, they further sent to the Military Control Commission the proposals of the German States for the organisation of their police,[15] pointing out that the basis of these proposals was the '*status quo* of 1913, conditions being adapted to the altered circumstances which have meanwhile set in'. The German Government offered also to give to the Military Control Commission verbal explanations of the necessity of these adaptations.

On the 30th May, 1922, the Military Control Commission pointed out[15] that the German Government's note of the 24th May, 1922, showed that 'measures had been taken for the maintenance of a State police in places where none existed in 1913'. Such a *fait accompli* without the previous authorisation of the Control Commission could not be admitted. The measures taken must therefore be cancelled. A reply on the other points at issue would follow at a later date.

ENCLOSURE 7 IN No. 238

Minute by Sir C. Hurst

September 12, 1921

The inter-Allied Commissions of Control are established by section 4 of Part V of the Treaty of Versailles. The scope of their functions is laid down with sufficient precision in article 203, which states that 'all the military, naval and air clauses contained in the present treaty, *for the execution of which a time-limit is prescribed*, shall be executed by Germany under the control of inter-Allied Commissions *specially appointed for this purpose* . . . '. An examination of the military, naval and air clauses shows that time-limits are prescribed in the following articles: Article 160, specifying the date by which the

German army must have been reduced to seven divisions; articles 166 and 167, dealing with munitions, and article 168, dealing with the closing down of munition factories; article 169, dealing with the surrender of surplus arms, and article 172, with the disclosure of the modes of preparation of toxic and other substances; article 176, dealing with the reduction in number of military schools; article 180, dealing with the disarmament and dismantling of fortifications; article 181, dealing with the reduction of the German naval forces; article 183, dealing with the reduction of the naval personnel; articles 185 and 188, dealing with the surrender and destruction of warships and submarines; article 192, dealing with the surrender of surplus naval munitions, and article 196 with the reduction of the stock of ammunition for the fortress guns; article 197 gives a control for a limited period over the wireless stations; articles 199, 201 and 202 contain aeronautical provisions for which a time-limit is provided. When the provisions in these various articles are fulfilled, the functions of the inter-Allied Commissions of Control are at an end. Their functions do not necessarily come to an end on the dates specified in the articles, because the object of their creation was to ensure that the articles should be carried out, and if Germany was not up to time in the execution of the provisions, it would be the duty of the Commissions of Control to see that the articles were carried out, and their existence must, therefore, last until the obligations Germany has undertaken in these articles are completed.

Articles such as 171, which prohibits the manufacture of poison gases, article 173, which prohibits compulsory military service in Germany, or article 191, which prohibits the construction of submarines, are articles imposing obligations on Germany, which are unlimited in duration, and which, therefore, do not concern the inter-Allied Commission of Control, at any rate after the primary functions of such commissions, namely, the execution of the time-limit clauses, have been fulfilled.

An article such as 204, which specifies with greater exactness the functions of the Commissions of Control in connection with the delivery, demolition and rendering things useless, provided for in the treaty, does not enlarge the scope of article 203; nor do articles 208, 209 and 210, which apportion the duties to be performed between the three commissions, military, naval and aeronautical. These articles are all subordinate to article 203, which contains the guiding principle that the functions of the commissions are limited to matters for the execution of which a time-limit is prescribed.

A comparison of the language of article 203 with that of article 213 will show the scheme which the framers of these military clauses must have had in mind, as the latter article imposes upon Germany the obligation to submit to any investigations considered necessary by the League of Nations *so long as the treaty is in force*, i.e., the enforcement of obligations where there is no time-limit, and which are imposed upon Germany so long as she is subject to the Treaty of Versailles, is a matter for the League of Nations and not for the inter-Allied Commissions of Control.

If for political reasons it is necessary to secure the establishment of some inter-Allied organisation as a substitute for the inter-Allied Commissions of

Control after the latter have ceased to exist, a distinction must be drawn between what can be done without German consent and what can be done only as the result of a new agreement with Germany.

Article 207 does not authorise the imposition on Germany of anything but the expenses of the Commissions of Control as set up by the treaty. If it is desired that Germany in future should bear all or part of the expense of the new organisation to be set up, a new agreement with Germany to that effect will be necessary; article 207 will not apply.

Similarly, under article 205 it is the inter-Allied Commissions of Control as set up by the treaty which the Allied Governments are entitled to maintain in Germany, and of which the members may be sent about in German territories. No new organisation could claim the right to have its headquarters in Germany or to send its members about German territory, unless Germany made an agreement to that effect, nor would it be entitled to claim the facilities which Germany is bound under article 206 to give to the Commissions of Control.

Without a new agreement with Germany, therefore, I think that a new organisation to be set up must be paid for by the Allied Governments, and will be limited to such activities as can be carried on outside German territory and without German assistance.

CECIL J. B. HURST

(N.B.—Sir C. Hurst having been asked with reference to the above minute whether article 211 of the Treaty of Versailles could be held to modify the conclusion there arrived at, i.e., does the fact that a time-limit is fixed in article 211 for modification of German laws, etc., bring all the other disarmament clauses within the category of time-limit clauses? replied as follows on the 19th June 1922:—

'Article 211 would only affect the question dealt with in my minute of September 1921 to this extent: the Commissions of Control would be concerned with ensuring that Germany did pass the necessary legislation within the time specified to carry the military, naval and air clauses into effect, because there is the time-limit of three months within which the legislation must be enacted. They would not be concerned with seeing to the enforcement and application of that legislation. Article 211 affords no ground for maintaining that the Commissions of Control must be continued indefinitely so long as the legislation is enforced.')

No. 239

Lord D'Abernon (Berlin) to the Earl of Balfour (Received July 13)

No. 532¹ [C 10002/8315/18]

BERLIN, *July 8, 1922*

Paris telegram 349 paragraph 8.²

I strongly endorse Sir M. Cheetham's objection to M. Cambon's proposal to reprove Dr. Wirth for statements made in his speech of June 25th.

Such reproof can do no possible good and may do considerable harm. All reasonable men have a strong interest to support and strengthen Dr. Wirth's Government as the best of available combinations in the present crisis.

Apart from expediency the speech under discussion contains, in my judgment, little which justifies censure. It was mainly directed against Nationalists and the Nationalistic spirit.

¹ This despatch was sent to the Foreign Office in telegraphic form by bag.
² No. 236.

No. 240

Lord Hardinge (Paris) to the Earl of Balfour (Received July 13)

No. 1596 [C 9987/6/18]

PARIS, *July 10, 1922*

My Lord,

With reference to my telegram No. 212 of the 14th April,¹ I have the honour to call Your Lordship's attention to the fact that the German Government have not yet replied to that part of the note addressed by the Conference of Ambassadors to the German Government on the 14th April,² in which it was proposed to set up a Military Committee of Guarantee in place of the present Military Commission of Control. This is all the more surprising in view of the opinion expressed by Lord D'Abernon in his telegrams to Lord Curzon, Nos. 104,³ 109⁴ and 112⁵ of the 26th April and the 8th and 12th May, to the effect that a speedy accept[ance] by the German Government might be reasonably expected. I should be glad to learn whether Your Lordship would like me to propose to the conference that the time has now come to press for a reply on this question.

I would remind your Lordship that the note contains a covert threat that until the German Government agree to the Allied Government's proposal, the Military Commission of Control will be maintained in Germany even though its work has been completed. As this threat might in certain circumstances constitute a violation of the Treaty of Versailles, which limits the duration of the Commission of Control, it would seem advisable to avoid if

¹ No. 207. ² See No. 208, Enclosure 1.
³ Not printed. ⁴ No. 216. ⁵ No. 221.

possible the occasion of applying it. A speedy settlement of this question on the lines proposed by the Allied Governments is therefore much to be desired. The French Government, on the other hand, who ask for nothing better than that the present Commission of Control should be kept on indefinitely, are quite prepared to let the question slide.

I have, etc.,
HARDINGE OF PENSHURST

No. 241

Memorandum by the Central European Department on the
Proposed Inter-Allied Enquiry into the Costs of the Rhineland Commission[1]

[C 10140/899/18]

FOREIGN OFFICE, July 11, 1922

In the course of its meeting in Paris in August 1921 the Supreme Council adopted the following resolution on the 13th August, 1921:—

'Each of the Governments represented at the Supreme Council shall send financial and military delegates to a commission which shall give its opinion on the cost of the armies of occupation and of the different civil commissions established by the treaties of peace, on the reduction to be made and on the date upon which each of these commissions should terminate its operations. This report should be transmitted to the aforesaid Governments on the 1st November, 1921.'[2]

2. The report of this commission, which was submitted on the 5th November, 1921,[3] was divided into two parts (1) dealing with the armies of occupation, and (2) dealing with the civil commissions set up under the Treaty of Versailles. It is with a matter arising out of the second part of this report—costs of the Rhineland High Commission—that this memorandum is concerned.

3. The recommendation of the commission with respect to the costs of the Rhineland High Commission was as follows:

'The commission considers that the Rhineland Commission might be asked by the Supreme Council:

(*a*) To devote a detailed study to the measures likely to reduce the expenses of all categories repayable by Germany to the minimum compatible with the mission with which the High Commissioners are charged.

(*b*) To fix an annual maximum for the expenses resulting from the supplies and services enumerated in articles 8, 9, 10, 11 and 12 of the arrangement annexed to the Treaty of Versailles (i.e., the Rhineland

---

[1] Papers (August 13, 1921–July 5, 1922) relating to this subject are in Confidential Print 12006, op. cit., pp. 557–94.

[2] See Vol. XV, p. 737.   [3] Not printed.

Agreement). (N.B.—The expenses arising under these articles of the Rhineland Agreement, so far as the armies of occupation are concerned, have been carefully studied by a special inter-Allied Commission, which reported on the 17th June, 1922.[3] In any similar enquiry which may eventually be conducted into the Rhineland Commission's share of these expenses, the report of this commission should be borne in mind).

(c) To address a joint report to the Supreme Council on the results obtained.'

4. It having been decided that the Ambassadors' Conference should deal with Part 2 of the report, and therefore with the section relating to the Rhineland High Commission, His Majesty's Ambassador at Paris was, on the 6th December, 1921, informed[4] that His Majesty's Government regarded the manner in which the commission had so far dealt with the question of the costs of the Rhineland High Commission 'as timid and tentative. When the report comes up for discussion, your Excellency should propose that further consideration should be given to this question, and should suggest that the civilian members of the commission (i.e., the Paris Commission) should be asked to undertake further enquiry into the matter.'

5. On the 24th December, 1921 (Coblenz despatch No. 493),[3] and again on the 17th January, 1922 (Coblenz despatch No. 515),[3] His Majesty's representative at Coblenz reported that the French representative on the Rhineland Commission was reluctant to take any action on the recommendations of the Paris Commission, pending the definite approval of those recommendations by the Allied Governments. Lord Kilmarnock, however, stated on the 24th December, 1921,[3] that 'it was most important that an inter-Allied committee should be set up to investigate the expenses of the Rhineland Commission as a whole'. This opinion was approved by the Foreign Office on the 5th January, 1922,[5] but the French High Commissioner at Coblenz definitely refused, on the 15th January, 1922,[6] to accept a proposal by Lord Kilmarnock to this effect. The French High Commissioner pointed out that 'the final report of the commission at Paris (which, moreover, has so far been communicated to the Rhineland Commission as a matter of courtesy only) does not contain any proposal regarding the establishment by the High Commission of a special committee. The High Commission is at liberty, therefore, in this as in other matters, to adopt whatever procedure it may consider expedient.' (N.B.—It will be noted that the action, which would at this stage have been technically correct, would have been the obtaining of the approval of the Allied Governments (i.e., the Ambassadors' Conference) to the report of the Paris Commission, the relevant passage in which read: 'The commission considers that the Rhineland Commission might be asked by the Supreme Council to devote a

---

[4] In Foreign Office telegram No. 702, not printed.
[5] In telegram No. 53 of January 5, 1922 to Lord Hardinge, not printed.
[6] As reported in Lord Kilmarnock's despatch No. 9 of January 24, not printed.

detailed study to the measures likely to reduce the expenses repayable by Germany to the minimum compatible with the mission with which the High Commissioners are charged.' Unfortunately, as events have shown, an attempt was made to go beyond this and to persuade the French Government to agree to the conduct of the enquiry by the Paris Commission itself, with a preliminary local enquiry in Coblenz by a committee to be set up, apparently, by the Rhineland Commission. It was really this attempt which has been responsible for the difficulties which have ensued.)

6. On the 10th March, 1922, Lord Hardinge, in accordance with his instructions, presented a memorandum[3] to the Ambassadors' Conference, and suggested that the report of the Paris Commission, in so far as the Rhineland Commission was concerned, 'should be referred back to the civilian members of that committee with instructions to undertake further and searching enquiry into the matter with a view to recommending substantial reductions in the present rate of expenditure. It may even be thought desirable that the conference should suggest to the Rhineland Commission that the representatives thereon of the Allied Governments should forthwith establish an inter-Allied sub-committee to collect the data which will be required by the civilian members of the special committee when they undertake the examination proposed.' Lord Hardinge's memorandum also drew attention to certain specific points in the existing organisation of the Rhineland Commission. These points were:

(a) The excessive number of superior personnel, liaison officers and 'Kreis' officers on certain of the national delegations; and

(b) The maintenance by certain delegations of economic sections whose work did not appear to fall within the scope of the High Commission.

7. This memorandum was considered by the Ambassadors' Conference on the 5th April, 1922,[7] and led to a fiery protest by M. Cambon, whose argument may be summarised as follows:

(a) The responsibility of the Rhineland Commission would be prejudiced by the conduct by another commission of an enquiry into its procedure, and each member of the Rhineland Commission, being directly responsible to his own Government, must remain responsible for reductions or increases in his own staff.

(b) All possible reductions had already been made in the French staff, and the French Government were inclined to think that increases rather than decreases, in view of the German attitude, were necessary in the staff of the whole commission.

(c) The French economic section was not paid out of the commission's funds.

(d) British expenses were higher than French expenses in relation to the size of the respective armies.

(e) If big reductions were really to be made, they had much better be made by (1) the suppression of the office of the German representative

[7] See No. 203.

494

attached to the commission, and (2) by the cessation of the excessive compensation paid by the German Government to German nationals whose property had been requisitioned by the Allied authorities under the Rhineland Agreement.

(N.B.—The conditions upon which the Allied Governments agreed to the appointment of Prince de Hatzfeld Wildenberg, the present German representative in the Rhineland, are laid down in a correspondence exchanged between the Ambassadors' Conference and the German Ambassador in Paris on the 27th July, 1921, the 16th August, 1921, and the 3rd September, 1921.[8] The Ambassadors' Conference only agreed to the appointment of this official on condition that he collaborated loyally with the Rhineland Commission; that the German Government suppressed the secret associations in the Rhineland, such as the Pfalzcentrale; that the German Government 'undertook to deliver at the earliest possible moment certain offenders whose persons were required by the Rhineland High Commission'; and that the German Government ceased to take steps to neutralise the effect of certain judicial measures taken by the Rhineland Commission. 'Should these conditions not be observed, the Allied Governments would feel obliged to consider whether it was not necessary to suppress purely and simply an institution (i.e., the office of the German representative attached to the Rhineland Commission), which is legalised by no agreement and the ineffectiveness of which the facts would in those circumstances themselves demonstrate.')

8. Lord Hardinge, realising after the Ambassadors' meeting of the 5th April, 1922, that there was likely to be great difficulty in persuading the French to agree to any reduction of the costs of the Rhineland Commission, suggested to the Foreign Office on the 6th April, 1922,[9] the strengthening and reorganisation of the original Paris Commission 'by appointing important and responsible representatives from each of the Allied Treasuries. The appointment of such persons would also save the face of the French Government, as they would be able to argue that it was a direct emanation from the Governments and thus capable of treating with the Rhineland Commission.' On the 23rd May, 1922 (Foreign Office despatch No. 1558 to Paris),[3] Lord Hardinge was instructed to place on the records of the Ambassadors' Conference a formal refutation of M. Cambon's statement (see Lord Kilmarnock's despatch No. 154 of the 9th May, 1922),[3] and at the same time to suggest the strengthening of the Paris Commission on the lines of his own proposal of the 6th April, 1922.

9. Accordingly on the 10th June, 1922, a new British memorandum[3] was deposited with the secretariat of the Ambassadors' Conference. This memorandum may be summarised as follows:

(a) It was pointed out, with reference to M. Cambon's statement, that each High Commissioner must remain responsible to his own

[8] Not printed. See however, Vol. XVI, No. 816.
[9] In a private letter of April 6 to Sir E. Crowe, not printed.

Government for reductions or increases in his own staff; that 'although the individual Commissioners are responsible to their own Governments for their actions and votes, there can be no question of the High Commissioners as individuals exercising any power or responsibility whatever'.

(b) M. Cambon's statements respecting the reductions already made in the French staff, the French economic section and the ratio borne by the British and French sections' expenses to the size of their respective armies, were again contested, and the general vagueness of the whole position was used as a fresh argument for the necessity of an immediate and thorough overhauling of the whole of the organisation of the Rhineland Commission.

(c) It was stated that the British Government were not prepared to agree to the suppression of the office of the German representative in the Rhineland. They were, however, ready to agree to a further enquiry into the amount of compensation paid by the German Government to their own nationals against the requisitions of the Allied authorities in the Rhineland, and it was suggested that this latter question might suitably be considered in connection with the whole question of the expenditure of the Rhineland Commission.

10. On the 26th June, 1922, the French Government submitted a further counter-memorandum,[3] in which they discussed the whole question in the greatest detail. The more important points raised in this memorandum were as follows:

(a) The necessity for the maintenance of the prestige and authority of the Rhineland Commission was again invoked against the British proposal to 'institute' a commission charged with examining the accounts of the Rhineland Commission. (N.B.—Lord Hardinge, in a private letter to M. Cambon of the 5th July, 1922,[3] pointed out that there was no question of 'instituting' a commission, but merely of strengthening the existing commission.)

(b) The question of the exact cost of the British and French sections of the High Commission and of the exact standing of the French economic section were argued at great length.

(c) The French Government maintained their proposal for the abolition of the office of the German representative attached to the High Commission. Note was in this connection taken of the statement contained in the last British memorandum to the effect that the Rhineland Commission had not, so far, protested against the failure of the German Government to deliver certain accused persons to the Allied authorities in the Rhineland, and it was stated that the French Government 'would be glad if the British Government would instruct their representative at Coblenz to support his French colleague, who was now ready to raise this question'. It was also pointed out that the Rhineland Commission had just unanimously declared that, contrary to the undertaking given in their note of the 16th August, 1921, the German Government were still taking measures designed to neutralise the judicial decisions of the Rhineland Commission. In these circumstances, the French Government considered that the time had arrived to suppress the office of the German representative in the Rhineland.

(d) The French Government, in deference to the strong views held by the British Government on the question of the need for an enquiry into the costs of the Rhineland Commission, whilst they could not agree to any independent commission or committee of enquiry of whatever nature, were ready to agree to the following compromise:

    (a) An undertaking at the Ambassadors' Conference by each of the Governments there represented to fix for its own High Commissioner, as the maximum of his budget in future years, a sum equal to his present budget.

    (b) A 'hearing' by the Ambassadors' Conference of the High Commissioners.

11. Lord Hardinge has now asked[10] for instructions respecting the attitude, which he should adopt, when the question again comes before the Ambassadors' Conference.

12. It will be seen from the above that after more than seven months of prolonged and, at times, acrimonious negotiations between the British and French Governments, the only result to date has been to bring the French Government—

(a) To propose the fixation of the figures of the present budgets of each High Commissioner as the maximum for such budgets in future years.

(b) To consent to the 'hearing' of the High Commissioners by the Ambassadors' Conference instead of the additional enquiry by the Paris Commission, which was unfortunately substituted by us for the original proposal of the Paris Commission to request the Rhineland Commission itself to undertake that enquiry.

(c) To raise a question, which it was entirely to our interest to allow to lie dormant—that of continuance of the office of the German representative in the Rhineland.

    [10] In his despatch No. 1558 of July 5, not printed.

No. 242

War Office to Foreign Office (Received July 12)

[C 9942/592/18]

Secret   WAR OFFICE, *July 11, 1922*

Sir,

I am commanded by the Army Council to forward herewith a copy of a list showing the discoveries of hidden war material[1] made by the Inter-Allied

    [1] Not printed.

Military Commission of Control in Germany and by the German police between the 4th September, 1920, and the 26th June, 1922.

Appended is a recapitulatory table showing—

(1) Hidden war material discovered by the Inter-Allied Military Commission of Control and by the German police.

(2) War material surrendered by the German Government to the Inter-Allied Military Commission of Control for destruction.

2. I am to state that this list has been compiled from reports received by the War Office in the past two years, and should not be taken as absolutely exhaustive; a comparison, however, between the vast amount of war material actually surrendered by the Germans to the Inter-Allied Military Commission of Control,[2] and the small amount of hidden war material recorded as discovered by the Inter-Allied Military Commission of Control and the German police, shows that the alarmist reports of hidden war material, which have appeared in the British press, appear to have very little foundation in fact.

I am, etc.,

B. B. CUBITT[3]

[2] See Vol. XVI, No. 836.
[3] Principal Assistant Secretary, War Office.

ENCLOSURE 2 IN No. 242

Comparative Statement of Hidden War Material Discovered and War Material Surrendered in accordance with the Peace Treaty up to June 2[6], 1922

Nature of War Material (1)	Hidden War Material Discovered by the Inter-Allied Military Commission of Control and the German Police (2)	War Material Surrendered by the German Government to the Inter-Allied Military Commission of Control for Destruction (Including Column 2) (3)
Guns	563*	33,484 (includes barrels)
Shells	4,780	37,926,222 also 10,678·3 tons
Trench mortars . . .	1	11,595
Machine guns . . .	288	87,377
Small-arms (including pistols, revolvers, &c.) . . .	31,868	4,525,358
S.A.A.	5,900,202	450,245,300[4]

* Includes 504 barrels, of which 150 were only partially manufactured; these were found between the 19th and 23rd November, 1921, at the Rockstroh Werke, Heidenau.

[4] According to a Memorandum dated December 7 (C 16778/6/18) this figure had risen to 460,305,400 by November 9. The figure in column (2) remained at 5,900,202.

498

Lord D'Abernon (Berlin) to the Earl of Balfour (Received July 15)

No. 536 [C 10091/725/18]

BERLIN, *July 12, 1922*

[My Lord,]

I had a long talk with the Chancellor this morning, walking about in the garden of the Chancellor's Palace, which he calls his prison. The threats of assassination are so numerous that the police will not allow him to go outside, except to the Reichstag.

The most important question discussed was the entry of Germany into the League of Nations. The Chancellor said he had already given his views to the Prime Minister at Genoa.[1] The whole thing really depended upon what the attitude of England towards Germany would be. Could Germany count on a continuation of English goodwill towards a restoration of Germany as a prosperous State and a prosperous commercial community? If, after Germany entered the League of Nations, England abandoned the attitude she now held, Germany would easily be put in a minority at Geneva, and would be out-voted by countries like Czechoslovakia and Poland, organised and marshalled by France. This would be infinitely worse than Germany's present position outside the League. He himself was a sincere friend of the idea of the League of Nations; if he could see clearly that Germany's interests would not be endangered by entering the League he would favour it, but he could not conceal from himself the fact that public opinion here was hostile to the idea. The wound of Upper Silesia was still too recent. 'Do you think that people have forgotten it? They will not forget it for a long time. That unfortunate decision[2] makes German opinion very suspicious of Geneva.' We discussed along these lines for some time, and finally agreed that the Chancellor should send me certain questions, to which he wanted an unofficial and private answer before he could take a decision on the question of the League of Nations.

The general impression the Chancellor's observations made on me was that personally he was anxious to see Germany admitted at Geneva. He is, however, apprehensive about the reception the proposal will meet with from German public opinion. He is also apprehensive about the position at Geneva, as he is suspicious of French action in conjunction with the *Petite Entente*. He has a particular distrust of Benes,[3] whom he regards as too active to be a very safe neighbour or a very comfortable colleague. 'You would have imagined at Genoa,' he said, 'that Benes represented the greatest country in the world.'

The Chancellor did not bring up any of the stock arguments against Germany applying for membership of the League of Nations. He said nothing about its being a tacit reaffirmation of the Treaty of Versailles, nor did he

---

[1] See Vol. XIX, No. 140. See also No. 223.   [2] See Vol. XVI, No. 329.
[3] Dr. Beneš was Prime Minister and Foreign Minister of Czechoslovakia.

raise the usual point that Germany must be represented *de jure* on the Council as a permanent member. His central preoccupation was—could he count on English support?

Turning to other subjects, the Chancellor told me that he had good hopes that the political crisis here would be solved fairly satisfactorily; that the three laws:—

(*a*) The Defence of the Republic Law;
(*b*) The Fidelity of Officials Law; and
(*c*) The Amnesty for 1920 Political Offences;

would all be passed, the Volkspartei voting for them.

He had seen Stresemann several times lately, and had found him reasonable. The Volkspartei were willing to join the Government, but the Majority Socialists had put their veto on this step. The Independent Socialists were also anxious to join the Government, and it had been suggested that an Independent Socialist should be appointed Minister for Foreign Affairs. That he was altogether against. The Minister for Foreign Affairs must be a *bourgeois*. For the present he would hold the post himself. The number of possible candidates was neither large nor very attractive, while with so much assassination about the number of those really anxious for the post was extremely limited.[4]

[I have, etc.,
D'ABERNON]

[4] Sir E. Crowe minuted (July 15): ' I hope Lord D'Abernon will be careful not to put H[is] M[ajesty's] G[overnment] in a difficult position by entering into any "unofficial and private" pact of a kind to fetter Great Britain's future freedom of action in the League of Nations.'

No. 244

Lord Hardinge (Paris) to the Earl of Balfour (Received July 14, 8.30 a.m.)

No. 364 Telegraphic: by bag [C 10029/289/18]

PARIS, *July 13, 1922*

The Conference of Ambassadors met this morning under the chairmanship of Monsieur Jules Cambon, the Belgian ambassador being also present, and considered the following questions:

. . .[1] 3. The Conference heard the experts who had been summoned from the Rhineland, on the question of the constitution of the proposed Rhineland Licensing Committee (see Lord Curzon's despatch No. 922 of March [31st]).[2] The French were at first entirely unwilling to make any concessions on the three points in dispute. I was, however, in all three strongly supported by my American, Italian and Belgian colleagues. As a result of a long discussion and with the concurrence of the British experts, I suggested in regard to point 1,

[1] The sections omitted referred to other matters.

[2] No. 197. This question of the Rhineland Licensing Committee is fully documented (March 7, 1921, to June 21, 1922) in a Foreign Office dossier which is printed in Confidential Print 12006, op. cit., pp. 672–762.

that the Commission should sit at Coblence provided that the General Officer commanding the American troops who is responsible for the billeting in Coblence was able to provide adequate accommodation for the Commission and its staff. If, however, General Allen should decide that there was no room at Coblence, then the French Government would waive further opposition and the entire Commission should sit at Cologne. I felt justified in suggesting this as I had good reason to believe that General Allen is very unlikely to agree that there is sufficient accommodation available in Coblence. Monsieur Cambon promised to consider this solution and to give his final opinion on Monday.[3]

With regard to point 2 in dispute, Monsieur Cambon finally agreed to accept the principle embodied in the text suggested by the Germans subject to the Committee of Allied Experts being instructed in their further negotiations with the German experts to use their best endeavours to extract some further concessions from the Germans which should satisfy the technical apprehensions of the French experts.

With regard to point 3, I had, before the meeting, prepared with the assistance of the British experts an alternative text which seemed to me to meet the French contention that they must be able to secure the issue of a license in the event of discrimination being established and their failing to obtain satisfaction from the Germans, and at the same time to avoid the issue of a blank license to which the German experts took such exception. My draft, copy of which is enclosed in my despatch No. 1639,[4] was accepted in principle by the French, subject to any slight verbal modifications which they might have to suggest after studying it between now and Monday.

It was only after a protracted and somewhat animated discussion that I succeeded in obtaining with the assistance of my Italian and Belgian colleagues the above concessions from the French Representatives, and under the circumstances I did not consider it either necessary or desirable to use the language contained in the 5th and 6th paragraphs of Lord Curzon's despatch No. 922 of the 31st March,[2] though I made it clear to Monsieur Cambon that his Majesty's Government were dissatisfied with the existing situation, that I had received rigid instructions from Your Lordship which I hoped he would not compel me to carry out, and that no concession on my part was possible.

[3] July 17.   [4] Of July 13, not printed.

No. 245

The Earl of Balfour to Lord Hardinge (Paris)

No. 2183 [C 95440/8315/18]

FOREIGN OFFICE, July 13, 1922

My Lord,

With reference to section 8 of Sir M. Cheetham's telegram No. 349 of June 30th[1] in regard to certain speeches made in Bavaria against the Treaty

[1] No. 236. See also No. 239.

of Versailles, Your Excellency is authorised to agree to the despatch of instructions to the allied ambassadors at Berlin, on the lines of the draft which was enclosed with Mr. Sargent's letter to Mr. Lampson of July 3rd,[2] for a remonstrance on the subject of the utterances of Herr von Kahr and Herr Schweyer.

2. His Majesty's Government consider it inexpedient that these official representations should include reference to the speech made by the Chancellor himself on June 25th 1922,[3] and they think it preferable that His Majesty's Ambassador in Berlin should be instructed to mention the matter privately to Dr. Wirth. I enclose for your information a copy of a despatch which has been addressed to Lord D'Abernon,[4] giving instructions in this sense.

I am, etc.,

BALFOUR

[2] Mr. Sargent had stated: 'The present draft represents the French draft considerably modified by ourselves. We have told the French that even in its present form we cannot accept it until we have received instructions from you. . . .'

[3] See No. 236.

[4] No. 1136 of July 13, not printed. In despatch No. 579 of July 24 Lord D'Abernon replied: 'I took an opportunity on July 21 of speaking to the Chancellor in the sense of Your Lordship's instructions. Dr. Wirth did not say much in reply, but he fully realises how much the difficulties of the situation may be increased by intemperate expressions in the Reichstag or in other public utterances.'

No. 246

Lord Hardinge (Paris) to the Earl of Balfour (Received July 15, 8.30 a.m.)

No. 367 Telegraphic: by bag [*C 10077/289/18*]

PARIS, *July 14, 1922*

My telegram No. 364 of July 13th.[1]

. . .[2] As regards the licensing question in the Rhineland and the decisions arrived at by the conference yesterday Monsieur Poincaré objected that they would provoke criticism in the chamber of deputies and that he considered that it was a question which should be decided by the prime ministers at their approaching meeting. This decision is to be conveyed by Monsieur Cambon to the conference of ambassadors on Monday.[3]

[1] No. 244.

[2] The section omitted referred to another matter.

[3] July 17.

No. 247

The Earl of Balfour to Lord Hardinge (Paris)

No. 235 Telegraphic [*C 10077/289/18*]

Urgent   FOREIGN OFFICE, *July 15, 1922, 9 p.m.*

Your telegram No. 367 (of July 14th: allied organisation for supervision of import and export licenses in the Rhineland).[1]

Please endeavour nevertheless to secure at conference meeting of July 17th cessation of payment of Italian delegation out of proceeds of customs sanction[2] (see my despatch No. 923)[3] or at least reduction proposed in Lord Kilmarnock's despatch No. 68.[4]

[1] See No. 246.

[2] See No. 197.

[3] Of March 31. This ran: 'While His Majesty's Government cannot admit that it is proper that the expenses of the Italian licensing experts should continue to be paid out of funds collected under the economic sanction they will, of course, continue to welcome Italian participation in the licensing negotiations.'

[4] Of March 14. This stated: '. . . The work connected with the economic sanctions has now become very much reduced. . . . The Italian delegation, however, continues to ask for 24,000 French francs per month, and I feel that this is excessive. . . . I suggest to your Lordship the advisability of steps being taken to reduce the cost of the Italian delegation to a minimum. I think that a reduction to 7,500 French francs per month should be possible.'

No. 248

Sir M. Cheetham[1] *(Paris) to the Earl of Balfour (Received July 16, 3.30 p.m.)*

No. 373 Telegraphic [*C 10103/289/18*]

PARIS, *July 16, 1922, 1.42 p.m.*

Your telegram No. 235.[2]

After careful consideration I venture to suggest that it would not be opportune to raise question of Italian delegation being paid from proceeds of customs sanction on July 17th. It is probable, if not certain, that strong support of Italian Foreign Minister will be required at discussion in London of licenses organization to overcome opposition of Monsieur Poincaré. As Italians are sure to resent our raising question of Italian delegation's expenses, it seems therefore better to defer mentioning matter until larger question of licenses organization is settled. Lord Hardinge I know is of this opinion and has for this reason consistently [deferred] acting on the Marquess Curzon's despatch No. 923:[3] matter has dragged on so long now that another fortnight's delay would not seem of great moment.

[1] See No. 232, n. 1.

[2] No. 247.

[3] See No. 247, n. 3.

No. 249

Sir M. Cheetham (Paris) to the Earl of Balfour (Received July 19, 8.30 a.m.)

No. 376 Telegraphic: by bag [C 10282/8315/18]

PARIS, *July 17, 1922*

The Conference of Ambassadors met this morning under the presidency of Monsieur Jules Cambon, the Belgian Ambassador being also present, and considered the following questions:

. . .[1]2. In accordance with instructions contained in Your Lordship's despatch No. 2183,[2] I informed the Conference of the conditions on which His Majesty's Government would agree to the despatch of instructions to the Allied Ambassadors at Berlin on the subject of the remonstrance against the utterances of Herr von Kahr and Herr Schweyer. The Belgian Ambassador asked that his colleague in Berlin might be allowed to associate himself with the remonstrance; this was agreed to. The Italian Ambassador asked that a paragraph should be added to the instructions calling attention to the support afforded by Bavarian State Authorities to the activities of the 'Andreas Hofer Bund'[3] and the latter's advocacy of the restoration of the Valley of the Adige to the Tyrol. This was agreed to. With regard to the question of the Chancellor's speech, it was decided that each Government should send appropriate instructions to its Ambassador in Berlin on the lines of Your Lordship's despatch to Lord D'Abernon No. 1136 of July 13th.[4]

. . .[1]7. The Conference had before it a Memorandum based on the instructions contained in Your Lordship's despatch No. 1749 of June 9th[5] regarding German military and naval personnel believed to be in the employ of the Soviet Government and a report from the A[llied] M[ilitary] C[ommittee of] V[ersailles] on the export of war material by ex-enemy Powers (copy enclosed in my despatch No. 1676).[6] General Desticker, representing Marshal Foch, read a report from General Nollet (copy enclosed in my despatch No. 1677)[6] on the general question of military control in Germany. It was stated that General Nollet was of opinion that the present crisis in Berlin would render any representations now fruitless and that it would be better to wait for some three or four weeks. These two questions were therefore adjourned on the understanding that they would be embodied in the general representations which will eventually be addressed to the German Government. This will give time for discussing with the French Government the proposals contained in Your Lordship's despatch No. 2101 of July 7th.[7]

. . .[1]9. The Conference considered a Memorandum by the Naval Advisers on the subject of the delivery to the Allies by Germany of certain war material for the cruisers and destroyers which had been incorporated in the French and Italian Fleet. Copy of this Memorandum, giving a summary of the

---

[1] The section(s) omitted referred to other matters. [2] No. 245.
[3] Named after a Tyrolese patriot who led a revolt against Bavarian rule in 1809.
[4] See No. 245, n. 4. [5] Not printed.
[6] Of July 17, not printed. [7] No. 238.

question and the views of the respective Naval Advisers, was enclosed in my despatch No. 1678 of today's date.[8] I said that I could not agree to the Allies demanding from the German Government a second instalment of material which had already been surrendered to the Allies and had been destroyed by the orders of our representatives (the Naval Commission). Monsieur Cambon and the Italian Ambassador, while agreeing with the views put forward by their Naval Advisers, were prepared to accept the Japanese solution 'that as the destruction of this material was due in part to the fault of the Germans and in part to that of the Naval Commission, the demands for the balance of the missing equipment should be reduced to a minimum'. Monsieur Cambon proposed to carry this solution by a majority decision of the Conference but the Italian Ambassador then suggested that, in the first instance, the French and Italian Ambassadors in London should be instructed to make a *démarche* with a view to persuading His Majesty's Government to accept the Japanese proposal. This was adopted and further discussion of this question was adjourned. Monsieur Cambon and Count Sforza, however, made it clear that, should the representations of their Ambassadors in London prove fruitless, they would insist on a majority decision when the question again came before the Conference, as the matter was considered a vital one by their Governments.

I would point out that an early settlement of this question is most desirable in order to enable the three Admirals at Berlin to be withdrawn (see section 8(c)). . . .[1]

[8] Not printed. This despatch (C 10279/7361/18) enclosed a memorandum of July 7 (not printed) by the Four Naval Advisers of the Principal Allied Powers.

No. 250

The Earl of Balfour to Lord Kilmarnock (Coblenz)

No. 183 [C 9621/899/18]

FOREIGN OFFICE, *July 17, 1922*

My Lord,

With reference to Lord Hardinge's despatch No. 1558 of the 5th July[1] (copy of which was forwarded to Coblenz direct) and to my despatch No. 181 of today's date,[1] I transmit to your Lordship herewith a copy of a memorandum[2] summarising the negotiations which have taken place on the question of an enquiry into the costs of the Rhineland High Commission.

2. The most important fact which emerges from this summary is the failure of the Allied Governments, either through the Supreme Council or through the Ambassadors' Conference, ever formally to approve the second part of the November report[3] of the Paris Commission, and therefore of the clauses of that report relating to the costs of the Rhineland High Commission.

3. It will be seen from paragraph 3 of the enclosed memorandum that the

[1] Not printed.   [2] No. 241.   [3] See Vol. XVI, No. 751, n. 4.

Paris Commission recommended that the Rhineland Commission might *inter alia* be asked by the Supreme Council (or by the Ambassadors' Conference, to whom, at the request of the French Government, the consideration of the report was referred) 'to devote a detailed study to the measures likely to reduce the expenses repayable by Germany to the minimum compatible with the mission with which the High Commissioners were charged, and to address a joint report to the Supreme Council on the results obtained'. Had the Paris Commission's report been approved by the Allied Governments, the proposal to set up an outside body to enquire into the costs of the Rhineland Commission would naturally not have been made, and the present dispute between the British and French Governments as to the effect of such a proposal on the prestige of the Rhineland Commission would never have arisen.

4. I am in complete agreement with your view, which I understand is shared by His Majesty's Ambassador in Paris, that it is most desirable to bring to an end this unfortunate controversy at the earliest possible moment, and I am inclined, therefore, to consider that the best course to pursue will now be as follows:—

5. I would propose to instruct Lord Hardinge, when this matter is again brought before the Ambassadors' Conference, to avoid any detailed reply to the French Government's memorandum of the 28th June[1] (enclosed in Lord Hardinge's despatch No. 1558).[1] His Excellency would be instructed to confine himself to recognising that this question has reached an *impasse*, and, in order to avoid further discussion in Paris, he would suggest that the Ambassadors' Conference should approve immediately that part of the Paris Commission's report which relates to the costs of the Rhineland Commission, thereby leaving it to the Rhineland Commission to report direct to the Allied Governments on its own internal economy. The adoption of this proposal could scarcely be held to prejudice in any way the authority of the Rhineland Commission, and its acceptance would appear to be all the more logical in that, in connection with such an enquiry, the position as regards the Rhineland Commission's requisitions under articles 8 to 12 of the Rhineland Agreement would also come under review. The Rhineland Commission would at the same time, if the French representative insists, naturally consider, too—at any rate in the first place—the question of the position of the German Reichskommissar in the Rhineland. I presume, however, that you agree that this is not a question which His Majesty's Government, so far as they are concerned, have any wish to raise at the moment.

6. I request that your Lordship will forward your observations on these suggestions at the earliest possible moment, and I should, in particular, be glad to learn whether you think that the French Government would oppose their adoption, in view of the statement to which M. Tirard at one time gave expression, to the effect that any reduction in the costs of each national delegation in the Rhineland must be left entirely to the individual High Commissioner concerned.

I am, etc.,
BALFOUR

The Earl of Balfour to Sir M. Cheetham (Paris)

No. 2289 [C 10125/1188/18]

FOREIGN OFFICE, *July 21, 1922*

Sir,

I have received your despatch No. 1500 of the 27th June,[1] in which you enclosed the French Government's amendments to the British draft reply (Enclosure 1 to the Marquess Curzon's note of the 2nd May to the French Ambassador at this Court)[2] to the demand made by the United States Government for the reimbursement of the costs of their army of occupation in the Rhineland.

2. The second amended draft reply submitted by the French Government (Enclosure 3 to your despatch No. 1500 of the 27th June) has been most carefully considered with the desire to do everything possible to reach an early agreement with the French Government in this matter. I am bound to state, however, that there are a number of points in this draft which His Majesty's Government would be very reluctant to accept.

3. The Treasury see, in particular, serious objection to the second paragraph, which may be taken to represent an attempt on the part of the French Government to obtain formal recognition of the principle of non-reimbursement to the common reparation fund of the value of payments, in cash as well as in kind, received by any Power in excess of its allotted share of the reparation payments. Moreover, the words included in this paragraph, 'et que, même pour les paiements en espèces, ils ont pu éviter jusqu'à présent les réajustements comportant reversement,' are not correct. It is therefore desirable that paragraph 2 of the original British draft should be substituted for paragraph 2 of the second French draft, with the omission, if the French Government so desire, of the words 'and were for practical purposes so distributed as far back as August 1921'.

4. I note also that paragraphs 3 and 4 of the original British draft have been omitted altogether from the second French draft. These paragraphs are of importance, and you should press for the restoration at least of their substance.

5. A revised British draft, which has been prepared on the lines of the two preceding paragraphs, is therefore transmitted herewith. You will observe that it contains also the original paragraph 1 of the first British draft, which, though not a matter of primary importance, is preferable to paragraph 1 of the second French draft. A new paragraph 5 has also been inserted in the new draft to meet Mr. Boyden's proposal[3] reported in the last paragraph of your despatch No. 1500.

6. The sixth paragraph of the new draft contains the substance of the third paragraph of the second French draft, although it omits all reference to the possible use of German sequestrated property in the United States

---

[1] No. 235.   [2] No. 213.   [3] Cf. *F.R.U.S.* 1922, vol. ii, p. 231.

as a means of recovering the costs of the United States army of occupation. There are objections, at the present stage of the negotiations, to any mention of this matter, which it would surely be wiser to allow to arise, if need be, in the course of the oral discussions.

7. As you will realise, however, the second and more important feature of paragraph 6 of the enclosed draft is the omission, in deference to the views of the French Government, of our original proposal to invite the United States Government to be officially represented on the Reparation Commission. Whilst the important results which would almost certainly ensue from the presence of an official delegate of the United States Government on the Reparation Commission have not been lost sight of, His Majesty's Government are the more disposed to defer to the French Government in this matter that the United States Government could not be officially represented on the commission without the conclusion of a new agreement to which the United States and Germany, as well as the Allied Powers, would have to be parties. The successful negotiation of such an agreement without the full support of the French Government would be exceedingly difficult, if not impossible, whilst the attitude of the United States Government themselves towards such a proposal is highly doubtful. Moreover, the proposal to negotiate such an agreement would directly raise the whole question of the juridical effects of the German–American Treaty,[4] a question upon which it has hitherto been the object of His Majesty's Government to avoid discussion. It would not be possible for the Allied Governments, in view of their commitments under the Treaty of Versailles, to recognise this treaty *in toto*, and there is no guarantee that refusal so to recognise it would not lead to serious difficulties between the Allied Governments and the Government of the United States. You will no doubt yourself decide at which point in the discussion at the inter-Allied meeting, and to what extent, it may be desirable to reveal to the French Government the change in the attitude of His Majesty's Government on this particular point.

8. As regards the sixth paragraph of the enclosed draft, you should make it clear to the inter-Allied meeting that, whilst, in the opinion of His Majesty's Government, the Allied delegates nominated to meet the representative of the United States Government should be the Allied delegates on the Reparation Commission, it is for technical reasons desirable that these delegates should be nominated as delegates of the Governments, and not in their capacity of members of the Reparation Commission.

9. In view of the report contained in my despatch No. 2290 of today's date,[5] I trust that the reply to the United States Government's notes of the 22nd[6] and 23rd March[6] will now be despatched with the least possible delay, and I request that you will accordingly arrange for the immediate consideration of this question by the inter-Allied meeting.

I am, etc.,
BALFOUR

---

[4] Of August 25, 1921 (see *F.R.U.S.* 1921, vol. ii, pp. 1–35).
[5] Not printed.   [6] See No. 196, n. 6.

Second British Draft Reply to the United States Notes as to the Reimbursement of the Costs of the United States Troops in Germany.

The memorandum of the 22nd March[6] and the supplementary note of the 23rd March,[6] containing the views of the Government of the United States concerning the reimbursement of the costs of their army of occupation on the left bank of the Rhine, have received the fullest consideration on the part of the Allied Governments concerned. These Governments have already indicated their willingness to find a practical means of meeting the manifestly just desires of the United States Government in this matter, so that it does not seem necessary at present to subject the reasoning contained in the United States notes to a detailed examination. The following observations to which the Allied Governments desire to confine themselves are therefore of a purely practical order, designed to expedite the solution of a problem as to which disagreement, if it exists at all, can only relate to the means and not to the end.

2. In the first place, it must be explained that receipts from Germany up to the present date, whether in cash or in kind, have already been actually distributed. Deliveries in kind have been made to specific countries and debited to those countries against the cost of their armies of occupation. These deliveries have in general been made for such specific purposes as the reconstruction of devastated areas. Deliveries in cash have been distributed to avoid useless and even dangerous accumulation in the hands of the Reparation Commission.

3. In the second place, to give effect to the claim of the United States Government in the precise form in which it is put forward would involve the complete reopening *ab initio* of all the complicated and difficult negotiations which eventually led to the solutions embodied in the Spa Agreement of July 1920[7] and the Paris Agreement of March 1922.[8]

4. These difficulties, however, do not detract from the completeness with which the Allied Governments concur in the equity of the claim of the United States Government to obtain payment of their costs of occupation from Germany in priority to further payments to other countries on account of reparations. The Allied Governments welcome the expressed readiness of the United States Government to consider suggestions for the reasonable adjustment of the matter, which will clearly have to take into account the *de facto* position and the financial and economic questions involved, regard being had in particular to the considerable proportion of Germany's payments in the near future, which will be made in kind rather than in cash.

5. As a practical suggestion for securing immediate progress towards a solution the Allied Governments desire to suggest that the costs of the United States army of occupation might conveniently be divided, as has been found necessary in the case of the similar costs of the British and French armies of occupation, into two parts, representing respectively expenditure incurred

---

[7] See Vol. VIII, No. 77, n. 3.   [8] See No. 11.

up to the 30th April, 1921, inclusive, and expenditure incurred since that date. If this were agreed to, arrangements might be made without further delay for meeting the current costs, including costs since the 30th April, 1921, out of the German deliveries in kind on lines similar to those now in force for the costs of the British, French and Belgian armies of occupation.

6. In order to examine the matter as a whole, however, the Allied Governments would be glad if the United States Government would be good enough to nominate a representative who could meet the Allied delegates at Paris forthwith. The presence of such a representative would enable the Allied Governments to complete their information on certain elements of the question respecting which they are at the moment insufficiently informed.

7. The Allied Governments feel sure that this procedure will make it possible to prepare for submission to the interested Governments a plan of a kind to solve in a satisfactory way the question discussed in the present communication.

No. 252

The Earl of Balfour to Lord D'Abernon (Berlin)

No. 1201 [C 10091/725/18]

FOREIGN OFFICE, *July 24, 1922*

My Lord,

The following observations may be of assistance to your Excellency with reference to your despatch No. 536 of the 12th July,[1] in which you report a conversation with the German Chancellor on the question of the entry of Germany into the League of Nations.

2. In the course of this conversation you state that Dr. Wirth enquired whether Germany, if she joined the League of Nations, 'could count on the continuation of English goodwill towards the restoration of Germany as a prosperous State'. Provided this enquiry is literally interpreted, there would be no difficulty in returning a favourable answer. His Majesty's Government certainly desire the restoration of Germany as a prosperous State. It is most important, however, to avoid giving the German Government any impression whatsoever that His Majesty's Government are prepared in any way to pledge themselves to guarantee loans to Germany, or otherwise to burden the British Exchequer in order to restore Germany's prosperity. Every concrete German proposal for furthering German prosperity would have to be considered on its merits, if and when brought forward.

3. From your Excellency's despatch Dr. Wirth also appears to suppose that, were Germany to enter the League of Nations, 'England might abandon the attitude (towards Germany) she now holds'. Of this, I think, there is no chance, nor do I understand the meaning of Dr. Wirth's statement, that

[1] No. 243.

'Germany could easily be put in a minority at Geneva, and would be outvoted by countries like Czechoslovakia and Poland organised and marshalled by France'. No doubt there are certain subjects—narrowly defined—on which the assembly and the council vote by majorities. On most questions, however—I really think on all, which vitally affect national prosperity—unanimity is required. In this matter, therefore, the fears of Dr. Wirth seem to be unfounded. Moreover, Dr. Wirth's idea that the League of Nations is controlled by the French Government is a complete delusion. I believe that in every case in which the French and British delegations at Geneva have been unable to agree the French delegation has been outvoted, or has had to withdraw. I am quite unable, therefore, to see why 'Germany's interests would be endangered by entering the League'.

4. As regards Dr. Wirth's reference to Upper Silesia, I imagine that it is impossible to induce German opinion to believe—what is actually a fact—that the decision, be it right or wrong, which the League arrived at in regard to Upper Silesia was absolutely impartial, and that its groundwork was prepared not by the ex-b[e]lligerents but largely by the 'neutral' members of the council. Moreover, in that decision every precaution was taken to preserve the rights of German capitalists and workmen, and to make the boundary follow as nearly as was practicable a line doing equal justice to the Polish and German populations.

I am, etc.,
Balfour

No. 253

Sir M. Cheetham (Paris) to the Earl of Balfour (Received July 25)

No. 1730 [C 10566/6/18]

PARIS, *July 24, 1922*

My Lord,

Before acting on the instructions contained in your Lordship's despatch No. 2101 of the 7th instant[1] regarding the winding up of the work of the Military Commission of Control in Germany, Lord Hardinge considered it advisable to consult the British member of the Allied Military Committee of Versailles in order to ascertain the attitude which the French military authorities were likely to adopt with regard to the proposals now put forward by His Majesty's Government. As anticipated, the French military authorities have been also examining this matter, and have since submitted to the Versailles Committee a statement of their views, copy of which is enclosed herewith.[2] In this statement they enumerate, as was to be expected, the whole of the outstanding questions which figure in categories (A), (B) and (C) of the War Office letter to the Foreign Office of the 13th June,[3] but it is to be noted that in the forefront of this enumeration they place the failure of

---

[1] No. 238.   [2] Not printed.   [3] No. 238, Enclosure 1.

the German Government to organise and recruit the Reichswehr on the lines laid down in the Treaty of Versailles. I observe that this particular question figures in category (B) in the War Office list—that is to say, it is considered to be one of the outstanding questions the complete execution of which the Army Council consider desirable, but which are actually of secondary importance only. From information furnished to me by Sir. C Sackville-West, I am satisfied that it will be difficult for this Embassy to induce either the French Government or the Conference of Ambassadors to accept this view, and I therefore venture to suggest that I should be authorised to add to the list contained in the War Office letter of the 13th June of outstanding questions 'the complete execution of which is considered of the utmost importance by the Army Council,' those further questions which deal with the organisation and recruiting of the German army, which at present appear as Nos. 3 and 4 of the second category of outstanding questions as given in War Office letter of the 13th June.

I fully realise that, generally speaking, these questions arise out of stipulations in the treaty for the execution of which no time limit is prescribed, and that the Commission of Control cannot therefore be kept in existence in order to supervise their continued execution. On the other hand, it is clear that, as the men who fought in the war are getting older, the German authorities are increasing their efforts to train young men, in addition to those regularly enlisted for twelve years army service, and the French Government, with recollections of the events which followed the battle of Iéna, naturally regard this development as a matter of vital importance to their national security. In these circumstances I trust that His Majesty's Government may see their way to adopt a sympathetic attitude towards the very natural anxiety which the French Government feel on this head. If authorised to add this question to the four outstanding questions 'the complete execution of which is considered of the utmost importance by the Army Council,' I would of course make it clear that, once the Commission of Control has been satisfied that recruiting is being regularly and properly carried out, and that the administrative establishments of the former German army have been alienated, the responsibility for the continued execution of these treaty stipulations must be left to the proposed Military Committee of Guarantee.

In one other point the situation has been somewhat modified since your Lordship's despatch under reply was written. I refer to the question of the reorganisation of the German police, which appears as one of the questions, 'the complete execution of which is considered of the utmost importance by the Army Council'. Negotiations have, as your Lordship is aware, been proceeding between the Commission of Control and the German Government on this subject, and General Nollet's letter to the German Government of the 11th July, copy[2] of which is enclosed herewith, shows that the commission has now authorised the formation of State police in twenty-two different localities, thus granting the most important of the concessions proposed by the War Office. Moreover, the commission has formally put forward certain demands as to the reorganisation of the police, and has made the granting of the concession referred to conditional on the execution of these demands. At the same time an increase in the number of State police schools has been authorised. In view of the above development, I would suggest, for your Lordship's consideration, that in taking up with the Conference of Ambassadors the general question of the state of the execution of the military clauses of the Treaty of Versailles, I should be authorised, in so far as the reorganisation of the German police force is concerned, to support the final proposals of the Commission of Control, as communicated to the German Government in General Nollet's letter of the 11th July. I make this suggestion after consultation with Sir. C. Sackville-West, on the following grounds:—

(a) The main concessions asked for by the German Government, and recommended by the War Office have been accorded.

(b) The demands of the commission have been set forth in simple and definite terms, and the submission to the German Government of fresh proposals, before even the receipt of a reply to the proposals of the commission, would inevitably weaken the authority of the commission.

(c) General Nollet's letter to the German Government presumably represents the unanimous opinion of the Commission of Control, including the chief of the British delegation.

Lastly, I would like to avail myself of this opportunity to obtain your Lordship's views with regard to the action I am to take with regard to the enforcement of the military clauses of the Treaty of Versailles, which forbid the export of war material from Germany (article 170) and the employment of German officers by foreign Governments (article 179). In the War Office letter of the 13th June, the first of these questions appears in the category of outstanding questions 'the complete execution of which the Army Council considers desirable, but which are actually of secondary importance only'. The second of them appears in the category of questions 'the complete execution of which is demanded by the French Government, but which the Army Council considers of no real importance'. On the other hand, your Lordship will recollect that Lord Hardinge has been instructed in your Lordship's despatches No. 1535 of the 19th May[2] and No. 1749 of the 9th June[2] to invite the conference to consider the question of strictly enforcing the treaty stipulations on these subjects. In fact these two questions had, as reported in my telegram No. 376, section 7 of the 17th July,[4] been placed at Lord Hardinge's request on the agenda of the last meeting of the Conference of Ambassadors, but were adjourned on the understanding that they would be embodied in the general representations which were eventually to be addressed to the German Government on the whole question of the military clauses of the treaty. I should be glad to know whether I am now to withdraw definitely these two questions from the agenda of the conference, on the

[4] No. 249.

ground that His Majesty's Government no longer consider them to be of sufficient importance to be taken up with the German Government in connection with the general representations which are to be made to them on the lines indicated in your Lordship's despatch under reply.

As regards the export of war material, it is perhaps well to bear in mind that the question is by no means purely military, and that its importance lies rather in its commercial and administrative aspects. It was in consideration of these aspects that I felt justified in informing the Conference of Ambassadors, as reported in my telegram No. 333, paragraph 6, of the 21st June,[5] that His Majesty's Government attached considerable importance to the question, and that it was their policy to enforce strictly article 170. As this can only be done by compelling the German Government to pass suitable legislation on the subject, your Lordship may perhaps be prepared, for political as distinct from military reasons, to add this question to those whose complete execution is considered by the Army Council to be of the utmost importance.

I have, etc.,
MILNE CHEETHAM

[5] No. 232.

No. 254

Lord Kilmarnock (Coblenz) to the Earl of Balfour (Received July 27)
No. 222 [C 10664/289/18]

COBLENZ, July 24, 1922

My Lord,

I have the honour to acknowledge the receipt of your Lordship's despatches Nos. 184[1] and 185,[2] together with copies of the correspondence noted in the margin relating to the establishment of the proposed Inter-Allied Committee of Supervision in the Rhineland.

2. I am of opinion that the agreement reached at the Ambassadors' Conference on the 13th July[3] in regard to the three points in dispute should be accepted. As regards the provisional decision to establish the Licence Office at Coblenz, there is no doubt that General Allen would report that there is no accommodation available in Coblenz for the Licence Office, its German staff and their families. If the French had accepted the Paris proposals,[4] therefore, the result would have been the establishment of the office in Cologne, and this is doubtless one of the reasons for their refusal.

[1] Of July 17, not printed.
[2] Of July 17, not printed. This asked Lord Kilmarnock for his observations on matters relating to the establishment of the proposed Inter-Allied Committee of Supervision in the Rhineland.
[3] See No. 244.
[4] Of August 13, 1921. See Vol. XV, No. 104, Appendix 8.

3. With regard to the two remaining points in dispute, I have no objection to offer to the new texts of the third paragraph of article 9 (b), regarding the question of names, and the second paragraph of article 10, regarding the action to be taken in the event of a case of discrimination being established. I think that there is a fair chance of the German representatives accepting the new text proposed for the third paragraph of article 9 (b). As to the new text for article 10, in my opinion Allied interests are sufficiently safeguarded by the stipulation that the German Government undertakes to issue a licence in favour of the injured party in cases where the Commission of Supervision is of opinion that the German Government has not taken satisfactory measures as a result of the protests transmitted by the commission. It has the great advantage of getting rid of the stipulation that a blank licence should be placed at the disposal of the new Allied body, which is very objectionable to the Germans.

4. In the event of the Allied Governments deciding to reopen negotiations with the German representatives, there would be reason to hope that the committee of experts would succeed in inducing the Germans to accept the new texts proposed in Paris. After the experts had sent in their report, the Germans asked for another meeting, from which, I think, it is reasonable to conclude that they were willing to make some further concessions in order to reach a settlement.

5. In regard to the continuance of the Ems organisation,[5] it is not at the present time a serious hindrance to Allied or German trade in the Rhineland. At the commencement of the sanctions very serious disorganisation resulted from the arbitrary transfer of the office to Bad Ems, but this has since been remedied. The placing of the licensing office under Allied authority has resulted in licences being given for the import of certain luxury articles which the German Government wished to prevent their nationals from buying, and for the export of goods which the German authorities considered could not be spared, or for which they considered the price asked was too low. Licences have been given freely for the importation of wines, cognac and other goods contrary to the wishes of the German authorities. The result of this has been that complaints from traders that they could not obtain licences have ceased. This has, however, nothing whatever to do with discrimination contrary to articles 264 to 267 of the Treaty of Peace. In fact, the question of discrimination scarcely arises under the Ems régime, as the Licence Office is forced to grant practically all Allied applications, and the applicant is not required to show that failure to do so would be discrimination.

6. I would mention, in passing, that the Allied trade which is advanced by these methods is not necessarily trade in the products of Allied countries. It is partly represented by the transactions of merchants of Allied nationality established here in goods the produce of or destined for neutral or ex-enemy countries. In fact, during the course of the negotiations the French have shown more desire to 'prevent discrimination against' firms than against products. The French are doing their utmost to establish here a body of

[5] See No. 197.

French traders and to throw into their hands as large a share of the trade in the occupied territory as possible. Actively supported by the Italian delegation, they lose no opportunity for pressing for more and more interference in the Ems Licence Office. The Belgians are inclined to side with the French. The British and Americans endeavour to limit Allied interference to cases where Allied trading interests are directly concerned. But even this goes far beyond the question of discrimination.

7. As an example of the length to which the French go, I would mention that they recently pressed for the adoption of a policy in the occupied territory hostile to the German Government's restrictions on imports from Switzerland.

8. The extreme importance attached to the three points in dispute is also significant. By holding out, the French hope to secure either the continuance of the present Ems régime or the acceptance of a new system which would give them complete information as to the foreign trade of every firm in the occupied territory. In conversation, the French say that political action is ineffective without economic penetration.

9. Another aspect of the question is that the Germans complain—with justification—that measures taken by them to prevent foreign exchange required for essential purposes from being used for the purchase of luxuries are overridden by the Bad Ems control—in other words, that the hole in the west is still partially open.

10. A continuance of the present state of affairs is in my opinion highly undesirable, not only because of its doubtful legality, but also because the German licensing system has given rise to many abuses, and all direct Allied responsibility for the Licensing Office should be terminated as soon as possible.

11. Although I agree with the opinion expressed by Mr. Kavanagh[6] that the maintenance of the Ems organisation contributes to a certain extent to remove certain difficulties encountered by British traders more quickly than the new method would do, I do not consider that we would be justified in continuing this sanction solely for this reason. This would in my opinion amount to a distinct breach of faith with the Germans, with whom we have made an agreement by which the sanctions were to be removed providing certain conditions were fulfilled. The only question that can arise is whether the Germans have fulfilled these conditions. In any case the new body will be confined to questions of discrimination contrary to articles 264 to 267 of the treaty. It will not be able to deal with refusals to grant licences where discrimination is not alleged.

12. As to the doubtful legality of the maintenance of the Ems organisation, the reason for the addition of article 11 to Ordinance 98 given in Colonel Ryan's despatch No. 410 of the 10th October, 1921,[7] was that the High Commission considered that it was undesirable in the economic interests of the occupied territories and countries with which they trade that there should be two changes of régime within a short interval, if that could be avoided.

[6] H.M. Commercial Commissioner at Cologne.   [7] Not printed.

(The Supreme Council's resolution[4] instructed the experts to submit proposals to the Governments before the 1st September, 1921.) Another reason given was that it was thought that the retention of control would facilitate the negotiations to be carried on with the Germans. It is, I think, perfectly clear that the High Commission would not have objected to the two changes of régime if they could have foreseen that the 'short interval' would last twelve months.

13. I would add that the original assumption by the High Commission of the control of the Licence Office and its transfer to Bad Ems in March 1921 was not ordered by the Allied Governments. Lord Curzon's telegram No. 13 to Mr. Robertson[8] of the 7th March, 1921[9] (page 1 of compilation of documents[10] respecting the negotiations for the establishment of an Allied Licensing Organisation in the Rhineland) instructing the High Commission to impose certain economic sanctions, includes no reference to the Licence Offices. The High Commission acted in this instance on its own responsibility and solely with the object of preventing the German authorities from interfering with the collection of customs duties by refusing licences for occupied territory.

14. By its resolution of the 13th August, 1921,[4] the Supreme Council decided to 'abolish the economic sanctions . . . , this decision to come into effect on the 15th September, 1921'. The decision was subject to three conditions which were to be previously accepted by the German Government, of which the first was the constitution of an inter-Allied body, the sole object of which is to ensure that the operation of the German system does not result in setting up discriminations contrary to the provisions of articles 264 to 267 of the treaty; the second is not relevant to the subject of this despatch; and the third was that the High Commission 'should have power to order and to carry out all executive measures during the period of transition as regards the decisions set out above'. At the end of July 1922, one of the economic sanctions is still in existence. The explanation of this state of affairs put forward by the French is that the Germans are not yet willing to accept a scheme for the new body in accordance with the terms of the Supreme Council's resolution of the 13th August, 1921. Now, the difference is on three points. As your Lordship is aware, the experts have negotiated with the German delegation a scheme which, in the opinion of all except the French, complies with the conditions laid down by the Supreme Council.

15. In these circumstances, I feel that the further continuance of the Bad Ems régime is unjustifiable (1) because its continuance was originally decided upon by the High Commission (in the exercise of its power of ordering executive measures during the period of transition) in order to avoid in the interests of traders two changes of régime within a short interval; (2) because the failure to constitute the new inter-Allied body within a short interval cannot be ascribed to the Germans, who as far back as in February

[8] British High Commissioner on the Rhineland High Commission, October, 1920–December, 1921. [9] See Vol. XV, No. 46, Appendix.
[10] C 10098/289/18 (in Confidential Print 12006, op. cit., pp. 673–4).

last accepted a scheme which, in the opinion of the majority of the Allied experts, fulfilled the conditions of the Supreme Council's resolution. Your Lordship agreed with this opinion and informed me[11] that His Majesty's Government were not prepared to instruct their experts to make further concessions (i.e., to the French point of view) which could only have the effect of travelling beyond the purpose that the Supreme Council had in view.

16. I realise that there are practical difficulties in the way of a solution, and, in particular, that it is unlikely that a settlement of this highly technical question could be reached at the forthcoming meeting of the Prime Ministers.[12] I trust, however, that His Majesty's Government will bring pressure to bear upon the French Government to induce them to accept the Paris proposals as a preliminary to a final meeting of the experts with the German delegation. The French will certainly object to the abolition of the present Ems régime before a final agreement has been reached with the Germans, on the ground that there will then be no inducement for the Germans to accept our scheme. This argument will be hard to resist, but, nevertheless, by pressing for the abolition of the Ems régime a settlement with the French Government on the points still under discussion should be facilitated.

17. I agree with the opinion expressed in Sir M. Cheetham's telegram No. 37[3] of the 16th July,[13] regarding the Italian delegation. If the Italians are likely to resent our raising the question of the Italian delegation's expenses now, it would be inadvisable to run the risk of losing their support. At the Ambassadors' Conference the Italian Ambassador in Paris rejected on two occasions the opinion of the Italian delegate, towards whom he appeared to be by no means well disposed. Perhaps, therefore, it would be possible for the question to be raised outside the conference with the Italians. The Italian delegation here loses no opportunity of assisting the French, who, in their turn, will give us no help in the question of the Italian delegation's expenses.

18. A copy of this despatch has been sent to His Majesty's Ambassadors at Paris and Berlin.

I have, etc.,
KILMARNOCK

[11] See No. 197, paragraph 5.   [12] See Chap. II.   [13] No. 248.

No. 255

Sir M. Cheetham (Paris) to the Earl of Balfour (Received July 28, 8.30 a.m.)
No. 394 Telegraphic: by bag [C 10728/32/18]

PARIS, *July 26, 1922*

The Conference of Ambassadors met this morning under the chairmanship of Monsieur Jules Cambon, the Belgian ambassador being also present, and considered the following questions:—

. . .¹8. The Allied Military Committee of Versailles have drawn up a further definition of the revolvers and pistols which are to be considered as war material and must therefore not be exported from ex-enemy countries (see Lord Hardinge's telegram No. 198 of April 5th, section 6,² and your despatches Nos. 1164 of April 22nd,² and 1018 of April 12th).² This definition, which was approved by the Conference, carries out the views of His Majesty's Government and replaces the former definition communicated to the German Government by the Military Commission of Control. Copy of the Versailles Committee's report² is enclosed in my despatch No. 1752 of today's date.²

. . .¹10. The Conference decided that certain naval material which had been left to the German Government in order to establish a rangefinding school, should be handed over to the Naval Commission, since it has been discovered that the proposed school is capable of being developed into the nucleus of a fortress.

11. As the result of the arrangements made between Your Lordship and the French Ambassador in London, as set forth in your despatch No. 1623 of the 27th May,³ the French government submitted to the conference a draft of the note to be addressed to the German government on the subject of German war criminals. Copy of this draft is enclosed in my despatch No. 1753 of today's date.⁴ I declined to discuss the draft at today's meeting, as I had only just received it, but I took the opportunity of pointing out that inasmuch as no demand for surrender of war criminals had ever been made, the German government could not be accused of defaulting in respect of article 228 of the treaty, and that, as moreover His Majesty's Government do not wish to put the German government in default over this article, I foresaw difficulty in agreeing to the wording of the last five paragraphs of the French note.⁵ I proposed therefore to submit a counter-draft at the forthcoming meeting. . . .¹

¹ The section(s) omitted referred to other matters.
² Not printed. See, however, No. 226.   ³ No. 225.   ⁴ Not printed.
⁵ These ran: 'Dans ces conditions, les Puissances alliées estiment, au vu des procédures et des jugements, que le Gouvernement allemand n'a pas tenu sa promesse de faire bonne et loyale justice. Elles déclarent ne tenir, dorénavant, aucun compte de la mise en jugement par l'Allemagne des inculpés, qui n'ont pas encore comparu devant la Cour de Leipzig, et, conformément à leur lettre du 7 mai 1920, elles considèrent que l'article 228 du Traité de Versailles doit désormais recevoir son plein et entier effet.

'Les Puissances alliées ont le regret de constater que les déclarations publiques faites le 26 janvier 1922 par le Chancelier d'Empire devant le Reichstag constituent un refus d'exécuter les articles 228 à 230 du Traité de Paix.

'Les Puissances alliée sse voient donc dans la nécessité de prendre acte de cette violation formelle d'une des clauses essentielles du traité. Elles protestent solennellement auprès du Gouvernement allemand contre l'impunité que, par son refus de livrer les coupables de guerre, celui-ci prétend assurer aux auteurs d'actes criminels, commis en violation des lois de la guerre et du droit des gens.

'Les Puissance salliées se réservent la liberté de poursuivre elles-mêmes, et s'il y a lieu par contumace, lesdits inculpés.

'Dès à présent, l'Allemagne, par son attitude, s'est exposée volontairement aux conséquences que le traité prévoit à son égard en cas de violation des clauses du Traité de Paix.'

Lord Kilmarnock (Coblenz) to the Earl of Balfour (Received July 28)
No. 224 [C 10697/899/18]

COBLENZ, *July 26, 1922*

My Lord,

With reference to your Lordship's despatch No. 183 of the 17th July,[1] relative to the costs of the Rhineland Commission, I have the honour to state that I have sounded the French High Commissioner unofficially as to whether the French Government would be likely to agree to the immediate approval by the Ambassadors' Conference of that part of the Paris Commission's report which relates to the costs of the Rhineland High Commission, thereby leaving it to the latter to report direct to the Allied Governments on its own internal economy. This proposal would certainly meet the objection of the French Government to an enquiry by an outside body which they consider would be prejudicial to the prestige and authority of the High Commission, but it seems a little doubtful whether the French Government would not consider that a joint report would impinge on the principle which they maintain, viz., that each High Commissioner is responsible solely to his own Government. M. Tirard made an alternative suggestion, to which he seemed to think he could secure the assent of his Government, viz., that each High Commissioner should be instructed to furnish a report to his own Government on the costs of his staff and the possibility of effecting reductions, and that these reports should then be communicated by each Government to the other Governments concerned. I do not think that there would be any objection raised by the French Government to a common enquiry and report into the contributions under article 8 of the agreement. This, of course, would not be so satisfactory a solution as your Lordship's proposal, and in any case if it were adopted as a *pis-aller* it would be important to avoid accepting the point of view of the French Government that each High Commissioner is responsible solely to his own Government. I dealt with this point in my despatch No. 154 of the 9th May.[2] I am anxious that no formula should be accepted which could be quoted by the French High Commissioner as justifying him in claiming any power in his own zone for himself, apart from the High Commission as a whole.

2. Whilst I cannot say that the suggestion contained in your Lordship's despatch, even if not modified in the sense proposed by M. Tirard, would, in my opinion, be likely to lead to any very direct results in the way of economy, it would, I think, afford a means of indirect pressure on the French which might induce them to make at all events some reductions in expenditure in order to forestall or avoid criticism. It would certainly provide a way out of the *impasse* which has been reached, but the best that can be expected from it would be that we should obtain some satisfaction instead of none, which would apparently be the result of the continuation of

[1] No. 250.   [2] Not printed.

the discussion on its present lines. Indirect pressure has proved by no means ineffective, since, as a result of the discussions of the past few months, M. Tirard has made substantial reductions in the expenses of the French Department.

3. With regard to the question of the position of the German Reichskommissar in the Rhineland, I am in entire agreement with your Lordship's opinion that this is not a question which it would be in the interest of His Majesty's Government to raise at the moment.

I have, etc.,
KILMARNOCK

No. 257

Lord D'Abernon (Berlin) to the Earl of Balfour (Received August 1)
No. 593 [C 10928/6/18]

BERLIN, *July 26, 1922*

My Lord,

With regard to the proposal made by the Conference of Ambassadors on the 14th April (forwarded under cover of Lord Hardinge's despatch No. 938 of the 14th April)[1] regarding the transformation of the Military Control Commission, I have the honour to report that Secretary of State von Haniel today informed me confidentially that before Dr. Rathenau's assassination[2] he had prepared a draft reply to this communication. Since then so many urgent questions had arisen that the matter had somewhat been lost sight of. He promised, however, to deal with it at the first opportunity.

In this connection, I took advantage of the opportunity to point out to Herr von Haniel that minor delays and acts of resistance which the present Military Commission of Control is encountering gravely prejudice Germany's case, when she presses for withdrawal of the commission. From information given me I was convinced that energetic action by the German Government for two or three months would clean the board. The matter, however, required the direction of some influential and energetic German official who could prevent subordinate officers obstructing. Herr von Haniel appeared impressed with this view, and it is not unlikely Dr. Peters[3] or some man of equal authority may be appointed to finish up the business.

I have, etc.,
D'ABERNON

[1] No. 208 (see also No. 207).
[2] See No. 234.
[3] Former German State Commissioner for Disarmament.

No. 258

Lord D'Abernon (Berlin) to the Earl of Balfour (Received July 28, 9.35 p.m.)
No. 139 Telegraphic [C 10742/336/18]

BERLIN, *July 28, 1922, 6.45 p.m.*

Chancellor is perturbed by rumours about Rhineland to the effect that England favours scheme of plebiscite there with a view to establishment of a buffer or semi-independent state. He requested me to telegraph about this as it would be of great assistance to him in dealing with internal political difficulties if he knew views of His Majesty's Government.[1]

[1] In telegram No. 67 of July 31, the Foreign Office replied: 'You may inform Chancellor that, so far as His Majesty's Government are concerned, rumours in question are without any foundation whatever.'

No. 259

The Earl of Balfour to Sir M. Cheetham (Paris)
No. 2403 [C 10697/899/18]

FOREIGN OFFICE, *July 31, 1922*

Sir,

With reference to your despatch No. 1709 of the 22nd July,[1] I transmit to you herewith a copy of a despatch[2] from His Majesty's representative at Coblenz on the question of the reduction of the expenses of the Rhineland High Commission.

2. In view of the attitude of the French Government, it is evident that it would serve no useful purpose to pursue further Lord Hardinge's proposal to the Ambassadors' Conference on the 10th March,[3] (*a*) to refer this question back to the civilian members of the Paris Financial Commission, and (*b*) to suggest to the Rhineland Commission the establishment of a sub-committee to collect the data which would be required by the Paris Commission.

3. The following three alternative lines of procedure therefore apparently remain open:—

(*a*) That indicated in paragraph 5 of my despatch No. 183 to Coblenz of the 17th July, i.e.,[4] that you should propose to the Ambassadors' Conference the approval by the conference of the suggestion in the report of the Paris Financial Commission to instruct the Rhineland Commission to report to the Governments direct on its own internal economy.

[1] Not printed. This transmitted a copy of a note dated July 20 from M. Cambon to Lord Hardinge.
[2] No. 256.
[3] Lord Hardinge's proposal was contained in a memorandum, a copy of which was transmitted to the Foreign Office in Paris despatch No. 847 of April 6, not printed.
[4] No. 250.

(b) That indicated in paragraph 8 of the French memorandum to the Ambassadors' Conference of the 28th June, 1922,[5] that the representatives of the Governments on the Ambassadors' Conference should each give an undertaking on behalf of their Governments that the present expenditure of their respective national delegations in the Rhineland would be taken as the maximum for future years, and that, if the conference considered it necessary, it should 'hear' the High Commissioners.

(c) That indicated in paragraph 1 of Lord Kilmarnock's despatch No. 224 of the 26th July,[2] whereby each High Commissioner would report to his own Government on the internal economy of his own delegation, the High Commissioners' reports being communicated by the respective Governments to the other Governments concerned.

4. Despite the fact that the financial results of the adoption of the line of procedure suggested by Lord Kilmarnock will no doubt be very small, this now seems the only line which it is politic to follow. The discussion of this question on the lines previously proposed has already resulted in a complete deadlock, and there is a real danger that the adoption of either of the other two alternative suggestions outlined in the preceding paragraph might result in raising, in an acute form, awkward questions, such as the exact responsibility of the French High Commissioner in his own zone or the continuance of the office of the Reichskommissar, both of which it is strongly to the general interest to allow to lie dormant.

5. Whilst expressing, therefore, to the French Government and to M. Cambon the appreciation of His Majesty's Government for the efforts which they have made to meet the views of His Majesty's Government in this matter—notably in the proposal to 'hear' the High Commissioners at the Ambassadors' Conference—you should inform the conference that His Majesty's Government, in view of the explanations which they have since received, and though they still consider that their proposals would most adequately and effectively have met the general interest, are yet ready to abandon the proposal made in Lord Hardinge's memorandum of the 10th March.[3] You should further explain that it seems sufficient if, in order to close the question, the report of each High Commissioner on the costs of his staff and the possibility of effecting reductions is communicated upon receipt to the other Governments concerned. In making this statement you will, no doubt, pay particular attention to the concluding sentence of paragraph 1 of Lord Kilmarnock's despatch No. 224.[2]

6. As regards the enquiry into the cost of the contributions under articles 8 to 12 of the Rhineland Agreement, you may inform the conference that I am in complete agreement with the proposal of the French Government, contained in paragraph 7 of their memorandum of the 28th June, that this matter should be considered by the High Commission.

[5] Not printed. A copy of this Memorandum was enclosed in Paris despatch No. 1558 of July 5, not printed.

7. Should the French Government make any further reference to the question of the continuance of the office of the Reichskommissar in the Rhineland, you should remind them of the concessions which have already been made to their point of view in the matter of the enquiry into the costs of the commission, and you should express the hope that they will leave this matter to be considered if they consider it necessary at Coblenz.

8. A copy of this despatch has been sent to His Majesty's representative at Coblenz.

I am, etc.,

BALFOUR

No. 260

The Earl of Balfour to Sir M. Cheetham (Paris)

No. 2421 [C 10566/6/18]

FOREIGN OFFICE, *August 1, 1922*

Sir,

I have received your despatch No. 1730 of July 24,[1] in which (1) you request authority, before laying the proposals contained in my despatch No. 2101 of July 7[2] before the French Government and the Ambassadors' Conference, to make certain amendments thereto, and (2) you ask for instructions respecting the action on my despatches No. 15[3]5[3] and No. 1749[3] of May 19 and June 9 relating to the enforcement of articles 170 and 179 of the Treaty of Versailles.

2. The amendments which you suggest to the proposals contained in my despatch No. 2101 are as follows: (*a*) The addition to the list of four outstanding questions, 'the complete execution of which is considered of the utmost importance by the Army Council', of the further questions of the organisation and recruitment of the German Army (Nos. B. (3) and (4) in paragraph 3 of the War Office letter of June 13),[4] and (*b*) the substitution of the police demands contained in the Military Control Commission's note to the German Government of July 11[5] for the proposals in the War Office letter of July 4.[6]

3. The War Office, who have been consulted,[7] deprecate the acceptance

---

[1] No. 253.   [2] No. 238.

[3] Not printed.   [4] No. 238, Enclosure 1.

[5] Not printed (see, however, No. 253).   [6] Not printed (see, however, No. 238).

[7] Mr. Lampson minuted on August 1: 'I have discussed this with Colonel Finlayson at the War Office. He concurs in the draft as now submitted.

'I gather from him that the W[ar] O[ffice] are not prepared to modify their views in any way; but so long as we make it clear that we do not claim that the question of recruiting is in any way a matter affecting the duration of the Commission of Control they agree to our doing what we can to meet the French on this point. He agreed to the passage on the subject as worded in the draft, and I gathered that in the event of the French holding out for more the War Office might wish to have a personal meeting with the French military advisers to thrash the whole thing out. But he wished that idea [be] held in reserve.'

of either of these amendments, and urge that the policy outlined in my despatch No. 2101 of July 7 and in their letters of June 13 and July 4 should for the present be maintained. As regards the question of the police, a copy of a War Office memorandum is enclosed comparing in detail the demands of the Control Commission with the proposals contained in the War Office letter of July 4. From a study of this memorandum it will be seen that, whilst in principle the War Office recommendations appear to have been generally followed, the demands made by the Control Commission on a number of points allow none of the concessions which the War Office have recommended, and which, in view of post-war conditions, they consider can be granted without prejudice to any necessary safeguards. In view of the fact that the Control Commission's note to the German Gov[ernmen]t has already been despatched, it would clearly not be politic, pending the German Gov[ernmen]t's reply thereto, to make any reference, in the general representations which are to be made to the German Government on the subject of control, to further concessions to the German point of view in this matter. For your own information, however, it is well that you should know that, if the German Government dispute the Control Commission's demands of July 11, H[is] M[ajesty's] G[overnment] may find it difficult to support the commission *in toto*. I understand that a communication to this effect has been sent by the War Office to the British representative on the commission, instructing him to refer home before consenting to the despatch by the commission of any further note on this subject.

4. As regards the organisation and recruitment of the German army, the War Office consider that (1) it will be impossible for the Military Control Commission ever effectively to check the recruitment of individuals, however long the commission remain in Germany; (2) whilst it will consequently be impossible to prevent the enlistment of a small number of men for short periods of service, short-service enlistment, if introduced on a large scale, will be bound soon to come to the notice of the Military Committee of Guarantee; (3) the situation after the battle of Jena, to which you refer in the second paragraph of your despatch, hardly offers an analogy, since at that time Germany had an army of 40,000 men only, and, by passing some 35,000 men through the ranks each year, was able to build up within a very short time a formidable reserve for the period; under modern conditions, however, even granted that Germany were able to pass 25,000 men through short-term service each year without the knowledge of the Military Committee of Guarantee, the resulting reserve would be very inadequate.

5. In these circumstances I am unable to authorise you to amend the proposals contained in my despatch No. 2101 in the manner you suggest. At the same time, whilst in no way desiring to dispute the War Office opinion with regard to a technical matter upon which they alone are capable of pronouncing, I am most anxious to work as harmoniously as possible with the French authorities on both these questions. I therefore request that you will, in discussing the question with the French Government and the Ambassadors' Conference, state (1) that, in the opinion of H[is] M[ajesty's]

G[overnment], the demands respecting the police made in the Control Commission's note of July 11 are not altogether consistent with the spirit of the general representations which they desire should now be made to the German Government on the whole question of military control, and that they would therefore prefer that, unless these representations can be deferred until the reply to that note has been received, no reference to the police question—except in general terms, as in the W[ar] O[ffice] letter of June 13—should therein be made beyond a request for an early reply to the Control Commission's note of July 11; (2) that, whilst His Majesty's Government are ready to add to the four points referred to in paragraph 5 (*a*) of my despatch No. 2101 of July 7 the taking of the legislative and administrative measures necessary to bring the German recruiting law and army organisation into conformity with the relevant articles of the treaty, they are not prepared to regard the supervision of the observance of these measures (a duty which is eminently one for the Committee of Guarantee) a reason for the continuance of the Control Commission; (3) that H[is] M[ajesty's] G[overnment] have in no way departed from their declared policy of strict insistence on the complete observance by the German Government of all the disarmament clauses of the treaty, and that it is because of their firm resolve to insist on such observance that H[is] M[ajesty's] G[overnment] are so anxious to take every precaution to ensure that the Allied Governments do not, by exposing themselves to the charge of exceeding their rights under the treaty, put the German Government in a position wherein they could claim that they were, by the action of the Allied Governments themselves, absolved from the execution of their obligations.

6. Considerations precisely similar to those outlined in the preceding paragraph apply to the question of the enforcement of article 170 of the Treaty of Versailles. I am prepared to allow the addition to the points mentioned in paragraph 5 (*a*) of my despatch No. 2101 of the passage of the legislative measures necessary to bring the German law on this matter into conformity with the stipulation of the treaty. I must, however, insist that the enforcement of the law shall be left to the Military Committee of Guarantee. I do not consider it desirable that any further action should be taken on my despatch No. 1749 pending a definite decision of the matters now under discussion.

I am, etc.,
BALFOUR

Note on the Inter-Allied Military Commission of Control Note No. 2107 of the 11th July to the German Government,[3] regarding the Reorganisation of the German Police

WAR OFFICE, *July 26, 1922*

Points demanded by the Inter-Allied Military Commission of Control	*Points recommended by the War Office Memorandum on the Police (27th June, 1922)[3]*

(*a*) Increase in State police.

The commission have allowed State police in 22 additional towns instead of in the 171 asked for by the Germans.

The Germans could hardly expect to get all they asked, but the above appears hardly a reasonable consideration of the German request. It is difficult to see why, except that it is in accordance with the principle you mentioned in your letter to the War Office, dated the 13th July, 1922,[3] such important Ruhr industrial centres as Düsseldorf, Duisburg, Horde, Hagen and Hamm in the neutral zone are not allowed some State police; in addition, such centres of unrest as Hof in Bavaria, the Saxon industrial towns, and some of the towns in Prussian Saxony, the scene of the Communist rising in 1921,[9] might be allowed State police.

The principle that the Inter-Allied Military Commission of Control have followed in this question appears reasonable on paper, but in practice it is not, and it is considered that each town should have been considered separately on its merits.

(*b*) Police to be composed and organised as in 1913.

Suppression of all police units not existing in 1913 is demanded.

Note.—No concession is made to the Germans.

The increase of 60,000 police sanctioned by the Boulogne note[8] is considered to have been intended to assist in dealing with large scale disorders. Therefore favourable consideration should be given to requests for an increase in State police in certain towns and for an introduction of State police in others in which there were only municipal police in 1913, each case being treated on its merits.

The Germans to be allowed to retain in the larger towns dismounted Hundertschaften and mounted detachments, also police armoured car detachments.

In view of the reduction of the German army, a certain proportion of the police to be located in barracks, to form a reserve in the hands of the higher

[8] See Vol. VIII, No. 33, Appendix 2, where the figure of 70,000 is given.
[9] See Vol. XVI, No. 594.

(c) All police officials to be given the legal status of 'Beamte': and
(d) Amendment of legislation regarding police terms of service.

Note.—This agrees with the War Office suggestion.

(e) Police administration and
(f) Police staffs.

Police administration to be exactly as in 1913. No staffs other than those existing in 1913 to be allowed.

Note.—This makes no concession to the Germans.

police authorities; the accommodation to be administered more in the nature of billets, like the London police, rather than [of] military barracks.

The German Government to be pressed to regularise police engagements and to enforce the 12 years' term of service.

The War Office memorandum does not discuss the question of police administration. A slight increase in the police administrative service is presumably necessitated by the changes in internal conditions since 1913 and the increase from 92,000 to 150,000 police.

War Office recommendations as regards staffs.

Insistence on the disbandment of the following military staffs:

Schupo staffs attached to Ministers of the Interior and to Oberpräsidenten of provinces.

Group staffs.

Abteilung staffs.

The following concessions to be permitted:

(i) Small administrative police staffs to be attached to Ministries of the Interior and to Oberpräsidenten of provinces.

(ii) A small executive police staff to be attached to the Regierungspräsident of a Bezirk or the Polizeipräsident of a town.

Note.—As regards staffs, the Prussian police decree of the 24th May (Part I, paragraph 2) states that from the 1st October, 1922, no special police officers are to be attached to Oberpräsidenten as technical police advisers; each Regierungspräsident of a Bezirk is only to have one higher police executive official as a technical police adviser.

Further, small executive police staffs

attached to Regierungspräsidenten and Landräte would appear to conform to the 1913 organisation.

(g) Police organisation in each locality.
The 1913 organisation is to be exactly maintained.

Note.—No concession is made.

The Germans to be allowed an increase of executive staff in Berlin, other very large towns, the Ruhr, and the whole neutral zone.

The Germans to be allowed to retain some form of constituted police unit (i.e., dismounted Hundertschaften and mounted detachments) in the larger towns.

(h) Local reserves.
To be drawn from the area police as required, as in 1913.

The Germans to be allowed to retain in the larger towns dismounted Hundertschaften and mounted detachments, also police armoured car detachments.

In view of the reduction of the German army, a certain proportion of the police to be located in barracks, to form a reserve in the hands of the higher police authorities; the accommodation to be administered more in the nature of billets, like the London police, rather than [of] military barracks.

(i) Military cadres of the Schupo.
To be abolished.

Note.—It is not quite understood what is meant by this sentence; it is thought that the dissolution of the staffs and units suggested in the War Office memorandum, and the surrender of all military transport, disposes of any danger of the police forming a military cadre.

Further, it is presumed that the personnel are not to be disbanded, but transferred to other police duties.

The abolition of all military Schupo staffs and technical Schupo units should deprive the police force of any military characteristics.

(j) Technical units.
Disbandment demanded.

Note.—Agreed to by the Germans.

Disbandment of Schupo M.T. units, signal units, aviation and wireless detachments recommended.

(k) Military training.
To be confined to individual training to the exclusion of all unit training.

As recommended by the War Office.

(*l*) Uniform.
   Non-military type to be adopted.
   Note.—Agreed to by the Germans.
	Not mentioned.

(*m*) Police schools. May be increased from the 1913 total (seven) to twelve.	A certain number to be permitted.
(*n*) Depots for material. To be limited to those already laid down by the commission.	Not mentioned.
(*o*) Delays in the reorganisation of the police. This is to be carried out by the 15th December, 1922, the periods asked for by the German Government being excessive.	Not mentioned.

No. 261

Sir M. Cheetham (Paris) to the Earl of Balfour (Received August 4, 8.30 a.m.)
No. 403 Telegraphic: by bag [C 11065/602/18]

PARIS, *August 2, 1922*

The Conference of Ambassadors met this morning under the chairmanship of Monsieur Jules Cambon, the Belgian Ambassador being also present, and discussed the following questions:—

1. I informed the Conference, in accordance with your telegram No. 253 of July 31st,[1] that I was now authorised to concur in the views of my colleagues to the effect that the German Government shall not be allowed to retain and reconstruct demilitarized warships for their post-war fleet. A decision to this effect was accordingly adopted and will be communicated to the Reparation Commission.

. . .[2]8. As reported in my telegram No. 394, section 11,[3] I submitted a counter-draft of the note to be addressed to the German Government on the subject of war criminals. Subject to certain modifications proposed by the French this was approved by the Conference *ad referendum*. The text as finally agreed upon is enclosed in my despatch No. 1807[4] and I shall be glad to learn as soon as possible whether His Majesty's Government are prepared to approve it. The French Government insisted upon maintaining the paragraph asserting their right of trying the war criminals *per contumacia*.

[1] This telegram was a reply to Paris despatch No. 1136 of May 10 (C 6969/602/18), not printed.
[2] The sections omitted referred to other matters.　　　　　　　　　　[3] No. 255.
[4] Of August 2, not printed. See No. 268, n. 2, below.

. . .²17. Monsieur Cambon reverted to the question of the equipment of the German allied cruisers and destroyers which are to be incorporated in the French and Italian fleets (see my telegram No. 376, section 9 of the 17th July)⁵ and suggested that as the representations made in London had been without effect the Conference should now adopt a majority decision in favour of the German Government being called upon to supply the equipment as desired by the French and Italian Governments. In accordance with Your Lordship's telegram No. 255,⁶ I at once informed the Conference that I could not accept a majority decision on a matter of this importance, and that His Majesty's Government could not agree to be bound in any way by such a decision. From a political point of view it is so desirable to bring naval control in Germany to an end as soon as possible, and at the same time to avoid further friction with the French and Italian Governments over this question, that I trust it may be possible to induce the Admiralty to modify their present views on this subject at an early date. . . .²

    ⁵ No. 249.
    ⁶ Of August 1, not preserved in the Foreign Office archives.

No. 262

Lord D'Abernon (Berlin) to the Earl of Balfour
(Received August 4, 8.30 a.m.)

No. 142 Telegraphic [C 11053/8315/18]

BERLIN, *August 3, 1922, 8.50 p.m.*

Meeting was held today of representatives of England, France, Italy, Belgium and Japan to consider action under decision of conference of ambassadors of July 17th.¹ Draft was presented by French ambassador embodying terms of protest as enclosed in your despatch No. 1136² but adding a paragraph protesting against attitude of Bavarian government towards Andreas Hofer Bund³ and against manifestations in favour of junction of Haut-Adige to Tyrol, see Paris telegram No. 376.⁴ Am I authorised to sign this as well as rest of documents?⁵ Next meeting will be held Monday.

Italian ambassador raised no objection to draft proposed but said he had not yet received instructions to sign protest against Herr Schweyer's speech although authorised regarding von Kahr and Andreas Hofer Bund. He has telegraphed for instructions.

Regarding Wirth's speeches I informed conference of my interview with Chancellor related in my despatch No. 579.⁶

    ¹ See No. 249.
    ² Of July 13, not printed (see, however, No. 245, n. 4).
    ³ See No. 249, n. 3.   ⁴ No. 249.
    ⁵ In telegram No. 70 of August 5, Lord Balfour replied: 'Yes'.
    ⁶ Of July 24 (see No. 245, n. 4).

531

No. 263

Foreign Office Memorandum on the Disarmament of Germany[1]
[C 11164/6/18]

FOREIGN OFFICE, *August 7, 1922*

Now that the aeronautical control commission has been withdrawn and that the naval disarmament of Germany is practically complete, the question of the further disarmament of Germany has been narrowed down to the final execution of the military clauses.

The position as regards these clauses is that the military control commission are endeavouring to clear up what His Majesty's ambassador at Berlin called last spring the 'shreds and patches' of military disarmament. Included in these shreds and patches are six points to the complete execution of which the British War Office attach importance. These shreds and patches also include a mass of unessential details which the French are constantly endeavouring to use as the pegs whereon to hang the tale of 'mauvaise volonté'.

The six points to which the British War Office attach importance are:

(*a*) the completion of the reorganisation of the German police forces in such a way as to deprive them of their centralised military character. The German government have, there is little doubt, been exceedingly slow in carrying out the demands of the military control commission on this point, but the control commission appear also to have made their own work more difficult by mixing up with the important points a number of minor points which were not essential. The control commission have, despite the efforts of the British War Office, continued this policy up to within the last few weeks and as recently as July 11 a note[2] on the old lines was sent to the German government. (N.B. It is important in the present discussions that the British government should not agree to regard this note as their last word on the police question, and nothing should be included in any note or ultimatum to the Germans which would finally commit us to giving support to this note.)

(*b*) the transformation of munition factories. No recent figures are available in the Foreign Office of the number of factories still untransformed. In May 1922, however, 6097 out of 6942 factories known to have manufactured munitions had been converted and passed by the control commission for the manufacture of non-military material.

(*c*) the surrender of outstanding unauthorised war material. The most recent figures available in the Foreign Office, dated March 9, 1922,[3] show that at that date the following quantities of war material remained to be

---

[1] A note on this document states: 'This statement is based on information communicated by the War Office.'

[2] Not printed (see, however, No. 260).

[3] A further report on the progress of the destruction and surrender of German war material was communicated by the War Office to the Foreign Office on August 15.

destroyed out of the following quantities surrendered (the latter being at that date believed to be the bulk of the material of that kind surplus to that allowed the German army under the treaty).

Guns and barrels.	122 out of 33,452.
Trench mortars.	8 out of 11,596.
Machine guns.	108 out of 87,076.
Small arms.	25,309 out of 4,366,090.
Shells loaded.	732 tons out of 11,410 tons.
Small arm munition.	43,125,600 out of 450,584,000.

(N.B. As far as is known the material still due for surrender consists mainly of gas-masks, harness, telephones and equipment of various kinds.)

(d) the surrender of the documents showing the munitions manufactured in factories in Germany during the war and the amount of German war material in existence in November 1918.

(e) the passage of certain additional laws prohibiting the export and import of war material.

(f) the passage of certain laws and administrative measures relating to recruiting.

In addition to the foregoing six questions the French government claim that the German government ought to

(a) pass further measures to prevent the illicit possession of war material by civilians. (N.B. In January 1922, 171 guns, 12,245 machine guns and $1\frac{1}{2}$ million rifles had been recovered from the civilian population and the War Office, although they acknowledged that a certain number of rifles were still scattered about the country, did not consider that the German government would be able to recover many more.)

(b) alienate definitely certain administrative establishments of the former German army; abrogate the laws relating to requisitions in time of mobilisation, certain powers possessed by the local and central authorities in time of mobilisation, certain measures relating to the military organisation of the German railway system; prevent the enlistment of German nationals in foreign armies and formally declare unfortified certain obsolete and dismantled fortification. (N.B. The War Office have pointed out that it is quite useless to insist on academic measures of this kind, as the German government could cancel such measures at exceedingly short notice.)

(c) dismiss certain excess staffs and N.C.Os in the hundred-thousand army. (N.B. the War Office point out that such measure is in practice useless as it is impossible to prevent the German authorities making changes in the distribution of their officers and N.C.Os.)

The policy of the British Government is now to persuade the other allied governments to drop for the moment insistence on all these minor details and to make a really strong effort—preferably through the allied ambassadors in Berlin—to get the German government to carry out the six important points. The British Government also think that abandonment for the moment of insistence on the minor details would be of real use, since, in return for such abandonment, the Germans might be willing to accept the military committe of guarantee.

This body, as is well known, was not foreseen by the treaty and therefore the allies cannot very well make its acceptance by the German government a prior condition of the withdrawal of the existing military control commission. Therefore if the allies go on insisting on the execution of minor details as well as of the six big points before they consent to the withdrawal of the control commission they may well one day find themselves in a position in which they will have under the treaty to withdraw the military control commission because its work will be complete and yet they will then have no means available of securing the consent of the German government to the military committee of guarantee.

No. 264

Lord D'Abernon (Berlin) to the Marquess Curzon of Kedleston
(Received August 12)
No. 626 [C 11493/8315/18]

BERLIN, *August 8, 1922*

My Lord,
With reference to the Earl of Balfour's despatch No. 1136 of the 13th July[1] and to your telegram No. 70 of the 5th instant,[2] I have the honour to transmit herewith copy of the note which has been signed by the five Allied representatives and despatched to the German Government today protesting against the speeches of Dr. Schweyer and Dr. von Kahr, and drawing attention to the tolerant attitude of the Bavarian authorities towards the activities of the Andreas Hofer Bund.

I have, etc.,
D'ABERNON

ENCLOSURE IN No. 264

Joint Note to German Government

BERLIN, *le [8] août 1922*

M. le Chancelier,
Conformément à une décision de la Conférence des Ambassadeurs, les représentants soussignés de la France, de l'Angleterre, du Japon, de l'Italie et de la Belgique ont l'honneur, d'ordre de leurs Gouvernements respectifs, d'attirer de façon pressante l'attention du Gouvernement allemand sur certains passages du discours prononcé par le Dr. Schweyer, Ministre de l'Intérieur dans le Cabinet bavarois, à la séance du Landtag du 1er juin 1922, ainsi que sur les propos tenus par le Dr. von Kahr, Préfet de la Haute-

[1] Not printed (see, however, No. 245, n. 4).　　　　[2] See No. 262, n. 5.

Bavière, le 31 mai 1922 à Munich, au cours d'une réunion des étudiants et fonctionnaires appartenant au parti populaire bavarois.

Le Dr. Schweyer a notamment affirmé qu' 'il faut mener une lutte décidée contre la base du Traité de Versailles et, avant tout aussi, contre le mensonge de la responsabilité, et que ce sera seulement le jour où le monde entier ne suivra plus la politique française et où la France se sentira complètement isolée moralement que l'édifice de la dette des réparations s'écroulera'.

D'autre part, le Dr. von Kahr a déclaré, d'après les comptes rendus donnés par la presse, que 'tous les efforts du peuple allemand doivent tendre au rétablissement de son armée malgré le Traité de Versailles'.

Les Puissances alliées s'attendent à voir le Gouvernement allemand désavouer formellement les paroles de MM. Schweyer et von Kahr qui, outre qu'elles vont directement à l'encontre des engagements signés par l'Allemagne, sont de nature à exercer sur l'opinion publique allemande une répercussion grave et à contrecarrer la politique que le Chancelier d'Empire a maintes fois déclaré vouloir suivre.

A cette occasion, les représentants soussignés croient devoir, au nom de la Conférence des Ambassadeurs, signaler au Gouvernement allemand l'attitude des autorités bavaroises, qui semblent non seulement tolérer, mais parfois même favoriser les manifestations de la presse et les agissements de l'Andreas Hofer Bund en faveur du rattachement du Haut-Adige au Tyrol. Ces manifestations et ces agissements, dont l'esprit est nettement contraire aux stipulations du Traité de Saint-Germain, ne sauraient en effet être admis par les Gouvernements alliés.

Veuillez, etc.,
D'ABERNON
CHARLES LAURENT
HIOKI
FRASSATI
COMTE DELLA FAILLE

No. 265

Memorandum by the Central European Department on the Administration of the Saar Valley

[*C 11752/116/18*]

FOREIGN OFFICE, *August 9, 1922*

It is perhaps desirable now to supplement Mr. Headlam Morley's memorandum of last February[1] on this question by considering constitutional developments in the Saar District since that date.

As a preliminary it is worth emphasising

(1) that the responsibility for the administration of the Saar basin rests with the League of Nations and with nobody else;

[1] See No. 190.

(2) that the constitution of the administration of this district was drawn up by the framers of the peace treaty with a view to compensating France for the wanton injury done during the war to French coal mines.

The constitution in the Saar is unique. The country has been German for the last 70 years. Its administration is now in the hands of the League of Nations; its mines are the property of the French state; its customs system is French; its governors are nationals of five different countries. With such a mixture it is not surprising to find that unprecedented problems arise and that intrigue has an open field. On one side Germany, with a view, of course, to the plebiscite in 1935, spares no efforts to persuade first the League of Nations and secondly such powers as might possibly bring influence to bear upon the League that the French spend their time in violating the provisions of the treaty which affect Saarland. France on the other hand knows that the treaty affords her singular opportunities in the Saar and she means to make the most of them. In these contests it is not surprising if the population sometimes suffer.

With these considerations in mind it is easier to estimate the value of the representations made during the last six months by the Saarlanders. Apart from somewhat vague charges of aggression against the French, these have been confined in the main to bringing before the League of Nations and the international conference at Genoa the objections which they feel to recent constitutional enactments promulgated by the commission which rules them. The developments which have caused special irritation have been (1) the appointment by the commission of advisory and technical committees, (2) the prolongation by the League of the period of office of the members of the commission.

Under section 19 chapter 2 of the annex to article 50 the governing commission will 'have all the powers of government hitherto belonging to the German Empire, Prussia or Bavaria, including the appointment and dismissal of officials and the creation of such administrative and representative bodies as it may deem necessary'. With this section in view the commission decided on March 24, 1922 to establish an advisory council and technical committee. Their intention, as stated by themselves, was to 'guarantee close and constant cooperation with the population, subject to maintenance of the constitution created by the treaty of Versailles and without detriment to the rights which the governing commission exercise in Saar territory in the name of the League of Nations'. Their decision was taken under the powers given, in addition to those in section 19 above, by section 23 of the annex to article 50, which states that 'if it is necessary to introduce modifications (into the laws and regulations of the Saar basin) they shall be decided on and put into effect by the governing commission after consultation with the elected representatives of the inhabitants'; and by section 26 of the annex, which says that 'the fiscal system existing on November 11, 1918, will be maintained as far as possible and no new taxes except customs duties may be imposed without previously consulting the elected representatives of the inhabitants'.

Accordingly they appointed (1) a provincial advisory assembly to approve laws coming under these sections, and (2) a consultative committee whose expert opinion should be invited by the governing commission in all cases in which it should deem it necessary. The provincial assembly was to consist of thirty members chosen by vote from native residents of the Saar. The consultative committee was to consist of at least eight persons nominated by the governing commission from native residents of the Saar.

To the disinterested observer these decrees appear to show a genuine attempt at cooperation within the limits of the treaty between the government and the Saarlanders. But this faint taste of freedom has inspired the latter, perhaps not unnaturally, to clamour for more. The decrees have succeeded in arousing quite exceptional hostility, of which we have only *a priori* grounds to suspect the German inspiration. It is claimed almost unanimously by the different political organisations in Saarland that the intention of the commission was to stifle the leading spirits in Saarland by bribing them with privileges which sounded well but meant nothing. They brought their complaints before the League of Nations and talked a great deal about the way in which they had been deprived of the elements of democracy, e.g. no taxation without consent, collaboration in the framing of the laws and immunity of elected representatives. Such protests are invalid, as the appointment of representative bodies is left, under Section 19, to the discretion of the governing commission, and at present, at all events, it is unnecessary to consider them.

Beyond noting the intentions of the governing commission in drawing up these decrees and the hostility with which the Saarlanders received them, it is perhaps unnecessary to make any further comment on the appointment of the advisory and technical committees.

The next point is the prolongation of the term of office of the members of the governing commission. The relative section of the treaty is included in section 17 of the annex which says: 'The members of the governing commission shall be appointed for one year and may be reappointed. They can be removed by the Council of the League of Nations which will provide for their replacement.'

Mr. Wellington Koo,[2] who was delegated by the Council of the League o. Nations to investigate conditions in the Saar district, reported in March 1922[3] that he felt that 'steps should be taken to assure a certain measure of permanence in the personnel of the governing commission . . . in order more fully to assure its authority and to allow its various members the certainty that they will be able successfully to carry out a programme of collaboration with the inhabitants of the territory and to avoid the discussions to which a possibility of new appointments gives rise each year'.

Mr. Wellington Koo advised, and the Council of the League of Nations on March 27 1922 accepted his recommendation, that the members of the

[2] Chinese delegate to the League of Nations.
[3] This report (C 4963/116/18) was communicated to the Foreign Office by the Cabinet Office on April 3.

governing commission should be assured that unless exceptional circumstances arose their term of office should be prolonged twice more, i.e. up to the beginning of 1925. In their decree adopting this recommendation, the Council, in order to make clear that they were acting in accordance with the section of the treaty referred to above, stated that they still 'reserved the right to make use of all powers conferred on them by the peace treaty, and to revoke or not to renew the appointments of this or that member of the commission'. In May 1922 they reaffirmed this view of their position when approached by the German government, who on April 25 1922 protested that the reappointment in such terms of the members of the commission involved a breach of the treaty.[4]

[4] A copy of the note of protest from the German Government to the League of Nations was transmitted to the Foreign Office by the German Ambassador on May 4 (C6842/116/18).

No. 266

Sir M. Cheetham (Paris) to the Marquess Curzon of Kedleston
(Received August 12, 8.30 a.m.)
No. 415 Telegraphic: by bag [C 11463/555/18]

PARIS, *August 11, 1922*

As foreseen in my telegram No. 403 paragraph 8 of August 2nd,[1] the French government have already taken measures to try their war criminals *in contumaciam*, and instructions have been sent to the 'Conseils de guerre' of the 1st, 6th, and 20th Army Corps districts to prepare the cases. It is intended that the trials should take place in October, presumably at Lille, Châlons sur Marne and Nancy.

[1] No. 261.

No. 267

The Marquess Curzon of Kedleston to Sir M. Cheetham (Paris)
No. 260 Telegraphic: by bag [C 11576/6/18]

FOREIGN OFFICE, *August 14, 1922*

Your despatch No. 1861 (of August 8th. Attack on military control officers at Stettin).[1]

[1] This despatch, in which it was reported that a member of the Military Commission of Control was forcibly obstructed (on July 17) in the performance of his duty by German officials, transmitted a draft of a Note to the German Government suggested by the French section of the Allied Military Committee of Versailles. In this same despatch Sir M. Cheetham expressed the opinion that French views on this incident should be respected: otherwise there could be no question of the French Government's 'agreeing to a comprehensive compromise with regard to the conclusion of the work of the Commission of Control'.

His Majesty's Ambassador at Berlin is being authorized to present to the German government note of which text was enclosed in your despatch as soon as his French, Italian and Belgian colleagues receive similar instructions.[2]

Date inserted in [9]th paragraph of note[3] should be a date one month subsequent to date of despatch of note.

[2] These instructions were communicated in Foreign Office despatch No. 1291 of August 15.

[3] This paragraph ran as follows: 'They [the Allied Governments] consequently request the German Government to take the following measures by the   August:—

1. Apologies shall be made to the president and members of the district committee of Stettin by a responsible local authority; a protocol covering these apologies to be subsequently drawn up by the president of the inter-Allied Military Commission of Control.

2. The authority responsible for the forcible expulsion of the control detachment shall be at once relieved of his duties.

3. The police officials guilty of violence against the control personnel, while in the exercise of its duties, shall be punished, as also the authorities who allowed these measures and prevented the execution of the proposed visit.

4. The members of the Verbindungstelle implicated in this matter shall be relieved of their duties.'

No. 268

The Marquess Curzon of Kedleston to Lord Hardinge (Paris)
No. 263 Telegraphic: by bag [C 11732/555/18]

FOREIGN OFFICE, *August 18, 1922, 1.45 p.m.*

Your telegram No. 403 Section 8. (War Criminals).[1]

You are authorized to accept text of note enclosed in your despatch 1807 of August 2nd.[2]

[1] No. 261. See also No. 266.

[2] Not printed. The text of this note, which was communicated to the German Embassy in Paris on August 23 and a copy of which was transmitted by Lord Hardinge to the Foreign Office in his despatch No. 2104 of September 8 (C 12710/555/18), ran as follows:

'Par une lettre du 14 février 1920, les Puissances alliées et associées ont constaté que le Gouvernement allemand se déclarait hors d'état de remplir l'obligation, résultant pour lui des articles 228 à 230 du Traité de Versailles, de livrer les Allemands dont la liste lui avait été communiquée le 3 février 1920. Elles ont, toutefois, pris acte de la déclaration faite par le Gouvernement allemand qu'il était prêt à ouvrir sans délai devant la Cour suprême de Leipzig une procédure pénale, entourée des garanties les plus complètes, contre toutes ces personnes; mais elles se sont réservé d'exercer leur droit dans sa plénitude tel qu'il est défini par les articles ci-dessus mentionnés du Traité de Paix et de saisir leurs tribunaux, si elles jugeaient au résultat des procédures et des jugements, institués en Allemagne, que l'offre faite par le Gouvernement allemand n'a eu d'autre effet que de tenter de soustraire les inculpés au juste et nécessaire châtiment des crimes qui seraient établis à leur charge.

'2. Les Puissances alliées ont, en conséquence, par une lettre du 7 mai 1920, fait parvenir au Gouvernement allemand une première liste contenant les noms des quarante-cinq accusés, choisis dans la liste générale des inculpés à leur remettre en vertu du traité. Elles ont demandé au Gouvernement allemand de prendre toutes dispositions en vue d'aboutir au jugement de ces individus, dans le plus bref délai possible.

'3. Les Puissances alliées ont, ainsi qu'il avait été prévu dans la lettre du 7 mai 1920, fait régulièrement exécuter les commissions rogatoires, délivrées par l'autorité judiciaire allemande dans les affaires appelées à leur requête. Elles ont facilité le voyage en Allemagne de leurs ressortissants, cités par le Procureur général allemand à comparaître comme témoins devant la Cour de Leipzig, sauf dans l'affaire Michelson, postérieure au rappel de la délégation française.

'4. Les Puissances alliées constatent que la Cour suprême de Leipzig a jusqu'ici statué en tout sur dix cas de coupables de guerre: quatre sur la notification du Gouvernement français, un sur la notification du Gouvernement belge, quatre sur la notification du Gouvernement britannique et un sur l'initiative des autorités allemandes. Le Gouvernement italien a, dans le courant de l'été, soumis à la cour des dossiers dans divers autres cas, mais il n'a été statué sur aucun de ces cas.

'5. En ce qui concerne la conduite de procédure devant la Cour de Leipzig, l'opinion unanime des Gouvernements alliés est que, sauf peut-être dans un petit nombre de cas, la cour n'a donné aucune satisfaction, en ce sens qu'il n'a pas été fait d'efforts suffisants pour parvenir à la vérité.

'6. En ce qui concerne les jugements rendus par la Cour de Leipzig, l'opinion unanime des Gouvernements alliés est que, dans presque tous les cas, la cour n'a donné aucune satisfaction, en ce sens que certains accusés ont été acquittés alors qu'ils auraient dû être condamnés et que, même dans les cas où les accusés ont été reconnus coupables, la peine appliquée n'a pas été suffisante.

'7. Les Puissances alliées ont, en outre le regret de constater que, dans les déclarations publiques qu'il a faites, le 26 janvier 1922, devant le Reichstag, le Chancelier d'Empire a adopté, à l'égard de cette question, la même attitude négative que ses prédécesseurs.

'8. Dans ces conditions, les Puissances alliées, estimant, au vu des procédures et des jugements, que le Gouvernement allemand n'a pas tenu sa promesse de faire bonne et loyale justice, déclarent ne tenir, dorénavant, aucun compte de la mise en jugement par l'Allemagne des inculpés qui n'ont pas encore comparu devant la Cour de Leipzig. Elles reprennent ou réservent, en conséquence, tous les droits actuels et futurs qui leur appartiennent en vertu du traité; elles se réservent, en particulier, la liberté de poursuivre elles-mêmes s'il y a lieu, par contumace, les coupables de guerre.'

No. 269

Lord Hardinge (Paris) to the Marquess Curzon of Kedleston
(Received August 23)
No. 1949 [C 11934/592/18]

PARIS, *August 22, 1922*

My Lord,

I have the honour to acknowledge receipt of Your Lordship's despatch No. 2506[1] (C 11090/592/18) forwarding copy of a letter of August 3 from War Office regarding the resumption of the manufacture of war material in Germany. I would refer Your Lordship to Sir Milne Cheetham's despatch on this subject No. 1898 of the 14th August[2] in which the view was expressed that it

---

[1] Of August 10, not printed.　　　　[2] Not preserved in the Foreign Office archives.

would be preferable to delay an answer to the German Government on this matter until the general question of future military control in Germany had been settled. On receipt of Your Lordship's despatch under reply, the French military authorities were again consulted in the matter and they have repeated their view that no reply should be made to the German Note[3] at present since the subject under the heading of 'transformation of factories' is already covered by the British proposals set forth in Your Lordship's despatch No. 2421 of August 1st[4] for the winding up of military control in Germany. In these circumstances, I propose to await further developments before submitting to the Conference of Ambassadors the proposal made in Your Lordship's Note to the Belgian Ambassador of the 10th August.[5]

I have, etc.,

HARDINGE OF PENSHURST

[3] Of July 7 (C 9950/592/18), not printed.
[4] No. 260.
[5] The proposal was that the Conference of Ambassadors should reply to the German government on the following lines: 'the refusal of the interallied military control commission to permit the resumption of the manufacture of war material for the German army is due to the failure of the German Government to comply with the instructions issued by the control commission respecting the conditions under which the future manufacture of such material shall be organised.'

No. 270

Lord Hardinge (Paris) to the Marquess Curzon of Kedleston
(Received August 28, 8.30 a.m.)

No. 443 Telegraphic: by bag [C 12121/6/18]

PARIS, *August 26, 1922*

Your despatches Nos. 2101[1] and 2421.[2] Military Control in Germany.

Allied Military Committee of Versailles has accepted His Majesty's Government's proposals as set forth in my Memorandum (copy of which is enclosed in my despatch No. 1986[3]) except for last paragraph[4] on which it was not competent to pronounce, and has drafted a notification to the German

[1] No. 238.   [2] No. 260.   [3] Not printed.
[4] This ran: 'Should the Conference of Ambassadors agree to the procedure proposed in paragraph 8 above, it will remain to decide upon the best method of approaching the German Government in the matter. The British Government are inclined to the opinion that in order to distinguish the present intervention of the Allied Governments from the many approaches addressed to the German Government through the Conference of Ambassadors or through the Military Commission of Control, it is desirable that the proposed representations to the German Government should, in this case, be made individually through the Allied Representatives at Berlin acting in co-operation. Such representations might be reinforced by similar and simultaneous representations to the German Ambassadors in Allied capitals.'

Government which after various modifications I have agreed to, and copy[5] of which is likewise enclosed in my despatch No. 1986 of today's date.[3]

French and Italians strongly object to proposal that this notification should

[5] This ran: '(A) Les Gouvernements alliés constatent, depuis plusieurs mois, un ralentissement considérable dans l'exécution des clauses militaires du Traité de Paix. Un nombre élevé de questions sont laissées en suspens par le Gouvernement allemand. Le contrôle exercé par les organes locaux de la Commission militaire interalliée se heurte à une obstruction sans cesse plus grave. Les Gouvernements alliés estiment qu'il convient de remédier sans plus tarder à cette situation, qu'ils ne sauraient admettre, et qui est d'ailleurs contraire aux intérêts de l'Allemagne elle-même.

'(B) Après un nouvel examen des diverses clauses, auxquelles satisfaction n'a pas encore été donnée, les Gouvernements alliés retiennent tout particulièrement les suivantes, auxquelles ils attachent une importance spéciale:

1. La réorganisation de la police (article 162 et Décision de la Conférence de Boulogne de juin 1920).

2. La transformation des usines (article 168).

3. La livraison du reliquat du matériel non autorisé (article 169).

4. La livraison des documents relatifs aux existants en matériel de guerre allemand à l'époque de l'armistice, et aux productions des usines allemandes pendant la guerre et après l'armistice (article 206, § 2, et article 208, § 4).

5. La promulgation de textes légaux (législatifs ou administratifs suivant le cas) nécessaires en vue de:

   (a) Interdire effectivement les importations et exportations de matériel de guerre (article 211 relativement à l'article 170).

   (b) Mettre le recrutement et l'organisation de l'armée en harmonie avec les clauses militaires du Traité de Paix (article 211 relativement aux articles 160, 161, 173, 174, 175 et 178, notamment en ce qui concerne l'abrogation des mesures diverses qui sont encore prévues actuellement et qui se rapportent à la mobilisation).

'(C) Le Gouvernement allemand est formellement invité à faire toute diligence pour régler dans le minimum de temps les questions énumérées au § (B) ci-dessus, et à donner à la C[ommission] M[ilitaire] I[nteralliée] [de] C[ontrôle] toutes facilités pour en assurer l'exécution (articles 206 et 208). Quant à la question No. 1 au sujet de la police, les Gouvernements alliés désirent en premier lieu connaître le plus tôt possible la réponse du Gouvernement allemand à la note de la C[ommission] M[ilitaire] I[nteralliée] [de] C[ontrôle] en date du 11 juillet.

'(D) Après avoir insisté de nouveau sur l'intérêt tout particulier qu'ils attachent à obtenir sans retard satisfaction sur les points visés ci-dessus, les Gouvernements alliés constatent qu'ils ont, d'autre part, le désir d'alléger les charges imposées à l'Allemagne par la C[ommission] M[ilitaire] I[nteralliée] [de] C[ontrôle] en retirant cette commission le plus tôt possible. Mais il est évident qu'un tel allègement ne pourra être réalisé que lorsque la C[ommission] M[ilitaire] I[nteralliée] [de] C[ontrôle] aura rendu compte que l'exécution des clauses rappelées ci-dessus est parvenue à un état d'avancement de nature à en assurer le règlement définitif. Ce moment venu, les Gouvernements alliés seront alors prêts, même si, aux termes du traité, le travail de la C[ommission] M[ilitaire] I[nteralliée] [de] C[ontrôle] n'est pas entièrement achevé, à mettre fin à l'activité de cette commission, sous la réserve que le Gouvernement allemand ait accepté au préalable l'institution du Comité militaire de Garantie envisagé dans la lettre de la Conférence des Ambassadeurs du 14 avril 1922 [see No. 208].

'(E) Il est entendu que ce Comité militaire de Garantie, dont les attributions ont été définies dans la lettre précitée, sera chargé de surveiller l'exécution finale des clauses qui seraient encore en suspens à la place de la C[ommission] M[ilitaire] I[nteralliée] [de] C[ontrôle] ainsi que le maintien en vigueur des engagements que le Gouvernement allemand aura pris au sujet des questions 1 et 5 visées au § (B).'

be made by the Allied Ambassadors in Berlin acting individually and urge that it should be made jointly, as has always been the procedure in the case of inter-allied decisions. If contrary to usual precedent the present communication is made separately by each Ambassador, the German Government may be led to draw all sorts of false deductions from this new procedure.

These objections seem to me so well founded that I trust that I may be authorised to agree that a joint communication should be made by the Allied Ambassadors in the name of the Allied Governments.

No. 271

The Marquess Curzon of Kedleston to Lord Hardinge (Paris)
No. 2694 [C 12080/32/18]

FOREIGN OFFICE, *August 29, 1922*

My Lord,

With reference to my despatch No. 2598 of the 18th instant,[1] relative to the export of war material from Germany,[2] I transmit to your Lordship herewith copy of a letter from the War Office.[3]

2. I request that when the Ambassadors' Conference meets again, your Lordship will make a proposal in the sense desired by the Army Council, and endeavour to obtain a decision by the conference to the effect that the export of military swords, bayonets and daggers from all ex-enemy countries shall be forbidden.

3. As regards the export of 'non-regulation' arms from Germany, the Board of Trade state that they have nothing to add to the observations contained in their letters of the 30th December, 1921, and the 24th May, 1922, copies[1] of which are for convenience of reference enclosed herein. On this point I request that your Lordship will again emphasise to the Ambassadors' Conference the importance of the adoption by the Allied Governments, including the Belgian Government, of a common procedure to deal with the export of these arms from Germany and the ex-enemy countries, and that you will endeavour to secure the adherence of the Allied Governments to the policy of His Majesty's Government as explained in the Board of Trade letter of the 30th December last.

I am, etc.,

CURZON OF KEDLESTON

[1] Not printed.
[2] See No. 255.
[3] Of August 24, not printed.

Lord D'Abernon (Berlin) to the Marquess Curzon of Kedleston
(Received September 4)
No. 699 [C 12464/6/18]

BERLIN, *August 30, 1922*

My Lord,

General Bingham has handed me the general note[1] of the German Government on the subject of disarmament, which they addressed to the Allied Governments through their Embassies abroad on the 19th[*sic*][2] August.

I have discussed this general note with General Bingham, and have come to the conclusion that not much practical result will be arrived at by a detailed discussion on the various points raised in the twelve annexes. Nor will much profit result from an examination of the charges by the Inter-Allied Commission of Control against the German Government regarding wilful obstruction, and the charges by the German Government against the Inter-Allied Commission of Control regarding an alleged excess of their powers.

The real practical plan to bring all this controversy to a close, and to clean up the shreds and remnants of disarmament, is for the German Government to appoint a superior official or officer to take the whole matter in hand. He should be charged with the duty of bringing the work of the Commission of Control to an end as rapidly as possible by carrying through such further measures of disarmament as are possible, and by freeing the Government from the charge of vexatious delay in carrying out with minimum delay the justifiable demands which it is within the power of the German Government to fulfil. He must have the fullest powers.

I have discussed this matter on several occasions with representatives of the German Government,[3] but have not pressed any specific recommendation. If, however, your Lordship gives the necessary instructions, I could urge the German Government to take action on the lines above indicated. It is General Bingham's opinion that this is the most practical solution.

I have, etc.,

D'ABERNON

[1] Not printed.
[2] This note (C 12456/6/18) was communicated to the Foreign Office by Herr Dufour-Feronce on August 30.
[3] See No. 257.

No. 273

Lord Hardinge (Paris) to the Marquess Curzon of Kedleston
(Received September 1, 8.30 a.m.)
No. 451 Telegraphic: by bag [C 12378/6/18]

PARIS, *August 31, 1922*

As a result of direct discussion between the French government and the various allied embassies, the following resolutions have been adopted in the name of the Conference of Ambassadors:—

. . .[1]2. It has been decided that the allied representatives at Berlin should be instructed to present the note drafted by the allied military committee of Versailles on the subject of the attacks on French members of the commission of control at Stettin. I gather from Your Lordship's telegram No. 260 of August 14th[2] that His Majesty's Ambassador at Berlin has already received instructions to join with his allied colleagues in presenting this note. . . .[1]

[1] The section(s) omitted referred to other matters.   [2] No. 267.

No. 274

The Marquess Curzon of Kedleston to Lord Hardinge (Paris)
No. 2876 [C 13250/7361/18]

FOREIGN OFFICE, *September 20, 1922*

My Lord,

With reference to your telegram No. 460 of the 12th September[1] in regard to the delivery by Germany of equipment for the light cruisers surrendered to France and Italy, I transmit to your Excellency herewith copy of further correspondence with the Admiralty.[1]

2. It will be observed that the Admiralty maintain their previous view that it would be in clear contravention of the treaty to demand the surrender of the material in question out of the stocks allocated to the German post-war fleet. Further, they do not admit that the date of the destruction of the material really influences the question, more especially as the majority of the material in question was, as far as can be ascertained, destroyed before the acceptance of the ultimatum of May 1921,[2] i.e., during the period when the treaty alone was binding. In any case, the fact that the only material to which it is thought the French Government attach any real importance, viz., the fire control apparatus, was destroyed even before the note of the 24th July, 1920,[3] was despatched, i.e., before the first notification to the German Government of the material they were to deliver, makes it impossible to press this point further merely on the ground that other less important portions of the material were destroyed at a date subsequent to the 24th

[1] Not printed.   [2] See Vol. XV, No. 85, Appendix 2.
[3] See Vol. X, No. 288.

July, 1920. Further, even if the material was destroyed after the German acceptance of the ultimatum the Admiralty hold that the only question would then be one of compensation, but not of the surrender of actual material from the stocks allocated to the post-war German fleet, with which the ultimatum has no connection.

3. In this connection it is important to place on record the inability of His Majesty's Government to accept the argument of the French Government that the acceptance of the ultimatum requires Germany to surrender the full equipment unconditionally, i.e., whether the actual material referred to has been destroyed or not. By reference to the Allied note of the 29th January, 1921,[4] which in turn referred to the previous Allied notes of July and September 1920,[3] it is clear that the ultimatum can only be held to cover the material mentioned in those notes. His Majesty's Government cannot therefore accept the French view that the term 'unconditionally' allows of the application of the ultimatum to any material now lying in Germany, e.g., the post-war fleet material.

4. His Majesty's Government do not consider that purely political considerations in favour of meeting the French and Italian Governments' views can be held to predominate to the extent of overriding the opinion of the Admiralty as to the just interpretation of the treaty. It will further be observed that the fire control apparatus would not have been on board the ships surrendered under article 23 of the armistice and articles 184 and 185 of the treaty, so that even on equitable, as distinct from legal, grounds the French case is weak.

5. I request therefore that you will inform the French Government that His Majesty's Government must adopt the Admiralty view, and that, at the first meeting of the Ambassadors' Conference in October, you will propose that, if the French and Italian Governments are unwilling to accept it, the whole question should be referred to the International Court of Arbitration at The Hague, in accordance with the suggestion in Admiralty letter of the 8th August.[1]

6. It is much to be hoped that the French and Italian Governments will adopt this solution and not attempt to obtain a settlement at the conference by a majority vote. In the unfortunate event of their following the latter course, you should appeal to the precedents referred to in the enclosed memorandum[5] and maintain the refusal of His Majesty's Government to be bound by a majority decision in a case of this kind.

7. At the same time your Excellency may think it well to emphasise the fact that His Majesty's Government have already made a concession in deference to the French Government's views, in agreeing to temporary retention of the admirals on the Naval Commission of Control (see your telegram No. 376, section 8 (c))[6] although the desirability or otherwise of their retention cannot really be held to be affected in any way by the

---

[4] See Vol. XV, No. 12, minute 1 and n. 2.
[5] Of August 15 (C 11760/11760/62), not printed.
[6] This section is not printed.

difficulties which have arisen in regard to the equipment of the light cruisers. If, therefore, your proposal to submit this question to The Hague Court is accepted, you should intimate that, in the view of His Majesty's Government, there is no longer any reason for the retention of the admirals, and should press for their withdrawal.

I am etc.,
CURZON OF KEDLESTON

No. 275

Lord Hardinge (Paris) to the Marquess Curzon of Kedleston
(Received September 29, 8.30 a.m.)

No. 488 Telegraphic: by bag [C 13593/1188/18]

PARIS, September 28, 1922

Your despatch No. 2289 of the 21st July.[1]

A meeting was held at the Quai d'Orsay this afternoon to endeavour to come to an agreement on the text of the draft reply to the demand made by the United States Government for the reimbursement of the costs of their army of occupation. General Goligher of the British delegation of the Reparation Commission and representatives from the Italian and Belgian Embassies were also present.

At the end of a long discussion it became clear that it would be impossible to reconcile the views held by the French government and the instructions contained in Your Lordship's despatch referred to above. Everyone was however agreed on the desirability of inviting the United States Government to send a qualified representative to discuss the question verbally. It was therefore suggested as a compromise, that the reply to the United States Government should be a short document reiterating the allies' desire to find a practical solution of this question and suggesting, with this object in view, that a United States representative should be sent at once. This note was to be presented by the allied representatives in Washington who should, at the same time, make a verbal communication to the United States Secretary of State explaining the difficulties of the situation and indicating the lines on which the allies considered conversations could be most usefully pursued. This communication was to contain the essential points raised in your Lordship's despatch under reference as well as certain points in the original French draft.[2] (We secured however French consent to the omission of any reference to Article 297 of the Versailles Treaty as well as of any phrase implying the formal recognition of the principle of non-reimbursement to the common reparation fund of the value of payments, in cash as well as in kind, received by any Power in excess of its allotted share of the reparation payments.) A further meeting will be held in the early days of next week to decide on the text of these two communications.

[1] No. 251.   [2] Not printed. See, however, No. 235.

I venture to hope that Your Lordship will agree that this is the best solution to the difficulty,[3] as the official note to the United States Government will contain nothing of a contentious nature which might be seized upon for anti-allied propaganda in the United States, and the verbal communication to be made by the allied representatives in Washington will indicate sufficiently clearly to the United States Government the considerations set forth in paragraphs 3 and 4 of the original British draft.[4]

[3] In his telegram No. 340 of October 2, Lord Curzon replied: 'I concur in the procedure proposed. Your Excellency should, however, only consent to both texts *ad referendum*.'
[4] No. 213, Enclosure.

No. 276

The Marquess Curzon of Kedleston to Lord Hardinge (Paris)
No. 338 Telegraphic: by bag [C 13600/6/18]

Urgent   FOREIGN OFFICE, *October 2, 1922*

Future of disarmament control in Germany.

His Majesty's Chargé d'Affaires Berlin[1] telegraphed on September 21st[2] that draft note[3] forwarded in your despatch No. 1986 of August 26[4] had not yet been presented to German Government owing to Italian ambassador being without instructions.

Please urge upon Italian representative extreme desirability of immediate issue of these instructions and take the opportunity to propose to the conference the issue to the German Government of an invitation at once to appoint a high official to clear up all outstanding matters with the control commissions (see Lord D'Abernon's despatch No. 699 of August 30).[5]

As regards the procedure for settlement of differences between the German Government and the control commissions (see my despatch No. 2881 of September 20),[4] there is, of course, no objection to the German Government being reminded that no protest against the decisions of the commissions can be considered by the conference except after consultation with the commissions themselves. In order therefore to avoid further delay in the progress of disarmament it is essential that the German Government should adhere to the established procedure and communicate copies of any such protests to the commission by whom they will be transmitted to the conference with the necessary comments.

[1] Mr. Addison (see No. 29, n. 1).
[2] No. 181, not printed.
[3] See No. 270, n. 5.
[4] Not printed.
[5] No. 272.

No. 277

Mr. Addison (Berlin) to the Marquess Curzon of Kedleston
(Received October 7)
No. 773 [C 13952/6/18]

BERLIN, *October 3, 1922*

My Lord,

I have the honour to forward to your Lordship herewith the text of the Allied note to the German Government[1] on the subject of future military control in Germany, the draft of which was enclosed in your Lordship's despatch No. 1352 of the 1st September.[2]

The note was handed to the Secretary of State for Foreign Affairs, in the absence of the Chancellor, by the Belgian Minister, as senior Allied representative, on the 30th ultimo.

I have, etc.,

J. ADDISON

[1] Of September 29, not here printed. See, however, No. 270, n. 5.
[2] Not printed.

No. 278

Lord Hardinge (Paris) to the Marquess Curzon of Kedleston
(Received October 7)
No. 2330 [C 13936/1188/18]

PARIS, *October 6, 1922*

My Lord,

With reference to your Lordship's telegram No. 340 of the 2nd instant[1] on the subject of the reimbursement of the costs of the United States army of occupation on the left bank of the Rhine, I have the honour to transmit to your Lordship herewith the text of the draft note[2] which it is proposed to communicate to the United States Government on the subject, together with a draft of the verbal communication to be made by the Allied Ambassadors in Washington when handing the note to Mr. Hughes. These texts were agreed on at a meeting held today at the Quai d'Orsay, and at which were also present representatives from the Belgian and Italian Embassies, and Mr. Goligher of the British delegation on the Reparation Commission. The texts were agreed on *ad referendum* to the respective Governments.

Your Lordship will observe that, taken together, the note to the United States Government and the verbal communication cover in all essentials the desiderata set forth in the first and second British drafts (see your Lordship's despatch No. 2289 of the 21st July last).[3] The third paragraph of the verbal

[1] See No. 275, n. 3.
[2] Not printed. The text of this note is in *F.R.U.S.* 1922, vol. ii, p. 232.
[3] No. 251.

communication, in which reference is made to the necessity of avoiding the repayment to a common fund of cash payments by Governments which may have received reparation in the form of deliveries in kind beyond their due share, was drafted by Sir John Bradbury, the British delegate on the Reparation Commission, and accepted textually by the French. Your Lordship will also observe that all reference to repayments from funds arising out of article 297 of the Treaty of Versailles has been omitted.

In these circumstances I venture to express the hope that your Lordship will be able to see your way to sanctioning the text as enclosed herewith, in order to avoid the delay which is bound to ensue if any considerable modifications thereof are made at this stage.

With regard to the procedure to be adopted at Washington, it is suggested that the Allied Ambassadors should jointly present the note in English, and that the doyen should read the verbal communication also in English. If this procedure meets with your Lordship's approval, the necessary instructions will be sent by their respective Governments to the French, Belgian and Italian Ambassadors in the United States.[4]

I have, etc.,
HARDINGE OF PENSHURST

ENCLOSURE 2 IN NO. 278

Draft Instructions to be addressed to the Ambassadors of Belgium, Great Britain, France and Italy at Washington

October 6, 1922

In handing to Mr. Hughes the annexed note, you should inform his Excellency verbally that the Belgian, British, French and Italian Governments consider it will be useful to indicate how, in their opinion, the problem of the reimbursement of the costs of the American troops in Germany appears when viewed from the purely practical point of view; they hope that the following observations may assist in arriving at the solution of a question where any difference of opinion, if it exists at all, can only relate to the means of execution and not to the end.

2. It appears in the first place to the interested Allied Governments that, to give effect to the claim of the United States Government in the precise form in which it was put forward would involve the complete reopening *ab initio* of all the complicated and difficult negotiations which eventually led to the solutions embodied in the Spa Agreement of July 1920[5] and the Paris Agreement of March 1922.[6] The receipts obtained from Germany up

---

[4] In his telegram No. 387 of October 18, Lord Curzon replied: 'You may accept texts of both communications. Necessary instructions are being sent to His Majesty's Ambassador at Washington by bag.' These instructions (despatch No. 1549 of October 18) ran: 'Immediately your French, Belgian and Italian colleagues receive similar instructions you may associate yourself with them in the communication to the United States Government of the joint note and verbal statement, the texts of which are enclosed in Lord Hardinge's despatch No. 2330 of the 6th October.'

[5] See Vol. VIII, No. 77, n. 3.   [6] See No. 11, n. 2.

to the present date, whether in cash or in kind, have as a matter of fact already been distributed in accordance with these agreements.

3. The agreements in question have up to the present been drafted so as to avoid the necessity of requiring cash payments to the common fund from Governments which have received reparation in the form of deliveries in kind and with a view to reducing to a minimum all readjustments of payments already received. The Governments concerned trust that the United States Government will recognise the inconvenience which would necessarily result from any retrospective interference with the application of these principles and the desirability of continuing to apply them in future, so far as may be practicable.

4. It also seems to them to be necessary to observe that a reasonable adjustment of the problem will clearly have to take into account the *de facto* position and the economic and financial questions involved, regard being had in particular to the fact that payments by Germany are at present being made, or should in the near future be made, to a greater extent in kind than in cash.

5. As a practical suggestion for securing immediate progress towards a solution, the Allied Governments desire to mention, for consideration by the United States Government, the method of settlement adopted in the case of the costs of occupation of the Belgian, British and French armies, which costs have been divided into two parts, comprising (1) those incurred up to the 30th April, 1921, inclusive, and (2) those incurred subsequently. If the United States Government should feel able to accept the application of a similar procedure to the costs of their army, arrangements might be made for making available, for the purpose of providing for the costs incurred since the 30th April, 1921, the value of deliveries in kind made by Germany to the United States, on the same lines as have been adopted in the case of the costs of the Belgian, British and French armies. Should the United States Government agree, this method of partial settlement might be put into force immediately and would form a useful introduction to the discussions which the Allied Governments propose should be held between the representatives of the Governments concerned.

No. 279

Lord Hardinge (Paris) to the Marquess Curzon of Kedleston
(Received October 13, 8.30 a.m.)
No. 514 Telegraphic: by bag [C 14155/7361/18]

PARIS, *October 11, 1922*

The Conference of Ambassadors met today under the chairmanship of Monsieur Jules Cambon, the Belgian Ambassador being also present, and considered the following questions:

. . .[1]4. The Conference had before it the proposal of His Majesty's

[1] The sections omitted referred to other matters.

Government as set forth in Your Lordship's despatch No. 2876,[2] to the effect that the question of the delivery by Germany of the equipment for the light cruisers surrendered to France and Italy, should be referred to the International Court of Arbitration at The Hague. Admiral de Marguerye entered on a discussion of the technical arguments raised in Your Lordship's despatch, which I had embodied in the memorandum submitted to the Conference, but I declined to be drawn into any further discussion on these points, and pressed for an immediate decision on the question of arbitration. It is, however, worth noting that Admiral de Marguerye, in the course of his remarks, stated that once this question was settled, the French Government would agree to the immediate withdrawal of the Naval Commission of Control. Both my French and Italian colleagues were opposed to the proposal of His Majesty's Government on the ground that it would be most unsuitable to refer an interallied dispute arising out of the disarmament of Germany to a tribunal drawn from countries which have been neutral during the war. The Italian Ambassador went on to say, however, that he recognised that the British Government were anxious to reach a decision which would be just and honourable, and, sympathising in general as he did with the principle of arbitration, he proposed that the question should be submitted for examination to an interallied Committee composed of Jurists and Naval Experts. I accepted this proposal on the express understanding that my proposal for arbitration should still remain before the Conference, and should be revived in the event of the proposed allied body failing to solve the question. It will of course be laid down that any decision by this interallied body would have to be unanimous. I understand that Sir C. Hurst is shortly coming to Paris and I trust it may be possible to send out at the same time a naval expert so that the proposed Committee may be constituted without delay.

No attempt was made at today's meeting to take a majority decision on the general question.[3]

. . .[1]18. On the advice of the Allied Military Committee of Versailles the Conference decided to inform the German Government through the Military and Naval Commissions of Control, that it does not propose to discuss the 12 memoranda[4] transmitted to Your Lordship in the German Embassy note of August 30th,[4] on the ground that the questions raised are fully dealt with in the joint Allied note of September 29th[5] regarding the execution of the military clauses of the Treaty and the winding up of the Commissions of

[2] No. 274.

[3] To this section Lord Curzon replied (telegram No. 385 of October 16): 'Proposal is accepted. It is, however, at present impossible to say whether Sir C. Hurst will have time to deal with matter in course of his approaching visit to Paris. Naval experts will be ready to proceed when called upon by you after consultation with Sir C. Hurst.' In telegram No. 532 of October 20, Lord Hardinge transmitted the following message from Sir C. Hurst: 'Please inform Admiralty that joint committee of lawyers and naval experts will meet on Monday October 23rd at 10 a.m. at the Ministry of Foreign Affairs. It is, therefore, desirable that the Admiralty representative should cross on Sunday.'

[4] Not printed.   [5] See No. 277, n. 1.

Control. My Military Representative had urged on the Versailles Committee the desirability of inviting the German Government at the same time to appoint a high official to clear up all outstanding matters, as suggested in Your Lordship's telegram No. 338 of October 2nd.[6] As, however, he had received no support I decided not to delay on this account the reply to the German Government. I propose in a separate despatch[7] to explain the objections which have been raised to Your Lordship's proposal.

The Conference adjourned until the next meeting the question of the procedure for settling difficulties between the German Government and the Commission of Control, which is dealt with in the last paragraph of your telegram No. 338[6]....[1]

[6] No. 276.

[7] This despatch was rendered unnecessary by Lord Curzon's despatch No. 3138 of October 17 (No. 282, below).

No. 280

The Marquess Curzon of Kedleston to Lord Hardinge (Paris)
No. 3118 [C 14135/3589/18]

FOREIGN OFFICE, *October 14, 1922*

My Lord,

With reference to your despatch No. 1986 of the 28th August,[1] I transmit to your Excellency herewith copies of three letters[2] from the War Office relating to the organisation of the German police.

2. You will recollect—

(a) That the despatch of the Military Control Commission's note of the 11th July, 1922,[3] made it impossible to include in the general scheme for the liquidation of outstanding disarmament matters, communicated to the German Government on the 29th September, 1922,[4] the plan, outlined in enclosure 5 to Lord Balfour's despatch No. 2101 of the 7th July, 1922,[5] for the settlement on similar lines of the question of the police;

(b) That no reference to this question was therefore made in the Allied note of the 29th September, 1922, beyond a request to the German Government to return an early reply to the Control Commission's note of the 11th July, 1922; and

(c) That paragraph 3 of Lord Balfour's despatch No. 2421 of the 1st August,[6] 1922, indicated that, were the German Government to refuse

[1] Not printed (see No. 270).   [2] Not printed.

[3] Not printed. See, however, No. 253.

[4] This communication, dated September 29, was handed to the German Government on September 30 (see No. 277). For the text, see No. 270, n. 5.

[5] No. 238.

[6] No. 260.

the Control Commission's demands, His Majesty's Government might find it difficult to support them *in toto*.

3. The German Government having refused these demands on the 11th September, 1922,[7] the situation envisaged in Lord Balfour's despatch No. 2421 has now arisen, and it becomes necessary to endeavour to secure a settlement of the question of the police on the lines so far successfully followed on the general question of disarmament.

4. I therefore request that you will take an early opportunity of submitting to the Ambassadors' Conference the memorandum (which forms enclosure 3[8] to the War Office letter of the 11th October) as the basis for a settlement of this question. Your Excellency will no doubt point out to the conference that reasons precisely similar to those already outlined to the conference in the general matter of disarmament in your memorandum of the 8th August, 1922,[2] hold good in this matter also.

5. A copy of despatch No. 773 from His Majesty's Chargé d'Affaires at Berlin[9] enclosing the text of the Allied note to the German Government of the 29th September, 1922, is enclosed for convenience of reference.

I am, etc.,

CURZON OF KEDLESTON

ENCLOSURE 9 IN NO. 280

British Memorandum on the Reorganisation of the German Police in accordance with the Treaty of Versailles and the Boulogne Note of June 1920[10]

In their note of the 11th September, 1922, to General Nollet,[7] the German Government have virtually maintained their position on the question of police reorganisation, and this question appears, therefore, to have reached a deadlock.

As with the general question of the military clauses of the treaty, so with the specific question of police organisation, the British Government consider it essential that a decision should be arrived at as to which are the important outstanding points relating to police, and then to press for their complete execution; on other points certain concessions may be made, as suggested below. It is considered that only by this procedure will it be possible to make real progress.

2. The principal points on which the Inter-Allied Military Commission of Control and the German Government have failed to reach a settlement fall under two heads:—

(*a*) Localities for which State police is authorised.

(*b*) Composition and organisation of the police.

These will be considered separately.

3. *Localities for which State Police is Authorised.*—In their note of the 11th

---

[7] In a note (not printed) to General Nollet.
[8] Enclosure 9.   [9] No. 277.
[10] See No. 260, n. 8.

554

July, 1922,[3] the Inter-Allied Military Commission of Control authorised State police for an additional twenty-two towns only, as against 171 as asked for by the German Government.

In the opinion of His Majesty's Government, the increase of 60,000 police sanctioned by the Boulogne note[10] was intended to assist in dealing with disorders on a large scale. It follows that favourable consideration should be given to requests for an increase of State police in certain towns, and for an introduction of State police in others in which only municipal police existed in 1913, each case being treated on its merits. The detailed settlement of this question can only be effected by the Inter-Allied Military Commission of Control after investigation of the local conditions; but on the basis of the above principle, His Majesty's Government consider that the concession should be extended to such important Ruhr industrial centres as Düsseldorf, Duisburg, Hörde, Hag[e]n and Hamm in the neutral zone, while in addition such centres of unrest as Hof in Bavaria, the Saxon industrial towns, and some of the towns in Prussian Saxony, the scene of the Communist rising in 1921, might also be allowed State police.

Provided the objectionable points in the present composition and organisation of the police are removed, it is difficult to see what objections there can be to the above proposal. The question of this composition and organisation is dealt with in the following paragraphs:—

4. *Composition and Organisation of Police.*—Under this head, the following are the more important of the demands made in the Inter-Allied Military Commission of Control note of the 11th July[3]:—

(*a*) The suppression of all police units not existing in 1913.
(*b*) Police administration to be exactly as in 1913.
(*c*) No staffs, other than those existing in 1913, to be allowed.
(*d*) Local police organisation of 1913 to be maintained.
(*e*) Local police reserves to be drawn from the area police as in 1913.

In the opinion of His Majesty's Government, the conditions in Europe now, as compared with those prevailing in 1913, justly permit a spirit of compromise in the consideration of this question, and the following paragraph indicates the views of His Majesty's Government as to how far the desires of the German Government on the above points can safely be met.

5. *Composition and Organisation of Police—Suggestions made on Behalf of His Majesty's Government.*—(*a*) The Germans to be allowed to retain in the larger towns dismounted Hundertschaften and mounted detachments; also police armoured-car detachments.

In view of the reduction of the German army, a certain proportion of the police to be located in barracks to form a reserve in the hands of the higher police authorities; the accommodation to be administered rather as billets than as military barracks.

The above would bring the German police in the larger towns on to a footing somewhat similar to that on which the London police is established;

the London police have never been considered as 'military' in any way, nor are they capable of being so at short notice.

(*b*) *Administration.*—A slight increase in the police administration service is presumably necessitated by the changes in the internal conditions since 1913, and the increase from 92,000 to 150,000 police.

(*c*) *Police Staffs.*—The disbandment of the following military staffs should be insisted upon:—

Schupo staffs attached to Ministers of the Interior and to Oberpräsidenten of provinces.

Group staffs.

Abteilung staffs.

The following concessions to be permitted:—

(i) Small administrative police staffs to be attached to Ministries of the Interior and to Oberpräsidenten of provinces.

(ii) A small executive police staff to be attached to the Regierungspräsident of a Bezirk or the Polizeipräsident of a town.

(*Note.*—This proposal appears to conform to the 1913 organisation.)

(*d*) *Local Organisation.*—The Germans to be allowed an increase of executive staff in Berlin, other very large towns, the Ruhr and the whole of the neutral zone.

(*e*) *Local Reserves.*—See proposal under (*a*) above.

6. *Police: Terms of Service.*—Pressure should be brought to bear on the German Government to regularise the engagements of the police, and to enforce the twelve years' term of service laid down for the police by the Inter-Allied Military Commission of Control.

With a shorter term than twelve years, it is possible to build up a reserve of young men. At present it is reported that many of the German police have no definite engagements or are engaged for short periods of service only. There is no period of service laid down in the Treaty of Versailles or in the Boulogne note, but after the London ultimatum, the 5th May, 1921, the German Government agreed that the period of service should be twelve years.

This arrangement should be adhered to, and if the German Government is acting in good faith in the matter of its police organisation, it should make no difficulty in the matter.

It may be noted that the German Foreign Minister, in a note to the Inter-Allied Military Commission of Control, dated the 15th March, 1922,[11] stated that all officials entering the German police have immediately to engage to serve for a period of twelve years.

7. *Abolition of Military Cadres.*—The abolition of all military Schupo staffs, and the disbandment of technical Schupo units, such as Schupo M.T. units, signal units, aviation units and of the transport of Schupo-Abteilungen, which corresponds to battalion transport, should be insisted on.

The Prussian Government has already issued instructions for the

---

[11] Not printed. See, however, No. 202.

disbandment of technical units, but the other German States have taken no action in the matter.

Training in the use of weapons of war should be strictly confined to individual training, to the exclusion of all forms of collective military training.

8. *Conclusion.*—It is suggested that the above proposals form a practical solution of the police question; they are not inconsistent with the stipulations of the treaty or of the Boulogne note,[10] while the demands of the Inter-Allied Military Commission of Control are met in all essential respects.

Further, it is desired to emphasise that the above proposals are presented in opposition to the demands of the Inter-Allied Military Commission of Control (see paragraph 4) by reason of the fact that the political and moral tone of the Germans, over whom the police have to exercise supervision, is—as in every other country—very different now from what it was in 1913.

No. 281

Lord D'Abernon (Berlin) to the Marquess Curzon of Kedleston
(Received October 19)
No. 802 [C 14413/6/18]

BERLIN, *October 15, 1922*

My Lord,

I have the honour to inform your Lordship, with reference to paragraph 2 of Lord Hardinge's telegram No. 501 of the 4th October,[1] that I signed yesterday, in conjunction with my French, Italian, Belgian and Japanese colleagues, a collective note to the German Government in regard to the incident at Stettin.

A copy of the note, which was handed to the German Government last night, is enclosed herein.

I have, etc.,
D'ABERNON

ENCLOSURE IN No. 281

Joint Note to German Government

BERLIN, *le 14 octobre, 1922*

Les Ambassadeurs de France, d'Angleterre et d'Italie, le Ministre de Belgique et le Chargé d'Affaires du Japon ont l'honneur de notifier au Gouvernement allemand que leurs Gouvernements respectifs, après avoir pris connaissance de l'avis exprimé par la Commission militaire interalliée de Contrôle sur les explications contenues dans la note allemande du 8 septembre[2] relative à l'incident de Stettin, ont décidé de maintenir

---

[1] Not printed. See, however, No. 273.   [2] Not printed.

intégralement les termes et les conclusions de la note collective adressée le 9 septembre[2] au Gouvernement allemand par leurs représentants à Berlin.

En s'acquittant de cette communication auprès de son Excellence le Chancelier, Ministre des Affaires étrangères, les soussignés lui renouvellent, etc.

CHARLES LAURENT
D'ABERNON
FRASSATI
MOLTKE
MATSUBARA

No. 282

The Marquess Curzon of Kedleston to Lord Hardinge (Paris)
No. 3138 [C 14344/6/18]

FOREIGN OFFICE, *October 17, 1922*

My Lord,

With reference to section 18 of your Excellency's telegram No. 514 of the 11th October,[1] I transmit to you herewith a copy of a letter from the War Office[2] on the subject of the proposed appointment by the German Government of an official to clear up outstanding questions of control.

2. In the circumstances outlined in General Sackville-West's letter,[3] I concur in the view expressed by the Army Council that it would be inadvisable to press any further for the adoption of this proposal.

I am, etc.,
CURZON OF KEDLESTON

[1] No. 279.

[2] Of October 13. This ran: 'I am to state that, as a result of General Sackville-West's letter and of a further telephone message from Colonel F. H. Kisch, employed with the Allied Military Committee of Versailles, the Army Council are of the opinion that it would be inadvisable to press for the acceptance of Lord D'Abernon's proposal, in view of the unanimous opposition of the Allied representatives.

'I am to add that Colonel Kisch stated today that political as well as military circles in Paris are resolutely opposed to this proposal.

'Further, Colonel Kisch is of opinion that an accommodating attitude by His Majesty's Government in this question would materially benefit the negotiations with the French authorities on the question of the War Office memorandum [No. 280, Enclosure 9] on the reorganisation of the German police, and might lead to the acceptance by the French of the latter proposal.'

[3] Of October 11, not printed.

No. 283

Lord Hardinge (Paris) to the Marquess Curzon of Kedleston
(Received October 22, 8.30 a.m.)
No. 535 Telegraphic: by bag [C 14510/6/18]

PARIS, *October 20, 1922*

The Conference of Ambassadors met this morning under the chairmanship of M. Jules Cambon, the Belgian ambassador being also present, and considered the following questions:—

1. General Nollet, president of the German [*sic*] military commission of control, made a detailed statement to the conference with regard to the growing obstruction placed by the German government in the way of the commission of control. This obstruction had been growing ever since the murder of Rathenau,[1] and had culminated in incidents, such as those at Stettin reported in my telegram No. 501, paragraph 2,[2] where members of the commission have been opposed by physical force in the performance of their duty. General Nollet argued that the position of the commission was so undignified that it could not continue indefinitely to work under existing conditions. In fact, a climax would be reached if the German government failed within the time limit now laid down to give satisfaction with regard to the Stettin incident. On the other hand, the commission had been required by the conference of ambassadors to settle certain specified questions, which could not be left to the proposed committee of guarantees, but it could only carry out this work if the German government [were] made to realise that the present obstruction must cease and the authority of the commission [be] respected. The fact was that the questions remaining to be settled all involved the destruction of institutions dear to the German nation, with the result that the opposition to the commission was bound to grow stronger as time went on.

I was somewhat surprised at the appearance of General Nollet before the conference, as I had been given no warning that he was to attend, and from enquiries I have made I have ascertained that his presence was asked for by the Ministry for Foreign Affairs, without Marshal Foch's staff being consulted. General Nollet, who spoke with considerable warmth, but not, I thought, with much conviction, failed in my opinion to prove that a crisis was impending in the affairs of the commission of control, and after a few questions by myself and the Italian and Belgian ambassadors, the discussion came to an inconclusive end.

Taking advantage of General Nollet's presence, the conference again considered the three protests by the German government enclosed in my despatch No. 2458 of today's date[3] regarding various questions connected with military control, and confirmed the decision taken at the last meeting of the conference, as reported in my telegram No. 514 of October 11th, section 18,[4] according to which the German government are to be informed

---

[1] See No. 234.   [2] Not printed. See, however, No. 273.
[3] Not printed.   [4] No. 279.

through General Nollet that all these questions are dealt with in the allied note of the 29th September.[5] As the German protests touch upon naval questions, Admiral Charlton is at the same time to inform the German government that, as these questions have already been settled by the conference, the latter does not propose to enter into a discussion with regard to them. At the same time it was decided, on the advice of the allied military committee of Versailles, to drop the proposal (see Your Lordship's despatch No. 3138 of October 17th)[6] that a special German official should be appointed to deal with the military commission of control. It was also definitely decided that the allied governments should abandon their demand for the surrender of the additional 119 pieces of fortress artillery referred to in Your Lordship's despatch No. 2898 of September 21st.[3] The German government are being informed in this sense.[7]

2. I made clear to the Conference that the Mixed Naval and Legal Committee will only be able to take unanimous decisions on the question of the equipment of the light cruisers to be ceded to France and Italy (see my telegram No. 514, section 4).[4] This was agreed to.

...[8]14. The Conference decided to supplement its decision reported in Sir Milne Cheetham's telegram No. 394 of July 26th, section 8,[9] regarding the prohibition to export, import or manufacture pistols and revolvers of certain dimensions in ex-enemy countries, by a further decision making it clear that this prohibition applies equally to ammunition suitable for the prohibited weapons. This is in accordance with the wishes expressed in Your Lordship's despatch No. 3069 of October 10th....[8]

[5] See No. 277, n. 1.
[6] No. 282.
[7] A copy of the note sent by the Conference of Ambassadors to the German Embassy in Paris on October 27 was transmitted to the Foreign Office in Paris despatch No. 2728 of November 22 (C 15983/592/18), not printed.
[8] The sections omitted referred to other matters.
[9] No. 255.

No. 284

The Marquess Curzon of Kedleston to Lord D'Abernon (Berlin)
No. 1532 [C 14435/336/18]

FOREIGN OFFICE, *October 23, 1922*

My Lord,
I transmit to your Excellency herewith a copy of a despatch[1] from His Majesty's representative on the Rhineland High Commission, regarding Nationalist meetings and demonstrations which have been held in places situated in close proximity to the boundaries of the occupied territories.

[1] No. 306 of October 18 (only the enclosure is here printed).

2. Immediately your French and Belgian colleagues receive similar instructions, you should join with them in presenting to the German Government a joint note on the lines suggested by the High Commission in the enclosure to Lord Kilmarnock's despatch.[1]

I am, etc.,
CURZON OF KEDLESTON

ENCLOSURE 2 IN No. 284

Draft Note from Rhineland High Commission to Allied Governments

COBLENZ, *le   octobre, 1922*

A diverses reprises les autorités alliées d'occupation se sont plaintes auprès du Commissaire d'Empire de ce que le Gouvernement allemand laisse organiser dans les localités de la zone neutre situées à proximité immédiate de la frontière des territoires occupés, des manifestations au cours desquelles les Gouvernements alliés ou des forces d'occupation sont violemment et grossièrement attaqués. Des faits de cette nature se sont produits à de nombreuses reprises, notamment à Caub (sur le Rhin à la limite de l'étroit couloir qui sépare la tête de pont de Coblenz et celle de Mayence), à Königswinter et à Elberfeld (à la limite immédiate de la tête de pont de Cologne).

De tels agissements ne manquent pas d'avoir leur répercussion dans les territoires occupés, où ils créent un état d'esprit contraire à l'ordre public, et ne peuvent que faire naître des incidents entre la population et les troupes alliées. En effet, à la demande du Gouvernement allemand la liberté de circulation a été autorisée sans restriction jusqu'à présent, entre les territoires occupés et le reste de l'Allemagne.

En outre, le choix de ces localités même s'il ne constitue pas un défi systématique à l'égard des autorités d'occupation, a pour effet d'engager les associations et groupements nationalistes interdits dans les territoires occupés à se réunir à proximité de leurs limites.

La Haute-Commission signale en particulier des discours violents prononcés par le Pasteur Korell, Député au Reichstag, qui, malgré l'avertissement qui lui a été adressé par les autorités alliées, a, le 9 octobre, au Rheinische Volkstag, à Elberfeld, attaqué violemment les Gouvernements alliés, particulièrement le Gouvernement français, et déclaré que 'l'Allemagne devrait exiger le départ des troupes d'occupation,' alors que l'occupation figure dans les clauses arrêtées dans le Traité de Paix. De tels propos ne peuvent qu'exciter l'opinion publique contre les Alliés.

Il y aurait peut-être lieu pour les Gouvernements alliés de faire connaître au Gouvernement allemand que, si ces faits venaient à se renouveler, les autorités d'occupation pourraient être obligées d'envisager des mesures spéciales de sécurité.

Lord Hardinge (Paris) to the Marquess Curzon of Kedleston
(Received October 28)

No. 548 Telegraphic: by bag [*C 14769/7361/18*]

PARIS, *October 26, 1922*

The Conference of Ambassadors met this morning under the presidency of Monsieur Jules Cambon, the Belgian Ambassador being also present, and considered the following questions:—

1. The Joint Legal and Naval Committee which has been meeting in accordance with the decision reported in my telegram No. 514 of October 11th, section 4,[1] to consider the question of the equipment for the light cruisers assigned to France and Italy, has failed to discover any solution of the present deadlock. In these circumstances my original proposal that the dispute, as between the Allies on the one hand and Germany on the other, should be referred to the Hague Tribunal again came before the Conference. Realising, however, that the French Government were determined not to accept such a course, I proposed as an alternative that Mr. Bassett Moore, the American judge at the Hague Court, should be invited to decide between the British and the Franco-Italian theses. The Italian Ambassador agreed at once to this proposal, but stipulated that the arbitration should have an entirely informal and private character. Monsieur Cambon likewise acquiesced and it was decided that the United States Ambassador in Paris should be asked to approach Mr. Bassett Moore semi-officially with a view to inviting him to take up the case. I had at first suggested that the invitation should be conveyed to him through the United States Government, but my colleagues preferred that it should pass through the United States Ambassador here, as indicating a more informal and private procedure.

I took this opportunity of suggesting that as soon as the equipment question was submitted to Mr. Bassett Moore, the Allied Admirals who have been kept on on account of this question (see my telegram No. 376, of July 17th, section 8c)[2] should be withdrawn from the Commission of Control and that the latter should be reduced to the smallest possible dimensions. This was agreed to.

2. The Legal Advisers submitted a report, copy of which was enclosed in my despatch No. 2435 of October 20th,[3] explaining that they had been unable to reconcile the divergent opinions which have been expressed in regard to the right of the Allied Governments to limit the calibre of guns for use in the post-war German fleet. I suggested that as Mr. Bassett Moore was to be invited to arbitrate on the equipment question he might equally be requested to arbitrate on this matter. Marshal Foch demurred to this proposal on the ground that an arbitral decision thus given might reopen the whole question of the manufacture of big guns for the German army. Monsieur Cambon thereupon asked that the question might be adjourned for further

[1] No. 279.   [2] This section is not printed.   [3] Not printed.

consideration at the next meeting on November 8th, by which time moreover it is possible that the Conference will know whether Mr. Bassett Moore is prepared to undertake to arbitrate on the equipment question.

. . .⁴6. The Legal Advisers having again examined the claim of the Belgian Government to the eight guns which formed the subject of my telegram No. 501 of October 4th, section 3,³ have now suggested as a compromise, that the cession to Germany of the 119 coastal guns decided by the Conference at the last meeting as reported in my telegram No. 535 of October 20th, section 1,⁵ should be made conditional on the German Government agreeing as a matter of equity to return to Belgium the four guns still in existence or to refund the money which the Belgian Government paid for these guns. I at once made it clear that I could only agree to this scheme being put forward to the German Government as a proposal and that I could not agree to its being made a condition to be fulfilled in order that the 119 coastal guns should be left to Germany. Marshal Foch at the same time objected strongly from a military point of view to the four guns being handed over to Belgium. As they are at present included in the guns which have been allowed to the German Government for their post-war army, if they are compelled to give them up they will be entitled to manufacture new and therefore better guns to replace them. He insisted therefore that the German Government should in any case be asked to make a money payment in lieu of the guns. The Belgian Ambassador agreed to this and it was finally decided to invite the German Government to reimburse the Belgian Government. But as this request can only be made on the grounds of equity and not in virtue of the Treaty of Versailles, I confess I do not foresee a favourable reply.

The further Belgian claim for compensation for the four other guns which were destroyed in the course of the War was rejected by the Conference. . . .⁴

⁴ The sections omitted referred to other matters.
⁵ No. 283.

No. 286

Memorandum by Sir Cecil Hurst
[C 14752/6/18]

FOREIGN OFFICE, *October 26, 1922*

My recent visit¹ to Paris for a series of meetings of the Committee of Legal Advisers of the Conference of Ambassadors has convinced me that our Peace Treaty machinery is beginning to work badly and that if we are to avoid increasing inter-Allied friction and also to avoid constant difficulties with the Germans, we must strengthen our machinery in London for supervising the action taken by the British members of the Military and Naval

¹ See No. 279, n. 3.

Commissions of Control and by the British member of the Military Committee at Versailles, so as to ensure that any decisions in which the British members of these bodies have concurred and which have in consequence been approved by the Conference of Ambassadors are decisions which H[is] M[ajesty's] G[overnment] will be prepared to back up.

To an increasing extent, decisions are being taken which fail to fulfil this condition. My attention was drawn to various notifications made by the Naval Commission of Control to the Germans of which the Admiralty disapprove. I have certainly seen myself various decisions taken by the Military Commission of Control which do not appear to me to be in accordance with the terms of the Treaty. The practice of the Conference of Ambassadors is that if a recommendation is made to them unanimously by the inter-Allied Committee at Versailles, it is approved as a matter of course as being a decision in which the representatives of all the Governments concerned have already signified their concurrence.

The cases in which decisions have been taken of which the Admiralty disapprove seem to be concerned with Article 196 of the Treaty, dealing with coast fortifications. This is a naval clause because the German practice was to man these coast fortifications with naval ratings, but the soldiers claim that in reality the questions are not naval questions, and it seems that the military and naval commissions agreed that the operative decisions should be taken by the Military Commission and the Naval Commission would carry them out. Consequently Admiral Charlton, as President of the latter, makes demands on Germany which are disapproved by the Admiralty. Apart from these, however, I am disposed to think that decisions are taken by one or other of these bodies with the concurrence of the Versailles Committee, and consequently approved by the Conference of Ambassadors, without adequate consideration of the legal aspects of the case. The Versailles Committee are probably quite unconscious of this, because they frequently ask that a question may be referred to the Committee of Legal Advisers in order that the legal aspects may be considered if it is a case about which they have doubts.

Another source of future difficulty is the increasing number of cases in which recommendations of the soldiers or of the sailors, approved by the Conference of Ambassadors, are being ignored by the Germans, who refuse to carry them out on the ground that they are not in accordance with the Treaty. These matters are frequently small matters which cannot be made the subject of heroic measures by the Allied Governments in threats to occupy territory or in decisions to despatch ultimatums to Berlin, but if one of the Departments of H[is] M[ajesty's] G[overnment] feels doubts about the validity of a decision of the Conference of Ambassadors which has been communicated to the Germans and is being ignored by them, it is quite certain that no steady pressure will be maintained on Germany to carry it out, and the Germans will find that they can ignore the decisions with impunity.

There appears to be very little co-operation between the Naval and Military Commissions of Control and the Germans are beginning to regard the decisions of the Military Commission as French decisions so that they are less and less disposed to accept them without criticism. On the other hand, the arrangement with regard to Article 196 is beginning to make increasing trouble with regard to the Naval Commission's decisions.

The difficulties which I have indicated above might, I think, be very sensibly diminished if there were instituted at the Foreign Office a small inter-departmental committee, consisting of representatives of the Admiralty, the War Office and this Department, at which the instructions to the Naval and Military members of these commissions would be co-ordinated, and considered also from the point of view of ensuring that they were in accordance with the Treaty. The institution of this committee would ensure that no decision was taken by the Commissions of Control or at Versailles which H[is] M[ajesty's] G[overnment] would not be able to support loyally when notified to the Germans. In the end I feel sure this would diminish the growing friction with the French as though it might provoke more discussion to begin with, when the decision was once taken, the French would know that they could count on the support of H[is] M[ajesty's] G[overnment] in backing it up. It would not in the least prejudice the possibility of the Committee at Versailles referring questions to the lawyers for advice in any case as to which they felt doubtful as to the correct interpretation of the Treaty.

The suggestion made above is the result of various conversations which I had in Paris, including one with the Ambassador who is quite in favour of the scheme.[2]

CECIL J. B. HURST

[2] Commenting on Sir C. Hurst's proposal, Mr. Cadogan stated (October 30): '. . . it would not get over the difficulty which arises in cases where the members of the Commissions, or the British rep[resentati]ve in the Versailles C[ommit]tee, concur in decisions not approved here, without reference home.' In fact, no interdepartmental committee was established. For the action taken, see No. 294, below.

No. 287

Lord D'Abernon (Berlin) to the Marquess Curzon of Kedleston
(Received October 30, 11.20 p.m.)
No. 193 Telegraphic [C 14925/6/18]

BERLIN, October 30, 1922, 9.30 p.m.

My despatch No. 773.[1]

German government have answered[2] allied note[3] expressing their satisfaction at proposal made by allied Powers for replacement of inter-allied military commission of control, by a military committee of guarantee as soon

[1] No. 277.

[2] A translation of the German answer dated October 27 was transmitted to the Foreign Office in Berlin despatch No. 833 of October 30, not printed.

[3] See No. 277, n. 1.

as execution of certain measures shall be so far advanced that their final settlement is assured.

In declaring themselves ready to enter at once into negotiations with this object, German government presume that these negotiations will prepare the way for limiting eventual control to extent foreshadowed in article No. 213 of treaty of Versailles.

No. 288

The Marquess Curzon of Kedleston to Lord Hardinge (Paris)
No. 3261 [C 14495/336/18]

FOREIGN OFFICE, *October 30, 1922*

My Lord,

I transmit to your Excellency herewith a copy of a note[1] from the German Ambassador at this court requesting that His Majesty's representative on the Rhineland High Commission may be instructed to move the commission to cancel the decree suspending the sentences passed in the German courts against Herr Smeets, a leader of a separatist movement in the Rhineland.

2. In view of the circumstances in which the decision of the commission was taken on this matter, I request that you will enquire of the French Government what reply should, in their opinion, be returned to M. Sthamer's communication.

3. A copy of the relevant portion of the minutes of the commission[1] and a Foreign Office memorandum[2] on the subject are enclosed for your information.

4. A similar despatch has been addressed to His Majesty's Ambassador at Brussels.

I am, etc.,
CURZON OF KEDLESTON

ENCLOSURE 7 IN No. 288

Note by Mr. Wigram respecting the History of the Smeets case

FOREIGN OFFICE, *October 24, 1922*

In April 1921, Smeets, the German leader of one of the separatist movements in the Rhineland, and, therefore, a protegé of the French officials, published three libels, (1) against the police president of Cologne, (2) against a German postal official and (3) against the President of the Reich.

2. Proceedings were taken against Smeets under German law. These proceedings were in some manner delayed for some months, but on the 5th December, 1921, Smeets was arrested by the German police on the ground of refusal to obey summons to attend at court.

---

[1] Not printed.   [2] Enclosure 7.

3. On the 8th December, 1921, the Rhineland Commission, acting under Ordinance No. 70 ordered Smeets's release, pending a final decision in his case, on the ground that Smeets claimed the benefit of certain provisions of this ordinance which provided that no judgment or punitive measures should be taken against any person by the German authorities for political acts committed during the armistice period.

4. The German Government protested against this action of the High Commission on the 15th December, 1921, claiming that the case was not covered by Ordinance No. 70.

5. Sentences were pronounced against Smeets on the 15th February, 1922, 3rd March, 1922, 12th June, 1922 and 19th June, 1922, and in August 1922 the German Commissioner in the Rhineland asked that the sentences, amounting to $8\frac{1}{2}$ months' imprisonment on all counts, might be put into force. On the 4th September, 1922, Lord Kilmarnock asked[3] what attitude he was to adopt when the matter came before the commission. On the 11th September, 1922, Lord Kilmarnock was instructed to oppose interference by the commission in the matter.[4]

6. On the 30th September the French High Commissioner, with the support of his Belgian colleague, proposed the suspension of the execution of the sentences passed against Smeets. The proposal was put to the vote and carried against the minority vote of the British representative.[5]

7. On the 18th October Lord Kilmarnock reported[6] the extreme dissatisfaction with which the commission's decision had been received in Germany.

8. On the 20th October, 1922, the German Ambassador in London protested against the decision, claiming that it was an insult to the German courts who had condemned Smeets, that the sentences passed on Smeets were only the sentences customary in German law and that the action of the commission was covered neither by Ordinance No. 70 (see paragraph 3 above) nor by Ordinance No. 90, since the offences with which Smeets was charged were in no way connected with matters concerning the Allied Rhineland authorities. The German ambassador therefore asked that instructions should be issued to the British representative on the Rhineland Commission to move the immediate cancellation of the decree suspending Smeets's sentences.

[3] In telegram No. 22, not printed.
[4] In Foreign Office telegram No. 16, not printed.
[5] This was reported by Colonel Ryan in despatch No. 289 of September 30 (C 13707/336/18), not printed.
[6] In his despatch No. 307 (C 14439/336/18), not printed.

No. 289

Lord D'Abernon (Berlin) to the Marquess Curzon of Kedleston
(Received November 6)
No. 839 [C 15163/6/18]

BERLIN, *October 31, 1922*

My Lord,

With reference to the German reply, transmitted under my No. 833 of yesterday,[1] I have the honour to state that, when this reply was first received, some members of the Commission of control stated that the German Government had refused the proposal of the Entente Powers almost insolently.

I had an opportunity in the course of yesterday of discussing the matter with General Bingham, and pointed out to him that the words used by the German Government were not open to the above interpretation; on the contrary, I regarded them as being a satisfactory acceptance of the principle of the Allied proposal, covered by the reserves which the Chancellor was obviously compelled to make in order to defend himself from the charge of having accepted permanent military surveillance in excess of that laid down in the Treaty of Versailles. Such a charge no German Government could possibly withstand, nor could they be expected to expose themselves to any such accusation.

The interpretation I give to the German answer is that the Government accept in principle the proposed commission under the conditions laid down, with the proviso or presupposition that the appointment of this commission is an intermediate stage leading to a final condition agreeable to the terms of article 213 of the Treaty of Versailles.

The German Government anticipate that the negotiations will take place at an early date, i.e. as soon as the antecedent conditions are fulfilled. I understand that they will propose either Geneva or Berlin as a suitable locality.

I have, etc.,
D'ABERNON

[1] See No. 287, n. 2.

No. 290

The Marquess Curzon of Kedleston to Lord Hardinge (Paris)
No. 3272 [C 14726/32/18]

FOREIGN OFFICE, *October 31, 1922*

My Lord,

With reference to section 14 of your telegram No. 535 of the 20th October,[1] I desire to remind your Excellency that no decision has as yet been taken by

[1] No. 283.

the Ambassadors' Conference respecting (*a*) the prohibition of the export of military swords, bayonets and daggers from ex-enemy countries, and (*b*) the adoption by the Allied Governments of a common procedure for the treatment of consignments of non-regulation weapons of ex-enemy origin imported into the Allied countries.

2. You will observe from the enclosed letter from the Board of Trade[2] that it is now desired somewhat to alter the procedure for dealing with the latter class of consignments, and I request that, in bringing these two matters before the conference, you will consider the instructions contained in my despatch No. 2694 of the 29th August[3] as modified accordingly.[4]

3. It would be convenient if these two matters, both of which have been some time outstanding, could be considered by the conference at an early date.

I am, etc.,
CURZON OF KEDLESTON

[2] Of October 26, not printed.   [3] No. 271.

[4] These modifications were summarised by the Board of Trade as follows:

'(*a*) The Board will henceforth refuse licences to import from ex-enemy countries pistols and revolvers of a barrel length exceeding 10 centim[etres], or of a calibre exceeding 6·5 millim[etres], and munitions capable of use with such weapons.

'(*b*) The Board are not at present prepared, on Peace Treaty grounds, to refuse import licences in any other case than (*a*) above, where an export licence issued in an ex-enemy country is produced.

'(*c*) The Board, subject to their being furnished with a definition of any other type of forbidden weapon as clear and simple to administer as that in (*a*) above, and subject to the adoption of a similar policy by the other Principal Allied Powers, will be prepared to refuse import licences for such a type of weapon.'

No. 291

Lord D'Abernon (Berlin) to the Marquess Curzon of Kedleston
(Received November 1, 10.10 p.m.)

No. 195 Telegraphic [C 15013/6/18]

BERLIN, *November 1, 1922, 8.30 p.m.*

My telegram No. 193.[1]

Answer of German government appears unexpectedly satisfactory and is certainly maximum Wirth could carry with public opinion here. I understand, however, that Nollet is not satisfied.

Modification of [agreement] is of course subject to fulfilment of disarmament conditions specified in allied note. I propose urging German government to carry out these with minimum delay if Your Lordship approves.

Once these conditions are fulfilled, there is not much to negotiate about as explicit terms have already been laid down by allied notes[2] and new régime could come into force at an early date.

[1] No. 287.   [2] See Nos. 208 and 277, n. 1.

No. 292

Memorandum by Mr. Dodds[1]
German protest against demands for surrender of material not properly classifiable as war material

[*C 15095/592/18*]

FOREIGN OFFICE, *November 1, 1922*

Article 169 of the Treaty of Versailles states that 'within two months from the coming into force of the present treaty, German arms, munitions and war material existing in Germany in excess of the quantities allowed must be surrendered (to the Allies) to be destroyed or rendered useless'.

On September 22, 1922 the German Government addressed a note[2] to the Allies protesting that the Military Commission of Control in their interpretation of this article had asked for the surrender of material which could not be considered war equipment as it included articles 'suitable for peace purposes, even semi-manufactured and raw materials'. The Military Control Commission on being remonstrated with by the Germans agreed to exempt from destruction certain of this material which should be sold and the proceeds handed over to the Reparation Commission. A branch of the Reparation Commission had been appointed in November 1920 to deal with such proceeds. This body, entitled the *Bureau de liquidation du Matériel de Guerre*, working with the Military Control Commission, had extended the list of war material to articles which had been sold to private purchasers and had deprived the latter of their purchases and the German Government of the money paid for them.

The latest ordinance of the Control Commission was to demand the surrender for destruction or sale of all material which had at any time been in the possession of the German Army. Protests by the German Government in regard to the economic effects which would result from such a demand had been ignored: they therefore asked that the allied Governments should recognise:

(a) The purely commercial character of certain articles which had been demanded as war material.

(b) The validity of all sales of army materials which had been carried out by the German Government before the *Bureau de liquidation du Matériel de Guerre* undertook that work.

(c) That material obtained on the dismantling of fortresses and on the removal of material for mobilisation should only be surrendered in the event of its being really war material.

2. On October 3rd we sent this protest to the Admiralty and War Office for observations.

On October 23rd the Admiralty replied:

1. That 'surrender' in Article 169 means that the material in question

---

[1] A member of the Central European Department of the Foreign Office.
[2] Not printed.

becomes the absolute property of the allies as from July 11, 1919. Moreover the Naval Commission is the authority to decide what constitutes naval war material and can add to the list at any time.

2. The 'arisings' from Naval Material destroyed or rendered useless come to the allies. If the material is destroyed, the allies (via the administrative organisation of the *Bureau de liquidation du Matériel de Guerre*) receive the money value of the 'scrap': if it has been rendered useless i.e. for war purposes, it is returned to Germany and does *not* come into the hands of the *Bureau de liquidation de Matériel de Guerre*.

3. That the Naval Control Commission might recognise the validity of sales of particular articles previously released by them as being commercial but that would not prevent them from prohibiting on another occasion the sale of similar articles.

The Admiralty considered that the procedure of the Naval Commission could not be objected to by the German Government, who had as a matter of fact confined themselves almost entirely to complaints about the procedure of the Military Commission, which is in many points different from that of the Naval.

3. On October 28th the War Office replied agreeing that some of the representations of the German Government should be favourably considered. They quoted the arguments presented by the Military Mission to the Versailles Military Committee on May 18th, 1922. The Mission argued that the German Government should under the Treaty surrender (a) war material disposed of prior to July 11, 1919 and still existing in Germany, (b) material which had been in the possession of the German army. The German Government replied that it could not be called on to account for such material and protested to the Conference of Ambassadors.

The Versailles Military Committee informed the Military Committee on October 6th that they felt that though the allies were legally entitled to claim material under (a) above it might be difficult to obtain it in practice, and that under (b) some material which had been in the possession of the German army could not be regarded as war material unless it were constituted in stocks which might present a military danger. They therefore asked the Commission for further information on the points on receipt of which the War Office will write to us again.

No. 293

The Marquess Curzon of Kedleston to Lord Hardinge (Paris)
No. 411 Telegraphic [C 15150/6/18]

FOREIGN OFFICE, *November 6, 1922, 9 p.m.*

Your despatch No. 2562 (of November 5th: attack on military control commission at Passau).[1]

I entirely endorse views of Marshal Foch and Your Excellency should give his proposals every support at the conference.

I would however suggest that it will almost certainly be more effective to embody allied demands regarding this matter in the communication to the German government which the German government's note of October 27th[2] on question of liquidation of control evidently renders imperative.

Whilst the German government in their note of October 27th declare themselves ready to enter into negotiations with the allied governments (presumably respecting the establishment of the military committee of guarantee, since this is the only matter on which negotiations are necessary) they have so far given no indication whatever that they intend to comply with the requirements of the military control commission respecting the 'five important points'[3] in the military clauses the execution of which is still outstanding.

[1] Not printed. This transmitted a translation of a report of November 3 by the Allied Military Committee of Versailles to the Conference of Ambassadors. This report ran:

'I [Marshal Foch] have the honour to forward herewith the dossier concerning an incident which occurred on the 24th October last at Passau, where, while engaged on their duties, two members of the Inter-Allied Military Commission of Control in Germany were insulted, molested and struck.

'General Nollet, as a result of this incident, has called upon the German Government to furnish, by the 6th November, the apologies of the local authorities and to punish the police authorities who failed to protect the members of the Commission of Control.

'The Inter-Allied Military Commission of Control has thought it necessary to mention that the moral responsibility for the trap organised on the 24th October falls on the Government of the Reich.

'The campaigns of provocation which this Government tolerates, in spite of repeated warnings, the impunity allowed to many offenders in the past, and, finally, the habit of shielding subordinates, even when their faults have been admitted, afford clear proof of the responsibility of the Government.

'Moreover, the Inter-Allied Military Commission of Control considers—

"That it would be just, opportune, and useful to call upon the German Government itself to apologise for the attitude of its nationals towards official representatives of the Allied Governments,"

and has asked, in consequence, for the question to be submitted to the Conference of Ambassadors, since the commission is not itself qualified to demand apologies from the German Government.

'On the 31st October the German Chancellor has, by his letter No. 7524 [not printed], expressed to General Nollet his regrets, while at the same time declaring that he reserves his reply to the demand for apologies and redress which have been made, without undertaking that this reply is to be furnished by the 6th November. The president of the Commission of Control, in acknowledging this letter, integrally maintained his demands for the date fixed.'

[2] See No. 287, n. 2.

[3] See No. 270, n. 5.

On the other hand their treatment of the allied governments' demand for satisfaction for the attack on the military control commission at Stettin[4] and now of the control commission's demands in connection with the Passau incident appear to indicate a distinct disinclination on the part of the German government to afford the commission the facilities which are a prior and necessary condition of the execution of the 'five points'.

Whatever communication therefore is now addressed to the German government should presumably lay stress upon this aspect of the question and, in demanding categorically a final and immediate settlement of the Stettin and Passau incidents, should also make it clear that (1) the only matter which the allied governments are prepared to negotiate with the German government is the constitution of the military committee of guarantee, upon the acceptance of which by the German government the allied governments will after the execution of the 'five points' be prepared to withdraw the military control commission, (2) the allied governments will not enter into negotiations with the German government respecting the execution of the 'five points', this being a matter entirely within the competence of the military control commission and (3) that, in accordance with this policy, the allied governments will in future refuse to receive, except through the control commissions, any note whatever from the German government respecting the execution of the 'five points' or the execution of any of the military and naval disarmament clauses of the treaty.

Repeated to Berlin No. 106.

4 See No. 267, n. 1.

No. 294

The Marquess Curzon of Kedleston to Lord Hardinge (Paris)
No. 412 Telegraphic [C 15081/6/18]

FOREIGN OFFICE, *November 6, 1922, 10 p.m.*

Liquidation of control in Germany.

Recent events have made it clear that the successful execution of the policy laid down in the allied note of September 29th, 1922,[1] will to a large degree be dependent on an even closer co-operation between the control commission, Ambassadors' Conference and allied governments, than that which has existed in the past.

I therefore request that in communicating to the conference the substance of my telegram No. 411 (of November 6th)[2] Your Excellency will propose as likely to contribute to the accomplishment of this purpose, that conference should decide:—

(a) to issue a reminder to naval and military control commissions that all German appeals to the conference must be referred to the conference with control commission's comments with least possible delay;

1 See No. 277, n. 1.   2 No. 293.

573

(b) to reject no German appeal to the conference without prior reference to the governments;

(c) to instruct the naval and military control commissions, in order to avoid these constant appeals to the conference, to exercise the utmost caution against making demands upon the German government to which that government can subsequently with reason object as not covered by the treaty.

I also request that, in order to put the process of liquidation of the naval control commission upon the same basis as that of the military control commission, Your Excellency will take this opportunity to propose the issue by the conference of an immediate instruction to the President of the naval control commission to report (1) upon the state of execution of the naval clauses and (2) whether in conformity with the line of policy laid down, as regards the military clauses, in the allied note of September 29th, there are matters, similar to the 'five military points', the execution of which is essential before the withdrawal of the naval control commission.

Repeated to Berlin No. 107.

No. 295

The Marquess Curzon of Kedleston to Lord D'Abernon (Berlin)
No. 108 Telegraphic: by bag [C 15013/6/18]

FOREIGN OFFICE, *November 6, 1922, 11 p.m.*
Your telegram No. 195 (of November 1st. Liquidation of military control commission).[1]

Please see my telegrams Nos. 411[2] and 412[3] to Paris. Pending decision of ambassadors' conference, it is unnecessary for you to make any further communication to German government on this matter.

Repeated to Paris No. 413.

[1] No. 291.   [2] No. 293.   [3] No. 294.

No. 296

Sir A. Geddes (Washington) to the Marquess Curzon of Kedleston
(Received November 9, 8 a.m.)
No. 441 Telegraphic [C 15355/1188/18]

WASHINGTON, *November 8, 1922*
Your despatch No. 1549.[1]

Four representatives called on Mr. Hughes today and French ambassador as doyen presented written document respecting Rhineland and spoke in the sense instructed.

[1] See No. 278, n. 4.

Secretary of State expressed his gratification and his appreciation of friendly spirit which animated our communication. He will study matter and reply later.[2]

Delay in making communication was due to Italian Embassy having only just received instructions.

[2] See *F.R.U.S.* 1922, vol. ii, pp. 232–3. Sir A. Geddes transmitted this reply, dated November 22, in his despatch No. 1294 of November 24, not printed. The reply stated that Mr. Eliot Wadsworth had been designated representative of the United States government to meet the Allied delegates in Paris.

No. 297

The Marquess Curzon of Kedleston to Lord Hardinge (Paris)
No. 3367 [C 15344/6/18]

FOREIGN OFFICE, *November 9, 1922*

My Lord,

With reference to the suggestion contained in my telegrams Nos. 411 and 412 of the 6th November,[1] respecting the procedure to be followed by the German Government in submitting to the Allied Governments any protests which that Government may in future wish to make against the decisions of the Military and Naval Control Commissions, there are still in the files of the Foreign Office four communications from the German Ambassador at this Court in which his Excellency, by instruction of his Government, protests against various decisions of the Military and Naval Control Commissions.

2. Protests of this nature will, in the event of the adoption by the Ambassadors' Conference of the procedure suggested in my telegrams Nos. 411 and 412, in future be refused by the Allied Governments, who will entertain such protests only upon their submission through the control commissions and the Ambassadors' Conference. But in the case of the protests already submitted direct to me by M. Sthamer and which have no doubt been submitted to the other Allied Governments represented on the conference and to which no reply has yet been made, I am of opinion that some reply is now desirable, if only in order that the German Government may have no excuse for continuing to refuse to execute the relevant instructions of the control commission affected.

3. The communications in question are as follows:—

(a) M. Sthamer's note of the 7th July, 1922,[2] dealing with the refusal of the Military Control Commission to permit the resumption of the manufacture of war material for the German army (see my despatch No. 2506 of the 10th August[2] and Paris despatches Nos. 1898[3] and 1949[4] of the 14th and 22nd August). It appears desirable that the communication, suggested in the War Office letter of the 3rd August[2] (enclosed

[1] Nos. 293 and 294 respectively.
[2] Not printed.
[3] Not preserved in the Foreign Office archives.
[4] No. 269.

with my despatch No. 2506), should now be made to the German Government.

(b) M. Sthamer's note of the 24th July, 1922,[2] respecting the demand of the Military Control Commission for the surrender of arms issued to German railway employees, a copy of which is enclosed together with a War Office letter of the 15th August, 1922,[2] on the subject. It appears desirable that the German Government should now be told, on the analogy of the reply[5] returned to their note of the 30th August,[6] 1922, that this matter is covered by the general policy laid down in the Allied note of the 29th September, 1922.[7]

(c) M. Sthamer's note of the 27th September, 1922,[2] respecting the demand of the Naval Control Commission for the removal of the engines from the motor boat 'Köro', a copy[2] of which is enclosed together with a copy[2] of the Admiralty letter on the subject. It appears desirable that the Naval Control Commission's reply to the German Government (if, indeed, that reply has been despatched) should be confirmed to the German Government by the Ambassadors' Conference, since the German Government's note was addressed to the Allied Governments and not to the Naval Control Commission.

(d) M. Sthamer's note of the 22nd September, 1922,[2] (of which a copy was enclosed in my despatch No. 3007 of the 3rd October),[2] protesting against the wide interpretation placed by the Military and Naval Control Commissions upon the meaning of the term 'war material'. The questions raised by this note are still under consideration here, and I am not yet in a position to communicate to your Excellency the views of His Majesty's Government, but it is evident that, in this matter, as in the three preceding cases, it will be proper for the conference eventually to take into consideration the German Government's communication and not through the control commissions.

4. I request that you will bring the foregoing matters to the notice of the conference and move them to reply without further delay to the German Government's communications quoted in paragraph 3 (a), (b) and (c) above and in the sense there suggested.

I am, etc.,
CURZON OF KEDLESTON

[5] Not preserved in the Foreign Office archives. See, however, No. 279, Section 18.
[6] Not printed. See, however, No. 272.
[7] See No. 277, n. 1.

No. 298

Lord Hardinge (Paris) to the Marquess Curzon of Kedleston
(Received November 11, 8.30 a.m.)

No. 580 Telegraphic: by bag [*C 15400/6/18*]

PARIS, *November 10, 1922*

Your telegram No. 412.[1]

Before submitting Your Lordship's suggestion to the Conference of Ambassadors I would like to offer the following observations:—

As regards (a) I was not aware that the commissions of control were delaying or preventing German appeals from reaching the Conference. Could I be supplied with instances for which I shall certainly be asked.

As regards (b) I have taken careful note of Your Lordship's wishes as regards myself, but it would be presumptuous on my part to suggest to my colleagues on the Conference that they must consult their governments before giving a decision with regard to a German appeal. In my own case I can think of no occasion where I have given such a decision without first obtaining the views of the War Office or the Admiralty through my military or naval advisers if the question was purely technical, or the instructions of Your Lordship if the matter had a political aspect. Only exceptions would be where appeal was merely a repetition of a previous appeal already rejected.

As regards (3) I have every reason to hope that the Conference of Ambassadors will fully agree with Your Lordship.

As regards the last paragraph of your telegram I would have preferred not to have reopened the question of the execution of the naval clauses of the treaty, which was fully dealt with in the annex to the allied Note to the German government of April 14th (see my despatch No. 938).[2] I fear if the question is reopened the opportunity will be seized to magnify the work still to be done in order to prolong the life of the commission. At present it is generally agreed that once the question of the equipment of the light cruisers is settled the naval commission can be withdrawn (cf. Admiral de Marguerye's remarks reported in paragraph 4 of my telegram No. 514).[3] I was under the impression that the Admiralty shared this view. Any fresh discussion in the Conference is likely to tend to prolong the existence of the commission.

[1] No. 294.　　　[2] No. 208.　　　[3] No. 279.

No. 299

Lord Hardinge (Paris) to the Marquess Curzon of Kedleston
(Received November 13, 8.30 a.m.)

No. 581 Telegraphic: by bag [*C 15434/7361/18*]

PARIS, *November 10, 1922*

The Conference of Ambassadors met this morning under the chairmanship of Monsieur J. Cambon, the Belgian Ambassador being also present, and considered the following questions:—

. . .[1]2. The United States Ambassador stated that Mr. John Basset Moore would owing to pressure of work be unable to undertake to arbitrate on the question of the equipment to be surrendered by Germany for the use of the light cruisers which had been handed over to France and Italy (see my telegram No. 548 of October 27th section 1).[2] It was decided that at the next meeting members of the Conference should submit names of other suitable persons who might be asked to undertake this arbitration. The United States Ambassador also offered to make enquiries.

I presume that His Majesty's Government would if necessary be ready to contribute towards the payment of a fee to the arbitrator.

. . .[1]4. The Conference approved the report of the Interallied Military Committee of Versailles enclosed in my despatch No. 2562[3] in which the Conference is requested to demand that the German Government apologise at once to the Military Commission of Control in addition to carrying out the demands made by the latter with regard to the apologies to be presented by the local authorities and the removal of the responsible local officials. Further correspondence with the Comm[ission]s of Control on this subject is enclosed in my despatch No. 2628.[4] I suggested that the Conference would do well to deal at the same time and on the same lines with the similar incident which had previously occurred at Stettin (see my telegram No. 501 of October 4th section 2)[5] and to frame its demand so that the apologies should cover both cases. This was agreed to, more especially as the time limit fixed in the case of the Stettin incident expires on the 11th instant. Further, on Marshal Foch's suggestion, it was decided to insist upon the German Government making the amends required of them before the 24th November. It was agreed in principle that if satisfaction is not given within this time limit, some sort of penalty will have to be applied. Marshal Foch suggested that a fine might be levied on the revenues of the occupied Rhineland, more particularly on those of the Palatinate as being in the province of Bavaria. I said that I would have to consult my Government on this matter and promised to inform the Conference of their views at the next meeting on the 15th instant. I should be grateful therefore for Your Lordship's instructions.

I thought it better not to attempt to link up, as suggested in Your Lordship's telegram No. 411 of November 6th,[6] the question of these attacks on members of the Commissions of Control with the general question of the execution of the military clauses of the Treaty of Versailles, more especially as the German Government's note of the 27th October[7] was not on the agenda today and has not even been circulated to the members of the Conference. It will no doubt be possible when replying to the German Government's note of October 27th (which will doubtless be considered at the next meeting) to make it clear that the systematic obstruction to which

---

[1] The section(s) omitted referred to other matters.   [2] No. 285.
[3] Of November 5 (see No. 293, n. 1).   [4] Of November 10, not printed.
[5] Not printed. See, however, No. 273.
[6] No. 293.   [7] See No. 287, n. 2.

the members of the Commissions of Control are being exposed is seriously delaying the whole scheme for withdrawing the Commissions of Control from Germany.

. . .¹6. Monsieur Cambon called attention to the growing habit of the German Government of appealing direct to the Allied Governments individually over the heads of the Commissions of Control and the Conference of Ambassadors. He proposed therefore that the German Government should be informed that the Allied Governments are determined not to reply to any notes addressed, either directly to one of them, or to the Conference of Ambassadors on subjects which the Commissions of Control are, in virtue of the Treaty, empowered to deal with, and that all such communications must be addressed direct to the Commissions of Control. I stipulated that in accordance with the original procedure laid down in April 1920, as reported in Lord Derby's telegram No. 486 of April 21st, section 1,⁸ the German Government should still be allowed to forward direct to the Conference copies of such communications. This addition was agreed to.

In view of the instructions contained in the last paragraph of Your Lordship's telegram No. 411,⁶ I was prepared to undertake that His Majesty's Government would not in future reply to any such notes addressed to them direct by the German Government. The Italian Chargé d'Affaires however demurred to giving any such undertaking on behalf of his Government, while assuring the Conference that in practice his Government always referred such communications to the Conference. It was accordingly agreed that in the communication to the German Government the Conference should merely state that the German Government were not to address the Allied Governments direct, while, on the other hand, the Conference should invite the Allied Governments to refuse in future to accept any such notes from the German Government. I propose at the next meeting to inform the Conference that His Majesty's Government have agreed to this course. In the meanwhile might I suggest that Your Lordship instead of answering the notes from the German Ambassador enumerated in your despatch No. 3367 of the 9th instant,⁹ should inform Dr. Sthamer that they have been referred to the Conference of Ambassadors. . . .¹

⁸ See Vol. X, No. 51.   ⁹ No. 297.

No. 300

Sir G. Grahame (Brussels) to the Marquess Curzon of Kedleston
(Received November 24)

No. 753 [C 15604/336/18]

Confidential   BRUSSELS, *November 10, 1922*

My Lord,

I have on various occasions, since I have been in Brussels, observed that the average Belgian—who may be described as on the whole a level-headed and sensible person—has at the back of his mind an uncomfortable impression that Belgium may one day be faced with the alternative either of watching France, freed from Allied tutelage, put herself into a position in the Rhineland, which would practically mean an *encerclement* for Belgium, or of having to enter into partnership with her. The average Belgian, unlike his light-headed Nationalist compatriot, sees strong objections to either alternative.

I have noticed that during the last few days the possibility of such a dilemma has been again brought to the attention of the Belgian public in various ways.

In the first place, the newspapers have published extracts from a report drawn up by the French Deputy M. Dariac, which, I understand, first appeared in the 'Manchester Guardian' of the 2nd instant,[1] in favour of a fundamental change in the present state of the Rhineland, the result of which would be that the control of this region would be taken over by France and Belgium. The Belgian public has also learnt that M. Loucheur declared in the French Chamber of Deputies a few days ago that the formula 'Rhineland for the Rhinelanders' was the only one which could assure the security of France, and shrewdly suspects that this in reality means 'Rhineland for the French'. In addition to these declarations, one by the French President of the Council has been noted, which was, I believe, made during the same sitting of the Chamber of Deputies, to the effect that France would not evacuate her positions in the Rhineland and across the Rhine until the Treaty of Versailles had been entirely executed, and that, as Germany had not yet begun to execute the treaty, the period during which, by that treaty, the Allies were to occupy the Rhineland had not yet begun to run.

There is, moreover, a feeling in Belgium that the French public are beginning fully to realise that the German Reich will not be able to make any cash payments in respect of reparations. The recent French budget of France has clearly revealed her deplorable financial situation,[2] and it is thought in many quarters in Belgium that this factor will result in irresistible pressure being brought to bear on the French Government to take the law into their own hands. It is not thought that such action can produce sums of

[1] See No. 123, n. 6. In his despatch No. 328 of November 20, Lord Kilmarnock commented: 'Whether this report is to be considered as official or not, it is clear that the opinions expressed by M. Dariac are shared by a certain section of French politicians, and similar views have been put forward from time to time by members of the French Commissariat. As far as I am in a position to judge locally from statements made by members of the French Department here, France is still desirous of securing her safety and at the same time of satisfying her financial demands to a very considerable extent out of German sources. This policy is a contradiction in terms, and its only possible solution in practice would be along the lines as indicated by M. Dariac. M. Dariac's conclusions are based on well-known facts. Should France acquire control of the Ruhr production, whether by means of an occupation of certain nodal traffic points, of which the most important are already in their hands (Duisburg–Ruhrort), or by some other means, she has Germany at her mercy. Eighty-five per cent. of the coal produced in Germany would then be placed completely under French control, and this would result in giving France complete economic hold over 62,000,000 Germans. It is unfortunate for Germany that fate has placed all her industrial eggs in one small basket, and it would appear probable that more will be heard in the future of the points raised by M. Dariac in his memorandum.' [2] Cf. No. 106.

money which do not exist, but if these cannot be obtained, the French at any rate feel that they have the power of eliminating for ever Germany as a dangerous enemy or rival to France. The possession by France of the richest fields of iron ore in Europe in her former and recently regained territory is regarded here as placing in her hands a potential power which can scarcely be exaggerated. Should she take over the control of the territory on the left bank of the Rhine and of the industries situated therein, and maintain her hold of the fluvial outlet from the Ruhr basin, it is thought that she could, if she so desired, achieve a practical hegemony on the European continent, not only in a military but eventually in an industrial sense, for her German competitors would be at her mercy and the screw could be turned on them at her will.

The prospect of such a position is calculated to fill Belgians with alarm. The term *encerclement* was first used to me in this connection by M. Delacroix when he was Prime Minister at the end of 1920. I have recently heard the same expression used by the present Prime Minister. They implied that Belgium might not only find a customs barrier as at present to the south, but probably in some form or another likewise to the east between herself and Central Europe. As M. Neuray, the editor of the 'Nation belge', declared in a leading article last February, Belgium would then become an enclave between France and a Rhineland subjected to French influence, and if the Belgian Government allowed France to act alone instead of going into partnership with her, she would infallibly fall into the position of a vassal of France.

I have on more than one occasion brought to your Lordship's notice the fact that certain circles here conceive that the course of events in Europe may bring the question of a Franco-Belgian condominium over the Rhineland into the region of practical politics.[3] It is true that such an eventuality has scarcely yet appeared even on the most distant horizon, but I think it my duty to mention the matter again to your Lordship in case events move faster than until recently has appeared to be in the least likely.

The present Belgian Ministers are far from being inclined to take any steps which might bring this eventuality any nearer. I believe them to be sincerely averse to it, but it might happen that, as the result of some kaleidoscopic change, events would prove to be too strong for them, and that they might find themselves obliged either to make way for some other Cabinet or to take steps urgently demanded by an overwhelming expression of public opinion to prevent Belgium from being shut off from the Rhine and from the markets in the Rhineland and further east.

Belgian Ministers have lately been told by the Francophil Belgian press that the time is not distant when England and France will come to some agreement about Germany, and that M. Theunis and his Cabinet, having then fallen between two stools, will be reprobated by the whole of Belgium for having, owing to their infatuation for English policy, missed the opportunity of a fruitful partnership with France.

[3] See No. 118.

Already vague and evanescent rumours, probably arising from a perusal of French newspapers, have been current here that some kind of a bargain between the British and French Governments may be struck, according to which Great Britain would obtain satisfaction in the Near East in return for giving to France a free hand in dealing with Germany.[4]

Nothing would be more conducive to rendering Belgian public opinion favourable to the idea of a partnership with France in enterprises against the Rhineland than the suspicion that His Majesty's Government might at some future date abandon opposition to French ambitions on the Rhine.

I have, etc.,

GEORGE GRAHAME

4 See No. 123.

No. 301

Lord Hardinge (Paris) to the Marquess Curzon of Kedleston
(Received November 15)
No. 2642 [C 15624/6/18]

PARIS, *November 14, 1922*

Lord Hardinge of Penshurst presents his compliments to the Secretary of State for Foreign Affairs, and has the honour to transmit herewith a copy of a note from the Conference of Ambassadors to the German Embassy in Paris, dated the 13th November, respecting the incidents at Stettin and Passau.

ENCLOSURE IN No. 301

M. Poincaré to Dr. Mayer

PARIS, *le 13 novembre, 1922*

M. l'Ambassadeur,

A la date du 28 octobre, le Président de la Commission militaire interalliée de Contrôle a fait connaître au Gouvernement allemand, sans préjudice des décisions que pourraient prendre, d'autre part, les Gouvernements alliés, les réparations et les sanctions jugées nécessaires à la suite des violences dont deux membres de la commission ont été l'objet à Passau le 24 octobre.[1]

Le Général Nollet, au nom de la commission, demandait que des excuses fussent présentées au Comité de District de Munich par le magistrat responsable de l'ordre public à Passau, la forme, la date et le mode de publication de ces excuses étant fixés ultérieurement; il demandait également que le chef de la police de Passau fût relevé de ses fonctions, ainsi que l'officier qui, à la date de l'incident, commandait le bataillon du 20e régiment d'infanterie dans le casernement duquel existaient les inscriptions offensantes que la Commission de Contrôle a signalées au Gouvernement allemand. La lettre du Général Nollet se terminait en invitant le Gouvernement allemand à faire tenir sa réponse avant le 6 novembre, dernier délai.

1 See No. 293, n. 1.

Ce délai a été maintenu dans la nouvelle communication que le Général Nollet a adressée, le 2 novembre,[2] au Gouvernement allemand. Néanmoins, aujourd'hui, 13 novembre, la Commission de Contrôle n'a pas encore reçu satisfaction.

Les Puissances alliées ont ainsi le regret de constater que le Gouvernement allemand n'a pas fait ce qui était en son pouvoir pour donner satisfaction au légitimes exigences, très modérées, d'ailleurs, de la Commission de Contrôle. Elles constatent en même temps qu'à la même date, et malgré l'intervention réitérée des Gouvernements alliés, l'incident de Stettin[3] n'a pas été réglé à leur satisfaction.

En conséquence, et au nom des Gouvernements représentés à la Commission de Contrôle, j'ai l'honneur de prier votre Excellence de bien vouloir transmettre au Gouvernement allemand la déclaration suivante:

'Indépendamment des réparations et sanctions visant les autorités locales de Passau et de Stettin que la Commission de Contrôle ou les Gouvernements alliés ont déjà exigées, les Gouvernements alliés ont l'honneur d'inviter le Gouvernement allemand à adresser à la Commission militaire interalliée de Contrôle, dès maintenant et sans attendre d'autres explications, des excuses pour l'attitude qu'ont eue ses nationaux *vis-à-vis* des représentants des Gouvernements alliés dans l'exercice de leur mission qu'a définie le Traité de Paix. Ces excuses devront porter aussi bien sur l'incident de Stettin que sur l'incident de Passau. Elles devront être adressées à la Commission de Contrôle avant le 24 novembre, dernier délai.

'A la même date, les réparations et sanctions déjà demandées par ladite commission ou par les Gouvernements alliés pour ces deux incidents devront avoir été accordées.

'Faute par le Gouvernement allemand d'avoir fait droit à ces différentes demandes à la date indiquée ci-dessus, les Gouvernements alliés se réservent de prendre telles mesures qu'ils estimeront convenables.'

Veuillez agréer, etc.,
POINCARÉ

[2] Not printed.   [3] See No. 267, n. 1.

No. 302

Lord Hardinge (Paris) to the Marquess Curzon of Kedleston
(Received November 17, 8.30 a.m.)
No. 604 Telegraphic: by bag [C 15705/6/18]

PARIS, November 15, 1922

The Conference of Ambassadors met this morning under the chairmanship of Monsieur Jules Cambon, the Belgian Ambassador being also present, and considered the following questions:—

....[1]5. Being without instructions from Your Lordship on the point raised

[1] The sections omitted referred to other matters.

in section 4 of my telegram No. 581 of November 10th,[2] I had to ask the Conference to adjourn the decision as to the 'sanctions' to be imposed on the German Government in the event of their failing to give satisfaction with regard to the Stettin and Passau incidents before the 24th instant.[3] I trust that I may be furnished with Your Lordship's views before the next meeting of the Conference on the 23rd instant, since the delay expires on the following day....[1]

[2] No. 299.   [3] See No. 301, Enclosure.

No. 303

Lord D'Abernon (Berlin) to the Marquess Curzon of Kedleston
(Received November 15, 12.50 p.m.)
No. 204 Telegraphic [C 15642/725/18]

BERLIN, *November 15, 1922, 12.10 p.m.*

Wirth resigned last night.

(? Ostensible) cause of government's fall was refusal of Socialist Party to agree to extension of government coalition so as to include Peoples Party. Wirth had demanded this extension as a condition of his remaining in office.

Underlying causes of Socialist attitude were distrust of sincerity of Peoples Party and of Stinnes regarding stabilization and of refusal of Socialist rank and file to abandon eight-hour day, which abandonment Stinnes regards as indispensable to economic restoration and conditional precedent of effective stabilization.

Future is uncertain.

Before resignation of government, all parties except Communist and Extreme Right had endorsed proposal which was sent to Reparations Commission yesterday.[1]

[1] See No. 113.

No. 304

Lord Hardinge (Paris) to the Marquess Curzon of Kedleston
(Received November 17)
No. 2683 [C 15724/6/18]

PARIS, *November 15, 1922*

Lord Hardinge of Penshurst presents his compliments to the Secretary of State for Foreign Affairs, and has the honour to transmit herewith a copy of a note from the Conference of Ambassadors to the German Embassy in Paris, dated the 15th November, respecting the German protests against decisions of the Commissions of Control.[1]

[1] See No. 299, section 6.

Conference of Ambassadors to German Ambassador

PARIS, *le 15 novembre, 1922*

M. l'Ambassadeur,

La Conférence des Ambassadeurs observe que le Gouvernement allemand croit devoir saisir des questions que pose l'exécution du contrôle tantôt les Commissions de Contrôle, tantôt chacun des Gouvernements alliés, tantôt la conférence elle-même.

Une telle procédure, par la confusion qu'elle crée, a nécessairement pour effet de retarder la solution des questions de litige et contribue à ralentir les opérations de contrôle, alors que le Gouvernement allemand a insisté à maintes reprises sur les lourdes charges que lui impose l'entretien des commissions alliées. Ces inconvénients ont frappé les Gouvernements alliés représentés à la Conférence des Ambassadeurs, qui ont estimé urgent de mettre fin à de tels errements. En conséquence, j'ai l'honneur de vous faire savoir en leur nom que ni ces Gouvernements eux-mêmes, ni la conférence n'examineront ni ne répondront désormais aux notes qui leur seraient directement adressées touchant des questions que les Commissions de Contrôle, de par le traité, ont compétence pour régler. Les observations que le Gouvernement allemand croira devoir présenter à ce sujet devront donc être adressées aux Commissions elles-mêmes. Le Gouvernement allemand aura, d'ailleurs, la faculté, s'il le juge utile, d'adresser copie de ces observations à la Conférence des Ambassadeurs, à laquelle il appartiendra de donner, s'il y a lieu, aux commissions les instructions nécessaires.

En invitant le Gouvernement allemand à observer cette procédure, la Conférence des Ambassadeurs a uniquement en vue de hâter l'achèvement des mesures de désarmement qui ont subi ces dernier mois un regrettable ralentissement. Elle attache la plus grande importance à obtenir satisfaction sur ce point essentiel et elle devra considérer comme une tentative d'obstruction toute démarche de la part du Gouvernement allemand qui ne serait pas conforme à la procédure indiquée ci-dessus.

No. 305

Lord D'Abernon (Berlin) to the Marquess Curzon of Kedleston
(Received November 18)
No. 881 [C 15778/144/18]

BERLIN, *November 15, 1922*

My Lord,

I have the honour to forward a memorandum by Mr. Addison on the near future in Bavaria and the activities of Herr Adolf Hitler.

I have, etc.,
D'ABERNON

Memorandum respecting Bavaria

November 13, 1922

Speculation as to what may or may not occur in the near future in Bavaria is again prominent in many press articles owing to the activities of the National Socialistic Workmen's Party, led by Herr Adolf Hitler. We know very little of Herr Hitler's past except that he is said originally to have been a designer of posters. The 'Acht-Uhr Abendblatt' published, in its edition of the 11th instant, an account of an interview with Herr Hitler by its special correspondent in Bavaria in which the latter was held up to ridicule. He would certainly appear to merit ridicule if his remarks have been accurately quoted, for they are mere verbiage. Herr Hitler is made to declare that the whole evil from which the world suffers comes from the Jews, and that he is fighting for the purity of race ('Rassenreinheit') of the German people and of the whole world. He went on to state that his adherents were not armed, but that if the Socialists were to attack them, they would reply with a terror such as the world had never seen. His followers were neither Monarchists nor Republicans; the particular form of government was merely a side issue, but they meant to get rid of all Jews and foreigners.

In a further conversation which this special correspondent had with a member of Herr Hitler's organisation, the latter is made to say that Jesus Christ was a German, but that the Pope Alexander VI, the Emperor Wilhelm II and King Edward VII were all Jews.

Although Herr Hitler would certainly appear to be an unbalanced person, it would yet be unwise to treat him as if he were a mere clown. In the first place, worthless demagogues have often caused trouble beyond what their attainments should have warranted. In the second place, Herr Hitler must have some sort of organising ability and some power for expressing the discontent of the time in a form accessible to the average intelligence, since he commands allegiance, funds and notoriety. It would therefore be a great mistake to neglect him altogether. In this connection, I cannot do better than quote the following from Mr. Seeds's[1] despatch No. 172 of the 2nd instant:—[2]

'During the last few months, however, Herr Hitler has developed into something much more than a scurrilous and rather comic agitator. Gifted with undoubted eloquence, he has never wearied in indiscriminate abuse. . . . But the middle-classes, who have seen his abuse apparently justified, now begin to look upon him as a very Mussolini, and he has more to offer them than mere words: he has succeeded in evolving out of his supporters an efficient and active organisation.'

Mr. Seeds points out that Herr Hitler would appear to be financed by the big industrials, that the money is efficiently spent and that—

[1] Mr. W. Seeds was Consul-General for Bavaria and the Bavarian Palatinate.
[2] Not printed.

'I have been greatly struck of late with the increasing reliance placed by Conservative circles here on Hitler's men as a safeguard against Communism, and, since recent events in Italy,[3] on Hitler himself as the rising political star.'

Whatever may have been the reasons which induced the Italian people on the whole to assist Signor Mussolini to his present position, the success of the Italian President of the Council could not fail to produce a certain effect in this country where people are weary, despair of good government, and are seeking a saviour. A German friend recently came here to tell me that he knew as a positive fact that emissaries from the Fascist organisation had come to Germany and placed themselves officially in communication with those who, for want of a better term, can be described as the leaders of reaction, but, as my informant is an excitable man who regularly predicts revolution and disaster for 10.30 on the next morning, I do not attach much importance to his unsupported statement. In any case, such co-operation could not of itself change much in the situation, which is plainly that Germany is discontented, and that, for very special reasons, Bavaria is more discontented than the rest of the country, also that such special discontent in Bavaria moves largely in a definite direction owing to the particularist and strongly Conservative views of the majority of the Bavarian population.

I do not for the moment think that anything particularly useful with regard to the situation in Bavaria can be said which would add anything to the information repeatedly conveyed home during the last year. To attempt to foreshadow future events is to attempt to prophesy, and prophecy must be left to soothsayers. We have received here during the past year innumerable items of information, and have heard innumerable expressions of views which have served as a basis for such opinions as we may have been able to form and transmit to the Foreign Office. Assuming that Bavaria were anxious to adopt an independent line and to dissociate herself, more or less completely, from the rest of Germany, it would be obviously very difficult for her to attempt to do so under present conditions. In despatch No. 1110 of the 3rd September of last year[4] I gave certain reasons in support of this opinion, which can be summarised thus:

1. Since Bavaria is being used by those who wish to return more or less to the conditions formerly obtaining, as a preserve of such conceptions and as a starting point from which to develop action throughout the Commonwealth, the utility of Bavaria to this end would largely disappear were she to become independent or semi-independent.

2. The Catholic Church would certainly view with disfavour the loss of power in Germany occasioned by such a separation.

3. Bavaria relies on the rest of Germany for her supplies of raw materials and, in particular, for her supplies of coal.

The situation in Bavaria again became one necessitating some comment at

[3] See No. 116, n. 2.
[4] See Vol. XVI, No. 825.

the beginning of December last. I then wrote[5] that I learnt, from information received from a very reliable source, that preparations for the restoration, or at least for a state of affairs leading to the restoration, of the Monarchy in Bavaria, had recently reached a very advanced stage, but concluded, largely on the same authority, that the movement had collapsed with the failure of the ex-Emperor of Austria to regain the Hungarian crown. Had the ex-Emperor succeeded it might have been possible—and it was probably the intention of the authors of the movement—to form a federation composed of Bavaria (plus perhaps one or two other South German States), Austria and Hungary, which would have acted as a counterpoise to a North German Federation. It appeared to me that such a plan was beyond the bounds of practical politics, but this did not necessarily lead to the conclusion that no such plan had ever been formed, nor that it might not have been attempted had encouragement been given in the shape of non-resistance to the attempt of the ex-Emperor to ascend the throne of Hungary. In a further despatch—No. 1385 of the 6th December last[2]—I commented on a report furnished to Major-General Sir Francis Bingham very much in the same sense, i.e., that a separatist movement in Bavaria could only be successful if that country could in fact, by combination with other territories, render herself independent of Northern Germany. I pointed out that it must not be forgotten that Bavaria had become a semi-industrial State; that she could consequently not do without German coal and raw materials, and that she therefore could not separate unless and until a strong political combination could be formed which could either command supplies from elsewhere or compel Northern Germany to continue to send supplies to an independent southern State. I added, however, that discontent, resulting in acts of violence in North Germany, might lead to some form of agitation in South Germany. I said that since unrest, due to bad conditions of living, was more likely to arise in the industrial north of Bavaria than in those parts of the country where the peasants found a ready market at good prices for their agricultural produce, disturbances would probably at the outset arise in support of advanced opinion, but that the work of restoring order might in turn serve to strengthen the idea of strong government, and the party of monarchical restoration might thus derive its greatest support from a movement primarily directed against its conceptions.

I do not think there is anything in the present situation which would cause one to modify these views. The situation is the same except for the facts that the discontent is probably greater, for obvious reasons, and that Herr Hitler has consequently been able to give more concrete form to public manifestations of such discontent. The problem, however, remains the same. Personally, for what my opinion is worth, I think that, although there is great political discontent, no movement, whether reactionary or communistic, can be attempted with any chance of ultimate success in any part of Germany, including Bavaria, except as a result of economic distress. Should such economic distress lead to disturbances, it is equally impossible to

[5] In despatch No. 1377 of December 3, 1921 (C 22982/416/18), not printed.

prophesy the result.[6] So far as Bavaria is concerned, we have a population at least three-fourths strongly Conservative, and undoubtedly desiring a return to a monarchical form of government. That part of the population is, however, the one which suffers least; therefore, if and when disturbances occur, they are more likely to occur in what one may call the Socialistic part of Bavaria, and will probably take the form of a Red revolt. The result of suppressing this Red revolt may well be to strengthen the Conservative cause, and consequently be exactly the reverse of that which the promoters of the original movement desired. This was said a year ago and appears to me still to be true. In a lesser degree it applies to the whole of Germany.

[6] In despatch No. 174 of November 5, Mr. Seeds had written: '. . . there is no concealing the fact that the economic situation has now reached a pitch of acuteness which justifies serious apprehensions, even taking the extraordinary patience of the German character into consideration. The Socialist Party does not seem, any more than the Government, to have any definite policy for dealing with the economic catastrophe and it is impossible to guarantee that the people will not in despair have recourse to the advice of Herr Hitler's organisation which . . . enthusiastically called for direct action with the view to the appointment of a popular dictator.'

No. 306

Lord Hardinge (Paris) to the Marquess Curzon of Kedleston
(Received November 22)
No. 2660 [C 15934/6/18]

PARIS, *November 15, 1922*

Lord Hardinge of Penshurst presents his compliments to the Secretary of State for Foreign Affairs, and has the honour to transmit herewith a copy of a note from the Conference of Ambassadors to the German Embassy in Paris, dated the 17th November, respecting military control in Germany (institution of a Military Committee of Guarantee in Berlin).

ENCLOSURE IN No. 306

M. Poincaré to Dr. Mayer

PARIS, *le 17 novembre, 1922*

M. l'Ambassadeur,

En réponse à la note collective remise par les Gouvernements alliés le 29 septembre dernier,[1] le Gouvernement allemand a fait connaître, par lettre en date du 27 octobre,[2] qu'il 'prenait acte avec satisfaction du désir des Gouvernements alliés d'entretenir le plus tôt possible des relations normales avec le Gouvernement allemand et d'alléger les charges imposées à l'Allemagne par la Commission militaire interalliée de Contrôle'. Le

[1] See No. 277, n. 1.   [2] See No. 287, n. 2.

Gouvernement allemand ajoute qu' 'il est prêt à entrer aussitôt en négocia-tions avec les Puissances alliées au sujet de la proposition formulée par elles'; en faisant cette déclaration, il 'suppose que ces négociations ont pour but de préparer la limitation de contrôle dans la mesure prévue par l'article 213 du Traité de Versailles'.

En réponse à cette communication, j'ai l'honneur de prier votre Excellence de bien vouloir transmettre à son Gouvernement, au nom des Puissances signataires de la note du 29 septembre, la note dont le texte suit:

'Les Gouvernements alliés rappellent tout d'abord que leur note collective du 29 septembre, signalait solennellement à l'Allemagne le ralentissement considérable intervenu depuis plusieurs mois dans l'exécution des clauses militaires du traité, en raison du nombre élevé de questions laissées en suspens par le Gouvernement allemand et de l'obstruction sans cesse plus grave opposée aux organes locaux de la commission.

'Après avoir déclaré ne pouvoir admettre une pareille situation, les Gouvernements alliés signalaient au Gouvernement allemand les clauses, d'une importance spéciale, restées inexécutées et l'invitaient à faire toute diligence pour régler ces questions dans le minimum de temps.

'C'est seulement après avoir obtenu satisfaction sur ces divers points que les Gouvernements alliés envisageaient la possibilité d'alléger les charges imposées à l'Allemagne par la Commission militaire interalliée de Contrôle.

'Le silence observé par le Gouvernement allemand sur l'objet essentiel de la note collective du 29 septembre ne peut évidemment être interprété comme le résultat d'un oubli ou d'un malentendu. Les Gouvernements alliés sont donc obligés de considérer ce silence comme la manifestation de l'intention du Gouvernement allemand de ne pas aller plus loin dans l'exécution des clauses militaires du Traité de Versailles.

'Ils sont d'autant plus fondés à tirer semblable conclusion que, depuis le 29 septembre, le Gouvernement allemand n'a effectivement donné satis-faction à la Commission militaire interalliée de Contrôle sur aucun des points signalés par la note collective des Gouvernements alliés. Bien plus, les incidents de Stettin et de Passau, survenus le 17 juillet et le 24 octobre,[3] ont montré que l'obstruction opposée aux organes locaux de la Commission de Contrôle, loin de cesser, prenait un caractère de gravité intolérable; l'attitude négative adoptée par le Gouvernement allemand à l'égard des demandes formulées par la commission au sujet de ces incidents donne l'impression que ce Gouvernement désire bien plutôt priver celle-ci des facilités qui lui sont nécessaires pour faire exécuter les cinq stipulations essentielles visées dans la note du 29 septembre et dont il est question ci-dessus.

'En présence d'une pareille situation, les Gouvernements alliés se voient obligés de faire clairement comprendre au Gouvernement allemand que la Commission militaire interalliée de Contrôle restera en fonctions, avec ses effectifs actuels, tant que les conditions fixées par la note collective du 29 septembre ne seront pas exactement remplies.

[3] See Nos. 267 and 293.

'C'est seulement lorsqu'ils auront eu pleine satisfaction sur l'exécution de ces conditions et que, en outre, ils auront reçu l'assurance formelle de l'acceptation par le Gouvernement allemand du Comité militaire de Garantie défini par la lettre de la Conférence des Ambassadeurs du 14 avril 1922[4] que les Gouvernements alliés pourront substituer ce Comité de Garantie à la Commission militaire de Contrôle.

'Quant aux négociations éventuelles que le Gouvernement allemand paraît envisager, il y a lieu de faire observer dès maintenant que la seule question au sujet de laquelle les Gouvernements alliés soi[en]t prêts à négocier est celle des modifications de détail qui pourront être apportées, le cas échéant, à la constitution du Comité de Garantie, telle qu'elle est décrite dans la note alliée du 14 avril. Les Gouvernements alliés n'entendent entamer aucune négociation avec le Gouvernement allemand au sujet des cinq stipulations essentielles que précise leur note du 29 septembre, puisque les questions qui y sont visées sont entièrement de la compétence de la Commission de Contrôle. Les Gouvernements alliés se refuseront donc à l'avenir à recevoir du Gouvernement allemand, sinon par l'entremise des Commissions de Contrôle, aucune communication au sujet de l'exécution de ces cinq stipulations. Cette voie est, d'ailleurs, celle que le Gouvernement allemand a été invité à suivre par la lettre de la Conférence des Ambassadeurs en date du 16 novembre 1922.[5]

'En conséquence, les Gouvernements alliés font connaître au Gouvernement allemand que la réponse qu'il leur a adressée à la date du 27 octobre[2] ne peut être considérée par eux que comme sans objet, et qu'ils attendent pour le 10 décembre, au plus tard, une réponse complète et définitive à la note collective du 29 septembre.'

Veuillez, etc.,
POINCARÉ

[4] See No. 208, Enclosure.
[5] See No. 304, Enclosure. This letter was dated November 15.

No. 307

The Marquess Curzon of Kedleston to Lord Hardinge (Paris)
No. 438 Telegraphic: by bag [C 15400/6/18]

FOREIGN OFFICE, *November 17, 1922*

Your telegram No. 580 (of November 10th: liquidation of control in Germany).[1]

Point (a). All we had in mind was that conference should issue *reminder* to control commissions to continue to refer all German appeals to conference with least possible delay. Certainty that all such appeals will be referred with expedition appears to be essential now that allied governments

[1] No. 298.

are in future to refuse to entertain appeals direct from German government. We did not mean to imply that control commissions were delaying or preventing appeals.

Point (b). Object of this suggestion was to ensure that if no German appeals against control commissions' decisions are to be received direct by allied governments, then *legal* aspect of any appeal should be considered by British legal adviser (who is not present in Paris) before at least appeal was finally rejected. In the light of your observations, however, it does not appear necessary to secure a decision from the conference on this point, though in order to ensure that British legal adviser has an opportunity of expressing his views, Your Lordship will no doubt agree that it will be advisable in future and in view of new procedure to refer all appeals before rejection.

Naval control. Admiralty is being consulted.[2]

[2] In a letter (C 15400/6/18) of November 17, not printed.

No. 308

Lord D'Abernon (Berlin) to the Marquess Curzon of Kedleston
(Received November 23)
No. 890 [C 16000/6/18]

BERLIN, *November 18, 1922*

My Lord,

With reference to my telegram No. 206 of last night,[1] I have the honour to transmit herewith to your Lordship a translation of the note which I have received from the German Government in regard to the Stettin incident. It would appear that full satisfaction has been given.

This view is taken by the chief staff officer to General Sir F. Bingham, whom I have consulted on the subject, in General Bingham's absence on leave.

I have, etc.,
D'ABERNON

ENCLOSURE IN No. 308

Dr. Wirth to Lord D'Abernon

(Translation)

BERLIN, *November 16, 1922*

M. l'Ambassadeur,

With reference to the note of the 14th October[2] signed by the Ambassadors of Great Britain, France and Italy, the Belgian Minister and the Japanese Ambassador, I have the honour to state that the German Government are

[1] Not printed.   [2] No. 281, Enclosure.

prepared to comply with the demands which were made in the note of the Allied Governments of the 9th September arising out of the incidents which occurred on the inspection of the police building at Stettin by members of the Inter-Allied Military Commission of Control.

In consequence the following measures are being taken:—

1. The president of police at Stettin is being ordered to make the desired apology.
2. The responsible official (*Regierungsassessor Tincauzer*) is being relieved of his duties at once.
3. The police officials concerned are being punished for the attitude they adopted towards the members of the commission.
4. The two liaison officers employed on control work have already been recalled from Stettin.

I avail, etc.,
WIRTH

No. 309

Sir E. Crowe to the Marquess Curzon of Kedleston (Lausanne)[1]
No. 6 Telegraphic [C 15705/6/18]

Urgent   FOREIGN OFFICE, *November 21, 1922, 7.30 p.m.*

1. On November 23rd a question comes before Ambassadors' Conference on which an immediate decision is required and as matters of high policy are involved I request your Lordship's instructions.

2. There have been two particularly bad cases of late in which officers of Military Control Commission in Germany have been interfered with and mishandled in the discharge of their official duties. First was at Stettin last August[2] and there now seems a prospect of settlement though details are not yet available here. The second occurred quite recently at Passau[3] in Bavaria and was of a particularly outrageous kind, shots being actually fired at two allied inspecting officers who narrowly escaped death at the hands of the mob. Commission of Control at once demanded satisfaction but without result, the German government always pleading that they must consult the Bavarian government. Ambassadors' Conference took the matter up and endorsed the conditions demanded by General Nollet which include an immediate apology by the German government and the removal of the responsible officials.[4] If satisfaction was not given by November 24th Conference agreed in principle that some sort of penalty would have to be

---

[1] Lord Curzon was attending the Conference of Lausanne which had begun on November 20 (see Vol. XVIII, No. 209).
[2] See No. 267.
[3] See No. 293.
[4] See Nos. 267, 281, 293, and 301.

applied, Marshal Foch suggesting that this should take the form of a fine on the revenues of the occupied Rhineland, more particularly on those of the Palatinate as being part of Bavaria.

3. Proposed penalty may possibly prove (1) ineffective and (2) of doubtful expediency from point of view of offering pretext for intensification of undesirable French activities in Rhineland.

Another point for consideration is whether it is not perhaps unwise to waste our powder on this one incident, serious though it is, when there are so many other matters that are bound before very long to reach a stage where allies will be forced to resort to even more drastic sanctions, for example reparations, systematic failure to comply with disarmament clauses of the treaty, etc., etc.

4. If I may express my opinion it is that Passau incident was so outrageous that we ought to make it clear we will stand no nonsense from Germany over it, and deal with it separately and at once, provided we can hit upon an appropriate penalty that will have a really deterrent effect without leading to grave economic or more generally political difficulties for the allies. On this point I have asked Lord D'Abernon by telegraph to furnish his observations and any practical suggestions.[5]

5. Should Your Lordship approve, Lord Hardinge might be instructed to say that His Majesty's Government approve in principle a special sanction for the Stettin and Passau outrages, but that before agreeing to particular measures, they desire to await suggestions from Lord D'Abernon as to the most suitable penalties to be imposed in the circumstances.

6. Lord Hardinge might at the same time invite the Ambassadors' Conference carefully to consider the question whether there would be an advantage in holding back the application of such penalties until the moment arrives when Germany's systematic failure to execute the treaty will compel the allies to resort to more comprehensive sanctions over a wider field and possibly of a severer character, a point on which His Majesty's Government would be ready eventually to conform with the views of the majority in the conference.

7. A copy of the present telegram goes to Lord Hardinge by tonight's bag. May I suggest to save time that Your Lordship telegraph your instructions to him direct?

Repeated to Berlin No. 110.

[5] Foreign Office telegram No. 111 of November 21 which ran as follows: 'It seems essential that Germany should give satisfaction at once and that if she does not we must bring her to reason. We are averse to agreeing to anything which might tend ultimately to complicate the position in the Rhineland which is already sufficiently delicate: but unless you can think of some effective substitute for French proposal it may be difficult not to accept it.

'As matter is pressing please repeat your reply to Paris.'

No. 310

Lord Hardinge (Paris) to the Marquess Curzon of Kedleston
(Received November 22, 8.30 a.m.)
No. 614 Telegraphic: by bag [C 15917/336/18]

PARIS, *November 21, 1922*

I am reading your telegram No. 440 of 18th November[1] (Anti-allied demonstrations in the Rhineland) to mean that I am authorised to agree to French government's proposal contained in my despatch No. 2641,[2] that the German government are to be told that if they don't take satisfactory measures the allied authorities in the Rhineland will set up an organisation for regulating the circulation between the occupied territories and the rest of Germany.

[1] This ran: 'No objection to despatch of note by Conference [of Ambassadors] if your colleagues think it desirable in addition to action at Berlin in which H[is] M[ajesty's] Ambassador there has already been authorised to participate [see No. 284].' The proposal that the Conference of Ambassadors should address a note to the German Government had been made on November 4. This proposed note, however, differed from that which had been drafted by the Rhineland High Commission (see No. 284, Enclosure 2) in that it contained the specific threat indicated in this telegram.

[2] Of November 13 (C 15588/336/18), not printed.

No. 311

Lord D'Abernon (Berlin) to the Marquess Curzon of Kedleston
(Received November 25)
No. 895 [C 16084/144/18]

BERLIN, *November 21, 1922*

My Lord,

With reference to my despatches Nos. 871[1] and 881[2] of the 14th and 15th instant, I have the honour to report that a notice appeared in the press on Sunday to the effect that the Prussian Government had forbidden the existence in Prussia of the National Socialist German Labour Party (Hitler's organisation) and of any branch unions connected with it on the ground that that party infringes in several respects the law for the protection of the republic, especially in the fact that the party contains a storm detachment (*Sturmabteilung*), which, under the command of Dr. Adolf Hitler, in Munich alone has a strength of 7,000 men, is divided into companies, and is said to be armed.

At the same time the existence in Prussia is forbidden of various unions working under innocent-sounding local names, which are in fact a continuation of the forbidden Rossbach[3] organisation, and are partly militarily

[1] Not printed.   [2] No. 305.
[3] Gerhard Rossbach commanded a Freikorps from November, 1918 to January, 1920.

595

organised and are in possession of arms or have knowledge of hidden depots of arms.

I have, etc.,
D'ABERNON

No. 312

Lord Hardinge (Paris) to the Marquess Curzon of Kedleston
(Received November 22)
No. 2710 [C 15936/6437/18]

PARIS, <i>November 21, 1922</i>

My Lord,

I have the honour to acknowledge receipt of Your Lordship's despatch No. 3400 (C 14944/6437/18) of the 14th instant[1] transmitting copies of correspondence relative to the establishment of civil air traffic between Great Britain and Germany. I gather from this correspondence that Your Lordship does not consider that the Allied Governments have any means of compelling the German Government, after the 1st January next, to continue to extend to allied aircraft the facilities stipulated for in Articles 313/319 of the Treaty of Versailles. I am afraid that once the impotence of the Allied Governments in this matter is acknowledged, the German Government will not be slow to avail themselves of their liberty of action in order to bring pressure to bear upon the Allied Governments to remove the various restrictions, such as the 'nine rules'[2] and the prohibition against German aeroplanes flying over and landing in the Rhineland, which have been placed in the way of the development of German aerial navigation. It is likely, therefore, at an early date that the Allied Governments will be called upon to choose between French interests which require the maintenance of the restrictive measures which have been imposed in order to guarantee the security of France, and British interests which involve the development of British civil aviation across German territory. The intention of the German Government to keep their hands quite free seems to be borne out by the fact that the contract for the maintenance of aeronautical installations for the use of international civil aviation has not been signed (see my telegram No. 324 of June 14th paragraph 7),[3] and that the Rules 8 and 9 have not been promulgated by the German Government.

In the meanwhile I should be grateful for Your Lordship's views as to the advisability of inviting ex-enemy countries forthwith to adhere to the Air Convention.[4] Such a course, which I could propose to the Conference of Ambassadors, would I think be useful whatever its results might be. If any of the ex-enemy Governments, more especially Germany, agreed to join the Convention, the difficulties of the present situation would be greatly reduced.

---

[1] Not printed.   [2] See No. 208, Enclosure 1, Annex (A).
[3] No. 230.   [4] See Vol. I, No. 55, minute 1, and No. 66, Appendix F.

In the more likely event of their refusing to join, since by so doing they would be assuming the obligations imposed by the Convention without obtaining any corresponding benefits, the Allied Governments would at any rate know what to expect and be able to draw their conclusions accordingly. I would suggest, therefore, that I should be authorised to propose at an early meeting of the Conference that Germany, Austria, Hungary and Bulgaria should be invited to adhere forthwith to the Air Convention, and in the event of their refusing that they should be pressed to give their reasons.

The French are not likely to take the initiative in this matter, as they seem in Treaty questions generally and especially in aeronautical matters, to be adopting the attitude that it is no use any longer to try to obtain satisfaction from Germany by means of the Treaty. In fact I have the impression that they have little wish to avert deadlocks and that they seem rather to welcome them as proving the breakdown of the Treaty provisions which were intended to guarantee Allied interests and French security.

I have, etc.,
HARDINGE OF PENSHURST

No. 313

Lord D'Abernon (Berlin) to the Marquess Curzon of Kedleston
(Received November 23, 8.30 a.m.)
No. 209 Telegraphic [C 16006/6/18]

BERLIN, *November 22, 1922, 5.40 p.m.*

Your telegram No. 110.[1]

Stettin incident I regard as practically settled to our satisfaction.

Passau incident I regard as aggravated case for which full amends must be made. Chancellor's letters expressing regret are partial satisfaction but not sufficient. Punishment of responsible officers must be exacted. While difficulties between Central and Bavarian governments are real they do not justify indefinite delay and we are entitled to demand suitable punishment by a specified not too distant date. Further as regards military officer in command he could be punished without intervention of Bavarian government. This distinguishes his case from that of police.

Difficulty is to hit really culpable parties. Apart from many obvious objections to them, measures in Rhineland would be matter of indifference to Bavaria. It is nationalist spirit in South Bavaria which is responsible and punishment of Central democratic government or some distant part of Germany is rather agreeable to this section of opinion than otherwise. They would be delighted to see Berlin government humiliated. Reply to your telegram No. 111[2] as a sanction in the event of non-punishment of guilty officers I suggest suspension of all negotiations for modification of commission of control. This would make Bavaria responsible for prolonged maintenance of control, responsibility they would particularly dislike. It

---

[1] No. 309.   [2] See No. 309, n. 5.

would also have secondary effect of proving to Germany that any proposal to modify commission of control is a concession and a favour. It would thus indirectly facilitate subsequent negotiations.

Sent to Paris No. 21.

No. 314

Sir E. Crowe to Lord Hardinge (Paris)
No. 444 Telegraphic: by bag [C 15917/336/18]

FOREIGN OFFICE, *November 22, 1922, 7 p.m.*

Your telegram No. 614 (of November 21st).[1]

We had not realised that the French intention was to use these words to German government and it would be better that Your Excellency should not consent to anything beyond last paragraph of draft note from Rhineland commission to allied governments enclosure No. 2 to Foreign Office despatch to Berlin No. 1532[2] (see my despatch No. 3429 of November 16th).[3]

[1] No. 310.   [2] No. 284.   [3] Not printed.

No. 315

Lord D'Abernon (Berlin) to the Marquess Curzon of Kedleston
(Received November 23, 10.50 p.m.)
No. 213 Telegraphic [C 16010/725/18]

BERLIN, *November 23, 1922, 8 p.m.*

Ministry is now complete,[1] von Rosenberg[2] having accepted Ministry of Foreign Affairs. Ministerial appointment which excites most comment is that of Becker as Minister of Economics. Becker was Minister of Finance in Hesse and is regarded with some suspicion by the Left.

Most popular appointment is that of Oeser, well known writer in *Frankfürter Zeitung* as Minister of Interior.

[1] See No. 303. In his telegram No. 212 of November 22, Lord D'Abernon had reported that Dr. Cuno had taken over the direction of affairs.
[2] German Minister at Copenhagen.

No. 316

Consul-General Seeds (Munich) to the Marquess Curzon of Kedleston
(Received December 1)
No. 183 [C 16401/425/18]

MUNICH, *November 23, 1922*

My Lord,

With reference to my despatch No. 172 of the 2nd instant,[1] I have the honour to report that the Landtag concluded yesterday a discussion, initiated by a Socialist interpellation, respecting the activities of Dr. Hitler and his National Socialists.[2]

The Socialists had no difficulty in quoting instances of aggression and provocation on the part of Hitler's bands, as, for example, a case not long ago when the town of Coburg was terrorised for a whole day, and they could show that the attitude of the authorities to that organisation was one of benevolent neutrality, if not worse. Two days ago a large Hitler detachment obtained from the railway administration a special train for a visit to Regensburg, which might well have caused serious disturbances, and the journey was only frustrated at the last moment by the refusal of the railway workmen to allow the train to proceed.

Although Hitler's organisation has now been formally recognised by the numerous patriotic associations as one of themselves, the Landtag debate showed to an interesting extent how the professional politicians of the conservative parties are apprehensive that their prestige is being undermined by the more activist attitude of the Bavarian Mussolini. On the other hand, the speech of the Minister of Interior might almost be regarded as a defence of the National Socialists.

Dr. Schweyer said that the great development of that organisation was the inevitable result of the pressure on Germany from abroad. The National Socialists had now and then been too ready to use their life preservers against their opponents, but there was no ground for proceeding against the party, as such, under the laws for the protection of the republic. As to the action which Prussia had recently taken, he would only say that many much more dangerous movements had been allowed to pass unforbidden in that State. Bavaria was less timid, and her Government felt itself quite able to deal with any subversive movement from whatever side it might come. Much had been heard lately of 'Putsches', for which dates had even been fixed, but no attempts to upset law and order were made except by the parties of the Left through their exaggerated preventive measures, which might easily have caused disturbances. It was not fair to say that Hitler's men had always been responsible for such troubles as had occurred at Coburg and other places; provocation often came from the Socialist side. Every party had the right of free assembly; the tendency of both sides to arm themselves and break up their opponents' meetings must be stopped, and an ordinance would be

---

[1] Not printed. See, however, No. 305, Enclosure.   [2] See No. 311.

issued restricting the practice of carrying weapons of self-defence such as life preservers. This last announcement of Dr. Schweyer's is of little comfort to the Socialists, as under such an ordinance they will find themselves prosecuted for their attempts to form organised bodies of roughs to oppose to the National Socialist bands.

Simultaneously with the Landtag debate Herr Hitler held a public meeting, filled to overflowing, at which he pointed out how neither the politicians of the Right nor the parties of the Left could offer Germany any hopes of salvation. The class-conscious proletariat with their 'Internationals' were as futile as the capitalist Governments with their Parliaments. Therefore, down with everybody, except with the National Socialists, whose numbers in Bavaria he now estimated at already 50,000 in spite of their short existence.

Speaking to me yesterday on the subject, the Prime Minister admitted that Hitler had now become a power in the land. His adherents were to be found in all classes, and included, Dr. von Knilling feared, Communists of the more ruffianly rather than of the political sort, besides many genuine patriots. The Premier was firmly of opinion, however, that the troops and the Green police could be relied upon to take action against Hitler's men if called on to do so. As regards the schemes attributed to the National Socialists, his Excellency said that they were probably exaggerated; in any case they were based on riots to be started by the workmen, but the latter were being kept well under control by the Socialists, whose fears as to an imminent reactionary 'Putsch' were, he could assure me, amusingly genuine. He compared their mentality in this respect to that of the spy-hunting maniacs at the outbreak of the war in 1914.

I have, etc.,
WILLIAM SEEDS

No. 317

Lord Hardinge (Paris) to the Marquess Curzon of Kedleston
(Received November 25)
No. 2729 [C 16057/6/18]

PARIS, *November 24, 1922*

My Lord,

I have read with interest your Lordship's despatch No. 3441 of the 17th instant[1] enclosing a letter from the Admiralty regarding the withdrawal of the Naval Commission of Control in Germany. As stated in my telegram No. 580,[2] I do not consider it necessary to consult the Naval Commission of Control in order to enable the Allied Governments to form an opinion as to the present state of the execution of the naval clauses of the treaty. An examination of the list attached to the note to the German Government of the

---

[1] Not printed.   [2] No. 298.

14th April (enclosed in my despatch No. 938 of that date),[3] which gives the work at that time still waiting to be done, shows clearly that all this work has now been completed, with the exception of the following points:—

1. The drafting of regulations regarding the manufacture of naval material in State factories.
2. The final release of the remaining Diesel engines.
3. The destruction of certain machinery in the event of it being decided that the calibre of guns carried by the post-war German fleet shall be limited.
4. The destruction of surplus war material belonging to coastal fortifications.
5. The settlement of the French and Italian Governments' claim for further equipment for their light cruisers.[4]

Of these outstanding questions, the only one of any importance is the last, and there is no indication that the French and Italians desire to keep on the Naval Commission until the final completion of the work indicated under the other headings. On the other hand, as your Lordship points out in your letter to the Admiralty of the 17th November,[5] the French and Italian Governments do desire to keep on the Naval Commission of Control, in order to strengthen their position in regard to the equipment question. They are frankly suspicious of the attitude adopted by His Majesty's Government in this matter, and are afraid that, if their claim is approved by the arbitrator, His Majesty's Government, moved by a desire to safeguard some supposed British naval interest, will still not support, and might even obstruct, their efforts to enforce it. If, however, they could be reassured on this head, they would probably no longer cling to the Commission of Control as they do at present. For instance, if they felt certain that, in the event of the arbitrator deciding this question in favour of the Franco-Italian claim, His Majesty's Government would whole-heartedly support them in enforcing this claim upon the German Government, I believe that they might be induced to agree to the withdrawal of the Commission of Control as soon as the equipment question is actually referred to arbitration.

As soon therefore as an arbitrator is found and approved by the Conference of Ambassadors, I would propose that I should be authorised to invite M. Cambon and the Italian Ambassador to give an assurance, on behalf of their Governments, to accept the decision of the arbitrator, whatever it may be, and that I should, on my part, go further, and undertake that His Majesty's Government will support the Franco-Italian claim whole-heartedly in the event of the arbitrator deciding in its favour. In return for this assurance, I would invite the Conference of Ambassadors to agree to the immediate withdrawal of the Naval Commission of Control. I would be inclined to make no special provision for the work still remaining to be completed. It might be safely abandoned without endangering the interests of the Allied Governments, but, if my colleagues insisted on its completion,

[3] No. 208.   [4] See No. 285.   [5] See No. 307, n. 2.

I would suggest that it should be transferred to the Military Commission of Control, on the clear understanding that the latter should be given no increase of staff on that account. The principal work would be the destruction under headings 3 and 4. In withdrawing the Commission of Control, the German Government would be notified that the Allied Governments reserved their final decision with regard to the equipment question, and that they claimed a right to send a special inter-Allied body to take over any further equipment in the event of the Allied Governments deciding to demand it. If, as is possible, my French and Italian colleagues urged that the Naval Commission of Control ought to be kept in existence in order to give effect to the arbitrator's decision, should he decide in favour of the Franco-Italian claim, I would press the argument contained in paragraph 7 of your Lordship's letter to the Admiralty of the 17th November,[5] to the effect that the equipment question does not arise under the treaty, and is therefore really outside the sphere of the Naval Commission. If they still insisted, I would, as a compromise, suggest that the life of the Naval Commission should be preserved by the retention of one junior officer from each country, who would remain in Berlin until the arbitrator's decision was given.

As I understand that a certain amount of naval material cannot be disposed of until the equipment question is settled, and is being stored at Kiel in the name of the Commission of Control, it might, in any case, be necessary to keep on the Naval Commission in such a skeleton form, if only to look after this material. It would be clearly understood, however, that these three officers would not be expected to perform any other of the functions of the Naval Commission.

I should be grateful for your Lordship's views with regard to this proposal.

I have, etc.,

HARDINGE OF PENSHURST

No. 318

Lord Hardinge (Paris) to the Marquess Curzon of Kedleston
(Received November 27, 8.30 a.m.)
No. 621 Telegraphic: by bag [C 16117/6/18]

PARIS, *November 25, 1922*

My telegram No. 604, paragraph 5 of November 15th.[1]

The Conference of Ambassadors considered this morning Stettin and Passau incidents, now complicated by further incident in Ingolstadt,[2] also in Bavaria, where same British and French officers have been attacked (see my despatch No. 2746).[3]

As regards punishment of and apologies by military and local officials, correspondence from the commission of control (see my despatch No. 2748)[3]

---

[1] No. 302.   [2] On November 22.   [3] Of November 24, not printed.

shows that in case of Stettin incident German Government have given adequate satisfaction. In the case of Passau a telegram had just been received from the commission of control to the effect that the German government had agreed to remove military officer involved. As, however, they appear to have given no undertaking as regards local officials, Marshal Foch suggested that the conference of ambassadors should await the arrival of a further report from the commission of control and should at the next meeting on the 29th examine as to how far the satisfaction offered by the German government should be accepted in both cases.

As regards the apologies which the German government were to make to the commission of control, the conference of ambassadors agreed that the regrets which they expressed in their recent letter to the commission[4] were insufficient (see my despatch No. 2747).[3] Inasmuch as the government were rendered directly responsible by presence of officials, it was necessary and according to precedent that they should offer apologies as well as regrets.

On the conference taking up the question of possible penalties, the French submitted a detailed scheme for the levy of a million gold marks. As a guarantee for this sum the Rhineland High Commission would collect and hold a certain number of taxes or income derived from state property in the occupied territories, and in order that this seizure of local revenue should not damage the local population, only the surplus revenue would be seized which would otherwise be paid either to the central German government or to various German states. It was argued that such a fine would hit Bavaria as it would be guaranteed in part by the revenue of the Palatinate.

I stated that we feared that this scheme might prove ineffective and complicate the delicate situation already existing in the Rhineland, and communicated the substance of paragraph 3 of Lord D'Abernon's telegram No. 209.[5] At the same time I invited the conference to consider the desirability of holding back for the present application of penalties for reasons given in your telegram to me No. 1 from Lausanne.[6]

Monsieur Cambon on behalf of the French government, rejected Lord D'Abernon's proposal to postpone negotiations for withdrawal of the commission of control as insufficient and pointed out that in practice it would be impossible to keep on the commission of control merely on account of these incidents when once these gradually began to be forgotten. I am

[4] The letter, dated November 16, ran as follows: 'En réponse à la lettre que la Conférence des Ambassadeurs a transmise, le 13 novembre dernier à l'Ambassadeur d'Allemagne à Paris au sujet des incidents de Stettin et de Passau, le Gouvernement allemand a l'honneur de déclarer qu'il a déjà souligné à plusieurs reprises, à l'occasion d'incidents analogues, qu'il désapprouve de la manière la plus expresse de tels actes de violence. Il ne manque donc pas, en ce qui concerne les incidents de Stettin et de Passau, d'exprimer également ses regrets pour la manière d'agir de ressortissants allemands envers des membres de la Commission militaire interalliée de Contrôle qui étaient en train de s'exécuter de fonctions leur incombant en vertu du Traité de Paix.'

[5] No. 313.

[6] The text of this telegram was transmitted to the Foreign Office by Lord Curzon in Lausanne telegram No. 17 of November 22, not preserved in the Foreign Office Archives. See, however, No. 309.

inclined to agree with him. Likewise he disapproved of the idea of postponing until some indefinite date in the future the application of the penalty. The incidents were sufficiently serious to require immediate attention and the expiry of the time limit on the 24th could not be ignored.

My Italian colleague was without instructions, but considered personally that if a penalty becomes necessary it should be applied at once, nor could he think of any better than that proposed by the French.

I was accordingly urged to obtain authority from my government to accept the French scheme at the next meeting on the 29th instant, should the reports which will by then have reached us from the commission of control show that the application of a penalty is unavoidable.

The French and Italian governments being of opinion that immediate sanctions should in that case be imposed, and His Majesty's Government being at the same time in favour of action of some kind being taken to obtain satisfaction for the recent incidents, repeated again within the last few days at Ingoldstadt, I am of the opinion that, no other effective course having been proposed, we should accept at once the French proposal, leaving other measures of a more drastic nature to be decided if and when it becomes necessary to deal with a wider and more general evasion of the treaty of Versailles by Germany. I shall be grateful therefore for immediate instructions. In the meanwhile I am consulting Sir John Bradbury as to whether he sees any objection from the point of view of reparations to the imposition of a fine as proposed.

No mention was made of the penalty taking the form of a military occupation of Bavarian territory, which in any case my military adviser says is impracticable.

Repeated to Lausanne.

No. 319

Lord Hardinge (Paris) to the Marquess Curzon of Kedleston
(Received November 28, 8.30 a.m.)
No. 624 Telegraphic: by bag [C 16218/336/18]

PARIS, *November 25, 1922*

The Conference of Ambassadors met this morning under the chairmanship of M. Jules Cambon, the Belgian Ambassador being also present, and considered the following questions:—

1. I have already reported in my telegram No. 621 of today's date[1] the discussion on the recent attacks on allied officers at Stettin and Passau.

2. The conference agreed that representations should be made to the German government as proposed by the Rhineland High Commission[2] in regard to the organisation of anti-allied demonstrations in the Rhineland

[1] No. 318.   [2] See No. 284.

neutral zone. I stipulated however in accordance with Your Lordship's telegram No. 444 of November 22nd[3] that no mention should be made of the French proposal that in the event of the German government failing to give satisfaction, an organisation should be set up for regulating the circulation between the occupied Rhineland and the rest of Germany. It was understood however that there is nothing to prevent this proposal being submitted to, and possibly adopted by, the Rhineland High Commission.

. . .[4]. As Mr. Basset Moore is unable to undertake to arbitrate on the question of equipment of the light cruisers (see my telegram No. 581 of November 10th section 2),[5] I suggested that Mr. Bayne, the legal adviser attached to the American unofficial delegation of the reparation commission, should be invited to undertake the task. This proposal was adopted and Mr. Bayne is to be approached accordingly. . . .[4]

[3] No. 314.   [4] The section(s) omitted referred to other matters.
[5] No. 299.

No. 320

Sir E. Crowe to the Marquess Curzon of Kedleston (Lausanne)
No. 23 Telegraphic [C 16117/6/18]

FOREIGN OFFICE, *November 27, 1922, 7.30 p.m.*

Lord Hardinge's telegram No. 621.[1]

French proposal to levy a fine of one million gold marks seems objectionable. Sum proposed works out at about fifteen hundred million paper marks, and would if paid mean so much less available for reparation thus serving further to aggravate the reparation problem.

When the French occupied the five German towns in 1920,[2] His Majesty's Government objected, but it did make Germany comply with the allies' demands. It is a question whether the best way of obtaining compliance in the present case is not to occupy some German, preferably a Bavarian, town. This may not be an ideal solution: but we can suggest nothing more effective which would not be open to the same objections as the French proposals.

I would suggest for consideration following alternative:

Germany having not so far completely met the allied demands with regard to Passau within the time limit fixed and a fresh incident having meanwhile occurred at Ingolstadt,[3] fines (of which the actual amount would be left to the Ambassadors' Conference), should be inflicted upon the towns of Passau and Ingolstadt, together with the insistence on the demands already made, and in addition upon formal apology by the appropriate officials at Ingolstadt and by the Prime Minister of Bavaria. The fine would be high enough to

[1] No. 318.   [2] See Vol. IX, No. 298.
[3] See No. 318, n. 2. Reports of this incident were enclosed in Lord Hardinge's despatch No. 2751 of November 26 (C 16185/6/18), not printed.

make the two towns feel it and yet not so high as to make payment impossible without seriously affecting state budgets. If not paid within say a week (or such time as might be required by the military authorities for the necessary preparations) a Bavarian town, say Wurzburg, to be and remain occupied until complete satisfaction as demanded is obtained.

Owing to the absence of Lord Cavan,[4] and the D[irector] [of] M[ilitary] I[ntelligence],[5] I have not attempted in the short time available to get an official War Office opinion; but from private discussion I gather it is not certain that War Office would endorse the opinion reported in last paragraph of Lord Hardinge's telegram. In any case would it not be worthwhile to put above plan before the Ambassadors' Conference, as an alternative to the French proposal? Its possibilities could at least be explored.[6]

Copy sent to Lord Hardinge by bag.

---

[4] Commander in Chief at Aldershot.
[5] Major-General J. T. Burnett-Stuart.
[6] In his despatch No. 2810 of November 30 (C 16396/6/18), Lord Hardinge transmitted to the Foreign Office the view of his military attaché Major-General Sackville West, that the occupation of a Bavarian town was militarily impracticable.

No. 321

Lord D'Abernon (Berlin) to the Marquess Curzon of Kedleston
(Received November 28, 2 p.m.)

No. 217 Telegraphic [C 16252/6437/18]

BERLIN, *November 28, 1922, 12 noon*

Your telegram No. 113.[1]

German Government agree to extension to end of the year of period during which British civil aircraft are provisionally permitted to land at Cologne.

They point out however that no further extension of this period can be granted unless equal facilities shall meanwhile have been obtained for similar machines in occupied territory and they urge conclusion of a general air traffic convention as suggested in their note of October 29th (my despatch No. 835).[2]

---

[1] Of November 24, not printed.
[2] Of October 31 (C 15121/6437/18), not printed.

No. 322

The Marquess Curzon of Kedleston (Lausanne) to Lord Hardinge (Paris)
No. 2 Telegraphic [C 16260/6/18]

LAUSANNE, *November 28, 1922, 10.40 p.m.*

Foreign Office telegram of November 27th.[1]
Passau and Ingolstadt incidents.

I have no idea whether Sir E. Crowe's suggestion has been submitted to anyone at home. Idea of fines might be worthy of consideration and in the event of their not being paid, some physical guarantee would be required. But occupation of a Bavarian town over 100 miles, and between two and three hours by rail, from nearest point of allied occupation seems to me a very startling proposal and to create a highly dangerous precedent. You might however consult ambassadors' conference on possible alternatives to French plan.

Repeated to Foreign Office No. 48.

[1] No. 320.

No. 323

Lord Hardinge (Paris) to the Marquess Curzon of Kedleston
(Received November 29, 8.30 a.m.)
No. 626 Telegraphic: by bag [C 16257/6437/18]

PARIS, *November 28, 1922*

My despatches Nos. 2533 of October 30th[1] and 2710 of November 21st.[2]

In reply to enquiries made by the French government, the French High Commissioner in the Rhineland has furnished his government with a confidential report which has been shown to my Air Attaché regarding separate negotiations between His Majesty's Government and the German government, which would involve giving German aircraft the right to land in occupied territory, thus endangering, according to M. Tirard, the security of the armies of occupation and violating the decision of the supreme council of January 5th 1920,[3] and those of the conference of ambassadors of July 24th 1920 (see Lord Derby's telegram No. 862, section 6)[1] and of the 15th and 27th December 1920 (see my telegrams Nos. 1394 section 7,[1] and 1420, section 11)'.[4] M. Tirard explains that the Rhineland commission intends subsequently to submit the whole question to the conference of ambassadors.

In view of increasing difficulties which I foresee in protecting British aircraft by means of separate agreements against unfavourable treatment by the German government after the 1st January next, I would again urge that

[1] Not printed.   [2] No. 312.
[3] See Vol. II, No. 51, minute 7, and Appendix I.
[4] This section is not printed.

I should be authorised to propose to the conference of ambassadors (1) that it should invite the German government to adhere at once to the air convention[5] which on the one hand would give them the right to land in and fly over occupied territory, and on the other hand would protect allied aircraft against unfair discrimination (see article 2), and (2) that the conference should consider joint action to protect allied interests in the event of the German government refusing to adhere to the convention and thereby proving their intention to penalise allied aircraft.

[5] See No. 312, n. 4.

No. 324

Lord Hardinge (Paris) to the Marquess Curzon of Kedleston
(Received November 29)
No. 2782 [C 16273/6437/18]

PARIS, *November 28, 1922*

Lord Hardinge of Penshurst presents his compliments to the Secretary of State for Foreign Affairs, and has the honour to transmit herewith a copy of a note from the French Ministry for Foreign Affairs, dated the 22nd November, respecting civil air traffic between Great Britain and Germany.

ENCLOSURE IN No. 324

French Government to British Embassy, Paris

PARIS, *le 22 novembre, 1922*

Le Ministère des Affaires étrangères a l'honneur d'accuser réception de la note de l'Ambassade britannique, en date du 7 novembre 1922,[1] au sujet d'autorisations spéciales et temporaires que le Gouvernement britannique se propose d'accorder à l'Allemagne en vue de permettre à des aéronefs civils allemands de survoler l'Angleterre.

Le Ministère des Affaires étrangères prend note de cette information, qui concerne l'usage, par le Gouvernement britannique, d'une faculté inscrite en l'article 5 de la Convention aérienne. Il est persuadé que, dans l'esprit du Gouvernement britannique, ces autorisations, destinées à faciliter les services aériens entre la Grande-Bretagne et l'Allemagne, ne sauraient rendre possible et légitime le survol, par des avions allemands, de territoires situés sur le parcours Allemagne–Angleterre et actuellement interdits à l'aviation allemande, notamment le survol des territoires rhénans.

[1] Not traced in the Foreign Office archives.

No. 325

Report[1] communicated by Gen[eral] Morgan to Sir W. Tyrrell privately and confidentially

[*C 17141/3589/18*]

November 28, 1922

In the reports (No. D.A.G. 807 of 1st July, 1922 and No. D.A.G. 837 of 3rd August, 1922) which I submitted on the subject of the Prussian Police Law and of the *Reichsgesetz über die Schutzpolizei* I pointed out that an examination of those laws disclosed a plan to make the Schutzpolizei[2] (a) identical with the Reichsheer, (b) interchangeable with it, and (c) interchangeable with the police forces of the other German States. In those reports I based my conclusions chiefly, though not entirely, on such provisions of the laws as related to *Versorgung* or maintenance.

I have now made a further examination of the same question from the point of view of civil employment on retirement (the *Anwärterschaft*), retiring pensions (*Ruhegehalt*), reward for long service, insurance (*Versicherung*), grading, pay and promotion. I have also re-examined the provisions as to *Versorgung*. The results of this investigation are set out below.[3] They are based on an examination of a large number of post-war laws, including, in particular, the *Besoldungsgesetze*. My conclusions may be summarized in a sentence by saying that they establish the complete identity of the *Reichsheer* and the *Schutzpolizei* for all purposes. They are not two forces but one. Practically every law relating to the Reichsheer passed during the last two years applies to the Schutzpolizei and with such completeness that wherever the word *Soldaten* occurs one can read for it the words *Angehörige der Schutzpolizei*. The *Reichsheer* and the *Schutzpolizei* have been organised on the basis of what engineers called 'standardization of parts' in such a way that any unit, any officer or any man of the *Schutzpolizei* can be incorporated at a moment's notice in the *Reichsheer*—in fact, legally, financially and administratively, a *Schutzpolizeibeamte* is indistinguishable from a *Soldat*.[4]

---

[1] This report, a copy of which was received in the Foreign Office on December 13, was addressed to General Nollet. Commenting on minutes by Mr. Wigram (December 23) and Mr. Lampson (December 27), Sir E. Crowe stated (December 28): 'The position as regards General Morgan [British representative on the effectives sub-commission of the military control commission] is unsatisfactory. He is probably right, and his chief, General Bingham probably wrong, in his view of German schemes and proceedings. But he places himself theoretically in the wrong by reporting behind the back of his chief to us, in the obvious hope that we shall not readily accept the War Office views based on General Bingham's reports. There is of course intense jealousy of General Morgan (who is really a civilian lawyer) in the War Office, and his rather underhand proceedings unhappily rather justify it.

'We had better keep clear of this personal question, meanwhile keeping careful note of General Morgan's reports.'

[2] A note on the original runs: 'Whenever the term *Schutzpolizei* is used in this Report it refers to the "Green" (or semi-military) police and not to the "Blue" (i.e. the ordinary) Police.'

[3] Not here printed.

[4] A note on the original runs: 'The process by which this has been effected is by applying

to the Prussian Police by Prussian laws every provision which applies to the Reichsheer by Imperial laws and then passing a law (the *Reichsgesetz über die Schutzpolizei*) standardizing most of these provisions for the police of all the other States.'

No. 326

Lord Hardinge (Paris) to the Marquess Curzon of Kedleston
(Received December 1, 8.30 a.m.)
No. 632 Telegraphic: by bag [C 16364/6/18]

PARIS, *November 29, 1922*

My telegram No. 621 of November 25th.[1]

Final reports from the Commission of Control with regard to the Stettin, Passau and Ingolstadt incidents (see my despatches Nos. 2751[2] and 280[5])[3] were before the Conference today.

In the case of Stettin the German Government have not apologised, but the demands for penalties against the local authorities have been accepted though not yet enforced. The Commission of Control has now been authorised to enforce them on the lines proposed in its telegram enclosed in my despatch No. 2748 of November 24th.[4]

In the case of Passau and Ingolstadt no apologies have been made by the German Government and the satisfaction offered as regards the local authorities is incomplete in the case of Passau and non-existent in the case of Ingolstadt. The immediate application of penalties was accordingly considered to be necessary in order to prevent a continuance of these incidents, and in order to enable the Commission of Control to continue its work in Bavaria.

In view of the opinion expressed in Your Lordship's telegram from Lausanne No. 2,[5] I made no mention of the suggestion that a town in Bavaria should be occupied. I had, however, before the meeting sounded Marshal Foch, who discountenanced the proposal on military grounds as being impracticable, except with a very large force which could not be provided.

The French proposal for a fine accordingly held the field at the meeting, and no alternative being forthcoming and a solution being urgent, I felt compelled to accept it. In order, however, to make the penalty fall more strictly on the two guilty towns, I proposed that each of them should be called upon to pay to the Commission of Control 500,000 gold marks within ten days, failing which the Allied Governments would take steps to levy the money on the resources of the Bavarian Government in the Palatinate, and if these resources proved insufficient on other state revenues in the Rhineland. This was agreed to.

In order to avoid any misunderstandings, the Allied Governments are to be

---

[1] No. 318.　　　[2] See No. 320, n. 3.　　　[3] Of November 29, not printed.
[4] Not printed. See, however, No. 318.　　　　　　　　　　　　　[5] No. 322.

610

invited to instruct their Representatives on the Reparation Commission to authorise the German Government to pay this fine and not to place the amount to Germany's credit on the reparation account, as has been suggested in the case of the fine imposed for the illegal export of aeronautical material. This is necessary as Sir John Bradbury has informed me that from a strictly reparation point of view the levying of a fine on Germany at the present moment was inopportune and in contradiction with the policy of granting a moratorium to Germany, and that in any case the German Government would have to ask the consent of the Reparation Commission in order to pay such a fine. I informed the Conference of Sir John Bradbury's views, but my colleagues insisted, I think rightly, that if the rights and authority of the Allied Governments are to be asserted and their agents supported, some penalty must be imposed which will strike public imagination, and as a fine seems to be the only practicable form for such a penalty to take, the Allied Governments ought to adopt it on purely political grounds, which in this instance must outweigh any technical financial objections. I trust, therefore, that instructions in this sense may be conveyed to Sir John Bradbury.

Lastly it was decided that the Conference of Ambassadors, while continuing to insist upon those of its previous demands which have not yet been carried out, should in addition require that the Bavarian Prime Minister should apologise to the Commission of Control for the Passau and Ingolstadt incidents, and that such penalties as the Commission of Control should prescribe should be inflicted on the local authorities of Ingolstadt.

A Note is being addressed to the German Ambassador in the sense of these decisions.

I am forwarding copy of this correspondence to the British High Commissioner at Coblenz for his views as to the best means of levying the fine on Bavarian Government revenues in occupied territory, should such a course become necessary.

Repeated to Lausanne.

No. 327

Lord Hardinge (Paris) to the Marquess Curzon of Kedleston
(Received December 1, 8.30 a.m.)
No. 633 Telegraphic: by bag [C 16375/7361/18]

PARIS, *November 29, 1922*

The Conference of Ambassadors met this morning under the chairmanship of Monsieur J. Cambon, the Belgian Ambassador being also present, and considered the following questions:—

1. I have dealt separately in my telegram No. 632[1] with the discussion as to the penalty to be imposed on Germany on account of the attacks on Allied officers at Passau and Ingolstadt.

2. The American representative informed the Conference that Mr. Bayne[2]

---

[1] No. 326.   [2] See No. 319, section 4.

has accepted the invitation of the Conference to arbitrate the question of the equipment to be handed over by the German Government for the light cruisers attributed to the French and Italian Governments. It was arranged that the Secretariat General shall communicate the relevant papers to Mr. Bayne and that the latter shall be invited to apply to the Naval Advisers in the case of his requiring any further explanations or information. The Conference also agreed to refer to the Financial Committee the question of paying Mr. Bayne a fee for his services (c.f. my telegrams Nos. 581 of November 10th[3] section 2 and 624 of November 25th section 4).[2] I shall be glad to know what line the British member of the Financial Committee is to adopt with regard to this question, which as an act of justice should in my opinion be accepted.

I regret that not having received a reply to my despatch No. 2729 of the 24th[4] instant I was unable to take this opportunity to make to the Conference of Ambassadors the declaration such as I proposed in the above despatch. I trust however that I shall be authorised to do so at the next meeting.

3. I took the opportunity of Mr. Bayne's appointment[2] to suggest that he should be likewise invited to arbitrate on the question of the calibre of guns to be allowed to the German post-war fleet. Monsieur Cambon asked for time to consider this proposal, but the French Military authorities were opposed to it.

4. The German Government agreed in their Note of the 11th May 1921[5] to accept whatever rules the Allied Governments might lay down in order to assure the application of Article 198 of the Treaty which forbids the maintenance of military aircraft in Germany. Of the nine rules thus drawn up by the Allied Governments, Germany has only so far promulgated the first seven which define the difference between civil and military aircraft. They have never promulgated Rules 8 and 9[6] which deal with the registration of German aircraft and the maintenance of stocks of engines and spare parts. At my suggestion, the Conference decided formally to summon the German Government to promulgate these rules without further delay, since it is important that they should have publicly accepted them before the 1st January next when they claim to resume full liberty of action in the matter of aerial navigation.

. . .76. The German Government have appealed to the Reparation Commission against various decisions of the Military Commission of Control regarding the transformation of German war factories. The Reparation Commission (copy of whose letter[8] is enclosed in my despatch No. 2803 of today's date)[8] have forwarded these protests to the Conference of Ambassadors. It was decided that they should be sent to the Commissions of Control to deal with and that the Conference should return no answer to the German Government direct. . . .[7]

---

[3] No. 299.   [4] No. 317.

[5] See Vol. XVI, No. 619, n. 2.

[6] See No. 208, Enclosure 1, Annex (A).

[7] The section(s) omitted referred to other matters.   [8] Not printed.

Lord D'Abernon (Berlin) to the Marquess Curzon of Kedleston
(Received December 2)
No. 913 [C 16452/6/18]

BERLIN, *November 29, 1922*

My Lord,

In my despatch No. 839 of the 31st October[1] I had the honour to express the opinion that the reply of the German Government of the 27th October[2] in regard to the question of future control in Germany should not be construed as a refusal to accept the Allied proposals.

I have now the honour to transmit herewith a translation of the note which the German Ambassador in Paris has been instructed to hand to the Conference of Ambassadors, from which it will be seen that the German Government fully realise that the settlement of the 'five points'[3] is a preliminary condition to the establishment of the Committee of Guarantee. In view, however, of the fact that the investigation of the 'five points' will occupy a certain time, the desire was expressed that the negotiations in regard to the Committee of Guarantee should be commenced at once in order that no time should be lost once the settlement of the 'five points' was concluded.

I have, etc.,
D'ABERNON

ENCLOSURE IN No. 328

(Translation)   BERLIN, *November 28, 1922*

The German Ambassador in Paris has been instructed to address the following note to the Conference of Ambassadors:—

'The German Government, to whose notice I have brought the note of the 17th November,[4] have instructed me to communicate the following: It has never been the intention of the German Government to ignore the five outstanding points mentioned in the joint note of the Allied Governments of the 29th September.[5] As the German Government are well aware, the settlement of these points is a preliminary condition to the establishment of the proposed Guarantee Committee. Inasmuch as the investigation and settlement of the five points will take a certain time the German Government deemed it advisable to express their readiness to enter into negotiations with regard to the contemplated Guarantee Committee in advance. These negotiations should, however, as is evident from the text of the note of the 17th November, deal merely with the Guarantee Committee and not with the five points. The German Government will make the five points which they are at present investigating the subject of a further communication in due course.—ROSENBERG.'

[1] No. 289.   [2] See No. 287, n. 2.   [3] See No. 270, n. 5.
[4] No. 306, Enclosure.   [5] See No. 277, n. 1.

No. 329

The Marquess Curzon of Kedleston to Lord Hardinge (Paris)
No. 3577 [C 15999/3589/18]

FOREIGN OFFICE, *December 1, 1922*

My Lord,

With reference to my despatch No. 3118 of the 14th October,[1] I transmit to your Excellency herewith a copy of a letter from the War Office[2] on the subject of the German police.

2. I request that you will take an early opportunity of informing the Ambassadors' Conference that I have learned the opinion of the Military Control Commission[3] on the British memorandum[4] presumably submitted to the Military Committee of Versailles by your military adviser in accordance with the policy outlined in my despatch under reference.

3. Your Excellency should make it clear to the conference that this memorandum was put forward by His Majesty's Government only with the object of reaching conclusions which, whilst adequately safeguarding the interests of the Allied Governments themselves, would at the same time be such as to be capable of acceptance and of immediate execution by the German Government.

4. Provided that this object be borne in mind, His Majesty's Government have no desire to urge on the conference any particular form of proposals in regard to the question of the German police. You are, in these circumstances, authorised to suggest the issue by the conference of an immediate reference to the Versailles Military Committee, asking them to report whether they recommend any further concessions to the German Government in the matter of the police, and to set out in definite form their proposals for the reply to be addressed by the Military Commission of Control to the German Government's note of the 11th September.[5]

I am, etc.,

CURZON OF KEDLESTON

ENCLOSURE 2 IN No. 329

British Section, Allied Military Committee of Versailles, to War Office

22, *Rue d'Aguesseau, Paris, November 10, 1922*

In forwarding a copy of the remarks on the British memorandum on the organisation of the police in Germany by the Commission of Control in Germany, I venture to make the following comments:—

The remarks are, with the exception of General Bingham, those of the commission in unanimity. This being so, there is no chance of acceptance by the Allied Military Committee of Versailles of the memorandum.

---

[1] No. 280.   [2] Of November 23, not printed.
[3] See Enclosure 3, which was enclosed in the War Office letter of November 23 (see n. 2).
[4] No. 280, Enclosure 9.   [5] Not printed.

2. Marshal Foch personally said he viewed the reply of the Germans[6] to the note of the 29th September[7] as being most unsatisfactory, if not as one of point-blank refusal. This situation does not make it easy to press for concessions.

3. In view of General Nollet's remarks, I see no use in pressing further for a consideration of the British memorandum by the Allied Military Committee of Versailles.

4. I therefore suggest that I be authorised to ask Marshal Foch whether he is prepared to make any concessions whatever in the matter of the police, and, if so, what. In other words, to get him to put up some form of memorandum, and, then see whether the proposals would in any way meet the desires of His Majesty's Government.

C. SACKVILLE-WEST, *Major-General,*
British Representative, Allied Military
Committee of Versailles

ENCLOSURE 3 IN NO. 329

Opinion of the Inter-Allied Military Commission of Control on the British Memorandum[4] of the 13th October, 1922, regarding the Reorganisation of the German Police in conformity with the Treaty of Versailles and the Boulogne Note of June 1920[8]

(Translation)

PART I—*Eventual Practical Consequences of the Adoption of the Various Suggestions Contained in the Memorandum*

(A) The memorandum proposes—

The extension of the principle of State control ('étatisation'), particularly in the industrial centres of the Ruhr, of Bavaria and of Saxony;

The maintenance of police units (Hundertschaften) in the larger towns;

The maintenance of police reserves quartered in barracks;

An increase of the administrative service of the police;

The maintenance of certain echelons of administrative or executive staffs; these latter, particularly in the larger towns and in the neutral zone;

The maintenance of military cadres, except as regards the only military staffs existing in the police;

Finally, the establishment of twelve years' service.

(B) The sum of these proposals would result in still further centralising the police, and in placing it in a position to be eventually used as a military force; for—

1. The State control of the police is a means of centralising it and of making it depend more completely on the State, and consequently of giving it with greater certainty such and such a character.

The German Government realised this when, in adding a fresh category of police to the categories which existed in 1913, it wished to avoid a fusion of the two categories and the material and moral consequences of such a

---

[6] See No. 287, n. 2.   [7] See No. 277, n. 1.   [8] See Vol. VIII, No. 36, n. 4.

615

fusion. The German Government's obstinacy in wishing to save the principle of State control and to extend its application is more easily explained by this consideration than by the general condition of Germany.

Further, the inconvenience of giving State control any extension is all the more serious, since the maintenance of homogeneous groups undoubtedly produces facilities for military instruction and for mobilisation.

2. Military instruction should, in theory, be reduced to the individual use of weapons of war, but would this restriction, in practice, prohibit the training of groups which would facilitate the maintenance of the units constituted? One is all the more disinclined to believe this since the German Government has always tried to prove that the instruction of groups is essential in order to repress troubles (attacks on villages, houses, etc.), and that the Government is actually giving this instruction to the police.

3. Military instruction would, moreover, be considerably facilitated by the maintenance of the cadres of the existing units (nearly 5,000 officers of the former army and of the provisional Reichswehr), the preservation of which is proposed in the memorandum.

4. The staffs would be able to organise the mobilisation of police units.

5. Finally, as is pointed out in the annexed note, the system of twelve years' service results, in practice, in a much reduced average service, because of the juggling with the annual discharges, whether anticipated (8 per cent.) or normal ($\frac{1}{12}$).

The result would be the automatic formation of police reserves—without insisting, moreover, on the eventual military training of volunteers.

(C) To sum up, and while observing what is the real attitude of the German Government and of the German authorities towards the military clauses of the Treaty of Peace, one arrives at the conclusion that—

'The effective military power of Germany would increase in proportion to the special police organisations authorised, such as units, staffs, etc.'

PART II—*The Memorandum considered from the point of view of the Treaty of Peace and the Boulogne Note*

(D) The Peace Treaty (article 162) only authorises local and municipal police. It forbids the meeting of employees and officials with a view to military drill.

The Boulogne note only admitted the old police force, which was allowed to be increased, special emphasis being laid on:—

1. That this increase should not be allowed to take place, under any pretext, by the maintenance of police of a military nature.
2. That on no account should the police have, in any way, a central organisation.

Those are the principles which were laid down for the German Government.

(E) Police of a military nature have been maintained.[9]

As, as has been shown in the first part of this letter, it cannot be admitted that this force has been changed if the following exist: numerous constituted units and groups in the form of military cadres and staff offices, whatever their theoretical function may be. Lastly, the facilities for instruction and mobilisation.

(F) On the other hand, it has been shown that the central organization, forbidden by the Boulogne note and by the Peace Treaty, would be maintained by the extension of State control and by the retention of staff offices.

(G) In these circumstances, the commission consider that the suggestions contained in the British memorandum amount to modifications of the principles of the Treaty of Peace and the Boulogne note.

The commission would like to point out that, for the maintenance of order and the suppression of serious trouble, Germany has in her possession a central force which she seldom mentioned, i.e., the Reichswehr, numbering 100,000 men, which, in accordance with the clauses of the Treaty of Peace, has for its sole object of existence the keeping of order in the interior and policing the frontiers (article 160).

The commission would point out that the Reichswehr is unnecessarily well armed for such a rôle. Further, if the information supplied by the German Government is true, the population is disarmed, and therefore the police and the Reichswehr cannot be called upon to oppose forces armed in any way to the same extent as themselves.

Conclusion

In conclusion, the commission is of opinion—

1. That the concessions mentioned in the British memorandum, in practice, would result in increasing the German forces which could be used in a military manner.
2. That the British memorandum modifies the spirit of the Treaty of Peace and the Boulogne note.

The commission consider they are not in a position to give an opinion on the advisability of such modifications, which is beyond their competence and responsibilities.

The commission consider it their duty to emphasise the fact that it seems impossible, in the light of the experience of the last three years, to chance, without danger, seeing how the German Government has carried out its obligations imposed on it, concessions which are bound to increase the number and variety of deceits at present practiced.

Further, these concessions will increase the difficulties, which are at present very great, in controlling the police, and would reduce the guarantee which might be obtained by control. The commission further think it fit

[9] A note on the original runs: 'The Sicherheitspolizei have only changed their name into Schutzpolizei. A mere glance at this "Schupo" is sufficient to show that they are in no way similar to the police of London or Paris.'

to point out that that which has just been said regarding the police as a whole in Germany, applies with still more force when it comes to a question of the neutral zone, in which no military organisation or facilities for mobilisation of any sort should exist, in accordance with the clauses of the Treaty of Peace.

GENERAL NOLLET

No. 330

Lord Hardinge (Paris) to the Marquess Curzon of Kedleston
(Received December 4)
No. 2812 [C 16499/6/18]

PARIS, *December 2, 1922*

Lord Hardinge of Penshurst presents his compliments to the Secretary of State for Foreign Affairs, and has the honour to transmit herewith a copy of a note from the Conference of Ambassadors to the German Embassy in Paris, dated the 30th November, respecting attacks on members of the Commission of Control at Stettin,[1] Passau,[2] and Ingolstadt.[3]

(Copies sent to Lausanne, Berlin, Munich and Coblenz.)

ENCLOSURE IN No. 330

M. Poincaré to German Ambassador

PARIS, *le 30 novembre, 1922*

M. l'Ambassadeur,

Par leur déclaration en date du 13 novembre,[4] les Gouvernements alliés avaient invité le Gouvernement allemand à présenter ses excuses à la Commission militaire de Contrôle en raison de l'attitude de ses nationaux à l'égard des membres de cette commission lors des incidents de Stettin et de Passau.

Ces excuses devaient être adressées à la Commission militaire interalliée de Contrôle pour le 24 novembre, dernier délai.

A la même date, les réparations et sanctions déjà demandées par ladite commission ou par les Gouvernements alliés pour ces deux incidents devaient avoir été accordées.

En ce qui concerne le premier point, par lettre en date du 16 novembre,[5] le Gouvernement allemand, au lieu d'adresser ses excuses à la Commission militaire interalliée de Contrôle, s'est contenté de lui exprimer des regrets qui ne sauraient être considérés comme suffisants, la responsabilité de fonctionnaires allemands étant directement engagée dans ces incidents.

---

[1] See No. 267, n. 1.   [2] See No. 293, n. 1.   [3] See No. 318.
[4] See No. 301, Enclosure.   [5] See No. 308, Enclosure.

Sur ce point, les Gouvernements alliés doivent constater qu'ils n'ont pas obtenu satisfaction.

Au sujet de l'incident de Stettin, le Gouvernement allemand a pris, par sa note du 16 novembre, l'engagement de donner à la Commission militaire interalliée de Contrôle les satisfactions réclamées par les Gouvernements alliés.

Pour l'exécution de ces mesures, la Commission militaire interalliée de Contrôle fera connaître au Gouvernement allemand, d'une part, la forme suivant laquelle doivent être présentées les excuses du Polizeipräsident de Stettin; d'autre part, les garanties à donner par le Gouvernement allemand à la Commission militaire interalliée de Contrôle pour les deux autres sanctions.

Au sujet de l'incident de Passau, le Bourgmestre de Passau s'est borné à adresser au Comité de District de Munich ses regrets, alors que les Gouvernements alliés, appuyant la lettre du Général Nollet en date du [28] octobre,[6] avaient réclamé des excuses, en spécifiant que la forme et la date en seraient fixées ultérieurement, ainsi que les conditions dans lesquelles ces excuses devraient être publiées dans la presse.

Sur ce point, satisfaction n'a pas été donnée à la déclaration des Gouvernements alliés en date du 13 novembre.

En outre, par lettre du 23 novembre,[7] le Gouvernement allemand a fait connaître que, s'il avait relevé l'officier commandant le bataillon de Passau, par contre, il n'avait pas encore satisfait à la demande de révocation du fonctionnaire de police.

D'autre part, à la date du 22 novembre, un nouvel incident grave s'est produit à Ingolstadt.[3] Les deux officiers alliés, déjà victimes de l'incident de Passau, étaient à nouveau l'objet d'injures et de voies de fait de la part de la population, et empêchés par elle de remplir leur mission.

Prenant acte aussi bien de l'insuffisance des satisfactions accordées par le Gouvernement allemand au sujet des incidents de Stettin et de Passau que du nouvel incident d'Ingolstadt, et considérant qu'il est devenu indispensable de mettre fin à l'obstruction opposée par les autorités allemandes à l'exécution des clauses militaires du traité, comme de protéger les membres de la Commission militaire interalliée de Contrôle dans l'exercice de leurs fonctions, les Gouvernements alliés ont décidé que, avant le 10 décembre prochain:

1. Les satisfactions non encore accordées par le Gouvernement allemand et ci-dessus rappelées devront avoir été exécutées;
2. Les réparations ou sanctions qui seront indiquées au Gouvernement allemand par la Commission militaire interalliée de Contrôle au sujet de l'incident d'Ingolstadt devront avoir été exécutées;
3. Le Premier Ministre de Bavière devra adresser par écrit à la Commission militaire interalliée de Contrôle ses excuses pour les incidents de Passau et d'Ingolstadt;

[6] Not printed. See, however, No. 301, Enclosure.
[7] Not printed. See, however, No. 318.

4. Chacune des villes de Passau et d'Ingolstadt sera frappée d'une amende de 500,000 marks-or, qui devra être versée à la Commission militaire interalliée de Contrôle.

Dans le cas où ce payement ne serait pas effectué ou ne le serait que partiellement à la date fixée, les Gouvernements alliés prélèveraient à leur profit la somme de 1,000,000 de marks-or ou le complément de cette somme sur les ressources que le Gouvernement bavarois tire du Palatinat, ou, en cas d'insuffisances, sur telles autres ressources qu'ils désigneront dans les pays rhénans occupés.

J'ai l'honneur de prier votre Excellence de vouloir bien porter ce qui précède à la connaissance de son Gouvernement.

Veuillez, etc.,
POINCARÉ

No. 331

Lord Kilmarnock (Coblenz) to the Marquess Curzon of Kedleston
(Received December 11)
No. 338 [C 16969/899/18]

COBLENZ, December 4, 1922

My Lord,

With reference to my despatch No. 337 of the 4th December, 1922,[1] I have the honour to bring to your Lordship's attention a method of effecting a substantial reduction of the expenditure of the Rhineland High Commission.[2]

The High Commission has delegates in the chief towns of each 'Bezirk' and 'Kreis'. They are given certain duties by ordinance, and are also required to furnish the High Commission with information useful to guide it in arriving at its decisions. These delegates are of the same nationality as the troops occupying the army zone in question. In the British zone, therefore, the High Commission is represented by officials of British nationality in sufficient numbers to undertake the whole of the work there. Nevertheless, the French High Commissioner maintains a special French staff as his personal representatives in the British zone. It is not clear what duties are performed by these officials. I understand that my predecessor[3] was of opinion that the separate representation of the French High Commissioner was unnecessary, and that his opinion was shared by the General Officer Commanding, British Army of the Rhine.[4] The French High Commissioner has no separate representation in the other two zones, nor have the other High Commissioners separate representatives of their own. I am of opinion that

---

[1] Not printed. Lord Kilmarnock had stated that he was not at that time able to put forward any suggestions for further reductions in the expenditure of the British Department.
[2] See No. 259.
[3] Mr. M. A. Robertson.
[4] Lieutenant-General Sir A. Godley.

the whole of the staff referred to could be abolished without in any way affecting the work of the High Commission.

I have, etc.,

KILMARNOCK

No. 332

Lord Hardinge (Paris) to the Marquess Curzon of Kedleston
(Received December 8, 8.30 a.m.)

No. 644 Telegraphic: by bag [*C 16804/2285/18*]

PARIS, *December 6, 1922*

The Conference of Ambassadors met this morning under the chairmanship of Monsieur Jules Cambon, the Belgian Ambassador being also present, and considered the following questions:—

1. I again raised the question of inviting Mr. Bayne to arbitrate on the armament of the German post-war fleet (see my telegram No. 548 of October 26th section 2)[1] and after a certain amount of hesitation Monsieur Cambon agreed. Marshal Foch, however, pointed out that should the arbitrator decide that the treaty does not limit the calibre of the guns in the German post-war fleet, a contradiction will arise between the naval and military disarmament clauses of the Treaty of Versailles which, in his opinion, would endanger the execution of the treaty stipulations limiting the size of guns allowed to the German army. He insisted on this consideration being taken into account by the arbitrator and was supported in his contention by the Italian Ambassador. I agreed therefore that Marshal Foch should draw up a statement of his views which should be annexed to the papers to be submitted to the arbitrator. The Admiralty may consider it desirable to prepare a counter statement. If so, I will arrange to have it likewise annexed to the case.

In the meanwhile the United States Ambassador has undertaken to invite Mr. Bayne to undertake this further arbitration under the same conditions as that of the equipment of the light cruisers.

...[2]5. In dealing with the question of the equipment for the German light cruisers handed over to France and Italy, the Supreme Council decided on the 29th January 1921[3] that such of the equipment as does not fall under article 192 is to be put to Germany's credit on the reparation account. The Conference decided to invite the Reparation Commission to carry out this decision which had not been communicated to them at the time....[2]

---

[1] No. 285.
[2] The sections omitted referred to other matters.
[3] See Vol. XV, No. 11, Appendix 2.

No. 333

Lieut.-Colonel Ryan[1] *(Coblenz) to the Marquess Curzon of Kedleston*
(Received December 7, 10.45 p.m.)
No. 38 Telegraphic [C 16776/6/18]

COBLENZ, *December 7, 1922, 6.10 p.m.*

Conference of Ambassadors has telegraphed this morning requesting High Commission to draw up plan for seizure of sum of one million gold marks from resources of Bavarian government in Palatinate and to put this plan into execution on the receipt of information from control commission in Berlin that German government have not paid by the evening of December 10th fines imposed upon towns of Ingolstadt and Passau.[2]

To effect the required seizure, High Commission has this morning approved provisionally two ordinances, copies of which follow by bag.[3]

As in case of Rhineland sanctions of March 1921,[4] this proposed action of High Commission is outside the scope of Rhineland agreement. I presume I am authorised by His Majesty's Government to concur in High Commission taking action as proposed by Conference of Ambassadors.

[1] See No. 129, n. 1.   [2] See No. 330, Enclosure.
[3] Despatch No. 349 of December 8, not printed.
[4] See Vol. XV, No. 46, Appendix.

No. 334

The Marquess Curzon of Kedleston to Lord Hardinge (Paris)
No. 3662 [C 16057/6/18]

FOREIGN OFFICE, *December 8, 1922*

My Lord,

I am in complete agreement with the views expressed in your Excellency's despatch No. 2729 of the 24th November[1] respecting the liquidation of the Naval Control Commission. You are accordingly authorised immediately to invite the French and Italian representatives at the conference to give an assurance on behalf of their Governments to accept the decision of the arbitrator, whatever it may be. You may give a similar assurance on behalf of His Majesty's Government, and you may further undertake that, in the event of the arbitrator deciding in favour of the Franco-Italian claim, His Majesty's Government will join the French and Italian Governments in pressing for its admittance by the German Government. I have some hesitation in agreeing to your proposal that we should, in that contingency, promise our 'whole-hearted support' in 'enforcing' the claim. Such an assurance might be construed as committing His Majesty's Government to take part in any forcible measure which France and Italy might propose in

[1] No. 317.

order to coerce Germany, a liability which might prove a most embarrassing commitment.

2. In return for the assurance, in the form above authorised, you may invite the Ambassadors' Conference to agree to the immediate withdrawal of the Naval Commission of Control.

I am, etc.,
CURZON OF KEDLESTON

No. 335

Memorandum[1] *on German Breaches of the Treaty of Versailles*
[*C 16839/8315/18*]

FOREIGN OFFICE, *December 8, 1922*

1. *Military Articles*

Unjustified delay on the part of the German Government in—

(*a*) Completion of transformation of munition factories.

(*b*) Surrender of remainder of war material in excess of quantities allowed to the post-war army.

(*c*) Delivery of statistics of German armistice war material and of German war munition factory production required to estimate and check quantity of war material still unsurrendered by Germany.

(*d*) Passage of legislative and administrative measures necessary to ensure prohibition of import and export of war material and to bring recruiting system and army organisation into conformity with the treaty.

(*e*) Organisation of police on the lines laid down by the Military Control Commission.

2. *Military Control Commission Articles*

The treaty lays upon the German Government the duty of 'giving all necessary facilities for the accomplishment of the mission of the Military

---

[1] A copy of this memorandum was sent to Mr. Sargent on December 8 in a private letter of Mr. Wigram. Mr. Wigram commented: 'It seems to me that it is very desirable that any action taken by the Ambassadors' Conference on these matters should, in view of the present circumstances, be taken at the very earliest possible moment; for if the Brussels Conference [see No. 108] does come off, and if the Allies were to agree to make any concessions to the Germans in the matter of reparations it seems to me that there might be a possibility of getting all these matters settled. We shall have to exercise pressure on the Germans if they are to accept our views on these questions and we might embody them all in a sort of ultimatum which the Germans would have to accept in return for the allied reparation concessions.

'This is only my own idea, but you may think, in view of possible developments, it will be well that the Ambassadors' Conference should deal with these outstanding points quickly so that we may know where we are with the Allies in regard to them before the Brussels Conference meets.'

Control Commission'. The German Government have, however, allowed attacks to be made upon the personnel of the Military Control Commission at Stettin (East Prussia)[2] on the 17th July, 1922, at Passau (Bavaria)[3] on the 15th October, 1922, and at Ingoldstadt (Bavaria)[4] on the 22nd November, 1922. The German Government have, in addition, so far failed to make to the Military Control Commission the full satisfaction required by the commission for these incidents.[5]

3. *Articles 323 and 327. Forbidding Discrimination against Allied Shipping Companies in the German Emigration Traffic*

Under German law, all ships using German harbours for the purpose of carrying emigrants must have an emigration licence. After the war the German Government, by raising difficulty after difficulty, attempted to avoid granting licences to British steamship lines. Finally, however, they gave way under compulsion and granted the licences. Such a licence, however, can only be utilised for the carriage of German passengers through inland booking agents, who themselves hold a licence. The Cunard Company have applied for licences for thirty inland booking agents. The authorities of Magdeburg, who alone, so far, have communicated their decision in the matter to the company, have refused the application on the ground that the licences already granted to the agents of the German and American lines were sufficient to cover the necessities of the district. Lord D'Abernon was instructed on the 13th October, 1922,[6] to bring the case to the notice of the German Government, and to request them to have the decision of the Magdeburg authorities reversed.

No reply to these representations has yet been received.

[N.B.—On the 29th August, 1922, the German Government endeavoured, by a deliberate misrepresentation of facts, to conceal the erection at Eydtkuhnen (East Prussia) of certain control stations for the sanitary examination of foreign emigrants, and which it was believed that the German Government intended (in violation of article 322) to allow to be used in a manner discriminatory to British shipping lines. His Majesty's Government have therefore demanded further explanations.[7] The German Government have so far confined themselves to disclaiming any intention of evading their obligations under article 322.]

4. *Article 276. Forbidding Discriminatory Treatment of Allied Nationals*

The German Government, in defiance of this article of the treaty, have allowed the Bavarian Government and other German State Governments to

---

[2] See No. 267, n. 1.   [3] See No. 293, n. 1.
[4] See No. 318.   [5] See No. 330, Enclosure.
[6] In Foreign Office despatch No. 1500 (C 13876/2/18), not printed.
[7] See Lord D'Abernon's despatch No. 711 of September 4 (C 12748/2/18), not printed. A report by Mr. Dilley, H.M. Consul at Kovno, on a visit to Eydtkuhnen, is preserved at C 14602/2/18.

levy on Allied nationals residence fees which are not levied upon German nationals and which are higher in the case of Allied nationals than in the case of Austrian and Hungarian nationals. No satisfaction has been given to the various representations made to them on the matter.

5. *Article 296. Clearing Offices*

Article 296 provides that pre-war debts due to Allied nationals by German nationals shall be collected from the debtors through the clearing offices in the currency of the Allied Power concerned at the pre-war rate of exchange. Despite the terms of this article, the German Clearing Office Law of the 24th April, 1920, absolved (*a*) German nationals owing debts in marks from the treaty obligation to valorise their debts at the pre-war rate of exchange, and (*b*) German nationals owing debts in Allied currency from the obligation arising both under the treaty and the contract of paying more than a sum in marks corresponding to the value of the debt in marks at pre-war rates of exchange. The German Government have in fact themselves assumed financial responsibility for the payment to the Allied clearing offices of the difference between valorisation at present and at pre-war rates, thereby utilising, in violation of the treaty, sums which would otherwise have been available for the payment of the reparation debt.

6. *Article 296. Payment of Pre-War Debts by Saar Residents of German Nationality*

Under the Treaty of Versailles, Saar residents of German nationality are, like other German nationals, liable for the payment through the clearing offices of the pre-war debts owed by them to Allied nationals. Whilst, however, the German Government, in the case of ordinary German nationals, assume the financial responsibility for the payment to the Allied clearing offices of the difference between valorisation of pre-war debts at present and at pre-war rates, they refuse to do so in the case of Saar residents of German nationality upon the ground that the latter do not pay German taxes. The Saar Governing Commission are therefore faced (entirely owing to the fact that the German Clearing Office Law does not conform with the treaty) with the alternative of themselves assuming this financial responsibility or of compelling Saar residents of German nationality, unlike other German nationals, to bear the whole burden of their pre-war debts. The Saar Governing Commission would then be exposed to the criticism that residents of the Saar are, under the government of a League of Nations Commission, receiving worse treatment than that meted out to ordinary German nationals. In these circumstances the pre-war debts due by Saar residents of German nationality to Allied nationals have remained unpaid, and Allied nationals are out of pocket owing to the maintenance by the German Government of a Clearing Office Law which is not in conformity with the treaty.

No. 336

Lord Hardinge (Paris) to the Marquess Curzon of Kedleston (Lausanne)
(Received December 9, 11.50 p.m.)
No. 650 Telegraphic [C 16893/6/18]

PARIS, *December 9, 1922, 10.10 p.m.*

Addressed to Lausanne, repeated to Foreign Office No. 650. . . .[1] Repeated to Berlin and Munich.

My telegram No. 632 to Foreign Office.[2]

It seems probable that Germans will offer apology in place of Bavarian Prime Minister and that German government will offer to pay fine of a million gold marks in place of Passau and Ingolstadt.

Subject to any observations which His Majesty's representatives at Berlin and Munich may desire to offer, I would suggest for your consideration that conference of ambassadors should continue to insist on distinction between Central government and Bavarian government being maintained in this matter. In that case Rhineland High Commission should notwithstanding any offer to pay by Reich proceed to levy fine on revenues of Palatinate (if unpaid by two towns on December 10th) and conference of ambassadors should refuse to accept apologies of German government as a substitute for those of Bavarian Prime Minister.

As question will probably come up before conference of ambassadors at its next meeting on December 13th, I should be glad of your views before that date.

I have as yet no information to show whether Bavarian government are ready to fulfil requirements of conference of ambassadors as regards punishment of local authorities at Passau and Ingolstadt.

[1] The text is here uncertain.   [2] No. 326.

No. 337

Sir E. Crowe to the Marquess Curzon of Kedleston (Lausanne)
Unnumbered Telegraphic [C 16893/6/18]

Urgent   FOREIGN OFFICE, *December 10, 1922, 2.15 p.m.*

My telegram No. 64[1]

Prime Minister's opinion rather inclines to accepting German offer as on the whole reasonable. He argues that is both our practice and our interest to hold the Central government at Berlin responsible for any obligations to other Powers. I expressed the view that whilst this was clearly right as

[1] Of December 10. This referred to No. 336 and continued: '(Sanctions for Passau and Ingolstadt outrages). Prime Minister with whom I have discussed the matter is anxious before forming an opinion to have Your Lordship's views.'

general principle, the position taken up by Bavaria in her resistance on the one hand to the central authority in Berlin and in her systematic defiance, on the other, to the allies, fully justifies the latter in insisting on responsibility and penalties being imposed definitely on the real culprit. I therefore thought there was much to be said for upholding the demand for apology from Bavarian Prime Minister and punishment of local officials.

As regards the fine on the two Bavarian towns, it must be admitted that we cannot in any case prevent Berlin from arranging to recoup the municipal authorities from central government funds. Moreover any payment requires ultimately, the sanction of the Reparation Commission. These considerations might be adduced either for or against maintaining demand for payment by the towns themselves. They cut either way.

There remains the superior consideration that it is not our interest to let France strengthen her economic hold over the occupied provinces and from this point of view it would be an advantage to accept the German offer of payment, rather than *distrain* on the Rhineland revenues.

I submit above for Your Lordship's consideration in arriving at a decision.

No. 338

Sir E. Crowe to Lord Hardinge (Paris)
No. 451 Telegraphic [C 16893/6/18]

Urgent   FOREIGN OFFICE, *December 10, 1922, 5.15 p.m.*
Your telegram No. 650.[1]

At this afternoon's meeting of allied Prime Ministers[2] M. Poincaré himself raised the question and expressed himself in favour of moderation.

As a result of his discussion with the Prime Minister it has been decided to accept the substitution of the central authorities at Berlin for the Bavarian authorities both as regards the payment of the fines imposed upon the towns of Passau and Ingolstadt and as regards the apologies demanded from the Bavarian Prime Minister. This consent is however subject to the distinct understanding that apologies are forthcoming from the Central Government as regards all three incidents, at Stettin, Passau, and Ingolstadt and that the payment of the fine of one million gold marks is outside and in addition to reparation payments.

This does not of course affect the punishment of the local officials at Passau and Ingolstadt for which the Ambassadors' Conference has already asked, in so far as that demand has not already been complied with.

Repeated to Lausanne No. 66, Berlin No. 114, Munich No. 22 and Coblenz No. 30.

[1] No. 336.   [2] See No. 133.

No. 339

Sir E. Crowe to the Marquess Curzon of Kedleston (Lausanne)
No. 67 Telegraphic [C 16893/6/18]

Urgent   FOREIGN OFFICE, *December 10, 1922, 5.30 p.m.*
My telegram No. 64.[1]

M. Poincaré having himself brought the matter up at this afternoon's meeting and expressed himself in favour of moderation, my telegram No. 451[2] to Paris (just repeated to Your Lordship) has been despatched on the instructions of the Prime Minister authorising Lord Hardinge to accept the expected offer of the German government as foreshadowed in the first paragraph of his telegram No. 650.[3]

[1] See No. 337, n. 1.   [2] No. 338.   [3] No. 336.

No. 340

Lord Hardinge (Paris) to the Marquess Curzon of Kedleston
(Received December 12, 8.30 a.m.)
No. 653 Telegraphic: by bag [C 17053/6/18]

PARIS, *December 11, 1922*
Your telegram No. 451 of December 10th[1] (sanctions for Passau and Ingolstadt incidents).

The German government's reply which is being sent to you in my despatch No. 2893[2] proposes, as we foresaw, that the central government should pay the fine of one million gold marks and offer their apologies in lieu of those of the Bavarian Prime Minister. The British and French governments have agreed to accept this solution on condition that:—

(1) the German government apologise for all three incidents,

(2) that the fine is outside and in addition to reparation payment.

As regards the first of these conditions, the present note does indeed contain an apology by the German government. It is very grudging, but I propose to accept it as adequate. It may be worth while considering at the Conference of Ambassadors whether it would not be a good thing to publish the two sentences[3] in the German note which contain this apology.

As regards the second condition, the German note makes no claim that the

[1] No. 338.   [2] Of December 11, not printed.
[3] These ran: 'Tout d'abord, en ce qui concerne la critique des déclarations du Gouvernement allemand, les termes dans lesquels celui-ci a exprimé sa réprobation et ses regrets n'impliquaient pas seulement, d'après l'idée et l'intention du Gouvernement allemand, la reconnaissance, en l'espèce, d'une infraction au droit des gens, mais, de plus, des excuses formelles. Toutefois, afin d'éviter tout conflit à ce sujet, le Gouvernement allemand constate formellement que les déclarations, qu'il renouvelle ici, contiennent et impliquent l'expression de ses excuses.'

fine shall be included in reparations and it only remains therefore for the Reparation Commission to make the position clear by adopting a definite resolution on the subject. I gather from the British delegation that the Commission do not like doing this, but the decision of the two Prime Ministers must override their objections.

As regards the payment of the fine of one million gold marks, the German note does not say whether the money has actually been paid to the Commission of Control or is going to be in the near future. I shall propose to the Conference that it should insist upon the money being forthcoming without delay.

As regards the apology by the Bavarian Prime Minister, it seems rather undignified for the Conference of Ambassadors to have to sit down under the flat refusal of the German government to obtain such an apology, but I do not see how he can be forced to apologise and that was always a weak point in the scheme.

There still remains the punishment of, and the apologies by the various local officials. We can leave the case of Stettin to be settled by the Commission of Control direct. In the case of Passau and Ingolstadt, the German note is unsatisfactory. It is probable that the German government have been faced with a flat refusal from the Bavarian government to give complete satisfaction. In these circumstances, if we continue to insist upon our full demands as regards the local officials, we shall be driven to apply further penalties to the German government. I propose therefore to recommend to the Conference of Ambassadors not to press any further our demands for the punishment of the local officials.[4]

Repeated to Lausanne.

[4] In minutes of December 12 and 13, Sir E. Crowe advocated that the German Government should be pressed to remove the Burgomasters concerned, but the Prime Minister remained opposed to 'making any further conditions'.

No. 341

The Marquess Curzon of Kedleston to Lord Hardinge (Paris)
No. 3736 [C 17036/2285/18]

FOREIGN OFFICE, *December 13, 1922*

My Lord,

With reference to section 1 of your Excellency's telegram No. 644 of the 6th December,[1] I transmit to you herewith a copy of a letter from the Admiralty[2] enclosing a statement[3] which the Admiralty desire should be communicated

[1] No. 332. [2] Of December 11, not printed.
[3] This statement, dated December 11, 1922, ran:
'The question of the calibre and number of guns for German warships is purely a naval one and is affected by the naval clauses of the treaty alone.

'2. The naval clauses (articles 181–197) of the Treaty of Versailles, reducing the naval

to the person appointed to arbitrate on the question of the calibre of the guns to be mounted on the German post-war fleet.

2. I request that you will act in accordance with the wishes of the Admiralty.

I am, etc.,

CURZON OF KEDLESTON

armament of Germany to the lowest point consistent with her national safety, were drawn up to limit—

(1) The number of war-vessels (article 181).
(2) The personnel (article 183).
(3) The size of warships and restrict the replacement of old vessels (article 190).
(4) The number and calibre of guns in naval fortifications (article 196).

'And to prohibit submarines altogether (articles 181 and 196).

'3. It was not considered necessary to place a limitation on the number and size of naval guns (other than those in the naval fortifications, *vide* article 196), as they would be naturally limited by the number and tonnage of the warships in which they would be used.

'Had it been intended further to restrict the power of the German warships, such restrictions would obviously have been embodied in article 190.

'4. Their Lordships are therefore of opinion that the only restrictions imposed on the guns of German warships, both in regard to their size and number, lies in the number and calibre of guns which it is possible to mount in the warships allowed to Germany by the treaty and the necessary proportion for spares.

'Article 192 dealt with the large stock of naval war material in the hands of the Germans at the time of the armistice and, by this article, the present armoured ships were allowed to retain their armament for which they were designed, which includes a definite number of 11-inch guns.

'5. In regard to the fears expressed by Marshal Foch, their Lordships consider that article 213, by which Germany undertakes to give every facility for any investigations "by the League of Nations", provides a safeguard against the abuse of the limitations imposed by the naval clauses of the treaty.

'6. It is the view of the British Naval Staff that the greater the size of the gun (after a certain point is reached) mounted in a vessel of limited size the more that vessel adopts the attributes of a coast defence vessel, and is therefore in conformity with the spirit of the limitations imposed upon Germany by the naval clauses.

'7. Their Lordships are desirous of limiting the German navy as far as possible, but in doing so they are unable to deviate from a strict and impartial interpretation of the naval clauses of the treaty.'

No. 342

Lord Hardinge (Paris) to the Marquess Curzon of Kedleston
(Received December 16, 8.30 a.m.)
No. 663 Telegraphic: by bag [C 17237/6437/18]

PARIS, *December 15, 1922*

The Conference of Ambassadors met this morning under the chairmanship of Monsieur Jules Cambon, the Belgian Ambassador being also present, and considered the following questions:—

1. I proposed to the conference as authorised in Your Lordship's despatch

No. 3729,[1] to invite the German government to adhere to the air convention before the end of the year and to consider immediately what joint action could be taken by the allied governments to protect the interests of allied aircraft in Germany in the event of the German government refusing to adhere to this convention and thereby showing that they intend to penalise allied aircraft. The conference agreed to this course and it was likewise decided on my suggestion that similar invitations should be addressed to the Austrian, Hungarian and Bulgarian governments.

I thought it preferable at this morning's meeting not to complicate the discussion by raising the question of the maintenance of the British air service to Cologne,[2] but I will take an early opportunity of impressing upon the French government the importance which His Majesty's Government attach to this service.

Likewise I did not think it necessary to inform the conference[3] that negotiations with the German government for the conclusion of an Anglo-German air agreement have been suspended for the time being, since the existence of these negotiations has never been made known to the conference and as long as they come within the terms of the air convention, there is no reason why the conference should concern itself with them. On the other hand, I am notifying the suspension of these negotiations to the French government since they were originally informed in accordance with Your Lordship's despatch No. 3276 of October 31st[4] that His Majesty's Government intended to enter into negotiations with the German government on this subject.

My Air Attaché will, at the same time, endeavour to ascertain what steps, if any, the French government are taking for the maintenance after the 1st January next of their civil air traffic from Strassburg to Prague.

2. Mr. Bayne has accepted to arbitrate on the question of the calibre of guns which the German government are to be allowed for their post-war fleet (see my telegram No. 644 of December 6th section 1).[5] Having received Your Lordship's despatch No. 3736 of December 13th[6] before the meeting, I took the opportunity of informing the conference that the British Admiralty proposed to put in a statement in reply to that furnished by Marshal Foch on the effect that a decision on this question may have on the execution of the military clauses of the treaty of Versailles.

. . .[7]6. As authorised by Your Lordship's despatch No. 3662,[8] I assured the conference that if the arbitrator decides the question of the equipment for the French and Italian light cruisers against His Majesty's Government,

---

[1] Of December 13, not printed. See, however, No. 312. [2] See No. 321.

[3] In despatch No. 3729 of December 13 (see n. 1) Lord Curzon had instructed Lord Hardinge as follows: 'You should take this opportunity to inform the conference that . . . the commencement of negotiations with the German Government respecting the conclusion of an Anglo-German air agreement have been suspended, and in making this announcement, you should ask what steps, if any, the French Government are themselves taking for the maintenance after the 1st January, 1923, of their civil air traffic from Strassbourg to Prague.' [4] Not printed. [5] No. 332.

[6] No. 341. [7] The sections omitted referred to other matters. [8] No. 334.

the latter will nevertheless join with the French and Italian governments in pressing for its execution by the German government. I urged that in these circumstances the equipment question might be considered as settled 'en principe' and that therefore in accordance with the resolution adopted on July 17th (see my telegram No. 376 of July 17th section 8 (c))[9] the three Admirals should be withdrawn at once. As moreover since the date when that resolution was taken the work of the commission has been practically completed, I urged that the whole commission should now be wound up. The French and Italians showed considerable opposition to my proposal, but I eventually got them to agree that the conference should inform the Naval Commission forthwith that it intends to reduce the commission within a month to three officers, one from each country, who are to be kept on until the equipment question is finally disposed of. The commission is at the same time to be asked whether beside the equipment question and the question of the calibre of guns in the post-war German fleet, there are any questions of importance for the settlement of which the conference ought to provide. It is hoped that the Naval Commission's reply will be received in time for a definite decision to be taken at the next meeting.

. . .[7]11. In view of the decision of the allied Prime Ministers reported in Your Lordship's telegram No. 451 of December 10th,[10] the conference arranged to accept the million gold marks which have now been paid by the German government to the Commission of Control instead of levying the fine on the property of the Bavarian government in the occupied Rhineland. It was also decided to accept the apologies offered by the German government in their note of the 10th December (copy of which is enclosed in my despatch No. 2893)[11] as being presented equally on behalf of the Bavarian government and of the local authorities of Passau and Ingolstadt. The German government are to be asked to publish these apologies.

The conference recognised that if it is impossible for the allied governments to demand apologies from the Bavarian Prime Minister, it was still less possible for them to insist on apologies from the local officials and it was readily agreed therefore that although the regrets expressed by the local authorities are quite inadequate, the conference should not insist any further on this point.

I was unable to persuade the conference equally to drop its demands for the punishment of Bavarian local officials in so far as these demands have not been executed, although I pointed out that the central German government were hardly likely in the face of the Bavarian government's opposition to be able to give the satisfaction demanded by the conference. The conference ran the risk therefore of stultifying itself, as there could be no question of imposing further penalties on the German government as the punishment for the sins of the Bavarian government and thereby further humiliating the central government in the eyes of Bavaria. The Italian Ambassador was inclined to agree with me, but the French government view the matter

[9] This section is not printed.   [10] No. 338.
[11] Of December 11, not printed. See, however, No. 340.

perhaps in a somewhat different light as they are apt to welcome anything which increases the ill-feeling between Berlin and Munich in the hopes that it may foster the separatist spirit in South Germany.

Marshal Foch in reply submitted to the conference a telegram[12] from the Commission of Control urging that the conference should insist upon complete satisfaction being given to its demands in order to put a stop to the campaign which has been started in the German press on this subject. In view of this appeal to maintain the prestige of the commission, I acquiesced in the decision that the conference should continue to press for the proper punishment of the local officials. But on Marshal Foch proposing that failing satisfaction a further fine should be imposed on the German government, I made it clear that His Majesty's Government would be most unlikely to agree to such a course and I can only trust that it may be possible ultimately to find some compromise which will save the face both of the allied and German governments.

Copies of all recent reports from the Commission of Control on this subject are enclosed in my despatch No. 2928 of today's date.[13]

[12] A copy of this telegram was enclosed in Lord Hardinge's despatch No. 2928 of December 15, not printed. [13] Not printed (see n. 12).

No. 343

Sir E. Crowe to Lord Hardinge (Paris)
No. 455 Telegraphic: by bag [C 17053/6/18]

FOREIGN OFFICE, December 15, 1922

Your telegram No. 653 (of December 11th. Passau and Ingolstadt incidents).[1]

Delay in replying is regretted: it has been due to necessity of submitting matter to Prime Minister, who has now approved course of action proposed in last paragraph of your telegram.

Copy sent to Lord Curzon.

[1] No. 340.

No. 344

The Marquess Curzon of Kedleston to Lord Kilmarnock (Coblenz)
No. 348 [C 16969/899/18]

FOREIGN OFFICE, December 15, 1922

My Lord,

With reference to your despatch No. 338 of the 4th December,[1] I do not feel that, in the light of past experience, it would be politic to take up at the

[1] No. 331.

Ambassadors' Conference or with the French Government through His Majesty's Ambassador at Paris the question of the abolition of the special French officials in the British zone of occupation.

2. It would be well, however, if your Lordship could find an opportunity of taking the matter up unofficially and in a friendly way with M. Tirard, and ascertain whether he attaches any importance to the retention of these French officials. If not, he might be prepared to recommend their withdrawal.

I am, etc.,
CURZON OF KEDLESTON

No. 345

The Marquess Curzon of Kedleston to Mr. Phipps[1] *(Paris)*
No. 3783 [C 16742/553/18]

FOREIGN OFFICE, *December 18, 1922*

Sir,

With reference to section 9 of Lord Hardinge's telegram No. 535 of the 20th October,[2] I transmit to you herewith a copy of a despatch from the British representative on the Inter-Allied Rhineland High Commission[3] together with a copy of a memorandum, prepared in the Foreign Office, on the demolition and modification of certain railways in the occupied territory.[4]

2. It was perhaps unfortunate that the Ambassadors' Conference, on the 19th May, 1922, requested the German Government to stop the construction of these railways and to undertake the destruction of certain other railways[5] without formally requesting the Allied Governments to consult the Rhineland Commission, who are, under article 2 of the Rhineland Agreement, 'the supreme representatives of the Allied Powers in the occupied territory'. Further, it seems questionable whether, technically, the conference ought to have issued, on the 20th October, direct instructions to the Inter-Allied Railway Commission attached to the Inter-Allied High Command in the occupied territory.

3. When, therefore, the letter addressed by the Rhineland Commission to the Ambassadors' Conference on the 30th November[4] (enclosure to Lord Kilmarnock's despatch No. 340) comes before the conference, I request that you will propose that the conference should, in accordance with the established procedure, invite the Allied Governments represented on the Rhineland Commission to transmit to their representatives at Coblenz a copy of the German Government's note of the 16th November, 1922,[4] with the suggestion

[1] See No. 144, n. 1.   [2] This section is not printed.
[3] No. 340 of December 4 (C 16742/553/18), not printed.   [4] Not printed.
[5] This was reported in Lord Hardinge's telegram No. 278 of May 17, section 3 (not printed).

that (unless they see anything in the German note of the 16th November to modify the decision reached by the conference on the 17th May) they should ask the Allied High Command to arrange for the execution of the decision notified by the conference to the German Government[5] on the 19th May, 1922.

4. For convenience of reference, a printed copy of the German note of the 16th November is enclosed.[4]

I am, etc.,
CURZON OF KEDLESTON

No. 346

Mr. Phipps (Paris) to the Marquess Curzon of Kedleston
(Received December 22, 8.30 a.m.)

No. 676 Telegraphic: by bag [C 17545/2285/18]

PARIS, *December 21, 1922*

The Conference of Ambassadors met this morning under the chairmanship of Monsieur Jules Cambon and considered the following questions:—

1. Mr. Bayne having agreed to arbitrate the question of the calibre of guns to be used in the post-war German fleet (see Lord Hardinge's telegram No. 663, section 2 of December 1[5]th),[1] I proposed that the conference should take a definite decision with regard to the procedure to be followed in the case of this arbitration. It was agreed that the case should be submitted to Mr. Bayne in the same manner as it has been decided to submit the case of the equipment for the Italian and French cruisers (see Lord Hardinge's telegram No. 633, section 2, of November 29th)[2] and that the fee to be offered to Mr. Bayne shall cover this arbitration as well as that of the equipment question. In view of the anxiety expressed by Marshal Foch with regard to the reaction which the decision of the calibre question may have on the execution of the (? military[3]) clauses of the treaty (see Lord Hardinge's telegram No. 644, section 1, of December 6th),[4] it was agreed that if Mr. Bayne decided in favour of the British view, this decision shall only be put into force after the allied military committee of Versailles have had an opportunity of examining the question and after the Conference of Ambassadors has agreed as to the best means of reconciling the military and naval clauses of the treaty in order to safeguard the rights of the allied governments. Although this arrangement is likely to cause delay in settling the question and as such may not I am afraid be welcome to the Admiralty, I felt bound on political grounds to agree to it as being the price which we are paying for the French government's consent to submitting to arbitration the interpretation of this particular naval clause.

[1] No. 342.
[3] This word was added in the Foreign Office.
[2] No. 327.
[4] No. 332.

...⁵3. In order to meet the wishes of the naval inter-allied commission of control, the conference agreed, on the advice of the naval advisers, to leave, after the 15th January next, two officers from each country instead of one, as originally proposed in Lord Hardinge's telegram No. 663, section 6.¹ The naval advisers have drawn up a list of the maximum staff to be retained by these officers which includes administrative and accountant officers to be kept on until the 31st January. In the meanwhile, the commission of control is to be instructed to hand over to the military commission of control the task of supervising the factories and machines for the manufacture of guns of large calibre, pending a decision by the conference in regard to the armament of the post-war fleet. The naval inter-allied commission of control report that besides the equipment and the gun calibre question, the only other outstanding question of any importance is that of the allied ownership of certain naval material disposed of by the German government before the entry into force of the treaty. This question is likely to be settled by the conference in consultation with the reparation commission in the near future.

...⁵9. The conference had before it the memorandum enclosed in Lord Hardinge's despatch No. 2698 of November 20th⁶ regarding the export of illegal German war material to allied countries as corrected in accordance with the instructions contained in Your Lordship's despatch No. 3668 of December 8th.⁶ Monsieur Cambon asked, however, that the question might be adjourned as he wished further to consult the French Ministry of Commerce on the subject. I pressed for a speedy decision on this long outstanding question and will not fail to bring the matter up again at an early date....⁵

⁵ The sections omitted referred to other matters.   ⁶ Not printed.

No. 347

The Marquess Curzon of Kedleston to Mr. Phipps (Paris)
No. 3848 [C 17178/1188/18]

FOREIGN OFFICE, December 21, 1922

Sir,

With reference to my despatch No. 3583 of the 1st instant,¹ I transmit to you herewith copies of a despatch² and a telegram³ from His Majesty's Ambassador at Washington in regard to the reimbursement of the costs of the United States army of occupation in the Rhineland.

2. In my despatch No. 2289 of the 21st July last,⁴ Lord Hardinge was

¹ Not printed.   ² No. 1294 of November 24, not printed.
³ No. 485 of December 2 reporting that the State Department had asked for the date of the proposed meeting (see No. 296, n. 2) and the names of the Allied delegates.
⁴ No. 251.

instructed to explain to the French Government and to the Belgian and Italian representatives at Paris that, whilst, in the opinion of His Majesty's Government, the Allied delegates nominated to meet the representative of the United States Government should be the Allied delegates on the Reparation Commission, it was, for technical reasons, desirable that these delegates should be nominated as delegates of the Governments, and not in their capacity of members of the Reparation Commission.

3. In bringing the enclosed documents to the notice of the French Government and to that of your Belgian and Italian colleagues, I request that you will say that His Majesty's Government have nominated Sir John Bradbury to act as their representative at the meetings with the representative of the United States Government. You should also suggest that a joint notification should be made to the United States Government concerning the date on which the proposed meeting in Paris can conveniently take place and the names of the delegates who will represent the Allied Powers thereat.

I am, etc.,

CURZON OF KEDLESTON

No. 348

Lord D'Abernon (Berlin) to the Marquess Curzon of Kedleston
(Received December 30)
No. 972 [C 17867/725/18]

BERLIN, *December 23, 1922*

My Lord,

I have the honour to report that Freiherr von Maltzan has now been appointed Secretary of State for Foreign Affairs, and has already taken over from Herr von Haniel.

Freiherr von Maltzan has been appointed, notwithstanding a certain hostility felt towards him by President Ebert—a hostility of long standing which originated in personal circumstances years ago, and was aggravated by divergences respecting the Treaty of Rapallo.[1]

Freiherr von Maltzan appears to have been appointed by the German Government for two reasons: first, because there was nobody else who appeared at all comparable in the matter of ability and intelligence; secondly, because Maltzan is well in with the Social Democratic Party and the Independent Socialist Party; the Cuno Government has, to some extent, made its peace with the Left by this appointment.

Compared with Herr von Haniel, Freiherr von Maltzan will be found quicker and more energetic, but probably less reliable and stable. His central idea has unquestionably been close agreement between Germany and

---

[1] See Vol. XIX, No. 75, n. 1.

Russia; a combination to which he would like to add England. But I imagine that he is essentially opportunist, so that he will not allow predilections or prejudices to stand in the way of any policy which he considers advantageous for the moment to Germany, and not detrimental to himself.

I should add that I have always found Freiherr von Maltzan extremely ready to give all the information in his power, and, with the exception of the Rapallo incident, anxious not to offend English susceptibilities.

I have, etc.,
D'ABERNON

No. 349

Mr. Phipps (Paris) to the Marquess Curzon of Kedleston
(Received December 26)
No. 2987 [C 17588/6/18]

PARIS, *December 23, 1922*

My Lord,

I have the honour to inform Your Lordship that the German Chargé d'Affaires called on me this morning and handed to me a copy of the communication, enclosed herein,[1] which is being addressed by him to the Conference of Ambassadors respecting the incidents at Stettin, Passau and Ingolstadt.[2]

I took advantage of Herr von Hoesch's visit to urge that the German Government should take all possible steps to comply with the sanctions imposed by the Conference of Ambassadors on the police officials responsible for the incidents in the two last-named places. I pointed out that a speedy compliance with those demands would not only produce a good effect in England but would render a recurrence of such incidents much less probable in the future. Herr von Hoesch expatiated upon what he described as the manifest desire of the French Government to stir up trouble between the Reich and Bavaria, but I gave him no encouragement to continue that line of argument.

I have, etc.,
ERIC PHIPPS

[1] This ran: 'Le Gouvernement a exprimé ses excuses en exerçant le droit de représentation qui lui est imparti dans le règlement des Affaires Etrangères pour toutes les parties du Reich, de sorte que, ainsi que la note du 10 décembre [see No. 340] l'a déjà fait remarquer, il ne reste pas de place pour des excuses particulières de la part de la Bavière; les excuses exprimées par le Gouvernement allemand valent aussi pour la Bavière.'

[2] See Nos. 338 and 339.

No. 350

Mr. Phipps (Paris) to the Marquess Curzon of Kedleston
(Received December 28)
No. 2993 [*C 17743/336/18*]

PARIS, *December 26, 1922*

My Lord,

I have the honour to transmit, herewith, copy of the Note[1] which I have received from the French Government in reply to the enquiry I addressed to them on receipt of Your Lordship's despatch No. 3261 (C 14495/336/18) of the 30th October[2] regarding the reply which in the opinion of the French Government ought to be returned to the Note[3] of the German Ambassador in London requesting the cancellation of the decree of the Rhineland High Commission whereby the sentence passed in the German Courts against Herr Smeets has been suspended. Your Lordship will observe that the French Government, in reply to a similar Note addressed to them by the German Ambassador here, have, in accordance with their usual practice, stated that the Note would be transmitted to the Rhineland High Commission, since this body is the supreme representative of the Allied Governments in the occupied territories.

The German Ambassador having, however, subsequently raised the question in conversation with the President of the Council, the latter has decided to return a reasoned reply to the arguments advanced by the German Government. The French Government now communicate for the observations of His Majesty's Government the draft of the Note[1] which they propose in these circumstances to address to the German Ambassador. I shall be glad to be informed of what reply I should return to the French Government.

I am forwarding copy of this despatch and previous correspondence to Lord Kilmarnock.

I have, etc.,
ERIC PHIPPS

[1] Not printed.   [2] No. 288.   [3] Of October 20, not printed.

No. 351

The Marquess of Crewe (Paris)[1] to the Marquess Curzon of Kedleston
(Received January 1, 1923)
No. 3026 [*C 12/12/18*]

PARIS, *December 30, 1922*

The Marquess of Crewe presents his compliments to the Secretary of State for Foreign Affairs, and has the honour to transmit herewith a copy of a note from the German Embassy to the Conference of Ambassadors, dated

[1] See No. 144, n. 1.

the 10th December, 1922, respecting the execution of the military clauses of the Treaty of Versailles.

ENCLOSURE IN No. 351

German Embassy to the Conference of Ambassadors[2]

PARIS, *le 10 décembre, 1922*

M. le Président,

Je suis chargé et j'ai l'honneur de faire connaître à votre Excellence ce qui suit :

Dans la note collective des Gouvernements alliés du 29 septembre dernier[3] et dans la lettre de la Conférence des Ambassadeurs du 17 novembre dernier,[4] le Gouvernement allemand a été invité à donner une réponse complète et définitive quant à l'exécution des dispositions militaires du Traité de Versailles.

La lettre du 17 novembre fit savoir simultanément que la réponse était attendue au plus tard pour le 10 décembre. A cette occasion, la plus grande importance a été attachée aux cinq points suivants :

1. Réorganisation de la police (article 162 et décision de la Conférence de Boulogne de juin 1920);
2. Transformation des usines (article 168);
3. Livraison du reliquat du matériel non autorisé (article 169);
4. Livraison des documents relatifs aux existants en matériel de guerre allemand à l'époque de l'armistice et aux productions des usines allemandes pendant la guerre et après l'armistice (article 206, alinéa 2, et article 208, alinéa 4);
5. Promulgation de textes légaux (législatifs ou administratifs suivant le cas) nécessaires en vue de :
   - (*a*) Interdire effectivement les importations et exportations de matériel de guerre (article 211 relativement à l'article 170);
   - (*b*) Mettre le recrutement et l'organisation de l'armée en harmonie avec les clauses militaires du Traité de Versailles (article 211 relativement aux articles 160, 161, 173, 174, 175 et 178), notamment en ce qui concerne l'abrogation des mesures diverses qui sont encore prévues actuellement et qui se rapportent à la mobilisation.

Le Gouvernement allemand a l'honneur de répondre ce qui suit :

Les Gouvernements alliés partent de l'opinion que depuis plusieurs mois un ralentissement serait intervenu dans l'exécution des clauses militaires du Traité de Versailles. Le Gouvernement allemand ne saurait partager cette manière de voir. Il est vrai que les progrès du désarmement réalisés dans ces derniers mois ne sont pas très sensibles. Mais la raison exclusive en est

---

[2] As reported in Paris telegram No. 45 of January 13, the Conference of Ambassadors considered this note on January 13, 1923.

[3] See No. 277, n. 1.

[4] No. 306, Enclosure.

que le désarmement de l'Allemagne est terminé, et ce non seulement dans le cadre du Traité de Versailles, mais encore au delà de ce cadre suivant l'extension des clauses militaires de ce traité en vertu de l'ultimatum de Londres. L'Allemagne peut faire valoir en sa faveur d'avoir exécuté le désarmement qui lui a été imposé dans une telle mesure et avec une telle rapidité que non seulement l'histoire le considérera comme un travail immense, mais encore qu'il constitue dans l'esprit et la lettre du Traité de Versailles l'exécution intégrale des dispositions de ce traité.

Le Gouvernement allemand n'a pas non plus laissé en suspens un nombre élevé de questions, comme l'estime la Conférence des Ambassadeurs. Au contraire, il s'est uniquement élevé auprès des Gouvernements alliés contre certaines exigences formulées par les Commissions interalliées de Contrôle, exigences qu'il considérait comme non fondées; il a prié les Gouvernements alliés de se prononcer sur les questions, ce qui n'a pas eu lieu jusqu'ici. C'est pourquoi il ne peut être question d'obstruction de la part d'organes allemands subordonnés; dans le cas où les autorités allemandes, conformément à l'instruction qu'ils ont reçue de s'en tenir aux clauses du Traité de Versailles, n'ont pas donné suite et n'ont pas pu donner suite aux exigences, il s'agit, en fait, exclusivement de questions en litige, au sujet desquelles une décision définitive n'avait pas été intervenus. Si des autorités locales devaient avoir outrepassé ces ordres et si une obstruction devait avoir eu lieu, contrairement aux lois allemandes et aux instructions du Gouvernement, le Gouvernement allemand prierait de vouloir bien lui communiquer les cas et, dès à présent, il se déclare prêt à prendre les mesures qui s'imposent pour remédier à de telles résistances.

En tant que les demandes principales, réunies par les Gouvernements alliés en cinq points, sont restés en suspens, la raison en est qu'elles ont pour objet des questions qui sont reliées étroitement à des nécessités vitales de la vie économique allemande ainsi qu'avec le maintien de la sécurité et de l'ordre dans le territoire du Reich. Sous ce rapport, le Gouvernement allemand doit faire remarquer qu'en présence de la situation du ravitaillement, devenue extraordinairement difficile, le peuple allemand se trouvera dans les mois à venir en présence de difficultés de politique intérieure, dont les effets ne peuvent nullement être appréciés à l'heure actuelle et qui nécessiteront d'une part de préserver la vie économique allemande de nouvelles et graves perturbations, d'autre part de ménager des moyens encore disponibles en vue du maintien d'une vie économique et politique régulière.

Si le Gouvernement allemand veut résoudre le problème fondamental dont dépend l'assainissement non seulement de l'Allemagne mais encore de l'Europe, savoir le problème des réparations, il doit réunir toutes les forces économiques de l'Allemagne. La majoration de la production est en l'occurrence la tâche la plus importante. Elle ne saurait être réalisée dans le cas où des objets indispensables à l'équipement des usines seraient détruits et que cette destruction provoquerait, au delà des cas concrets, l'insécurité de toute la production. C'est ainsi qu'il s'agit, en ce qui concerne les points encore en litige sous le titre 'Transformations des Usines' d'objets indispensables tout aussi bien à la production industrielle qu'indirectement aussi la production agricole; il faudrait donc, en cas de destruction, procéder sans retard à leur nouvelle fabrication. La conséquence en serait que l'industrie, au lieu de pouvoir se vouer à des tâches purement productives, devrait tout d'abord s'appliquer à le reconstruction des moyens accessoires indispensables à la production proprement dite. Le Gouvernement allemand lui-même a le plus grand intérêt à la réglementation de ces questions pour pouvoir passer enfin de l'activité improductive de la destruction au travail positif de la reconstitution de la vie économique.

Pour autant donc que les intérêts économiques entrent en considération pour les cinq points, le Gouvernement allemand les a traités dans l'Annexe I[5] dans l'ordre des différents points.

Au sujet des questions purement militaires, le Gouvernement allemand se place sur le point de vue, déjà exposé antérieurement à différentes reprises, que dans l'exécution des clauses militaires du Traité de Versailles il est allé loin au delà de ce qui pouvait être réclamé en vertu du texte de ce traité. Mais en ce qui concerne ces questions, il est prêt à faire preuve d'un esprit très large de conciliation, étant donné qu'il s'efforce lui-même de faire conclure le fonctionnement des Commissions interalliées de Contrôle.

Dans l'Annexe II,[5] le Gouvernement allemand a exposé les questions militaires non encore réglées et il a traité tous les cas isolés soulevés jusqu'ici par les Commissions interalliées de Contrôle pour informer la Conférence des Ambassadeurs de ses raisons et pour lui fournir l'occasion d'apprécier ces raisons aussi dans leurs détails.

Si les Gouvernements alliés devaient estimer que l'exposé de cette annexe contient encore des lacunes, le Gouvernement allemand serait très désireux de recevoir à ce sujet des explications étendues et complètes. Mais il est convaincu qu'après examen de toute la documentation les Gouvernements alliés reconnaîtront que le Gouvernement allemand n'essaye d'éluder d'aucune manière les dispositions du Traité de Versailles, mais qu'il a fait et qu'il fait tout ce qui est de son pouvoir pour les exécuter loyalement.

Veuillez, etc.,

DR. MAYER

[5] Not printed.

No. 352

The Marquess of Crewe (Paris) to the Marquess Curzon of Kedleston
(Received January 1)
No. 3030 [C 13/13/18]

PARIS, *December 30, 1922*

My Lord,

With reference to my despatch No. 30[6]7 of yesterday's date[1] I have the honour to transmit to Your Lordship, herewith, the text of a note[2] which will

[1] Not printed.   [2] Not printed. See, however, Nos. 324 and 342.

be addressed today to the German Embassy, announcing the intention of the Allied Governments to continue for the present the running of their air services in Germany.

It is just possible that the Italian Embassy may refuse to agree to the terms of this note and in that case it will be addressed to the German Embassy on behalf of His Majesty's Government and that of France alone.

I have, etc.,
CREWE

CHAPTER V

Russia

March 22–December 31, 1921

No. 353

Sir A. Geddes[1] (Washington) to Earl Curzon (Received April 4)
No. 274 [N 4088/5/38]

WASHINGTON, *March 22, 1921*

My Lord,

I have the honour to state that the Trade Agreement recently concluded between His Majesty's Government and the Russian Soviet Government[2] has aroused widespread interest in this country.

I transmit herewith, for Your Lordship's information, copies of an article in the 'New York Times' of March 22nd[3] which contains a statement issued by Mr. Herbert Hoover, United States Secretary of Commerce, on this subject.

There can be little doubt that Mr. Hoover voices the opinion of the new Administration,[4] so far as such opinion may be said to have been formed at all, when he states that the question of trade with Russia at the present time is a political rather than an economic one. He believes that trade between Russia and foreign countries cannot be carried on in any appreciable volume since, with the exception of confiscated gold, platinum and jewellery now in the hands of the Soviet Government, Russia has no commodities available for export in payment for the goods she needs. This condition would, in his view, continue to exist so long as the Bolshevist economic system persisted, since large-scale production, whether industrial or agricultural, is impossible under a communistic régime. Under the influence of economic stagnation events in Russia are, he thinks, slowly but surely developing towards the downfall of the Soviet Government, nor could the Trade Agreement now concluded prevent the occurrence of that event if it resulted in nothing more than a small exchange of commodities. It seems likely, however, that the Trade Agreement will be worked in such a way as to enable British capitalists who formerly owned or operated mines and factories in Russia to resume their industrial activity in that country. Their example will soon be followed by German capitalists in a like position

---

[1] See No. 137, n. 1.
[2] For a summary of this agreement, which was signed on March 16, see Vol. XII, No. 845 and for the text, see *B.F.S.P.*, vol. 114, pp. 373–9.
[3] Not printed.
[4] President Harding's administration took office on March 4, 1921.

and production will revive to an extent sufficient to prolong the life of the Trotsky–Lenin régime. Two main results may therefore be expected to flow from the Agreement, first, the indefinite postponement of the overthrow of the Soviets and secondly, a partial, but only a partial economic recovery in Russia. Moreover, if British and German capitalists succeed in securing a restoration of the Russian plants and properties which they formerly operated, a strong demand will arise in this country for the negotiation of similar opportunities for American capital and the hand of the United States Government will be forced.

Mr. Hoover's views are not so definitely set forth in the statement he made public, but they were expressed in the form above summarised in a casual conversation with a member of this Embassy from whom he did not attempt to conceal his disapproval of the step taken by His Majesty's Government. That disapproval is made equally clear in his public statement which is generally endorsed in the press and interpreted to mean that the Republican Administration will adhere to the Russian policy of their predecessors. For some time, as Your Lordship is aware, that policy has met with a strong undercurrent of dissent actuated by varying motives and now reinforced to some extent by reports of speeches made by Lenin[5] offering a cordial welcome to foreign capitalists and promising radical modifications in the whole Bolshevik structure of Government, political as well as economic. The principal responsible opponent of the attitude heretofore adopted towards Bolshevik Russia by the American Government is Senator France of Maryland, who finds in the conclusion of the Anglo-Russian Commercial Agreement a strong reason for the immediate recognition by the United States of the Soviet Government.[6]

The Hearst press claims that Great Britain is endeavouring to persuade Japan to follow her example in reopening commercial relations with Russia and asserts that the signing of the agreement will relieve Great Britain of the necessity of making concessions to France 'in order to create a solid front against the United States'.

The American press correspondents in London represent the attitude of His Majesty's Government as being one of watchful waiting. The correspondent of the Associated Press claims to have been informed officially that, even in the event of the British courts authorising the seizure of Bolshevik gold brought into England,[7] the agreement will not be allowed to lapse but will be renegotiated.

I have, etc.,
A. GEDDES

[5] See No. 41, n. 8.

[6] On the American attitude towards trade relations with Soviet Russia, see *F.R.U.S.* 1921, vol. ii, pp. 760–90.

[7] See Vol. XII, Nos. 741, 828, and 845. For the views of the U.S.A. Treasury Department on Russian gold, see *F.R.U.S.* 1921, vol. ii, pp. 764–8, 771, and 774–5.

Lord Kilmarnock[1] *(Berlin) to Earl Curzon (Received March 29)*
No. 475 [N 3871/105/38]

BERLIN, *March 23, 1921*

My Lord,

With reference to my despatch No. 446 of the 18th instant,[2] I have the honour to report that, according to information said to be from Bolshevik sources which is reproduced in the *Vossische Zeitung*, the following are further particulars of the Russo-German Agreement:—[3]

Both Governments agree to hand over to the existing representatives the protection of their respective subjects until normal relations are restored between the two countries. Special trade representatives will be attached to the existing missions for commercial purposes. Missions will be accredited to the respective Foreign Offices. Members of the Missions will enjoy diplomatic privileges. Those attached or on special duty will enjoy special legal protection. All such persons are free from public taxes and duty to work. Diplomatic courier's luggage is to be immune. Missions in both countries are entitled to use wireless and the postal and telegraph systems both for ordinary and cypher correspondence. Consuls are to be empowered to issue permits to reside and passports, and to legalise documents, signatures and translations.

A special paragraph is devoted to the rights of subjects of both States and deals with the conditions regulating travel between Germany and Russia. Every German citizen who travels to Russia in order to take up any duty as

---

[1] H.M. Chargé d'Affaires at Berlin.

[2] This reported that the Head of the Russian Department of the Ministry for Foreign Affairs [Baron von Maltzan] and the Soviet Government agent in Berlin had signed on March 17 a protocol containing two agreements. It continued: 'The first agreement relates to the release of civilian prisoners of war, the restitution of the private property of such prisoners and of the private property of German citizens which had been seized in Russia. It does not involve the repayment of any public debts. The agreement further guarantees the personal safety of German citizens who may visit Russia for the purposes of trade.

'The second agreement concerns the establishment of Delegations (not Legations) in each country. These Delegations will consist of a consular agent and a commercial agent, charged with the protection of their nationals and of the interests of private traders.

'The protocol had been drawn up a month ago, but the Head of the Russian Department would not sign it until he had received confirmation of the signature of the Anglo-Russian Convention in London [see No. 353, n. 2], which Germany is bound to recognise under the terms of the Treaty of Peace (Article 117). In the course of a conversation confirming this statement, Baron Maltzan said he was anxious to follow the lead of England and to work with her in the development of Russian trade.

'The protocol has not yet come into force, as it has first to be submitted to the Cabinet and then to Parliament; but Baron Maltzan did not anticipate that this would entail more than a week's delay or would involve any material change in the draft. He promised to communicate to me copies of the final text as soon as it had been passed.'

(As will be seen from No. 362, below, these agreements were not signed until May 6, 1921.)

[3] For the sources of the two Russo-German Agreements signed on May 6, 1921, see Slusser and Triska, p. 21.

the result of the Treaty is guaranteed immunity for all property that he takes into or acquires in that country. The Russian Government undertakes to transport to Germany former German subjects who, according to German laws, can again take up German citizenship. As regards Russian citizens in Germany, the existing laws in Germany apply as far as concerns their person and property.

The activity of the Trade Missions is to be treated separately according to the different economic systems in both countries. The Bolshevist Trade Mission in Germany represents the State organ for Import and Export; it enjoys in Germany the rights of a juridical person; such valuables, goods and other property as are in its possession are declared immune as far as legal claims and debts are concerned, if such obligations arose before the conclusion of the present Treaty. The German Trade Mission in Russia assumes the economic interests of the German State and German citizens. It is to deal with all public offices who carry on trade according to Russian law; it is to register all contracts which are made with German subjects on Soviet territory. Such contracts are not liable to taxation, but both Missions reserve to themselves the right to compensate by special surcharges the loss in taxation which arises from the monopolistic character of the Bolshevik trade system.

I have, etc.,
KILMARNOCK

No. 355

Mr. Gregory[1] to M. Kopwillem[2]
[N 4101/5/38]

FOREIGN OFFICE, *April 4,* [*1921*]

Dear Monsieur Kopwillem,

You told me on Saturday that you had received a telegram from your Government to the effect that the preamble to the Russian Trade Agreement[3] was being interpreted in Esthonia to mean that in the event of a Bolshevik attack on the Border States Great Britain had formally undertaken to observe neutrality.

I replied to you that the terms of the preamble were perfectly clear and in no sense justified an interpretation of the kind described, and added that the clause in question must be taken literally and unreasonable deductions must not be drawn.

I have much pleasure in confirming what I said, and you will no doubt telegraph to Professor Piip[4] to that effect.

J. D. GREGORY

[1] Head of the Northern Department of the Foreign Office.
[2] Esthonian Chargé d'Affaires in London.
[3] See No. 353, n. 2.   [4] Esthonian Foreign Minister.

No. 356

Mr. Wise[1] to Mr. O'Malley[2] (Received April 11)
[N 4369/5/38]

BOARD OF TRADE, *April 7, 1921*

Dear O'Malley,

The enclosed is a copy of the telegram from Chicherin,[3] as passed to me by Klishko.[4] A copy had previously been transmitted to Sir Robert Horne.[5]

Yours sincerely,

E. F. WISE

ENCLOSURE IN NO. 356

M. Chicherin to M. Krassin[6]

March 31, 1921

Telegraphic

Letter with trade agreement[7] and Sir Robert Horne's letter[8] received. Please assure British Government of our firm resolve to execute strictly all engagements entered into by agreement. Our departments are engaged in studying the agreement, and shortly the instructions provided for by the agreement will be issued. Special study is made of questions put before us by Sir Robert Horne's Afghanistan note,[8] and shortly results will be made known. On our part the agreement will be fully adhered to. We expect same from the British Government, and hope to hear what is done as to engagements of the British Government towards us.—CHICHERIN

[1] Acting Assistant Secretary at the Board of Trade.
[2] A senior member of the Northern Department of the Foreign Office.
[3] People's Commissar for Foreign Affairs.
[4] A member of the Russian trade delegation in London.
[5] Former President of the Board of Trade; Chancellor of the Exchequer from April 5, 1921. [6] Head of the Russian Trade Delegation in London.
[7] See No. 353, n. 2. [8] See No. 361, n. 8, below.

No. 357

Foreign Office to the Law Officers of the Crown
[N 4720/1221/38]

FOREIGN OFFICE, *April 13, 1921*

Gentlemen,

I am directed by Earl Curzon of Kedleston to inform you that he is anxious to obtain your views as to the effect on the relations between His Majesty's Government and the Soviet Government of the signing of the recent Trade Agreement entered into between Sir Robert Horne, on behalf of His Majesty's Government, and M. Krassin, on behalf of the Soviet

Government. This question, which is bound to arise in various connections, has been expressly raised in the accompanying letter from Messrs. Coward, Hawkesley Sons and Chance.[1]

2. In this connection, I am to refer you to a report of a speech by the Prime Minister in the House of Commons on the 22nd March last, which appears in No. 28, Vol. 139, of the official report of the Parliamentary Debates in the House of Commons on p. 2518, where Mr. Lloyd George states: 'This is purely a trading agreement recognising the Soviet Government as a *de facto* Government of Russia—which undoubtedly it is.'

3. I am also to remind you that, in response to an enquiry made before the signature of the Agreement, a firm of solicitors were informed, after reference to the Attorney-General, 'that His Majesty's Government, for a certain limited purpose, regarded the Soviet Government as a State Government in Russia'.

4. If it were held to be the case that there has been *de facto* recognition, the position would appear to Lord Curzon to be similar to that created by the *de facto* recognition of the Governments of the republics of Latvia and Esthonia, when representatives of those Governments resided in London and conducted diplomatic negotiations with the Foreign Office, although their final recognition as envoys to the Court of St. James was deferred until full *de jure* recognition was accorded.[2] The creation of such a situation would entail consequences of grave importance.

5. Lord Curzon would therefore be grateful of your opinion on the following questions:—

(1) Would it be correct to inform Messrs. Coward, Hawkesley Sons and Chance that His Majesty's Government recognise the Soviet Government as the *de facto* Government of Russia?

(2) If the answer to (1) is in the negative, should Messrs. Coward and Hawkesley be informed that His Majesty's Government recognise that, for a certain limited purpose, the Soviet Government is a State Government in Russia?

(3) If the answer to (1) is in the affirmative, does it necessarily follow that direct diplomatic relations can be established between representatives of the Soviet Government and the Secretary of State for Foreign Affairs as in the case of the representatives of Latvia and Esthonia referred to in paragraph 4 of this reference?

(4) Generally.[3]

> I have, etc.,
>
> J. D. GREGORY

[1] Of March 21, 1921 (N 3632/1221/38), not printed.
[2] On January 26, 1921 (see Vol. XV, No. 6).
[3] The Law Officers replied on April 18 as follows: 'In our opinion—(1) It would be correct to inform Messrs. Coward, Hawkesley Sons and Chance that His Majesty's Government recognise the Soviet Government as the *de facto* Government of Russia. (2) Does not arise. (3) Yes; we think it necessarily follows that direct diplomatic relations can be established between representatives of the Soviet Government and the Secretary of State for Foreign Affairs.'

No. 358

Record by Mr. Gregory of a conversation with M. Krassin
[N 4625/5/38]

FOREIGN OFFICE, *April 14, 1921*

Monsieur Krassin came to see me yesterday evening and we went through the various subjects on which I had to speak to him. The result was in each case, I think, satisfactory. He is returning to Moscow next week and will take up the questions at once with Chicherin.

i. *Repatriation of Russian refugees*

Monsieur Krassin said that he thought that there would be no difficulty about coming to an arrangement for the repatriation of the bulk of the 6,000 odd for whom His Majesty's Government are responsible. It was only reasonable, however, he said, to require that they should be examined and passed by an official of the Soviet Government, as there would undoubtedly be some disturbing elements who could not be readmitted to Russia. I said that was probably reasonable, but we should also require a guarantee that those who were readmitted would not be shot or maltreated in any way. Monsieur Krassin agreed that there should be something of this nature. He would, he said, take up the matter with Chicherin immediately on his return to Moscow, and was sure that we could establish the principle of repatriation without any delay. As regards practical steps, we considered, after some discussion, that the best way for the Soviet Authorities to check the refugees would be for them to attach two or three officials for the purpose to their Trade Delegation at Constantinople. I gave him a short memorandum[1] with the main figures and distribution of the refugees; and promised some further details for which he asked. In reply to his enquiry, I said that we only wished at present to negotiate on behalf of the particular refugees for whom we have assumed liability.

ii. *Disposal of the Russian Cruiser and destroyers under our control*

I explained to Monsieur Krassin the position created with regard to these ships by Article 10 of the Trade Agreement[2] and said that it had been decided to offer them to him. He was at first somewhat overcome by our apparently generous offer and said he would then ask permission to bring over Russian crews to take the ships back to Russia. When, however, it was explained to him that all three ships were in such a rotten condition that the destroyers could hardly be kept afloat in the port and that the cruiser would almost certainly fall to pieces directly anyone attempted to move her, his face fell considerably. He said that he would consult Chicherin as to what to do with them.

---

[1] Not traced in the Foreign Office archives.   [2] See No. 353, n. 2.

iii. *The Treaty between the Soviet Government and Afghanistan*[3]

I drew Monsieur Krassin's attention to the text which had appeared a short time ago in the *Manchester Guardian*[4] and asked whether he could vouch for its authenticity. Better still—as he was just going to Moscow, could he possibly procure a real copy of the treaty and bring it back to me? He said that certainly he would—and that I should have it as soon as possible.

iv. We finally touched on a few minor questions, among which I mentioned the Salvation Army people alleged to be in prison in Moscow—though I said that, as they were not British Subjects, we had no right to make any demands. The point merely was that the Salvation Army were good non-political people, whom it was a pity to molest. Monsieur Krassin said that, if they were in prison, it was for something else not because they were Salvationists—but he would enquire. I said the Salvation Army here were anxious to get into touch and enquire into their organisation. He said that could eventually be arranged, since, as soon as Russia was opened up, they would be treated on an equality with kindred religious and philanthrophic bodies.

J. D. GREGORY

[3] Signed in Moscow on February 28, 1921. For sources, see Slusser and Triska, p. 19. For an English text, see *B.F.S.P.*, vol. 123, pp. 706–9, and Jane Degras, *Soviet Documents on Foreign Policy* (Oxford, 1951), vol. i, pp. 233–5.

[4] See the *Manchester Guardian*, March 31, 1921, p. 8.

No. 359

Earl Curzon to Sir H. Rumbold[1] *(Constantinople)*
No. 234 Telegraphic [*N 4417/2866/38*]

FOREIGN OFFICE, April 16, 1921, 6 p.m.

Your telegram No. 166.[2]

Now that trade agreement has been signed you should treat Soviet representative in a similar manner to that in which German representatives are treated, viz.: to return but not to initiate any courtesies and not to refuse to transact official business.[3]

Should any wireless stations under British control receive any messages addressed to the Soviet Delegation they should be transmitted to M. Koudich.[4]

[1] British High Commissioner in Constantinople.

[2] Of March 8, not printed.

[3] These instructions were repeated in a circular telegram of May 13 to His Majesty's Representatives at Kovno, Helsingfors, Warsaw, Berlin, Stockholm, Copenhagen, Christiania, Rome, and Prague.

[4] Representative of the All Russian Central Union of Consumers' Societies (Soviet Trade Delegation).

No. 360

Sir H. Rumbold (Constantinople) to Earl Curzon (Received May 4)
No. 419 [N 5355/2866/38]

CONSTANTINOPLE, April 26, 1921

My Lord,

I have the honour to transmit to Your Lordship herewith copy of a letter[1] from M. Koudich, the Representative here of the so-called All Russian Central Union of Consumer's Societies, or Soviet Trade Delegation, requesting my intervention with a view to protection from insults offered to him by members of General Wrangel's Army.[2]

2. M. Koudich bases his claim for my protection on the terms of the Trade agreement concluded between Great Britain and Soviet Russia.

3. I fail to perceive in that agreement any justification for this claim. Articles 5 and 6 refer to the position of the agents of the two parties in our respective territories but the immunities and rights enjoyed under those two clauses cannot be said to extend to the position of such agents in Turkey or in any other country.

4. My own view is that M. Koudich is entitled here to exactly the same measure of police protection as would be afforded to any other individual whose presence is tolerated in Constantinople. I am accordingly forward[ing] a copy of his letter to the General Officer Commanding-in-Chief, Army of the Black Sea,[3] and to the President of the Allied Police Commission[4] for their information. I am also communicating to General Sir Charles Harington a copy of this despatch.

5. Subject to Your Lordship's approval I propose to reply to M. Koudich in the above sense and I have in the meantime confined myself to simply acknowledging his letter.

6. A good deal of information has reached me from various sources lately in regard to the undesirable activities in Constantinople of this individual, who is a prominent communist and who prior to his arrival here was connected with the Extraordinary Commission at Kharkow.[5]

7. Ostensibly his mission here is purely commercial. Beyond however buying a motor-car and living in considerable style at first at an expensive hotel and now in a luxurious office, none of his commercial transactions [has] as yet materialised, the negotiations always breaking down at the last moment owing to some impossible condition put forward by M. Koudich himself. The relations of his trade delegation with other commercial institutions or individuals are apparently restricted to those of Jewish nationality

[1] Not printed.

[2] See Vol. XII, Nos. 824, 829, and 832, Vol. XIII, No. 174 and Vol. XVII, Nos. 70 and 77.

[3] Lieutenant-General Sir Charles Harington.

[4] Colonel C. R. Ballard.

[5] The reference is to the Extraordinary Commission for Struggle against the Counter-Revolution, commonly known as the *Cheka* (see Vol. XV, p. 780).

or doubtful character, or at most to firms eager for business of any kind in a period of commercial stagnation.

8. The political activities of the Trade Delegation are however far wider and even more obscure, but they undoubtedly comprise such diverse fields of work as agitation, propaganda, political and military intelligence, registration, etc. M. Koudich appears to be himself directly responsible for the work of all the different political and revolutionary Sovietist organisations in Constantinople, such as the Revkom (revolution committee), the Cheka (extraordinary commission), as well as of the political intelligence centre which concentrates and checks the work of the different communist sections, British, German, French, Cossack, Polish, etc. in Constantinople.

9. In short, and in so far as Constantinople is concerned, the Trade Delegation is the professedly respectable cloak under the many intricate folds of which M. Koudich conceals his other designs.[6]

I have, etc.,

Horace Rumbold

[6] In reply (May 26) to M. Klishko, who had raised the same issue in his note of May 3, not printed, Mr. Gregory stated: ' . . . there is nothing in the trade agreement which could be construed as entitling Soviet representatives in foreign countries generally or in Turkey in particular, to the protection of the British Mission. The position at Constantinople is complicated by the fact that the existing Russian Consular Court is the only court recognised by the local government as competent to afford redress in disputes between two parties both of whom are of Russian nationality. The British authorities in Constantinople are not competent to enquire into the status of the existing Russian Consular Court at that capital, nor would the intervention of the British High Commissioner on the Armistice Commission be justified.'

No. 361

Minutes of a Meeting held at the Board of Trade, April 26, 1921
[N 5286/5/38]

PRESENT: The Rt. Hon. Stanley Baldwin, M.P.[1]
Sir Sydney Chapman[2]
Mr. E. F. Wise
Mr. C. Litchfield[3]
Mr. W. Peters[4]
Mr. R. C. Clively[5]

M. Krassin ⎫
M. Klishko ⎬ Russian Trade Delegation.

[1] President of the Board of Trade.
[2] Permanent Secretary to the Board of Trade.
[3] Private Secretary to the President of the Board of Trade.
[4] Commercial Secretary for Siberia in the Department of Overseas Trade, who had been recalled to London in 1920 to assist in the negotiations with the Russian Trade Delegation.
[5] Formerly in charge of the office of the Permanent Committee of the Supreme Economic Council.

M. KRASSIN stated that he was leaving for Moscow on the 27th April and desired to raise certain points before he left. He had received information from his Government that he was appointed the official agent for England, and the formal declaration to that effect would be handed to the British Government in the near future. M. Klishko, in his absence, would act for him.

He had also recently submitted names of additional experts with which he wished to augment his present staff in this country, as their presence here would greatly facilitate the progress of trade and he would like the granting of their visas expedited as much as possible.

He had had an interview at the Foreign Office recently[6] in connection with the repatriation of soldiers who had served with Denikin. He wished to raise the question as to which channels of approach the British Government preferred him to use—whether he should communicate direct with the Foreign Office on purely diplomatic questions and with the Board of Trade on questions relating to trade, or whether the British Government preferred him to use only one recognised channel.

Mr. BALDWIN stated that at present the Delegation had better refer to the Foreign Office any diplomatic matters, and to the Board of Trade any matters connected with trade, as they had been doing in the past, but M. Krassin's question would be considered and no doubt settled before his return.

M. KRASSIN handed to Mr. Baldwin copy of telegram[7] received from M. Tchitcherin in reply to the letter handed by Sir Robert Horne[8] to M. Krassin on the signing of the Agreement.[8]

Mr. BALDWIN, after reading the telegram, remarked that if it was carried out, as he trusted it would be, in the spirit and the letter, the better relations between the two countries which both sides hoped for would be much assisted.

M. KRASSIN stated that he had received further evidence that the Soviet Government had changed their policy towards Great Britain in a great many ways. All Commissariats and all Agents abroad had received instructions with regard to this matter, and he was convinced that there would be no cause for dissatisfaction in the future as to the carrying out of the agreement both in letter and spirit. In London he had himself taken certain steps with

[6] See No. 358.

[7] This telegram (April 18), which is printed in *Degras*, vol. i, pp. 245–6, contained the following passage: 'Since the agreement was signed everything on our part will be avoided in particular in quarters referred to by which would involve hostile action or propaganda, or support of such, against British interests in the sense provided against by the treaty. We value too highly the relations newly established with Britain and strive too strongly for peace and trade. In particular, all the representatives and agents in Afghanistan are instructed not to conduct any anti-British policy. Of course, we maintain in full our right to preserve amicable neighbourly relations with Afghanistan, and the activities of our consulates in that country as well as those of other agents will be strictly limited to such actions as in conformity with the British agreement and not directed against Britain.'

[8] Of March 16, not printed. See *The Times*, March 17, 1921, p. 11. See also No. 353, n. 2.

regard to the gold question and the general financial situation. He was at present endeavouring to arrange for the formation in London of a Russo-English Bank, through which the operations of the Russian delegation in this country would be carried out. Although the shares at the Bank would, as at present proposed, belong to Russia, the Managers would be one-half Russian and one-half English and the Bank would have at its head an English Director, nominated by one of the English Banks. Under the control of this proposed Bank would be other minor organisations, or limited companies, dealing with shipping, the sale in this country of goods exported from Russia, the purchase of machinery, etc. The personnel of this organisation had not yet been decided, and of this it was too early to speak, especially on the finance side, but the name of Mr. Jones[9] had been recommended to him by Lloyds Bank as a suitable Managing Director.

M. Krassin further stated that, before a final decision was reached in this matter, he would like to trouble the Board of Trade to advise him on the whole scheme, particularly in regard to personnel, as it was of primary importance that the scheme should be acceptable to them and have their approval. He would like to point out, however, how all his operations had been delayed by the gold case.[10] During the time he has been in England, both before and since the signing of the Trade Agreement, he had placed orders for about four millions sterling, but further orders depended upon the settlement of the gold test case. The position as regards exports from Russia was, of course, worse, for the reason that all attempts to import anything into the United Kingdom had ended hitherto in the goods being arrested and, as the settlement of the gold case would not be reached until June or July, he was afraid there was a risk of losing half the navigation period before business settled down.

Mr. Wise explained that M. Krassin was, in his opinion, too pessimistic as to delay that might take place. All cases depended on two issues—whether the goods were identifiable, or not identifiable. Some time ago the Soviet Government had lost a case dealing with identifiable goods. An appeal had been lodged and was likely to be heard in a very few days. The issue of the appeal would be much affected by the fact that the British Government had recognised the Soviet Government as the de facto Government of Russia. If the appeal was successful, cases of a similar kind would probably lapse.

M. Krassin stated that he would be very glad if things turned out in the way suggested by Mr. Wise, but at the present moment the fear of attachment stopped the export of goods from Russia, and this in turn stopped orders, as trade could not be based solely on gold. In his opinion, normal trading conditions were not possible until full recognition of the Soviet Government had been accorded.

M. Krassin now came to what he considered the most important question, and one which presented the most difficulty. This was the question of credit. He saw daily a great many British traders who told him that their

[9] Presumably Mr. L. E. Jones of Helbert Wagg and Co. Ltd., merchant bankers.
[10] See Vol. XII, No. 828.

warehouses were full of such goods as tractors, ploughs, etc., of which they would like to dispose. The trade depression in this country prevented their disposal, but there was a colossal demand for them in Russia. He could not place orders for these goods on the scale he would desire without credit, and he suggested that if the British Government supported a credit scheme it would be in the interests of their own trades as much as it was in the interests of Russia. One of the problems he was going to Moscow to decide was the wider purchase programme in all countries. He hoped during the course of the next few days to place a contract for 30,000 tons of steel rails, and he also hoped to make a contract for a million pounds of rubber sleeves in connection with vacuum brakes used on railways, but if he had some other basis except cash he could place infinitely larger orders immediately.

M. Krassin stated that he quite realised that the question of credit was a very big and very difficult one, and one that could not be settled in a few days. What he was asking was merely that it might be considered by the British Government during his absence, and in connection with it he thought that the Russo-British Finance Organisation, to which he had referred, might help, as it would give the British Government confidence that Russian financial matters were in the hands of the right people.

Mr. Baldwin thanked M. Krassin for his statement. The points M. Krassin had made would receive careful consideration by the Government, as it was the wish of the British Government to make the Trade Agreement fully effective and to clear away the difficulties that stood in the way as far as it lay in their power to do so.

Mr. Baldwin told M. Krassin that his son[11] was at present a prisoner in Bolshevist hands in Armenia, and he wanted him released and sent to this country as soon as possible. He, therefore, asked M. Krassin to use any influence he had in the matter as soon as he got back to Moscow.

M. Krassin asked that he might be furnished with as full particulars as it was possible with regard to Mr. Baldwin's son and undertook to do anything in his power to expedite his release and return to England.

[11] Lieutenant O. R. Baldwin, who had been arrested by the Bolsheviks in Erivan.

No. 362

Lord D'Abernon (Berlin)[1] *to Earl Curzon (Received May 17)*
No. 691 [N 5773/105/38]

BERLIN, *May 10, 1921*

My Lord,

With reference to Lord Kilmarnock's despatch No. 446 of March 18th last,[2] I have the honour to report that the final texts of the two agreements between Germany and the Soviet Government of Russia were signed at

[1] See No. 3, n. 1.   [2] See No. 354, n. 2.

Berlin on the 6th instant;[3] and to enclose herewith a translation of these agreements,[4] copies of which have been communicated to me by Baron Maltzan of the Ministry for Foreign Affairs, the official chiefly responsible for their conclusion.

The only paper that has as yet produced the full text of the agreements is the *Deutsche Allgemeine Zeitung*, which also publishes an explanatory article on the subject, of which the following is a summary.

The writer begins by pointing out that the relations between Germany and Russia differed from those between Great Britain and Russia. The recent trade agreement between England and Russia involves for the first time the recognition by England of the Soviet Government as de facto rulers of Russia. Germany's relations with the Soviet Government date from the Treaty of Brest-Litovsk of March 1918.[5] Although Germany renounced this Treaty by the Treaty of Versailles, her renunciation could only be one-sided so long as Russia was not a party to the Versailles Treaty. In April 1920 the German Government concluded an agreement[6] with the Soviet Government for the exchange of prisoners of war, and offices for the purpose were established at Berlin and Moscow in May of that year. Later the Russian Office in Berlin was allowed to assist trade between Germany and Russia. As this trade developed, a German commercial agent was attached to the German prisoners of war bureau at Moscow at the end of last year. Since many German prisoners of war still remained in Russia, it became necessary to extend the previous agreement and the opportunity was taken at the same time to conclude a commercial agreement.

Under the present agreements the activities of the prisoners of war bureau are extended to include the protection of their respective nationals and the furtherance of trade relations between the two countries. Article VI gives the representatives certain consular powers and privileges. Article VIII is of importance as guaranteeing the property of German nationals in Russia. Article XV forbids the representatives to undertake any propaganda.

Of greater importance for German commerce with Russia are articles XII and XIII. In contrast to the provisions of the Anglo-Russian agreement, the purely political character of which is emphasised by the absence of analogous conditions, the attempt is here made to bring into harmony with free trade the fundamental differences of the Russian economic system. Only practice can show if this attempt will succeed. The difficulty to be overcome lies in the fact that hitherto the Russian Government as sole contracting party with the German merchant could not be held responsible for the fulfilment of business contracts. By virtue of this article the Russian Government recognises all contracts entered into by its representatives as

---

[3] For the sources of these agreements, see Slusser and Triska, p. 21.

[4] Not printed.

[5] See *B.F.S.P.*, vol. 123, pp. 740–4.

[6] This agreement was signed at Berlin on April 19, 1920. It was confirmed on April 25, 1921, and was supplemented by agreements of July 7, 1920, January 22, and May 6, 1921. For the sources of these agreements, see Slusser and Triska, pp. 9, 11, 17, and 21.

binding on itself; and, so far as such contracts are concluded in Germany, submits itself to be bound by German legislation. Contracts concluded in Russia are subject to the decision of a court of arbitration. This latter provision renders possible, in disputes over contracts concluded in Russia, not only an appeal, but the intervention of the German representation. The submission of contracts concluded in Germany to German law ensures the right of taxation of the Treasury.

There will of course be no lack of attacks against this agreement. Such attacks have already been made, chiefly from circles which object to the establishment of official relations with the Soviet Government and which fear the possibility of Bolshevik propaganda. Such people overlook the fact that the agreement is merely an extension and legalisation of existing relations and that it renders possible the return to Germany of thousands of German prisoners of war. It remains for German merchants to prove whether Russia really has any produce to offer in exchange for German manufactures. German firms will anyhow no longer be obliged to conduct their negotiations with Russia through roundabout channels. The agreement is a step in the right direction. In contrast to the Anglo-Russian, it is in no way political but purely commercial. It is to be hoped that it will prove beneficial to both countries.

The *Freiheit* also welcomes the conclusion of the German-Russian agreement. It points out that it is a happy augury that the agreement should have been signed on the same day as the presentation of the Allied ultimatum,[7] for it indicates that there are still constructive forces at work in the Government, and holds out a hope that amends may be made to German and Russian labour for the political mistakes of the last three years.

I have, etc.,
D'ABERNON

[7] The Allied Ultimatum (see Vol. XV, No. 85, Appendix 2) was dated May 5, 1921.

No. 363

Earl Curzon to Sir M. Cheetham[1] *(Paris)*

No. 1416 [N 5732/62/38]

FOREIGN OFFICE, *May 23, 1921*

Sir,

I have received Lord Hardinge's despatch No. 1056 (P. 478) of April 7th,[2] transmitting a further communication from the Ministry for Foreign Affairs on the subject of the French financial claims against Russia.[3]

2. The first part of the letter of November 25th[4] sets forth the view of the

[1] See No. 11, n. 11. He acted as Chargé d'Affaires from May 16 to May 23.
[2] Not printed.   [3] Of April 6, not printed.
[4] Not printed. This letter was communicated to the Foreign Office in Paris despatch No. 3520 of November 25, 1920.

French Government that the resumption of trade with Russia, and the recognition of Russian debts should not be dealt with independently. His Majesty's Government were unable to agree with this view and, for reasons which have been publicly stated and which must be well known to the French Government, the trade agreement between this country and Russia was concluded on March 16th and it would therefore appear unnecessary to reply in any detail to this part of the letter.

3. The second part of the letter sets forth the following general principles on which the question of Russian indebtedness should be dealt with:—

(1) Russia should undertake to fulfil all her foreign debt obligations without distinction.

(2) Such obligations should be shared by all states possessing territory of the former Russian Empire.

(3) Effective guarantees should be obtained, but the internal affairs of Russia should not be interfered with.

(4) Article 116 of the Treaty of Versailles and analogous clauses in other treaties should be strictly observed.

(5) An international body should be appointed to regulate the distribution of Russian debt and liability for damages.

(6) The burden on Russia should be made as light as possible.

4. These principles are of so general a nature that His Majesty's Government can readily express their agreement with them though naturally there will need to be considerable discussion as to the details of the procedure whereby they may be given practical effect.

5. With regard to the note of the 6th April, Article 9 of the trade agreement was only intended to make it clear that His Majesty's Government would not initiate any steps to attach or take possession of gold, funds, securities or commodities exported from Russia in payment for imports, with the sole exception of articles identifiable as the property of His Majesty's Government. There is, however, nothing in the agreement which prevents legal action being taken in the courts of this country by persons of any nationality, who desire to put forward a claim in respect of such gold, funds, securities or commodities exported from Russia. French nationals having claims to any such articles brought to this country will be able to take action in the courts, should they so desire, in the same way as British subjects.

6. So far as concerns seizures of goods, etc., in Russia by the Soviet authorities, and the action taken by those authorities in regard to immovable property and rights of any description, the declaration of recognition of claims appended to the trade agreement provides not for restoration but for compensation to private persons who have supplied goods or services to Russia, for which they have not been paid, and the equitable settlement in the peace treaty contemplated in the preamble to the trade agreement of all claims of British nationals against the Russian Government.

7. His Majesty's Government have taken note of the French declaration that in the event of French immovable property or rights of any description

in Russia having been taken over by the Soviet authorities and disposed of, or rights therein conceded, to say a British subject, the French Government would refuse to recognise the validity of the transaction. His Majesty's Government would however point out that any British subject who acquired rights of property in Russia claimed by any person, whether French or British, would clearly do so at his own risk, and could be called upon to defend himself against the claimant in the local courts.

8. I should be glad if you would communicate the sense of these observations to the Minister for Foreign Affairs.

I am, etc.,
(For the Secretary of State)
J. D. GREGORY

No. 364

Mr. Wise to Mr. O'Malley (Received May 27)

[*N 6170/5905/38*]

BOARD OF TRADE, *May 26, 1921*

Dear O'Malley,

Here is a copy of the Memorandum prepared in the Marine Department of the Board of Trade, with reference to the telegram from Chicherin,[1] concerning fishing in the White Sea.

The view of that Department is that unless the Ministry of Agriculture attach great importance to maintaining British rights to fish in the White Sea the protest should not be pressed too far for the present.

Yours sincerely,
E. F. WISE

ENCLOSURE IN No. 364

Note on Russian Territorial Waters

May 23, 1921

From 1910 to 1912 attempts were made by the Russian Government to secure a 12 mile territorial limit for Russian waters and Bills were introduced into the Duma for this purpose. Representations were made to the Russian Authorities and the Bill of 1912 was finally withdrawn in the face of considerable opposition to the withdrawal.

A Decree of the North Russian Provisional Government of 20th January, 1919 prohibited trawling within 12 miles of the Russian coast. The Russian Authorities were informed that the British Government could not recognise

---

[1] Not printed. On June 2, M. Krassin transmitted to the Foreign Office a copy of a Russian decree on the protection of fisheries and kindred trades in the Arctic Ocean and White Sea.

the jurisdiction of the Provisional Government outside the 3 mile limit and in the British representations reference was made to the case of the 'Onward Ho'. The Russians arrested this vessel in July 1920 under a new law, the provisions of which were similar to those of the Decree of January 1919. As a result of representations the Russian Government paid £400 compensation on account of the arrest of the vessel. The Provisional Government agreed to refrain from applying the Decree of January 1919 to British subjects outside the three mile limit.

The Russian Government now seems disposed to enforce a Decree, of which notice was given to the Norwegian Government on the 15th April, 1920, for the prohibition from 1st May, 1920 of fishing and hunting in Russian territorial waters. We have no information as to the extent of this prohibition though from M. Chicherin's note it seems that more than the three mile limit is claimed, and in fact jurisdiction over the whole of the White Sea. It seems necessary to press our position as to the maintenance of the three mile limit, but it is doubtful to what extent reference to precedents under the Czarist or Provisional Government regimes would carry weight. It would probably be safe to reply[2] to M. Chicherin that British fishermen understand that they are prohibited from fishing within the three mile limit recognised by international agreement, and that no support could be given to British vessels within these limits. The British Government have always maintained the generally recognised limit of three miles and it is presumed that the present Russian Government will, in conformity with previously established practice, not enforce its prohibitions against vessels carrying on fishing operations outside the limit of three miles from the Russian coast.

[2] A reply was sent by Mr. Gregory to M. Krassin (N 6432/5905/38) on June 10. It ran: 'Pending a complete reply which will be forwarded to you when the competent departments of His Majesty's Government have had time to study the decree in detail, I am to point out that His Majesty's Government must expressly reserve their rights in regard to territorial waters, and they cannot concur in any extension of territorial limits beyond the existing limit of three nautical miles.'

No. 365

Earl Curzon to Mr. Barclay[1] (Stockholm)
No. 34 Telegraphic [N 6096/5901/38]

Confidential   FOREIGN OFFICE, *May 28, 1921, 5 p.m.*

Your telegram No. 92 (of 19th May).[2]
(Congress of Third International in Moscow).

[1] H.M. Minister at Stockholm.
[2] This ran: 'Minister for Foreign Affairs tells me that he is refusing to give passports to Swedish extremists who wish to proceed to Moscow to attend . . . Congress of . . . Internationale on June 1st. . . .
'He would be glad to know if possible what attitude His Majesty's Government are adopting in this respect.'

You may inform Swedish Government that His Majesty's Government intend to refuse similar applications.

No. 366

Department of Overseas Trade to Foreign Office (Received May 30)
[N 6223/5/38]

Confidential   DEPARTMENT OF OVERSEAS TRADE, *May 28, 1921*

The Comptroller-General of the Department of Overseas Trade presents his compliments to the Under-Secretary of State for Foreign Affairs and transmits herewith copy of a note by Mr. Peters of a conversation with M. Karakhan on the 5th May respecting Soviet activity in Afghanistan.

ENCLOSURE IN No. 366

Note by Mr. Peters of a Conversation on May 5, 1921, with M. Karakhan, Assistant Commissary for Foreign Affairs in the Soviet Government

Jerram[1] and I saw Karakhan on the 5th May at 4 p.m. I presented my letter of instructions[2] and left a copy with him.

As regards the question of the housing of the mission, Karakhan said arrangements were being made, and instructed his assistant, Florinsky, to arrange for us to inspect the premises they propose to offer. Florinsky was also told to acquaint us with the rules and regulations governing Soviet relations with foreign missions. From the narrow issues raised by my instructions the talk passed to an exchange of hopes for the success of the trade agreement. Karakhan, as directly in charge of Soviet Eastern foreign policy, said that the British Government need not fear any acts of aggression or any infringements of the agreement on the part of Soviet agents in Eastern countries. In particular, as regards Afghanistan, although the Russo-Afghan Treaty[3] gave Russia the right to establish six consulates, only three would in fact be set up—at Herat, at a second place, the name of which I did not catch (Mazari Sherij), and (a little later) at Kandahar. Karakhan remarked that the two periods—before the agreement and after the agreement —were quite distinct. Although the Soviet Government had not sent a note to the British Government on the lines of that handed to Krassin by Sir Robert Horne,[4] none the less they were perfectly well aware of many acts

---

[1] Mr. C. B. Jerram, a Vice-Consul in the Levant Consular Service. In a letter of April 23, the Foreign Office had notified M. Krassin that Mr. Peters and Mr. Jerram would proceed to Moscow to make preliminary arrangements for the British Mission to be sent to Russia in accordance with the terms of the Anglo-Soviet Trade Agreement.

[2] Not traced in the Foreign Office archives. A similar letter of April 26 to Mr. Jerram is preserved at K 6083/5275/238.

[3] See No. 358, n. 3.   [4] See No. 361, n. 8.

of the British Government and its agents directed against the Soviet Government before the signing of the agreement. Since the agreement they had had no cause for complaint, although certain events (e.g., in Persia the *coup d'État* and the invitation to British officers to enter Persian service)[5] indicated the necessity of watchfulness.

One point Karakhan raised as regards the courier service. Under present conditions only 3 kilog[rams] are allowed to be taken in sealed packets not subject to examination. The Soviet Government wishes to bring books and newspapers from London and finds that the countries through which couriers pass delay matters by wishing to examine all printed matter. Karakhan suggested that the arrangement already in force between Soviet Russia and certain other countries might be adopted, viz., in the case of books from the United Kingdom, these should be submitted to the British Government, who, after examination, would place their own seal on the packet. I said that presumably the point would be raised by Krassin in London. I thought that possibly some arrangement on the lines indicated might be concluded, and would in any case report in London that the question was likely to be brought up.

I enquired as to the possibility of arranging for me to meet Kamenev[6] and Miliutin,[7] whom I had met en route for England. Karakhan promised to arrange meetings, and said there was in any case no objection to my seeing anyone I liked. I said I would like to have a collection of Soviet literature and decrees, and this Karakhan said Florinsky would arrange. Florinsky is to be liaison officer with Jerram and myself.

[5] A reference to the Cossack *coup d'état* in Persia of February 21–2, 1921, which resulted in the formation of a government under Sayyid Zia-ed-Din on March 2. Although this government denounced the Anglo-Persian Agreements of 1919 (see *B.F.S.P.*, vol. 112, pp. 761–3), it asked for British officials to reorganise the military and financial administrations.

[6] President of the Moscow Municipal Soviet.

[7] Vice-President of the All-Russia Supreme Economic Council.

No. 367

Department of Overseas Trade to Foreign Office (Received May 30)
[*N 6216/69/38*]

Confidential   DEPARTMENT OF OVERSEAS TRADE, *May 28, 1921*

The Comptroller-General of the Department of Overseas Trade presents his compliments to the Under-Secretary of State for Foreign Affairs and transmits herewith a copy of a report by Mr. Peters respecting the attitude of the Soviet Government towards the resumption of relations with Western Europe.

Copy also sent to Board of Trade.

Mr. Peters to Comptroller-General, Department of Overseas Trade

DEPARTMENT OF OVERSEAS TRADE, *May 26, 1921*

Sir,

I have the honour to enclose a short report embodying certain information obtained in Moscow on the subject of the attitude of the Soviet Government towards the resumption of relations with Western Europe, and in particular regarding their attitude on the question of concessions.

I have, etc.,
WILLIAM PETERS

ENCLOSURE 2 IN No. 367

Memorandum respecting attitude of Soviet Government towards the resumption of Trade with Western Europe

Although my instructions[1] were simply to carry out a preliminary investigation of the arrangements to be made for the transport, accommodation and subsistence of the British Trade Mission to Russia, I endeavoured to obtain as much information as possible regarding the general attitude of the Soviet Government in the matter of the resumption of relations with Western Europe. My information was secured—

1. From various informal conversations with M. Krassin, and in particular from an interview with him at Moscow. A record of this interview is attached.

2. From conversations in Moscow with a number of leading Soviet officials. These included:—

(*a*) M. Karakhan, Assistant Commissary for Foreign Affairs. As, however, the trend of my conversation with M. Karakhan was, naturally, mainly political, I am putting forward a separate minute on the subject.

(*b*) M. Miliutin, vice-president of the Supreme Economic Council, which controls Russian industries. A record of my conversation is attached.

(*c*) M. Lomov, head of the External Relations Department of the Supreme Economic Council. M. Lomov's Department deals in particular with the question of concessions. I attach a short note of my conversation.

(*d*) M. Nogin, who is President of Slavtextil, the Department of the Supreme Economic Council which controls the Russian textile industry (note of conversation is attached).

3. From talks with minor officials in the Commissariat for Foreign Affairs and the Commissariat for Foreign Trade.

The records of the interviews, I think, almost speak for themselves, but I may perhaps underline one or two points:—

[1] See No. 366, n. 2.

1. The past two months have been marked by a complete change in the Soviet internal economic policy. This change is principally the work of Lenin, and has been explained and defended by him in masterly fashion in an article which he wrote at the end of April for the first number of a new Soviet periodical.[2] When I left Russia, this periodical had not yet made its appearance, but the article had been issued in pamphlet form. M. Lomov kindly supplied me with a copy of this pamphlet. I attach also a translation of an abridged version of the article which appeared in one of the Soviet newspapers.[3]

Briefly, Lenin's argument is that, in order to save Russia, the position of the peasant must be improved. This can only be done by allowing him freedom in disposing of his produce. This freedom of trade means capitalism, and the Soviet Government are therefore consciously encouraging the development of capitalism. Capitalism, however, is a step in advance as compared with the existing system described by Lenin under the terms of 'patriarchalism' and 'small-scale production by isolated small producers'. To render this development of capitalism safe, it must be guided into the channels of co-operation and of concessions which render State control easy.

2. The change in internal policy is naturally accompanied by a change in external policy. In particular as regards concessions, the Soviet Government seem to be prepared to go a considerable way. From what Krassin and others told me, it would appear that the Soviet Government will be prepared to come to some form of arrangement with British capitalists who formerly owned undertakings in Russia. This does not mean that undertaking X which formerly belonged to capitalist A will necessarily simply be handed back to A. More probably, an arrangement might be devised whereby capitalist A would set up a syndicate B, who would receive as a concession from the Soviet Government undertaking X plus perhaps other undertakings—Y and Z. The Syndicate B could then come to some arrangement with A and with the owners of Y and Z. I should emphasise that no arrangement of this kind was described to me, and that I am merely recording the impression left in my mind after various interviews in Moscow.

As regards the general policy of concessions, Lenin's remarks in the article above referred to are worth quoting, and, as they did not appear in the abridged version in the Soviet press, I attach a translation of the relevant extract from his pamphlet.[4]

[2] *Krasnaya Nov*, published in Moscow by the *Glavpolitprosvet* (Chief Political Educational Committee).

[3] Not printed.

[4] Not printed. In this article, Lenin defined concessions as follows: 'What do concessions mean under the Soviet system, from the point of view of the social-economic strata and their co-relation? They mean a treaty, a union, an alliance of Soviet, i.e. of proletarian, State power with State capitalism against the small proprietorship (patriarchal and small-bourgeois) system. The concessionnaire is, in fact, a capitalist. He does his work in a capitalist fashion, for the sake of profit; he consents to enter into an agreement with the proletarian power owing to the prospect of obtaining a special profit above the ordinary, or of obtaining such raw materials as would otherwise be impossible, or extremely difficult, for him to

3. In their external policy, the Soviet Government undoubtedly and indeed openly reckon on competition between capitalists for Soviet concessions. International competition there undoubtedly will be, but it is of the utmost importance that steps should be taken to eliminate as far as possible competition between various British groups. Those applying for concessions will have to deal with a single organisation, and this unity of direction on the Soviet side will enable them to play one foreign group off against another unless precautions are taken. It is desirable, therefore, that the Department of Overseas Trade should be in the closest possible touch with groups interested in Russian opportunities. I should like to suggest that, before the departure of the British Trade Mission, an opportunity should be taken to call together, preferably perhaps informally, the representatives of British groups formerly interested in Russia, e.g., the Urquhart Group, the Spassky Copper Company and the New Russia Company, etc. It would then be possible for the members of the mission to talk matters over and to understand the attitude which these British groups propose to take up in the matter of the restoration to them in one form or other of their former Russian interests.

4. I should like to call attention to M. Krassin's remarks (see note of conversation with him)[5] regarding the possibility of something being done in the matter of loans. As this question is closely linked up with the question of concessions, the same procedure might be followed as suggested above in 3, i.e., that we should get into touch with individual bondholders or with an organisation representing bondholders' interests.

ENCLOSURE 3 IN No. 367

Record of Interview with M. Krassin

May 9, 1921

I called on Krassin today at the Commissariat for Foreign Affairs. He was in extraordinarily good spirits, absolutely immersed in work, with a constant stream of callers *wishing* to see him and a permanent pool of some twenty persons *waiting* to do so.

I informed him of the position with regard to our search for a house for the mission,[6] and also referred to my conversations at the Commissariat for Foreign Affairs on the subject of allowing all the mission's baggage to come in free of all examination. Krassin had, as I remarked to him, himself suggested this in London in the course of the trade negotiations. He now at once said that he would 'insist' on this being done.

He asked my impressions of Moscow, and, on my replying that they were 'mixed', said: 'Ah, good in the theatre and bad in the streets.' He proceeded to describe with great animation and evident satisfaction the change in

obtain. The Soviet power gains an advantage in respect of the development of productive forces and of an immediate increase in the quantity of products.'

[5] Enclosure 3, below.   [6] See No. 366.

attitude which he had discovered in Moscow. The change was much greater than he had expected. As he put it: 'People aren't now in the least afraid of talking about State capitalism' (compare Miliutin's remarks on the subject).[7] I said that I had seen Miliutin, who had also referred to the change in policy, and Krassin at once said that it was a surprising feature that those who formerly used to be considered, and were, narrowly theoretical and had no practical experience of affairs—those of the Miliutin type—had now been brought into line with the new policy. This was Lenin's work. I asked whether there was not some opposition to such a big change of policy. Krassin said that on this point—as regards economic policy—Trotsky[8] was as much of a 'Right' as Lenin was. The opposition came mainly from the workers, who had assimilated theories but had not a sufficiently wide outlook to enable them to 'modify their position and policy when it was evident that things actually were different from what one wanted them to be'. Shliapnikov[9] was an important leader of this 'labour opposition'.

The change was so great that he now felt confident that real business could be done. For example, he had been negotiating in London with a British company that was interested in Hughesovka (he refers to the New Russia Company), in a concession of Hughesovka, and this company wished to send their representative, Mr. Glass, to Hughesovka to make an investigation on the spot. M. Krassin found on arrival in Moscow that this proposal was welcomed with open arms: the Soviet Government was prepared to give not only Hughesovka but an adjoining area as a concession. Krassin therefore proposed to attach to Mr. Glass a Russian (Communist) engineer who would go over the ground with him.

Again, when he was approached in London by Mr. B. Said on behalf of Mr. Leslie Urquhart,[10] he had said that he very much doubted whether Moscow would be prepared to enter into negotiations. When, however, he spoke to Lenin on the subject, Lenin said that the Ural industry was of such importance that something must be done. Hence when Krassin got back to London he would be prepared immediately to open negotiations, and he hoped some agreement might be arrived at.

Further, Krassin said that with the changed state of affairs he had even hopes that it might be possible to arrange something in regard to the question of loans. He, however, added that it was, of course, perfectly clear that not a kopek would be paid in respect of the war loans, but, as regards pre-war loans for railway and other purposes, he was more confident. One difficulty was the attitude of France, who absolutely refused to recognise the Soviet Government. I suggested that the Soviet Government might perhaps find that making an arrangement whereby British holders would receive something would be the best means of bringing France into line.

---

[7] Enclosure 4, below.　　　　[8] People's Commissar for Military and Naval Affairs.

[9] Leader of the Workers' Opposition Group in 1921: see I. Deutscher, *The Prophet Armed* (Oxford, 1954), pp. 507–10 and 518–20.

[10] Chairman of Russo-Asiatic Consolidated Ltd., and President of the Committee for British Industrial Interests in Russia.

The conversation then turned to a general talk on the advantages the trade agreement had already brought. I remarked that he had himself said in his speech to the Russian Supreme Economic Council (on the 5th May) that so far no big orders had been placed in England. He argued that more orders—for 4,000,000*l.* or 5,000,000*l.*—had been placed in the United Kingdom than in Germany, where, he said, the orders paid for did not exceed 1,500,000*l.* (300,000,000 M.). This was, he admitted, without reckoning the locomotives, but these had not yet been paid for.

Krassin said that he had news from London that a fresh campaign had been opened in press and Parliament against the trade agreement, one ground of attack being that an agreement had been concluded without the negotiators of the agreement knowing to what area (in the case of Russia) the agreement was to extend. Certain formal difficulties did, of course, exist, but he was convinced that there would be no difficulty in having the agreement extended to cover the Ukraine, the Far Eastern Republic and so forth.

Krassin also referred to Mr. Baldwin's request regarding his (Mr. Baldwin's) son.[11] Krassin had telegraphed both to Tiflis and Baku on the matter, and had also asked a friend of his who was proceeding on a separate mission to the Caucasus to take the matter up. Everything that could be done was being done; the difficulty was one of communication.

I asked what the position was regarding the list of names of proposed British representatives in Moscow which I had handed to him unofficially. He replied that he was to discuss the matter tonight with Chicherin.

I asked whether, in view of the fact that I should probably be having frequent relations with his department (Krassin is, of course, still Commissar for Foreign Trade), he thought it would be desirable for me to meet some of the officials with whom the mission would have to deal. Krassin said that unfortunately his vice-commissary, Lezhava, was at present lying ill in a sanatorium some 20 miles from Moscow, and that I therefore would not be able to see him. He called in Voikov (Peter Zakharevitch), Lezhava's second in command, and introduced him to me.

Voikov said there was one matter which he would like to take up on the spot as one of urgency, viz., that of our sending representatives to Petrograd, particularly representatives of Lloyd's, who could report that the port was once more in a fit state to receive vessels. I said to Krassin that our original plan had been to send someone to Petrograd at once, but he (Krassin) had, I thought, rather taken the view that no one should go to Petrograd until after the mission had established itself in Moscow. Krassin said that was so, that Chicherin had raised difficulties formerly, but that under present circumstances he now considered our representatives at ports should come out soon. Voikov said he hoped we would send out as many 'consuls' as possible to the ports. I asked what the position was in the Black Sea, and Voikov said that, as a matter of fact, many more ports were ready for trade, and that probably a supplementary decree enumerating these would be issued shortly. Krassin said they would discuss with the Commissariat for Foreign

[11] See No. 361.

668

Affairs the question of giving me a memorandum on the ports. In saying good-bye, Krassin said how glad he was as Commissary for Foreign Trade to see a British official visiting him for business purposes.

In the course of the talk arrangements for our accompanying Krassin as far at least as Helsingfors were also discussed.

ENCLOSURE 4 IN No. 367

Record of Interview with M. Miliutin

May 9, 1921

I called on Miliutin, vice-president of the All-Russian Supreme Economic Council, today. I had already made his acquaintance when accompanying Kamanev from Reval to London. He received me very courteously, and agreed to the various requests I made.

1. As Miliutin is a well-known authority on economic matters from the theoretical Bolshevik side, I arranged with him that when, and if, I came back to Russia with the mission, he would give me a note authorising me to obtain books on economic questions. In Russia at present the private individual is unable to buy books; they are reserved for public bodies and institutions.

2. He promised to send me copies of the decrees embodying the new economic policy of the Soviet Government.

3. I briefly touched on these decrees, or rather on the comments I had seen in the Soviet press. I said that so far as one could judge without having the actual text of the decrees, they appeared to constitute a bold step. Miliutin agreed that they meant a distinct change in economic policy, and said the effect would be a development of State capitalism. He remarked: 'We know perfectly well where we are going. State capitalism has no terrors for us.'

This remark of his is typical of the change in attitude: such an expression would have been inconceivable as coming from a high Soviet official a few months ago.

4. I enquired what the procedure was in the case of concessions. He replied that these were dealt with by his department, but that after completion of negotiations the actual agreements had to be approved by the Soviet of People's Commissars. He indicated in reply to an enquiry that the Soviet Government were proceeding very cautiously as regards the actual grant of concessions, as they realised that a great many of the offers received were not serious. One or two concessions were, however, practically arranged.

5. I enquired with whom I should have to deal in his department if I returned to Moscow with the mission. He replied that there was an 'external relations sub-department' with M. Lomov at its head, through which all external questions (e.g., the grant of concessions) had to pass. I might get into touch with M. Lomov.

Record of Interview with M. Lomov

I called on M. Lomov, head of the External Relations Department of the Supreme Economic Council, on the 12th May. M. Lomov deals particularly with the question of concessions, and our conversation turned largely on that question. He said that he had had several talks with Krassin on the matter since Krassin's return to Moscow. As illustrating the general attitude in concessions, he provided me with one or two booklets on the question, saying that although these were of a popular type, they would indicate the difficulties which the Soviet Government had to overcome in securing support for its policy amongst the workers. As regards concessions, he said that they would be prepared to offer large tracks of timber land in North-Western Siberia. As regards coal, they were to offer two large concessions, one in the extreme east of the Donets basin, which would be linked up with the Kerch iron ore deposits, and another in the west, which would include the Hughe-sovka district. The actual conditions on which these concessions were to be granted had not been quite definitely laid down. There had been a big fight with the trades unions on the subject of the rates of wages to be paid by con-cessionnaires. Finally, the trades unions had agreed to the tariff rates being abandoned, that was to say, that foreign capitalists would be allowed to pay higher wages than prevailed in the rest of Russia. This would, of course, also apply to foreign workmen and foreign technical personnel introduced by the concessionnaire. I pointed out the difficulty of inducing one section of the British capitalist world to sink fresh capital in Russia at a time when another section, which had already sunk much capital in Russia, had been deprived of all it had invested. M. Lomov thought that M. Krassin, when he returned to London, would be able to negotiate some satisfactory arrangement which would overcome this difficulty.

As regards general policy, he said that it was absolutely essential to read Lenin's new article[12] on the subject, explaining and defending the change inaugurated by the introduction of the food tax, or rather of the tax in kind, in place of the former system of forcible requisitioning. M. Lomov later sent me a copy of this article.

Record of Interview with M. Nogin

May 9, 1921

Today I called on V. P. Nogin, president of Slavtextil—the central Soviet organisation for the textile industry. He was one of the original mem-bers of the Krassin Mission, so that my acquaintance with him dates from April 1920.

Our talk turned on two subjects:—

[12] See n. 4.

1. The new economic policy of the Soviet Government.
2. The state of the textile industry in Russia.

Naturally, the two subjects were not kept distinct, as illustrations of the working of 1 were taken from the textile industry described in 2.

As regards the textile industry, Nogin is a comparative optimist. The crisis in the industry was due not to lack of raw materials, but to lack of fuel. Owing to the lack of fuel the production programme has had to be reduced. The original plan was to produce 650,000,000 arshines[13] of cotton fabric. The fuel crisis meant that the production of the first half year had to be specially cut down, since fresh supplies of oil will only be available in the second half of the year (when the oil begins to reach the industrial centres from the oil distributing ports on the Volga). None the less, it is expected that with only 1,000,000 spindles working the output of cloth for the first half year will be 180,000,000 arshines. The original intention was to have 4,500,000 spindles working by the end of the year. Even with the increased spindleage the supplies of raw cotton are sufficient to last for two years.

I enquired whether there was not a shortage of technical men, and M. Nogin replied in the negative. He explained that the Englishmen who formerly managed the cotton mills were men without higher technical education. The Russians, who had this education, used to work under these Englishmen. When the latter left their Russian assistants filled their posts satisfactorily. M. Nogin agreed, however, with my suggestion that at present it was comparatively easy to run the industry so far as technical management was concerned, but that matters would be complicated if the industry were once more to run at full capacity (8,000,000 spindles).

As regards workers, the country factories retain much the same class of workers as before: now, as before the war and revolution, most of the workers in, say, the Ivanovo–Voznesensk district are recruited from the local peasants. In the towns most of those with country connections have left the factories. Most of the younger men—who were the most intelligent and best trained—were mobilised for the Red army. There were left only the older workers of the more purely proletarian type—with no connection with the land.

I enquired regarding the manner in which it is proposed to apply the new economic legislation, explaining that I had as yet not seen the text of the actual decrees. Nogin said that what had happened amounted to a change in policy: now that the war was over it was possible to loosen the reins slightly.

I put the question to Nogin quite simply: what difference is this going to make to, say, one of your cotton mills? Nogin explained that the general idea was that a certain proportion of the output of a factory should be allocated to the workers themselves. The percentage had not yet been fixed. In a draft instruction which he had prepared and which was to be put forward to the Soviet of People's Commissars, the percentage for textile mills was fixed at 15 per cent. The percentage would vary in different industries roughly in

[13] A measure of length used in Russia: 1 arshine—28 inches.

correspondence with the variations in the free market price of the respective products. Nogin explained at some length that although the labour cost of, say, a piece of cloth and a piece of machinery might be the same, the 'free market' price might be different in the two cases, and it was intended in fixing the percentage to make allowance for this difference.

The important thing to notice is that, as Nogin said, the percentage allocated to the worker is his own property. Each man will receive in proportion to his own individual productive capacity, or rather his actual production. It is proposed that a certain proportion of what the worker receives should actually be handed over to him for his own use and that of his family. For example, in a cloth factory a worker will receive cloth. The general principle proposed in this connection is that a worker should actually receive, should actually have handed over to him, sufficient cloth to meet the needs of himself and his family. If he were to get more, said Nogin, the worker would really become a small trader, and this possibility it is desired to avert. The remainder of the, say, 15 per cent. allocated to the worker is handed over, not to the worker himself, but to a co-operative organisation. According to Soviet legislation, all the members of a community are *ipso facto* members of the co-operative unit, the 'consumer's co-operative' embracing that area. Now, however, workers and others have received the right to form separate co-operative units inside the larger geographical one. Thus, while all inhabitants of a town or other area are *nolens volens* members of a big co-operative grouping, they may, in addition, voluntarily group themselves into any number of smaller co-operative units. It is to a voluntary organisation of this sort that it is intended to pass over the remainder of the worker's share (after he has received enough for his own and his family's use). This organisation will exchange the goods fund so constituted for products (food, etc.) required by the workers, and the amount of these which each worker will receive will depend on his contribution to the goods fund, i.e., ultimately on his personal output.

This arrangement is to apply to industries producing goods of mass consumption. Nogin admitted that it will be more difficult to apply it to industries producing other commodities, e.g., producing machinery, railway engines, etc.

The exchange of industrial goods for agricultural produce will be effected by the co-operative organisation. Originally, it was intended that each voluntary organisation should have the right to effect such exchanges with the peasants direct, but, Nogin said, the central co-operative bodies said that such a procedure would ruin the whole co-operative fabric. Hence, the voluntary organisations will only act as part of the big co-operative movement which in turn will work hand in hand with the Commissariat of Food.

As illustrating some of the work done by the Russian textile industry in the revolutionary period, M. Nogin showed me specimens of—

(a) Paper prepared from the pith of the hemp plant.
(b) Cloth woven with a mixture of 'cottonised flax' and wool.

Samples of (*a*) and (*b*) were given me and are attached.

May 10, 1921

I should add that Nogin told me that he had taken part in the campaign preceding the election of the Moscow Soviet, and that he had then had an opportunity to convince himself that the masses of the population welcomed the fresh departure in economic policy.

The political opponents of the Bolsheviks—the Mensheviks and the Social Revolutionaries—were also in favour of the new policy, but took up the position that they had long advocated this change and that only now the Bolsheviks had been forced to make it.

No. 368

Sir H. Dering (Bucharest)[1] *to Earl Curzon (Received June 13)*
No. 272 [N 6813/217/38]

BUCHAREST, *May 31, 1921*

My Lord,

With reference to my despatches Nos. 231[2] and 265[2] Confidential of the 14th and 26th instant respectively, relating to peace negotiations between the Roumanian and Soviet Governments, I learnt last night from the Minister for Foreign Affairs that owing to the continued absence from Reval of Litvinov[3] he had after all again delayed the departure of Monsieur Filality[4] for Reval. He informed me that the day before yesterday he had received another telegram from Chicherin stating that Litvinov would not be available for the negotiations in question and proposing that his assistant, whose name I do not recall but will report at a later date, should take his place. The latter was now engaged in terminating at Warsaw with the Polish Government details of the recent Russo-Polish Treaty.[5] When they were completed it was further suggested that the negotiations with Roumania should take place at Warsaw instead of Reval.

Monsieur Take Jonescu said he had sent a reply accepting the change of Russian negotiator and of venue, adding that as soon as he heard the Russian representative was at liberty he would instruct Monsieur Filality to start for Warsaw.[6]

I asked if Chicherin had ever shown any desire to have the negotiations take place at Moscow, and received a reply in the negative. Monsieur Take

---

[1] H.M. Minister at Bucharest.   [2] Not printed.

[3] Assistant Commissar for Foreign Affairs in charge of Western European countries.

[4] Roumanian Representative at Constantinople.

[5] Signed on March 18, 1921 at Riga. For sources, see Slusser and Triska, p. 20.

[6] In his despatch No. 285 of June 4, Sir H. Dering reported that M. Jonescu had stated (June 3) that, as the new Soviet negotiator, who was to be Russian Minister to Poland, had not yet reached Warsaw, the date of M. Filality's departure was still uncertain.

Jonescu observed that he should never have agreed to a suggestion to despatch Monsieur Filality to any place in Russia. If anything were to happen to him there it would mean that Roumania would have to declare war on Soviet Russia, which he was determined to avoid at all costs. I also enquired whether he attached any importance to the presence of a certain number of Soviet divisions in the neighbourhood of Kiev, of which I had heard unconfirmed reports. He replied that he thought it likely that the Soviet Government, as was their wont, would use the presence in those regions of their troops for purposes of pressure in the conduct of negotiations, but that this would have no effect. He considered it possible, however, that after the Roumanian harvest in Bessarabia had been garnered, the Soviet troops might attempt raids across the Dniester to carry off what they could. He has mentioned this possibility to me before.

In the course of the same evening, which was spent at the French Legation, I took the opportunity, during conversation with General Gorsky, Sub Chief of General Staff, of enquiring whether he had confirmation of reports of the arrival of three new divisions of Soviet cavalry for manœuvres south of Kiev, and whether he was in any way apprehensive that any offensive movement from the other side of the Russian frontier was in contemplation. He replied that he did not think anything except manœuvres was projected, but that he had just supplied two agents, one of whom would go to Kiev, with funds to investigate the conditions over the border. I should explain that the unconfirmed reports respecting the arrival of new cavalry divisions came from a Roumanian source in Jassy and had just been written to me, for what they were worth, by Colonel Duncan,[7] who is on a tour of investigation there and had obtained the intelligence from Corps Headquarters in that town. He had recently had similar indication thereof from a British officer in Lemberg, whom he will meet during his tour in order to compare notes.

I have, etc.,

HERBERT G. DERING

[7] Military Attaché to H.M. Legation at Bucharest.

No. 369

Mr. Gregory to the Liquidation Committee[1]

[*N 6000/1221/38*]

FOREIGN OFFICE, *June 10, 1921*

Sir,

I am directed by Earl Curzon of Kedleston to acknowledge the receipt of your letter No. F.1/231 of the 23rd May,[2] enquiring as to the effect of the

[1] The reference is to the Liquidation Committee of the British Supply Mission, Archangel, and Murmansk.
[2] Not printed.

recent judgment of the Court of Appeal in the 'Sagor' case,[3] on the work of your Committee.

2. As at present advised Lord Curzon considers that you should proceed on the assumption that the decision of the Court of Appeal is binding, in view of the fact that judgment in this case was not only unanimous, but each of the three Judges delivered considered judgments of considerable length disposing of practically every argument and precedent which had been put up by Counsel in the course of the arguments. Moreover considerable time must elapse before the appeal can be heard in the House of Lords, and it does not appear to His Lordship that any material advantage would be derived by delaying the proceedings of your Committee until the hearing in the House of Lords.

3. At the same time I am to point out the advisability of your Committee consulting the Legal Adviser in all cases where the final decision depends primarily upon the recognition or *de facto* existence of any Russian government.

4. With regard to the cases referred to in paragraph three of your letter under reply, where you suggest resisting claims on the ground that they were incurred under an administration which had not been recognised by the British Government, no general rule of procedure can be laid down. Each case will have to be considered on its own merits. One of the points on which the Court of Appeal expressly refrained from deciding was the actual date on which the Soviet Government came into real *de facto* being as the government of Russia. The Court was also concerned to point out that whereas they regarded the Soviet decrees duly passed by the executive of the Government as acts of state which could not be questioned in British courts, they were careful to guard themselves against the interpretation that this covered either individual acts of members of that Government, or even acts of individual ministries.

5. Subject to the remarks in the foregoing paragraphs, your interpretation, that the decision of the Court is to the effect that the Government of Russia must now be considered as having been continuous since the revolution, is correct. I am to mention, however, that certain cases are now pending in the King's Bench division which turn almost exclusively upon the date on which the Soviet Government may be considered to have assumed *de facto* power, and the date from which therefore the decrees of that Government may be recognised in British Courts.

6. For your information I am to transmit a copy of a letter written to Messrs. White, Child and Beney Ltd.,[4] together with its enclosures.

I have, etc.,
J. D. Gregory

[3] For this case, *Aksionairnoye Obschestvo* A. M. Luther v. James Sagor and Co., see *The Times*, May 13, 1921, p. 9.

[4] Of June 10, 1921, not printed.

No. 370

Lord D'Abernon (Berlin) to Earl Curzon (Received June 15)
No. 818 [N 6902/4/38]

BERLIN, *June 11, 1921*

My Lord,

I have the honour to forward a memorandum of a conversation which I had with Baron von Maltzan, the Head of the Russian Department of the German Foreign Office.

The views expressed therein regarding the internal condition of Russia, the Soviet Army, and, more particularly, regarding the prospects of Communism in Germany now as compared with a year ago, may be of interest to Your Lordship.

I have, etc.,
D'ABERNON

ENCLOSURE IN No. 370

Memorandum on Conversation

BERLIN, *June 9, 1921*

I had a conversation today with Baron von Maltzan, the Head of the Russian Department of the Foreign Office, who is considered the best authority here on all that concerns Moscow or emanates from it.

Baron von Maltzan said:—

'The Soviet Government is still spending a large amount of money on propaganda in Germany. There is no good in attempting to stop this. If I stop them in one direction it will be spent in another. I don't think, however, they are making much head-way or many converts. But they are none the less continuing to spend money and to appoint agents. I see no reduction of their propaganda expenditure nor any sign that they are getting near the end of their available resources for evangelistic purposes. Jewels and other valuables are still going to Holland and America. They would sell them here but our people cannot afford to pay the price. The danger from communism in Germany is certainly less than it was, but it must not be neglected. Compared with last August there is improvement—great improvement. Last year the whole of Germany would have become Bolshevistic if Warsaw had fallen.[1] That is quite certain. I can prove it by documents—chapter and verse. At that time the Bolsheviks had succeeded in capturing or hoodwinking the Nationalist organisers here, telling them Russia and Germany must work together to throw off the Western yoke. All our extremists on the Right took the bait. At the same time Moscow told their communist friends in Germany: "We will only employ the Nationals until we have won the position—then we will cut their throats and enjoy pure

[1] See Vol. XI, Nos. 373 to 482 *passim*.

676

communism".' Maltzan has a list of the proposed communistic committees which were to rule Germany. Radek[2] was to be the head. In Danzig the organisation was complete and the communists were already marching out to meet their brothers from Russia.

Curiously enough a letter has just come into my hands from another source giving an account of a recent interview between General Ludendorff[3] and an envoy from Moscow—an ex-Officer of the Russian army, which goes to show that the same combination is being engineered again.

As to the present condition of the Russian army, Maltzan's statement is that they have no capacity for fighting outside Russia, and generally speaking are war-weary and unwilling to engage in foreign adventures. Otherwise they could not have resisted the temptation of falling on the Poles during the trouble in Upper Silesia since hatred and contempt for the Poles are ingrained in all Russians, whether they are communists or imperialists.

As regards the attribution or partition of Upper Silesia,[4] Maltzan's view is that Moscow favours the Polish solution, merely because it is the worst available. The Poles are certain to mismanage the industry—its collapse would be another capitalist failure, which would redound to the advantage of communism.

[2] M. Karl Radek was Secretary of the Executive Committee of the Communist International.
[3] Formerly First Quartermaster-General of the German Army.
[4] See Vol. XVI, Chap. I.

No. 371

Earl Curzon to Lord Hardinge[1] (Paris)
No. 1614 [N 6246/62/38]

Confidential   FOREIGN OFFICE, *June 11, 1921*

My Lord,

I have received your despatch No. 1569 of the 27th ultimo[2] transmitting a note from the French Government respecting the effect of the Anglo-Russian Trade Agreement on French subjects whose property or rights in Russia have been nationalised by the Soviet Government.

2. The only point in this new note which is not covered by my despatch No. 1416 of the 23rd ultimo[3] is that raised by the recent decision of the Court of Appeal.[4] It appears to me that what the French Government are in effect asking for, is that His Majesty's Government should take such steps as would secure judgment in the English courts being given in favour of French claimants.

3. His Majesty's Government have taken every step that lay open to them to secure the rights of French nationals. French subjects still possess the same

[1] See No. 2, n. 1.   [2] Not printed.
[3] No. 363.   [4] See No. 369, n. 3.

right as British subjects who have lost property or rights in Russia to sue in the British courts, should any of their property be sold in this country by or through the Russian Trade Delegation. The fact that, if the judgment of the Court of Appeal is upheld in the House of Lords, judgment would probably be given against them may be regrettable, but with the best will in the world His Majesty's Government are powerless to interfere with the course of justice in the courts of this country.

4. It must, moreover, be remembered that the French Government had an equal opportunity with us for securing from the Soviet Government a declaration of the recognition of claims, since the original negotiations were started by the Permanent Committee of the Supreme Economic Council, upon which body a French representative sat.[5]

5. The French Government preferred, however, to essay another solution of the Russian problem, and the Permanent Committee was eventually dissolved,[6] leaving each country free to conclude its own trade agreement with the Soviet Government. His Majesty's Government have, however, throughout the proceedings deliberately refrained from endeavouring to secure any preferential treatment for British claims as opposed to those of France or any other country; indeed, His Majesty's Government inserted in the declaration of the recognition of claims a clause specifically withholding from the British claims any preferential treatment, and this clause, together with the Prime Minister's statement in the House of Commons on the 22nd March[7] that, when there is a general discussion with a view to establishing peace between Russia and the Western Powers, French claims will have the support of His Majesty's Government, is a clear proof that His Majesty's Government have taken every practicable step to avoid prejudicing French interests.

6. His Majesty's Government are prepared once more to assure the French Government that they will continue to adopt this attitude so long as there is a reasonable chance of obtaining French co-operation in the general treaty between Russia and such of the Western Powers as are willing to negotiate with Soviet Russia.

7. There is, however, one further alteration which I should be glad if you would make to my despatch above quoted: in paragraph 3, sub-section 5, the statement 'an international body should be appointed to regulate the distribution of Russian debt and liability for damages' should be deleted, and a new paragraph should be inserted between paragraphs 4 and 5 of the original despatch to the effect that 'with regard to the principle enunciated that an international body should be appointed to regulate the distribution of Russian debt and liability for damages, His Majesty's Government are in general agreement with the principle, but they consider that the

[5] See Vol. II, No. 74, minute 2 and Appendix 1, No. 76, minute 1, No. 77, minute 1; Vol. VII, No. 16, minute 4, No. 17, minute 1, No. 22, No. 23, minute 1, No. 61, minute 2; Vol. VIII, No. 14, note 10.

[6] In telegram No. 49 of January 22, 1921 (C 1770/332/62) Lord Hardinge reported that the French and Italian Governments had agreed to the dissolution of the Supreme Economic Council, including the Permanent Committee.

[7] See 139 H.C. Deb. 5 s., col. 2508.

international body should be formed by representatives from those countries which are ready either to take part in or to recognise as valid the first general treaty with the Soviet Government of Russia'.

8. I should be glad, therefore, if you would embody the views expressed in this despatch, together with those in my despatch No. 1416,[3] into a note for communication to the French Government.[8]

I am, etc.,

CURZON OF KEDLESTON

[8] Lord Hardinge embodied this despatch in a Note of June 14 to M. Briand [see No. 390, n. 3], copies of which he transmitted to the Foreign Office in his despatch No. 1775 of June 14, 1921 (N 6949/62/38), not printed.

No. 372

Mr. Barclay (Stockholm) to Earl Curzon (Received June 21)
No. 335 [N 7146/86/38]

Confidential
STOCKHOLM, June 14, 1921

My Lord,

With reference to your Lordship's telegram No. 29, Confidential, of the 20th ultimo,[1] I have the honour to report that the enquiries which I have caused to be made in various quarters have so far failed to substantiate the information that large quantities, or, in fact, any quantities, of German gold coin are being melted in Sweden and stamped with Swedish marks. For the purpose of financing commercial transactions, such operations would appear to be somewhat improbable, as Germany presumably has a considerable amount of Swedish currency at her disposal on account of her large exports to Sweden.

Your Lordship will, however, recollect that, in my despatches No. 233 of the 23rd April[1] last and No. 242, Confidential, of the 27th April,[2] I reported

[1] Not printed.

[2] Not printed. In this despatch, Mr. Barclay transmitted the following Memorandum respecting the export of Russian gold to Sweden, written by the Commercial Secretary at Stockholm, Mr. H. Kershaw: 'With reference to the articles which have appeared recently in the Swedish press announcing that Russian gold, aggregating about 600,000,000 kronor, was consigned to Sweden last year, in addition to a further nineteen tons which is reported to have been dealt with by the Swedish mint, I have to report as follows:—

'I learn from enquiries which I have made privately in various reliable quarters that the gold, valued at 200,000,000 kronor, which is reported as having passed through Sweden to other countries, was probably mainly composed of Czar roubles, and that this gold, along with any gold which was disposed of in Stockholm on account of Swedish purchases on behalf of the Soviet authorities, was consigned to Switzerland, Holland, France and the United States of America. This gold did not presumably bear the stamp of the Swedish mint, but was melted down in other countries and accordingly stamped by the local authorities. These transactions have been veiled in mystery, but certain facts emerge which are of interest. When this trafficking in Russian gold commenced, much timidity was exhibited by the various Governments, and dealers were compelled to get the gold to the most lucrative

on the large quantities of Russian gold and gold coin which had passed and were passing through Stockholm to other countries, and more particularly to the United States. I also drew attention to the great increase this year in the amount of gold handled by the Swedish Mint.

Presumably considerable quantities of gold have reached Germany from Russia in payment of locomotives, agricultural machinery, etc., for which large orders are said to have been placed with German firms by the Soviet, and it seems probable that the holders of such Russian gold would make every effort to send it directly or indirectly to New York as the principal or most attractive market for gold at the present time.

I find that German agents in Stockholm have for some time been engaged in Russian gold, and probably platinum, transactions, and that the United States authorities here were approached by them about two months ago with a view to ascertaining whether Russian gold bearing the stamp of the German Mint would be accepted in the United States. It was not, however, market through any circuitous channels. It seems fairly certain that, owing to the attitude adopted in England towards this question, America has proved, and is still proving, to be the most profitable market for Russian gold. This commodity found its way to America last year through Switzerland, Holland and France. Owing to the fact that the American authorities have now announced that the United States will receive Russian gold bearing the stamp of any neutral country [see *F.R.U.S.* 1921, vol. ii, pp. 764–8 and p. 771] (the Germans have endeavoured to sell Russian gold bearing the German stamp, but the United States authorities have refused it), practically all the gold which is now finding its way to America is being melted down and assayed by the Swedish mint. This would appear to be substantiated by the statement contained in the "Aftonblad" of the 22nd April, attributed to the director of the Swedish mint, that about 70 tons of Russian gold have already been delivered to the mint for treatment this year, and there is little doubt that the major part thereof is destined for the United States. Another reason of the large increase this year in the amount of gold handled by the Swedish mint is that, as I am given to understand, the Americans have become dissatisfied with the gold-testing methods of the authorities in Amsterdam. It appears also that the Esthonian assays of Russian gold are not generally accepted.

'I am informed on good authority that Russian coins (1,000 per cent. fineness) can be purchased f[ree] o[n] b[oard] [in] Sweden for 610 dollars per kilog[ram], to which should be added 6 dollars for refining and remelting and 9 dollars for freight and insurance, bringing the total cost up to 625 dollars per kilog[ram] c[ost] i[nsurance] f[reight] Washington. As Washington is offering ex-Treasury 664 dol[lars] 60 c[ents] per kilog[ram] it will be seen that these transactions yield a profit of about 39 dol[lars] 60 c[ents] per kilog[ram], which, needless to say, is very lucrative business for the dealers. (I calculate that 664 dol[lars] 60 c[ents] per kilog[ram] is equivalent to about 104s. per ounce, which is approximately the current market rate on London.) I am informed confidentially that up to a week or two ago Russian gold aggregating about 50,000,000 kronor had been exported to the United States.

'The United States authorities are not perturbed about Bolshevik propaganda for the reason that every effort is made to control the despatch and the destination of the gold. Here in Stockholm invoices in triplicate are presented in each case to the American consul-general for certification, and the information is forthwith telegraphed to the authorities in Washington, who in turn take all the necessary precautions to control the movements of the gold when it reaches the United States. One result of these gold sales is that every shipment tends to improve the Swedish exchange as against the dollar.

'I am informed that during the last week or two a German syndicate has been established in Stockholm, having for one of its objects the purchase and disposal of Russian gold, but I have not been able to obtain information regarding detailed operations.'

until the 23rd April that instructions reached the American consulate-general here that the German stamp would be recognised by the United States Mint, while the mark of the Swedish Mint and that of certain other neutral countries had been recognised by an Order issued by the United States Mint about the end of February.

In view of all these circumstances, I am disposed to think that the gold mentioned in your Lordship's telegram under reference is not German gold and coin, but gold of Russian origin, melted down in Sweden on behalf of German nationals and shipped by the latter, bearing the Swedish mark, to the United States.

I have, etc.,

COLVILLE BARCLAY

No. 373

Mr. Gregory to Mr. Fountain[1]

[*N 6245/62/38*]

FOREIGN OFFICE, *June 15, 1921*

My dear Fountain,

Many thanks for your letter of the 27th ultimo.[2] We have given very careful consideration to your suggestion that some form of conversations might be begun with Monsieur Krassin on the subject of Russian claims, but, after consultation with the India Office, we do not really feel justified in giving our sanction to any steps, however unofficial, which might be considered by the Russians as the preliminaries to a general peace treaty. The situation is not yet sufficiently clear, and while we have no absolute proof that the Soviet Government is not carrying out its undertakings, we do feel that more time is required to allow confidence in the Soviet Government to develop. No final treaty can be negotiated in the atmosphere of mutual suspicion which still unfortunately exists, and of which Monsieur [Chicherin's] latest note[3] (on Japan and the Far Eastern Republic) is a glaring example.

With regard to French claims on Russia, we have sent you a copy of our last despatch to Lord Hardinge,[4] which I think clearly explains our view. We have accorded all support we could to the French, short of tying ourselves to their chariot-wheels in perpetuity.

Yours sincerely,

J. D. GREGORY

[1] An Assistant Secretary in the Commercial Relations and Treaties Department of the Board of Trade.

[2] Not printed.

[3] Of June 1. See Degras, vol. i, pp. 246–8.

[4] No. 371.

No. 374

Mr. Gregory to M. Krassin
[N 6752/5381/38]

FOREIGN OFFICE, *June 17, 1921*

Sir,

I am directed by Earl Curzon of Kedleston to refer to your note No. NK/4276 of the 3rd ultimo,[1] alleging that the offices of the Russian Trade Delegation had been under the observation of a certain Mr. Tractenberg.

2. His Lordship has caused enquiries to be made into this incident, and is informed that a British police officer was directed to make enquiries regarding the whereabouts of a certain Russian who was believed to be in the country, but who had failed to register, and for this purpose it was necessary for him to take with him a Russian who could identify the man. As it was thought likely that he might call at the Russian Trade Delegation offices, the police officer kept observation with the Russian in Bond Street for a couple of days.

3. In no case has the assistance of British police officers been given to ex-Tsarist officials in maintaining a watch over the offices of the Russian Trade Delegation.

I am, etc.,
J. D. GREGORY

[1] Not printed.

No. 375

Lord Kilmarnock (Berlin) to Earl Curzon (Received June 27)
No. 856 [N 7330/6510/38]

BERLIN, *June 20, 1921*

My Lord,

I have the honour to transmit herewith to Your Lordship a memorandum drawn up by the Commercial Secretary to His Majesty's Embassy on the subject of Anglo-German co-operation with regard to trade with Russia.

I have, etc.,
KILMARNOCK

ENCLOSURE IN NO. 375

Memorandum on Anglo-German Co-operation with regard to Russia

Confidential   BERLIN, *June 15, 1921*

I

Since the conclusion of the Commercial Treaties between England and Russia and Germany and Russia,[1] activity with regard to the possibility of

[1] See No. 354, n. 3.

trading with the latter has received a considerable impetus in the United Kingdom and in Germany with the result that intrigues and rumours have become rife. It may be as well, therefore, to give a brief summary of the situation as far as it is known to me. I am informed that most of the articles in the *Berliner Tageblatt* which are now appearing on the subject of Russian International Trade are inspired by the Russian Mission here and must, therefore, be read with caution, as they are propaganda. My general enquiries tend to confirm this.

II

Purely German-Russian trade has been seriously interfered with since Bolshevism became supreme in Russia and was very nearly brought to a standstill in the early part of the German Revolution when production in Germany was reduced to a minimum and the fear of the introduction of Bolshevist agents into Germany was at its height. The commercial connection between the two countries has, however, I believe, never been completely lost and with the return of order in Germany, activity in this direction has steadily increased. Trade has gradually worked up from comparatively small consignments of such things as milk cans, light agricultural machinery, boots, etc. to the recent placing of considerable orders for locomotives, electrical machinery, oil engines, etc. This traffic has so to speak received official sanction and been placed on a more or less sound basis by the conclusion of the commercial treaty between Germany and Russia which followed immediately after that between England and Russia.

When Monsieur Krassin was last in Berlin on his way to England, he was visited by the leading Representatives of German Industry, amongst whom were Geheimrat Deutsch of the A[llgemeine] E[lektrizitäts] G[esellschaft], Herr Firmann, representing Stinnes' Russian interests, Dr. Guggenheimer of the Augsburg–Nürnberg Maschinenfabrik, and others. These gentlemen asked Krassin for his views as to the reconstruction of Russia and the part that Germany might play in it. Monsieur Krassin replied that that was the very point upon which he expected to receive proposals from the Germans. Geheimrat Deutsch thereupon said that no serious reconstruction could be attempted unless the Soviet Republic recognised the right to possess private property. Monsieur Krassin retorted that the two greatest achievements of the Revolution had been the abolition of capital and of private ownership and that *for the time being* it would be impossible to restore either. In this reply, of course, the words 'for the time being' are of the greatest importance. In summing up Geheimrat Deutsch stated that as long as neither capital nor private property of any kind were recognised, the real reconstruction of Russia was impossible and trade with her would have to be confined to more or less limited transactions on a cash or very short credit basis. Both for the carrying out of this business and more particularly for the much greater enterprise of building up Russia when the time came, Geheimrat Deutsch considered the co-operation of all the leading nations of the world necessary and he expressed the intention of taking the necessary steps at once to ensure such collaboration.

The foregoing is of course a very brief sketch of the main lines upon which the conversation took place, as I believe there were several meetings and no doubt the participation of German industry both in any immediate business and the future development of Russia was discussed in some detail.

III

The views expressed by Geheimrat Deutsch naturally raise the question of Anglo-German co-operation in Russia. So far I believe there are only four groups of any importance which have approached this matter:

(*a*) Vickers with Krupps and certain concerns connected with the latter,

(*b*) Dudley Docker with the A[llgemeine] E[lektrizitäts] G[esellschaft],

(*c*) The General Electric Co[mpany] with the A[llgemeine] E[lektrizitäts] G[esellschaft],

(*d*) Mr. Tilden Smith with Stinnes,

but in none of these cases, I believe, has any definite arrangement been come to. The whole question may, therefore, still be considered an open one.

I think the view expressed by Geheimrat Deutsch in the meeting with Krassin and also to me privately that the Russian task is much too great a one to be tackled by any nation singly is correct; moreover, for the various nations to obtain the greatest advantage out of the rebuilding of Russia it is imperative that they should collaborate and not make a vastly difficult problem still more difficult by competition. The urgency and the importance of reopening the Russian market to International Trade need not be emphasised here. It is of course obvious that the loss of the free purchasing power of Russia is one of the chief reasons for the general industrial depreciation and stagnation which at present exist throughout the world.

The reasons why British manufacturers should co-operate with the Germans in the Russian market have already been given by me on previous occasions, as well as the benefits which both parties might derive from such co-operation:— The Germans possess the knowledge of the market, of the people and of the general conditions of the country and they have the advantage of cheapness; we can assist them by financing the transactions where necessary and through political support.

As already pointed out in my Memorandum concerning the delivery of Turbo-Generators to Russia, forwarded with my despatch T/A 4342 of the 14th instant,[2] the inclination in this country for such co-operation is very strong. Moreover, I think the time has come when there should be as little delay as possible in beginning negotiations on this subject. No doubt there are very great attractions in entering upon enterprises in Russia independently, but I feel sure that any such undertakings will be much more expensive and much less likely to succeed than if other nations are partners to them. It must, of course, be understood that I primarily advocate co-operation with

---

[2] Not printed.

Germany not only because she has the most experience in Russian trade, but also because I am chiefly concerned in this country; but the idea is of course that all the great nations should participate. In this connection it is interesting to note that Mr. V[on] Wiegand, the Representative of the Hearst press, has been trying to rouse the interests of the Americans in this matter, and I understand that with this object in view he was responsible for some of the articles which have appeared recently in the German Press, stating that definite agreements had already been made between British and German groups for joint action in Russia. As Mr. Otto Kahn is on his way to Berlin, no doubt the question of American co-operation will be thoroughly discussed between him and his brother-in-law, Geheimrat Deutsch.

IV

If, as I hope, the foregoing suggestions meet with favourable consideration in England, I shall have no difficulty in securing the leading Representatives of German Industry and Finance to meet similar English Representatives.[3]

F. THELWALL

[3] In his despatch No. 765 of July 26, Lord Curzon referred to Mr. Thelwall's Memorandum, and instructed Lord D'Abernon as follows: ' . . . 2. I should be glad if you would adopt a benevolent attitude towards projects either for co-operation between British and German groups for trade with Russia, or alternatively for British participation in the formation of International Syndicates for trading with Russia.

'3. You should, however, refrain from committing His Majesty's Government to affording any active support in the formation of such syndicates.

'4. The Department of Overseas Trade is being requested to inform any enquirers or interested parties in this country that His Majesty's Government have no objection to co-operation between individual firms interested in Russian trade whatever their nationality.'

No. 376

Earl Curzon to Mr. Hodgson[1] (Moscow)

[*N 6993/3779/3⁸*]

Confidential   FOREIGN OFFICE, *June 22, 1921*

Sir,

It has been decided, in accordance with clause 5 of the Trade Agreement between His Britannic Majesty's Government and the Government of the Russian Socialist Federal Soviet Republic, signed on the 16th March last, to despatch to Russia a mission for the purpose of protecting and furthering British interests in Russia generally, and more particularly for supervising the operation of the Trade Agreement, and keeping His Majesty's Government informed on such matters as may be of importance as having a bearing upon the resumption and development of political and commercial relations with Russia.

[1] Commercial Counsellor in Russia from November 1, 1919.

2. This mission will be styled the 'British Commercial Mission to Russia', and you have been selected to be at its head, with the official designation of 'British Agent'. The headquarters of the mission will be in Moscow.

3. You will have under your immediate orders as members of your staff a commercial secretary, a political secretary and three assistants of vice-consular standing. It is also intended to create various consular posts in Russia as circumstances may render advisable. For the present a consul-general is to be appointed for Moscow and a consul for Petrograd. A vice-consul will be attached to both posts. These, and such other consulates as may be created in the future, will be subordinate to the Commercial Mission in Moscow. The official designation of officers appointed in a consular capacity, as well as that of your assistants, will be 'Assistant Official Agents'.

4. In view of the peculiar conditions obtaining in Russia it is not proposed to give you detailed instructions as to the scope of your duties. Their range will be largely governed by local circumstances, the importance of which it is impossible from here to appreciate.

5. You will, however, bear in mind the necessity of His Majesty's Government being kept fully informed on questions of political, social and industrial importance, and you will do all in your power to assist British subjects who may have need of your help for the purpose of safeguarding their property or establishing commercial interests. You will pay special attention to cases where British subjects have been detained against their will in Russia, and will make such representations on their behalf as you may deem opportune.

6. You will use your best efforts to ensure that the Soviet Government execute loyally their engagements under the Trade Agreement, and you will not fail to report to this Office on any violation of the agreement, as well as on any obstacles or impediments that may be placed in the way of its operation by the Soviet Government or its officials.

7. You will use every endeavour to ensure that such British subjects as shall be admitted into Russia under clause 4 of the agreement shall have proper protection and shall enjoy all the privileges and immunities to which they are entitled under that clause.

8. You will keep closely in touch with matters affecting merchant shipping, and will endeavour to obtain for vessels under the British flag all proper facilities and protection such as are habitually granted to merchant vessels in foreign ports.

9. You will convey to the official agents under your orders such instructions in harmony with the foregoing as you may deem necessary to guide them in the execution of their duties.

10. You will report on all matters direct to this Office, forwarding despatches intended for the Department of Overseas Trade or other Departments of His Majesty's Government 'under flying seal' to the Secretary of State.

I am, etc.,

CURZON OF KEDLESTON

No. 377

Memorandum¹ by Mr. Roberts² on Bolshevik Propaganda and the Trade Agreement

[N 7646/7023/38]

FOREIGN OFFICE, *June 22, 1921*

Since the signing of the Trade Agreement on March 16th there has been little evidence of any sincere intention on the part of the Soviet Government to abandon their propaganda campaign. They have been prompt to declare that they regard the conclusion of the Agreement as a turning-point in Anglo-Russian relations and that they have instructed their agents abroad, particularly in Afghanistan, to conform to its provisions. It is also reported that Krassin telegraphed to the Central Executive Committee to stop all propaganda in the near East and to exclude all Indian revolutionaries who were British subjects from the special schools of instruction at Tashkent and elsewhere. This was apparently agreed to and the Soviet Government agents warned accordingly, but at the same time Zinoviev, as President of the Executive Committee of the Third International, was instructed to take over the control of the propaganda in the whole of the East and to transfer the majority of the existing Government agents to his service.

Apart from this ingenuous subterfuge, the Bolsheviks have continued to act as if the preamble to the agreement did not exist. We have recently received from Sir B. Thomson³ a detailed summary⁴ of the evidence for the introduction of propagandist literature into this country and for the supply of funds to agitators. A typical instance of the former is a manifesto issued on May 19 from Moscow and addressed by the delegates of the All Russian Congress of Trade Unions to the British miners. It ends with the words 'Long live the revolutionary advance on Capitalism! Long live the revolutionary miners of England!' Similar telegrams have been sent by various labour organizations and also from the Third International. In all cases they have been despatched by wireless or telegram and as all transmitting stations in Soviet Russia are state-owned, it is idle for the Soviet Government to disclaim responsibility. If it is intended to insist upon the strict adherence to the letter of the Agreement, and to seize the first legitimate occasion to denounce it, here is evidence enough; but if there are any real advantages to be gained from it, then before this extreme step is taken, it will be necessary to show that the Bolsheviks are undermining our position in some vital quarter.

In endeavouring to trace the sources from which agitators in this country are believed to have received funds, the police have investigated the banking

---

¹ On June 22, Mr. Gregory minuted: 'This memorandum embodies the material which *we* have got. The India Office are collecting all their evidence and will let us have a memorandum as soon as possible.'

² A member of the Northern Department of the Foreign Office.

³ Director of the Special Branch from 1919.

⁴ Not printed.

687

accounts of Krassin and Klishko, together with those of the British bureau of the Red Trade Union International and of the Communist Party. While the evidence tends to confirm the suspicion that considerable sums are being received by extremists from Soviet Russia, it has not yet been possible to trace any single transaction in all its stages and, although it is clear that Klishko has something to conceal, there is no direct evidence that the Delegation has financed revolutionary bodies in this country. The police investigation has been seriously hampered by the fact that in consequence of an order of the late Postmaster-General no record is any longer kept of the numbers of £5 banknotes.

Special efforts have been made to trace the relations of the Bolsheviks with Sinn Fein, but here too the results are disappointing. An agent at Reval has obtained from one of the staff of the Soviet Delegation there copies of telegrams which have passed during April and May between Bukharin[5] and Litvinov relating to two Communist germ cells in Ireland. One of the telegrams is an order to Litvinov to subsidize germ cells in Dublin with £50,000 through Krassin. These telegrams are considered in all probability to be genuine, but it has not yet been possible to establish this, as no reference to them has been traced in the telegrams received by or despatched from the delegation in London and there is no evidence of any money being sent from its funds to suspected quarters in Ireland. The agent at Reval is endeavouring to obtain facsimiles of the telegrams in the Soviet delegation, but this is likely to prove very difficult. It is known that agents of Sinn Fein have been in Moscow and a White Paper[6] containing copies of captured documents regarding the relations between Bolshevism and Sinn Fein was recently laid by the Irish Office. This paper gives the draft of a proposed agreement between the Irish 'Republic' and the Soviet Government, and the comments of de Valera[7] thereon. Unfortunately there is not a shadow of evidence to show that the Soviet Government have discussed such a proposal with the Sinn Feiners: whatever, therefore, may be its advantage to us as a means of discrediting the Sinn Fein movement, it certainly puts us in a very foolish position *vis-à-vis* the Bolsheviks, by giving them an excellent opportunity of expatiating upon the perfidy of the British Government.

There remains the Near East; and here undoubtedly we have stronger material upon which to base a case for denouncing the Agreement. The arrival at Teheran of the new Soviet Minister, who has taken with him a staff large enough to set up a Consulate in every town of Persia, has inspired the utmost misgiving in the mind of our own Minister. Mr. Norman[8] states that Rothstein is flagrantly and consistently violating the Trade Agreement and he fears that the disappearance of the South Persia Rifles will pave the way for the spread of Bolshevik propaganda over the whole of Persia. He has

[5] A member of the Executive Committee of the Communist International, and Editor of *Pravda*.

[6] Cmd. 1326 (1921), *Intercourse between Bolshevism and Sinn Fein*.

[7] President of Sinn Fein.

[8] H.M. Minister at Teheran.

already reported that Rothstein attributes the alleged tyrannical measures of the late Persian Government[9] to the influence of the British Legation and that he has assured the released prisoners that Mr. Norman was responsible for their incarceration. He has now been asked to formulate the whole evidence on this point.

The Bolsheviks have for a long time past openly stated their intention of helping all those whose aim is the overthrow of the British rule in India, and the treaty with Afghanistan[10] which was signed at Moscow at the end of February and still awaits ratification is designed to further their scheme for stirring up trouble on the North-West frontier and creating an advanced base for propaganda in India. This treaty provides for the opening of Russian Consulates in Eastern Afghanistan and for a subsidy of a million gold roubles; we also know that the Bolsheviks have agreed to supply the Afghans with arms and ammunition. Meanwhile the Government of India have also been negotiating a treaty with the Amir and these negotiations have now reached a stage at which it appears probable that in consideration of military and financial assistance from us the Afghan Government will be prepared to reverse their policy and abandon entirely their treaty with the Soviet Government. If the Afghan Government are induced to make a clean cut of the Russian treaty, there is of course no guarantee that we shall not still have to reckon with the possibility of propaganda from that quarter conducted through underground channels, but provided that the Afghans carry out their engagements, this danger will be reduced to a minimum. If the above assumption is correct, it is submitted that the present is not a suitable opportunity to reopen the question of propaganda with the Soviet Government. It would, I think, be wiser to wait at any rate until the Afghan situation becomes clearer and in the meanwhile to collect further evidence with which to strengthen our case.[11]

[9] The government of Sayyid Zia-ed-Din (see No. 366, n. 5), which was overthrown on May 22, 1921.

[10] See No. 358, n. 3.

[11] On June 24, Mr. Montagu (Secretary of State for India) wrote to Lord Curzon as follows: 'I have in the course of the last fortnight sent you a memorandum [not printed] about Bolshevism by Major Bray [India Office: see No. 379, below], and a Cabinet Memorandum [not printed] largely based upon this Memorandum, in which I sought to draw the attention of my colleagues to the menace of what I feel to be the indisputable purpose of the Russian Government to destroy the prestige of the British Empire, and even to assail our territories in the East.

'I think that the problem is urgent, for I think the public should at the earliest possible opportunity be informed of the existence of this danger and His Majesty's Government's recognition of the fact.

'I, therefore, suggest to you now that we should appoint an Inter-departmental Committee [see No. 379, below] of experts to collate this India Office information with the information which could be provided by your Office with a view to a combined Memorandum by us to the Cabinet.

'I say again that in my opinion the matter is urgent.

'I am sending a similar letter to the Secretary of State for War, the Secretary of State for the Colonies, and the Secretary of State for Home Affairs.'

No. 378

Mr. Norman (Teheran) to Earl Curzon
(Received July 1, 2.20 p.m.)
No. 357 Telegraphic [N 7570/1/38]

TEHERAN, *June 30, 1921, 1.10 p.m.*

Your telegram No. 253 of June 17th received June 25th.[1]

Russian Minister is unlikely to give me chance of acquiring documentary proof of his activities, and much of the oral evidence in my possession cannot be used without compromising those who have supplied it, so that any representation made at Moscow would have to be in general terms. Facts however are universally known and undisputed here.

Please see my despatches Nos. 58 of May 1st,[1] 73 of May 23rd,[1] 82 of June 1st,[1] 86 of June 9th,[1] and 89 of June 10th.[1] Propaganda amongst released prisoners mentioned in penultimate paragraph of last named, which is now on its way to Your Lordship, has given rise to quite a formidable agitation against Legation amongst governing class and in Mejliss,[2] and offensive references have even been permitted to appear in official newspaper.

Following facts have not been reported in above mentioned despatches. Russian Minister warned late Prime Minister[3] against co-operation with Great Britain.

He told Minister of War that he would finance Cossack Division on sole condition that all British officers were removed from it. This information comes from a secret source which has hitherto always proved trustworthy.

He spent two hours in trying to dissuade present Prime Minister[4] from opening Mejliss on the ground that, a large proportion of the deputies having been elected under auspices of this Legation (which is universally known to be the case), it would be amenable to British influence. Having failed in his endeavour, he said that if Mejliss behaved unneutrally it would be the worse for Persia, by which he could only have meant that if Mejliss engaged British officers and officials, Russia would intervene. His language throughout interview was threatening. Prime Minister is my informant, but source of information must on no account be disclosed.

There are in the field three communist groups, Persian, Russian and Armenian, with all of which he is certainly in close touch. First named, seal of which bears an inscription in Russian as well as Persian, has just published for the first time a violently anti-British manifesto.

Activities of all three have greatly increased of late.

He is importing large sums in Persian silver coin minted in Russia, much of which he is known to spend on propaganda. He has a staff of nearly 100 people, mostly propagandists, and is expecting more.

He and his staff visit personally all Persians of importance for the purpose

---

[1] Not printed (see, however, No. 377).
[2] The Persian Consultative Assembly.
[3] Sayyid Zia-ed-Din (see No. 366, n. 5 and No. 377, n. 9).
[4] Kawam-es-Sultaneh, who formed a Cabinet on June 5.

of exciting hostility against us. For conclusive evidence of determination of Russian Soviet Government to continue propaganda in spite of Treaty see Director of Military Operations' secret letter of April 27th to Military Attaché No. 0162 $\frac{498}{3}\times$ (?S) (M.O.2),[5] and for their general designs against us in the East see Constantinople intelligence report No. 1930 of April 23rd.[5]

He is equally violating Russo-Persian treaty[6] by (? open) propagation of (? Bolshevism) but Persian Government (? dare not) take steps to prevent this.

If it is decided to approach Russian Soviet Government may I be told beforehand?

[5] Not traced in the Foreign Office archives.
[6] Signed in Moscow on February 26, 1921. For sources, see Slusser and Triska, pp. 18–19.

No. 379

Minutes of meeting of July 1, 1921, of Interdepartmental Committee on Bolshevik Menace to the British Empire

[*N 7648/7023/38*]

An Interdepartmental Committee[1] meeting was held in Sir W. Tyrrell's[2] room at the Foreign Office on July 1st to discuss the evidence of Bolshevik anti-British activity available and to suggest what action could be taken to meet the situation.

In the absence of Sir W. Tyrrell through illness the Hon. R. C. Lindsay[2] was in the chair. The following were present.

Sir E. Blackwell K.C.B.	Home Office
Sir B. Thomson K.C.B.	,,
Sir A. Sinclair Bart	Colonial Office
Mr. Clausen	,,
Major Bray	India Office
Mr. J. D. Gregory C.M.G.	Foreign Office
Mr. E. Forbes Adam	,,
Mr. R. A. Leeper	,,

Mr. Lindsay proposed that the first matter for consideration should be any instances of Bolshevik activity which were clearly an infringement of the Trade Agreement, such as propaganda in Great Britain or hostile action directed against the interests of the British Empire in the East.

Sir B. Thomson mentioned four cases of attempted propaganda in this country which were undoubtedly a violation of the spirit if not the letter of the Trade Agreement.

(1) The purchase of £60,000 in English and French currency already sent to Moscow. This was probably intended for the British and French delegates at the Congress of the 3rd International at present being held in

[1] See No. 377, n. 11.   [2] An Assistant Under Secretary of State for Foreign Affairs.

Moscow, but it was impossible so far to prove that the notes in question had been set aside for propaganda here.

Sir B. Thomson pointed out that he had complete proof that Russian money had been used to prevent a settlement of the coal strike and he was most anxious to prevent any further money being brought from Russia for purposes of agitation. Although he recognised the extreme difficulty of intercepting this money on its way to England he felt that a protest made to the Soviet Government before any attempt was made to import the money might act as a sufficient deterrent.

After discussion it was agreed that it was impossible to convict the Soviet Government of the intention of importing this money and that it was therefore advisable to take no immediate action in the matter. Sir B. Thomson subsequently agreed that though some action was urgent it would be more effective if Mr. Hodgson protested on his arrival in Moscow[3] than if a remonstrance were made with M. Krassin in London.

(2) The transmission of money from Russia to England via Berlin. A Russian of the name of Berats who without officially being a member of the Soviet Delegation in Berlin frequented Kopp's office[4] there was known to have transmitted a sum of money to English Communists. Sir B. Thomson explained that in this case he had a complete chain of evidence the publication of which he thought possible.

A further consideration of the facts, however, made it clear that there was no proof implicating any official member of the Soviet Government and it was finally agreed that publication was not desirable.

(3) The next items considered were two propagandist messages sent (a) May 19th, from the 4th All-Russian Congress of Trade Unions to the British miners, (b) May 21st, from the Executive Committee of the 3rd International to the Daily Herald.

These two telegrams are attached to the present report.[5]

It was generally agreed by the Committee that these 2 messages were distinct breaches of the conditions in the Preamble to the Trade Agreement, because, although despatched by private bodies in Russia, they were sent across the Russian wireless which is in the hands of the Soviet Government. It was felt that these 2 messages were proper subjects for representations to Moscow.

The Committee then turned to the consideration of the India Office memorandum.[5] Major Bray, the author, was asked whether the sources of his information were such that publication would be possible. Major Bray replied in the negative and said that he would deplore the sources being compromised,[6] as they inevitably would be, if any use were made of his information,

---

[3] See No. 376.

[4] M. Vigdor Kopp was acting unofficially as Soviet Representative in Berlin.

[5] Not printed.

[6] Major Bray annotated the draft minutes to the effect that there was documentary evidence which would 'prove complicity of the Soviet Gov[ernmen]t with Indian Revolutionaries'.

either through direct representations to the Soviet Government or through publication in the press. He said, however, that he hoped before long to be in possession of documents (a) relating to the financing of Indian revolutionaries by the Soviet Government (see p. 4 of India Office memorandum) (b) showing the secret instructions sent to K[o]udich's mission at Constantinople[7] which had been seized a few days ago when the military Authorities had raided and arrested the mission.

Major Bray then referred to a clause contained both in the Turco-Afghan[8] and in the Turco-Russian[9] Treaties recognising the independence of all Eastern peoples. He added that this clause was obviously directed against British interests in India. The signature of these treaties was, however, *prior*[10] to the conclusion of the Trade Agreement and the Committee thought that ratification[11] alone would constitute a breach.

He also drew the attention of the Committee to the fact that the Soviet Gov[ernmen]t was carrying on its propaganda in the East principally through the medium of Bokhara, Azerbaijan and Georgia and that Chicherin had instructed Klishko that these states were *not* included in the R.S.F.R., were responsible for their own foreign policy [and] were not bound by agreements made by the Soviet Gov[ernmen]t. That from our point of view this was most important, because although it permitted the Soviet Gov[ernmen]t to carry on its anti-British propaganda through mediums over which it could claim no responsibility, the fact that these states were responsible for their own acts would enable H[is] M[ajesty's] G[overnment] to take any action deemed neccessary in direct communication with these states.

On reviewing the case against the Soviet Government Mr. Lindsay doubted whether the evidence was sufficiently strong to base on it effective representations to the Soviet Government or sufficiently sensational to impress the public. Mr. Gregory then suggested that a possible line of action would be to instruct Mr. Hodgson on arrival in Moscow to make a statement to the Soviet Government, somewhat on the following lines; that he had been sent out by His Majesty's Government to carry out the terms of the Trade Agreement and was prepared to do his best to make it successful, that this must, however, depend on the manner in which they carried out the conditions attached to the Agreement but that unfortunately he had information that propaganda was still continuing. The continuance of his mission in Moscow would necessarily depend upon the cessation of these activities. Mr. Gregory added that the alternative which was to present Monsieur Krassin with a list of Bolshevik iniquities would merely lead to a long drawn-out

[7] See No. 359.

[8] Of March 1, 1921. For text, see *B.F.S.P.*, vol. 118, pp. 10–11.

[9] Of March 16, 1921. For sources, see Slusser and Triska, p. 20.

[10] The Turco-Russian Treaty was signed on the same day as the Anglo-Soviet Trade Agreement.

[11] The Soviet-Afghan Treaty of February 28, to which Major Bray may have intended to refer, was ratified by the Soviet Government on April 20, 1921 and by Afghanistan on August 13. The Turco-Russian Treaty of March 16 was ratified by Russia on March 20 and by Turkey on July 21.

controversy in the course of which the Soviet Government would make the usual counter-charges covering Japanese action in the Far East, French action towards Wrangel, our protection of the 'counter-revolutionaries' in Europe and other lies, whereas Mr. Hodgson on the spot would be in a position to test the professions of the Soviet Government as well as to gauge the effect of representations and protests. Mr. Hodgson would be in Moscow in 3 weeks' time and a short delay would seem not to make much difference and in fact we should be in a better position, as by that time we should be in possession of the stronger evidence which Major Bray expected.

Mr. Gregory further suggested that in the meantime the establishment of an Interdepartmental vigilance Committee would enable the chief departments concerned to collate and sift the evidence which reached us from time to time and to report on the opportuneness of taking any action.

Mr. Lindsay enquired whether these suggestions met with the approval of the committee, and after a little further discussion they were unanimously adopted. It was finally agreed that the Foreign Office should receive the reports from the other departments and should be represented for this purpose by Mr. Leeper who would prepare a report and call fortnightly meetings of the Committee.[12]

[12] Mr. Lindsay minuted (July 4): '*Interdepartmental Committee*

'The conclusions were arrived at unanimously that there was not enough material (if it was desirable) on which to come to a breach with Moscow, and that representations should be made to Moscow about their tendencies. The only point on which the Committee was at all divided was on the question whether representations should be made immediately to Krassin, or 3 weeks hence by Hodgson in Moscow. Sir B. Thomson wanted the former because he had some vague hope it might stop Moscow from giving the money (dealt with in (1) in the report) to the British Communists; but he had not much faith in his own hope and assented to having the representations made by Hodgson.

'I was struck by the extreme anxiety of the experts present to do nothing which would make the Bolsheviks suspect we are still reading their telegrams. This of course makes it difficult to cite facts in support of our charges against the Moscow Gov[ernment]. Sir B. Thomson said he did not at all like the prospect of having to face even three weeks without intercepts.'

On July 8, Mr. Lindsay minuted that Mr. Churchill [Secretary of State for the Colonies] had suggested enlarging the scope of the Committee's researches, and that he himself thought that a representative of the Secret Intelligence Service should be added to the Committee.

Lord Curzon minuted, on July 9: 'Mr. Churchill and Mr. Montagu are alike dissatisfied both with the composition and with the findings of the Committee.

'The report is so meagre that a similar doubt prevails in my mind.

'It is said that the D[irector of] M[ilitary] I[ntelligence] should have been invited to attend or to be represented.

'As the Committee intends to meet fortnightly I trust that the S[ecret] I[ntelligence] S[ervice] man and possibly a representative of the D[irector of] M[ilitary] I[ntelligence] should be added.

'In a little while when Major Bray has his fresh evidence it might be possible to draw upon a fresh and more useful report.

'I concur with Mr. Churchill's view and with Mr. Leeper's [*sic*] suggestion.'

Mr. Montagu wrote on July 9 to Lord Curzon as follows: 'I have received the Minutes of the Interdepartmental Meeting which was held in Sir William Tyrrell's room at the Foreign Office on July 1st.

'As I understood it, this Committee was intended to collate together for discussion by the

Cabinet, or a Committee of Cabinet, the case against the Bolsheviks from the various Government departments. That was what I had in my mind; that all the evidence against the Bolsheviks would, as a result of the deliberations of this Committee, be distributed in what has come to be called the K.K. distribution to the Cabinet, and either that body, or a Committee of it, would discuss what, if any, action should be taken by way of publication so as to inform public opinion and protest to the Bolsheviks for denunciation of the Trading Agreement.

'We want to get the evidence from each department. When we have got it, surely it is Ministerial decision as to what we should do with it. I cannot regard, and I am sure you will not regard, the decision of this Committee as decisive on such grave questions of policy. I notice in particular that the Colonial Office, which must have obtained evidence of what is going on in Mesopotamia and elsewhere, contributed no material, and that the War Office was not there at all.'

No. 380

Mr. Ovey[1] to M. Krassin
[N 6987/5/38]

FOREIGN OFFICE, *July 1, 1921*

Sir,

I am directed by Earl Curzon of Kedleston[2] to refer to the Note which you were good enough to address to me on the 16th ultimo,[3] and in which exception is taken to certain statements made in Parliament[4] on the subject of the relations of the Russian Soviet Government with the Angora Government and with the Government of Persia.

2. His Majesty's Government take note of the assurance of the Soviet Government that no representations were made to the Angora Government in connection with the execution of a British Indian subject[5] by the Turks, and that there is no connection between the arrival of Mr. Rothstein at Teheran and the resignation of the Persian Prime Minister.[6] They are pleased to note, further, the declaration of the Soviet Government that its attitude in both cases is one of strict non-interference in the internal affairs of these two Governments.

3. I am to point out, however, that the answers given to the two questions referred to in your Note were statements of fact and, in Lord Curzon's opinion, not liable to give rise to any misunderstanding.

4. I am to add that, for practical reasons, it would not be possible normally to consult you with regard to the answers to be given to questions addressed to His Majesty's Ministers in Parliament. Moreover, His Majesty's Government do not consider that there is any ground for claiming this privilege

[1] A senior member of the Northern Department of the Foreign Office.
[2] Earl Curzon was created 1st Marquess Curzon of Kedleston on June 28, 1921.
[3] Not printed.
[4] See 142 *H.C. Deb. 5 s.*, col. 1022.
[5] See Vol. XVII, No. 198.
[6] See No. 377 n. 9.

under Article 13 of the Trade Agreement, if indeed your Note under reply is intended to put forward such a claim.

I am, etc.,
ESMOND OVEY

No. 381

Note from Sir E. Crowe to M. Krassin
[N 7816/2866/38]

FOREIGN OFFICE, July 7, 1921

The Under Secretary of State for Foreign Affairs presents his compliments to Monsieur Krassin, and is directed by the Marquess Curzon of Kedleston to acknowledge receipt of the communication of the 5th instant,[1] respecting the arrest of members of the Russian Delegation at Constantinople.[2] Lord Curzon notes Monsieur Krassin's assurance that this Delegation represents the Russian Centrosoius,[3] and that it has no political standing or objects.

2. From telegrams now received at the Foreign Office it appears that unimpeachable evidence reached General Sir C. Harington to the effect that a plot aimed at creating a revolution in Constantinople was being hatched, which involved the use of terrorist methods including his own assassination. Acting as Commander-in-Chief of the troops under martial law prevalent in Constantinople, General Harington caused the persons indicated to him as implicated in this plot to be arrested, and the places used for these purposes to be searched. In this manner the offices of the Russian Delegation were searched and eighteen members of the Delegation arrested, of whom nine were subsequently released.[4]

[1] Not printed.
[2] See Vol. XVII, No. 282, n. 2.
[3] The Central Consumers' Co-operative Association.
[4] On July 19, General Harington wrote to the Secretary to the War Office as follows: 'I have the honour to inform you that on June 29th 1921 I gave orders for the arrest and deportation of certain individuals whose presence in Constantinople I considered dangerous to the security of the Allied troops under my command.

'The town . . . is an ideal centre in which to conduct and from which to distribute inflam[m]atory propaganda. This fact has been known for a long time, but with the advent of the "Bolshevik Trade Delegation" it became apparent that the disunited efforts of such bodies as the District Communist Committee, small Communist "Cells" and independent agents for propaganda and espionage, were being co-ordinated and regulated with a view to anti-Entente military activity in Anatolia. This co-ordination had assumed the proportions of a serious menace to the safety of the troops in Constantinople and the population itself in the event of military operations occupying my numerically weak forces upon my immediate front.

'I, therefore, decided to forestall any action calculated to produce the outbreak of a revolutionary and terrorist rising in Constantinople which I have reason to believe was intended to coincide with a Unionist revival in Anatolia, the effect of which would eventually be to bring the Turkish troops in Anatolia into direct conflict with my forces.

'Among the people arrested and deported were certain members of the "Bolshevik Trade

3. On the information at present at his disposal Lord Curzon cannot see that the action of General Harington, who is immediately responsible for the maintenance of law and order in Constantinople, was other than entirely justifiable.

Delegation" (or, as it should be more correctly designated, the "Constantinople Branch of the Soviet Centrosouz of Ukrania")... . Neither the nationality nor race of the individuals concerned came into the question and I should have acted as unhesitatingly against them had they been British. . . .

'I would add that when my plans for arrest were ready I decided only within 24 hours of putting them into execution to include the Trade Delegation offices. Had I thought that I could have dealt adequately with the situation without their inclusion I should have done so, but after serious consideration I decided that I could not.'

No. 382

Mr. Rattigan[1] *(Constantinople) to the Marquess Curzon of Kedleston*[2]
(Received July 9, 11.40 a.m.)
No. 507 Telegraphic [N 7906/2866/38]

CONSTANTINOPLE, *July 8, 1921, 8 p.m.*

Your telegram No. 425.[3]
I have asked General Officer Commanding what proofs he has obtained of Bolshevik plots. He informs me that he has ample evidence which he is forwarding to War Office at once.[4] I think it desirable I should keep entirely

[1] H.M. Chargé d'Affaires at Constantinople.
[2] See No. 380, n. 2.
[3] Of July 7. This, in view of questions in Parliament and the likelihood of further discussions (see 144 *H.C. Deb. 5 s*, cols. 367–9, 409–11, 644–5, and 892–4) requested fullest information on the arrest of the members of the Russian Trade Delegation (see No. 381).
[4] On July 9, at 4.20 p.m., General Harington telegraphed to the War Office as follows: 'Following were grounds for carrying out arrest and subsequent deportation.

'1. Persistent agent's report confirmed by independent information and news from other sources.

'2. Presence of notorious individuals in Constantinople, reported on reliable information to have come for definite purposes of terrorist activity and anti-Allied propaganda.

'3. Very strong local evidence, supported by absolutely reliable information from indisputable genuine Russian sources, which will not be divulged, of deep laid plot to engineer local rising against allied forces of occupation by Russian and Turkish elements simultaneously.

'4. Close connection between member of so-called Bolshevik Trade Delegation in Constantinople, one Musabekoff, and self-confessed member of local communist terrorist organisation.

'5. Established connection between employees in General Staff Intelligence and agent known to be working for trade delegation with definite purpose of obtaining military and political information of a secret nature.

'6. Effort to depreciate local currency by circulation of forged notes on large scale.

'7. Direct threat to the public security of Constantinople caused by steady agitation of those agents amongst large population of Russian refugees, the position of which refugees

out of this matter. As Your Lordship is aware I was not consulted though I am satisfied that arrests were necessary to ensure security and . . .[5] allied troops.

will, when French stop relief of those in Constantinople on July 15th, shortly become very much more grave.'

On July 12, General Harington telegraphed to the War Office as follows: 'I have given following additional information to High Commissioner in answer to request from Foreign Office.

'A. ? Motor was seized on receipt from garage in which it was housed to prevent inter-communication and to prevent its use for escape of wanted persons who evaded arrest. To ensure against use ? by anybody, working ? party went and it was placed in Army garage. It will be returned to the delegation with other office effects. At the same time money that remained in the office will be returned untouched. All other money has been returned against receipt. Every effort was made to collect all personal effects before the departure of H.M.S. Splendid. This was done ? from addresses and particulars supplied by individuals concerned under supervision of British Officers. Owners nominated agents for collection of baggage left behind.

'B. Guard of Turkish police has been retained at delegation office, pending complete investigation of documents, which will be completed today. Office will be handed over tomorrow July 13th together with effects including any money in the office.

'C. At signed request of his tutor Pavlovitch Koudish's 7 years old son was taken on board.

'D. H.M.S. Splendid s[l]ipped the tow from the vessel containing the 9 deported ? members at 0430 hours July 4th well in sight of land 14 miles 140 degree true from Cape Astodar. The deportees are shown to have reached the port of Yalta in safety by subsequent evidence to observation of Destroyer.

'E. I have decided to hand office back at once and to forego going through trade papers. I had secured impartial technical assistance but the work could ? only be done by a reliable Russian interpreter and would take another week.'

[5] The text is here uncertain.

No. 383

Minutes of meeting of July 15, 1921 of Interdepartmental Committee on Bolshevism

[N 8328/7023/38]

FOREIGN OFFICE, *July 15, 1921*

The second meeting of the Interdepartmental Committee on Bolshevism was held in Sir W. Tyrrell's room at the Foreign Office on July 15th. The Hon. R.C. Lindsay acted as Chairman. The following were also present:—

Gen. Bartholomew, C.B., C.M.G., D.S.O.	War Office
Sir B. Thomson, K.C.B.	Home Office
Sir A. Sinclair, Bart.	Colonial Office
Mr. Clausen	,,
Major Bray	India Office
Mr. R. A. Leeper[1]	Foreign Office
Mr. O. Harvey[1]	,,
Mr. L. G. M. Gall	S[ecret] I[ntelligence] S[ervice]

[1] Members of the Northern Department of the Foreign Office.

1. Mr. Lindsay in his preliminary remarks explained that when the first meeting had been held on July 1st[2] he was not in possession of any clear terms of reference, but that he was now in a position to explain that the task of the Committee was to sift all the available evidence on Bolshevik anti-British activities and to present a concise report for the consideration of the Cabinet. This report would contain a summary of the evidence classified according to reliability and importance and drawing special attention to any attempts made by the Bolsheviks to evade either the letter or the spirit of the Trade Agreement.

2. The question of procedure was then discussed. It was decided to form a Sub-Committee consisting of Sir A. Sinclair, Major Bray, Mr. Leeper, Mr. Gall and Mr. Liddell (acting for Sir B. Thomson) whose duty it would be to prepare a detailed report for submission to the full Committee at its next meeting on July 22nd. Sir B. Thomson urged the importance of losing no time in getting the first report ready as the British Communists who had been attending the meeting of the Third International would soon be on their way home and that, if any action were to be taken, the available evidence should be in the hands of the proper authorities without delay.

3. During the discussion which followed on the main lines of the report it was agreed that the Committee should set itself the task of answering two questions[3]:— (1) Is the Soviet Government hostile to the British Empire? (2) If so, in what respect is it showing its hostility? It was agreed that the two most important aspects of the hostile action being taken by the Soviets was (a) the financing of Communists and Communist propaganda in this country (b) the work carried on by the Third International. It was agreed that attention should be called to the responsibility of the Soviet Government for the actions of the Third International on the ground that the latter body was financed by the former. Information was also to be collected about other attempts being made by the Soviet Government to take refuge under any other organisations such as the Trade Unions, Arcos[4] etc. in order to continue their work of propaganda.

4. It was finally decided that the sub-Committee should meet on July 18th.

---

[2] See No. 379.
[3] In a letter to the Foreign Office of July 13, the India Office communicated Mr. Montagu's suggestion that, at its next meeting, the Committee should deliberate and report on Bolshevik anti-British activities under the following headings:
'I Has the Soviet Government designs against the British Empire?
'II If so in which directions is it proposed that these designs be put into operation?
'III In what spheres is any hostile action they may contemplate most likely to be effective?
'IV Are there any indications as to the time when such action may take place?
'V What form is it likely to take?'
[4] The All-Russian Co-operative Society Limited, a Russian Company registered in Great Britain and the first organisation to be established after the resumption of Anglo-Soviet trading relations.

to draw up the preliminary report which was to be shown to a Legal Adviser before submission to the main Committee.[5]

[5] In a letter of August 4, Sir A. Hirtzel, Deputy Under Secretary of State at the India Office, wrote to the Under Secretary of State for Foreign Affairs as follows: 'The Secretary of State for India has had under consideration the report of the interdepartmental Committee presided over by the Hon. R. C. Lindsay on Bolshevism as a menace to the British Empire, and he understands that copies of it have been furnished to the other Secretaries of State concerned.

'Mr. Montagu is greatly impressed by the evidence which the Committee have marshalled, and by the necessity for taking immediate action on it. He would accordingly suggest for the consideration of the Marquess Curzon of Kedleston that the Secretaries of State personally should meet to discuss the question as soon as possible.

'He would also suggest that the Committee should be kept in being for the purpose of collating fresh evidence as it comes in, and he would be glad if it could meet again at a very early date to examine a report further on the eastern aspect of Bolshevik and kindred intrigues. . . .'

On August 9, Mr. Ovey replied: 'I am directed by the Marquess Curzon of Kedleston to acknowledge the receipt of your letter No. P.3378 of 4th. instant, relative to the Interdepartmental Committee on Bolshevik Activities.

'2. Lord Curzon regrets that his duties in connection with the Supreme Council [see Vol. XV, Chap. VI] will prevent him for the present from discussing in person the report with Mr. Secretary Montagu.

'3. Arrangements have been made, however, for all fresh information bearing on the subject to be collected and collated from day to day; and it is proposed shortly to call a fresh meeting of the Committee with a view to the production of a second report.'

To this letter Sir A. Hirtzel replied on August 15: 'With reference to Mr. Ovey's letter No. N. 894.9/ of the 9th instant, I am directed by the Secretary of State for India to say that he understands from the public press that the Supreme Council had concluded its business [on August 13] and that the Secretary of State for Foreign Affairs has now returned to town. He trusts therefore that the Marquess Curzon of Kedleston will be able to arrange a meeting with the other Secretaries of State at a very early date. He regards such a meeting as the more important because, for his own part, he is entirely unable to learn what the policy of His Majesty's Government towards Bolshevism at present is, and because the instructions recently issued by the Soviet Government to their agent at Kabul, and officially communicated [on August 5: N 9064/9064/97] to the Prime Minister by M. Berzin [see No. 384, n. 1, below], make it necessary to define the attitude of the representative of the Government of India in Afghanistan in his negotiations with the Afghan Government.'

No. 384

Mr. O'Malley to M. Berzin[1]

[N 8491/2866/38]

FOREIGN OFFICE, *July 29, 1921*

Sir,

I am directed by the Marquess Curzon of Kedleston to refer to Monsieur Krassin's notes of July 7th and 8th,[2] concerning the arrest and deportation of certain members of the Russian Trade Delegation,[3] and quoting a

[1] Assistant Official Agent of the Russian Soviet Government in Great Britain.
[2] Not printed.
[3] See No. 381.

statement made on this subject in the House of Commons[4] by the Parliamentary Under Secretary of State for Foreign Affairs[5].

2. As between the Allied Governments and Turkey the position is that of a state of war with a suspension of hostilities in virtue of the armistice of October 30th, 1918;[6] the troops of the Allied Governments are in occupation of Constantinople and under the command of General Sir C. Harington. In this position Sir C. Harington possesses all the powers of a commander of a belligerent force in occupation of enemy territory, and the special powers derived from the terms of the armistice. He is responsible to the Allied Governments not only for the execution of the duties incumbent upon an officer in that position—in particular for the safety of the troops under his command —but also for the maintenance of order under martial law in the occupied territory. In these circumstances the Commander-in-Chief is obviously not only competent, but is obliged, to suppress any disturbance of the peace irrespective of the nationality and profession of the persons creating and abetting or suspected of creating and abetting such disturbance.

3. As regards the actual evidence on which Sir C. Harington's action was based it should be noted that one of Sir C. Harington's own clerks, not a British subject, was involved in the plot, and correspondence was found which established the fact that he had been supplying an agent employed by the Russian Trade Delegation with secret political information. Further a member of the Trade Delegation named Musabekoff was closely identified with a local terrorist organisation, whose plans came into the possession of the Commander-in-Chief.

4. This information seems to Lord Curzon completely to justify the action which Sir C. Harington took against certain members of the delegation, who, incidentally, did not number one third of the persons arrested.[7]

5. Monsieur Krassin appears to labour under the delusion that this measure was aimed specially at the Trade Delegation, but you will observe that this is not the case. Indeed the above comparison of the proportion of its members to the total number of arrests makes this clear. Moreover, the office with all its papers and effects including the money and the motor car referred to in Monsieur Krassin's note of 8th instant, was returned to the delegation on the 13th instant[8] and there should be no further hindrance to the normal work of the Trade Delegation, provided that its members confine themselves to what Monsieur Krassin defines as their proper function, namely to engage solely in matters connected with trade and not to mix themselves up in political affairs.

I am, etc.,

Owen O'Malley

---

[4] See 144 *H.C. Deb. 5 s.*, col. 368.

[5] Mr. C. B. Harmsworth.

[6] Signed at Mudros. For text, see *B.F.S.P.*, vol. 111, pp. 611–13.

[7] See No. 381. In his telegram No. 580 of July 11, General Harington informed the War Office that he had arrested 52 people altogether.

[8] See No. 382, n. 3.

No. 385

Record by Mr. Ovey of a conversation with the American Commercial Counsellor

[*N 9835/8614/38*]

FOREIGN OFFICE, *August 2, 1921*

The American Commercial Counsellor, Mr. Post Wheeler, called on me today with reference to a recent rumour in the 'Evening Standard' that the Soviet Government were going to acknowledge the Russian debt in return for relief to the starving.

Mr. Wheeler thought he read into this the first symptoms of negotiations on our part to take up this question. I assured him that nothing of the sort had been considered here and that at present our policy was confined to carrying out the Trade Agreement.

As regards our policy with regard to relief I referred him to a reply given by Mr. Harmsworth in the House of Commons and to the Prime Minister's statement[1] that the matter would probably be discussed at the forthcoming meeting of the Supreme Council. I was unable to give him the considered views of His Majesty's Government on this point as I was not yet aware of them although I was *personally* not in favour of the question being placed on the Agenda of the Supreme Council.

Mr. Wheeler expressed his view that a discussion by the Supreme Council might lead to raising still more important questions of Bolshevik recognition and such like.[2] The American people might, if the Bolsheviks released their nationals (he knew nothing officially of the Hoover negotiations[3]) and if a larger scheme of relief came into force, suddenly be swayed towards a new and friendly feeling towards the Bolsheviks. He agreed that this was probably one of the Bolsheviks' main motives in making a widespread appeal.

ESMOND OVEY

[1] See 145 *H.C. Deb. 5 s.*, col. 928.
[2] Cf. *F.R.U.S.* 1921, vol. ii, pp. 818–19.
[3] See No. 386, n. 2 and No. 396, below.

No. 386

Sir G. Clerk[1] (Prague) to the Marquess Curzon of Kedleston
(Received August 5, 3.55 p.m.)

No. 93 Telegraphic [*N 8971/8614/38*]

PRAGUE, *August 5, 1921, 9 a.m.*

Minister for Foreign Affairs informs me Czechoslovak Government has decided to give material assistance to combat famine in Russia. It is proposed

[1] H.M. Minister at Prague.

to send mission of doctors several fully-equipped hospital trains, etc. and Government is beginning to collect clothing and food. Czechoslovak Government has asked for assistance of different public and political organizations and hope that the entire population will help in alleviating the distress of their fellow-creatures. Government is anxious that this undertaking should develop into an international[2] one and invites the collaboration of other countries. International Red Cross has already been approached. Czechoslovak Government is prepared to place at the disposal of any international organization many medical men and others who know Russia and the language.

Motives are not only humanitarian but also inspired by the wish to prevent the spread of contagious diseases especially cholera to neighbouring countries.

[2] The Council of the International Committee of the Red Cross and the League of Red Cross Societies met on August 4 and in a resolution proposed that 'an international relief organisation should be formed to centralize both the action taken by the Governments for provisioning Russia and the work of the voluntary organisations'. The resolution continued: 'The Joint Council welcomes the steps already taken by Dr. Nansen [Head of the Norwegian Delegation to the League of Nations], by Mr. Hoover, in the United States, and by the International Credits Committee with various States, and is convinced that *only a powerful International Organisation* recognised by all the Governments, and specially by the Soviet Government and acting with the authorisation of the latter, would be able to organise relief measures, to co-ordinate the various efforts made, to collect funds, and to supervise the distribution of foodstuffs in Russia.

'The Joint Council, therefore, invites representatives of all the European and American Associations, which are willing to take action in aid of Russia, to meet at Geneva on August 15th, to draw up the constitution of this international organisation. It hopes by this means to be able to furnish the Governments desiring to participate in international action on a large scale in Russia, and willing to appoint representatives to this Conference, with an absolutely neutral platform for the discussion of their further plans.

'The International Red Cross Committee and the League of Red Cross Societies will endeavour to assist this International Organisation, either by sending delegates, or by organising the technical side of the relief work for children and of the measures to combat diseases and epidemics, or by issuing an appeal for the active co-operation of all the national Red Cross Societies.'

On August 17, Dr. Haden Guest, representing the Imperial War Relief Fund at the Russian Famine Relief Conference at Geneva, reported that the Conference had ended that afternoon.

His report continued: 'Conference agreed [to] form International Committee Russian relief to be appointed by Joint Council Red Cross and to represent all Governments private associations and Red Cross organisations willing to work for alleviation of Russian famine. This International committee to be advisory. Executive action confided to two commissioners Dr. Nansen and Mr. Hoover or his representative. Joint Council Red Cross given full power to take any necessary action in case either commissioner cannot accept office. The two commissioners were given full power [to] conclude necessary arrangements [with] Russian Government and Russian voluntary organisations and to make other arrangements necessary for relief. Measures taken to secure co-ordination action voluntary organisations and Committee formed by Supreme Council. General discussions very harmonious and basis of action of relief committee definitely agreed as non-political and purely humanitarian. International Committee will shortly issue appeal [to] all charitable organisations in world to assist Russia. Need for co-operation of Governments recognised but also need for intense voluntary action. Many Governments and chief Relief Organisations represented and also for the first time at Geneva a representative of Soviet Red Cross. . . .'

Minister for Foreign Affairs asks whether His Majesty's Government will be ready to join in any such action.[3]

Copy of note by bag.[4]

[3] The Foreign Office replied (despatch No. 254 of August 12):
'Please inform the Czecho-Slovak Government that the matter is being considered by the Supreme Council and that we hope to be in a position to reply more fully when the Council have come to a decision.' (See Vol. XV, Chap. VI).

[4] Prague despatch No. 182 of August 5, not printed.

No. 387

Note of interview with Members of the Russian Trade Delegation at 10, Downing Street, S.W., August 5, 1921

[N 9536/8614/38]

PRESENT:

British: The Prime Minister, Mr. E. F. Wise, C.B., Sir Edward Grigg.

Russian: M. Berzin, M. Klishko.

Sir Robert Horne and Sir Maurice Hankey were present during part of the meeting.

THE PRIME MINISTER asked M. Berzin to begin.

M. BERZIN (translated throughout by M. Klishko) said that he had asked for an interview because he had been informed that the subject of relief for the Russian famine was to be discussed by the Supreme Council in Paris[1] the following week. He made a statement on the extent and gravity of the famine, handing in certain maps and statistics.

THE PRIME MINISTER asked what, in M. Berzin's opinion, the Supreme Council could do.

M. BERZIN replied that they had to come to ask that. He explained that they thought they could get sufficient grain for sowing next Spring, but could not deal with the immediate need for food. Transport was the main difficulty, but they were also unable to get grain from some Russian provinces which had a surplus because the peasant would only surrender it in return for goods—such as woollen clothing, boots, agricultural implements, etc.—which he needed. Could the British people help in supplying goods?

THE PRIME MINISTER pointed out that this raised the question of credit. Would the Soviet Government acknowledge the Russian debt?

M. BERZIN said he would make enquiries.

Some discussion followed as to whether Russia had any produce such as timber and jute available for export.

THE PRIME MINISTER then adjourned to discuss the subject privately with the Chancellor of the Exchequer, for whom he had sent.

On returning, the Prime Minister said he would like MM. Berzin and

[1] For the minutes of the meeting of the Third Conference of Paris (August 8-13, 1921), see Vol. XV, Chap. VI.

Klishko to state their case to Sir Philip Lloyd-Greame,[2] whom he had instructed to make a report to him on the possibility of giving assistance. The Prime Minister then referred to the propaganda and hostile activity of the Soviet Government, contrary to the Trade Agreement.

M. BERZIN said individual Russians, whom the Government could not control, might be doing so, but not the Government itself. As evidence of *bona fides*, he handed in a copy of M. Chicherin's instructions to the Soviet delegates in Afghanistan.

THE PRIME MINISTER said it was acknowledged that Russians on the Third International, including M. Trotski, were stirring up trouble against us.

M. BERZIN said some members of Russian Government were also members of the Third International but only as individuals. They were forbidden even to take any action inconsistent with the obligations of the Government, such as the Trade Agreement.

THE PRIME MINISTER said he hoped they would endeavour to exercise better control and play the game. The British people wanted peace throughout the world. They had no quarrel with the Russian people, and they believed that the only way of improving the lot of humanity, particularly of its more stricken millions, lay in the attainment of as large a measure of fraternity as humanity was capable of.

He said he would communicate any particular instances of bad faith on the part of the Soviet Government which were reported to him.

The delegation then withdrew, Mr. Wise taking the maps and statements on the famine for communication to Sir Philip Lloyd-Greame.

[2] Secretary of the Department of Overseas Trade and Additional Parliamentary Under Secretary of State for Foreign Affairs.

No. 388

Minutes of a Meeting on Relief for Russian Famine held at the Board of Trade, August 6, 1921

[*N 9054/8614/38*]

PRESENT: Sir P. Lloyd-Greame, Sir E. A. Crowe, Sir S. J. Chapman, Mr. Payne,[1] Mr. Wise, Commander Maxse,[2] Mr. Reyntiens,[3] Captain Clively. Also: MM. Berzin, Klishko, Krysin.[4]

1. *Area in question.* Maps were shown in which were indicated

   (a) the famine area,
   (b) area of inadequate harvest,
   (c) area of normal harvest,
   (d) harvest which allowed of surplus.

   [1] Second Secretary at the Board of Trade.
   [2] A member of the Northern Department of the Foreign Office.
   [3] An Assistant Director in the Department of Overseas Trade.
   [4] An expert with the Russian Trade Delegation.

Sir P. Lloyd-Greame suggested that there appeared to be sufficient wheat in Russia in the aggregate to meet immediate needs, but the Russian Delegates demurred, pointing out that there had not been enough for last year and there was still an adverse balance to be made up.

The Delegates pointed out that their desire was to have grain imported into the ports such as Petrograd, Odessa, and the Crimea, for the supply of the adjacent areas, so that the corn grown there might be moved into the famine-stricken districts.

As regards Southern Russia, the proposal was to import supplies both from abroad and from Siberia. As regards the region about Kiev (Southern Ukraine) this part was self-sufficing and a certain proportion of the grain would be taken from there to go into the famine area. Further the area round the Sea of Azof, and also Siberia, were destined to supply the famine territory.

2. *Difficulties involved.* Sir P. Lloyd-Greame said that it appeared to be mainly a question of transport, but The Russian Delegation pointed out that, in addition, there was the question of insufficiency of supply, and they said that if the ports could be put into as good a trim as possible for the handling of imports of grain, then that would provide a partial solution of the transport difficulty.

As regards the rivers and canals, they were mainly frozen from October to April, and the almost sole means of transport would be by railway.

The Railways in Northern Russia were as follows:–

(a) Murmansk–Petrograd Line, which served the North, including Vologda.
(b) The Archangel Line.
(c) Reval–Petrograd.
(d) Riga–Moscow.
(e) Libau–Moscow, and
(f) Line from the Finnish Ports to Petrograd.

From Petrograd there was a double line to Moscow.

In all these cases the permanent way is in a fairly good condition, but there is a shortage of locomotives. The total pre-war number was 17,000 and this has now been reduced to 5,000 or 6,000. The Russians have placed an order in Germany for 500 or 600, for delivery to begin this month and extend over the next twelve months. Some of these locomotives were said to be ready, but Poland was making a difficulty about their transit.

As regards waggons, the question had not been closely looked into, but it was thought that there were as many as their existing locomotives could haul. It was also stated that 3,000 or 4,000 waggons had been built in Canada for the late Russian Government and were held there by the Disposals Board. Also there were about 100 locomotives in the United States, which could not be delivered pending settlement as to price.

The centre and south of the famine area are comparatively (for Russia) well served in respect of railways by the lines Moscow–Simbirsk–Ufa, Moscow–Simbirsk–Samara, Moscow–Saratov, Moscow–Tsaritsyn–Astrakhan. Viatka is only indirectly connected with Moscow, by a branch line meeting the Petrograd–Viatka–Perm railway at Vologda. There is a north to south connecting line running from Kazan to the Crimea, a little to the west of the famine area.

There were also the following lines:—

Odessa–Kharkov.
The lines from the Azof ports to Kharkov.
Krementchug–Kharkov line.

3. *Fuel*. A difficulty had arisen through having to change the fuel for the locomotives. On certain lines the engines had originally been designed for oil fuel but they had had to be converted for coal, and again in the case of these and some other locomotives wood fuel eventually had to be adopted in lieu of coal. On the whole it would be difficult to make up the wastage of locomotives by repair work. On the other hand, SIR P. LLOYD-GREAME pointed out that it would be useless to give out contracts for new locomotives because it would be from 9 to 12 months before they would be ready for delivery, and the Russian delegation laid stress on the need of their repair shops for spare parts, fittings and fuel.

4. *Transport difficulties this year and last.* MR. WISE pointed out that the situation as regards locomotives was much the same this year as last year but that the rolling stock would be less absorbed in military operations.

SIR EYRE CROWE suggested that supplies for troops were now being moved to the Caucasus for the support of the Turkish Nationalists. This fact complicated difficulties in transporting food to famine areas. MR. KLISHKO said an official denial had been given by the Russian Government to the report that military movements were taking place.[5]

5. *Distribution*. SIR P. LLOYD-GREAME pointed out that in the south there appeared to be four lines of railways running approximately parallel by which the famine area could be served, separated each from the other by areas of from 50–120 miles broad. How then would the food, which was conveyed by rail, be distributed throughout the country? MR. KLISHKO suggested that the peasants would transport [it] with horses. SIR P. LLOYD-GREAME asked whether the horses were not all dying of famine. MR. KLISHKO said no doubt many were dying and that motor transport would be required for this purpose; they had some but not enough. There was by the way plenty of petrol available. How far motor transport could be used in winter required consideration.

6. *Means of securing surplus supplies*. Mr. Klishko said that they did not intend to make compulsory requisitions of corn beyond the statutory levy. They proposed to persuade the peasants to surrender the further surplus by giving them goods in exchange.

[5] At M. Klishko's request, the following amendment was made: '—which official denial was thereupon handed to Sir Eyre Crowe by M. Klishko.'

The goods required would be cloth, boots, tools and smaller agricultural and other implements. Larger agricultural implements would be distributed to Co-operative Societies.

7. *Goods required.* THE DELEGATES gave the following rough figures as to their requirements:—

Wheat, for food	2,000,000	Tons
Wheat, for seed	80,000	,,
Coal	£1,000,000	worth
Cloth	£2,000,000	,,
Boots	£1,500,000	,,
Agricultural implements and machinery . .	£4,000,000	,,
Motor Lorries, —amount not certain.		
Chemicals including fertilisers		
etc. and medicines	£1,000,000	,,
Cattle for breeding	. . .	

Of these goods the Russians propose to purchase the wheat outside this country as they understood it would be impossible to make purchases here. They could buy in the United Kingdom the coal, cloth, boots and motor lorries, and the small agricultural implements up to £750,000. The remainder, which would consist of such implements as threshers, binders, etc., would be obtained from the United States and Canada. They would supply a complete list on Monday. The list might include British goods up to £10,000,000.

7 [*sic*]. *Proposals for obtaining goods.* THE RUSSIANS suggested that the Export Credits Scheme should be extended to their country, and they offered to pay 15% down on the price of the goods they were to obtain, with 85% credit.

SIR P. LLOYD-GREAME put the following questions to them

(a) Would they acknowledge their existing debts?

In reply they [THE RUSSIANS] said that they could not go beyond the Trade Agreement, and that this could be discussed at Peace Treaty negotiations. Pressed further on this, they said that they would refer the question to Moscow.

(b) What security would they give, supposing the Scheme should be extended to Russia?

They offered Bills of the Russian Co-operative Society Limited (Arcos Ltd.) the capital of which they declared to be £100,000—the Bills to be endorsed by M. Krassin as Commissar of Foreign Trade. The Bills would be promises to pay in £s sterling within three years, according to the provisions of the Act.

(c) What collateral could they supply?

They offered to obtain, if possible, the signature to the Bills of the Central Union of Russian Co-operative Societies, which they explained was an entirely separate concern from the Company in this country, but they could not give any assurance as to the assets of this concern. They were of opinion that the credit offered was sufficient, but they could not offer any tangible security which could be realised in event of default.

SIR PHILIP pressed the delegation as to whether they could not offer tangible collateral security which could be realised in case of default, e.g. gold or the proceeds of sale of timber and other exports. THE DELEGATION stated that they were not prepared to offer any security beyond the endorsement of the Soviet Government.

They required their gold and other resources for other purchases, particularly of grain. They could make no further offer without reference to Moscow.

8. *Conclusion.* SIR P. LLOYD-GREAME summed up the position by pointing out that they could not, at least at present, undertake to acknowledge their debts, but that at the same time they were asking for further credit on the word of the Soviet Government. He went on to point out that every application under the Export Credit Scheme had to be submitted to and scrutinised by the Advisory Committee which consisted of Bankers and Merchants. This Committee put a value on the security offered and it was an essential part of the Scheme that half the uncovered risk was to be taken by the Exporter in this country. He added that the proposition put forward by the delegation did not appear to afford a security which a Business Committee would regard as adequate.

THE DELEGATION said that they would endeavour to lay before the Board shortly revised and detailed figures about their requirements and as to their plans for relieving the famine. They also stated that they would communicate with Moscow as to the recognition of debts and the provision of security, and that if they had a further proposal to make they would ask for a further interview.[6]

Board of Trade, August 6, 1921.

[6] At M. Klishko's request the following was added: 'At the conclusion of the meeting M. Berzin asked whether the Board of Trade consider[ed] the proposal put by the Russian Trade Delegation as unacceptable, and [was], therefore, refused, to which Sir Philip Lloyd-Greame replied that this proposal [was] neither accepted nor refused, and the purpose of this meeting was to collect all the information for the purpose of the report to the Prime Minister.'

No. 389

Mr. Hodgson (Moscow) to the Marquess Curzon of Kedleston
(Received August 16)
No. 2 [N 9386/4/38]

Confidential   MOSCOW, *August 8, 1921*
My Lord,

I have the honour to transmit, herewith, situation report for the week ended the 6th August.

I have, etc.,
R. M. HODGSON

Situation Report for the Period July 17 to August 7, 1921

On Sunday, the 17th July, the British Commercial Mission to Russia[1] left London and, travelling through Berlin, arrived at Riga on the following Thursday.

M. Bisseneek, the Lettish Minister in London, was in Riga on leave. He described various difficulties which the Lettish Mission in Moscow had had, and advised the British Mission to expect a treatment of continual petty obstruction from the Soviet authorities.

The attitude of M. Ganetsky, Soviet representative at Riga, seemed to give immediate justification to this warning. He produced a telegram from Moscow stating that the rent of the house reserved for the British Mission in Moscow had been fixed at 5,000*l.* per annum instead of 700*l.* or 800*l.*, the amount which had been suggested to M. Klishko in London, and which he promised to recommend for favourable consideration.

M. Ganetsky further declared that he had orders to charge the preposterous rate of four (4) gold roubles per pood[2] on all the stores of the mission for the transport from the Lettish frontier to Moscow. His behaviour generally in matters of detail was such as to give the impression that he was far from being anxious to assist the mission to arrive in Moscow at an early date. Finally it was arranged, on receipt of a telegram from Moscow, that the mission should proceed on the understanding that the house originally proposed was reserved for occupation on condition that if the mission could not come to an agreement on the matter of rent, it should move into other premises.

The mission left Riga on Thursday, the 28th July. At the Russian frontier it was found necessary, on account of the bad state of the baggage waggons, to detach the mission cars from the fast train and proceed with the post train. Moscow was reached on the 31st July.

The mission was met by a junior official from the Commissariat for Foreign Affairs and driven in motor cars to the house prepared in the Povarskaya.

The house was found to contain fine spacious rooms, but not spacious enough to accommodate suitably the personnel of the mission.

A guard of eight Red army soldiers is on duty at the house, and the Soviet authorities had provided a domestic staff, a Commandant and a house steward.

Official visits have been paid to M. Litvinov, Assistant Commissar for Foreign Affairs in charge of Western European countries: to other officials of the same Department; to M. Krassin, now on a visit to Moscow; M. Kamenev, President of the Moscow Municipal Soviet and of the Committee of Aid to the Famine Areas: also the Esthonian, Lettish, Lithuanian and Finnish Missions.

It would be obviously premature to form an opinion on the political situation in Moscow. Some light, however, is thrown on the working of the

[1] See No. 376. [2] 1 pood = 40 lb.

710

political machine by experiences of the mission in so far as it has yet been in contact with it. The official-in-charge of the sub-Department of the Ministry for Foreign Affairs dealing with British and American affairs received the mission with the utmost suavity, and volunteered his assistance in obtaining for the mission all facilities and conveniences which might be required. Various requests were put to him, such as providing newspapers, telephones, diplomatic cards, photograph permits, etc. In every case this official undertook immediate fulfilment. In no case up till now have his promises been fulfilled.

Permission to see the American prisoners was at first promised, but subsequently it was stated that no such permission would be given. This, and a number of other incidents of a similar nature, are indicative of an attitude on the part of the Soviet institutions which the mission will, in all probability, have to confront throughout. How far this attitude is dictated by the intention to obstruct, how far by ineptitude and incompetency, it is yet too early to say.

Representatives of the Baltic States—Latvia, Esthonia and Lithuania—who, on account of the presence of large numbers of their nationals in various districts of Russia, are well informed as to the course of events throughout the country, differ little in their estimate of the situation.

They allude to the all-pervading influence of the Extraordinary Commission, whose spies are everywhere, and without whose sanction no step can be taken by the Government; whose ramifications extend into every department and from whom no individual is safe. Even the highest officials in the Commissariat for Foreign Affairs are mere cyphers and have agents of the 'Cheka'[3] attached to them. Some twenty of such agents, male and female, are specially designated for watching the foreign missions. The Lettish Minister showed photographs of these persons and promised copies.

Much stress was laid on the difficulty experienced in protecting the nationals of the smaller States, who are liable to be arrested on trivial charges and sentenced to some years' imprisonment without trial. The Government Departments are apt to express regret at such occurrences and promise to deal with them, but, in practice, the condemned persons remain indefinitely in jail, and any attempt at intervention is stultified by obstruction on the part of officials.

With regard to the position of the Soviet Government, the Baltic representatives are sceptical of any possibility of its being overthrown by internal agencies. The rule is brutal, stupid and universally disliked, but it is a strong autocratic rule which the country is in too depressed and disjointed a state to resist. Accounts of the famine received from this and other sources seem to establish the fact that catastrophe is impending. Twenty-one Governments—fourteen in Russia and seven in Ukraine—are affected and their population is in danger of annihilation. The stricken area extends eastward from the Dnieper to the Ural river and northwards to Viatka and Ufa. Some 18 million people are said to be affected. In the Moscow neighbourhood the

3 See No. 360, n. 5.

situation is better, but prices for foodstuffs are very high and quite out of reach of the population. Reports from Siberia are somewhat conflicting but it appears that the towns are at all events in a disastrous condition of want. The local press speaks of the intention of Germany to send a relief expedition with stores and supplies. The Lettish and Esthonian Ministers state that their Governments signify their intention of sending help on similar lines.

Prospects of trade do not appear encouraging. According to the statements of a variety of persons with whom members of the mission have discussed the situation, the country has nothing whatever to offer in exchange for goods imported. The Baltic representatives assure me that, in spite of the fact that their countries have in abundance precisely the products of which the Russian Government is in most urgent need, namely, grains and fats, no business whatsoever is being done, Russia having no financial resources with which to effect purchases. The Lettish Minister states definitely that the balance of gold still remaining at the disposal of the Government only totals 125,000,000 gold roubles. The financial crisis is reflected in other directions. M. Krassin now says that it will be impossible to conclude the Armstrong-Whitworth contract for repairing locomotives.[4] The projected despatch of engines to be repaired in England is regarded unfavourably here, and it is now impossible on financial grounds to execute it. Such funds as were available are required for purchasing foodstuffs abroad. In reply to the observation that the failure to carry out a project that has been definitely accepted would have a disastrous effect upon commercial circles in England, M. Krassin replied that it was preferable to repudiate the business at once rather than to sign the contract and then be unable to effect the necessary payments.

The general aspect of the town of Moscow is deplorable. There are now a few small provision shops open, a café here and there, some ladies' hat shops and a florist or two. There are also a fair number of little shops where repairs of almost every conceivable article are carried on. The restrictions on private trade having been relaxed, it is possible that the number of retail shops will increase. The appearance of such as are open is pitiable in view of the almost complete absence of goods for sale. Whole streets of offices and shops show nothing but windows broken and boarded up, with chaos and rubbish inside. Many houses have been destroyed as the result of civil war and no effort has been made to rebuild them or to repair the buildings which have suffered.

[4] See *The Times*, February 1, 1921, p. 10.

No. 390

Lord Hardinge (Paris) to Sir E. Crowe[1] *(Received August 11)*
No. 591 Telegraphic [N 9220/8614/38]

Confidential   PARIS, *August 10, 1921*

Following for Cabinet:—

'Question of Russia's relief was also discussed at this evening's sitting.[2]

'M. Briand[3] proposed that this should be encouraged through Red Cross.

[1] In the absence of Lord Curzon, who was in Paris, Sir E. Crowe was in charge of the Foreign Office.

[2] Of the Supreme Council (see Vol. XV, No. 95, minute 3). On August 5, the British Cabinet had met and had reached the following conclusions [Cab. 64(21), copy in N 9036/8614/38]: 'The Cabinet had a short discussion in regard to the attitude to be taken up by the British representatives at the forthcoming meeting of the Supreme Council in Paris on the subject of the Russian famine, which will be raised by the French and Belgian representatives.

'Misgivings were expressed as to whether, in view of the stringent financial situation, when all classes of the community were being asked to make great sacrifices, the British Government would be justified in asking Parliament to vote such a sum as would meet the needs of the situation.

'In the unavoidable absence of the Chancellor of the Exchequer, the Lord Privy Seal [Mr. A. Chamberlain] summarised the main features of the financial outlook. He pointed out that existing taxation must, in present financial and industrial conditions, produce less money than in the past. Additional taxation was out of the question. A loan could only be floated for renewing debt falling due, and then only if it could be convincingly demonstrated that expenditure was reduced to a minimum. Consequently the utmost difficulty would be met even in dealing with such essentials as unemployment relief. It was imperative that, if money were required, Parliament should be asked to vote it before prorogation. But, in the conditions outlined above, this would be very difficult.

'The Cabinet were reminded, however, that the Bolsheviks might possess sufficient gold to pay for all the food that could be imported; that, even if gold was not available, there might be other resources which might be hypothecated to the raising of a loan; that possibly it was facilities rather than money that was required; that, even though the Soviet at present ruled in Russia, the famine districts were those which had longest resisted the Bolsheviks; that when Bolshevism had disappeared, the Russian people would remain, and it would be a wise policy to give so emotional a people reason for gratitude; that, even if money were required, the raising of a great voluntary fund might be more effective than Government assistance, and that possibly the best manner in which the Government could help would be by creating a favourable atmosphere for raising such a fund.

'A suggestion, which met with much support, was that Roumania, where a good harvest was reported, should be permitted to pay a part of her debt to this country by sending grain to Russia.

'The view was strongly pressed that in any event Government funds should not be put at the disposal of the Bolshevist Government, which had flagrantly broken the Trade Agreement and had given so many examples of bad faith.

'The general trend of the discussion was to the effect that, while the Prime Minister and Lord Curzon should have reasonable latitude to negotiate, it was undesirable, in existing financial conditions, to promise Government funds, but that there was no objection to giving facilities in return for payment, or to the raising of a voluntary fund, or to the proposal to allow Roumania to send wheat to Russia in discharge of her debt, provided that the administration of any form of relief to be provided by this country, whether in one of the above forms or in any other, should be British.'

[3] French President of the Council and Minister for Foreign Affairs.

'The Prime Minister considered this would not be sufficient, and suggested that matter should be studied rather on more immediately practical basis of inducing Ukraine and other districts which had corn on the spot to part with it to starved regions in return for clothing, finances, etc., to be supplied by Allies.

'M. Bonomi[4] agreed with M. Briand in thinking Red Cross most practical channel of relief already existing.

'Japanese representative declared that Japanese Red Cross would co-operate with other similar bodies for this purpose.

'Colonel Harvey[5] said American relief societies were already interested, though he could not say exactly what was being done. He offered to obtain this information.

'M. Jaspar[6] thought problem too great for Red Cross. He proposed appoint-ment of an international commission to study it in consultation, if desirable, with Red Cross and other similar bodies having experience of such matters.

'Lord Curzon gave account of solution of similar but vaster problem in India during his Viceroyalty, and described the practical measures necessary for any success. He suggested this difficulty must and could only be similarly met; but consent of Soviets to accept and work with foreign personnel was essential to this. He welcomed proposal of M. Jaspar to study the question on these lines.

'Following resolution was adopted:

'"Le Conseil suprême a décidé de créer une commission internationale pour étudier les possibilités de porter secours d'urgence aux populations affamées de la Russie."'

---

4 Italian President of the Council and Minister of the Interior (see No. 2, n. 5).
5 See No. 204, n. 1.
6 See No. 8, n. 2.

No. 391

Mr. Hodgson (Moscow) to the Marquess Curzon of Kedleston
(Received August 12, 4.30 p.m.)
No. 14 Telegraphic [N 9266/8614/38]

MOSCOW, *August 11, 1921, 9.30 a.m.*

Your telegram No. 2 August 3rd.[1]

1. I have discussed Russian famine with patriarch of [*sic*] Tikhon, Monsieur Kishkin formerly Minister (? under) Kerensky[2] now member of Council of

---

1 Not printed. This instructed Mr. Hodgson, in view of the forthcoming discussions in the Supreme Council in Paris (see No. 390), to report on famine conditions in Russia, the political effects of giving or withholding relief, and the most practical form foreign assistance could take.
2 Head of the Provisional Government of Russia, July–November, 1917.

all Russian Committee[3] for assistance to famine stricken . . .[4] Professor Procopovich[5] and others. Area affected by famine extends from Tambov Government to Orenberg Government and from Astrakan to Viatk. Districts bordering Volga which are normally richest in Russia are those which are suffering the most while crops in neighbouring districts are barely sufficient to satisfy local needs. Estimated population affected is continually increasing as reports from various areas come in. It is now calculated that 35,000,000 persons will require relief. Inhabitants of famine stricken districts seeing that there is no possibility of help reaching them in time to prevent starvation are moving in large masses in different directions. Those who were settled in Volga region as a result of the evacuation of Poland during the war see their only hope in returning to Poland. Rest are mostly moving eastwards towards Siberia and Turkestan. Poland is unable to accept the former since the districts from which the people came are still unfit for habitation. Latter travelling through the Steppes, where there are no food supplies and no shelter, appear to be doomed to annihilation. Of these migratory bodies only some twenty per cent are able-bodied and more than thirty per cent children. Condition of these last is piteous as they are without clothing or food. Many of them are being abandoned to their fate by their parents. The people are eating grass, bread made from roots, (? horses) and other rubbish.

2. I am strongly of opinion that relief should be given and submit the following considerations.

A. All neighbouring states as well as Germany are making preparations to send assistance. Great Britain having concluded an agreement with a view to commercial advantage would be placed in an invidious position by standing aloof.

B. Bolshevik Government is largely responsible for the present catastrophe having for three years past by its policy of confiscation prevented accumulation of reserves. It is now obliged to have recourse to help of moderate political elements whose position is accordingly strengthened. Assistance rendered by us should aid those with whom we are in sympathy.[6]

C. Economic blockade of Russia caused maximum privation precisely to those who most deserved our help. To withhold relief now would have similar results.

[3] The All-Russian Famine Relief Committee was set up by a decree of July 21, 1921 of the All-Russian Central Executive Committee. An English text of this decree is preserved at N 9366/8614/38.   [4] The text is here uncertain.

[5] Former Minister of Trade and Industry in the Provisional Government (see n. 2).

[6] In a minute of August 12 (N 9153/8614/38), Mr. Harvey wrote: 'It is extremely likely that the famine will cause among the ignorant Russian peasants a revulsion of feeling against the Soviet Government.

'To divert this and to strengthen its own position, the Soviet Government is to be expected to endeavour to start the intervention-scare again and to make out that the bourgeois-capitalist Powers are on the warpath.

'This shews how important it is in any relief proposals not to attach any conditions that can be interpreted as "intervention": otherwise the Soviet Government will be able to reassert its authority as the only alternative to anarchy or White restoration; and any hope of a change *from within* in an anti-Bolshevik sense would be scotched.'

D. A neutral attitude which I assume to mean allowing private organizations to render assistance without Government approval seems to me to have nothing in its favour. Our inaction would be used for propaganda purposes as proving that the people of England are friendly to Russia whereas the Government alone is antagonistic. Moreover, it is advisable in order to avoid friction and misunderstandings that the British Government exercise a guiding influence over voluntary organizations.

E. Great Britain in spite of great sacrifices she made in order to help political groups in Russia has lost, owing to failure of enterprises with which she was associated herself, the sympathy of all classes. It is doubtful whether by signing trade agreement she has improved her position; an opportunity now occurs of regaining ground by giving aid which cannot be criticised as having political or financial objectives. It would, I think, be a misfortune were it allowed to pass.

3. Problem of relief may be divided into two parts.

A. Relief of immediate suffering, and

B. Provision of seed next . . . .[4]

For the purpose of A. are required principally warm clothing for children —winter will be beginning in Volga districts in two (? months) from now— foodstuffs, particularly milk and flour, waterproof material for making temporary shelters at concentration points, and medical supplies, of which there are none in the country. Doctors too are required as the mortality during the wars has seriously depleted the number of Russian doctors available.

Most effective form of help would be, I believe, despatch of a relief mission having its headquarters at Moscow, transit depots in Petrograd and Novorossisk and distributing centres in such localities as experience may recommend. Organization should postulate as conditions preliminary to its undertaking relief operations that it should be allowed to work through its own representatives have freedom of transport for personnel and goods and be allowed to bring its members freely into Russia.

It is too late to import grain for the winter sowing. What is required is grain for spring 1922.[7]

Repeated to Paris No. 1.

[7] In his despatch No. 14 of August 18 (N 9925/8614/38), Mr. Hodgson transmitted to Lord Curzon a detailed report on the famine situation in Russia.

No. 392

Lord Hardinge (Paris) to Sir E. Crowe
(Received August 14, 9.10 p.m.)
No. 607 Telegraphic: by bag [N 9288/8614/38]

PARIS, *August 13, 1921*

Following from Lord Curzon for Cabinet:—
Russian relief.

At today's meeting of supreme Council[1] it was agreed that each Power should appoint three Representatives to Committee[2] which should meet at Paris as soon as possible. I undertook that selection of British Representatives should be proceeded with on my return. The Committee should have power to add to its numbers by selection of representatives from Border and other interested States, and should decide what other organisations working for the same purpose should be co-ordinated with it. This was accepted. All the other representatives at the Supreme Council referred to probable Soviet obstruction to any efficient system of supervision, without which any project must fail. I said that this need not be anticipated at this stage, but that this would be one of the first questions the Committee would have to consider. Meanwhile first business was to get it constituted.

I also raised question of protecting Europe against grave danger of typhus and cholera from Russia.[3] The League of Nations had appointed a Commission last year to Border States with protection measures against typhus. Contributions of £50,000 had been made by larger States, and smaller ones by other countries. Commission had now come to end of its resources and unless renewed would disappear in face of the even greater danger this year. I proposed that Supreme Council should invite all contributory Powers to renew subscriptions. This was agreed to.

> [1] See Vol. XV, No. 103, minute 4. [2] See No. 390.
> [3] See Vol. XV, No. 103, minute 5.

No. 393

Mr. Hodgson (Moscow) to the Marquess Curzon of Kedleston
(Received August 14, 11 p.m.)
No. 20 Telegraphic [N 9396/9395/38]

MOSCOW, *August 14, 1921, 8.35 p.m.*

My telegram No. 19 of August 1[4]th.[1]

Policy of Soviet Government as elaborated in recently published decrees is to retain in their own hands only a few of the best equipped nationalised undertakings and to lease all others to co-operative societies and private individuals. There is a danger that properties of foreign owners who do not

> [1] Not printed

claim their return may fall . . .[2] hands of others who are likely to ruin under-takings by mishandling of stocks and machinery.

Such British firms as contemplate entering into negotiations with Soviet Government with a view to recovering their property would be well advised to:

1. Act as far as possible jointly.

2. Keep Department of Overseas Trade informed of their action and furnish reports for communication to Moscow where negotiations will tend to concentrate.

Report on developments in the economic policy follows by bag.[3]

[2] The text is here uncertain.
[3] Mr. Hodgson's despatch No. 13 of August 17 (N 9924/4/38), not printed.

No. 394

The Marquess Curzon of Kedleston to Lord Hardinge (Paris)
No. 471 Telegraphic [N 9288/8614/38]

FOREIGN OFFICE, *August 16, 1921, 3.40 p.m.*

Your telegram No. 607.[1]

Inform French Government that British delegates[2] on Committee will be Sir Philip Lloyd-Greame,[3] Sir John Hewett[4] and Mr. Oliver Wardrop[5] with Mr. Leeper as Secretary. Please instruct Wardrop to be prepared to come to Paris at a moment's notice.

Two former will go over Thursday[6] or Friday and will require rooms if Committee is not to be guest of French Government.[7]

[1] No. 392.
[2] These were nominated at a Cabinet Meeting held on August 15 at 12 noon.
[3] See No. 387, n. 2.
[4] Lieutenant-Governor of the United Provinces of Agra and Oudh, 1907–12.
[5] H.M. Consul-General at Strasbourg, who had been entrusted with a Special Political Mission to Transcaucasia in 1919.
[6] August 18.
[7] Following a request by Sir Philip Lloyd-Greame for decisions on certain points, the Cabinet at their meeting of August 17 resolved: 'That the British representatives (a) should support the representation of Germany on the Commission: (b) should generally shape their policy so as not to fall behind that of other nations in rendering assistance: (c) should not offer any money grants, even if other nations do so, without first obtaining the consent of the British Government: (d) should indicate a general willingness to contribute certain goods in kind, such as tents and medical stores, on the same scale as other countries, but should obtain the approval of the British Government to the particular quantities to be granted: (e) should examine the application of the Export Credits Scheme to the problem of relief, subject to the Soviet Government being willing to recognize their obligations for supplies already sent to Russia, as indicated in the Prime Minister's speech in the House of Commons on August 16, 1921 [see 146 *H.C. Deb. 5 s.*, cols. 1241–2].'

No. 395

The Marquess Curzon of Kedleston to Mr. Hodgson (Moscow)
No. 14 Telegraphic [N 9155/3779/38]

Confidential   FOREIGN OFFICE, *August 17, 1921*

Your telegram No. 9:[1] Relations with representatives in Moscow of Governments not recognised by His Majesty's Government.

India Office are being consulted regarding Afghanistan.

There is no objection to, and in fact it would seem difficult for you to avoid, establishing some sort of unofficial relations with the representatives of first six countries mentioned, if you are to obtain the information regarding their status, the conditions prevailing in them, and their relations with the Soviet Government, in which we are particularly interested.

Nor is there any objection to your seeing the representative of the Angora Government, should he seek an interview, since its representatives were received at the London Conference last March,[2] but you should bear in mind that no treaty of peace has been signed between Great Britain and Turkey.

We leave entirely to your discretion the nature of the unofficial relations into which you enter.

[1] Of August 9. This ran: 'Besides recognised Governments the following States have representatives here: Ukraine, Georgia, Azerbaijan, Bokhara, Khiva, Armenia, Angora and Afghanistan. I presume that I should neither visit them nor have any official relations with them.'

[2] See Vol. XV, Chap. II.

No. 396

Mr. Hodgson (Moscow) to the Marquess Curzon of Kedleston
(Received August 19, 10.30 a.m.)
No. 31 Telegraphic [N 9511/8614/38]

MOSCOW, *August 18, 1921, 6.25 p.m.*

My telegram No. 14.[1]

I learn from Chicherin that negotiation between Mr. Hoover's[2] representative in Riga[3] and Litvinov are progressing satisfactorily. Only obstacle now is the question of Government control. Soviet Government does not see its way to allowing entire freedom from control to the American relief organisation though it appears prepared to reduce it to the minimum.

With regard to the proposed assistance of other powers Chicherin expressed the opinion that this would be more efficacious if given by individual nations rather than as a result of combined action. He alluded to the discussions of the Supreme Council[4] which he thought hampered the action of

[1] No. 391.   [2] See No. 353.
[3] Walter Lyman Brown. For his negotiations, see *F.R.U.S.* 1921, vol. ii, pp. 812–17.
[4] See Vol. XV, No. 95, minute 3, No. 102, minute 2, and No. 103, minutes 4 and 5.

Great Britain in compelling her to subordinate her policy to that of France. He believes that France wishes to withhold support being under the impression that by so doing she will hasten disruption in Russia and so weaken the Soviet Government.

Repeated to Riga No. 5.

No. 397

The Marquess Curzon of Kedleston to Lord Hardinge (Paris)
No. 479 Telegraphic [N 9550/8614/38]

FOREIGN OFFICE, *August 19, 1921, 4 p.m.*

British Delegation to International Committee for Russian Relief considers it of highest importance that Committee should meet at once: first duty of Committee will undoubtedly be despatch of small body of experts to famine area in Russia: private committees are already in the field and there is considerable danger of overlapping.

Please bring these considerations to notice of French Government and request them to expedite summoning of first meeting.

If delay is due to reluctance of other Governments to co-operate I will instruct His Majesty's representatives abroad to approach the Governments concerned.

Repeated to Rome No. 357 and Brussels No. 114, to whom please repeat your reply.

No. 398

Lord Hardinge (Paris) to the Marquess Curzon of Kedleston
(Received August 20, 5.25 p.m.)
No. 628 Telegraphic [N 9556/8614/38]

PARIS, *August 20, 1921, 1.15 p.m.*

Your telegram No. 479¹ has crossed my telegram No. 625² from which Your Lordship will see that delay in convoking Russian Relief Commission is chiefly due to failure of Belgian, Italian, Japanese, and United States Governments to reply to enquiries of French Government regarding appointment of delegates. I gather that persons invited to act as French delegates will in all probability accept.

This morning I hear that Italian and Belgian delegates³ are appointed,

---

¹ No. 397.   ² Of August 19, not printed.

³ In his telegram No. 155 of August 20, Mr. Phipps (First Secretary at H.M. Embassy at Brussels and Acting Chargé d'Affaires from July 25 to September 1, 1921) informed the Foreign Office that the Belgian members of the International Commission for Russian Relief were M. Delacroix (Belgian delegate to the Reparation Commission), M. Charlier (former Belgian Consul-General at Moscow), and M. Widmeur.

though names have not yet been communicated officially to Ministry of Foreign Affairs. Latter entirely agree as regards desirability of Commission meeting at once[4] and will be grateful if Your Lordship could instruct British Ambassadors at Tokyo and Washington to impress urgency of matter on Japanese and United States Governments.

Repeated to Rome and Brussels.

[4] On August 25, Lord Hardinge communicated to the Marquess Curzon of Kedleston (telegram No. 650) the following: 'Ministry for Foreign Affairs now informs me that since my conversation with M. Briand yesterday it has been found impossible for Russian relief commission to meet on Monday, as Monsieur Noulens chief French delegate will not reach Paris in time. Date is therefore fixed provisionally for Tuesday [August 30], but this is not yet certain as Monsieur Delacroix has to leave Paris on Wednesday, and no answer has yet been received from Washington regarding appointment of United States delegates. It therefore seems (? useless) for our delegates to come to Paris till Monday at earliest.'

No. 399

Mr. Hodgson (Moscow) to the Marquess Curzon of Kedleston
(Received August 23, 9.50 a.m.)
No. 34 Telegraphic [N 9619/9619/38]

MOSCOW, *August 23, 1921, 3.15 a.m.*

Please inform Armstrong-Whitworth that Krassin has expressed himself to the effect that there is very little probability of contract[1] for repair of locomotives being executed. Excuse is extremely critical financial position of Russia rendered more dangerous owing to necessity for purchasing supplies abroad in view of famine.

Possibly it would assist matters if Armstrong were to urge on Russian Trade delegation harmful consequences in England to reputation of Soviet Government more particularly when railway material to value of some 40 million pounds has been bought within the last few months in Germany. Mr. Glass[2] recommends this course. It would be advisable to act at once as Krassin is leaving for London in about a week's time and it is necessary that decision be forced while he is still here.[3]

[1] See No. 389, n. 4.   [2] Of the New Russian Company.

[3] In a minute of August 23, Lieutenant-Commander Maxse, describing a meeting with representatives of Armstrong-Whitworth's and Boulton Brothers' stated: 'I think this is essentially a case in which we can afford the firm all the support that we possibly can. The contract has been on the tapis for very nearly two years, and it was this country which first signed a Trade Agreement. His Majesty's Government cannot sit idly by while the Russians use their gold to buy railway material in Germany and food from America and leave British firms with whom they have concluded definite contracts stranded.'

Mr. Gregory commented (August 23): 'This is a new departure—namely supporting a British firm in obtaining a contract from the Soviet Gov[ernmen]t—and is certainly not very congenial. But the Trade Agreement is in existence, and, that being so, we can hardly stand by while large Russian orders are given in Germany and a British firm is left in the lurch.'

No. 400

Mr. Hodgson (Moscow) to the Marquess Curzon of Kedleston
(Received August 25, 10 a.m.)
No. 37 Telegraphic [N 9733/9619/38]

MOSCOW, *August 25, 1921, 2 a.m.*

My telegram No. 34.[1]

Mr. Glass informs me that Ministry of Ways and Communications definitely decided yesterday to proceed with Armstrong contract. Krassin and Lomonossov[2] have been deputed to negotiate for modifications in terms of agreement in view of difference in cost of repairing locomotives under this contract and in Germany.

Relative cost is Armstrong 41, Germany 25.

Chief obstacle remaining is indemnity stipulation which Russians regard as derogatory. They will endeavour to get this condition deleted and point out that Leeds Forge Company to whom it was decided at same session to give an order for 1,000 cistern cars costing £1,000,000 made no such stipulation.

Please advise Armstrong and ask them to inform Ivitski.

Please notify New Russian Company that Mr. Glass leaves for Uzovo August 26th.

Progress so far favourable.

[1] No. 399.
[2] Professor Lomonossov, head of the Russian Railway Purchase Mission abroad.

No. 401

The Marquess Curzon of Kedleston to Mr. Hodgson (Moscow)
No. 22 Telegraphic [N 9619/9619/38]

FOREIGN OFFICE, *August 25, 1921, 3.30 p.m.*

Your telegram No. 34.[1]

I have discussed position with Armstrong-Whitworth and Boultons who are collaborating in contract.

They fully appreciate Krassin's difficulty regarding the famine but in view of their long-standing contract and in view of much larger contracts placed in Germany they will rely upon Krassin carrying out the contract, it may be in somewhat modified form to meet the special circumstances. But in any case they consider the gold necessary for payment should be earmarked and retained.

Meanwhile they will do all possible to facilitate any further arrangements to meet M. Krassin in his present difficulty. But they naturally emphasize their legal rights under the contract.

[1] No. 399.

Please inform M. Krassin of the Company's point of view which I fully support and urge upon him the importance of carrying through this contract. It would be fatal to all chances of working and developing the Trade Agreement if M. Krassin's return to this country were to synchronise with an action for breach of contract against Arcos Ltd.

Directors are seeing Mr. Ber[z]in tomorrow.

No. 402

Mr. Hodgson (Moscow) to the Marquess Curzon of Kedleston
(Received August 26, 11 p.m.)
No. 38 Telegraphic [N 9798/8614/38]

MOSCOW, *August 26, 1921, 9.15 a.m.*

My telegram 15.[1]

Government, at last moment before their departure, has withdrawn permission for [? Famine] Delegation to leave Russia.[2] Pretext is that unity of effort is needed immediately for Bolshevik Russia and that journey of party has become unnecessary now that agreement has been reached with Mr. Hoover[3] and other Foreign organizations. I think it is case that journey would not have achieved any great practical result in the way of enlisting aid for famine districts, but it would have had some importance as advertisement to the outside world of the readiness of Bolshevik Government to accept collaboration of its (? inveterate adversaries).

Press continues truculent and publishes a variety of noxious articles attacking the policy of allied countries in connection with the famine situation regardless of the tendency its attack may have to alienate foreign sympathy.

[1] Of August 11. This stated: '. . . delegation from All Russian Committee for assistance to the famine stricken, which is to visit England, are awaiting permission to proceed.'

[2] In his despatch No. 20 of August 29, Mr. Hodgson reported as follows: 'On the 18th August the Presidium of the All-Russian Executive Committee decided that, "as the Soviet Government is already in pourparlers with Western European societies, the despatch abroad of a delegation of the All-Russian Committee for Helping the Famine Areas cannot be considered as indispensable, and would lead to the dispersion of our force". At the same time it instructed the Famine Committee sharply to concentrate its energies on the famine area and to turn the maximum number of their staff on to local work.

'The Famine Committee replied that this decision was a hindrance to their work and a violation of their rights, and that as all their information confirmed the impossibility of fighting the famine without speedy help from abroad, if their delegation were still refused permission to leave the country, they would be forced to conclude their labours on account of the impossibility of carrying out their task under such conditions. A meeting to discuss the situation on the 27th August was interrupted by the intrusion of agents of the All-Russian Executive Committee, and all persons present were arrested.'

[3] See *F.R.U.S.* 1921, vol. ii, pp. 813–17.

No. 403

Mr. Hodgson (Moscow) to the Marquess Curzon of Kedleston
(Received August 27, 12 noon)
No. 40 Telegraphic [N 9828/8614/38]

MOSCOW, *August 26, 1921, 9.15 a.m.*

Doctor Nansen arrived at Moscow yesterday as High Commissioner for Geneva Conference.[1] He is accompanied by Messrs. Gorvin,[2] Lodge,[2] and Frick.[2] He is placing before Chicherin two proposals. First is to create an (?international) Russian relief executive consisting of representatives of Geneva Conference and Russian Government for handling such relief resources as shall be forthcoming from private organizations. Second is that Russian Government approaches through him Governments of foreign countries with a request to grant to Russia credits for ten million pounds to be repaid by bonds bearing six per cent. interest repayable in ten years to be a first charge on national assets.

Nansen does not appear to hope much of Paris conference[3] which he thinks will waste too much time before getting to work. He criticises American relief plan[4] under which operations are to commence in Petrograd and then in Moscow, whereas it is obviously vital that relief should begin in districts where it is most required namely Volga.

[1] See No. 386, n. 2.
[3] Cf. No. 398 and No. 404, below.
[2] See No. 410, below.
[4] See No. 402, n. 3.

No. 404

The Marquess Curzon of Kedleston to Lord Hardinge (Paris)
No. 491 Telegraphic [N 9816/8614/38]

FOREIGN OFFICE, *August 26, 1921, 3.45 p.m.*

Your telegram No. 650.[1]

British delegates on Russian Relief Commission will come to Paris on Sunday with the object of getting into touch informally with other foreign delegates on Monday[2] before formal meeting on Tuesday.[3]

You should inform French Government that His Majesty's Government feel that further postponement would be regrettable and request it to do what it can to get the other delegates to Paris by that date.[3]

[1] See No. 398, n. 4.
[2] August 29.
[3] In his telegram No. 364 to Rome, of August 26, Lord Curzon instructed Mr. Kennard (Counsellor of H.M. Embassy at Rome, acting as Chargé d'Affaires from July 16 to September 15, 1921) as follows: 'British delegates on International Commission for Russian Relief are going to Paris on Sunday. .... You should request Italian Government to make every effort that Italian delegates should arrive on the same date to avoid any further delay in meeting of Commission.'

No. 405

Mr. Hodgson (Moscow) to the Marquess Curzon of Kedleston
(Received August 27, 12.10 p.m.)
No. 41 Telegraphic [N 9827/8614/38]

MOSCOW, *August 26, 1921*

My telegram No. 40.[1]

Dr. Nansen asks me to state that he is leaving Moscow on 27th August, arriving at Riga 29th August, and leaving for Berlin same day. He is very anxious to see Mr. Lloyd George in order to report on famine situation and explain the project which he has put before the Russian Government suggesting an appeal to foreign Governments for a loan. If Mr. Lloyd George is able to receive him, he would arrange to arrive in London 2nd September from Berlin, leaving for Geneva 4th September in time to arrive for the opening of Congress on 5th September.

Please reply to British Legation, Riga, and British Embassy, Berlin.[2]

[1] No. 403.
[2] In his telegram No. 209 of August 29, Lord Curzon replied: 'Please inform Dr. Nansen that the Prime Minister is unfortunately away and will therefore be unable to receive him on the dates proposed but that he would be well advised to proceed to Paris and see Sir Philip Lloyd-Greame, the British Representative on the International Commission now sitting to study the Russian famine question.'

No. 406

Mr. Hodgson (Moscow) to the Marquess Curzon of Kedleston
(Received September 6)
No. 18 [N 10169/9619/38]

MOSCOW, *August 26, 1921*

My Lord Marquess,

I have the honour to transmit, herewith, for the information of the Comptroller General of the Department of Overseas Trade, a note on observations made by Professor Lomonosov, head of the Russian Railway Commission abroad, to Mr. Peters, Commercial Secretary to this Mission, and to me in the course of a conversation.

I have, etc.,
R. M. HODGSON

ENCLOSURE IN No. 406

Interview with Professor Yury Vlad. Lomonosov

Present: Mr. Hodgson and Mr. Peters.

MOSCOW, *August 25, 1921*

Prof[essor] Lomonosov referred to the Armstrong contract[1] which, he said, would be carried through. M. Krassin and he had been empowered to

[1] See No. 389, n. 4.

negotiate with the firm certain changes in the agreement. In particular, the Soviet Government resented the provision for an indemnity of £150,000. Orders were at present being executed for the Soviet Government to a total value of 240 or 250 million gold roubles, and not one of these contained this humiliating indemnity provision. This was the main objection to the contract as it now stood, and would be pressed. As regards prices, those in the contract were undoubtedly too high; but the agreement provided for their being reviewed after one year, and it would not then pay Messrs. Armstrong to take up an unreasonable attitude, particularly in view of possible future contracts for the repair of Russian ships.

Prof[essor] Lomonosov refused to admit that he could with justice be accused of placing orders in Germany rather than in England. He had given considerable orders in the British Empire and was very satisfied with the material so far supplied. He mentioned:—

In Great Britain

1. Armstrong contract.
2. Leeds Forge Co[mpany], contract for 1000 (oil) Cistern Cars @ £750.

This is a joint contract with the Leeds Forge Co[mpany] and a German firm. The British firm will make the upper parts of the cars and the German firm the lower. Delivery will be at the rate of 150–250 a month. Payment is 30% with order, and the final instalment is payable against shipping documents.

3. Considerable quantities of tool steel ordered in Sheffield, and other miscellaneous orders.

An order for rails was lost because the British firm refused to lower its price till a fortnight after the final date fixed by Prof[essor] Lomonosov, who in the interval placed the order in Germany.

4. Negotiations are proceeding in England and in other countries for the supply of rubber piping and equipment required for the conversion of locomotives for burning oil. Prof[essor] Lomonosov is working through Mr. Glass of the New Russia Co[mpany] in this matter, and has been put in touch with two syndicates of rubber manufacturers and with the Westinghouse Co[mpany]. Prof[essor] Lomonosov noted that the British Westinghouse Co[mpany] quoted prices 25% above those quoted by the German concern of the same name.

In Canada

A contract for 500 cistern cars placed with the Canadian Car & Foundry Co[mpany].

This contract is on much the same lines as that with the Leeds Forge Co[mpany] and also provides for delivery within six months.

Prof[essor] Lomonosov considers the transport position in Russia as showing a tendency to improve, although conditions in the Ukraine are bad owing to trouble with peasant bands. There are more trucks than the available stock of locomotives will haul, and there are 1,700 locomotives which might work but do not owing to lack of fuel. Prof[essor] Lomonosov referred to criticisms of the policy of buying new locomotives abroad (700 in Germany and 1000 in Sweden (of the latter lot 18 are ready)) and said that many of the locomotives considered as 'healthy' in Russia would be counted as 'sick' in Great Britain.

As regards fuel, the position is very serious. The output of coal is insignificant, the Donetz Basin being particularly affected. Prof[essor] Lomonosov is very hopeful as regards oil, particularly after delivery of the cistern cars ordered abroad. There are 7 or 8 million poods of benzine lying at Grozny. A commencement will be made with export in February, and this export will provide liquid resources. Nearly all lines south and east of Moscow are burning oil and the Petrograd–Moscow line will soon join this number.

Prof[essor] Lomonosov will probably visit England in about three weeks' time, and he is also shortly to visit Canada.

No. 407

Lord Hardinge (Paris) to the Marquess Curzon of Kedleston
(Received August 27, 6.50 p.m.)
No. 655 Telegraphic [N 9824/8614/38]

PARIS, *August 27, 1921, 3.15 p.m.*

Your telegram No. 491.[1]

Ministry of Foreign Affairs inform me that they have just heard from Washington that United States delegate will be Mr. Brown who signed agreement with Litvinov at Riga; they are consequently summoning first meeting of Russian Relief Commission for Tuesday[2] at 3 p.m. and telegrams are being sent to French embassies in London, Brussels and Rome in this sense. They further tell me that Italian Government have suggested postponement till early in September as Monsieur Turatti, first Italian delegate, is ill; French Government have telegraphed to Rome saying that matter is too urgent to admit of further delay and urging that other Italian delegates should attend meeting on Tuesday without fail. In order to avoid any possible hitch it might be well for His Majesty's Embassy at Rome to support French representations to this effect.

Repeated to Rome.

[1] No. 404.
[2] August 30.

No. 408

Mr. Hodgson (Moscow) to the Marquess Curzon of Kedleston
(Received August 31, 11.30 a.m.)
No. 44 Telegraphic [N 9984/8614/38]

MOSCOW, *August 30, 1921, 7.45 p.m.*

My telegram No. 38.[1]

Meeting of All (? Russian) Committee for aid to famine-stricken to discuss action to be taken in view of withdrawal of permission for its representatives to go abroad was interrupted by agents of Extraordinary Commission who arrested all persons present, some 40 in number. The majority were released subsequently.[2]

Press continues to be extremely bitter in its attitude towards allied countries which it accuses of most diabolical schemes for exploiting the misery of Russia. Towards Germany and America it shows friendly dispositions.

Yesterday 'Na Pomosch', a special organ published by the Government to create interest in famine situation, gave prominence to a telegram[3] from H. G. Wells[4] in which he speaks of famine which has fallen upon 'districts

[1] No. 402.

[2] Under cover of his despatch No. 26 of September 3, Mr. Hodgson, transmitting a résumé of the speeches delivered by Kamenev and Trotsky at the Extraordinary Meeting of the Moscow Soviet on August 30, stated:

'It will be observed that Kamenev confined himself to questions arising directly out of the famine, but took occasion to justify the action of the Government in dissolving the Committee for Aiding the Famine Stricken. He did not mention the arrest of its members. No evidence was adduced, nor, I believe, does any exist, in support of his proposition that the refusal of the members of the committee to accept the Government's veto on their departure demonstrated their political insincerity. Their arrest seems to be merely an incident in the perpetual struggle between moderate groups and the extreme "left" parties in the Government. The Cadets and their colleagues allowed themselves to be used as pawns in this struggle and to be thrown aside when they were no longer necessary and their impotence had been exhibited. . . .'

[3] This telegram (not printed) was transmitted under cover of Mr. Hodgson's despatch No. 21 of August 31. Mr. Hodgson commented as follows: 'It is misleading in that:—

'1. The districts mainly affected by famine—the Samara, Saratov, Simbirsk, Kazan and Viatka Governments—have, in reality, suffered comparatively little from civil war. They were not devastated either by Kolchak [see n. 5, below] or by Denikin [see n. 6, below].

'2. The Polish invasion did not destroy the Russian railway system; civil war, though it resulted in damage to the railways in the extreme south of Russia, certainly did not ruin the lines in the famine area or its communications with the rest of Russia, which are working now as satisfactorily as the supply of fuel admits.

'3. The catastrophe is not "sudden". The population over much of the famine territory has been starving ever since March of the present year. It has been obvious for months past that famine was inevitable.

'4. The implication that, were the Russian railways working normally, the Government would be able to deal effectively with the situation, is untrue. Internal traffic being practically at a standstill the rolling stock available is amply sufficient—as is now being demonstrated—to convey supplies to the suffering districts. Lack of fuel alone is liable to hinder the movements of trains.'

[4] Mr. H. G. Wells, the novelist, who had visited Russia in October, 1920, and had recorded his impressions in his book *Russia in the Shadows*, published in December, 1920.

728

laid waste by Kolchak[5] and Denikin'[6] and renders 'vacillating and inhuman policy of Entente' responsible for inability of Russian Government 'to deal effectively with this sudden catastrophe'.

[5] Admiral Kolchak, former Head of the White Russian Administration in Siberia.

[6] Commander in Chief of the White Russian forces in South Russia.

No. 409

The Marquess Curzon of Kedleston to Lord Hardinge (Paris)
No. 2347 [N 9818/8614/38]

FOREIGN OFFICE, *August 30, 1921*

My Lord,

I transmit to Your Lordship herewith a copy of a memorandum,[1] regarding a request from the Georgian representative for the assistance of His Majesty's Government in relieving the present distress in Georgia, together with a copy of a telegram received by Prince Soumbatov[2] from the former Minister of the Interior.

2. I shall be glad if Your Lordship will inform the British delegates on the International Commission for the relief of Russia that there is no objection to relief being given to the Caucasian republics, provided that they are satisfied that the famine conditions in these states justify their inclusion.

3. The British delegates should, however, be careful, in framing any proposals, not to compromise the political principles of His Majesty's Government with regard to the Caucasian States by allowing their inclusion in a Russian relief scheme to imply some sort of recognition that they form part of Russia.

I am, etc.,
(For the Secretary of State)
J. D. GREGORY

[1] Not printed.　　　　[2] Georgian Representative in London.

No. 410

Mr. Wilton[1] to the Marquess Curzon of Kedleston
(Received September 6)
No. 25 [N 10150/8614/38]

Confidential　　　　　　　　　　　　　　RIGA, *August 30, 1921*

My Lord,

With reference to my telegrams Nos. 30 and 33,[2] I have the honour to enclose copy of an agreement concluded on the 27th August[3] between the

[1] H.M. Representative at Riga and Reval.

[2] Of August 22 and August 30 respectively, not printed.

[3] Not printed. For sources of this agreement, signed in Moscow, see Slusser and Triska, p. 23.

Bolshevik Foreign Minister and Dr. Nansen (appointed High Commissioner for Russian Relief by the Geneva Conference of the 15th August). The agreement empowers the latter to raise a loan of 10,000,000*l.* from the European Governments for purposes of famine relief. I have also the honour to forward Annex 'A'[4] referred to in the agreement and a supplementary agreement,[4] defining the principles for the regulation of the European voluntary and official efforts to help the famine-stricken population in Russia.

2. Dr. Nansen left Riga for Moscow on the 22nd August. He was accompanied by Mr. Gorvin (British), secretary to the International Committee for Relief Credits; Mr. Lodge (British); M. Frick (Swiss), representing the Joint Council of Red Cross Societies; Mr. Mackenzie (British), secretary of Save the Children Fund; and M. Schlesinger (German). M. Litvinov, who was at Riga when Dr. Nansen arrived, did not appear anxious for him to go to Moscow, but on a reference to the Government the necessary visas were at once given.

3. Dr. Nansen informed me that in his negotiations with M. Chicherin he had endeavoured to obtain the nomination of a representative of the All-Russian Hunger Relief Committee in place of the Government representative on the International Russian Relief Executive. The Executive is defined in article 1 of the Supplementary Agreement (Annex 'A'), and the constitution of the All-Russian Hunger Relief Committee is defined in the enclosure (section 3A) enclosed in my despatch No. 23 of the 24th instant.[4] M. Chicherin had fallen in with Dr. Nansen's views, but on this point he stood out strongly. I hear on good authority that the Committee, which was called into being on the 21st July, may shortly be dissolved. It is probable that not only is the committee not a good working organization, but also it has served its purposes, as far as the Bolshevik Government is concerned, in having brought 'official' Russia into touch with Western Europe and America by means of the famine appeal. Dr. Nansen did not conceal from me the gravity of the task of famine relief, but he believed, from his former experiences in Russia last year while he was engaged in the repatriation of prisoners, that the agreement would be workable if the money were forthcoming. He expressed some anxiety lest the French Government might endeavour to thwart the scheme, and he hoped that the Governments concerned would consent to allow the balance of the relief credits, amounting, I understand, to about 6,000,000*l.*, to be utilised as an advance for the famine relief.

4. Dr. Nansen stated that he had no doubt that the Bolshevik Government regarded the situation as desperate, and would render all possible assistance to make the famine relief measures successful. These measures may be divided into two separate categories, viz., the supply of foodstuffs and the supply of seed. As regards the former, Dr. Nansen estimates the shortage of grain required to be imported from abroad for the actual needs of human consumption at 2,000,000 tons; as against this the Soviet Government have two grain ships on the way from Canada, and the first relief ship of the

[4] Not printed.

American Relief Administration is expected to arrive at Petrograd today. As regards seed (rye-seed), the shortage required from abroad is estimated by Dr. Nansen at 100,000 tons, and it is imperative that this should reach the sowing areas not later than the 15th September. Dr. Nansen has opened negotiations with the States of Esthonia, Latvia and Lithuania for rye-seed, either on purchase or on loan, but he is hampered through lack of funds. Chicherin has promised to open credits for him at Stockholm, but he can obtain nothing until this is done. With no available data at hand it is difficult to estimate the amount of rye-seed which these three States could spare, but I conjecture the amount at not less than 20,000 tons. But time is slipping by, and unless immediate measures are taken it will be too late to utilise a part even of this amount. The Esthonian Government has already permitted the sale of over 3,000 tons of rye-seed to Russia, and is ready to release another 2,500 tons on condition of replacement. I have put Dr. Nansen into direct communication with the proper Lithuanian authorities with a view of obtaining seed in that State also, which should be in a position to supply larger quantities than either Esthonia or Latvia. I hear on excellent authority that M. Ganetsky, the Bolshevik representative at Riga, has been haggling over details for the purchase of 7,000 tons of seed offered to him by the Lettish authorities several days ago, and did not even report the offer to Moscow. If an adequate supply of seed is not forthcoming in time it is probable that a repetition of the famine will also have to be feared next year. From the estimate of the amount of rye required for food and seed it would appear that the sum of 10,000,000l. represents little more than one-quarter of the amount required; nor does this take into consideration the necessary fodder for cattle or agricultural machines to take the place of the numbers of plough animals which have already died.

5. In addition to his work on behalf of the Joint Council of Red Crosses, Dr. Nansen arranged at Moscow for the despatch of Mr. Webster[5] (British) to Saratov in connection with Save the Children Society. Dr. Nansen told me there were sufficient funds in hand to feed 10,000 children for four months. On the 29th August Dr. Nansen received a telegram at Riga stating that Mr. Lloyd George wished him to proceed at once to the Supreme Council Committe sitting at Paris 29th August–1st September.[6] After consideration, he decided that he would proceed to England to lay the whole matter before the Prime Minister. He left on the 29th August for London via Berlin, accompanied by Mr. Lodge, whom he is detaching to report direct to Sir P. Lloyd-Greame at Paris.[7]

6. In my telegram No. 30 I had the honour to report that my French colleague had received instructions (20th August) to make enquiries whether

[5] Mr. Laurence Webster was in charge of the work of the Save the Children Fund in Russia; his observations on conditions in the Saratov districts were transmitted to the Foreign Office under cover of Mr. Hodgson's despatch No. 55 of September 26 (N 11345/8614/38), not printed.

[6] A reference to Foreign Office telegram No. 209 to Berlin of August 29 (N 9827/8614/38), not printed.

[7] Cf. No. 405, n. 2.

Litvinov was willing to conclude an agreement with the French Red Cross on similar lines to the Hoover Agreement reported in my despatch No. 19 of the 22nd August.[8] Litvinov had already left for Reval to visit his family, and Mlle. Weiss, editor of the 'Europe nouvelle' and correspondent of the 'Petit Parisien' has told me that she is trying to arrange with the Bolshevik representative at Riga for permission to go to Moscow, and that she is authorised to sound the authorities there for a relief agreement with the French Red Cross. M. Frick has informed me confidentially that he believes the French Government would not be well disposed towards any relief scheme which does not provide for the recognition of the pre-war Russian debts to France. According to my information, the Bolsheviks will certainly refuse to conclude any agreement of this nature.

7. In the course of conversation, Dr. Nansen's companions, who had not visited Moscow since the revolution, gave gloomy impressions of the conditions of existence at Moscow. Dr. Nansen, however, who was in Moscow last year, told me that he had noticed some general improvement in the city. Apparently no attempt was made to shadow any of the party. Supplies of food were publicly vended in the streets, and it was observed that the large congregations in the churches included numbers of soldiers and officers. Neither Dr. Nansen nor his party was impressed by the methods of the Government Departments with which they had dealings, and they remarked that a good deal of Chicherin's time was occupied in the performance of trivial tasks usually left to an office servant.

A copy of this despatch, with enclosures, is being sent to Mr. Hodgson, at Moscow.

I have, etc.,

E. C. WILTON

[8] Not printed. See No. 402, n. 3.

No. 411

The Marquess Curzon of Kedleston to Mr. Hodgson (Moscow)
No. 29 Telegraphic [N 10128/9395/38]

FOREIGN OFFICE, *September 1, 1921, 4.30 p.m.*

Your telegram No. 20.[1]

Circular has been issued to all former owners of industrial property known to Department. Group principally centered in Manchester will probably be formed among owners of textile mills.

You may expect offer at early date to negotiate for leases; meantime please ascertain what date if any fixed as latest on which former owners may put forward claims for preferential treatment in matter of lease.[2]

[1] No. 393.

[2] In his telegram No. 48 of September 5, Mr. Hodgson replied: 'Your telegram No. 29 of September 1st. Decrees regarding leases make no provision for preferential treatment of former owners.'

No. 412

Record by Mr. Lindsay of Conversation with Dr. Nansen
[N 10180/8614/38]

FOREIGN OFFICE, *September 2, 1921*

I today saw Dr. Nansen who arrived last night from Russia. He had been to 10 Downing Street, and had sent messages to the Prime Minister and tomorrow he is seeing Sir P. Lloyd-Greame who is coming over from Paris tonight.[1]

Dr. Nansen said Mr. Hoover had set himself a comparatively easy task, confining himself to feeding children. The tests in this case were simple; the recipient must be a child, and hungry; and the relief is just cooked food. Only a small staff would be wanted, especially as Mr. Hoover was starting work in Moscow and Petrograd where conditions though bad were, Dr. Nansen said, better than last year.

He himself was embarking on the far more complex problem of giving relief on a different scale involving the distribution not only of food, medicines, clothing, but also of seed corn. Obviously a far greater staff on the spot would be wanted and he had come to the conclusion that he must use the machinery of the Soviet Government. He believed it was sufficiently well organised to carry out the work, but to prevent abuses he had provided for a personnel in the districts of his own men to act, I imagine, as supervisors and inspectors, reporting to a Central Executive in Moscow which he regarded as the keystone of his scheme. It was to consist at first of two people, one his man, the other nominated by the Soviet Government. In case of any abuse or failure of the two to agree on questions of capital importance, he would be able to stop all relief. He also provided that to this Board of Two should be added three more, the representatives of the Governments who might grant credits for Famine Relief, who, on behalf of their Governments, would have the power, if dissatisfied with the administration of relief, of closing the credit at once.

Dr. Nansen was eloquent on the urgent (and obvious) necessity of setting to work at once, and the futility of sending out an International Mission of Enquiry.[2] The winter sowings have to be in the ground by September 15th, and water transport ends by November! He detailed some preliminary steps that had already been taken for the purchase of seed in the Baltic States and Prussia and for the collection of it in various parts of Russia not affected by famine. There were, he said, large areas where there was an abundant surplus of grain. Travelling west from Moscow he had himself everywhere seen good crops and large areas being prepared for winter sowing. He said that the recent authorization of trading had made an extraordinary difference. Peasants could be seen in the streets of Moscow selling their potatoes. This and the cessation of requisitions had restored the confidence of the peasantry and he seemed to believe that the Soviet Government would have

---

[1] Cf. Nos. 405, n. 2 and 410.   [2] See No. 413, below.

no difficulty in obtaining from these non-stricken regions all the help that might reasonably be expected of them.

I was greatly struck by Dr. Nansen's sanguine views, especially as, only five minutes earlier, I had been reading in Mr. Hodgson's report[3] of the 'general demoralization which prevails, with an incompetent and corrupt administration, a suspicious and hostile peasantry in the prosperous regions, and a chaotic transport system . . .'. I received the impression that the Bolsheviks had thrown dust in Dr. Nansen's eyes.

Dr. Nansen laid great stress on the political importance of the Governments of Europe providing credits for the relief of Russia. He did not think it possible for them to stipulate for the recognition of debts as a condition; and a mere refusal of credits he considered would have the effect of strengthening the Soviet Government. The latter, he said, were already preaching that the Capitalist States had no intention of providing anything more than fair words, and by trying to incite in the sufferers hatred of Europe hoped to succeed in obtaining toleration or something more for themselves.

[3] Enclosed in his despatch No. 14 of August 18, not printed (see No. 391, n. 7).

No. 413

Report on International Commission on the Russian Famine, by Sir P. Lloyd-Greame (Received September 5)

[*N 10107/8614/38*]

Confidential   *September 3, 1921*

The commission held its first meeting on the 30th August. The personnel of the delegations of the countries represented is set out in Appendix (A)[1] to this report. The American delegate, Mr. Lyman Brown, stated that he was in the position of holding a watching brief. The commission appointed M. Noulens[2] president of the conference.

2. The British delegation arrived in Paris on the 28th August. This enabled them to devote the following day to discussions with the French Foreign Office and with such members of other delegations as they were able to meet. This was fortunate, as no programme had been arranged, and as a result of these informal conversations a definite plan was agreed upon and considerable delay avoided.

3. The resolutions, which are fully set out in Appendix (B) to this report, were passed by the commission. The resolutions dealing with the despatch of the Mission of Enquiry to Russia and the activities of charitable organisations formed the subject of detailed investigation and report by two sub-committees.

[1] Not printed.
[2] M. Joseph Noulens, formerly French Ambassador in Petrograd (1917–18).

The telegram set out in Appendix (B) was despatched by M. Noulens to M. Chicherin on the evening of the 1st September.

There was complete unanimity on all the resolutions adopted.

4. The commission considered what action should be taken according as the reply of the Soviet Government took the form of either (*a*) acceptance of the proposal to send a mission, (*b*) refusal, (*c*) was of a dilatory character. They decided that in the event of acceptance the mission should be despatched forthwith. In the event of a refusal, it was felt that, as the commission considered the report of the Mission of Enquiry an essential condition precedent to making any recommendations (other than those contained in the resolutions of the present session), no useful purpose would be served by the various delegations reassembling; and that M. Noulens should be given authority to publish the reply of the Soviet Government and to make a statement on the position in accordance with the views expressed by the delegations in agreeing to the necessity for the mission. In the event of the Soviet Government sending a reply of a dilatory character, it was felt that this might either involve explanations merely on points of detail or might raise questions of principle. It was, therefore, decided that each delegation should appoint one of their number to serve on a sub-committee, which could be summoned by M. Noulens at short notice to assist him in framing his reply. Mr. Wardrop,[3] who can come quickly at short notice from Strasburg to Paris, will represent the British delegation on this sub-committee.

5. It is proposed that the British members of the Mission of Enquiry should consist of the following:—

Sir John Campbell: Famine;
General Mance and Colonel Hull: Transport;
Mr. MacDougal: Agriculture;
Mr. Wise: Administration;
   together with Mr. Preston[4] as interpreter.

It was stated at the commission that other nations would have no difficulty in appointing doctors, and it is therefore felt that, in view of Colonel Hull's knowledge and experience of the railways in Southern Russia and of the importance of the transport problem, it is desirable that he should be associated with General Mance.

It is understood that all these gentlemen are prepared to serve on the mission, and they have already been advised to hold themselves in readiness.

6. *Credits.*—The British delegation opened a discussion on credits, and submitted a proposal which is set out in Appendix (C). This proposal deals with the question purely from the economic point of view, and follows the lines of the Prime Minister's speech of the 16th August.[5] The terms of this draft resolution were agreed between M. Loucheur[6] and Sir Philip Lloyd Greame, and they were also approved in principle by the Japanese and Belgians prior to the formal discussion.

[3] See No. 394, n. 5.
[4] Formerly Acting Consul at Vladivostok. See also No. 470, below.
[5] See No. 394, n. 7.   [6] French Minister for Reconstruction of the Liberated Regions.

At the discussion on the commission the Italian delegates stated that they were not authorised by their Government or prepared to discuss the question of the recognition of debts at this stage. It was pointed out that any recommendation as to credits involved by implication a recommendation, tacit or expressed, on the subject of debts. This reasoning was admitted, but no decision was reached for the following reasons:—

(a) Some delegates doubted if a recommendation as to credits was within the scope of the commission.

(b) The feeling was expressed in some quarters that this subject involved a great political question and ought to be dealt with by the Supreme Council.

(c) Other delegates again felt a difficulty in making any recommendation without further reference to their Governments.

(d) It was suggested that any decision on the question of credits ought to be postponed until the Mission of Enquiry had reported.

In these circumstances, while it was impossible to secure a unanimous decision, there was little doubt that the French, Belgian and Japanese delegations agreed with the British proposal. The Italians were doubtful. In this connection it may be remembered that the Italians have only a small interest in Russian debts and claims. Accordingly, as it was impossible to arrive at a decision, the British delegation agreed to the desire of the other delegations that the question should be adjourned.

7. Mr. Lodge[7] arrived in Paris on the 1st September, and communicated to the British delegation Dr. Nansen's agreement with the Soviet Government and his proposals for credits.[7] This information was at once placed before the commission by the British delegation.

As stated above, the commission failed to arrive at any decision on the question of credits, but it was clear that there was the strongest opposition in all quarters to Dr. Nansen's proposals for credits. Even the Italian delegation regarded the provision of full security as essential to any credit proposal.

8. During the meetings of the commission, the news arrived that the non-Bolshevik members of the All-Russian Committee had been arrested.[8] There was some disposition, expressed for the most part outside the conference room, that this precluded further discussions. The British delegation opposed this view, which was not pressed, but it was generally agreed that this action rendered the despatch of a Mission of Enquiry more than ever necessary as the condition precedent of any detailed recommendations by the commission to their respective Governments.

9. The proceedings of the commission were marked by a signal degree of unanimity. All the delegates clearly approached the question as an economic and humanitarian problem, and without any political considerations, and the interchange of views between the various delegations, both formally and informally, was throughout full and frank.

[7] See No. 410.   [8] See No. 408.

10. A *procès-verbal* of the proceedings of the commission is being prepared by the French secretariat, and will be forwarded from Paris in the course of a few days.[9]

Appendix (B) to No. 413

The following resolutions were passed by the International Commission on the 1st September:—

1. *Mission of Enquiry.*—It was resolved that a Mission of Enquiry should be sent to Russia to examine the famine conditions on the spot. The constitution of the mission and scope of the enquiry, together with the text of the telegram despatched to M. Chicherin, are as follows:—

(i) *Constitution.*—Each delegation will nominate at most five persons and one interpreter.

The experts will be specialists in the following subjects:—

1. Famine relief.
2. Transport.
3. Medical and sanitary questions.
4. Agriculture.
5. Administration.

The interpreters must know Russian and, as far as possible, two other European languages.

There will further be included in the Mission of Enquiry a member nominated by the Mixed Commission of the International Committee of the Red Cross and of the League of the Red Crosses.

(ii) *Telegram to the Soviet Government.*—'The mission nominated by the Supreme Council to make proposals on the best way of helping the Russian people suffering from famine and epidemics has unanimously decided, with the sole object of organising effective assistance, that it is essential in order to fulfil its task to send to Russia a committee of experts to conduct on the spot a rapid and thorough enquiry into the question of what is necessary and the resources available as quickly and as thoroughly as possible.

'Consequently the commission has decided to address itself to the Soviet Government to obtain for the Mission of Enquiry—of which the composition and the scope of the investigations to be carried out are set forth below—the necessary facilities in order to proceed with its enquiries with the object of presenting a report as quickly as possible.

'The information in the possession of the committee leads it to suppose that the experts would conduct their enquiry most quickly if they travelled first to Novorossisk, and from there to Moscow across the famine area.

'The commission cannot doubt that its proposal will meet with the approval of the Soviet Government. The experts will be ready to start for Russia as soon as the Soviet Government gives its consent to the proposal, and gives an assurance that the experts will meet with the necessary facilities in order to proceed with their enquiry.

'The Mission of Enquiry will be composed of some thirty individuals belonging to the nationalities of the five Powers represented on the International Commission

[9] Transmitted to the Foreign Office by the International Commission on the Russian Famine on September 6 (N 10244/8614/38), not printed.

and will be chosen for special knowledge on questions of famine, transport, sanitation, agriculture and administration. There will also be attached to them a representative of the Red Cross and interpreters.

'The scope of the enquiry is given in the following memorandum:—

(1) Area and extent of the famine and number of persons affected.
(2) Present importance and possible developments of the emigration of the population threatened by the famine.
(3) Extent and possible development of epidemic diseases.
(4) In what measure sowing can be effected this year and next year in the famine area.
(5) Importance and destination of the reserves of food and the surplus of crops which could be used in the famine area. Also the losses and available number of live-stock.
(6) State of transport in general, and particularly between the provinces disposing of a surplus and the territories subjected to famine, as well as the state of the ports.
(7) Measures taken by the Soviet Government to deal with the above problems. Existing organisations or those to be created for the following objects:—
    (a) Collection of grain in the provinces with a surplus.
    (b) Distribution of food and seed-corn in the districts subjected to the famine.
    (c) Treatment of sick persons suffering from epidemics or from lack of sufficient food. Preventive methods against epidemics.
    (d) Special care for children.
    (e) Agricultural work in the famine area.
    (f) Distribution of foodstuffs and objects of primary necessity in the interior and exchange against products.
    (g) Measures to be undertaken to make the organisation of relief more effective, especially as concerns those products and instruments the importation of which by the Soviet Government is particularly necessary. Designation of the areas where they must be distributed.
    (h) Examination of the possibilities of establishing special territorial zones to be supplied with food from abroad.

'The above instructions, which are given to the Mission of Enquiry, cannot be carried out unless the Soviet Government gives the members of the mission all facilities for moving freely in the districts which they will have to visit, and unless the local authorities are invited to provide all useful information and give the assistance necessary that the enquiry may obtain useful results.'

(iii) The commission trust that within seven days experts will be chosen, and that their departure will take place on the 15th September at the latest.

2. It was resolved that the Mission of Enquiry should make a report within three weeks of their arrival in Russia.

3. *League of Nations and Prevention of Epidemics.*—The conference is convinced of the necessity of preventing diseases from gaining ground in the States bordering on Russia. This cannot but be a serious problem not only in Europe but also in the Caucasus. The commission is of the opinion that the organisation under the League of Nations, which has already undertaken this work, is particularly qualified to continue it. The commission, therefore, expresses the hope that the League of Nations will continue its task.

In order to avoid overlapping and to benefit by mutual experience, it would be desirable if the organisation of the League of Nations remained in close contact with the Mixed Commission of the Red Cross and all other bodies engaged in sanitary work in Russia.

The conference considers that the activity of the organisation under the League of Nations will be most usefully confined to the States bordering upon Russia. When it will consider that any action be usefully undertaken in Russia, the organisation will ask constituted bodies working in Russia to proceed there.

4. *Co-ordination of Charitable Relief.*—The commission, which has taken note of the resolutions adopted at the assembly called together by the Mixed International Commission of the Red Cross at Geneva on the 15th and 16th August, associates itself with the appeal addressed to the public for the collection of charitable funds for Russia. It insists that the delegates of each country should do everything in their power to encourage the different charitable organisations in their respective countries to unite their funds and their products which are necessary for the Russian population affected by the famine.

Without prejudging the plan of action, the direct organisation of which it will be able to recommend to Governments, the commission recommends to the Red Crosses to take measures to act as quickly as possible.

It draws the attention of the Governments to the opportunity of each assisting its national Red Cross, especially by furnishing to it all the surplus medical and sanitary material available in order to co-operate in the work of helping Russia.

The commission has heard with satisfaction the news given by the representative of the American Relief Administration, namely, that, while reserving its liberty of action, the organisation could work in complete accord with its other organisations as to the best means of avoiding overlapping.[10] While recognising that the private charitable organisations which are already bringing help to Russia must continue to provide their help by the ways hitherto adopted, the commission considers it essential, in order to obtain the best result from the activities and resources employed in order to alleviate the famine in Russia, that the organisations of all the countries represented should take account of the directions which the commission will be in a position to give when it is in possession of the report of its Mission of Enquiry.

The commission considers it advisable to invite the Mixed Commission of the Red Cross in Geneva to send a representative to take his place among its members.

5. The commission considered the question of credits. Doubt was expressed by some of the delegations as to the competence of some of the members to deal with the question. The commission accordingly agreed to adjourn the discussion and to take the instructions of their respective Governments.

6. It was resolved that, as soon as the Mission of Enquiry has reported, the commission will invite to join it representatives of all nations, which are able and willing, to render assistance to the Russian famine.

Appendix (C) to No. 413

Credits

The conference feels a difficulty in making specific suggestions in the absence of the necessary information which the Mission of Enquiry is designed to obtain.

---

[10] See *F.R.U.S.* 1921, vol. ii, pp. 819–21.

But, in view of the fact that requests have been made by the Soviet Government for credits in one form or another, the conference considers it at once within its province and within its competence to record the following conclusions:—

1. Whatever the precise dimensions of the present famine, no adequate or final solution can be found, unless conditions are established in which the internal distribution and exchange of grain and commodities in Russia can take place effectively, and unless a degree of confidence is established which will induce foreign exporters to send their goods into Russia.

2. Credit must rest on confidence; and no confidence can be created or maintained among the trading communities of the world unless debts and obligations are recognised, and advances are sufficiently secured. Nor is there any difference in the principle upon which credits can be given by Governments from those upon which credit is given and obtained by private traders.

In these circumstances, the conference is forced to the conclusion that the effective creation of credits for assisting exports to Russia will only be practicable under two conditions:—

(a) That the Russian Government should recognise its responsibility for the discharge of existing debts and other obligations and liabilities.

(b) That adequate security should be afforded for any credit given in future.

3. If credits are given on these conditions they should be devoted to assisting the import into Russia of such commodities as the conference consider most essential, after taking into consideration the report of the Mission of Enquiry.

4. The conference desires to emphasise as strongly as possible the fact that in coming to these conclusions they are actuated by no political motive. But they feel bound to express their conviction, based solely on economic considerations, that the conditions herein stated are vital if either public or private credit is to be extended to Russia with any hope of effectively alleviating the existing distress and preventing a recurrence of the present disaster.[11]

[11] In a letter to M. Delacroix of October 1, Sir P. Lloyd-Greame stated: 'I am convinced, as I think you are, that both the reasoning and the conclusions stated in the Resolution on Credits which I submitted to the Commission, are sound. The reasoning and the conclusions are based on purely economic considerations; and I feel that in dealing with this question the International Commission would be well advised to confine itself to the economic aspects of the situation. I think therefore that the wiser course for the Commission would be to adopt the resolution which I proposed or one in similar terms and based on similar reasons. Such action would make it clear both to the Soviet Government and to the countries of the world, that the restoration of economic conditions is essential to the recovery of Russia whatever form of Government may be established there.

'It is not within the province of the Commission to dictate to Russia what form of Government she should adopt; but it is clearly their function to explore and advise their Governments on the economic issues; and I think that a reasoned resolution based, not on any political considerations but purely upon the basic economic factors, which must exist and operate whatever the political constitution of a country, would carry more weight and would conform more to the purpose for which the Commission was appointed and the scope of its activities.

'There is a clear distinction between the broad question of commercial credits, and the charitable assistance which private individuals and Governments can give to the Red Cross and other charitable organisations. The former can only be dealt with on an economic basis; the latter is pure charity. I think the two should be kept clearly distinct. We have maintained this distinction hitherto in our deliberations and in our recommendations; and I think it is important to continue to observe it.'

No. 414

The Marquess Curzon of Kedleston to Mr. Hodgson (Moscow)
No. 64 [N 10221/5/38]

Confidential FOREIGN OFFICE, *September 7, 1921*

Sir,

For some time past His Majesty's Government have viewed with grave concern the failure of the Soviet Government to give effect to the obligations laid upon it by the trade agreement, and they have had under consideration the necessity of drawing its attention to the objectionable activities and to the inevitable consequences of their continuance.

2. The accompanying note records the more flagrant violations of the agreement of which His Majesty's Government have to complain, and is based on evidence which has been most carefully examined by an inter-departmental committee,[1] and which must be regarded as irrefutable. You should present the note to M. Chicherin with a request that a reply may be received without delay.

3. It is not proposed to communicate the text of the note to the press unless after a reasonable time no reply has been received from the Soviet Government.

I am, etc.,

CURZON OF KEDLESTON

ENCLOSURE IN No. 414

Note to Soviet Government[2]

By the terms of the preamble of the trade agreement concluded between His Majesty's Government and the Russian Soviet Government on the 16th March, each party undertook to 'refrain from hostile action' or undertakings against the other and from conducting outside of its own borders any official propaganda, direct or indirect, against the institutions of each other, and more particularly the Russian Soviet Republic undertook to refrain from any attempt by military or diplomatic or any other form of action or propaganda to encourage any of the peoples of Asia in any form of hostile action against British interests or the British Empire, especially in India and in the independent State of Afghanistan.'

[1] For the first two meetings of this Committee, see Nos. 379 and 383.

[2] The text of this note was published in Cmd. 2895 of 1927, *A Selection of Papers dealing with the relations between His Majesty's Government and the Soviet Government, 1921–27*. On August 19, the Cabinet had before them a draft Note to the Russian Soviet Government circulated by the Secretary of State for India, and, after a short discussion, agreed: 'That the draft despatch by the Secretary of State for India should be utilised as the basis of a despatch to be prepared by the Secretary of State for Foreign Affairs and approved by the Prime Minister before being actually sent. The despatch should contain instances of breaches of the Agreement, press for explanations, and demand that these breaches of the Trade Agreement should cease, but should stop short of an actual threat of cancellation of the Trade Agreement, which should at this stage be held in reserve.'

In a letter handed by Sir Robert Horne to M. Krassin on the signature of the agreement,[3] the attention of the Soviet Government was drawn to certain specific activities of a hostile nature which were then known to be proceeding, and upon the cessation of which His Majesty's Government insisted as an essential corollary of the resumption of trading relations.

M. Chicherin, in his note of acknowledgment of the 20th April,[4] stated that the Soviet Government regarded the signature of the agreement as a turning-point in its relations with Great Britain, and that everything would be avoided on its part which would involve hostile action or propaganda or support of such against British interests in the sense provided against by the treaty. He added that all the representatives and agents of the Soviet Government in Afghanistan in particular were instructed not to conduct any anti-British policy.

His Majesty's Government thus felt entitled to believe that the signature of the trade agreement would, in fact, inaugurate a new era in Anglo-Russian relations.

It is with profound disappointment that His Majesty's Government are obliged to register the fact that, although five months have elapsed since M. Chicherin's assurance was given, the hostile activities, upon the cessation of which the successful working of the agreement depends, still continue unabated. His Majesty's Government are, moreover, in possession of indisputable evidence that the objectionable activities are due to the direct instigation of the Soviet Government.

The first charge which His Majesty's Government have to make is concerned with the part played by the Third International in the propagation of subversive principles. Reports on the work of this organisation delivered in Moscow by prominent officials during the recent congress leave no doubt as to the fact that one of its foremost aims is to undermine British institutions, particularly in the East.

A few instances of the recent proceedings of the Third International will suffice to substantiate this charge. On the 1st June, M. Stalin, President of the Eastern Section of the Third International, in the course of his report to the Central Committee, stated that 'the general guiding purpose of the Eastern Secretariat in all its work lies in exerting pressure upon the political authority of the capitalist Powers of Western Europe through their colonies, discrediting them in the eyes of the native population and simultaneously preparing the latter to emancipate themselves from an alien yoke. The problems connected with the class struggle in the West will be incomparably easier of solution if the external power of France and England can be undermined'.

Again, in reviewing the work of the Eastern Secretariat during the period from the 1st February, 1921, to the 1st June, 1921, M. Stalin, in commenting on the recent Russo-Afghan treaty,[5] stated that it guaranteed friendly

3 See No. 361, n. 8.
4 Dated April 18, but received on April 20. See No. 361, n. 7.
5 See No. 358, n. 3.

relations with Afghanistan, 'through which the Communist International maintains direct communication further south with British India, propaganda in which area is the primary objective of the Eastern Secretariat'. He added that continuous though unofficial relations had been maintained with several native leaders in the Indian provinces.

On the 5th June, M. Eliava,[6] in a similar report to the Central Committee of the Third International, stated: 'It is natural that we should have to pursue a path of partial compromise, refraining from an imposition by force, and that we should have been placed under the necessity of cloaking the aims of the Communist International in a nationalist guise. The policy pursued by us has already proved its expediency, and it is sufficient to point to the fact that, in combating British imperialism, we succeeded in 1919 in defending Turkestan from British influence, whereas, in 1921, we are already taking the offensive against the foundations of capitalism in India itself.'

Finally, on the 20th June, M. Nuorteva, Director of the Department of Propaganda under the Third International, after drawing attention to 'the gigantic work accomplished by the Eastern Secretariat during the past six months,' stated: 'The whole attention of our agency at the present moment is directed to elaborating a system for supplying the Eastern organisations with all they require. Up to the present time, the work has been considerably interfered with by the alertness of the Colonial administration, but, in the near future, with the inevitable changes in the life of Persia, we shall have at our disposition in the immediate neighbourhood of India, a base amply sufficient for our task.'

It is unnecessary to point out the essentially subversive character of these aims, for they have been proclaimed in countless manifestos and reports sent out by the Moscow official wireless station. If the plan of campaign for the fulfilment of its aims has been discussed in secret, the aims themselves have been made known to all the world.

These speeches and proclamations emanate no doubt nominally from the Third International as such and not directly from the Soviet Government. But it is impossible for the latter to disprove its close association, if not its absolute identity, with the former. MM. Lenin and Trotsky are, for instance, members of the Executive Committee of the Third International; M. Stalin, whose report has already been quoted, is both President of the Eastern Secretariat and also People's Commissar for Nationalities. It is evident, moreover, that the Congress of the Third International could only take place on Russian soil with the approval of the Soviet Government. Further, M. Nuorteva, whose report has already been referred to, himself complained of the 'perpetual confusion of party and public policy' as a result of which the Council of People's Commissars had imposed upon the Third International the task of promoting armed demonstrations and strikes for 'considerations of State policy'. Nor is it possible to account for its possession of such funds as must be necessary in view of the extent of its organisation,

[6] A prominent Georgian Bolshevik. In 1919, he had been elected president of a mission to Turkestan.

except on the assumption that the Soviet Government, which does not permit of the accumulation of capital in private hands, has assigned them to the Third International for its work. The plea, indeed, that the Soviet Government is one authority and the Third International another, and that the former has no connection with or responsibility for the latter, is not only belied by all the facts of the case, but is of so transparent a character as not to deceive anyone who has the slightest acquaintance with the case.

The activities of the Third International are, however, not the only subject of which His Majesty's Government have cause to complain. The spokesmen and representatives of the Soviet Government even in their official capacity have not scrupled in repeated instances to contravene the written undertaking of their Government. M. Lenin himself has not refrained from using language on a public occasion which cannot but be regarded as contrary to the spirit of the agreement, as, for instance, on the 8th June, when speaking at the Congress of the Third International, he used the following words: 'We must use this breathing space in order carefully to prepare the revolution in capitalist States. A very important factor for the development of the world revolution is the awakening of millions of workers in the colonies and dependencies. This fact presents us with a most important task which consists in helping these enormous masses of backward individuals on the road to world-revolution.'

INDIA

His Majesty's Government also have evidence of continued intrigue with Indian revolutionaries in Europe, of which complaint was made in Sir R. Horne's note. After lengthy negotiations between the Soviet Government and Chattopadhyaya,[7] some of these individuals, who were then taking refuge in Berlin and other places in Europe, were invited by the Soviet Government to attend a meeting in Moscow on the 25th May, 1921, in order to discuss the best means of provoking a revolution in India. They were supplied with funds through M. Kopp, the official [sic] representative of the Soviet Government in Berlin, who also supplied them with visés to their passports.

Chattopadhyaya has been assisted financially by the Soviet Government to the extent of 15,000 Swedish kronen, whilst in addition every member of the Indian Revolutionary Society who attended the Moscow meeting had all his expenses paid and received additional monetary assistance in amounts varying from 5,000 to 15,000 M.

His Majesty's Government are likewise aware that the Soviet Mission in Berlin have afforded facilities for communication between members of the Indian Revolutionary Society in Berlin, which, as is well known to the Soviet Government, is plotting against British rule in India, and their associates in Moscow, thus directly assisting anti-British intrigue.

[7] Virendranath Chattopadhyaya, an Indian political refugee, who had lived in Sweden from 1917 until early in 1921.

744

For some considerable time the Soviet Government has been trying to persuade a well-known Indian anarchist, Dr. Hafiz, who has been studying the manufacture of bombs in Vienna, to proceed to Afghanistan to supervise a bomb depot on the borders of India in order to facilitate their importation into India. Dr. Hafiz has now, with the assistance of the Soviet Government, undertaken the task of manufacturing smokeless powder in Kabul, and has received from the Soviet Government the sum of 10,000 kronen for expenses connected with his wife and children.

PERSIA

As regards Persia, His Majesty's Government have the strongest reasons for believing that the policy of the Soviet Government is directed principally against British interests.

M. Rothstein, the representative of the Soviet Government in Tehran, is importing large sums of money, much of which he is known to spend on propaganda; he has a staff of nearly 100 persons, many of whom are actively engaged in propaganda, and he and his staff, by personal visits and other means, have sought to influence members of the Mejliss and other Persians of good standing against His Majesty's Government. He is also known to subsidise certain Persian newspapers in order to carry on a press campaign against Great Britain.

It is clearly recognised that M. Rothstein is doing everything possible to conceal his real activities, and seeks to place the responsibility of anti-British action and the formation of revolutionary bodies on to third parties; as, for instance, when a protest was made to him by the Persian Government on the 4th July, 1921, on the occupation of Resht, he stated that this was carried out by the Azerbaijan Soviet Government, whose activities the Moscow Government had difficulty in controlling, whereas His Majesty's Government are fully aware that the Soviet Government is in a position to control the policy of the Azerbaijan Government should it so desire.

That the Soviet Government itself is cognisant of M. Rothstein's activities admits of no doubt, and M. Chicherin has approved his suggestion to set up a revolutionary committee in Tehran.

Finally, not content with his own activities, M. Rothstein seeks the co-operation of the newly-appointed Soviet representative at Kabul, with whom he wishes to work in harmony and with whose assistance he seeks to obtain the dismissal of the present Afghan representative in Tehran in order to make room for another more actively hostile to Great Britain.

TURKESTAN

In Sir R. Horne's note the attention of M. Krassin was invited to the obnoxious work of the Tashkend propaganda school, the temporary base for Indian work, in which emissaries were trained before despatch to India.

745

Instructions issued, as is known to His Majesty's Government, in March from Moscow for the intensification of Eastern propaganda, particularly in Turkestan and on the Indian frontier, have not been cancelled; a special allocation of 2,000,000 gold roubles was sanctioned for the purpose, and Tashkend and, if possible, Kabul were selected as the bases for the work. His Majesty's Government are aware that the base at Tashkend has not yet been transferred, as was intended, to Kabul; they are no less well aware that the anti-British endeavour, of which the Tashkend base was the 'centre', has not ceased. Natives of India returning through Afghanistan who have within the last two months been intercepted on the Indian frontier have made no secret of the fact that they had been sent to Tashkend by Soviet Govenment officials for training in propaganda methods and had been provided with money and other facilities to make their way to India.

ANGORA

His Majesty's Government[8] are fully aware of the real motives underlying the policy of the Soviet Government in supporting the Turkish Nationalists and affording them considerable assistance in money and arms of every description. Of the facts of this assistance His Majesty's Government received convincing proof at the very moment when M. Klishko was assuring the Prime Minister that no such assistance was being given. The Soviet Government have used every persuasion in order to prevent the Angora Government from arriving at a peaceful solution with the *Entente* Powers, and, in order to exert still stronger pressure, have assembled considerable forces on the borders of Anatolia, and have suggested to the Angora Government that these forces should be sent into Anatolia for their active support.

The reason for this action is clearly apparent; Turkey is regarded in M. Stalin's words as 'the citadel of the Mohammedan world representing the most real threat to the power of Europe in general and the *Entente* in particular'. Whilst M. Karakhan, in his recent report upon 'The situation in the Near East,' states that 'Angora, with its branches in Samarkand in the East and Cairo in the West, is the spiritual and administrative centre of the united front of oppressed natives spreading from the Ganges in the East to the Nile in the West. The revolutionary enthusiasm of the Moslem population of this continent, inspired by Angora, is disciplined to such an extent that no important event can take place without the sanction and knowledge of the Angora centre, which in its turn completely co-ordinates and regulates its instructions in accordance with our proposals and desires.' Similarly, M. Eliava, in his report quoted previously, says: 'The Angora Government, for example, can serve as a unifying force. The extension of its influence to Afghanistan and the Mohammedan tribes of India is now essential, for without that the separate races will never be in a position independently to raise the standard of open struggle against their oppressors.'

[8] For British policy in the Near East during 1921, see Vol. XVII, Chaps. I and II.

But the most serious charge of all which His Majesty's Government have to make against the Soviet Government still remains to be recorded. Reference has already been made to M. Stalin's mention of the Russo-Afghan treaty as an instrument to guarantee friendly relations with a State whose territory is an important channel by which 'the Communist International maintains direct contact with' India. Article 10 of this treaty (which is a public document and has been officially communicated to His Majesty's Government by M. Krassin) and the supplementary clause amplifying this article show how these friendly relations, so necessary to the Communist International for the execution of its policy, are guaranteed, namely, by the annual payment of a free subsidy of 1,000,000 roubles in gold or silver coin or bullion; by the construction of a telegraph line from Kushk through Herat and Kandahar to Kabul, and by the readiness of the Russian Republic to place at the disposal of the Afghan Government 'technical and other specialists'. And, in fact, cash—no doubt part of the first instalment of the annual subsidy—is known to have arrived in the capital of Afghanistan.

Further, this treaty contains two articles—Nos. 4 and 5—providing for the establishment of Russian consulates at selected places in Afghanistan, and specifically at Herat, Maimana, Mazar-i-Sharif, Kandahar and Ghazni; to the question of these establishments special attention was drawn in Sir R. Horne's note of the 16th March, but His Majesty's Government are aware that quite recently M. Chicherin laid particular emphasis on the importance of retaining the clause in the Afghan treaty, which provides for the opening of consulates in the eastern districts of Afghanistan, alleging economic reasons for their importance: yet no one knows better than the Russian Commissary for Foreign Affairs that there are no economic reasons to justify the opening of Russian consulates in these districts. Apart from the inference to be legitimately drawn from M. Stalin's expression of view, already quoted, of the importance of the Russo-Afghan treaty, His Majesty's Government possess indisputable evidence that the former throughout have regarded these consulates as prospective centres of propaganda, and that their utility in this respect is the reason for which they have continuously pressed for the Afghan Government's consent to their establishment. In spite of the protest made by Sir R. Horne in March, M. Suritz[9] was able to inform the Afghan Foreign Minister in May that the incumbents designated for these consulates with full personnel were accompanying M. Rosenberg, who shortly after arrived in Kabul.

The above are not the only activities of the Soviet Government and its agents in Afghanistan to which His Majesty's Government must take exception. His Majesty's Government hold a mass of ind[i]sputable evidence that Jamal Pasha[10] (to whose activities also specific objection was raised in

[9] Expelled from Denmark, M. J. Z. Suritz was appointed Soviet representative in Afghanistan.
[10] A member of the Young Turk Committee of Union and Progress War Government and leader of a special Turkish mission to Kabul (see Vol. XVII, No. 4, n. 4).

Sir R. Horne's note of the 16th March) was despatched to Afghanistan by the Soviet Government, and that the lines of policy he is following were dictated to him from Moscow, and that its execution is supervised by the Russian Legation in Kabul.

In the late summer of 1920, Jamal Pasha was on his way to Kabul from Moscow and he was introduced to M. Suritz by the intimation that he and his companions (including the notorious Indian revolutionary, Barkatullah) were being sent by the Eastern Department of the Moscow Commissariat for Foreign Affairs, and that particular reliance was placed in him as representing both the Russian Soviet Government and the Turkish Revolutionary Government. Jamal's activities in Afghanistan were, and are, financed by funds provided by the Soviet Government, as is evident from the fact that from time to time they have been impeded, temporarily, by the non-receipt of remittances—amounting on one occasion to half a million roubles at the expected date. His Majesty's Government are aware that the funds were remitted to Jamal through the hands of the Soviet Minister in Kabul, to whom also was entrusted the task of supervising Jamal's activities. His Majesty's Government's knowledge of the nature of these activities is precise. One of his principal tasks, and one to which His Majesty's Government take particular objection, lay amongst the tribesmen of the Indo-Afghan frontier, particularly amongst those of Waziristan, from whom a representative was summoned in January of this year to Kabul to confer with Jamal on a plan of action. Besides devoting himself (indirectly through this 'representative' and certain tribal Maliks and directly by personal visits to the frontier districts) to propaganda amongst the tribes (for which purpose he has received on occasion sums as large as Rs. 1, 50, 000 [sic] from M. Suritz), Jamal has set himself to furnish the tribesmen with arms and ammunition, so far as possible of British make, and he and the Soviet Minister have budgetted for an expenditure of up to Rs. 10,00,000 [sic] for this purpose.

The identity of the 'Waziristan representative' is well known to British officers on the north-west frontier of India, as are those of his principal assistants. Their actions are closely followed, and the Indian Government is informed of their receipt from time to time of supplies of money, arms and ammunition for distribution to the tribes now in arms against the British forces. These activities are continuing with unabated energy to the present time.

Of Jamal's efforts under the inspiration and with the support of Moscow to form a *corps d'élite* in Afghanistan, of the cost of maintenance of his Mission, including the Turkish officers assisting him, of allowances from the Soviet Government to his family, of all these and other points His Majesty's Government have equally indisputable evidence.

It is obvious from the terms of his letter of credentials to the Amir of Afghanistan that Jamal's selection for the work he has undertaken was due largely to the appeal which his nationality and religion might be expected to make to the sympathies of the people of Afghanistan and the fanaticism of the frontier tribesmen; it was, in fact, but an incident in what M. Eliava describes as the gradual approach of the Soviet Government and Third International to their fundamental object, the creation of a powerful united Moslem movement which would deal the final blow against the power of capital and destroy the colonial system upon which the power of Western European capital rests. That the direction of this movement, of which Jamal is but the instrument, lies with the Soviet Government is clearly shown by the fact that when Bedri Bey[11] and Ali Faud Pasha[12] make suggestions or give directions to Jamal as to the policy to be pursued by him, they only do so after consultation with official members of the Soviet Government and officials of the Third International.

On the above review of the history of the last five months, it is abundantly clear that the conditions on which His Majesty's Government undertook to renew relations with Soviet Russia by the conclusion of the trade agreement remain unfulfilled. In spite of all the professions of good faith on the part of the Soviet Government, there have been unabated indications of bitter hostility towards this country and its dominions and dependencies. Even apart from the specific considerations to which it is pledged, it seems utterly to have failed to grasp the elementary principles which ordinarily underlie the relations between Governments professedly at amity with one another and naturally jealous of any attack on their own particular institutions. It still appears quite incapable of realising that a constant flow of inflammatory invective delivered by its leading representatives against the existing institutions of this country is an absolute barrier to the renewal of correct relations, and that actual hostile activities by its agents must necessarily prompt the belief that its desire for such relations is insincere.

His Majesty's Government have long been loth to believe that the Soviet Government was not as anxious as they themselves to create a more favourable atmosphere than previously existed, in which Anglo-Russian relations could be gradually cultivated till they finally became entirely normal. It has been their sincere desire that the trade agreement should not only be carried out, but should be the prelude to better relations between the Governments and peoples of the two countries. Such a future is, however, incapable of realisation if the conditions which have been described in this note are to continue; and His Majesty's Government must ask for a definite assurance that the Soviet Government will cause these activities which constitute breaches of the trade agreement to cease.[13]

[11] A leader of the Committee of Union and Progress and member of Jamal Pasha's mission to Kabul.

[12] Kemalist Ambassador at Moscow from 1920 until his recall in April, 1922.

[13] M. Litvinov's reply (September 27, 1921) to this Note was published in Cmd. 2895 of 1927, op. cit. The text will be found also in Degras, vol. i, pp. 257–62.

No. 415

Sir M. Findlay[1] (Christiania) to the Marquess Curzon of Kedleston (Received September 14)
No. 366 [N 10419/3687/38]

CHRISTIANIA, *September 9, 1921*

My Lord,

With reference to my despatch No. 352 of the 2nd instant,[2] I have now the honour to enclose herewith copy in English[2] of the trade agreement which was recently signed between the Norwegian and Soviet Governments.[3] This copy has been supplied to me by the Norwegian Ministry for Foreign Affairs.

Having failed to find any clause in this agreement respecting the right of previous approval of official representatives on either side, I enquired this morning by telephone from the Acting Under-Secretary at the Ministry for Foreign Affairs where this clause could be found. He informed me that in notes exchanged between the Norwegian Minister of Commerce and M. Kerzhentsev,[4] which have not yet been published, but of which he promised to send me copies in a few days, it was provided that either party had the right of previous approval of official representatives appointed by the other, and of demanding the withdrawal of such representatives should they think fit. I am informed that the notes exchanged are to be regarded as a final protocol of the agreement itself.

It would appear that on various points the agreement between Norway and the Soviet Government goes considerably further than the Krassin-Horne Agreement. I would draw your Lordship's attention to the following points: Article 1, paragraph 4, providing that the official delegation of the R.S.F.S.R. in Norway should be regarded as the only representative of the Russian State, and paragraph 5, providing for the appointment of trade agents to reside and carry out the functions of consular officers outside the capital of the respective country. Further, article 2, paragraphs 1 and 2, and paragraph 3, respecting the right to use the flag and other official emblems; article 5, paragraph 1; article 9, paragraph 2, respecting transit; and article 13, respecting ratification.

I would point out, with regard to article 9, paragraph 2, that as the Norwegian Government have recently repealed their prohibition of the import of Russian literature, which was held to be incompatible with the existing law, there would appear to be nothing to prevent the transit of such literature destined for other countries in virtue of this paragraph, i.e., if literature be held to come under the heading of 'goods', as I suppose it may be.

I have, etc.,

M. DE C. FINDLAY

[1] H.M. Envoy Extraordinary and Minister Plenipotentiary at Christiania.

[2] Not printed.

[3] Signed at Christiania on September 2. For sources, see Slusser and Triska, p. 23; for the text, see *B.F.S.P.*, vol. 114, pp. 882–6.

[4] Head of the Russian Trade Delegation in Sweden. M. Kerzhentsev also acted as Soviet representative in the negotiation of the trade agreement with Norway.

No. 416

The Marquess Curzon of Kedleston to Lord Hardinge (Paris)
No. 508 Telegraphic [N 10387/8614/38]

FOREIGN OFFICE, *September 12, 1921, 5 p.m.*

I understand that Soviet Government may follow up refusal to admit Mission of Enquiry[1] by making separate proposals to His Majesty's Government including recognition of purely British debts and admitting British mission.[2]

You should inform French Government that His Majesty's Government desire to co-operate most closely on question of famine relief and will listen to no separate proposals the object of which is merely to divide the Allies.[3]

[1] This refusal was contained in a Russian note of September 7 (not printed), a copy of which was transmitted by M. Berzin to Lord Curzon in a letter of September 8 (received in the Foreign Office on September 12). After this telegram was drafted, Mr. Gregory minuted (September 9): 'We have not yet received the text of the Soviet reply either directly or indirectly. All we have to go on is the "Daily Herald" [September 9] account and information from Mr. Wise [see No. 356] which confirms it.' In his unnumbered telegram of September 13, Lord Hardinge reported: 'Press announces that the French section of Russian Relief Commission met yesterday, and pronounced in favour of liquidating Commission altogether in view of Soviet reply.'

[2] A marginal note by Mr. Gregory to a minute of September 9 of Mr. Leeper runs: 'This is information received indirectly from Mr. Wise who, as is well known, is in daily, if not hourly, touch with the Bolsheviks.'

[3] Lord Hardinge carried out these instructions in a Note of September 13. In a letter of September 16, M. Berthelot (Secretary General of the French Ministry of Foreign Affairs) replied: 'Je serai reconnaissant à Votre Excellence de vouloir bien être auprès du Gouvernement Britannique l'interprète des sincères remerciements du Gouvernement français pour l'attitude qu'il a décidé d'observer dans cette affaire.'

No. 417

Memorandum by Mr. Leeper on the Political Aspects of the Russian Famine
[N 10364/4/38]

FOREIGN OFFICE, *September 12, 1921*

The question of giving relief to Russia has already ceased to be discussed from a purely humanitarian point of view and demands have been made for a reconsideration of our policy towards Russia as laid down by the Trade Agreement on March 16th.[1] Though the International Commission which met at Paris on August 30th[2] was careful to avoid all political questions and confine itself to the purely economic problem of the best method of distributing food to the population of Russia, the request of the Soviet Government for credits and the reply of the Soviet Government[3] to the telegram asking

[1] See No. 353, n. 2.   [2] See No. 413.   [3] See No. 416, n. 1.

for permission for the Mission of Enquiry to enter Russia have made it impossible to ignore the political issues which are now at stake.

It may be useful therefore to summarise:— (1) the actual political position in Russia (2) the arguments for and against supporting the Soviet Government on the ground that it is the only possible Government (3) the proposals which have been made for giving it this support and facilitating the distribution of food to the population by using the existing Soviet organization.

1. The main object in concluding the Trade Agreement was to promote trade with Russia. It was argued that the immediate result of this policy would be the disappearance of Communism and the gradual evolution of the Soviet Government towards something resembling democracy. The abandonment of the former food policy of the Soviet Government, the granting of concessions to foreigners and the recognition of private property by admitting free trade were welcome signs of moderation, whether they were prompted by a genuine desire on the part of the moderate wing of the Soviet Government to adopt reasonable methods of Government or whether they were concessions wrung from the Government by fear. Subsequent events, however, have not justified this optimism. The changes in the policy of the Soviet Government have been more apparent than real, as is shown by:— (1) the continual propaganda in the East in direct violation of the Trade Agreement (2) the material support given by the Soviet Government to the Third International (3) the maintenance of the Extraordinary Commission and the failure on the part of the Government to curtail its powers (4) the way the famine has been exploited by the Government for purely political ends and the refusal to cooperate with non-Bolsheviks in Russia. These charges against the Soviet Government are set forth in detail in the note which has been prepared for despatch to Moscow[4] and in Mr. Hodgson's recent telegrams[5] explaining the significance of the arrest of the non-Bolshevik members of the Famine Committee and the execution of numerous individuals in Petrograd. On the basis of this information it is not too much to say that the Soviet Government in all essentials still maintains its former policy of revolutionary intrigue abroad and oppression at home.

2. Those who advocate the granting of credits to the Soviet Government insist on the necessity of keeping the present Government in existence on the ground that the only alternative is chaos. The spectre of chaos in Russia has been constantly held up before Western Europe as the main argument for supporting the Soviet Government. So long as there were any reasonable hope that that Government, bad as it might be, could be the means of restoring Russia it was an intelligible course to try to avoid any action which would overthrow the Government without having anything to put in its place. But after 6 months' experience of the Trade Agreement and the policy of the Soviet Government since it was thereby given a reasonable chance to mend its ways it is time to consider whether it is still profitable or reasonable, on the bare hypothesis that the Government will yet reform itself, to continue to bolster it up in order to avoid the danger of anarchy.

[4] No. 414, Enclosure.   [5] See, for example, No. 408.

752

In order to justify taking the responsibility of giving any active support to the Soviet Government at the present moment it would be necessary to point to some concrete improvement in the position in Russia due to the action of the Government. The granting of a few concessions to foreigners, the opening of a few boutiques in the towns, the institution of the food tax instead of requisitions and the abolition of a limited number of decrees prohibiting private property are not much to go upon as against the charges already made against the Soviet Government. Anarchy in Russia is not yet complete, it is true, but it is already an accomplished fact over a large part of Russia and it would be difficult to say that the Soviet Government was actually reducing the area where its writ does not run at all or where its writ is merely nominal. On the contrary the available evidence, which it must be admitted is far from complete, tends to show that the efficiency of the Soviet Government is waning rather than waxing.

The Soviet rulers are themselves at variance, corruption is rife and the famine has now come to disorganise still more thoroughly what little authority is still exercised outside the principal cities.

In these circumstances it is not easy to put much trust in the Soviet Government as the instrument for the restoration of Russia. In spite of certain favourable signs it has used the opportunities afforded it for political and revolutionary ends and has put political considerations before economic even when so vital a question as famine relief was concerned. If any further confidence is to be shown it the next step lies with it and not with Western Europe. The Soviet Government is perfectly well aware that Western Europe is anxious to promote the return of normal economic conditions in Russia, and it knows equally well that this return depends upon confidence abroad. Its future, therefore, is in its own hands and the best way of bringing it to reason is to make this perfectly clear to the world at large and refrain from any official intervention in Russian affairs whether in a sense favourable or unfavourable to the Soviet Government until it makes a radical change in its present attitude and offers the only guarantees which will admit of credit and confidence being given to it. Until the Soviet Government provides these guarantees it must remain a useless instrument for the restoration of Russia, and any attempt to support it without them can only postpone for a short period the inevitable disruption of Russia into a number of small communities until such time as the Russian people themselves can come together again under a reasonable form of Government.

3. The proposals made by the Soviet Government for the granting of credits by foreign Governments are contained in the Nansen agreement[6] attached[7] to this memorandum. These proposals were before the International Commission in Paris and were considered as unacceptable on the ground that no credits could be given by Governments until two principles had been recognised by the Soviets viz. full recognition of debts and the provision of real tangible security.[8]

Dr. Nansen on the other hand wishes to persuade the Governments to put

[6] See No. 410.   [7] Not printed.   [8] See No. 413.

aside these principles for the time being on the plea of the necessity of feeding the starving population. He considers that he is in a position to guarantee the distribution of food to the population if once the Governments would provide the necessary credits.[9] The security which he proposes and which he considers satisfactory is the potential wealth of Russia. His argument is that no future Government of Russia can refuse to recognise a loan made under the present conditions and that even if previous debts are not recognised the debts now contracted will be.

Dr. Nansen's proposals would establish a very dangerous precedent in international relations. If once Governments were prepared to ignore the elementary principles upon which credit is given all the world over they would be striking at the very foundations of confidence between nations. If one Government in Russia is tacitly allowed to refuse its obligations, there is no reason why a future Government in that country should recognise them. It could plead the same excuses and it would be difficult to know where to draw the line. Dr. Nansen would have succeeded in obtaining the money needed for solving a problem which may not be soluble at all, for it is extremely doubtful whether (1) the money he demands could be used effectively to save Russia from the present famine (2) the Soviet Government itself is capable of being used as an effective instrument for restoring Russia and averting a period of anarchy. The nations of Europe are themselves in sufficiently difficult financial straits to require better security for a loan of such dimensions than can be given them by Dr. Nansen or anybody else.

[9] See No. 412.

No. 418

Mr. Hodgson (Moscow) to the Marquess Curzon of Kedleston
(Received September 20)
No. 41 [N 10605/9395/38]

MOSCOW, *September 12, 1921*

My Lord,

I have the honour to transmit, herewith, for the information of the Comptroller-General of the Department of Overseas Trade, a report by Mr. Peters, commercial secretary to this mission, showing the principles on which the Soviet Government contemplates the leasing of concessions to be exploited by foreign capital.

I have, etc.,
R. M. HODGSON

Memorandum respecting the Grant of Concessions by the Soviet Government

Why is the Soviet Government giving Concessions?

1. The Soviet Government is granting concessions because it has found itself unable to run Russian industry without foreign aid.

Russian industry always depended largely on foreign technical personnel and foreign capital. The nationalisation of industry in 1918 led to the breaking off of relations with abroad; foreign engineers left and foreign supplies ceased. The effect of nationalisation (combined with that of Bolshevik legislation in general and of general disorganisation) was a catastrophic decline in production which may be seen from the following table giving production in 1920, as compared with pre-war output:—

	Per cent.
Iron ore	$2\frac{1}{4}$
Copper	0·6
Salt	17
Coal	20
Naphtha	40
Cast iron	2·3
Agricultural machinery	1·5 to 13·7
Linen	25
Woolwork	15
Rubber	5
Matches	15
Paper	22
Sugar	6

Hence the concession policy as regards industry is the counterpart of the new economic policy as regards agriculture where the confiscatory system has been replaced by the payment of produce taxes. Both constitute a tacit admission of failure.

Is the Soviet Government likely to keep Faith with Concessionnaires?

2. This is the crux of the whole question of concessions. Can a Communist Government be expected to keep a bargain made with representatives of the capitalist system they condemn? Trotsky, in a recent speech, supplies at least part of the answer. Replying to critics of the Soviet Government's policy he remarked that in signing agreements the Soviet Government pledged only themselves—they gave no pledge for the course of history. In other words, if matters turned out in such a way that concessionnaires were superfluous they would soon be got rid of without ceremony.

But, on the other hand, as pointed out elsewhere (see 1), concession policy is a result of the failure of Communist principles as applied to industry. It has been forced on the Bolsheviks by the pressure of events, and there seems little chance of their being able to put the clock back and to carry out a fresh *coup* of nationalisation.

The answer to the question may, therefore, be stated: Events are not likely to allow the Soviet Government deliberately to break faith with concessionnaires, although there is no doubt that at least a large section of the Communist Party is bitterly opposed to the idea of granting concessions.

Hence, for intending concessionnaires the question is more or less reduced to one of the concrete conditions under which they will have to work. These may be such that it may prove impossible for a capitalist oasis to exist in the midst of a quasi-Communist desert. Various aspects of the working of a concessional undertaking are discussed elsewhere.

What Classes of Undertaking does the Soviet Government propose to give to Concessionnaires?

3. The declared policy of the Soviet Government is to retain in its own hands transport and the key industries (in particular, the so-called heavy industry).

There would thus be available concessions not classed as belonging to the key industries.

Further, since the Soviet Government depends for support mainly on the 'proletariat of Central and Northern Russia', it wishes, as far as possible, to prevent foreign capitalists from obtaining a hold there. It is afraid that concessionnaires would be able to put their workmen in a much better position than those of State undertakings, and thus discredit Communism in the eyes of the workers. Hence it is intended that concessions should be confined, as far as possible, to the outlying parts of Russia, e.g., to the northern timber areas, Siberia and the Urals, the Caucasus, etc.

In point of fact, however, the Bolshevik Government is not in a position to carry out these schemes in its [*sic*] entirety, and it is probably not going too far to say that it would grant a concession for almost any undertaking if a concessionnaire could be found willing to take it. No list of available concessions exists.

One may note here that so far as the Soviet Government is concerned there is no distinction between a nationalised undertaking owned by foreigners and one owned by Russians.

What is the Attitude of the Soviet Government towards the Return of Property to Private Owners?

4. Officially there can be no question of returning property to former owners. The view of the Soviet Government is that nationalisation was carried out by a sovereign act of the Soviet State, and that all nationalised undertakings are, and will remain, State property.

Provision is, however, made for leasing properties to their former owners, although officially such owners come into the last category of applicants for leases. Officially it is stated simply that if no co-operative society or

756

association of workers is willing to lease an undertaking, it may be leased to private owners, not even excluding former owners.

Practically matters stand otherwise. The Soviet Government wishes to retain in its hands only the undertakings which are the most easily supplied with fuel and food, and which in general are most easily worked. The undertakings which may be leased are therefore those which have to work under most difficult conditions. In practice Soviet officials quite understand that former owners with their knowledge of local conditions are the persons who are most likely to make a success of an enterprise.

In particular, as regards foreign owners there can be no doubt that the Soviet Government will certainly not refuse to consider proposals for the restoration of properties to their former management on a leasehold basis.

What Payment will the Soviet Government exact for Concessions?

5. Payment will, in all cases, take the form of a percentage of the production of the enterprise. The Soviet Government wishes in general to receive a percentage of the gross output either in nature or in foreign currency on the basis of prices realised for the commodity produced in some foreign market.

Obviously there is room for negotiation here, as a percentage of gross output might have to be paid on an unprofitable concession. Possibly the Soviet Government might on occasions agree to accept a percentage of net profit.

What is the Attitude of the Soviet Government in the matter of Compensation for Damage done to Nationalised Properties taken as Concessions by their former Owners?

6. In general, the Soviet Government denies the existence of any right to compensation. The Soviet State exercised its sovereign rights in nationalising undertakings, and the question of compensation does not arise.

But this official attitude is not preserved in actual practice. The Soviet Government knows that it will not be able to induce former owners to come back to Russia unless some recognition of their losses is made. The plan proposed is that 'compensation' (the actual word is avoided) should be involved in the terms of payment for the concession. Thus payment might be in the form of 10 per cent. of the gross output, together with freedom from all taxes. This might mean that the undertaking paid considerably less every year than it did before the revolution, and to this extent the owner would be receiving compensation.

All concession contracts will include a clause stating that the concessionnaire renounces all claims against the Soviet Government in respect of damage done to his property by nationalisation.

How are Concessionnaires to Dispose of their Products?

7. This question raises a series of difficulties. At present there is no free market in Russia, and the main purchase[r] will, therefore, in the majority of cases, be the State. The Soviet Government therefore introduces into concession contracts a clause giving the Government the right to preserve the

output of the enterprise. But so far as concessionnaires are concerned, they are interested in making a profit in foreign currency—their need of Russian roubles is confined to the sums required for payment of workmen, etc. They will demand at least part payment in foreign currency or an equivalent.

In some cases the Soviet Government may be forced to abandon its preferential claim and to allow concessionnaires to dispose of part of their output to private purchasers. Everything in this case depends on the extent to which the free market develops—at present, as stated above, it is practically non-existent. Further, will the free market command foreign currency or its equivalent? In this connection it may be mentioned that in the case of agricultural machinery factories, the original Government proposal was to link up the concession with a concession for a grain-producing area in the Kuban region, the idea being that all agricultural machinery would have to be disposed of inside Russia (some talk of export possibilities to Balkan countries may be dismissed as absurd under present conditions), and that the foreign currency required by the concessionnaire could be obtained by the export of grain from the Kuban concession.

This plan is fantastic, but illustrates the lines on which the Soviet Government thinks of working. A later plan involves the abandonment by the Government of its prior right to purchase. The concessionnaires will be allowed to sell direct to peasants in exchange for agricultural produce, and this produce they would be free to export. The concessionnaire's profit on the manufacture of machinery in Russia would thus be obtained from the sale of agricultural produce abroad.

Will Concessionnaires be allowed Freely to Import and Export from Soviet Government or what Limits are imposed in this connection?

8. Concessionnaires are given the right freely to import equipment and stores required for their undertakings. As regards customs duties, it is proposed that special conditions should be inserted in the concession agreements.

As regards export, this is linked up with the question of disposal of output, treated under 7. In general, concessions will be for the production of goods which find a sale abroad (timber, ores, oil, etc.), and, since the concessionnaire must be placed in a position to make a profit in foreign currency, he must be given the right either to export his products or to be paid in foreign currency or its equivalent (other goods, e.g., peasant produce saleable abroad).

Obviously this point is one which will require careful consideration in each case.

It may be noted here that one of the conditions imposed on concessionnaires is that they should import food and articles of prime necessity for their workers from abroad. This, again, is a subject for negotiation, as it would clearly be absurd if a concessionnaire were to import food products such as could be obtained more cheaply in Russia. The object of the Soviet Government in imposing this condition is to enable Soviet factories to obtain food more easily and cheaply by removing the competitive demand of concessionnaires.

What Guarantees does the Soviet Government give that they will fulfil Concession Agreements?

9. No guarantees other than the signature of the Concession Agreement by the Soviet Government will be forthcoming. Hence, in general, the question for concessionnaires reduces itself into:—

(*a*) The question of the sincerity of the Soviet Government (a question which has already been treated under 2).

(*b*) The question of the political stability of the Soviet Government.

The position may be summarised as follows:
Politically the Soviet Government is strong in the sense that there are no signs of the existence of any organised political grouping which might overturn the present political régime. There is much discontent, but it is of an apathetic kind—the discontent of the cowed. But the economic fabric on which the Soviet Government rests is crumbling. The concession policy itself is, as has been pointed out in 1, a confession of failure. It is more correct to say that the ground beneath the Soviet Government is changing rather than that the Government is changing its ground. The effect, however, is the same. We may describe what is going on in Russia today as a process of forced evolution.

The Soviet Government is more likely to fall rather than to be struck down. When it falls the criterion as to the permanence (or continuity) of the concessions it granted will be the criterion of usefulness to Russia; if a concession is in the interests of Russia it will be recognised by the successors of the Bolsheviks, who will be quite as dependent upon the support of foreign capital as the Bolsheviks themselves have admitted themselves to be. In the above it has been assumed that no British group will take over an enterprise which formerly belonged to others without entering into an understanding—which putting it on the lowest grounds would serve as a measure of insurance—with the former proprietors.

What Control will the Soviet Government exercise over Concessional Undertakings?

10. The actual form of control exercised by the Soviet Government will be laid down in each Concession Agreement, and will vary according to the character of the enterprise.

It will be for concessionnaires to secure that there should be no harassing political control, and that such control as is exercised should be of a purely technical character. As regards timber concessions, the Central Timber Committee will, of course, supervise operations; in the case of mines, the Mining Department.

What Powers will a Concessionnaire have as regards his Employees?

11. The problem of labour is perhaps the most difficult practical problem which the concessionnaire will have to solve, and it is over this question that disagreement with the Soviet Government is most likely to arise during negotiations.

The trade union movement in Russia is a powerful political factor, and in many ways the All-Russia Central Committee of Trade Unions, which links up all unions in Russia, may almost be regarded as a State within State. When the new concession policy was elaborated the trade unions insisted that concessions should be subject to general Soviet labour legislation. It has only been after a strenuous struggle that the industrial departments interested in concessions have forced the All-Russia Central Committee of Trade Unions to agree to a series of exceptions being made from general legislation.

The actual draft rules embodying these exceptions regarding labour conditions are attached hereto.[1] It should be noted that these will probably be considerably altered in the course of negotiations with intending concessionnaires. No copy of a draft 'collective agreement', i.e., the agreement between the concessionnaire and the trade union is at present available.

What Obligations as regards Production will be imposed on Concessionnaires?

12. In all cases a minimum programme of production is laid down. In case of the concessionnaire failing to carry out this programme, penalties will be imposed. This, again, is a very difficult point, as the actual conditions of working will make it by no means easy to estimate possible production.

[1] Not traced in the Foreign Office archives.

No. 419

Lord Hardinge (Paris) to the Marquess Curzon of Kedleston
(Received September 16, 9.15 a.m.)
No. 681 Telegraphic [N 10459/8614/38]

PARIS, *September 15, 1921, 11.30 p.m.*

Following from Sir P. Lloyd-Greame.

The Inter-allied Commission for Russian Relief which met today at Quai d'Orsay resolved that, notwithstanding refusal of Soviet Government to admit Mission of Enquiry into Russia,[1] the work of Commission should continue. No reply will be returned to telegram of Soviet Government but an invitation will be issued to all Governments, including Germany, directly interested in Russian question to send representatives to a further meeting of Commission[2]

[1] See No. 416, n. 1.

[2] In a minute of September 12 (N 10365/8614/38) Mr. Gregory wrote: 'It is in any case within the competence of the Commission to summon representatives of the non-Allied States to join them, and they were only waiting for the reply of the Soviet Gov[ernmen]t before taking this action. But an admirable opportunity is now afforded for bringing all the European Powers into line against the Soviet Gov[ernmen]t and besides destroying the pet weapon of the latter—which is to play off one Power against another—would assist us very materially in defeating the pro-Bolsheviks at home. An international combine against the Soviet Gov[ernmen]t has been impossible so far but, if the French Gov[ernmen]t are prepared to be accommodating now, the thing becomes realisable and we ought to take swift advantage of it.'

to be held at Brussels on October 6th.[3] Invitation will explain reasons which decided Commission to propose Mission of Enquiry and will request collaboration of other Governments in recommending what methods should be adopted in giving relief to the population in the famine area. Text of invitation will be drawn up at tomorrow's meeting.[4]

[3] See No. 430, below.

[4] In Paris telegram No. 686 of September 16, Sir P. Lloyd-Greame reported: 'International Commission for Russian Relief today drew up text of letter of invitation to international meeting at Brussels on 6th October which is being addressed to following States: United States, Germany, Argentine, Brazil, Bulgaria, China, Denmark, Spain, Esthonia, Finland, Lithuania, Latvia, Norway, Holland, Poland, Portugal, Roumania, Yugoslavia, Sweden, Switzerland (? Czechoslovakia), Vatican.'

'I return to London tonight.'

On September 19, M. Chicherin telegraphed to the Governments of Great Britain, France, Italy, and Belgium a Note dated September 18 which, having stated that the Russian Government had learned from the Press of the intention to invite other states to send representatives to the international commission, went on to say: 'Le gouvernement russe se voit obligé (? de déclarer) que l'adjonction de nouveaux participants ne rendra point plus acceptable pour lui le plan d'investigation de la commission de Monsieur Noulens, dont le gouvernement russe a déjà révélé le caractère inadmissible dans sa note circulaire du sept Septembre [see No. 416, n. 1]. Chaque jour nous apporte des nouvelles preuves de l'existence des plans d'intervention forgés par certains gouvernements contre la république Sovietiste. La politique du gouvernement français en Pologne et Roumanie, qui s'exprime en préparatifs de guerre contre la Russie et en aide et protection accordée aux gardes blancs et aux organisations contre-révolutionaires, est suffisamment montrée par les faits. Les bandes d'adhérents de Savinkov et Petlura, qui viennent de Pologne et Roumanie et traversant les frontières des républiques Sovietistes y empêchent le collectionnement du blé, y détruisent les stocks de grains et s'y attaquent aux trains de ravitaillement, font clairement réssortir le véritable degré d'intérêt porté par ceux qui les arment et les protégent au tort des affamés en Russie. Dans ces conditions et vu la situation politique générale actuelle, l'envoi en Russie de la commission internationale de l'investigation projetée par la commission de Monsieur Noulens où participent des Gouvernements hostiles à la Russie équivaudrait à rendre possible à ces derniers de préparer l'accomplissement de leurs plans.'

Mr. Leeper commented (September 20): 'M. Chicherin has not quite understood the object which the International Commission in Paris had in view when it sent the letter of invitation to the Governments enumerated in Sir P. Lloyd-Greame's report. It was not intended to send another Mission of Enquiry into Russia, but to bring all the other Governments into line on the plan of action to be followed in giving relief and above all in the general attitude to be adopted on the question of credits.'

No. 420

Mr. Max Muller[1] *(Warsaw) to the Marquess Curzon of Kedleston*
(Received September 26)
No. 540 [N 10779/36/38]

WARSAW, *September 15, 1921*

My Lord Marquess,

In the course of a conversation which I had with the Minister for Foreign Affairs the day before yesterday, on which I have already had the honour to

[1] H.M. Envoy Extraordinary and Minister Plenipotentiary at Warsaw.

report to Your Lordship in my telegram No. 3[7]7[2] and my despatch No. 535[3] Confidential, both of September 13th, I enquired of His Excellency whether his information from Moscow pointed to the probability of fresh military aggression on the part of the Bolsheviks against Poland. Monsieur Skirmunt replied that, though it was obvious that the constant exchange of recriminatory notes must retard the re-establishment of normal conditions of peace, such as he had hoped would ensue on the renewal of diplomatic relations, still neither he, nor the Minister of War, nor the Polish representative in Moscow anticipated the resumption of active hostilities by the Soviet Government, at all events this year.

I was able to tell His Excellency that this impression was shared by our Military Mission here, and also by myself, so far as my opinion on such a question counted for anything. At the same time I felt bound to add that the news which reached me from Lemberg as to the possibility of fresh disturbances in the Ukraine and concentrations of the Bolshevik troops on the Bessarabian frontier was such as to cause me some preoccupation.

Major Grant, a member of our Military Mission stationed at Lemberg, wrote on September 9th[4] that there was a general feeling of uneasiness prevalent in those parts owing to the reported concentration of Bolshevik cavalry in the angle of the rivers Zbrucz and Niester. There was definite information, he said, that at least two new divisions of Bolshevik cavalry had arrived in that region, but no infantry, and in any case it was certain that the Bolsheviks were adopting a very provocative attitude towards the Roumanians. There was much talk about various plans for a cavalry attack on the Roumanians in those parts, but General Haller, who is in command of the Polish forces in Eastern Galicia, did not believe in the possibility of such an attack in view of the Polish Roumanian military convention;[5] he was inclined rather to regard the movement of Red troops as a bluff directed against Roumania in the hope of influencing the negotia-

[2] In this telegram Mr. Max Muller reported that he had warned M. Skirmunt seriously concerning the continued activities of M. Savinkov (a former member of the Kerensky Government who was organising the military formation of Russian refugees in Poland), and continued: 'I told his Excellency that so long as M. Savinkov remained in Poland there could be no stable peace with Russia, as he was a born conspirator and would continue to plot against Soviet Government, whatever promises he might give to the contrary. M. Skirmunt told me that Soviet Government had renewed to Polish representative in Russia their complaints about activities of M. Savinkov and other White Guard organisations, and had produced documents proving complicity of certain [members] of Polish Ministry of War. Many of these documents were found to be forgeries, but still M. Skirmunt admitted that there was some justification for Russian complaints. This he was determined to remove, and as a first step it had been decided that the Political Director was to leave Poland. I expressed my pleasure at this, which I hoped might result in reducing tension between Russia and Poland. M. Skirmunt replied that he hoped so also, but he had his doubts, as Polish Government had far greater ground for complaint against Soviet Government, who were carrying on extensive revolutionary propaganda against Polish State, and showed no signs of executing terms of Treaty of Riga [of March 18, 1921, see Slusser and Triska, p. 20].'

[3] Not printed.   [4] Not traced in the Foreign Office archives.
[5] Of March 3, 1921. See B.F.S.P., vol. 114, pp. 916–17.

tions which are about to commence in Warsaw.[6] Previous experience of Bolshevik strategy lends colour to General Haller's explanation. Major Grant added that he also attached but little importance to the concentration of Bolshevik forces on the Roumanian frontier which he was inclined to ascribe to the fear of fresh Ukrainian uprisings and to the hope of being able to requisition supplies of food for both men and horses.[6]

A subsequent letter from Major Grant[4] talks of further reinforcements of Red troops in the Kamienec region, the whole force there being estimated by the Polish staff at Lemberg at about 10,000 men, while there were also rumours of large arrivals of Red troops further south on the Roumanian frontier.

The air at Lemberg appears to be full of rumours, but it is impossible to elicit any definite information except that every one in those parts is expecting a rebellion in the Ukraine, though personally I am inclined to doubt whether such a movement is possible on a large scale without the assistance, or at all events the tacit connivance, of the Polish military authorities. I can only repeat that the British Military Mission here are not inclined to attach much importance to the rumours of preparations for active aggression on the part of the Soviet Government.

This view seems to receive corroboration from the general tenor of Mr. Hodgson's recent despatches and telegrams as communicated to me. In his despatch No. 20 of August 29th[3] Mr. Hodgson stated that the Soviet Government had addressed a note to the Roumanian Government accusing it of supporting Petlura[7] and the so-called national republic of the Ukraine, requesting it to break off all relations with the latter and warning it that if Petlura's troops coming from Roumanian territory crossed over the Russian–Ukrainian frontier the Red Army would chase them back and pursue them into Roumania. Mr. Hodgson added that a similar threatening policy was being adopted against Poland. At first sight it might be thought that the Soviet Government was preparing a *casus belli* against Roumania and Poland, but Mr. Hodgson goes on to say that in all probability this truculent attitude is dictated by the desire to keep the minds of the Russian people off internal affairs and to stimulate national feeling in the face of an invented foreign menace.

Again in his telegram No. 52 of September 6th[3] Mr. Hodgson reported that Trotsky had left for the Roumanian frontier, that large forces of the Red Army were being assembled there and that the continuous despatch of troops to various destinations was causing a general feeling of nervous tension. Nevertheless Mr. Hodgson gives it as his opinion that these troops are not destined for an attack on one of the neighbouring states but are rather meant to overawe the discontented peasants of the Ukraine, and that the Soviet Government was trying to strengthen its position at home by exaggerating the dangers threatening it from outside.

[6] See No. 368.
[7] General Petliura was Head of the Ukrainian Directory and Commander-in-Chief of Ukrainian forces.

In his telegrams Nos. 58[8] and 59[8] of September 11th Mr. Hodgson stated that he had learned that the despatch of troops from Moscow towards Poland and Roumania was continuing but he again repeats that this step need not necessarily be taken as indicating hostile intentions and that in his opinion the Soviet Government was working for two objects—firstly to provide justification for its failure to execute the Riga Treaty[9] and secondly to arouse national feeling at home and thus render its own position more secure.

It is not surprising that the Roumanian Government should feel some anxiety regarding these movements of Bolshevik troops. In the conversation which I had with Monsieur Skirmunt on the 13th His Excellency said that the Roumanian Government did not share the Polish view that there was no immediate military menace to be feared from Russia and that on the contrary there was wide-spread anxiety in Roumania in regard to the aggressive intentions of the Bolsheviks.[10] Nevertheless the Roumanian

[8] Mr. Hodgson's telegram No. 58 of September 11 ran: 'I called on M. Litvinov yesterday at his request.

'He raised the question of Poland, whose Government, he said, was aiding and abetting M. Savinkov in anti-Soviet agitation amongst peasantry in [text uncertain] regions. Complete information is in their hands as to M. Savinkov's organisation, and it is of a nature incriminating very seriously Polish Government.

'Exchange of notes of increasing acerbity gave no good results, but only made situation more critical. Their proposal to form Mixed Commission at Warsaw to examine evidence which they possessed had been met with refusal on the ground that acceptance would involve infringement of Poland's rights. Their demands for expulsion of M. Savinkov were ignored.

'In the meantime, incursions of armed bands into Soviet territory might at any time provoke [text uncertain]. Russia was anxious to avoid war, and he thought that Poland also wished peace, but was profiting by presumed weakness of Russia. He is convinced that Great Britain would view with disfavour an outbreak of hostilities, and therefore spoke to me on the matter in the hope that by my intervention Polish Minister might be brought to understand gravity of situation. As long as Poland countenances anti-Soviet agitation of M. Savinkov, it is no use for her to expect that Russia will fulfil obligations under the Treaty of Riga.'

Telegram No. 59 (September 11) ran: 'Following is continuation of my telegram No. 58:

'View of Polish Legation is, of course, diametrically opposed to that of Litvinov. They maintain that Moscow is carrying on violent propaganda in Poland, evidence of which is supplied by discovery of an organisation emanating from Ukraine Government known as Zakordot, members of which have been arrested with diamonds and gold objects in their possession.

'Their instructions, which were seized at the same time, were to foment agitation in Poland, and failing this to join Petlura for purpose of manufacturing evidence of a nature to implicate Polish Government in anti-Soviet movement. They ridicule accusation of supporting Savinkov, whose influence is nil, who has no following, and is himself on the point of leaving the country.

'My belief is that Soviet Government is working for two objects: firstly, to provide justification for not observing terms of Polish treaty; secondly, to create national feeling and so strengthen internal position.

'I learn from sources which I believe to be reliable that despatch of troops from Moscow to Polish and Roumanian frontiers is continuing. Details by despatch [No. 39 of September 12, not printed].'

[9] See n. 2.

[10] Cf. No. 368.

Government was sending to Warsaw Monsieur Filality as its delegate to commence negotiations with Monsieur Karakhan[11] for the conclusion of a Treaty with the Soviet Government, and he hoped that this might conduce towards relieving the present tension between the two countries.

Finally, though with some diffidence, I venture to express my belief that relations between the Polish and Soviet Governments are not really so critical as might appear from accounts in the newspapers, at all events so far as the probability of an outbreak of regular hostilities in the near future is concerned. At the same time I am convinced that nothing can prevent the Soviet Government from continuing to wage war against Poland and the other neighbouring states by every sort of indirect and secret means, short of open military operations—that is to say by the dissemination of revolutionary propaganda, by the fomenting of strikes and disorders, and by terrorism. In spite of Monsieur Karakhan's assertions to the contrary there can be no doubt that a vigorous campaign on these lines is being conducted from Moscow against Poland, and I can only hope that the Polish Government will show the necessary patience and sagacity in dealing with this form of underhand warfare, without either breaking off diplomatic relations or having recourse to violent acts of reprisal, which might lead to an outbreak of active hostilities. The question of the recall of the Polish Legation from Moscow has been under consideration but Monsieur Skirmunt, I believe, shares my view that such action would effect nothing and would only result in leaving the eastern frontier in the same state of uncertainty as it was in before the signature of the Treaty of Riga.

Monsieur Chicherin, while protesting the most strictly pacific intentions towards Poland, has told Mr. Hodgson that Russia will not fulfil her obligations under the Treaty of Riga so long as Poland encourages anti-Russian agitation on her territories, while Monsieur Karakhan has stated repeatedly that the only factor preventing the re-establishment of good relations between the two Governments was the presence in Poland of the White Guard organisations and that as soon as this grievance was removed the Soviet Government would be prepared to carry out the clauses of the Riga Treaty. Up till now, however, Monsieur Karakhan's verbal promises have, according to Monsieur Skirmunt, proved worthless and his statements devoid of foundation, and even though the Polish Government may in return for the removal from Polish soil of the various White Guard organisations receive material advantages from the execution of certain clauses of the Treaty of Riga, it is too much to expect that the Soviet Government will ever renounce the use of subversive propaganda or cease to incite to revolution the proletariat in the neighbouring countries.

I have, etc.,

W. G. Max Muller

11 Soviet representative at Warsaw (see No. 366).

No. 421

Mr. Hodgson (*Moscow*) to the Marquess Curzon of Kedleston
(*Received September 18, 7.10 p.m.*)
No. 66 Telegraphic [N 10515/5/38]

MOSCOW, *September 17, 1921, 11.46 a.m.*

I presented note of September 7th[1] to Chicherin today in the presence of Monsieur Litvinov. Chicherin qualified contents as a mass of forgeries and inventions. Pronouncements attributed to Stalin are not genuine. Nuorteva never occupied post with which he is credited and having been in gaol since March could not have played the part ascribed to him. Lenin and Trotsky are the only members of the Government who are liaison members of executive of Third Internationale and this fact no more identifies the Third Internationale with Russian Government policy than did the fact that Vandervelde[2] belonged to Second Internationale identify policy of that body with policy of Belgian Government. All relations with Indian revolutionaries have been broken off and propaganda school at Tashkent has long been abolished. No anti-British agitation has been undertaken in Persia where Chicherin understands that relations between British Minister and Russian representative are friendly. It is not the fact that troops have been sent or promised for Anatolia.

With regard to Afghanistan it is the case that Consulates are to be created but for trade purposes only. Relations with Afghanistan are friendly but have not been utilised for purposes of detraction of Great Britain.

I expect to have detailed reply to note[3] in the course of a few days and will forward it with report by next bag.[4]

---

[1] No. 414, Enclosure.   [2] Belgian Minister of Justice.   [3] See No. 414, n. 13.

[4] The report was transmitted in Mr. Hodgson's despatch No. 59 of September 29 and the English text of the Russian Note (of September 27) in his despatch No. 61 of the same date. On September 30 Mr. Hodgson transmitted in his telegram No. 87 a long summary of this Russian Note (see No. 428, below). In a communication of September 26 to Lord Curzon, M. Berzin wrote: 'M. Berzin presents his compliments to the Marquess Curzon of Kedleston, and begs leave to refer to the note addressed to the Commissar for Foreign Affairs of the Russian Socialist Federal Soviet Republic (M. Chicherin) on the 7th September.

'M. Berzin understands from his Government that its reply to this note is being handed to Mr. Hodgson in Moscow.

'The Russian Government, while fully convinced that the accusations contained in Lord Curzon's note have no foundation in fact, is making fresh enquiries in order to be able to refute in detail the statements upon which the charges in Lord Curzon's note are based.

'Meanwhile, M. Berzin feels that no time must be allowed to pass before pointing out that many of these statements will not bear even the most superficial examination. For instance, M. Nuorteva is said by Lord Curzon to have issued a statement as Director of the Department of Propaganda under the Third International on the 20th June last. In fact, he has been in prison since March, and has never held any position under the Third International. Similarly, the other reports attributed to Eliava, Karakhan and others have never existed. M. Rothstein, the Ambassador of the Russian Socialist Federal Soviet Republic at Tehran, has never been engaged in the forming of revolutionary committees in Persia. Dr. Hafitz has never been sent to Moscow or to any other place by the Soviet Government.

'These examples should serve, pending the receipt of a full reply from the Russian

Government, to convince the British Government that the charges made are based upon inaccurate information.

'There can be no doubt that Lord Curzon and the Foreign Office have fallen victims to the false rumours spread by the Russian White Guards and of French origin. It will be recalled that the French press a short while ago was full of similar statements and insinuations.

'M. Berzin wishes to impress upon the Foreign Office that the Russian Government wishes more than ever to promote friendly and sincere relations with His Britannic Majesty's Government, and that it has given the best proof of its good intentions in taking steps, immediately after the signing of the trade agreement, to cease all activity and to dissolve any organisation in the East which might be construed as likely to give offence to His Britannic Majesty's Government or to constitute a breach of the agreement.'

No. 422

Mr. London[1] (Geneva) to the Marquess Curzon of Kedleston
(Received September 20, 10 p.m.)
No. 34 Telegraphic [N 10650/8614/38]

GENEVA, *September 20, 1921, 7.45 p.m.*

Following for Sir M. Hankey from Mr. Balfour.[2]

Debate on Russian famine must take place soon in Assembly and Nansen is sure to make an impassioned appeal for help, pointing out that in his opinion any report by Brussels Conference will be too late owing to approach of Russian winter. He will probably also comment on fact that while Brussels meeting must be too late League of Nations meeting, if turned to account, might possibly be in time.

Personally I am not anxious to see the League involved in this difficult business and I shall keep out of the debate if possible. But as this may not be possible please send me Government views on the question and in particular let me know whether we are going to give any financial contribution to relief fund,[3] and if so on what conditions. I understand Nansen has told

[1] H.M. Consul at Geneva.   [2] See No. 214, n. 3.

[3] In a letter of September 21 to Mr. Leeper, Sir P. Lloyd-Greame stated: 'The attitude of the Gov[ernmen]t is stated in Cabinet Minutes 69. (21) of 17 August [No. 394, n. 7]. The Chancellor is increasingly unwilling to find money for Russia; [and] he should be asked to telegraph his views to Mr. Balfour. . . .

'I hold very strongly that the Nansen proposal is pure charity, [and] in no sense an economic or business proposition. If Gov[ernmen]ts are to find credits on Nansen's terms, it must be done as charity, and no pretence must be made that it is anything else. I adhere absolutely to the Prime Minister's speech [see No. 394, n. 7] [and] to the reasoning set out in my draft Resolution on Credits [see No. 413, Appendix C].

'I believe that nothing but credit can save the situation; but I am convinced that credit on any large scale can only be given if properly used [and] bear fruit in the future, if the Russians accept the basic economic essentials of the recognition of debts [and] the provision of security. There is no half-way house, because the object of Gov[ernmen]t credit is to pave the way for commercial credit; [and] that is only possible if conditions of confidence are restored.

'Anything else is charity [and] must be voted as such.

'I would not myself oppose offering to give the Relief Credit balance to Nansen and/or

Soviet that if they will pay in gold he will undertake to send them surplus of rye harvest of Bulgaria.[4]

the Red Cross as charity, providing France [and] Italy w[oul]d give similar sums. There w[oul]d be this advantage in such a course. If H[is] M[ajesty's] G[overnment] give a limited sum in charitable famine relief, it strengthens their position to insist on economic credits being treated on a strictly economic basis.

'If Soviet Bonds were to be taken for this limited charitable advance, it w[oul]d be preferable that they sh[oul]d be given to the International Red Cross [and] not to the individual Gov[ernmen]ts.'

Mr. Leeper stated (September 22): 'I have spoken to Mr. Fass of the Treasury about the balance of £1,260,000 of the British vote for Relief Credits. He says that it could not be allocated to Russia without Parliamentary sanction [and] that in any case they are most anxious to keep it for Austria. This is apparently the only financial contribution which Sir P. Lloyd-Greame thinks might be possible, but in view of the Treasury's statement it clearly could not be given at once.'

Mr. Gregory commented (September 22): 'I am sure we should oppose anything in the nature of a grant, let alone credits. The Soviet Gov[ernmen]t has got plenty of money to spare, and in the present state of unemployment in this country it is hardly credible that even Labour can want us to contribute to Russia.'

Lord Curzon minuted his agreement (September 23).

[4] On September 24, Sir E. Crowe transmitted to Sir M. Hankey the following: 'The Under Secretary of State for Foreign Affairs presents his compliments to the Secretary to the Cabinet and, with reference to Mr. Balfour's telegram from Geneva of September 20th on the question of Dr. Nansen's proposals for Russian relief, begs leave to state that Lord Curzon considers that, in view of the great difficulty in finding the sum required for the unemployed in this country, no financial contribution towards Dr. Nansen's relief fund is possible. Lord Curzon understands that he is in full agreement with Sir R. Horne on this matter.

'His Lordship is, however, of the opinion that it would be desirable to contribute a small supply of medicaments to the British Red Cross from the surplus stocks of the Disposals Board in accordance with the recommendation of the International Commission in Paris.'

No. 423

Mr. Hodgson (Moscow) to the Marquess Curzon of Kedleston
(Received October 4)

No. 49 [N 11086/7452/38]

Confidential   MOSCOW, *September 22, 1921*

My Lord Marquess,

Mr. Leslie Urquhart,[1] who arrived in Moscow towards the middle of June for the purpose of continuing his negotiations for the return of the property of the Russo-Asiatic Consolidated Mining Corporation, left for London a week ago without having reached an agreement with the Soviet Government.

He was at first inclined to take a favourable view of his prospects of success, as he found a disposition on the part of the local officials to meet him on the various points at issue. Latterly he modified this opinion in the face of the

[1] See No. 367, n. 10.

difficulties he experienced in coming to an understanding on certain essential points.

The attitude of the Government appeared to vary during the course of the negotiations. Mr. Urquhart's arrival had been widely advertised as heralding the commencement of a new era in the economic relations between Russia and the outside world. Private information was to the effect that Lenin himself showed a keen interest in the negotiations and had given orders that they were to be brought to a successful conclusion at any cost.

Subsequently this favourable disposition of the officials gave way to an attitude of obstruction.[2] The change of front synchronised with the outbreak of the activity of the Extraordinary Commission in Petrograd and other centres towards the end of last month.[3] The political outlook here is very sensitive to outside events and it is quite possible that the signature of the Hoover Agreement[4] had an influence upon the Urquhart negotiations by lending stiffening to the Bolshevik resistance to his demands.

Whatever may have been the cause of this change of front, there is no doubt but that the attitude of the Bolshevik officials was variable. At one time it was darkly insinuated to Mr. Urquhart that, in his personal interests, it was advisable for him to sign the contract before leaving Russia. Later he had a private intimation that under no circumstances were the Bolsheviks willing to come to an agreement (about this time information was received that an important American financial group was on the way to Moscow). Finally he learnt that the Government had made up its mind not to break off the negotiations but to leave certain oustanding points for settlement in London, with the obvious intention of yielding or not as the political outlook might render this advisable or the reverse.

It was this last attitude which prevailed when Mr. Urquhart left. The points remaining for decision were the following:

1. The Soviet Government offers a 72 years' lease of the properties of the Urquhart Company. Mr. Urquhart holds out for a 99 years' lease.

2. The Soviet Government has accepted the principle that it should pay for the work necessary to bring the undertaking back to the condition in which the Government found it on nationalisation, but would not come to terms on details.

3. The Soviet Government, over and above a definite percentage of output, demands an 'excess profits tax' on sales of metals at prices above a certain level. Mr. Urquhart absolutely declines to agree to any excess profit payments and stands out also for a lower percentage of output.

---

[2] In his telegram No. 55 of September 9, Mr. Hodgson reported as follows: 'Urquhart negotiations are (? delaying) consideration of other concession schemes. Desirability of restarting agricultural machinery factories is recognised and draft contract is being now prepared as basis of discussion.

'Mission should receive this next week and will telegraph essential points. Pending receipt I do not recommend persons interested coming to Moscow.

'Present Russo-Asiatic negotiations are doing much to make clear the main obstacles to be overcome.'

[3] Cf. No. 408. [4] See No. 402, n. 3.

4. There is disagreement as to the terms on which the Soviet Government might buy out the concessionnaire.

5. No agreement could be reached on the labour question and fresh proposals are to be drawn up by the Concessions Committee and the Central Council of Trade Unions.

6. Since Soviet laws are expressly stated to be on a class basis all disputes in connection with the agreement are, according to the Concession Agreement, to be settled by an Arbitration Committee. Mr. Urquhart insists that the neutral chairman of this Committee should not be a Russian, but the Soviet Government has not yet agreed to this.[5]

I have, etc.,
R. M. Hodgson

[5] In a note of September 20 Sir W. Tyrrell stated: 'Mr Leslie Urquhart called today on his return from Moscow, where he has been attempting to negotiate with the Soviet Government for the future management of his properties and concessions in Russia on behalf of the company which he has formed here for their exploitation.

'In the course of his negotiations and dealings with the Bolsheviks he very soon realised that he had been brought out there by Krassin for propaganda purposes, and that his main chance of obtaining a satisfactory settlement depended on his playing up to the Russians for that purpose. As he was unwilling to play their game, he made up his mind not to sign any agreement, and towards the end of his stay his task was rendered easy by the fact that the Bolsheviks were taking no further interest in his business, as their attention was diverted to the negotiations with foreign Powers for the relief of the famine.'

No. 424

Mr. Hodgson (Moscow) to the Marquess Curzon of Kedleston
(Received October 4)
No. 52 [N 11089/4/38]

Confidential   MOSCOW, *September 22, 1921*
My Lord,

I have the honour to transmit herewith situation report for the ten days ending the 21st September, 1921.

I have, etc.,
R. M. Hodgson

ENCLOSURE IN No. 424

Situation Report for the Ten Days ending September 21, 1921

No improvement is visible either in the internal or the external situation. There is certainly a lull in the activity of the Extraordinary Commission, though it claims to have unearthed a pro-Polish and pro-*Entente* conspiracy in Kiev. It is admitted that eighty-nine persons have been executed in connection with this plot. The atmosphere in Petrograd is still one of terror and suspicion. In Smolensk a whole family was butchered because a boy of 16 made a disparaging remark about the 'Cheka' while at a cinematograph. In Rostov a number of persons have been arrested, including two Frenchmen, on charges of espionage, and efforts are evidently being made to create in connection with these arrests a concerted anti-Bolshevik movement.

The economic position continues to be disastrous, nor is there any reason to think that an improvement is in sight. The approaching exhaustion of the gold reserve is visible in the efforts that are being made by the Commissariat for Foreign Trade to accumulate jewellery, gold and precious articles, such as can be utilised for obtaining foreign currency. No doubt the purchases effected by the Commissariat are responsible to some extent for the rapid fall in the value of the Soviet rouble.

New shops continue to open in Moscow and slightly relieve the depressing monotony of the streets, but stocks are miserably small and cannot be re-newed in the absence of supplies in the country and the impossibility of purchasing from abroad. A few small factories are said to be starting work under private management, but great difficulty is experienced in obtaining raw materials, and in surmounting other difficulties which stand in the way of the resumption of work. The new economic policy has not so far given tangible results, for the restrictions imposed by the situation or by the com-plete breakdown of industry make it next to impossible for the principles enunciated by Lenin to be put into force. Mr. Leslie Urquhart, of whose advent much was expected, returned to London after protracted negotiations without having achieved any definite result.[1] There is, however, a possibility of his conversations with the Soviet Administration being continued in London.

The political horizon is still clouded by the Polish menace, to which the Commissariat for Foreign Affairs continues to give an importance which it can hardly possess in reality. Two incidents have occurred in this connection. The first is the publication in the Polish press of the revelations of Myslovsky,[2] who claims to have forged a correspondence implicating the Polish Government in the support of Savinkov,[3] and to have used it for deceiving Karakhan.[4] As the complaints against Poland made by the Russian Government are mainly based on the former's alleged connection with Savinkov and Petlura, Myslovsky's revelations should have tended to do away with the difficulties of the position as it is at present. The Bolsheviks naturally affected to attach no credence to the disclosures of Myslovsky, and Karakhan treats them as ridiculous and maintains that even the Poles did not take them seriously. The second incident of importance as affecting the Russo-Polish relations is the disclosure of a note which the French Govern-ment is alleged to have sent to Poland and the Ukraine inciting them to take advantage of the Russian weakness at the present time to present demands couched in the form of an ultimatum and promising to take similar action

[1] See No. 423.
[2] See *The Times*, September 16, 1921, p. 7.
[3] See No. 420, n. 2.
[4] See ibid., n. 11.

herself.[5] Trotsky and the whole press have seized upon this note and are fulminating against Poland and more particularly against France. Chicherin has addressed to Poland an interminable note of which a résumé is attached hereto.[6] The derailing of a provision train in the Ukraine has provided the Bolsheviks with a concrete cause for complaint, and it is being used by Trotsky as a ground for accusing Poland and Roumania, at the instigation of France, of striving to increase the difficulties caused by the famine by destroying the railway system in the Ukraine.

Although the Russo-Polish situation remains acute, France has become the main object of Bolshevik attack. The 'Pravda' sees in Paris the centre of a widespread anti-Soviet movement, whose leaders, among them English and Japanese, he [sic] calls 'national bandits'. The arch-bandit is Noulens, who is resuming his old bandit activities, viz., destruction and blackmail. The attacks on Finland which appeared in the press some time ago have ceased. It is probable that the scarecrow of a Finnish invasion was used to justify the despatch of Red troops to the Petrograd neighbourhood in view of the outbreak by the Extraordinary Commission there.

A growing tendency is noticeable to emphasise the difference between the attitude of France and Great Britain. Trotsky, in his tirade against Poland and Roumania, contrasted the policy of France with that of America, England, Norway and Germany, all of whom are sending food to the famine area. The 'Economisheskaya Zhizn' of the 16th September points out that the greatest quantity of food for the famine has been obtained from England. But the best example of this tendency appears in a long article by Radek on the [policy] of England and France towards Soviet Russia. He began by observing that France's policy has always been one of open and uncompromising hostility to the Soviet Government. England, he continued, desired the ultimate destruction of the Soviet power no less than France, but the difference was that she sought to postpone the moment of

[5] In a minute of September 16 Mr. Gregory stated: 'M. Berzin and M. Klishko, who came to see me yesterday about other (routine) matters, produced the Litvinov telegram now published in the "Daily News" and said that it was largely owing to this information that the Soviet Gov[ernmen]t had replied as it had to the International Commission on the Russian famine.

'I said that it was the first time I had heard any allegation of the kind, that there was nothing that had come to my knowledge which could lend colour to the report, that I did not believe there was a word of truth in it and that I could not accept their statement.

'At the same time it is more than probable that the Soviet Gov[ernmen]t is going to make the most of its charge ag[ain]st the French Gov[ernmen]t and that it will form the basis of every communication to us in reply to our recent note, to any further attempts to get guarantees for famine relief and in fact to any and every remonstrance or request that we may have to make in the course of the next few weeks.

'There is probably some slight foundation: but I imagine what must have happened is that the Polish and Roumanian Gov[ernmen]ts, feeling themselves menaced again by the Bolsheviks, as we know they do, applied hypothetically to the French Gov[ernmen]t for assistance in case of attack and were answered in the affirmative. There is not much harm in that. But this is, of course, pure conjecture.'

[6] Not printed. An English text of this Note of September 22 is given in Degras, vol. i, pp. 254–7.

that destruction, because, fearing the alliances which a White Russia would make with France and America, she wished to secure her position in the East and to place her relations with France on firmer ground before a White Government returns to power in Russia. It was for this reason that England never gave sufficient assistance to Kolchak, Denikin or Yudenitch,[7] but inclined towards Lord Curzon's Asiatic policy. Radek further sees in France the beginning of a new movement in favour of trade with Russia as being the only means of recovering a portion of the Imperial and Kerensky debts. But France is endeavouring to force Soviet Russia to enter into trade relations by means of blackmail. This, says Radek, the Soviet Government will never accept, and the result is that England remains the one country with whom we can enter into any agreement.

As regards other countries, the new representative of the German Government, Dr. Wiedenfeld, presented his letter of credit to M. Kalinin[8] on the 19th instant.

M. Pikko, the representative of the Italian Government, passing through Riga on his way to Moscow declared that his mission had no political, but only a commercial character. He had no doubt, however, that diplomatic recognition of the Soviet Government would soon follow.

The All-Russian Ukrainian Central Executive Committee, on the 17th September, signed an agreement with Turkey[9] regarding the repatriation of prisoners and *internés*, and on the 19th September ratified the Treaty of Peace between the Ukraine and Latvia.[10]

A Roumanian delegate of the name of [Filality][11] has left Bucharest to negotiate with Karakhan at Warsaw.

An American Commercial Mission is reported to have left America for the Far Eastern Republic.[12]

A translation is attached of a note from Mongolia[13] and of M. Chicherin's reply thereto, concerning the establishment of relations between Mongolia and China.[13]

The accounts of peasants returning from the famine area make it possible to form an idea of the actual situation. The picture is thoroughly depressing. Child mortality is enormous, and whatever measures are taken the needs of the population can only be partly relieved. The American Relief Association[14] is already at work on the spot.

---

[7] See No. 408, nn. 5 and 6. M. Yudenitch was formerly Commander-in-Chief of the White Russian North West Army.

[8] M. M. I. Kalinin was Chairman of the All-Russian Central Executive Committee, March, 1919–December, 1922.

[9] See Slusser and Triska, p. 24.

[10] Signed in Moscow on August 3, 1921 (see Slusser and Triska, p. 22).

[11] See No. 368.

[12] See *F.R.U.S.* 1921, vol. ii, pp. 745 ff.

[13] Not printed.

[14] This consisted of several American organisations which worked in Europe under the name of the European Relief Council. The work in Russia was under the direction of Colonel William N. Haskall (see *F.R.U.S.* 1921, vol. ii, pp. 821–2).

It is difficult to establish how far the measures taken by the Soviet Government to relieve the situation are in reality efficacious, but it is claimed that of 10,000,000 poods of seed corn despatched to the famine area 5,000,000 have already reached their destination. Eye-witnesses state that the peasants, at all events in the Samara and Kazan districts, are in receipt of their portion and are busily engaged in sowing it. It is to be noted that no one speaks of a movement of resentment against the Government in these districts. On the contrary it appears that the local Bolshevik Administration is working in close sympathy with the people and is gaining their gratitude by supplying to some extent their needs. The complete lack of medical stores renders the combating of famine and disease a matter of extreme difficulty, while the sudden change of temperature of the approach of winter finds thousands of peasants homeless and starving.

The efforts of the Government to collect funds for the famine relief have not met with an encouraging welcome. The financial department of the All-Russia Central Executive Committee has received only, so far, 326,492,000 roubles, of which 120,000,000 roubles were contributed by a British subject, Mr. Urquhart. So far, according to public figures, 38,000,587,000 roubles have been expended in the famine area.

Nor have the attempts made to stimulate the generosity of the world proletariat so far met with an enthusiastic reception. Up to now only 300,000 fr. have been subscribed by the proletariat in France, 300,000 lire by that in Italy, 10,000 gulden by that in Holland, and 100,000 M. by that in Germany. The Executive Committee of the Third International and the Famine Committee of the All-Russia Central Executive Committee have accordingly formed a temporary foreign committee to co-ordinate and centralise the assistance of the world proletariat. This committee has started work in Berlin, and is composed of: Clara Tsetkin, Professor Einstein and seven other Germans, four Scandinavians, Bernard Shaw and one other Englishman, Anatole France, Barbusse, Frossart and Varkant Couturier for France, two Swiss, two Dutch, one Austrian, one Italian and one Czechoslovak. The committee publishes daily bulletins in German and French, and brochures with articles by Lenin, Kamenev and Hauptmann. Local committees have also been formed in Germany, Switzerland, Austria, Hungary, Italy, England, France, Holland, Spain, Portugal, Belgium, Latvia and Lithuania.

In an official report the Ministry of Health claims that cholera has been mastered throughout Soviet Russia. While 74,750 cases were registered in July, only 16,781 were registered in the first fortnight of August.

Mr. London (Geneva) to the Marquess Curzon of Kedleston
(Received September 23, 3.15 p.m.)
No. 37 Telegraphic [N 10738/8614/38]

GENEVA, *September 23, 1921, 12.40 p.m.*

Following for Sir M. Hankey from Mr. Balfour.
Russian famine.
Following is substance of communication just received from Nansen.
Argentine possesses exportable quantity of wheat up to approximately £4,000,000 worth. He suggests that Argentine Government, who have statutory power to control export of wheat and who are showing great interest in famine question, should be asked to provide, through intermediary of National Bank of Argentine, wheat and other foodstuffs against bonds to be given by Russian Government on condition that other Governments should guarantee bonds which would be secured on any real assets which Russian Government possess or on liens on customs etc. He enquires whether British Government would be willing to participate in such a guarantee, pointing out that liability might be postponed for four or five years when general economic situation should have improved all round. He is sanguine of securing the participation of other Governments if His Majesty's Government would agree to proposal, but cannot, of course, guarantee acceptance of Argentine Government.[1]

[1] In a note to Sir M. Hankey of September 27, Sir E. Crowe stated: 'The Under Secretary for Foreign Affairs presents his compliments to the Secretary to the Cabinet, and begs leave to refer to telegram No. 37 of the 23rd instant from His Majesty's Consul at Geneva, transmitting a message from Mr. Balfour regarding the utilization of Argentine wheat for famine relief in Russia.
'Sir E. Crowe would be grateful if Sir M. Hankey would inform Mr. Balfour that His Majesty's Government are unable to adopt the proposals made by him.'

The Marquess Curzon of Kedleston to Mr. Hodgson (Moscow)
No. 54 Telegraphic [N 10713/5/38]

Confidential   FOREIGN OFFICE, *September 26, 1921, 7 p.m.*

Your telegram No. 72 of 22nd September[1]: Violations of Trade Agreement.
It is most unfortunate that you should have said anything to Chicherin about publication. You were not authorised to give any undertaking.

[1] This ran: 'Your despatch No. 64 of September 7th [No. 414].
'Chicherin states that contents of note have been divulged and have appeared in English press. In virtue of paragraph three of your despatch I gave assurance that note would not be published. Please place me in position to explain matters to Chicherin.'

My original idea was indeed, as indicated in paragraph 3 of your instructions, to allow a certain interval to elapse before publication, though I never intended to pledge myself to M. Chicherin. As, however, the latter's preliminary comments on the note foreshadowed a frivolous reply from the Soviet Government,[2] a copy of the note was communicated to M. Berzin[3] with an intimation that it would be published forthwith.

Past experience has unfortunately taught us that it is safer to forestall premature publication in the 'Daily Herald' of correspondence between the Soviet Government and His Majesty's Government, and we felt all the more justified in doing so in this instance owing to the close association between the newspaper mentioned and the Russian trade delegation having of late become even more pronounced than before.

But more important than this is the fact that within the last fortnight the Soviet Government itself has launched a public polemic, indirectly against this country and directly against its allies, firstly in its provocative reply to the telegram of the International Famine Commission,[4] and secondly in its unfounded allegations against the French Government of inciting Poland and Roumania to attack Russia.[5] The Soviet Government cannot have it all its own way as regards the methods of conducting diplomacy, and, if it does not scruple to publish its attacks on foreign Governments, it can hardly expect the latter to withhold their legitimate complaints from the public.

You should use the above arguments at your discretion in answering M. Chicherin, should he return to the charge.[6]

[2] On September 27 (see No. 414, n. 13). For M. Berzin's reply, see No. 421, n. 4.
[3] By Mr. Gregory on September 20.
[4] See No. 419, n. 4.
[5] See No. 424, n. 5.
[6] In his telegram No. 82 of September 30, Mr. Hodgson replied as follows:
'My assurance was given to Litvinov in strict accordance with paragraph three of my instructions and only in reply to question by Litvinov as to whether it was the intention of His Majesty's Government to publish the note. No undertaking against eventual publication was given.

'Contention of Soviet Government is that quotations from speeches in British note have their origin in compilations of secret service agency in Berlin managed by group (? of exiles). I have been shown large mass of printed matter purporting to emanate from this source and containing passages which are almost identical with some of those quoted in British note. It is certain that this printed matter cannot have been concocted subsequently to presentation of note in order to meet the occasion. Government maintains that fabrications of this bureau have been hawked about for sale and that they themselves purchased them some months ago. They accuse British secret service of having been duped by them.

'Presentation of note at the time of crisis in Russo-Polish relations is taken as proof that Great Britain has changed her policy and has joined France in views with which she is credited of (? advocating) intervention, with Poland as its instrument.'

Mr. Hodgson (Moscow) to Mr. Gregory
[*N 11451/5/38*]

MOSCOW, *September 29, 1921*

My dear Gregory,

Many thanks for your kind note of the 7th[1] which I received on the 15th. No, I certainly bore you no malice for not wishing the Mission good luck on its departure. I knew you were on leave and was very glad you got away into an atmosphere where the word Russia was never likely to be mentioned. You doubtless paid for your momentary immunity by a period of intensified misery on your return.

We had no trouble worth talking about on the way here and have settled down in a comfortable though exiguous house. The Soviet people promise us additional accommodation but that does not necessarily imply that we shall get it.

We have now our own domestic staff, having succeeded in chasing out the staff provided for us. Now it only remains to get rid of the Red Guard which protects our threshold. I have made a final *démarche* on this matter and, if it fails, I propose to suggest that Krassin's portals also be protected by stout policemen who will not budge from them day or night.

Generally I have no cause to complain of the behaviour of the Soviet Government towards the mission; they spy upon us fairly consistently but that appears to amuse them and is harmless. Chicherin is a strange individual. He is a peculiar sort of *illuminé*, extraordinarily shy and nervous. He is to be met at odd times in the disgusting staircases and corridors of the commissariat for foreign affairs, wandering about with a telegram or looking for a bit of blotting paper—too shy to send for the office boy or the Soviet substitute for one. He has no idea of time or space—is quite likely to promise to come and dine and change his mind on your doorstep and go home again. You probably know that he was heir to one of the finest estates in Russia, known as Karaul, with magnificent artistic collections. His uncle from whom he was to inherit it was in a state of senile decay and did not realise that his nephew had disgraced the family traditions by becoming a socialist. When he died, Chicherin, then a student in Berlin, refused to accept his heritage, knowing that his uncle, had he been aware of his nephew's divagations, would inevitably have disinherited him. 'Anyhow,' he said, 'it is of no importance, for Karaul, like everything else in Russia, is soon to become the property of the Russian nation.' The other day a Russian was dining here who remembered staying at Karaul when Chicherin was a child. He said he could still see the infant Chicherin with his small sister, putting their hands together and saying grace in English before being allowed to leave the table. He has developed into a strange furtive little creature, who looks nervously at the door every two minutes when he is talking to you and

---

[1] Not traced in the Foreign Office archives.

has a horrid little cough from somewhere round his diaphragm. He lives in one room in the commissariat for foreign affairs and I have not yet definitely located his *cabinet de travail*, if indeed he has a permanent one. Last time I went to see him he could not be found for about a quarter of an hour. Wherever he is disorder reigns—mountains of correspondence heaped up on all sides. He has a peculiarly receptive brain and will talk for hours on end in a small and not unpleasant voice, discussing theories of socialism, agriculture, the Near East or any other subject, with attention and understanding. His English is almost perfect; his French and German, I believe, quite perfect while he knows quite a number of uncanny languages. It is not very clear how far he has a real influence upon the policy of the Soviet Government. He is regarded as an eccentric who is to be humoured, as possessing assets rarely combined in supporters of the Soviet cause—fanatical devotion to the party, the training, education and associations of a man of birth and culture and absolute honesty. I should say that he is the mouthpiece of Lenin and is in accord with Lenin on matters of foreign policy, but I believe that he drafts and composes his notes himself. He has at his elbow Menzhinsky, commissary for Northern Europe and representative of the Cheka in the Narkomindel (People's Commissariat for Foreign Affairs), as well as Gorboonov, a member of the collegium and an influential communist. It is clear that the Cheka, in these assistants of Chicherin, keep a strong hand over the conduct of affairs.

Now for the Note.[2] Its presentation did not produce the paralysing effect which might have been expected. Neither Chicherin nor Litvinov bore themselves like convicted criminals. Chicherin read it through rapidly in my presence, commenting on the various points as he went along and pointing out allegations the justice of which he disputed and details the accuracy of which he challenged. The denunciation of Nuorteva provoked even a vestige of levity as Nuorteva, who was arrested in March, is said—and as far as I can find out it is the truth—to be still in gaol. A charge against him is I believe that of being a spy in British employ! I saw Litvinov yesterday and he promised me the official reply to the Note[3] in time to catch today's bag, but I am afraid there will be no time for me to examine it at any length before despatching it. I would say however that everything points to our having been unfortunate in the selection of some of the data advanced in support of our allegations. The matter of Nuorteva is one instance and a second instance is the speech attributed to Lenin on the 8th June. I have secured newspapers dealing with the congress mentioned and Lenin certainly does not appear as a speaker. I am sending translations of all the articles which have appeared so that you will see the line of defence which the Soviet Government is taking up. I have actually seen the reports in German from which, according to Chicherin, our information has been gleaned. You will of course know how our data is obtained at home and will be able to appreciate Chicherin's defence at its true value. I am sorry that we have, as seems evident, introduced statements the veracity of which can be

[2] See Nos. 414 and 426.   [3] See No. 414, n. 13.

challenged as this obviously weakens very much the authority of the document.

The Note, coming at the moment when the trouble with Poland[4] was at its most acute stage, has produced an effect the desirability of which I am not of course competent to judge. It has—coupled with the exhumation of Mrs. Harding,[5] the visit of the British fleet to Helsingfors[6] and other matters of small importance—convinced the Bolsheviks that the interventionists are again to the front at home and that we are parties to the horrible conspiracies of which France, Poland and Roumania are accused.

Upon the signing of the Trade Agreement secret instructions were issued to the press throughout the country that Great Britain was to be exempted in its attacks upon the bandit western nations. These instructions have hitherto been obeyed so far as the essential spitefulness of the Bolshevik soul made obedience possible, but since the Note the floodgates have been re-opened and we are again the object of universal opprobrium.

Yours ever,

R. M. Hodgson

[4] See No. 424.

[5] Mrs. Stan Harding, a journalist, had been imprisoned on false charges by the Bolsheviks in the summer of 1920. His Majesty's Government had taken up her case (see file N 6395/38 for 1921; see also Cmd. 1602 of 1922, *Correspondence with the Russian Soviet Government respecting the imprisonment of Mrs. Stan Harding in Russia*).

[6] In September, 1921.

No. 428

Mr. Hodgson (Moscow) to the Marquess Curzon of Kedleston
(Received October 3)

No. 87 Telegraphic [N 11058/5/38]

Confidential   MOSCOW, *September 30, 1921*

Reply of Soviet Government to note of 7th September[1] was despatched by bag yesterday.[2] Contents are as follows:—

Though Commissary of Foreign Affairs realised on cursory glance that charges were unfounded or based on false information, he refrained from precedent of Foreign Office in returning note and subjected it to careful investigation.

Reports and speeches quoted are inventions, and conclusions drawn from them that it is the policy of Russian Government, in collaboration with Third International, to undermine influence of British Government abroad are worthless.

Fact that Third International has its seat in Russia in no wise implicates Russian Government in activities of this organisation any more than presence of Second International in Brussels incriminates the Belgian Government.

Neither Stalin nor Eliava was ever connected with the Third International. Eastern section of International ceased to exist in the autumn of 1920.

[1] No. 414, Enclosure.   [2] See No. 414, n. 13 and No. 421, n. 4.

779

Karakhan never made report ascribed to him. Nuorteva has been in prison since March, and no department of propaganda existed in June 1920. Lenin did not speak on 8th June.

Various quotations in note have appeared from time to time in Russian counter-revolutionary papers. Government, in endeavouring to trace source of these and similar forgeries, traced them to a bulletin printed in Germany under title of 'Ostinformation.' Address of printing works is A. Winser, Wilhelmstrasse 11, Berlin S.W. 48; and bank's, Westerhagen-Potsdamstrasse 127, Berlin. This bureau supplied secret information on Soviet Russia to various Governments. Sample photographs of its production are transmitted with Soviet Government's reply. It is regretted that British Government should have based charges against friendly Government on documents issuing from this bureau. Apocryphal speeches, etc., in British note are repeated in bulletin almost word for word. Had Foreign Office realised the dubious source of information, Soviet Government is confident that note never would have been sent.

Soviet Government states most emphatically that since the conclusion of Anglo-Russian Agreement it has had no dealings, direct or indirect, with any Indian revolutionaries. No propaganda school exists in Tashkend for preparing emissaries for India. Government has had no contact with Hafiz, nor has it any knowledge of his present . . .[3] but Indian who proposed to organise traffic in arms in Kabul has been arrested and is still in prison. Government disclaims any responsibility for actions of Jemal Pasha, to whom no assistance is being given. Crossing of Russia by Indians on their way to Afghanistan does not violate agreement any more than hospitality extended in England to counter-revolutionaries. Soviet Government has not tried to prevent Angora Government from coming to an agreement with Great Britain, nor has it assembled forces on Anatolian frontier. Chicherin himself brought Angora Ambassador into contact with British agent to allow discussion of differences.

Strict instructions were issued by Soviet Government to its representatives on the conclusion of trade agreement to adapt their activities to the new relationship between the two countries. It is believed that these instructions are being followed, and that Russian representatives are confining themselves to protection of Russian interests without infringing those of Great Britain. True to principle of self-determination, Russia respects the independence of the Eastern countries, and is abandoning privileges and concessions extorted by Imperial Russia. Any help given to Afghanistan in accordance with a treaty brought to the knowledge of His Majesty's Government by M. Krassin cannot be construed as an unfriendly act. Rothstein has not set up a revolutionary committee or attempted to secure dismissal of Afghan representative, with whom he is on friendly terms.

If Russian representatives have . . .[3] infringed British interests it is because these have not been defined. Repeated requests during negotiations . . .[3] agreement for full discussion of contracting parties' mutual obligations in order to

[3] The text is here uncertain.

prevent future misunderstandings were repulsed. Russian Government has done its best to honour its undertakings and obviate causes of friction, but could not prevent malefactors forging documents and deceiving His Majesty's Government, nor could it expect that Foreign Office would use such documents in order to discredit it.[4]

British attitude recently has been far from friendly, witness arrests in Constantinople, co-operation with France on Russian question, support of French schemes tending to frustrate famine relief, and presentation of note at time when France was inciting Poland and Roumania to make war on Russia.

His Majesty's Government is well aware of the readiness of the Russian Government to discuss in a friendly manner means for removing hindrances to the re-establishment of normal relations. When, instead of resorting to baseless charges to impugn Russian good faith and deter other countries from concluding agreements with Russia, England will show similar disposition, she will find ready response.

[4] In a memorandum of September 30 [N 11182/7023/38], Mr. Gregory stated: 'In accordance with the instructions of the Secretary of State I at once instituted an examination or rather a re-examination of the evidence produced for the note and particularly of the sources from which it was derived.... We are at all events entitled to stick to our assertions about Nuorteva, Stalin and the rest—which are much more incriminating on the whole than Hafiz and his bombs.

'But where we are on the strongest ground of all is in regard to Lenin's speech. We have actually got this from the Wireless and from the "Rote Fahne" . . . . We can convict the Bolshevists practically out of their mouths. ·

'Consequently I would suggest as a general principle—though we have still to see what else the detailed reply of the Soviet Government contains—that we should take this one instance of Lenin's speech to prove that the Bolsheviks are liars and—without going into the rest of their denials—argue from that single instance that everything else they say is false and insist on the accuracy of the charges which appeared in the original note.'

Lord Curzon commented (October 2): 'I am much obliged to Mr. Gregory for his careful and on the whole reassuring analysis altho[ugh], likewise, I do not feel completely satisfied.

'One point he does not appear to have noticed. I see subsequently that Mr. Ovey has pointed it out. The Soviet reply says "Dr. Hafiz has never been sent to Moscow or to any other place by the Soviet Gov[ernmen]t."

'But this was not our charge. We did not even mention Moscow in this context. We said that the Soviet Gov[ernmen]t had "tried to persuade" Hafiz to proceed to Afghanistan, and that they had afterwards "assisted him" in his task.

'So that the Soviet reply is a reply to an allegation that had not been made.'

No. 429

The Marquess Curzon of Kedleston to Lord D'Abernon (Berlin)
No. 220 Telegraphic [N 11068/8614/38]

FOREIGN OFFICE, *October 3, 1921, 7 p.m.*

I understand from private sources that German Government is doubtful about accepting invitation to Brussels Conference on October 6th sent by

International Commission for Russian Relief.[1] Apparently Germans are surprised at being invited by French and fear there may be some trap.

It would help if you explained privately to Chancellor the importance of Germany being represented and the set-back it would give to the work of the Conference if she refused to cooperate. Any scheme for helping Russia must be international if it is to be successful.

Confidential

His Majesty's Government attach great importance to German co-operation as otherwise Soviet Government will continue game of playing off one country against another. Unless latter is faced with united front of European Powers, there is little hope of bringing it to reason.[2]

[1] See No. 419, n. 4.

[2] In his telegram No. 475 of October 4, Lord D'Abernon replied that the Minister of Foreign Affairs had agreed to send Geheimrat Hausschild to Brussels as the German delegate. Lord D'Abernon added that the Foreign Minister had stated that Germany 'was anxious not to go beyond the medical aid she has already promised Russia'.

No. 430

Report on Meeting of International Commission for Russian Relief at Brussels
(Communicated by Cabinet Office [October] 14, 1921)

[*N 11673/8614/38*]

Secret   *October 11, 1921*

The International Commission for Russian Relief met at Brussels on the 6th, 7th and 8th October. The following countries were represented:—

Belgium, China, Czechoslovakia, Denmark, Esthonia, Finland, France, Germany, Great Britain, Holland, Italy, Japan, Latvia, Lithuania, Poland, Roumania, Spain, Sweden, Switzerland, United States, Yugoslavia.

The representatives of Germany and the United States were only present with a watching brief, and did not vote. M. Ador represented the *Commission mixte* of Geneva.

The full personnel of the delegations is given in Appendix (A).[1]

2. M. Delacroix, the head of the Belgian delegation, acted as chairman, and it was largely owing to his tact and skill in that capacity that the commission succeeded in passing the resolutions attached to this report in Appendix (B) with very little dissent. The fact that twenty-one countries took part in the proceedings on so highly contentious a question as that of Russia, and passed resolutions dealing with the broad economic aspects of the Russian famine, is a distinct step forward in international co-operation which it was the object of the conference to achieve. It was unfortunate that the German delegate had not received instructions from his Government to vote on any of the resolutions, but both at the conference itself and in informal

[1] Not printed.

conversations it was made clear to him that it was the unanimous desire of the commission that, in the future, Germany would be fully represented, and would co-operate whole-heartedly in any work that was undertaken in connection with the Russian famine.

3. There was a good deal of discussion on the rival merits of the Hoover[2] and Nansen[3] agreements. It was clear that a majority of the delegations attached great importance to the provision in the Hoover agreement for sole control as against the Nansen provision of control jointly with the Soviet Government. A resolution was actually passed in this sense; but in deference to M. Ador's representations the modified expression of opinion contained in the latter part of the first resolution was substituted.

4. The most important progress made since the first meeting of the commission in Paris[4] is shown by the fact that the resolution (No. 5) on credits was adopted. It will be remembered that this resolution was discussed at Paris, and the further consideration adjourned for the deliberation of the full International Commission. The Italian delegation declined to accept the clause relating to the recognition of debts. Otherwise they accepted the general principles which, in the opinion of the commission, should regulate any granting of credits to the Soviet Government.

The question of credits was very fully discussed, and it was agreed that the commission would be shirking its duty unless it faced the economic question and expressed its opinion in the form of a resolution. The resolution is similar in its reasoning and its conclusions to the views expressed by the Prime Minister in the House of Commons on the 16th August last.[5]

5. Each nation was requested to state the action taken by private charity, and the extent of Government assistance afforded. The reports under this head put in by the various delegations are set out in Appendix (C).[1]

6. It will be seen that the assistance given by the British Government largely exceeds that hitherto undertaken by other European Governments.

7. It was unanimously agreed that the work which has thus been initiated on an international scale should be continued, and that every effort should be made to keep the nations of Europe in close contact with one another throughout the different phases of the Russian question. This object has for the present been secured by the establishment of a secretariat in Paris. It will depend on the course of events when the International Commission will again assemble.

P. Lloyd-Greame

Appendix (B)

Resolutions Passed by the Russian Relief Commission

The International Commission for Russian Relief, which met at Brussels on the 6th, 7th and 8th October, passed the following resolutions:—

First—Notwithstanding that efforts have already been so devotedly undertaken

---

[2] See No. 402, n. 3. [3] See No. 410, n. 3.
[4] See No. 413. [5] See No. 394, n. 7.

by certain national Red Cross Societies, by the American Relief Administration, and by the Geneva Conference, called the Mixed Commission, the Russian people are suffering from a famine of such gravity that the commission, renewing and confirming the appeals made at previous meetings at Paris, declares that the immediate assistance in supplies and money on the part of the various Governments is necessary, in order to assist the private organisations in their purely humanitarian and charitable work. The distribution of relief should be accompanied by the widest possible guarantees of control that can fairly be demanded. To each Red Cross Society especially must be reserved the right to have its supplies accompanied to their destination by its own agents, with the object of controlling distribution.

Second—In order to obtain the full co-ordination of the efforts undertaken by private organisations, the International Commission considers it indispensable to know the total amount of resources to be distributed by private organisations of each country. To this end Governments are asked to communicate by the 1st November the quantity and the description of the assistance they are according to humanitarian associations and Red Cross Societies. The latter are also invited to furnish information about their own resources and programmes of work by the same date.

Third—The commission further records its opinion that systematic relief covering the full scope of the problem of the food supply through the critical period, and the task, not only of giving momentary relief from the effects of the famine, but also of suppressing its causes, requires a previous study into the extent of the famine area, the surplus stocks of corn which can be collected in the regions not affected by the famine, the means of transport, the best methods of distribution, the plans for the next harvest and the numbers of the people affected. It therefore resolves that only after the despatch of a mission of specialists appointed by the commission, can the latter, having seen the documented report, advise Governments as to the credits which may be necessary to protect effectively the Russian population against famine.

Fourth—The International Commission calls the attention of the Red Cross Societies to the importance of saving the greatest possible number of Russian children by methods which will be considered best by these societies.

Fifth—The commission feels the difficulty of making specific suggestions in the absence of the necessary information which the Mission of Enquiry proposed at the first meeting was designed to obtain. But in view of the fact that requests have been made by the Soviet Government for credits in one form or in another, the commission considers it is within its competence to record the following conclusions:—

(a) Whatever are the precise dimensions of the famine, no final solution can be found unless economic conditions are established in which normal production and a regular exchange of goods of all sorts are guaranteed within Russia itself; unless the growth of prosperity is stimulated by intensive work; unless confidence exists to a degree sufficient to induce foreign exporters to send goods to Russia.

(b) Commercial and financial credit must be based on confidence, and this can only be created and maintained among commercial communities provided debts and obligations are recognised and advances sufficiently secured. These principles apply equally to credits granted by Governments as to private commercial credits.

(c) The commission is, therefore, forced to the inevitable conclusion that the creation of credits to assist exports to Russia will only be practicable on the following conditions:—

    (i) The Russian Government must recognise existing debts and other obligations arising from established claims.

    (ii) Adequate security should be afforded for any credit given in the future.

(*d*) If credits are given on these conditions they should be devoted to assisting the import into Russia of those commodities which the commission judges to be most essential after taking into consideration the report of the Mission of Enquiry.

(*e*) The commission desires to emphasise that in coming to these conclusions it is actuated by no political motive. Its conviction is founded solely on economic considerations of a vital character, and the commission is convinced that only in the manner herein stated will it be possible to extend to Russia public or private credit for the purpose of alleviating the existing distress in Russia and preventing a recurrence in the future.

The Italian delegation does not associate itself with section (*c*) (i).

The delegates of certain Governments holding a watching brief for this reason abstained from voting on the resolutions.

No. 431

Mr. Max Muller (Warsaw) to the Marquess Curzon of Kedleston
(Received October 17, 4 p.m.)

No. 413 Telegraphic [N 11593/1917/55]

WARSAW, *October 16, 1921*

My telegrams Nos. 400[1] and 403.[2]

Considerable opposition has developed to execution of agreement[3]

[1] Of October 8. This ran: 'Minister for Foreign Affairs informs me that conversations between M. Dabski [see n. 4] and M. Karakhan have been resumed and led to an agreement for enforcing terms of treaty.

'I understand that Polish Government will expel some more leaders of White Guard organisations, and Soviet Government will commence work of re-evacuation and payment of gold. When first payment has been made, Polish Government will expel remaining members of anti-Soviet organisations whose removal has been demanded by Soviet Government.

'It remains to be seen how far this arrangement will be executed.'

[2] Of October 10. This ran: 'My telegram No. 400 [see n. 1].

'Minister for Foreign Affairs tells me that number of leaders of White Guard organisations to be expelled is fifteen. Work on evacuation commission in Moscow has already commenced, and Soviet Government will forbid further removal or sale of objects to be returned to Poland. First payment of gold by Soviet Government is to be made on 20th October provided that necessary financial arrangements can be made.

'President of the Council, in the name of Polish Government, is to circularise all officials, military and civil, to abstain from all encouragement or support of organisations directed against the Soviet Government.'

[3] This agreement had been signed on October 7. For sources, see Slusser and Triska, p. 25.

concluded between M. Karakhan and M. Dabski,[4] especially as regards expulsion from Poland of leaders of anti-Soviet organisations.

This opposition has been strongest in ranks of Socialist Party, who say that proposed expulsion violates Poland's right to offer asylum to political refugees. There is, however, a suspicion that expulsion has secret support of Marshal Pilsudski.[5]

Question was discussed in . . .[6] Commission for Foreign Affairs, when only very qualified approval was given to agreement, and it was definitely laid down that in future Government could not expel foreign political refugees on the strength of agreement with foreign Governments.

Minister for Foreign Affairs told me that at first the fourteen [sic] leaders made no difficulty about leaving the country, but that subsequently they raised all kinds of objections, and he was convinced that this change of attitude was due to some secret influence. Polish Government, however, were determined that agreement concluded with M. Karakhan should be executed and the fifteen leaders made to leave the country.

I had previously mentioned to Minister for Foreign Affairs M. Savinkov's intention to return, as reported in Lord Hardinge's telegram No. 712 of 30th September.[7] His Excellency had explained that, though M. Savinkov claimed the right to return, he would only be permitted to do so for a few days to settle up his private affairs and then leave Poland for good. I pointed out the imprudence of granting M. Savinkov even this favour, but Minister for Foreign Affairs replied that he would explain the matter beforehand to M. Karakhan.

He agreed with me that French influence might be at the bottom of M. Savinkov's desire to return, and also possibly the sudden change in the attitude of anti-Soviet leaders.

[4] Polish Under Secretary of State for Foreign Affairs and head of the Polish delegation at Riga.

[5] Polish Head of State and Commander-in-Chief of the Polish armies.

[6] The text is here uncertain.

[7] Not printed.

No. 432

Mr. Ovey to M. Krassin

[*N 11704/10242/38*]

FOREIGN OFFICE, October 19, 1921

Sir,

The Marquess Curzon of Kedleston is informed by Colonel J. W. Boyle[1] that the Royal-Dutch-Shell Group are anxious to obtain a concession from

[1] Colonel J. Boyle (see Vol. XII, No. 332) had been appointed by the Royal Dutch Shell Group, the Shell Transport and Trading Company and the Royal Dutch Petroleum Company as their plenipotentiary in negotiations with His Majesty's Government and the

the Soviet Government for the production of oil from their properties in South Russia and Caucasia.

I am directed to inform you that it is with the full approval and support of His Majesty's Government that Colonel Boyle has addressed himself to you on this subject. His Majesty's Government trust that these negotiations may result in an early and satisfactory settlement.[2]

I am, etc.,

Esmond Ovey

Soviet Government concerning their Russian properties. (For the history of these concerns, see S. H. Longrigg, *Oil in the Middle East* (Third Edition, London, 1968), pp. 12–44 *passim*.) In a Foreign Office Memorandum of September 13 (N 10279/10242/38) Commander Maxse stated: 'Colonel Boyle has assured Sir John Cadman [formerly Director of H.M. Petroleum Executive and Chairman of the Inter-Allied Petroleum Council] and myself that he has British interests very strongly at heart, and he is prepared to work in the interests both of his employers and His Majesty's Government as he is convinced that their interests are identical. Briefly, Colonel Boyle's idea is that if he can secure, on terms to be agreed upon, the transfer of these Russian properties to British control, he hopes to show such a result as will pave the way for the transference of other Royal Dutch properties outside Netherlands jurisdiction to British control, and thus achieve one of the main objectives of the oil policy of His Majesty's Government.

'The first proposal from Colonel Boyle was that His Majesty's Government should accord their diplomatic support to him in Russia when he was negotiating regarding these properties on account of the very large British interests involved. As a result of preliminary conversations between Sir Philip Lloyd-Greame, Sir John Cadman, Mr. Weakley [of the Eastern Department of the Foreign Office] and myself, which took place at various times, Colonel Boyle was definitely informed by the Petroleum Department that His Majesty's Government could not actively intervene with the Soviet Government on behalf of a foreign corporation, however large the British minority. This is in accordance with the ordinary practice.

'Colonel Boyle now proposes that these Companies should be brought under British control as soon as possible, but this of necessity will take a little while, and that in the meantime His Majesty's Government should afford them such support as they could. After a prolonged discussion the proposal to give effect to this suggestion was tentatively agreed upon by Sir J. Cadman, Colonel Boyle and myself. (I, of course, made it clear that I had no power to commit the Foreign Office.)'

[2] On October 25, M. Krassin replied: 'M. Krassin wishes to assure the Marquess Curzon of Kedleston that, as far as the Russian Trade Delegation is concerned, it has taken every step necessary to deal promptly and satisfactorily with the matter raised by Lieutenant Colonel Boyle . . . . M. Krassin begs leave to take this opportunity of enquiring whether the Foreign Office is prepared and in a position to give an assurance that Lieutenant Colonel Boyle and the firms represented by him are seriously interested in the granting of a concession and that the negotiations initiated by him have no ulterior motive.

'M. Krassin is prompted to make this enquiry by a recent case. The representative of a large British firm, with whom the Russian Government had entered into negotiations, without any reason broke off those negotiations, although they were progressing normally, and utilised this rupture for a political campaign of insinuation and ridicule against the Soviet Government, the State, and the social order existing in Russia, thus revealing that the prevailing motive with him and his associates was anything but a business-like solution of the question regarding concessions.'

The allusion in the last paragraph of M. Krassin's note was to Mr. Leslie Urquhart's circular to the shareholders of Russo-Asiatic Consolidated Limited (transmitted to the Foreign Office on October 12) giving the reasons for the breakdown of his negotiations with M. Krassin.

No. 433

Mr. Ovey to M. Krassin

[*N 11313/216/38*]

FOREIGN OFFICE, *October 20, 1921*

Sir,

I am directed by the Marquess Curzon of Kedleston to inform you that His Majesty's Government have had under consideration the number of Russian citizens at the Russian Trade Delegation who may be considered 'reasonably necessary' in the sense of Article 4 of the Trade Agreement for the purpose of giving effect to that agreement.

2. Lord Curzon is informed that the personnel of the Russian Trade Delegation numbers about one hundred persons, of whom about forty have joined the staff since March 16th, and he is of opinion that adequate effect could be given to the agreement without a further increase in numbers.

3. I am therefore to state that in future applications for the admission of Russians to this country can only be considered, if the capacity in which the individual in question will be employed is stated together with full particulars of the nature of the work for which he is required.

4. I am to request that this information may be furnished in respect to the following applications:—

(1) Mr. Andre Leshava and daughter.
   (L.K. 1179, of October 10th, 1921.)
(2) Miss Bertha Tsypkin.
   (L.K. 1224, of October 12th, 1921.)
(3) Mr. Mark Tamarkin.
   (L.K. 1202, of October 11th, 1921.)
(4) Miss Alla Grosjean.
   (L.K. 1184, of October 11th, 1921.)[1]

I am, etc.,
ESMOND OVEY

---

[1] On October 25 M. Krassin replied: 'However undeveloped the trading relations between the two countries may still be, the Russian Trade Delegation and The All-Russian Co-operative Society Ltd. (Arcos), working under its instructions, have been able to place during the last year orders to the value of about £6,000,000. For the proper appreciation of this figure it must be recalled that in 1913 the total British exports to Russia amounted to about £14,000,000. This £14,000,000 worth of goods was dealt with through the intermediary of a number of private individuals and organisations and there is no doubt that the number of Russian citizens sojourning in this country in connection with trading matters during that period was counted not in hundreds, but in thousands. . . . The suggestion in Mr. Esmond Ovey's note that the personnel of the Delegation in this country could not be further increased without exceeding the actual needs, is, therefore, obviously not well founded.

'The trade between the two countries is now at the beginning of its development and, in particular, Russia is just now beginning to export timber, flax, bristles, furs, peasant products, etc. The Russian trade representation in this country requires for each of these branches special experts fully conversant with the particular trade. The sale of timber requires its experts, and so does the sale of flax, caviar, peasant products and so on, and naturally each of these experts requires his own assistants and clerical staff. . . .

'M. Krassin cannot help pointing out that at the present moment there are in England and particularly in London thousands of well-to-do Russians, of the class of the late land-owners, bankers, merchants, grand dukes etc. who do not pursue here any useful trade or profession and who are certainly doing nothing to help the reestablishment of sound economic and trading relations between the two countries.'

No. 434

Mr. Hodgson (Moscow) to the Marquess Curzon of Kedleston (Received November 8)
No. 100 [N 12376/3779/38]

MOSCOW, *October 24, 1921*

My Lord Marquess,

By Mr. Ovey's despatch No. 111 (N 10829/3779/38) of the 8th inst.[1] I was instructed to submit to Your Lordship any observations I might have to offer on the proposed appointment of

(1) a British Agent in Petrograd and
(2) an Agent of the Russian Railway Commission to reside at Leeds and/ or Newcastle.

In the matter raised in the first question I am of the opinion that an Agent should most certainly be appointed and that he should proceed to his post as expeditiously as possible. The grounds on which I base this opinion are the following:—

i. Petrograd has always been a port visited by large numbers of British ships. The trade is already reviving and ship-masters, under conditions now prevailing, will find the presence of a consular officer indispensable. Apart from the immediate need of having a consular officer to protect the shipping interests which already exist it may be safely anticipated that local authorities will use the opportunity to introduce practices in the handling of foreign shipping which will be prejudicial to the trade in the future and which, once established, it will be difficult subsequently to contest.

ii. There are in and around Petrograd a large number of factories owned, wholly or partly, by British subjects. These have been, in the great majority of cases, nationalised, but events are rapidly moving in the direction of the liberation of private commercial enterprise in Russia. It is imperative that there should be a British official on the spot who can look into the condition of factories, take such action as may be possible to protect the interests of the lawful owners and give advice and assistance to such of them as may be contemplating negotiations for the return of their property.

[1] Not printed.

iii. There is in Petrograd a British community of some 150 persons, most of whom are destitute, old or infirm. They have been living for some four years past in miserable conditions. It is true that many of them have little British but their passports, but even so it is impossible to leave them any longer entirely without official help or to have to utilise the kind offices of the American Relief Administration or the German Red Cross in order to preserve contact with them.

iv. Many British subjects have personal property in the Petrograd district, which they hope at some time to recover, but which can be neither traced nor protected unless there is some British representative in Petrograd.

v. Moscow is cut off from Petrograd to an extent which is, I think, hardly realised at home. Consequently the Moscow Mission is dependent upon the accounts of casual visitors from Petrograd for forming an opinion upon the actual situation prevailing there. This acts prejudicially upon the proper working of the Mission, which requires to be kept fully and accurately informed on matters of a political nature in Petrograd.

I think the study of these considerations will render it abundantly clear that the appointment of a permanent Agent in Petrograd in the immediate future is not only desirable but essential in the public interest.

I am also strongly in favour of acceding to the request of the Soviet Government for permission to appoint a representative of the Railway Commission in Leeds or Newcastle, or indeed in any other centre where the Russians may wish to appoint representatives, provided that such appointments have a clearly demonstrable commercial utility and that reasonable measures of precaution be taken to control the actions of such persons as may be appointed.

In the present instance I consider that the proposed appointment is most distinctly justifiable on the grounds of commercial utility for, in addition to the Armstrong Whitworth contract[2] for the repair of locomotives, which is either signed or is on the point of being signed, an important order has been placed in Leeds recently for cistern cars. Moreover a representative of the Russian Government, M. Cotomin, has just left Moscow for England in the company of Mr. Glass of the New Russia Company, with powers to place very considerable orders for files, tool steel, etc.,—orders which were to have been diverted to England as a result of representations made by Mr. Glass, during his recent visit to this country.

It seems to me that to refuse the request of the Moscow Government to be allowed to appoint an Agent to look after the execution of these and other orders in prospect would be equivalent to the renunciation of such small advantages to British trade as the Trade Agreement confers.

It is from this angle that I regard the situation. The Trade Agreement once signed, it remains to us to make the most of what cannot be regarded as anything but a thoroughly unsatisfactory instrument. It was signed with a Government upon whose form we had every reason to look with the strongest disfavour and whose members are living exponents of doctrines

[2] See No. 389, n. 4.

which we regard as subversive and noxious. But, having compounded with them, it obviously behoves us to get the greatest advantage possible from our compact. I do not believe that the method of dealing with Bolshevism which the Home Office would have us adopt would have that result. Confining the members of the Russian Trade Delegation to their Bond Street quarters, forbidding them to have representatives in the manufacturing centres of Great Britain, hindering their courier service by vexatious regulations and generally subjecting them to harassing and restrictive measures will not stop communist propaganda. It will however deflect it—supposing it does come from this source—into more secret channels and will compel it to take a more insidious and a more dangerous form. It will moreover drive abroad trade which should come to Great Britain and will, incidentally, by creating perpetual conflicts on small issues, render the work of this Mission sterile.

It is my personal conviction, based on my own observation and on numerous conversations which I have had with persons who have every reason to view the matter objectively, that the Bolshevik Government is not wilfully violating the terms of the Trade Agreement and that such apparent violations of the Agreement as have given rise to complaint are the work of communists who are either sheltering themselves behind the name of the Moscow Government or who, being employed by it, are acting contrary to instructions. Instances of the kind are unavoidable in view of the fundamental antagonism to our whole social system of the ideas which Moscow represents. That Moscow should wittingly ignore the obligations which interest commands it so obviously to observe is, on the face of it, unlikely for the fact that Russia is economically broken is now patent to the most ardent communists and the necessity of arriving at an understanding with Europe is recognised by all who have any remnant of the reasoning faculty left to them. The Russian Government is, to the best of my belief, endeavouring to carry out its engagements, not because it is drawn to Great Britain by the bonds of sympathy, but because it has everything to gain by doing so.

Moreover, I believe the attitude which the Home Office advocates to be harmful in that it weakens the position of the more moderate Bolsheviks as opposed to the intransigent elements of the Communist Party. It is no secret that the signature of the Trade Agreement was strongly opposed by the extreme wing of the Communist Party, who saw in it a sordid compromise with bourgeoisie and imperialism. If successful in its result, the Trade Agreement accentuates the cleavage between the two factions in the Communist party: if it is a failure, it justifies the opposition in their attitude of antagonism to it and facilitates their ascendancy.

The position would be otherwise were there any reason to anticipate the overthrow of the Bolshevik Government as the result either of a revolutionary movement within Russia or of the action of Russian anti-Bolshevik groups from outside. But there is no indication that anything of the kind is likely to happen. The 'white' groups outside Russia have already had various opportunities of demonstrating their futility and have used them to the utmost: they have alienated any support they had in the country itself and their return is not desired even by those who were sympathetic to them formerly from ties of family or political creed, but who, having survived four years of the present regime, have accommodated themselves more or less to the new order of things and believe that they stand to lose all they have left to them by the reappearance of those whose ideas they at one time shared.

As to the possibility of an internal movement causing the downfall of the present regime, I think that this eventuality may be dismissed for the present. The country is too depressed, too apathetic and too miserable to allow of anything more than sporadic outbursts of discontent to take place. The organisation of counter-revolution on a scale which could seriously menace the stability of the Soviet Government is hardly conceivable. The sole alternative to the continuance in power of the present administration—and it is one, the possibility of which cannot be ignored—is the chaos which would ensue from its breakdown as the result of organic rottenness.

Nor do I think that it is to our interest that another upheaval in Russia should take place, for the operation of elementary economic laws is rapidly destroying the whole basis on which the communist structure was founded. One after another of the party axioms have been abandoned in practice and the Government is rapidly becoming communist in little but the name. Till now the sacrifices of the principles in virtue of which the whole of Russia has been brought to a state of collapse, have been masked for the benefit of a duped proletariat: in their most recent utterances the leaders of Bolshevik thought have torn away this mask and admitted with cynical frankness the completeness of their failure.

I have, etc.,
R. M. Hodgson

No. 435

Mr. Hodgson (Moscow) to the Marquess Curzon of Kedleston
(Received November 8)
No. 110 [N 12382/9395/38]

moscow, *October 26, 1921*

My Lord Marquess,

With reference to my telegrams No. 55 of September [9]th[1] and No. 111 of October 24th,[2] I have the honour to transmit herewith, a copy of the draft contract referred to therein, with translation.[3]

[1] See No. 423, n. 2.
[2] This ran: 'Following are main points:—
  1. Twenty-five years lease.
  2. Stipulated output for five years.

The Concession Committee have taken a long time to produce this draft, but the delay is partly explained by the absence of Mr. Bogdanov, Chairman of the Supreme Council of National Economy, who has been absent in the Ukraine.

As regards the formal approval of the Ukrainian Government, in whose territory the factories in question lie, this has not been obtained by the Moscow Authorities as yet, but the Ukrainian Government was notified some time ago that negotiations on the subject of a concession for these factories were impending, and raised no objections.

The draft of the Collective Agreement governing conditions of labour, which will stand as an appendix to the Concession Contract, is not available yet, but the Concession Committee are confident, with what justification I am not prepared to say, that it will be reasonable. Whatever form it takes, however, it is likely to be a source of continual friction and to make harmonious working practically impossible.

It will be evident from the draft that the principle of compensation for losses caused is not yet admitted.

The Concessions Committee promised two further 'variants' of the Concession Contract shortly, the only difference being as regards the disposal of the output of the works.

According to variant No. 2 it is proposed to give the contractor the right of free sale of his output, and according to variant No. 3 the Concession is to be linked up with an agricultural concession a certain amount of the proceeds of which would be payable to the Government and enable it to pay for machinery purchased from the contractor.

I have, etc.,

R. M. HODGSON

3. This output to be purchased by Government who refund actual cost of production in whatever currency outlay incurred plus 8 to 15 per cent profit payable in foreign currency.
4. Amortisation and interest to be included in cost of production.
5. Excess of output over (? stipulated) amount to be at disposal of contractor.
6. Contractor to provide factory requirements and workmen's supplies obtaining them in Russia as far as possible.
7. Remainder (? can be) imported duty free during three years.
8. Government to supply articles of state monopoly against payment.
9. Contract to contain provision for premature redemption of factories by Government and conditions for appointment of expert and arbitration commissions.
10. Labour (? conditions) to be drawn up as Appendix 9⁵.

'Two further variations of contract are promised first leaving sale of manufactures in hands of contractor, second linking up agricultural concessions with this proposal.'

³ Not printed.

No. 436

Mr. Hodgson (Moscow) to the Marquess Curzon of Kedleston
(Received November 8)
No. 115 [N 12386/12386/38]

MOSCOW, *October 27, 1921*

My Lord Marquess,

I have the honour to report that Mr. A. G. Marshall, of the British Baltic Shipbuilding and Engineering Works Ltd., and Colonel Bonner, London representative of Sir William Beardmore and Company, have left for London, having arrived at a preliminary understanding with the Soviet Government.

The negotiations were conducted on behalf of Sir William Beardmore and Company, who have made an arrangement with the British Baltic Company by which they would be able to take over the works at Libau and Reval controlled by the latter. The original offer made to the Soviet Government was to repair 2,000 locomotives, 10,000 freight wagons and 1,000 passenger wagons at the Esthonian and Latvian works within five years.

M. Krassin, with whom the matter was first taken up, indicated that in view of the strain on Russia's resources imposed by the famine situation, it would be difficult to pay cash. Colonel Bonner and Mr. Marshall then intimated that they were prepared to accept payment in the form of an oil concession at Grozny, the balance of 25% of the output, after deduction of the cost of the repair work in Reval (or Libau) to be paid over to the Soviet Government.

The Soviet authorities were quite prepared to discuss the grant of an oil concession, but their attitude as regards the question of rolling-stock repairs varied almost from day to day. At first the proposal was welcomed, but later the Railway Department decided that all rolling-stock repairs could be carried out in Russia—a decision which was, however, received with the utmost scepticism by other Government departments acquainted with the past record of the Railway Department as regards repair work. The Kremlin (read 'Lenin') decided that it was politically desirable that Mr. Marshall's proposal should be accepted in principle, but the actual receipt of an intimation to that effect was delayed from day to day and week to week.

The Mission finally requested that the matter should be settled without delay. A decision, conveyed in a letter from the President of the Supreme Council of National Economy, was to the effect that:

(a) The question of locomotive repairs is postponed.
(b) The Soviet Government is prepared to discuss an arrangement for repairs of passenger and freight wagons.
(c) The arrangement will be dependent on the grant of an oil concession.

Colonel Bonner and Mr. Marshall have returned home to report. Later Mr. Marshall expects to return with an oil engineer to examine the Grozny property. No active steps as regards repair work will in any case be taken before next spring.

A copy of this despatch is being sent to His Majesty's Minister at Riga.

I have, etc.,

R. M. Hodgson

No. 437

The Marquess Curzon of Kedleston to the Cabinet Office

[*N 12040/5/38*]

Confidential   FOREIGN OFFICE, *October 27, 1921*

I circulate to my colleagues the reply which I propose to send to M. Litvinov's attack[1] upon my former note[2] (approved by the Cabinet), which called the attention of the Soviet Government to their repeated violation of the pledge about propaganda given in the text of the Trade Agreement.

I should not have desired to continue the correspondence were it not that M. Litvinov, in his reply, deliberately challenged the truth of the statements contained in my former note, and declared them to be either forgeries or fabrications. Silence in answer to such a challenge would be held to imply acceptance of the charge, or at least inability to meet it.

I have made my reply as precise and concise as possible, and it should be issued without delay.[3]

C[URZON] OF K[EDLESTON]

Draft Reply to the Soviet Government

In their letter of the 7th September[2] His Majesty's Government complained that the hostile activities of the Soviet Government against British interests in the East and elsewhere continue unabated, and added that they are in possession of indisputable evidence that these activities have been due to the direct instigation of the Soviet Government.

In his reply of the 27th September[1] M. Litvinov declared that the charges contained in the British note were either unfounded or were based on false information and forgeries.

His Majesty's Government had not made these charges without a prolonged and careful investigation in each case into the sources of their information—sources which it is necessarily impossible in many cases to disclose. They see no reason to recede from or even to qualify a single one of these charges now. Nor would any further statement have been required, were it not that specific allegations have been made by M. Litvinov in his rejoinder which it is necessary to repel.

---

[1] See No. 428.   [2] No. 414, Enclosure.

[3] This draft reply was approved and was transmitted to Mr. Hodgson in Foreign Office despatch No. 156 of November 2 (see No. 444, below). Memoranda and minutes referring to the drafting of this reply are to be found at N 11182/7023/38, N 11337/5/38, and N 12040/5/38.

It is impossible to accept M. Litvinov's attempt to dissociate the Russian Government from the Third International. That the Second International should have included in its executive such men as M. Vandervelde or Mr. Henderson is wholly irrelevant.[4] On the other hand, that the Third International, established in Moscow under the protection of the Russian Government, from whom it draws constant support and resources, should include in its executive MM. Lenin and Trotsky, the two most prominent members of the Russian Government, establishes so close an identity between the two bodies that each must be answerable to charges against the other. Moreover, the procedure adopted in this case has long since become familiar. When the Russian Government desire to take some action more than usually repugnant to normal international law and comity, they ordinarily erect some ostensibly independent authority to take the action on their behalf. So it was when at Russian instigation the Tashkent Government destroyed the independent Khanate of Bokhara,[5] when Russian troops, under the mask of the Azerbaijan Government, occupied a province of Persia,[6] when Azerbaijan itself demolished the Dashnak Republic of Armenia,[7] and when Armenia in her turn attacked the State of Georgia.[8] So it is today, when, through the Third International, the Russian Government seeks to spread its propaganda throughout the world. The process is familiar, and has ceased to beguile.

His Majesty's Government acknowledge one error in their note of the 7th September. A quotation was made from a speech by M. Lenin stated to have been delivered on the 8th June. M. Litvinov has denied the delivery of any such speech. It was in fact delivered by M. Lenin on the 8th July, and the words quoted in the British note were actually disseminated broadcast to the world by the Russian official wireless news from Moscow. Further, none of the information on which His Majesty's Government based their note of the 7th September or on which Lord Emmott founded his report[9] was drawn from 'Ost Information,' as conjectured by M. Litvinov.[10] They have better and

[4] M. Litvinov had stated: '... the mere facts of the Third International having for obvious reasons chosen Russia as the seat of its executive committee as the only land which allows full freedom to the spreading of communist ideas and personal freedom to Communists, and of some of the members of the Russian Government in their individual capacity belonging to the executive committee, give no more justification for identifying the Third International with the Russian Government than the Second International, having its seat in Brussels or counting among the members of its executive M. Vandervelde, a Belgian Minister, and Mr. Henderson, a British Cabinet Minister, gave justification for rendering identical the Second International with the Belgian or British Government.'

[5] In August, 1920. The Moscow Government maintained a commission in Tashkent, the capital of the Turkestan Republic.

[6] See Vol. XIII, No. 543.

[7] The Dashnak Republic had come into being in February, 1921 (see Vol. XV, No. 26, n. 5). [8] See Vol. XII, No. 662.

[9] For the report of Lord Emmott's committee, see Cmd. 1240 of 1921.

[10] M. Litvinov had written:

'It is quite obvious that all the reports, speeches and utterances quoted in the British note have been invented, forged and falsified for some purpose. They have appeared some time ago in various Russian counter-revolutionary papers, which have also reproduced a

more reliable sources of information. Lord Emmott's report was based in the main on official Soviet publications supplied to him by the Soviet delegation in London or, in a less degree, received from Russia direct.

His Majesty's Government knew long since that M. Nuorteva had been found guilty of malversation of funds; but they also know of the Bolshevik system under which persons under conviction for such an offence are permitted to remain at liberty at the goodwill of the local authorities. Whether he is or is not in prison, his condemnation does not preclude the presentation of reports on his work, as to which His Majesty's Government repeat their former statement. M. Eliava's appointment is, or was till recently, in the Transcaucasus. M. Stalin holds the post of People's Commissar for Nationalities, and in the last few days it has been confirmed that he is in charge of Eastern propaganda. Of none of these was it said that they belonged to the Third International—though the point is immaterial—nor that they submitted reports at Moscow in person; their reports were, however, quoted, and as to the authenticity of these His Majesty's Government entertain no doubt.

M. Litvinov denies that the Soviet Government has had any relations, direct or indirect, with Indian revolutionaries. This is not in accordance with the facts. The Soviet Government cannot deny the presence in Moscow of some twenty or more well-known Indian revolutionaries, invited to Moscow by the Soviet Government itself, where they remained as its guests for a period of three months—from the end of May to the beginning of September—attending various conferences, the object of which was to decide on measures for fomenting revolution in India. The names of many of those who attended these conferences are known.

M. Litvinov returns little more than a general denial to the paragraphs in the British note concerning Persia, Turkestan, Anatolia and Afghanistan. The statements there made are, however, in the majority of cases a matter of common knowledge in those countries, where His Majesty's Government are

number of other documents, circulars and letters purporting to come from the Third International, various Soviet institutions or from MM. Lenin, Trotsky, Chicherin, Litvinov, Preobrajensky or other Russians connected with the Soviet Government. In an attempt to follow up these forgeries to their sources, the Russian Government came across a bulletin published in Germany under the title "Ostinformation," published by an anonymous group of detectives and supplied mostly to counter-revolutionary papers and to secret agents of various Governments anxious to obtain secret documents on Soviet Russia. Though stamped "very secret," the bulletin does not conceal, and prints the address of the printing office (A. Winser, Wilhelmstrasse II, Berlin, S.W. 48), and in one of its issues gives the name and address of its bankers—Westerhagen and Co., Potsdamerstrasse, 127, Berlin (Appendix I) [not printed], to whom subscriptions are to be sent. Mr. Hodgson has been shown at the Commissariat for Foreign Affairs original copies of this bulletin, and attached to this note are photographic copies of some pages of the bulletin [not printed]. It is this bulletin that circulates the majority of forged sensational documents, such as instructions, circulars, personal letters, confessions, &c., from Soviet leaders. It is probably from this source that emanates the false information on Soviet Russia and Soviet leaders in the official report of the Parliamentary Commission under Lord Emmott. It is, however, mostly to be regretted that such trumped-up reports and speeches should have found their way into an official note of the British Foreign Office, to form the basis of a series of charges against the Government of a friendly country.'

797

not without excellent sources of information. M. Rothstein's activities in Tehran, his subsidies to the Persian press and his expenditure on propaganda do not admit of denial. The fact that a Revolutionary Committee has not been set up in Tehran does not disprove the allegation, now repeated, that M. Rothstein advocated and M. Chicherin approved this step. Within the last few days a reliable eye-witness of neither British nor Russian nationality has confirmed the regular despatch of the so-called propaganda train to the East, and the continued printing of propaganda in all the languages of the Orient. M. Litvinov denies the concentration of troops on the Anatolian frontier; yet the movement of such bodies of men cannot take place secretly, and reliable confirmation of the information was easily secured. The attitude of M. Nazarenus, the Soviet emissary to the Nationalist Government, is well known in Angora, and his activities in the direction mentioned in the note of the 7th September have been accentuated since it was delivered. The caravans of Russian arms on their way to the Turkish forces have been seen by reliable witnesses. M. Litvinov's references to the allegations concerning Afghanistan are particularly scanty; there is a denial as to Russian assistance and co-operation with Jemal Pasha as to which His Majesty's Government, who possess unimpeachable evidence to the contrary, must retain their opinion. His Majesty's Government continue to take the strongest exception to the general policy of the Soviet Government in Afghanistan as being aimed against the interests of the British Empire; and in particular they observe, as a further instance, that no attempt is made by M. Litvinov to disprove the purely propaganda purposes to be served by the suggested Russian consulates in Eastern Afghanistan.

M. Litvinov signally fails to produce any evidence in favour of his counter-charges against His Majesty's Government. The latter have consistently and faithfully conformed their conduct and policy to the conditions of the Trade Agreement, and are entitled to insist upon a similar degree of loyalty from the Soviet Government. They note with regret that the assurances for which they asked that the Russian breaches of the agreement shall cease have not been forthcoming, and they are accordingly left to consider whether the conclusion of the agreement has in any material degree been followed by the mutual advantage which they had the right to expect.

No. 438

Mr. Gregory to M. Krassin
[*N 12085/12085/38*]

FOREIGN OFFICE, *November 1, 1921*
Sir,
 I am directed by the Marquess Curzon of Kedleston to acknowledge the receipt of your memorandum of October 28th,[1] enclosing a copy of a

[1] Not printed. For an English text, see Degras, vol. i, pp. 270–2.

communication from Monsieur Chicherin on the subject of Russia's foreign indebtedness. Monsieur Chicherin alludes to the resolution 5 (c) (i) passed by the Brussels conference (copy annexed)[2] and declares that the proposal to recognize 'the old debts under certain conditions', corresponds with the intentions of the Soviet Government at the moment. The note goes on to state that the Soviet Government is ready to recognise the obligations towards other states and their citizens which arise from state loans concluded by the Czarist Government before 1914, on the express condition that the Great Powers conclude a definite peace with, and recognise the Government of the Soviet Republic. For this purpose it is stated to be essential that an International Conference should be assembled.

2. His Majesty's Government feel that in making this announcement the Soviet Government have set their feet upon the only path by which they can attain to the goal they here profess to desire, namely economic co-operation with other nations. But it contains passages of which the exact purport is not clear to them: and in respect to some of these they would desire further information before they can, in consultation with the Governments with whom they are associated in the International Famine Commission, decide what their attitude towards the declaration as a whole should be.

3. You indicate that the recognition of what the Brussels conference defined as 'existing debts and other obligations arising from established claims' corresponds with the intentions of the Soviet Government, at the moment, but on the other hand your concrete proposition confines recognition to one particular class of debts or obligations. His Majesty's Government wish to know whether recognition of other classes of obligations, e.g. loans to the Czarist Government since 1914, municipal and railway loans and claims by foreign owners of property in Russia confiscated or destroyed by the Soviet Government, also corresponds with the intention of the Soviet Government at the moment; and they invite that government explicitly to define their attitude in regard to all such other classes of claims.[3]

---

[2] See No. 430, Appendix B.

[3] In a memorandum of November 4 Mr. O'Malley stated: 'A rough classification of the categories and amounts of claims against Russia is annexed. I also annex a classification of the foreign debt of Russia taken from a pre-war year book by the Russian Ministry of Finance. The Russian declaration does not make it clear whether they admit liability for all or only part of these debts.'

CLAIMS AGAINST RUSSIA

There are 38,000 claimants on the Register, and fresh claims are coming in at the rate of from 50 to 60 per week. As regards the total amount involved it is only possible to make a rough estimate, as the work of tabulation has necessarily been slow. It is thought however that the total amount *claimed* is probably somewhere between £300,000,000 and £350,000,000 sterling. The total represents the claims as stated by claimants themselves and is obviously an inflated figure, particularly in the case of the claims in respect of Mining and Oil Properties and of Private properties confiscated.

The following figures show roughly the distribution of the total under various heads. Those as regards Traders Claims, Bank Balances, Municipal Securities, Business and

4. There are other phrases in Monsieur Chicherin's note inviting comment, such for instance as the passage which imputes to His Majesty's Government the intention to support hostile interventions against the

Private Properties may be taken to be fairly near the mark. The others are estimates based on the results obtained from such work as has been done on them.

Claims by Traders
 (a) In respect of goods supplied and services rendered to customers in
  Russia   —about £7,500,000
 (b) Goods supplied and services rendered to Russian Government—about £1,500,000
  (Note: In addition to the above figures, many traders who were
  unable to transfer their money to this country left it on Deposit or
  invested it in Treasury Bills or other Government Securities.
  See below.)
 (c) Advances for goods purchased   —about £1,000,000
 (d) Goods requisitioned or nationalized   —about £4,000,000

Claims in Respect of Bank Balances and Deposits
  about Rbls. 250,000,000   —say £25,000,000
  (of which probably about two-thirds to three-fifths are trade or
  business claims)

Other Business Claims, Banks, Discount Houses, Insurance Companies, etc.
 (exclusive of Securities. See below)   —say £5,000,000

Securities
 (a) *State Loans, Guaranteed Railways, etc.*
  (The tabulation of these claims is not yet completed.)
  May be estimated at from £40,000,000 to   £50,000,000
 (b) *Municipal*   —about £16,000,000
 (c) *Other Investments* (Shares in Russian Companies, Municipal Credit
  Societies, Land Banks, Commercial Banks, etc.) —say £10,000,000

Business Properties
 (a) Mining and Oil   —about £180,000,000
  (These are considerably inflated.)
 (b) Industrial and Manufacturing   —about £30,000,000
Private Properties (real and personal) (exclusive of securities) —say £5,000,000
Miscellaneous including imprisonment, personal injury, forced payments, etc.
             —say £1,000,000
Claims by His Majesty's Treasury against the Russian Government in
 respect to credits granted since 1914 (August) —about £650,000,000
Claims by His Majesty's Treasury against the Russian Government in
 respect to guarantees given to traders in the United Kingdom who sup-
 plied traders in Russia with munitions etc. since August 1914 —about £7,000,000

RUSSIAN DEBT
The following classification is taken from the Year Book of the Ministry of Finance.
1. State Debts
 These are classified under (a) Debts contracted for general Imperial requirements, and (b) Debts on Railway Bonds. This latter class includes both loans directly issued by the State for railway purposes (such as, e.g. the Consolidated Railway Loans of 1889–90), and bonds issued by private railways and subsequently declared to be incorporated into the State Debt when these railways were purchased by the State.

Soviet Government and the further passage which implies that the obligation to meet a debt grows less binding with the lapse of time; but His Majesty's Government do not consider any useful purpose would now be served by going beyond the terms of this letter.

I am, etc.,

J. D. GREGORY

2. *Railway Shares and Bonds guaranteed by the Government*
These are loans of Railways which were still in private ownership. It is perhaps notice-able that the word used here is Pravitelstvo (Government) not Gosudarstvo (State).

The $4\frac{1}{2}$% Armavir Touapse Railway Loan, which was a sterling loan issued in London in June 1909, is stated to be 'unconditionally guaranteed by the Russian Government' and probably the other guaranteed loans which were issued here subsequently are in similar form.

3. *Other Securities (papers) State or guaranteed by the Government*
This includes mortgage securities issued by the Imperial Land Bank of the Nobility and the Peasants' Land Bank. The number of British holders of these is comparatively small.

No. 439

Mr. Max Muller (Warsaw) to the Marquess Curzon of Kedleston
(Received November 14)
No. 654 [N 12576/217/38]

WARSAW, *November 3, 1921*

My Lord Marquess,
With reference to the statements regarding the Russo-Roumanian negotia-tions contained in the summaries of events for the weeks ending October 11th and October 25th enclosed respectively in my despatches No. 601 of October 11th[1] and No. 640 of October 25th,[1] I have the honour to inform Your Lordship that I have learnt from the Roumanian Minister that the con-versations between Monsieur Karakhan and Monsieur Filality have been suspended *sine die* and that there is little chance of their resumption in the near future.

As Your Lordship is aware from my telegram No. 386 of September 24th[2] the Roumanian Government made it a condition *sine qua non* of entering upon any negotiations with the Soviet Government that the question of Bessarabia should not be raised and Monsieur Chicherin accepted this condition. However soon after the negotiations were opened here at the end of September it became apparent that the Soviet representative did not intend to adhere to this undertaking as he at once began to discuss the question of Roumania's right to Bessarabia. Negotiations were suspended in order to permit of the representatives consulting their respective Governments and on their being resumed Monsieur Karakhan informed Monsieur Filality that he was instructed not to raise the question of Bessarabia provided the Roumanian Government would consent on their part not to raise that of the

[1] Not printed.   [2] Not printed (see, however, No. 420).

Roumanian gold treasure,[3] the property of Roumanian banks and private individuals, which had been deposited in Moscow during the war merely for purposes of safe custody. As this condition was obviously impossible of acceptance the Roumanian Government decided to break off the conversations and postpone further discussion with the Soviet Government until the latter was in a more reasonable frame of mind.[4]

I have, etc.,

W. G. MAX MULLER

[3] See Vol. XIX, No. 47, n. 3.
[4] A copy of this despatch was sent to Bucharest.

No. 440

Mr. Gregory to M. Krassin
[N 11984/216/38]

FOREIGN OFFICE, *November 3, 1921*

Sir,

I am directed by the Marquess Curzon of Kedleston to acknowledge the receipt of your memorandum marked L.K./1442 of October 26th,[1] relative to a case now pending in the Court of Appeal[2] which involves your position under the Diplomatic Privileges Act of 1708.[3]

[1] Not printed.
[2] Fenton Textile Association Ltd. v. Krassin and others. The minutes of a Conference of Ministers held on November 2 (copy in N 12267/216/38) explain the position as follows: 'The plaintiffs had sought to join M. Krassin as a defendant and the Master in Chambers had refused on the ground that M. Krassin had an ambassadorial status. The plaintiffs took the case to a Justice in Chambers who had sent it on to the Court of Appeal. Before proceeding further the Court had asked the Foreign Office to reply to the two following questions:—

(1) Whether H.M. Government had had any dealings with M. Krassin other than those on questions relating to trade;
(2) Whether he had been received as Representative of the Soviet Government in any capacity other than head of the Russian Trade Delegation.

'The question was whether the Foreign Office should in their reply state directly whether or not M. Krassin was regarded by H.M. Government as a full representative of the Soviet Government, or whether an answer should be given setting out the facts and leaving the decision as to M. Krassin's status to the Court of Appeal.

'General agreement was expressed with the view that no direct statement of opinion should be made by H.M. Government as to the status of M. Krassin, but that the facts should be placed before the Court and the decision left to them.

'The proposed draft reply by the Foreign Office was read to the Committee, the effect of which was that M. Krassin had been received by H.M. Government solely in his capacity as Chief Official Agent in connection with the Trade Agreement although the opportunity had been taken of his presence in this country to discuss the question of the famine in Russia and the exchange of prisoners. The draft reply went on to state that M. Krassin had never been received as Ambassador by H.M. Government. This reply, it was stated, represented

2. Your letter to me of June 1st last,[1] enquiring when and to whom you could transfer your credentials addressed to the Prime Minister, was carefully considered by this department; but the fact that no exact precedent could be found for the presentation of credentials by the head of a Trade Delegation rendered it difficult for them to return an early answer to it. Before the reply which I am now directed to make was ready to be despatched, you had left England, on what proved to be an absence of three months.

3. On your return at the end of September, Lord Curzon was in doubt as to whether you would still desire to present the credentials addressed to the Prime Minister, and it was considered probable that a fresh communication would be received from you on this subject.

the facts as known to the Foreign Office. It would be impossible to recognize M. Krassin as Ambassador because such recognition would carry with it recognition of the Soviet Government as a *de jure* Government, whereas the recognition so far accorded to that Government had been more or less that of a *de facto* Government.

'It was pointed out that in a case of this importance, the decision of which might involve the suspension of trade with Russia since British traders would certainly refuse to do further business with a trading agent who had been declared by the Courts to possess diplomatic immunity from being sued, it was essential that the Court should have before it the full facts of the case. As a matter of fact M. Krassin had on certain occasions been treated informally as the representative of the Soviet Government. Discussions, for instance, had been held with him regarding Poland, and the War Office had put forward in June 1920 various proposals for discussion with him regarding military matters. The Prime Minister had himself seen M. Krassin at the time of the discussions on the subject of Poland when there had been a question of a general European Conference. The assent of the French Government had been obtained at Boulogne by the Prime Minister and Lord Curzon to the calling of such a Conference and definite proposals had been put before M. Krassin and M. Kamenev by the Prime Minister [see Vol. VIII, Chaps. IX and X].

'The Committee agreed:— That the Cabinet Secretariat should examine the records of the discussions with M. Krassin and communicate details of them to the Secretary of State for Foreign Affairs for inclusion, of such as are relevant, in the reply to the enquiry from the Court of Appeal.'

Lord Curzon's reply of November 7 to Lord Justice Bankes (N 12333/216/38) ran as follows: 'I beg to state that Monsieur Krassin has not at any time been received by His Majesty. Monsieur Krassin is present in this country in consequence of an agreement with the Soviet Government. It is not the practice of the Sovereign to receive the representatives of States which have not been recognized *de jure* and, therefore, quite apart from the question of Monsieur Krassin's position, no representative of the Soviet Government would be received by His Majesty, because the Soviet Government has not been recognized *de jure* as a State.

'Since the signature of the Russian Trade Agreement, Monsieur Krassin has been received by the officials of my department as an official agent of the Soviet Government under the provisions of Article 5 of that Agreement for purposes covered by the Agreement. This will, I think, give Your Lordship the information in reply to your first question.

'Apart from this, advantage has been taken of the presence of Monsieur Krassin in London by the officials of this department, acting with my authority, on certain occasions, to discuss with him such questions as the repatriation of Russian refugees and the famine in Russia, and on one occasion, during the temporary absence of Monsieur Krassin, his representative was invited to take part in a Conference at the Board of Trade on the subject of the credits required for famine relief.

'I trust that the above information may be sufficient for Your Lordship's guidance.'

[3] See *B.F.S.P.*, vol. 1, part 2, pp. 993–5.

4. I am to state that it would be entirely contrary to the procedure customary in the case of foreign representatives of heads of states or governments or official bodies, that you should present credentials to the Prime Minister. Credentials can only be presented at the Foreign Office, and will be acknowledged by the Secretary of State if you decide to transmit them to him. If on the other hand you prefer to deposit them personally, I shall be happy, in accordance with His Lordship's instructions, to accept them from your hands.

5. I am to add that you are under a misapprehension in thinking that there has been any deviation, or at any rate an intentional deviation from the canons of courtesy.

I am, etc.,
J. D. GREGORY

No. 441

Lord D'Abernon (Berlin) to the Marquess Curzon of Kedleston
No. 1310 [N 12555/8614/38]

BERLIN, *November 6, 1921*

My Lord Marquess,

I have the honour to acknowledge receipt of Your Lordship's despatch No. 1088 of October 29,[1] and to state that I spoke to Dr. Wirth on this matter yesterday, and impressed upon him the importance which His Majesty's Government attach to continued German co-operation in the Russian question, as initiated at the Brussels Conference.[2]

Dr. Wirth replied that the German Government had no intention of receding from their policy in this matter. So far as he knew the Soviet Representative in Berlin had not shown any inclination to criticise the German attitude as stated above.

I have, etc.,
D'ABERNON

[1] Of October 29. This ran: 'As Your Excellency is aware, it is a part of Soviet policy to sow dissension among the Western Powers and more especially to prevent Germany from coming into line with the policy of the Allies towards Russia. There is reason to believe that the Soviet Government is much exercised at the invitation made to the German Government to participate in the International Committee for the Relief of Russia.'

[2] See No. 430.

No. 442

Mr. Ovey to M. Krassin
[N 11913/10242/38]

FOREIGN OFFICE, *November 7, 1921*

Sir,

I am directed by the Marquess Curzon of Kedleston to acknowledge the receipt of your letter of October 25th,[1] relative to the negotiations between yourself and Colonel Boyle in regard to the oilfields of Russia and Caucasia.

2. Lord Curzon believes that Colonel Boyle and the firms represented by him are seriously interested in the grant of a concession and that the negotiations initiated by him have no ulterior motive. Neither Colonel Boyle nor the interests for which he acts however have any special connection with His Majesty's Government which would permit them to control or render them responsible for the policy or actions of the firms with whom you are in negotiation. In these circumstances it would be impossible for His Lordship to give assurances going beyond the terms of this letter.

I am, etc.,
ESMOND OVEY

[1] See No. 432, n. 2.

No. 443

Lord Hardinge (Paris) to the Marquess Curzon of Kedleston
(Received November 10)
No. 3089 [N 12449/12085/38]

PARIS, *November 8, 1921*

My Lord,

I have the honour to transmit to Your Lordship herewith a copy of a communication[1] in which the French Government make the offer[2] by the Soviet Government to acknowledge the obligations contracted by their predecessors an opportunity for a lengthy expression of their own views as the attitude to be adopted towards Russia.

They claim with great complacency that the present more accommodating frame of mind of the Soviet Government is due to the firmness of the French policy, which they are happy to think is in conformity with the theory and practice of the United States Government. The Note maintains that the Soviet offer must be unconditional, and criticizes Monsieur Chicherin's overtures as being too vague. It then proceeds to explain the conditions essential to a resumption of relations with the Soviet Government. It concludes with an enquiry as to the views of His Majesty's Government on the

[1] Of November 8.
[2] In a telegram of October 28 addressed by M. Chicherin to France, Great Britain, Italy, Japan and the United States, not printed (see No. 438, n. 1).

considerations set forth by the French Government. I am aware, from Your Lordship's despatch No. 2883 of November 7th,[3] that a copy of your reply to Monsieur Chicherin[4] has been communicated to the French Ambassador; but you will doubtless consider that it would be desirable to make a specific reply to this communication which, as Your Lordship will observe, the French Government propose to publish like its predecessors (see my telegram No. 592 of August 11th)[5] and previous correspondence.[6]

I have, etc.,

HARDINGE OF PENSHURST

ENCLOSURE IN NO. 443

PARIS, *le 8 novembre, 1921*

A la date du 28 octobre dernier, M. Tchitcherine, Commissaire du Peuple pour les Affaires extérieures, a exposé, dans un télégramme adressé aux cinq grandes Puissances, que les Soviets étaient disposés, sous certaines réserves, à faire face aux payements correspondant aux engagements contractés par les Gouvernements russes précédents avant 1914, mais qu'il subordonnait cette mesure à la reconnaissance du Pouvoir des Soviets par toutes les Puissances qui ne sont pas entrées jusqu'ici en relations politiques avec ce Pouvoir.

En raison de la forme nouvelle que revêt ainsi l'effort constant fait par les Soviets pour obtenir leur reconnaissance il a paru nécessaire au Gouvernement français de faire connaître une fois de plus au Gouvernement britannique ses vues, tant au sujet de cette reconnaissance même, que de la valeur des déclarations de M. Tchitcherine. Aussi bien, le Gouvernement de la République ne peut s'empêcher de considérer que les déclarations du Commissaire du peuple aux Affaires Étrangères sont un heureux résultat de la constance et de la fermeté dont a été empreinte la politique suivie par la France vis-à-vis des Soviets de que ces déclarations marquent un premier pas dans le sens désiré par tous.

A plusieurs reprises, notamment, par les notes adressées à l'Ambassade britannique en 1920 et 1921, documents qui ont été publiés le 15 août dernier,[6] le Gouvernement de la République a d'ailleurs déjà défini les principes dont il n'a cessé de s'inspirer dans le règlement de sa conduite à l'égard de la Russie soviétique. Il a déjà indiqué au Gouvernement britannique les raisons pourquoi il lui paraissait à la fois vain et dangereux d'essayer une prise de contact, même économique, avec les territoires soumis à la dictature des chefs communistes.

Au surplus, le Gouvernement britannique n'ignore pas qu'une telle

---

[3] Not printed.   [4] No. 438.   [5] See n. 6.

[6] In telegram No. 396 of July 14, Lord Curzon had stated: 'I see no objection to the publication of the correspondence particularly as one or two questions have been asked in Parliament.' In telegram No. 592 Lord Hardinge reported that the correspondence would be published in the French Press on August 16. On that same date this correspondence was published as a White Paper (Cmd. 1456 of 1921) in Great Britain (see *The Times*, August 16, 1921, p. 7).

attitude est conforme à celle qu'a adoptée le Gouvernement fédéral nord-américain et qui a été définie, avec une précision ne permettant aucun conteste, par Messieurs Norman H. Davis, en janvier 1921, Bainbridge Colby, en août 1921, et plus récemment par le Président Harding lui-même. L'expérience, du reste, a justifié le bien fondé de cette ligne de conduite, et le Gouvernement français se plait à rappeler les termes mêmes où dans une lettre écrite à M. Krassine, M. Leslie Urquhart a exposé, avec une clarté parfaite, l'échec d'une tentative loyale de collaboration avec les Soviets et signalé les obstacles insurmontables que les principes et les procédés des maîtres actuels de la Russie opposent au succès de toute entreprise de cet ordre.

Ainsi, s'est établie, et se confirme, la conviction unanime que la régénération de la Russie reste subordonnée à l'abandon sincère et complet des expériences tentées et du système appliqué jusqu'ici et au respect des principes et des règles morales adoptés par tous les peuples civilisés.

A cet égard, le Gouvernement de la République croit devoir signaler au Gouvernement britannique que la reconnaissance des dettes russes est présentée, dans le télégramme de M. Tchitcherine, comme une concession, dont l'octroi dépend de la reconnaissance du Pouvoir Soviétique. Or, il s'agit là, non point d'une concession susceptible de faire l'objet d'un marché, mais de l'application d'un principe de droit commun qui n'a jamais été contesté par aucun Gouvernement. Il serait donc indispensable que le Gouvernement des Soviets proclamât, sans réticence ni réserve, sa volonté de se conformer désormais à un principe qu'il a renié jusqu'à présent. Seuls les moyens et les garanties de paiement peuvent donner lieu à discussion, encore devraient-ils être indiqués.

La suggestion esquissée par le Commissaire du Peuple est d'ailleurs trop limitée pour pouvoir être considérée comme une reconnaissance par les Soviets de leurs obligations financières suivant les règles universellement suivies par tous les Gouvernements. M. Tchitcherine ne parle, en effet, ni des dettes de guerre, ni des emprunts des municipalités, ni des prêts consentis avant la guerre à des sociétés soutenues par l'État, Sociétés dont les Soviets ont confisqué les biens. Il exclut également les dédommagements dûs aux ressortissants étrangers qui ont été depossédés de leurs avoirs, et la remise en la possession de leurs légitimes propriétaires des usines; immeubles et valeurs de toutes sortes qui subsistent, en attendant que la question d'une équitable indemnisation puisse être envisagée.

Cette acceptation de l'ensemble des règles qui dominent les rapports des peuples civilisés, règles qui sont l'expression, non d'une contrainte ou d'une diminution de souveraineté, mais bien des nécessités internationales, comporte, comme le rappelaient les notes américaines mentionneés ci-dessus, la mise en application de plusieurs garanties fondamentales, aussi bien dans le domaine politique que dans le domaine financier.

Le Gouvernement doit représenter la volonté nationale. Cette représentation régulière de la nation peut seule assurer, avec la puissance partout admise du pouvoir central, le respect des autorités qu'il délègue. Faute de ces conditions, le témoignage de M. Urquhart en fait foi, les décisions du pouvoir de Moscou se heurtent aux volontés pratiquement indépendantes et souvent contraires d'organismes spéciaux tels que la Commission extraordinaire ou les Unions professionnelles.

En ce qui concerne spécialement les étrangers, ils doivent pouvoir compter, aussi bien pour leurs personnes que pour leurs biens, sur l'application du traitement qui leur est assuré dans tous les pays civilisés. Un tel régime implique le respect de la propriété individuelle.

Enfin l'acceptation par les Soviets de leurs obligations internationales devrait se marquer par l'abandon de toute propagande bolchévique, de toute ingérence dans les affaires intérieures des autres pays, de toute subvention des organismes hostiles aux Gouvernements étrangers, dans le but de détruire les fondements constitutifs mêmes des autres états. Il serait indispensable que le pouvoir des Commissaires donnât toute garantie, qu'il a renoncé à entretenir ou à en encourager, par ses agents officiels ou officieux, toute action subversive hors de ses frontières.

Le Gouvernement de la République reste profondément convaincu que la renaissance de l'activité économique russe ne saurait se produire si ces conditions ne sont pas réalisées. Il croit fermement que ce rétablissement de la vie normale permettra seule à la Russie de faire face, par des moyens réguliers et d'une manière durable, à tous les engagements financiers, sans exception, que les Gouvernements russes ont contractés. Toute tractation tendant à obtenir des avantages immédiats et exclusifs n'aurait qu'un caractère trompeur et risquerait, en outre, d'aller au détriment de l'un ou de l'autre pays, en retardant l'application des mesures générales, qui, seules, peuvent rétablir définitivement et dans tous les domaines, la vie de la nation russe.

Quand ces conditions essentielles auront été remplies par le Gouvernement de Moscou, le Gouvernement de la République française sera disposé à envisager la possibilité d'entrer en pourparlers avec lui, alors que, dans les circonstances actuelles, l'organisme permanent international, créé par la Conférence de Bruxelles, suffit pour entamer les conversations qui peuvent être nécessitées pour secourir les affamés. Agir autrement serait mal servir, à la fois, les intérêts du peuple russe, dont la restauration dans la plénitude de sa vie nationale et économique, n'a cessé d'être un but de la politique française, et les intérêts des porteurs étrangers qui n'ont, jusqu'ici, aucune garantie de l'exécution sincère et continue d'un programme encore illusoire.

Le Ministère des Affaires Étrangères serait heureux que l'Ambassade britannique voulût bien lui faire connaître les vues du Gouvernement anglais, touchant les considérations exposées dans la présente note, que le Gouvernement français a l'intention de publier, comme l'ont été les précédentes notes anglaises et françaises relatives à la Russie.

Mr. Hodgson (Moscow) to the Marquess Curzon of Kedleston
(Received November 22)

No. 147 [N 12863/5/38]

Confidential   MOSCOW, *November 13, 1921*

My Lord,

I have the honour to report that, in accordance with the instructions conveyed in Mr. Gregory's despatch No. 156 of the 2nd instant,[1] received on the 9th instant, I called upon M. Chicherin by appointment yesterday and presented to him the note of His Majesty's Government.[2] M. Chicherin had expressed his inability, owing to pressure of business, to receive me at an earlier date.

As in the case of the note of the 7th September,[3] M. Chicherin read through the text rapidly in my presence. He repeated with emphasis his denial of the identity of the Third International with the Russian Government, saying, 'Not one of us will admit that.' Throughout the interview he exhibited signs of considerable nervous irritation, and at one time he expressed surprise that 'a serious Government like the British Government' should allow itself to be influenced by such ill-supported evidence, revealing, as he maintained, complete misunderstanding of the situation. 'If Great Britain is anxious to quarrel with us, she should find a better pretext.'

I pointed out that I could not admit that the charges in the British note could be qualified as groundless or ill-supported, and His Majesty's Government would most certainly not have made accusations of this gravity unless in possession of absolute proof of their justice. I added that, if it was desired to maintain the contention that the data in the British note relating to the activities of the Third International and its connection with the Soviet Government were erroneous, it was to be regretted that the reports tending to support this contention promised by M. Litvinov in the course of my interview with him and M. Chicherin on the 1[7]th September[4] had not been forthcoming.

In connection with the remark in the British note as to the anti-British attitude of M. Nazarenus, M. Chicherin repeated the statement made in the Soviet note of the 27th September[5] to the effect that the Russian Government, never having been granted an opportunity of learning the scope of British interests, could not be expected to know how or when they were infringing them. He was doubtful whether the action of France in Angora was compatible with them.[6] I replied that I had no knowledge of negotiations

---

[1] Not printed. See, however, No. 437, n. 3.
[2] See No. 437.
[3] No. 414, Enclosure.
[4] See No. 421.
[5] Not printed (see No. 421, n. 4 and No. 428).
[6] The reference is presumably to the Franklin-Bouillon Angora Agreement of October 20, 1921 (see Vol. XVII, Nos. 422 and 423).

between France and the Angora Government, and that I did not see, in any case, how his insinuation could affect the conduct of Russia.

I have, etc.,

R. M. Hodgson

No. 445

The Marquess Curzon of Kedleston to Mr. Rennie[1] (Helsingfors)
No. 62 Telegraphic [N 12615/12266/38]

FOREIGN OFFICE, November 15, 1921, 10 p.m.

Your telegram No. 154.[2]

You should neither encourage nor even receive M. Pokrovski. His Majesty's Government, after concluding a Trade Agreement with the Soviet Government, are precluded from taking any interest in a financial scheme which is based on the downfall of that Government.

Private British financial interests are, of course, free to take what action they choose.

[1] See No. 171, n. 2.

[2] Of November 3. This ran as follows: 'Nicolas Nicolaevitch Pokrovski, former Russian Assistant Minister of Finance and well-known in international financial circles, is at present at Rev[a]l. He is working on scheme of formation of strong Russian financial group, strictly non-political for *re-creation* of Russia economically after downfall of present régime, which he believes to be not far off. He considers that only Russian group will be acceptable to Russia. As however sufficient Russian capital is not available, he proposes to invite participation of foreign capitalists as shareholders. Project appears to be favoured by Americans who have already sent representative acquainted with details from Reval to United States. French Minister at Reval has so far shown no active interest but Pokrovski expects that scheme may be taken up in Paris through Russian organisations there. Pokrovski is shortly coming here.

'Would it be useful if I saw him in order to obtain further details regarding his project with a view to eventually increasing British finance?'

No. 446

The Marquess Curzon of Kedleston to Lord Hardinge (Paris)
No. 2988 [N 12449/12085/38]

FOREIGN OFFICE, November 15, 1921

My Lord,

I have received your despatch No. 3089 of 8th November,[1] enclosing a copy of a memorandum from the Ministry for Foreign Affairs commenting upon the recent declaration of the Soviet Government of their readiness conditionally to recognise certain classes of foreign liabilities.

2. Your Excellency suggests the desirability of making a specific reply

[1] No. 443.

to this communication because the French Government intend that the correspondence shall be published; but unless you consider that public opinion in France would be unfavourably affected by a somewhat perfunctory answer, I should be averse from entering upon a lengthy public discussion of the principles upon which relations with Russia should be conducted.

3. Subject to any suggestions Your Excellency may wish to make on this head, I request that you will inform the French Government that His Majesty's Government share their anxiety that the Soviet Government should fully recognise all her foreign liabilities, a step which they have repeatedly stated is essential to the re-establishment of normal economic relations between Russia and the rest of the world. They do not feel able, however, to express a definite opinion on the merits of the Russian memorandum of October 29th[2] until a reply to my note of November 1st to Monsieur Krassin[3] is received.

I am, etc.,
(for the Secretary of State)
J. D. Gregory

[2] See No. 438, n. 1. This Memorandum was dated October 28.
[3] No. 438.

No. 447

Mr. Rennie (Helsingfors) to the Marquess Curzon of Kedleston
(Received November 21, 9 p.m.)
No. 163 Telegraphic [N 12869/4/38]

HELSINGFORS, *November 21, 1921, 8 p.m.*

My telegram No. 162, November 19th.[1]

Minister for Foreign Affairs[2] told me last night that he had been approached by representatives of white or reactionary party who had asked whether Finnish Government would be willing to close their eye to passage of arms and ammunition for Karelian rebels. He had replied that Finnish Government were determined to maintain strictest neutrality.[3] They would only permit food supplies to be brought up to certain spots close to the frontier to assist starving refugees who may be expected to cross into Finland.

Minister for Foreign Affairs seems to fear that attempt is being made by reactionaries to make trouble between Finnish Government and Russia and to create difficulties which may have serious consequences next spring.

[1] Not printed. This had reported that the region between the Finnish frontier and the White Sea was in revolt against the Soviet Government.
[2] Dr. Holsti.
[3] Lord Curzon replied in telegram No. 66 of November 24: 'You may inform Dr. Holsti of the satisfaction with which we learn of the strong line he is taking in insisting on strict neutrality.'

No. 448

Memorandum of Conference held at the Foreign Office on November 22, regarding admission of Russians to this country

[*N 12951/216/38*]

PRESENT: Mr. Gregory (*in the Chair*) Foreign Office
Mr. O'Malley   ,, ,,
Commander Maxse   ,, ,,
Mr. Reyntiens   Department of Overseas Trade
Mr. Davis   Home Office
Mr. Mugliston   ,, ,,
Captain Miller   Scotland House
Mr. Parkin   Passport Control
Mr. Peters   British Mission to Moscow

After considerable discussion as to the practicability of laying down the numbers to be considered as 'reasonably necessary' for the legitimate work of the Russian Trade Delegation, it was decided that it was not practicable to ask Mr. Krassin, as desired by the Board of Trade, to put forward a specified establishment of numbers required, nor to ask him for further information as to the amount of trade done by his Delegation.

The procedure agreed upon was that each case should be considered on its merits, and that reference should be made to the Department of Overseas Trade, who would probably be in a position to say whether the amount of trade being done was sufficient to justify any particular appointment, or the total number in the country at any time.

The Home Office produced figures to show that the personnel of the Trade Delegation proper, including wives and children, was fifty (this number does not include couriers). The total number of Russians employed directly and indirectly by the Soviet Trade Delegation and Arcos Limited amounted to approximately two hundred.[1]

The Home Office representative stated the conditions under which Russians other than those connected with the Russian Trade Delegation were admitted to this country. The first requirement was that such persons should be able to support themselves, or produce evidence that they would be supported in this country; the general rule was, however, to refuse admission to all non-Trade Delegation Russians, with the exception of those who had,

(1) British connections,
(2) Genuine trade interests,
(3) Previous long domicile in this country, and
(4) In certain very special cases, young persons for education.

Arising out of this point, was the position of directors and members of the newly-formed Russian trading companies. It was explained that the Soviet Government now sanctioned the formation of private companies, who were

---

[1] Cf. No. 433.

allowed to buy and sell both in Russia and abroad on a commission basis, under licence from the Soviet Government. It was pointed out that it was distinctly to British interest to encourage this more free and natural form of trade, which it was anticipated would eventually undermine the position of the Russian Commissariat for Foreign trade, consequently it was decided to authorise Mr. Hodgson to refer home any applications for visas which he might receive from such Companies, provided that they had the licence of the Soviet Government to trade, and the permission of the Soviet authorities to leave the country, and also provided that in all cases he was satisfied with their bona fides.

(N.B. Mr. Hodgson's previous instructions had been to refuse, out of hand, all applications for visas which were not made directly by the Soviet authorities.)

The question of the nature of the visa to be granted to the Russian Official Agent in this country, and the Soviet Officials of equivalent rank, was discussed. It was ascertained that the Home Office and Scotland House had no objection to the diplomatic visas which had already been granted, as a matter of personal privilege, to Mr. Krassin and Professor Lomonosov being retained, but in view of the practical facilities to which a diplomatic visa entitles the holder, they requested that no fresh diplomatic visas should be issued without previous consultation with them, and that the general question might perhaps stand over till the decision of the High Courts on the status of Mr. Krassin.[2]

The Home Office was adamant that Mr. Hodgson must refer every application for a visa for Home Office approval.[3] It was pointed out that it was very necessary to speed up if possible the existing machinery, and that at the present moment it took us anything from three to eight weeks to obtain a Home Office decision. Mr. Davis on behalf of the Home Office definitely promised that they would speed up the decisions as much as possible, and he referred to the possibility of letting us have a definite answer within two or three days to any application which contained full particulars.

As regards couriers it was decided to suggest to Mr. Krassin that he should submit a fresh list of twelve names (including those who had previously been on the couriers list), and that once these names had been approved by the Home Office, visas could be granted without any further necessity for consultation.

The question of the Soviet Representatives being allowed to reside in other parts of the country than London was also discussed together with the question of the effect of any decision arrived at upon the possibility of sending British representatives to Petrograd or Novorossisk. But it was decided that this Conference had no powers to decide such an important question, and that the matter should be pursued by means of interdepartmental correspondence.

[2] See No. 440.
[3] Instructions to this effect were despatched to Mr. Hodgson in Foreign Office despatch No. 232 of November 28 (N 12951/216/38), not printed.

No. 449

Mr. Rennie (Helsingfors) to the Marquess Curzon of Kedleston
(Received November 28, 9.10 p.m.)
No. 174 Telegraphic [N 13115/4/38]

HELSINGFORS, *November 28, 1921, 8 p.m.*

My telegram No. 170 of 25th November.[1]

Minister for Foreign Affairs has shown me note that Finnish Government are sending today to League of Nations. After recapitulating events leading to the creation of Eastern Karelia under the Treaty of Dorpat,[2] note states promises to the population have not been fulfilled, and rising[3] has accordingly been provoked. Finnish Government draws attention of League to complications threatened by the state of war in adjoining country. They ask whether League will send commission to examine the case of Karelians and their rights as a national minority.[4]

Copy of note by bag.[5]

[1] Not printed.
[2] Of October 14, 1920. For sources, see Slusser and Triska, p. 15.
[3] See No. 447, n. 1.
[4] In his telegram No. 177 of December 1, Mr. Rennie reported: 'I have received note from Finnish Government requesting support of British representative at Council of League of Nations for proposals made in Finnish note regarding Karelia.'

Sir W. Tyrrell, commenting on Mr. Rennie's telegram No. 174 in a minute of November 29, with which Lord Curzon concurred, stated: 'For the present we are doing enough by sending the proposed telegram of warning to Helsingfors [see No. 450, n. 3 below].'

[5] Despatch No. 390 of November 28 (N 13406/4/38), not printed.

No. 450

The Marquess Curzon of Kedleston to Mr. Hodgson (Moscow)
No. 106 Telegraphic [N 12976/4/38]

FOREIGN OFFICE, *November 30, 1921*

From information received from Helsingfors,[1] it appears that the Karelian revolt, if spontaneous in origin, is now being exploited by White Russian and monarchist German elements from outside, and that it is spreading.

Dr. Holsti has already expressed the determination of the Finnish Government to maintain strictest neutrality, and he has been informed by H[is] M[ajesty's] Minister of our satisfaction at this policy.[2]

As it now appears that White elements are nevertheless sending military supplies to the rebels from Finland, strong representations are being made to Dr. Holsti by H[is] M[ajesty's] Minister, that steps be at once taken to

[1] In Helsingfors telegrams Nos. 166, 167, and 168 of November 23, not printed.
[2] See No. 447, n. 3.

stop all such supplies, as otherwise Finnish neutrality cannot be regarded as serious.[3]

Above is for your private information only.

[3] Instructions to this effect were communicated to Mr. Rennie in Foreign Office telegram No. 68 of November 30 (N 12976/4/38), not printed.

No. 451

Mr. Rennie (Helsingfors) to the Marquess Curzon of Kedleston
(Received December 2, 3.10 p.m.)
No. 180 Telegraphic [N 13278/4/38]

HELSINGFORS, *December 2, 1921, 2.10 p.m.*

My telegram No. 179.[1]

I have seen Prime Minister, Minister of War and Minister for Foreign Affairs. All assure me that Finland will take every possible step for safe-guarding her neutrality. They declare that government are doing all they can to prevent organisation of forces to assist [K]arelians. Owing to the length of frontier however it is impossible to prevent individuals or isolated small bands from crossing. They consider they cannot or should not prevent organisation of humanitarian assistance for feeding refugees, ambulances, etc., and it is better to allow Finnish supporters of Karelia to have this outlet for their sympathy. The existing base of organisation at Karelia though suspected cannot so far be proved nor is any undue activity of foreigners apparent there. Minister of war declares that volunteers at Viborg have done nothing but prepare organisation of humanitarian help. Minister for Foreign Affairs also has told me that Finnish passport control officers have been instructed to control more stringently applications for visas to enter Finland.

I have said that in order to support Finnish government's request to League of Nations[2] for commission of enquiry His Majesty's government must be able to state definitely that Finnish Government were doing all in their power to prevent Finland becoming a base of operations. All these ministers assured me that suspects were being watched and were being prevented from exercising their activities, difficult though this was, owing to geographical conditions.

[1] Of December 1. This ran: 'British vice-consul at Viborg states that he learns from reliable source connected with Karelian League, that active assistance is being given to movement, and that volunteers, including officers and men of local forces, are said to be joining Karelians.

'I have spoken to Minister for Foreign Affairs in the sense of your telegram No. 68 [see No. 450, n. 3], and hope to see Prime Minister later.'

In his preceding telegram (No. 178 of December 1) Mr. Rennie, citing press reports, stated that Soviet troops had been despatched to crush the rebellion in Karelia.

[2] See No. 449.

No. 452

Mr. Rennie (Helsingfors) to the Marquess Curzon of Kedleston
(Received December 2, 8.50 p.m.)

No. *181 Telegraphic* [N *13279/4/38*]

HELSINGFORS, *December 2, 1921, 7.45 p.m.*

My telegram No. 180.[1]

Minister for Foreign Affairs told me last night that he had just received information that 200 Russian officers belonging to staff of army of General Miller[2] had escaped from confinement at Solovetski monastery on White Sea and had arrived at Kem. He had just been asked by local representative of White Russians recognised by Finnish Government, whether supplies or money could be sent to enable them to remain at Kem. Minister for Foreign Affairs said that this confirmed his suspicion that understanding existed between White Russians, through Bermondt and German reactionaries, with regard to intention to utilise Karelian rising for their own purposes.

Minister for Foreign Affairs will probably reply that supplies, &c., may not be sent to them, but that they may come into Finland, where they will be interned in concentration camp or watched, as are other Russian refugees.

Request of Finnish Government to League of Nations[3] that International Commission of Enquiry may be sent is made in order that commission may be able to prove *bona fides* of Finnish Government and prevent greater difficulties of an international character. Minister for Foreign Affairs therefore . . .[4] His Majesty's Government will see their way to support the Finnish Government request to the League of Nations. He also thinks that the activities of the reactionaries and the White Russians outside Finland will thereby be watched and restrained. In view of strong sympathies that exist here towards Karelians, Finnish Government are in difficult situation, and wish to clear themselves of all suspicion of being responsible for breaches of neutrality. Hence their request for presence of impartial international commission, which would also investigate the general Karelian situation.

Minister for Foreign Affairs had made similar request for support to Italian Minister, and proposes to address French and Polish representatives similarly.

[1] No. 451
[2] White Russian general, formerly General Wrangel's military representative in Paris.
[3] See No. 449.
[4] The text is here uncertain.

No. 453

Mr. Rennie (Helsingfors) to the Marquess Curzon of Kedleston
(Received December 6, 8.30 a.m.)
No. 183 Telegraphic [N 13388/4/38]

HELSINGFORS, *December 5, 1921, 11 p.m.*

Finnish government received this afternoon note[1] addressed to Finnish legation at Moscow. Note is couched in very strong language. Following is summary:

Soviet government protest against appeal made to league of nations regarding Karelian rising[2] as league consists of group of nations hostile to Russia, notably France and Japan. Appeal is considered as an hostile act violating treaty of peace. Russian government possesses proof that Finnish government had long prepared movement and were only waiting for favourable moment to act; this is shown by the fact that attacks took place solely in communes touching Finnish frontier. Finnish government is said on November 22nd to have given Savinkov[3] permission to enter Finland and has also permitted acts of aggression by corps of counter-revolutionaries who participated in Kronstadt rising.[4] Soviet Government insist on Finnish government taking the following steps:—

1. Immediate and effective closing of frontier.

2. Cessation of all support of organizations or individuals preparing acts of aggression against Russia.

3. Dissolution of all organizations and bureaux on Finnish territory which directly or indirectly participate in organization of incursions.

4. Dissolution of all organizations formed by Russian counter-revolutionaries and expulsion of those who directed them.

Unless measures are executed Russian government will . . .[5] other steps to ensure observation by Finnish government of the treaty[6] concluded with Soviet Russia.

---

[1] See Degras, vol. i, pp. 280–2. In his despatch No. 406 of December 6 (N 13654/4/38) Mr. Rennie transmitted a copy of this note to the Foreign Office, and reported: 'Dr. Holsti . . . does not appear to be greatly perturbed at the contents of the Russian note.'

[2] See No. 449.   [3] See No. 420, n. 2.

[4] See Vol. XI, No. 701, n. 1.   [5] The text is here uncertain.

[6] i.e. the Treaty of Dorpat (see No. 449, n. 2). In a minute of December 8, Sir Cecil Hurst stated: 'Finland, as a party to the treaty of Dorpat, is entitled to claim the fulfilment of the provisions of Articles 10 and 11 of that treaty, which assure a certain autonomous status to the territory of East Karelia and provide for certain special rights in favour of the local population. If Finland is in a position to establish any failure on the part of the Soviet authorities to carry out the obligations of these Articles, she would be entitled to maintain that the subjects of the dispute were not solely within the domestic jurisdiction of the Russian authorities. I see that attached to the treaty of Dorpat (page 11 of the print) is a declaration by the Russian plenipotentiaries concerning self-government for East Karelia which seems to promise to the inhabitants rights which are rather larger than those contained in Article 11. As this declaration was made formally by the Russian plenipotentiaries at a session of the Conference, I think the Finnish Government would be entitled to claim its fulfilment as part of the agreement between the two Governments. If the questions, therefore, out of

I understand that reply will not be sent before Wednesday night as various members of the cabinet are absent in connection with municipal elections.

Copy of note by bag tomorrow.[7]

which the East Karelian rising has originated consist of breaches by the Soviet authorities of Article 11 or of the declarations made by the Russian plenipotentiaries, I think the League of Nations would be entitled to intervene.'

Sir W. Tyrrell added, in a minute of December 8 initialled by Lord Curzon: 'It is quite clear that Finland is entitled to appeal to the League of Nations [and] the latter is entitled to intervene.

'As regards Finland we should continue to advise her to maintain strict neutrality in the dispute [and] to leave the matter as much as possible in the hands of the League.

'I venture to doubt very much any willingness on the part of the Soviets to go to Geneva.'

[7] See n. 1.

No. 454

Mr. Rennie (Helsingfors) to the Marquess Curzon of Kedleston
(Received December 12, 6.15 p.m.)

No. 185 Telegraphic [N 13578/4/38]

HELSINGFORS, *December 11, 1921, 4.53 p.m.*

My telegram No. 183 of December 5th.[1]

Following summary of reply of Finnish government to Soviet notes of November 18th,[2] November 28th,[2] and December 5th[3] despatched yesterday.

Finnish government maintain it is their right as well as their duty to address themselves to league of nations regarding events occurring on their frontier, which threaten to provoke various difficulties. If impartial enquiry proves that Soviet government has fulfilled her promises to population of eastern Karelia, this result can only be to their advantage. Finnish government in general terms categorically deny that they are responsible for rising in Karelia, adding that, although Soviet government state that they have confirmatory documentary evidence, latter have produced nothing to justify their accusations. As to the demand that certain measures should be taken with a view to putting an end to the rising, Finnish government renew their declaration of absolute neutrality, and state that directly the news reached them they issued orders to prevent any violation of the peace treaty[4] and forbade all recruiting, organization of bands, and transport of *matériel* on Finnish territory. They cannot refuse the right of asylum to political refugees, but armed refugees will be disarmed. They cannot consider as justified demand that private persons are to be prevented from sending humanitarian assistance, food, medicines, etc, to civilian population of Karelia, especially in view of the fact that Soviet government is already receiving such help from other foreign countries including Finland. As regards those demands of the Soviet government which imply an interference in Finnish

[1] No. 453.
[2] Not printed.
[3] See No. 453.
[4] The Treaty of Dorpat.

sovereign rights, government will maintain full liberty of action. Note concludes by stating that the best means of restoring order in Karelia is for the Soviet government to execute provisions of treaty of Dorpat and its annexed declaration.

Copy of note by bag.[5]

[5] Despatch No. 414 of December 12 (N 14010/4/38), not printed.

No. 455

Mr. Hodgson (Moscow) to the Marquess Curzon of Kedleston
(Received December 14, 4.20 p.m.)
No. 143 Telegraphic [N 13731/8614/38]

MOSCOW, *December 13, 1921, 12.20 p.m.*

Your telegram No. 111 of December 9th.[1]

No statement of the kind has been made in Izvestia or elsewhere and allegations attributed to Bolshevik representative of American relief committee have no foundation in fact.

Americans state:—

1. Rail transport has not held up food supplies which are reaching their destination regularly.

2. Food is being consumed by children only and sick in hospitals.

3. 35,000 children are being fed in Petrograd and Moscow as against 800,000 in famine districts.

4. Some delay in distribution occurs locally as a result of inefficiency of officials but this is not wilful.

5. Loss owing to pilferage on the way will probably not exceed $\frac{1}{100}$ per cent.

6. Helsingfors report is . . .[2] but they are continually having to contradict statements of this kind.

Nansen who has just returned from Saratov and Samara areas confirms above.[3]

[1] This ran: 'Central News message from Helsingfors given wide publicity in today's press states that Bolshevik representative on American relief committee admits in Izvestia that food supplies sent from abroad to Russia are mostly distributed to the organised communists and red guards in Petrograd and Moscow, that owing to disorganised transport, impossible for food to reach real famine areas and better for food to be eaten up than let it rot.

'Please telegraph whether there is any truth in this statement and whether American relief administration in Moscow are satisfied that distribution is proceeding satisfactorily.'

[2] The text is here uncertain.

[3] Cf. the report, enclosed in Mr. Hodgson's despatch No. 218 of December 13 (N 14149/ 8614/38), of Dr. R. Farrar, who accompanied Dr. Nansen on his tour of the Saratov and Samara areas. Dr. Farrar stated: 'As regards the work of the A[merican] R[elief] A[dministration], it must be noted that, though they have established a large number of posts, their work covers only a fringe of the need. There is danger that a glance at the map of Samara district dotted over with American relief stations may convey the impression that the famine

His local representative states that distribution proceeding satisfactorily.
Owing to enormous mortality amongst horses it is to be feared that in the near future it will be impossible to deliver supplies. . . .² To cope with this motor transport will be greatly needed.

needs are sufficiently covered by the A[merican] R[elief] A[dministration]. This is not so. They only meet a fraction of the need. I think they make a mistake in spreading their work too wide, instead of dealing more thoroughly with a smaller area.

'Nansen is convinced that, without Government help from the different Governments of Europe on a large scale, large districts in the famine area will become practically depopulated.'

No. 456

The Marquess Curzon of Kedleston to Mr. Rennie (Helsingfors)
No. 69 Telegraphic [N 13649/4/38]

FOREIGN OFFICE, *December 16, 1921, 10 p.m.*

Your despatch No. 398 (East Karelia).¹

His Majesty's Government do not propose to support the Finnish appeal to the League of Nations² which they regard entirely as a matter for the League to decide upon.

In the meanwhile you should continue to urge the maintenance of strictest neutrality.

Repeated to Moscow No. 117.

¹ Of December 3 (N 13649/4/38), not printed. This transmitted a copy of a note from Dr. Holsti requesting British support at the Council of the League.
² See No. 449, n. 4.

No. 457

Mr. Hodgson (Moscow) to the Marquess Curzon of Kedleston
(Received December 20, 8.30 a.m.)
No. 145 Telegraphic [N 13927/4/38]

MOSCOW, *December 17, 1921*

Your telegram No. 106.¹

Russian government professes to regard relations with Finland as having reached a very critical stage. They appear satisfied that Finnish government is not in favour of movement in Karelia but attribute it to machinations of reactionary Finnish groups receiving their inspiration from Mannerheim² and aiming at the acquisition of Karelia. They insist on complicity of

¹ No. 450.
² General Mannerheim, former Commander-in-Chief of the Finnish Army and Regent of Finland from December, 1918 to July, 1919.

Savinkov[3] and White Russian organisation. They will not admit rising could be the result of spontaneous outburst of discontent but maintain that it had been long prepared and only rendered over [sic] possible by help from Finland in the shape of volunteers and military supplies. Monsieur Litvinov declares that Russian members of mixed commission sitting in Helsingfors have been recalled and that the government is contemplating the recall of diplomatic mission.[4] Probably Monsieur Litvinov's statements are designed to lend enhanced gravity to the situation for it is untrue that commission has been recalled but Russians are so obsessed with the idea that they are the object of conspiracy that a diplomatic rupture is not impossible.

Result however would not necessarily be serious for, according to Finnish Chargé d'Affaires's information, Russian troops cannot move forward from Petropavodsk[5] for several months owing to lack of skis and other winter equipment. As a precautionary measure all ladies attached to Finnish legation have been sent home.

[3] See No. 453.
[4] In his telegram No. 146 of December 19, Mr. Hodgson reported: 'Russian members of mixed commission have now been recalled and Finnish minister is of the opinion that recall of diplomatic mission may very likely follow. There seems however to be no intention on the part of the Russian government, even if diplomatic rupture should occur, of taking matters further.'
[5] Cf. No. 451, n. 1.

No. 458

Mr. Rennie (Helsingfors) to the Marquess Curzon of Kedleston
(Received December 20, 9.10 p.m.)

No. 193 Telegraphic [N 13940/4/38]

HELSINGFORS, *December 20, 1921, 8.5 p.m.*

My telegram No. 185.[1]

On December 17th Soviet government addressed further note to Finnish government in reply to latter's note of December 11th,[2] stating that they possess proof of negative value of assurances given by Finnish government. They declare recruiting centres are (? working) in Helsingfors and other named places and that organization of bands received help from Schutz corps and that bands numbering three hundred, seven hundred and even a thousand men have crossed the frontier, and their (? activity) now has been transferred from northern to southern parts of Karelian frontier, with connivance of frontier authorities, and that bands possess arms of Finnish origin. Further that movement is actively supported by Finnish journalists, politicians, officers and even members of the government. Note adds that

[1] No. 454.   [2] See No. 454. This note was dated December 10.

government are evidently pursuing a policy contrary to wishes of majority of Finnish population, reiterates assertion that government is responsible for movement and in conclusion declares that if Finnish government persists in refusal to take steps demanded in Soviet government's preceding note[3] responsibility of menace to peace with Russia will rest with Finnish government.

Tone of note is less threatening than that of previous one. Finnish government will not reply for a few days but, meanwhile, Finnish minister has been already instructed to reply to more obvious misstatements in a note verbale.

[3] See No. 453.

No. 459

Sir R. Graham[1] (Rome) to the Marquess Curzon of Kedleston
(Received December 27, 6.40 p.m.)
No. 516 Telegraphic [N 14062/2041/38]

ROME, *December 27, 1921, 3.20 p.m.*

My despatch No. 1031.[2]

Vorovski[3] suddenly modified his obstructive attitude after vote in chamber favourable to Italian government which dashed his hope of any successful political manœuvre and unexpectedly expressed readiness to sign agreement without further discussion.

Agreement was therefore signed yesterday.[4] It follows the general lines of British agreement, and the only important differences are that the Italian government definitely agree that the property of Russian government in Italy shall not be sequestrated, and that provision is also made for conclusion of further commercial agreement six months hence. Identic agreement with Ukraine was also signed.[5]

Italian Ministry for Foreign Affairs have promised me a copy to send by bag[6] on Friday.

[1] See No. 15, n. 1.
[2] Of December 22, not printed.
[3] Soviet Agent at Rome.
[4] For the sources of this preliminary agreement between Italy and Soviet Russia, see Slusser and Triska, p. 28.
[5] See ibid.
[6] Rome despatch No. 1046 of December 30 (N 57/57/38), not printed. Also enclosed was a memorandum giving a detailed comparison of the Anglo- and Italo-Soviet agreements.

Mr. Rennie (Helsingfors) to the Marquess Curzon of Kedleston
(Received January 9, 1922)
No. 431 [N 240/2/38]

HELSINGFORS, *December 27, 1921*

My Lord,

With reference to my despatch No. 430 of yesterday's date,[1] I have the honour to report that the representatives of the *Entente* Powers and the Baltic States were asked by Dr. Holsti to come again to his house, when he promised that he would give the latest information regarding the military movements and any decisions which the Government meanwhile might have taken.

As regards the military situation on the other side of the frontier, the Finnish Chief of the Staff had reported as follows:—

Three Russian regiments of artillery were *en échelon* along the frontier— one regiment was rather further eastward in the village of Toksovo. Some artillery had been unloaded at the railway stations along the line. The 5th regiment belonging to the division in question (the 11th) was still at Petrograd, the arrival of the full number of troops having apparently been somewhat delayed. Yesterday morning the field-artillery guns fired a few rounds.

Subsequent to our meeting at Dr. Holsti's house in the afternoon a Cabinet meeting was held, and the following statement to be communicated to the representatives of the Allied and Associated Powers and of the Baltic States was agreed upon:—

'The Finnish Government, which on its side has respected and will continue to respect the Treaty of Dorpat,[2] trusts that peace will not be violated on the part of Russia. But if, contrary to expectation, a surprise attack be made against Finland, the latter will defend herself. In that event, and also if Russia, in consequence of the dispute that has arisen out of the Karelian question, presents to the Finnish Government an ultimatum such as the latter could not accept from the point of view of national interests and honour, the Finnish Government will ask Great Britain, either alone or with her Allies (also France, Italy, "either alone," etc.) (also the Government of Esthonia, either alone or in concert with other Border States on Russia's western frontier . . . . Latvia, Poland, Roumania, "either alone," etc.) to support Finland in order that the dispute in question between Finland and Russia be solved in a pacific manner.'

Dr. Holsti further gave the following information: Immediately the Finnish Government received news of the outbreak of the rising in Karelia they issued to Government and frontier authorities instructions that neutrality must be observed. With this object the following measures were taken:—

1. All recruiting and organising of troops on Finnish territory was forbidden.

[1] Not printed.   [2] See No. 449, n. 2.

2. The crossing of the frontier by armed individuals and groups was forbidden.
3. The sending across the frontier of munitions and warlike material was forbidden.
4. Any of the armed individuals or groups coming from East Karelia, refugees or otherwise, were to be disarmed.
5. Individuals near the frontier with the evident intention of proceeding to East Karelia to take part in the fighting were to be sent back from the frontier districts.

Dr. Holsti made a further declaration on the part of the Government that no organisation, either Russian or Karelian, exists on Finnish territory with the object of organising armed activity against Russia. Nor, so far as the Finnish Government are aware, does any such Finnish organisation exist.

Dr. Holsti stated that, as the result of the steps taken by the Government, the enlistment of volunteers, which possibly had been attempted on a small scale when the news of the outbreak of the rising arrived, had ceased, and no enlistment, so far as he knew, was going on. Among other instances he mentioned that of a group of men who had arrived at the town of Joensuu, near the frontier, and had been made to reenter the train and return. He added that the so-called Karelian Government, which has been representing Karelian interests in Finland and consisted of two individuals, had been told to leave the country, and had last week crossed back into the Repola commune.

I have, etc.,
ERNEST RENNIE

No. 461

The Marquess Curzon of Kedleston to Mr. Hodgson (Moscow)
No. 127 Telegraphic [N 14061/4/38]

FOREIGN OFFICE, *December 29, 1921, 7 p.m.*
According to information which we have just received from the Finnish government,[1] the situation between Finland and Russia has become serious, if not critical, and the possibility of an outbreak of hostilities is not to be excluded.

We are satisfied, on the data at our disposal, that the behaviour of the Finnish government in the face of the obvious difficulties arising for it out of the Karelian revolt has been correct and that it has done its best to prevent the perpetration of unneutral acts from Finnish territory. As you have already been informed,[2] His Majesty's Government have not failed from the beginning of the dispute to give advice in this sense to the Finnish government.

[1] See No. 460.   [2] See No. 450.

The Soviet government now however appears to be presenting demands with which the Finnish government may not unreasonably find it impossible to comply, and at the same time Russian troops are being concentrated either on or near the Finnish frontier.[1] The peace may therefore at any time be broken and His Majesty's Government feel it a matter of urgency to take any step that may be possible to avert such a disaster.

The Finnish government, as you are aware, has appealed to the league of nations[3] for an enquiry into the dispute and it may be that the league will send an invitation to the Soviet government to state its case. Only the interpretation of the treaty of Dorpat would of course be at issue and there would be no question of disturbing the status quo. In these circumstances the Soviet government would, in its own interests, be well-advised not to reject an invitation from the league off-hand, and in fact it must be of advantage to a government which not merely professes to desire peace but has an obvious need of it at the present moment to find this pacific way out.

You alone are in a position to judge what effect advice in this sense to M. Chicherin would be likely to have, but, if you see no objection, you should endeavour to see him at once and dissuade him from taking any steps likely to bring the dispute to a head before all possible means of arriving at a peaceful settlement have been tried.

Repeated to Helsingfors No. 70.[4]

[3] See No. 449.

[4] Referring to this telegram, Lord Curzon, in his telegram No. 71 of December 29, instructed Mr. Rennie as follows: 'Please inform Minister for Foreign Affairs that we are using such influence as we possess at Moscow to restrain the Soviet government from breaking the peace, and urge him once again to do everything in his power to prevent any acts that might lend colour to the charges of a lack of neutrality on the part of the Finnish government.'

No. 462

Mr. Max Muller (Warsaw) to the Marquess Curzon of Kedleston
(Received January 3, 1922, 8.30 a.m.)
No. 470 Telegraphic [N 67/2/38]

WARSAW, *December 31, 1921, 8.30 p.m.*

My despatch No. 783.[1]

Minister for Foreign Affairs has just read telegram from Polish Minister at Helsingfors, dated the 28th December, reporting conversation which had

[1] In this despatch, dated December 30, Mr. Max Muller reported: 'Monsieur Zaleski, Political Director of the Ministry for Foreign Affairs, informed Mr. Kimens [Commercial Secretary to H.M. Legation at Warsaw] last night that in the event of the breaking off of diplomatic relations between Finland and Soviet Russia, the Polish Government will be invited to act as intermediary. Monsieur Zaleski added that his Government will not refuse the mandate.'

taken place between Finnish Minister for Foreign Affairs and Soviet Chargé d'Affaires[2] about the situation in Karelia. Tenor of conversation has doubtless been telegraphed to you.[3]

Polish Minister terminated by statement that situation between Finland and Russia at end of this conversation was not far from rupture of relations, and that there was feeling akin to panic in Helsingfors.

Minister for Foreign Affairs, while doubtful as to likelihood of Soviet Government proceeding to extremes at present juncture of affairs in Russia, had instructed Polish representatives at Moscow and Helsingfors, when presenting to Russian and Finnish Governments new year congratulations, to express earnest desire for reestablishment of peace and stability in Eastern Europe, and to offer assistance of Polish Government, if desired, in arriving at peaceful solution of present tension between Russian and Finnish Governments.

Repeated to Helsingfors and Riga.

[2] M. Chernik.
[3] In Mr. Rennie's telegram No. 202 of December 29 (N 14214/4/38), not printed.

CHAPTER VI

Russia

January–December, 1922

No. 463

Mr. Rennie (Helsingfors) to the Marquess Curzon of Kedleston
(Received January 2, 3.55 p.m.)
No. 1 Telegraphic [N 61/2/38]

HELSINGFORS, *January 2, 1922, 3.6 p.m.*

My telegram No. 205.[1]

Minister for Foreign Affairs told me last night he had had conversation yesterday with Bolshevik representative regarding attitude of Finland towards Karelian rising. Latter's tone comparatively reasonable and conciliatory, and Minister for Foreign Affairs gathers that Soviet Government are anxious to find a formula that will save their face. Conversations will be resumed today. According to Minister for Foreign Affairs's private information Soviet Government have been very seriously perturbed by alarmist reports received from their agents at Berlin, Warsaw and Riga, which have now been sent to Bolshevik agent here for report and comment.

Offer of mediation in Karelian question was communicated here yesterday by Polish Minister.[2] Also chief of general staff received letter, which was described as very satisfactory, from Polish military attaché promising Finland support in certain eventualities.[3]

[1] Of December 30, not printed.
[2] Cf. No. 462. In his telegram No. 2 of January 2, Mr. Rennie stated: 'Reply will probably not be returned for two or three days, and will be to the effect that Finnish Government, having already suggested mediation of third country, will accept offer of Polish Government provided acceptance of Government of Poland's good offices has been previously signified.

'Finland's hands, however, are naturally rather tied by their appeal to the League of Nations.'

[3] Mr. Max Muller, in Warsaw telegram No. 5 of January 3, reported: 'Minister for Foreign Affairs expressed great surprise concerning letter alleged to have been written by Polish military attaché to Finnish Chief of General Staff, as policy of Polish Government is entirely opposed to any such promise of support to Finland.

'He thinks that there must be some misunderstanding, and will see Polish Chief of General Staff on the subject tomorrow.'

No. 464

Mr. Rennie (Helsingfors) to the Marquess Curzon of Kedleston
(Received January 24)
No. 1 [N 753/2/38]

Confidential   HELSINGFORS, *January 2, 1922*
My Lord Marquess,

I called on Dr. Holsti immediately on receipt of Your Lordship's telegram No. 71[1] and told him that the British Representative at Moscow had been instructed[2] to use his influence with the Bolshevik Government with a view to obtaining a peaceful solution of the present dispute regarding the attitude of the Finnish Government in the Karelian question. At the same time I did not fail to impress upon him that the Finnish Government must do all that they could to avoid anything which might lend colour to the Soviet accusations that they were in any way giving assistance to the insurgents.

Dr. Holsti expressed his warmest thanks for this friendly intervention on the part of His Majesty's Government and said that he felt sure that it would have its effect. Indeed, he seemed to think that this was already the case, as he told me confidentially that he had already received a message from the Bolshevik representative here to the effect that the Russian Government did not intend to push their demands, and suggesting that confidential negotiations by means of private conversations should be initiated with a view to reaching an amicable settlement. To this he had readily agreed. The President[3] who received me yesterday on the occasion of the New Year's receptions, also expressed to me his warm thanks, and appeared to be in good spirits as if his mind had been relieved of a great weight of responsibility. Owing to Dr. Holsti's indisposition on the 31st, and press of Cabinet business he was unable to receive Chernik[4] until yesterday afternoon, and in the course of the evening he gave me a short account of the conversation he had had that day.

I gather that the talk had been only on general lines regarding the attitude of Finland towards the Karelian rising and that Dr. Holsti had pointed out to Chernik which of the Soviet's demands were possible of fulfilment and in what way it was possible to meet their wishes. Chernik's tone had been comparatively reasonable and conciliatory, and Dr. Holsti gathered that the Soviet Government were very anxious to find some formula that would save their face. The conversation was to be resumed today on the more special points raised in the Soviet notes.

According to Dr. Holsti's private information, the Soviet Government have lately been very seriously perturbed by the reports which they have received from their agents at Berlin, Warsaw and Riga, and have been genuinely under an impression that some combined White attack upon Russia was brewing and was indeed imminent. A number of these reports have

---

[1] See No. 461, n. 4.   [2] See No. 461.
[3] Dr. K. J. Ståhlberg.   [4] See No. 462, n. 2.

now been sent here for Chernik to comment on and investigate, and Dr. Holsti said he expected that the latter would describe them as at least exaggerated and misleading.

As regards the possibility of White Russian or German officers coming to this country in order to join the Karelian insurgents, Dr. Holsti told me on December 30th that renewed categorical instructions had already been sent to the Finnish Legations and Passport Offices abroad to refuse to grant visas to any persons suspected of such intentions who may present themselves.

I had some talk last night with the Prime Minister regarding the speech he had made on the 29th in the Diet and his declarations regarding the policy of the Finnish Government. Dr. Vennola seemed very satisfied with the results of his declarations and said that the pacific intentions of the Government had been approved by all parties and sections. According to him the numbers of Finns now with the Karelian forces amounted to between 3 and less than 4 hundred men, who had contrived to elude the vigilance of the frontier guards by passing over individually or in very small groups. These numbers were very small in comparison with those of Communists who, it was known, the Russian Government had sent into Finland, and which, according to him, amounted to over 2,000. Many of these men had been found to be in possession not only of propaganda material, but also of arms and bombs. The so-called Finnish help to the Karelians was therefore nothing in comparison with the Russian interference in this country.

As regards the money collected for the Karelian insurgents, Dr. Vennola said that it was impossible to prevent such action on the part of private persons. He was rather vague about the amount which had been so far thus obtained, but thought it amounted to about Fmks. 600,000 (roughly £2,500), an infinitesimal sum, he said, on the calculation that it cost the Finnish Government Fmks. 6,000 a year to maintain each single refugee.

As I have mentioned in my Despatch No. 435 of December 29th,[5] the Communists here have of late been showing activity, a fact to which attention was called at one of the meetings of the Allied Representatives last week. Dr. Holsti now maintains that these Communist efforts had led to little result here. He said emphatically that they had utterly failed among the railway officials, and their effect in the army was also practically nil. He further stated that this propaganda had now quite discredited itself in the eyes of the Government employees and troops, as the latter, in addition to their innate contempt for the Russian working classes, had had their eyes very considerably opened of late regarding the results of communism in Russia. The danger of internal revolution here appeared to him now to be remote. His remarks were somewhat borne out by another member of the Cabinet with whom I talked last night, and who is specially interested in social affairs.

Dr. Holsti also told me last night that the Polish Minister, when presenting his New Year's congratulations yesterday to the President, had made the offer of good offices in the Karelian question, as described in Mr. Max

[5] Not preserved in the Foreign Office archives.

Muller's telegram No. 470 of December 31st,[6] and he further said that the Chief of the General Staff had also received from the recently arrived Polish Military Attaché, what he described as a very satisfactory letter,[7] containing an offer of assistance to Finland in certain eventualities. He could not tell me exactly what answer would be given, much as the offer was appreciated. Finland's hands were somewhat tied by the appeal she had made to the League of Nations,[8] which would come before that body within the next few days. I gathered that a few days might elapse before the Finnish Government gave their reply in order to allow time for the fresh conversations which he had initiated with Chernik to develop.

I have, etc.,
ERNEST RENNIE

[6] No. 462.   [7] See No. 463, nn. 2 and 3.   [8] See No. 449.

No. 465

*The Marquess Curzon of Kedleston to Lord Hardinge (Paris)
and Sir R. Graham (Rome)*

No. 4[1] Telegraphic: by bag [N 14031/4/38]

FOREIGN OFFICE, *January 4, 1922, 6 p.m.*

East Karelian dispute.

As soon as relations between Russia and Finland became strained over the Karelian revolt, His Majesty's minister in Helsingfors was instructed[2] to impress upon the Finnish government the paramount importance of the maintenance of the strictest neutrality.

When asked to support the Finnish appeal to the League of Nations, His Majesty's Government replied[3] that they regarded it as a matter entirely for decision by the league on its merits and again urged the necessity for the strictest neutrality.

Finally, in view of the increased tension, the British representative in Moscow has been instructed,[4] at his discretion, to approach the Soviet government and endeavour to ascertain whether an invitation from the league in accordance with article 17 of the covenant would be acceptable. Mr. Hodgson was to point out the obvious advantages of such a course, more especially as there would be no question of disturbing the status quo but only of the interpretation of the treaty of Dorpat. He was to add that on the data available to His Majesty's Government, the attitude of the Finnish government had been correct, and to urge the importance of the utmost caution.

His Majesty's Government would welcome the intervention of the league in the dispute, although the attitude hitherto adopted towards the league by

[1] No. 4 to Paris, No. 5 to Rome.
[2] See Nos. 450 and 456, and No. 461, n. 4.
[3] See No. 456.   [4] See No. 461.

Soviet Russia does not justify sanguine expectations of acceptance of its good offices. On the other hand, Poland has offered herself as a mediator[5] and her offer may prove acceptable to both parties, in which case it would be open to the league to remain aloof from the dispute.

Please inform the French/Italian government of the above, and add that, if any information is received as the result of Mr. Hodgson's representations in Moscow, it will be at once communicated. In the meanwhile, I would suggest that it would be for the consideration of the council whether the usual invitation to Soviet Russia, as a non-member, should be despatched, in the absence of any information as regards the probable attitude of the Soviet government.

Repeated to Helsingfors No. 1 and Moscow No. 5.

[5] See Nos. 462 and 464. In his telegram No. 7 of January 7, Mr. Rennie reported that the Soviet Government had rejected the Polish Government's offer of mediation.

No. 466

Mr. Rennie (Helsingfors) to the Marquess Curzon of Kedleston
(Received January 8, 9.30 p.m.)
No. 9 Telegraphic [N 283/2/38]

HELSINGFORS, *January 8, 1922, 8 p.m.*

My telegram No. 1[1] and Warsaw telegram No. [5][2]

According to copy of letter addressed by Polish military attaché to Finnish Chief of General Staff, dated 31st December, which I have seen, it is stated that writer had heard from Polish General Staff that Polish Government could not remain indifferent in the event of threat of war against Finland on the part of Russia, and that it was for Finland to ask for help if diplomatic or military aid were desired.

This was considered here as implying assurance of assistance.

(Repeated to Warsaw and Moscow).

[1] No. 463.   [2] See No. 463, n. 3.

No. 467

Mr. Hodgson (Moscow) to the Marquess Curzon of Kedleston
(Received January 16)
No. 20 [N 480/11/38]

MOSCOW, *January 9, 1922*

My Lord,

The opening of the 9th All-Russia Congress of Soviets, which was announced for the 20th December, was delayed and ultimately took place on the 24th. The Congress was held in the Moscow Opera House, which has

831

seating space for 1,740 people, but for the occasion accommodated some 1,900 delegates, besides the foreign representatives, the Third International, and Government officials, for whom boxes were set apart. The foreign missions and relief organisations had each two tickets assigned to them and were given one of the stage boxes, facing the Third International. The meetings were well attended throughout, the audience being remarkably well disciplined, obviously interested in the proceedings and attentive, though much of what was said must certainly have been beyond the comprehension of a considerable number of the delegates. No sounds of opposition at any stage of the proceedings were audible: the violent outburst, expected by some from the 'Left' groups with Communistic consciences outraged by the new economic policy, had been effectively stifled, and the 9th Congress, like its predecessors, ended in a triumph for the organised discipline of the 'party'. Lenin emerges from it with his personal prestige enhanced and a position more nearly approximating to absolutism than he has held at any previous time in his career. The 'unmoral Asiatic policy' in which he is believed to pride himself has again succeeded, for, having reversed all the processes of Communism preached for three years at the cost of lives innumerable and the economic ruin of the country, he has carried over the 'party'—less numerous now owing to the exclusion of unworthy adherents, but stronger in unity and decision—to his new positions, satisfied that the change of front is one of tactics only and that the ultimate objective is surer than ever of attainment.

The subjects down for discussion were the following:—

1. Report of the All-Russian Executive Committee and the Soviet of People's Commissars on the internal and external policy of the Republic.
2. Report on famine relief.
3. Preliminary results of the new economic policy.
4. Position of industry.
5. Restoration of agriculture and, particularly, of the famine stricken districts.
6. Finance and the budget.
7. Co-operation and co-operative legislation.
8. Report on the international situation.
9. Questions of the construction of the Red army.
10. Soviet construction.
11. Elections to the All-Russian Executive Committee.

I have the honour to transmit, herewith, digests[1] of the principal speeches made. Those of Lenin and Trotsky, being of particular importance, are given at considerable length. Chicherin, who was to have spoken on foreign politics, did not put in an appearance, the subject having been sufficiently exhausted by Lenin and Trotsky. Kamenev, speaking on the new economic policy, Bogdanov on the state of Russian industry and Hinchuk on

[1] The digest of Lenin's speech only is here printed.

co-operation, did little more than repeat the speeches they had made at the Communist Conference, though Hinchuk added a strong plea for a restriction of Government interference in the operations of the Co-operatives.

Lack of opposition robbed the proceedings to some extent of interest. The care which had been taken to achieve this triumph of discipline was betrayed by Litvinov who, in a casual conversation, rather naïvely spoke of Bukharin—the most redoubtable of the pure Communists—as 'of course unable to speak, being in the opposition'.

The new economic policy is naturally, to a greater or less extent, the theme of every speech. Lenin dwelt upon it at length, defining the attitude of the Soviet Government towards this *volte-face* in Communism in the following sentence: 'We have universally stated that we have adopted this policy in all seriousness and for a considerable time to come; but of course, as it has been rightly said on previous occasions, not for always. It has been dictated by our present poverty and ruin and by the very marked enfeeblement of our large scale industry. But the new economic policy can only prosper provided it takes root on ground adapted to its growth, and in order to meet these requirements, it is essential that the international situation should be favourable to Russia.'

Lenin's speech, though it gave a clear *exposé* of the aims of the new economic policy and the circumstances which rendered its introduction essential, added little or nothing to what has been said by him and by other Soviet orators on the same subject before. His declaration regarding the restriction of the powers of the Extraordinary Commission was an announcement having the merit of novelty. If—as there is every reason to believe will be the case—his promise is translated into fact by the promulgation of new criminal legislation and of decrees guaranteeing the security of the person a very great step will have been taken towards the internal pacification of Russia.

Trotsky's speech on the Red army constituted a masterly exposition of the case for the retention and strengthening of the force. By the aid of huge diagrams on the stage, on which were shown the Russian frontiers traversed by an infinity of small red arrows 'pointed at the heart of the Russian People,' he persuaded an easily-convinced audience of the necessity of maintaining an army ever ready to repel the attacks of imperialism, using at one time Poland, at another Roumania, and now Finland, as its tools for the destruction of Communist Russia.

I have, etc.,
R. M. Hodgson

ENCLOSURE IN No. 467

Digest of Lenin's Speech on December 23, 1921

With regard to the international situation, a certain equipoise has come about which is undeniable, although it is still unstable.

Those of us who have watched affairs from the beginning have observed in what an extraordinary fashion they have worked themselves out. We all expected a simpler and more direct development, and we said that there could be no other issue from the accursed and criminal imperialist slaughter-house than that provided by revolution, but it appeared that this simple path, which in fact, led us out of imperialism, did not succeed in other countries—at all events as quickly as we had expected.

We are now solitary Socialist Soviet Republic surrounded by a series of hostile Powers incomparably more powerful than ourselves both economically and militarily—the question arises: How can it be? How can it be that the efforts of three years to crush us have all come to nothing? The answer is that, although we did not receive the speedy direct support of an [sic] from the labouring masses of the world on which we had reckoned, still we received support of another sort, namely, the sympathy of those labouring masses even in countries most hostile to us—a fact which rendered futile all attacks directed against us. This is the explanation of the strange and unintelligible position in which we find ourselves, namely, that although incomparably weaker than all the other Powers in the economic agricultural and military sense, at the same time we are stronger than all.

We must remember, however, that we are still surrounded by peoples, classes and Governments who are openly hostile to us, and are ever in imminent danger of new attacks. We must therefore do all we can to avert such a misfortune and must constantly be on our guard.

We are ready to make the greatest concessions and sacrifices in order to keep the peace, but there is a limit, and let this fact be borne in mind by the adherents—fortunately few in numbers—of the militarist parties in Finland, Poland and Roumania.

We have seen that it is possible for a Communist country to subsist militarily and diplomatically in the midst of capitalist Powers, but can this be accomplished in the economic sense? All the capitalist Powers have endeavoured to stifle us economically, but the economic position was stronger than they were. Foreign countries are compelled to assist in the reconstruction of our economic life. We are receiving locomotives and cars from abroad, and our foreign trade is developing. There is a power greater than the desire, the will and the decision of any hostile Government or class. It is the general economic world situation.

With regard to our internal economic position, the fundamental question is the relation of the working class to the peasantry, and the ability of the former to win over to its side the mass of peasants crushed by capitalism, landowners and their own misery. This can only be accomplished if industry is restored and can supply the [peasant] with the products which he needs, thus establishing a correlation between the products of agriculture and the products of industry. Only then will the peasant be fully satisfied, recognise the force of our system and admit that our order is better than that of capitalism. This is the foundation of our new economic policy and on to this path we are led by absolute necessity.

We have advanced in the political and military sphere much further than we were able to do in the economic relations between the working men and the peasants. We were forced to do this in order to defeat our enemies, and our justification lies in the fact that we did defeat them, although in the economic field we suffered heavy losses. That is why we have had to retreat to State capitalism, to concessions and to trade. Otherwise we ran the risk that the front line of revolution would advance so far that it would break the link with the peasantry, and thus destroy the revolution.

We can win in the economic sphere too, but we must remember that progress here is at a different rate, that circumstances are different and that success is harder to obtain than it was in the political or military field. Stages are reckoned here by tens of years.

With regard to the famine and foreign assistance, I would point out that we have received in contributions from abroad 2,500,000 poods of food and 600,000 gold roubles. These miserable figures show how greedily the European bourgeoisie have behaved towards us in the matter of the famine. You have probably all of you read how pompously the bourgeois leaders declared at the start that to utilise the famine in order to raise the question of our old debts would be a diabolic game. I do not know whether the devil is more terrible than the contemporary imperialism, but I do know that, as things turned out, the imperialists endeavoured to extort from us our old debts on the hardest possible terms. We do not refuse to pay, and declare ourselves ready to discuss the matter in a business-like way, but in no case will we allow ourselves to be enslaved.

We have lately received a promise of food supplies to the value of 40,000,000 gold roubles from the United States Government on condition that we ourselves expend 20,000,000 gold roubles, and we have at once agreed to this condition. This is real assistance. But in spite of it and of all that we have done ourselves, enough has not yet been provided, and we must state clearly that in no case are we ourselves able to cover our own needs.

With regard to the tax in kind, the point is not what quantity of grain has been taken from the peasants, but that the peasants feel themselves secured by this tax and more interested in the question of agricultural production. Nevertheless, we must not forget that the collection of the tax in kind falls very heavily on the peasantry. But in the name of the Government I must say to you that this tax must be carried out, that we must face this difficulty and assume this burden, for otherwise it is impossible to guarantee the existence of either our industry or our transport. The very existence of our Soviet Republic depends upon this, and our extremely modest plan for restoring transport and industry is based on the completion of our general food collection programme. For this reason the tax in kind must be collected to the full.

As regards fuel, our figures show that, great as were the difficulties of the past year and great as were the burdens which fell upon the working men and the peasants, nevertheless we are improving our position. We are upon the right road, and by exerting all our efforts we can hope to raise ourselves still higher.

I should also like to give you figures concerning the progress of electrification. I had hoped to be able to congratulate this Congress on the opening of a second big electric station which we had counted on opening in December. Unfortunately, this has had to be postponed for a few weeks. The figures for the years 1918 and 1919 show that during this period fifty-one large stations were opened, while in the past year there were opened no less than 221. Naturally, these figures are miserable in comparison with those of Western Europe, but nevertheless they show that we are going ahead in spite of circumstances of extreme difficulty.

The amount of peat which we secured in 1920 was 93,000,000, and in the past year, 139,000,000 [sic]. This is the sole sphere in which we have exceeded the pre-war figures, and in this sphere we have immeasurable wealth, such as no other country in the world has. In the past year we were working in Russia two hydraulic plants—our own invention—for securing peat, and we have now on order in Germany for the coming year another twenty such plants. An enormous amount can be accomplished, if only we can elaborate the idea that through the mechanisation of labour we can rise from our economic crisis as no other country in the world.

From 1917 to 1920 we solved with heroism and success a series of military and political problems. Now a different task lies before us. We worked well in the political and military spheres, but in that of national economy we worked badly. We must recognise this and work better. I say to you: Cease chattering, do something productive and cease writing beautiful resolutions about raw material and saying that you represent the proletariat. For what is the proletariat? A class which is occupied with heavy industry. But where is the heavy industry? Why have you collected no raw material? Why have you only written resolutions for collecting it? And why do you continue sitting in your puddle? History has laid a task upon us.

The greatest political revolutions require to run a long course before they can be digested. Our work is not to accomplish rapid reorganisation, but to digest the political transformation which has been accomplished in such a way as to acquire a new level of economic culture. All the peasantry must help us in digesting the great political conquest which we have made. At this point we must be sober and face facts. The revolution has not yet entered into the flesh and blood of the everyday economic life of the masses. Here is a work of tens of years which requires the greatest exertion of our strength, a work which cannot be accomplished with that rapidity with which we performed our task in the military and political spheres.

Before finishing, I would say a word about the All-Russian Extraordinary Commission. You all know, of course, what hatred this institution inspires in our enemies. But you all know that, without it, and without the rapid and merciless means of suppression which it provides, the power of the labouring classes could not have subsisted. Nevertheless, we also recognise that this institution must be limited to the purely political sphere, to which its functions, competence and energies must all be restricted. Such a general reform of the Extraordinary Commission must be accomplished.

In conclusion, I must say that the task upon which we have decided—the task of welding the working classes and peasantry into a lasting economic union—has been decided correctly. We are upon the right lines: of this there can be no doubt.

No. 468

Mr. Rennie (Helsingfors) to the Marquess Curzon of Kedleston
(Received January 24)
No. 9 [N 760/2/38]

HELSINGFORS, January 9, 1922

My Lord Marquess,

As reported in my telegram No. 7 of January 7th,[1] the Minister for Foreign Affairs has had various conversations last week with the Bolshevik representatives.

The principal subject dealt with was the question of the expulsion from Finland of White Russians, supposed to be implicated in the Karelian rising, and Chernik vainly endeavoured to get Dr. Holsti to consent, on principle, to a demand on the part of the Soviet Government that the persons whose names they brought forward, should be ordered to quit Finland. Dr. Holsti appears to have taken up the line that he considered such a demand as an infringement of Finnish rights and an unwarrantable interference in Finnish internal affairs, and told the Bolshevik representatives that he must refuse to be treated as if he were a Soviet official. He told Chernik, however, that he would be glad to receive and examine a list of persons suspected and to decide on the merits of each case, and he mentioned to me that the information which he hoped thus to obtain from Bolshevik sources would be useful in the case of certain undesirables, whom the Government suspected of anti-Russian intrigues, but against whom evidence was not sufficiently strong to warrant severe measures being taken. He subsequently, on Saturday afternoon[2] said that he greatly doubted whether the Bolshevik representative intended to present such a list. As to the further demands that Chernik had made, namely, that the Finnish Government should return all arms, etc. taken from refugees crossing the Finnish frontier and should pay the expenses of the present expedition now being undertaken against the Karelians, he told Chernik this was a matter he was really unable to discuss. He told me that the Finnish Government would send a further reply to the Soviet complaints, which would also answer these two demands in the negative, but that this could not be done before the middle of this week because, as was the case a fortnight ago, so many members of the Cabinet were absent in the country and the Note accordingly would not be sent before the 12th or 13th.

Although he frequently complains of the difficulty he has in discussing

---

[1] See No. 465, n. 5.   [2] January 7.

questions with the Soviet Representative, who apparently declines to talk about facts, and indulges in generalities and lectures on Bolshevist principles, he appeared to think that the general disposition of the Soviet Government was disposed to be more conciliatory. The impression here seems to be that the Soviet Government knowing that their case against the Finnish Government is far from a strong one, would be quite satisfied if they were able to obtain some outward show of a diplomatic success, and thereby satisfy various parties at Moscow. The Finnish Government, on their part would, I think, be prepared to contribute towards this end.

I informed Dr. Holsti today of portions of the contents of the telegrams Nos. 1[3] and 3[4] of January 2nd and 5th, addressed to Your Lordship by His Majesty's Chargé d'Affaires at Moscow, as it seemed well to impress upon him the Russian view of the situation, and I said that Mr. Hodgson had stated that he had good reason to believe that a show of conciliation on the part of Finland might put an end to the present crisis. Dr. Holsti assented but said that this was by no means easy owing to Chernik's inexperience in customary diplomatic methods, and his habit of making every show of concession an excuse for putting forward fresh demands.

The news of the crossing of the frontier by 250 men and 2 machine guns of the Bolshevik forces on Friday,[5] created some sensation here, especially in the Swedish press. Dr. Holsti and the Chief of the General Staff, whom I saw yesterday, were disposed to regard it only as an almost inevitable incident in a desolate country where the frontier is ill-defined and a mistake could easily occur. Three or four days previously General Enkell had told me that he had no apprehensions in this respect, as he knew that the Bolshevik forces had instructions to be very careful not to violate Finnish territory. The affair shows how fortunate it was that the concentration of Bolshevik troops took place just before Christmas, when the press and the population in general had their thoughts turned towards holiday-making.

Colonel Gyllenbögel, the Finnish Minister at Moscow, arrived at Helsingfors on the morning of the 7th. I saw him for a few minutes in Dr. Holsti's room on that afternoon, but he had no special information of interest. He has given an interview to the Press in which he has spoken of the difficulties of intercourse with the Soviet representatives at Moscow, which has considerably annoyed the Government, and Dr. Holsti said that he would probably not return to his post.

[3] Not printed.

[4] The reference is to No. 5 of January 3, not printed.

[5] In his telegram No. 6 of January 7, Mr. Rennie had reported: 'Bolshevik detachment crossed Finnish frontier last night, south of Repola, and penetrated short distance beyond. Shots were exchanged with Finnish frontier guards. Minister for Foreign Affairs has protested to Bolshevik representative, who happened to be calling when news arrived. He does not appear to attach much importance to the affair, which he seems to regard as an accident.'

In a further telegram, No. 11 of January 9, he stated: 'Bolsheviks, who had occupied village of Megri on Finnish side of frontier due west of Porajävo, withdrew to Karelian side on approach of Finnish frontier guards and Schutz corps.'

A copy of this despatch has been sent to His Majesty's Representative at Moscow.

I have, etc.,

ERNEST RENNIE

No. 469

Mr. Hodgson (Moscow) to the Marquess Curzon of Kedleston
(Received January 12, 11.50 a.m.)
No. 15 Telegraphic [N 400/2/38]

MOSCOW, *January 10, 1922, 6.30 p.m.*

My telegram No. 1 of 1st January.[1]

M. Litvinov complains that Finland . . .[2] reasonable and conciliatory mood a few days ago have now assumed arrogant attitude, and refuse even to discuss demands put forward by Soviet representative. Dr. Holsti, according to this version of events, has postponed matters indefinitely on the plea that Finland is relying on support from League of Nations and is therefore intent on protracting. Russia on her side is determined that a treaty[3] which affects only her and Finland should be decided by these countries without any interference from outside, and if Great Britain is anxious for assistance in terminating crisis the best way in which she can help is by making Finland understand that she cannot count upon foreign help. M. Litvinov seems nervous of the warlike preparations which are, according to reports of agents, being made in the Baltic States, particularly Esthonia.

If M. Litvinov's accusations no longer have any foundation in fact, I believe that Finnish Government would be well advised to abandon this attitude. Soviet Government are, I believe, still genuinely anxious to avoid war (I learn from a private source that stringent orders have been sent to Commander-in-chief to avoid violation of Finnish territory), but complete preparations for hostilities have been made, and I should be disinclined to rely too much upon pacific intentions of Kremlin.

(Repeated to Helsingfors and Warsaw.)

[1] Not printed. It was dated January 2.
[2] The text is here uncertain.
[3] The Treaty of Dorpat (see No. 449, n. 2).

No. 470

The Marquess Curzon of Kedleston to Mr. Grove[1] *(Moscow)*
No. 19 Telegraphic [*N 14052/216/38*]

FOREIGN OFFICE, *January 12, 1922, 6 p.m.*

My despatch No. 111 (of October 8th).[2]

His Majesty's Government have decided to permit members of the Russian trade delegation to reside in such parts of England as may be necessary to enable them to supervise contracts, etc. This clears the way to the appointment of British agents in other parts of Russia.

The first appointment we propose to proceed with is Petrograd. Please, therefore, approach the Soviet government and inform it that we desire to appoint a British agent at Petrograd to look after British shipping and trade interests. It is proposed to send Mr. Preston[3] in this capacity with Mr. Jordan[4] to assist him, and a clerical staff of one. If these names are acceptable to the Soviet government it is proposed that Mr. Preston should start forthwith.

As Mr. Hodgson will see Mr. Preston here before the latter leaves, I do not propose to send him via Moscow, unless you especially desire it.

[1] Senior Assistant Agent on the British Commercial Mission to Russia. Mr. Hodgson had left Moscow for London on January 10.
[2] Not printed. See, however, No. 434.
[3] See No. 413, n. 4.
[4] Formerly on the staff of the British High Commission in Vladivostok.

No. 471

Mr. Rennie (Helsingfors) to the Marquess Curzon of Kedleston
(Received January 14, 6.10 p.m.)
No. 19 Telegraphic [*N 448/2/38*]

HELSINGFORS, *January 14, 1922, 2.50 p.m.*

My telegram No. 17.[1]

Minister for Foreign Affairs communicated yesterday verbally to Bolshevik representative reply of Finnish Government to various Russian demands,[2] which is to following effect:—

1. Finnish Government already on 28th December announced that all recruitment and sending of military assistance across frontier was forbidden. Finnish citizens could, however, be punished for such action directed against friendly State only when there are reciprocal arrangements between Finland and States concerned.

2. As regards expulsion of White Russians now resident in Finland, and dissolution of their secret organisations, Finnish Government reserves

[1] Of January 13, not printed.   [2] See Nos. 453, 454, 458, 461, 464, and 468.

to itself liberty of action, but Russian Government can make any communication they may think necessary through diplomatic channel.

3. Finnish Government have declared that they will disarm and intern refugees from Karelia, and have already acted on these lines in accordance with international usage. They cannot, however, admit claim that refugee Karelian chiefs must be expelled, and Finnish Government must be free to decide which of such persons may enjoy right of asylum in Finland, and to which it will be refused. As regards return of arms taken from refugees this will be subject for future negotiations.

4. Finnish Government will not be responsible for costs of expedition against Karelia, as this would be admission of responsibility of Finland for rising.

5. Finnish Government cannot accept proposal for mixed commission to supervise execution of orders given by Finnish Government to protect their neutrality.

Minister for Foreign Affairs told me that tone of Bolshevik representative yesterday was less uncompromising. He also heard last night from Finnish Chargé d'Affaires at Moscow, whom he had instructed to communicate above-mentioned reply in most conciliatory manner, that attitude of Russian Foreign Office appeared to be, these last few days, much less stiff.
(Repeated to Moscow).

No. 472

Mr. Rennie (Helsingfors) to the Marquess Curzon of Kedleston
(Received January 24)
No. 20 [N 770/2/38]

HELSINGFORS, *January 17, 1922*

My Lord Marquess,

With reference to my telegram No. 20 of January 15th,[1] in which I forwarded to Your Lordship Dr. Holsti's request that His Majesty's Government should use their good offices at Moscow with the object of supporting, either the recommendation of the League, or, the further suggestion of the intervention of a third state, with a view to arranging an amicable settlement between the Finnish and the Soviet Governments with regard to the Karelian question, I have the honour to state that Dr. Holsti received a further Note on the afternoon of the 14th from Moscow, copy of which is enclosed.[1]

I met him yesterday afternoon and he said that the Bolshevik representative here was coming to see him today, and he asked me what I thought he ought to say, pending an answer to this latest Note, which would probably not be sent for three or four days' time. I told him that it seemed to me he should

[1] Not printed.

explain, in the most conciliatory manner he could, all that Finland was doing to protect her neutrality and meet such of the Soviet demands as seemed reasonable, and which the Finnish Government were, in fact, trying to meet, and to show general goodwill and, at the same time, to avoid the more controversial sides of the question. A talk on these lines ought to tend to remove the impression that the Finnish Government were trying to gain time until further action was taken by the League of Nations.

Dr. Holsti repeated his former statement concerning the trouble he had in holding conversations with Chernik,[2] and said he knew the latter was not transmitting to his Government correct accounts of what passed between them, and was evidently trying to create rather than smooth over difficulties. Matters were not made any easier by the absence from Moscow of Colonel Gyllenbögel,[2] who has now resigned his post, and with Finnish affairs in charge of a comparatively young Secretary. The personnel of the Finnish Legation would be reinforced, but some delay must inevitably occur in selecting a suitable new representative. Meanwhile, therefore, the intervention of some third disinterested party, who would be able to bring together the two Governments, was all the more desirable. He would be most grateful if His Majesty's Representative at Moscow would continue to do what he had been doing, namely, to exercise a moderating influence on the Soviet Foreign Office, until some more formal method of mediation was arranged.

I have, etc.,
ERNEST RENNIE

[2] See No. 468.

No. 473

Mr. Grove (Moscow) to the Marquess Curzon of Kedleston
(Received February 2, 8.30 a.m.)[1]
No. 22 Telegraphic [*N 1067/2/38*]

MOSCOW, *January 25, 1922*

Your telegram No. 25.[2]

I had interview with Chicherin last night. He absolutely refuses any intervention by any third party between Russia and Finland. He states that Finland is not disarming or interning invaders, but allows them to return into Karelia from various points, thanks to use of Finnish railways. He says also that movement is White Guard one, and is largely engineered by Sir Paul Dukes,[3] who is or who was very recently in Finland. He points out that simultaneously similar movement also started in Poland and Roumania. He states

[1] This telegram was repeated on February 1 (despatched at 5.30 p.m.).
[2] Of January 20 not printed.
[3] Journalist and lecturer, formerly Chief of the British Secret Intelligence Service in Russia.

further that Finland has not accepted any demand Russia has made. He said that status of Karelia was clearly defined in supplementary declaration to Dorpat Treaty,[4] and Russia refused any intervention by mixed foreign commission or otherwise to inspect Russian carrying out in Karelia of treaty, that being purely Russian internal concern, but agrees to appointment of such commission solely to control Finland's disarmament and internment of returned invaders of Karelia. I have reason to believe that, thanks to the importance of invitation to attend international conference,[5] Karelian question has lost its predominance. Each Government complains of accredited representative of the other, and holds that new representatives will probably clear channel for more friendly discussion.

(Repeated to Helsingfors No. 4 and Warsaw No. 5.)

[4] See No. 449, n. 2.
[5] i.e. the Genoa Conference (see Vol. XIX, No. 19, Appendix 1).

No. 474

Mr. Rennie (Helsingfors) to the Marquess Curzon of Kedleston
(Received January 28, 8.30 a.m.)
No. 25 Telegraphic [N 915/2/38]

HELSINGFORS, *January 27, 1922, 8.5 p.m.*

Moscow telegram No. 22.[1]

M. Chicherin's views regarding causes of Karelian rising appear to be based on inaccurate and prejudiced information. Reports here indicate that the movement was due to Bolshevik oppression, and was spontaneous outbreak. Finnish Government have done and are doing their best to prevent armed support from reaching the insurgents, but the nature of the frontier prevents it being absolutely closed. Soviet army has also received support from Finnish Reds, and today there are probably nearly as many Finns in Karelia with Red army as with the insurgents. Nothing is known here of movement stated to have been engineered here by Duk[es]. My despatches . . .,[2] telegram regarding conversations between Finnish Minister for Foreign Affairs and Bolshevik representative here and notes exchanged show how far Finnish Government have tried to meet such of Bolshevik demands as are reasonable.

Minister for Foreign Affairs tells me that in his recent conversations with Bolshevik representative here latter has shown himself much more . . .[2] reasonable and conciliatory, and that in his latest . . .[2] regarding list of persons whose expulsion Soviet Government have demanded, something like an understanding was reached as regards Russian refugees therein named.

[1] No. 473. This telegram had not been received in the Foreign Office: it was repeated on February 1 and reached the Foreign Office on February 2.
[2] The text is here uncertain.

It is evident, however, that Bolshevik representative does not report to his Government the tenor of his conversations with Minister for Foreign Affairs, nor keep them properly informed regarding the situation. Minister for Foreign Affairs now telegraphs to Finnish representative at Moscow full particulars of each conversation for communication to Russian Government.

He tells me that Finnish Government are sending to Moscow on temporary mission M. Hackzell, late member of Russo-Finnish Mixed Commission, who will have greater standing and speak with more authority than present Chargé d'Affaires. He leaves for Moscow week after next.

It would be very desirable that Soviet Government should also replace their present representative here with someone of greater knowledge of affairs. Discussion between the two Governments would then probably assume a different tone and lead to result.

(Repeated to Moscow).

No. 475

Mr. Grove (Moscow) to the Marquess Curzon of Kedleston
(Received February 15)
No. 56 [N 1470/380/38]

MOSCOW, *January 31, 1922*

My Lord Marquess,

I have the honour to report that a Congress of the Oil Industry was held in Moscow from December 31st 1921 to January 10th 1922. A general account of the proceedings, summarised from reports which have appeared in the press, is appended.[1]

The centre of interest for British financial circles lay in the attitude which the Congress adopted towards the concessions question. The final resolution adopted in this connection declared definitely against the granting of oil concessions in the Baku and Grozny areas. In this matter the Congress acted in accordance with the views strongly expressed by both Smilga, head of the Central Fuel Department (so-called 'GUT') and Liadov, head of the Central Oil Department (so-called 'TsUNP').

This was not the first occasion on which M. Smilga had expressed himself in this sense. When the position in the fuel industry became acute last autumn, M. Smilga was sent down to the Donetz Basin, Grozny and Baku. On his return he expressed the definite view that there was no necessity for concessions in the oil industry and that the State was perfectly well able to cope with the flooding problem without external assistance.

The fact that these responsible officials took so definite a line lent a certain degree of importance to the resolutions of the Congress, and the Commercial Secretary of this Mission consequently took an opportunity of raising the

[1] Not printed.

question with M. Bogdanov, President of the Supreme Council of National Economy.

M. Bogdanov stated that the resolution of the Congress reflected the atmosphere of confidence resulting from the success of the past few months' working of the oilfields. It had been conclusively proved that, before the Revolution, the fields were not worked on rational lines. No attention, for example, had been paid to the advice of geologists and the result had been the waste of millions of gallons of oil, owing to premature tapping of big oil reservoirs. The oil companies had held small plots, distributed in patchwork fashion, and had exploited them, not in the interests of the industry but in the interests of their pockets. If the State had sufficient resources there would, therefore, be no question of returning to the old methods of working. As, however, State resources were not sufficient for the big development work required, it would be necessary to allow foreign capital to come in.

He himself had not yet received a detailed statement of the proceedings at the Congress, but he could state that the question of oil concessions was not pre-decided. In connection with the Genoa Conference,[2] instructions were being sent to M. Krassin as to the possibility of granting oil concessions. Concessions would not be given for small plots which could not be rationally exploited but for larger areas where it would be possible to centralise various services, e.g. water, electricity and pipe lines.

In view of the Genoa Conference the views of Russian official circles may be not without interest. In the oil industry, as elsewhere, State management has been on its trial. Notwithstanding the statements made as to the success which has attended the working of the industry by the State it seems probable that, even if other factors be neglected, the difficulties encountered in the execution of the State supply plan will, of themselves, compel the Soviet Government to come to terms with the oil companies, however difficult it may be to reconcile this action with the confident assertions of the State officials who are now running the industry.

I have, etc.,

H. Montgomery Grove

[2] See Vol. XIX, Chap. III.

No. 476

Sir C. Barclay[1] *(Stockholm) to the Marquess Curzon of Kedleston*
(Received February 14)
No. 42 [N 1407/252/38]

STOCKHOLM, *January 31, 1922*

My Lord,

In the last paragraph of my despatch No. 24 of the 18th instant,[2] I stated that Mr. Branting[3] had told me that in view of the impending Conference at

[1] Mr. Barclay had received a Knighthood on January 2, 1922.
[2] Not printed.   [3] Swedish Prime Minister.

Genoa Sweden would not single herself out by coming to a separate Agreement with the Soviet pending that Conference.

As reports were being published in the press respecting the continuation of negotiations with Kerzhentsev,[4] I asked Mr. Branting today how matters really stood. His Excellency replied that his previous statement to me holds good in so far as an agreement involving any political recognition of the Soviet Government is concerned, but that it does not preclude the conclusion of a trade agreement on the lines of those already concluded by other countries. The present position, he went on to say, was that the Swedish representatives had laid their proposals and the Russian proposals before the Swedish Government, requesting instructions as to whether there were any points on which they could meet the Russian demands. The Swedish Government had given certain directions to their representatives and the negotiations were to have been resumed today but Kerzhentsev was not well so they have been put off for a few days. More than this Mr. Branting did not say.

I gather from another source that while the Swedish Government are anxious not to be behind Great Britain, Italy, Germany, Norway and others who have already concluded trade agreements they are not disposed to come to an agreement which would be one-sided like the Norwegian Agreement,[5] and they are still working with a view to negotiating an agreement as far as possible on the lines of ours.[6]

I have, etc,
COLVILLE BARCLAY

[4] Soviet Representative in Sweden (see No. 415, n. 4).
[5] See No. 415, n. 3.
[6] In telegram No. 24 of March 2, Sir C. Barclay reported that a provisional trade agreement between Soviet Russia and Sweden had been signed on March 1. For the sources of this temporary treaty, which was not ratified, see Slusser and Triska, p. 399.

No. 477

Mr. Rennie (Helsingfors) to the Marquess Curzon of Kedleston
(Received February 7, 8.30 a.m.)
No. 28 Telegraphic [N 1177/1171/38]

Secret   HELSINGFORS, *February 6, 1922, 8.30 p.m.*

Minister for Foreign Affairs leaves probably this week to attend Warsaw conference.[1] I understand from him that he will submit to Polish Government proposal for understanding which will take the form of military alliance to come into force in the event of trouble between Finland or Poland with Russia and mediation of League of Nations (or ?) third parties proving unavailing. Minister for Foreign Affairs tells me that public opinion and political groups in diet have lately become seriously perturbed at recent

[1] See No. 479, below.

846

Bolshevik threats and uncompromising attitude of Soviet Government to the Karelian difficulty and are now urging government to seek friendships which may guarantee Finland against sudden attack. He will propose to Polish government that alliance should come into force only in above eventuality of attack against either Poland or Finland after mediation has failed and considers that this proviso will be accepted at Warsaw and will meet exigencies of the situation here without causing undue alarm. His idea is then to proceed with military understanding with Latvia and Esthonia.

Repeated to Warsaw.

No. 478

Mr. Wilton (Riga) to the Marquess Curzon of Kedleston
(Received February 7, 11.15 p.m.)
No. 10 Telegraphic [N 1171/1171/38]

RIGA, *February 6, 1922, 9 p.m.*

Minister for Foreign Affairs informed me today that he had received telegraphic news from his representative at Moscow that secret orders had been issued on February 4th to move two additional divisions, Nos. 33 and 51, to Finnish front. Representative believed that Moscow desired to exercise pressure on Finland to prevent attendance at proposed Warsaw conference.

Minister for Foreign Affairs stated that Polish government had invited Latvia, Esthonia and Finland to a conference at Warsaw to discuss subjects of joint interest preliminary to Genoa conference.[1] He thought Moscow was apprehensive that the object of Warsaw conference was to conclude a military alliance aimed against Russia. He seemed to think that the tendency of the present Bolshevik step might induce Finland to seek an alliance.

Repeated to Helsingfors and Warsaw.

[1] Cf. No. 479, below.

No. 479

Mr. Max Muller (Warsaw) to the Marquess Curzon of Kedleston
(Received February 8, 9.30 p.m.)
No. 29 Telegraphic [N 1218/1171/38]

WARSAW, *February 7, 1922, 7.15 p.m.*

Riga telegram No. 10.[1]

Minister for Foreign Affairs tells me that invitations to conference to be held shortly at Warsaw were issued in consequence of arrangement come to

[1] No. 478.

at Helsingfors last July (see my despatch No. 553)[2] and previous to Cannes conference[3] so that it was mistake to describe it as preliminary to Genoa conference.[4] Original object was to discuss common policy towards Russia both political and economic as had been done at Helsingfors, but naturally advantage would now be taken of meeting to co-ordinate as far as possible policy of four states at Genoa. He was not aware that Russian government were apprehensive of purpose of Warsaw conference, but he was taking precaution of keeping their representative informed of progress of negotiations and objects of meeting.

I asked His Excellency if it would not be possible to include Lithuania, pointing out what a good impression such action on the part of Polish government would produce. He replied that if only Lithuanian reply to his last note[5] was satisfactory he would recognise Lithuania *de jure* and invite her to the conference.

Repeated to Riga, Helsingfors, Moscow.

[2] Of September 21, not printed.   [3] See Vol. XIX, Chap. I.
[4] Ibid., Chap. III.
[5] Presumably a reference to the Polish note of February 7, a copy of which was enclosed in Warsaw despatch No. 74 of February 9 (N 1363/69/55), not printed.

No. 480

Mr. Rennie (Helsingfors) to the Marquess Curzon of Kedleston
(Received February 9, 9.20 p.m.)
No. 33 Telegraphic [N 1262/2/38]

HELSINGFORS, *February 9, 1922, 7.30 p.m.*

Your telegram No. 12.[1]

In reply to Soviet note of 12th January,[2] Finnish Government have sent reply dated 7th February, stating that Finnish Government will agree to formation of mixed commission, composed of four members to be chosen equally by Russia and Finland, provided that it is charged with examination of Karelian question from point of view of Dorpat Treaty,[3] and at the same time of any remarks which Soviet Government wish to make in this connection with regard to attitude of Finnish Government.

Finnish Government consider investigation would be best carried out under auspices of League of Nations, but if Russian Government prefer another arrangement, e.g., institution of mixed commission composed of subjects of neutral countries, Finnish Government is disposed to taking such a plan into consideration.

Copy of note by next bag.[4]

(Repeated to Riga and Moscow.)

[1] Of January 20, not preserved in the Foreign Office archives.
[2] This note was received by Dr. Holsti on January 14 (see No. 472).
[3] See No. 449, n. 2.   [4] Not traced in the Foreign Office archives.

Memorandum by Mr. Gregory on the Soviet Government and Genoa[1]

[*N 4293/646/38*]

FOREIGN OFFICE, *February 12, 1922*

As a general rule I have not thought it worth while to send up casual information on the position and intentions of the Soviet Government, as it is mostly founded on unreliable or biased reports and hardly ever adds to what is public property. I am making an exception, however, today and submitting notes that I have made on a report which has just come into my hands founded on the investigations of Czecho-Slovak Secret Agents in Russia and which I believe to represent the truth, the Czechs being really the only non-Russians who understand the Russian mentality. It is, too, of particular importance as disclosing or purporting to disclose the attitude which the Bolsheviks intend to adopt at Genoa and afterwards. The report is of a highly confidential nature and it is requested that knowledge of it and its contents may not go outside the Foreign Office.

The Communist party, the report states, was in straits in the middle of last year, but was saved owing to its efforts in dealing with the famine. But differences still survive, notably in regard to the Genoa Conference. The Left wing regard the Conference merely as an opportunity for propaganda, and are utilising the Third International to promote this idea in the press which it controls. In this connection it is interesting to note that the Third International, at the head of which, as is well known, is Zinoviev, the intimate friend of Lenin, subsidises 298 newspapers in the various countries in Europe—42 in Germany, 41 in Norway, 28 in Italy, 20 in Czecho-Slovakia, 19 in England, 12 in France, etc. The lines of this propaganda are to represent the invitation to the Soviet Government to come to Genoa, first as being tantamount to *de jure* recognition, and secondly as a complete victory of the Soviet Government over the Governments of the West. The party that is running this policy would equally like to use Genoa as a means of ventilating pro-Bolshevik opinions, crying up the Soviet system and running down the Capitalist.

At the same time the Central Executive Committee, which was convoked to consider the questions connected with the invitation to Genoa, took, at Lenin's instance, two decisions; the first was that the Soviet delegation should be furnished with full powers to give any undertaking that might be necessary; the second was to refrain from all propaganda.

In the face of these two contradictory tendencies it is very difficult to foretell what will actually be the attitude of the Soviet delegation at Genoa: whether it will refrain not merely from making propaganda at Communist meetings but from pro-Bolshevik and subversive speeches at the Conference itself for the benefit of the working-classes abroad—or whether it will maintain an only outwardly correct attitude while carrying on subterranean

[1] i.e. the Genoa Conference (see Vol. XIX, Chap. III).

propaganda through its entourage. A good deal will depend on whether the Conference itself makes a firm stand against these things and also whether the delegation is able to score a success by obtaining its principal object, viz. *de jure* recognition.

At all events the Soviet Government is preparing with all its might for the Conference, and has already prepared a programme dealing with the following points:—pre-war debts, war debts, indemnity for material losses arising out of the various foreign invasions of Russia, return of the warships and merchant vessels evacuated from Russian ports by Denikin and Yudenitch, international settlement of the East, international settlement of the question of the economic reconstruction of Russia on a basis elaborated at Moscow, the details of which are not yet known, settlement of commercial, industrial and financial relations, Consular arrangements, question of nationalities—and exchange.

The Soviet delegation will also present in connection with debts a bill for damage inflicted on Russia by the Allies in the Civil wars of Kolchak, Denikin, Yudenitch, Wrangel, etc. As soon as the Cannes decision[2] reached Moscow, orders were given, all over Russia, to prepare this bill as quickly as possible, and by the methods employed by the Peace Conference in regard to Germany and her Allies. The object is threefold (a) to prove that the Allied Powers owe Russia more than she owes them: (b) to make Germany's position easier in the matter of reparations and give her an opportunity of raising that question: (c) as a means of stirring up trouble in the various countries against Governments and making them weaker vis-à-vis the Soviet Government. In this connection the 'Pravda' states that Soviet Russia will never consent to take advantage of Article 116 of the Treaty of Versailles, which gives her the right to demand reparations from Germany. 'Russia', it says, 'would discredit herself in the eyes of the German proletariat if she made use of this right! She prefers to dispense with the Treaty of Versailles.'

Chicherin in an interview given to the 'Novi Mir', a paper edited at Berlin (Jan. 25, 1922), explained that the attitude of the Soviet Delegation at Genoa [was] to be:— 'The French press, in its anxiety to *sabotage* the International Economic Conference, says that the Soviet Government is going to Genoa not for negotiations but in order to create a centre at Genoa for revolutionary propaganda. This information is entirely inaccurate. The Russian Government has been trying for ages to enter into peaceful relations with other States and is endeavouring to arrange these relations in such a way that Russia can take her part in the general economic life of the world.' The 'Pravda' of January 12th had however in the meantime explained that the Genoa Conference represented merely another phase of the struggle against foreign Imperialism; whereupon Chicherin declared that, the 'Pravda' not being an official organ of the Soviet Government, the latter could not be responsible for its opinions. This in the face of the known intimate relations between Radek, the editor, and the Soviet Government.

Trotsky, on his side, has given an interview, which was published in the

[2] See Vol. XIX, No. 6, Appendix.

English press on January 22nd, in which he also asserts that the Bolsheviks are going to Genoa with a conciliatory programme. Red Russia, he says, would be perfectly ready to disarm, if only the other countries, including France, would do likewise. In this case she would limit her forces to the equivalent of those maintained by the Little Entente. Counter claims on account of Allied intervention in Russia will certainly be put forward as a set off to the demand for a recognition of her debts: but a claim for damage caused by the German invasion will also be made and no deduction will be allowed on account of the Russian invasion of East Prussia. This is in contradiction to the statement previously mentioned that the Soviet Government does not intend to demand reparations under Article 116 of the Treaty of Versailles. Yet the same object may be achieved, namely to give Germany an opportunity of bringing up the question of reparations by showing at the instance of the Soviet delegation the defects in the allied calculations under the Treaty of Versailles. As, however, present day Russia is really not in a position to make serious demands on Germany, as the battle fields were all on what is now non-Russian territory, it may be that Trotsky's real object is to destroy an impression created by the entire Soviet press that the Soviet delegation and the German delegation are going to work hand in hand. The pacific utterances with regard to the reduction of the Red Army are in striking contrast to a speech made by him in December 1921 in which he insisted on the maintenance of a great army not merely for the defence of Russia but for revolutionary purposes and also with a secret circular of the Third International dated December 8th, 1921 instructing its agents to work for a reduction of foreign armies and the formation of revolutionary centres among the new recruits, who are easier than the old men to deal with.

The inference from all this is that the Soviet leaders are merely throwing dust in the eyes of the Western world and that the real intentions of the Soviet Government at Genoa will be other than they profess. Both wings of the Communist party will really be regarding the Conference as a further step in their struggle to bring about a world revolution. There is nothing extraordinary about this, as it is in accord with their character, both as Russians and Bolsheviks. Students of Russian mentality are never tired of pointing out that the essential characteristic of the Russian is to concern itself with the world rather than with Russia and the Russian people. The latter is essentially Messianic and its desire to bring happiness to humanity as a whole invariably prevents Russians from being happy themselves. The main success of Bolshevism has been its appeal to the romanticism of the Russian people—the belief that Russia was predestined to save the world by setting an example and bearing the sacrifice it entails. To expect therefore a cessation of propaganda is to expect the Russians to change their nature.

At the present moment the resources of the Soviet Government are in a bad way, and in order to improve its organisation and obtain funds for its struggle with the outer world, it wishes to get hold of foreign capital. The latter is in fact indispensable to it, if it is to survive. But capital can only be introduced into Russia on its own conditions, and these conditions are political rather than economic. The economic disorder is the result of political disorder and the remedy must therefore be political. The Russian people of all classes and shades of opinion is still, however, extremely sensitive and national pride is by no means dead. Conditions calculated to wound that pride will result only in uniting all Russians in defence of their country. But a demand for civic liberty and a minimum of personal security, not merely for foreigners, but for Russians themselves who must collaborate in the economic reconstruction of their country, far from being regarded as an undue interference in the internal affairs of Russia, will be actually welcomed by the people. It is moreover essential. A foreign capitalist cannot invest his capital in large enterprises without being certain that he will get a return. He cannot rebuild a factory or a railway without being certain that one fine day the Cheka will not descend on his engineers and workmen and lock them up. A proper judicial system is then absolutely a pre-requisite to trade, and the Soviet Government will be bound in the end, if the Powers are firm, to accept this as a condition. But it will nevertheless constitute a distinct practical danger for the Soviet régime. If a number of foreign enterprises are introduced into Russia and, at any rate at the beginning, there is a special jurisdiction guaranteeing personal liberty against the arbitrary action of Bolshevik officials and if these little oases of civilisation flourish and compare favourably with their communist surroundings, public opinion may easily agitate for an extension of the system throughout the country. Should the Bolsheviks thereupon try and destroy these oases, then they will have to forego the help of foreign capital. Once the Cheka loses its power, one of the chief supports of the Soviet régime will have disappeared.

The final consideration refers to the elements on which the Soviet Government is counting at Genoa to achieve the maximum of success with the minimum of sacrifice. Both the Bolshevik press and the Soviet leaders have disclosed them on various occasions. Their intention is to try and obtain *de jure* recognition first and credits afterwards, and to be able to dispose of these credits themselves. In this they will no doubt be grievously disappointed. But where they may partially succeed, if the plans of the principal Governments represented are not carefully laid beforehand and faithfully carried out, is to play off one Power against another, if not in the political, at least in the economic field. An essential condition of any economic arrangement is a common plan whereby the capital of all countries will collaborate. The Soviet Government hopes to attract foreign capital group by group and remain absolute master of its disposal, and it will be on the lookout for and take advantage of every jealousy that exists between countries and between the finance of each country and try and set one against another. Unity of front is therefore vital.

The Soviet Government is counting on the general weakness of the Powers who will confront it at Genoa. But it is singularly ill-informed. *Inter alia* it is convinced that England will be obliged to make terms with it for three reasons: (a) because she regards the Soviet Government as a formidable adversary in the world of Islam with which she wishes to be on good terms: (b) because the British working classes are so powerful and ready to revolt that they have been able to impose their will on the British Government: (c) because the economic condition of England is so disastrous and British trade in such a bad way that it can only be saved by an agreement with Russia at any price. The Soviet Government is, besides, counting on the support of Germany and close collaboration with the Germans. It thinks it can bring about the formation of a Russo-German-British-Italian *bloc* which will impose its ideas on the Conference. It is not bothering much about France, thinking that she is too absorbed in her own reconstruction to help Russia effectively. Politically the Bolsheviks are under the impression that if they can succeed in releasing Germany from the payments which she has to make under the Treaty of Versailles, that will isolate France from England on one side, and from Italy and the United States on the other, and will completely paralyse her. With the smaller Powers in Central Europe, the Soviet Government is not concerning itself, believing that their political and economic disorder will prevent them from taking part in any political or economic scheme. As regards Japan it thinks that she can be paralysed in her dealings with Russia by the jealousy between herself and America. This is why the Bolsheviks attach so much importance to American participation in the Conference. They also think that the economic reconstruction of Europe is impossible without American help.

As a result of all this the Bolsheviks hope to score an easy victory at Genoa by gaining *de jure* recognition (which is all they care about) without having to give effective guarantees, and they think they will be able to postpone all discussions on the economic reconstruction of Russia with its consequences and conditions to a later date when with their new recognised status they will be in a better position to deal with the Powers and pursue their object of dividing them in order to triumph over the capitalist world. The Russian Communists who formerly were fiercest in their denunciations of France are now saying that they wish for nothing better than close and friendly collaboration with her. This is simply a manœuvre for being able to put pressure on Germany by threatening her with a rapprochement with France. This theory is being developed at length in the German papers which Radek can either control or influence. It may also be that another object is to bring pressure on England and also to place the French Government in a difficult position with the French working classes over the Genoa Conference.[3]

---

[3] Lord Curzon minuted on February 15: 'One may differ as to the tactics that will be employed (I do not believe e.g. that the Russians mean first and foremost to propagandise) but that their one cardinal object is recognition seems to be indisputable.'

No. 482

Mr. Grove (Moscow) to the Marquess Curzon of Kedleston
(Received March 1, 10.05 p.m.)
No. 48 Telegraphic [N 1999/1999/38]

MOSCOW, *March 1, 1922, 7.15 p.m.*

Press today publishes an order issued by Trotsky February 28th to Red army and fleet, warning them that owing to postponement of Genoa conference[1] they can have no assurance regarding safety of their frontiers, calling on all their energy in work of preparation of armies,[2] and reminding them that inviolability of Soviet Russia depends on their might.

Translation following by bag.[3]

[1] See Vol. XIX, No. 34, minutes 6 and 16.
[2] In reply to a Parliamentary Question of March 2, Mr. Harmsworth stated: 'As far as His Majesty's Government are aware, the numerical strength of the Russian standing army was on the 1st of January last about 1,200,000.'
[3] No. 117 of March 1 (N 2394/1999/38), not printed.

No. 483

The Marquess Curzon of Kedleston to Mr. Grove (Moscow)
No. 71 Telegraphic [N 2189/1185/38]

FOREIGN OFFICE, *March 10, 1922, 1 p.m.*

Your telegram No. 42.[1]

A telegram[2] has been received from Murmansk dated 5th March from British trawler 'St. Hubert' of Hull reporting that she had been arrested and taken to Murmansk.

Both 'St. Hubert' and 'Magneta' were, when arrested, nine or ten miles from the shore and at no time approached within three mile limit.[3]

His Majesty's Government cannot recognise Russian claim to extend territorial waters beyond three miles. They have on previous occasions insisted that British fishing vessels must not be interfered with outside that limit. His Majesty's Government have moreover specifically protested against Soviet decree of 24th May 1921 prohibiting fishing by foreign vessels within twelve-mile limit.[4]

You should immediately protest in strongest terms against this unjustifiable interference with British shipping and demand an assurance that such interference will not be repeated. You should ask for the immediate release of the 'St. Hubert' and her crew and claim compensation for any loss incurred by her detention, and demand compensation for the owners of the 'Magneta', the two survivors and the families of the ten men drowned.

[1] Of February 22 (N 1759/1185/38), not printed. [2] Not printed.
[3] The 'Magneta' had been arrested on January 31, and the 'St. Hubert' on March 3, 1922.
[4] See No. 364, n. 1.

854

Mr. Rennie (Helsingfors) to the Marquess Curzon of Kedleston
(Received March 20)
No. 90 [N 2639/2/38]

HELSINGFORS, *March 14, 1922*

My Lord Marquess,

With reference to my despatch No. 77 of February 27th,[1] I have the honour to report that there appear to be no fresh developments in the relations between Finland and Russia regarding the Karelian question,[2] the conversations between Dr. Holsti and the Soviet Representative here being temporarily suspended with the former's departure last week to attend the Warsaw Conference.[3] The general situation has, however, improved; trade, which was forbidden at the end of last year, is now being resumed, the Soviet Government have agreed to the repatriation of some 5,000 Finnish citizens still in Russia, the Mixed Commission will shortly, it is stated, resume work and another Commission is to be instituted to examine questions relating to frontier difficulties and, further, the Finnish Government is to be allowed to send corn and flour into East Karelia.

Although the scare that prevailed here among the general public, occasioned by the Bolshevik attitude at Christmas time, has now greatly subsided, it would appear that the higher military authorities are not yet fully assured that the threat of a military move may not be renewed in the course of the spring. The Chief of the General Staff told me yesterday that he had received information that the Soviet Government had brought out a cavalry brigade to the neighbourhood of Petrograd, within an easy distance of the Finnish frontier. The Russian authorities, too, had been trying to purchase oats in considerable amounts. These two facts were, General Enckell contended, in themselves suspicious. Moreover, he added, the staff had received information of large consignments of arms being shipped to Petrograd; he asked if nothing could be done to prevent this, and whether I had not received from the Foreign Ministry the evidence he had submitted to that Department. I told him the only information I had received under this heading related to the two vessels mentioned by His Majesty's Consul at Reval in his Telegram No. 109 of December 24th, 1921.[4] General Enckell replied that these were not the only consignments, and said he would send me further details. In the course of our brief talk, it was evident that he was considerably preoccupied as to the course which events might take on the

---

[1] Not printed.

[2] Mr. Ovey minuted (March 23): 'The Karelian dispute is gradually fizzling out.' In his despatch No. 351 of October 30, 1922, Mr. Ogilvie-Forbes (Chargé d'Affaires at Helsingfors) transmitted to the Foreign Office a Green Book (*Livre Vert: Actes et Documents Concernant la Question Karélienne*, Helsinki, 1922) published by the Karelian Delegation. Part I consists of Karelian official documents; Part II contains translations into French of Russian official documents; Part III gives official documents concerning the Karelian question as an international issue.

[3] See No. 479.

[4] Not printed.

Eastern frontier in the spring, in the event of the Bolshevists being dissatisfied with their reception at the Genoa Conference[5] and the results.

The French Military Attaché here takes a much less serious view of the situation. He has told me that he considers that the Bolshevist threat against Finland had been intentionally magnified for purposes connected with interior politics, in order to assist the Government in the Diet in the matter of the Bill regulating the period of military service—which has now been postponed until after the coming elections—and contends that general conditions in Russia, and particularly the state of the railways, must prevent any offensive movement on a large scale. He admits, however, that the state of mind of 'des fous' must always be taken into account, especially if they return from the Genoa Conference with nothing to enable them to prolong the now precarious existence of the present régime.

I have, etc.,
ERNEST RENNIE

[5] See Vol. XIX, No. 67.

No. 485

Mr. Grove (Moscow) to the Marquess Curzon of Kedleston
(Received March 18, 8.30 a.m.)
Unnumbered Telegraphic [*N 2599/246/38*]

MOSCOW, *March 17, 1922, 6 p.m.*

Warsaw No. 57 of March 15th.[1]

There is some evidence to show that extremists of communistic party are gaining upper hand in the government. Split in party (see my telegram No. 56 of March [10]th[2] and my despatch No. 127 of March 7th[2] and 154 of March 17th)[2] appears to have been caused by invitation to Genoa.[3] Difficulties created by postponements of conference[4] and elaborate preliminary conditions seem to have made position of Soviet government more precarious and to have enabled extremists to rally to the call of danger and thereby extend their influence.

Evidence of this can be seen in Trotsky's order to Red army and fleet (see my despatch No. 117 of March 1st),[5] Lenin's speech to Moscow metal workers (see my telegram No. 56 of March [10]th),[2] Trotsky's speech to Moscow Soviet (see my despatch No. 155 of March 17th)[2] Krassin's interview to a Soviet newspaper (see my despatch No. 144 of March 13th),[2] and in recent attitude of the press (see my despatch No. 156 of March 17th).[2]

Whether this influence of extremists will continue to extend or not, probably depends largely on the state of Lenin's health regarding which

[1] Not printed. This reported that the Polish Minister of Foreign Affairs had stated that on March 14 he had received a note from the Soviet Government threatening measures would be taken if the Polish Government failed to prevent violation of the frontier by bands.

[2] Not printed.　　　　　　　　　　　　　[3] See Vol. XIX, No. 19, Appendix 1.
[4] See ibid., No. 34, minutes 6 and 16.　　　[5] Not printed. See, however, No. 482.

I have hitherto been unable to obtain authentic information. It is possible that their influence is already sufficient to assist the work of any delegation sent to Genoa and that if it extends further policy of economic co-operation with capitalism may be supplanted by more aggressive tactics.

Repeated to Warsaw, Helsingfors and Riga.

No. 486

Mr. Grove (Moscow) to the Marquess Curzon of Kedleston
(Received March 25, 8.30 a.m.)

No. 70 Telegraphic [N 2861/1185/38]

MOSCOW, *March 24, 1922, 5.7 p.m.*

My telegram No. 65 of March 21st.[1]

In official reply Commissary of Foreign Affairs after quoting records of international conference at Geneva in October 1921[2] and of sub-committee of Barcelona conference in the spring of 1921[3] to show that question of mileage limit of territorial waters remains unsettled in international law, states that Soviet government felt itself free to issue decree setting a twelve-mile limit on northern coast of Russia. Two ships in question having been arrested in conformity with this decree,[4] Soviet government cannot entertain any claim for compensation or give assurances required by British government.

Commissary of Foreign Affairs has again been asked for release of the 'St. Hubert' and her crew and information regarding the two survivors of 'Magneta' concerning which there is no mention in their reply, copy of which follows by next bag.[5]

[1] Not printed.

[2] It was at this conference that the Convention respecting the Non-Fortification and Neutralisation of the Åland Islands was concluded (see *B.F.S.P.*, vol. 114, pp. 421–6).

[3] The Barcelona Conference was held between March 10 and April 20, 1921. The reference is to the records of the sub-commission on territorial waters.

[4] See No. 483.

[5] Despatch No. 188 of April 4 (N 3690/1185/38), not printed.

No. 487

Mr. Rennie (Helsingfors) to the Marquess Curzon of Kedleston
(Received March 25, 7.30 p.m.)

No. 58 Telegraphic [N 2867/246/38]

HELSINGFORS, *March 25, 1922, 6.40 p.m.*

Following from Naval Attaché[1] (begins).

From different most reliable sources news has been received of projected extent of mobilization in Soviet Russia. In addition to classes of 1899, 1901

[1] Captain J. Wolfe-Murray.

and part of 1902 still under arms, orders to prepare to mobilize have been issued to classes of 1897 and 98, and preliminary work has been done to call in men of 1891 class and onwards. All ex-officers, ex-non-commissioned officers have been told to prepare for instant mobilization and in frontier districts all men up to 1886 [class] have been registered.

It is further stated that Bolsheviks intend to commission ten extra torpedo boats now under repair. Two German ex-officers Neumann and Treckell are stated to be members of revolutionary war council. It is further rumoured that Soviet intend to move twenty torpedo boats with German sailors. Please inform Admiralty (ends).²

Chief of General Staff confirms most of above which I have also heard from other reliable diplomatic source. He added that some 160 hospital stations have been organised along the Russian west front and that military stores are being collected along Petrograd-Moscow railway. It is somewhat curious that German Military Attaché yesterday telephoned to Finnish staff headquarters and volunteered warning that reports regarding mobilisation in Russia were not to be credited.

Repeated to Moscow.

² On March 27 Mr. Ovey minuted: 'The Admiralty view is that they have nothing to fear from the Bolshevik fleet so long as it is manned and organised entirely by Russians.

'The introduction into it of German officers would however entirely alter the situation: its improvement by means of German material would also be serious.

'I have consulted the Central European Department who point out that by Article 179 of the Treaty of Versailles: "Germany agrees to take appropriate measures to prevent German nationals from leaving her territory to become enrolled in the Army, Navy or Air Service of any foreign power, or to be attached etc., or otherwise for the purpose of giving military, naval or air instruction in any foreign country."

'They feel, and I agree, that it would be practically impossible, however, to enforce this in the case of Russia, where the army probably contains many German officers.'

No. 488

Mr. Wilton (Riga) to the Marquess Curzon of Kedleston
(Received March 25, 8.55 p.m.)
No. 33 Telegraphic [N 2868/1171/38]

RIGA, *March 25, 1922, 7 p.m.*

My telegram No. 29.¹

I have gathered in private conversation with Lettish Foreign Minister that secret discussion took place between the four foreign ministers² on two subjects

¹ Of March 20, not printed.

² i.e. of the four powers meeting in Warsaw (see No. 479). In his telegram No. 34 of March 25, Mr. Wilton reported: 'Foreign Minister has given me very confidentially copy of secret protocol concluded at Warsaw. It is in two parts, (A) and (B): (A) Economic questions and adoption of common diplomatic front at Moscow as regards Russian treaties; (B) General co-ordination of policy and concerted action at Genoa. Polish Government engages to endeavour to secure support at Genoa of her allies, especially Little *Entente*, to common programme of Warsaw and three other States.'

of international spheres of economic influence in Russia and of Russian debts. No minutes of this discussion were recorded. According to Minister for Foreign Affairs both proposals were inspired by French and introduced apologetically by Polish Minister for Foreign Affairs.

First embraced four zones.

1. Petrograd (industrial)
2. Vologda (timber)
3. Caucasus (oil)
4. Don Basin (coal)

Four ministers agreed in principle to general exploitation of Russia by international syndicates but declined to support zone proposition.

As regards Russian debts, Polish minister shared view that Russian treaties[3] absolved Esthonia and Latvia.

I am informed from a trustworthy source that Foreign Minister in conversation with French minister March 22nd suggested that claim against Baltic States for share of Russian debts should not appear on Genoa agenda.[4] Otherwise, he hinted, it would be opposed by a block consisting of Little Entente and signatories of Warsaw agreement.

Repeated to Warsaw and Helsingfors.

[3] A reference to the treaties of peace between Russia and Esthonia of February 2, 1920, and Russia and Latvia of August 11, 1920. For sources, see Slusser and Triska, pp. 8–9 and 12 respectively.
[4] Cf. Vol. XIX, Nos. 56 and 61.

No. 489

The Marquess Curzon of Kedleston to Mr. Hodgson[1] (Moscow)
No. 90 Telegraphic [N 2861/1185/38]

FOREIGN OFFICE, *March 31, 1922, 6.30 p.m.*

Your telegram No. 70.[2]

You should inform Soviet government that His Majesty's Government are arranging to send without delay a vessel to protect their fishing interests in these waters.

You should add that the officer in command of His Majesty's ship will have instructions to take such action as may be necessary to prevent interference with any British vessel fishing outside the three-mile territorial limit.

[1] Mr. Hodgson had resumed his duties in Moscow on March 27.
[2] No. 486.

No. 490

Lord D'Abernon (Berlin) to the Marquess Curzon of Kedleston
(Received April 5, 8.30 a.m.)
No. 94 Telegraphic [N 3234/646/38]

BERLIN, *April 4, 1922, 10 p.m.*

Chicherin publishes interview warmly praising the Prime Minister's allusion to disarmament[1] and stating that Soviet will support this policy at Genoa.

Agreement already come to between Russia and Polish border states[2] is an earnest of Russia's intentions.[3]

[1] In his speech in the House of Commons on April 3 (see 152 *H.C. Deb. 5 s*, cols. 1885–1904).

[2] See Vol. XIX, No. 47, n. 2.

[3] Mr. Leeper minuted (April 6): 'The Soviet promise to disarm would certainly be made to depend upon obtaining *de jure* recognition all round. As they are not likely to obtain this, the promise will merely be used for propaganda purposes against France.'

No. 491

Mr. Hodgson (Moscow) to the Marquess Curzon of Kedleston
(Received April 18)
No. 207 [N 3625/1185/38]

MOSCOW, *April 11, 1922*

My Lord Marquess,

I have the honour to transmit, herewith, copy of a communication which, in accordance with instructions conveyed in Your Lordship's telegram No. 90 of April 1st last,[1] I addressed to M. Karakhan—now replacing M. Chicherin—on the 4th instant with regard to the protection of British fishing interests on the northern coast of Russia.

I discussed the matter with M. Karakhan in the course of interviews on the 5th and 8th instant, and have been promised an official reply to my communication within the next few days.

My conversations did not reveal any change in the attitude of the Soviet Government.

M. Karakhan maintained the argument that in the absence of any International Act, universally agreed, regulating the extent of territorial waters, the Soviet Government, like any other, was entitled to fix a limit in accordance with what it conceived to be the interests of Russia: the fisheries off the Northern Coast of Russia were the property of the Russian people just as much as her forests: Great Britain had no justification in international law to support her contention in favour of the three-mile limit—indeed, she had herself established a closed zone around her coasts exceeding three miles

[1] No. 489. This telegram was dated March 31.

860

in breadth. He added that he had of course communicated to M. Chicherin the announcement that Great Britain intended to have recourse to armed force in order to establish her views, and that this news would certainly create a most unfortunate impression in Genoa. Russia's Naval Forces in the North were, he admitted, insignificant, but they would do what they could to protect Russia's rights.

I urged that international law was created by the custom of nations, and it was impossible to admit that an individual nation could by a simple declaration establish its rights over what was recognised by general practice to be the property of the whole world. The ocean was the property not of one nation but of all, and the principle which Russia sought to uphold would enable any nation to declare exclusive rights over whatever area of the high seas might happen to suit it. Russia could fix today a limit of her territorial waters at 12 miles, tomorrow at 25 miles, and so on ad infinitum. A country with a powerful fleet could declare all the surrounding seas to be necessary for its exclusive use. As a fact, all countries, even those which, like Norway, were dependent largely upon the fishing industry, had fallen into line with universal usage and had disallowed the occasional attempts made, e.g. by Spain, to extend arbitrarily her territorial waters.

In reply to his observation that Great Britain had herself insisted at times on her territorial zone extending beyond three miles, I stated that he was misinformed in this matter, and that, though for revenue and sanitary purposes we exercise rights beyond three miles from our coasts, this had nothing to do with the question of territorial waters as to which we had never varied our practice.

I further submitted that not the Soviet Delegation at Genoa alone would be painfully impressed by the recent incident, but that the position taken up by Russia in insisting upon maintaining an attitude in conflict with an international custom definitely established and universally practised was unlikely to meet with the sympathy of the other nations participating in the Conference.[2]

I have, etc.,
R. M. HODGSON

[2] See Vol. XIX, Chap. III.

No. 492

Mr. Rennie (Helsingfors) to the Marquess Curzon of Kedleston
(Received May 2)

No. 145 [N 4181/646/38]

HELSINGFORS, *April 22, 1922*

My Lord Marquess,

Dr. Holsti came to see me today, in order to talk over the general situation and, in particular, to ask whether I had any special information regarding the situation that had arisen, owing to the signature of the German-Russian Commercial Agreement.[1] I told Dr. Holsti that I knew nothing beyond the telegrams I had seen in the papers and that I was, therefore, unable to give him any inside news. I said that it seemed to me that the evident object of the announcement made at Genoa was to bring new elements into the proceedings of the conference and was an attempt to show that the Soviet were in a stronger position than the Allied Powers anticipated. It had for some time been evident that Germany was trying to get into closer touch with Russia, e.g., it seemed an undoubted fact that German officers had been employed on the General Staff in reorganising the Russian Army, and that there were other, but rather indefinite, stories of a growing co-operation between the two countries which was, at least, greater than that between Russia and any other foreign State.

Dr. Holsti said that he was considerably preoccupied by the German-Russian *rapprochement*, and he thought that one of the principal lines of communication between the two Governments was the German Legation and the Russian Delegation at Helsingfors, in both of which Missions were German officers who had formerly been employed in Russia, and he mentioned in this connection Captain von Kotze, of the German Legation, who acts as Attaché and Press Agent, and Captain Hoffman, who is in charge of the passport section of the Bolshevik delegation, who had formerly been employed by the German Government on a mission to Moscow. He then repeated what I have already reported in previous despatches, namely, that the German Legation here was extremely active and was also making use of the Lithuanian Chargé d'Affaires. Their policy seemed to be a revival of the German policy of two years ago. They were spreading rumours that a German-Russian entente had the object of putting an end to the existence of the newly-formed States on the southern shores of the Baltic, which would be pressed to renounce their independence in favour of some system of federation with Russia which would give the latter a complete outlet to the Baltic, while Germany would be allowed to regain her former economic and cultural predominance in these States. The Socialists were, accordingly, being told here that they must await events, as a couple of years would show how dangerous a formal alliance with Latvia and Esthonia would be to this country, while the Swedish parties here were being urged to oppose the Polish connection and to advocate the need for Finland to enter into closer connections with Sweden and, through Sweden, with Germany. In this manner, Finland, for the present, was to be deterred from engaging herself in any 'entangling alliances' and would then later on be in a position to associate herself with any Russo-German understanding which might grow up in the near future. Dr. Holsti seemed to think that there thus seemed to be nothing new in the Russo-German Treaty so far as Finland was concerned; the present position was merely a revival, in a rather more acute form, of the situation of a few years ago. As to the question of ratifying the Warsaw Agreement,[2] much, he said, would depend on the attitude of Dr. Vennola,

[1] See Vol. XIX, No. 75. [2] See No. 488, n. 2.

who was expected to return from Genoa in the early days of May, in order to answer the interpellations in the Diet regarding the Warsaw Conference, and to communicate the impressions which he would have derived of the Genoa Conference. Nevertheless, he could not but feel a certain amount of anxiety regarding the Russian-German propaganda which was here being circulated. (I may mention in this connection that, though the German propaganda in this country does not receive funds directly from the German Government, substantial sums for this purpose are derived from the German Cinema Company, who own several theatres and who, I am told on good authority, devote the profits to propaganda purposes.) Events of the last months certainly all tend to show that a strenuous attempt is now proceeding to divert the policy of President Ståhlberg and his Cabinet from Entente to a German-Russian orientation.

The press, for the first days after the news became known of the German-Russian Treaty, seemed at a loss as to how to comment on the situation. The 'Iltalehti' (Finnish Right) of today now states that the treaty cannot have come as a surprise, as the attitude of the Western Powers towards Germany could not but compel the latter to seek for Russian support and a field for commercial development; while their tactics towards Communistic Russia could only result in the latter seeking an alliance with Germany, which was suffering under the Versailles Treaty.

The 'Svenska Press' (now allied with the 'Hufvudstadsbladet', but more actively pro-German) asks whether Finland has been pursuing a proper course in her policy of hatred towards Russia and also towards Germany, who saved her from the Red Terror.

The 'Sosialidemokraatti' considers that the Treaty is the natural result of the Allied policy towards both States and declares that, come what may of the Genoa Conference, the capitalistic States will be compelled to come to terms with both Germany and Russia.

A copy of this despatch is being sent to His Majesty's Ambassador at Berlin.

I have, etc.,
ERNEST RENNIE

No. 493

Mr. Hodgson (Moscow) to the Marquess Curzon of Kedleston
(Received May 1)
No. 239 [N 4119/155/38]

MOSCOW, *April 24, 1922*

My Lord Marquess,
    With reference to my despatch No. 199 of April 10th,[1] I have the honour to report that I was in error in stating that the Concessions Committee of the

---
[1] Not printed.

Supreme Council of National Economy has been dissolved. Both this Committee and those established by the People's Commissariat of Land and the People's Commissariat of Ways and Communications still exist and report on concessions in their respective spheres, but the ultimate decision is now taken by the Central Committee referred to in my despatch No. 215 of the 13th instant.[1]

2. From a reliable but confidential source, I have received the following information regarding applications for concessions from various countries now under consideration by the Supreme Council of National Economy.

(i) A German group representing the Deutsche Bank is negotiating for a concession in Grosny. The area covers two plots, each of approximately 250 acres of undeveloped but proved land in the 5th Section of old Grosny. This land is State land and it is reported that Mr. Smilga[2] has been sent to Berlin to carry on these negotiations. He is understood to have arrived at an agreement.

It will be remembered (see my despatch No. 56 of January 31st)[3] that Mr. Smilga was one of the opponents of the concession policy as regards the oil industry. His conversion is believed to be due to direct instructions from the Political Bureau of the Communist Party.

(ii) The *Gutehoffnungshütte* has filed an application for the Kramatorsky Iron Works, some iron mines in the Krivoi Rog district and coal mines in the basin of the Donetz.

There was a hitch for a long time over the question of exporting the very valuable Krivoi Rog ore. The Russians were not inclined to permit the export of more than 15% of the output, to which the Germans would not agree. However, direct orders were received from the Political Bureau of the Party that the Germans were to be permitted to export 50% of the output. Lenin is understood to have written a personal letter to Bogdanov[4] in this sense.

(iii) The German firm of Karo, Michael and Company is negotiating for a concession for fisheries and hunting in the White Sea, with a view to fish and seal oil production. It is suggested that this concession should be combined with the operation of the Krestovnikov Soap and Candle Works at Kazan.

3. It is of interest to note that although as a general rule applications are only considered for definite propositions, in these two latter [*sic*] cases the propositions were put forward by the Supreme Council of National Economy to the Germans in accordance with special instructions from the Political Bureau of the Communist Party.

4. Other German applications under consideration are:

from a shipbuilding concern (the name is given as 'Gotebocker Werf') for shipbuilding plant at Nikolaiev;

from Rabetke and Giesekke for the return of their sugar beet seed plantations on a concession basis;

from Konig for a sugar refinery;

[2] Vice-President of the Supreme Council of National Economy (see also No. 475).
[3] No. 475.   [4] See Nos. 435 and 475.

from Rudgers for a concession for 16 sleeper impregnating factories; and seven other applications of less interest and in a more nebulous state.

5. It is reported that within the last three weeks definite instructions have been issued by the Political Bureau of the Communist Party to give favourable replies to German applications and to override the objections of the Russian interests.

6. Two French applications are under consideration. One from Paul Sicault (Paris) for a concession for the Renault works at Rybinsk, the construction of which was commenced during the war with funds advanced by the Ministry of War; a second from the firm of Ferrar and Gontran of Marseilles for sericulture in the Caucasus. The latter firm had a very extensive concession from the Menshevik Government of Georgia and paid in advance a sum of one million francs. This concession gave the firm a practical monopoly of the silk grain and filature industry in the Caucasus.

7. The application of the Belgian Société Petrole de Grozny for a return on a concession basis of its holdings has been refused.

8. A Norwegian group headed by Arensen has proposed to establish factories to produce 20,000 standard wooden houses per year in return for a timber concession.

9. Two American proposals are under consideration, one from an engineer named Deitrichs for an irrigation scheme in the Ili Valley in Turkestan, which he proposed to develop in conjunction with a coal concession from the Chinese Government in the Kuldya territory, and a recent application from the Associated Welding Corporation for a monopoly for electric welding in Petrograd for a period of five years.

10. Two applications from Russians are being considered, one from Kuznetsov (of the Pereaslavskaya Manufactures) now in Berlin, for an irrigation concession in Ferghana. This application is believed to be backed by French capital. The second is from a group of Russian engineers under Masloff for a railway from Petschore to Petropavlovsk, including the exploitation of the timber and minerals along the line.

11. The only concession so far granted in a final form remains the Asbestos Concession in the Urals. A preliminary agreement has been concluded with an American group for the operation of the Kousnetski coalmines in Siberia and it is reported that work is to be commenced on this proposition. The Anglo-Russian and Dutch-Russian timber concession (Anglo-Russko Les and Gollando-Russko Les) are on the point of signature.

The above information has been obtained from a member of the Concessions Committee whose identity would be disclosed were it to become public property. I have the honour to request that, for this reason, it should not be made available for other than official purposes.

I have, etc.,

R. M. HODGSON

No. 494

The Marquess Curzon of Kedleston to Mr. Gregory (Genoa)
No. 57 Telegraphic [N 4146/646/38]

Urgent　　　　　　　　　　　　FOREIGN OFFICE, *May 1, 1922, 4.50 p.m.*
Following for Prime Minister from Lord Privy Seal.
Confidential.
Press telegrams from Rev[a]l dated April 27th announce that at a meeting of Third International held at Moscow it was decided to intensify Communist propaganda in Great Britain and France and that the sum of five million gold roubles was allocated for this purpose.

Most Secret
I learn from secret and very reliable source that some such sum has been sent from Russia one-third to Genoa delegation for expenditure there and two-thirds for Western Europe propaganda.

No. 495

Mr. Hodgson (Moscow) to the Marquess Curzon of Kedleston
(Received May 8)
No. 264 [N 4418/2169/38]

Confidential　　　　　　　　　　　　MOSCOW, *May 2, 1922*
My Lord Marquess,
　In my despatch No. 239 of April 24th[1] I mentioned that, in accordance with secret instructions received from the Political Bureau, the Concessions Committee has recently adopted an attitude favourable to proposals emanating from German groups.
　The Soviet Government, having succeeded in concluding the recent agreement with Germany,[2] would now appear to have definitely embarked upon a course leading to the establishment of intimate relations with that country. I am not, however, prepared yet to venture an opinion as to how far the new attitude of the Soviet Government indicates a real change of policy and how far it is of a provocatory nature designed to impress other countries with a sense of impending peril.
　In Mr. Grove's despatch No. 159[3] was mentioned a scheme, which appears to have been under consideration for several months, for restoring the Bolshevik fleet by the aid of Germany. According to this plan the ships were to be sold to Germany who would place crews on board and at once set about repairing them, with a view to using them for joint action in the event of complications between France and Germany leading to the outbreak of hostilities. I was informed a few weeks ago that, though these negotiations

---

[1] No. 493.　　　[2] See Vol. XIX, No. 75, and No. 492, above.
[3] Of March 21, not printed.

had not been concluded, it was probable that an agreement would be reached. The point under discussion at the time was whether the Germans should take over the whole fleet of 38 or 40 units or whether they should take only the half of that number. I have since been told that they have taken twenty ships and it is reported that at all events a part of the personnel has arrived at Kronstadt. The matter has, of course, been kept a strict secret, and even now I cannot definitely state that the transaction has taken place, but the reports in circulation are so circumstantial that it is impossible to dismiss them lightly. The fact that Admiral Hin[t]ze[4] spent a considerable time here during the last few months may very possibly have a connection with this matter.

I am, moreover, informed that arrangements have been made between Russia and Germany for the supply by the latter of artillery, and that preparations are being made in the shape of special instruction in the military schools for dealing with the guns when they arrive. The breech blocks have, it is said, already been received and the guns are expected via Petrograd by early sailings.

The Czecho-Slovak Representative here, who mentioned this matter to me the other day, was of opinion that the artillery would be shipped through Sweden but I do not know what ground he has for this suggestion.

Preparations have, it is believed, been made for dealing with the position which will arise in the event of an advance of the Red Army into Poland. Special 'Cheka' officials have been designated—naturally the most barbarous and vindictive which this organisation can provide—for taking charge of the different centres on the line of march and there exercising unrestricted 'terror'.

The question of the supply of small arms by Germany for Russia came up in connection with the Berchielli contract[5] of last year. I gather that no confirmation of the existence of the arrangement reported at the time was received. However, a former officer of the Russian Navy, now an Esthonian subject, who is in close touch with the General Staff here, asserts that the contract was, in fact, signed and, at all events, partly executed. He maintains that the arms were brought down the Rhine and shipped via Hamburg in the fall of last year on vessels loaded with timber.

In payment for the vessels which Russia is to cede to Germany the latter country is, it is believed, to supply aeroplanes and other military requirements. Enquiries have recently been made for timber urgently required for the construction of aeroplane sheds. It is, of course, possible that these are needed for housing the aeroplanes which, in connection with the services recently inaugurated, are to carry mails to and from Berlin.

I am not, myself, of the opinion that these preparations necessarily presage

---

[4] Admiral von Hintze, former German Military Plenipotentiary in Imperial Russia and State Secretary for Foreign Affairs in 1918.

[5] A copy of the contract alleged to have been made in October, 1921 by Signor Berchielli for the supply of arms to Russia was transmitted by Mr. Wilton in his despatch No. 1 of January 11, 1922. Papers relating to this contract are preserved in file 51 (of 1922).

aggression on the part of Russia. As far as can be judged the army itself is not in the least enthusiastic for a campaign on any front, nor are there indications of bellicose intentions among the superior officers or at headquarters. Moreover, though by expending special care on the improvement in morale and equipment of certain units on which it mainly relies for its own security, the Soviet Government has managed to bring these forces to a fair degree of efficiency, the Red Army remains as a whole much as it was some months ago—ragged, poorly fed and ill disciplined. The demobilisation of the 1899 class is proceeding rapidly and will soon be complete. As to the feeling of the population generally, it is entirely pacific and opposed to any military adventure.

Such danger as there is lies, first, in the suspicious Bolshevik mentality, convinced of hostile designs on the part of its neighbours; secondly in the access of truculence born of the Russo-German agreement[2] and what the Bolsheviks regard as their diplomatic success in Genoa and, thirdly, in the possibility that Lenin, from bad health or waning influence, may lose his control of affairs.

I have, etc.,

R. M. HODGSON

No. 496

The Marquess Curzon of Kedleston to Mr. Gregory (Genoa)
No. 84 Telegraphic [N 4498/646/38]

Very Urgent and Secret FOREIGN OFFICE, *May 9, 1922, 1 p.m.*

Following for Prime Minister from Chamberlain:—

1. President Chambers of Commerce[1] has obtained approval of his Committee to clause [VII][2] as it stands but spoke to me yesterday with great anxiety of possibility that its terms might be in any way weakened by subsequent alterations or explanations. In that case Chambers would turn against you.

2. Horne has received most interesting account from Fred Cripps[3] who has just returned from Moscow where he has put through big deal for rebuilding. Cripps says life at hotel luxurious. Shops doing large trade often in luxuries. No difficulty in private firms doing business. Does not need guarantee and says all business can be done without it.

3. Horne and I feel that you will in any case meet with considerable difficulty in getting proposed additional 25 millions and altering

---

[1] Sir Arthur Shirley Benn.

[2] Of a draft agreement submitted to Russia at the Genoa Conference on May 2, 1922 (see Vol. XIX, pp. 700–1 and 790–6).

[3] Colonel Hon. F. Cripps. In his despatch No. 249 of April 25, Mr. Hodgson had reported: 'Colonel Cripps left Moscow on the 21st instant. Before his departure he concluded an agreement on behalf of the "Beecham Trust" with the Moscow Commune for repairing house property in this city.'

conditions so as to make them available for Russia, and if Cripps account is at all correct we shall do as much business without agreement as with it.

4. We are both strongly of opinion that you should on no account weaken on clause VII which is the absolute minimum acceptable here.[4]

Cripps has large business experience in Russia dating from before the war.

[4] In telegram No. 89 of May 10, the Foreign Office transmitted the following message from Mr. Urquhart (see No. 367, n. 10) to Sir P. Lloyd-Greame at Genoa: 'Association of British creditors of Russia, after full discussion, authorised me to inform you they approve Russian memorandum including clause 7, and greatly appreciate Prime Minister's efforts to further British interests. Am personally confident that if clause 7 proves unacceptable to Russians, I can carry commercial opinion here in favour of alternative formula we discussed of perpetual possessive titles to be granted by Soviet state.'

No. 497

Lord D'Abernon (Berlin) to the Marquess Curzon of Kedleston
(Received May 15)
No. 365 [N 4684/2169/38]

BERLIN, *May 10, 1922*

My Lord Marquess,

I have read with great interest Mr. Hodgson's Despatch 264 of May 2,[1] and note his opinion that the Soviet Government, having succeeded in concluding the recent Agreement with Germany,[2] appears to have definitely embarked on a course leading to the establishment of intimate relations with that country. He adds that he is not prepared to venture an opinion as to how far this new attitude of the Soviet Government indicates a real change of policy and how far it is of a provocatory nature designed to impress other countries with a sense of impending peril.

So far as the question can be judged from here, I incline rather to the latter view. I have always considered that the signature of the Treaty of Rapallo[2] was certainly on the part of the Germans and possibly on the part of the Russians rather a provocatory or retaliatory demonstration than the outcome of any serious belief in a policy of lasting cooperation.[3] Judged by

[1] No. 495.   [2] See Vol. XIX, No. 75.

[3] Lord D'Abernon sent many telegrams and despatches to this effect to the Foreign Office, largely in response to Lord Curzon's telegram No. 32 of April 20 which ran: 'We are somewhat concerned at extent to which you appear to have been kept in dark by Germans as to recent negotiations of Russo-German treaty which must have reached its penultimate stage in Berlin.' The gist and in many cases the details of Lord D'Abernon's communications concerning the Treaty of Rapallo will be found in his *An Ambassador of Peace* (3 vols., London, 1929–30), vol. i, pp. 296–322 *passim*, and vol. ii, pp. 117–35 *passim*. On November 27, 1922, in his despatch No. 909 (cf vol. ii, pp. 134–5) he wrote to Lord Curzon as follows: 'It is now abundantly evident that the Rapallo Treaty was really signed by German representatives in a moment of panic, and not as the result of a deliberate policy. The panic which caused them to sign it was created by the idea, skilfully exploited by the Russian delegates, that a close union was being negotiated at Genoa between the Western Powers and Russia:

ordinary standards of bourgeois commercialism, there is almost always in the attitude of the Soviet a strange element of mockery. They appear to enjoy playing a trick on capitalistic Powers to an extent which frequently mars the success of their own policy, and I do not think they regard the Germans— at any rate the present German Government—as possible collaborators in their schemes for reforming the face of the world. It is noticeable that since signing the Russo-German Agreement, so far from abstaining from propaganda, they have accentuated it and have already come into conflict with the German Government on this subject. Radek has been particularly active in this agitation.

There is fairly reliable information to the effect that the communist scheme is to take advantage of any aggressive action on the part of France in the Ruhr to declare a general strike. The calculation is that the mass of the German people would be favourable to a general strike on nationalistic grounds if it was resorted to as a reply to French violence. Once a general strike is let loose, the field is open for unlimited communistic agitation.

The signature of the Russo-German Agreement has produced an extraordinary crop of documents purporting to be military conventions between Russia and Germany, contracts for sale of arms by Germany to Russia, contracts for naval reorganisation in Russia by German intermediary, contracts for the development of German trade in Russia, etc. The majority of these documents are forgeries—some are genuine. Wherever there is a chance of a lucrative commercial deal without undue political risk, German firms will be found ready to enter upon it, but I am sceptical of any wide and general compact involving officially the German Government.

The attitude of the military class in Germany and of German parties connected with the military class is too violently anti-communistic to allow much prolonged cooperation. Stories of German officers in Russia have been current for the last two years, but no solid foundation has ever been discovered for them, and so far as I know, nobody has yet seen a German officer in any authoritative position in the Russian army. During the Soviet attack on Poland in 1920,[4] no German officers were found among the thousands of Russian troops who surrendered.

Similarly, large official contracts for the delivery of war material by German firms must be viewed with suspicion if they involve direct violation of Germany's obligations under the Treaty of Peace. I quite believe in a good deal of smaller trading, and it is obvious that any German having to choose between the destruction of old armaments by the Commission of Control and a possible sale to anybody—in Russia, Turkey, Afghanistan or India—will prefer to run a certain amount of risk in the hope of gain rather than lose his property and get no compensation. In my judgment it is extraordinary that the Commission of Control have been able to obtain the

that this union would be used against Germany; and that if Russia did not sign with Germany she would sign with the Western Powers and would become an instrument of pressure in the hands of those Powers.'

[4] See Vol. XI, Chap. II.

destruction of such vast quantities of guns and munitions,[5] and that larger quantities of these have not found their way out of Germany.

Apart from ordinary considerations of gain, it must be constantly remembered that in Germany there are a large number of small Jewish traders, who are specialists and experts in second-hand dealing, and who are strongly attracted by the large profits obtainable on such transactions in arms. In a certain section of their complicated mentality these classes have more than a sneaking affection for the Bolsheviks. Many of them are inclined to regard their co-religionaries at Moscow as rather fine fellows who have done something to avenge the misfortunes of the Jewish race—they consider Trotsky and the Cheka somewhat as the apostolic successors to Judith and Deborah. The conjunction of this idealistic hero-worship with the possibility of a high percentage of gain, forms an almost irresistible temptation to such as happen not to be endued with an exceptional austerity in regard to international obligations.

The German Government is cognisant of the folly of allowing operations of this kind to be carried on, but its police is not very efficient—its officials are ill-paid and open to bribery—its authority not very strong. Weakness is shown in high quarters rather than ill-will and many officials outside corrupt influences are politically recalcitrant.

What I have said above regarding the non-probability of prolonged and close cooperation is subject to this reserve—that the two Governments are not driven together by external forces, and by exposure to a common danger.

I have, etc.,
D'ABERNON

[5] See Chap. IV.

No. 498

Mr. Hodgson (Moscow) to the Marquess Curzon of Kedleston
(Received May 12, 3.30 p.m.)

No. 108 Telegraphic [N 4622/2965/38]

MOSCOW, *May 12, 1922, 12.26 a.m.*

My telegram No. 106.[1]

Acting Commissary of Foreign Affairs told me today that there was every prospect that death sentence would be carried out. Condemned persons had been found guilty by a properly constituted tribunal and penalty was deserved; to commute it would be taken as a sign of weakness.

I told him I was not charged to make any representation on behalf of these persons but that he would do well to remember that extreme sentence had been pronounced at time when Soviet delegation at Genoa is trying to

[1] Of May 9, not printed. This referred to telegram No. 105, which reported that on May 8 the death sentence was pronounced on eight priests and three other persons for spreading provocative reports in connection with the requisition of church property.

persuade western nations that they are wrong in distrusting judicial system at present in force in Russia.[2]

[2] See Vol. XIX, No. 89, Annex I.

No. 499

Mr. Hodgson (Moscow) to the Marquess Curzon of Kedleston
(Received May 22)
No. 285 [N 4947/246/38]

MOSCOW, *May 15, 1922*

My Lord,

I have the honour to acknowledge receipt of Mr. Ovey's despatch No. 353 of the 1st instant.[1]

2. I am not in a position to verify Mr. Hackzell's[2] statement that 2,500,000 gold roubles were allocated in the secret budget of the Soviet Government for the use of the Third International,[3] but he has repeated this statement to me, and there is, I think, every probability that some such sum has in fact been contributed by the Soviet Government for the purpose stated, since it is clear that without financial help from the Bolsheviks the Third International could not exist. But the ruinous financial condition which prevails in Russia has reacted upon the relations between the Government and the Third International, with the result that this organisation is receiving very much less help now than before.

3. All information on the economic situation points to the correctness of the conclusion reached by Mr. Hackzell in his conversation with Mr. Rennie. For months past the State has been unable to pay salaries to its employees, even in military and naval services; the Treasury is empty, industry is stagnant and the expedients which have been improvised to replace the ordinary processes of trade and commerce have failed; nearly three months have still to run before the harvest becomes available for the people, and, although favourable climatic conditions have so far prevailed, it is highly doubtful if the small area of land sown will suffice to give even a minimum of sustenance for the coming winter.

4. I do not share the alarmist views expressed to Mr. Rennie by the Finnish General Staff,[4] though they are undoubtedly held widely in circles here which should be well informed. The representatives of the Baltic States in Moscow have good opportunities for getting into touch with the inner working of the Bolshevik system, but they are, I think, apt to magnify trifles and to draw wrong conclusions. A case in point is the story of the restoration of the Russian fleet by Germany, mentioned in my despatch No. 264 of the 2nd May.[5] It would now look as if a number of Russian vessels of the Baltic fleet are indeed to be handed over to Germany, but only for breaking up as

[1] Not printed.   [2] Finnish Chargé d'Affaires in Moscow.
[3] Cf. No. 494.   [4] See No. 487.   [5] No. 495.

scrap. It is quite probable that the rumour reported in my despatch was only a distorted version of this transaction.

It is hard to see how a war against either Poland or Roumania, or against both, would furnish to the Russian Communists a means of escaping from their present situation. The railway system is so broken down that it is, I am assured, impossible for a mere diversion of troops to be made, let alone the transport of forces on the large scale required for a campaign abroad. The efficiency of the Red army is still low, except in units which can ill be spared from the duty of maintaining internal order, while there are no signs in the country of a desire for military adventure.

I have, etc.,

R. M. HODGSON

No. 500

Mr. Hodgson (Moscow) to the Marquess Curzon of Kedleston
(Received May 22)

No. 293 [N 4953/1185/38]

MOSCOW, *May 16, 1922*

My Lord Marquess,

With reference to my despatch No. 227 of April 18th on the matter of the arrest of the 'St. Hubert',[1] I have the honour to report that I have just received from the Commissariat for Foreign Affairs a communication dated May 13th as follows:—

'I am instructed by M. Karakhan to send you the following information concerning the trawler "St. Hubert" detained pending trial by the Russian authorities for illicit fishing in our territorial waters.

'The trial took place in the People's Court at Murmansk on the 8th March and the verdict rendered reads as follows:

The trawler together with its equipment and the fish on board—except 10 per cent of the fish which is to go to the crew—to be confiscated; the crew to be released and sent to England.

'This verdict was however set aside by the Department of Judicial Control of the People's Commissariat for Justice and the case was returned to the People's Court for new trial. The crew of the "St. Hubert" were placed on board the ship "Ruslan" which left for Vardo, Norway, on the 10th March.'

I am now in receipt of Your Lordship's telegram No. 119 of the 13th instant,[2] and am at once making further representations with a view to securing the release of this vessel, at the same time adverting to the extraordinary delay there has been in furnishing this mission with information as

---

[1] Not printed. See, however, Nos. 483, 486, 489, and 491.

[2] This ran: 'Interests concerned are much perturbed by failure of Soviet government to give reply to your reiterated demands for release of "St. Hubert". . . . You should insist on receiving an immediate reply to your representations.'

to the court proceedings, which could certainly have been obtained at a much earlier date.[3]

On receipt of the evidence mentioned in Your Lordship's telegrams Nos. 98[4] and 119,[2] I shall be in a position to press the case from the point of view that the arrest of the vessel was, even on the basis of the Russian pretensions, inadmissible.

I am transmitting, herewith, a copy of a further letter which I addressed on April 21st,[1] to the Acting People's Commissariat for Foreign Affairs in the sense of the enclosure to Your Lordship's despatch No. 277.[5]

I have, etc.,

R. M. HODGSON

[3] In his letter of May 17 to M. Karakhan, Mr. Hodgson stated: '... I have repeatedly, both in writing and verbally, requested that full information should be given to me as to the procedure followed in dealing with this case, the action of the Courts, and the fate of the crew. Yet two and a half months have elapsed without any information on these matters being supplied to me. The delay might be explained were communications with Murmansk interrupted, but the fact that the verdict of the Murmansk Court has been received in Moscow, examined here, and sent back to Murmansk for reconsideration, shows that this is not the case. It was, as I have previously mentioned, only through the British press that I learned accidentally that the crew of the "St. Hubert" were repatriated in March.'

[4] Of April 10. This ran: 'Evidence (copies being sent you) shows that "St. Hubert" was arrested 14 miles off coast. Please renew demand for instant release mentioning above new factor without prejudice to our claim against interference within 12 mile limit.'

[5] Of April 3 (N 2861/1185/38), not printed.

No. 501

Mr. Rennie (Helsingfors) to the Marquess Curzon of Kedleston
(Received May 30)

No. 179 [N 5269/1999/38]

HELSINGFORS, *May 19, 1922*

My Lord,

With reference to Your Lordship's Despatch No. 101 of April 1st[1] and to my despatch No. 152 of April 28th,[1] relative to German military and naval personnel in the employ of the Soviet Government, I have the honour to transmit the following information which has been received from a reliable source.

There are approximately 1,700 Germans in Moscow. This number includes the 600 members of the 'German Executive Committee' of the Komintern (Western Section). Practically all the individuals are military men.

In the All-Russian General Headquarters there are eighteen German officers:— Captain Romul Heinze, Major Sezemann, Kircher, Lutz, Taube, Count Adlerberg and Lieutenant Krause.

[1] Not printed. See, however, No. 487.

The majority of these officers have taken Russian names. Major Sezemann works under the name of Bistritsky.

A German Major Kruger is in charge of the topographical Department of the General Staff. He also acts as adviser to the 'People's Commissariat for War'. Kruger has been awarded the Order of the Red Ensign (*Prikaz* of 24th September, 1921).

It is also reported that a number of German naval officers and mechanics have arrived at Kronstadt. According to Bobrischev, Military Attaché of the Bolshevik Delegation in Helsingfors, a project has been accepted to widen the Kronstadt port and 500,000 gold roubles have been assigned for this purpose. An engineer called Stradesch, a Czech, will supervise the work of the German mechanics.[2]

In the Seventh Department of the Russian General Staff, there are several German agents who are working on behalf of Russia and collecting information about Poland, Roumania and France.

The chief of the 'Intelligence Department' of the General Staff is General Snesarev.

I have, etc.,
ERNEST RENNIE

[2] In a letter of June 9 the Admiralty forwarded the following comments: 'Though considerable German personnel will doubtless find its way into Russia by small instalments, it is assumed that the German Government will avoid a breach of Article 179 of the Treaty of Versailles.

'As regards the immediate naval result of the employment of Germans in the Russian Navy, German influence and ideas will appear in the various fleets and produce increased efficiency.

'The Russian-Baltic fleet can no longer be regarded as practically non-effective, but may become the most powerful force in the Baltic, greatly to the disadvantage of Finland and the Baltic States.'

No. 502

Mr. Hodgson (Moscow) to the Marquess Curzon of Kedleston
(Received May 29)
No. 308 [N 5217/4058/38]

Secret   MOSCOW, *May 20, 1922*
My Lord Marquess,

In my despatch No. 264 of May 2nd,[1] I mentioned that Admiral Hintze had been recently in Moscow. I now learn from reliable sources that his stay here was connected with negotiations which he had been conducting and which have as their object the reestablishment of the Russian war industry with German assistance. It has been arranged that various factories of munitions of war and artillery—among them the Molotilovka and Zlatoust Works—will be reorganised with German help. Two aeroplane factories will

[1] No. 495.

also come under the arrangement. The output of the factories will, according to my information, be shared between the two countries.

Weekly meetings are being held at the Kremlin under the presidency of Trotsky to examine various projects arising in connection with the realisation of this plan of operations. The German Consultative Mission is headed by General Bauer, of whom I know nothing but that he is said to be of the German General Staff. He was mentioned recently in the local press as being present at the review of the Red troops on May 1st.

I understand that two Russian commissions are dealing with this matter, one being Russo-German in its composition and the other purely Russian. Proceedings are being carried on in secret.

I have, etc.,
R. M. Hodgson

No. 503

Mr. Hodgson (Moscow) to the Marquess Curzon of Kedleston
(Received May 23, 8.30 a.m.)

No. 113 Telegraphic [N 5057/2965/38]

MOSCOW, *May 22, 1922, 9.30 p.m.*

Your telegram No. 123.[1]

Patriarch, who has been isolated for some time past, has been transferred to Donskoi monastery, where he is closely confined.[2] Soviet press report, that he

[1] Of May 18. This ran: 'Some anxiety is felt here as to fate of Patriarch. Please telegraph circumstances of his arrest and trial and probable outcome. Would joint protest from religious bodies here or wide publicity improve or endanger his position?'

[2] In his despatch No. 329 of May 22, Mr. Hodgson stated: 'On February 23rd the Presidium of the All Russian Central Executive Committee published a decree to the effect that within one month all valuable objects made of gold and silver or containing precious stones should be removed from ecclesiastical establishments and churches of all religions and presented to a special famine fund. It was stipulated that the decree should not apply in the case of "objects the removal of which would essentially affect the interests of the cult".

'According to the law of the Orthodox Church, consecrated objects cannot be touched by lay persons, and the execution of the above decree would therefore have involved sacrilege. The Patriarch accordingly issued a second circular to the clergy, reminding them of the terms of the Canon Law and warning them that if they took part in handing over the consecrated property they would be liable to excommunication. No suggestion was made that the clergy should offer resistance to the orders of the Government, but they were warned not to sign *procès-verbaux* recording the confiscation of consecrated ecclesiastical property.

'. . . The decisive measures adopted by the Government to cope with any possible trouble and the condemnation to death of two of the priests responsible for the opposition at Shouya seem to have discouraged any idea of active resistance which the Orthodox may have nourished. Moreover, opposition was very much weakened, first by the violent, but skilful, campaign in the press accusing the hierarchy of the Church of counter-revolution and treachery towards the starving population of Russia, and secondly, by the defection of a certain portion of the Orthodox clergy itself—notably the Bishop Antonin of Moscow.

'. . . The Soviet Government has been able not only to carry out with success the

has resigned his office, has been again denied in well informed quarters where it is stated he has refused to sign resignation in spite of great pressure put upon him, and (? in any case) such (? resignation) without consent of conclave would be invalid. It is not clear how his trial will take place.

(? Vatican) would, I think, be favourable to him but I question wisdom of protest from religious organisations which are already regarded with suspicion by Bolshevik government and whose interference would be interpreted as anti-Soviet.

confiscation of Church property, but it has used to its own advantage the false position in which it placed the Orthodox Church. Priests and other persons who signed protests against the spoliation of the Church property, or who in other manner showed themselves opposed to it, have been arrested. A number have been tried and condemned, and at the present moment most of the best-known ecclesiastics of Moscow are in prison awaiting trial, while the provincial papers report daily arrests and occasionally death sentences.

'. . . The Bolsheviks are now directing their attacks against the Patriarch and have announced their intention of bringing him to justice, as responsible for the anti-Soviet conspiracy which they have themselves invented. He is now confined in the Donskoi monastery. They have profited by discords which have arisen within the Church itself and found a party subservient to their purpose, having as its most prominent member Bishop Antonin—an ecclesiastic of heterodox views and little standing. Tikhon is reported in the Soviet papers to have signed his resignation as Patriarch, but there is some doubt as to how far this statement is in accordance with the facts.'

No. 504

Mr. Gregory (Genoa) to the Marquess Curzon of Kedleston
(Received May 23, 11.30 a.m.)
No. 234 Telegraphic [N 5024/57/38]

Urgent   GENOA, *May 23, 1922, 8.45 a.m.*

In conversation today Contarini late permanent head of Italian foreign office intimated to me that his government was on the point of signing the commercial treaty with Soviet government to which Schanzer drew attention[1] during discussion on the Hague proposals. I understand that signature will take place before departure of Chicherin. This treaty is renewal in slightly expanded form of trade agreement concluded December 2[6]th last[2] and which will lapse June 2[6]th unless more comprehensive arrangements have been arrived at. Treaty will not cover subjects comprised in terms of reference to Hague commissions.

I pointed out to Contarini that although no objection had been made at meeting above mentioned I foresaw that great capital would be made out of this in French press which might well say, no sooner had British delegation departed than Italy broke loose and came to separate agreement with Soviet

[1] See No. 459. See also Vol. XIX, No. 130.
[2] See No. 459, n. 4. Under Article 13, a trade convention was signed in Genoa on May 24, but was not ratified by the Soviet Government.

government. I therefore suggested that it would be well if action of Italian government were properly presented to public.

Repeated to Paris and Rome.

No. 505

Mr. Addison[1] *(Berlin) to the Marquess Curzon of Kedleston*
(Received May 29)

No. 410 [*N 5197/646/38*]

BERLIN, *May 24, 1922*

My Lord Marquess,

I have the honour to acknowledge the receipt of Your Lordship's despatch No. 818 of the 18th instant[2] in which you transmit the text of a military convention between Germany and Russia and request that I should endeavour to ascertain whether such a convention has in fact been concluded.

The document enclosed in the despatch from His Majesty's Chargé d'Affaires at Paris was also published in 'The Times' on the 8th instant and His Majesty's Ambassador has reported the various specific official assurances given to him that no such convention is in existence, while the German Ambassador in London, as stated in Your Lordship's despatch No. 765 of the 13th instant,[2] has made a similar declaration to Sir William Tyrrell. I also enclose translation of a semi-official statement to the same effect published in the German press of the 20th instant.[2]

I readily admit that assurances emanating from German official circles at the present time may not be deserving of full credit or implicit confidence, but other persons, on whose word I have reason to place more reliance, have assured me that nothing of the nature of a definite military understanding is in existence between Germany and Russia. I would also draw Your Lordship's attention to the opinion on this subject expressed by His Majesty's Ambassador in his despatch No. 342 of the 29th ultimo.[2]

It has been stated to me on various occasions that discussions relating to military problems have taken place between the Representatives of the German and Soviet Governments and one of my informants even went so far as to declare, on the authority of General Ludendorff, that a military convention, signed by General von Seeckt, was in existence at the Ministry of War.[3] It does not seem likely that the non-existence of an arrangement of this nature will ever accurately be ascertained, since it is almost impossible to prove a negative, while even the production of a copy of an agreement would be no conclusive proof of its existence, since the demand for the

---

[1] See No. 29, n. 1.   [2] Not printed.

[3] In May, 1922, General von Seeckt, German Chief of Staff, denied the existence of any military agreement between Germany and Soviet Russia. See John Erickson, *The Soviet High Command* (London, 1962), p. 156.

document would create a ready supply. So far as it is possible for me to make any addition to the views adumbrated by His Majesty's Ambassador in his despatch above-mentioned, I would suggest that the truth is probably to be found halfway between the two extremes of a formal written agreement and no understanding at all, and that, while no definite convention has in fact been signed, the conversations and tacit arrangements between the Representatives of the German and the Representatives of the Soviet Governments did more than relate merely to the subject matter of the Treaty of Rapallo.[4] From conversations which I have had with persons of reliability it would seem clear that the Soviet Representatives at various times used the weapon of military danger from Russia, in case no understanding were reached, and held out the allurement of a benevolent neutrality and possible military assistance from Russia provided the relations between the two countries were made closer. It is not a far step from such conversations in negotiation to the conclusion of a tacit understanding that any terms of friendship between the two countries should imply military assistance and help, as and when time permits, and that meanwhile such military supplies as can be smuggled out of Germany and such technical help as Russia is able and willing to absorb should be provided.

As an example of the exaggerated nature of the reports which are freely being circulated at the present time and as an indication of the necessity of caution in this connection, I would draw Your Lordship's attention to the fact that the report that Germany had taken over the reconstruction and equipment of the Russian Fleet has now, according to His Majesty's Representative in Moscow,[5] dwindled down to the proportion of a sale of a certain number of Russian vessels of the Baltic Fleet to Germany for the purpose of being broken up as 'scrap'.

This exercise of proper caution, together with a due mood of regard for certain indications of cumulative force would appear to lead one to form the opinion that, while it is impossible to assert that a military convention does not exist, it is difficult to resist the conclusion that all the evidence points to the non-existence of a formal document on the subject but rather to the fact that the new-born understanding between Germany and Russia implies that the former country will do all in its power to assist the latter, even in military matters, in the hope that it may somehow by these means improve its own position.

As an aside I would mention that I have repeatedly heard that the Soviet Representatives consistently laid stress on the fact that Russia was much more dangerous, from a military point of view, to Germany than France and that, incredible as it may sound, they actually used the argument, which apparently was to a certain extent believed, that, while the Red Army was willing and eager to fight, the French Army was so war-weary and permeated with Socialistic and Bolshevik principles that it was rapidly becoming almost a negligible quantity for war-like operations against this country. It is difficult to understand how such foolish talk should have gained any

4 See Vol. XIX, No. 75. 5 See No. 499.

879

credence but the German mind is still so permeated with the idea of a possible Russian danger and so eager to believe what it wishes to believe that the assurances and threats of the Soviet Delegation may well have been one of the factors of determination.

I have, etc.,
JOSEPH ADDISON

No. 506

Mr. Hodgson (Moscow) to the Earl of Balfour[1]
(Received June 1, 8.30 p.m.)
No. 124 Telegraphic [N 5356/2965/38]

MOSCOW, *June 1, 1922, 5 p.m.*

My telegram No. 108.[2]
Cassation committee of supreme tribunal confirmed finding of Moscow Court and referred petition for pardon to presidium of all Russian executive committee. Latter have rejected petition in case of 5 condemned priests but have commuted sentence on 6 others to 5 years' imprisonment.

[1] See No. 24, n. 1.   [2] No. 498.

No. 507

Sir C. Barclay (Stockholm) to the Earl of Balfour
(Received June 6)
No. 255 [N 5472/252/38]

STOCKHOLM, *June 1, 1922*

My Lord,
With reference to my despatch No. 254 of yesterday,[1] I have the honour to report that the Government Bill relating to the Russo-Swedish Agreement of 1st March 1922[2] after a lengthy discussion was last night rejected in both chambers. The votes in the Second Chamber were 105 to 94, and in the First Chamber 81 to 47. The minority votes represented the Socialist and Communist parties. The only non-Socialist speaker that supported the Bill was Herr Vennersten (Conservative) one of the negotiators of the Agreement.

The arguments brought forward in the debate by the speakers on either side were, generally speaking, a reiteration of those adduced in the findings of the Committee and the dissentient opinion of the minority, respectively. The reasoning of the Government supporters was on the whole very weak. The speeches made by the Opposition showed that the principal motive for the negative vote was the feeling of insecurity and lack of confidence arising

[1] Not printed.   [2] See No. 476, n. 6.

from the non-recognition in the Agreement of Sweden's claims on Russia. The risks of the admission of Bolshevists into Sweden which had been dilated on in the Conservative press were placed in the background.

The debate in both Chambers was opened by the Minister of Commerce with a not very effective speech. He criticised the Committee for allowing themselves to be influenced by the opinions of Swedes with interests in Russia who were naturally prejudiced, and asserted that the Committee's recommendations would relegate the question of Sweden's commercial relations with Russia into the indefinite future. The Minister of Commerce was supported by the Prime Minister, who pointed out that other countries were making preparations for relations with Russia without awaiting guarantees, which, he said, would certainly be worked out. He announced that he was in receipt of information regarding the contents of the new Italian Agreement with Russia,[3] but that he was under obligation not to disclose its details. He was, however, at liberty to say that it was an advancement on the previous series of agreements with Russia, and involved a *de facto* recognition of the Russian Government so close to the *de jure* recognition that the difference was almost negligible. Mr. Branting thought it possible that the Hague Conference[4] might lead to more tangible results than that at Genoa;[5] but, he added, that if Sweden stakes all relations with Russia on the Hague Conference, an agreement such as that desired by the Committee might be long delayed. This delay might be dangerous. Now that great Powers were concluding agreements with Russia that country could scarcely view the Krassin agreement with satisfaction. He feared that, whilst Sweden was hesitating, she would be left in the lurch. Sweden ought not to set up a barrier between herself and Russia which would create an unfriendly atmosphere between the two countries.

In the latter part of the debate in the Second Chamber, Mr. Branting endeavoured to make capital of supposed differences between the Liberal and Conservative Parties. The Conservative leader denied that there was any difference of opinion between him and Herr Eden.

Herr Nylander, the director of the Swedish Export Association, expressed the opinion that the risks which would be incurred by business men in Russia were by no means small. Even if their goods were not requisitioned they might be subjected to maximum prices, without the possibility of re-exporting them.

Herr Kilbom, one of the Communist leaders, asserted that the Krassin Agreement had already been denounced and, when pressed for an explanation, declared that in any case it would be denounced. He moreover threatened the withdrawal of the Russian orders for locomotives.

One of the Liberal speakers stated that the Government had been warned by members of the bourgeois parties not to lay the Bill before the Riksdag.

The defeat of the Russian Agreement was probable from the very first day of its publication, and a foregone conclusion when the Riksdag committee

[3] See No. 509, below.
[4] See Vol. XIX, Chap IV.
[5] See ibid., Chap. III.

issued their report. Mr. Branting when I saw him a couple of days ago did not conceal his disappointment at the attitude taken up by the Socialist parties. He thought they were making a grave mistake in not following the lead given by others. Sweden's geographical position made it all the more imperative for her to be on good terms with Russia. The market, which they had been at pains to open with Russia during the past 2 years, might now be jeopardised and Russian orders placed elsewhere to the detriment of the Swedish working classes.

On the whole there seems to be no doubt that the rejection of the Agreement reflects the opinion of the country generally with the exclusion of the working classes.

As I indicated some time ago the Government did not make the question a Cabinet one. In fact the Social Minister in his speech in the course of the debate on the unemployment question, which also took place yesterday, stated that he did not consider the substantial advantages of the Russo-Swedish Agreement to be such that the Government should stake their existence on it.

I have transmitted a copy of this despatch to His Majesty's Ministers at Copenhagen and Christiania.

I have, etc.,
COLVILLE BARCLAY

No. 508

The Earl of Balfour to Sir A. Geddes (Washington)
No. 201 Telegraphic [N 5169/1999/38]

FOREIGN OFFICE, June 2, 1922, 10.15 p.m.

Your telegram No. 251[1] has been submitted to Prime Minister who desires following statement of his views to be telegraphed[2] to you for communication at your discretion to Mr. Hughes.

[1] Of May 27. This ran: 'If I could be furnished with reliable evidence to show that Russian army is really a formidable force for offensive operations as seemed to be implied by Mr. Lloyd George's words [in his speech in the House of Commons of May 25: see 154 *H.C. Deb. 5 s*, col. 1466] in form that they appeared in American press, I should not be without hope of being able to persuade United States government to modify its policy to the extent that they might be willing to participate in international conference with regard to Russia.

'View of United States government with regard to Russian army is that it is incapable of taking the field as an army, though it might carry out raids into neighbouring territory. American intelligence department has, I know, placed its strength at about 700,000 effectives badly provided with means of transportation and transport (sic).'

[2] This telegram was drafted by Sir E. Grigg on instructions from Mr. Lloyd George. Sir E. Crowe minuted (June 2): 'Sir E. Grigg's draft may represent the views of the Prime Minister, and I presume we must send the telegram. But I very much doubt whether those views harmonize with the information at the disposal of either the War Office or the Foreign Office.'

Earl Balfour added: 'The telegram must be sent. The question is one on which private

Rakowsky[3] made following statement on April 12th to Finance Sub-Commission at Genoa:

'Russia spent 24 per cent of its receipts on the maintenance of the army, although it had been greatly reduced in strength during the past year. While on 1st January 1920 there were 5½ million men in the army, on 1st January 1921 there were only 1,450,000. Practically the whole of this force was stationed on the frontiers of the Republic. General disarmament was essential, if effective results were to be obtained.'

Importance of facts thus disclosed is threefold.

One. Rakowsky's statement putting strength at 1,450,000 coincides with our estimate of total men under arms. How many of these would be available for operations would depend of course on impulse behind them and on nature of campaign, but Western estimates of Russian fighting capacity have hitherto been very incorrect. Very considerable campaigns have been organised against Red Army from Siberia, the Don, Archangel, Poland and Odessa.[4] All have ended in absolute failure despite very confident predictions of success. While therefore Russian Army is no doubt deteriorating by comparison with Western standards, to the Border States it does appear and in fact is a formidable instrument of war necessitating the maintenance of large forces on their side. From a purely military standpoint this is dangerous, as all experience proves that when conflicts are apprehended on disturbed frontiers they ultimately occur.

Two. In our opinion, however, the danger from Russian armed forces is not to be calculated solely by the standards of organised and scientific warfare. There is also danger of marauding movements which can be very formidable even to a well-organised defence if led by capable men. An armed rabble such as fringes the Russian border is a grave menace to the health and security of neighbouring countries when driven from behind by famine and despair. Military leaders have often made their profit from such conditions, as Napoleon did when he first invaded Italy. But whether any such leader appears or not, the condition of Russia will make armed incursions into foreign territory inevitable if famine and pestilence continue to increase. At the least these would be made by large marauding bands which would carry desolation, pestilence and political unrest across the frontiers wherever they spread, and which even when defeated would unless exterminated aggravate the serious existing burden cast upon the Border States by Russian refugees. The Russian cavalry though poor is a particular danger in this respect.

speculation is most [?permissible]. My personal view is that lack of communication, famine, and disease, prevent the Soviets being formidable enemies at the present moment. The same causes also defer any hopes of commercial revival. As soon as such a revival takes place, the Soviets will become more formidable foes—on the other hand they may be less disposed to fight.'

[3] President of the Council of People's Commissars and Commissar for Foreign Affairs in the Ukrainian Soviet Government.

[4] See J. Bradley, op. cit., pp. 211–14.

Three. Rakowsky's statement that 24 per cent of Russian Government's receipts are still spent on army shows how grave in a financial sense the continuance of these conditions on both sides must be. Russia herself faces aggression as much as her neighbours do, and while these conditions remain the dangers described in one and two above will steadily increase. There is no remedy in military measures however provident for a situation of this kind. On the contrary the military remedy merely aggravates the disease. Russia is a plague-spot and the plague of Russian conditions will inevitably spread across the frontiers of Russia and drag down the condition of her neighbours unless the condition of Russia herself is improved. This is the essence of the argument which has impelled His Majesty's Government to regard the Russian problem as one in which the possible disadvantages of forcing the pace towards a solution is greatly less than the certain dangers to be apprehended from indifference and delay.

.

No. 509

Sir R. Graham (Rome) to the Earl of Balfour
(Received June 6)
No. 496 [N 5422/57/38]

ROME, *June 2, 1922*

My Lord,

In amplification of my telegram No. 196 of the 27th [ultimo][1] I have the honour to report that, according to statements in the press, the Italo-Russian treaty, which was signed at Genoa on the 23rd ultimo[2] contains provisions assuring:—

1. Full liberty of circulation and employment to Italians going to Russia.

2. Most favoured nation treatment as regards the carrying on of commercial enterprises, professions and trades by Italians in Russia and by Russians in Italy.

3. The early conclusion of a special treaty about labour and emigration questions.

4. The validity in Russia of contracts which contain an 'arbitration clause'.

5. Reciprocal freedom for the transit trade of each country across the territory of the other.

6. A free-port for Russia at Trieste and for Italy at the principal Black Sea ports.

7. Facilitation of trade in produce and, with limitations, for that in Italian wines.

8. Most Favoured Nation treatment for Italy in all branches of commerce.

9. A Right of option for Italy in regard to oil wells not yet ceded to other countries.

10. Agricultural grants of about 100,000 hectares in the Ukraine and the

[1] Not printed.   [2] See No. 504, n. 2.

Kuban, under a lease of 24 years renewable on expiry, and to be paid for 'in natura' and by means of a percentage of 70% including taxes.

I am informed by the Ministry of Foreign Affairs that a copy of the treaty will not be available until it has been ratified.[3]

I have, etc.,
R. GRAHAM

[3] In his despatch No. 444 of June 27, Mr. Hodgson reported: '... the Soviet Government, having refused to ratify the Treaty of the 24th May, has now decided to renew the preliminary agreement concluded with Italy on the 2[6]th December last [see No. 459].'

No. 510

Sir A. Geddes (Washington) to the Earl of Balfour
(Received June 8, 8.30 a.m.)
No. 262 Telegraphic [N 5541/1999/38]

WASHINGTON, *June 7, 1922*

Your telegram No. 201.[1]

I spoke today to Secretary of State in the sense desired. Since our earlier conversation[2] he appears to have received confidential information from Russia reporting that Russian military position is much weaker than statistics quoted by Prime Minister seemed to show. He appears, therefore, to have receded somewhat from position which he took up on earlier occasion. On pressing him Secretary of State promised to see whether it would be possible to communicate this information.

[1] No. 508.
[2] Reported by Sir A. Geddes in his telegram No. 251 of May 27 (see No. 508, n. 1).

No. 511

The Earl of Balfour to Lord Hardinge (Paris)
No. 1749 [N 5269/1999/38]

FOREIGN OFFICE, *June 9, 1922*

My Lord,

I transmit herewith a copy of a despatch from His Majesty's Minister at Helsingfors[1] giving particulars of German military and naval personnel believed to be in the employ of the Soviet Government.

2. I should be glad if Your Excellency would bring this information to the notice of the Conference of Ambassadors. A copy of Mr. Rennie's despatch is

[1] The reference is to No. 501.

also being communicated to His Majesty's Chargé d'Affaires at Berlin[2] for the information of the Inter-Allied Commission of Control.

I am, etc.,

(for the Earl of Balfour)

J. D. GREGORY

[2] Mr. Addison.

No. 512

Sir G. Clerk (Prague) to the Earl of Balfour (Received June 13)

No. 140 [N 5659/242/38]

PRAGUE, *June 9, 1922*

My Lord,

In continuation of my despatch No. 134 of June 2nd,[1] I have the honour to transmit herewith copy of an official resumé[1] in French of the Provisional Commercial Agreement between Czecho-Slovakia and Russia.[2]

This 'resumé' is almost identical with the summary which I transmitted to Your Lordship in my above-mentioned despatch, but it states definitely that the final solution of the question of the recognition *de jure* of the two Governments will not be prejudiced by this agreement and Article 9 establishes the principle of most favoured Nation treatment for the civil rights of the subjects of the two countries.

I have, etc.,

GEORGE R. CLERK

[1] Not printed.

[2] On August 22, the Foreign Office received from Sir G. Clerk the text of the Russo-Czechoslovak provisional treaty signed at Prague on June 5. For sources, see Slusser and Triska, p. 32.

No. 513

Mr. Hodgson (Moscow) to the Earl of Balfour (Received June 19)

No. 390 [N 5901/2169/38]

MOSCOW, *June 10, 1922*

My Lord,

With reference to Mr. Ovey's despatch No. 448 (4501/2169/38) of May 19th,[1] I have the honour to report as follows on the questions raised therein.

2. I am now informed that Messrs. Krupps' project for taking over a large

[1] Not printed.

agricultural concession in the Kuban district has fallen through. Their representative was a month and a half in Moscow negotiating an agreement, and affairs went so far that on April 6th the German Agent here, Herr Wiedenfeld, informed me that the contract was signed. I am not aware of the circumstances which led to the agreement breaking down.

A report on this matter from a reliable source is to the effect that the German agriculturists who were to have settled on the land were to have the right to carry arms, as it was thought that the Soviet Government, by colonising this territory—which is hostile to their rule—would simplify the task of government.

3. The German Chargé d'Affaires here informs me that no agreement between the Ukraine and Germany has been signed. The representative of the Ukrainian Government has no knowledge of any agreement of the kind having been concluded.

4. I have no information regarding the reported formation of the Russo-German Trading Company mentioned in paragraph 2 of the despatch under reply, though there are rumours current that some combination such as outlined is projected. It would seem unlikely that any organisation would take over land situated partly in the Samara government, partly in the Chernigov government and partly in the Crimea, since these districts are very widely separated and belong, the first to the Moscow Government, the second to the Ukrainian Government and the third to the Crimean Government.

5. It would appear that the Ukrainian Government has shown readiness to give an agricultural concession in the Nicolaev-Odessa district, and negotiations with a Czecho-Slovak group on the subject have been instituted. It is not clear yet whether any agreement has been reached.

6. I will keep in touch with these matters and will not fail to communicate any information of interest that may come to my knowledge.

I have, etc.,

R. M. Hodgson

No. 514

Mr. Leeper to Mr. Hodgson (*Moscow*)

[*N 5347/1691/38*]

FOREIGN OFFICE, *June 10, 1922*

My dear Hodgson,

We are interested to see that the case of the twenty six Baku commissaries who were murdered in Trans-Caspia,[1] which has from time to time since 1918 been given such wide prominence in the Bolshevik press and wireless, has at last been brought up by them against us officially (your despatches Nos. 134[2] and 345[2] of the 9th of March and the 27th of May about the execution of

---

[1] See n. 7, below.   [2] Not printed.

Mr. Charles Davisson).[3] I see from your telegram No. 121,[4] too, that you anticipate the possibility of the matter being brought up in connection with the impending trial of the Social Revolutionaries.[5] We have authorised you by our telegram No. 134[6] to give a most categorical denial of the complicity of any British authorities in the murder.

I enclose a copy of a minute by McDonell,[7] now in this office, who was at that time in those parts, and also a letter[8] addressed to the India Office by

[3] Mr. Davisson was executed on the night of January 16, 1920 by decree of the Extraordinary Commission of Petrograd. He was alleged to have been involved in a counter-revolutionary conspiracy with Sir Paul Dukes (see No. 473, n. 3).

[4] Of May 31. This ran: 'There is a probability that in the course of trial of social revolutionaries question of murder of 26 commissaries on September 26th 1918 mentioned in correspondence on Davisson case will be brought up. Pravda writes that commissaries were assassinated by social revolutionaries on initiative taken by British military mission in Trans-Caucasus.'

[5] See No. 524, n. 2, below.

[6] Of June 2 (N 5347/1691/38), not printed.

[7] Former Vice Consul at Baku. The minute (dated June 2) ran: 'The 26 Commissaries were members of the Baku Bolchevik Government which was replaced by the Social Revolutionary Organ "Centrocaspie" on the arrival of the British force under General Dunsterville. These people were interned on their own ships, but their batteries placed themselves under General Dunsterville and did good work against the invading Turks.

'On our evacuation of Baku these Commissaries and the officers of their batteries sailed from Baku and my impression is that General Dunsterville hoped that they would escape to their friends at Astrachan. It is certain that we had quite enough to do to look after ourselves as the Turkish guns had knocked G.H.Q. about and were reaching our ships, while our former friends the "Centrocaspie" had their guns trained on our transports. However the Commissaries' ships, instead of sailing to Astrachan or to Enzeli to be interned by the British, sailed to Krasnovodsk. It is supposed that the Captain and crew were bribed by the Social Revolutionaries.

'Kum, the S.R. Commissar at Krasnovodsk interned them on arrival at that port.

'They were subsequently sent under guard to Askahbad but never arrived. They were murdered at Kizyl Avat by their guard.

'Kum and his Social Revolutionaries were friendly to the British and it was immediately reported that the murders had been planned by the British and that the actual instruction had been issued by Captain Teague Jones, Intelligence officer under General Mallesson.

'Some weeks later I sailed from Krasnovodsk with General Andrews who instructed me to endeavour to find out from Kum what had happened to the Commissaries.

'After a dinner given to us at the Club I approached Kum who told me that as he had no machinery for trying them at Krasnovodsk he had sent them under guard to Askahbad. Before their departure he had told the captain of the guard that the Commissaries, 26 in number, were on one waybill and the other prisoners on another. That if anything happened to the goods on No. 1 W/B he had better tear it up. He continued that after no news of the party for 4 days he telegraphed down the line and received a reply from the captain of the guard which read: "I apologise for the delay but the three shovels you sent me with the party were not enough." He, Kum, then added: "You see when I make up my mind I do it properly; they will never say of me, as they do of the British, that I talk of armies and arrive with 2 batmen, a ford van and a general".'

[8] Not printed. On June 13 Mr. Ovey wrote to Mr. Wakely of the India Office as follows:
'Teague Jones has been round here again this morning and tells me that he is under orders to return to India immediately. He says that he proposes to send in his papers but that nevertheless, as things at present stand, he will have to return to India. He thinks however that the India Office would be prepared to try and arrange for him to stay on in

Teague Jones whose name has been very prominently mixed up in this matter. You will see that the charge against the British authorities in general and Teague Jones in particular is entirely trumped up, and rests exclusively on the authority of a certain Chaikin.[9] We think now that the accusation has been officially made against us by the Soviet Government it is the time to have the matter out and to clear the British authorities and Teague Jones in particular of the very gross and entirely baseless accusations which have been so widely broadcasted during the last few years.

Before, however, we instruct you to take the matter up officially with the Soviet Government we should like to obtain a copy of the book produced by Chaikin[10] (under official auspices, I gather) containing the whole of his story with facsimiles of the documents on which it is based, in order that we may see exactly what sort of evidence the Bolsheviks have got. I should be glad if you could, as soon as possible, get and send me a copy of this book, without attracting undue attention. After receiving it we shall be in a position to furnish you with very full particulars to enable you to take the matter up effectively.

I am not sending you any of the enclosures mentioned in Teague Jones's letter as they are at present with the India Office.

Yours sincerely,

R. A. LEEPER

this country if it would be convenient in connection with the case of the twenty-six Baku commissars.

'We are on the point of taking this case up with the Soviet Government and it would certainly be handy to have Teague Jones within reach to enable him to answer the points which will undoubtedly crop up as time goes on. If, therefore, it could be arranged for him not to return to India at present, it would undoubtedly be helpful as far as we are concerned. Of course we do not wish to have the appearance of interfering in what after all is your pidgin, but I undersand that the India Office would really be glad to have the matter threshed out as thoroughly as may be.'

[9] Vadim Chaikin, a former lawyer who had made an investigation into the Baku case.

[10] A copy of a section of this book, entitled 'The Execution of the 26 Baku Commissaries', was transmitted to the Foreign Office in Moscow despatch No. 1691 of June 19 (N 6141/1691/38), not printed.

No. 515

Mr. Hodgson (Moscow) to the Earl of Balfour
(Received June 19)

No. 400 [N 5909/5909/38]

MOSCOW, *June 13, 1922*

My Lord,

There is a marked feeling of nervousness and uncertainty in the air here at present which, I think, may be ascribed to the failure of the Genoa Conference,[1] the illness of Lenin and the growing economic chaos.

[1] See Vol. XIX, Chap. III.

That Genoa would give no result seemed likely from the moment of the signature of the agreement with Germany,[2] though it is hard to estimate how far the obduracy of the Soviet Government should be ascribed to new confidence born of this agreement and how far to the exigencies of the internal situation.

Scepticism as to the results of the Conference was expressed in government and in private circles for some time before its inception, yet there was a real hope that an agreement with Western Europe would be reached, and the negative result was a bitter disappointment to many.

Best-informed opinion here is to the effect that the German agreement and the initial success won by the Bolshevik delegation emboldened Chicherin to take up a position from which he found it afterwards impossible to recede; that the Soviet Government did—as it loses no opportunity of impressing upon the world—obtain certain tactical advantages—the sympathy aroused in the masses by the appeal for disarmament, the rebuff to the League of Nations and the creation of dissension among the Entente Powers—but that, having obtained neither credits nor recognition, it is fully conscious that the tactical successes to which it lays claim are poor compensation for the failure to obtain material advantages.

Profound secrecy is maintained as to the health of Lenin, with the result that an infinity of rumours are circulating. According to many who have opportunities of getting inside information, he is completely paralysed, deaf, dumb, and condemned to death within the next few weeks; according to others, with equally good means of obtaining information, his general state is much improved, and, though there is yet danger from a clot of blood which, it is feared, may go to the brain, there is every reason to believe that he will shortly be convalescent and again able to take interest in affairs of State. It is probable that the truth lies somewhere between the two extremes and that Lenin, whether he recovers now or not, is a broken man and will never be able to play an important rôle in Russia again. It is not necessary to insist upon the importance which his disappearance from the stage would have upon Communist Russia, and it is natural that the secrecy maintained as to the truth over so long a period and the speculation as to the consequences which will ensue from his removal have engendered a universal feeling of apprehension and disquiet.

The economic situation also gives cause for serious alarm. The trusts, the nature of which has been described in other despatches,[3] have every appearance of being on the point of breakdown. As long as they could work on accumulated stores and supplies taken over by the State they could continue production, but these supplies are in nearly every case coming to an end, and no new raw material is forthcoming to replace them. They have found it impossible to pay their workmen and impossible to sell their products, even at prices, at times, fifty per cent. below the cost of production. All of them

[2] See Vol. XIX, No. 75.
[3] Not printed. The trusts were created to deal with certain branches of industry (see No. 516, below).

are bankrupt or on the verge of bankruptcy, and, as they can get no more relief from the State, the closing down of the majority of them in the near future seems inevitable. In the meantime, they are continually casting out such subsidiary undertakings as to have exhausted their resources, offering them to private enterprise on a concession basis—generally forty-nine years. But machinery and plant not having been replaced or kept up to efficiency level, and no raw material being available, concessionnaires are unwilling to accept doomed undertakings. Unemployment has already assumed alarming proportions, and there is every prospect in the immediate future, as the trusts cease operations, that it will become a problem with which the State in its crippled condition will be unable to deal.

That much good will come of the Hague Conference[4] is not expected, though the more enlightened of the Bolshevik leaders have no illusions as to the absolute necessity of coming to an agreement, even at the cost of their principles, with Western Europe. But a wave of violent Communist feeling is now prevailing—witness the recent executions of the priests and the trial of the Social Revolutionaries[5]—hostile to the truce with the bourgeois Powers, which cannot in any case give the credits which the Soviet Government requires.

Were Lenin in a position to take the lead himself, he might be able to curb this movement, but without his influence it is hardly to be hoped that the more sane opinion, represented by Chicherin, will prevail. Private property and denationalisation are still likely to prove obstacles which will defeat any prospects of a formal settlement, though the former is already beginning to be recognised in fact in Russia, and the latter is coming about automatically by the breakdown of the systems improvised by the Soviets.

I have, etc.,

R. M. HODGSON

4 See Vol. XIX, Chap. IV.　　　　5 See Nos. 498, 503, 506, and 524 n. 2, below.

No. 516

Mr. Hodgson (Moscow) to the Earl of Balfour (Received June 26)
No. 403 [N 6153/155/38]

MOSCOW, *June 14, 1922*

My Lord,

The mixed company, that is, the combination of State and private capital which is now regarded by the Communist party as the present solution of their economic difficulties, is not to be confined merely to the field of foreign trade, but is to be extended to include all of Russia's home trade and industry. This form of enterprise was, indeed, suggested as the way for the economic restoration of Russia in the memorandum addressed to the Allied Powers[1]

1 See Vol. XIX, No. 46, Enclosure.

just prior to the Genoa Conference, and again in the protocols of the Riga Conference of March 29th and 30th last,[2] where the participating States (Russia, Poland, Esthonia and Latvia) were invited to 'facilitate the establishment of mixed companies for the purpose of satisfying the special requirements of these countries'.

It is, perhaps, not without interest to trace the development of the idea of mixed companies in Russia. Apart from the financing of private railway companies by State loans and guarantees, where the State, in general, took no part in the management of the concerns, the idea of the direct participation of the State in the management of industrial undertakings was first developed in approaching the problem of the management of the German undertakings in Russia which were sequestered after the declaration of war in 1914. For example, a scheme was confirmed just before the Revolution for the formation of a new company to take over the Russian General Electric Company—formerly a subsidiary of the Allgemeine Elektrizitäts Gesellschaft. The concern was to have a capital of twenty-four million roubles, divided into 240,000 shares, of which 84,000 were to belong to the State, 40,000 to the American General Electric Company, which was to assume the technical direction, 30,000 to the former Russian, allied and neutral shareholders, 40,000 to the Petrograd International Bank and 46,000 to the Moscow Industrial Bank (Junker). In actual fact the State ultimately retained two-thirds of the shares in the undertaking, but even this overwhelming control did not affect the management of the concern, which really remained in the hands of the persons who had formerly been in charge of its destinies. Similar results followed the formation of the 'Siemens' concern and the Vyksynsky Metallurgical Works.

These schemes were not abandoned even in the early days of the Soviet regime, and in January, 1918 a scheme was put forward by Meshtchersky, director of the Sormova works, for the organisation of a gigantic locomotive and rollingstock trust which would combine 85% of the locomotive works and 70% of the rollingstock works of the country.

The adoption by the Supreme Council of National Economy of the principle of the nationalisation of all industry put an end to these negotiations and organisations.

The question of mixed companies was not raised again until 1921, when experience had convinced the technical advisers of the Communist party of the impossibility of organising industry in accordance with the scientific plans of the Government without the correcting influences and help of competition and personal initiative. As a result probably of suggestions from Russo-German interests, the People's Commissariat for Foreign Trade was the first to proclaim the new doctrine, and the German-Russian Transport Company was formed and a number of other German-Russian concerns (see my despatch No. 395 of June 13th last).[3] Krassin hailed this step as a great advance in Soviet economic politics and praised the farsightedness of the Germans.

[2] See Vol. XIX, No. 47, n. 2.   [3] Not printed.

The idea of mixed companies was approved at the IXth Congress of Soviets. Krassin started pushing his idea with great vigour, maintaining the principle that the People's Commissariat for Foreign Trade shall always hold half the shares and have a majority on the Board. He claimed 'the most serious capitalists will follow this path as soon as it is clearly shown that hope is lost of a breakdown of the monopoly of foreign trade'.

Standard articles of association were worked out for a 'Russian Export and Import Company, Limited'. In one project the People's Commissariat for Foreign Trade was to receive 52% of the shares, 25% being without payment, as compensation for the rights of foreign trade; in a second project they were to hold 51% of the shares, which were to be paid for.

All the mixed companies which have been formed for dealing with the foreign trade of Russia were enumerated in my despatch No. 395[3] above referred to. The idea has now spread to the other Commissariats, and the Commissariat of Finance suggests that all the State trusts should be transformed into private mixed companies—principally in order to relieve the State budget. It would appear that few of these schemes have yet proceeded beyond very preliminary conversations, as in actual fact there is no such thing as Russian private capital, and foreign capital is even less attracted by the mixed company idea applied to Russian industry than it is to the concerns for foreign trade where there is the prospect of being able to influence business to suit the interests of the foreign capitalists.

The following list of companies known to be under discussion may be of interest:—

(1) 'Prodasilikat' for the sale of glass, cement, ceramics and building materials of mineral origin. The capital of five million gold roubles is to be held, 60% by the State and 40% by private capital.

(2) 'Porechye' for operating an electric power station in two neighbouring districts of the Moscow and Smolensk governments.

(3) South-Eastern Bank at Rostov-on-the-Don. The statutes were approved by the Council of Labour and Defence in February, 1922, and it is stated that the capital is to be subscribed by the State Bank and by English capitalists.

(4) Bank of Commerce and Industry. Scheme approved by the Supreme Council of National Economy in March, 1922. The capital is to be subscribed by the Supreme Council of National Economy, the State Bank, the large State trading and industrial trusts and by private capital.

There is also talk of the formation of a Russo-Esthonian and a Russo-Mongolian Bank.

I have, etc.,
R. M. HODGSON

No. 517

Mr. Hodgson (Moscow) to the Earl of Balfour (Received July 3)
No. 438 [N 6373/2965/38]

Copy   MOSCOW, *June 27, 1922*

My Lord,

I have the honour to submit the following observations upon the reply of the Soviet Government to the protest of the Archbishop of Canterbury[1] in the matter of the campaign against the Orthodox Church.

1. The statement that 'there has been no attack upon the Church' is not in accordance with facts. The Soviet Government has from the outset pursued a definitely anti-clerical policy, never losing an opportunity of holding religion up to ridicule. Its latest legislation on the subject of religious education is particularly illuminating, as showing its attitude in this connection. Clause 121 of the New Criminal Code runs as follows:— 'The teaching of religious beliefs in State or private educational establishments and schools to children of tender age and minors is punishable by forced labour for a period not exceeding one year.' Innumerable articles in the official press testify to the desire of the Bolsheviks to crush the hierarchy of the Orthodox Church, which they accuse of counter-revolution and conspiracy against the Soviet power, although the evidence given at the recent trials of various ecclesiastics and others gives no support whatsoever to this charge.[2] It is, indeed, common knowledge that the Orthodox Church, far from organising rebellion against the present Government, has exhibited under persecution a passivity which only the complete demoralisation of the population of this country can explain. The contention that a campaign is being directed against certain individuals only and not against the Church itself is, in view of the general attitude of hostility which the Government has throughout exhibited to the Church, a subterfuge which can deceive nobody.

Having concealed up till August 1921 the existence of a famine[3] which had begun to make itself felt six months earlier, which could not, even if measures had been taken in time, have been prevented from assuming the proportions of a gigantic calamity, and which moreover was the result mainly of its own tyrannous and inept legislation, the Soviet Government refused the offers of co-operation made by the Church in the autumn of last year and in the early part of the present year, and now utilises the situation to hold up to the execration of the masses the leaders of the Church for withholding the help of which it flouted the offer.

As for the proposition that the measures which have led to the present conflict were designed 'to save the lives of tens of millions of human beings including children', it should be said that these measures were as tardy as they were inadequate. Not till December 1921—when the famine had been in progress for nearly a year—did the Bolsheviks, stimulated thereto by the

---

[1] See *The Times,* June 1, 1922, p. 10. For M. Krassin's reply, see ibid., June 8, p. 7. Cf. No. 503.

[2] See No. 503, n. 2.   [3] See No. 385.

generous proposal of the American Government,[4] make any serious financial contribution to the cause of famine relief, and only in February last did they order the confiscation of the treasures of the Church.[2] Yet the crying need for help in the famine-stricken regions was established many months earlier; while they could certainly not be unaware that the results of the spoliation of the Church—by which possibly some thirty to forty million roubles may be realised—could do little to alleviate the situation.

Having accepted foreign relief for some nine millions[5] out of the eleven millions of persons, who according to their own estimates are being assisted, and having despoiled the churches for the ostensible object of collecting resources which they knew beforehand would represent an insignificant amount, they have recently exhibited to Governor Goodrich[6] [a] crown and other jewels in the Kremlin of a value which they themselves state to be one milliard gold roubles, and which Mr. Goodrich considers do not fall short of that amount.

2. Nor can the statement of the Soviet Government that the vast majority of the clergy sides with it in the conflict with the Patriarch bear investigation. Though it is not possible to refute this assertion by the production of statistics, it has been made abundantly clear by the reception given to ecclesiastics of Antonine's[2] group on all occasions when they have appeared in public that they enjoy no sympathy among the people. Hostility breaks out in the churches where they minister; the meetings which they address almost invariably refuse to hear them. As for the priesthood, though individuals can doubtless be produced who will, either by conviction or through fear of offending the powers existing, subscribe to the doctrines of the new party, such represent only a fraction of the whole number. The implication that the Patriarch and the priests who have recently been judged and condemned are apostles of imperialism is singularly infelicitous when it is borne in mind that Tikhon after his long sojourn in America brought away ideas so democratic as to cause him to be the object of the suspicions of the old regime; whereas the condemned priests were from among the humble parochial clergy who were certainly not in league with those in high places.

Nor is the Soviet Government happier when it alludes to the impression made by the Archbishop's protest on public opinion in a country where during five years it has so successfully stifled every expression of independent thought by terrorism and misuse of the press that no semblance of public opinion exists.

3. The blockade[7] did not as the Soviet Government maintains 'strangle

---

[4] A reference to Executive Order No. 3601 of December 24, 1921 (see *F.R.U.S.* 1921, vol. ii, pp. 822–3).

[5] In his situation report of June 13 (despatch No. 392, N 5902/472/38), Mr. Hodgson reported that the Americans were feeding more than 7,000,000 people.

[6] Mr. J. P. Goodrich, former Governor of Indiana, was working in Moscow with the American Relief Administration.

[7] In a minute of June 2 Mr. O'Malley stated: 'No blockade of Russia, in the technical sense of the term, was ever proclaimed. What is generally referred to as the "blockade" of Russia consisted in measures taken by His Majesty's Government and the allied governments

Russian workers, peasants and children'. As far as it had any results at all, its effects were felt precisely by those classes of the population which were sympathetic to the Allied cause. On the other hand, the monopoly of foreign import and export trade, of which Mr. Krassin is the chief supporter, creates a most effectual blockade which renders nugatory every attempt to improve the situation in Russia by delaying indefinitely the return to normal commercial relations with countries abroad.

4. The supplementary statement made by Mr. Krassin that no arrest of Patriarch Tikhon has taken place is deliberately untrue and can be justified only by the quibble that the Patriarch's removal to the Donskoi Monastery was undertaken on his own volition. He was under close home arrest for a considerable period previously, and in the Monastery he is kept in a state of close confinement.[2] Nor is it true that he laid down his office; only that he has transferred to the ecclesiastics designated by the Holy Synod the administrative powers which owing to the measures taken by the Soviet Government he himself was no longer able to exercise. They in their turn have been prevented from fulfilling their functions and the affairs of the Church have been placed in the hands of a new organisation created to serve the purposes of the Government.

I have, etc.,

R. M. HODGSON

to prevent goods being exported from their territories to Russia. The Supreme Council also invited the "neutral powers" to take similar measures, but, generally speaking, those powers took no special steps to prevent trade between themselves and Russia. These steps to prevent trade with Russia virtually constituted a "blockade", but His Majesty's Government have always strenuously insisted that no blockade of Russia ever existed. . . .'

No. 518

Mr. Hodgson (Moscow) to the Earl of Balfour (Received July 6, 10.20 p.m.)
No. 145 Telegraphic [N 6512/2965/38]

MOSCOW, *July 6, 1922, 5.5 p.m.*

My despatch No. 438.[1]

Three weeks' trial of Petrograd priests and others in connection with requisitioning of church property concluded with following sentences:—
11 condemned to death,[2] of whom metropolitan Benjamin, one bishop, several priests and (? professors)s: fifty-three to 5 years' imprisonment and lesser sentences.

Court also decided to start criminal proceedings against Tikhon.

[1] No. 517.
[2] In his telegram No. 163 of July 31, Mr. Hodgson reported: 'Appeal against sentence of death has been rejected by Court of Cassation and Soviet government presidium of all Russian central executive committee.'

No. 519

Mr. Hodgson (Moscow) to the Earl of Balfour (Received July 17)
No. 468 [N 6835/4058/38]

MOSCOW, *July 8, 1922*

My Lord,

In the 'Ekonomicheskaya Zhisn' of the 5th instant there is a report from the delegation of the North-Western Economic Council, which has recently sent delegates from Petrograd to Germany to discuss there the possibilities of concessions.

It appears that the following questions were discussed:— (1) The organisation of a system of motor transport with the central management in Petrograd. (2) The organisation of steamer passenger and freight services on the Neva and the Merinsky Canal systems. (3) The amalgamation of the Baltic Steamship Trust, which is now being organised in Petrograd, with important steamship companies in Germany and other countries. (4) The employment of foreign capital in the repair, equipment and extension of the Petrograd Port. (5) The introduction of foreign capital into the hotel business. (6) The repair and completion of houses. (7) Sewers. (8) The restoration of the gasworks. In addition, the question was raised of the participation of foreign capital in the kinematograph business in Petrograd and in certain other branches of industry.

The delegation remained in Berlin only a comparatively short time, and no concessions have actually been completed and it was only possible to enter into preliminary discussions.

As regards the first proposal, the discussions took place with a banking group through one Schlesinger, of the Merkator Company. The delegation has asked permission to continue the negotiations. As regards the second point, discussions took place with a group in which the Deutsche Bank and the Stakheev group were interested. The delegation suggest that a mixed company should be formed for dealing with this question. Regarding the third proposal, discussions took place with the Hamburg-Amerika Company and also with the Harriman group. The discussions regarding the Petrograd Port were with one Friedlieb, who was interested in the supply of the necessary cranes, and with the firm of Julius Berger, regarding the construction work. Discussions regarding the hotel business were carried on with the director of the Esplanade Hotel, Mr. Kremer, who is supported by Stinnes, and also with a Swiss group under one Heki. These negotiations are still in a preliminary stage. Discussions regarding the repair of houses and drainage were carried on with representatives of two important firms, Stecker and Heinicke, but again no conclusions have been reached. The above-mentioned Friedlieb was also interested in the questions of the gasworks; and this matter was also discussed with the firm of Julius Pintsch.

Representatives of all the above-mentioned groups are expected in Petrograd shortly, when it is hoped to bring these discussions to a conclusion.[1]

[1] See No. 534, below.

I regard with some scepticism the result of these negotiations. German groups have been visiting Russia, more particularly since the Rapallo Agreement, in large numbers, and an infinity of commercial, financial and industrial projects have been discussed. In many cases negotiations have advanced to a stage where there seemed to be every probability of their coming to a final issue; but, in every instance of which I am aware, unreasonable demands on the Russian side have compelled the Germans to withdraw. I do not, however, wish to minimise the importance which this German activity is likely to have in the future: the Germans are obtaining extensive and intimate knowledge on the spot, but so far have been unsuccessful in achieving anything of importance, first, because they have not the necessary capital, secondly, because the Bolsheviks have not yet abandoned an impractical attitude towards foreign capital. Neither of these obstacles is likely to stand in the way indefinitely, when both sides have so much to gain by coming to terms.

I have, etc.,
R. M. HODGSON

No. 520

Mr. Hodgson (Moscow) to the Earl of Balfour (Received July 17)
No. 491 [N 6841/1999/38]

MOSCOW, *July 11, 1922*

My Lord,

The conclusions reached by the persons who have compiled the report upon the Red Army transmitted under cover of Foreign Office despatch No. 597 (N 5897/1999/38)[1] coincide generally with those which I have myself reached.

The Red Army is not a formidable fighting machine—it is not animated by an aggressive spirit, is, except for a small proportion of its effectives, badly trained and badly equipped and is extremely short of artillery, stores and munitions of all kinds.

Nor is it possible to improve its military qualities at the present time. The factories for the production of artillery are without exception lying idle, while those which should be turning out small arms and ammunition share in the general stagnation which affects the industry of this country as a whole.

As to the numerical strength of the army which since Trotsky's speech last December[2] it has been customary to estimate at one and a half million men, it is not possible to establish this with any certainty. It is undoubtedly far lower than this number and in all probability does not exceed some eight

[1] Of June 27, not printed. This confidential report, transmitted to the Foreign Office in Washington despatch No. 689 of June 9, had been communicated to Sir A. Geddes by the Secretary of State following their conversation of June 7 (see No. 510).
[2] See No. 467.

hundred thousand.[3] Of these, the great majority are useless, or next to useless, and it is, I think, fairly safe to say that not more than two hundred thousand men could be relied upon to form an effective, trained attacking force. Even these troops, with the demoralisation in their rear and the lack of military resources, would be quite unable to face a campaign of any length.

As I have said above, there is no aggressive spirit in the army—the whole country is tired of war and revolution, and the army merely reflects the general mental attitude of the nation. The Soviet forces can only be a danger to their neighbours should the Government, by fair means or foul, succeed in creating a situation which would induce in the country the belief that the national safety is imperilled by the menace of an attack from outside. Such a situation might conceivably arise out of ill-considered action by Poland, such as the incursions into Russian territory which took place last year,[4] or as the result of propaganda based upon the reported efforts of France to stimulate the Baltic States into active hostilities towards this country.[5]

I have, etc.,

R. M. Hodgson

[3] Cf. No. 508.   [4] See No. 485, n. 1.   [5] Cf. No. 424.

No. 521

Mr. Hodgson (Moscow) to the Earl of Balfour (Received July 17, 10.30 p.m.)
No. 153 Telegraphic [N 6920/5909/38]

MOSCOW, *July 17, 1922, 3.10 p.m.*

Your telegram No. 163.[1]

Failure of conference was discounted beforehand and I do not anticipate any serious internal developments will arise out of it. Karakhan regards rupture with equanimity. He has formed the opinion that Great Britain and Italy intended to wreck the conference in order to get rid of their obligations towards France and Belgium and then pursue policy of independent agreement with Russia. Only on this theory can he explain that Great Britain having accepted at Genoa principle of compensation in lieu of restitution[2] should have insisted at The Hague on integral restitution.[3] This opinion is widely held in circles which have throughout viewed with distrust Great Britain's attitude of compromise with Bolsheviks.

Soviet government now hopes to reach arrangements with individual states and with private interests. I learn on good authority that proposals emanating from British groups would be particularly welcome.

Policy to be followed in the near future will be, I believe, one of pure

[1] Of July 14. This ran: 'The Hague conference [see Vol. XIX, Chap. IV] has now definitely broken down. Please report by telegraph on developments in Moscow and how your situation is likely to be affected by failure of conference.'

[2] See Vol. XIX, No. 71, Appendix.

[3] See ibid., No. 148, Enclosure, and No. 191.

opportunism. The harvest being imminent it is felt that there is no immediate cause for anxiety, and before the autumn comes on and question of resumption of industry again becomes vital, it is hoped either individual negotiations will have succeeded in alleviating Russian economic difficulties or that political developments in Europe will have created a situation favourable to aspirations of the Communists. In this connection events in Germany are being followed with close attention and with the hope that any concession of a nature to relieve her economic position, such as moratorium, will be withheld. It is thought that discontent in Germany may lead to outbreak which will react on proletariat (? of) . . .,[4] that Austria is ripe for new experience (? in) communism and that inter-indebtedness amongst the allies may become fertile source of trouble between peoples affected. A special session of Russian Communist party opens on August 3rd and is likely to be important. Educated members of the party are alive to the necessities of economic situation, but unintelligent communists still clamour for literal fulfilment of doctrine of revolution. As Lenin is rapidly recovering and already taking interest in affairs it is probable that decisions will be taken in direction of moderation and concessions of a nature to attract foreign capital . . .[4] (? is) adoption of aggressive attitude possibly culminating in military adventure against Baltic States but there is no reason to fear this unless (? politics) in Germany or Poland give favourable opening.

[4] The text is here uncertain.

No. 522

Record[1] *by Sir G. Clerk (Prague) of a conversation with Dr. Beneš*[2]
[*N 9694/646/38*]

July 19, 1922

The Prime Minister said that he had for some time wished to speak to me on the subject of his relations with Mr. Lloyd George in Genoa,[3] and he was moved to do so now by information which he had just received from President Masaryk (who is spending a holiday in Italy) that Mr. Lloyd George had spoken to the Italians—presumably to Signor Schanzer—in somewhat harsh and, Dr. Beneš felt, unmerited terms of Dr. Beneš's attitude at the Genoa Conference.

At that Conference itself Sir Edward Grigg had told Dr. Beneš that Mr. Lloyd George was deeply disappointed at Dr. Beneš's failure to support the British point of view, as he had gathered in the early stages of the Conference that Dr. Beneš entirely shared that view.[4] Dr. Beneš had pointed out that he

[1] This document was not received in the Foreign Office until October 26.
[2] Czechoslovakian Prime Minister and Minister for Foreign Affairs.
[3] See Vol. XIX, Chap. III.
[4] On October 27 Mr. Gregory minuted: 'Mr. Lloyd George became firmly convinced about halfway through the Conference that M. Beneš was playing a double game and inciting

had pursued an open and consistent policy throughout. He had agreed with the British view that relations of some sort must if possible be set up with the Bolshevik Government, though he was, as he had always been and remained, opposed to a 'de jure' recognition. But he had very early become convinced that the Russians at Genoa would not accept the conditions discussed at the Conference and he had so informed Mr. Lloyd George, at the same time suggesting that the Conference should not be definitely broken up but should be, so to say, transformed into a purely business conference meeting after a decent interval at some other place. In fact, he was the author of the idea of the Hague Conference[5] and he knew from Monsieur Barthou himself that Mr. Lloyd George had quoted him as such when first suggesting the Hague Conference to Monsieur Barthou.[5]

Convinced as Dr. Beneš was that the Russians meant nothing serious at Genoa, he felt very strongly that the progressive divergence of view between France and England was not only most unfortunate in itself but provided increasing grist to the Russian mill and weakened the prospects of a satisfactory conclusion to any subsequent conference. Since in his view the Russian question at the Genoa Conference was practically eliminated, he considered that its main purpose had gone and he refused to allow himself to take sides in the differences between Great Britain and France, for to do so would only tend to aggravate the situation, which he deplored in itself and as weakening the position of the Allies in their dealings with the Russians.

Moreover, he had striven his utmost to preserve the outward unity of the Conference. When it looked as though France would withdraw, Poland and Roumania had intended to shew their solidarity with France by also leaving, but Dr. Beneš had told them that he was resolved to remain until the end, even if France left, and had thereby arrested this intention.

His attitude had throughout been consistent and open and he was deeply pained to find it not only not appreciated by the British Prime Minister but to hear it qualified in the terms which Mr. Lloyd George applied to it in speaking to the Germans, as the latter had taken careful occasion to tell him, and to the Italians, as he had just heard from President Masaryk.

Dr. Beneš felt also that even though, as he realised, the progress of events in Genoa had obliged him to adopt an attitude which might have disappointed the hopes of the British members of the Conference, that attitude had not been judged fairly on its merits but had been prejudiced by his association with Mr. Wickham Steed.[6] Dr. Beneš confessed that he had seen more of Mr. Wickham Steed than he himself personally welcomed, but Mr. Wickham Steed was not only an old personal friend but a man who had done work during the war for which the Czecho-Slovak Republic owed him a debt of

---

the Bolsheviks to resist our proposals in order to leave the ground clear for a separate agreement between his Government and them. This is indeed what happened. Within a few hours of the breakdown of the Conference he was busy negotiating an agreement [see No. 512]: and I must say that the information about his activities which reached me from quite independent and reliable sources was not altogether to his credit.'

[5] See Vol. XIX, No. 123.   [6] Editor of *The Times*.

gratitude and he, Dr. Beneš, would have thought himself unworthy if he had allowed his political disapproval of much that Mr. Wickham Steed was doing at Genoa to prejudice his personal relations. As a matter of fact, he had on nearly every occasion when he saw Mr. Wickham Steed begged him to be more moderate and sensible and had pointed out the folly and danger of his perpetual attacks on the British Prime Minister, and he had so far impressed Mr. Wickham Steed as to secure some moderation.

I told Dr. Beneš that I was not in a position to judge of what happened at Genoa, nor was I aware of the terms in which the British Prime Minister might have criticized the policy of Czecho-Slovakia, but I was certain that Mr. Lloyd George would not have made such criticism unless he considered them justified. But I reminded Dr. Beneš that the Secretary of State for Foreign Affairs had already (Mr. Vansittart's Private telegram of June 16th)[7] expressed his own and the Prime Minister's high opinion of Dr. Beneš's honesty and ability. In fact, if I might say so, it seemed to me that the attitude of the British Delegation at Genoa was one of disappointment, and not of reprobation. I would however take occasion, should it offer, to submit Dr. Beneš's explanation to my Chief.

[7] Not traced in the Foreign Office archives.

No. 523

Mr. Gregory to the India Office
[N 6673/2458/38]

FOREIGN OFFICE, *July 20, 1922*

Sir,

I am directed by the Earl of Balfour to acknowledge the receipt of your letter No. P 2208 of the 11th July[1] with reference to the possible bearing upon Indian interests of any arrangements entered into with the Soviet government.

2. I am to state that recent information from The Hague[2] does not point to the probability of an arrangement of any kind being come to with the representatives of the Russian Soviet government; consequently, the question of reviving any treaty arrangements affecting Indian interests is not likely immediately to arise.

3. If however the question of the revival of the arrangements with the late Imperial government of Russia were raised at a conference designed to place relations with the existing Government of Russia on a normal diplomatic basis, and if the renewal of these relations became dependent on the revival of one or more of the treaties with the late government of Russia, the matter would have to be considered in all its bearings, and the Government of India would be given full opportunity of expressing their view on such aspects of the problem as might affect them.

[1] Not printed.   [2] See Vol. XIX, No. 203.

4. I am to add that the Secretary of State will not fail to bear in mind, for his future guidance, the views of the India Office on this matter. In the meantime it would be desirable for the Secretary of State for India to explain his point of view to any delegate who may in future attend conferences with representatives of the Russian Government on behalf of the Government of India, so that he on his side may watch the proceedings with a view to ensure that the Government of India are not committed to a course of action inconsistent with their existing interests.

5. A copy of this correspondence is being sent[3] to the British Delegation at The Hague.

I am, etc.,
J. D. GREGORY

3 In despatch No. 48 of July 20, not printed.

No. 524

Mr. Hodgson (Moscow) to the Earl of Balfour (Received July 31)
No. 522 [N 7263/1691/38]

MOSCOW, *July 22, 1922*

My Lord,

With reference to Mr. Ovey's despatch No. 640 (N 6240/1691/38) of the 4th instant,[1] I have the honour to state that in my opinion, any action which I might take here on behalf of the Social Revolutionaries under trial[2] would be more likely to do harm than good. No efforts are being spared by the Soviet authorities to establish connection between the accused and foreign

1 This ran: 'I transmit herewith, for your information, a copy of a memorandum [not printed] which has been addressed to the Foreign Office by Mr. MacCallum Scott, M.P., and am to inform you that you are authorised, at your discretion, to use your good offices unofficially on behalf of the Socialist Revolutionaries now undergoing trial in Moscow, provided that you are of opinion that you can thereby do anything to help them.'

2 These alleged counter-revolutionaries, thirty-four in number, had been arrested over the preceding two years. In his Situation Report, May 31 to June 13 (see No. 517, n. 5), Mr. Hodgson stated: 'The trial . . . continues to fill the columns of the local press. The excitement it causes has every appearance of being worked up, for the events which led to the trial occurred so long ago, and so many things have happened since, that anything in the nature of spontaneous interest in the matter is out of the question. The press campaign seeks to implicate all political creeds other than the Bolshevik in the conspiracies of the S[ocial R[evolutionist]s, and is exhuming every conceivable incident in the counter-revolutionary movement to give colour to its charges. Every possible precaution has been taken to prevent the foreign advocates from coming into contact with the outside world. Vandervelde especially is the object of surveillance, being described as "the representative of one of the Governments most hostile to Russia".'

'It is still a matter of speculation as to what the sentences will be, but as the three judges are members of the Communist Party, and the counsel for the defence is partly composed of Communists, who contradict on all occasions their non-Communist colleagues, while the Public prosecutor is at the same time president of the Supreme Revolutionary Tribunal, the accused would appear to have little chance of an acquittal.'

governments. Intervention from abroad would, therefore, be liable only to play into the hands of the prosecution.

I have, etc.,
R. M. Hodgson

No. 525

The Earl of Balfour to Mr. Hodgson (Moscow)
No. 170 Telegraphic [N 6953/6953/38]

FOREIGN OFFICE, *July 24, 1922, 4.50 p.m.*

Your telegram No. 156 (of July 18th.[1] Closing of White Star offices in Moscow).

Last [sentence]. In no way whatever.

You should make suitable protest and insist on written explanation from Soviet government, and take such other steps for protection of company's agents and property as you can and report fully by despatch.[2]

[1] This ran: 'Moscow office of White Star Line was closed July 15th by militia and all correspondence seized. In discussions between commissaries of Foreign Affairs and Foreign Trade, the view was expressed that nothing was to be got by trade with Great Britain and that retaliation was justified in view of hostile attitude adopted in England towards Arcos. Inform me if operations of Arcos have been in any way curtailed by British authorities.'

[2] On July 26, Mr. Hodgson, in his telegram No. 159, reported: 'Offices were reopened on July 21st and all correspondance returned. Incident may be regarded as closed.'

No. 526

The Earl of Balfour to Mr. Hodgson (Moscow)
No. 762 [N 7102/567/38]

FOREIGN OFFICE, *July 29, 1922*

Sir,

As a result of an application submitted by the High Commissioner for Canada[1] notes[2] have recently been exchanged between this department and the Russian Trade Delegation in London providing for the adherence of the Dominion of Canada to the Anglo-Russian Trade Agreement. This arrangement is regarded as having been completed with full effect as from July 3rd.

2. In this connection I transmit herewith the enclosed copy of a letter No. 32721/22 of the 24th instant from the Colonial Office,[2] together with its enclosure,[2] submitting the name of Mr. Leonlyn Dana Wilgress for the post of Canadian trade representative in Russia.

3. I should be glad if you will submit Mr. Wilgress' name to the Soviet Government for this appointment and inform me, provided that a favourable

[1] The Rt. Hon. P. C. Larkin.   [2] Not printed.

reply is received, of your views as to when Mr. Wilgress might with advantage proceed to Russia.

4. It is regretted that the information contained in the first paragraph of this letter should not have been communicated to you sooner.

I am, etc.,
(for the Earl of Balfour)
J. D. Gregory

No. 527

Mr. Hodgson (Moscow) to the Earl of Balfour (Received August 9)
No. 555 [N 7541/2965/38]

MOSCOW, *July 31, 1922*

My Lord,

By telegram No. 165 of July 15th,[1] I was asked to express an opinion as to whether the intervention of the Prime Minister on behalf of the Patriarch Tikhon would be likely to serve a useful purpose. I replied[2] deprecating this action, which might, I thought, only lead to an insulting answer such as that recently given through the Russian Trade Delegation in London to the Archbishop of Canterbury.[3]

The fact that the Metropolitan Anthony was responsible for the suggested intervention would be an additional reason for withholding action. Anthony, who is, I believe, the ex-Metropolitan of Kiev, became prominent some months ago in connection with the convocation at Karlowitz of what was known as the Supreme Church Administration. This assembly, which was intended to unite Russian emigrants abroad, advocated the re-establishment of the monarchy and the restoration of the Romanovs. Any gesture instigated by the Metropolitan would be liable to produce results contrary to those which it is hoped to attain.[4]

I have, etc.,
R. M. Hodgson

[1] This ran: 'Metropolitan Anthony has appealed to Prime Minister and also to the President of the French Republic for their intervention with the Soviet authorities on behalf of the Patriarch Tikhon [see Nos. 503 and 517].

'Please telegraph whether in your opinion such intervention would serve any purpose or whether it would only be likely to make matters worse.'

An appeal had also been made to the American Government (see *F.R.U.S.* 1922, vol. ii, pp. 835–40).

[2] In telegram No. 158 of July 22. This ran: 'I do not consider intervention on behalf of patriarch at this time would have any good result and it might be indeed harmful. The patriarch is still kept in a state of close seclusion under armed guard. It is not yet certain whether he will be actually brought before a court. Any protest from foreign countries is liable to be met by an affront and will certainly be utilised to demonstrate solidity of bourgeois powers with the enemies of proletariat.'

[3] See No. 517, n. 1.

[4] In his despatch No. 621 of August 21 (N 8069/2965/38), not printed, Mr. Hodgson

transmitted to the Foreign Office a translation of a long report drawn up by priests and lay-men describing the initial conflict between the Soviet Government and the Orthodox Church. Mr. Hodgson commented: 'The feeling that the Church should become again a living force was widely spread, but the priesthood was incompetent to take advantage of it and the people too apathetic, too depressed and too ignorant to take the lead themselves. The Soviet Government has stepped in and utilised for its own ends the failure of the Church to mend its ways. With a brutality which has effectually crushed sporadic efforts at resistance it has set itself to destroy the Church hierarchy; with an ingenuity which would be admirable in a better cause it has profited by the situation arising out of the famine to discredit the old Church administration, and it has seized an opportune moment to direct in channels useful to itself the perfectly natural and healthy desire of the people for a Church more in harmony with its present needs.

'It has selected Bishop Antonin and his colleagues as its instruments, and it has facilitated by its support the coming into being of the so-called "Living Church," of which these ecclesiastics are the initiators.

'The "Living Church" has become a power in the land. It has its headquarters in the Patriarch's residence, has usurped all the functions of the old Church administration, and the number of its adherents is rapidly growing.'

No. 528

Mr. Hodgson (Moscow) to the Earl of Balfour
(Received August 2, 7.50 p.m.)
No. 164 Telegraphic [N 7358/2965/38]

MOSCOW, *August 1, 1922, 5.50 p.m.*

Your telegram No. 176.[1]

It is not yet clear whether Patriarch[2] will be actually brought before a court or not. Should he be tried I see no objection to my seeking permission for a member of my staff to attend. Though I think it unlikely that foreign interest would influence favourably course of trial yet there is no reason to believe that it would prejudice position of Patriarch.

[1] Of July 28. This ran: 'Archbishop of Canterbury enquires whether His Majesty's government could secure presence of impartial observer at impending trial of Patriarch Tikhon. Telegraph your views as to desirability of requesting permission for one of your staff to attend.'

[2] See Nos. 503, 517, 518, and 527.

No. 529

Mr. Hoare[1] (Warsaw) to the Earl of Balfour (Received August 8)
No. 358 [N 7478/1999/38]

WARSAW, *August 2, 1922*

My Lord,

With reference to my despatch No. 270 of June 1st,[2] regarding the rumoured reorganisation of the Red Army, I have the honour to transmit herewith

[1] Acting Chargé d'Affaires at Warsaw.
[2] Not printed. See, however, Nos. 508 and 520.

a short summary of a report on the subject prepared by the Polish General Staff.[3] The Military Mission, to whom I am indebted for the loan of this document, have already forwarded copies in extenso to the War Office.

The report, if well-founded, disposes of the rumours, mentioned in the last sentence of my despatch, that the Soviet military authorities intended to form a larger number of divisions with lower effectives, and the Polish General Staff appear to be considerably impressed by the reorganisation which is taking place.

I have, etc.,

R. H. HOARE

[3] The summary ran: 'The simplicity and suitability of the new organisation, and the progress which has already been effected, indicate that trained officers of "a western power" (Germany) are lending their co-operation. Of this there is, however, no definite evidence. . . . The Soviet General Staff have shown energy and common sense; they have abandoned their prejudice against the European system, which they have adopted and even simplified. The Red Army is thus being raised gradually to the level of the armies of western Europe, and is becoming a factor to be reckoned with, especially by the states bordering on Russia.'

No. 530

Mr. Millington-Drake[1] *(Bucharest) to the Earl of Balfour*
(Received August 10, 2 p.m.)

No. 91 Telegraphic [N 7582/4287/38]

BUCHAREST, *August 9, 1922, 10 p.m.*

My telegram No. 86.[2]

Secretary-general of Ministry of Foreign Affairs called today and told me that Roumanian government had now informed Soviet government that they were prepared to participate in disarmament conference with other states bordering on Russia but on express condition that existing frontiers were recognised. This information was also being communicated to my French colleague.

Secretary-general added (which Minister for Foreign Affairs had not mentioned) that overture was made by Litvinov to Roumanian representative at the Hague who submitted it to his government on his return. See my despatch No. 422.[3]

[1] Acting Chargé d'Affaires at Bucharest.

[2] Of August 4. This ran: 'Minister for Foreign Affairs informed me today unofficially and confidentially that Roumanian government have received overtures from Soviet government for negotiations regarding disarmament, and recovery of Roumanian treasure.

'He was going to refer matter to King [Ferdinand] at first opportunity next week. He thought that Roumanian government could not do otherwise than express willingness to negotiate, but would then wish His Majesty's Government to be informed at once.'

[3] Of August 2 (N 7480/646/38), not printed.

The Marquess Curzon of Kedleston[1] to Mr. Hodgson (Moscow)
No. 793 [N 7372/155/38]

Confidential   FOREIGN OFFICE, *August 10, 1922*

Sir,

Mr. Krassin was received by Mr. Lloyd George on the 28th of July,[2] immediately prior to his departure for Moscow.

2. Mr. Lloyd George impressed on Mr. Krassin the importance of obtaining a direct and unequivocal answer from the Soviet Government to the questions submitted to it as the outcome of The Hague Conference.[3] Mr. Krassin, in reply, referred to the proposal made by the Russian Delegation at The Hague[4] that the governments concerned should express their opinion whether, in the event of the desired assurances being given by the Soviet Government, they would consider this satisfactory. Mr. Lloyd George pointed out that as far as Great Britain was concerned this point was answered by the reply which he had given to Mr. Wise in the House of Commons on the 27th of July[5] (my despatch No. 759 of July 29th).[6] Mr. Lloyd George explained that this reply meant that the British government would encourage their nationals to return to Russia and would give them the advantages of the export credits and trade facilities schemes.

3. Mr. Krassin then touched on the question of *de jure* recognition of Russia, the absence of which he said was an obstacle in the way of large capitalists embarking in Russian trade. Mr. Lloyd George pointed out that for trading purposes Russia was recognised under the Anglo-Russian Trade Agreement, but Mr. Krassin urged that this was not really sufficient, and alluded to certain negotiations in regard to, e.g. oil concessions, which would not come to a successful conclusion until Russia was recognised. Mr. Lloyd George, however, was unable to admit that the absence of *de jure* recognition could be the cause why these negotiations were still pending. He believed that, once the two governments could come to an understanding on the points at issue, all negotiations of this nature would be easily put through. Mr. Krassin agreed, but urged that, in this event, some further arrangement might be formally concluded between the two countries and the result made generally known. Mr. Lloyd George, in reply, pointed out that the idea of His Majesty's Government was to effect recognition by degrees; in the first instance a chargé d'affaires might be appointed in London and in Moscow, with full authority, and later full recognition might be achieved, when the position had been proved satisfactory. If during this interim period the Soviet Government were able to come to arrangements with British capitalists, the latter would no doubt bring pressure to bear in favour of granting

[1] See No. 24, n. 1.

[2] The British Secretary's Note of this conversation held at 10 Downing Street, London, at 6.50 p.m. on July 28 (S 54) is preserved at N 7372/155/38.

[3] See Vol. XIX, No. 202.   [4] See ibid., Nos. 202 and 203.

[5] See 157 *H.C. Deb.*, 5 s, cols. 687–8.   [6] Not printed.

full recognition and of exchanging Ambassadors. Mr. Krassin, urging that the existing Trade Agreement could be broken at any moment, said that his government was anxious for something more definite which would be tantamount to absolute recognition. After some further discussion Mr. Lloyd George accepted the suggestion that, in the event of the Soviet Government's reply to the questions now under their consideration being satisfactory, it might be necessary for some further agreement to be signed between His Majesty's Government and the Soviet Government, and expressed the view that in the event of such a favourable issue arrangements might be made for an exchange of chargés d'affaires, preliminary to the grant of full recognition which would follow if the position developed satisfactorily. Sir Philip Lloyd-Greame, who was present at the interview, informed Mr. Krassin that it would be possible to take this next step towards recognition without awaiting a further general conference. Mr. Lloyd George then read to Mr. Krassin the enclosed extract from his speech in the House of Commons on the 3rd of April,[7] prior to the Genoa Conference, showing the attitude of His Majesty's Government towards the question of recognition of the Soviet Government.

4. Mr. Lloyd George then alluded to the unfortunate actions on the part of the Soviet Government which were apt to disturb the favourable development of the situation. He referred, for example, to the issue by the Russian Delegation at Genoa of the memorandum defending the doctrine of repudiation of debts.[8] He said that this had not only had a most unfavourable effect on the other states represented at the conference, but had been wholly unnecessary. Mr. Krassin replied that it was primarily designed for consumption in Russia.

5. Mr. Krassin said that he expected to be back in a fortnight's time, and the conversation then closed.

I am, etc.,
(for the Secretary of State)
Esmond Ovey

[7] See No. 490, n. 1.
[8] See Vol. XIX, No. 89, Annex. See also ibid., No. 122.

No. 532

Mr. Hodgson (Moscow) to the Marquess Curzon of Kedleston
(Received August 22)
No. 597 [N 7893/12/38]

moscow, *August 14, 1922*

My Lord,
 A copy has been produced to me of a telegram from Dr. Nansen in Christiania addressed to M. Kamanev, who is at the head of the Russian Famine Relief Organisation, of which the following is a translation:—

 'Litvinov stated at The Hague that Russia will this year be in a position to export grain.[1] This declaration he repeated on the 25th July to the press. Unless a categorical *démenti* is issued, propaganda for help with the Russian famine in Europe and in South America is quite useless, and we must give up all work. Our position will as a result become quite untenable. Please reply and save our work.'

M. Kamanev has avoided replying to this telegram, but a Mr. Lander, who has taken the place of Mr. Eiduk as intermediary between the foreign relief associations and the Russian Government, has communicated to Mr. Gorter, of the Nansen organisation, an answer the tenor of which is stated by M. Kamanev's secretary to represent his views.

This reply explains that M. Litvinov's statement 'was based on the fact that this year's crop is a fairly good one, and is absolutely better than last year's'; that the need for further help is still, however, very great, as thousands of children have been left homeless and in need of care; that the peasants have been ruined, and gigantic efforts are required to enable them again to cultivate an adequate area; that parts of Russia have again suffered from drought and locusts, particularly the Crimea, the Odessa, Nicolaiev and Zaparog Governments, the Tartar Republic and other parts of the Volga area; that Dr. Nansen is requested again to apply his energies for the organisation of relief in Russia during the coming winter.

Recently there was held in Berlin a meeting called by M. Krestinsky,[2] attended by representatives of the various bodies interested in relief in this country. Dr. Nansen, I believe, was represented at it by Mr. Frick. At this meeting Mr. Eiduk drew an optimistic picture of the position of this country, saying that the lean period was now over and charity was no longer required. The period of reconstruction was now upon them, and the co-operation for this purpose of Dr. Nansen and his colleagues would be warmly welcomed.

Officials of the American Relief Administration, of the Nansen organisation and of various bodies affiliated thereto confirm the statements of Mr. Lander, and, indeed in some instances assert that the distress in large areas of Russia is likely this year to be at least as severe as it was during 1921–22. Even so, I do not think that there is any call for another altruistic effort on the part of Great Britain. If the distress does attain such dimensions that, as a matter of common humanity, it is impossible to stand aloof, I am strongly of opinion that another figure-head than Dr. Nansen should be selected and that no connection should be had with any organisation under his guidance.

I am against the continuation of help to the Russian famine districts, because, in the first place, the Russian Government, both through its official press and through the mouths of its representatives abroad, has declared insistently that help is no longer needed. Doubtless these declarations—as to the accuracy of which neither M. Litvinov nor Mr. Eiduk can have any illusions—were designed to impress Western Europe at The Hague Conference with a sense of Russia's independence of the outside world; but, whether this

[1] Cf. Vol. XIX, No. 173.   [2] Accredited Soviet representative in Berlin.

is so or not, I consider there is every reason for taking responsible representatives of the Soviet Government—in this instance, at all events—at their word. If what they say is true, grain can be exported, and the money realisable from export should be utilised for purchasing medical supplies, &c., of which the country is denuded; if, as I imagine is the case, they purposely distorted the facts and relief is really required, it should be given only when the Government admits its necessity, and then only on terms agreeable to the donors.

The position might be different had the Russian Government shown any disposition to be grateful for the foreign aid extended in the past; it has, on the contrary, been blatantly and consistently ungrateful. No opportunity has been lost of decrying the efforts of foreign organisations or of creating suspicion as to the motives which inspired their actions; the agents of foreign relief societies have been faced everywhere with the obstructiveness of officials sent to the famine areas by the Central Government, and have everywhere had to overcome an insistent propaganda directed to inducing the belief in the mind of the people that the foreigners are in reality doing nothing, but that all credit for assistance is to be rendered to the Soviet Administration.

In the second place, I believe that from the point of view of the development of the general situation in Russia further assistance would be ill-advised, as tending to interfere with the normal course of events. Experience has abundantly shown that the individuals who control the destinies of Russia at the present time are refractory to reason; that it is only the driving force of circumstances that can impel them to adopt a policy in harmony with that of the outside world—in other words, that evolution is taking place in Russia, not with their goodwill, but in spite of their efforts to retard it. This being so, anything that makes their task easier for them at home is harmful in the end, and tends to prolong a situation which the folly of those who have created it is steadily determining.

I am against any further association with Dr. Nansen or any organisation connected with him, because, in the first place, the work done hitherto in his name has been badly done, and there is no reason to think that it will be better done in the future; secondly, because any British effort made through him loses its individuality; and, thirdly, because I distrust the motives which underlie the actions, if not of Dr. Nansen himself, at all events of his close associates.

That the work of the Nansen organisation has been badly done hardly needs demonstration; its defects are already known in England. The individuals in charge on the spot have been, as a rule, badly selected and inefficient; the distribution of relief has been attempted over an area larger than the resources available justified—with results that might be anticipated; individual groups working under the Nansen agreement have indeed been successful, but the work generally has lacked harmony and has been piecemeal and unbusinesslike.

The assistance rendered by Great Britain to the cause of famine relief has been considerable, and, particularly in the case of the 'Save the Children

Fund,' has been efficiently organised in the country and satisfactory in its results. It has, however, been successful rather in spite of than on account of its connection with Dr. Nansen. It has suffered in that its individuality has been merged in that of the larger organisation by which it was nominally controlled, but of which it found it necessary in practice to be independent. Without wishing to utilise for purposes of national propaganda an organisation which is purely humanitarian in its objects, I think that it is obvious that an arrangement is faulty which deprives of credit due to it the country whose contributions have made the operation of the organisation possible.

The last objection which I have to further connection with Dr. Nansen entails treading on more delicate ground, but I think that recent developments show that it is well grounded. A very clearly defined tendency exists to use the Nansen agreement for putting on foot projects which, on examination, prove to be not altruistic but commercial. At the Berlin meeting mentioned above, Mr. Frick's attitude was particularly instructive. He gave whole-hearted support to the proposal to transfer to reconstruction the energies so far devoted to charity. By reconstruction, as understood by the Dutch, Swedish and Czechoslovak organisations, is meant the exploitation of land in Russia on commercial lines—an excellent object, and one of which the execution will assist powerfully this country's recovery from the state of depression into which she has been plunged by war, famine, pestilence and the folly of her rulers, but not one with which, I think, Dr. Nansen's organisation is competent to deal, or one which is likely to commend itself to the charitable public in England.

I have, etc.,
R. M. Hodgson

No. 533

Mr. Hodgson (Moscow) to the Marquess Curzon of Kedleston
(Received August 22)

No. 601 [N 7896/1691/38]

MOSCOW, *August 15, 1922*

My Lord,

As reported in my telegram No. 169 of the 9th August,[1] the trial of the Social Revolutionaries[2] came to an end on the 7th instant with the condemnation to death of fifteen persons (of whom three, who turned informers, were recommended to mercy), the acquittal of two, and sentences of various terms of imprisonment, ranging from two to ten years, on the rest.

The trial lasted fifty days, and was characterized from beginning to end by a series of incidents which demonstrated how completely the idea of proletarian justice, as administered in Bolshevik Russia, is at variance with the principles of justice as understood in the civilised world outside. Communist

<hr>

[1] Not printed.　　　[2] See No. 524, n. 2.

judges sat in a packed court to try a group of representatives of the political party which Communists regard as that of their most dangerous and most irreconcilable foes. There was really no pretence of administering justice, for in response to the demands of a popular demonstration—also arranged by the party—the judges openly declared their intention of discarding *bourgeois* precedents, and, in deference to the will of the people as expressed by the manifestants, of deciding the case impartially as regards facts, but partially as regards the personality of the accused.

The resolution of the Presidium of the All-Russia Central Executive Committee, which approved the sentences of the court but decided that the twelve persons condemned to death shall be detained indefinitely as hostages for the good behaviour of the Social Revolutionary Party as a whole, is a fitting termination to the proceedings.

I am transmitting herewith a résumé of the sentences taken from the local press.[1]

I have, etc.,
R. M. Hodgson

No. 534

Mr. Hodgson (Moscow) to the Marquess Curzon of Kedleston
(Received August 28)
No. 629 [N 8074/4058/38]

MOSCOW, *August 22, 1922*

My Lord Marquess,

I have the honour to transmit herewith translation of a speech[1] pronounced by M. Krassin on the occasion of the first meeting of the Special Commission appointed to prepare the Russo-German Commercial Treaty.[2]

The speech does not hold out great hopes of important economic results accruing to Russia from the signature of the prospective agreement and admits that the primary benefit which it can bring to Russia will be the breaking down of the wall which the Entente has built around her. In order to reach an agreement with Germany which will accomplish this object, Russia is prepared to go to the utmost limit in the matter of concessions.

The attitude of members of the German mission in Moscow, as revealed in their conversation, is not without interest. They lose no opportunity of asserting that it is only by the force of circumstances that Germany is driven towards closer relations with Russia: they admit that the two parties to the projected treaty are not at present in a position to assist one another materially and state that so far, at all events, the Russian Government has not shown an inclination to yield on the essential principles which make a compact with a bourgeois state impossible: yet, in the position to which Germany has been

[1] Not printed. The speech was printed in the *Ekonimicheskaya Zhizn* of August 17.
[2] See No. 519.

reduced, she is driven by her isolation to come to terms with a Government with which she has nothing in common.

I will not fail to keep in touch with the progress of events and will report to Your Lordship in due course.

I have, etc.,

R. M. HODGSON

No. 535

Mr. Hodgson (Moscow) to the Marquess Curzon of Kedleston
(Received August 28)

No. 630 [N 8975/6953/38]

MOSCOW, *August 22, 1922*

My Lord Marquess,

With reference to my despatch No. 568 of August 4th,[1] I have the honour to report that the Moscow Office of the White Star Line, though it has now resumed operations, has not yet been able to rid itself of the disagreeable attentions of the secret police. One of the office employees, a young girl, has been continually pestered by the same police agent who has distinguished himself in other matters referred to in my despatch No. 609,[2] while a boy of eighteen, son of a general of the Russian Army, who is also working in the office, was recently dragged off to prison, treated abominably and finally, under threats, compelled to sign an undertaking to act as a spy upon the doings of the Company in Russia. He was told that Major Bustard was a secret service agent and that the White Star Office in Moscow was nothing but an organisation for collecting confidential information.

I took the matter up yesterday with M. Karakhan, pointing out that the procedure of the secret police with regard to the White Star Line was stupid and entirely inexcusable. I did not mention, for obvious reasons, the names of the persons who had been approached by the police, but pointed out that, as long as foreign firms which started operations in Russia were exposed to persecution of this kind, it was impossible to expect commercial relations between Russia and the outside world to develop. M. Karakhan agreed with me that the attitude of suspicion adopted by the police towards the White Star Line was absurd and wrong and asked that details of the actions of the police of which I had cause to complain should be communicated to the head of the Anglo-American Department of the Commissariat.

I am following up this matter and will not fail to communicate to Your Lordship the results of my action.

I have, etc.,

R. M. HODGSON

---

[1] Not printed. See, however, No. 525.
[2] Of August 17 (N 8065/5429/38), not printed.

No. 536

Mr. Hodgson (Moscow) to the Marquess Curzon of Kedleston
(Received August 24, 7.30 p.m.)
No. 183 Telegraphic [N 7987/1691/38]

MOSCOW, *August 24, 1922, 1 p.m.*

Soviet government has within last few days arrested numerous professors of all branches in Moscow and Petrograd, also leading scientists, engineers, co-operators and others (? to total of) one hundred of whom seventy from Moscow are being expelled the country and given seven days in which to cross the frontier. These wholesale arrests are in harmony with views expressed by Zinoviev at recent conference[1] and are obviously effort to reassert authority of communist party by getting rid of persons whose influence is feared as being leaders of thought in directions hostile to communist system. Advocates who defended social revolutionaries[2] are kept in solitary confinement and are being banished to Archangel district.

[1] The All-Russian Conference of the Communist Party. In his Situation Report for August 23–9 enclosed in his despatch No. 660 of August 29 (N 8243/472/38), Mr. Hodgson stated: 'Zinoviev's speech . . . made it clear that the propaganda weapon was to be vigorously employed in order to gain popular support for the Government by persuading the nation that its enemies were again endeavouring to encompass the downfall of the country.'

[2] See Nos. 524, n. 2, and 533.

No. 537

Lord D'Abernon (Berlin) to the Marquess Curzon of Kedleston
(Received September 5)
No. 700 [N 8257/1999/38]

BERLIN, *August 30, 1922*

My Lord Marquess,

The following telegram appeared in a recent copy of 'The Times'[1]:—

'General Braun, of the German Army, with one hundred German officer specialists, has completed several months' study of the Russian situation on the spot, and it is now reported that Trotsky is undertaking an aeroplane trip to Germany with the plan of a definite military convention to lay before the German General Staff.'

I have made enquiry here regarding this, through General Bingham,[2] who reports that he has been able to ascertain nothing of a nature to confirm it, and that he entirely discredits the statements made. Personally I regard any extended co-operation between German officers and the Soviet Army organisation as in the last degree improbable, the temperament and the tenets

[1] See *The Times*, August 24, 1922, p. 7.
[2] See No. 202, n. 9.

of the two parties being fundamentally opposed.[3] The last thing that Trotsky would willingly admit into the Soviet organisation are foreigners whom he regards as potential spies, and ex-German officers whom he regards, with some justice, as politically hostile to the whole Soviet conception.

Extreme external pressure exercised simultaneously upon Germany and Russia might finally weld the two military organisms together but it would be a task of almost superhuman difficulty. The military sphere is the last in which co-operation will be achieved. There is much greater sympathy in the financial and industrial worlds (notably between the Jews of both countries) than is the case among those engaged in the profession of arms.

In this connection I enclose summary of an article[4] in the 'Frankfurter Zeitung', which gives information regarding the present condition of the Russian Army.[5]

I have, etc.,
D'ABERNON

[3] Cf. Nos. 501, 502, 505, and 529. Cf. also John Erickson, op. cit., Chap. 6.
[4] Not printed.
[5] See Nos. 508, 510, and 520.

No. 538

Memorandum
[*N 8210/13/38*]

FOREIGN OFFICE, *September 4, 1922*

It has been noted that a large number of applications are being regularly received for the admission of Russians into this country under the Trade Agreement. It would, *prima facie*, appear to be a matter of considerable doubt whether the large proportions which the number of such applications has assumed are in any way commensurate with the amount of trade that has taken place between Great Britain and Russia under the Trade Agreement.

2. It is therefore requested that the Foreign Office may be furnished at an early date with such information as the Department of Overseas Trade may have in their possession, or may be able to procure, which would show the total value in pounds sterling of such contracts as have been completely executed up to the present date between this country and Russia under the Trade Agreement.

3. It is desirable that any figures quoted in this connection should be derived from data other than those supplied by the Russian Trade Delegation or the interests connected with it.[1]

[1] On September 9 the Department of Overseas Trade transmitted to the Foreign Office a statement showing the value of United Kingdom trade with Russia from April 1, 1921 to June 30, 1922, and with Latvia and Esthonia during the same period. Lord Curzon minuted (September 14): 'The figures show that more is being done than I at least expected.'

No. 539

Mr. Hodgson (Moscow) to the Marquess Curzon of Kedleston
(Received September 18)
No. 676 [N 8578/5429/38]

Confidential   MOSCOW, *September 6, 1922*

My Lord Marquess,

In my despatch No. 609 of the 17th August[1] I reported upon the activity recently displayed by the State Political Department in connection with this mission.

I now learn from a reliable source that the reason for this outburst of interest in the working of this mission was a report sent in by M. Litvinov from The Hague,[2] drawing attention to the fact that the British Delegation there was in possession of information on economic matters which showed an acquaintance with facts too close to have been obtained through normal channels. It was assumed that this material was obtained from the British Mission in Moscow—consequently, that this mission must have secret sources of information which needed investigation. M. Dzerzhinski, head of the State Political Department, was accordingly instructed to take necessary action in order to establish with what persons or organisations I was in contact.

The Commissariat for Foreign Affairs has laid it down as a fast rule that foreign missions should approach no government departments or institutions except through its intermediary: moreover, any individual in Russia who gives information to foreigners, or even to Russians abroad, on commercial or industrial matters is liable to be charged with a mysterious offence known as 'economic espionage' for which till recently the death penalty, and even now very heavy sentences of imprisonment, can be pronounced. In spite of this, as it is practically unheard of for the Commissariat for Foreign Affairs ever to communicate any information of any use to anyone, foreign missions are compelled either to transgress consistently the rule laid down by the Commissariat or to remain ignorant. The fact that the British Delegation at The Hague was in possession of information obtained in Moscow otherwise than through official channels should not have shocked M. Litvinov.

2. In my despatch under reference I mentioned that I had already complained in general terms to M. Karakhan of the obnoxious methods adopted by the agents of the Soviet Government in their efforts at espionage upon foreign missions here. I again took up this matter with him on the 4th instant from the point of view that, though foreign missions are not concerned in the unpleasant methods followed by the Russian secret police in its dealings with Russian citizens in Russia, yet it could, I thought, hardly be agreeable to the Soviet Government to know that foreign representatives were aware that Russians, among other things, were being dragged to prison and forced by threats to act as spies upon them.

[1] Not printed.
[2] M. Litvinov had attended The Hague Conference (see Vol. XIX, Chap. IV).

M. Karakhan appeared to be impressed by this argument and assured me that my previous observations on the subject had been borne in mind, but I do not suppose that, in reality, he is desirous or indeed able to interfere seriously with the operations of the State Political Department.

I have, etc.,

R. M. HODGSON

No. 540

Mr. Hodgson (Moscow) to the Marquess Curzon of Kedleston
(Received September 19)
No. 683 [N 8605/573/38]

MOSCOW, *September 8, 1922*

My Lord Marquess,

I have the honour to report that a group of ten persons, supposed to be representing French commercial interests, has recently arrived in Moscow.

I learn that this visit is the outcome of negotiations conducted by M. Chicherin in Berlin, the intermediary being a M. Olshansky, a Pole from Paris, who has close but somewhat obscure relations with the Bolshevik Government.

The Russian press is inclined to attach to the appearance in Moscow of this group greater importance than it would seem in reality to possess. It sees in it an indication that the Soviet policy has triumphed and French capital is on the point of abandoning its attitude of reserve towards Russia.

In fact the party is visiting Russia mainly for purposes of obtaining information, and its composition is not such as to justify the expectations it has aroused. The ten arrivals include, I believe, only two Frenchmen—one an engineer, formerly employed by the Makeyevka Iron and Coalfields (Belgian), and one representing the Salmson Motors—the rest being of various nationalities, including an Englishman (Mr. Bloomfield, who represents Consortium Pathé and various French medical specialities), a Swede, an American and one or two Belgians, acting on behalf of commercial interests not of first rate importance.[1]

I have, etc.,

R. M. HODGSON

[1] In his despatch No. 715 of September 22 Mr. Hodgson reported the arrival in Moscow on September 20 of M. Herriot, the Mayor of Lyons. He went on to say: 'Much is being made by the Bolshevik press of Monsieur Herriot's visit to which important signification is given and which is interpreted as heralding a complete change in the attitude of France towards the Soviet Government.'

Mr. Hodgson (Moscow) to the Marquess Curzon of Kedleston
(Received September 18)
No. 697 [N 8585/2965/38]

MOSCOW, *September 11, 1922*

My Lord Marquess,

Since my last despatch on the subject of the conflict between the Orthodox Church and the Soviet Government (No. 621 of August 21st)[1] several cases have been decided arising out of charges brought by the Government against ecclesiastics and laymen of opposing the confiscation of church treasures.

The Smolensk trial (Situation Report accompanying my despatch No. 660 of August 29th)[2] concluded with the condemnation of four laymen to death. At Rostov Bishop Arsenius and a number of clergy and laymen were condemned to various terms of imprisonment. The bishop, who is said to have made a confession of guilt, had the death sentence commuted to one of ten years' imprisonment.

An important development in the conflict has been a split within the 'Living Church'.[1] Bishop Antonin who, at the time of the congress of the Living Church in August had dissented upon the question of allowing married priests to become bishops and, on his proposal being rejected, resigned his position as chairman of the supreme church administration, has now definitely seceded from the Living Church, placing himself at the head of a group styled 'Church Regeneration'. The new group, which has a prominent supporter in N. Bogoluibsky, professor of theology in the Theological Academy, declares its desire to return to the democratic state of the original Christian Church and the simplification of ritual: it is prepared to admit both 'white' and 'black' priests to the episcopate, but holds that the question of the second marriage of ecclesiastics must be settled by the General Assembly and demands that all church appointments be filled by election: it admits the monastic life as a means of spiritual refuge but not as a method of obtaining temporal advantage.

'Church Regeneration', which acknowledges the Soviet Government and admits the righteousness of the social revolution, has already come into actual being and has formed its own administration, consisting of six priests with Bishop Antonin at its head. It is at enmity with the Living Church, which has demanded unsuccessfully that the bishop be expelled from Moscow. In many quarters it is believed that the dissension which has led to the creation of this new sect has been staged in order to multiply divisions in the Church and so increase its weakness.

For a government which is professedly atheistic and which has lost no opportunity of harrying religion, the Bolsheviks find themselves in a singularly incongruous position. By protecting and encouraging the Living Church they have identified themselves with this new religious body and

---

[1] See No. 527, n. 4.   [2] See No. 536, n. 1.

have become responsible for it—in fact, the Living Church has become the established church: by the strong stand they have taken in their *démêlés* with the Polish Government (vide my despatches Nos. 573[3] and 651[3] of August 7th and 28th respectively) they have emerged as the champions of oppressed religious minorities abroad.

I have, etc.,

R. M. HODGSON

[3] Not printed.

No. 542

Mr. Ovey to M. Berzin
[N 8258/153/38]

FOREIGN OFFICE, *September 18, 1922*

Sir,

With reference to your letter No. I.B/8866 of May 5th last[1] I am directed by the Marquess Curzon of Kedleston to inform you that His Majesty's Government are now prepared to hand over to the Russian Government the S.S. 'Marie Rose' and the S.S. 'Ethelaida'.[2]

2. It is desired that the formalities for effecting this transfer may be completed in the customary manner.

3. I am therefore to request that some person may be delegated on behalf of the Russian Government to make the necessary arrangements with the Board of Trade direct for taking an inventory of these vessels and that similarly when the vessels are placed in drydock by the Soviet Government the Board shall be granted the necessary facilities for inspecting and agreeing the condition of their bottoms and underwater fittings.

4. At the same time I am to point out that there are at present detained in Petrograd three ships, the property of His Majesty's Government namely the 'Flour', 'Moscow' and 'Saltburn'.[3]

5. It is presumed that the Russian Government is prepared to grant reciprocal treatment in respect of these ships and I am to request that immediate arrangements may be made for handing over these vessels, free of all liens and encumbrances, to the Board's nominee in Petrograd.

I am, etc.,

ESMOND OVEY

[1] Not printed.

[2] These vessels had belonged to the Imperial Russian Government and had been requisitioned by H.M. Government during the war.

[3] Negotiations were in progress for the evacuation of these damaged British steamers from Petrograd.

No. 543

Mr. Ovey to the Home Office
[N 7802/13/38]

FOREIGN OFFICE, *September 16, 1922*

Sir,

With reference to the letter from this department No. 6863/13/38 of the 14th ultimo,[1] I am directed by the Marquess Curzon of Kedleston to transmit herewith a copy of a letter from Monsieur Berzin[1] enclosing:—

(1) revised lists of the staff of the Russian Trade Delegation and Arcos Limited, and

(2) lists of those officials to whom he has requested that permanent visas may be issued.

2. The question of granting to certain members of the above organisations facilities which would enable them to journey to and from this country without each time completing the formalities which are at present in force formed the subject of an Interdepartmental Conference which was held at the Home Office on July 28th last.[2] It was generally agreed at this

---

[1] Not printed.

[2] This question had long been under discussion. A Foreign Office Memorandum (N 6863/13/38) of August 4 states: 'On the 21st of March Mr. Berzin, in response to a request from this office, furnished two lists of staff; (1) for the office of the Official Agent of the Russian Socialist Federal Soviet Republic, 128 New Bond Street, and the Information Bureau and Publishing Department, 68 A. Lincoln's Inn Fields, and (2) for the Russian Trade Delegation proper, Soviet House, 49 Moorgate.

'On the 20th of June, in reply to a protestation which we had addressed to him, owing to the presentation to Mr. Charnock of a questionnaire on the occasion of his rejoining the British Mission in Moscow, Mr. Klishko stated that the Trade Agreement provided at present for diplomatic treatment of three persons on each side only. He continued that no questionnaire was laid before Mr. Hodgson, Mr. Grove, or Mr. Peters; and that in the case of Mr. Charnock and the other members of the staff the question of diplomatic treatment and visas did not arise. Article 5 on the Trade Agreement is worded as follows:—"Either party may appoint one or more official agents to a number to be mutually agreed upon . . .". There has been, so far as I am aware, no formal agreement that this number shall be fixed at three, but as a matter of fact (apart from Professor Lomonosov, who does not belong to the Trade Delegation and is a case apart) diplomatic visas have been granted only to Krassin, Berzin, and Klishko. The question of diplomatic treatment of the staff of the Trade Delegation has, as far as I am aware, arisen only as regards diplomatic visas. I understand that, nevertheless, as a matter of courtesy the whole of the staff of the Moscow Mission are, in Moscow (though not in London), granted diplomatic visas.

'In the same letter Mr. Klishko proposes that the formality of filling in a questionnaire should be waived for the whole of the staff of the Moscow Mission if we are prepared to accord "similar treatment" to the members of the Trade Delegation staff, who appear on the two lists furnished on the 21st of March. It appears, however, that the term "similar treatment" should not be interpreted too closely. What was apparently intended was that, provided Mr. Hodgson is authorised to grant visas to persons on those lists who are returning from Russia to London without prior reference to London, the Trade Delegation in this country will issue visas to members of the Moscow Mission returning from here to Moscow on the request of this department without any further formality.

'On the 15th of July Mr. Berzin requested that no difficulty should be made for the staff

Conference that it was desirable to grant permanent visas which should be valid for six or twelve months up to as wide limits as were reasonable, but that no definite decision could be taken in the matter until Monsieur Berzin should have furnished the names of those individuals for whom this privilege was desired.

3. In view of the information which has now been obtained, I am to enquire whether the Home Office is prepared in principle to sanction the grant, to a limited number of members of the Russian Trade Delegation and of Arcos of the necessary facilities to enable them to journey to and from this country without each time applying for a fresh visa and if so, to which of the individuals other than British subjects named on the enclosed lists shall a permanent visa be issued and for what period will such a visa be valid.

4. In this connection a further question has arisen with regard to the grant of diplomatic visas, which formed the subject of a communication from the Home Office on July 29th.[1] As matters stand at present the whole staff of the British Mission in Moscow receive such visas, whereas (apart from Professor Lomonosov, who does not belong to the Trade Delegation and is a case apart) diplomatic visas have been granted only to Messrs. Krassin, Berzin and Klishko of the Russian Trade Delegation. Indications have not been lacking to show that the Russian authorities intend to enforce strict reciprocity of treatment in this respect as between the Trade Delegation in this country and the British Mission in Moscow. Such action would cause serious embarrassment to the British Mission, who are dependant on the issue of diplomatic visas in order to obtain the special train accommodation provided between the Polish frontier and Moscow, and to enable them to travel to and from Russia in any degree of security or comfort, whereas the Russian Delegation would not be affected.

5. In these circumstances it is felt that it would be more satisfactory for all parties concerned if, as a matter of courtesy, and not as a privilege, diplomatic visas were granted to a number of the higher officials of the Russian Trade Delegation, corresponding to the number of the British Mission who at present receive this privilege. It would of course be made clear that, except in the case of the three official agents, the grant of diplomatic visas involves no recognition whatever of the holders' right to any other form of diplomatic privilege.

6. I am to request that His Lordship may be furnished at an early date with the observations of the Home Office on the various points raised in this letter.

I am, etc.,
Esmond Ovey

of the Delegation when returning from Russia to London. He proposed that they should be granted visas for six or twelve months enabling them to travel between Great Britain and Russia, as frequently as may be necessary. The persons to whom he would wish this privilege extended are those shown on list No. (1) submitted on the 21st of March (i.e., the staff of the New Bond Street office) and the higher officials only of list No. (2) (the Moorgate office) and also the higher officials of Arcos. Mr. Berzin offered to send in the requisite list of these persons.'

No. 544

Sir H. Dering (Bucharest) to the Marquess Curzon of Kedleston
(Received September 30, 11.35 p.m.)
No. 127 Telegraphic [N 8967/4287/38]

BUCHAREST, *September 30, 1922, 8 p.m.*

Telegram dated September 26th[1] signed Karakhan on behalf of Soviet Government expresses astonishment that invitation at Hague Conference to Roumania to participate in Moscow disarmament conference[2] should have received reply that Roumania can only be represented provided that Russia agrees to compensate her by abandoning considerable extent of territory.[3] Message intimates that reply can only denote aggressive intentions or obligations towards other states to maintain present armament. Demand for special compensation may be considered as refusal to contribute to consolidation of peace.

Regret is expressed that Roumania shows no desire, beyond giving pacific assurances, to act in proof of sincerity of desire for peace.

Referring to Roumanian declaration of readiness to discuss questions pending between the two countries, Russia, who inaugurated proposals preliminary to peace, which by fault of Roumanian Government have been without result, is ready to commence such discussion. But she cannot admit that fundamental matters to be discussed should be decided in advance in favour of Roumania.

Warsaw discussions in 1921[4] remained without result because Roumania declined to participate in peace conference without acceptance by Russia of all her territorial and material pretensions.

Russian Government confirm previous attitude by declaring readiness to send delegates to a conference but advises Roumanian Government in the interests of establishing normal relations not to make any preliminary ultimatory conditions for their representatives thereat.

Refusal to take part in disarmament conference without territorial compensation makes Soviet Government realise that Roumania is her only neighbour refusing to make peace with Russia. Russian Government declare they will hold Roumanian Government responsible for all difficulties in the path of securing disarmament owing to nonparticipation of Roumania in conference.

Above communicated to me yesterday by Minister for Foreign Affairs.[5]

---

[1] This telegram, under the date September 27, is printed in Degras, vol. i, pp. 336–7.

[2] In his telegram No. 128 of June 14 (N 5783/5783/63), Mr. Hodgson reported that the Moscow Press had that morning published a proposal by M. Litvinov that Latvia, Poland, Finland, and Esthonia should be invited to attend a conference to discuss proportional disarmament. Mr. Millington-Drake, in Bucharest telegram No. 91 of August 9 (N 7582/4287/38), reported that an overture had been made to Roumania at the Hague Conference, and that the Roumanian Government had replied that Roumania would only participate in the proposed conference if her existing frontiers were recognised (see n. 3).

[3] i.e. Bessarabia.   [4] See No. 439.   [5] M. Duca.

He had despatched very conciliatory reply and will communicate it to me today.

French text by bag.[6]

[6] See No. 545, below.

No. 545

Sir H. Dering (Bucharest) to the Marquess Curzon of Kedleston
(Received October 9)
No. 519 [N 9176/4287/38]

BUCHAREST, *September 30, 1922*

My Lord,

With reference to my telegram No. 127 of this day's date[1] I have now the honour to transmit the text[2] of Monsieur Karakhan's telegraphic message to the Roumanian Government on the subject of the latter's alleged attitude towards the Soviet Government. Monsieur Duca, who communicated it to me, was anxious that I should bring it to Your Lordship's notice in order that His Majesty's Government should clearly understand the difficulties with which the Roumanian Government is surrounded. Given this somewhat aggressive attitude of the Soviet Government, and a similar attitude of the Ukraine Government, evinced by the telegram which formed the subject of my despatch No. 496 of 20th instant,[2] no choice is left to the Roumanian Government which, as Monsieur Duca desired me to point out, must remain keenly on the alert on the Bessarabian frontier and therefore retain troops and material there to guard against possible surprises. I saw the Minister for Foreign Affairs yesterday and again today.

He appeared to me rather over apprehensive of Bolshevist intentions, so I endeavoured to show him that so far as our own information went, there was no present indication of any movement of troops by these in the direction of Bessarabia, and expressed the hope that the threatening language of the last telegrams from the Soviet Government was merely for the purpose of preventing Roumania from taking an active part in the defence of Constantinople.[3] After all, I observed, Roumanian Governments should by now be accustomed to these insultingly worded messages. Monsieur Take Jonesco[4] had received many of them, had returned conciliatory and purposely dilatory replies, and nothing serious had resulted.

Monsieur Duca stated that he also intended to despatch a conciliatory reply, which he would in due course communicate to me. This he has now done, and copy thereof is enclosed[2] herewith for Your Lordship's information. It refutes the assertions as to Roumania's uncompromising attitude in regard to the disarmament Conference, reasserts her policy of non-aggression as

[1] No. 544.   [2] Not printed.   [3] See Vol. XVIII, Nos. 29, 51, and 71.
[4] Roumanian Minister for Foreign Affairs in the Averescu Cabinet, which had resigned on December 13, 1921.

regards her Russian neighbour, but declares that discussion respecting disarmament can only take place if the Roumanian frontier is clearly defined in advance. Once more Roumania's desire for peace is emphasised. The tone of the message, if argumentative, is wholly conciliatory. We agreed that as the Soviet Government and that of Angora seem to be in close relation, nothing was more probable than that it had been arranged between them that Russia should divert Roumania's attention at this juncture. I mentioned that I had seen a press report today that Monsieur Karakhan was leaving for Angora, which would seem to confirm the above view.

The Minister for Foreign Affairs said that he keenly regretted that Roumania should be compelled just now to pay such attention to her Russian frontier, sharing as he did entirely the point of view of Great Britain in regard to the defence of the Straits and Constantinople until the peace conference[5] had time to meet and make other dispositions. He was almost apologetic for Roumania's inability to take steps which might be construed as offensive action, and which he anticipated would bring about the aggression by Russia which he was so desirous of avoiding at the present time.

He discussed the latest news of communications[6] which have passed between the British Commander-in-Chief and Kemal Pasha,[7] expressing his conviction that the latter was playing a double game in protesting that he had no desire to attack British troops, while at the same time Turkish forces were penetrating the neutral zone and entrenching themselves there. In his opinion the Soviet Government were responsible for advising this attitude and he thought it likely that Soviet emissaries at Angora were actively engaged in encouraging an offensive by the Turks, in furtherance of their own ulterior aims at Constantinople and in the Straits.

I have, etc.,

HERBERT G. DERING

[5] i.e. the Lausanne Conference (see Vol. XVIII).
[6] See Vol. XVIII, No. 62.   [7] Turkish nationalist leader.

No. 546

Sir C. Marling (The Hague) to the Marquess Curzon of Kedleston
(Received October 10)

No. 471 [N 9226/646/38]

Immediate   THE HAGUE, *October 9, 1922*
My Lord,

M. [van] Karnebeek[1] informed me this morning that he proposed to notify the Powers that had not participated in the Hague Commission of the resolution proposed by M. Cattier[2] and adopted at the Fourth Plenary Meeting of the 20th July last.[3] The requisite documents had been prepared,

[1] Netherlands Minister for Foreign Affairs.
[2] Belgian delegate at The Hague Conference.   [3] See Vol. XIX, No. 205.

and he was anxious to make the communication at a very early date, but he was loath to do so without having ascertained previously the views and wishes of Great Britain. I told His Excellency that I had reported to your Lordship the steps taken by the Italian and Belgian chargés d'affaires (see my telegram No. 55 of the 14th ultimo)[4] but though quite three weeks must have elapsed I had no reply. The oversight was no doubt due to the pressure of work resulting from the situation in the Near East.[5]

M. van Karnebeek went on to say that it was his intention merely to notify the non-participating Powers of the resolution, and also of the interpretation given to it by Dr. Giannini on behalf of Italy,[3] but for various reasons he felt it impossible to invite the adhesion of those powers as had been suggested by the Italian and Belgian Governments. In the first place, he felt that he had no mandate to give such an invitation. The resolution had been adopted by the Commission for recommendation to the Governments represented at it, and so far these latter had not formally expressed their approval. Further, an invitation might very well have practical disadvantages. It was quite possible that one (or even more) of the participating powers themselves might wish to attach some reserves to its approval and he, M. van Karnebeek, was by no means confident that all the non-participating countries were ready to give in their adhesion. If either of these contingencies should occur, a very awkward situation would be created, and of course, His Excellency added, Germany will always be standing out. If however it was desired that the adhesion of the non-participating Powers should be sought, he would readily undertake to ask for it, but on condition of course that he received a clear formal mandate to do so.

M. van Karnebeek said that he has spoken in this sense to the Belgian Minister who was disposed to agree with his views and had promised to recommend them to the consideration of the Belgian Government.

I said I would lay his views before your Lordship and would ask for an

---

[4] Not printed. On October 12 Mr. O'Malley summarised the negotiations from July 20 as follows: 'Nothing further occurred until August 11, when the Belgian Ambassador informed us that his government were going to raise with the Netherlands government the question of what action was to be taken in regard to the proposed recommendation. On September 6 the French government informed Lord Hardinge that they thought publicity ought to be given to the proposed recommendation without waiting for the German government to subscribe to it. On September 18 the Italian Chargé d'Affaires in London asked us to join in urging the Dutch government to communicate the proposed recommendation to the governments not represented at The Hague.

'On September 20 we asked Sir Philip Lloyd-Greame what he thought we ought to do about all this, and he replied that he thought we ought to hold our hand till we knew what the French were doing in Russia. His information was that the French were, in fact, in negotiation with the Soviet government, and that if this were so, it would be inexpedient for us to take any further action which might commit us to the proposed recommendation. I understand Sir Philip's point to be that the French might be anxious to tie our hands to some extent with the proposed recommendation, while not hesitating themselves to act contrary to that recommendation where their own interests dictated. On October 10 we instructed Lord Hardinge to ask the French government what their attitude towards the proposed recommendation was at the present moment.'

[5] See Vol. XVIII, Chap. I.

early reply.[6] M. van Karnebeek thanked me and said he would be very grateful if I could give him an answer within a week.

I have, etc.,

CHARLES M. MARLING

[6] In a minute of October 12 Mr. O'Malley stated: 'If it is desired to back the "recommendation" in its present form, it might be desirable to send the papers again to the Prime Minister, who on a former occasion had rather special views about it. Otherwise, I do not see why we should not tell the Dutch government that we think the whole thing might be allowed to drop.'

Mr. Gregory added: 'We have referred the matter to the French and I suggest that for the moment we might throw the onus on them and the Belgians of proposing the next step.'

No. 547

Mr. Peters[1] (Moscow) to the Marquess Curzon of Kedleston
(Received October 16)

No. 795 [N 9398/573/38]

MOSCOW, *October 9, 1922*

My Lord Marquess,

With reference to Mr. Hodgson's despatch No. 715 of September 22nd[2] last regarding Monsieur Herriot's visit to Russia, I have the honour to report that simultaneously with the publication of the decision of the Council of People's Commissaries not to ratify the concession agreement with Russo-Asiatic Consolidated Limited,[3] and doubtless with a view to emphasising the political aspects of that decision, the Soviet press commenced to devote considerable attention to the possibility of a Russo-French rapprochement.[4]

Prominence has been given to reports of speeches by and interviews with M. Herriot. The latter is represented as very much impressed with what he has seen in Soviet Russia.

In the course of a long interview which appeared in the 'Pravda' of 7th October, the following statements are attributed to him:—

(1) The first step towards putting Russo-French relations on a sound basis should be the exchange of Trade Delegations:

(2) Political recognition of Soviet Russia should not be considered now but after a commencement has been made with trade between the two countries:

(3) M. Herriot is satisfied that the position of the Soviet Government is extremely stable:

(4) M. Herriot has written M. Poincaré to the effect that in the question of the Dardanelles the interests of France and Russia coincide. 'Russia requires real freedom of the Straits: we require the same. Russia must participate in the conference[5] on the Near Eastern question. France does not want the straits only for herself, which is what others are aiming at.

[1] Mr. Hodgson had left Moscow on October 3 on leave.
[2] See No. 540, n. 1.   [3] See No. 548, below.   [4] Cf. No. 540.
[5] i.e. the Conference of Lausanne (see Vol. XVIII, Chap. II).

Here, too, French policy coincides with Russia. As for the Russian policy of Great Britain, it is far from sincere. Having concluded a trade agreement with you the British are thinking only of making money.'

M. Herriot's secretary hereupon interjected: 'We are against the Russian policy of Poincaré; but we are also against Lloyd George. We stand for the policy of M. Herriot, for the policy of the France of tomorrow.'

With reference to the above, I learn privately that M. Herriot has expressed himself as very much disappointed with what he has seen here, in particular during his visits to Nijni Novgorod and to Petrograd. I understand, further, that he has received a message from M. Poincaré apparently hinting that the possibility of an agreement between France and Russia on the Near Eastern question is not excluded. This leads me to doubt the accuracy of the report of the interview which may none the less be interesting as indicating the direction which the Russian Government desires to give to the discussion of the possibility of a Russo-French rapprochement.

I have, etc.,

WILLIAM PETERS

No. 548

Mr. Peters (Moscow) to the Marquess Curzon of Kedleston
(Received October 16)

No. 794 [N 9397/50/38]

MOSCOW, *October 10, 1922*

My Lord,

I have the honour to refer to my telegram No. 218 of the 8th October,[1] reporting the rejection by the Council of People's Commissaries of the draft agreement between the Russo-Asiatic Consolidated Company and the Soviet Government, signed in Berlin by Mr. Leslie Urquhart[2] and by M. Krassin.

The question of the expediency of ratifying the preliminary agreement has been actively discussed in Moscow ever since M. Krassin's arrival. I am informed on excellent authority that M. Krassin was much disappointed by his reception here. He had anticipated that the signature of the concession would be hailed as a distinct Soviet victory. Instead of this, when the question of the concession was submitted for consideration it was made clear that the signature of M. Krassin was not to be considered as even morally binding in any degree for the Soviet Government, and was not to fetter freedom of discussion. From the beginning a strong current of opposition made itself manifest. In the Presidium of the All-Russian Central Executive Committee ('Vtsik') the general feeling was decidedly against the concession, and a definite decision in this sense was avoided only owing to an impassioned appeal by M. Krassin, who declared that he would regard such a

---

[1] Not preserved in the Foreign Office archives.
[2] See No. 367, n. 10 and No. 423.

result as a vote of no confidence, and would tender his resignation. It was obvious from the first that the real decision would be taken by the political bureau of the Russian Communist Party, which decides all important questions of policy. When the matter was first discussed there no definite views were expressed, but on the 5th October it was decided to reject the concession.[3]

On the following day the matter came before the Council of People's Commissaries. According to information from a private source, which I have no opportunity of checking, a vote took place on the question and the concession was rejected by 14 votes to 7, a few (I understand four) abstaining from voting. Lenin is known to have decided the issue by declaring against ratification. He is said to have declared that the granting of a concession for ninety-nine years involved a return to the system of private property. When the Government heads of State Economic Departments referred to the gravity of the industrial situation in Russia, he declared that Russia would yet be able to show the world what she could do by her own efforts.

The importance which the Soviet Government attaches to the Urquhart agreement is shown by the fact that the unusual course was taken of publishing the decision on the question in the form of a resolution of the Council of the People's Commissaries, i.e., in the form in which most laws are now published in Russia. Incidentally it may be observed that the resolution was published the very day after the meeting of the council, an honour reserved for few Russian laws.

As will be seen from the terms of the resolution, a translation[1] of which is transmitted herewith, the motive advanced for the rejection of the contract is the unsatisfactory nature of the political relations existing between Soviet Russia and Great Britain. In other words, those responsible for Soviet policy announce that the rejection of the Urquhart agreement is to be regarded as punishment for British action in the Near Eastern question.[4] It is known that the Soviet Government considers that Mr. Leslie Urquhart has in Berlin been acting as representative of the British Government.

[3] Mr. Gregory minuted on October 27: 'Mr. Urquhart . . . gave me confidentially the following distinctly amusing piece of information: (a) Mr. Clynes [Chairman of the Parliamentary Labour Party]; (b) The Council of Action; (c) The Hands Off Russia Committee had all been to him to say that the non-ratification of his agreement had finally destroyed any case they had left for making capital out of the Russian question in the coming elections. The failure of Genoa and The Hague had been bad enough, but this was the last straw. They would now be quite unable to put up any proper fight, as the Foreign Office—or the present Government and its supporters—could now successfully demolish any arguments in favour of recognition or renewing relations. They had consequently sent urgent telegrams to Moscow saying: "For God's sake reverse your decision of the other day", and they begged Mr. Urquhart on his side to do all he could to reopen negotiations and get his agreement ratified as soon as possible. Mr. Urquhart said that, while he thought that would come about in the future, there was not the slightest chance of its happening in time to be of use for Labour electioneering purposes.'

Sir E. Crowe added: 'Prime Minister to see.' On October 28 Lord Curzon minuted: 'Pity the late P[rime] M[inister] cannot see also.'

[4] See Vol. XVIII, Chap. I.

The rejection of the concession is thus ostensibly based on other than economic grounds, and the way is left clear for the resumption of negotiations when political conditions are more favourable. It is probable that the Soviet Government were not sorry to avail themselves of a suitable political pretext to postpone the decision of the question as to the actual advisability of granting the concession. Leading Communists—even the all-powerful political bureau—have shown noticeable reluctance to declare themselves on the subject.

The reason is obvious. Russian agriculture, and, in consequence, the purchasing power of the Russian peasant, is impoverished. Russian industry is suffering a severe financial crisis and is working at a loss. Yet the existence of the dictatorship of the proletariat depends on the existence of that proletariat. The Communist Party therefore emphasise the necessity of developing Russian industry, but at the same time proclaim that key industries must remain in the hands of the State, and see very clearly the political dangers involved in allowing big industrial enterprises to be run efficiently by private capitalists. If account is further taken of the vested interests which have grown up in connection with nationalised undertakings —in particular, the interests of the Red specialists who have obtained and now occupy comparatively comfortable posts—it will be seen that the concession question bristles with difficulties, which have so far prevented the elaboration of a settled policy. The fundamental fact, however, appears to be that industry is now being run at a loss and that it will continue to be so run unless fresh capital and new methods are introduced. It is, I think, to do Russia no good service to conceal the patent fact that Russia has need of outside assistance and that this need is more urgent in character than Europe's need for Russia.

I refer in a separate despatch[5] to hints at the possibility of a Russo-French rapprochement as a result of British policy in the Near East and in connection with the refusal of the Urquhart concession.[6]

The immediate effect of the refusal has been greatly to weaken M. Krassin's position. It is known that a section of the Communist Party, of which Radek is a representative, has long considered M. Krassin too accommodating. It would, they consider, be better that a real Communist of high party standing should be sent to London, as he would, in the first instance, be less likely to mislead the British Government; while, in the second place, his reports would be received with more trust than those of M. Krassin.

The latter is known to have expressed his intention of resigning, but no reliable information is available as to whether his resignation has actually

[5] See No. 547.

[6] In his despatch No. 790 of October 11, Lord D'Abernon transmitted a translation of an interview given by M. Litvinov to several journalists and commented as follows: 'In the interview under review Litvinov professes that the refusal to ratify the Urquhart Convention was due to information which the Soviet Government had, or professed to have, that England had taken a leading part at the recent Paris Conference [see Vol. XVIII, Nos. 106–8] in refusing Russian participation in the Dardanelles [Lausanne] Conference.'

been tendered or accepted. He leaves Moscow on the 11th instant, travelling via Helsingfors and Stockholm.

I have, etc.,
WILLIAM PETERS

ENCLOSURE IN No. 548

Decree of the Council of People's Commissaries

(Translation)

The Council of People's Commissaries, acknowledging, in accordance with its repeated declarations, the extreme desirability of the participation of foreign capital in the economic restoration of Soviet Russia, and, in particular, recognising the desirability of the conclusion, on agreed terms, of a contract with the Russo-Asiatic Consolidated Company (Urquhart), recognises that the exceptionally vast extent of the concession, its political and economic importance, demands, above all, friendly, stable and defined relations between the Soviet Republic and the Government of the country in which the Russo-Asiatic Consolidated Company is domiciled. Meanwhile, the recent action of the English Government, which in fact denies to Soviet Russia equal rights with other nations in discussing her vital and economic interests in the Near East and in the Black Sea, clearly indicates the absence of the above-mentioned desirable relations. In these circumstances, the Council of People's Commissaries decrees that the confirmation of the preliminary agreement signed in Berlin on the 9th September, 1922, by Mr. L. Urquhart and L. B. Krassin is refused.

V. ULIANOV (LENIN)
President of the Council of People's Commissaries
N. GORBUNOV
Chief Secretary of the Council of People's Commissaries
L. FOTIEVA
Secretary of the Council of People's Commissaries
Moscow, October 6, 1922.

No. 549

Lord D'Abernon (Berlin) to the Marquess Curzon of Kedleston
(Received October 17)
No. 794 [N 9404/2169/38]

Secret   BERLIN, *October 11, 1922*
My Lord Marquess,

I have the honour to enclose a Memorandum of a recent conversation with Baron Maltzan regarding Russian affairs and others.

Notwithstanding criticism of the Rapallo Treaty[1] when it was signed, and disappointment with it since, Baron Maltzan remains the head of all Russian affairs of the Auswärtiges Amt.

I have, etc.,
D'ABERNON

ENCLOSURE IN No. 549

Secret BERLIN, *October 11, 1922*

Baron Maltzan called on me this morning and discussed the position, particularly as regards Russia.

He said he had been intentionally away from Berlin during the last two months as he did not want to go on with the negotiations regarding the extension of the Rapallo Treaty to the Ukraine and other Associated States of Russia.

He considered that the Russian Government was much more firmly in the saddle than a year ago, and that the Turkish success[2] had undoubtedly done a great deal to consolidate it. Apart from partiality for this or that Western Power, there was doubtless a growing feeling of solidarity of Eastern or Asiatic peoples versus the West.

I drew Baron Maltzan's attention to the statement made in 'The Times' of Monday[3] that there had been great joy in German circles at the failure of the Urquhart negotiations,[4] and that German representation at Moscow had been against ratification. He said: 'Nothing in the world could be more false. Not for English reasons, but for German reasons, we have been strongly in favour of ratifying Urquhart's Agreement. In the first place he has German participants, in the second it is quite clear that Germany can develop her commerce with Russia much more rapidly in the wake of the Urquhart Convention than if it is abandoned. Not only have we urged strongly in Moscow that the Treaty should be ratified, but there was genuine disappointment here when it was rejected. You can ask any of your people who are in touch with the Russians in Berlin.'

I replied: 'If the news is false, it would be foolish of you not to have it contradicted widely and officially. These statements make a considerable impression on public opinion in England.' Baron Maltzan said: 'I have already taken steps in this matter.'

He added: 'Personally I consider that negotiations with Urquhart will begin again rapidly and will probably succeed. Krassin and Stomoniakov[5] are certainly in favour and I believe that Lenin is also, but Lenin is ill and the moderate section in Moscow has been recently under a cloud. The negotiations of the Russians with Krupp and with Stinnes have also broken down, probably temporarily. Of course, there is a section in Moscow strongly against any modification of communism, and another section which is

[1] See Vol. XIX, No. 75. [2] See Vol. XVIII, Chap. I.
[3] See *The Times*, October 9, 1922, p. 12. [4] See No. 548.
[5] Soviet trade representative in Berlin.

anti-English. The latter includes Radek and also Litvinov, although he has an English wife of whom he is very proud. Zinoviev is fanatically against any departure from the Communistic gospel. As for Chicherin, it is difficult to say quite what he is, but he is certainly not pro-English.'

Baron Maltzan continued: 'Herriot is a clever fellow and is undoubtedly working hard to create a Russo-French agreement.[6] He has been all over the place in Russia, to Petersburg and to the Ukraine. In the latter place he made great friends with Rakowsky. At one time, in the early part of the year, I was very frightened of a Russo-French rapprochement. Now that Article 116 of the Treaty of Versailles has no terrors for us, I am much less frightened. A Russo-French Trade Agreement would not be anti-German. We feel already that the French are beginning to prepare to change sides, and to be pro-Russian rather than pro-Polish. The Poles feel it too, and we see the reaction in our negotiations in Dresden[7] with them for a commercial treaty.'

'Regarding a possible combination between Enver Pasha[8] and Kemal Pasha, German agents at Moscow say any such event is impossible, owing to personal hostility between these two. The Russians certainly believed that Enver was dead, for they found a dead body in a General's uniform with letters from Enver's wife in the pocket. It appears, however, that the corpse must have been a fake, for Enver does not go nearer the front line than he can help, and his wife, who is in Berlin, received a letter from him only ten days ago.'

[6] See No. 547.

[7] These negotiations, dealing with outstanding points of difference between Germany and Poland, had been opened after the conclusion of the economic convention of May 15, 1922 (see Vol. XVI, No. 393, minute 4). A series of conferences were held at Dresden during 1922 and 1923 following agreement on a preliminary agenda at Warsaw on July 24, 1922.

[8] Ex-Minister and pro-German leader of the Young Turks.

No. 550

The Marquess Curzon of Kedleston to Lord Hardinge (Paris)
No. 3109 [N 9208/573/38]

FOREIGN OFFICE, *October 13, 1922*

My Lord,

Reports which have recently appeared in the press and other information from private sources indicate that M. Herriot, who, as Your Excellency is aware, recently paid a visit to Moscow[1] with the tacit approval of the French Government, has now concluded or is possibly about to conclude some kind of agreement with the Soviet Government.

2. One report in particular states that the text of an agreement between

[1] See No. 540, n. 1 and No. 547.

M. Herriot and M. Karakhan has already been received at the Quai d'Orsay and that the main points of the agreement are the following:—

(1) Russia undertakes to recognise the whole of the Imperial Debt to France while leaving open to discussion later the apportionment of certain parts of it to Poland and other States originally part of the Russian Empire.

(2) Russia undertakes to restore to their properties, or else to indemnify, all French property owners in Russia, it being understood that compensation might take the form of new concessions.

(3) France undertakes to see that Russia is represented in the final settlement of the question of Constantinople and the Straits.[2]

(4) France undertakes to recognise the Russian Government as a *de jure* Government immediately.

3. It is further stated that the object M. Poincaré has in view is to isolate this country completely in Europe by diplomatic means, that France intends to secure co-operation with Russia over a wide field and also to make her own terms with Germany.

4. I should be glad if Your Excellency would enquire, if necessary from M. Poincaré himself, as to the truth of these rumours and request to be informed as to the real nature of M. Herriot's mission in Russia. Recent experience of M. Franklin-Bouillon's visits to Angora[3] renders it necessary to make sure that we are not faced with a repetition of these tactics.

I am, etc.,

(For the Secretary of State)

J. D. GREGORY

[2] See Vol. XVIII, Chap. I.
[3] See Vol. XVII, No. 423, and Vol. XVIII, No. 51, n. 9.

No. 551

Lord D'Abernon (Berlin) to the Marquess Curzon of Kedleston
(Received October 19)

No. 803 [N 9489/2169/38]

BERLIN, *October 15, 1922*

My Lord Marquess,

With further reference to the subject of Germany's relations with Russia,[1] it is now clear that the German Government will proceed to negotiate for the extension of the Rapallo Agreement[2] to the Associated States of the Ukraine, Georgia, etc. They will also negotiate for a detailed commercial treaty between Germany and Russia.

Baron Maltzan has been criticised in the German Press—notably in 'Der Tag' and 'Germania'—for not having pushed these negotiations more

[1] See No. 549.   [2] See Vol. XIX, No. 75.

rapidly. His defence is that criticism of the Rapallo Treaty, mainly from English sources, had deterred him from pushing along the Rapallo lines too rapidly. The effect produced at Genoa[3] by the treaty had been too bad.

Now, however, it is thought that things are different. Italy[4] and Czecho-slovakia[5] have signed some convention with Russia; France is active in semi-official negotiation;[6] England has been pressing the Urquhart Agreement.[7] No-one could throw a stone at Germany if she pursues Russian negotiations.

I have, etc.,

D'ABERNON

[3] See ibid., Nos. 75 and 76.   [4] See No. 509.
[5] See No. 512.   [6] See No. 550.   [7] Cf. No. 548.

No. 552

Mr. Peters (Moscow) to the Marquess Curzon of Kedleston
(Received October 16, 7.35 p.m.)

No. 220 Telegraphic [N 9409/1185/38]

MOSCOW, *October 16, 1922, 5.20 p.m.*

With reference to Mr. Hodgson's despatch No. 759,[1] reply just received from commissary of foreign affairs in the main recapitulates argument of Mr. Karakhan's note of April 13th, copy of which was transmitted with Mr. Hodgson's despatch No. 227.[2]

Course of action decided on by British government is declared incapable of solving problem, in contra-distinction to proper method, stated to be adopted by Norway, viz., 'of negotiations, meanwhile warning Norwegian vessels against fishing in Russian territorial waters'.

Commissary of foreign affairs concludes by calling attention to final paragraph of Karakhan's note above referred to, which deals with armed escorts, and 'must insist that carrying out of above decision of British government[3] can only provoke incidents, consequences of which may gravely affect relations of the two countries'.

Despatch follows next bag.[4]

[1] Of October 2. This referred to Foreign Office despatch No. 908 of September 15, not printed, in which Mr. Hodgson was instructed to address a note to the Soviet Government, referring to his previous note of April 4 (see No. 491) and stating that the British Government had decided to send to North Russian waters a ship to protect British fishing vessels. The despatch continued: 'I have advised the Acting Commissary for Foreign Affairs of the intention of His Majesty's Government to maintain their attitude in the matter of the protection of British fishing vessels off the Northern coasts of Russia.' (Cf. Nos. 483, 486, 489, and 491.)

[2] Of April 18 (N 3846/1185/38), not printed.

[3] See No. 491.

[4] No. 816 of October 20 (N 9776/1185/38), not printed. This transmitted a copy of M. Karakhan's note of October 14.

No. 553

Lord D'Abernon (Berlin) to the Marquess Curzon of Kedleston
(Received October 23)
No. 809 [N 9569/2169/38]

BERLIN, *October 19, 1922*

My Lord Marquess,

I have the honour to inform Your Lordship that I am informed from a fairly reliable source that the negotiations between Germany and Russia relative to the extension of the Treaty of Rapallo[1] are making tardy progress. Six Commissions have been formed of representatives of both countries to deal with such questions as shipping, legal status, postal, trade, consular arrangements and customs agreements. It is expected that the most important of these agreements will be drafted before the end of this year.

The question of the extension of the Rapallo Treaty to the other Soviet Federal States continues to encounter difficulties. With the exception of the Social Democrats no party is definitely opposed to extension. The German National Party is prepared to admit the necessity of establishing economic relations with the Ukraine, but for propaganda reasons they are reluctant to admit this in public. The Volkspartei has criticised the dilatory methods of the Foreign Office, but the attitude of the industrials does not quite coincide with that of the party leaders. Stinnes and Krupp are obstructive factors, though not definite opponents. The Allgemeine Electrizitäts Gesellschaft, Strauss and Wolff, as well as the great export firms, are likewise in favour, but opinion is divided within the new united Socialist party, Hilferding favouring and Breitscheid opposing extension, while Hermann Müller is neutral. The Government itself has not taken any initiative as the Chancellor is averse to entering into fresh conflict with President Ebert, who has been the most energetic opponent of the Rapallo Treaty from the outset. The attitude of the Socialists may be ascribed to their opposition to the Moscow Communists who expelled the Social Revolutionary Government in Georgia[2] by force of arms.

It is expected, however, that negotiations respecting extension will begin sometime this year, as the Georgian Government have recently rescinded certain unfriendly measures enacted against German nationals.

Graf Brockdorff-Rantzau will take up his post in Moscow[3] by the end of this month at latest.

I have, etc.,
D'ABERNON

[1] See No. 551 and cf. No. 554, below.
[2] See Vol. XII, Nos. 514, 518, 523, and 531.
[3] As German Ambassador.

No. 554

Mr. Peters (Moscow) to the Marquess Curzon of Kedleston
(Received November 6)

No. 815 [N 9949/4058/38]

MOSCOW, *October 20, 1922*

My Lord Marquess,

With reference to Foreign Office despatch No. 574 (C 8073/2370/18) of June 21st,[1] I have the honour to report that the contract signed at Berlin on October 9th, 1922, by Boris Stomoniakov on behalf of the Soviet Government and by Otto Wolff, has been confirmed by decree of the Council of People's Commissaries dated October 19th, 1922.

According to a note in 'Izvestia' of today's date, Otto Wolff represents a group of large German works, including 'Phoenix' and 'Rheinstahl'. A 'mixed' company, called the Russo-German Trading Company, Limited, is to be formed, with a capital of three hundred thousand gold roubles—one half furnished by the Russian Government and the other half by the German group.

The company is granted a trading concession with the right to open offices all over Russia and to carry out under the control of the People's Commissariat for Foreign Trade import operations, primarily in iron and steel wares, and the export of Russian raw products. The German group undertakes to open a credit account in goods in favour of the new company to the extent of 7,500,000 gold roubles and in favour of the Russian Government to the extent of 5,000,000 gold roubles.

The Russian Government and the group nominate an equal number of members of the Board of Directors and 'Aufsichtsrat'.[2]

The goods which the Company will be allowed to import and export will be specified by the Government. The contract provides for limitation of profits.

I am making enquiries through private sources in order to obtain fuller information, which I will report without delay.

I have, etc.,

WILLIAM PETERS

[1] Not printed. Cf., however, No. 553.
[2] Board of Trustees.

Mr. Wilton (Riga) to the Marquess Curzon of Kedleston
(Received October 22, 4.30 p.m.)

No. 66 Telegraphic [*N* 9538/50/38]

RIGA, *October 22, 1922, 3.40 p.m.*

Minister for Foreign Affairs informs me that Latvian Minister at Moscow has reported that Herriot[1] did his best to oppose ratification of Urquhart agreement[2] and that German influence inspired by Maltzan[3] also worked in the same direction. Minister for Foreign Affairs added that Soviet representative at Riga had declared in recent conversation with him that non-ratification was due to political motives, and representative believed ratification would eventually take place subject to minor modifications.

[1] See Nos. 547 and 550.
[2] See No. 548.
[3] Cf. Nos. 549 and 551.

No. 556

Lord Hardinge (Paris) to the Marquess Curzon of Kedleston
(Received October 25)

No. 2491 [*N* 9662/573/38]

PARIS, *October 24, 1922*

My Lord,

With reference to Your Lordship's despatch No. 3109 (N 9208/G) of the 13th instant[1] I have the honour to transmit to Your Lordship herewith copy of Monsieur Poincaré's reply to my enquiry as to the exact nature of Monsieur Herriot's mission to Russia.

Your Lordship will observe that Monsieur Poincaré denies that Monsieur Herriot was charged with any official or unofficial mission by the French Government, and that he is stated to have undertaken his journey purely for private commercial reasons.

I have, etc.,
HARDINGE OF PENSHURST

ENCLOSURE IN No. 556

M. Poincaré to Lord Hardinge

PARIS, *octobre 23, 1922*

Monsieur l'Ambassadeur,

Par votre lettre du 14 de ce mois,[2] vous avez bien voulu me faire connaître que le Gouvernement de Sa Majesté britannique s'était ému des nouvelles

[1] No. 550.
[2] Not traced in the Foreign Office archives.

publiées dans la presse au sujet du voyage de M. Herriot en Russie et qu'il serait désireux de savoir ce qu'il y a de fondé dans les bruits qui représentent le Député, maire de Lyon, comme chargé de conclure un arrangement avec le Pouvoir des Soviets.

J'ai l'honneur de vous informer que M. Herriot n'a reçu aucune mission officielle ni officieuse du Gouvernement de la République, qu'il a entrepris son voyage de sa propre initiative, dans l'intérêt du commerce lyonnais et principalement, d'après ce que je crois savoir, pour s'occuper de la Foire de Lyon.

Veuillez agréer, etc.,

R. POINCARÉ

No. 557

Lord Hardinge (Paris) to the Marquess Curzon of Kedleston
(Received October 27)

No. 2499 (C) [N 9714/573/38]

PARIS, *October 25, 1922*

My Lord,

With reference to the commercial relations between France and Russia,[1] I have the honour to inform Your Lordship that Monsieur Skobelev, the semi-official representative of the Soviet Government in France, who is at present in Moscow, has stated to Press representatives in that city, according to a telegram published in *L'Information Financière* of today's date, that his office in Paris has bought in the course of this year French goods to the value of ten million francs. These goods consisted mainly of motor accessories and vegetable seeds. Russia has sold in the same period goods to approximately the same value. Commercial exchanges had also taken place in the Black Sea region. 'The improvement in the political relations between the two countries gave ground for hoping that in the near future commercial relations would assume large dimensions.'

At the conclusion of the general meeting of the Lyons Fair Company on the 23rd instant Monsieur Herriot, in the course of his account of his recent voyage in Russia,[1] stated that he had carried away from that country the best impressions, especially as regards the economic revival now being manifested there. He warmly advocated the establishment of a French commercial delegation at Moscow and the establishment of a similar Russian delegation at Paris. He was convinced that France, after an entente with Russia, would assume a predominant position in that country. On high political and economic grounds France should therefore support the Russian demand to participate in the Conference[2] which would deal with the question

---

[1] See Nos. 547, 550, and 556.
[2] The forthcoming Lausanne Conference (see Vol. XVIII, Chap. I).

of Constantinople. It was vital in fact for Russia to obtain an entry to the Mediterranean by the maintenance of the liberty of the Straits.

'It would no doubt be an exaggeration to claim that everything is now perfect in Russia, but it would be also going too far to affirm that we should hold aloof from all the happenings in the land of the Soviets. It is for the French to see whether they ought to leave the field free for Germans and English. Moreover, the rulers of Russia are neither fools nor ignorant persons. Russia will soon have put her finances in order and will be a peasant republic established on a solid basis. No Soviet statesman moreover refuses to recognize the debts contracted by the Government of the Czar.'

I have, etc.,
HARDINGE OF PENSHURST

No. 558

Lord Hardinge (Paris) to the Marquess Curzon of Kedleston
(Received October 27)
No. 2508 [N 9705/573/38]

PARIS, October 26, 1922

My Lord,

I have the honour to acknowledge receipt of Your Lordship's despatch No. 3914 (N 9472/573/38) of the 23rd instant[1] regarding the rumoured intention of the French Government to conclude some kind of agreement with the Soviet Government.

As Your Lordship is aware Monsieur Herriot has since his return from Russia been conducting an active campaign in favour of a resumption of relations with Russia. My despatch No. 2499 (C) of October 25th[2] summarises a speech made by Monsieur Herriot at Lyons in which he advocated a start being made by the despatch of a commercial mission on the lines of the existing British mission already established in Moscow. Monsieur Herriot repeated his proposal (adding that the mission should be in charge of a Consul, not a Diplomat) in an address last night before the 'Ligue National des Intérêts Français en Russie,' a body composed of Frenchmen who lived or had business interests in Russia before 1914, including French holders of Russian bonds.

Considerable prominence has been given to Monsieur Herriot's remarks by the Press but comments have generally been along the lines of an article by 'Pertinax'[3] in the 'Echo de Paris' (copy enclosed)[1] which concludes by urging that in all dealings with Soviet Russia, France 'should only give in the measure in which she receives and that only when she has actually received'.

This morning's Press reports that Monsieur Herriot was received yesterday

---

[1] Not printed. [2] No. 557.
[3] M. André Géraud (see No. 14, n. 3).

by Monsieur Poincaré and the fact that Monsieur de Lasteyrie, French Minister of Finance, was also present at the interview is taken by some papers to mean that the Government are considering the expediency of encouraging French private interests to initiate commercial dealings with the Soviet Government, though entirely at their own risk.[4] This may be true but it is open to some doubt whether Monsieur Poincaré will take so decisive a step as the despatch of an official commercial mission to Russia until public opinion has been educated sufficiently to pronounce definitely in favour of Monsieur Herriot's thesis.

I have, etc.,
HARDINGE OF PENSHURST

[4] Cf. No. 556.

No. 559

Lord D'Abernon (Berlin) to the Marquess Curzon of Kedleston
(Received November 4)

No. 832 [N 9937/2169/38]

BERLIN, *October 27, 1922*

My Lord Marquess,

It may be convenient if I review briefly the relations between Germany and Russia[1] which have resulted from the Rapallo Treaty.[2]

This treaty has now been in force some six months, and there is disappointment both in German and Russian circles at the scanty results so far attained. As regards commercial business, the amount of goods exchanged remains meagre. As regards future contracts, most of the German representatives who have been to Russia have come back disappointed. They find the process of negotiation invariably long and tedious, for signature, after appearing certain, is often delayed or refused. As has been graphically said, 'The Soviets are Jews in making a contract, and Russians in carrying a contract out: i.e., in the first case minute and punctilious, in the second lax and unreliable'.

It is now reported that Messrs. Wolff have concluded a contract with the Soviet Government,[3] providing for the establishment of a new company with a capital of £30,000—half to belong to Messrs. Wolff and half to the Soviet Government. Under this contract Messrs. Wolff engage to make large advances in Russia for the purchase of goods.

Similarly a contract between Messrs. Krupp and the Soviet Government is on the point of conclusion.

Negotiations are, further, in progress between the Moscow Government and the Mitropa Company for a service of restaurant and sleeping cars on through-trains.

[1] See Nos. 549, 551, 553, and 554.
[2] See Vol. XIX, No. 75. See also No. 497, n. 3.   [3] See No. 554.

These contracts, however, are not very important, and it is by no means certain what their ultimate development will be. Time alone can show.

It is remarkable that in the case of Messrs. Wolff and of Messrs. Krupp, these firms seem anxious to co-operate with Mr. Urquhart, and, to some extent, to come under the Urquhart umbrella. Further—the Mitropa Company is owned to a considerable extent in England. I see, therefore, no reason to apprehend that any of the three contracts need be regarded with anything but favour from the English standpoint.

The view originally taken at Genoa and in other places was that the Rapallo Agreement would lead to military co-operation of a dangerous character between Germany and Russia,[4] but this opinion has so far proved fallacious. As I expressed at the time (see my despatch No. 342 of April 29th last)[5] the political tendencies of the military elements in the two countries are so diverse and opposed that there is nothing either would dislike as much as close connection with the other. German military circles are essentially monarchical and reactionary. Russian military circles are progressive, if not communistic. These two forces can only be welded together by extreme pressure from outside forces.

If, however, the Rapallo Treaty has produced little or no military result, it has served to increase largely the number of Russians of the 'Red' persuasion in Berlin and in Germany. The German Foreign Office continues to deliver passports to these gentlemen, notwithstanding the protests of the German police and secret police. The latter hold that Bolsheviks cannot be brought in without increasing the forces of disorder, and accentuating the danger of social and labour trouble. In any estimate of the probabilities of the winter, the presence of these elements of agitation in most large German centres must not be lost sight of. Apparently the argument of the German Foreign Office is that the presence of the Bolsheviks they admit is indispensable to develop trade, but even trade may be bought too dear.

It is certainly to be hoped that in future considerable discrimination will be used in granting more Russians visas for residence in Germany.

In connection with the relations of Germany and Russia, it may be noted that, although disappointment has been felt about the result of Rapallo, Freiherr von Maltzan, who had a good deal to do with the Rapallo Treaty, is one of the favourites for the succession to Herr von Haniel as State Secretary at the Foreign Office. Herr von Haniel will probably be moved to be German Representative at Munich early in the New Year, if not before.

If Freiherr von Maltzan is in fact appointed it must be taken as a sign that the German Government intend to develop still further their relations with Russia, Freiherr von Maltzan being a pronounced advocate of this policy.

The explanation of the apparent contradiction between the failure of the Rapallo Treaty and the popularity of its author is to be found in the fact that Germany is seriously alarmed at the Herriot mission[6] and that the

[4] Cf. Nos. 495, 497, and 505.
[5] Not printed.
[6] See Nos. 547, 550, and 555–8.

Russians are again suggesting, as they did at Genoa, that Germany will be left out in the cold if she does not consolidate and extend the Moscow connection.

I have, etc.,

D'ABERNON

No. 560

*Lord D'Abernon (Berlin) to the Marquess Curzon of Kedleston
(Received November 9)*

No. 851 [N 10088/2169/38]

BERLIN, *November 4, 1922*

His Majesty's Ambassador presents his compliments to His Majesty's Secretary of State for Foreign Affairs, and has the honour to forward Note of a conversation with Baron Maltzan, of the German Foreign Office.

ENCLOSURE IN No. 560

Note of conversation with Baron Maltzan of the German Foreign Office

Confidential   BERLIN, *November 4, 1922*

The German Government are negotiating with the Russians for the extension of Rapallo to the Ukraine, Georgia and Chita.[1] Germany has refused to extend the Treaty to Khiwa and Bokhara; partly on the ground that it might offend English susceptibilities; partly on the ground that they regarded Central Asia as the future objective of the Turks, and that they were unwilling to treat it as exclusively Russian. They had found various reasons for this attitude—the influence of Enver, etc. etc.

The German Government are discussing a Commercial Treaty with Lithuania, also on the basis of Rapallo.

The German Government are about to appoint Count Schulenberg as Minister to Persia. Maltzan said Schulenberg was a quiet sensible man with country tastes. He had previously been at Warsaw and in Roumania.

In further conversation I asked Baron Maltzan his view regarding the Herriot Mission[2] and the working of the Rapallo Treaty. He said: 'Had we not signed the Rapallo Treaty we should have been very alarmed by the Herriot Mission. We should have feared joint action by France and Russia under Article 116 of the Treaty of Versailles, to our detriment, and we should have expected some agreement with France, under which she obtained in Russia special rights. The Rapallo Treaty, however, protects us

[1] In his telegram No. 197 of November 5, Lord D'Abernon reported that that day the German Government had signed a treaty with the Soviet Republics of Ukraine, White Russia, Georgia, Azerbaijan, Armenia and the Far East, and in his despatch No. 853 of November 5 transmitted to the Foreign Office a translation of the text of the treaty (for sources see Slusser and Triska, p. 36). The treaty was ratified on various dates between December 1, 1922 and February 1, 1923 and entered into force on October 25, 1923.

[2] See Nos. 547, 550, and 555–8.

943

from any danger under Article 116, and it further gives us most-favoured-nation rights, so that anything the Russians may give to France they have to extend to us. So, although according to our information Herriot gained considerable influence in Russia, and made an excellent impression, we are not so much alarmed as we otherwise should have been. I still, however, think that within a short space of time there will be a French official representative at Moscow.'

No. 561

The Marquess Curzon of Kedleston to Mr. Knatchbull-Hugessen[1] *(The Hague)*

No. 585 [N 9800/646/38]

FOREIGN OFFICE, *November 16, 1922*

Sir,

I have received Sir C. Marling's despatch No. 471 of the 9th of October,[2] enquiring the views of His Majesty's Government with regard to communicating to the non-participating Powers the resolution proposed by Monsieur Cattier[3] and adopted at the concluding meeting of The Hague Conference.

2. On receipt of Sir C. Marling's telegram No. 55 of the 14th of September[4] and of a note from the Belgian Ambassador dated the 18th of September,[4] I requested His Majesty's Ambassador at Paris in a despatch,[5] a copy of which was transmitted to Sir C. Marling under cover of my despatch No. 527 of the 12th of October,[4] to ascertain what steps the French Government were taking in this matter. I enclose a copy of the reply[6] which I have now received from Lord Hardinge, and also a copy of an earlier note from the French Government on this subject, dated the 6th of September.[4]

3. You will observe that the French Government has instructed the French Minister at The Hague to propose that the non-participating governments should be invited to adhere to the Cattier resolution. I consider, however, that it would be amply sufficient merely to bring this resolution to the knowledge of these governments, as proposed by Monsieur van Karnebeek (Sir C. Marling's despatch No. 471 of the 9th of October[2]). You should therefore inform the Netherlands Government that His Majesty's Government have no objection to the proposed notification being made to the non-participating governments. I am not disposed in any way to press the Netherlands Government in this question, and I am content to leave the initiative to the French and Belgian Governments.

[1] 1st Secretary in H.M. Embassy at The Hague, acting as Chargé d'Affaires.
[2] No. 546.   [3] See Vol. XIX, No. 205, n. 2.   [4] Not printed.
[5] No. 3079 of October 11 (N 8947/50/38), not printed.
[6] Paris despatch No. 2529 of October 29, which enclosed a copy of M. Poincaré's note of October 27 to Lord Hardinge.

4. I have no objection to this notification including the interpretation placed upon the resolution by Signor Giannini.[3] As, however, this interpretation is in itself somewhat obscure, it would be desirable to explain to the Netherlands Government the sense in which it is understood by His Majesty's Government, who consider that it is intended solely to cover cases of which the following would be typical. A particular property belonged either to a Russian or to a foreign national; after the 1st of November, 1917, but before the property had been nationalised, it was purchased *bona fide* by a foreign national, and subsequently nationalised. In such circumstances the property in question would, under the Italian interpretation, come within the scope of the resolution; and to this His Majesty's Government have no objection.

I am, etc.,
(For the Secretary of State)
Esmond Ovey

No. 562

Mr. Peters (Moscow) to the Marquess Curzon of Kedleston
(Received November 27)

No. 903 [N 10526/2169/38]

moscow, *November 18, 1922*

My Lord Marquess,

With reference to my despatches No. 860 of the 4th[1] and No. 882 of the 10th instant,[1] I have the honour to report that the press continues to pay much attention to the newly appointed German Ambassador.

The 'Izvestia' of the 11th instant produced an interview with Count Brockdorff-Rantzau,[2] in which the latter, after alluding to the great impression made on him by his reception by M. Kalinin and also by the public manifestations on the anniversary of the Bolshevik revolution, affirmed that the sympathies of the German people had during the past five years been all the time on the side of revolutionary Russia. 'Unfortunately,' he added, 'Germany could not and cannot actively help Soviet Russia.'

Questioned as to the attitude of Germany towards the Near Eastern problem,[3] the Ambassador was reported to have replied: 'Germany cannot for the moment take an active part in the solution of this question. She cannot allow herself in this connection the luxury of sending Poincaré and Curzon notes such as those sent by Soviet Russia[4] with such dignity. But Germany is not smashed and at the first opportunity will support Russia's just demands.'

The 'Izvestia' of the 15th instant published a note to the effect that the above interview corresponds neither in form nor in context to the few

---

[1] Not printed.
[2] See No. 553, n. 3.
[3] See Vol. XVIII, Chap. I.
[4] See ibid., No. 138, n. 3.

words exchanged between the German Ambassador and the journalist to whom the interview was given. The latter had, in consequence, been dismissed.

Finally, on the 17th instant, the 'Izvestia' printed a further interview with Count Brockdorff-Rantzau, on this occasion signed, and purely colourless.

I have, etc.,

WILLIAM PETERS

No. 563

Mr. Preston[1] (Petrograd) to Mr. Leeper (Received November 28)
[N 10565/5431/38]

PETROGRAD, *November 19, 1922*

My dear Leeper,

I am writing you a private letter in the hopes that, should you be on leave, somebody else in the Northern Department will read it.

I have not had time to digest my impressions, nor could I in any case prepare a report in time for the courier, as since my arrival most of my time has been taken up in looking for suitable accommodation. There is also so much of interest at Petrograd that it is difficult to know what to write about in a short letter.

As in almost every branch of life in Russia, the new economic policy has brought about great changes in Petrograd. By the denationalisation of internal trade, it has brought back from between 200,000 and 300,000 people, a great many of whom have returned here to open their shops. The Nevsky—which is now renamed October 25th Prospect—is well lit and almost as crowded as before the war. The Europe Hotel is almost in pre-war condition; the appointments are well preserved but the food is, of course, not up to pre-war standard. Bourgeois and Bolshevik who, a few months ago, were at each other's throats, are now to be seen dining together in first class restaurants, of which quite a number are opening, both as private and State undertakings.

Similarly, in the trusts,[2] experts (former professional men) work side by side with Communists. Nep,[3] I am informed, has also had the effect of actually reducing the numbers of the 'party', especially of the Jewish Communists, who readily abjure the tenets of Bolshevism and find their real métier in raking in speculative profits at the emporium of free trade.

The chances of any strong reactionary movement amongst the bourgeois civilian population are very remote, and as long as the labourers are allowed

---

[1] See No. 470. Mr. Preston, Assistant Agent of the British Commercial Mission since August, 1922, had left Moscow to take up his post in Petrograd on November 4.
[2] See No. 516.   [3] New Economic Policy.

to sell articles, such as benzine cigarette lighters, which they make out of government material at the Government works, and put the proceeds into their pockets, they are likely to continue sweetly dreaming that the Government is mainly concerned in protecting their interests. The émigrés living in Europe and elsewhere are, with their reactionary ideas, politically four years behind their own kith and kin in Russia and would get a very bad reception from everybody.

The army here seem to be getting into extraordinarily good fettle. The general staff, I am informed, consists almost exclusively of officers of the ancien régime and the soldiers absolutely refuse to admit Jewish Communists into the regimental germ cells. In fact, politics are taboo and it is generally becoming an essentially Russian army. The time is probably not far off when the authorities will have to decide whether they can maintain their control of a militarily disciplined army or whether they can afford the risky experiment of continuing to make the peasant soldier 'conscientious' by inoculating him with the serum of Bolshevik propaganda. It is still believed in some quarters that the army here (in Petrograd) may yet be the centre from which may emanate new political ideas which will spread—as, indeed, did the Revolution and Bolshevism—throughout Russia. This theory is probably based on the fact that the abortive rising at Kronstadt in 1921,[4] which was in favour of soviets but also of properly conducted elections, was started by sailors and had the sympathy of a part of the Petrograd garrison.

The inevitable effect in Russia of reaction in Europe and the gradual evolution which, th[r]ough sheer force of economic circumstances, is taking place in Russia, should however make things move in the right direction and at a pace that should placate Russian opinion—feeble as it is; moreover, the people, at any rate for the present, have absolutely made up their minds to have peace.

As far as the town of Petrograd itself is concerned, the main thoroughfares are in good condition and well lit. I am told that a great deal has been done in improving the roads within the last year. Ninety per cent of the houses have been leased in blocks by the Communal Town Council to groups of old householders called Domoviya Tovarischestva, who run them and are responsible for their repair. This is a most glaring case of how the Soviet Government, by pursuing their idiotic policy have cut their own throats economically. A tremendous number of houses in Petrograd are going to rack and ruin for want of repair and the Soviet Government are only too glad to rid themselves of the burden of keeping them from tumbling to pieces altogether. The new departure of the Domoviya Tovarischestva system has left everybody in a quandary as to which way the cat is going to jump next, that is, back to nationalisation when the houses have been repaired, or to the return of private property. The latter course is, at any rate, anticipated as a lot of property is illegally changing hands.

I am told that of the royal palaces the Anichkov, where the Dowager Empress used to live, and Tsarskoe Selo, are practically just as they were when

4 See Vol. XI, No. 701.

947

vacated, whilst the Hermitage has become richer during the revolution by objets d'art from the churches and private collections.

In view of Hodgson's despatch No. 223 of December 14th, 1921,[5] I have carefully avoided the Embassy,[6] which, I am informed, is being looked after by Burobin.[7] I should be grateful for a line on this question. I am sure there would be no difficulty in my visiting it, if necessary. At the Rectory the central heating is out of order; the house is otherwise in good condition.

Kindest regards to Gregory and Ovey.

Yours ever,
THOMAS PRESTON

[5] Not printed.   [6] The former British Embassy.

[7] An organization under the Commissariat for Foreign Affairs concerned with supplying needs of foreigners in Moscow.

No. 564

Mr. Gregory to M. Berzin

[*N 9319/13/38*]

FOREIGN OFFICE, <i>November 22, 1922</i>

Sir,

With reference to your memorandum No. I.B./11494 of the 16th of August,[1] transmitting revised lists of the staff of the Russian Trade Delegation in this country and of affiliated organisations, I am directed by the Marquess Curzon of Kedleston to inform you that it has now been decided that visas valid for six months may be granted to members of the staff of the official agent of the Soviet Government in this country, and to those higher officials of the Moorgate Street office of your delegation and of Arcos, Limited, whose names appear in the lists numbered 1, 3 and 4 enclosed with your letter under reference, and who are of Russian nationality.

2. In this connection I am to point out that the following persons whose names appear in the lists transmitted by you have not yet fulfilled the formalities of registration with the police, which are incumbent on all aliens within two months of entering this country:—

Mr. Peter Miller   ⎫
Mr. Simeon Schwartz   ⎬ List 1.
Miss Henrietta Rozanova ⎭

Miss Fanny Rappoport   ⎫
Mrs. Marie Kouprianova ⎬ List 2.
Mr. John Gagarin   ⎭

With the exception of M. Krassin, M. Berzin and M. Klishko the obligation to register is incumbent on all alien members of the staff of the Russian Trade

[1] Not printed (see, however, No. 543).

Delegation and affiliated organisations; and I am to request that you will be good enough to instruct the persons whose names appear above to fulfil this formality without delay. In the event of a change of residence, or absence from their place of residence exceeding two months, aliens are, as you are doubtless aware, obliged to report the fact to the police, but apart from this no further formality of this nature is imposed after the first registration.

3. On production of evidence that they have complied with the registration formalities, visas valid for six months will be issued by the competent authorities to the persons mentioned in the first paragraph of the present letter. In the event, however, of a new member of your staff being appointed whose name does not appear on these lists, it will still be necessary for the application for a visa on his behalf to be referred in the first instance to the competent authorities in this country, who will, if satisfied, authorise the issue of a visa for the single journey. After his arrival in this country the proper procedure will be that your delegation should report that he has joined its permanent staff and should be added to the lists of staff, when, on production of evidence of police registration, he will be granted a visa valid for six months.

4. The competent departments of His Majesty's Government have also had under consideration the inconvenience created by the fact that only three members of the staff of your delegation and of the British Mission in Moscow are entitled to diplomatic visas. They are disposed to grant a further number of diplomatic visas to the staff of your delegation (lists 1 and 3), up to a total, including those already held, of seventeen; provided that a similar courtesy is extended to the members of the British Mission in Moscow, and that it is clearly understood that this further concession is granted solely on grounds of courtesy and must not be held to involve any sort of recognition of the holder's right to any other form of diplomatic privilege.

5. In the event of application being made by the Soviet authorities for a diplomatic visa for a new member to join the staff of your delegation, the application should be submitted in the same way as prescribed in paragraph 3 above. In the event of the visa being approved a diplomatic visa would then be granted, provided the total allotment of seventeen is at no time exceeded.

6. I am to suggest that arrangements should be made for a representative of your delegation to call at the Foreign Office with a view to fixing the names of the further persons to whom the courtesy of a diplomatic visa is to be extended (as proposed in paragraph 4 above).

I am, etc.,

J. D. GREGORY

No. 565

Mr. Knatchbull-Hugessen (The Hague) to the Marquess Curzon of Kedleston (Received November 24)

No. 520 [N 10477/646/38]

THE HAGUE, *November 22, 1922*

My Lord,

In accordance with the instructions in Your Lordship's despatch No. 585 (N 9800/646/38) of November 16th,[1] I informed Monsieur van Karnebeek at his weekly reception yesterday of the attitude of His Majesty's Government in regard to the proposal to communicate to the non-participating Powers the Cattier resolution[2] adopted at the concluding meeting of the Hague Russian Conference. I gave His Excellency an aide-memoire which included the view of Signor Giannini's interpretation set forth in the final paragraph of Your Lordship's despatch.

His Excellency, who expressed himself as entirely in agreement with the attitude of His Majesty's Government, informed me that he should proceed to notify the resolution to the Governments concerned but should go no further.[3]

I have, etc.,
H. M. KNATCHBULL-HUGESSEN

[1] No. 561.

[2] See Vol. XIX, No. 205, n. 2.

[3] In a private letter of November 23 to Mr. Ovey, Mr. Knatchbull-Hugessen stated: 'Your note to Moncheur of November 18th [not printed] tells him that you have told me to join with my Belgian, French and Italian colleagues in requesting the Netherlands Government to communicate the resolution. This seems to go beyond your instructions to me, which seem particularly to avoid any direct request to the Neth[erlands] Gov[ernmen]t.

'The two don't seem absolutely to tally and I gathered from the previous correspondence that you did not agree with the Belgian proposal, which went further than suited us.

'I don't think it makes any difference and I only mention it to you because I imagine my colleagues will ask me to join with them and may assume that I have been instructed to go as far as they. If I am approached, I shall tell them what I have done and shall not go any further.'

Mr. Gregory replied (November 30): 'I fear we have perhaps given the Belgian Ambassador rather an exaggerated idea of the lengths to which we are prepared to go. You are quite right in thinking that we do not want you to go any further than the terms of our despatch No. 585. I agree that there seems no need for you to take any further steps, over and above those reported in your despatch No. 520 of the 22nd of November [not printed]. I don't suppose that your colleagues will want to insist on your taking part in a joint representation to the Netherlands Government.'

No. 566

The Marquess Curzon of Kedleston to Lord Hardinge (Paris)
No. 3523 [N 10158/573/38]

Secret   FOREIGN OFFICE, *November 24, 1922*

My Lord,

With reference to Your Excellency's despatch No. 2508 of the 26th ultimo,[1] I have recently received a report[2] from a secret and confidential source which tends to indicate that certain powerful influences are at work with the object of improving the relations, both political and economic, between France and Russia.[3]

2. According to this report the French are making a determined effort to get into touch with the Soviet Government, with the primary object of re-establishing trade relations and thereby paving the way towards a definite political agreement between the two countries.

3. This policy is alleged to have been initiated on the French side about the time of the Genoa Conference, when certain financial, commercial and Jewish circles in Paris, who enjoyed the support of the government, enlisted the services of Markotun, President of the Ukrainian National Committee in Paris, as intermediary in arriving at an understanding with the Soviet Government.

4. In pursuance of this arrangement Markotun drew up an agreement with Rakowsky, Chairman of the Ukrainian Council of People's Commissaries, whereby the Ukrainian National Committee was to be accepted by the Soviet Government as a legal political party and ally, in return for the recognition by the committee of the Soviet Government.

5. This agreement was duly signed at the time, much to the surprise of all Russian circles, since the Ukrainian National Committee had been regarded as definitely anti-Bolshevik, and it was incorrectly assumed that this rapprochement with the 'enemy' was due to Germanophile influences.

6. Use was next made of the mission of Monsieur Herriot[4] to Russia to send to Moscow Monsieur Henri Rollin, a correspondent of the 'Temps' and member of the French secret service, who was given instructions by Markotun, with the sanction of the French authorities, to get into touch with prominent Bolsheviks and to work out a detailed scheme for a Franco-Soviet agreement of a political, as well as economic, character. Rollin was to have returned to Paris with Herriot and the whole future negotiations are stated to depend on the nature of his report and on the attitude of the Bolshevik leaders whom he has seen.

7. It is further alleged that in the meanwhile subsidiary negotiations were initiated by the French in Constantinople with the Soviet Trade Delegation,

[1] No. 558.

[2] Secret Intelligence Service Report No. 951 of November 8: *Franco-Russian Relations*, not printed.

[3] Cf. No. 557.   [4] See No. 559, n. 6.

through the medium of Dankovsky, the local representative of the Ukrainian National Committee, and that on Markotun's suggestion the plan was adopted of forming a Franco-Ukrainian trust which was to function under cover of Ukrainian commercial organisations, and which was to mask the political side of the negotiations. This plan proved unsuccessful, and in its place a scheme was elaborated whereby certain French banks were to approach the Soviet Trade Delegation in Constantinople through their agents, with a view to obtaining acceptance of the project which Dankovsky had been commissioned to put forward. This compromise met with greater success and resulted in the despatch to Paris of Anikiev, a member of the Soviet Trade Delegation in Constantinople, to discuss the matter further. Dankovsky is reported in the meanwhile to have been granted a French diplomatic visa, and to be about to proceed to Paris for participation in these discussions. He is also stated to be furthering French interests in the Near East generally.

8. Although it has not been found possible, for obvious reasons, to verify the accuracy of the information given above, I have deemed it to be of sufficient interest to communicate it to Your Excellency for what it is worth.

I am, etc.,
(For the Secretary of State)
J. D. GREGORY

No. 567

Sir E. Crowe to Lord Hardinge (Paris)
[*N 10413/252/38*]

FOREIGN OFFICE, *November 27, 1922*

My dear Hardinge,

With reference to your letter of the 20th instant,[1] I have ascertained that we have no information that the Swedish Government are about to commence negotiations with the Soviet Government for the recognition of the latter 'de jure', the latest report from Barclay being that Branting intends to resume negotiations with it merely for a trade agreement. I see no objection to you informing the Norwegian Minister accordingly.

2. The action of the Norwegian Minister for Foreign Affairs in instructing Wedel Jarlsberg[2] to enquire of you the views of His Majesty's Government as to the course of action contemplated by Sweden is, as you say, quite irregular and, if you do not object, you might tell him that we should prefer that any further enquiries which his Government may wish to make should be addressed to the Foreign Office.

3. While, of course, we cannot advise other Powers as to the attitude which they may henceforth see fit to adopt towards the Soviet Government, we should nevertheless view with regret any departure from the policy of the

---

[1] Not printed. [2] Norwegian Minister in Paris.

united front pursued at Genoa[3] and The Hague,[4] which we have tried to make the basis of the relations between Europe and the Soviets.

Yours sincerely,
EYRE A. CROWE

[3] See Vol. XIX, Chap. III.   [4] See ibid., Chap. IV.

No. 568

Mr. Gregory to M. Berzin

[*N 10346/155/38*]

FOREIGN OFFICE, *November 27, 1922*

Sir,

I am directed by the Secretary of State for Foreign Affairs to inform you that, according to information which has reached this department, restrictions have recently been placed on the importation of cargoes into Russian ports, and that, in consequence, Messrs Arcos, Limited, have informed British business firms that no goods may in future be loaded on board ship unless they are accompanied by a licence, or unless such a licence has been previously lodged by them with the British firm concerned, specifically detailing the order number and quantity of goods to be shipped.

2. I am to enquire whether this information is correct, and in particular whether Messrs Arcos have been appointed by you as the sole authority to issue the requisite licences for the importation of goods into Russia.

3. I am also to enquire whether, if this is the case, any powers delegated by you to Messrs Arcos for this purpose would apply to independent or autonomous Soviet republics.[1]

I am, etc.,
J. D. GREGORY

[1] M. Berzin replied to this communication in a letter of December 15 (N 11051/155/38), enclosing two memoranda, one on Regulations for Private Trade with Russia, the other on the Foreign Trade Monopoly (Export and Import Licences). M. Berzin drew attention to the Russian state monopoly of foreign trade and continued: 'This monopoly in practice signifies, apart from a small percentage of trade done directly by the State, the exercise of supervision and control over trading operations conducted by private firms.' To render this control efficient, a system of licences for import and export trade has been established, similar to but wider in application than that partially introduced in Great Britain during the war.

'The principles underlying the issue of these licences, which in practice do not restrict but rather facilitate the development of trade between Russia and other countries, are to be found summarised in the two statements issued by this Delegation and appended to the present letter. The first was issued in September last, and the second about a week ago . . . the Russian Trade Delegation remains the sole authority for the issue of licences for the importation of goods into Russia, and has not delegated such powers to Messrs. Arcos Limited, or any other firm.

'Messrs. Arcos Limited are the Commercial Agents of the Russian Government in Great Britain, and issued the statement referred to in the Foreign Office letter as a friendly communication to their clients, with the object of facilitating business and preventing unnecessary misunderstandings.

'Licences for trade with the independent or autonomous Soviet Republics should also be applied for at the offices of the Russian Trade Delegation.'

No. 569

Memorandum by Mr. Gregory on the 'Pact of Non-Aggression'
[N 10819/646/38]

FOREIGN OFFICE, December 1, 1922

Mr. Fisher[1] asked the Prime Minister in the House of Commons on the 24th ultimo[2] what steps would be taken for renewing the Pact of Genoa (which was entered into on the 19th May).[3] It will be observed from article 6 of this pact[3] that it had special reference to the commissions which were to be set up at The Hague to continue the examination of, and, if possible, to settle the Russian question, and that the various Governments pledged themselves to observe it 'for a period of four months from the closing of the work of the commissions.'

This arrangement was, as is well known, a makeshift to cover the failure of the Genoa Conference and was hurriedly put together without any regard for logic or consequences. The inference would be, for instance, that once the four months were up, or alternatively if the work of the commissions broke down, the parties to the arrangement would be free to attack one another without incurring even the moral sanction implied in the pact. There were, in any case, to be no other sanctions. Doubtless this was not the intention of the authors, but the general impression was, I think, that the thing was a farce from beginning to end.

So little in fact have the parties to it—they were not signatories—taken this instrument seriously that, as far as I know, no one of them has suggested the need of regularising or renewing it. The work of the commissions at The Hague,[4] of course, came to nothing, and, as stated, no provision was made in the pact for that eventuality. Consequently the whole position of it is entirely ambiguous.

I doubt if we need worry. Moreover, the point of the pact, as far as it had one, was to restrain only the East European nations from flying at one another's throats. It was hardly intended or likely to apply to Franco-German relations—in fact Germany was not a party—or Italian–Serb relations. But the East European nations are now engaged on endeavouring to come to some pacific arrangement among themselves, as shown in the annexed memorandum.[5] It therefore seems that our reply to an enquiry, such as Mr. Fisher's, is a reference to the negotiations now proceeding between them, and a statement to the effect that we trust the object aimed at in

[1] Mr. H. A. L. Fisher (see No. 190).   [2] See 159 *H.C. Deb. 5 s*, col. 201.
[3] See Vol. XIX, No. 142.   [4] See ibid., Chap. IV.
[5] Not traced in the Foreign Office archives.

the Genoa Pact will be attained, and indeed more effectively attained, by an agreement for disarmament or some other device for keeping the peace among the nations for whose benefit the original pact was concluded.

J. D. GREGORY

No. 570

The Marquess Curzon of Kedleston to Mr. Peters (Moscow)

No. 1148 [N 10421/1185/38]

FOREIGN OFFICE, *December 4, 1922*

Sir,

I have received your despatch No. 818 of the 24th October,[1] transmitting a copy of the reply returned by the Soviet Government to the claim advanced by you in connection with the loss of the S.T. 'Magneta'.[2]

2. You should reply to the Soviet Government reiterating the refusal of His Majesty's Government to admit that the S.T. 'Magneta' was within territorial waters when seized. You should add that His Majesty's Government cannot accept the Soviet Government's view that the loss of the vessel was due to 'vis major', but that they consider that the direct cause of the loss was the action of the Soviet patrol vessel in compelling the 'Magneta' to anchor in a dangerous position when a gale was impending. It seems in fact clear that if the 'Magneta' had been left alone with plenty of sea room she would have ridden out the gale in perfect safety, as did the other trawlers in the vicinity.

3. You should therefore inform the Soviet Government that His Majesty's Government must continue to hold it responsible for the loss of the vessel, and that, in view of this unsatisfactory attitude of the Soviet Government in this respect they find themselves obliged to give full publicity to the matter.

I am, etc.,
(For the Secretary of State)
J. D. GREGORY

[1] Not printed.   [2] See No. 483.

No. 571

The Marquess Curzon of Kedleston to Sir R. Graham (Rome)

No. 1443 [N 10717/57/38]

Confidential   FOREIGN OFFICE, *December 4, 1922*

Sir,

Dr. Giannini, head of the Italian Commercial Mission in this country, recently had a conversation with a member of this Department, the substance of which appears to me to deserve communication to your Excellency, in view of the numerous suggestions now in the air that Italy will shortly conclude an agreement with the Soviet Government.[1] I understand that Dr. Giannini is on intimate terms with Signor Mussolini,[2] who has installed him in an office of his own at the Consulta, and takes his advice on matters connected with Russia.

2. Dr. Giannini stated quite definitely that he was engaged on working out the basis of an agreement with the Soviet Government. He said that such an agreement was necessary for Italy, because they were obliged to have practical dealings with Russia, and yet one of the parties to these dealings had no legal existence. It was most necessary, for instance, to conclude a commercial agreement, a shipping agreement and an agreement defining the status of Italian subjects of Russia, of whom there are already a considerable number working on railways and other undertakings in the neighbourhood of Odessa. There was a certain trade going on with the South Russian ports, and out of that numerous disputes arose which could not be settled owing to the ambiguity of Italian–Russian relations.

3. In answer to the suggestion that it would be strange if one of the first acts of a Government founded on hostility to Communism should be to recognise *de jure* a Communist Government, Dr. Giannini said that anti-Communism was no longer the *raison d'être* of the Fascista Government, as the Fascisti had killed Italian Communism. Signor Mussolini's object was now the welfare of Italy in other directions, and, as he was determined that no other country should interfere in her internal administration, so he felt it only right to treat other countries as entitled to the Government they had chosen.

4. He seemed surprised on learning that His Majesty's Government did not share this view. He was told that it was naturally impossible to foretell developments in the policy of His Majesty's Government, but that, on present information, they could see no reason for taking the initiative in resuming negotiations with the Soviet Government. As he knew himself, since he had played so prominent a part at Genoa[3] and The Hague,[4] His Majesty's Government had gone to the limit of concessions—or, according to the opinion of some, actually beyond—and the Soviet Government had shown itself utterly intractable. The best plan now was to leave it severely alone. Besides which, His Majesty's Government had evidence that the Bolsheviks were utterly impenitent as regards their theory of world revolution and their propaganda was actually on the increase. It seemed the worst possible moment to negotiate with them again, and there appeared to be no reason for it.

5. Dr. Giannini said that he now quite saw this point of view. The position of His Majesty's Government was different from that of Italy. His Majesty's Government had to think primarily of debts and property, whereas the main preoccupation of Italy was with her workmen and her shipping. Accordingly there was every reason for separate action. The

[1] For earlier agreements, see Nos. 504 and 509. [2] See No. 116, n. 2.
[3] See Vol. XIX, Chap. III. [4] See ibid., Chap. IV.

Italian Government considered that since The Hague everyone was free to act for himself. Dr. Giannini was thereupon informed that, while there was no doubt no longer any actual obligation on the Powers to continue to act together, it must evidently weaken everyone's position *vis-à-vis* Russia if the united front policy were abandoned, and that it was accordingly to be hoped that the Italian Government would go slowly.

I am, etc.,
CURZON OF KEDLESTON

No. 572

Mr. Peters (Moscow) to the Marquess Curzon of Kedleston
(Received December 11)

No. 961 [N 10893/50/38]

MOSCOW, *December 5, 1922*

My Lord,

With reference to Mr. Gregory's despatch No. 1110 of the 21st November,[1] I have the honour to submit the following observations regarding the last paragraph of Lord D'Abernon's telegram No. 185 of the 8th October,[2] addressed to the Foreign Office.

I may state at once that I do not share the view that the Soviet Government would be prepared to make really serious concessions in order to obtain speedy *de jure* recognition. I base this opinion on the following considerations.

In foreign policy, and in domestic policy alike, the Soviet Government is guided entirely by 'Real Politik'. It is quite true that its calculations are often based on entirely false premises, and that it has numerous obsessions. In this connection I need only refer to the entirely disproportionate importance which it has always attached, and which it continues to attach, to the question of oil. But none the less, in estimating the probable course of procedure of the Soviet Government, it is essential to examine the concrete advantages which speedy *de jure* recognition might be expected to yield.

As regards its internal position, the Soviet Government is independent of recognition by foreign Powers. Whatever opinion may be held of the present Moscow Government, there can be no doubt that it is in point of fact the one and only Government of Russia, and that there does not appear to be any prospect of its being replaced by some alternative Government in the measurable future. It controls the entire political machine. No organised political opposition is allowed, and although there is and will continue to be a great deal of discontent, this discontent is confined to grumbling, and does

---

[1] Not printed.

[2] This paragraph ran: 'Private reports from Moscow state that Soviet Government consider speedy recognition so vital that it would consent to almost any sacrifice to obtain it.'

not show signs of finding expression in action. It is true that the economic basis on which the Soviet Government rests is not sound, and the Government itself recognizes that unless it can run the main branches of industry, which are still directly controlled by the State, at a profit, its position will become still weaker. Adaptability is, however, the keynote of Soviet policy, and no considerations of abstract principle will be allowed to interfere with the granting of any concessions in the economic sphere which it may be necessary to make in order to retain power. I do not think that *de jure* recognition by foreign Powers will have any considerable effect in this connection.

As regards the foreign interests of Russia, the Soviet Government has certainly begun to speak more in the manner of a Government of Russia and less in the manner of a Communist organisation aiming at Communist world revolution, but so long as Europe presents a picture of political dissension it is less necessary for Soviet Russia to obtain admission on an equal footing to the conferences of the Powers. At present Soviet Russia is in some ways at an advantage in being able to stand outside and to point to the differences which exist between the policies of the great European Powers.

To sum up, I consider that the Soviet Government might easily hint at concessions which it would be prepared to make if political recognition were granted, but I do not think that it would in practice make any considerable concessions.

I have, etc.,
WILLIAM PETERS

No. 573

Sir R. Graham (Rome) to the Marquess Curzon of Kedleston
(Received December 11)
No. 1123 [N 10901/57/38]

Confidential   ROME, *December 7, 1922*
My Lord,

With reference to my despatch No. 1118 of the 5th instant,[1] on the subject of Signor Mussolini's interview with Krassin, and to your Lordship's despatch No. 1443 of the 4th instant,[2] I have the honour to report that on the day after the interview in question the following Stefani communiqué was published in the press:—

'In accordance with arrangements made with the Russian commercial organisations, and after a final interview with M. Krassin and M. Feinstein,[3] Commendatore Gavazzi and Dr. Marinotti, president and manager respectively of the Compagnia Industriale per il Commercio Estero, of Milan, have started for Moscow. This company, which is supported by the principal industrials in Italy, has already established important trade

---

[1] Not printed.   [2] No. 571.
[3] A member of the Soviet trade delegation in Rome.

connections with Russia, and is hopeful of coming to an agreement with the Russian authorities concerning a vast programme of work.'

On the 6th December Krassin gave an interview to the press at Rome, in the course of which he referred to the steps which had already been taken in order to re-establish trade connections between the two countries. He stated that he had come to Italy for a rest and for change of climate, and had only asked for an interview with Signor Mussolini to pay his respects. On the other hand, I am credibly informed that Signor Mussolini really sent for Krassin to come to Rome, and this appears quite probable in view of the information which I have now received in your Lordship's despatch No. 1443 of the 4th instant.[2]

Russia, Krassin said, had this year sold merchandise of every description, from tobacco to building materials and from Persian carpets to 8,000 tons of anthracite. Italy, on the other hand, had exported textiles and machinery, in particular motor-cars and camions. He praised the work which had been done by the Italian merchant navy and by the Lloyd Triestino Company in re-establishing shipping services, and mentioned the concessions to Italy of 150,000 hectares of agricultural land. With reference to the protection of foreign traders, he said that under the new Russian Civil Code, which would come into force on the 1st January, 1923, full protection would be assured for property acquired through trade. It was in the interest of Russia herself, desirous as she was to re-establish her commerce abroad, to see that this guarantee was maintained. He is reported to have added:—

'The fear has been expressed that the Russian Government may one day take away that which it now concedes. But the experience of the last few years is not such as to encourage an action of this kind, which would offer small and temporary advantages as compared with the grave and irreparable evil which it would occasion.'

In replying to a question regarding the failure of the Soviet Government to ratify the trade agreement with Italy,[4] Krassin said that no agreement was popular in Russia which did not contain a recognition of the Soviet Government. When reminded of the *modus vivendi* with England, he answered that this agreement was concluded in 1921,[5] and that in 1922 the Russian Government, which had been in the meantime recognised *de jure* by Poland,[6] Norway,[7] Germany,[8] and other States,[9] was now in a position to be more exacting. Moreover, the agreement with England represented an exceptionally important step in Russia's foreign policy as indicating the first

[4] The reference is to the trade convention signed at Genoa on May 24, 1922 (see Nos. 504 and 509) under Article 13 of the Preliminary Agreement signed at Rome on December 26, 1921 (see No. 459). The convention was not ratified, but the Preliminary Agreement was extended by an exchange of notes, dated June 22, 1922 (see Slusser and Triska, p. 28).

[5] See No. 353, n. 2.

[6] By the Treaty of Riga (see No. 368, n. 5).

[7] By the treaty of September 2, 1921 (see No. 415, n. 3).

[8] By the Treaty of Rapallo (see Vol. XIX, No. 75).

[9] For other treaties, see Slusser and Triska, pp. 21–37, *passim*.

re-establishment of her international relations. When interrogated with regard to the sequestration of Italian ships in the Black Sea, Krassin retorted by a reference to the sequestration of Russian sulphate of ammonia in Italy, and added that the policy of reprisals would do no good to either country. According to one report, Krassin is said to have concluded the interview by saying, 'I am truly happy to have found Signor Mussolini so favourably disposed (in così favorevole disposizione).'

The 'Corriere della Sera', in commenting on these proposals, expresses the opinion that Krassin takes too optimistic a view of Russian resources, and points out that the commercial treaty which he offers to negotiate will be conditional on the *de jure* recognition of Russia. The newspaper is not hopeful regarding the prospects of an agreement with Russia after the failure of previous attempts, and in connection with the concession of agricultural land in Russia (see my despatch No. 865 of the 25th September)[1] asks who will be called upon to finance so large and risky an undertaking. The article concludes by saying that until the Government of Moscow re-establishes normal conditions of life, all treaties of commerce between Russia and other nations are worthless.

I have, etc.,
R. GRAHAM

No. 574

Lord Hardinge (Paris) to the Marquess Curzon of Kedleston
(Received December 8)
No. 2864 (C) [N 10832/573/38]

PARIS, *December 7, 1922*

My Lord,

With reference to my despatch No. 2800 (C) of the 29th ultimo[1] with regard to the question of sending a French commercial mission to Russia, I have the honour to acquaint Your Lordship that, according to the weekly commercial review 'Les Echos' of the 6th instant, the Ministry for Foreign Affairs has intervened and vetoed the proposal of the Minister of Commerce (Monsieur Dior) to send a commercial mission to Russia.

The newspaper recalls the fact that, in accordance with the suggestion of the President of the Marseilles Chamber of Commerce, the question of the despatch of such a mission was considered at the assembly of the Presidents of the Chambers of Commerce of France, and that it was decided to appoint a committee to investigate the matter.[2]

The committee discussed the question with the Minister of Commerce, who stated that he had already taken action. He remarked that MM. Herriot and

---

[1] Not preserved in the Foreign Office archives. See, however, No. 558
[2] See No. 576, below.

Daladier[3] on their return from Moscow[4] had suggested that a mission of a commercial, financial and intellectual character should visit Russia, but that he proposed to limit himself to his sphere and to send a mission with the sole object of making enquiry into the commercial possibilities of Russia at the present time and to provide guidance for French merchants in view of possible business. He added that the mission would no doubt be headed by Monsieur de Chevilly, Commercial Attaché, and Monsieur Bayard, Director of the Commercial Office for Russia and formerly chief engineer of a manganese mine in the Caucasus.

The newspaper states that this was the position when the Ministry for Foreign Affairs laid their veto on the proposal.

I have, etc.,

HARDINGE OF PENSHURST

[3] Radical-Socialist deputy for Vaucluse.　　　[4] See Nos. 557 and 558.

No. 575

Sir C. Barclay (Stockholm) to the Marquess Curzon of Kedleston
(Received December 20)

No. 524 [N 11141/252/38]

Confidential　　　　　　　　　　　　　　STOCKHOLM, *December 12, 1922*

My Lord,

On several occasions during the past two months I have asked the Prime Minister how matters stood as regards the renewal of negotiations for a Trade Agreement with Russia.[1] On each occasion Herr Branting replied that the Special Committee which had been appointed under the Chairmanship of the Minister of Commerce to investigate certain points with a view to finding a new basis for contact had not yet terminated their labours.

It will be remembered that in the Trade Agreement signed in March and rejected by the Riksdag in May,[2] the question of private claims had been only touched upon; Article XV merely stating that they would be equitably dealt with in a subsequent Treaty. The small attention paid to these claims had been strongly reported against by the Riksdag Committee on Foreign Affairs and had not a little contributed to the rejection of the Agreement. The principal work of the present Special Committee has been to collect and investigate the various claims of Swedish subjects and much time has, it appears, been necessary to sift and cut them down.

The departure of Monsieur Kerzhentsev, Head of the Russian Trade Delegation here, for Moscow on the 7th instant, gave me the opportunity yesterday of once more asking Herr Branting whether there were any fresh developments. His Excellency replied that it was very probable that two Swedish experts would unofficially proceed to Russia shortly after Christmas to report on present conditions, and if their report were favourable the

[1] See Nos. 507 and 567.　　　[2] See No. 507.

resumption of negotiations for an Agreement would be renewed. I remarked that I took it for granted that it would only be a Trade Agreement and there was no question of any *de jure* recognition of the Soviet. His Excellency seemed to hesitate a little but replied that it was only a question of a Trade Agreement as conditions for the moment were not ripe for a *de jure* recognition. I remarked that Sweden would probably not care to depart from the line of conduct towards the Soviet adopted at Genoa[3] and The Hague.[4] The conversation, which took place at a dinner, was then interrupted.

As regards the forthcoming visit of experts to Russia I learn from a reliable source that Monsieur Kerzhentsev, when he left, was the bearer of a Memorandum to the effect that if the Soviet Government were agreeable, two Swedish experts would be sent unofficially to Moscow to discuss matters generally and to furnish a report as to present conditions in Russia and as to the opportuneness of renewing negotiations for an Agreement; this report to be submitted to the Riksdag Committee on Foreign Affairs and to be used eventually as a basis for new negotiations.

The experts selected, I am informed, are Herr Eliel Löfgre, former Minister of Justice in Herr Eden's Cabinet, and Herr Joseph Sachs, Director of the Nordiska Company, the largest stores in Stockholm with branches in Russia before the revolution. Herr Sachs has also been the Vice-Chairman of the Special Committee that has been investigating the Swedish claims. The report is confidently expected by the Swedish Government to be 'favourable', an opinion which will be prompted not only by the Government's avowed desire to discover any effective means of concluding a working arrangement, but also because Herr Sachs, as a prominent leading industrialist, represents the views of other powerful Swedish concerns possessing large interests in Russia (L. M. Ericsson, Kullager Fabrik, Almänna Svenska Elektricitets A/B, etc), who have nothing to lose and everything to gain by the resumption of trade relations.

I have, etc.,
COLVILLE BARCLAY

[3] See Vol. XIX, Chap. III.   [4] See ibid., Chap. IV.

No. 576

Lord Hardinge (Paris) to the Marquess Curzon of Kedleston
(Received December 14)
No. 2905 (C) [N 10982/573/38]

PARIS, *December 12, 1922*

My Lord,
With reference to Mr. Peters' telegram No. 258 of the 6th December[1] from Moscow, in which he stated that a Soviet trade mission will proceed to France

[1] Not printed.

in a month's time, I have the honour to inform you that I have not observed as yet any public announcement to that effect in this country. Monsieur Herriot on his return from Russia[2] stated that he had invited the Russians to come to the Lyons Fair[2] which is held in the first half of March; and it is possible that this mission may have some connection with that invitation. The Monsieur Rollin alluded to in the telegram is no doubt the correspondent of *Le Temps*, who is now representing that journal at Lausanne, and who is referred to in paragraph 6 of Your Lordship's despatch No. 3523 (N 10158/ 573/38) of the 24th November last.[3]

As to the general question of the inception of a Franco-Russian rapprochement whether of a political or an economic nature, it appears to me that certain circumstances now visible should converge towards the facilitation of any such projects. The presence of an important Russian delegation at Lausanne[4] for a prolonged period offers opportunities of useful conversations; and the reported reception of Monsieur Krassin by the Italian Prime Minister in Rome on the 5th instant [*sic*][5] for the purpose of discussing the question of a commercial agreement between Italy and Russia may encourage the French Government to adopt a bolder Russian policy in this respect. This forward movement may be further stimulated by the constant reports (brought back among others by Monsieur Skobelev the semi-official Soviet trade representative in France)[6] of the growing imports from Germany, America, and Great Britain into Russia, and by the persistency of the endeavours of Mr. Urquhart and others[7] to make arrangements on a large scale with the Soviets.

In France the public are growing more and more accustomed to the idea of the initiation of some form of accommodation with Russia. In Lyons and Marseilles, two leading personalities, Monsieur Herriot and Monsieur Giraud (president of the Marseilles Chamber of Commerce and deputy for the Bouches-du-Rhône), are warm advocates of the despatch of a commercial mission to Russia. More than one of the leading banks in Paris which have large commitments (especially in the Ukraine) are desirous of some *modus vivendi* being realised; and several of the metallurgical and engineering firms or groups, such as the Schneider, St. Chamond, and de Wendel, which had relations with Russia and are now more than formerly desirous of large export markets owing to their greater productive powers, are anxious not to allow their competitors to obtain too firm a foothold in Russia before their advent. Important textile (linen, silk, clothing), wine, perfumery, and luxury articles interests are also concerned for the Russian market.

The Minister of Commerce is reported (see my despatch No. 2864 (C) of the 7th instant)[8] to be in favour of sending a commercial mission to Russia, but to be discountenanced in this matter by the Ministry of Foreign Affairs. The President of the Marseilles Chamber of Commerce moved at the last meeting of all the presidents of French Chambers of Commerce that these Chambers should take the initiative in sending collectively a permanent

---

[2] See Nos. 557 and 558.   [3] No. 566.   [4] See Vol. XVIII, Chap. II.
[5] Cf. No. 573.   [6] See No. 557.   [7] See Nos. 548, 555, 558, 559, and 566.
[8] No. 574.

commercial delegation to Moscow, after obtaining the sanction of the French Government; this proposal was not accepted mainly owing to the intervention of Monsieur Touron, a Senator, who pleaded that it would embarrass the action of the Government.

These circumstances and these manifestations of French opinion, to which I draw attention, appear to me to afford indications that, should the Soviet trade mission due to arrive in France in about a month's time be not merely a delegation for the Lyons Fair, but one of large scope, the French Government is not unlikely to adopt a less uncompromising attitude than it has shown in the past.

I have, etc.,
HARDINGE OF PENSHURST

No. 577

The Marquess Curzon of Kedleston to Sir R. Graham (Rome)
No. 1053 [N 10991/57/38]

FOREIGN OFFICE, *December 15, 1922*

Sir,

In my despatch No. 1443 of the 4th December[1] I informed your Excellency of an interview between Dr. Giannini, head of the Italian Commercial Commission in this country, and a member of this Department, on the possibility of the conclusion in the near future of an agreement between Italy and the Soviet Government.

2. In a subsequent interview with Dr. Giannini the arguments previously used against recognising the Soviet Government at the present moment were developed at some length. They appeared, however, to make no impression upon Dr. Giannini, and all that could be extracted from him was an undertaking that the Italian Government would not spring a surprise on His Majesty's Government at Lausanne.[2] Dr. Giannini promised to discuss the question further with this Department after he had consulted with Signor Mussolini, and added that he would give 'ample warning' before any definite step was taken.

I am, etc.,
CURZON OF KEDLESTON

[1] No. 571.
[2] See Vol. XVIII, Chap. II.

No. 578

Mr. Gregory to M. Berzin
[N 10951/13/38]

FOREIGN OFFICE, December 16, 1922

Sir,

I am directed by the Secretary of State for Foreign Affairs to acknowledge receipt of your memorandum No. JB/14423 of the 12th of December,[1] and to inform you that authorisation cannot be given for Mr. Karl Radek to enter this country.

I am, etc.,
J. D. GREGORY

[1] In this memorandum, M. Berzin had requested a visa for Karl Radek (see No. 370, n. 2), who wished to stay in England for one month in order to read in the British Museum.

No. 579

Mr. McNeill[1] to Mr. Morel[2]
[N 10833/3/38]

FOREIGN OFFICE, December 16, 1922

Dear Mr. Morel,

I have carefully considered your letter of the 6th December[3] setting forth the grounds for your assertion that the absence of normal diplomatic relations with Russia is an obstacle to the development of Anglo-Russian trade relations.

In my reply to your question in the House of Commons on the 27th November[4] I undertook to go into the facts of any specific case you might put forward where the absence of *de jure* recognition of the Soviet Government by His Majesty's Government was the obstacle to the completion of a proposed commercial transaction. But it was not then my intention, and I could not now agree, to enter fully into the more general considerations put forward in your letter. The Government's attitude on those questions can more properly be debated on the floor of the House, and I will, therefore, confine my answer to the only specific case which you mention, viz., the Urquhart–Krassin Agreement.[5]

The Foreign Office are familiar with every stage of the negotiations for the conclusion of this agreement; but I should draw from the facts conclusions which are the opposite of yours. The draft agreement was brought to completion in Berlin and initialled by both parties in the full expectation that it would be ratified and carried into effect forthwith. The existing political, financial and commercial relations of the two countries were clearly such as render ratifications and fulfilment of the draft agreement practicable.

[1] Parliamentary Under Secretary of State for Foreign Affairs since November 17, 1922.
[2] Member of Parliament for Dundee.   [3] Not printed.
[4] See 159 H.C. Deb. 5 s, col. 255.   [5] See No. 548.

No physical or legal obstacle was found to exist. If we are to believe the statements of the spokesmen of the Soviet Government, its rejection was decided upon as a means of bringing pressure to bear upon His Majesty's Government in order to induce them to grant *de jure* recognition and to invite Russian participation in all as well as in some sections of the Lausanne Conference. In short, the Soviet Government demanded recognition as the price of its consent to the resumption of trading relations with us, and this is the only sense in which it is true to say that the absence of *de jure* recognition proved an obstacle to the fulfilment of the agreement in question.

Now what is the expectation that, even if we had yielded to this pressure, the Urquhart–Krassin Agreement would be ratified and satisfactorily implemented? For months previous to the conclusion of the trade agreement, the Soviet Government and its friends in this country attacked the policy of His Majesty's Government on the ground that they were preventing the resumption of trade with Russia. The Soviet Government declared that Russia was being blockaded; that the blockade was ruining her industries and her commerce, and that His Majesty's Government were *pro tanto* responsible for the starvation and misery of the Russian people. The trade agreement was concluded, and in due course negotiations were begun between M. Krassin and the Russo-Asiatic Consolidated. Those negotiations were initiated and conducted and successfully concluded on the basis of the trade agreement, and on that alone. But the Soviet Government, by refusing ratification on grounds quite foreign to the proposed concession or to the manner in which we had carried out our part of the trade agreement, has put in doubt the honesty of its intentions in concluding the trade agreement, and its action in this case renders it difficult to believe that it would cordially and consistently co-operate with Mr. Urquhart in the operation of his concession even if His Majesty's Government were to pay the price which they ask for ratification.

It is a fact that Mr. Urquhart told the shareholders of the Russo-Asiatic Consolidated that he was in favour of giving full and public recognition to the Soviet régime; but I should be surprised to learn that such recognition should, in his view, be accorded unconditionally. Indeed, in a letter to 'The Times' on the 25th October Mr. Urquhart says that he has 'no doubt a bargain could be struck between Moscow and Downing Street,' but that 'the basis of it would be full political recognition in return for Russia's acknowledgement of her national debts and of her liability to foreign owners for the nationalisation of their properties.' This expression of Mr. Urquhart's opinion is inconsistent with the course which I understand you to recommend, namely, immediate recognition with or without conditions.

I need hardly say that His Majesty's Government are no less anxious than Mr. Urquhart to see Russia re-enter the comity of nations and come to terms with foreigners, like Mr. Urquhart, who have contributed so much to the development of Russia's resources and of Russia's foreign trade. During the last two years the conditions upon which it was open to her to do so have been made abundantly clear to her and to the whole world by speeches in the

House of Commons, by diplomatic correspondence, and by the unanimous resolutions of conferences at which twenty-six States were represented. No sign of willingness to agree to those conditions has, however, been forthcoming from the Soviet Government.

I agree that this correspondence should be given to the press.[6]

Yours very truly,
R. McNEILL

[6] Extracts from the press concerning this correspondence are preserved at N 11193/3/38.

No. 580

The Marquess Curzon of Kedleston (Lausanne) to Sir E. Crowe
(Received December 19, 8.30 a.m.)
No. 130 Telegraphic: by bag [N 11110/3/38]

LAUSANNE, *December 17, 1922*

M. Chicherin asked to see me this afternoon and we spent more than an hour in conversation. Setting aside the question of recognition, he asked me what were the intentions of the present British government towards Russia. Did we desire by methods of conciliation and compromise to arrive at a friendly understanding, starting from the basis of the trade agreement and proceeding to co-operation over a wider area? His government had the impression that we were more hostile than our predecessors. In reply I welcomed the opportunity of speaking with perfect frankness to M. Chicherin. I said that he knew as well as I did what were the conditions of such an understanding. No Prime Minister could have been more disposed towards close relations with Russia and certainly none had worked harder to achieve them than Mr. Lloyd George, both because of his broad conception of European policy, and because his personal attitude towards the Soviet government had been more elastic than that of some of his colleagues. But Russia herself by her behaviour at Genoa[1] and The Hague[2] seemed to have deliberately thrown away the opening, and to have only produced irritation where she pleaded for friendship. As regards the present government, the conditions on which friendship could be attained had been restated a few days ago by Prime Minister in House of Commons.[3] Until these were satisfied, how could advance be made? To one of them I called special attention. I had been personally responsible for paragraphs in trade agreement renouncing political propaganda against British Empire, notably in East. Nevertheless, I had overwhelming evidence up till present hour to show that in every part of East, Afghanistan, Persia, Mesopotamia, Anatolia, Soviet Russia had been persistently intriguing and spending large sums of money in anti-British policy and propaganda.[4] How could we be expected

[1] See Vol. XIX, Chap. III.   [2] See ibid., Chap. IV.
[3] See 159 *H.C. Deb.*, 5 s, col. 3136.
[4] Cf. Nos. 377–9, 383, 414, Enclosure, and 437.

to embrace a would-be friend who thus stabbed us in the back? Until there was an absolute desistence from this pestilent activity, there could be no real reconciliation, although present British government were not less anxious than their predecessors that Russia should play her due part in scheme of world reconstruction, and realised that her permanent estrangement was an international loss.

Chicherin in reply made only the feeblest defence. He denied all my charges, which he said were based on worthless secret service reports; he actually accused us of intriguing against Russia in Afghanistan, Northern Persia and Caucasus, whereas as I pointed out under system in which Caucasian states had been absorbed in the caresses of Russia, we had no agent and no information there at all, Moscow having ignored our request to send a trading representative. He declared that Soviet government were not responsible for what irregular Russian agents might do, and that it was necessary here as elsewhere to establish a compromise between our two points of view.

I replied that where one of two parties was exclusively guilty of propaganda, while the other was wholly innocent, no mid-way house or compromise appeared to be possible, and I challenged him, though without result, to name a single part of world in which we were doing towards Russia what Russia was daily and weekly doing towards us. Even while I was here he was putting out malicious articles in the press attacking the British, and trying to embroil me with Labour Party in England; while simultaneously he succeeded in exasperating the latter by such follies as the Stan Harding case.[5] I gave these replies in presence of Sir William Tyrrell, who can corroborate that Chicherin found no response except repetition of formulas about communistic principles and necessity for Russia of following what he called a diagonal line.

We then turned to Lausanne situation. . . .[6]

[5] See No. 427, n. 5.

[6] The greater part of the remainder of this telegram is printed in Vol. XVIII, No. 282, n. 3.

No. 581

Mr. Addison (Berlin) to the Marquess Curzon of Kedleston
(Received December 27)
No. 966 [N 11243/4058/38]

Confidential   BERLIN, *December 20, 1922*

My Lord Marquess,

I have the honour to acknowledge receipt of Your Lordship's despatch No. 1743 (N 10805/4058/38) of the 14th instant[1] and to transmit to you

[1] Not printed. This requested Mr. Addison to endeavour to obtain details of any agreement reached between Messrs. Krupp and the Russian Government for an agricultural concession.

herewith copies of a confidential memorandum prepared by Mr. Thelwall regarding the Krupp concession in Russia.

I have, etc.,

JOSEPH ADDISON

ENCLOSURE IN No. 581

Memorandum

With reference to the attached Foreign Office despatch,[1] relative to the Krupp concession in Russia, the following is the latest information which I possess:—

The terms which have been agreed upon between Messrs. Krupp and Monsieur Stomoniakov, the Russian Commercial representative in Berlin, are in broad outline as follows: They are not a new contract, but represent alterations to the original one proposed in March of this year. It will be remembered that the agreement has been the subject of endless disputes, as the Russians asserted that Krupps had definitely accepted, while the latter maintain that they had only signed provisionally. The real difficulty, however, seems to have been that Krupps did not feel themselves financially sufficiently strong to carry out the terms of the original agreement.

The modifications are as follows: The total concession is to be a purely agricultural one for the production of grain and there is to be no stock raising, as originally proposed by the German firm. The payments to be made by Messrs. Krupp to the Russian Government are to be based on the gross earnings, and there are to be no preliminary deductions from these earnings, as originally demanded by Krupps. As compensation for these less favourable terms, the area which the German firm is to work is to be reduced from 50,000 to 25,000 desjatins.[2] The agreement has only been signed in Berlin and is still awaiting ratification by the Moscow Government.

As stated in my first despatch on this subject, Overseas Trade (B) 105, of the 11th April, 1922,[3] the concession is in respect of land in the neighbourhood of Rostow on the Don, and reports have reached me that the Don Cossacks may raise objection to its being carried out.

A few days ago I had a conversation with Dr. Sorge, the resident Director of Messrs. Krupp in Berlin and one of the leading persons in German industrial life.[4] He assured me that the provisional signature of the agreement had only become possible through the participation of British capital and he said that this participation was being provided by or through Major Dunning[5] who had been brought into touch with Krupps through Boris Said. The English participation is to amount to 70 or 75%. What the total sum involved is I do not know, but from various indications believe it is between £80 and 100,000.

[2] One dessiatine = 109.254 acres.   [3] Not printed.
[4] A marginal note stated: 'Please treat particularly confidentially.'
[5] Of Messrs. James Dunning and Co., who also were negotiating for an oil concession in Russia.

No. 582

Mr. Gregory to the Board of Trade
[*N 10831/50/38*]

FOREIGN OFFICE, *December 21, 1922*

Sir,

I am directed by the Secretary of State for Foreign Affairs to acknowledge the receipt of your letter No. P.D. 853 of the 7th instant,[1] and to inform you that he concurs in the views taken by the Board of Trade of resolutions 2 and 3 passed in the conference recently held in Paris by companies interested in the Russian oilfields.

2. The Secretary of State approves of what he understands to be the spirit of resolution No. 1, but he anticipates that various difficulties may arise in its application.

3. The course adopted by the Foreign Office hitherto has been to urge an intending concessionnaire to secure agreement in advance with the former owners of any plot not formerly in his own possession but included by the Soviet government in the proposed concession. Where such agreement has not been reached in advance the Foreign Office have intimated to the intending concessionnaire that they would withhold their support unless he offer to the former owners of plots inside his concession equitable terms for participation in the concession or for a sub-lease from the concessionnaire; and have stated that in case of doubt the question of what constituted 'equitable terms' would have to be submitted to an arbitrator.

I am, etc.,

J. D. GREGORY

[1] This ran: 'As Lord Curzon is probably aware, a meeting was recently held in Paris at which most of the existing South Russian oil interests were represented, the only important exception so far as is known to the Board of Trade being the Baku Consolidated Oilfields, Limited. At this meeting resolutions in the following sense were passed unanimously:

'(1) That it is inadmissible for any of the parties interested to prejudice directly or indirectly existing interests and acquired rights of other owners dispossessed by the Soviet legislation.

'(2) That the exploitation of petroliferous lands is only possible on condition that their former rights and properties be restored on equal terms to all the persons concerned.

'(3) That the petroliferous lands belonging to the State are necessary for the development of the industry as a whole, and in consequence they are not to be accepted by any one of the parties interested as an individual concession without common consent.

'No. (1) of these resolutions appears to be in accord with the general view of H.M. Government in the matter. Resolutions (2) and (3), which appear to involve respectively insistence on the recognition by the Soviet authorities of property rights of Russians as well as of foreign subjects and a demand by the existing owners for the partition among them of hitherto undeveloped State lands, go considerably further and make claims in respect of which the British companies concerned are hardly entitled to expect support. The Board of Trade would be glad to learn Lord Curzon's views on this subject.'